Gender and Law

Gender and Law
Theory, Doctrine, Commentary
Third Edition

Katharine T. Bartlett
Dean and A. Kenneth Pye
Professor of Law
Duke University
School of Law

Angela P. Harris
Professor of Law
University of California, Berkeley
School of Law (Boalt Hall)

Deborah L. Rhode
Ernest W. McFarland
Professor of Law and Director of the
Keek Center on Legal Ethics and the
Legal Profession
Stanford Law School

Aspen Law & Business
A Division of Aspen Publishers, Inc.
New York   Gaithersburg

ISBN 0-7355-2548-X

1 2 3 4 5 6 7 8 9 0

Library of Congress Cataloging-in-Publication Data

Bartlett, Katharine T.
    Gender and law : theory, doctrine, commentary / Katharine T. Bartlett, Angela P. Harris, Deborah L. Rhode. — 3rd ed.
        p. cm.
    Includes index.
    ISBN 0-7355-2548-X
    1. Women — Legal status, laws, etc. — United States — Cases. 2. Sex and law — United States — Cases. 3. Sex discrimination against women — Law and legislation — United States — Cases. 4. Feminist jurisprudence — United States. I. Harris, Angela P., 1961-II. Rhode, Deborah L. III. Title.

KF478.A4 B37 2002
346.7301'34 — dc21

                                                                2001056178

About Aspen Law & Business Legal Education Division

With a dedication to preserving and strengthening the long-standing tradition of publishing excellence in legal education, Aspen Law & Business continues to provide the highest quality teaching and learning resources for today's law school community. Careful development, meticulous editing, and an unmatched responsiveness to the evolving needs of today's discerning educators combine in the creation of our outstanding casebooks, course-books, textbooks, and study aids.

ASPEN LAW & BUSINESS
A Division of Aspen Publishers, Inc.
A Wolters Kluwer Company
www.aspenpublishers.com

Summary of Contents

Contents

4 ≡ *Nonsubordination* 533

5

Women's Different Voice(s) 805

Preface

Many topics from traditional law school courses such as employment law, family law, criminal law, and constitutional law have special relevance to women. Studying these topics within their conventional legal categories can provide systematic coverage of those substantive areas of law that are central to women's lives. Some excellent courses on gender and law proceed in this fashion. The risk of this approach, in the view of the authors of this book, is that it reinforces some questionable assumptions about the relationship between law and gender. Among these questionable assumptions are (1) that sex discrimination law can be sliced off from the larger fields of law of which it is but one of many parts, (2) that once removed and consolidated, the parts form a coherent body of law worthy of separate academic study, and (3) that the salient categories in that body of law are the different spheres of women's life to which law is (separately) applied, that is, the workplace, the family, the jury box, public benefits, and the like.

The insights of feminist legal theory over the past two decades pose an implicit challenge to a cut-and-paste approach to the field of sex-based discrimination, by demonstrating the importance of the overall structure and assumptions of law, including the categories it uses to divide one area of law from another, in maintaining a gendered society. The organization of this book into different perspectives, each of which has different theoretical claims and practical aspirations, reflects the authors' view that what makes gender and law an academic subject worthy of a separate course of study is less the specific content of laws that are thought to have particular relevance to women, than the different ways of thinking about what the relationship between law and gender is, and ought to be, across legal categories.

The perspectives represented in this book are not mutually exclusive, nor are they fully formed or "total" theories of law and gender. They draw from and play off one another. The field is still in a healthy stage of evolution and has been changing through the life of each edition of this book. We have maintained the same six categories used in the first edition: formal equality, substantive equality, nonsubordination (or dominance theory), women's different voice(s), autonomy, and anti-essentialism. Each perspective draws on cases and readings from a cross-section of legal materials. Thus, for example, while much of Title VII is covered in Chapter 2 on formal equality, the issue of affirmative action is covered as an example of substantive equality in Chapter 3, issues of work and family are covered both in Chapter 3 and in relation to different voice theory in Chapter 5, the topic of sexual harassment appears in Chapter 4 as an example of nonsubordination theory, and the issue of bifurcating race and sex claims in Title VII cases exemplifies one type of "essentialism" in Chapter 7. Similarly, while the conventional "women's" subjects such as family law, employment, reproductive rights, and rape are well covered, the book also includes topics in civil procedure, legal ethics, federal sentencing guidelines, tort remedies, and other subject areas and interdisciplinary materials that help demonstrate the implications of the various frameworks at issue.

A few principles have guided the preparation of these materials. Their order is, for the most part, cumulative. For example, a student must understand the principles of formal equality before fully appreciating the impulse toward, and potential limitations of, substantive equality; similarly, knowledge of both formal and substantive equality is a prerequisite to a firm grasp of the concepts incorporated in the nonsubordination approach. The book is also interactive. In early chapters, the student is asked to consider questions for which later materials may give fuller answers; as the book progresses, the student is asked to return to questions previously examined under an earlier perspective. In this sense, the book is an ongoing unraveling and reweaving of interconnected designs, rather than a straight-seamed assembly of a single, finished fabric.

The approach of this book works best if the student attempts to be both open to, and critical of, each approach studied. As will become clear in this book, we find significant value *and* serious limitations in each of the perspectives presented. We urge students to join in the creative effort begun in these course materials to formulate approaches that offer the greatest potential for constructive social change. Toward this end, we welcome disagreement with whichever of our own preferences may surface in the textual notes or in the choice of cases and readings. On the other hand, it is our hope that the search for the *best* approach — an enterprise that usually emphasizes distinctions and contrasts — does not blind the student to the overlap and similarities between the various perspectives offered. It seems unlikely that social progress will be made on gender issues as a consequence of one perspective trumping another. The premise of this book is that a fuller understanding, and at least partial acceptance, of numerous perspectives on law and gender is the most promising precondition for meaningful reform.

A comment on the title of this book. Why "gender and law" instead of "sex and law"? The usual distinction between sex and gender is that sex refers to the biological basics distinguishing men and women, whereas gender refers to those cultural attributes that have come to be associated with the biological facts of sexual identification. This book is about both sex and gender, insofar as it addresses many rules and practices that make classifications based on an individual's sex — whether one *is* a man or a woman — and also attends to the social consequences of sex or gender. The deeper one gets into the sex-gender distinction, however, the more problematic it seems to be. As will be clear as the book proceeds, much about sex that is assumed to be biologically determined turns out to have social dimensions hidden from view. Moreover, even when the state refers in its laws unambiguously to men, or women, its decisions to do so are political or cultural acts, which both reflect and reinforce certain gendered under-standings and relationships. The book's title reflects its emphasis on the nature of these decisions.

Finally, a word on the editing of this book. Additions to, deletions from, and other alterations to quoted material are indicated by brackets and ellipses, except that footnotes and citations are deleted without notice. Where retained, the original footnote numbers are used. Paragraph breaks and the order of paragraphs are occassionally modified without notice to make edited excerpts coherent. Fuller presentation of the statutes most often referred to, usually in abbreviated form, in the text is found in the Statutory Appendix at the end of the book.

Katharine T. Bartlett
Angela P. Harris
Deborah L. Rhode

February 2002

Acknowledgments

With every edition, the circle of friends, colleagues, and students who have contributed to this book enlarges. I give special thanks to users who take the time to give us constructive suggestions. My research assistants this round — Julie Baldassano, Gina Dizzia, and Orit Gayerman — were, like their predecessors, wonderfully exact and hard working. I acknowledge also faculty, students, and staff of the Duke Law community who are understanding when my needs as a scholar sometimes crowd out my duties as dean.

With every edition, I also learn more and more. My coauthors helped me to see past my rather rigid notions of what this book ought to be while making major improvements to this edition. While this was a truly collaborative endeavor, Angela Harris took primary responsibility for Chapters 1 and 7, for the section in Chapter 3 on work and family, the section in Chapter 4 on domestic violence, and the introductory sections to Chapter 5. Our new collaborator for this edition, Deborah Rhode, added important material throughout the book on the legal profession and professional responsibility issues, and took primary responsibility for the sections in Chapter 4 on sexual harassment and pornography, and for the sections in Chapter 6 on rape and prostitution. I retained primary responsibility for Chapters 2 and 3, for the sections in Chapter 4 on same-sex marriage and gay and lesbian parenthood, for the sections in Chapter 5 on women jurors, criminal sentencing, and civil remedies, and for the sections in Chapter 6 on reproductive rights and poverty. The result is a book of intertwining visions and ideas about how the law does, and should, impact individuals on account of their gender, which we hope encourages students to form their own.

K.T.B.

My gratitude to the large, scattered, sometimes impromptu support system that kept me going while I worked on this third edition, providing me with music, encouragement, sympathy, and babysitting. I would also like to thank the many colleagues and friends who provided thoughtful criticism and ideas about how to make the book better, among them Kathy Abrams, Marjorie Shultz, Stephanie Wildman, and Joan Williams. Special thanks to my research assistants Robert Brayer, Andria Janos, and Donna Maeda, all of them pearls beyond price. The Boalt Hall Fund and Dean John Dwyer provided much-appreciated financial support. Finally, I would like to thank Ayn Lowry, my assistant, who spent many hours beyond the call of duty tracking down fugitive copyright holders, checking my cites, and raising my political consciousness.

A.P.H.

I am deeply grateful for the research assistance of David W. Knight, Marti McCausland, and Jonathan Sanders, and the manuscript preparation assistance of Mary Tye and Christian Steriti. I owe far greater debts to Kate Bartlett and Angela Harris for including me in a publication that I have admired from a distance and a collaborative relationship that has immeasurably enriched my personal and professional life.

D.L.R.

Katharine T. Bartlett & Jean O'Barr, The Chilly Climate on College Campuses: An Expansion of the "Hate Speech" Debate, Duke L.J. 574 (1990). Reprinted by permission.

Katharine T. Bartlett, Feminist Legal Methods, 103 Harv. L. Rev. 829 (1990). Copyright © 1990 by the Harvard Law Review Association. Reprinted by permission.

Norma Basch, In the Eyes of the Law: Women, Marriage, and Property in Nineteenth-Century New York. Copyright © 1992 by Cornell University. Used by permission of the publisher, Cornell University Press.

Mary E. Becker, Patriarchy and Inequality: Toward a Substantive Feminism, 1999 U. Chi. L. F. 21. Reprinted by permission.

Leslie Bender, A Lawyer's Primer on Feminist Theory and Tort, 38 J. Legal Educ. 3 (1988). Copyright © 1988 by the Association of American Law Schools. Reprinted by permission.

Leslie Bender, From Gender Difference to Feminist Solidarity: Using Carol Gilligan and an Ethic of Care in Law, 15 Vt. L. Rev. (1990). Reprinted by permission.

Bethany R. Berger, After Pocahontas: Indian Women and the Law, 1830 to 1934, 21 Am. Indian L. Rev. 1 (1997). Reprinted by permission.

Sharon Block, Lines of Color, Sex, and Service, in Sex, Love, Race: Crossing Boundaries in North American History (Martha Hodes ed., 1999). Reprinted by permission.

Mary A. Boutilier & Lucinda SanGiovanni, The Sporting Woman (1983). Reprinted by permission of authors.

Kingsley R. Browne, Sex and Temperament in Modern Society: A Darwinian View of the Glass Ceiling and the Gender Gap, 37 Ariz. L. Rev. 974 (1995). Copyright © 1996 by the Arizona Board of Regents. Reprinted by permission.

Martha Chamallas, Listening to Dr. Fiske: The Easy Case of *Price Waterhouse v. Hopkins*, 15 Vt. L. Rev. 89 (1990). Reprinted by permission.

Sumi K. Cho, Converging Stereotypes in Racialized Sexual Harassment: Where the Model Minority Meets Suzie Wong, 1 J. Gender, Race & Justice 177 (1977). Reprinted by permission.

Donna K. Coker, Heat of Passion and Wife Killing: Men Who Batter/Men Who Kill, 2 S. Cal. L. & Women's Stud. 71 (1992). Reprinted by the permission of the author and the Southern California Review of Law and Women's Studies.

Mary Coombs, Interrogating Identity, 11 Berkeley Women's L.J. 222 (1996). Copyright © 1996 by Berkeley Women's Law Journal. Reprinted by permission.

Nancy F. Cott, Public Vows: A History of Marriage and the Nation. Reprinted by permission of the publisher, Harvard University Press, Cambridge, Mass. Copyright © 2000 by Nancy F. Cott.

Shannon DeRouselle, Welfare Reform and the Administration for Children's Services: Subjecting Children and Families to Poverty and The Punishing Them For It, 25 N.Y.U. Rev. L. & Soc. Change 403 (1999). Reprinted by permission.

Ellen Carol Dubois, Outgrowing the Compact of the Fathers: Equal Rights, Woman Suffrage, and the United States Constitution, 1820-1878, 74 J. Amer. History 836 (Dec. 1987). Reprinted by permission of the Organization of American Historians.

Mary C. Dunlap, Sexual Speech and the State: Putting Pornography in Its Place, 17 Golden Gate U. L. Rev. 359 (1987). Reprinted by permission of the author and Golden Gate University Law Review.

Maxine Eichner, On Postmodern Feminist Legal Theory, 36 Harv. C.R.-C.L. L. Rev. 1 (2001). Reprinted by permission.

Richard A. Epstein, Gender Is for Nouns, 41 DePaul L. Rev. 981 (1992). Reprinted by permission.

Susan Estrich, Rape, 95 Yale L.J. 1087 (1986). Reprinted by permission of the author, The Yale Law Journal Company, and Fred B. Rothman & Company.

Holly B. Fechner, Three Stories of Prostitution in the West: Prostitutes' Groups, Law, and Feminist "Truth," 4 Colum. J. Gender & L. 26 (1994). Permission granted by the Columbia Journal of Gender & Law.

Lucinda Finley, Female Trouble: The Implications of Tort Reform for Women, 64 Tenn. L. Rev. 847 (1997). Reprinted by permission of the author and the Tennessee Law Review Association, Inc.

Martha Albertson Fineman, Cracking the Foundational Myths: Independence, Autonomy, and Self-Sufficiency, 8 Am U. J. Gender Pol'y & L. 13 (1999). Reprinted by permission.

Martha Albertson Fineman, Societal Factors Affecting the Creation of Legal Rules for Distribution of Property at Divorce. Reprinted from At the Boundaries of Law: Feminism and Legal Theory (Martha Albertson Fineman & Nancy Sweet Thomadsen eds., 1990), by permission of the author and Routledge, Inc., part of the Taylor & Francis Group.

Karla Fischer, Neil Vidmar, & Rene Ellis, The Culture of Battering and the Role of Mediation in Domestic Violence Cases, 46, SMU L. Rev. 2117 (1993). Reprinted by permission from the SMU Law Review and the Southern Methodist University School of Law.

Katherine M. Franke, Becoming a Citizen: Reconstruction Era Regulation of African American Marriages, 11 Yale J.L. Human. 251 (1999). Reprinted by permission of the author and the Yale Journal of Law & the Humanities.

Marilyn Frye, The Politics of Reality. Reprinted by permission from The Politics of Reality (Marilyn Frye ed., 1983). Copyright © 1983, The Crossing Press, Freedom, California.

Neil Gilbert, The Phantom Epidemic of Sexual Assault. Reprinted by permission from The Public Interest, No. 103 (Spring 1991), 54-61. Copyright © 1991 by National Affairs, Inc.

Evelyn N. Glenn, The Racial Division of Reproductive Labor, 18 Signs 1 (1992). Reprinted by permission of the author and the University of Chicago Press.

Ellen Goodman, Value Judgements. Reprinted by permission of International Creative Mangements, Inc. Copyright © 1993 by Ellen Goodman.

Ariela J. Gross, Beyond Black and White: Cultural Approaches to Slavery, 101 Colum. L. Rev. 640 (2001). Reprinted by permission.

Isabelle R. Gunning, Arrogant Perception, World-Traveling, and Multicultural Feminism: The Case of Female Genital Surgeries, 23 Colum. Human Rts. L. Rev. 189 (1991-1992). Reprinted by permission.

Heidi I. Hartmann, Patricia A. Roos, & Donald Treiman, An Agenda for Basic Research on Comparable Worth. Reprinted from Comparable Worth: New Directions for Research (Heidi I. Hartmann ed.) Reprinted by permission of the authors and National Academy Press, Washington, D.C.

L. Camille Hébert, The Economic Implications of Sexual Harassment for Women, 3 Kan. J. L. & Pol'y 41 (Spring 1994). Reprinted by permision.

Ronald K. Henry, "Primary Caretaker': Is It a Ruse?, 17 Fam. Advoc. 53 (Summer 1994). Copyright © 1995 American Bar Association. Reprinted by permission.

Tracey E. Higgins, "By Reason of Their Sex": Feminist Theory, Postmodernism, and Justice, 80 Cornell L. Rev. 1536 (1995). Reprinted by permission.

Joan W. Howarth, Deciding to Kill: Revealing the Gender in the Task Handed to Capital Jurors, 1994 Wis. L. Rev. 1345 (1994). Copyright © 1994 by the Board of Regents of the University of Wisconsin System. Reprinted by permission of the Wisconsin Law Review.

Nan D. Hunter & Sylvia A. Law, Brief Amici Curiae of Feminist Anti-Censorship Taskforce et al. In *American Booksellers Association v. Hudnut*, 21 U. Mich. J. L. Ref. 69 (Fall 1987-Winter 1988). Reprinted by permission.

Rosemary Hunter, Afterword: A Feminist Response to the Gender Gap in Compensation Symposium, 83 Geo. L.J. 147 (1993). Reprinted with the permission of the publisher, Georgetown University and Georgetown Law Journal, Copyright © 1994.

Emma Coleman Jordan, Race, Gender, and Social Class in the Thomas Sexual Harassment Hearings: The Hidden Fault Lines in Political Discourse, 15 Harv. Women's L.J. 1 (1992). Copyright © 1992 by the President and Fellows of Harvard College. Reprinted with permission.

Jonathan Ned Katz, Gay/Lesbian Almanac (1983). Reprinted in William Rubenstein, Lesbians, Gay Men, and the Law 50-51 (1993). Reprinted by permission.

Herma Hill Kay, Equality and Difference: The Case of Pregnancy, 1 Berkeley Women's L.J. 1 (1985). Copyright © 1985 by California Law Review. Reprinted by permission.

Alice Kessler-Harris, Out to Work: The History of Wage-Earning Women in the United States. Copyright © (1982) by Alice Kessler-Harris. Used by permission of the author and Oxford University Press, Inc.

Karen M. Kramer, Note, Rule by Myth: The Social and Legal Dynamics Governing Alcohol-Related Acquaintance Rape, 47 Stan. L. Rev. 115 (1994). Copyright © 1994 by the Board of Trustees of the Leland Stanford Junior University.

Linda Hamilton Krieger, The Content of Our Categories, 47 Stan. L. Rev. 1161 (1995). Reprinted by permission.

Jane E. Larson, "Women Understand So Little, They Call My Good Nature 'Deceit'": A Feminist Rethinking of Seduction, 93 Colum. L Rev. 374 (1993). Reprinted by permission.

Gerda Lerner, The Meanings of Seneca Falls, 1848-1998, 45 Dissent 34 (Fall 1998). Reprinted by permission of the author.

Nancy Levit, Feminism for Men: Legal Ideology and the Construction of Maleness. Reprinted with permission of the author. Originally published in 43 UCLA L. Rev. 1037. Copyright © 1996, The Regents of the University of California. All Rights Reserved.

Dorchen Liedholdt, Prostitution: A Violation of Women's Human Rights, 1 Cardozo Women's L.J. 133 (1993). Reprinted by permission.

Catharine A. MacKinnon, Disputing Male Sovereignty: On *United States v. Morrison*, 114 Harv. L. Rev. 135 (2000).

Catharine A. MacKinnon, Feminism Unmodified: Discourses on Life and Law. Reprinted by permission from Feminism Unmodified: Discourses on Life and Law by Catharine A. MacKinnon, Cambridge, Mass: Harvard University Press. Copyright © 1987 by the President and Fellows of Harvard College.

Catharine A. MacKinnon, Pornography as Defamation and Discrimination, 71 B.U. L. Rev. 793 (1991). Reprinted with permission of the author and Boston University Law Review.

Catharine A. MacKinnon, Sexual Harassment of Working Women (1979). Reprinted by permission of the author and Yale University Press.

Catharine A. MacKinnon, Toward a Feminist Theory of the State. Reprinted by permission from Toward a Feminist Theory of the State by Catharine A. MacKinnon, Cambridge, Mass: Harvard University Press. Copyright © 1989 by Catharine A. MacKinnon.

Martha R. Mahoney, Legal Images of Battered Women: Redefining the Issue of Separation, 90 Mich. L. Rev. 4 (1991). Copyright © 1991 by

The Michigan Law Review Association. Reprinted with permission of the author and Michigan Law Review.

Toni M. Massaro, Gay Rights, Thick and Thin, 49 Stan. L. Rev. 45 (1996). Copyright © 1996 by the Board of Trustees of the Leland Stanford Junior University.

Mari J. Matsuda, Beside My Sister, Facing the Enemy: Legal Theory Out of Coalition, 43 Stan. L. Rev. 1183 (1991). Reprinted by permission.

Linda C. McClain, The Domain of Civil Virtue in a Good Society: Families, Schools, and Sex Equality, 69 Fordham L. Rev. 1617 (2001). Reprinted by permission.

Eileen L. McDonagh, My Body, My Consent: Securing the Constitutional Right to Abortion Funding, 62 Albany L. Rev. 1057 (1999). Reprinted by permission.

Carrie Menkel-Meadow, Portia in a Different Voice: Speculation on a Woman's Lawyering Process, 1 Berkeley Women's L.J. 39 (1985). Copyright © 1985 by California Law Review, Inc. Reprinted by permission.

Carlin Meyer, Sex, Sin, and Women's Liberation: Against Porn-Suppression, 72 Tex. L. Rev. 1097 (1994). Copyright © 1994 by the Texas Law Review Association. Reprinted by permission.

Jennifer Nedelsky, Reconceiving Autonomy: Sources, Thought, and Possibilities, 1 Yale J.L. & Feminism 7 (1989). Reprinted by permission of the author and the Yale Journal of Law and Feminism, Inc.

Note, Invisible Man: Black and Male Under Title VII, 104 Harv. L. Rev. 749 (1991). Reprinted by permission.

Michelle Oberman, Turning Girls Into Women: Re-evaluating Modern Statutory Rape Law, 85 J. Crim. & Criminology 15 (1994). Reprinted by special permission of Northwestern University School of Law, Journal of Criminal Law and Crimonology, vol. 85, issue 1, 32-33, 65-66, 70 (1994).

L. Amede Obiora, Bridges and Barricades: Rethinking Polemics and Intransigence in the Campaign Against Female Circumcision, 47 Case W. Res. L. Rev. 275 (1997). Copyright: Case Western Reserve Law Review. Reprinted by permission.

Nell Irvin Painter, Sojourner Truth: A Life, A Symbol (1996). Copyright © 1996 by Nell Irvin Painter. Reprinted by permission of W. W. Norton & Company, Inc.

Peggy Pascoe, Race, Gender, and the Privileges of Property, in New Viewpoints in Women's History (Linda K. Kerber & Jan Sherron De Hart eds., 2000). Reprinted by permission.

Theda Perdue, Cherokee Women and the Trail of Tears, 1 J. Women's History 14 (Spring 1989). Copyright © 1989 Journal of Women's History. Reprinted with permission of author and the Indiana University Press.

Richard A. Posner, Conservative Feminism 1989 U. Chi. Legal F. 191. Reprinted by permission.

Margaret Jane Radin, The Pragmatist and the Feminist, 63 S. Cal. L. Rev. 1699 (1990). Reprinted with the permission of the author and Southern California Law Review.

Milton C. Regan, Jr., Divorce Reform and the Legacy of Gender, 90 Mich. L. Rev. 1453 (1992). Reprinted by permission.

Judith Resnik, On the Bias: Feminist Reconsiderations of the Aspirations for Our Judges, 61 S. Cal. L. Rev. 1877 (1988). Reprinted with the permission of the Southern California Law Review and the author.

Deborah L. Rhode, Speaking of Sex: The Denial of Gender Inequality (1997). Reprinted by permission of the Harvard University Press. Copyright © 1997 by Deborah L. Rhode.

Deborah L. Rhode, Occupational Inequality, Duke L.J. 1207 (1988). Reprinted by permission.

Cookie Ridolfi, Statement on Representing Rape Defendants, unpublished manuscript, July 26, 1989, Santa Clara University School of Law. Reprinted by permission.

Dorothy E. Roberts, Punishing Drug Addicts Who Have Babies: Women of Color, Equality, and the Right of Privacy, 104 Harv. L. Rev. 1419 (1991). Copyright © 1991 by the Harvard Law Review Association. Reprinted with permission of the author and the Harvard Law Review.

Dorothy Roberts, Spiritual and Menial Housework, 9 Yale J. L. & Feminism 51 (1997). Reprinted by permission of the Yale Journal of Law & Feminism, Inc., from the Yale Journal of Law & Feminism.

Cristina M. Rodriguez, Clearing the Smoke-Filled Room: Women Jurors and the Disruption of an Old-Boys' Network in Nineteenth-Century America, 108 Yale L.J. 1805 (1999). Reprinted by permission of The Yale Law Journal Company and William S. Hein Company.

Katie Roiphe, The Morning After. Copyright © 1993 by Katherine Anne Roiphe. By permission of Little, Brown and Company, Inc.

Carol M. Rose, Women and Property: Gaining and Losing Ground, 78 Va. L. Rev. 421 (1992). Reprinted with permission of the author, Virginia Law Review Association, and Fred B. Rothman & Company.

Gayle Rubin, The Traffic in Women, in Toward an Anthropology of Women (Rayna R. Reiter ed., 1995). Reprinted by permission.

Judy Scales-Trent, Black Women and the Constitution: Finding Our Place, Asserting Our Rights, 24 Harv. C.R.-C.L. L. Rev. 9 (1989). Copyright © 1989 by the President and Fellows of Harvard College and the Harvard Civil Rights-Civil Liberties Law Review.

Judy Scales-Trent, Equal Rights Advocates: Addressing the Legal Issues of Women of Color, 3 Berkeley Women's L.J. 34 (1998). Reprinted by permission.

Kim Lane Scheppele, The Re-Vision of Rape Law, 54 U. Chi. L. Rev. 1095 (1987). Reprinted by permission.

Elizabeth M. Schneider, The Violence of Privacy, 23 Conn. L. Rev. 973 (1991). Reprinted by permission of the author and Connecticut Law Review.

Vicki Schultz, Life's Work, 100 Colum. L. Rev. 1881 (2000). Copyright © Vicki Schultz. Reprinted by permission.

Marjorie Maguire Shultz, Reproductive Technology and Intent-Based Parenthood: An Opportunity for Gender Neutrality, 1990 Wis. L. Rev. 297. Copyright © 1990 by Wisconsin Law Review. Reprinted by permission.

Reva Siegel, Reasoning from the Body: A Historical Perspective on Abortion Regulation and Questions of Equal Protection, 44 Stan. L. Rev. 261 (1992). Copyright © 1992 by the Board of Trustees of the Leland Stanford Junior University.

Katharine Silbaugh, Turning Labor into Love: Housework and the Law, 91 NW U. L. Rev. 1 (1996). Reprinted by permission.

Jana B. Singer, Alimony and Efficiency: The Gendered Costs and Benefits of the Economic Justification for Alimony, 82 Geo. L.J. 2428 (1994).

Rickie Solinger, Wake Up Little Susie: Single Pregnancy and Race before *Roe v. Wade* (1992). Copyright © 1992. Reproduced by permission of Routledge, Inc., part of The Taylor & Francis Group.

Elizabeth Cady Stanton, Susan B. Anthony, & Matilda Joslyn Gage, eds., History of Women's Suffrage (1985 reprint edition), Declaration of Sentiments: Address of Elizabeth Cady Stanton to the New York Legislature, Feb. 14, 1854; Reminiscences by Frances D. Gage of Sojourner Truth & Susan B. Anthony's trial comments. Reprinted by permission of Ayer Company Publishers, Inc., P.O. Box 958, Salem, N.H., 03079.

Susan Sturm, Second Generation Employment Discrimination: A Structural Approach, 101 Colum. L. Rev. 458 (2001). Reprinted by permission.

Susan Sturn & Lani Guinier, The Future of Affirmative Action: Reclaiming the Innovative Ideal, 84 Cal. L. Rev. 953 (1996). Copyright © 1996 by California Law Review, Inc. Reprinted by permission.

Rena K. Uviller, Father's Rights and Feminism: The Maternal Presumption Revisited, 1 Harv. Women's L.J. 107 (1978). Copyright © 1978 by the President and Fellows of Harvard College.

Leti Volpp, Feminism Versus Multiculturalism, 101 Colum. L. Rev. 1881 (2001). Reprinted by permission.

Amy L. Wax, Against Nature — On Robert Wright's "The Moral Animal," 63 U. Chi. L. Rev. 307 (1996). Reprinted by permission.

Carol Weisbrod, Images of the Woman Juror, 9 Harv. Women's L.J. 59 (1986). Copyright © 1986 by the President and Fellows of Harvard College. Permission granted by the author and the Harvard Women's Law Journal.

Robin L. West, The Difference in Women's Hedonic Lives: A Phenomenological Critique of Feminist Legal Theory, 3 Wis. Women's L.J. 81 (1987). Reprinted by permission.

Robin L. West, Feminism in the Law: Theory, Practice, and Criticism, 1989 U. Chi. Legal F. 59. Reprinted by permission.

Robin L. West, Jurisprudence and Gender, 55 U. Chi. L. Rev. 1 (1988). Reprinted by permission.

Robin L. West, The Supreme Court 1989 Term, Foreword: Taking Freedom Seriously, 104 Harv. L. Rev. 43 (1990). Reprinted by permission.

Joan Williams, Toward a Reconstructive Feminism: Reconstructing the Relationship of Market Work and Family Work, 19 N. Ill. U. L. Rev. 89 (1998). Reprinted by permission.

Joan Williams, Unbending Gender: Why Family and Work Conflict and What Do To About It. Copyright © 1999 by Oxford University Press. Used by permission of Oxford University Press, Inc.

Wendy W. Williams, The Equality Crisis: Some Reflections on Culture, Courts, and Feminism, 7 Women's Rts. L. Rep. 175 (1982). Reprinted with permission of the author and the Women's Rights Law Reporter.

Gender and Law

1

Foundations of Women's Legal Subordination

A. THEORIZING SUBORDINATION

This chapter examines the foundations of women's subordinate status in American law. These foundations have roots in many religious and secular sources, including Judeo-Christian traditions, English common law, the frontier conditions of colonial America, and the American plantation economy of the eighteenth- and nineteenth-century South. The materials in this chapter do not present a comprehensive overview of women's legal history. Instead, the readings offer a series of snapshots, many taken in the mid- to late-nineteenth century — a time of ferment that arguably did much to shape women's status today.

Before examining these historical sources, however, it may be helpful to consider the meaning of the term "subordination" itself and its common synonyms, such as "oppression." What do these words mean? Are women oppressed? If so, what does women's oppression look like?

Marilyn Frye, *The Politics of Reality:*
Essays in Feminist Theory
1-2, 8-10, 13 (1983)

It is a fundamental claim of feminism that women are oppressed. The word "oppression" is a strong word. It repels and attracts. It is dangerous and dangerously fashionable and endangered. It is much misused, and sometimes not innocently. . . .

. . . Human beings can be miserable without being oppressed, and it is perfectly consistent to deny that a person or group is oppressed without denying that they have feelings or that they suffer. . . . [I]f one wants to determine whether a particular suffering, harm or limitation is part of someone's being oppressed, one has to look at it in context in order to tell

1

whether it is an element in an oppressive structure: one has to see if it is part of an enclosing structure of forces and barriers which tends to the immobilization and reduction of a group or category of people. One has to look at how the barrier or force fits with others and to whose benefit or detriment it works. As soon as one looks at examples, it becomes obvious that not everything which frustrates or limits a person is oppressive, and not every harm or damage is due or contributes to oppression.

A great many people, female and male and of every race and class, simply do not believe that woman is a category of oppressed people, and I think that this is in part because they have been fooled by the dispersal and assimilation of women throughout and into the systems of class and race which organize men. Our simply being dispersed makes it difficult for women to have knowledge of each other and hence difficult to recognize the shape of our common cage. The dispersal and assimilation of women throughout economic classes and races also divides us against each other practically and economically and thus attaches interest to the inability to see: for some, jealousy of their benefits, and for some, resentment of the others' advantages.

To get past this, it helps to notice that in fact women of all races and classes are together in a ghetto of sorts. There is a women's place, a sector, which is inhabited by women of all classes and races, and it is not defined by geographical boundaries but by function. The function is the service of men and men's interests as men define them, which includes the bearing and rearing of children. The details of the service and the working conditions vary by race and class, for men of different races and classes have different interests, perceive their interests differently, and express their needs and demands in different rhetorics, dialects and languages. But there are also some constants. . . .

The boundary that sets apart women's sphere is maintained and promoted by men generally for the benefit of men generally, and men generally do benefit from its existence, even the man who bumps into it and complains of the inconvenience. That barrier is protecting his classification and status as a male, as superior, as having a right to sexual access to a female or females. It protects a kind of citizenship which is superior to that of females of his class and race, his access to a wider range of better paying and higher status work, and his right to prefer unemployment to the degradation of doing lower status or "women's" work.

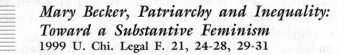

Mary Becker, Patriarchy and Inequality: Toward a Substantive Feminism
1999 U. Chi. Legal F. 21, 24-28, 29-31

Allan Johnson, a sociologist working in masculinities, calls our male-centered, male-identified, male-dominated social structure "patriarchy" and identifies male distrust and fear of other men as patriarchy's core motivating force. Patriarchal culture values "control and domination" most, because control and domination of other men ensures one's own safety from them. In Allan Johnson's words:

> What drives Patriarchy as a system — what fuels competition, aggression, and oppression — is a dynamic relationship between control and fear. Patriarchy encourages men to seek security, status, and other rewards through control; to fear other men's ability to control and harm them; and to identify being in control as both their best defense against loss and humiliation and the surest route to what they need and desire. In this sense, although we usually think of patriarchy in terms of women and men, it is more about what goes on among men. The oppression of women is certainly an important part of patriarchy, but, paradoxically, it may not be the point of patriarchy.[1]

Although oppression of women is not the point of patriarchy, a social system that is male-identified, male-controlled, male-centered will inevitably value masculinity and masculine traits over femininity and feminine traits. In such a system, men (and women) will be encouraged to regard women as beings suited to fulfill male needs. . . .

Women's inequality cannot be adequately addressed simply by working to get women "a bigger piece of the pie."[2] If this is all we do, some women will succeed. But the women who succeed will be those who are male-centered and male-identified; who conform to patriarchal values; and who do not seriously threaten the patriarchal order. Moreover, these women will themselves contribute to the oppression of other races, classes, and ethnicities, and of women who are less male-centered and male-identified and who are therefore more threatening to the status quo.

Although women as well as men are encouraged to adopt patriarchal values and perspectives, patriarchy is not a stable, all-powerful system. Countless opportunities for resistance exist. An individual man can refuse to participate in discussions rating women as "babes" or in terms of body parts. Or he can insist that the point made by a female colleague at a meeting is a good one when others ignore it (until it is made by a man). He can even do his share of the housework, cleaning, and child care. A woman can refuse to interact with male colleagues in flirtatious ways, assuaging male egos. Or she too can insist that a point made by a female colleague at a meeting (and ignored) is an important one.

As this analysis suggests, patriarchy is not stable, but ever-changing in response to resistance. It is also resilient. Patriarchal social structures have been tribal, monarchical, and totalitarian; dictatorial and democratic; nomadic, feudal, capitalist, and socialist; religious and atheistic; primitive and post-modern; tolerant and repressive of pornography. . . .

---

1. [Allan G. Johnson, The Gender Knot: Unraveling Our Patriarchal Legacy 26 (Temple 1997).]
2. Id. at 249.

Although the subjugation of women is not the central dynamic driving patriarchy, patriarchal culture is deeply misogynistic and valorizes masculinity. . . .

Women play a number of important roles in patriarchal culture, though those roles often vary with race, class, and other "differences." Perhaps most basic is the use of women and femininity to define men and masculinity. Men are men to the extent they are not women: masculine, independent, invulnerable, tough, strong, aggressive, powerful, commanding, in control, rational, and non-emotional. "Real women" (that is, middle- or upper-middle-class white women) are dependent, vulnerable, pliant, weak, supportive, nurturing, intuitive, emotional, and empathic. "Real women" and "real men" are essentially different in patriarchal culture.

A woman can be a trophy, symbolizing and signaling a man's success against and to other men. Most men are far from the top of the patriarchal hierarchy of control and power; women are important as consolation prizes, giving men who have little someone over whom they have rights of power and control. In patriarchy, women are expected to "take care of men who have been damaged by other men."[3] When men fail, as they must, "women are also there to accept the blame and receive men's disappointment, pain, and rage."[4]

Women assuage male egos, reflecting men back at "twice their natural size." Women assure men that they are real men by deferring to them, by allowing them to set the agenda and do most of the talking, and by stroking their egos in countless other ways. In women's eyes, men see themselves as they should be: independent, autonomous, strong, and successful. Heterosexual men expect to see only themselves and their own needs reflected back in relationships with individual women. But it is not ultimately women who confirm manhood; in the end, men depend on other men — "coaches, friends, teammates, co-workers, sports figures, fathers, or mentors" — for such assurances.[5]

Men use women to bond with each other through shared participation in demeaning and devaluing women. This can be done through extreme means, such as gang rape, or more subtle ones, such as telling sexist jokes or judging women's bodies or rating them as "babes." Participation in college fraternities, football teams, and other male groups that demean women is basic training for masculinity under patriarchy. Even men who don't actively participate in such rituals are complicit: rare is the man who always objects to such camaraderie. Whether active or passive in these all-male groups, men are pressured to adopt demeaning attitudes toward women in order to confirm their membership in the masculine brotherhood. . . .

3. Id. at 37.
4. Id.
5. Id. at 31.

In a patriarchal culture, there is a strong tendency to deny conflicts of interest between women and men despite obvious inequalities in the allocation of responsibilities and scarce resources. For example, Arlie Hochschild has documented the tendency of working parents to deny inequality in their marriages, despite the fact that the women in the families she studied worked the equivalent of an extra month a year.[6] Because women and men live together in intimate relationships as parents and children or husbands and wives, we are reluctant to admit conflicts of interest. And it is easy to deny conflicts of interest because patriarchy justifies inequalities and injustices, even violence, in terms of women's choices and defects: if women get what they choose or deserve, we need not worry about conflicts of interest nor that mostly male decisionmakers divide the pie.

As the dominant group, men (still) fear women: women can rebel and retaliate. This fear, along with guilt, fosters misogyny, a condition which "can be seen as a cultural result of men's potential to feel guilty about women's oppression." But men love and need women as well, creating a dangerous emotional mix: "When love and need are bound up with fear and envy, hate and resentment, the result is an explosive mixture that can twist our sense of ourselves and one another beyond recognition."[7] Sadistic pornography and much domestic violence are more understandable when one considers how love, need, fear, envy, hate, and resentment combine in the feelings of many men toward women. . . .

Although men cannot be oppressed as men in a patriarchal society, men tend not to feel privileged. Part of the explanation is that patriarchal power has become increasingly institutionalized. In pre-capitalist patriarchies, power "was often directly exercised by individual patriarchs. . . ." In our late capitalist patriarchy, "men collectively exercise power over women, but are themselves as individuals increasingly under the domination of [increasingly institutional] patriarchal powers."[8] Most men, even white men, are far from the top of the patriarchal order, particularly at work. Many men are severely oppressed as members of certain racial or class groups. And some of the ways in which men feel less than powerful are attributable to the costs of conforming to patriarchal ideals of manhood, such as basing self-worth on performance, hiding doubts and vulnerabilities, and repressing feelings. But the fact that many men do not feel privileged does not prove that men are not privileged.

Those with privilege are often oblivious; it is those without privilege who are likely to notice. Privilege is not a pronouncement from on high that

6. [Arlie Hochschild, The Second Shift: Working Parents and the Revolution at Home 33-58 (1989) (discussing a family in which wife does more than husband but the arrangement is described as "equal" because of their commitment to equality).]

7. Johnson, The Gender Knot, at 41.

8. Harry Brod, Pornography and the Alienation of Male Sexuality, in Larry May, Robert Strikwerrda and Patrick D. Hopkins, eds., Rethinking Masculinity: Philosophical Explorations in Light of Feminism 237, 245 (1996).

"this is my Son, my Beloved, on whom my favour rests; listen to Him." As Allan Johnson has noted, "Privilege can be something as simple as being heard and taken seriously when we say something, of being served promptly and courteously in a store or restaurant, or of being free to move around or express an opinion."[9] Common courtesy becomes privilege when it is unevenly distributed between groups, elevating some over others.

Gayle Rubin, The Traffic in Women: Notes on the "Political Economy" of Sex, in Toward an Anthropology of Women
157, 179-180, 182, 184-185, 193, 199-200, 209-210 (Rayna R. Reiter ed., 1975)

At the most general level, the social organization of sex rests upon gender, obligatory heterosexuality, and the constraint of female sexuality.

Gender is a socially imposed division of the sexes. It is a product of the social relations of sexuality. Kinship systems rest upon marriage. They therefore transform males and females into "men" and "women," each an incomplete half which can only find wholeness when united with the other. Men and women are, of course, different. But they are not as different as day and night, earth and sky, yin and yang, life and death. In fact, from the standpoint of nature, men and women are closer to each other than either is to anything else — for example, mountains, kangaroos, or coconut palms. The idea that men and women are more different from one another than either is from anything else must come from somewhere other than nature. Furthermore, although there is an average difference between males and females on a variety of traits, the range of variation of those traits shows considerable overlap. There will always be some women who are taller than some men, for instance, even though men are on the average taller than women. But the idea that men and women are two mutually exclusive categories must arise out of something other than a nonexistent "natural" opposition. Far from being an expression of natural differences, exclusive gender identity is the suppression of natural similarities. It requires repression: in men, of whatever is the local version of "feminine" traits; in women, of the local definition of "masculine" traits. The division of the sexes has the effect of repressing some of the personality characteristics of virtually everyone, men and women. . . .

Furthermore, individuals are engendered in order that marriage be guaranteed. . . . If biological and hormonal imperatives were as overwhelming as popular mythology would have them, it would hardly be necessary to insure heterosexual unions by means of economic interdependency. More-

9. Johnson, The Gender Knot, at 175.

over, the incest taboo presupposes a prior, less articulate taboo on homosexuality. A prohibition against some heterosexual unions assumes a taboo against non-heterosexual unions. Gender is not only an identification with one sex; it also entails that sexual desire be directed toward the other sex. The sexual division of labor is implicated in both aspects of gender — male and female it creates them, and it creates them heterosexual. The suppression of the homosexual component of human sexuality, and by corollary, the oppression of homosexuals, is therefore a product of the same system whose rules and relations oppress women. [Rubin acknowledges that some societies recognize third genders (neither male nor female); others allow men to take on female roles, or vice versa; and still others permit individuals ritually to change their originally assigned sex. However, she argues, these societies still treat the division between men and women as fundamental.]

Kinship systems dictate some sculpting of the sexuality of both sexes. But . . . more constraint is applied to females when they are pressed into the service of kinship than to males. If women are exchanged, in whatever sense we take the term, marital debts are reckoned in female flesh. A woman must become the sexual partner of some man to whom she is owed as return on a previous marriage. If a girl is promised in infancy, her refusal to participate as an adult would disrupt the flow of debts and promises. It would be in the interests of the smooth and continuous operation of such a system if the woman in question did not have too many ideas of her own about whom she might want to sleep with. From the standpoint of the system, the preferred female sexuality would be one which responded to the desire of others, rather than one which actively desired and sought a response. . . .

. . . Psychoanalysis contains a unique set of concepts for understanding men, women, and sexuality. It is a theory of sexuality in human society. Most importantly, psychoanalysis produces a description of the mechanisms by which the sexes are divided and deformed, of how bisexual, androgynous infants are transformed into boys and girls. . . .

The Oedipal crisis is precipitated by certain items of information. The children discover the differences between the sexes, and that each child must become one or the other gender. They also discover the incest taboo, and that some sexuality is prohibited — in this case, the mother is unavailable to either child because she "belongs" to the father. Lastly, they discover that the two genders do not have the same sexual "rights" or futures.

[Rubin notes that the much popularized theory of "penis envy" posits that little girls feel deprived by not having a penis. However, in Freudian and Lacanian theory little boys and girls wish for penises only because of the sexual and social power and status that the physical organ represents. Psychoanalysts use the word "phallus" to describe the power of male social status symbolized by the physical penis. To possess "the phallus" is to possess all of the social-sexual-cultural-familial rights and privileges accorded to anatomical males in Western society. Understood this way, the Oedipal crisis is the moment when little boys and little girls alike realize that only people with penises are going to inherit this powerful set of rights and privileges. Moreover, from this perspective, "penis envy," lesbianism, and tomboyism are all strategies a little girl may adopt to express resentment at — or challenge — this injustice. Thus, Rubin argues, "Freud suggests that there are three alternate routes out of the Oedipal catastrophe. The girl may simply freak out, repress sexuality altogether, and become asexual. She may protest, cling to her narcissism and desire, and become either 'masculine' or homosexual. Or she may accept the situation, sign the social contract, and attain 'normality.'"]

Human sexual life will always be subject to convention and human intervention. It will never be completely "natural," if only because our species is social, cultural, and articulate. . . . But the mechanisms and aims of this process need not be largely independent of conscious choice. Cultural evolution provides us with the opportunity to seize control of the means of sexuality, reproduction, and socialization, and to make conscious decisions to liberate human sexual life from the archaic relationships which deform it. Ultimately, a thoroughgoing feminist revolution would liberate more than women. It would liberate forms of sexual expression, and it would liberate human personality from the straightjacket of gender. . . .

[S]exual systems cannot, in the final analysis, be understood in complete isolation. A full-bodied analysis of women in a single society, or throughout history, must take everything into account: the evolution of commodity forms in women, systems of land tenure, political arrangements, subsistence technology, etc. Equally important, economic and political analyses are incomplete if they do not consider women, marriage, and sexuality. Traditional concerns of anthropology and social science — such as the evolution of social stratification and the origin of the state — must be reworked to include the implications of matrilateral cross-cousin marriage, surplus extracted in the form of daughters, the conversion of female labor into male wealth, the conversion of female lives into marriage alliances, the contribution of marriage to political power, and the transformations which all of these varied aspects of society have undergone in the course of time.

Notes

1. Defining Oppression. What is "oppression"? Are there differences in the definitions these authors use?

Iris Marion Young points out that due to the influence of "the new left social movements of the 1960s and 1970s," the meaning of oppression has shifted. The term originally referred to political tyranny, as in a dictatorship.

> In its new usage, oppression designates the disadvantage and injustice some
> people suffer not because a tyrannical power coerces them, but because of the

everyday practices of a well-intentional liberal society. . . . In this extended structural sense oppression refers to the vast and deep injustices some groups suffer as a consequence of often unconscious assumptions and reactions of well-meaning people in ordinary interactions, media and cultural stereotypes, and structural features of bureaucratic hierarchies and market mechanisms — in short, the normal processes of everyday life.

Iris Marion Young, Justice and the Politics of Difference 41 (1990). Young identifies five "faces" of oppression — exploitation, marginalization, powerlessness, cultural imperialism, and violence. Exploitation refers to "a steady process of the transfer of the results of the labor of one social group to benefit another." Id. at 49. Marginalization involves the expulsion of a category of people from "useful participation in social life," thus making them vulnerable to "severe material deprivation and even extermination." Id. at 53. Powerlessness names the situation of people who "must take orders and rarely have the right to give them." Id. at 56. Powerless people lack the authority, status, and sense of self that professionals have, and lack access to "respectability." Id. at 57.

To experience cultural imperialism, Young argues, is "to experience how the dominant meanings of a society render the particular perspective of one's own group invisible at the same time as they stereotype one's group and mark it out as the Other." Id. at 58-59. Finally, by violence Young refers not only to forms of physical violence to which certain groups are uniquely vulnerable, but also to verbal and nonverbal harassment.

Can you identify social groups in contemporary life that suffer one or more of these "faces" of oppression? Are women oppressed under this account, and, if so, in what ways? Young suggests that her account of oppression makes comparative analysis potentially richer, because rather than asking simply whether one group is more or less oppressed than another, it becomes possible to compare and contrast various types of oppression.

Can individuals be described as "oppressed"? Young argues that only groups of people can experience oppression or privilege, not individuals. Would you describe yourself as a member of one or more groups that are "oppressed"? If so, what are those groups and in what ways are they oppressed?

Can you identify groups in contemporary social life that fit Frye's or Young's understanding of oppression, whether or not you are a member? How would you analyze that oppression using Young's categories? Are Young's categories useful? Do they leave certain "faces" of oppression out? To what extent can women be plausibly described as oppressed under Young's analysis?

2. Men, Oppression, and Patriarchy. Are men an oppressed group? If not, are they an oppressing group? A privileged group? Becker suggests that "patriarchy" is a social institution that primarily structures relationships among groups of men. Are low-status men nevertheless "privileged"?

Can individual men reject their male privilege? Can a man be a feminist?

3. Multiple Oppression and Social Theory. What is the relationship between the oppression of women and the oppression of other groups, such as groups oppressed along lines of race, class, and sexuality? The attempt to understand this relationship has led to highly contentious divisions among feminists. For more on this issue, see Chapter 7.

4. Oppression and Group Identity. Is the central problem of oppression that groups are treated unequally? Or is it that organizing people into groups is inherently problematic? Classic liberal theory suggests that treating people as members of groups rather than as individuals is an injustice. On this account,

> social groups are invidious fictions, essentializing arbitrary attributes. . . . [P]roblems of prejudice, stereotyping, discrimination, and exclusion exist because some people mistakenly believe that group identification makes a difference to the capacities, temperament, or virtues of group members. . . . Eliminating oppression thus requires eliminating groups. People should be treated as individuals, not as members of groups, and allowed to form their lives freely without stereotypes or group norms.

Young at 46-47.

While many people in the present day are willing to argue that we should stop treating racial minorities as members of groups and that in an ideal world "race" would be meaningless, far fewer people seem willing to argue that classifying people by gender is an inherent injustice, or that sexual difference would be meaningless in an ideal world. Is this a failure of imagination? Should gender itself be abolished? Rubin's article suggests that sexual difference is exaggerated to serve social purposes. What would life be like without that exaggeration? Would men and women be exactly the same? In the ideal society, would there be less emphasis on classifying everyone in terms of male and female? Would sex be something like eye color?

For a classic legal and philosophical comparison of these two views of sexual equality — equality as the meaninglessness of sexual difference, and equality as fair treatment of admittedly "different" genders — see Richard A. Wasserstrom, Racism, Sexism, and Preferential Treatment: An Approach to the Topics, 24 UCLA L. Rev. 581 (1977); Alison Jaggar, On Sexual Equality, 84 Ethics 275, 291 (1974) ("And when people complain that you can't tell the boys from the girls nowadays, the feminist response must be to point out that it should make no difference. As Florynce Kennedy demanded, 'Why do they want to know anyway? So that they can discriminate?' ").

Of course, as Jaggar notes, whether feminists should strive for a society in which sexual difference is meaningless depends in part on whether there are irremediable biological differences between males and females. For readings that tackle this question, see Chapter 5.

5. Identifying the Aim of Feminism.   So, is the task of feminism to abolish the sex/gender system? Or does being a feminist mean simply to fight for the category "women" to have the same dignity and respect as the category "men"? For more on this question, see Chapter 7.

Do you describe yourself as a feminist? Why or why not? How should feminism be defined? Ask yourself this question again at the end of the course.

B. ELEMENTS OF WOMEN'S LEGAL SUBORDINATION

As the previous section suggested, subordination may take many forms. Sometimes the forms subordination takes are *material*: members of a subordinated group have less money, cannot own property, or are themselves classified as property. Sometimes subordination takes *symbolic*, or *ideological* forms, as when subordinated groups are said to possess certain characteristics that make them less valuable to society than dominant groups or are excluded from certain social rituals.

As you examine the historical materials that follow, ask yourself several questions. Within what kinds of structures of subordination have women found themselves? To what extent have women been divided, as well as united, by experiences of subordination, and what constitutes those lines of division? How has the law contributed to women's subordination in United States history? To what extent are those contributions ideological and to what extent material? To what extent is the past not really past at all?

The readings in this section cluster around the theme of marriage in American legal history. In many ways, the institution of marriage has been the central defining institution in Anglo-American women's political and economic lives, as well as in their personal lives. Marriage has helped determine the economic fate of individual women, and regulated the access to wealth of women as a class. In tandem with immigration policy, marriage policy has helped shape the body of "We, the People" of the United States. Marriage has also long been an important ideological institution. As historian Nancy F. Cott points out, "By incriminating some marriages and encouraging others, marital regulations have drawn lines among the citizenry and defined what kinds of sexual relations and which families will be legitimate." Nancy F. Cott, Public Vows: A History of Marriage and the

Nation 4 (2000); see generally Herma Hill Kay, From the Second Sex to the Joint Venture: An Overview of Women's Rights and Family Law in the United States During the Twentieth Century, 88 Cal. L. Rev. 2017 (2000).

1. Introduction

Forbush v. Wallace
341 F. Supp. 217 (M.D. Ala. 1971)

PER CURIAM:

Plaintiff brings this class action challenging the unwritten regulation of the Alabama Department of Public Safety which requires that each married female applicant use her husband's surname in seeking and obtaining a driver's license. The thrust of the complaint is that the refusal of the Department to issue plaintiff Forbush a driver's license in her maiden name because she is married is a denial of equal protection as guaranteed by the Fourteenth Amendment to the United States Constitution. Also under attack is Alabama's common law rule that the husband's surname is the wife's legal name. . . .

We may commence our analysis of the merits of the controversy by noting that Alabama has adopted the common law rule that upon marriage the wife by operation of law takes the husband's surname. . . . Apparently, in an effort to police its administration of the issuance of licenses and to preserve the integrity of the license as a means of identification, the Department of Public Safety has required that each driver obtain his license in his "legal name." Thus, in conformity with the common law rule, the regulation under attack requires that a married woman obtain her license in her husband's surname.

. . . [T]he state has a significant interest in maintaining close watch over its licensees. The confusion which would result if each driver were allowed to obtain licenses in any number of names he desired is obvious. This would be true not only of the maintenance of driving records, but also of the identification purposes to which a license is put, whether traffic-related or otherwise. Thus, it is reasonable for the Department of Public Safety to require each driver to secure a license only in his "legal name."

This determination, however, does not dispose of the case since the plaintiff has also attacked the Alabama Supreme Court's adoption of the common law rule which requires a wife upon marriage to take her husband's surname. This judicial pronouncement, as with any state statute or regulation, must have a rational basis. It is well settled that "the Equal Protection Clause does not make every minor difference in the application of laws to different groups a violation of our Constitution." Williams v. Rhodes, [393 U.S. 23, 30 (1968)]. Thus, as a general rule, a law is not violative of the Fourteenth Amendment, despite the existence of discrimination in the technical or broad sense, where the law at issue maintains some rational connection with a legitimate state interest. . . .

Certainly the custom of the husband's surname denominating the wedded couple is one of long standing. While its origin is obscure, it suffices for our purposes to recognize that it is a tradition extending back into the heritage of most western civilizations. It is a custom common to all 50 states in this union. Uniformity among the several states in this area is important.

An additional basis exists for finding a rational connection between Alabama's law and a legitimate state interest. The administrative convenience, if not a necessity, is an important consideration.[10]

The evidence in this case reflects that the State of Alabama's system of issuing drivers' licenses and maintaining control over its licensees represents a considerable investment. In balancing the interest of the plaintiff and the members of plaintiff's class against the interest of the state, this Court concludes that the administrative inconvenience and cost of a change to the State of Alabama far outweigh the harm caused the plaintiff and the members of plaintiff's class. In balancing these interests, this Court notes that the State of Alabama has afforded a simple, inexpensive means by which any person, and this includes married women, can on application to a probate court change his or her name. . . . Thus, on balance, plaintiff's injury, if any, through the operation of the law is *de minimis.*

We conclude, therefore, that the existing law in Alabama which requires a woman to assume her husband's surname upon marriage has a rational basis and seeks to control an area where the state has a legitimate interest. . . .

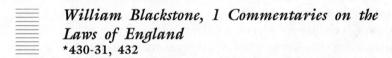

William Blackstone, 1 Commentaries on the Laws of England
*430-31, 432

By marriage, the husband and wife are one person in law: that is, the very being or legal existence of the woman is suspended during the marriage, or at least is incorporated and consolidated into that of the husband; under whose wing, protection, and cover, she performs everything; and is therefore called in our law-french a *feme-covert, foemina viro co-operta;* it is said to be *covert-baron,* or under the protection and influence of her husband, her *baron,* or lord; and her condition during her marriage is called her *coverture.* Upon this principle, of a union of person in husband and wife, depend almost all the legal rights, duties, and disabilities, that either of them acquire by the marriage. I speak not at present of the rights of property, but of such

---

10. Administrative factors have often been considered rational bases for challenged statutes. See, e.g., Hoyt v. Florida, [368 U.S. 57, 64 (1968)]; Wells v. Civil Serv. Commn., [225 A.2d 554 (Pa. 1967), cert. denied, 386 U.S. 1035 (1967)].

as are merely *personal*. For this reason, a man cannot grant any thing to his wife, or enter into covenant with her; for the grant would be to suppose her separate existence; and to covenant with her would be only to covenant with himself; and therefore it is also generally true, that all compacts made between husband and wife, when single, are voided by the intermarriage. A woman indeed may be attorney for her husband; for that implies no separation from, but is rather a representation of, her lord. And a husband may also bequeath any thing to his wife by will; for that cannot take effect till the coverture is determined by his death. The husband is bound to provide his wife with necessaries by law, as much as himself; and, if she contracts debts for them, he is obliged to pay them; but for anything besides necessaries he is not chargeable. Also if a wife elopes, and lives with another man, the husband is not chargeable even for necessaries; at least if the person who furnishes them is sufficiently apprised of her elopement. If the wife be indebted before marriage, the husband is bound afterwards to pay the debt; for he has adopted her and her circumstances together. If the wife be injured in her person or her property, she can bring no action for redress without her husband's concurrence, and in his name, as well as her own; neither can she be sued without making the husband a defendant. . . . In criminal prosecutions, it is true, the wife may be indicted and punished separately; for the union is only a civil union. But in trials of any sort they are not allowed to be evidence for, or against, each other: partly because it is impossible their testimony should be indifferent, but principally because of the union of person; and therefore, if they were admitted to be witnesses for each other, they would contradict one maxim of law, "*nemo in propria causa testis esse debet*"[11] and if *against* each other, they would contradict another maxim, "*nemo tenetur seipsum accusare*."[12] . . .

But though our law in general considers man and wife as one person, yet there are some instances in which she is separately considered; as inferior to him, and acting by his compulsion. And therefore all deeds executed, and acts done, by her, during her coverture, are void; except it be a fine, or the like matter of record, in which case she must be solely and secretly examined, to learn if her act be voluntary. She cannot by will devise lands to her husband, unless under special circumstances; for at the time of making it she is supposed to be under his coercion. And in some felonies, and other inferior crimes, committed by her, through constraint of her husband, the law excuses her; but this extends not to treason or murder. . . .

11. [No one ought to be a witness against his own cause.]
12. [No one is bound to accuse himself.]

Norma Basch, In the Eyes of the Law
17, 19-20, 22-23 (1982)

From the time of the Norman Conquest, the common law developed a complex body of theory based on the simple presumption that "in the eyes of the law" the husband and wife were one person — the husband. Common law jurisprudence perpetuated this legal fiction as a convenient device for ordering the legal and economic relationship of the two parties to the marriage and of the married couple with third parties. At marriage a wife assumed her husband's name and his rank; she came under her husband's wing or protective cover in a condition designated as coverture. As a result of this condition, a husband and wife could not contract with one another, nor could they testify in court for or against one another. More important, coverture imposed serious procedural and substantive disabilities on the wife. She could neither sue nor be sued in her own name, she was limited in making contracts and wills, and all of her personal property as well as the management of her real property went to her husband. . . .

The doctrine of marital unity . . . was not unique to the common law. The wife's inferior status had a religious and metaphysical foundation in Western culture. Both the Old and New Testaments supported the wife's subordinate status, and the doctrine of marital unity had a specific canonical equivalent in the doctrine of the unity of the flesh. This doctrine shaped decisions in the ecclesiastical courts. In England, by the twelfth century, cases of adultery, bigamy, separation, and the few complete divorces the church allowed came within the jurisdiction of ecclesiastical courts. . . . The common law generally reserved for itself the right to adjudicate land-related problems. The church courts tended to deal with the succession of "movables" as well as areas touching the sexual morality of the family. They set the rules on the degree of consanguinity permitted between the marrying couple. In cases concerning legitimacy, the common law declared that the child who was capable of inheriting was the child whom the church deemed to be legitimate. Similarly, in cases concerning dower, the common law abided by the church's estimate of whether or not a marriage was valid.

On the other hand, the English legal heritage, which placed harsh restrictions on the wife and allowed spacious powers to the husband, had an alternate side. Situations arose to confound the secular doctrine of absolute marital unity. . . . First of all, the common law afforded a certain amount of leeway in the wife's activities; she could buy "necessaries" and enter into contracts as long as she represented her lord. Thus out of necessity a primitive theory of agency developed. Second, the common law recognized the wife's contingent interest in the husband's realty through its championship of dower, and it functioned during marriage to protect her potential interests as a widow. By allowing the wife a life interest in one-third of her husband's realty if she survived him, the common law did have some limited notion of a community of goods. Third, the common law accommodated the woman who resided in a center of trade and participated in local commerce, either as a matter of custom or through "sole-trader statutes." Thus a married woman might contract business debts and engage in trade if she had her husband's permission. Finally, the common law recognized some specific emergencies in which a married woman would need to act as if she were a single woman, such as when her husband "abjured the realm," or when he was judged to be civilly dead. . . .

. . . The legal status of married women in colonial America remains somewhat ambiguous, varying geographically from colony to colony and chronologically over more than a century and a half of development. . . . The question of whether frontier conditions, a shortage of labor, the presence of dissenting religious sects, uneven sex ratios, and non-English influences improved the legal status of wives has not been answered yet in a comprehensive way. . . . [However,] there can be no doubt that in the English colonies of North America, the English common law model of marital property, along with its ameliorating exceptions, did take root, grow, and flourish until it eventually crowded out most informal non-English practices.

Notes

1. The Uses of History. Are you satisfied with the court's finding that the Alabama statute had a rational basis? The court describes the source of Alabama's custom as "obscure." Does legal history provide any insight?

How important was the lawsuit in Forbush v. Wallace? Would you, as an attorney in 1971, have encouraged the bringing of this lawsuit? Does some knowledge of legal history help answer this question? What else might you need to know?

2. Coverture and Ideology. Is coverture a symbol of women's subordination? Certainly there is support for the notion that women have long been considered inferior to men in the Western European tradition. For example, Gustave Le Bon, a nineteenth-century writer who began his career as an anthropologist and archaeologist and helped invent the field of social psychology, put the popular prejudices of his time in scientific language when he asserted the following:

In the most intelligent races, as among the Parisians, there are a large number of women whose brains are closer in size to those of gorillas than to the most developed male brains. This inferiority is so obvious that no one can contest it for a moment; only its degree is worth discussion. All psychologists who have studied the intelligence of women, as well as poets and novelists, recognize today that they represent the most inferior forms of human evolution and that they are closer to children and savages than to an adult, civilized man. They excel in fickleness, inconstancy, absence of thought and logic, and incapacity to reason. Without doubt there exist some distinguished women, very superior to the average man, but they are as exceptional as the birth of any monstrosity, as, for example of a gorilla with two heads; consequently, we may neglect them entirely.

Recherches Anatomiques et Mathématiques sur les Lois des Variations du Volume du Cerveau et sur Leurs Relations avec L'Intelligence, in Revue d'Anthropologie, 2d Series, vol. 2, at 60-61 (1879), as quoted in Stephen Jay Gould, The Mismeasure of Man 104-105 (1981).*

Do past sentiments like this one have any relevance for the meaning of practices like that of the State of Alabama?

3. Marriage, Slavery, and the State. Although in contemporary times we tend to think of marriage as a "private" relation between individuals, historically the state has played an active role in defining and shaping the meaning and implications of marriage, as the preceding excerpts suggest. A second social institution that has had a profound influence on American economic, political, and personal life is slavery. Where the implications of marriage for gender relations are obvious, slavery has had a more indirect but nevertheless pervasive effect. By defining slaves as property rather than persons, slavery made possible the widespread sexual exploitation of women, de-legitimated consensual relations between slaves and free persons, and vastly complicated the Southern planter family. The ideologies and practices of caste racism that emerged from the practice of African slavery, interacting with marriage policy, produced miscegenation laws that would thrive long after slavery was abolished, and channeled wealth into the hands of "legitimate" — often white — families.

Intertwined with this legacy is the United States' history of nativism. As this multicultural nation has struggled to define itself, gender norms have played an important role in the effort to assimilate or exclude peoples considered culturally alien, from Indians to Mormons to Asian immigrants. Moreover, anxieties about interracial sexuality and procreation have frequently shaped United States family and immigration policy.

As you read these materials, think about how the institutions of marriage and slavery have affected public ideology, economics, politics, and intimate relations. How did they interact with one another? To what extent can they be understood as forms of oppression? What role did the law play in reinforcing or altering these institutions? How have these institutions shaped feminist movement?

---

* Gustave Le Bon, who began his career as an anthropologist and archaeologist, helped to invent the field of social psychology. His assessment of women based on both psychological and anatomical criteria was part of a larger project to establish a hierarchy of races and nationalities. See Gustave Le Bon, Psychology of Peoples (1894).

2. Gender and the Economy in United States Legal History

a. Women, Labor, and Property

Act XVI (Dec. 1662), 2 The Statutes at Large: Being a Collection of all the Laws of Virginia from the First Session of the Legislature, in the Year 1619, 170 (William W. Hening ed., 1823).

WHEREAS some doubts have arrisen whether children got by any Englishman upon a negro woman should be slave or free, *Be it therefore enacted and declared by this present grand assembly*, that all children borne in this country shalbe held bond or free only according to the condition of the mother. . . .

≡≡≡ *Potts v. Merrit & Potts*
    53 Ky. (14B. Mon.) 406 (1854)

Chief Justice HISE delivered the opinion of the court.

[This case concerns the enforceability of the] verbal agreement between the complainant, Priscilla, and her husband, Jonathan Potts, made before their marriage, to the effect that she should retain the title to her slaves, and have the control and the power of disposition of them after marriage as before. . . .

By the marriage of the complainant with Jonathan Potts, her slaves became his property, and the legal title and absolute right to them vested in him. . . . Her right to them having been thus divested, she could not of course, as a *feme covert*, without right, maintain an action against her husband, his vendee, or even donee, to recover the said slaves. If the sale and conveyance from Jonathan Potts to William W. Merrit, of the slaves which had belonged to the wife before her marriage with Potts, had been procured by Merrit fraudulently from Potts, who was, either by incapacity to contract, or by the deceit practiced upon him by Merrit, overreached in the sale or gift and delivery of them, then Potts, but not his wife, could maintain an action to avoid the contract. . . . [B]ut in no event, during the life of Potts, can his wife demand the interposition of a court of law or equity to enforce a parol marriage contract, or to recover the slaves — all her right and title to which had been transferred by operation of law to Jonathan Potts upon his marriage with the complainant.

Potts does not complain of fraud, or seek to avoid the sale to Merrit, but on the contrary, gives sound reasons and adequate motives which led him to convey the slaves to Merrit, for what appears to be a mere nominal consideration. No creditors of Potts or subsequent innocent purchaser from him, contests Merrit's title. Potts, who had the right, might give or vend the slaves to another, though not related to himself or wife, and who would thereby hold them against the claim and suit of the wife, instituted in the lifetime of her husband.

The paper executed by Potts, dated 28th February, 1848, purporting to be a conditional ratification, or rather adoption of a will, which had been previously signed and acknowledged by the complainant, and by which she vainly devises the slaves in question to her brother, Samuel Hasslip, did not and could not have the effect to transfer from Potts to his wife his right to the slaves; and if the same was even valid and irrevocable, it could not divest Potts or his vendee of the title to, and possession of the slaves during the joint lives of Potts and wife. For the paper does not create a present separate estate, or right in his wife to the slaves; he does not divest himself thereby of his own title acquired by his marriage, but it amounts to nothing more than a will, by which he devises the slaves, in conformity with the will and desire of his wife, as indicated in her own abortive will, to Samuel Hasslip, and by which he confesses, (say, for the sake of argument,) that he had agreed with his wife before marriage, that those slaves should be so devised; yet this document, thus devising the slaves, or adopting the disposition thereof as made in the paper dated 17th October, 1846, signed by complainant, did not disturb or affect Potts' right to the slaves during his own life at least, and the complainant could not acquire to herself thereby any such right or title as would enable her to recover, herself, the slaves from Potts' vendee, whilst her husband lived.

But the paper referred to is in fact nothing but a will, which being revocable at the pleasure of Potts, was actually revoked by him impliedly and effectually, first, by selling the slaves devised, to Merrit, by which the devise to Hasslip was defeated, and, secondly, by an express revocation in writing. So that it seems to this court that there is no settled doctrine of law, or established principle of equity, upon which the complainants claim to the slaves in question can be sustained.

Bethany Ruth Berger, After Pocahontas: Indian Women and the Law, 1830 to 1934
21 Am. Indian L. Rev. 1, 15-19 (1997)

[T]he assumption that a woman was not the head of the family, and even the attempts to displace women who acted as the heads of families, were both reflections of a policy which appears in federal enactments of the period. Some treaties were as explicit as the 1861 Treaty with the Pottawatomie, which declared that when the President determined "that any adults, being males and heads of families . . . are sufficiently intelligent and prudent to control their affairs and interests," he might convey those Indians, land to them in fee simple and they would thereafter be citizens. Though less explicit, an article inserted in all of the major treaties with the Indians of 1868 clearly envisions assimilation through male heads of families:

> If any individual . . . being the head of a family, shall desire to commence farming, he shall have the privileges to select . . . a tract of land within the reservation not exceeding three hundred and twenty acres [which shall be] held in the exclusive possession of the person selecting it, and of his family.

The gender-specific language was deliberate. Within the same article, such treaties used both male and female pronouns to refer to those who were not heads of families and were entitled to only one quarter of the land that male heads of families were entitled to: "Any person over eighteen years of age, not being the head of a family, may in like manner select and cause to be certified to him, or her . . . a quantity of land not exceeding eighty acres in extent. . . ." The 1887 Dawes Act also initially excluded married women from allotments of tribal land. Only after much protest was it modified in 1891.

Such legislation was often motivated by a desire to improve the lives of both the Indian people and of the women themselves. As expressed here by a prominent "Friend of the Indian," it was believed that this would improve the lot of both these "less-favored" women and of their race as a whole:

> The Indian woman has so far been only a beast of burden. . . . The Indian wife was treated by her husband alternately with animal fondness, and with the cruel brutality of the slave-driver. Nothing will be more apt to raise the Indians in the scale of civilization than to stimulate their attachment to permanent homes, and it is the woman that must make the atmosphere and form the attraction of the home.

Similarly, William Strong, a former Supreme Court Justice, spoke against allotting land to married women under the impending Dawes Act: "I want the Indians brought together in families. There can never be any civilization without families. I would have the head of the family have the land, and have it descend to his wife and children."

. . . [S]uch well-meaning policy makers were motivated by a misunderstanding of the role of the Indian woman within many tribes. Women were almost uniformly responsible for a greater share of the productive labor of American Indian communities than their white nineteenth century counterparts. Ironically, despite the frustrated attempts of federal officials to turn Indian men into farmers, it was women who had responsibility for cultivating the land in most American tribes. White observers and federal officials rejected such female participation in what they conceived of as the male sphere of work as a sign of ignoble savagery and of the debasement of the Indian male.

These traditional responsibilities, however, gave Indian women a degree of autonomy unknown to their white counterparts. Women controlled what food would be grown, how it would be prepared, what clothes, shoes, and blankets would be made. Sitting Bull, the powerful Chief of the Sioux, well recognized the power that productive labor gave women when he pleaded with a white woman administrating the Dawes Act. "Take pity on my women. . . . The young men can be like the white men, can till the soil, supply the food and clothing. They will take the work out of the hands of women. And the women . . . will be stripped of all which gave them power."

Women's task-based responsibility translated into property rights. In contrast to the white nineteenth century woman whose property transferred by law to her husband upon marriage, it was a "maxim" that among the Indians, everything belonged to the women, "except the Indian's hunting implements and war implements, even the game the Indian brought home on his back." The Cherokees memorialized this understanding in their earliest written laws.

Indian women also exercised relatively greater control over the descent of property and the family name. The commonplace that all Indian tribes were matrilocal — or that couples lived with the woman's family — and matrilineal — or that kinship was traced and inherited from the woman — is probably somewhat overstated. The Navajo and Iroquois were matrilineal and matrilocal, the Cheyenne and Arapaho were generally matrilocal, the Pamunkey were matrilineal, but the Blackfoot and many of the Great Lakes tribes were patrilineal and patrilocal, and the Crow and Sioux appear to have been either. Nor were tribes perfect models of feminist culture. The double standard, for example, was alive and well among the Sioux and some other Plains tribes — adolescent girls spent their nights tied to their beds to preserve their chastity, and unfaithful wives might have their noses cut off or be otherwise mutilated to discourage infidelity. But while tribes might differ in the amount of autonomy given to women, women typically exercised legal and political powers that sat very uneasily with judges of the nineteenth and early twentieth centuries.

Coleman v. Burr
93 N.Y. 17 (1883)

EARL, J.

This action was brought to set aside a deed of sixty-two acres of land, made by the defendant Isaac C. Burr, to Franklin P. Smith, and by him to Ellen A. Burr, the wife of Isaac, on the ground that the deeds were made with intent to hinder, delay, and defraud the creditors of Isaac, of whom the plaintiff was one. The facts, as they appear from the findings of the referee, upon which alone this appeal is based, are as follows: In the year 1869, the defendant Isaac lived upon the land conveyed, and had a family consisting of himself, his wife, the defendant Ellen, two children of his wife by a former husband, his two children by his wife Ellen, and his mother, who lived in a part of his house and whom he had engaged to support in consideration of a conveyance by her to him of twenty-six of the sixty-two acres of land. His mother was about eighty years of age, and in the month of January of that year she had an attack of paralysis which rendered her partially helpless. She had another attack in the month of February, and still another in the month of April, which substantially rendered her helpless. After the last attack she could not walk or feed herself for a year or more. The care of her devolved mainly upon Mrs. Burr, and her services in such care were onerous, exacting, and disagreeable. Soon after the last attack it was considered in the family that it would be a most unpleasant and disagreeable duty to take charge of the mother, and provide for and administer to all her wants in her helpless condition, and it was agreed between Mr. Burr and his wife that if she would undertake to discharge such duty she would be paid by him for her labor and services the sum of five dollars a week, which, in view of the very irksome, laborious, and disgustful duty she performed during the residue of the life of the mother, was no more than a fair and reasonable compensation for such labor and services. The mother lived after the last attack of paralysis, and after this agreement was made, eight years and four months, and the compensation agreed upon amounted to $2,175.

The referee found that the contract between Mr. and Mrs. Burr was a fair, just, and honest one, made at a time when there was little expectation on their part that the life of the mother would be so greatly prolonged, considering her advanced age, her disease, and helpless condition. For the purpose of paying the sum which it was claimed thus became due to his wife on the 29th day of December, 1877, Isaac and his wife conveyed the sixty-two acres of land to the defendant Smith for the nominal consideration of $1.00, and on the same day Smith executed and delivered a deed of the same land to the wife for the same nominal consideration. The deeds were both delivered at their date, and acknowledged and recorded. Prior to the execution of these deeds Isaac C. Burr was indebted in the various sums mentioned in the complaint, for which, before the commencement of this action, judgments had been obtained against him, upon which executions had been issued and returned unsatisfied.

The referee decided that, as a matter of law, the contract established by the proof between the husband and wife, indicated a clear and explicit election on her part, with his consent, to render the labor and services performed by her as nurse, in taking care of her husband's mother in her sickness, on her sole and separate account, and to claim the fruits of her labor and services for herself, and showed her intention to avail herself of the privilege conferred upon her by the statute [the Married Women's Property Act]; and that the agreement on the part of her husband to pay her for such services was an abandonment on his part of his marital rights to claim or require such services and labor, and created a valid contract in law, and gave her a right to the stipulated price and value of her services which constituted them, or the amount due her for such services, a valid debt against her husband, which was sufficient in law and equity to form the consideration for the deed executed to her as before stated; and he decided that the deeds were not fraudulent and void, and that the complaint should be dismissed.

The sole question for our determination now is, whether the conveyance of the land to Mrs. Burr is sustained by a consideration good as against the creditors of the husband. It must be conceded that the contract between the wife and the husband, in reference to these services, would, at common law, have been void, as she could make no contract with her husband, and her services, whether rendered in her husband's family or elsewhere, absolutely belonged to him. . . . But modern legislation in this State has enlarged the powers of married women. By the acts of 1848 and 1849, for the protection of the property of married women, a husband was deprived of that right to and control of his wife's property which the common law gave him. The purpose of those acts was to protect married women against unkind, thriftless, or profligate husbands, by securing to them the separate and independent control of all their own property. But those acts went no further.

By chapter 90 of the Laws of 1860, still further protection was given to married women, and a wife was authorized to carry on any trade or business, and to perform any labor or services on her sole and separate account, and her earnings from her trade, business, labor, or services thus carried on or performed were declared to be her sole and separate property. It was the purpose of those provisions to secure to a married woman, free from the control of her husband, the earnings and profits of her own business and of her own labor and services, carried on or performed on her sole and separate account, which at common law would have belonged to her husband. It was not their purpose, however, to absolve a married woman from the duties which she owes to her husband, to render him service in his household, to care for him and their common children with dutiful affection when he or they need her care, and to render all the services in her household which are commonly expected of a married woman, according to her station in life. Nor was it the purpose of the statute to absolve her from due obedience and submission to her husband as head and master of his household, or to depose him from the headship of his family, which the common law gave him. He still remains liable to support and protect his wife and responsible to society for the good order and decency of his household. He is to determine where he and his family shall have a domicile, how his household shall be regulated and managed, and who shall be members of his family. The statutes referred to touch a married woman in her relations to her husband only so far as they relate to her separate property and business, and the labor she may perform on her sole and separate account. In other respects the duties and responsibilities of each to the other remain as they were at common law. . . .

Whatever services a wife renders in her home for her husband cannot be on her sole and separate account. They are rendered on her husband's account in the discharge of a duty which she owes him or his family, or in the discharge of a duty which he owes to the members of his household.

It would operate disastrously upon domestic life and breed discord and mischief if the wife could contract with her husband for the payment of services to be rendered for him in his home; if she could exact compensation for services, disagreeable or otherwise, rendered to members of his family; if she could sue him upon such contracts and establish them upon the disputed and conflicting testimony of the members of the household. To allow such contracts would degrade the wife by making her a menial and a servant in the home where she should discharge marital duties in loving and devoted ministrations, and frauds upon creditors would be greatly facilitated, as the wife could frequently absorb all her husband's property in the payment of her services, rendered under such secret, unknown contracts. . . .

. . . But it is sought to make a distinction between such services of the wife and those which she renders for one not strictly a member of the husband's family. Such a distinction does not stand upon principle. A line drawn there would be merely an arbitrary one. While the wife cannot demand or receive payment as against creditors for services rendered in the care of her husband and children, can it upon principle be said that she can demand and receive payment for every service she renders in caring for visitors, from time to time, in her husband's house upon his invitation? Whenever she aids him in the discharge of a duty which he owes to an inmate of his house, who is yet not strictly a member of his family, can she stipulate for compensation? Whenever she nurses in sickness, one of his children of a former marriage, a member of his family, can she lawfully demand a share of his property for her services? But in this case the mother was properly part of the household. The husband was under a natural, legal, and contract obligation to support her. It would have shocked the moral sense of every right-minded person, if he had not supported her in his own household where she could have the tender care, suitable to her age and feeble condition, of her son and his wife and her grandchildren. He was under just as much natural, legal, and moral obligation to support his mother as he was to support his own children. When, therefore, the wife rendered service in caring for her, she was engaged in discharging a duty which her husband owed his mother, and precisely the same kind of duty which he owed to his children and to his wife. In discharging that duty she earned no money, she brought no increase to her husband's property and no income into the family. The services were rendered simply in the discharge of a duty which the husband owed to his mother, and in rendering them she simply discharged a marital duty which she owed to him. . . .

. . . Here, the wife during the eight years and four months, it must be presumed, received from her husband a home, shelter, food, raiment, and, if needed, medical attendance, and yet, at the end of the time, she had over $2,000 in property taken from him, and he nothing but clamorous creditors . . . .

Order affirmed and judgment accordingly.

Notes

1. Women's Labor and the Law. Slavery, marriage, and the Indian treaties described in the Berger excerpt arguably all served to transfer the fruits of women's labor to men's ownership and control. Is the law in each situation facilitating oppression? If so, who is being oppressed, and for whose benefit? Do these excerpts begin to suggest a common "woman's place"?

Imagine, as might have been the case, that one of the Potts' slaves was a woman. In what ways did the law of property disempower both Mrs. Potts and her unnamed slave? In what ways did their disempowerment differ? Did Mrs. Potts and her slave share a common women's fate? Is it important that marriage could be freely entered into, whereas slavery was a condition one was born into? Why could not Priscilla and Jonathan Potts modify their marriage contract?

2. Slavery, Gender, and Women's Labor. Slave labor was central to the economic growth of the colonial and nineteenth-century United States. In the "triangle trade," goods manufactured in Britain, such as cloth and guns, were traded for slaves in Africa; slaves were sold to planters in the American colonies and forced to produce agricultural products; and planters exported these products and imported manufactured and luxury goods from Britain. Slave labor also sustained the master's household. Slave men chopped wood, cleared land, and plowed; slave women nursed and cared for white children, sewed and spun, did the washing, and served as personal servants for white ladies. Gender lines were not always rigidly observed, particularly on small plantations; it was not uncommon, for example, for slave women to serve as field hands, working alongside the men.

Legal rules were central to the development and maintenance of black slavery as an economic system. These rules both used sexual difference as the basis for economic exploitation, and built a system of racial caste on gender difference. The most important rule, of course, was that a slave was not legally a full human being but a form of property. In Louisiana, and in Kentucky before 1852, slaves were treated as a form of real estate; everywhere else they were considered personal property ("chattels personal"). As property, slaves were not only bought and sold; they were "bartered, deeded, devised, pledged, seized, and auctioned. They were awarded as prizes in lotteries and raffles; they were wagered at gaming tables and horse races. They were, in short, property in fact as well as in law." See Kenneth Stampp, "Chattels Personal," in Lawrence M. Friedman and Harry N. Scheiber, *American Law and the Constitutional Order: Historical Perspectives* 203, 205 (enlarged ed. 1988).

Nearly as important to the maintenance of black slavery, however, was the law that children took the status of their mothers, derived from the Roman rule *partus sequitur ventrem.* As Margaret Burnham notes, "The justification for the rule was the same as that offered by its Roman originators: 'From the principles of justice, the offspring, the increase of the womb, belongs to the master of the womb.'" Margaret A. Burnham, An Impossible Marriage: Slave Law and Family Law, 5 L. & Ineq. J. 187, 215 (1987). Burnham observes:

> In providing that the fruits of the bondwoman's womb were the "property" of her master, slave law echoed early non-slave domestic law. The master was deemed to "own" his wife and her children, just as he "owned" the slave woman and her children. Thus, the genesis of the rule involved two entangled proprietary relations: the master's marriage (a property relation) produced property for him (children), and his slave property also produced more property (slave children). . . .
>
> This use of a commercial principle to vitiate a social relationship led to a confusing legal situation. . . . Courts were, for example, perplexed by questions having to do with the legal status of the children of an enslaved but soon to be emancipated mother, and the fate of children born to a fugitive or momentarily free mother.
>
> . . . [A]nother highly litigated issue was who owned the child. The courts debated whether in determining ownership disputes, slave children could be treated like the offspring of farm animals. At common law, animal offspring were "natural fruits" which were deemed the property of the mother animal's owner. Yet, since the judges were dealing with the relationship between mother and child, a relationship which the culture deemed sacred and fundamental, the commercial analogy to farm animals was not altogether satisfying. As one court put it, "the law . . . treats [slaves], as human beings, deprived, doubtless for wise purposes, of their freedom . . . and in our opinion the rule which applies to [the disposition of animals' issue] has no application to them."

Id. at 215-217.

3. Slavery and Gender Distinctions. In a study of colonial Virginia, historian Kathleen Brown argues that gender subordination was the foundation upon which racial subordination was built. For Brown, the "seventeenth-century Virginia lawmakers began to define the social meaning of racial difference by reserving the privileges of womanhood for the masters and husbands of English women." Kathleen Brown, Good Wives, Nasty Wenches, and Anxious Patriarchs: Gender, Race, and Power in Colonial Virginia 128 (1996). For example, English women who worked in the tobacco fields were legally classed as dependents on the assumption that, like children and old men, they were too weak to produce much. African women, however, were classed as "tithables," individuals who performed taxable labor. Id. at 118. Examining tax-exemption petitions in several county courts, Brown found that a free black woman had to "demonstrate dependent status by proving her physical disability" in order to "enjoy the privileges of English women." Id. at 125. The notion that white women were physically delicate and sexually chaste, whereas black women were physically strong and sexually promiscuous, would serve to reinforce both inequalities of sex and of race in the antebellum United States and beyond. It also served the interests of slaveholders, who relied on African women's labor to create property for themselves.

Notions of gender not only shaped how property was created, but who could control property. Under the common law tradition, the institution of coverture in marriage ensured that the labor and the property of a married woman were under the control of her husband. Berger argues that the United States government's attempt to make Indians more like whites in this respect had the effect of disempowering Indian women. Coverture, moreover, was by no means uncontested among Americans. Women's right to control property after marriage was one of the central goals of the early American feminist movement. For example, at the First National Woman's Rights Convention held in 1850 at Worcester, Massachusetts, the participants resolved:

> That the laws of property, as affecting married parties, demand a thorough revisal, so that all rights may be equal between them — that the wife may have, during life, an equal control over the property gained by their mutual toil and sacrifices, be heir to her husband precisely to the extent that he is heir to her, and entitled, at her death, to dispose by will of the same share of the joint property as he is.

Reva B. Siegel, Home as Work: The First Woman's Rights Claims Concerning Wives' Household Labor, 1850-1880, 103 Yale L.J. 1073, 1113 (1994).

4. Feminism and the Slavery-Marriage Analogy. Many antebellum feminists received their political education from working in the abolitionist movement; and in shaping their demands for property rights they often likened marriage to slavery. Reva Siegel argues:

> [F]eminists used the marriage-as-slavery argument to expose contradictions between the ideology of domesticity and the institution of marriage, to pierce the veil of sentimentality shrouding the relation and to reveal its economic logic. More precisely, the argument demonstrated the role of law in perpetuating women's economically dependent status. In political antislavery, then, antebellum feminists found a discourse of wide popular appeal that allowed them to analyze woman's situation in marriage and to dramatize it in compelling form.

Id. at 1101. See also Serena Mayeri, "A Common Fate of Discrimination": Race-Gender Analogies in Legal and Historical Perspective, 110 Yale L.J. 1045 (2001). Does *Potts* illustrate the limitations of the sex-race analogy?

5. The Married Women's Property Acts. Antebellum feminists were successful in challenging the legal fiction of marital unity. As early as 1839 in Mississippi, "married women's property acts" passed in several states granted married women the right to own property they owned prior to marriage and even property they received after marriage if acquired by gift or bequest. Basch, In the Eyes of the Law, supra, at 27. Ownership and control, however, were often split between husband and wife. For example, Basch notes: "The Mississippi statute . . . stipulated that slaves owned by the wife at the time of marriage or acquired afterward should be her property, but their control and management, along with the profits from their labor, were reserved to the husband." Id.

Perhaps the farthest-reaching married women's property act was the New York Earnings Act of 1860, which gave wives the right to sue and be sued and included their wages as part of their separate estate. Even this statute, however, did not establish shared rights in all marital property, as movement leaders had sought; instead, it merely accorded married women a separate property right in their own labor. Moreover, the end of the Civil War altered feminist priorities. Feminist activists began to focus on suffrage as the linchpin of gender equality rather than property rights. Meanwhile, courts and legislatures began to develop a new body of law designed to protect a husband's property rights in the paid and unpaid labor his wife performed in the household. *Coleman* is an example of this new jurisprudence. Was Mrs. Burr any better off than Mrs. Potts? If so, in what way?

6. The Cooperative Housekeeping Movement. As Katharine Silbaugh notes, some late nineteenth-century feminists sought structural solutions to Mrs. Burr's predicament.

> "[M]aterial feminists" sought wages for housework as well as economies of scale that would move housework out of the home and into a mass production context in which it would be managed by women. This Cooperative Housekeeping movement, which garnered substantial support around the turn of the century, envisioned community kitchens and laundries that would allow women's work to be subjected to the same modernization and efficiencies that had come to men's work in a capitalist economy.

Katharine Silbaugh, Turning Labor Into Love: Housework and the Law, 91 Nw. U. L. Rev. 1, 24 (1996). For contemporary legal examples of the problem of valuing women's work in the home, see chapter 3, section 2 (a).

b. Women, Labor, and Wage Work

Joan Williams, Unbending Gender: Why Family and Work Conflict and What To Do About It
21, 23-25 (2000)

As of the early nineteenth century, . . . the key unit [of the family] still was the household, not the biological family. Many households were composed not only of a mother, a father, and their children but of apprentices, bound servants (often children themselves), other relatives (aunts, orphans, grandmothers), boarders, and others as well. A significant portion of the population spent part of their lives in other families' households. . . .

Though men and women typically did different work in the era before domesticity, women often did work associated with men. If the husband had a trade, the wife often worked with him, sewing the uppers on the shoes or tending the shop he owned. Throughout the eighteenth century, wives acted as "deputy husbands" when their husbands were away and often did work traditionally done by men in this capacity. We find reports of women as blacksmiths, wrights, printers, tinsmiths, beer makers, tavern keepers, shoemakers, shipwrights, barbers, grocers, butchers, and shopkeepers. Women doing "men's work" did not jar contemporary sensibilities because men and women were not primarily defined by their separate spheres. Women were defined, instead, by their inferiority. . . .

Though paternal power persisted long after 1750, open hierarchy diminished. By 1776 all men had been declared equal. This had a profound influence on the development of domesticity. While the market economy reorganized work in ways that set the economic structure within which domesticity arose, the notion that men and women belonged in spheres that were separate but (in some sense) equal reflected the influence of Enlightenment ideals. Domesticity explained that women were not inferior; they were just different. In fact, they were equally important in their distinctive domestic sphere.

Domesticity not only bifurcated the work of adults into a women's sphere of the home and men's market work outside of it; it justified that reorganization through new descriptions of the "true natures" of men and women. To quote historian Christine Stansell:

> In eighteenth-century Europe and early nineteenth-century America, a striking rearrangement of gender identities and stereotypes occurred. To men were assigned all the character traits associated with competition: ambition, authority, power, vigor, calculation, instrumentalism, logic, and single-mindedness. To women were assigned all the traits associated with cooperation:

gentleness, sensitivity, expressivism, altruism, empathy, personalism, and tenderness.[14]

Men belonged in the market because their natural competitiveness suited them for it. Women remained at home as "moral mothers" whose selflessness suited them to provide the moral uplift men needed when they staggered home to their haven from the heartless world. . . .

Under patriarchy, men's authority was based on their role in the structure of governance: "Household authority was the basis of the political order." [Id. at 83]. To achieve the ideals of masculinity, a man had only to use the weapons placed at his disposal (violence, property, and threat of damnation) to "govern" his household and other social inferiors. This changed under domesticity. The association of masculinity with breadwinning, so that manhood became contingent on success in market work, was a sharp shift whose significance is often underestimated. . . .

With the shift from patriarchy to domesticity, "a man's work t[ook] on a separate meaning and provide[d] the chief substance of his social identity," according to historian E. Anthony Rotundo. According to historian Robert Griswold, "Despite men's differences, breadwinning has remained the great unifying element in fathers' lives. Its obligations bind men across the boundaries of color and class, and shape their sense of self, manhood, and gender." A law student in 1820 noted that business engages a man's "mind and occupies his thoughts so frequently as to engross them almost entirely and then it is upon his employment that he depends almost entirely for his happiness of life." "I often think it is so different for men from what it is with us women," a woman told her suitor in 1868; "[l]ove is our life, our reality, business yours."

≣≣≣ ### Bradwell v. Illinois
≣≣≣ #### 83 U.S. (16 Wall.) 130 (1872)

Mrs. Myra Bradwell, residing in the State of Illinois, made application to the judges of the Supreme Court of that State for a license to practice law. . . .

The statute of Illinois on [this] subject . . . enacts that no person shall be permitted to practice as an attorney or counsellor-at-law . . . without having previously obtained a license for that purpose from some two of the justices of the Supreme Court. . . .

[The Supreme Court of Illinois denied the application because she was a married woman.]

[Mr. Justice Miller delivered the opinion of the court, affirming the denial, on grounds that "the right to control and regulate the granting of

---

14. See Stephanie Coontz, The Social Origins of Private Life 58 (1988).

license to practice law in the courts of a State is one of those powers which
are not transferred for its protection to the Federal government, and its
exercise is in no manner governed or controlled by citizenship of the United
States in the party seeking such license. . . ."]

Mr. Justice BRADLEY:

I concur in the judgment of the court in this case, by which the
judgment of the Supreme Court of Illinois is affirmed, but not for the
reasons specified in the opinion just read.

The claim of the plaintiff, who is a married woman, to be admitted to
practice as an attorney and counsellor-at-law, is based upon the supposed
right of every person, man or woman, to engage in any lawful employment
for a livelihood. The Supreme Court of Illinois denied the application on the
ground that, by the common law, which is the basis of the laws of Illinois,
only men were admitted to the bar, and the legislature had not made any
change in this respect. . . .

The claim that, under the fourteenth amendment of the Constitution,
which declares that no State shall make or enforce any law which shall
abridge the privileges and immunities of citizens of the United States, the
statute law of Illinois, or the common law prevailing in that State, can no
longer be set up as a barrier against the right of females to pursue any lawful
employment for a livelihood (the practice of law included), assumes that it is
one of the privileges and immunities of women as citizens to engage in any
and every profession, occupation, or employment in civil life.

It certainly cannot be affirmed, as an historical fact, that this has ever
been established as one of the fundamental privileges and immunities of the
sex. On the contrary, the civil law, as well as nature herself, has always
recognized a wide difference in the respective spheres and destinies of man
and woman. Man is, or should be, woman's protector and defender. The
natural and proper timidity and delicacy which belongs to the female sex
evidently unfits it for many of the occupations of civil life. The constitution
of the family organization, which is founded in the divine ordinance, as well
as in the nature of things, indicates the domestic sphere as that which
properly belongs to the domain and functions of womanhood. The
harmony, not to say identity, of interests and views which belong, or should
belong, to the family institution is repugnant to the idea of a woman
adopting a distinct and independent career from that of her husband. So
firmly fixed was this sentiment in the founders of the common law that it
became a maxim of that system of jurisprudence that a woman had no legal
existence separate from her husband, who was regarded as her head and
representative in the social state; and, notwithstanding some recent
modifications of this civil status, many of the special rules of law flowing
from and dependent upon this cardinal principle still exist in full force in
most States. One of these is, that a married woman is incapable, without her
husband's consent, of making contracts which shall be binding on her or

him. This very incapacity was one circumstance which the Supreme Court of Illinois deemed important in rendering a married woman incompetent fully to perform the duties and trusts that belong to the office of an attorney and counsellor.

It is true that many women are unmarried and not affected by any of the duties, complications, and incapacities arising out of the married state, but these are exceptions to the general rule. The paramount destiny and mission of woman are to fulfil the noble and benign offices of wife and mother. This is the law of the Creator. And the rules of civil society must be adapted to the general constitution of things, and cannot be based upon exceptional cases.

The humane movements of modern society, which have for their object the multiplication of avenues for woman's advancement, and of occupations adapted to her condition and sex, have my heartiest concurrence. But I am not prepared to say that it is one of her fundamental rights and privileges to be admitted into every office and position, including those which require highly special qualifications and demanding special responsibilities. In the nature of things it is not every citizen of every age, sex, and condition that is qualified for every calling and position. It is the prerogative of the legislator to prescribe regulations founded on nature, reason, and experience for the due admission of qualified persons to professions and callings demanding special skill and confidence. This fairly belongs to the police power of the State; and, in my opinion, in view of the peculiar characteristics, destiny, and mission of woman, it is within the province of the legislature to ordain what offices, positions, and callings shall be filled and discharged by men, and shall receive the benefit of those energies and responsibilities, and that decision and firmness which are presumed to predominate in the sterner sex.

For these reasons I think that the laws of Illinois now complained of are not obnoxious to the charge of abridging any of the privileges and immunities of citizens of the United States.

Mr. Justice SWAYNE and Mr. Justice FIELD concurred in the foregoing opinion of Mr. Justice BRADLEY.

The CHIEF JUSTICE dissented from the judgment of the court, and from all the opinions.

≡≡≡ *In re Goodell*
≡≡≡ **39 Wis. 232 (1875)**

RYAN, C.J. . . .

This is the first application for admission of a female to the bar of this court. And it is just matter for congratulation that it is made in favor of a lady whose character raises no personal objection: something perhaps not always to be looked for in women who forsake the ways of their sex for the ways of ours. . . .

[We] find no statutory authority for the admission of females to the bar of any court of this state. And, with all the respect and sympathy for this lady which all men owe to all good women, we cannot regret that we do not. We cannot but think the common law wise in excluding women from the profession of the law. The profession enters largely into the well being of society; and, to be honorably filled and safely to society, exacts the devotion of life. The law of nature destines and qualifies the female sex for the bearing and nurture of children of our race and for the custody of the homes of the world and their maintenance in love and honor. And all life-long callings of women, inconsistent with these radical and sacred duties of their sex, as is the profession of the law, are departures from the order of nature; and when voluntary, treason against it. The cruel chances of life sometimes baffle both sexes, and may leave women free from the peculiar duties of their sex. These may need employment, and should be welcome to any not derogatory to their sex and its proprieties, or inconsistent with the good order of society. But it is public policy to provide for the sex, not for its superfluous members; and not to tempt women from the proper duties of their sex by opening to them duties peculiar to ours. There are many employments in life not unfit for female character. The profession of the law is surely not one of these. The peculiar qualities of womanhood, its gentle graces, its quick sensibility, its emotional impulses, its subordination of hard reason to sympathetic feeling, are surely not qualifications for forensic strife. Nature has tempered woman as little for the juridical conflicts of the court room, as for the physical conflicts of the battle field. Womanhood is moulded for gentler and better things. And it is not the saints of the world who chiefly give employment to our profession. It has essentially and habitually to do with all that is selfish and malicious, knavish and criminal, coarse and brutal, repulsive and obscene, in human life. It would be revolting to all female sense of the innocence and sanctity of their sex, shocking to man's reverence for womanhood and faith in woman, on which hinge all the better affections and humanities of life, that woman should be permitted to mix professionally in all the nastiness of the world which finds its way into courts of justice; all the unclean issues, all the collateral questions, of sodomy, incest, rape, seduction, fornication, adultery, pregnancy, bastardy, legitimacy, prostitution, lascivious cohabitation, abortion, infanticide, obscene publications, libel and slander of sex, impotence, divorce: all nameless catalogue of indecencies, *la chronique scandaleuse* of all the vices and all the infirmities of all society, with which the profession has to deal, and which go towards filling judicial reports which must be read for accurate knowledge of the law. This is bad enough for men. We hold in too high reverence the sex without which, as is truly and beautifully written, *le commencement de la vie est sans secours, le milieu sans plaisir, et le fin sans consolation,*[15] voluntarily to commit it to such studies and such occupations. *Non tali auxilio nec defensoribus istis,*[16] should juridical contests be upheld. Reverence for all womanhood would suffer in the public spectacle of woman so instructed and so engaged. This motion gives appropriate evidence of this truth. No modest woman could read without pain and self abasement, no woman could so overcome the instincts of sex as publicly to discuss, the case which we had occasion to cite supra, King v. Wiseman. And when counsel was arguing for this lady that the word, person, in §32, ch. 119, necessarily includes females, her presence made it impossible to suggest to him as *reductio ad absurdum* of his position, that her same construction of the same word in §1, ch. 37, would subject woman to prosecution for the paternity of a bastard, and in §§39, 40, ch. 164, to prosecution for rape. Discussions are habitually necessary in courts of justice, which are unfit for female ears. The habitual presence of women at these would tend to relax the public sense of decency and propriety. If, as counsel threatened, these things are to come, we will take no voluntary part in bringing them about.

By the Court. — The motion is denied.

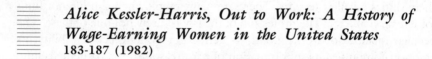

Alice Kessler-Harris, *Out to Work: A History of Wage-Earning Women in the United States* 183-187 (1982)

When the Knights of Labor introduced demands for the eight-hour day in 1871, its founder, Uriah Stephens, argued the advantages of shorter hours for workers who would "have time for social enjoyment and intellectual improvement, and be enabled to reap the advantages conferred by the Labor-saving machinery which their brains have created."[17] A sprinkling of states responded to such pressure. South Carolina and Maryland passed laws mandating a ten-hour day for all industrial workers. Eleven more states declared eight- or ten-hour "legal" days — but without enacting enforcement machinery. Some states asserted the right to regulate working relations on the most general grounds of health and police power regulation.

But states that tried to legislate working conditions for adult males found their laws unceremoniously struck down in the courts. The New York State Supreme Court decision that voided an 1884 act prohibiting the manufacture of cigars in tenement houses illustrates the point. The court could not see how "the cigarmaker is to be improved in his health or his

---

15. [The beginning of life is without help, the middle without pleasure, and the end without consolation.]

16. [Not by such help nor by such defenders.]

17. Quoted in Norman Ware, The Labor Movement in the United States, 1860-1890: A Study in Democracy (New York: Vintage, 1964 [1929]), p. 300.

morals by forcing him from his home and its hallowed associations and beneficent influences to ply his trade elsewhere."[18] It left open the question of whether states had special interest in the health of their citizens, and subsequent legal battles turned on the issue of whether the state's police power could properly be used to protect workers.

The U.S. Supreme Court dealt this doctrine a mortal blow in 1905 when it decided against a New York state law limiting the hours of bakers to ten per day. The issue was not the hours of labor, the Court argued in Lochner v. New York [198 U.S. 45 (1905)], but the bread itself. "Clean, and wholesome bread does not depend upon whether a baker works but 10 hours per day," said the Court, concluding that the statute was therefore "an illegal interference with the rights of individuals to make contracts."[19] The decision reflected prevailing opinions. It decisively rejected the idea that a shared sense of justice ought to influence working hours and conditions. Legislators and courts by and large agreed that freely negotiated contracts were necessary to success in a society that offered readily attainable upward mobility.

Under these circumstances only skilled trade unionists managed to achieve significant reductions in hours or to play a role in determining their own work practices. By the 1890s, such groups as cigar makers, builders, and machinists regularly worked only fifty hours a week. But there were precious few women among them. Textile mills, laundries, and the garment industry, all heavily women-employing, still averaged twelve-hour days, and five-and-a-half- or six-day weeks.

While the use of state power to limit hours and to regulate work conditions in the interest of the general welfare was still in question, special arguments based on notions of female domesticity began to emerge for restricting women workers. Since the courts rejected the assertion that the general welfare demanded regulation for all workers, proponents moved to the position that women in their capacity as child bearers and rearers served the state's welfare in a special way. The idea that their service to the state entitled women to special protection spread rapidly.

Tactically, the argument grew out of the difficulty in getting any kind of protective legislation past lawmakers and courts. Much of the energy behind attempts to limit the hours of women and children in the 1880s and 1890s came from those who believed that women could be an "opening wedge" in obtaining laws for all the unorganized. Shorter hours for some, they argued, along with adequate factory sanitation and safety devices, would inevitably lead to better conditions for all workers. Economist Elizabeth Brandeis acerbically concluded that Massachusetts workers had decided to "fight the

18. [Elizabeth Faulkner Baker, Protective Labor Legislation with Special Reference to Women in the State of New York, Columbia University Studies in History, Economic and Public Law, Vol. 116, no. 2 (New York: AMS Press, 1969 [1925]), p. 27.]
    19. [198 U.S. at 42.]

battle behind the women's petticoats."[20] But a substantial amount of pressure for such legislation came from those who genuinely felt that women's peculiarly vulnerable position demanded special protection. When this argument was made by unskilled workers competing with each other for jobs, it carried conviction. Their pressure, for example, encouraged Massachusetts lawmakers in 1874 to limit the labor of women and children to sixty hours per week.

Arguments for special protection for women were marked by sympathy and genuine concern. But there was ideological danger in asserting women's weakness. Originally the organized feminist movement staked its claim to women's rights, including the suffrage, firmly on the conviction that women were more like men than unlike them and were therefore entitled to all human rights. By the 1880s, an important wing of the woman suffrage movement had reversed its position. Woman's special sphere, her special sensibilities nurtured in the home, feminists like Lucy Stone argued, developed unique attributes that required representation in the political process. Reformers like Helen Campbell and Annie McLean held that these same attributes — compassion, nurturance, a better-developed sense of morality — unfitted her for the competitive economic struggle. In the unfortunate event that women were forced into the wage labor force the special sensibilities must be preserved.

The argument provided justification not merely for regulating, but for prohibiting altogether, the work of women in certain occupations. If wage work was necessary it had to be bounded by regulations that would preserve woman's body, mind, and morals for home roles. The argument was implicit in all the official investigations of this period, and became the articulated basis of legislation after 1900. Agitation for protection of wage-earning women now rested squarely on the assumption that all women were homemakers without sufficient skill to compete in the labor market. Proponents of protection did not declare all workers in need of it. Rather, they claimed special privilege for the home and motherhood.

A growing eugenics movement and concern for "race suicide" provided additional ammunition around 1900. No selfish employer could be allowed to undermine the strength of the race by threatening the health of future mothers or tempting the morality of future homemakers. All semblance of the class solidarity that had informed the search for protective legislation in the mid-nineteenth century disappeared. By 1900 special protection for women was the rule.

In this climate, legally imposed limitations on the kinds of work women could do took form. Elizabeth Faulkner Baker assigns the first such law to California; in 1881 that state passed a measure denying women the right to

---

20. [Elizabeth Brandeis, "Labor Legislation," in John R. Commons, A History of American Labor (New York: Macmillan, 1936), 3: 462.]

work in places that sold alcoholic beverages. The state Supreme Court quickly invalidated it. The state constitution, it ruled, prohibited legislation "either directly or indirectly incapacitating or disabling a woman from entering or pursuing any business, vocation, or profession" open to men. But courts in Ohio and Washington upheld similar statutes as valid exercises of police power, and other forms of prohibition emerged quickly. Most were based on physical and moral grounds. Selling liquor might expose women to lewd men and threaten their innocence. Grinding and polishing metal might clog women's lungs with dust. Work in underground mines (never prevalent in the United States) would coarsen women's gentle natures. Later women were denied work as messengers because Western Union could not guarantee who might open the door to them. Operating elevators, reading meters, becoming letter carriers, and driving taxis were among the erratic series of occupations sporadically denied to women.[21]

A surprising absence of controversy about such legal prohibitions reveals the strength of popular beliefs in women's assigned roles. More often than not, such legislation merely confirmed custom, and courts readily upheld it. Protests tended to be individual—like those of women who disguised themselves as men in order to obtain jobs—and quickly stifled. When successful, such instances never found their way into the public record. But once caught, women who had tried to pass as men received stiff punishments. One young woman drew six months' imprisonment in New York's Blackwell's Island for dressing like a man. . . .

More controversy surrounded legislation that attempted to regulate the conditions under which women could earn wages. Ohio passed the first maximum-hour law for women—a ten-hour day—in 1852. Minnesota, Massachusetts, and Illinois followed after the Civil War. The first legal restrictions against night work for women appeared in Massachusetts in 1890. These were at first isolated instances which state judicial opinion generally upheld. The Pennsylvania Superior Court, in an 1896 decision, the first on the sixty-hour week and twelve-hour day for women, declared: "Surely an act which prevents the mothers of our race from being tempted to endanger their life and health by exhaustive employment can be condemned by none save those who expect to profit by it." The court went on to say, "Adult females are a class as distinct as minors, separated by natural conditions from all other laborers, and are so constituted as to be unable to endure physical exertion and exposure to the extent and degree that is not harmful to adult workers."[22]

In rapid succession, legislators in Nebraska, Washington, and Oregon passed statutes limiting the workday for women. State courts upheld them. Shared assumptions about women's natural weakness underlay their actions.

21. Baker, Protective Labor Legislation, p. 58.
22. Quoted in Baker, Protective Legislation, pp. 61, 62.

"That which must necessarily affect any great number of women who are the mothers of succeeding generations must necessarily affect the public welfare and morals," argued the Washington Supreme Court in 1902. It was no surprise to many and an enormous relief to proponents when in 1908 the U.S. Supreme Court set its seal on the motherhood argument in response to the famous Brandeis brief in the case of Muller v. Oregon.

Louis Brandeis and his sister-in-law Josephine Goldmark, working at the time for the national Consumers' League, correctly reasoned that to persuade the court that shorter hours for women were in fact conducive to the general welfare required evidence that long hours were inimical to health and safety. In their carefully prepared argument, presented to the Court in defense of Oregon's ten-hour law, they asserted that woman's "special physical organization," her child-bearing and maternal functions, and the need to prevent "laxity or moral fibre," which "follows physical debility" all required restricting her hours of labor to ten per day. The authors used strong language: "women are fundamentally weaker than men in all that makes for endurance: in muscular strength, in nervous energy, in the powers of persistent attention and application." Quoting extensively from state and federal labor officials, the brief argued: "They must have vacations, and they break down in health rapidly." It cited physicians who asserted "the periodic semi-pathological state of health of women" and their greater predisposition to disease. It dwelt on "pale, crooked, and sickly-looking" women and children who worked sixty or more hours per week. It pointed to women who spent "a good part of their Sundays . . . in bed and recuperating for the next week's demands." Neurasthenia, back troubles, pyrosis, constipation, vertigo, and headaches were the least of the problems identified. Edema, varicose veins, displacement of the uterus, throat and lung diseases were said to follow from excessive work.

Muller v. Oregon
208 U.S. 412 (1908)

Mr. Justice BREWER delivered the opinion of the court.

On February 19, 1903, the legislature of the State of Oregon passed an act, . . . the first section of which is in these words:

> SEC. 1. That no female (shall) be employed in any mechanical establishment, or factory, or laundry in this State more than ten hours during any one day. . . .

Section 3 made a violation of the provisions of the prior sections a misdemeanor, subject to a fine of not less than $10 nor more than $25. On September 18, 1905, [defendant was charged with violation of the statute for ordering Mrs. E. Gotcher to work more than ten hours per day in defendant's laundry]. . . .

A trial resulted in a verdict against the defendant, who was sentenced to pay a fine of $10. The Supreme Court of the State affirmed the conviction . . . whereupon the case was brought here on writ of error.

The single question is the constitutionality of the statute under which the defendant was convicted so far as it affects the work of a female in a laundry. . . .

It is the law of Oregon that women, whether married or single, have equal contractual and personal rights with men. . . .

It thus appears that, putting to one side the elective franchise, in the matter of personal and contractual rights they stand on the same plane as the other sex. Their rights in these respects can no more be infringed than the equal rights of their brothers. We held in Lochner v. New York, 198 U.S. 45 [1905], that a law providing that no laborer shall be required or permitted to work in a bakery more than sixty hours in a week or ten hours in a day was not as to men a legitimate exercise of the police power of the State, but an unreasonable, unnecessary and arbitrary interference with the right and liberty of the individual to contract in relation to his labor, and as such was in conflict with, and void under, the Federal Constitution. That decision is invoked by plaintiff in error as decisive of the question before us. But this assumes that the difference between the sexes does not justify a different rule respecting a restriction of the hours of labor. . . .

. . . In the brief filed by Mr. Louis D. Brandeis, for the defendant in error, is a very copious collection of all these matters, an epitome of which is found in the margin.[23] . . .

The legislation and opinions referred to [above] may not be, technically speaking, authorities, . . . yet they are significant of a widespread belief that woman's physical structure, and the functions she performs in consequence thereof, justify special legislation restricting or qualifying the conditions under which she should be permitted to toil. Constitutional questions, it is true, are not settled by even a consensus of present public opinion, for it is the peculiar value of a written constitution that it places in unchanging form limitations upon legislative action, and thus gives a permanence and stability to popular government which otherwise would be lacking. At the same time, when a question of fact is debated and debatable, and the extent to which a special constitutional limitation goes is affected by the truth in respect to that fact, a widespread and long continued belief concerning it is worthy of consideration. We take judicial cognizance of all matters of general knowledge.

That woman's physical structure and the performance of maternal functions place her at a disadvantage in the struggle for subsistence is obvious. This is especially true when the burdens of motherhood are upon her. Even when they are not, by abundant testimony of the medical

---

23. [Legislation from 19 states and 7 foreign countries is cited.]

fraternity continuance for a long time on her feet at work, repeating this from day to day, tends to injurious effects upon the body, and as healthy mothers are essential to vigorous offspring, the physical well-being of woman becomes an object of public interest and care in order to preserve the strength and vigor of the race.

Still again, history discloses the fact that woman has always been dependent upon man. He established his control at the outset by superior physical strength, and this control in various forms, with diminishing intensity, has continued to the present. As minors, though not to the same extent, she has been looked upon in the courts as needing especial care that her rights may be preserved. Education was long denied her, and while now the doors of the school room are opened and her opportunities for acquiring knowledge are great, yet even with that and the consequent increase of capacity for business affairs it is still true that in the struggle for subsistence she is not an equal competitor with her brother. Though limitations upon personal and contractual rights may be removed by legislation, there is that in her disposition and habits of life which will operate against a full assertion of those rights. She will still be where some legislation to protect her seems necessary to secure a real equality of right. Doubtless there are individual exceptions, and there are many respects in which she has an advantage over him; but looking at it from the viewpoint of the effort to maintain an independent position in life, she is not upon an equality. Differentiated by these matters from the other sex, she is properly placed in a class by herself, and legislation designed for her protection may be sustained, even when like legislation is not necessary for men and could not be sustained. It is impossible to close one's eyes to the fact that she still looks to her brother and depends upon him. Even though all restrictions on political, personal and contractual rights were taken away, and she stood, so far as statutes are concerned, upon an absolutely equal plane with him, it would still be true that she is so constituted that she will rest upon and look to him for protection; that her physical structure and a proper discharge of her maternal functions — having in view not merely her own health, but the well-being of the race — justify legislation to protect her from the greed as well as the passion of man. The limitations which this statute places upon her contractual powers, upon her right to agree with her employer as to the time she shall labor, are not imposed solely for her benefit, but also largely for the benefit of all. Many words cannot make this plainer. The two sexes differ in structure of body, in the functions to be performed by each, in the amount of physical strength, in the capacity for long-continued labor, particularly when done standing, the influence of vigorous health upon the future well-being of the race, the self-reliance which enables one to assert full rights, and in the capacity to maintain the struggle for subsistence. This difference justifies a difference in legislation and upholds that which is designed to compensate for some of the burdens which rest upon her.

We have not referred in this discussion to the denial of the elective franchise in the State of Oregon, for while it may disclose a lack of political equality in all things with her brother, that is not of itself decisive. The reason runs deeper, and rests in the inherent difference between the two sexes, and in the different functions in life which they perform.

For these reasons, and without questioning in any respect the decision in Lochner v. New York, we are of the opinion that it cannot be adjudged that the act in question is in conflict with the Federal Constitution, so far as it respects the work of a female in a laundry, and the judgment of the Supreme Court of Oregon is affirmed.

Evelyn Glenn, The Racial Division of Reproductive Labor
18 Signs 1, 6-8, 10-12 (Autumn 1992)

Both the demand for household help and the number of women employed as servants expanded rapidly in the latter half of the nineteenth century. This expansion paralleled the rise of industrial capital and the elaboration of middle-class women's reproductive responsibilities. Rising standards of cleanliness, larger and more ornately furnished homes, and sentimentalization of the home as a "haven in a heartless world," and the new emphasis on childhood and the mother's role in nurturing children all served to enlarge middle-class women's responsibilities for reproduction at a time when technology had done little to reduce the sheer physical drudgery of housework.

By all accounts middle-class women did not challenge the gender-based division of labor or the enlargement of their reproductive responsibilities. Indeed, middle-class women — as readers and writers of literature; as members and leaders of clubs, charitable organizations, associations, reform movements, and religious revivals; and as supporters of the cause of abolition — helped to elaborate the domestic code. Feminists seeking an expanded public role for women argued that the same nurturant and moral qualities that made women centers of the home should be brought to bear in public service. In the domestic sphere, instead of questioning the inequitable gender division of labor, they sought to slough off the more burdensome tasks onto more oppressed groups of women.

Phyllis Palmer observes that at least through the first half of the twentieth century, "most white middle class women could hire another woman — a recent immigrant, a working class woman, a woman of color, or all three — to perform much of the hard labor of household tasks." Domestics were employed to clean house, launder and iron clothes, scrub floors, and care for infants and children. They relieved their mistresses of the heavier and dirtier domestic chores. White middle-class women were thereby freed for supervisory tasks and for cultural, leisure, and volunteer activity or, more rarely during this period, for a career. . . .

Who was to perform the "dirty work" varied by region. In the Northeast, European immigrant women, particularly those who were Irish and German, constituted the majority of domestic servants from the mid-nineteenth century to World War I. In regions where there was a large concentration of people of color, subordinate-race women formed a more or less permanent servant stratum. . . .

Where more than one group was available for service, a differentiated hierarchy of race, color, and culture emerged. White and racial-ethnic domestics were hired for different tasks. In her study of women workers in Atlanta, New Orleans, and San Antonio during the 1920s and 1930s, Julia Kirk Blackwelder reported that "[A]nglo women in the employ of private households were nearly always reported as housekeepers, while Blacks and Chicanas were reported as laundresses, cooks, or servants." . . .

Despite their preference for European immigrant domestics, employers could not easily retain their services. Most European immigrant women left service upon marriage, and their daughters moved into the expanding manufacturing, clerical, and sales occupations during the 1910s and twenties. With the flow in immigration slowed to a trickle during World War I, there were few new recruits from Europe. In the 1920s, domestic service became increasingly the specialty of minority-race women. Women of color were advantageous employees in one respect: they could be compelled more easily to remain in service. There is considerable evidence that middle-class whites acted to ensure the domestic labor supply by tracking racial-ethnic women into domestic service and blocking their entry into other fields. Urban school systems in the Southwest tracked Chicana students into homemaking courses designed to prepare them for domestic service. . . .

The education of Chicanas in the Denver school system was similarly directed toward preparing students for domestic service and handicrafts. Sarah Deutsch found that Anglo women there persisted in viewing Chicanas and other "inferior-race" women as dependent, slovenly, and ignorant. Thus, they argued, training Mexican girls for domestic service not only would solve "one phase of women's work we seem to be incapable of handling" but it would simultaneously help raise the (Mexican) community by improving women's standard of living, elevating their morals, and facilitating Americanization. One Anglo writer, in an article published in 1917 titled "Problems and Progress among Mexicans in Our Own Southwest," claimed, "When trained there is no better servant than the gentle, quiet Mexicana girl."

Notes

1. Law and the Regulation of Working Class Women's Labor. According to Kessler-Harris, Muller v. Oregon

> electrified the field of protective legislation, reviving long-dormant restrictive measures. Hours were the first and prime target. Between 1909 and 1917, nineteen states passed laws restricting women's working day. Regulations differed not only from state to state but from industry to industry within each state. Manufacturing and mercantile enterprises were the first statutory targets, with laundries and telegraph and telephone companies running a close second.

Kessler-Harris, Out to Work, supra, at 187.

In addition to hours regulations, wage regulations for women were upheld on grounds similar to those spelled out in Muller v. Oregon. For example, in West Coast Hotel Co. v. Parrish, 300 U.S. 379 (1937), the Supreme Court had no difficulty upholding the constitutional validity of Washington state's minimum wage law for women. In the Court's view, "The legislature of the State was clearly entitled to consider the situation of women in employment, the fact that they are in the class receiving the least pay, that their bargaining power is relatively weak, and that they are the ready victims of those who would take advantage of their necessitous circumstances." Id. at 398.

Women were also explicitly barred from certain jobs. For example, in Goesaert v. Cleary, 335 U.S. 464 (1948), the Supreme Court upheld a Michigan statute barring a woman from working as a bartender unless she was "the wife or daughter of the male owner" of a licensed liquor establishment. The Court began by affirming Michigan's power, if it wished, to bar all women from the job. Nor was it irrational for Michigan to make distinctions among women:

> Since bartending by women may, in the allowable legislative judgment, give rise to moral and social problems against which it may devise preventive measures, the legislature need not go to the full length of prohibition if it believes that as to a defined group of females other factors are operating which either eliminate or reduce the moral and social problems otherwise calling for prohibition. Michigan evidently believes that the oversight assured through ownership of a bar by a barmaid's husband or father minimizes hazards that may confront a barmaid without such protecting oversight.

335 U.S. at 466.

Not all jobs in which women worked became subject to wages and hours limitations, however. As Kessler-Harris notes, hotels, restaurants, and cabarets often escaped regulation entirely. Domestic service and agriculture, the two leading female occupations and occupations that were physically arduous, also remained unregulated. See Kessler-Harris, Out to Work, supra, at 188. Consider, on this point, Glenn's excerpt. Which women did the argument from domesticity help, and which did it hurt? What other facts would be useful to know to answer this question?

For a contemporary instance in which women were barred from holding certain industrial jobs out of concern for their reproductive health, see UAW v. Johnson Controls, Inc., 499 U.S. 187 (1991), (set forth at pages 236-245 below).

2. Law and the Regulation of Upper Class Women. As Bradwell v. Illinois and In re Goodell suggest, the rhetoric of domesticity could be used both to deny women access to industrial work and to bar them from entering the professions. The Glenn excerpt, however, suggests that relegating women to "the home" had different consequences for women in different places in class and ethnic hierarchies. For contemporary examples of "women's work" dividing women by race and class, see Chapter 3 (Work and Family).

3. Gender and Intimate Life in United States Legal History

a. Law and the Regulation of Non-Marital Relations

Plymouth Sodomy Case
Taken from William Rubenstein, Lesbians, Gay Men, and the Law 85-86 (1993)

1649, March 6

Plymouth: Sara Norman and Mary Hammon

"Lewd behavior . . . upon a bed"

Plymouth colony records included the accusation against two women, Sara Norman and Mary Hammon (or Hammond):

> We present [charge] the wife of Hugh Norman, and Mary Hammon, both of Yarmouth, for lewd behavior each with [the] other upon a bed. . . .

Recent research by J. R. Roberts in the Plymouth manuscript records provides background information on Norman and Hammon. At the time of the above charges Mary Hammon was fifteen years old, and recently married. Sara Norman's age is unknown, but she was apparently somewhat older, as she had been married in 1639. About the time of the court's first charge, 1649, Hugh Norman, Sara's husband, deserted his wife and children.

A marginal note in the Plymouth court record of March 6, 1649, reported that Mary Hammon was "cleared with admonition" — perhaps because of her youth. Sara Norman's case was evidently held over for later judgment.

A year after the first charge, on March 6, 1650, Sara Norman was cited again in the Plymouth court records, this time accused of "unclean practices" with a male, Teage Jones. This charge was subsequently dropped, when her accuser pleaded guilty of perjury.

On October 2, 1650, the records report the outcome of the original charge against Sara Norman. The court punished her with a warning, and asked her to acknowledge publicly her "unchaste behavior" with Mary Hammon. This punishment, though publicly humiliating, was lenient compared to the death penalty imposed for male-male "sodomy."

Patriarchal custom was evident in the fact that court records in this case referred to "the wife of Hugh Norman"; although Sara Norman was publicly charged with a serious crime, her whole name was used only once in the documents.

The court record of 1650 said:

> Whereas the wife of Hugh Norman, of Yarmouth, hath stood presented [in] divers Courts for misdemeanor and lewd behavior with Mary Hammon upon a bed, with divers lascivious speeches by her also spoken, but she could not appear by reason of some hindrances unto this Court, the said Court have therefore sentenced her, the said wife of Hugh Norman, for her wild behavior in the aforesaid particulars, to make a public acknowledgement, so far as conveniently may be, of her unchaste behavior, and have also warned her to take heed of such carriages for the future, lest her former carriage come in remembrance against her to make her punishment the greater.

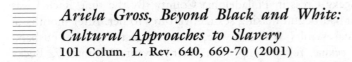

Ariela Gross, *Beyond Black and White:*
Cultural Approaches to Slavery
101 Colum. L. Rev. 640, 669-70 (2001)

While fornication cases in the mid-seventeenth century appear to have been handled similarly whether the offenders were African, English, or an "interracial" couple, racial differentiation became evident when women serving life terms gave birth. Beginning in 1662, legislation decreed that children followed the condition of their mother, and in the same act, that "if any christian shall committ fornication with a negro man or woman, hee or shee soe offending shall pay double the fines imposed by the former act." "Christian" did not long remain adequate as a legal marker of difference; by 1667, baptism was no longer enough to free one who was born a slave.

The earliest restrictions on sexual activity aimed their discipline at white women; in 81 percent of the cases enforcing a 1662 law banning interracial intimacy, white women bore the brunt of the expense and punishment for the transgression. But existing laws regulating white women's sexuality were increasingly used by lawmakers "to refine the legal meanings and practical consequences of racial difference." Over the course of the late seventeenth century, a shift occurred in punishments for bastardy, from penance rituals to secular punishments, especially money damages to masters, treating sexual wrongdoing less as a sin and more as a crime. There was a "growing overlap between patriarchal privilege and racial domination." In rape cases, women lost their suits against white men, but won against black men.

Court records from the seventeenth century demonstrate the linkage made between race and sexuality, for example, in the insult that a woman was "such a whore that she would lye with a negro." Over the course of the seventeenth and eighteenth centuries, the typical sexual slander suit changed from a white man suing a white woman after she claimed that he had slept with her and then abandoned her to a white woman suing someone, often another white woman, alleging that she had slept with a black man. Allegations of interracial sex were enough to threaten the white status of an English woman.

Sharon Block, Lines of Color, Sex, and Service: Comparative Sexual Coercion in Early America, in Sex, Love, Race: Crossing Boundaries in North American History
141-43, 148-49, 150, 151-52, 156, 157 (Martha Hodes ed., 1999)

Rachel Davis was born a free white child in the Pennsylvania mountains in 1790. She was fourteen years old when she became an indentured servant to William and Becky Cress in Philadelphia County. By the time Rachel was fifteen, William had begun making sexual overtures to her. After months of continuing sexual assaults, William's wife, Becky, suspected that her husband was having a sexual relationship with their servant. Ultimately, Becky demanded that Rachel be removed from the house. William continued to visit Rachel at her new home, again trying to have sex with her. In 1807, Rachel's father found out what had occurred and initiated a rape prosecution against William, who was found guilty and sentenced to ten years in prison.

Harriet Jacobs was born an enslaved black child in Edenton, North Carolina, in 1813. In 1825, she became a slave in James and Mary Norcom's household. By the time Harriet was sixteen, James had begun making sexual overtures to her. After months of continuing sexual assaults, James's wife, Mary, suspected that her husband was having a sexual relationship with their slave. Ultimately, Mary demanded that Harriet be removed from the house.

James continued to visit Harriet at her new home, again trying to have sex with her. In 1835, Harriet became a runaway slave, and spent the next seven years a fugitive, hiding in her free grandmother's attic crawlspace.

If we were to focus on the conclusions to these stories, we would frame a picture of the contrasting consequences for masters who sexually coerced black and white women: the master of the white servant was sent to prison, while the black slave imprisoned herself to escape her abuser. But these opposing ends tell only part of the story. Until their conclusions, both women engaged in nearly parallel struggles with masters, mistresses, and unwanted sexual overtures. This contrast between the laborers' similar experiences and their stories' opposing conclusions suggests that the practice of sexual coercion and the classification of the criminal act of rape were differently dependent on status and race. . . .

Legally, the endings to Harriet Jacobs's and Rachel Davis's stories were foregone conclusions: Rachel had an opportunity for institutional intervention that was unequivocally denied to Harriet. Enslaved women in early America did not have access to legal redress against white men who raped them. While no colonial or early republic statute explicitly excluded enslaved women from being the victims of rape or attempted rape, many mid-Atlantic and Southern legislatures passed statutes setting harsh punishments for black men's sexual assaults on white women, thus implicitly privileging white women as victims of rape. At the same time, enslaved people could qualify as witnesses only in cases with nonwhite defendants, so an enslaved woman could not testify against a white man who had raped her. Accordingly, no historian has recorded a conviction of a white man for the rape of a slave at any point from 1700 to the Civil War, let alone a conviction of a master for raping his own slave. Rape in early America was a crime whose definition was structured by race. . . .

How did a master sexually coerce a servant or slave in early America? Unlike a surprise attack where an assailant might use explicit physical force, a master did not have to rely on physical abilities to force his dependents into a sexual act. Instead, he might use the power of his position to create opportunities for sexual coercion, backing a woman into a corner where capitulation was her best option. A servant or enslaved woman often recognized this manipulation and tried to negotiate her way around her master's overtures rather than confront him with direct resistance. But that compromise came at a high price: when a dependent negotiated with a master, sexual coercion could be reformulated into a consensual relationship. Negotiation implied willingness, and a woman's willingness contrasted with the early American legal and social code that rape consisted of irresistible force. Despite its surface counterintuitiveness, it was precisely women's attempts to bargain their way out of sexual assaults that made these sexual encounters seem consensual. . . .

After attempting sexual overtures toward their laborers, masters had to contend with the possibility that the women would tell others about their masters' behavior. Harriet Jacobs's and Rachel Davis's masters attempted to threaten their laborers into silence about their sexual interactions. Harriet wrote that her master "swore he would kill me, if I was not as silent as the grave." Similarly, William told Rachel that if she told "any body, he wd be the death of me." When Rachel threatened to tell his wife what William had been doing, "he sd if I did, I shd repent." By demanding her silence, each master tried to dictate the parameters of his sexual interactions with his servant or slave without outside interference that might contradict his interpretation or stop his sexual pursuit.

But each woman also believed that her master was afraid of the damage she could do by publicizing his sexual behavior. . . . From each woman's vantage point, then, her master's concern about his public image again allowed her some room for negotiation: he needed his servant or slave to conceal their sexual interactions. But by not telling anyone about her master's sexual assaults, a woman increased the likelihood that their sexual relationship would not appear to be a rape. This double-edged sword made the servant or slave an unwilling accomplice in the masking of her own sexual coercion. . . .

. . . Each woman had to deal with a mistress who ultimately took her displeasure at her husband's sexual relationship out on her servant or slave. Each mistress also used her position of secondary mastery to create a temporary alliance with her servant or slave. Once this alliance outlived its usefulness, it became another tool with which the mistress could assist in redefining or denying the sexual relationship between the master and the slave or servant. . . .

If mistresses could not personally control their husbands' behavior, how could they stop the sexual relationship between master and laborer that was making a mockery of their marital vows? Theoretically, mistresses could turn to the legal system to petition for a divorce from their husbands. By the early nineteenth century, most states had divorce laws that allowed wives to apply for divorce on the grounds of their husbands' adultery, but women's petitions for divorce were more commonly based on charges of desertion. Furthermore, proving adultery with a slave might be difficult without firsthand witnesses to the sexual interactions since the slave was limited in her ability to testify against the white man. Married women also had a vested interest in their husbands' social and economic standing. Divorce or incarceration would most probably result in a woman's economic downturn from the loss of her husband's labor. . . .

Ultimately, Rachel Davis's and Harriet Jacobs's mistresses concentrated their energies on removing their laborers from the household. Instead of bringing charges against her husband or applying for a divorce on the grounds of adultery, Becky Cress told Rachel Davis that she must "leave the house." Rachel recalled that "they then hired me out." . . .

Mary Norcum demanded that Harriet Jacobs leave the house once she learned that Harriet was pregnant, believing that conception was proof of their slave's sexual relationship with her husband. . . .

By not telling others what had happened to her, Harriet was at the mercy of other people's versions of events. James's wife, Mary, went to the house of Harriet's free grandmother to tell her that Harriet was pregnant with James's baby. Molly Horniblow then turned on Harriet, apparently believing Mary's story that Harriet had consented to the relationship: "I had rather see you dead than to see you as you now are," she told her granddaughter. "You are a disgrace to your dead mother . . . Go away . . . and never come to my house, again." . . . Later, Harriet's grandmother learned that Harriet had chosen to become pregnant with another man's baby to try to force her sexually abusive master to leave her alone or sell her. Once her grandmother understood "the real state of the case, and all I had been bearing for years. . . . She laid her old hand gently on my head, and murmured, 'Poor child! Poor child!' " . . .

Both Harriet Jacobs and Rachel Davis fought similar battles against the veil of silence surrounding their masters' treatment of them. Both were confronted by relatives and neighbors who had limited authority over another household's problems. Both women turned to another powerful figure — father or free grandmother and elite white lover, respectively — to rescue them from their masters' sexual abuse. When Rachel finally told her father about her master's sexual assaults, Jacob Davis successfully encouraged the local legal system to begin a criminal prosecution. But neither Harriet Jacobs's ultimate confession to her grandmother nor her involvement with a white lover could lead to legal intervention. The legal system marked an irreversible disjuncture in the two women's experiences.

Notes

1. Law and the Regulation of Lesbian Sexuality. Ruthann Robson asserts that as of the early 1990s, "About half the jurisdictions in the United States ha[d] statutes that criminalize[d] lesbian sexual expressions, and virtually every state . . . had a statute as recently as 1968 that would imprison someone for lesbian sexual expression." Ruthann Robson, Lesbian Out(law): Survival Under the Rule of Law 47 (1992). Yet reported cases involving criminal prosecutions of women for lesbian sexual activity are few. See id. (describing cases). Moreover, the original English term "sodomy" described only anal intercourse between males; thus, in states that punished only "sodomy," "the exclusion of oral sex effectively excepted female homosexuality from the realm of the criminal law, even though copulation between males was punished as a very grave offense." Model Penal Code §213.2, Comment 1 (1962, comments revised 1980). Why might the law be so much more concerned with male than female homosexuality? Why has the law been more concerned about proscribing various expressions of heterosexual relations than lesbian relations?

2. Law and the Regulation of Women's Non-Marital Sexuality. Gross's excerpt suggests that women's sexuality was frequently the subject of legislation. What dangers did women's sexuality pose?

3. Sexual Harassment and the Tort of Seduction. As Jane Larson describes it, the common law tort of "seduction" provided one remedy for the sexual exploitation of women and girls.

> The origins of the action for seduction lie in the Roman law notion that some individuals may hold property interests in the bodies and sexuality of others. The seduction action exemplified the proprietary character of master-servant law, which allowed a master to sue someone who injured his servant (defined to include his child) for loss of services. By the mid-seventeenth century in Britain, a father's common-law right to sue his daughter's seducer — typically, when a pregnancy had resulted — was established under this "loss of services" framework.
>
> A working-class family faced serious financial hardship when an unmarried daughter earning wages outside the home became pregnant and lost her income. Moreover, because access to the marriage market was economically crucial for women, the daughter's loss of opportunity to marry was of still greater consequence. As a result, working-class and poor families brought the greater number of seduction actions. Nineteenth-century seduction plaintiffs thus sought both a remedy for economic loss and a recompense for injured social status.
>
> In the late nineteenth century, the tort of seduction was among the most common civil actions. Appellate case records for the United States indicate that all-male juries were sympathetic to claims made by fathers of seduced women. . . .
>
> As the nineteenth century wore on, however, the relationship between fathers and daughters began to change in ways that eventually undermined this broad social acceptance of the seduction tort. Urbanization and expanding wage labor opportunities took young women outside the home to work, eroding fathers' control over their daughters' activities. Many unmarried women gained unprecedented personal and economic independence by taking work in factories and domestic service, and some began to live apart from their families before marriage. . . .
>
> Against this background, the familial and social tensions created by young women's growing independence also led to changes in the law of seduction. Between 1846 and 1913, nineteen states enacted seduction statutes that codified the cause of action and altered key elements of the tort. All but one state explicitly abandoned the original property basis for the tort and recognized seduction as a personal injury. The loss of services requirement was removed, and the moral and emotional investment in sexual chastity was recognized as a legally protected interest. Damages could be awarded apart from any economic loss. Beginning with the Iowa statute enacted in 1851,

most (but not all) reform statutes also allowed the seduced woman to sue in her own name, replacing her father as the plaintiff and real party in interest. Thus, legislation in about half of the states brought the seduction action into line with its real social basis in that era: the prevailing sexual morality and economic reality that made premarital sexual experience or single motherhood an obstacle to a woman's chance to work and to marry, and therefore a devastating social injury. . . .

Once a seduced woman was allowed to sue on her own behalf, the circumstances of her sexual consent became the most contested factual issue in the dispute. She was required to prove that her apparently willing consent to sexual relations had been compromised by the defendant's wrongdoing. Reformulated as a moral injury to the seduced woman herself, the paradigmatic seduction case evolved into a claim of fraud: By means of an intentional deception, the seduced woman had yielded a valuable interest — her consent — only in reliance on "deception, enticement, or other artifice." Pregnancy — a critical element of the tort when economic loss of services had been the gravamen of the cause of action — now brought only an additional measure of damages. The wrong remedied by the tort was the woman's loss of sexual chastity per se, and the courts presumed that a sexually active woman had no virtue to lose. In the latter part of the nineteenth century, the plaintiff's prior virtue and spotless sexual reputation thus became critically important to a successful seduction claim.

Jane E. Larson, "Women Understand So Little, They Call My Good Nature 'Deceit'": A Feminist Rethinking of Seduction, 93 Colum. L.Rev. 374, 382-87 (1993).

b. Law and the Regulation of Marital Relations

William Blackstone, 1 Commentaries on the Laws of England
*432-433

The husband . . . , by the old law, might give his wife moderate correction. For, as he is to answer for her misbehaviour, the law thought it reasonable to intrust him with this power of restraining her, by domestic chastisement, in the same moderation that a man is allowed to correct his apprentices or children; for whom the master or parent is also liable in some cases to answer. But this power of correction was confined within reasonable bounds, and the husband was prohibited from using any violence to his wife. . . . The civil law gave the husband the same, or a larger, authority over his wife. . . . But with us, in the politer reign of Charles the Second, this power of correction began to be doubted; and a wife may now have security of the peace against her husband; or, in return, a husband against his wife. Yet the lower rank of people, who were always fond of the old common law, still claim and exert their ancient privilege; and the courts of law will still permit a husband to restrain a wife of her liberty, in case of any gross misbehaviour.

State v. Rhodes
61 N.C. 453 (1868)

The defendant was indicted for an assault and battery upon his wife, Elizabeth Rhodes. Upon the evidence submitted to them the jury returned the following special verdict:

"We find that the defendant struck Elizabeth Rhodes, his wife, three licks, with a switch about the size of one of his fingers (but not as large as a man's thumb), without any provocation except some words uttered by her and not recollected by the witness."

His Honor was of opinion that the defendant had a right to whip his wife with a switch no larger than his thumb, and that upon the facts found in the special verdict he was not guilty in law. Judgment in favor of the defendant was accordingly entered and the State appealed.

READE, J. The violence complained of would without question have constituted a battery if the subject of it had not been the defendant's wife. The question is how far that fact affects the case.

The courts have been loath to take cognizance of trivial complaints arising out of the domestic relations — such as master and apprentice, teacher and pupil, parent and child, husband and wife. Not because those relations are not subject to the law, but because the evil of publicity would be greater than the evil involved in the trifles complained of; and because they ought to be left to family government. . . .

In this case no provocation worth the name was proved. The fact found was that it was "without any provocation except some words which were not recollected by the witness." The words must have been of the slightest import to have made no impression on the memory. We must therefore consider the violence as unprovoked. The question is therefore plainly presented, whether the court will allow a conviction of the husband for moderate correction of the wife without provocation. . . .

We have sought the aid of the experience and wisdom of other times and of other countries.

Blackstone says "that the husband, by the old law, might give the wife moderate correction, for as he was to answer for her misbehavior, he ought to have the power to control her; but that in the polite reign of Charles the Second, this power of correction began to be doubted." 1 Black., 444. Wharton says, that by the ancient common law the husband possessed the power to chastise his wife; but that the tendency of criminal courts in the present day is to regard the marital relation as no defense to a battery. . . . Chancellor Walworth says of such correction, that it is not authorized by the law of any civilized country; not indeed meaning that England is not civilized, but referring to the anomalous relics of barbarism which cleave to her jurisprudence. . . . The old law of moderate correction has been questioned even in England, and has been repudiated in Ireland and Scotland. The old rule is approved in Mississippi, but it has met with but little favor elsewhere in the United States. . . . In looking into the discussions of the other States we find but little uniformity.

From what has been said it will be seen how much the subject is at sea. And, probably, it will ever be so: for it will always be influenced by the habits, manners and condition of every community. Yet it is necessary that we should lay down something as precise and practical as the nature of the subject will admit of, for the guidance of our courts.

Our conclusion is that family government is recognized by law as being as complete in itself as the State government is in itself, and yet subordinate to it; and that we will not interfere with or attempt to control it, in favor of either husband or wife, unless in cases where permanent or malicious injury is inflicted or threatened, or the condition of the party is intolerable. For, however great are the evils of ill temper, quarrels, and even personal conflicts inflicting only temporary pain, they are not comparable with the evils which would result from raising the curtain, and exposing to public curiosity and criticism, the nursery and the bed chamber. Every household has and must have, a government of its own, modeled to suit the temper, disposition and condition of its inmates. Mere ebullitions of passion, impulsive violence, and temporary pain, affection will soon forget and forgive, and each member will find excuse for the other in his own frailties. But when trifles are taken hold of by the public, and the parties are exposed and disgraced, and each endeavors to justify himself or herself by criminating the other, that which ought to be forgotten in a day, will be remembered for life.

It is urged in this case that as there was no provocation the violence was of course excessive and malicious; that everyone in whatever relation of life should be able to purchase immunity from pain, by obedience to authority and faithfulness in duty. And it is insisted that in S. v. Pendergrass, 2 D.&B., 365, which was the case of schoolmistress whipping a child, that doctrine is laid down. It is true that it is there said, that the master may be punishable even when he does not transcend the powers granted; i.e., when he does not inflict permanent injury, if he grossly abuse his powers, and use them as a cover for his malice. But observe, the language is, if he grossly abuse his powers. So that every one would say at once, there was no cause for it, and it was purely malicious and cruel. If this be not the rule then every violence which would amount to an assault upon a stranger, would have to be investigated to see whether there was any provocation. And that would contravene what we have said, that we will punish no case of trifling importance. If in every such case we are to hunt for the provocation, how will the proof be supplied? Take the case before us. The witness said there was no provocation except some slight words. But then who can tell what significance the trifling words may have had to the husband? Who can tell what had happened an hour before, and every hour for a week? To him they may have been sharper than a sword. And so in every case, it might be impossible for the court to appreciate what might be offered as an excuse, or no excuse might appear at all, when a complete justification exists. Or, suppose the provocation could in every case be known, and the court should undertake to weigh the provocation in every trifling family broil, what would be the standard? Suppose a case coming up to us from a hovel, where neither delicacy of sentiment nor refinement of manners is appreciated or known. The parties themselves would be amazed, if they were to be held responsible for rudeness or trifling violence. What do they care for insults and indignities? In such cases what end would be gained by investigation or punishment? Take a case from the middle class, where modesty and purity have their abode, but nevertheless have not immunity from the frailties of nature, and are sometimes moved by the mysteries of passion. What could be more harassing to them, or injurious to society, than to draw a crowd around their seclusion? Or take a case from the higher ranks, where education and culture have so refined nature, that a look cuts like a knife, and a word strikes like a hammer; where the most delicate attention gives pleasure, and the slightest neglect pain; where an indignity is disgrace and exposure is ruin. Bring all these cases into court side by side, with the same offense charged and the same proof made; and what conceivable charge of the court to the jury would be alike appropriate to all the cases, except that they all have domestic government, which they have formed for themselves, suited to their own peculiar conditions, and that those governments are supreme, and from them there is no appeal except in cases of great importance requiring the strong arm of the law, and that to those governments they must submit themselves.

It will be observed that the ground upon which we have put this decision is not that the husband has the right to whip his wife much or little; but that we will not interfere with family government in trifling cases. We will no more interfere where the husband whips the wife than where the wife whips the husband; and yet we would hardly be supposed to hold that a wife has a right to whip her husband. We will not inflict upon society the greater evil of raising the curtain upon domestic privacy, to punish the lesser evil of trifling violence. Two boys under fourteen years of age fight upon the playground, and yet the courts will take no notice of it, not for the reason that boys have the right to fight, but because the interests of society require that they should be left to the more appropriate discipline of the school room and of home. It is not true that boys have a right to fight; nor is it true that a husband has a right to whip his wife. And if he had, it is not easily seen how the thumb is the standard of size for the instrument which he may use, as some of the old authorities have said; and in deference to which was his Honor's charge. A light blow, or many light blows, with a stick larger than the thumb, might produce no injury; but a switch half the size might be so used as to produce death. The standard is the effect produced, and not the manner of producing it, or the instrument used. . . .

No error.

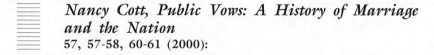

Nancy Cott, *Public Vows: A History of Marriage and the Nation*
57, 57-58, 60-61 (2000):

Marriage values and practices animated the rhetoric of both sides [of the slavery debate in the antebellum period]. Abolitionists, forcefully rejecting slavery for turning human beings into chattel, harped on the way it deformed marriage. They called the denial to slaves of legally recognized and binding marriages a human tragedy, and a crying affront to American pretensions to value the purity of family life. When abolitionists vituperated that slavery caused "a complete extinction of all the relations, endearments and obligations of mankind, and a presumptuous transgression of all the holy commandments," they were referring unmistakably to violations of Christian monogamy: the master's power to sever relationships between slave couples and families; the inability of enslaved women to prevent unwelcome white masters, overseers, and sons from using their bodies sexually; and slave men's inability to act effectively as protectors or defenders. . . .

In response to abolitionists' attacks, southern defenders "domesticated" slavery, rather than treating it simply as a labor regime. They portrayed it as a benevolent practice in which the white master protected and spoke for "my family black and white." In this counterattack, proslavery spokesmen legitimated the inequalities of slavery by praising all the domestic relations of domination and subordination — master-servant, parent-child, and husband-wife — as one and by seeing the three types as indivisible. . . .

The domestic emphasis remade slavery as a set of relationships intended to foster qualities desirable in family members. Parental wisdom, protection, support, and discipline were expected from masters and cheerful, childlike obedience from slaves. . . .

The southern elite believed that God and nature intended women to be the subordinates in marriage. Individual competence did not matter. Working from that premise, proslavery spokesmen argued that God had ordained for slaves, as for wives, a position in the inevitable hierarchy of society, with particular rights and duties attached. Notions of universal or inherent rights faded in significance as southern spokesmen emphasized particular obligations in given roles. In the case of marriage, southern defenders specified that the position of the wife was suitable and noble, not to be misunderstood as demeaning her personally or labelling her inferior. Just as women were fitted by nature and God to conform to their place as wives, enslaved African Americans were suited for slavery; and slavery, like marriage, was a relationship of unequals benefiting both parties. Both women as a sex and blacks as a race flourished best where they were guided and protected, it was said.

State v. Samuel, a Slave
19 N.C. 177 (1836)

[A slave, whose name is not recorded in this opinion, was murdered, and another slave, Samuel, was arrested for the crime. The state called as a witness a slave named Mima, who was the only eyewitness to the incident in which the victim was killed. The defense counsel objected on the ground of marital privilege, and introduced in support of the objection the testimony of one A.M. Lea, Mima's owner. Lea testified that Samuel and Mima had lived together as man and wife for about ten years and had five children together. Lea also testified that she overheard a quarrel between the two, during which she heard Samuel announce his intention to leave Mima and saw him pick up a bundle of his clothes. Lea intervened, telling Samuel to get an order from his master if he wanted the clothes. Within two weeks Samuel returned with the order, took his clothes, and was told by Lea not to return. Soon thereafter the murder victim applied to Lea for permission to take Mima as his wife, and upon being given permission, he did so.

The trial judge overruled the objection to Mima's competency as a witness, and Samuel was convicted and sentenced to death. This appeal followed.]

RUFFIN, Chief Justice: . . .

. . . The objection to the competency of the witness is, that she is the wife of the prisoner, and cannot be compelled or allowed to give evidence against him. The novelty of the attempt to apply this rule of the law of evidence, to this relation between slaves, is, perhaps, a sufficient reason for not yielding to it. The inclination of the courts now, is, to hear every person, who is not clearly excluded by a positive rule precisely embracing the witness offered; and thus leave the weight and effect to the jury. . . .

The disqualification of husband and wife, to testify for or against each other, is merely of civil institution, upon reasons of general policy. That policy has regard in the common law of England, chiefly to the peace of families, by avoiding all causes of dissension between those who, according to that law, are indissolubly joined together. No code could justly, by one of its edicts, pronounce that a union between two persons once formed, should by no means be severed, and yet, by another of its edicts, coerce them to acts necessarily productive of dissensions, that would deprive their union of all cordiality, separate them in feeling, and make their connexion intolerable. This privilege, accorded by the law, seems manifestly, therefore, to owe its origin to the duration of the legal obligation of the contract of marriage. . . .

The rule is thus stated . . . in [an English common law case] in which after a long cohabitation as man and wife, and the birth of children, the woman was received as witness for the man. There can be no other rule, with certainty enough to entitle it to the name. For at what period of an illicit cohabitation shall the incompetency begin? Or how long after the cohabitation terminates, before the competency shall be restored?

It being thus the common law of England, that no length of cohabitation, and no recognition by the parties merely, of each other as man and wife, invests them, for this purpose, with that character; it is next to be considered whether a like cohabitation between slaves, constitutes, in this state, a marriage, or rather such a marriage as produces incompetency to give evidence. It has been argued at the bar, that it does; because our laws have not prescribed any ceremony or formality for the celebration of marriages among persons of any colour or degree; and because slaves are human beings, with passions and senses impelling them to this union, and with a natural capacity to contract it, which no municipal regulation can annul, or at least, which no regulation in this state professes to annul. It has been urged that the essence of this, as of other contracts, consists in the consent of the parties; which if expressed before any witnesses, in any words, or by any acts, fully denoting present consent, renders the contract obligatory by the law of nature and of reason; and it was thence inferred, that it is necessarily binding in our law, in the absence of positive provisions to the contrary.

If every position in this chain of reasoning were true, it would not follow that to such a marriage contracted in this state, the effect is to be given of excluding the parties as witnesses. But the court is entirely satisfied, that some of those positions are not correct. We do not agree that persons *sui juris* are legally married merely in virtue of their own consent, however explicitly expressed . . . While as to other contracts, security is provided in various ceremonies and solemnities, a well regulated state could not leave that of marriage — the most important of all, in reference to the happiness of the parties and their issue, and to the right of succession to estates — to be established or denied upon the loose testimony of perhaps a single witness, speaking entirely from memory, of the words of the parties. . . . [I]t is plain from the earliest period of our legislation, that in consequence thereof, it has been constantly required as an essential requisite of a legal marriage, that it should either be celebrated by some person in a sacred office, or be entered into before some one in a public station and judicial trust. . . .

If that be the law of marriage between free persons, upon what principle or pretext can a marriage between slaves, not thus contracted, be sustained as a marriage *de jure*? . . . If it be said, that the statutes relate only to the cases of free persons, and therefore do not require the marriages of slaves to be thus celebrated; the reply is obvious, that the marriage of slaves, then, is wholly pretermitted, and hence a legal marriage cannot be contracted between them. Such, indeed, may unfortunately be the law; and may have been intended by the legislature to be the law, upon the general ground of the incapacity of a slave to enter into this, as into other contracts, upon the presumption of the want of free consent, and upon the further ground of the difficulty of giving legal validity to the marriage, in respect to its most important legal incidents, without essentially curtailing the rights and powers of the masters. If it be so, it may be a fit subject for legislative interposition, to avert this melancholy addition to the misfortunes and legal disabilities of this depressed race. The subject is too full of perplexities, to authorize the court to express an opinion upon that point, without duly considering it in a case in which it shall directly arise. . . . It cannot be judicially determined, that a wife by cohabitation, shall not give evidence against the man with whom she lives, more than that the other marital rights shall be accorded to them; nor, more than we can pronounce, that a man has incurred the guilt of bigamy, or cohabiting with one woman, under the name of his wife, after abandoning, or being forcibly separated from another, with whom he had once lived on the like terms. Unless the one consequence would follow, the other cannot; and the court is not prepared, without a mandate from a higher authority than our own, to apply to this class of our population a rule, which would in innumerable instances, either subject them to legal criminality of a high grade, or deprive them almost entirely of their greatest solace — that of having families of their own, frail as may be the right, and temporary the enjoyment, dependent, as they are, upon the caprice of the parties themselves, and yet more upon the necessities or caprice of their owners. The opinion of the court therefore is, that the witness was never in law, the wife of the prisoner.

This conclusion is in no degree shaken by the incidental notices of this connection between slaves, which is found in some of our statutes. In the act of 1729 . . . , for instance, which provides against hunting by slaves, their travelling by night, and collecting in quarters among other persons' negroes, the ninth section, by way of proviso to those enactments, declares, that nothing in that act shall be construed to hinder neighbours' negroes intermarrying together, license being first had of their several masters. This does not profess to say what shall constitute their marriage, nor what consequence such a marriage shall draw after it. . . . Thus viewed, and in reference to the general law of marriage, and also the known usages and modes of forming this connection between slaves, this proviso can mean only that concubinage, which is voluntary on the part of the slaves, and permissive on that of the master — which, in reality, is the relation, to which these people have ever been practically restricted, and with which alone, perhaps, their condition is compatible.

[Judge Ruffin finally notes that even if the contract of marriage between Mima and Samuel had been valid, the marriage had come to an end by mutual agreement and Mima had married the victim.]

Judgment affirmed.

Katherine Franke, Becoming a Citizen: Reconstruction Era Regulation of African American Marriages
11 Yale J.L. & Human. 251, 276-78, 280-82, 283-84, 294-96, 300-01, 304, 307-08 (1999)

As early as 1774, enslaved people identified the inhumanity of slavery as lying, in significant part, in the inability to marry: "[W]e are deprived of every thing that hath a tendency to make life even tolerable, the endearing ties of husband and wife we are strangers to for we are no longer man and wife than our masters or mistresses thinkes proper marred or onmarred." Abolitionist Angelina Grimké argued that both positive and natural legal principles required that the United States "[n]o longer deny [African Americans] the right of marriage, but let every man have his own wife, and let every woman have her own husband." In 1850, Henry Bibb, an enslaved person, observed: "I presume that there are no class of people in the United States who so highly appreciate the legality of marriage as those persons who have been held and treated as property." Arguing in favor of the 1866 Civil Rights Act, Senator Trumbull specifically identified the right to marry as a necessary aspect of citizenship.

Thus, the right to marry figured prominently in the bundle of rights understood to have been denied to enslaved people, and was considered necessary to any robust conception of liberty. Marriage

> provided a way to establish the integrity of their relationships, to bring a new security to their family lives, and, to affirm their freedom . . . . If the prohibition on marriage had underscored their dependent position and the precariousness of their family ties in slavery, the act of marriage now symbolized the rejection of their slave status.[24]

Formerly enslaved people and abolitionists generally deemed the right to marry one of the most important ramifications of emancipation.

After emancipation, formerly enslaved people traveled great distances and endured enormous hardships in order to reunite families that had been separated under slavery. Shortly after the end of the war, southern states acted quickly to amend their constitutions or enact statutes validating marriages begun under slavery. Laws that simply legitimized slave marriages if the couple were cohabiting as husband and wife when the law went into effect were quite common. Mississippi's 1865 civil rights law was typical: "All freedmen, free negroes and mulattoes, who do now and have

---

24. [Laura Edwards, "The Marriage Covenant is at the Foundation of all Our Rights': The Politics of Slave Marriages in North Carolina after Emancipation, 14 L. & Hist. Rev. 81, 101 (1996).]

heretofore lived and cohabited together as husband and wife shall be taken and held in law as legally married."

Some states took a different approach to the marriage of former slaves, giving "all colored inhabitants of this State claiming to be living together in the relation of husband and wife . . . and who shall mutually desire to continue in that relation," nine months to formally re-marry one another before a minister or civil authority. These laws further required newly married couples to file a marriage license with the county circuit court, a bureaucratic detail that carried a prohibitively high price for many freedpeople. In every state with such laws, failure to comply with these requirements while continuing to cohabit would render the offenders subject to criminal prosecution for adultery and fornication. North Carolina gave the freed people just under six months to register their marriages with the county clerk. Each month they failed to do so constituted a distinct and separately prosecutable criminal offense.

While many formerly enslaved people merely allowed the law to operate upon them, automatically legitimizing their marriages, others "swamped public officials with demands to validate old and new unions." Thus, the right to marry for African Americans in the immediate postbellum period had both symbolic and practical significance — symbolic in the sense that enjoyment of the right signaled acceptance into the moral community of civil society, and practical to the extent that social and economic benefits flowed from being legally married.

However, the right to marry was not merely an unconstrained liberty enjoyed by African Americans independent of state interest or control. Even prior to the end of the war, state and federal officials played an active role in impressing upon Black people the responsibilities, rather than the rights, that marriage imposed. . . .

In its reports to the Secretary of War, the American Freedmen's Inquiry Commission reflected the view dominant among whites that Black people were uncivilized, degraded, undisciplined, and lived in wholly unchristian ways, but that the rule of law as well as patient guidance from whites would tame and civilize them. Thus the Commission observed that "[t]he law, in the shape of military rule, takes for him the place of his master, with this difference — that he submits to it more heartily and cheerfully, without any sense of degradation." Urging an active role for the federal government in the moral cultivation of Black character, the Commission's Final Report concluded on an optimistic note: "[T]hey will learn much and gain much from us. They will gain in force of character, in mental cultivation, in self-reliance, in enterprise, in breadth of views and habits of generalization. Our influence over them, if we treat them well, will be powerful for good." In support of this claim, the Commission referred to a Canadian high school principal who maintained that proximity to whites could even "whiten" Black people's unattractive physical features. . . .

Much of the rhetoric of the time related to the need to civilize the freed men and women. Gutman summarized these beliefs as follows: "As slaves, after all, their marriages had not been sanctioned by the civil law and therefore 'the sexual passion' went unrestrained."[25] White officials informed African American audiences that "[t]he loose ideas which have prevailed among you on this subject must cease," and that "no race of mankind can be expected to become exalted in the scale of humanity, whose sexes, without any binding obligation, cohabit promiscuously together."

Freedmen's Bureau agents had their hands full dealing with the systemic violence suffered by African Americans at the hands of white people, including lynchings, rapes, beatings, and other brutal assaults, and "outrages," as well as overwhelming white resistance to honoring labor contracts with the newly freed Blacks. Their weekly and monthly reports, however, are replete with exasperation regarding the manner in which Blacks were flaunting the institution of marriage. Agents complained that the freed men and women persisted in "the disgusting practice of living together as man and wife without proper marriage," "living together and calling themselves man and wife as long as it conveniently suits them," and maintaining bigamous or adulterous relationships. In "many instances," wrote one agent, "where after being legally and lawfully married they live together but a short time. Separate and marry again or live together without any obligation at all." Time and again, the agents complained that Blacks continued to "act as they did in time of slavery," clinging to "old habits of an immoral character." They were particularly outraged by the habit of "taking up" with a person, and then separating when they tired of one another. "It would appear to be more difficult to change their ideas in this matter than on any other affecting their welfare," wrote Alvan Gillem, Bureau agent in charge of Mississippi, in 1868. Gillem took a particular interest in the problem of marriage among African Americans, requiring his agents in the Mississippi sub-districts to provide a detailed account of the freedmen's marital relations each month. . . .

Even though some state laws were silent on the question of multiple spouses, state and federal officials forced freed men and women to choose one and only one spouse as a matter of practice. In some cases where a freed man or woman was unwilling or unable to choose, Bureau agents felt free to do so for them. An agent in North Carolina reported that "[w]henever a negro appears before me with two or three wives who have equal claim upon him . . . I marry him to the woman who had the greatest number of helpless children who otherwise would become a charge on the Bureau."

Many Bureau agents felt that moral suasion was insufficient to gain African American compliance with marriage laws and determined that the

25. [Herbert G. Gutman, The Black Family in Slavery and Freedom 1750-1925, 295 (1979).]

law must be looked to to solve this problem. Their frustration led them to turn adulterers, bigamists, and fornicators over to the local authorities for prosecution under local criminal laws. Some Freedmen's Bureau agents also encouraged white planters to punish Blacks for adultery and fornication. Gillem informed the Washington Bureau office in September 1868 that "I have caused the proper steps to be taken to bring this matter before the Civil Courts and shall urge that offenders be brought to trial and punished." Other officers followed suit. "The courts alone can establish a radical cure," wrote Gillem in October 1867. . . .

Despite the general acceptance of common-law marriage by the judiciary, legislative reformers of this era voiced concern about a crisis of the family provoked by the perceived ease with which divorce could be obtained, the prevalence of male promiscuity, the incidence of polygamy amongst certain social groups, and the nascent feminist movement, which was diminishing the traditional role of the husband as the head of the household. "Each departure from orthodoxy . . . undermined needed domestic division of labor, sexual restraints, paternal authority, and household economic responsibilities." Increasingly, marriage was positioned as an institution that would "save the race from moral ruin." This anxiety about moral chaos reflected reformers' more general preoccupation with the perceived disintegration of social order.

Attacks on common-law marriage formed one of the centerpieces of the marital reform movement of this era. These attacks were grounded in the notion that marriage was not like other contracts, which the parties can create and dissolve at will, but was rather a special kind of status-creating compact in which society had a particular interest. As a consequence, state after state enacted positive laws setting forth the terms of valid marriages and limiting the means of dissolution.

Undergirding these reform efforts lay two important norms of particular relevance to the application of these marriage laws to newly freed African Americans. First, formal marriage, it was believed, performed the very important social function of taming wanton licentiousness and civilizing uncontrollable desire: "[T]he first object of marriage still is to regulate [sexual passion]." For some reformers and courts of this period, common-law marriage was too fluid an institution to accomplish this crucial disciplinary function: "These loose and irregular contracts, as a general thing, derive no support from morals or religion but are most generally founded in a wanton and licentious cohabitation."

Second, reformers increasingly convinced both legislatures and courts of the public stake in marriage. While marriage was treated as a civil contract, it was a special kind of contract insofar as the state was obligated to enact laws prescribing who could marry and according to what positive legal requirements, as well as imposing significant restraints upon the terms of exit, or divorce. . . .

All of these views of marriage were invoked by the Supreme Court in 1888, when Justice Field summarized the status of marriage during the era of reform: "Marriage, as creating the most important relation in life, as having more to do with the morals and civilization of a people than any other institution, has always been subject to the control of the legislature."[26] Thus the Court concluded that marriage "is an institution, in the maintenance of which in its purity the public is deeply interested, for it is the foundation of the family and of society, without which there would be neither civilization nor progress."[27] For Victorian legislators and jurists alike the question of legal marriage involved "the best interests of society, and the preservation of the home and family — the foundation of all society."[28] . . .

As the rhetoric surrounding the institutional reform of marriage invoked widespread concerns about immorality and respectability, it did so in the service of installing marriage and the household as the principal sites of private dependency. To be a husband necessarily entailed the status of head of household, while to be a wife rendered one structurally dependent upon the husband's support. The neat trick of this ideology was at once to affirm the wife's dependence upon the husband for support, and to deny the husband's dependence upon the wife's unpaid household labor "without which he could never maintain the facade of independence." As Nancy Cott observes of this period, "[h]aving and supporting dependents was evidence of independence."[29] Thus, the self-governing free man of the antebellum era was, or could be, master to his slaves, whilethis same man became master over a household of dependents in the postbellum period. This domestic grouping — a household headed by a free man — emerged in the late nineteenth century as the fundamental unit of both consumption and production.

Since "[i]ndependence inhered in the self-governing individual who could dispose of his own labor profitably,"[30] it would be disastrous for white masculinity if Black men could exercise that self governance in a way that undermined the stability of marriage as the institution that bounded dependence in the home and in femininity. Thus the freedom that African Americans enjoyed by virtue of the Thirteenth and Fourteenth Amendments had to be filtered through larger liberal notions of freedom that were being renegotiated during this era. Just as liberal reformers rejected the call from some feminists to liberalize marriage laws, so too postbellum officials were

---

26. Maynard v. Hill, 125 U.S. 190, 205 (1888) (arguing that a legislative grant of a divorce, without the consent of the wife, to a husband who had breached the marriage contract by abandoning his wife, was an impairment of contract).

27. Id. at 211.

28. Id. at 588.

29. [Nancy F. Cott, Marriage and Women's Citizenship in the United States, 1830-1934, 103 Am. Hist. Rev. 1440, 1452 (1998).]

30. Id. at 1453.

shocked that African Americans thought they were free to organize their intimate and family lives as they wished. Freedmen's Bureau agents were aghast that "[l]iving together in a state of concubinage they have come to look upon as a privilege, in fact, a right which no one has a right to interfere with." An agent in Mississippi commented incredulously that "the men contend that they had a right to have as many women as they could support."

Thus, one of the overarching projects of the postbellum era was the task of making women into wives and men into husbands. . . .

These postbellum statutes are typical of the ways in which southern legislatures permitted African Americans to participate in the institution of marriage, but did so on terms that respected the integrity of households they created only in so far as (1) the father or husband performed his proper role as provider and head of household, and (2) the household itself was the place where the needs of dependents were met privately. To the extent that poverty or some "moral infirmity" hindered African American men from performing the role of republican husband or father, they were categorically denied the privilege of participation in this exalted institution. . . .

My aim has been to demonstrate the complexity of rights discourses in movements for personal and political emancipation. Rather than simply liberating a people to make autonomous decisions free from state-imposed constraints, the granting of rights signals the inauguration of a new relationship with the state. Rights both shape political culture and produce political subjects. In the postbellum era, African Americans acquired an identity as rights holders and entered the "bureaucratic juridical apparatus" through which those rights were negotiated. Wendy Brown frames this dynamic in the following way: "Rights . . . may subject us to intense forms of bureaucratic domination and regulatory power even at the moment that we assert them in our own defense."[31]

Notes

1. The Right To Marry: A Mixed Blessing? Given Franke's argument, was the African American determination to win the right to marry justified? Was the legal invisibility of lesbian relations in some ways a blessing?

2. Marriage and Domestic Violence. As the Blackstone excerpt and State v. Rhodes suggest, marriage did not completely protect women from violence. Indeed, marriage made women uniquely vulnerable to one form of violence: rape by her husband. Sir Matthew Hale, Chief Justice of the Court

31. Wendy Brown, States of Injury 121 n.41 (1995).

of King's Bench from 1671 to 1675, stated the position of English common law that was incorporated into American law: "[T]he lawful husband cannot be guilty of a rape committed by himself upon his lawful wife, for by their mutual matrimonial consent and contract the wife hath given up herself in this kind unto her husband, which she cannot retract." 1 The History of the Pleas of the Crown 628 (1st American ed. 1847) (1st ed. (posthumous) 1736).

For contemporary issues concerning domestic violence, see Chapter 4, section C.

3. Critiquing Marriage: The Free Love Movement. Beginning in the 1850s, some women and men began to attack the institution of marriage in the name of "free love." Nancy Cott observes:

> Most free lovers gave at least lip service to woman's rights, and some were fierce partisans. At a meeting called the Free Convention held in Rutland, Vermont, in 1858, where the nature of government, free trade, slavery, woman's rights, marriage, maternity, land reform, immortality, and the Sabbath were all subjects of discussion, Julia Branch announced herself a free lover and proposed a controversial resolution "that the slavery and degradation of woman proceed from the institution of marriage: that by the marriage contract she loses control of her name, her property, her labor, her affections, her children, and her freedom."

Nancy Cott, Public Vows: A History of Marriage and the Nation 68-69 (2000).

Needless to say, "free love" was reviled by most mainstream observers and institutions. Nevertheless, free love principles influenced many of the intentional communities that sprang up in the decades following the Civil War. These communities saw the abolition of private property and communal living as a route to greater equality and freedom. Id. at 71.

4. Critiquing Marriage: American Polygamy. The Church of Jesus Christ of Latter-Day Saints was also publicly attacked in the mid-nineteenth century as a threat to the political and moral character of the nation. Their leader, Joseph Smith, had received a revelation in 1843 mandating "plural marriage," but it was not until 1852, when the church had migrated to the western territory of Utah, that the revelation was made public. Antislavery advocates equated polygamy with slavery; proslavery advocates argued that polygamy was the result of Northern liberalism. The controversy continued following the Civil War. The Morrill Act of 1862 made bigamy a federal crime punishable by up to five years in prison, but proved unenforceable — Mormon juries refused to convict. Members of Congress sought alternatives. One bill would disenfranchise Mormon men; a second would enfranchise its women on the theory that Mormon women with the ballot would vote polygamy out of existence. Cott, Public Vows, supra, at 112. But

Mormon women demonstrated in support of plural marriage. One spokes-woman, Harriet Cook Young, declared: "Wherever monogamy reigns, adultery, prostitution, free-love and foeticide, directly or indirectly, are its concomitants. . . . The women of Utah comprehend this and they see in the principle of a plurality of wives, the only safeguard against adultery, prostitution, free-love and the reckless waste of pre-natal life." Id.

The Poland Act of 1874 permitted federal courts in the Utah territory to try federal crimes, including cases under the Morrill Act, and non-Mormon juries began to convict Mormons of bigamy. In Reynolds v. United States, 98 U.S. 145 (1879), the Supreme Court held that such prosecutions did not violate the first amendment's guarantee of religious freedom. In Mormon Church v. United States, 136 U.S. 1 (1889), the Court upheld the Edmunds-Tucker Act of 1887, which repealed the act of incorporation of the Church of Jesus Christ of Latter-Day Saints, disenfranchised Mormon women (who had received the vote in 1870), and created federal jurisdiction for crimes involving adultery, incest, and fornication. The church ultimately gave way to government pressure and issued a manifesto officially disapproving of plural marriage, and in 1896 Utah finally became a state. Id. at 119-120.

c. Law and the Economic Functions of Marriage

In re Estate of Fred Paquet, Deceased
200 P. 911 (Ore. 1921)

GEORGE R. BAGLEY, Judge.

[On September 30, 1919, Ophelia Paquet filed a petition in the County Court of Tillamook County, Oregon to be appointed as administrator of the estate of Fred Paquet, declaring herself the deceased's widow. The petition was granted. Fred's brother, John B. Paquet, then filed his own petition seeking to be appointed administrator, and alleged that the Paquets' marriage was a nullity because Fred Paquet was a white man and Ophelia Paquet a full-blooded Indian woman. The County Court consequently removed Ophelia as administrator and appointed John instead. Ophelia appealed to the Circuit Court, which affirmed the County Court's ruling. Meanwhile, one I. N. Henkle, a creditor of the estate, filed a petition claiming that John Paquet was "of unsound mind, insolvent, of immoral character and . . . not competent to administer the estate," and seeking his own appointment instead. Following a hearing, the County Court removed John as administrator; the Circuit Court reversed and reinstated him; and Henkle appealed. The cases were consolidated.]

Johns, J. — It is conceded that John is a brother of Fred Paquet, deceased, that both of them were bona fide residents of Tillamook County and that if Ophelia was not the lawful wife of Fred Paquet, John is his only living relative residing in the State of Oregon. The primary questions involved here are: (1) Whether or not Fred and Ophelia were husband and wife and (2) whether John is a competent and suitable person to administer upon the estate. Although the evidence is conclusive that Ophelia and Fred lived together as husband and wife and that he recognized and treated her as such, it is not claimed that they were ever legally married under the statutory law of any state. It is also conceded that Fred Paquet was a white man and that Ophelia was a full-blooded Indian woman. Section 2163, Ore. L., provides:

> Hereafter it shall not be lawful within this state for any white person male or female, to intermarry with any negro, Chinese, or any person having one fourth or more negro, Chinese, or Kanaka blood, or any person having more than one half Indian blood; and all such marriages, or attempted marriages, shall be absolutely null and void.

Section 2164 enacts that if any white person or Indian within the degree forbidden in Section 2163 shall knowingly intermarry under any of the forms legalized by the state, upon conviction they "shall be punished by imprisonment in the penitentiary or county jail not less than three months nor more than one year." Section 2165 provides:

> If any person authorized to license marriages or to solemnize marriages within this state shall willfully or knowingly license, marry, or attempt to marry any of the persons forbidden to marry by Section 2163, such person or persons, upon conviction thereof, shall be imprisoned in the penitentiary or county jail not less than three months nor more than one year, and be fined not less than $100, nor more than $1,000.

The appellant contends that such statutory provisions are unconstitutional and void. R. C. L., Volume 8, Section 381, says: "Miscegenation is a purely statutory offense, consisting in the intermarriage of a person of the white race with a negro or a colored person. Most states in which the negro or colored people form an appreciable element have enacted these laws inhibiting intermarrying between the white and black races, and the offense thereby created is usually of the grade of a felony. There can be no doubt as to the power of every country to make laws regulating the marriage of its own subjects; to declare who may marry, how they may marry, and what shall be the legal consequences of their marrying; and accordingly although miscegenation statutes have been persistently attacked on the ground that they are violative of the United States Constitution they have been universally upheld as a proper exercise of the power of each state to control its own citizens."

Appellant also contends that "an Indian has the same right as a white person, and any statute of the state, attempting to abridge their rights of marriage, in any manner, is void." It will be noted that the statute does not discriminate. It applies alike to all persons either white, negroes, Chinese, Kanaka or Indians. . . . Ophelia, claiming to be the wife of Fred Paquet, a white man, and it being admitted that she is a full-blooded Indian, the duty devolves upon her to allege and prove that she was his lawful wife.

Appellant relies upon Leefield v. Leefield, 85 Ore. 287 (166 P. 953). That decision construed and was founded upon Sections 7017, 2098, and 502, L. O. L. The parties there were first cousins and notwithstanding the provisions of the statute, they were married in the State of Washington. . . .

In the instant case there is no claim that the parties were married in another state. In fact, it is claimed that they were married in Tillamook County, Oregon, in accord with an Indian tribal custom and that such marriage is valid. There is some indefinite, uncertain testimony tending to show that Fred Paquet paid Ophelia's mother $50 for her daughter and that under the Indian custom, followed by marital relations, this would constitute a valid marriage and make them husband and wife. Upon that point appellant relies upon McBean v. McBean, 37 Ore. 195 (61 P. 418), and Kalyton v. Kalyton, 45 Ore.122-124 (74 P.491, 78 P. 332). On page 202, in McBean v. McBean, this court says:

> As a general proposition, it is well settled that a marriage valid according to the law or custom of the place where it is contracted is valid everywhere: Story, Confl. Laws, at 113. And it is the adjudged policy of the law to treat the Indian tribes who adhere to their peculiar customs, as separate communities or distinct nationalities, with full and free authority to manage their own domestic affairs, and to pursue their own peculiar habits and customs, especially as it concerns the marriage relation. And this is so although their territory is located within the state lines, and the federal government manages their affairs through agencies designated for the purpose. Nor are they regarded as subject to the state laws.

On page 203, it is said:

> At the time of the alleged marriage the Territory of Washington had been set apart by Congress and provided with a form of government, but some of the Indian tribes, yet maintaining their distinct tribal customs, among whom may be designated the Cayuses, Walla Wallas, Umatillas, and Nez Perces, still occupied, without relinquishment of the Indian title, a large portion of the territory, which included Fort Walla Walla within its boundaries.

That is not this case. Ophelia was one of a small remnant of what is known as the Clatsop Indians, who once lived in and around Seaside in Clatsop County. At the time of the alleged marriage she was living with her mother at Garibaldi in Tillamook County. She was not living on a reservation and was not a ward of the United States government, in fact the alleged marriage took place within Tillamook County and at a place where the state would have original and exclusive jurisdiction over any marriage contract between them, and both parties then lived and mingled with the white people as ordinary citizens of the state. Neither the government nor any Indian tribe had any control or jurisdiction over the place of the alleged marriage. Under appellant's contention, if an Indian woman without regard to her actual residence was a member of one tribe and should marry a white man under an Indian custom, such a marriage would be valid and Section 2163 would be a nullity. That is not the law. As in this case where both parties and the alleged marriage were within the original and exclusive jurisdiction of the state, they are subject to and are bound by the state law. Such a marriage would only be valid where Indians lived together under the tribal relation and a tribal form of government and for the reason that they would then be subject only to the jurisdiction of Congress. After the appeal was taken from the County Court to the Circuit Court and based upon affidavits, the appellant asked for leave to offer testimony that she was a member of a tribe of Indians in and around Tillamook Bay at the time of her marriage and that there was a chief of the Indian tribe. We have carefully read the affidavits and assuming all the facts therein stated to be true, it would not bring the instant case within the law of this court in McBean v. McBean, above quoted. Upon the record, we hold that Ophelia was never the lawful wife of Fred Paquet.

Being the only relative in the state, if otherwise qualified, John was entitled to administer upon his brother's estate. Henkle was never a personal creditor of Fred Paquet. His only claim against the estate is for funeral expenses. Upon the petition of Henkle, the County Court removed John Paquet as administrator, which ruling was reversed by the Circuit Court. It is true that there is some testimony against his ability and reputation, but a large number of respectable citizens testified that he was an honorable man and well qualified to act as administrator. The main value of the estate is in real property which cannot be sold without an order of the probate court and we must assume that it would protect the interests of all parties.

In both appeals, the opinion of the lower court is affirmed.

Legally, Ophelia was not the lawful wife of the deceased, yet the record is conclusive that she lived with him as a good and faithful wife for more than thirty years. Although the question is not before this court, the writer feels that in the interests of justice, a fair and reasonable settlement should be made. In the case of Ophelia Paquet v. John Paquet, neither of the parties will recover costs. Costs will be allowed to the respondent in the Henkle case.

Affirmed.

Peggy Pascoe, Race, Gender, and the Privileges of Property: On the Significance of Miscegenation Law in United States History, in New Viewpoints in Women's History: Working Papers from the Schlesinger Library 50th Anniversary Conference
101, 101-106, 107-110, 112-113 (Susan Ware ed., 1994).

Although miscegenation laws are usually remembered (when they are remembered at all) as a Southern development aimed at African Americans, they were actually a much broader phenomenon. Adopted in both the North and the South in the colonial period and extended to western states in the nineteenth century, miscegenation laws grew up with slavery but became even more significant after the Civil War, for it was then that they came to form the crucial "bottom line" of the system of white supremacy embodied in segregation.

The earliest miscegenation laws, passed in the South, forbade whites to marry African Americans, but the list of groups prohibited from marrying whites was gradually expanded, especially in western states, by adding first American Indians, then Chinese and Japanese (both often referred to by the catchall term "Mongolians"), and then Malays (or Filipinos). And even this didn't exhaust the list. Oregon prohibited whites from marrying "Kanakas" (or native Hawaiians); South Dakota proscribed "Coreans"; Arizona singled out Hindus; and Georgia prohibited whites from marrying "West" and "Asiatic" Indians. . . .

Many states packed their miscegenation laws with multiple categories and quasi-mathematical definitions of "race." Oregon, for example, declared that "it shall not be lawful within this state for any white person, male or female, to intermarry with any negro, Chinese, or Kanaka blood, or any person having more than one half Indian blood." Altogether, miscegenation laws covered forty-one states and colonies. They spanned three centuries of American history: the first ones were enacted in the 1660s, and the last ones were not declared unconstitutional until 1967.

Although it is their sexual taboos that have attracted most recent attention, the structure and function of miscegenation laws were . . . more fundamentally related to the institution of marriage than to sexual behavior itself. In sheer numbers, many more laws prohibited interracial marriage than interracial sex. And in an even deeper sense, all miscegenation laws were designed to privilege marriage as a social and economic unit. Couples who challenged the laws knew that the right to marry translated into social respectability and economic benefits, including inheritance rights and legitimacy for children, that were denied to sexual liaisons outside marriage. Miscegenation laws were designed to patrol this border by making so-called miscegenous marriage a legal impossibility. Thus criminal courts treated offenders as if they had never been married at all; that is, prosecutors charged interracial couples with the moral offense of fornication or other illicit sex crimes, then denied them the use of marriage as a defense. . . .

. . . The Paquet case, like most of the civil miscegenation cases of this period, was fought over the estate of a white man. . . . Fred and Ophelia's relationship had a long history. In the 1880s, Fred had already begun to visit Ophelia frequently and openly enough that he had become one of many targets of a local grand jury which periodically threatened to indict white men who lived with Indian women. Seeking to formalize the relationship — and, presumably, to end this harassment — Fred consulted a lawyer, who advised him to make sure to hold a ceremony which would meet the legal requirements for an "Indian custom" marriage. Accordingly, in 1889, Fred not only reached the customary agreement with Ophelia's Tillamook relatives, paying them $50 in gifts, but also sought the formal sanction of Tillamook tribal chief Betsy Fuller (who was herself married to a white man); Fuller arranged for a tribal council to consider and confirm the marriage. Afterwards Fred and Ophelia lived together until his death, for more than thirty years. Fred clearly considered Ophelia his wife, and his neighbors, too, recognized their relationship, but because Fred died without leaving a formal will, administration of the estate was subject to state laws which provided for the distribution of property to surviving family members. . . .

. . . John Paquet had little to recommend him to the court. Some of his neighbors accused him of raping native women, and he had such an unsavory reputation in the community that at one point the county judge declared him "a man of immoral habits . . . incompetent to transact ordinary business affairs and generally untrustworthy." He was, however, a "white" man, and under Oregon's miscegenation law, that was enough to ensure that he won his case against Ophelia, an Indian woman. . . .

As the Paquet case demonstrates, miscegenation law did not always prevent the formation of interracial relationships, sexual or otherwise. Fred and Ophelia had, after all, lived together for more than thirty years and had apparently won recognition as a couple from many of those around them; their perseverance had even allowed them to elude grand jury crackdowns. They did not, however, manage to escape the really crucial power of miscegenation law: the role it played in connecting white supremacy to the transmission of property. In American law, marriage provided the glue which allowed for the transmission of property from husbands to wives and their children; miscegenation law kept property within racial boundaries by invalidating marriages between white men and women of color whenever ancillary white relatives like John Paquet contested them. . . . [P]roperty, so often described in legal sources as simple economic assets (like land and capital) was actually a much more expansive phenomenon, one which took various forms and structured crucial relationships. . . . [R]ace is in and of itself a kind of property. As Derrick Bell . . . explains, most whites did — and still do — "expect the society to recognize an unspoken but no less vested property right in their 'whiteness.'" "This right," Bell maintains, "is

recognized and upheld by courts and the society like all property rights under a government created and sustained primarily for that purpose."[32]
. . .

The second property relationship [is] illuminated by the etymological connection between the words "property" and "propriety." Miscegenation law played on this connection by drawing a sharp line between "legitimate marriage" on the one hand and "illicit sex" on the other, then defining all interracial relationships as illicit sex. The distinction was a crucial one, for husbands were legally obligated to provide for legitimate wives and children, both men owed nothing to "mere" sexual partners: neither inheritance rights nor the legitimacy of children accompanied illicit relationships. . . .

It was all but impossible for women of color to escape the legacy of these associations. Ophelia Paquet's lawyers tried to find a way out by changing the subject. Rather than refuting the association between women of color and illicit sexuality, they highlighted its flip side, the supposed connection between white women and legitimate marriage. Ophelia Paquet, they told the judge, "had been to the man as good a wife as any white woman could have been." In its final decision, the Oregon Supreme Court came as close as any court of that time did to accepting this line of argument. . . . But in the Paquet case, as in other miscegenation cases, sexual morality, important as it was, was nonetheless still subordinate to channelling the property along racial . . . lines. Ophelia got a judicial pat on the head for good behavior, but John and his siblings got the property.

Which brings me to the third form of property relationship structured by miscegenation laws — and, for that matter, marriage laws in general — and that is women's economic dependence on men. Here the problems started long before the final decision gave John Paquet control of the Paquet estate. One of the most intriguing facts about the Paquet estate is that everyone acted as if the estate in question belonged solely to Fred Paquet. In fact, however, throughout the Paquet marriage, Fred had whiled away most of his time; it was Ophelia's basket-making, fruit-picking, milk-selling, and wage work that had provided the income they needed to sustain themselves. And although the deed to their land was made out in Fred Paquet's name, the couple had used Ophelia's earnings, combined with her proceeds from government payments to Tillamook tribal members, both to purchase the property and to pay the yearly taxes on it. It is significant . . . that, although lawyers on both sides of the case knew this, neither they nor the Oregon Supreme Court judges considered it a key issue at the trial in which Ophelia lost all legal right to what the courts considered "Fred's" estate.

Indeed, Ophelia's economic contribution might never have been taken into account if it were not for the fact that in the wake of the Oregon

32. Derrick Bell, Remembrances of Racism Past, in Hill and Jones, Race in America: The Struggle For Equality 78 (1992). See also Bell, White Superiority in America: Its Legal Legacy, Its Economic Costs, 33 Villanova L. Rev. 767-779 (1988).

Supreme Court decision, United States Indian officials found themselves responsible for the care of the now impoverished Ophelia. Apparently hoping both to defend Ophelia and to relieve themselves of the burden of her support, they sued John Paquet on Ophelia's behalf. Working through the federal courts that covered Indian relations and equity claims, . . . they eventually won a partial settlement. Yet their argument, too, reflected the assumption that men were better suited than women to the ownership of what the legal system referred to as "real" property. Although their brief claimed that "Fred Paquet had practically no income aside from the income he received through the labor and efforts of the said Ophelia Paquet," they asked the Court to grant Ophelia the right to only half of the Paquet land. In the end, the court ordered that Ophelia should receive a cash settlement (the amount was figured at half the value of the land), but only if she agreed to make her award contingent on its sale. To get any settlement at all, Ophelia had to relinquish all claims to actual ownership of the land, although such a claim might have given her legal grounds to prevent its sale and so allow her to spend her final years on the property. It is not even clear that she received any payment on the settlement ordered by the court. As late as 1928, John Paquet's major creditor complained to a judge that Paquet had repeatedly turned down acceptable offers to sell the land; perhaps he had chosen to live on it himself. . . .

Today, most Americans have trouble remembering that miscegenation laws ever existed . . . [and] are incredulous at the injustice and the arbitrariness of the racial classifications that stand out in [such] . . . cases. [Yet] few . . . notice that one of the themes raised in the Paquet case — the significance of marriage in structuring property transmission — not only remains alive and well, but has, in fact, outlived both the erosion of traditional patriarchy and the rise and fall of racial classifications in marriage law.

More than a generation after the demise of miscegenation laws . . . the drawing of exclusionary lines around marriage [continues]. . . . The most prominent — though hardly the only — victims are lesbian and gay couples, who point out that the sex classifications currently embedded in marriage operate in much the same way that the race classifications embedded in miscegenation laws once did: that is, they allow courts to categorize same-sex relationships as illicit sex rather than legitimate marriage and they allow courts to exclude same-sex couples from the property benefits of marriage, which now include everything from tax advantages to medical insurance coverage.

Both these modern legal battles and the earlier ones fought by couples like Fred and Ophelia Paquet suggest . . . that focusing on the connections between property and the political economy of marriage . . . offer a revealing vantage point from which to study both the form and power of analogies between race and sex classifications in American law and the relationships between race and gender hierarchies in American history.

Notes

1. The Ideological Consequences of Anti-Miscegenation Laws. As Rachel Moran notes, anti-miscegenation laws typically served an ideological function, creating and maintaining power differentials between racialized groups.

> In the colonial era and during the early years of nationhood, bans on intermarriage were critical to drawing the color line between indentured white servants and blacks. Once the color line was in place, the statutes became a way to enforce racial hierarchy by barring blacks from assimilating through marriage to whites. Interracial sex continued to occur on a widespread basis, but it did not threaten white identity and privilege because the one-drop rule classified any illegitimate offspring as black. Nor did the extramarital liaisons jeopardize white superiority since white men could have their way with black women, but black men faced severe sanctions for having sex with white women.

Rachel F. Moran, Interracial Intimacy: The Regulation of Race and Romance 39-40 (2001).

As Pascoe argues, however, both the ideology of white superiority and nonwhite inferiority and the relationship between property and whiteness were potentially disrupted when a nonwhite intimate partner claimed property rights through private law doctrines such as executorship, intestate succession, and testamentary transfer. In such situations, Adrienne Davis argues, courts faced a difficult dilemma:

> Both before and after slavery, southern courts dealing with the wills of white men who tried to leave property to their black concubines were faced with a series of apparently insoluble ideological conflicts. The legal consciousness of the nineteenth century set great store on the power of the sovereign rights-holder to dispose of his property, at the same time that it was built around a series of racial hierarchies — explicit and formal during the antebellum period, implicit and substantive during the postbellum period. What is to be done when the ideal of the sovereign property-holder apparently conflicts with the racial hierarchies around which the law is built?

Adrienne Davis, The Private Law of Race and Sex: An Antebellum Perspective, 51 Stan. L.Rev. 221, 285 (1999). Examining ante- and post-bellum cases where white men attempted to transfer property to black women with whom they were sexually involved, Davis concludes that judges tiptoed through this minefield by preventing sexual relationships from ever yielding economic rights while opining that — as a matter of charity — the concubines deserved some material support.

2. Anti-Miscegenation Laws and Ethnic Communities. Moran notes that miscegenation laws had different effects on different ethnic groups in the late nineteenth and early twentieth centuries. For example, "Blacks could form same-race families, but Chinese men often remained single and childless for life because of the shortage of Chinese women." Moran, Interracial Intimacy, supra, at 40. This shortage was the result both of social patterns in China and restrictive immigration laws in the United States. Moreover, Chinese men seldom became sexually involved with white women, despite being portrayed in the popular press as lascivious and sexually degraded. Id. In contrast, thanks to the 1908 "Gentleman's Agreement" between Japan and the United States, Japanese male immigrants were permitted to bring their wives and families to the United States. Anti-miscegenation laws thus did not hinder the determination of Japanese American families to build "prosperous, autonomous communities." Id. at 36.

Filipino men, arriving on the West Coast in the 1920s and 1930s not from a foreign country but from an American territory, alone among Asian immigrant groups openly defied miscegenation laws and mores. Moran reports: "Filipinos confounded their critics by reveling in their depiction as sexually powerful and threatening. In 1936, a San Francisco municipal court judge wrote in *Time* magazine that Filipinos 'have told me bluntly and boastfully that they practice the art of love with more perfection than white boys.' " Id. at 37. Filipinos were also more likely than Chinese or Japanese immigrants to enter intimate relations with non-Filipino, nonwhite partners; by 1946, over half of Filipino immigrant children were biracial. Id. at 39.

3. The Economic Consequences of Anti-Miscegenation Laws. Pascoe argues that marriage was a profoundly economic institution. What incentives did anti-miscegenation laws create for the transmission of wealth?

If anti-miscegenation laws concentrated property in families deemed legally "white," in the West interracial intermarriage could be a way to accomplish the same goal. Tomas Almaguer, examining nineteenth-century California, notes:

> . . . European Americans . . . were not oblivious to the advantages of marrying into wealthy [Mexican land-holding] families. With eligible white women being scarce in the territory, fair-complexioned, upper-class Mexican women were among the most valuable marriage partners available. While white men derived a degree of status from marrying the Californio's daughters, more important were the tangible political and economic opportunities that such unions afforded. These marriages provided strategic access to land held by the old elite. Thousands of acres passed into the hands of Anglo men as part of the inheritances some Californio women brought to marriage. Moreover, Anglo sons-in-law were often the first ones given access to land sold by rancheros desperately needing cash.

Tomás Almaguer, Racial Fault Lines: The Historical Origins of White Supremacy in California 58-59 (1994).

Indeed, it was not altogether clear that such marriages were "interracial." As Almaguer notes, elite Mexicans often emphasized their European ancestry to distinguish themselves from pure-blooded Indians, contemptuously viewed both by Anglos and Mexicans as "savages." Id. at 55. In several Western states, Mexicans as a group were even legally defined as "white." See Ian Haney Lopez, Race and Erasure: The Salience of Race to LatCrit Theory, 85 Cal. L. Rev. 1143 (1997), 10 La Raza L.J. 57 (1998).

4. Gender, Political Rights, and Citizenship in United States Legal History

a. Law and Women's Citizenship

Linda K. Kerber, No Constitutional Right to Be Ladies: Women and the Obligations of Citizenship
xx-xxi, xxiii-xxiv (1998)

Women have been citizens of the United States as long as the republic has existed. Passports were issued to them. They could be naturalized; they could claim the protection of the courts. They were subject to the laws and were obliged to pay taxes. But from the beginning American women's relationship to the state has been different in substantial and important respects from that of men. . . .

Although the founding generation brilliantly revised the definition of citizenship for their new country, they did not have the heart or the energy to reconstruct the entire legal system. . . . Thirteen state constitutions, the Northwest Ordinance, and the Constitution of 1787 radically changed the relationship of state and citizen. But the United States absorbed, virtually unrevised, the traditional English system of law governing the relationship between husbands and wives. . . .

By treating married women as "covered" by their husbands' civic identity, by placing sharp constraints on the extent to which married women controlled their bodies and their property, the old law of domestic relations ensured that — with a few exceptions, like the obligation to refrain from treason — married women's obligations to their husbands and families overrode their obligations to the state.

. . . The assumption that married women owe their primary civic obligation to their husbands persisted long after the Revolution. It continued to define relationships among men, women, and the state. It lurks behind what many people take to be the common sense of the matter in our own time.

Mackenzie v. Hare
239 U.S. 299 (1915)

Mr. Justice MCKENNA delivered the opinion of the court:

The facts are not in dispute and are stated by Mr. Justice SHAW, who delivered the opinion of the [California Supreme Court], as follows:

> The plaintiff was born and ever since has resided in the state of California. On August 14, 1909, being then a resident and citizen of this state and of the United States, she was lawfully married to Gordon Mackenzie, a native and subject of the kingdom of Great Britain. He had resided in California prior to that time, still resides here, and it is his intention to make this state his permanent residence. He has not become naturalized as a citizen of the United States and it does not appear that he intends to do so. Ever since their marriage the plaintiff and her husband have lived together as husband and wife. On January 22, 1913, she applied to the defendants to be registered as a voter. She was then over the age of twenty-one years and had resided in San Francisco for more than ninety days. Registration was refused to her on the ground that, by reason of her marriage to Gordon Mackenzie, a subject of Great Britain, she thereupon took the nationality of her husband and ceased to be a citizen of the United States.

Plaintiff in error claims a right as a voter of the state under its Constitution and the Constitution of the United States.

The Constitution of the state gives the privilege of suffrage to "every native citizen of the United States," and it is contended that under the Constitution of the United States every person born in the United States is a citizen thereof. The latter must be conceded, and if plaintiff has not lost her citizenship by her marriage, she has the qualification of a voter prescribed by the Constitution of the state of California. The question then is: Did she cease to be a citizen by her marriage?

On March 2, 1907, that is, prior to the marriage of plaintiff in error, Congress enacted a statute the third section of which provides: "That any American woman who marries a foreigner shall take the nationality of her husband. At the termination of the marital relation she may resume her American citizenship, if abroad, by registering as an American citizen within one year with a consul of the United States, or by returning to reside in the United states, or, if residing in the United States at the termination of the marital relation, by continuing to reside therein." [34 Stat. at L. 1228, chap. 2534, Comp. Stat. 1913, §3960.]

Plaintiff contends that "such legislation, if intended to apply to her, is beyond the authority of Congress." . . .

An earnest argument is presented to demonstrate its invalidity. Its basis is that the citizenship of plaintiff was an incident to her birth in the United States, and, under the Constitution and laws of the United States, it became a right, privilege, and immunity which could not be taken away from her except as a punishment for crime or by her voluntary expatriation.

The argument to support the contention and the argument to oppose it take a wide range through the principles of the common law and international law and their development and change. Both plaintiff and defendants agree that under the common law originally allegiance was immutable. They do not agree as to when the rigidity of the principle was relaxed. . . .

It would make this opinion very voluminous to consider in detail the argument and the cases urged in support of or in attack upon the opposing conditions. Their foundation principles, we may assume, are known. The identity of husband and wife is an ancient principle of our jurisprudence. It was neither accidental nor arbitrary, and worked in many instances for her protection. There has been, it is true, much relaxation of it, but in its retention as in its origin it is determined by their intimate relation and unity of interests, and this relation and unity may make it of public concern in many instances to merge their identity, and give dominance to the husband. It has purpose, if not necessity, in purely domestic policy; it has greater purpose, and, it may be, necessity, in international policy. And this was the dictate of the act in controversy. Having this purpose, has it not the sanction of power?

. . . It may be conceded that a change of citizenship cannot be arbitrarily imposed, that is, imposed without the concurrence of the citizen. The law in controversy does not have that feature. It deals with a condition voluntarily entered into, with notice of the consequences. We concur with counsel that citizenship is of tangible worth, and we sympathize with plaintiff in her desire to retain it and in her earnest assertion of it. But there is involved more than personal considerations. As we have seen, the legislation was urged by conditions of national moment. And this is an answer to the apprehension of counsel that our construction of the legislation will make every act, though lawful, as marriage, of course, is, a renunciation of citizenship. The marriage of an American woman with a foreigner has consequences of like kind, may involve national complications of like kind, as her physical expatriation may involve. Therefore, as long as the relation lasts, it is made tantamount to expatriation. This is no arbitrary exercise of government. It is one which, regarding the international aspects, judicial opinion has taken for granted would not only be valid, but demanded. It is the conception of the legislation under review that such an act may bring the government into embarrassments, and, it may be, into controversies. It is as voluntary and distinctive as expatriation and its consequence must be considered as elected.

Judgment affirmed.

Theda Perdue, Cherokee Women and the Trail of Tears
1 J. Women's Hist. 14, 15-17, 20-21 (Spring 1989)

Traditionally, women had a voice in Cherokee government. They spoke freely in council, and the War Woman (or Beloved Woman) decided the fate of captives. As late as 1787, a Cherokee woman wrote Benjamin Franklin that she had delivered an address to her people urging them to maintain peace with the new American nation. She had filled the peace pipe for the warriors, and she enclosed some of the same tobacco for the United States Congress in order to unite symbolically her people and his in peace. She continued:

> I am in hopes that if you Rightly consider that woman is the mother of All — and the Woman does not pull Children out of Trees or Stumps nor out of old Logs, but out of their Bodies, so that they ought to mind what a woman says.

The political influence of women, therefore, rested at least in part on their maternal biological role in procreation and their maternal role in Cherokee society, which assumed particular importance in the Cherokee's matrilineal kinship system. In this way of reckoning kin, children belonged to the clan of their mother, and their only relatives were those who could be traced through her. . . .

As late as 1785, women still played some role in the negotiation of land transactions. Nancy Ward, the Beloved Woman of Chota, spoke to the treaty conference held at Hopewell, South Carolina to clarify and extend land cessions stemming from Cherokee support of the British in the American Revolution. She addressed the assembly as the "mother of warriors" and promoted a peaceful resolution to land disputes between the Cherokees and the United States. Under the terms of the Treaty of Hopewell, the Cherokees ceded large tracts of land south of the Cumberland River in Tennessee and Kentucky and west of the Blue Ridge Mountains in North Carolina. Nancy Ward and the other Cherokee delegates to the conference agreed to the cession not because they believed it to be just but because the United States dictated the terms of the treaty.

The conference at Hopewell was the last treaty negotiation in which women played an official role, and Nancy Ward's participation in that conference was somewhat anachronistic. In the eighteenth century, the English as well as other Europeans had dealt politically and commercially with men, since men were the hunters and warriors in Cherokee society and Europeans were interested primarily in military alliances and deerskins. As relations with the English grew increasingly important to tribal warfare, women became less significant in the Cherokee economy and government. Conditions in the Cherokee Nation following the American Revolution accelerated the trend. In their defeat, the Cherokees had to cope with the destruction of villages, fields, corn cribs, and orchards which had occurred during the war, and the cession of hunting grounds which accompanied the peace. In desperation, they turned to the United States government, which proposed to convert the Cherokees into replicas of white pioneer farmers in the anticipation that they would then cede additional territory (presumably hunting grounds they no longer needed). While the government's so-called civilization program brought some economic relief, it also helped produce a transformation of gender roles and social organization. The society envisioned for the Cherokees, one which government agents and Protestant missionaries zealously tried to implement, was one in which a man farmed and headed a household composed only of his wife and children. The men who gained power in eighteenth-century Cherokee society — hunters, warriors, and descendants of traders — took immediate advantage of this program in order to maintain their status in the face of a declining deerskin trade and pacification, and then diverted their energy, ambition, and aggression into economic channels. As agriculture became more commercially viable, these men began to farm or to acquire African slaves to cultivate their fields for them. They also began to dominate Cherokee society, and by example and legislation, they altered fundamental relationships.

In 1808, a Council of headmen (there is no evidence of women participating) from Cherokee towns established a national police force to safeguard a person's holdings during life and "to give protection to children as heirs to their father's property, and to the widow's share," thereby changing inheritance patterns and officially recognizing the patriarchal family as the norm. Two years later, a council representing all seven matrilineal clans, but once again apparently including no women, abolished the practice of blood vengeance. This action ended one of the major functions of clans and shifted the responsibility for punishing wrongdoers to the national police force and tribal courts. Matrilineal kinship clearly did not have a place in the new Cherokee order. . . .

As the Cherokee government became more centralized, political and economic power rested increasingly in the hands of a few elite men who adopted the planter lifestyle of the white, antebellum South. A significant part of the ideological basis for this lifestyle was the cult of domesticity, in which the ideal woman confined herself to home and hearth while men contended with the corrupt world of government and business. The elite adopted the tenets of the cult of domesticity, particularly after 1817, when the number of Protestant missionaries, major proponents of this feminine ideal, increased significantly, and their influence on Cherokee society broadened. . . .

. . . In 1826 the council called a constitutional convention to draw up a governing document for the nation. According to legislation which provided for election of delegates to the convention, "No person but a free male citizen who is full grown shall be entitled to vote." The convention met and drafted a constitution patterned after that of the United States. Not surprisingly, the constitution which male Cherokees ratified in 1827 restricted the franchise to "free male citizens" and stipulated that "no person shall be eligible to a seat in the General Council, but a free Cherokee male, who shall have attained the age of twenty-five." Unlike the United States Constitution, the Cherokee document clearly excluded women, perhaps as a precaution against women who might assert their traditional right to participate in politics instead of remaining in the domestic sphere.

Notes

1. Women in the Constitution. The original Constitution of the United States did not mention women directly. As historian Rogers Smith adds:

> [The Constitution] did, however, use masculine pronouns thirty times in describing U.S. Representatives, Senators, the Vice-President, and the President. Later these pronouns would be used to argue on the floor of Congress and in state courts that the Constitution denied federal office-holding to women. To be sure, no federal court ever confirmed that position. Among other things, this claim confronted the difficulty that a masculine pronoun is also employed in Article IV, section 2, requiring states to extradite fugitives charged with treason, felonies, or other crimes, a provision no one wished to confine to men. And the Constitution's preferred nouns were invariably gender-neutral, referring to "persons," "members," or "parties," never "men." Those usages might in the abstract have been taken to permit women various political rights.

Rogers M. Smith, Civic Ideals: Conflicting Visions of Citizenship in U.S. History 131 (1997).

Walter Dellinger notes that the only use of the female pronoun in the draft versions of the Constitution appears in the next-to-last draft of the document:

> At the conclusion of the compromise over navigation and slavery, Mr. Butler moved to insert the following clause: "If any person bound to service or labor in any of the U[nited] States shall escape into another State, he or she shall not be discharged from such service or labor . . . but shall be delivered up to the person justly claiming their service or labor." Throughout the Constitution and all its drafts, "he" is used to refer to President, Vice-President, Senator; "she" appears but once in the evolving drafts of the Constitution, and "she" can be one, and only one thing: a fugitive slave.

Walter E. Dellinger III, 1787: The Constitution and "The Curse of Heaven," 29 Wm. & Mary L. Rev. 145, 153 (1987) (footnote omitted) (quoted in Martha Craig Daughtrey, Women and the Constitution: Where We Are at the End of the Century, 75 N.Y.U. L. Rev. 1, 4 (2000)).

2. Marriage and Women's Citizenship. As the Mackenzie case suggests, at common law the marriage relation had no effect on citizenship. The first federal statutes concerning the citizenship of children born abroad, passed in 1790, 1795, and 1802, withheld citizenship from children whose fathers had never resided in the United States, but it was unclear whether citizenship could pass through mothers as well as fathers. See Miller v. Albright, 523 U.S. 420, 460 (1998) (Ginsburg, J., dissenting). A bill proposed by Daniel Webster that would have clarified the law by granting citizenship to children born abroad to United States-born citizen mothers as well as fathers was unsuccessful. Id. Instead, the federal naturalization act of 1855 provided that citizenship would pass to children born abroad only when the father was a United States citizen. The act also provided that a woman of any origin or nationality would become a citizen of the United States upon marrying an American man, but not the converse. Thus, notions of coverture influenced naturalization policy. See Candice Lewis Bredbenner, A Nationality of Her Own: Women, Marriage, and the Law of Citizenship 19 (1998); Nancy Cott, Public Vows, supra, at 133.

Naturalization under the 1855 act also required that the woman marrying a United States citizen meet the general requirements for naturalization, including that she be "white." Thus, in 1868 the Supreme Court held that only white women could gain citizenship by marrying a citizen. Kelly v. Owen, 74 U.S. 496, 498 (1868). Moreover, naturalization was denied to noncitizen women who married men racially ineligible for citizenship, even if they themselves were legally "white." The automatic naturalization of a foreign-born woman upon her marriage to a citizen or upon the naturalization of her husband did not end until 1922. Ian F. Haney López, White By Law: The Legal Construction of Race 46-47 (1996).

Regarding the statute discussed in Mackenzie, Haney López notes:

> The citizenship of American-born women was also affected by the interplay of gender and racial restrictions. Even though under English common law a woman's nationality was unaffected by marriage, many courts in this country stripped women who married noncitizens of their U.S. citizenship. Congress recognized and mandated this practice in 1907, legislating that an American woman's marriage to an alien terminated her citizenship. Under considerable pressure, Congress partially repealed this act in 1922. However, the 1922 act continued to require the expatriation of any woman who married a foreigner racially barred from citizenship, flatly declaring that "any woman citizen who marries an alien ineligible to citizenship shall cease to be a citizen." Until Congress repealed this provision in 1931, marriage to a non-White alien by an American woman was akin to treason against this country: either of these acts justified the stripping of citizenship from someone American by birth. Indeed, a woman's marriage to a non-White foreigner was perhaps a worse crime, for while a traitor lost his citizenship only after trial, the woman lost hers automatically.

Id. at 47.

From 1790 until 1870, only "white" persons were permitted to become naturalized citizens. In 1870, Congress amended the racial prerequisites for naturalization, allowing persons of African nativity or descent to become citizens. In 1882, however, the Chinese Exclusion Act explicitly disqualified Chinese persons from becoming naturalized citizens; this ban was not lifted until 1943. The 1940s also saw naturalization opened to "descendants of races indigenous to the Western Hemisphere," and to persons from the Philippines and India. It was not until 1952, however, that Congress revised the naturalization statutes to provide that "the right of a person to become a naturalized citizen of the United States shall not be denied or abridged because of race or sex or because such person is married." Id. at 43-46 (1996).

The government's link between marriage and citizenship also affected Indian women. Bethany Berger notes that in 1888 Congress passed an act declaring that Indian women who married white men would thereby become American citizens.

> The law was ostensibly designed to protect Indian women from unscrupulous white men who would marry them only to gain rights to Indian land. Although the statute responded to a real problem, it equally addressed the fear raised by Rogers that white men would assimilate with their wives' tribes. The amendment was intended to ensure that the effect of the Dawes Act [breaking up common ownership in Indian reservation lands and distributing it to households in the form of "allotments"] to Indians would be to "make citizens of the United States instead of making Indians of our citizens." The legislative history presents a unwitting contrast between the two paths for intermarriage, the approved path in which the Indian woman left her tribe for an allegiance with the United States, and that in which her husband joined her people:
>
> Mr. Ezra B. Taylor: Is not the object of this bill to prevent the marriage or miscegenation of these degenerate whites with the Indian squaws?
> . . . .
> Mr. Weaver: The effect of the bill is to encourage Indians to marry white men and become citizens of the United States.
> In gaining United States citizenship, intermarried Indian women were to lose their bonds with their tribes.

Berger, After Pocahontas, supra, at 30.

It was often taken for granted in nineteenth-century American discourse that foreign nations and civilizations treated their women more poorly than did Anglo-Americans. See Leti Volpp, Feminism versus Multiculturalism, 101 Colum. L.Rev. 1181, 1196-97 (2001). As the Purdue excerpt suggests, however, assimilation into the legal and social culture of the United States meant fewer rights of political participation for women from many native

American nations. Berger suggests that assimilation also meant economic losses for Indian women.

3. Restrictions on Women Immigrants. Immigration has also been subject to racial and gender restrictions throughout United States history. For instance, the first federal restriction on immigration, the Page Act of 1875, targeted Chinese women. Far more Chinese men immigrated to the United States than Chinese women during the first wave of Chinese immigration, in the mid-1800s. See Ronald Takaki, A Different Mirror: A History of Multicultural America 209-210 (1993). Of the Chinese women who did come to America during this period, many were prostitutes, some forcibly transported to the United States. Id. at 210. The Page Act prohibited and criminalized the entry or importation of all prostitutes, and required the U.S. consul to make sure that any immigrant arriving from an Asian country was not under contract for "lewd and immoral purposes." Cott, Public Vows, supra, at 136. Asian women seeking to emigrate to the United States, then, were automatically placed under suspicion of being prostitutes.

The Gentlemen's Agreement of 1908 between Japan and the United States, which reduced Japanese immigration, provided in return that the United States would admit wives and children of Japanese men already in the country. The family-building efforts of Japanese immigrants were fostered by the subsequent popularity of "picture brides" — Japanese women linked with Japanese American men by matchmakers. By 1919, however, with racist and nativist sentiments running high, the Japanese government agreed to prohibit picture brides from emigrating to the continental United States. In the Immigration Act of 1924, Congress provided that "the terms 'wife' and 'husband' do not include a wife or husband by reason of a proxy, or picture marriage."

b. Law and Women's Suffrage

United States v. Anthony
(1873)
History of Women's Suffrage, vol. II, 1861-1876, at
688-689 (Elizabeth Cady Stanton, Susan B. Anthony &
Matilda Joslyn Gage eds., reprint ed. 1985)
(1881-1922)

[The following is an excerpt of comments made by Susan B. Anthony, in open court, the day after a verdict was directed against her for voting in violation of section 19 of the Civil Rights Act of 1870, 16 Stat. 144, a statute intended to prohibit multiple voting by white voters in order to dilute black votes.]

Miss ANTHONY: All my prosecutors, from the 8th Ward corner grocery politician, who entered the complaint, to the United States Marshal, Commissioner, District Attorney, District Judge, your honor on the bench, not one is my peer, but each and all are my political sovereigns; and had your honor submitted my case to the jury, as was clearly your duty, even then I should have had just cause of protest, for not one of those men was my peer; but, native or foreign, white or black, rich or poor, educated or ignorant, awake or asleep, sober or drunk, each and every man of them was my political superior; hence, in no sense, my peer. Even, under such circumstances, a commoner of England, tried before a jury of lords, would have far less cause to complain than should I, a woman, tried before a jury of men. Even my counsel, the Hon. Henry R. Selden, who has argued my cause so ably, so earnestly, so unanswerably before your honor, is my political sovereign. Precisely as no disfranchised person is entitled to sit upon a jury, and no woman is entitled to the franchise, so, none but a regularly admitted lawyer is allowed to practice in the courts, and no woman can gain admission to the bar — hence, jury, judge, counsel, must all be of the superior class.

Judge HUNT: The Court must insist — the prisoner has been tried according to the established forms of law.

Miss ANTHONY: Yes, your honor, but by forms of law all made by men, interpreted by men, administered by men, in favor of men, and against women; and hence, your honor's ordered verdict of guilty, against a United States citizen for the exercise of "that citizen's right to vote," simply because that citizen was a woman and not a man. But, yesterday, the same man-made forms of law declared it a crime punishable with $1,000 fine and six months' imprisonment, for you, or me, or any of us, to give a cup of cold water, a crust of bread, or a night's shelter to a panting fugitive as he was tracking his way to Canada. And every man or woman in whose veins coursed a drop of human sympathy violated that wicked law, reckless of consequences, and was justified in so doing. As then the slaves who got their freedom must take it over, or under, or through the unjust forms of law, precisely so now must women, to get their right to a voice in this Government, take it; and I have taken mine, and mean to take it at every possible opportunity.

Judge HUNT: The Court orders the prisoner to sit down. It will not allow another word.

Miss ANTHONY: When I was brought before your honor for trial, I hoped for a broad and liberal interpretation of the Constitution and its recent amendments, that should declare all United States citizens under its protecting aegis — that should declare equality of rights the national guarantee to all persons born or naturalized in the United States. But failing to get this justice — failing, even, to get a trial by a jury not of my peers — I ask not leniency at your hands — but rather the full rigors of the law.

Judge HUNT: The Court must insist — (Here the prisoner sat down.)

Judge HUNT: The prisoner will stand up. (Here Miss Anthony arose again.) The sentence of the Court is that you pay a fine of one hundred dollars and the costs of the prosecution.

Miss ANTHONY: May it please your honor, I shall never pay a dollar of your unjust penalty. All the stock in trade I possess is a $10,000 debt, incurred by publishing my paper — *The Revolution* — four years ago, the sole object of which was to educate all women to do precisely as I have done, rebel against your man-made, unjust unconstitutional forms of law, that tax, fine, imprison, and hang women, while they deny them the right of representation in the Government; and I shall work on with might and main to pay every dollar of that honest debt, but not a penny shall go to this unjust claim. And I shall earnestly and persistently continue to urge all women to practical recognition of the old revolutionary maxim, that "Resistance to tyranny is obedience to God."

Remarks of Senator George G. Vest in Congress (1887)
18 Cong. Rec. 986 (1887)

MR. VEST . . . If this Government, which is based on the intelligence of the people, shall ever be destroyed it will be by injudicious, immature, or corrupt suffrage. If the ship of state launched by our fathers shall ever be destroyed, it will be by striking the rock of universal, unprepared suffrage. . . .

. . . I speak now respecting women as a sex. I believe that they are better than men, but I do not believe they are adapted to the political work of this world. I do not believe that the Great Intelligence ever intended them to invade the sphere of work given to men, tearing down and destroying all the best influences for which God has intended them.

The great evil in this country to-day is in emotional suffrage. The great danger to-day is in excitable suffrage. If the voters of this country could think always coolly, and if they could deliberate, if they could go by judgment and not by passion, our institutions would survive forever, eternal as the foundations of the continent itself; but massed together, subject to the excitements of mobs and of these terrible political contests that come upon us from year to year under the autonomy of our Government, what would be the result if suffrage were given to the women of the United States?

Women are essentially emotional. It is no disparagement to them they are so. It is no more insulting to say that women are emotional than to say that they are delicately constructed physically and unfitted to become soldiers or workmen under the sterner, harder pursuits of life.

What we want in this country is to avoid emotional suffrage, and what we need is to put more logic into public affairs and less feeling. There are spheres in which feeling should be paramount. There are kingdoms in which the heart should reign supreme. That kingdom belongs to woman. The realm of sentiment, the realm of love, the realm of the gentler and the holier and kindlier attributes that make the name of wife, mother, and sister next to that of God himself.

I would not, and I say it deliberately, degrade woman by giving her the right of suffrage. I mean the word in its full signification, because I believe that woman as she is to-day, the queen of the home and of hearts, is above the political collisions of this world, and should always be kept above them. . . .

It is said that the suffrage is to be given to enlarge the sphere of woman's influence. Mr. President, it would destroy her influence. It would take her down from that pedestal where she is to-day, influencing as a mother the minds of her offspring, influencing by her gentle and kindly caress the action of her husband toward the good and pure.

Ellen Carol DuBois, Outgrowing the Compact of the Fathers: Equal Rights, Woman Suffrage, and the United States Constitution, 1820-1878
74 J. Am. Hist. 836, 839-840, 852 (1987)

The notion of political equality for women was so radical that for a long time it was virtually impossible even to imagine woman suffrage. Within the democratic political tradition, the emphasis on independence as a condition for possession of the suffrage worked to exclude women, who were dependent on men almost by definition. Women had an honored place in early republican thought, but they were never considered men's equals, nor was it regarded as appropriate to demand political rights for them. During the 1820s and 1830s, as popular passions increased, so did the obstacles to the political inclusion of women. Who besides women could provide the "virtue" needed to protect the republic from the rampant but necessary self-interest of men?

The barrier to the proposition of equal political rights for women was broken within a movement that was not initially political, but within which female activism flourished — abolitionism. Whereas the labor reformers of the 1820s and 1830s advocated women's rights without having much faith in women's own activism, the evangelical movements of the 1830s depended on women's activism. Of the moral reform movements, abolitionism was the most radical and contributed the most to the emerging sensibility of female self-assertion. The abolitionists' indictment of the absolute immorality of slaveholding established a much stronger political language than did workingmen's republicanism for describing the tyrannical abuse of power; women quickly put that language to good use in indicting men's tyranny over them. As arguments against the institution of chattel slavery, abstract ideas about equality and individual rights gained real social meaning. In particular, abolitionists paid attention to the misuses of the slave's body, thus illuminating themes of sexual and marital abuse among free women as well.

. . . The woman who articulated the proposition that women should have the same political rights as men had equally strong links to female and to political abolitionism. She was Elizabeth Cady Stanton, protege of Lucretia Mott, cousin of Gerrit Smith, and wife of Henry B. Stanton. She came to understand that a fundamental change in women's political status was the key to their comprehensive equal rights. . . .

By inscribing the freedmen's political rights firmly in the Constitution, the ratification of the Fifteenth Amendment threatened to bring the process of constitutional revision, and the strategic possibilities of winning women's political rights, to an end. When the amendment passed Congress in February 1869, it created what looked like a strategic dead end for woman suffrage. Then in October, a husband and wife team of Missouri suffragists, Francis Minor and Virginia Minor, came up with a different approach that relied on what was already in the Constitution, rather than requiring an additional amendment.

The Minors argued that the Constitution, properly understood, already provided for women's political rights; women were already enfranchised and had only to take the right that was theirs. Their argument rested on the link in the pending Fifteenth Amendment between national supremacy and equal political rights. Although the first section of the Fourteenth Amendment had defined national citizenship, the second section had left suffrage under control of the individual states. The Fifteenth Amendment shifted that control to the national level, thus intensifying the nationalizing aspect of the Fourteenth Amendment and extending its scope to the franchise. Much of the subsequent woman suffrage case was based on that relationship between the two amendments.

Minor v. Happersett
88 U.S. (21 Wall.) 162 (1875)

Mr. Chief Justice WAITE delivered the opinion of the court:

The question is presented in this case, whether, since the adoption of the fourteenth amendment, a woman, who is a citizen of the United States and of the State of Missouri, is a voter in that State, notwithstanding the provision of the constitution and laws of the State, which confine the right of suffrage to men alone. . . .

It is contended that the provisions of the constitution and laws of the State of Missouri which confine the right of suffrage and registration therefor to men, are in violation of the Constitution of the United States, and therefore void. The argument is, that as a woman, born or naturalized in the United States and subject to the jurisdiction thereof, is a citizen of the

United States and of the State in which she resides, she has the right of suffrage as one of the privileges and immunities of her citizenship, which the State cannot by its laws or constitution abridge.

There is no doubt that women may be citizens. They are persons, and by the fourteenth amendment, "all persons born or naturalized in the United States and subject to the jurisdiction thereof" are expressly declared to be "citizens of the United States and of the State wherein they reside.". . .

. . . [S]ex has never been made one of the elements of citizenship in the United States. In this respect men have never had an advantage over women. The same laws precisely apply to both. The fourteenth amendment did not affect the citizenship of women any more than it did of men. In this particular, therefore, the rights of Mrs. Minor do not depend upon the amendment. She has always been a citizen from her birth, and entitled to all the privileges and immunities of citizenship. This amendment prohibited the State, of which she is a citizen, from abridging any of her privileges and immunities as a citizen of the United States; but it did not confer citizenship on her. That she had before its adoption.

If the right of suffrage is one of the necessary privileges of a citizen of the United States, then the constitution and laws of Missouri confining it to men are in violation of the Constitution of the United States, as amended, and consequently void. The direct question is therefore presented whether all citizens are necessarily voters.

The Constitution does not define the privileges and immunities of citizens. For that definition we must look elsewhere. . . .

It certainly is nowhere made so in express terms. The United States has no voters in the States of its own creation. The elective officers of the United States are all elected directly or indirectly by State voters. The members of the House of Representatives are to be chosen by the people of the States, and the electors in each State must have the qualifications requisite for electors of the most numerous branch of the State legislature. Senators are to be chosen by the legislatures of the States, and necessarily the members of the legislature required to make the choice are elected by the voters of the State. . . . Congress may at any time, by law, make or alter such regulations, except as to the place of choosing Senators. It is not necessary to inquire whether this power of supervision thus given to Congress is sufficient to authorize any interference of voters, for no such interference has ever been attempted. The power of the State in this particular is certainly supreme until Congress acts.

The amendment did not add to the privileges and immunities of a citizen. It simply furnished an additional guaranty for the protection of such as he already had. No new voters were necessarily made by it. Indirectly it may have had that effect, because it may have increased the number of citizens entitled to suffrage under the constitution and laws of the States, but it operates for this purpose, if at all, through the States and the State laws, and not directly upon the citizen.

It is clear, therefore, we think, that the Constitution has not added the right of suffrage to the privileges and immunities of citizenship as they existed at the time it was adopted. This makes it proper to inquire whether suffrage was coextensive with the citizenship of the States at the time of its adoption. If it was, then it may with force be argued that suffrage was one of the rights which belonged to citizenship, and in the enjoyment of which every citizen must be protected. . . .

When the Federal Constitution was adopted, all the States, with the exception of Rhode Island and Connecticut, had constitutions of their own. . . . Upon an examination of those constitutions we find that in no State were all citizens permitted to vote. . . .

In this condition of the law in respect to suffrage in the several States it cannot for a moment be doubted that if it had been intended to make all citizens of the United States voters, the framers of the Constitution would not have left it to implication. So important a change in the condition of citizenship as it actually existed, if intended, would have been expressly declared.

But if further proof is necessary to show that no such change was intended, it can easily be found both in and out of the Constitution. By Article 4, section 2, it is provided that "the citizens of each State shall be entitled to all the privileges and immunities of citizens in the several States." If suffrage is necessarily a part of citizenship, then the citizens of each State must be entitled to vote in the several States precisely as their citizens are. This is more than asserting that they may change their residence and become citizens of the State and thus be voters. It goes to the extent of insisting that while retaining their original citizenship they may vote in any State. This, we think, has never been claimed. And again, by the very terms of the amendment we have been considering (the fourteenth), "Representatives shall be apportioned among the several States according to their respective numbers, counting the whole number of persons in each State, excluding Indians not taxed. But when the right to vote at any election for the choice of electors for President and Vice-President of the United States, representatives in Congress, the executive and judicial officers of a State, or the members of the legislature thereof, is denied to any of the male inhabitants of such State who are twenty-one years of age and citizens of the United States, . . . the basis of representation shall be reduced in the proportion which the number of such male citizens shall bear to the whole number of male citizens twenty-one years of age in such State." Why this, if it was not in the power of the legislature to deny the right of suffrage to some male inhabitants? And if suffrage was necessarily one of the absolute rights of citizenship, why confine the operation of the limitation to male inhabitants? Women and children are, as we have seen, "persons." They are counted in the enumeration upon which the apportionment is to be made, but if they were necessarily voters because of their citizenship unless clearly excluded, why inflict the penalty for the exclusion of males alone? Clearly, no such form of words would have been selected to express the idea here indicated if suffrage was the absolute right of all citizens.

[The Court reasons further that the Fifteenth Amendment, providing that the suffrage not be denied or abridged on account of race, color, or previous condition of servitude would not have been necessary if suffrage had been already one of the privileges and immunities of citizenship.]

It is true that the United States guarantees to every State a republican form of government. . . .

. . . No particular government is designated as republican, neither in the exact form to be guaranteed, in any manner especially designated. . . .

. . . [That all citizens were not given the right to vote when the Constitution was adopted is] unmistakable evidence of what was republican in form, within the meaning of that term as employed in the Constitution. . . .

. . . No new State has ever been admitted to the Union which has conferred the right of suffrage upon women, and this has never been considered a valid objection to her admission. On the contrary, . . . the right of suffrage was withdrawn from women as early as 1807 in the State of New Jersey, without any attempt to obtain the interference of the United States to prevent it. . . .

Certainly, if the courts can consider any question settled, this is one. For nearly ninety years the people have acted upon the idea that the Constitution, when it conferred citizenship, did not necessarily confer the right of suffrage. If uniform practice long continued can settle the construction of so important an instrument as the Constitution of the United States confessedly is, most certainly it has been done here. Our province is to decide what the law is, not to declare what it should be. . . . If the law is wrong, it ought to be changed; but the power for that is not with us. . . . No argument as to woman's need of suffrage can be considered. We can only act upon her rights as they exist. . . .

Being unanimously of the opinion that the Constitution of the United States does not confer the right of suffrage upon any one, and that the constitutions and laws of the several States which commit that important trust to men alone are not necessarily void, we affirm the judgment.

Notes

1. **Women and the Right To Vote.** In New Jersey in the earlier days of the republic (from 1783 to 1807), women had enjoyed the right to vote, see Catherine Clinton, The Other Civil War: American Women in the Nineteenth Century 14-16 (1984), but except for that short experiment (and that of the Utah Territory, see above at page 66), woman suffrage was apparently a nonexistent concept in the nineteenth-century United States. In the minds of Stanton, Anthony, and other early feminists, however, the

equal rights principle compelled not only women's suffrage, but also women's right to own property, make contracts, serve on juries, testify in court, receive an education, and achieve legal equality with husbands in marriage. While this broader social agenda provided early momentum for the suffrage movement, it lacked the popular support needed to sustain it.

This lack of popular support doomed the effort to enshrine woman suffrage in the Fourteenth Amendment. Despite a petition drive begun by Stanton and Anthony, the Fourteenth Amendment not only failed to explicitly give women the vote, but section 2 "made the Constitution appear to embrace female disfranchisement openly for the first time." Rogers M. Smith, Civic Ideals: Conflicting Visions of Citizenship in U.S. History 311 (1997). Smith notes:

> Similarly, in 1867 the nation's leading reform journalist, Horace Greeley, persuaded a New York constitutional convention to endorse suffrage for blacks but not women. Shortly thereafter, Kansas considered separate constitutional reforms that would have extended the vote to black men and all women. Without expressing opposition, such abolition leaders as Frederick Douglass and Wendell Phillips refused to work for women's suffrage there, fearing that it would jeopardize support for black enfranchisement. It was, they insisted, the "Negro's hour." As a result, an infuriated Susan B. Anthony accepted the aid of a wealth, ambitious, and rabidly antiblack Democrat, George Francis Train, in an ugly Kansas campaign in which both campaigns for franchise extension lost.

Id. at 311-12.

As Minor v. Happersett indicates, the argument that the Reconstruction Amendments affected in any way women's political status was soundly rejected by the courts. See also Ward Farnsworth, Women Under Reconstruction: The Congressional Understanding, 94 Nw. U. L. Rev. 1229 (2000) (arguing that the legislative history of the Fourteenth Amendment suggests that the Reconstruction Congress believed that the amendment would leave women's legal status undisturbed).

Susan B. Anthony did not live to see women receive the vote. She "died at age eighty-six in 1906, fourteen years before the Nineteenth Amendment, the 'Susan B. Anthony Amendment,' was finally ratified in 1920." Martha Craig Daughtrey, Women and the Constitution: Where We Are at the End of the Century, 75 N.Y.U. L. Rev. 1, 5-6 (2000).

Daughtrey continues:

> Three years later, in 1923, the original Equal Rights Amendment was first introduced into Congress. The initial language, changed in 1943, provided: "Men and women shall have equal rights throughout the United States and every place subject to its jurisdiction." It had been drafted by the radical suffragist Alice Paul, whose National Woman's Party had split from the ranks of mainstream suffragism, led by Anthony and later by Catt. It was Alice Paul

and her sisters-in-arms who chained themselves to the White House gates and were force-fed in prison when their protests took the form of hunger strikes. Once the Nineteenth Amendment took effect in 1920, Paul's followers continued to agitate for the expansion of women's rights, convinced that the vote would not be sufficient to bring about equality between the sexes. The old-line suffragists formed the League of Women Voters, convinced to the contrary that they could rally newly enfranchised women to vote in the reforms they deemed necessary to protect women and children in post-war America.

Id. at 6.

Alice Paul's National Woman's Party, though never garnering broad public support, effectively lobbied in the 1920s and 1930s for women's full political and civil equality. In addition to supporting the Equal Rights Amendment, the Party campaigned for reforms in immigration and naturalization law, custody rights over children, "property rights, the reinstatement of maiden names after marriage, divorce rights, estate administration, guardianship rights, contract powers, civil liability, and jury service. The party claimed that about half of the six hundred bills it authored were adopted." Richard F. Hamm, Mobilizing Legal Talent for a Cause: the National Woman's Party and the Campaign to Make Jury Service a Federal Right, 9 Am. U.J. Gender Soc. Pol'y & L. 97, 100 (2001).

The more moderate branch of the women's movement shifted the arguments for women's suffrage from the egalitarian arguments represented in the readings in this section to arguments based on women's special characteristics and strengths. Rather than resisting women's domestic role, many women reformers of the Progressive Era such as Carrie Chapman Catt and Jane Addams built upon it, arguing that society would benefit from the distinctive contributions women had to make in resolving the social problems of crime, government corruption, poverty, child abuse, alcohol abuse, lack of sanitation, and poor health:

> The suffragists' acceptance of female distinctiveness represented the departure point for [a] new strategy. In the past feminist leaders had championed the principle that the two sexes had exactly identical rights to engage in worldly activity. Now, they frequently argued that women deserved the vote precisely because they were different. The suffragists brilliantly exploited traditional assumptions about woman's unique place. Females were primarily spiritual creatures, they claimed. Hence their participation in politics would elevate the moral level of government. Men possessed special talents to cope with material problems based on their experience in the business world. But women had special abilities to cope with human problems based on their experience in the home. Each sex occupied its own particular sphere, but the two were complementary rather than incompatible. Just as the creation of a good family required the contribution of both husband and wife, so the establishment of effective government depended upon the equal participation of male and female citizens. Politics dominated by men alone constituted a half-finished social instrument. Involvement by women was essential to complete it.

William Chafe, The American Woman: Her Changing Social, Economic, and Political Roles, 1920-1970, at 13 (1972). Although Stanton and Anthony represented a more radical potential than that offered by Progressive Era reformers, note that even these figures seemed to assume, on occasion, that there are some important differences between men and women. What do you make, for example, of Stanton's discussion of women's "maternal instincts"? Is women's strongest claim for suffrage that they are just like men, or that they are different? This dichotomy, and its role in women's subordination, is a central theme of this book.

2. Women and Jury Service. Although many had assumed that the right to serve on juries would follow automatically from passage of the Nineteenth Amendment, ten years after the passage of the amendment only about half the states allowed women to serve on juries. Hamm, Mobilizing Legal Talent, supra, at 102. Where women were permitted to serve on juries, they were frequently given easy exemptions; jury commissioners in many jurisdictions also used their broad discretion in compiling jury lists to keep women out of jury pools. It was commonly said in support of such policies that jury service would cause women to neglect their household duties. See Linda K. Kerber, No Constitutional Right To Be Ladies: Women and the Obligations of Citizenship 146 (1998).

In Hoyt v. Florida, 368 U.S. 57 (1961), the Court considered the constitutionality of Florida's jury statute under the equal protection clause. Florida's statute gave women, but not men, an absolute exemption from jury service on account of sex. It also provided that women would not be called for service unless they had voluntarily registered, whereas men were to be considered eligible unless they had filed a written claim of exemption. The Court upheld the statute:

> Despite the enlightened emancipation of women from the restrictions and protections of bygone years, and their entry into many parts of community life formerly considered to be reserved to men, woman is still regarded as the center of home and family life. We cannot say that it is constitutionally impermissible for a State, acting in pursuit of the general welfare, to conclude that a woman should be relieved from the civic duty of jury service unless she herself determines that such service is consistent with her own special responsibilities.

Id. at 61-62.

In Taylor v. Louisiana, 419 U.S. 522 (1975), the Supreme Court finally held that a statute that required women to "opt in" to jury service violated the Sixth Amendment's requirement of a jury pool that reflects a cross-section of the community. Three years after Taylor, "Ruth Bader Ginsburg convinced the Supreme Court in Duren v. Missouri, 439 U.S. 357 (1979) to invalidate Missouri's 'opt-out' provision, which allowed any woman, in response to a prominently placed notice on the jury summons, to decline service by returning the summons or by simply not reporting for jury duty." Daughtrey, Women and the Constitution, supra, at 19.

C. THE HISTORY OF FEMINIST LEGAL MOVEMENT

Feminism as a social and legal movement in the United States emerged in two waves. The Seneca Falls Convention of 1848 is generally credited as marking the beginning of the first wave; the second wave of feminism is said to have emerged in the 1960s.

Both the first and second waves of feminism were intertwined with other social struggles that gripped the nation. Many of the early suffragettes, like the South Carolina-born Sarah and Angelina Grimké, were abolitionists; indeed, the idea for the Seneca Falls Convention was inspired at the Anti-Slavery Convention in London a few years earlier when two of its organizers, Lucretia Mott, a Quaker minister, and Elizabeth Cady Stanton, were barred from participation in the Convention and required to sit behind a curtain. Sara M. Evans, Born for Liberty: A History of Women in America 81 (1989). Similarly, many pioneering feminists in the second wave of women's movement in the United States had previously participated in labor organizing, the "New Left," or civil rights work. See Ruth Rosen, The World Split Open 58-59 (2000).

This section excerpts some famous texts from first-wave legal feminism. As you read these documents, ask yourself how first-wave feminists framed their claims of oppression, and what vision of sex equality they hoped to achieve.

Declaration of Sentiments, Seneca Falls Convention, Seneca Falls, New York
(July 1848)
History of Women's Suffrage, vol. I, 1848-1861, at 70-71
(Elizabeth Cady Stanton, Susan B. Anthony & Matilda Joslyn Gage eds., reprint ed. 1985)
(1881-1922)

When, in the course of human events, it becomes necessary for one portion of the family of man to assume among the people of the earth a position different from that which they have hitherto occupied, but one to which the laws of nature and of nature's God entitle them, a decent respect to the opinions of mankind requires that they should declare the causes that impel them to such a course.

We hold these truths to be self-evident: that all men and women are created equal; that they are endowed by their Creator with certain inalienable rights; that among these are life, liberty, and the pursuit of happiness; that to secure these rights governments are instituted, deriving their just powers from the consent of the governed. Whenever any form of government becomes destructive of these ends, it is the right of those who suffer from it to refuse allegiance to it, and to insist upon the institution of a new government, laying its foundation on such principles, and organizing its powers in such form, as to them shall seem most likely to effect their safety and happiness. Prudence, indeed, will dictate that governments long established should not be changed for light and transient causes; and accordingly all experience hath shown that mankind are more disposed to suffer, while evils are sufferable, than to right themselves by abolishing the forms to which they were accustomed. But when a long train of abuses and usurpations, pursuing invariably the same object evinces a design to reduce them under absolute despotism, it is their duty to throw off such government, and to provide new guards for their future security. Such has been the patient sufferance of the women under this government, and such is now the necessity which constrains them to demand the equal station to which they are entitled.

The history of mankind is a history of repeated injuries and usurpations on the part of man toward woman, having in direct object the establishment of an absolute tyranny over her. To prove this, let facts be submitted to a candid world.

He has never permitted her to exercise her inalienable right to the elective franchise.

He has compelled her to submit to laws, in the formation of which she had no voice.

He has withheld from her rights which are given to the most ignorant and degraded men — both natives and foreigners.

Having deprived her of this first right of a citizen, the elective franchise, thereby leaving her without representation in the halls of legislation, he has oppressed her on all sides.

He has made her, if married, in the eye of the law, civilly dead.

He has taken from her all right in property, even to the wages she earns.

He has made her, morally, an irresponsible being, as she can commit many crimes with impunity, provided they be done in the presence of her husband. In the covenant of marriage, she is compelled to promise obedience to her husband, he becoming, to all intents and purposes, her master — the law giving him power to deprive her of her liberty, and to administer chastisement.

He has so framed the laws of divorce, as to what shall be the proper causes, and in case of separation, to whom the guardianship of the children shall be given, as to be wholly regardless of the happiness of women — the law, in all cases, going upon a false supposition of the supremacy of man, and giving all power into his hands.

After depriving her of all rights as a married woman, if single, and the owner of property, he has taxed her to support a government which recognizes her only when her property can be made profitable to it.

He has monopolized nearly all the profitable employments, and from those she is permitted to follow, she receives but a scanty remuneration. He closes against her all the avenues to wealth and distinction which he considers most honorable to himself. As a teacher of theology, medicine, or law, she is not known.

He has denied her the facilities for obtaining a thorough education, all colleges being closed against her.

He allows her in Church, as well as State, but a subordinate position, claiming Apostolic authority for her exclusion from the ministry, and with some exceptions, from any public participation in the affairs of the Church.

He has created a false public sentiment by giving to the world a different code of morals for men and women, by which moral delinquencies which exclude women from society, are not only tolerated, but deemed of little account in man.

He has usurped the prerogative of Jehovah himself, claiming it as his right to assign for her a sphere of action, when that belongs to her conscience and to her God.

He has endeavored, in every way that he could, to destroy her confidence in her own powers, to lessen her self-respect, and to make her willing to lead a dependent and abject life.

Now, in view of this entire disfranchisement of one-half the people of this country, their social and religious degradation — in view of the unjust laws above mentioned, and because women do feel themselves aggrieved, oppressed, and fraudulently deprived of their most sacred rights, we insist that they have immediate admission to all the rights and privileges which belong to them as citizens of the United States.

In entering upon the great work before us, we anticipate no small amount of misconception, misrepresentation, and ridicule; but we shall use every instrumentality within our power to effect our object. We shall employ agents, circulate tracts, petition the State and National legislatures, and endeavor to enlist the pulpit and the press in our behalf. We hope this Convention will be followed by a series of Conventions embracing every part of the country.

Gerda Lerner, The Meaning of Seneca Falls, 1848-1998
Dissent, Fall 1998, at 35, 37-39

. . . By selecting the Declaration of Independence for their formal model and following its preamble almost verbatim, except for the insertion of gender-neutral language, the organizers of the convention sought to base their main appeal on the democratic rights embodied in the nation's founding document. They also put the weight and symbolism of this revered text behind what was in their time a radical assertion: "We hold these truths to be self-evident: that all men and women are created equal."

The feminist appeal to natural rights and the social contract had long antecedents on the European continent, the most important advocate of it being Mary Wollstonecraft. Her work was well known in the United States, where the same argument had been well made by Judith Sargent Murray, Frances Wright, Emma Willard, Sarah Grimke and Margaret Fuller.

The second fundamental argument for the equality of women was religious. As stated in the Declaration:

> Resolved, That woman is man's equal — was intended to be so by the Creator, and the highest good of the race demands that she should be recognized as such.

And one of the "grievances" is:

> He [man] has usurped the prerogative of Jehovah himself, claiming it as his right to assign to her a sphere of action, when that belongs to her conscience and her God.

The feminist argument based on biblical grounds can be traced back for seven hundred years prior to 1848, but the women assembled at Seneca Falls were unaware of that fact . . . They did know the Quaker argument, especially as made in her public lectures by Lucretia Mott. They had read Sarah Grimke's Letters on the Equality of the Sexes, and several of the resolutions in fact followed her text. They knew the biblical argument by Ann Lee of the Shakers and they echoed the anti-slavery biblical argument, applying it to women.

The Declaration departed from precedent in its most radical statement:

> The history of mankind is a history of repeated injuries and usurpations on the part of man toward woman, having in direct object the establishment of an absolute tyranny over her.

The naming of "man" as the culprit, thereby identifying patriarchy as a system of "tyranny," was highly original, but it may have been dictated more by the rhetorical flourishes of the Declaration of Independence than by an actual analysis of woman's situation. . . .

The Declaration claimed universality, even though it never mentioned differences among women. Future woman's rights conferences before the Civil War would rectify this omission and pay particular attention to the needs of lower class and slave women.

While grievances pertaining to woman's sexual oppression were not explicitly included in the Declaration of Sentiments, they were very much alive in the consciousness of the leading participants. Elizabeth Cady Stanton had already in 1848 begun to include allusions to what we now call "marital rape" in her letters and soon after the Seneca Falls convention made such references explicit, calling on legislatures to forbid marriage to "drunkards." She soon became an open advocate of divorce and of the right of women to leave abusive marriages. Later woman's rights conventions would include some of these issues among their demands, although they used carefully guarded language and focused on abuses by "drunkards." This was a hidden feminist theme of the mainstream woman's temperance movement in the 1880s and caused many temperance women to embrace woman suffrage. What we now call "a woman's right to her body" was already on the agenda of the nineteenth-century woman's rights movement.

It was the confluence of a broad-ranging programmatic declaration with a format familiar and accessible to reformers that gave the event its historical significance. The Seneca Falls convention was the first forum in which women gathered together to publicly air their own grievances, not those of the needy, the enslaved, orphans or widows. The achievement of a public voice for women and the recognition that women could not win their rights unless they organized, made Seneca Falls a major event in history.

Elizabeth Cady Stanton, Address to the Legislature of the State of New York
(February 14, 1854)
History of Women's Suffrage, vol. I, 1848-1861, 595, 595-599, 602-605 (Elizabeth Cady Stanton, Susan B. Anthony & Matilda Joslyn Gage eds., reprint ed. 1985)
(1881-1922)

The tyrant, Custom, has been summoned before the bar of Common-Sense. His majesty no longer awes his multitude — his sceptre is broken — his crown is trampled in the dust — the sentence of death is pronounced upon him. All nations, ranks and classes have, in turn, questioned and repudiated his authority; and now, that the monster is chained and caged, timid woman, on tiptoe, comes to look him in the face, and to demand of her brave sires and sons, who have struck stout blows for liberty, if, in this change of dynasty, she, too, shall find relief. Yes, gentlemen, in republican America, in the nineteenth century, we, the daughters of the revolutionary heroes of '76, demand at your hands the redress of our grievances — a revision of your State Constitution — a new code of laws. Permit us then, as briefly as possible, to call your attention to the legal disabilities under which we labor.

1st. Look at the position of woman as woman. It is not enough for us that by your laws we are permitted to live and breathe, to claim the necessaries of life from our legal protectors — to pay the penalty of our crimes; we demand the full recognition of all our rights as citizens of the Empire State. We are persons; native, free-born citizens; property-holders, tax-payers; yet we are denied the exercise of our right to the elective franchise. We support ourselves, and, in part, your schools, colleges, churches, your poor-houses, jails, prisons, the army, the navy, the whole machinery of government, and yet we have no voice in your councils. We have every qualification required by the Constitution, necessary to the legal voter, but the one of sex. We are moral, virtuous, and intelligent, and in all respects quite equal to the proud white man himself and yet by your laws we are classed with idiots, lunatics, and negroes; and though we do not feel honored by the place assigned us in fact, our legal position is lower than that of either; for the negro can be raised to the dignity of a voter if he possess himself of $250; the lunatic can vote in his moments of sanity, and the idiot, too, if he be a made one, and not more than nine-tenths a fool; but we, who have guided great movements of charity, established missions, edited journals, published works on history, economy, and statistics; who have governed nations, led armies, filled the professor's chair, taught philosophy and mathematics to the savants of our age, discovered planets, piloted ships across the sea, are denied the most sacred rights of citizens, because, forsooth, we came not into this republic crowned with the dignity of manhood! . . .

Now, gentlemen, who would fain know by what authority you have disfranchised one-half the people of this State? You who have so boldly taken possession of the bulwarks of this republic, show us your credentials, and thus prove your exclusive right to govern, not only yourselves, but us. . . . Can it be that here, where we acknowledge no royal blood, no apostolic descent, that you, who have declared that all men were created equal — that governments derive their just powers from the consent of the governed, would willingly build up an aristocracy that places the ignorant and vulgar above the educated and refined — the alien and the ditch-digger above the authors and poets of the day — an aristocracy that would raise the sons above the mothers that bore them? Would that the men who can sanction a Constitution so opposed to the genius of this government, who can enact and execute laws so degrading to womankind, had sprung, Minerva-like, from the brains of their fathers, that the matrons of this republic need not blush to own their sons!

. . . [Y]ou place the negro, so unjustly degraded by you, in a superior position to your own wives and mothers; for colored males, if possessed of a certain amount of property and certain other qualifications, can vote, but if they do not have these qualifications they are not subject to direct taxation; wherein they have the advantage of woman, she being subject to taxation for whatever amount she may possess. (Constitution of New York, Article 2, Sec. 2.) But, say you, are not all women sufficiently represented by their fathers, husbands, and brothers? Let your statute books answer the question.

[W]e demand in criminal cases that most sacred of all rights, trial by a jury of our own peers. . . .

Shall an erring woman be dragged before a bar of grim-visaged judges, lawyers, and jurors, there to be grossly questioned in public on subjects which women scarce breathe in secret to one another? Shall the most sacred relations of life be called up and rudely scanned by men who, by their own admission, are so coarse that woman could not meet them even at the polls without contamination? [A]nd yet shall she find there no woman's face or voice to pity and defend? Shall the frenzied mother, who, to save herself and child from exposure and disgrace, ended the life that had but just begun, be dragged before such a tribunal to answer for her crime? How can man enter into the feelings of that mother? How can he judge of the agonies of soul that impelled her to such an outrage of maternal instincts? How can he weigh the mountain of sorrow that crushed that mother's heart when she wildly tossed her helpless babe into the cold waters of the midnight sea? Where is he who by false vows thus blasted this trusting woman? Had that helpless child no claims on his protection? Ah, he is freely abroad in the dignity of manhood, in the pulpit, on the bench, in the professor's chair. The imprisonment of his victim and the death of his child, detract not a tithe from his standing and complacency. His peers made the law, and shall law-makers lay nets for those of their own rank? Shall laws which come from the logical brain of man take cognizance of violence done to the moral and affectional nature which predominates, as is said, in woman?

Statesmen of New York, whose daughters guarded by your affection, and lapped amidst luxuries which your indulgence spreads, care more for their nodding plumes and velvet trains than for the statute laws by which their persons and properties are held — who, blinded by custom and prejudice to the degraded position which they and their sisters occupy in the civil scale, haughtily claim that they already have all the rights they want, how, think ye, you would feel to see a daughter summoned for such a crime — and remember these daughters are but human — before such a tribunal? Would it not, in that hour, be some consolation to see that she was surrounded by the wise and virtuous of her own sex; by those who had known the depth of a mother's love and the misery of a lover's falsehood; to know that to these she could make her confession, and from them receive her sentence? If so, then listen to our just demands and make such a change in your laws as will secure to every woman tried in your courts, an impartial jury. At this moment among the hundreds of women who are shut up in prisons in this State, not one has enjoyed that most sacred of all rights —

that right which you would die to defend for yourselves — trial by a jury of one's peers.

2d. Look at the position of woman as wife. Your laws relating to marriage — founded as they are on the old common law of England, a compound of barbarous usages, but partially modified by progressive civilization — are in open violation of our enlightened ideas of justice, and of the holiest feelings of our nature. If you take the highest view of marriage, as a Divine relation, which love alone can constitute and sanctify, then of course human legislation can only recognize it. Men can neither bind nor loose its ties, for that prerogative belongs to God alone, who makes man and woman, and the laws of attraction by which they are united. But if you regard marriage as a civil contract, then let it be subject to the same laws which control all other contracts. Do not make it a kind of half-human, half-divine institution, which you may build up, but can not regulate. Do not, by your special legislation for this one kind of contract, involve yourselves in the grossest absurdities and contradictions.

. . . . The wife who inherits no property holds about the same legal position that does the slave on the Southern plantation. She can own nothing, sell nothing. She has no right even to the wages she earns; her person, her time, her services are the property of another. She can not testify, in many cases, against her husband. She can get no redress for wrongs in her own name in any court of justice. She can neither sue nor be sued. She is not held morally responsible for any crime committed in the presence of her husband so completely is her very existence supposed by the law to be merged in that of another. Think of it; your wives may be thieves, libelers, burglars, incendiaries, and for crimes like these they are not held amenable to the laws of the land, if they but commit them in your dread presence. For them, alas! there is no higher law than the will of man. . . .

[The discussion of the position of the widow is deleted.]

. . . 4th. Look at the position of woman as mother. There is no human love so strong and steadfast as that of the mother for her child; yet behold how ruthless are your laws touching this most sacred relation. Nature has clearly made the mother the guardian of the child; but man, in his inordinate love of power, does continually set nature and nature's laws at open defiance. The father may apprentice his child, bind him out to a trade, without the mother's consent — yea, in direct opposition to her most earnest entreaties, prayers and tears.

He may apprentice his son to a gamester or rum-seller, and thus cancel his debts of *honor*. By the abuse of this absolute power, he may bind his daughter to the owner of a brothel, and, by the degradation of his child, supply his daily wants; and such things, gentlemen, have been done in our very midst. Moreover, the father, about to die, may bond out all his children wherever and to whomsoever he may see fit, and thus, in fact, will away the guardianship of all his children from the mother. The Revised Statutes of New York provide that "every father, whether of full age or a minor, of a child to be born, or of any living child under the age of twenty-one years, and unmarried, may by his deed or last will, duly executed, dispose of the custody and tuition of such child during its minority, or for any less time, to any person or persons, in possession of remainder." . . . Thus, by your laws, the child is the absolute property of the father, wholly at his disposal in life or at death.

In case of separation, the law gives the children to the father; no matter what his character or condition. At this very time we can point you to noble, virtuous, well-educated mothers in this State, who have abandoned their husbands for their profligacy and confirmed drunkenness. All these have been robbed of their children, who are in the custody of the husband, under the care of his relatives, whilst the mothers are permitted to see them but at stated intervals. . . .

. . . By your laws, all these abominable resorts are permitted. It is folly to talk of a mother moulding the character of her son, when all mankind, backed up by law and public sentiment, conspire to destroy her influence. But when woman's moral power shall speak through the ballot-box, then shall her influence be seen and felt. . . .

Many times and oft it has been asked us, with unaffected seriousness, "What do you women want? What are you aiming at?" Many have manifested a laudable curiosity to know what the wives and daughters could complain of in republican America, where their sires and sons have so bravely fought for freedom and gloriously secured their independence, trampling all tyranny, bigotry, and caste in the dust, and declaring to a waiting world the divine truth that all men are created equal. What can woman want under such a government? Admit a radical difference in sex, and you demand different spheres — water for fish, and air for birds.

It is impossible to make the Southern planter believe that his slave feels and reasons just as he does — that injustice and subjection are as galling as to him — that the degradation of living by the will of another, the mere dependent on his caprice, at the mercy of his passions, is as keenly felt by him as his master. If you can force on his unwilling vision a vivid picture of the negro's wrongs, and for a moment touch his soul, his logic brings him instant consolation. He says, the slave does not feel this as I would. Here, gentlemen, is our difficulty: When we plead our cause before the law-makers and savants of the republic, they can not take in the idea that men and women are alike; and so long as the mass rest in this delusion, the public mind will not be so much startled by the revelations made of the injustice and degradation of woman's position as by the fact that she should at length wake up to a sense of it.

If you, too, are thus deluded, what avails it that we show by your statute books that your laws are unjust — that woman is the victim of avarice and power? What avails it that we point out the wrongs of woman in social life; the victim of passion and lust? You scorn the thought that she has any natural love of freedom burning in her breast, any clear perception of justice urging her on to demand her rights.

Would to God you could know the burning indignation that fills woman's soul when she turns over the pages of your statute books, and sees there how like feudal barons you freemen hold your women. Would that you could know the humiliation she feels for sex, when she thinks of all the beardless boys in your law offices, learning these ideas of one-sided justice — taking their first lessons in contempt for all womankind — being indoctrinated into the incapacities of their mothers, and the lordly, absolute rights of man over all women, children, and property, and to know that these are to be our future presidents, judges, husbands, and fathers; in sorrow we exclaim, alas! for that nation whose sons bow not in loyalty to woman. The mother is the first object of the child's veneration and love, and they who root out this holy sentiment, dream not of the blighting effect it has on the boy and the man. The impression left on law students, fresh from your statute books, is most unfavorable to woman's influence; hence you see but few lawyers chivalrous and high-toned in their sentiments toward woman. They can not escape the legal view which, by constant reading, has become familiarized to their minds: "*Femme covert*," "dower," "widow's claims," "protection," "incapacities," "incumbrance," is written on the brow of every woman they meet.

But if, gentlemen, you take the ground that the sexes are alike, and, therefore, you are our faithful representatives — then why all these special laws for woman? Would not one code answer for all of like needs and wants? Christ's golden rule is better than all the special legislation that the ingenuity of man can devise: "Do unto others as you would have others do unto you." This, men and brethren, is all we ask at your hands. We ask no better laws than those you have made for yourselves. We need no other protection than that which your present laws secure to you.

In conclusion, then, let us say, in behalf of the women of this State, we ask for all that you have asked for yourselves in the progress of your development, since the Mayflower cast anchor beside Plymouth rock; and simply on the ground that the rights of every human being are the same and identical. You may say that the mass of the women of this State do not make the demand; it comes from a few sour, disappointed old maids and childless women.

You are mistaken; the mass speak through us. A very large majority of the women of this State support themselves and their children, and many their husbands too. . . .

Now, do you candidly think these wives do not wish to control the wages they earn — to own the land they buy — the houses they build? To have at their disposal their own children, without being subject to the constant interference and tyranny of an idle, worthless profligate? Do you suppose that any woman is such a pattern of devotion and submission that she willingly stitches all day for the small sum of fifty cents, that she may enjoy the unspeakable privilege, in obedience to your laws, of paying for her husband's tobacco and rum? Think you the wife of the confirmed, beastly drunkard would consent to share with him her home and bed, if law and public sentiment would release her from such gross companionship? Verily, no! Think you the wife with whom endurance has ceased to be a virtue, who, through much suffering, has lost all faith in the justice of both heaven and earth, takes the law in her own hand, severs the unholy bond, and turns her back forever upon him whom she once called husband, consents to the law that in such an hour tears her child from her — all that she has left on earth to love and cherish? The drunkards' wives speak through us, and they number 50,000. Think you that the woman who has worked hard all her days in helping her husband to accumulate a large property, consents to the law that places this wholly at his disposal? Would not the mother whose only child is bound out for a term of years against her expressed wish, deprive the father of this absolute power if she could?

For all these, then, we speak. If to this long list you add the laboring women who are loudly demanding remuneration for their unending toil; those women who teach in our seminaries, academies, and public schools for a miserable pittance; the widows who are taxed without mercy; the unfortunate ones in our work-houses, poor-houses, and prisons; who are they that we do not now represent? But a small class of the fashionable butterflies, who, through the short summer days, seek the sunshine and the flowers; but the cool breezes of autumn and the hoary frosts of winter will soon chase all these away; then they, too, will need and seek protection, and through other lips demand in their turn justice and equity at your hands.

Sojourner Truth: Reminiscences by Frances D. Gage
Akron Convention (May 28-29, 1851)
History of Women's Suffrage, vol. I, 1848-1861, at
115-117 (Elizabeth Cady Stanton, Susan B. Anthony &
Matilda Joslyn Gage eds., reprint ed. 1985)
(1881-1922)

The leaders of the movement trembled on seeing a tall, gaunt black woman in a gray dress and white turban, surmounted with an uncouth sun-bonnet, march deliberately into the church, walk with the air of a queen up the aisle, and take her seat upon the pulpit steps. A buzz of disapprobation was heard all over the house, and there fell on the listening ear, "An abolition affair!" "Woman's rights and niggers!" "I told you so!" "Go it, darkey!"

I chanced on that occasion to wear my first laurels in public life as president of the meeting. At my request order was restored, and the business of the Convention went on. Morning, afternoon, and evening exercises came and went. Through all these sessions old Sojourner, quiet and reticent as the "Lybian Statue," sat crouched against the wall on the corner of the pulpit stairs, her sun-bonnet shading her eyes, her elbows on her knees, her chin resting upon her broad, hard palms. At intermission she was busy selling the "Life of Sojourner Truth," a narrative of her own strange and adventurous life. Again and again, timorous and trembling ones came to me and said, with earnestness, "Don't let her speak, Mrs. Gage, it will ruin us. Every newspaper in the land will have our cause mixed up with abolition and niggers, and we shall be utterly denounced." My only answer was, "We shall see when the time comes."

The second day the work waxed warm. Methodist, Baptist, Episcopal, Presbyterian, and Universalist ministers came in to hear and discuss the resolutions presented. One claimed superior rights and privileges for man, on the ground of "superior intellect"; another, because of the "manhood of Christ; if God had desired the equality of woman, He would have given some token of His will through the birth, life, and death of the Saviour." Another gave us a theological view of the "sin of our first mother."

There were very few women in those days who dared to "speak in meeting"; and the august teachers of the people were seemingly getting the better of us, while the boys in the galleries, and the sneerers among the pews, were hugely enjoying the discomfiture, as they supposed, of the "strong-minded." Some of the tender-skinned friends were on the point of losing dignity, and the atmosphere betokened a storm. When, slowly from her seat in the corner rose Sojourner Truth, who, till now, had scarcely lifted her head. "Don't let her speak!" gasped half a dozen in my ear. She moved slowly and solemnly to the front, laid her old bonnet at her feet, and turned her great speaking eyes to me. There was a hissing sound of disapprobation above and below. I rose and announced "Sojourner Truth," and begged the audience to keep silence for a few moments.

The tumult subsided at once, and every eye was fixed on this almost Amazon form, which stood nearly six feet high, head erect, and eyes piercing the upper air like one in a dream. At her first word there was a profound hush. She spoke in deep tones, which, though not loud, reached every ear in the house, and away through the throngs at the doors and windows.

"Wall, chilern, whar dar is so much racket dar must be somethin' out o' kilter. I think dat 'twixt de niggers of de Souf and de womin at de Norf, all talkin' 'bout rights, de white men will be in a fix pretty soon. But what's all this here talkin' 'bout?

"Dat man ober dar say dat womin needs to be helped into carriages, and lifted ober ditches, and to hab de best place everywhar. Nobody eber helps me into carriages, or ober mud-puddles, or gibs me any best place!" And raising herself to her full height, and her voice to a pitch to like rolling thunder, she asked, "And a'n't I a woman? Look at me! Look at my arm! (and she bared her right arm to the shoulder, showing her tremendous muscular power). I have ploughed, and planted, and gathered into barns, and no man could head me! And a'n't I a woman? I could work as much and eat as much as a man — when I could get it — and bear de lash as well! And a'n't I a woman? I have borne thirteen chilern, and seen 'em mos' all sold off to slavery, and when I cried out with my mother's grief, none but Jesus heard me! And a'n't I a woman?

"Den dey talks 'bout dis ting in de head; what dis dey call it?" ("Intellect," whispered some one near.) "Dat's it, honey. What's dat got to do wid womin's rights or nigger's rights? If my cup won't hold but a pint, and yourn holds a quart, wouldn't ye be mean not to let me have my little half-measure full?" And she pointed her significant finger, and sent a keen glance at the ministers who had made the argument. The cheering was long and loud.

"Den dat little man in black dar, he say women can't have as much rights as men, 'cause Christ wan't a woman! Whar did your Christ come from?" Rolling thunder couldn't have stilled that crowd, as did those deep, wonderful tones, as she stood there with outstretched arms and eyes of fire. Raising her voice still louder, she repeated, "Whar did your Christ come from? From God and a woman! Man had nothin' to do wid Him." Oh, what rebuke that was to that little man.

Turning again to another objector, she took up the defense of Mother Eve. I can not follow her through it all. It was pointed, and witty, and solemn; eliciting at almost every sentence deafening applause; and she ended by asserting: "If de fust woman God ever made was strong enough to turn de world upside down all alone, dese women togedder (and she glanced her eye over the platform) ought to be able to turn it back, and get it right side up again! And now dey is asking to do it, de men better let 'em." Long-continued cheering greeted this. "Bleeged to ye for hearin' on me, and now ole Sojourner han't got nothin' more to say."

Amid roars of applause, she returned to her corner, leaving more than one of us with streaming eyes, and hearts beating with gratitude. She had taken us up in her strong arms and carried us safely over the slough of difficulty turning the whole tide in our favor. I have never in my life seen anything like the magical influence that subdued the mobbish spirit of the day, and turned the sneers and jeers of an excited crowd into notes of respect and admiration. Hundreds rushed up to shake hands with her, and congratulate the glorious old mother, and bid her God-speed on her mission of "testifyin' agin concerning the wickedness of this 'ere people."

Nell Painter, Sojourner Truth: A Life, a Symbol
125-126, 170-171, 174 (1996)

A much later report would attribute a dominant role to Sojourner Truth. In fact she was only one of several self-possessed, competent, and experienced antislavery feminists who conducted this meeting so boldly — and with the support of the men who were there. Her remarks did not bring the meeting to a halt or even change its course, but they engrossed the audience. Her friend and host, Marius Robinson, was used to her way of speaking and was also serving as secretary of the convention. He printed his report of her whole address:

> One of the most unique and interesting speeches of the Convention was made by Sojourner Truth, an emancipated slave. It is impossible to transfer it to paper, or convey any adequate idea of the effect it produced upon the audience. Those only can appreciate it who saw her powerful form, her whole-souled, earnest gestures, and listened to her strong and truthful tones. She came forward to the platform and addressing the President said with great simplicity:
>
>> May I say a few words? Receiving an affirmative answer, she proceeded; I want to say a few words about this matter. I am a woman's rights. I have as much muscle as any man, and can do as much work as any man. I have plowed and reaped and husked and chopped and mowed, and can any man do more than that? I have heard much about the sexes being equal; I can carry as much as any man, and can eat as much too, if I can get it. I am as strong as any man that is now. As for intellect, all I can say is, if a woman have a pint and man a quart — why cant she have her little pint full? You need not be afraid to give us our rights for fear we will take too much, — for we cant take more than our pint'll hold. The poor men seem to be all in confusion, and dont know what to do. Why children, if you have woman's rights give it to her and you will feel better. You will have your own rights, and they wont be so much trouble. I cant read, but I can hear. I have heard the bible and have learned that Eve caused man to sin. Well if woman upset the world, do give her a chance to set it right side up again. The lady has spoken about Jesus, how he never spurned woman from him, and she was right. When Lazarus died, Mary and Martha came to him with faith and love and besought him to raise their brother. And Jesus wept — and Lazarus came forth. And how came Jesus into the world? Through God who created him and woman who bore him. Man, where is your part? But the women are coming up blessed by God and a few of the men are coming up with them. But man is in a tight place, the poor slave is on him, woman is coming on him, and he is surely between a hawk and a buzzard. . . .

In Gage's scenario, Truth addresses male critics and antiblack women, not a meeting full of people who agreed with and supported her. Gage does two things with her set-up: She reiterates a familiar Christian narrative in which a lone preacher — like Sojourner Truth against the rowdies at Northampton — subdues and converts a body of unruly non-believers. And she plays on the irony of white women advocating women's rights while ignoring women who are black. White feminists' hostility is the bedrock of the emblematic Sojourner Truth who emerges from Gage's narrative. Their antagonism proves the power of Truth, the preacher able to convert them. . . .

Gage's Truth speaks in an inconsistent dialect that may have been inspired by the South Carolinians around Gage in 1863 . . . [T]he dialect serves primarily to measure the distance between Truth and her white audience. . . .

"Ar'n't I a woman?" was Gage's invention. Had Truth said it several times in 1851, as in Gage's article, Marius Robinson, who was familiar with Truth's diction, most certainly would have noted it. . . .

One of only a few black women regulars on the feminist and antislavery circuit, Truth was doing in Gage's report the very same symbolic work of her personal presence in these meetings: she was the pivot that linked two causes — of women (presumed to be white) and of blacks (presumed to be men) — through one black female body. One phrase sums up the emblematic Sojourner Truth today: "ar'n't I a woman?" . . .

We cannot know exactly what Truth said at Akron in 1851, an unusually well reported appearance. We know even less of what she said most other times she spoke. She put her soul and genius into extemporaneous speech, not dictation, and lacking sound recordings or reliable transcripts, seekers after Truth are now at the mercy of what other people said that she said. Accounts of her words in 1851 differ, and today the one that historians judge the more reliable — because it was written close to the time when Truth spoke — is Marius Robinson's.

Unlike professional historians, whose eyes are fixed on accuracy, Truth's modern admirers almost universally prefer the account that Gage presented twelve years after the fact. It fits far better with what we believe Truth to have been like. But this is testimony to the role of symbol in our public life and to our need for this symbol. To Robinson's contemporaneous report in standard English, we prefer the Sojourner Truth in dialect of a skilled feminist writer.

Notes

1. Racial Tensions in the First Wave of Feminism. Sojourner Truth's speech at the Akron Convention in 1851, as well as the reporting of it, represents some continuing tensions in the women's movement, prefiguring a complex and still-troubled relationship between white and non-white women. As a former slave and abolitionist missionary, Sojourner Truth was a strong voice for the rights of all women, and yet in order to assert her claims she had to overcome resistance from women who were willing to exploit racial fears and to align themselves with pro-slavery advocates in order to advance the cause of white women. See bell hooks, Ain't I a Woman: Black Women and Feminism 127-131 (1981); Ellen Carol DuBois, Feminism and Suffrage: The Emergence of an Independent Women's Movement in America 1848-1869, at 95-96 (1978). This continuing struggle reappears in other forms throughout this book.

Note the compound references to slaves and slavery by Stanton. Women are like slaves to the extent they are subject to the unjust laws of men, and thus women are justified in resisting their oppression. But they are also higher than slaves; thus Stanton is outraged that (white) men place the "negro . . . in a superior position to [their] own wives and mothers." Later suffragettes used even more explicit arguments about the desirability of diluting the Negro vote as a rationale for supporting women's suffrage. As an example, historian Sara Evans quotes one Southern suffragist at a 1903 NAWSA convention as saying that "[t]he enfranchisement of women would insure immediate and durable white supremacy, honestly attained." Evans, Born for Liberty, supra, at 155.

The limitations of the analogy between slavery and women's subordination are examined in other chapters of this book, especially Chapter 7. See generally Serena Mayeri, A Common Fate of Discrimination: Race-Gender Analogies in Legal and Historical Perspective, 110 Yale L.J. 1045 (2001); bell hooks, supra, at 139 ("white women have used comparisons between 'women' and 'blacks' to exclude black women and to deflect attention away from their own racial caste system"); Joyce E. McDonnell, Beyond Metaphor: Battered Women, Involuntary Servitude, and the Thirteenth Amendment, 4 Yale J.L. & Feminism 207, 207-208 (1992) ("No matter how rhetorically useful [the metaphor of women as slaves] may have seemed then or may seem now, it was and remains grossly inaccurate and inherently racist"). In the nineteenth-century context, is the analogy between women's status and that of slaves ever useful?

Note that some of the cases set forth in this chapter represented efforts to obtain rights for women based on constitutional amendments passed to remove the vestiges of slavery after the Civil War. In both Bradwell v. Illinois and Minor v. Happersett, for example, advocates for women asserted that women's rights were compelled by the privileges and immunities clause of the Fourteenth Amendment; Minor v. Happersett also involved a claim under the Fifteenth Amendment prohibiting involuntary servitude. Were these efforts "inherently racist"?

2. The Second Wave of Feminism. In 1963, a housewife and former labor union journalist named Betty Friedan published The Feminine Mystique. The book, which became an instant best-seller, reported the results of Friedan's interviews with affluent graduates of Smith College, now suburban housewives. Despite their material privilege, these women were deeply unhappy: desperately in search of stimulation and challenge, some had sexual affairs, others spent their time shopping and accumulating consumer goods, and still others "gulped tranquilizers, cooked gourmet meals, or scrutinized their children as though they were rare insects." Ruth Rosen, The World Split Open 4 (2000). Friedan called their common, pervasive unhappiness "the problem that has no name." Id.

The 1950s had been a time in which domesticity rhetoric — celebrating the heterosexual nuclear family with a male breadwinner and female housewife as the source of American prosperity and happiness and as a bulwark against world Communism — was all-pervasive. Experts agreed that homemaking was one of the highest professions a woman could aspire to, and harshly criticized women who worked outside the home. Ruth Rosen reports, for example:

> In their influential anti-Communist best-seller, *The Modern Woman: The Lost Sex* (1947), Ferdinand Lundberg and Marya Farnham typically laid society's problems on women's defiant determination to pursue outside interests and careers. The authors argued that an "independent" woman was an oxymoron, single women were sick, and childless women were "emotionally disturbed." "All spinsters," they concluded, "[should] be barred by law from having anything to do with the teaching of children on the ground of emotional incompetence."

Id. at 26.

Yet even throughout the quiescent 1950s, women active in labor unions and other left-wing movements had preserved a familiarity with "the woman question." In the 1960s and 1970s, younger women working in the civil rights movement and the new student Left movements began increasingly to turn their organizing skills and intellectual and political radicalism to espousing "women's liberation." For an engrossing account of what happened next, see generally Rosen, supra; see also William H. Chafe, The Road to Equality: 1962-Today, in Nancy F. Cott (ed.), No Small Courage: A History of Women in the United States 529-86 (2000).

In their quest for liberation, contemporary feminists have both attacked existing legal doctrines and institutions, and enlisted legal principles and procedures in their own work.[33] Martha Chamallas divides feminist legal theory into three stages: the Equality Stage, the Difference Stage, and the Diversity Stage. Martha Chamallas, Introduction to Feminist Legal Theory 23 (1999). These stages correspond roughly to the decades in which they emerged most forcefully: the Equality Stage is associated with the 1970s, the Difference Stage with the 1980s, and the Diversity Stage with the 1990s. However, as Chamallas notes, this is an oversimplification, for all three perspectives on feminism and the law may co-exist at any given moment.

Chamallas describes the 1970s Equality Stage as a moment when feminists "concentrated primarily on dismantling the intricate system of sex-based legal distinctions which had been established purportedly to protect women." Chamallas, supra, at 24. Their principal tool was the argument

---

33. The account that follows draws heavily on Martha Chamallas, Introduction to Feminist Legal Theory 23-29 (1999); see also Katharine T. Bartlett, Gender Law, 1 Duke J. Gender L. & Pol'y 1 (1994). For other periodizations of feminist theory, see Alison M. Jagger, Feminist Politics and Human Nature (1983); Rosemarie Tong, Feminist Thought: A Comprehensive Introduction (1989); Alison M. Jaggar and Paula S. Rothenberg, Feminist Frameworks: Alternative Theoretical Accounts of the Relations Between Women and Men (2d ed. 1984). For other periodizations of feminist legal theory, see Patricia A. Cain, Feminist Jurisprudence: Grounding the Theories, 4 Berkeley Women's L.J. 191, 198-205 (1989-90); Clare Dalton, Where We Stand: Observations on the Situation of Feminist Legal Thought, 3 Berkeley Women's L.J. 1 (1987-88); Carol Smart, Feminist Jurisprudence, in Law, Crime & Sexuality 162 (1995).

that men and women, rather than being inherently different, were inherently the same. "Because women were the same as men in all relevant respects, they deserved access to all public institutions, benefits and opportunities on the same terms as men." Id. And, because men and women were the same in all relevant respects, people should be treated as individuals. Stressing the similarities between men and women allowed 1970s feminists to attack the pervasive sex-segregation of society, from want ads classified by sex to male-only clubs, restaurants, and other public accommodations. Stressing that persons should be treated as individuals, not members of a class, permitted feminists to attack the many social and legal rules drawn up to "protect" women as a group, including rules excluding women from higher education, the professions, and sports.

The focus of the Equality Stage on "sameness" and individual rather than group rights makes it compatible with classical political liberalism, which also stresses the sovereignty of the individual. For this reason, the dominant arguments of the Equality Stage are often associated with so-called liberal feminism. Liberal feminism, in turn, is highly compatible with United States legal doctrine, which has a similar focus on individual rights. The legal version of liberal feminism is often called "formal equality."

As Chamallas argues, "The 1980s brought to the forefront of discussion the feminization of poverty, the gender gap in politics, the 'glass ceiling,' and other phenomena, which made it clear that, in many ways that mattered, men and women were different." Id. at 25. Toward this end, feminist legal theorists began revising their theories of equality, to suggest that "to be treated as equals, women whose lives differed from those of men paradoxically needed to be treated differently. Rather than requiring women to act more like men to achieve equality, feminist theorists argued that the norms themselves should be changed." Id. at 26. This new version of equality is often called "substantive equality." Rather than identifying equality as identical treatment under the law, substantive equality seeks fair outcomes, even when it means different legal treatment.

The 1980s also saw a critique of liberal feminism that focused on the power relations between men as a class and women as a class. "Dominance theory" or "nonsubordination" feminists argued that liberal feminism, like liberalism more generally, was assimilationist: it permitted a few privileged women to play by men's rules, but left men's rules in place. Moreover, liberalism's commitment to concepts such as privacy, objectivity, neutrality, and individual rights, and liberalism's aversion to thinking about group status, helped obscure the reality that contemporary law functioned to disempower women as a class and to privilege men as a class. For example, 1980s feminists began to bring to the fore issues like rape, domestic violence, and pornography, which could not be eradicated by a commitment to identical treatment under the law. Only a group domination analysis could reveal how these social realities functioned to keep women as a class living in fear of men.

Finally, the 1980s also saw a rise in the influence of so-called cultural feminism. As Chamallas notes, "feminists debated how women's 'different voice' — with its concern for human relationships and for the positive values of caring, nurturing, empathy, and connection — could find greater expression in law. In contrast to liberal feminism's de-emphasis of the mothering role, cultural feminists sought ways to support maternal and other traditional activities associated with women." Id. at 27.

In the 1990s, Chamallas argues, "feminist preoccupation with comparing the situation of men and women began to be eclipsed by a new focus on diversity among women. . . . The hallmark of the Diversity Stage is its attention to differences among women. This shift was impelled by powerful critiques by women of color and lesbians who claimed that they had been left out of the now-classic feminist analyses." Id. Feminist theorists in the 1990s "tried to explain how race, class, and gender intersected in multiple ways to create distinctive forms of discrimination for specific subgroups of women." Id. at 28. Feminist activists struggled with conflicts and coalitions among women. Lesbians and gay men coined the term "heterosexism" to describe the ideology that privileges heterosexual relations over same-sex ones and that works in tandem with male dominance. Feminists influenced by postmodernism called into question the category "woman" itself. The increasing complexity and, perhaps, the very success of feminism meant that "feminism" was also called into question as a unitary term. Some young women identified themselves as "post-feminists" or as non-feminists who, nevertheless, believed in equal pay for equal work. Others "longed for simpler times when the feminist agenda was unitary, focused on equality, and not so clearly linked to politics of race and sexual orientation." "Anti-essentialism" is often a key word used to refer to these multiple and overlapping concerns; for more on anti-essentialism, see Chapter 7.

As feminist legal theory moves into the twenty-first century, it has increasingly been concerned with understanding the connections between the liberation of women and the liberation of other subordinated groups. As Chamallas emphasizes, however, the concerns of the Equality Stage and the Difference Stage have not been lost. Indeed, from the beginning feminism has been fought on many fronts at once, as the following excerpt makes clear.

Gerda Lerner, *The Meaning of Seneca Falls, 1848-1998*
Dissent, Fall 1998, at 35, 37-39

It is useful to think of women's demands as encompassing two sets of needs: women's rights and women's emancipation.

Women's rights essentially are civil rights — to vote, to hold office, to have access to education and to economic and political power at every level of society on an equal basis with men. . . . These rights are demanded on the basis of a claim to equality: as citizens, as members of society, women are by rights equal and must therefore be treated equally. All of the rights here listed are based on the acceptance of the status quo; . . . These are essentially reformist demands.

Women's emancipation is freedom from oppressive restrictions imposed by reason of sex; self-determination and autonomy. Oppressive restrictions are biological restrictions due to sex, as well as socially imposed ones. Thus, women's bearing and nursing children is a biological given, but the assignment to women of the major responsibility for the rearing of children and for housework is socially imposed.

Self-determination means being free to decide one's own destiny, to define one's own social role. Autonomy means earning one's status, not being born into it or marrying it . . . It means freedom to define issues, roles, laws and cultural norms on an equality with men. The demands for emancipation are based on stressing women's difference from men, but also on stressing women's difference from other women. They are radical demands, which can only be achieved by transforming society for men and women, equalizing gender definitions for both sexes, assigning the repro-ductive work of raising the next generation to both men and women, and reorganizing social institutions so as to make such arrangements possible.

Women, just like men, are placed in society as individuals and as citizens. They are both equal and different. The demand for women's emancipation always includes the demand for women's rights, but the reverse is not true. Generally speaking, women's rights have been won or improved upon in many parts of the world in the past 150 years. Women's emancipation has not yet been won anywhere.

The movement started at Seneca Falls . . . from the start embraced both [concepts] by demanding legal, property, civil rights; and by demanding changes in gender-role definition and in woman's rights to her own body. As the nineteenth-century movement matured, there developed some tension between advocates of these two different sets of demands, with the mainstream focusing more and more on legal and property rights, while radicals and outsiders, like sex reformers, birth control advocates, and socialist feminists, demanded more profound social changes.

. . . But the same distinctions and tensions . . . have appeared [in the twentieth-century women's movement]. One wing focused mainly on women's rights — adoption of ERA, legal/political rights and representation and civil rights for women of different classes, races and sexual orientations. The other wing began as "radical women's liberation" and later branched off into many more specialized groups working on abortion rights; protection of women against violence and sexual harassment; the opening up to women of nontraditional occupations; self-empowerment and the creation of women's cultural institutions, ranging from lesbian groupings to women's music festivals and pop culture. The two informally defined wings of the movement often overlapped, sometimes collaborated on specific narrow issues, and recently have worked more and more on bridge-building. . . .

The cultural transformation on which demands for woman's emancipation build has been enormous. Many demands that seemed outrageous 150 years ago are now commonly accepted, such as a woman's right to equal guardianship of her children, to divorce, to jury duty, to acceptance in nontraditional occupations. Female police and fire officers and female military personnel are accepted everywhere without question. Women's participation in competitive sports is another area in which progress has been great, though it is far from complete. Many other feminist demands that seemed outrageously radical thirty years ago have become commonplace today — the acceptance of lesbians as "normal" members of the community; single motherhood; the criminal character of sexual harassment and marital rape. The acceptance of such ideas is still uneven and different in different places, but generally, the feminist program has been accepted by millions of people who refuse to identify themselves as "feminists." What critics decry as the splintering and diffusion of the movement is actually its greatest strength today.

It should also be recognized that the aims of feminism are transformative, but its methods have been peaceful reform, persuasion and education. For 150 years feminists have organized, lobbied, marched, petitioned, put their bodies on the line in demonstrations, and have overcome ancient prejudices by heroic acts of self-help. Whatever gains were won had to be won step by step, over and over again. Nothing "was given" to women; whatever gains we made we have had to earn. And perhaps the most precious "right" we have won in these two centuries, is the right to know our own history, to draw on the knowledge and experience of the women before us, to celebrate and emulate our heroines and finally to know that "greatness" is not a sexual attribute.

Putting Theory into Practice

1-1. An Oregon statute in the mid-1950s makes it a crime for women to "participat[e] in wrestling competition and exhibition." A woman is charged under the statute and offers the defense that the statute violates her constitutional rights under the Fourteenth Amendment. *Defend* the statute, and her prosecution under it, using arguments based on the concepts presented in this chapter.

1-2. There is evidence that in enacting the statute described above,

[the Oregon legislature] intended that there should be at least one island on the sea of life reserved for man that would be impregnable to the assault of woman. It had watched her emerge from long tresses and demure ways to bobbed hair and almost complete sophistication; from a creature needing and depending upon the protection and chivalry of man to one asserting complete independence. She had already invaded practically every activity formerly considered suitable and appropriate for men only. In the field of sports she had taken up, among other games, baseball, basketball, golf, bowling, hockey, long distance swimming, and racing, in all of which she had become more or less proficient, and in some had excelled. In the business and industrial fields as an employe[e] or as an executive, in the professions, in politics, as well as in almost every other line of human endeavor, she had matched her wits and prowess with those of mere man, and . . . in many instances had outdone him.

State v. Hunter, 300 P.2d 455, 458 (Or. 1956). Does this evidence help or hurt your defense of the statute?

1-3. You are approached by a lesbian rights organization and asked to work on an amicus brief supporting same-sex marriage and incorporating women's legal history. Would you accept the assignment? Why or why not? If you would accept the assignment, what kinds of arguments would you make, using what historical evidence? What arguments and evidence would you downplay or leave out?

2

Formal Equality

Formal equality is a principle of equal treatment: individuals who are alike should be treated alike, according to their actual characteristics rather than assumptions made about them based on stereotypes. It is a principle that can be applied either to a single individual, whose right to be treated on his or her own merits can be viewed as a right of individual autonomy, or to a group, whose members seek the same treatment as members of other similarly situated groups. What makes an issue one of *formal* equality is that the claim is limited to treatment *in relation to* another, similarly situated individual or group and does not extend to a demand for some particular, *substantive* treatment.

Most of the materials in this chapter explore the development of constitutional and statutory doctrines since the early 1970s, when the U.S. Supreme Court began applying principles derived from earlier civil rights cases to challenges to sex-based discrimination. After some experimentation with the appropriate standard of review that should be applied to sex discrimination under the Fourteenth Amendment of the Constitution, the Court came to settle on the standard that a classification based on sex "must serve important governmental objectives and must be substantially related to achievement of those objectives," Craig v. Boren, 429 U.S. 190, 197 (1976), or, as later stated, that it be supported by "an exceedingly persuasive justification." See J.E.B. v. Alabama ex rel. T.B., 511 U.S. 127, 136 (1994). Within this "intermediate" standard of review, courts have responded to challenges to state-created sex-based classifications by examining the underlying assumptions of these classifications and how well the classification based on these assumptions "fits" the purposes used to justify them. In a sense, both questions are designed to identify the extent to which two individuals or groups are similarly situated and thus entitled to equal treatment. Once the underlying assumptions are identified, the assumptions are tested empirically to determine if they are factually accurate or based on overbroad or archaic stereotypes about women.

If a classification is based on inaccurate empirical assumptions, it fails. Even where the assumptions are *to some extent* accurate, however, standard formal equality analysis does not end. First, the assumptions may be true *of women in general*, but not true *of each individual woman*; in such cases, the equality principle incorporates the concept of individual autonomy, requiring that each woman be given the opportunity to show eligibility for the desired benefit on the same basis as men. Second, classifications based on stereotypes may be impermissible even if true (or partially true) because they help to perpetuate the stereotypes, thereby reinforcing the conditions that make those classifications plausible. Third, even if the classifications identify accurate differences between men and women, they may violate formal equality principles if their use is not substantially related to the purposes they purport to serve.

Some problems of sex equality are masked because the rule or practice is based on criteria that appear to be sex-neutral, such as height and weight requirements, but impact disproportionately upon women. While formal equality might appear to provide no grip on such criteria, the principle that likes be treated alike requires that such criteria be justified by the actual requirements of the job, lest stereotyped expectations (airline stewardesses = beautiful women; firefighters = strong men) govern, perhaps unconsciously, what are viewed as reasonable job qualifications. Formal equality insists not only that those who are similarly situated be treated alike, but that stereotypes and overgeneralizations not dictate who is determined to be similarly situated to whom.

Formal equality applies to sex-based classifications that discriminate against men, as well as those that discriminate against women. In formal equality terms, the goal is equal treatment for all, not just women. Extending formal equality principles to rules that discriminate against men, or favor women, might also be justified on the ground that such rules, even when they may appear to benefit women, promote attitudes and expectations about women, including their dependency or status as victims, that disadvantage them across a wide spectrum of social contexts. Those who offer this rationale may favor formal equality as a strategy, but insofar as their choice of principle is based on its woman-centered results or outcomes, they already have their foot in the door of substantive equality, examined in Chapter 3.

Throughout this chapter it is important to keep in mind both the benefits and the limitations of formal equality. As will be apparent, much has been accomplished and many societal inequities can be addressed most readily on formal equality grounds. But what is left after formal equality has done its work? Look critically not only at formal equality as an analytical tool of gender reform but at the criticisms made against it. To what extent do these criticisms identify defects in formal equality analysis, and to what extent might they reflect, instead, the failure to apply formal equality analysis properly? Which objections are ones of principle? Which ones differences of strategy? Is there a distinction?

A. FORMAL EQUALITY AND THE CONSTITUTIONAL RIGHT TO EQUAL PROTECTION OF THE LAW

1. The Right to Equal, Individualized Treatment

≣ *Reed v. Reed*
≣ 404 U.S. 71 (1971)

Mr. Chief Justice BURGER delivered the opinion of the Court.

Richard Lynn Reed, a minor, died intestate in Ada County, Idaho, on March 29, 1967. His adoptive parents, who had separated sometime prior to his death, are the parties to this appeal. Approximately seven months after Richard's death, his mother, appellant Sally Reed, filed a petition in the Probate Court of Ada County, seeking appointment as administratrix of her son's estate.

Prior to the date set for a hearing on the mother's petition, appellee Cecil Reed, the father of the decedent, filed a competing petition seeking to have himself appointed administrator of the son's estate. The probate court held a joint hearing on the two petitions and thereafter ordered that letters of administration be issued to appellee Cecil Reed. . . . The court treated §15-312 and §15-314 of the Idaho Code as the controlling statutes and read those sections as compelling a preference for Cecil Reed because he was a male.

Section 15-312 designates [in order of priority] the persons who are entitled to administer the estate of one who dies intestate. In making these designations, that section lists 11 classes of persons who are so entitled[2] and provides, in substance, that the order in which those classes are listed in the section shall be determinative of the relative rights of competing applicants for letters of administration. One of the 11 classes so enumerated is "[t]he father or mother" of the person dying intestate. Under this section, then, appellant and appellee, being members of the same entitlement class, would seem to have been equally entitled to administer their son's estate. Section 15-314 provides, however, that:

---

2. [Priority was in the following order: (1) Surviving husband or wife. (2) Children. (3) Father or mother. (4) Brothers. (5) Sisters. (6) Grandchildren. (7) Next of kin entitled to share in distribution of estate. (8) Any kindred. (9) Public administrator. (10) Creditors. (11) Any legally competent person.]

[o]f several persons claiming and equally entitled [under §15-312] to administer, males must be preferred to females, and relatives of the whole to those of the half blood.

In issuing its order, the probate court implicitly recognized the equality of entitlement of the two applicants under §15-312 and noted that neither of the applicants was under any legal disability; the court ruled, however, that appellee, being a male, was to be preferred to the female appellant "by reason of Section 15-314 of the Idaho Code." In stating this conclusion, the probate judge gave no indication that he had attempted to determine the relative capabilities of the competing applicants to perform the functions incident to the administration of an estate. It seems clear the probate judge considered himself bound by statute to give preference to the male candidate over the female, each being otherwise "equally entitled."

Sally Reed appealed [and the Idaho Supreme Court upheld the statute]. . . .

. . . [W]e have concluded that the arbitrary preference established in favor of males by §15-314 of the Idaho Code cannot stand in the face of the Fourteenth Amendment's command that no State deny the equal protection of the laws to any person within its jurisdiction.

In applying that clause, this Court has consistently recognized that the Fourteenth Amendment does not deny to States the power to treat different classes of persons in different ways. . . . The Equal Protection Clause of that amendment does, however, deny to States the power to legislate that different treatment be accorded to persons placed by a statute into different classes on the basis of criteria wholly unrelated to the objective of that statute. A classification "must be reasonable, not arbitrary, and must rest upon some ground of difference having a fair and substantial relation to the object of the legislation, so that all persons similarly circumstanced shall be treated alike." Royster Guano Co. v. Virginia, [253 U.S. 412, 415 (1920)]. The question presented by this case, then, is whether a difference in the sex of competing applicants for letters of administration bears a rational relationship to a state objective that is sought to be advanced by the operation of §15-312 and §15-314.

In upholding the latter section, the Idaho Supreme Court concluded that its objective was to eliminate one area of controversy when two or more persons, equally entitled under §15-312, seek letters of administration and thereby present the probate court "with the issue of which one should be named." The court also concluded that where such persons are not of the same sex, the elimination of females from consideration "is neither an illogical nor arbitrary method devised by the legislature to resolve an issue that would otherwise require a hearing as to the relative merits . . . of the two or more petitioning relatives. . . ." [465 P.2d at 638].

Clearly the objective of reducing the workload on probate courts by eliminating one class of contests is not without some legitimacy. The crucial question, however, is whether §15-314 advances that objective in a manner consistent with the command of the Equal Protection Clause. We hold that it does not. To give a mandatory preference to members of either sex over members of the other, merely to accomplish the elimination of hearings on the merits, is to make the very kind of arbitrary legislative choice forbidden by the Equal Protection Clause of the Fourteenth Amendment; and whatever may be said as to the positive values of avoiding intrafamily controversy, the choice in this context may not lawfully be mandated solely on the basis of sex. . . .

Reversed and remanded.

Frontiero v. Richardson
411 U.S. 677 (1973)

Mr. Justice BRENNAN announced the judgment of the Court in an opinion in which Mr. Justice DOUGLAS, Mr. Justice WHITE, and Mr. Justice MARSHALL join.

The question before us concerns the right of a female member of the uniformed services to claim her spouse as a "dependent" for the purposes of obtaining increased quarters allowances and medical and dental benefits under 37 U.S.C. §§401, 403, and 10 U.S.C. §§1072, 1076, on an equal footing with male members. Under these statutes, a serviceman may claim his wife as a "dependent" without regard to whether she is in fact dependent upon him for any part of her support. . . . A servicewoman, on the other hand, may not claim her husband as a "dependent" under these programs unless he is in fact dependent upon her for over one-half of his support. . . . [T]he question for decision is whether this difference in treatment constitutes an unconstitutional discrimination against servicewomen in violation of the Due Process Clause of the Fifth Amendment. A three-judge District Court for the Middle District of Alabama, one judge dissenting, rejected this contention and sustained the constitutionality of the provisions of the statutes making this distinction. 341 F. Supp. 201 (1972). . . . We reverse. . . .

In an effort to attract career personnel through reenlistment, Congress established . . . a scheme for the provision of fringe benefits to members of the uniformed services on a competitive basis with business and industry. [Under this scheme] a member of the uniformed services with dependents is entitled to an increased "basic allowance for quarters" and . . . a member's dependents are provided comprehensive medical and dental care.

Appellant Sharron Frontiero, a lieutenant in the United States Air Force, sought increased quarters allowances, and housing and medical benefits for her husband, appellant Joseph Frontiero, on the ground that he was her "dependent." Although such benefits would automatically have been granted with respect to the wife of a male member of the uniformed services, appellant's application was denied because she failed to demonstrate that her husband was dependent on her for more than one-half of his support.[4] Appellants then commenced this suit, contending that, by making this distinction, the statutes unreasonably discriminate on the basis of sex in violation of the Due Process Clause of the Fifth Amendment. In essence, appellants asserted that the discriminatory impact of the statutes is twofold: first, as a procedural matter, a female member is required to demonstrate her spouse's dependency, while no such burden is imposed upon male members; and, second, as a substantive matter, a male member who does not provide more than one-half of his wife's support receives benefits, while a similarly situated female member is denied such benefits. Appellants therefore sought a permanent injunction against the continued enforcement of these statutes and an order directing the appellees to provide Lieutenant Frontiero with the same housing and medical benefits that a similarly situated male member would receive.

Although the legislative history of these statutes sheds virtually no light on the purposes underlying the differential treatment accorded male and female members, a majority of the three-judge District Court surmised that Congress might reasonably have concluded that, since the husband in our society is generally the "breadwinner" in the family — and the wife typically the "dependent" partner — "it would be more economical to require married female members claiming husbands to prove actual dependency than to extend the presumption of dependency to such members." [341 F. Supp. 201, 207 (1972).] Indeed, given the fact that approximately 99% of all members of the uniformed services are male, the District Court speculated that such differential treatment might conceivably lead to a "considerable saving of administrative expense and manpower." Ibid.

At the outset, appellants contend that classifications based upon sex, like classifications based upon race, alienage, and national origin, are inherently suspect and must therefore be subjected to close judicial scrutiny. We agree and, indeed, find at least implicit support for such an approach in our unanimous decision only last Term in Reed v. Reed [404 U.S. 71 (1971)]. . . .

[The Court reviews the attitude of "romantic paternalism" discussed in *Reed*.] As a result of notions such as these, our statute books gradually became laden with gross, stereotyped distinctions between the sexes and, indeed, throughout much of the 19th century the position of women in our society was, in many respects, comparable to that of blacks under the pre-Civil War slaves codes. Neither slaves nor women could hold office, serve on

---

4. Appellant Joseph Frontiero is a full-time student at Huntingdon College in Montgomery, Alabama. According to the agreed stipulation of facts, his living expenses, including his share of the household expenses, total approximately $354 per month. Since he receives $205 per month in veterans' benefits, it is clear that he is not dependent upon appellant Sharron Frontiero for more than one-half of his support.

juries, or bring suit in their own names, and married women traditionally were denied the legal capacity to hold or convey property or to serve as legal guardians of their own children. . . . And although blacks were guaranteed the right to vote in 1870, women were denied even that right . . . until adoption of the Nineteenth Amendment half a century later.

It is true, of course, that the position of women in America has improved markedly in recent decades. Nevertheless, it can hardly be doubted that, in part because of the high visibility of the sex characteristic, women still face pervasive, although at times more subtle, discrimination in our educational institutions, in the job market and, perhaps most conspicuously, in the political arena. . . .

Moreover, since sex, like race and national origin, is an immutable characteristic determined solely by the accident of birth, the imposition of special disabilities upon the members of a particular sex because of their sex would seem to violate "the basic concept of our system that legal burdens should bear some relationship to individual responsibility. . . ." Weber v. Aetna Casualty & Surety Co. [406 U.S. 164 (1972)]. And what differentiates sex from such non-suspect statuses as intelligence or physical disability, and aligns it with the recognized suspect criteria, is that the sex characteristic frequently bears no relation to ability to perform or contribute to society. As a result, statutory distinctions between the sexes often have the effect of invidiously relegating the entire class of females to inferior legal status without regard to the actual capabilities of its individual members.

We might also note that, over the past decade, Congress has itself manifested an increasing sensitivity to sex-based classifications. In [Title VII] of the Civil Rights Act of 1964, for example, Congress expressly declared that no employer, labor union, or other organization subject to the provisions of the Act shall discriminate against any individual on the basis of "race, color, religion, sex, or national origin." Similarly, the Equal Pay Act of 1963 provides that no employer covered by the Act "shall discriminate . . . between employees on the basis of sex." And §1 of the Equal Rights Amendment, passed by Congress on March 22, 1972, and submitted to the legislatures of the States for ratification, declares that "(e)quality of rights under the law shall not be denied or abridged by the United States or by any State on account of sex." Thus, Congress itself has concluded that classifications based upon sex are inherently invidious, and this conclusion of a coequal branch of Government is not without significance to the question presently under consideration. . . .

With these considerations in mind, we can only conclude that classifications based upon sex, like classifications based upon race, alienage, or national origin, are inherently suspect, and must therefore be subjected to strict judicial scrutiny. Applying the analysis mandated by that stricter standard of review, it is clear that the statutory scheme now before us is constitutionally invalid.

The sole basis of the classification established in the challenged statutes is the sex of the individuals involved. . . .

Moreover, the Government concedes that the differential treatment accorded men and women under these statutes serves no purpose other than mere "administrative convenience." In essence, the Government maintains that, as an empirical matter, wives in our society frequently are dependent upon their husbands, while husbands rarely are dependent upon their wives. Thus, the Government argues that Congress might reasonably have concluded that it would be both cheaper and easier simply conclusively to presume that wives of male members are financially dependent upon their husbands, while burdening female members with the task of establishing dependency in fact.[22]

The Government offers no concrete evidence, however, tending to support its view that such differential treatment in fact saves the Government any money. In order to satisfy the demands of strict judicial scrutiny, the Government must demonstrate, for example, that it is actually cheaper to grant increased benefits with respect to all male members, than it is to determine which male members are in fact entitled to such benefits and to grant increased benefits only to those members whose wives actually meet the dependency requirement. Here, however, there is substantial evidence that, if put to the test, many of the wives of male members would fail to qualify for benefits. And in light of the fact that the dependency determination with respect to the husbands of female members is presently made solely on the basis of affidavits rather than through the more costly hearing process, the Government's explanation of the statutory scheme is, to say the least, questionable.

In any case, our prior decisions make clear that, although efficacious administration of governmental programs is not without some importance, "the Constitution recognizes higher values than speed and efficiency." Stanley v. Illinois, 405 U.S. 645, 656 (1972). And when we enter the realm of "strict judicial scrutiny," there can be no doubt that "administrative convenience" is not a shibboleth, the mere recitation of which dictates constitutionality. . . . We therefore conclude that, by according differential treatment to male and female members of the uniformed services for the sole purpose of achieving administrative convenience, the challenged statutes violate the Due Process Clause of the Fifth Amendment insofar as they require a female member to prove the dependency of her husband.

Reversed.

22. It should be noted that these statutes are not in any sense designed to rectify the effects of past discrimination against women. . . . On the contrary, these statutes seize upon a group — women — who have historically suffered discrimination in employment, and rely on the effects of this past discrimination as a justification for heaping on additional economic disadvantages. . . .

Mr. Justice STEWART concurs in the judgment, agreeing that the statutes before us work an invidious discrimination in violation of the Constitution. Reed v. Reed [404 U.S. 71].

Mr. Justice REHNQUIST dissents for the reasons stated by Judge Rives in his opinion for the District Court, Frontiero v. Laird, 341 F. Supp. 201 (1972).

Mr. Justice POWELL , with whom THE CHIEF JUSTICE and Mr. Justice BLACKMUN join, concurring in the judgment.
. . . It is unnecessary for the Court in this case to characterize sex as a suspect classification, with all of the far-reaching implications of such a holding. Reed v. Reed, [404 U.S. 71 (1971)], which abundantly supports our decision today, did not add sex to the narrowly limited group of classifications which are inherently suspect. . . . In my view, we can and should decide this case on the authority of *Reed* and reserve for the future any expansion of its rationale.
There is another, and I find compelling, reason for deferring a general categorizing of sex classifications as invoking the strictest test of judicial scrutiny. The Equal Rights Amendment, which if adopted will resolve the substance of this precise question, has been approved by the Congress and submitted for ratification by the States. If this Amendment is duly adopted, it will represent the will of the people accomplished in the manner prescribed by the Constitution. . . . It seems to me that this reaching out to pre-empt by judicial action a major political decision which is currently in process of resolution does not reflect appropriate respect for duly prescribed legislative processes. . . .

≡≡≡ **Orr v. Orr**
≡≡≡ 440 U.S. 268 (1979)

Mr. Justice BRENNAN delivered the opinion of the Court.
The question presented is the constitutionality of Alabama alimony statutes which provide that husbands, but not wives, may be required to pay alimony upon divorce.
On February 26, 1974, a final decree of divorce was entered, dissolving the marriage of William and Lillian Orr. That decree directed appellant, Mr. Orr, to pay appellee, Mrs. Orr, $1,240 per month in alimony. On July 28, 1976, Mrs. Orr initiated a contempt proceeding in the Circuit Court of Lee County, Ala., alleging that Mr. Orr was in arrears in his alimony payments. On August 19, 1976, at the hearing on Mrs. Orr's petition, Mr. Orr submitted in his defense a motion requesting that Alabama's alimony statutes be declared unconstitutional because they authorize courts to place an obligation of alimony upon husbands but never upon wives. The Circuit Court denied Mr. Orr's motion and entered judgment against him. . . .

Relying solely upon his federal constitutional claim, Mr. Orr appealed the judgment. . . . We now hold the challenged Alabama statutes unconstitutional and reverse.

I. . . .

. . . The fact that the classification expressly discriminates against men rather than women does not protect it from scrutiny. Craig v. Boren, [429 U.S. 190 (1976)]. "To withstand scrutiny" under the Equal Protection Clause, " 'classifications by gender must serve important governmental objectives and must be substantially related to achievement of those objectives.' " Califano v. Webster, [430 U.S. 313, 316-317 (1977)]. . . .

Appellant views the Alabama alimony statutes as effectively announcing the State's preference for an allocation of family responsibilities under which the wife plays a dependent role, and as seeking for their objective the reinforcement of that model among the State's citizens. . . .

The opinion of the Alabama Court of Civil Appeals suggests other purposes that the statute may serve. Its opinion states that the Alabama statutes were "designed" for "the wife of a broken marriage who needs financial assistance," 351 So. 2d at 905. This may be read as asserting either of two legislative objectives. One is a legislative purpose to provide help for needy spouses, using sex as a proxy for need. The other is a goal of compensating women for past discrimination during marriage, which assertedly has left them unprepared to fend for themselves in the working world following divorce. We concede, of course, that assisting needy spouses is a legitimate and important governmental objective. We have also recognized "[r]eduction of the disparity in economic condition between men and women caused by the long history of discrimination against women . . . as . . . an important governmental objective," Califano v. Webster [supra]. It only remains, therefore, to determine whether the classification at issue here is "substantially related to achievement of those objectives." Ibid.

Ordinarily, we would begin the analysis of the "needy spouse" objective by considering whether sex is a sufficiently "accurate proxy," Craig v. Boren [supra], for dependency to establish that the gender classification rests " 'upon some ground of difference having a fair and substantial relation to the object of the legislation,' " Reed v. Reed, [404 U.S. 71, 77 (1971)]. Similarly, we would initially approach the "compensation" rationale by asking whether women had in fact been significantly discriminated against in the sphere to which the statute applied a sex-based classification, leaving the sexes "not similarly situated with respect to opportunities" in that sphere, Schlesinger v. Ballard, [419 U.S. 498, 508 (1975)]. Compare Califano v. Webster, [supra] and Kahn v. Shevin, [416 U.S. 351, 353 (1974)], with Weinberger v. Wiesenfeld, [420 U.S. 636, 648 (1975)].

But in this case, even if sex were a reliable proxy for need, and even if the institution of marriage did discriminate against women, these factors still would "not adequately justify the salient features of" Alabama's statutory scheme. . . . Under the statute, individualized hearings at which the parties' relative financial circumstances are considered already occur. . . . There is no reason, therefore, to use sex as a proxy for need. Needy males could be helped along with needy females with little if any additional burden on the State. In such circumstances, not even an administrative-convenience rationale exists to justify operating by generalization or proxy. Similarly, since individualized hearings can determine which women were in fact discriminated against vis-à-vis their husbands, as well as which family units defied the stereotype and left the husband dependent on the wife, Alabama's alleged compensatory purpose may be effectuated without placing burdens solely on husbands. Progress toward fulfilling such a purpose would not be hampered, and it would cost the State nothing more, if it were to treat men and women equally by making alimony burdens independent of sex. "Thus, the gender-based distinction is gratuitous; without it, the statutory scheme would only provide benefits to those men who are in fact similarly situated to the women the statute aids," Weinberger v. Wiesenfeld [420 U.S. at 653], and the effort to help those women would not in any way be compromised.

Moreover, use of a gender classification actually produces perverse results in this case. As compared to a gender-neutral law placing alimony obligations on the spouse able to pay, the present Alabama statutes give an advantage only to the financially secure wife whose husband is in need. Although such a wife might have to pay alimony under a gender-neutral statute, the present statutes exempt her from that obligation. Thus, "[t]he [wives] who benefit from the disparate treatment are those who were . . . nondependent on their husbands," Califano v. Goldfarb, [430 U.S. 199, 221 (1977)] (Stevens, J., concurring in judgment). They are precisely those who are not "needy spouses" and who are "least likely to have been victims of . . . discrimination," id., by the institution of marriage. A gender-based classification which, as compared to a gender-neutral one, generates additional benefits only for those it has no reason to prefer cannot survive equal protection scrutiny.

Legislative classifications which distribute benefits and burdens on the basis of gender carry the inherent risk of reinforcing the stereotypes about the "proper place" of women and their need for special protection. . . . Thus, even statutes purportedly designed to compensate for and ameliorate the effects of past discrimination must be carefully tailored. Where, as here, the State's compensatory and ameliorative purposes are as well served by a gender-neutral classification as one that gender classifies and therefore carries with it the baggage of sexual stereotypes, the State cannot be permitted to classify on the basis of sex. And this is doubly so where the choice made by the State appears to redound — if only indirectly — to the benefit of those without need for special solicitude.

III....

Reversed and remanded.

[The concurring opinions by Justices Blackmun and Stevens are omitted. The dissenting opinion by Justice Powell urging abstention, and the dissenting opinion by Justice Rehnquist, with whom the Chief Justice joined, urging that the plaintiff has no standing because he is a nondependent spouse who is not in a position to benefit from a sex-neutral statute, are also omitted.]

2. The Right to Equal Group Treatment

≣ *Stanton v. Stanton*
≣ 421 U.S. 7 (1975)

Mr. Justice BLACKMUN delivered the opinion of the Court.

This case presents the issue whether a state statute specifying for males a greater age of majority than it specifies for females denies, in the context of a parent's obligation for support payments for his children, the equal protection of the laws guaranteed by §1 of the Fourteenth Amendment.

[The case is an appeal arises from divorce proceedings, following a stipulated judgment requiring, among other things, that the father pay child support to the mother for a daughter and a son. The father discontinued support payments for the daughter when she turned 18, even though under Utah Code Ann. §15-2-1 (1953) he was required to support the son until he reached the age of 21. Pursuant to the challenged statute establishing different support obligations toward female and male children, the Supreme Court of Utah affirmed the denial of the mother's motion for further support.] . . .

We find it unnecessary in this case to decide whether a classification based on sex is inherently suspect. . . .

Reed, we feel, is controlling here. . . . "A classification 'must be reasonable, not arbitrary, and must rest upon some ground of difference having a fair and substantial relation to the object of the legislation, so that all persons similarly circumstanced shall be treated alike.'" . . .

The test here, then, is whether the difference in sex between children warrants the distinction in the appellee's obligation to support that is drawn by the Utah statute. We conclude that it does not. It may be true, as the Utah court observed and as is argued here, that it is the man's primary responsibility to provide a home and that it is salutary for him to have education and training before he assumes that responsibility; that girls tend to mature earlier than boys; and that females tend to marry earlier than males. The last mentioned factor, however, under the Utah statute loses whatever weight it otherwise might have, for the statute states that "all minors obtain their majority by marriage"; thus minority, and all that goes with it, is abruptly lost by marriage of a person of either sex at whatever tender age the marriage occurs.

Notwithstanding the "old notions" to which the Utah court referred, we perceive nothing rational in the distinction drawn by §15-2-1 which, when related to the divorce decree, results in the appellee's liability for support for Sherri only to age 18 but for Rick to age 21. This imposes "criteria wholly unrelated to the objective of that statute." A child, male or female, is still a child. No longer is the female destined solely for the home and the rearing of the family, and only the male for the marketplace and the world of ideas. . . . Women's activities and responsibilities are increasing and expanding. Coeducation is a fact, not a rarity. The presence of women in business, in the professions, in government and, indeed, in all walks of life where education is a desirable, if not always a necessary, antecedent is apparent and a proper subject of judicial notice. If a specified age of minority is required for the boy in order to assure him parental support while he attains his education and training, so, too, is it for the girl. To distinguish between the two on educational grounds is to be self-serving: if the female is not to be supported so long as the male, she hardly can be expected to attend school as long as he does, and bringing her education to an end earlier coincides with the role-typing society has long imposed. And if any weight remains in this day to the claim of earlier maturity of the female, with a concomitant inference of absence of need for support beyond 18, we fail to perceive its unquestioned truth or its significance, particularly when marriage, as the statute provides, terminates minority for a person of either sex. . . .

[Whether the common law age of 21 applies to both children or the remedy for the unconstitutional inequality is to treat males as adults at age 18] is an issue of state law to be resolved by the Utah courts on remand. . . .

[The dissenting opinion by Mr. Justice Rehnquist is omitted.]

≡≡≡ *Craig v. Boren*
≡≡ 429 U.S. 190 (1976)

Mr. Justice BRENNAN delivered the opinion of the Court.

The interaction of two sections of an Oklahoma statute . . . prohibits the sale of "nonintoxicating" 3.2% beer to males under the age of 21 and to females under the age of 18. The question to be decided is whether such a gender-based differential constitutes a denial to males 18-20 years of age of the equal protection of the laws in violation of the Fourteenth Amendment.

This action was brought in the District Court for the Western District of Oklahoma on December 20, 1972, by appellant Craig, a male then between 18 and 21 years of age, and by appellant Whitener, a licensed vendor of 3.2% beer. The complaint sought declaratory and injunctive relief against enforcement of the gender-based differential on the ground that it constituted invidious discrimination against males 18-20 years of age. A three-judge court . . . sustained the constitutionality of the statutory differential and dismissed the action. . . . We reverse. . . .

To withstand constitutional challenge . . . classifications by gender must serve important governmental objectives and must be substantially related to achievement of those objectives. . . . We accept for purposes of discussion the District Court's identification of the objective underlying [the statutes in question] as the enhancement of traffic safety. Clearly, the protection of public health and safety represents an important function of state and local governments. However, appellees' statistics in our view cannot support the conclusion that the gender-based distinction closely serves to achieve that objective and therefore the distinction cannot under [Reed v. Reed, 404 U.S. 71 (1971)] withstand equal protection challenge.

The appellees introduced a variety of statistical surveys. First, an analysis of arrest statistics for 1973 demonstrated that 18-20-year-old male arrests for "driving under the influence" and "drunkenness" substantially exceeded female arrests for that same age period.[8] Similarly, youths aged 17-21 were found to be overrepresented among those killed or injured in traffic accidents, with males again numerically exceeding females in this regard. Third, a random roadside survey in Oklahoma City revealed that young males were more inclined to drive and drink beer than were their female counterparts. Fourth, Federal Bureau of Investigation nationwide statistics exhibited a notable increase in arrests for "driving under the influence."[11] Finally, statistical evidence gathered in other jurisdictions, particularly Minnesota and Michigan, was offered to corroborate Oklahoma's experience by indicating the pervasiveness of youthful participation in motor vehicle accidents following the imbibing of alcohol. Conceding that "the case is not free from doubt," 399 F. Supp. at 1314, the District Court nonetheless concluded that this statistical showing substantiated "a rational basis for the legislative judgment underlying the challenged classification." Id., at 1307.

Even were this statistical evidence accepted as accurate, it nevertheless offers only a weak answer to the equal protection question presented here. The most focused and relevant of the statistical surveys, arrests of 18-20-year-olds for alcohol-related driving offenses, exemplifies the ultimate

8. The disparities in 18-20-year-old male-female arrests were substantial for both categories of offenses: 427 versus 24 for driving under the influence of alcohol, and 966 versus 102 for drunkenness. Even if we assume that a legislature may rely on such arrest data in some situations, these figures do not offer support for a differential age line, for the disproportionate arrests of males persisted at older ages; indeed, in the case of arrests for drunkenness, the figures for all ages indicated "even more male involvement in such arrests at later ages." 399 F. Supp. at 1309. See also n.14, infra.

11. The FBI made no attempt to relate these arrest figures either to beer drinking or to an 18-21 age differential, but rather found that male arrests for all ages exceeded 90% of the total.

unpersuasiveness of this evidentiary record. Viewed in terms of the correlation between sex and the actual activity that Oklahoma seeks to regulate — driving while under the influence of alcohol — the statistics broadly establish that .18% of females and 2% of males in that age group were arrested for that offense. While such a disparity is not trivial in a statistical sense, it hardly can form the basis for employment of a gender line as a classifying device. Certainly if maleness is to serve as a proxy for drinking and driving, a correlation of 2% must be considered an unduly tenuous "fit."[12] Indeed, prior cases have consistently rejected the use of sex as a decisionmaking factor even though the statutes in question certainly rested on far more predictive empirical relationships than this.

Moreover, the statistics exhibit a variety of other shortcomings that seriously impugn their value to equal protection analysis. Setting aside the obvious methodological problems,[14] the surveys do not adequately justify the salient features of Oklahoma's gender-based traffic-safety law. None purports to measure the use and dangerousness of 3.2% beer as opposed to alcohol generally, a detail that is of particular importance since, in light of its low alcohol level, Oklahoma apparently considers the 3.2% beverage to be "nonintoxicating." . . . Moreover, many of the studies, while graphically documenting the unfortunate increase in driving while under the influence of alcohol, make no effort to relate their findings to age-sex differentials as involved here. Indeed, the only survey that explicitly centered its attention upon young drivers and their use of beer — albeit apparently not of the diluted 3.2% variety — reached results that hardly can be viewed as impressive in justifying either a gender or age classification.[16]

12. Obviously, arrest statistics do not embrace all individuals who drink and drive. But for purposes of analysis, this "underinclusiveness" must be discounted somewhat by the shortcomings inherent in this statistical sample, see n.14, infra. In any event, we decide this case in light of the evidence offered by Oklahoma and know of no way of extrapolating these arrest statistics to take into account the driving and drinking population at large, including those who avoided arrest.

14. The very social stereotypes that find reflection in age-differential laws, see Stanton v. Stanton, 421 U.S. 7, 14-15 (1975), are likely substantially to distort the accuracy of these comparative statistics. Hence "reckless" young men who drink and drive are transformed into arrest statistics, whereas their female counterparts are chivalrously escorted home. . . . Moreover, the Oklahoma surveys, gathered under a regime where the age-differential law in question has been in effect, are lacking in controls necessary for appraisal of the actual effectiveness of the male 3.2% beer prohibition. In this regard, the disproportionately high arrest statistics for young males — and, indeed, the growing alcohol-related arrest figures for all ages and sexes — simply may be taken to document the relative futility of controlling driving behavior by the 3.2% beer statute and like legislation, although we obviously have no means of estimating how many individuals, if any, actually were prevented from drinking by these laws.

16. The random roadside survey of drivers conducted in Oklahoma City during August 1972 found that 78% of drivers under 20 were male. Turning to an evaluation of their drinking habits and factoring out nondrinkers, 84% of the males versus 77% of the females expressed a preference for beer. Further 16.5% of the men and 11.4% of the women had consumed some alcoholic beverage within two hours of the interview. Finally, a blood alcohol concentration greater than .01% was discovered in 14.6% of the males compared to 11.5% of the females. "The 1973 figures, although they contain some variations, reflect essentially the same pattern."

There is no reason to belabor this line of analysis. It is unrealistic to expect either members of the judiciary or state officials to be well versed in the rigors of experimental or statistical technique. But this merely illustrates that proving broad sociological propositions by statistics is a dubious business, and one that inevitably is in tension with the normative philosophy that underlies the Equal Protection Clause. Suffice to say that the showing offered by the appellees does not satisfy us that sex represents a legitimate, accurate proxy for the regulation of drinking and driving. In fact, when it is further recognized that Oklahoma's statute prohibits only the selling of 3.2% beer to young males and not their drinking the beverage once acquired (even after purchase by their 18-20-year-old female companions), the relationship between gender and traffic safety becomes far too tenuous to satisfy *Reed*'s requirement that the gender-based difference be substantially related to achievement of the statutory objective.

We hold, therefore, that under *Reed*, Oklahoma's 3.2% beer statute invidiously discriminates against males 18-20 years of age. . . .

[The opinion of Mr. Justice Powell, concurring, is deleted.]

Mr. Justice STEVENS, concurring.

There is only one Equal Protection Clause. It requires every State to govern impartially. It does not direct the courts to apply one standard of review in some cases and a different standard in other cases. Whatever criticism may be leveled at a judicial opinion implying that there are at least three such standards applies with the same force to a double standard. . . .

In this case, the classification is not as obnoxious as some the Court has condemned,[1] nor as inoffensive as some the Court has accepted. It is objectionable because it is based on an accident of birth, because it is a mere remnant of the now almost universally rejected tradition of discriminating against males in this age bracket, and because, to the extent it reflects any physical difference between males and females, it is actually perverse.[4] The question then is whether the traffic safety justification put forward by the State is sufficient to make an otherwise offensive classification acceptable.

---

399 F. Supp., at 1309. Plainly these statistical disparities between the sexes are not substantial. Moreover, when the 18-20 age boundaries are lifted and all drivers analyzed, the 1972 roadside survey indicates that male drinking rose slightly whereas female exposure to alcohol remained relatively constant. Again, in 1973, the survey established that "compared to all drivers interviewed, . . . the under-20 age group generally showed a lower involvement with alcohol in terms of having drunk within the past two hours or having a significant BAC (blood alcohol content)." [Id.] In sum, this survey provides little support for a gender line among teenagers and actually runs counter to the imposition of drinking restrictions based upon age.

1. Men as a general class have not been the victims of the kind of historic, pervasive discrimination that has disadvantaged other groups.

4. Because males are generally heavier than females, they have a greater capacity to consume alcohol without impairing their driving ability than do females.

The classification is not totally irrational. For the evidence does indicate that there are more males than females in this age bracket who drive and also more who drink. Nevertheless, there are several reasons why I regard the justification as unacceptable. It is difficult to believe that the statute was actually intended to cope with the problem of traffic safety,[5] since it has only a minimal effect on access to a not very intoxicating beverage and does not prohibit its consumption. Moreover, the empirical data submitted by the State accentuate the unfairness of treating all 18–20-year-old males as inferior to their female counterparts. The legislation imposes a restraint on 100% of the males in the class allegedly because about 2% of them have probably violated one or more laws relating to the consumption of alcoholic beverages. It is unlikely that this law will have a significant deterrent effect either on that 2% or on the law-abiding 98%. But even assuming some such slight benefit, it does not seem to me that an insult to all of the young men of the State can be justified by visiting the sins of the 2% on the 98%. . . .

Mr. Justice REHNQUIST, dissenting.

. . . I think the Oklahoma statute challenged here need pass only the "rational basis" equal protection analysis . . . and I believe that it is constitutional under that analysis.

Most obviously unavailable to support any kind of special scrutiny in this case, is a history or pattern of past discrimination, such as was relied on by the plurality in [Frontiero v. Richardson, 411 U.S. 677 (1973)] to support its invocation of strict scrutiny. There is no suggestion in the Court's opinion that males in this age group are in any way peculiarly disadvantaged, subject to systematic discriminatory treatment, or otherwise in need of special solicitude from the courts.

The Court does not discuss the nature of the right involved, and there is no reason to believe that it sees the purchase of 3.2% beer as implicating any important interest, let alone one that is "fundamental" in the constitutional sense of invoking strict scrutiny. . . .

It is true that a number of our opinions contain broadly phrased dicta implying that the same test should be applied to all classifications based on sex, whether affecting females or males. . . . However, before today, no decision of this Court has applied an elevated level of scrutiny to invalidate a statutory discrimination harmful to males, except where the statute impaired an important personal interest protected by the Constitution.[1] There being

---

5. There is no legislative history to indicate that this was the purpose. . . . [This discrimination] represented nothing more than the perpetuation of a stereotyped attitude about the relative maturity of the members of the two sexes in this age bracket. . . .

1. In Stanley v. Illinois, 405 U.S. 645 (1972) . . . the Court struck down a statute allowing separation of illegitimate children from a surviving father but not a surviving mother, without any showing of parental unfitness. The Court stated that "the interest of a parent in the companionship, care, custody, and management of his or her children 'come[s] to this Court with a momentum for respect lacking when appeal is made to liberties which derive merely from shifting economic arrangements.'"

no such interest here, and there being no plausible argument that this is a discrimination against females,[2] the Court's reliance on our previous sex-discrimination cases is ill-founded. It treats gender classification as a talisman which — without regard to the rights involved or the persons affected — calls into effect a heavier burden of judicial review.

The Court's conclusion that a law which treats males less favorably than females "must serve important governmental objectives and must be substantially related to achievement of those objectives" apparently comes out of thin air. The Equal Protection Clause contains no such language, and none of our previous cases adopt that standard. I would think we have had enough difficulty with the two standards of review which our cases have recognized — the norm of "rational basis," and the "compelling state interest" required where a "suspect classification" is involved — so as to counsel weightily against the insertion of still another "standard" between those two. How is this Court to divine what objectives are important? How is it to determine whether a particular law is "substantially" related to the achievement of such objective, rather than related in some other way to its achievement? Both of the phrases used are so diaphanous and elastic as to invite subjective judicial preferences or prejudices relating to particular types of legislation, masquerading as judgments whether such legislation is directed at "important" objectives or, whether the relationship to those objectives is "substantial" enough. I would have thought that if this Court were to leave anything to decision by the popularly elected branches of the Government, where no constitutional claim other than that of equal protection is invoked, it would be the decision as to what governmental objectives to be achieved by law are "important," and which are not. As for the second part of the Court's new test, the Judicial Branch is probably in no worse position than the Legislative or Executive Branches to determine if there is any rational relationship between a classification and the purpose which it might be thought to serve. But the introduction of the adverb "substantially" requires courts to make subjective judgments as to operational effects, for which neither their expertise nor their access to data fits them. And even if we manage to avoid both confusion and the mirroring of our own preferences in the development of this new doctrine, the thousands of judges in other courts who must interpret the Equal Protection Clause may not be so fortunate. . . .

In Kahn v. Shevin, 416 U.S. 351 (1974) . . . the Court upheld Florida's $500 property tax exemption for widows only. The opinion of the Court appears to apply a rational-basis test. . . .

2. I am not unaware of the argument from time to time advanced, that all discriminations between the sexes ultimately redound to the detriment of females, because they tend to reinforce "old notions" restricting the roles and opportunities of women. As a general proposition applying equally to all sex categorizations, I believe that this argument was implicitly found to carry little weight in our decisions upholding gender-based differences. See Schlesinger v. Ballard, 419 U.S. 498 (1975); Kahn v. Shevin, 416 U.S. 351 (1974). Seeing no assertion that it has special applicability to the situation at hand, I believe it can be dismissed as an insubstantial consideration.

Notes

1. Individualized-Based and Group-Based Equality. Cases such as *Reed* and *Orr*, involving matters as to which individualized hearings already take place, presented relatively favorable sites for the origins of modern constitutional sex discrimination law. In a context of individualized decisionmaking, it is easy to see the offense to the individual of not being treated as an individual. And from the state's point of view, prohibiting use of sex as a basis for decision would not burden it with having to hold fact-finding hearings it was not already holding. Moreover, in both cases, use of sex as a criterion would often produce inaccurate results, given the legitimate state purposes involved. Likewise, the classification in *Frontiero* had as its declared purpose the identification of dependent spouses, yet it served to exclude some spouses who were dependent, and include others who were not.

Craig and *Stanton* arose not in the context of individualized decision-making, but in the context of matters that the state typically determines in a group-based manner because they do not lend themselves easily to individualized fact-finding. There are many such matters, including the right to vote, marry, drive, serve in the military, and attend public schools, as well as to drink alcoholic beverages (*Craig*) and to receive financial support from one's parents (*Stanton*). All the state can rely on in drawing lines as to such matters are group-based judgments; individualized decision-making is not an alternative. Moreover, sex may be as accurate — even more accurate — than the available alternatives. At stake in these cases is more than administrative convenience; the state's ability to meet its substantive purpose is at issue, as well. With these cases, then, the Court begins to confront the problems with stereotypes even if they are true and even if they do aid in accurate decisionmaking: they reinforce themselves, and hence the circumstances that make the stereotypes true. Putting sex-based stereotypes out of play is said to be necessary even when they are at least partially accurate and even when some stereotypes are necessary because it is undesirable, as a matter of constitutional law, for the state to participate in the perpetuation of stereotypes and the truths they reflect.

2. The Role of Stereotyping. The articulated standard in these cases, at least from *Craig* forward, is that the challenged classification serve important governmental objectives and be substantially related to the achievement of those objectives. At the same time, note the frequency with which the Supreme Court's analysis focuses on the harm of stereotyping, rather than on the imperfect fit between valid objectives and the classification. Consider the following:

> . . . [T]he components of the intermediate scrutiny standard — a practice "substantially related to an important governmental objective" — have rarely

been the moving parts in a Supreme Court sex discrimination decision. Rather, the bulk of work in these decisions has been done by what readers of the opinions may be tempted to treat as mere decorative rhetorical flourish — the proposition that there are constitutional objections to "gross, stereotyped distinctions between the sexes," that is to say, to "classifications based on sex . . . premised on overbroad generalizations." To determine whether there is unconstitutional sex discrimination, one need generally ask only two questions: (1) Is the rule of practice at issue sex-respecting, that is to say, does it distinguish on its face between males and females? and (2) Does the sex-respecting rule rely on a stereotype?

In the constitutional . . . law of sex discrimination, "stereotype" has become a term of art by which is simply meant any imperfect proxy, any overbroad generalization. For a sex-respecting rule to withstand constitutional scrutiny by the Court, it seems to be at least necessary and usually sufficient that it embody some perfect proxy. That is to say, the assumption at the root of the sex-respecting rule must be true of either all women or no women or all men or no mean; there must be a zero or a hundred on one side of the sex equation or the other.

Mary Anne Case, "The Very Stereotype the Law Condemns": Constitutional Sex Discrimination Law as a Quest for Perfect Proxies, 85 Cornell L. Rev. 1447, 1449-50 (2000).

Does Case's analysis fit the cases set forth so far? Reconsider the analysis after reading Personnel Administrator of Massachusetts v. Feeney, supra, and United States v. Virginia, supra.

3. Remedying Formal Equality Defects. Formal equality defects often can be eliminated in more than one way. Formal gender neutrality could be achieved in *Orr* either by eliminating alimony for both husbands and wives, or by leaving the state's system of individualized alimony determinations in place and extending eligibility to dependent husbands. 440 U.S. at 282. The latter alternative, which is the option Alabama chooses, presents the classic "won the battle but lost the war" scenario for Mr. Orr: he prevails on the constitutional point, but remains liable for alimony (albeit under a different, gender-neutral regime). The formal equality principles applied in *Craig* and *Stanton* also did not compel any particular resolution: the state could use the higher age or the lower age or some other age altogether, just so long as they used the same age for both males and females.

Frontiero also presents the rule-maker with options — either require all employees to demonstrate dependency, or extend dependency benefits to all spouses. The first option would have the same effect as the ultimate result in *Orr*: All spouses would have to show dependency in order to receive the attendant benefits. Instead, however, the court decided to extend the presumption of dependency to all spouses, putting the burden on Congress to eliminate the presumption if it so chose. Thus while, as in *Orr*, a benefit previously available only to members of one sex was extended to both, in *Frontiero* the effect of extending the benefit is to give a windfall to some employees — female as well as male. It seems clear enough why Mr. Orr should not have the relief to which he was not entitled — escape from alimony obligations — simply because other husbands (dependent ones) were victims of unconstitutional discrimination: Mr. Orr was not like those other, dependent husbands. It may seem less clear that Sharron Frontiero and her husband should receive dependency benefits when her husband was not a dependent, simply because some other potential claimants, who also were not dependent, were receiving them. Another way of looking at this issue is that while in *Reed*, *Orr*, *Craig*, and *Stanton* the Court forces the state to abandon gender-based stereotypes and adopt an approach that is *more accurate*, in *Frontiero* extension of the presumption actually renders the fringe-benefit scheme *less accurate*. Is this a problem, constitutionally speaking? Is it consistent with the analysis set forth in Note 2, above, by Mary Anne Case?

4. Distinguishing Employment-Based Dependency Benefits from Social Welfare. Subsequent to *Frontiero*, two cases challenged sex-based classifications in the Social Security Act. Weinberger v. Wiesenfeld, 420 U.S. 636 (1975), concerned a provision that provided spousal benefits only to widows, not widowers, without respect to need and without the opportunity for a widower to show that he was dependent on his wife. The Court, in an opinion also written by Justice Brennan, held that "given the purpose of enabling the surviving parent to remain at home to care for a child, the gender-based distinction . . . is entirely irrational." 420 U.S. at 651. Amendments following *Wiesenfeld* extended survivors' benefits to widowers, but only if they showed that they received at least one-half of their support from their deceased wives. In the case challenging the extra burden imposed on widowers, Califano v. Goldfarb, 430 U.S. 199 (1977), the plaintiff-widower could not establish dependency according to this standard, which he claimed violated equal protection since a similarly situated nondependent widow was eligible for benefits without such a showing. As in *Frontiero*, the person challenging the statute sought dependency benefits even though he wasn't a dependent, on the grounds that a similarly situated person of the other sex, by virtue of the sex-based presumption, would have received (equally undeserved) benefits.

In defense of the statutory presumption in *Goldfarb*, the government attempted to distinguish the case from *Frontiero* by arguing that the benefit in question was not a contractual benefit that impermissibly used sex as a proxy for dependency but rather a social welfare scheme defining different standards of eligibility based on the differing social welfare needs of widowers and widows. Support for this argument was sought from a prior United States Supreme Court case, Kahn v. Shevin, 416 U.S. 351 (1974), which had upheld a $500 property tax exemption for widows, but not widowers, on the grounds that women faced financial needs at the death of their spouses not equal to those faced by men. (This case is excerpted in Chapter 3 at page 266.) Rather than face the reasoning of *Kahn* directly, Justice Brennan, writing for the Court in *Goldfarb*, distinguished the case by determining that the purpose of the statutory scheme at issue was to determine dependency, not need, and thus that *Frontiero*, rather than *Kahn*, controlled.

While the result in *Goldfarb* may have been compelled by *Frontiero* and *Wiesenfeld*, the manner of distinguishing the case from *Kahn* was, at best, highly questionable. Both involved presumptions based on sex. What *Goldfarb* did, at least in the context of state benefit plans (contractual or otherwise), was to kick the legs out from under *Kahn*. The desirability of such a result should be considered after you have read the relevant materials in Chapter 3.

Justice Stevens, in a separate concurring opinion in *Goldfarb*, applied the single-standard form of equal protection review he urged in *Craig*. Under this standard, a sex-based classification may sometimes be sufficiently rational to pass constitutional muster, but not if its actual purposes, as may be revealed by its actual effects, are improper ones. In *Goldfarb*, Justice Stevens found the presumption irrational after determining that for the administrative convenience of processing the applications of the estimated 90 percent of widows who are dependent, "perhaps $750 million" in payments are made to the remaining, nondependent widows. 430 U.S. at 220. Given this costly trade-off, Justice Stevens concluded that the "actual reason" for the presumption was neither administrative convenience nor redressing the "legacy of economic discrimination" against women; it was, rather,

> the accidental byproduct of a traditional way of thinking about females. . . . In my judgment, something more than accident is necessary to justify the disparate treatment of persons who have as strong a claim to equal treatment as do similarly situated surviving spouses.

430 U.S. at 223. Following this line of analysis, Justice Stevens found nothing worth salvaging in *Kahn* and noted that it was effectively ignored, if not explicitly overruled, by *Wiesenfeld*. See also Wengler v. Druggists Mut. Ins. Co., 446 U.S. 142 (1980) (Missouri statute granting worker's compensation death benefits to widows, but not widowers, without proof of actual dependency violates equal protection).

Further amendments by Congress to the Social Security Act eliminated the need to prove dependency for widowers, but to avoid the possible windfall for plaintiffs such as Goldfarb who may have pensions based both on their own previous employment and that of their wives, Congress imposed a requirement that an individual's own pension be set off against any entitlement acquired through one's spouse's employment. In order to protect the reliance interests of female employees who may have planned their retirements based on the "double" benefits potentially available to them under pre-1977 law, this offset provision was delayed for *women* for five years. This sex-based, five-year exemption from the pension offset requirement was challenged in Heckler v. Mathews, 465 U.S. 728 (1984). In an opinion written also by Justice Brennan, the exemption was upheld as a "temporary" effort to protect "reasonable reliance interests" through "reasoned analysis" rather than "archaic generalizations about the roles and abilities of men and women." 465 U.S. at 750. Is this reasoning persuasive? Does it meet the requirements of formal equality? Is the exemption an example of a "perfect proxy"?

5. Who Is the Protected Victim? One question in some of these cases is who is being discriminated against. In *Goldfarb* and *Frontiero*, for example, is it the female wage-earner whose benefits are reduced by the fact that her husband is not presumed to be a dependent, or the male dependent himself? Justice Brennan in *Goldfarb* determined that since the benefits were based upon contributions made by a female employee on the basis of her earnings, the discrimination was, as in *Frontiero*, a discrimination against women. Justice Rehnquist, in a part of his dissenting opinion in *Goldfarb* that was joined by four other justices, reasoned that the discrimination at issue was a discrimination against those for whom dependency benefits were sought, i.e., men.

What are the consequences? None, if you think that discrimination against men should be analyzed the same as discrimination against women. But Justice Rehnquist's view in his dissenting opinion in *Craig* (and other early cases) is that when the "victim" of the discrimination is male, the constitutional standard of review appropriate to other forms of "social welfare legislation" — i.e., the rational basis test — is all that is required (and that administrative convenience satisfies this standard). Consider this position, in light of the current Court's view, shared by Chief Justice Rehnquist, that affirmative action plans designed to eliminate the effects of past discrimination against racial minorities be evaluated by the same strict standard as rules and practices that exclude or disadvantage those minorities. See pages 284-285.

One approach to the "victim" problem is reflected in such cases as *Orr* and *Craig*, but found frivolous by Justice Rehnquist in footnote 2 to his dissent in *Craig*: to assume that women are harmed by discriminations that favor them as well as those that disfavor them when they are based on traditional stereotypes. How would you evaluate this proposition?

6. The Equal Rights Amendment. The Equal Rights Amendment (the "ERA") referred to in both Justice Brennan's and Justice Powell's opinions in *Frontiero* failed by three states to gain the support of two-thirds

(38) of the states by the Congressional deadline of June 30, 1982 (a date already extended three years beyond the original 1979 deadline). The simple language of the proposed amendment read: "Equality of rights under the law shall not be denied or abridged by the United States or by any state on account of sex." It was assumed that the passage of the ERA would have mandated a stricter review of classifications based on sex, amounting in effect to the kind of "strict scrutiny" favored by four Justices in *Frontiero*. For a comprehensive analysis of how the ERA would have been applied, see Barbara A. Brown et al., The Equal Rights Amendment: A Constitutional Basis for Equal Rights for Women, 80 Yale L.J. 871 (1971). The ERA did not itself resolve fundamental issues about when sexual differences warrant different treatment. See Ruth Bader Ginsburg, Sexual Equality Under the Fourteenth and Equal Rights Amendments, 1979 Wash. U.L.Q. 161, 176 ("No one can predict with complete assurance how the Amendment will be interpreted and applied . . ."). As a result, the significance of its passage — or its loss — was perhaps more symbolic than anything else. Id. at 177.

The viability of the ERA almost 20 years after it failed the ratification process is still a debated topic. The ratification of the 27th Amendment (Congressional Pay Amendment) in 1992, more than 200 years after it was originally proposed, may offer encouragement for a revival of the ERA. See Brannon P. Denning & John R. Vile, Necromancing the Equal Rights Amendment, 17 Const. Comment 593 (2000); Allison L. Held et al., The Equal Rights Amendment: Why the ERA Remains Legally Viable and Properly Before the States, 3 Wm. & Mary J. Women & L. 113 (1997). Some scholars contest whether there is still a need for the ERA in light of the significant advancement of women since its failure. See Martha Craig Daughtrey, Seventy-five Years Madison Lecture: Women and the Constitution: Where We Are at the End of the Century, 75 N.Y.U. L. Rev. 1 (2000); David A. Strauss, Comment, The Irrelevance of Constitutional Amendments, 114 Harv. L. Rev. 1457 (2001).

A number of individual states have enacted their own versions of the ERA into their constitutions: Utah in 1896, Wyoming in 1890, and fourteen others between 1970 and 1977. See Beth Gammie, State ERAs: Problems and Possibilities, 1989 U. Ill. L. Rev. 1123, 1125-1126 (1989).

3. The Right to Be Free of Indirect Discrimination

Personnel Administrator of Massachusetts v. Feeney
442 U.S. 256 (1979)

Mr. Justice STEWART delivered the opinion of the Court.

This case presents a challenge to the constitutionality of the Massachusetts veterans' preference statute . . . on the ground that it discriminates against women in violation of the Equal Protection Clause of the Fourteenth Amendment. Under [this statute], all veterans who qualify for state civil service positions must be considered for appointment ahead of any qualifying nonveterans. The preference operates overwhelmingly to the advantage of males.

The appellee Helen B. Feeney is not a veteran. She brought this action pursuant to 42 U.S.C. §1983, alleging that the absolute preference formula established in [the Massachusetts statute] inevitably operates to exclude women from consideration for the best Massachusetts civil service jobs and thus unconstitutionally denies them the equal protection of the laws. The three-judge District Court agreed, one judge dissenting. . . .

The Federal Government and virtually all of the States grant some sort of hiring preference to veterans. The Massachusetts preference, which is loosely termed an "absolute lifetime" preference, is among the most generous. It applies to all positions in the State's classified civil service, which constitute approximately 60% of the public jobs in the State. It is available to "any person, male or female, including a nurse," who was honorably discharged from the United States Armed Forces after at least 90 days of active service, at least one day of which was during "wartime." Persons who are deemed veterans and who are otherwise qualified for a particular civil service job may exercise the preference at any time and as many times as they wish. . . .

The appellee has lived in Dracut, Mass., most of her life. She entered the workforce in 1948, and for the next 14 years worked at a variety of jobs in the private sector. She first entered the state civil service system in 1963, having competed successfully for a position as Senior Clerk Stenographer in the Massachusetts Civil Defense Agency. There she worked for four years. In 1967, she was promoted to the position of Federal Funds and Personnel Coordinator in the same agency. The agency, and with it her job, was eliminated in 1975.

During her 12-year tenure as a public employee, Ms. Feeney took and passed a number of open competitive civil service examinations. On several she did quite well, receiving in 1971 the second highest score on an examination for a job with the Board of Dental Examiners, and in 1973 the third highest on a test for an Administrative Assistant position with a mental health center. Her high scores, however, did not win her a place on the certified eligible list. Because of the veterans' preference, she was ranked sixth behind five male veterans on the Dental Examiner list. She was not certified, and a lower scoring veteran was eventually appointed. On the 1973 examination, she was placed in a position on the list behind 12 male veterans, 11 of whom had lower scores. Following the other examinations that she took, her name was similarly ranked below those of veterans who had achieved passing grades.

Ms. Feeney's interest in securing a better job in state government did not wane. Having been consistently eclipsed by veterans, however, she eventually concluded that further competition for civil service positions of interest to veterans would be futile. In 1975, shortly after her civil defense job was abolished, she commenced this litigation. . . .

The sole question for decision on this appeal is whether Massachusetts, in granting an absolute lifetime preference to veterans, has discriminated against women in violation of the Equal Protection Clause of the Fourteenth Amendment.

. . . The cases of Washington v. Davis, [426 U.S. 229 (1976)], and Arlington Heights v. Metropolitan Housing Dev. Corp., [429 U.S. 252 (1977)], recognize that when a neutral law has a disparate impact upon a group that has historically been the victim of discrimination, an unconstitutional purpose may still be at work. But those cases signaled no departure from the settled rule that the Fourteenth Amendment guarantees equal laws, not equal results. *Davis* upheld a job-related employment test that white people passed in proportionately greater numbers than Negroes, for there had been no showing that racial discrimination entered into the establishment or formulation of the test. *Arlington Heights* upheld a zoning board decision that tended to perpetuate racially segregated housing patterns, since, apart from its effect, the board's decision was shown to be nothing more than an application of a constitutionally neutral zoning policy. Those principles apply with equal force to a case involving alleged gender discrimination.

When a statute, gender-neutral on its face, is challenged on the ground that its effects upon women are disproportionably adverse, a twofold inquiry is thus appropriate. The first question is whether the statutory classification is indeed neutral in the sense that it is not gender-based. If the classification itself, covert or overt, is not based upon gender, the second question is whether the adverse effect reflects invidious gender-based discrimination. . . . In this second inquiry, impact provides an "important starting point," [429 U.S. at 266], but purposeful discrimination is "the condition that offends the Constitution." Swann v. Charlotte-Mecklenburg Board of Education, [402 U.S. 1, 16 (1971)]. . . .

. . . The District Court made two central findings that are relevant here: first, that [the statute] serves legitimate and worthy purposes; second, that the absolute preference was not established for the purpose of discriminating against women. The appellee has thus acknowledged and the District Court has thus found that the distinction between veterans and nonveterans drawn by [the statute] is not a pretext for gender discrimination. . . .

. . . Veteran status is not uniquely male. Although few women benefit from the preference the nonveteran class is not substantially all female. To the contrary, significant numbers of nonveterans are men, and all nonveterans — male as well as female — are placed at a disadvantage. Too many men are affected by [the statute] to permit the inference that the statute is but a pretext for preferring men over women. . . .

. . . The dispositive question, then, is whether the appellee has shown that a gender-based discriminatory purpose has, at least in some measure, shaped the Massachusetts veterans' preference legislation. . . .

. . . Discriminatory intent is . . . either . . . a factor that has influenced the legislative choice or it is not. The District Court's conclusion that the absolute veterans' preference was not originally enacted or subsequently reaffirmed for the purpose of giving an advantage to males as such necessarily compels the conclusion that the State . . . intended nothing more than to prefer "veterans." Given this finding, simple logic suggests that an intent to exclude women from significant public jobs was not at work in this law. To reason that it was, by describing the preference as "inherently nonneutral" or "gender-biased," is merely to restate the fact of impact, not to answer the question of intent. . . .

. . . The basic distinction between veterans and nonveterans, having been found not gender-based, and the goals of the preference having been found worthy, [the statute] must be analyzed as is any other neutral law that casts a greater burden upon women as a group than upon men as a group. The enlistment policies of the Armed Services may well have discriminated on the basis of sex. . . . But the history of discrimination against women in the military is not on trial in this case.

. . . The decision to grant a preference to veterans was of course "intentional." So, necessarily, did an adverse impact upon nonveterans follow from that decision. And it cannot seriously be argued that the Legislature of Massachusetts could have been unaware that most veterans are men. It would thus be disingenuous to say that the adverse consequences of this legislation for women were unintended, in the sense that they were not volitional or in the sense that they were not foreseeable.

"Discriminatory purpose," however, implies more than intent as volition or intent as awareness of consequences. . . . It implies that the decisionmaker, in this case a state legislature, selected or reaffirmed a particular course of action at least in part "because of," not merely "in spite of," its adverse effects upon an identifiable group.[25] Yet, nothing in the record demonstrates that this preference for veterans was originally devised or subsequently re-enacted because it would accomplish the collateral goal of keeping women in a stereotypic and predefined place in the Massachusetts Civil Service.

---

25. This is not to say that the inevitability or foreseeability of consequences of a neutral rule has no bearing upon the existence of discriminatory intent. Certainly, when the adverse consequences of a law upon an identifiable group are as inevitable as the gender-based consequences of [the statute at issue in this case], a strong inference that the adverse effects were desired can reasonably be drawn. But in this inquiry — made as it is under the Constitution — an inference is a working tool, not a synonym for proof. When, as here, the impact is essentially an unavoidable consequence of a legislative policy that has in itself always been deemed to be legitimate, and when, as here, the statutory history and all of the available evidence affirmatively demonstrate the opposite, the inference simply fails to ripen into proof.

To the contrary, the statutory history shows that the benefit of the preference was consistently offered to "any person" who was a veteran. That benefit has been extended to women under a very broad statutory definition of the term veteran. The preference formula itself, which is the focal point of this challenge, was first adopted — so it appears from this record — out of a perceived need to help a small group of older Civil War veterans. It has since been reaffirmed and extended only to cover new veterans. When the totality of legislative actions establishing and extending the Massachusetts veterans' preference are considered . . . the law remains what it purports to be: a preference for veterans of either sex over nonveterans of either sex, not for men over women.

Veterans' hiring preferences represent an awkward — and, many argue, unfair — exception to the widely shared view that merit and merit alone should prevail in the employment policies of government. After a war, such laws have been enacted virtually without opposition. During peacetime, they inevitably have come to be viewed in many quarters as undemocratic and unwise. Absolute and permanent preferences, as the troubled history of this law demonstrates, have always been subject to the objection that they give the veteran more than a square deal. But the Fourteenth Amendment "cannot be made a refuge from ill-advised . . . laws." . . . . The substantial edge granted to veterans by [the Massachusetts statute] may reflect unwise policy. The appellee, however, has simply failed to demonstrate that the law in any way reflects a purpose to discriminate on the basis of sex.

The judgment is reversed, and the case is remanded for further proceedings consistent with this opinion. . . .

Mr. Justice STEVENS, with whom Mr. Justice WHITE joins, concurring. . . . If a classification is not overtly based on gender, I am inclined to believe the question whether it is covertly gender-based is the same as the question whether its adverse effects reflect invidious gender-based discrimination. However the question is phrased, for me the answer is largely provided by the fact that the number of males disadvantaged by Massachusetts' veterans' preference (1,867,000) is sufficiently large — and sufficiently close to the number of disadvantaged females (2,954,000) — to refute the claim that the rule was intended to benefit males as a class over females as a class.

Mr. Justice MARSHALL, with whom Mr. Justice BRENNAN joins, dissenting. . . .

That a legislature seeks to advantage one group does not, as a matter of logic or of common sense, exclude the possibility that it also intends to disadvantage another. Individuals in general and lawmakers in particular frequently act for a variety of reasons. . . . Absent an omniscience not commonly attributed to the judiciary, it will often be impossible to ascertain the sole or even dominant purpose of a given statute. . . . Thus, the critical constitutional inquiry is not whether an illicit consideration was the primary or but-for cause of a decision, but rather whether it had an appreciable role in shaping a given legislative enactment. . . .

Moreover, since reliable evidence of subjective intentions is seldom obtainable, resort to inference based on objective factors is generally unavoidable. . . . To discern the purposes underlying facially neutral policies, this Court has therefore considered the degree, inevitability, and foreseeability of any disproportionate impact as well as the alternatives reasonably available. . . .

In the instant case, the impact of the Massachusetts statute on women is undisputed. Any veteran with a passing grade on the civil service exam must be placed ahead of a nonveteran, regardless of their respective scores. The District Court found that, as a practical matter, this preference supplants test results as the determinant of upper level civil service appointments. . . . Because less than 2% of the women in Massachusetts are veterans, the absolute-preference formula has rendered desirable state civil service employment an almost exclusively male prerogative. . . .

As the District Court recognized, this consequence follows foreseeably, indeed inexorably, from the long history of policies severely limiting women's participation in the military. . . .

. . . The legislative history of the statute reflects the Commonwealth's patent appreciation of the impact the preference system would have on women, and an equally evident desire to mitigate that impact only with respect to certain traditionally female occupations. Until 1971, the statute and implementing civil service regulations exempted from operation of the preference any job requisitions "especially calling for women." . . . In practice, this exemption, coupled with the absolute preference for veterans, has created a gender-based civil service hierarchy, with women occupying low-grade clerical and secretarial jobs and men holding more responsible and remunerative positions. . . .

Thus, for over 70 years, the Commonwealth has maintained, as an integral part of its veterans' preference system, an exemption relegating female civil service applicants to occupations traditionally filled by women. Such a statutory scheme both reflects and perpetuates precisely the kind of archaic assumptions about women's roles which we have previously held invalid. . . . The Court's conclusion to the contrary — that "nothing in the record" evinces a "collateral goal of keeping women in a stereotypic and predefined place in the Massachusetts Civil Service" — displays a singularly myopic view of the facts established below.[3]

---

3. Although it is relevant that the preference statute also disadvantages a substantial group of men, see [opinion of Stevens, J., concurring], it is equally pertinent that 47% of Massachusetts men over 18 are veterans, as compared to 0.8% of Massachusetts women. Given this disparity, and the indicia of intent noted, . . . the absolute number of men denied preference cannot be dispositive, especially since they have not faced the barriers to achieving veteran status confronted by women. . . .

To survive challenge under the Equal Protection Clause, statutes reflecting gender-based discrimination must be substantially related to the achievement of important governmental objectives. . . . Appellants here advance three interests in support of the absolute-preference system: (1) assisting veterans in their readjustment to civilian life; (2) encouraging military enlistment; and (3) rewarding those who have served their country. . . . Although each of those goals is unquestionably legitimate, the "mere recitation of a benign, compensatory purpose" cannot of itself insulate legislative classifications from constitutional scrutiny. Weinberger v. Wiesenfeld, [420 U.S. 636, 648 (1974)]. And in this case, the Commonwealth has failed to establish a sufficient relationship between its objectives and the means chosen to effectuate them.

With respect to the first interest, facilitating veterans' transition to civilian status, the statute is plainly overinclusive. . . . By conferring a permanent preference, the legislation allows veterans to invoke their advantage repeatedly, without regard to their date of discharge. As the record demonstrates, a substantial majority of those currently enjoying the benefits of the system are not recently discharged veterans in need of readjustment assistance.

Nor is the Commonwealth's second asserted interest, encouraging military service, a plausible justification for this legislative scheme. In its original and subsequent re-enactments, the statute extended benefits retroactively to veterans who had served during a prior specified period. . . . If the Commonwealth's "actual purpose" is to induce enlistment, this legislative design is hardly well suited to that end. . . . For I am unwilling to assume what appellants made no effort to prove, that the possibility of obtaining an *ex post facto* civil service preference significantly influenced the enlistment decisions of Massachusetts residents. Moreover, even if such influence could be presumed, the statute is still grossly overinclusive in that it bestows benefits on men drafted as well as those who volunteered.

Finally, the Commonwealth's third interest, rewarding veterans, does not "adequately justify the salient features" of this preference system. . . . Where a particular statutory scheme visits substantial hardship on a class long subject to discrimination, the legislation cannot be sustained unless " 'carefully tuned to alternative considerations.' " . . . Here, there are a wide variety of less discriminatory means by which Massachusetts could effect its compensatory purposes. For example, a point preference system, such as that maintained by many States and the Federal Government, or an absolute preference for a limited duration, would reward veterans without excluding all qualified women from upper level civil service positions. Apart from public employment, the Commonwealth, can, and does, afford assistance to veterans in various ways, including tax abatements, educational subsidies, and special programs for needy veterans. . . . Unlike these and similar benefits, the costs of which are distributed across the taxpaying public generally, the Massachusetts statute exacts a substantial price from a discrete group of individuals who have long been subject to employment discrimination, and who, "because of circumstances totally beyond their control, have [had] little if any chance of becoming members of the preferred class." 415 F. Supp. at 499. . . .

I would affirm the judgment of the court below.

NOTE ON NONDISCRIMINATORY AND DISCRIMINATORY INTENT

Did the Idaho and Alabama legislatures in *Reed* and *Orr* "intend" to disadvantage people because of their sex? Probably not, but the point of these cases is that laws based on stereotyped thinking about women, even if — perhaps *especially* if — unintentional, are unacceptable.

Why, then, in *Feeney*, does the Court allow to stand a system that has a substantially disproportionate impact against women — a much greater practical impact, indeed, than the statutes in *Reed* and *Orr*? One explanation is that when a rule or practice is facially neutral it is not clear that discrimination *on the basis of sex* has actually occurred. A showing of discriminatory intent establishes discrimination when it is not otherwise evident.

Should intent be required in order to establish the presence of sex discrimination in cases such as *Feeney*? On the one hand, as noted above, without such a requirement we may be unsure whether discrimination based on sex has actually occurred or whether there is a more benign explanation. On the other hand, rules and practices that are not explicitly sex-based but have a disproportionate, negative impact against women may be even more dangerous than cases of explicit sex-based discrimination, in that the stereotypes that guide decisionmaking in such cases may be more hidden and thus easier to perpetuate. In fact, Title VII of the Civil Rights Act of 1964, explored later in this chapter, requires that rules and practices in the employment context that have a disparate impact on women be justified by their job-relatedness, regardless of the "intent" of the employer. See Dothard v. Rawlinson, 433 U.S. 321 (1977) (finding height and weight requirements for prison guards that had a discriminatory impact on women a violation of Title VII).

Ironically, some direct or explicit sex-based classifications are actually "saved" by the intention to discriminate. For example, in Rostker v. Goldberg, 453 U.S. 57 (1981), the Supreme Court upheld a male-only draft registration system on the theory that, since females could not be used in combat, they were not likely to be subjected to future drafts. The fact that the reasons for the exclusion of women were well reviewed in the legislative history meant that the statute was not an "accidental by-product" of narrow, outmoded stereotypes about women, but a deliberate, reasoned choice. 453 U.S. at 74. Similarly in Mississippi University for Women v.

Hogan, 458 U.S. 718 (1982), the Court's conclusion that an all-female state-supported nursing school was a violation of equal protection turned in part on the origins of the school and stereotyped notions about what it was appropriate to train women to do. Justice O'Connor suggests in her opinion for the court that if the intent had been to compensate women for disadvantage they experienced in their educational or employment opportunities, another result might have followed. See 458 U.S. at 728-729.

To the extent a showing of discriminatory intent seems analytically desirable, what should be required to establish it? In *Feeney*, the fact that few women performed military service was a "neutral fact" used to disprove discriminatory intent. Was this analysis sound? The issue of intent is explored further in this chapter in the context of employment discrimination cases in which the motives are "mixed," see Price Waterhouse v. Hopkins, and later in Chapter 6 in an exploration of the general subject of consent.

Putting Theory into Practice

2-1. The following exchange is reported as part of a voir dire examination conducted by a judge in a criminal case in a municipal court in California:

> *The Court*: Miss Bobb, what is your occupation?
> *Miss Bobb*: I'm an attorney.
> *The Court*: And in your practice do you practice criminal law as well as civil law?
> *Miss Bobb*: No, I practice entirely bankruptcy law.
> *The Court*: All right. Is there a Mr. Bobb?
> *Miss Bobb*: I have some difficulty with that question because I've noticed only the women have been asked to answer that.
> *The Court*: Yes, I know. Do you have a Mr. Bobb — is there a Mr. Bobb?
> *Miss Bobb*: Are you going to [poll] the men to see if they care to disclose —
> *The Court*: No, I'm just going to ask you if you have a husband or not. Do you have a husband?
> *Miss Bobb*: I don't care to answer it then. What's relative to women is relative to men.
> *The Court*: Yes, I know. What is your husband's occupation?
> *Miss Bobb*: I don't care to answer that.
> *The Court*: I instruct you to answer.
> *Miss Bobb*: I don't think I should.
> *The Court*: I've got — you understand that you'll be in contempt of Court — jury — you're an attorney, you understand these rules, don't you?
> *Miss Bobb*: No, I do not understand why only the women are asked certain questions and the men aren't asked the same questions.

The Court: The question to you, Mrs. Bobb — you're an attorney at law, you understand the rules and regulations of — of — of being an attorney. And the question to you now simply is: What is your husband's occupation?

Miss Bobb: I refuse to answer.

The Court: You're held in contempt of Court, Mrs. Bobb.

Bobb v. Municipal Court, 192 Cal. Rptr. 270, 270-271 (Cal. App. 1983). To what extent will formal equality principles provide relief to Mrs. Bobb? What are the possible limitations of those principles in this context?

2-2. In response to acts of violence in and around school occurring between warring factions of rival gangs, a school board instituted a ban on students wearing or displaying any gang symbol. This ban is interpreted in one school to bar males, but not females, from wearing earrings, because some males who wear earrings do so as a sign of gang allegiance while earrings on females do not have any gang significance. Does the rule offend formal equality principles?

2-3. A Veterans Administration rule requires that all chaplains at VA hospitals be "ordained" clergy members. The requirement is shown to have a disparate impact on women since in some churches, including the Roman Catholic church, women cannot be ordained as priests. Does the rule offend formal equality principles?

B. FORMAL EQUALITY IN EMPLOYMENT

1. The Equal Pay Act: Formal Equality Paradigm?

EEOC v. Madison Community Unit School District No. 12
818 F.2d 577 (7th Cir. 1987)

POSNER, Circuit Judge.

The Equal Employment Opportunity Commission brought this suit against the school district of Madison, Illinois, charging that the district was paying female athletic coaches in its high school and junior high school less than male coaches, in violation of the Equal Pay Act of 1963. That Act . . . forbids an employer to discriminate . . . between employees on the basis of sex by paying wages to employees . . . at a rate less than the rate at which he pays wages to employees of the opposite sex . . . for equal work on jobs the performance of which requires equal skill, effort, and responsibility, and which are performed under similar working conditions, except where such payment is made pursuant to [(i) a seniority system; (ii) a merit system; (iii) a system which measures earnings by quantity or quality of production; or] (iv) a differential based on any other factor other than sex: Provided, That an employer who is paying a wage rate differential in violation of this subsection shall not, in order to comply with the provisions of this subsection, reduce the wage rate of any employee.

29 U.S.C. §206(d)(1). . . .

The trial brought out the following facts:

[Luvenia] Long was paid substantially less for coaching girls' track than Steptoe, a man, was paid for coaching boys' track. Although the boys' track program included more students and had more meets than the girls', Steptoe had two assistant coaches compared to Long's one, and as a result Long and Steptoe devoted approximately equal time to their coaching jobs. Long also coached the girls' tennis team, and Jakich, a man, the boys' tennis team; and Jakich was paid more than Long even though there were no significant differences between the teams in number of students, length of season, or number of practice sessions; however, the boys' team played almost twice as many matches as the girls' team. Long was also assistant coach of the girls' basketball team one year and received lower pay than Tyus, the male assistant coach of the boys' track team. The district judge found that the work of the two assistant coaches was substantially equal and required the same skill, effort, and responsibility — except that Long worked longer hours than Tyus.

[Carol] Cole, who coached the girls' volleyball, girls' basketball, and girls' softball teams, was paid less for coaching volleyball than the male coach of the boys' soccer team, less for coaching basketball than the male coach of the boys' soccer team, and less for coaching softball than the male coach of the boys' baseball team. Also, as assistant coach of the girls' track team she was paid less than the assistant coach of the boys' track team. In all of these cases the judge found that the work of the female coach and her male counterpart was the same in skill, effort (including time), and responsibility. Any potential differences in effort and responsibility stemming from the fact that the boys' teams were sometimes larger and played longer seasons were, he found, offset by the fact that the head coaches of the boys' teams had more assistants than their female counterparts. . . .

The first question we must decide is whether the pairs of jobs that the district judge compared in finding unequal pay are sufficiently similar to be "equal work" within the meaning of the Equal Pay Act. The Act is not a general mandate of sex-neutral compensation. It does not enact "compara-ble worth" — the principle that wages should be based on "objective" factors, rather than on market conditions of demand and supply which may depress wages in jobs held mainly by women relative to wages in jobs held mainly by men. See American Nurses' Assn. v. Illinois, 783 F.2d 716, 718-20 (7th Cir. 1986). A female secretary paid less than a male janitor cannot complain under the Equal Pay Act that the disparity in their wages is not justified by "objective" factors such as differences in skill, responsibility, and effort. . . . The Act requires equal pay only when men and women are performing "equal work on jobs the performance of which requires equal skill, effort, and responsibility, and which are performed under similar working conditions." 29 U.S.C. §206(d)(1). The working conditions of a janitor are different from those of a secretary, and so are the skills and responsibilities of the two jobs. The Act does not prohibit paying different wages even if the result is to pay a woman less than a man and by doing so "underpay" her because the difference in the wage rate is greater than necessary to compensate the male for any greater skill, effort, or responsibility required by, or any inferior working conditions encountered in, his job.

Thus the jobs that are compared must be in some sense the same to count as "equal work" under the Equal Pay Act; and here we come to the main difficulty in applying the Act: whether two jobs are the same depends on how fine a system of job classifications the courts will accept. If coaching an athletic team in the Madison, Illinois school system is considered a single job rather than a congeries of jobs, the school district violated the Equal Pay Act prima facie by paying female holders of this job less than male holders, and the only question is whether the district carried its burden of proving that the lower wages which the four female coaches received were lower than the wages of their male counterparts because of a factor other than sex. If on the other hand coaching the girls' tennis team is considered a different job from coaching the boys' tennis team, and *a fortiori* if coaching the girls' volleyball or basketball team is considered a different job (or jobs) from coaching the boys' soccer team, there is no prima facie violation. So the question is how narrow a definition of job the courts should be using in deciding whether the Equal Pay Act is applicable.

We can get some guidance from the language of the Act. The Act requires that the jobs compared have "similar working conditions," not the same working conditions. This implies that some comparison of different jobs is possible. It is true that similarity of working conditions between the jobs being compared is not enough to bring the Act into play — the work must be "equal" and the jobs must require "equal" skill, effort, and responsibility, as well as similar working conditions. But since the working conditions need not be "equal," the jobs need not be completely identical.

Estimating and comparing the skill, effort, responsibility, and working conditions in two jobs are factual determinations. . . . We can overturn them, therefore, only if they are clearly erroneous. . . . The district judge found (among other things) that coaching a girls' tennis team is sufficiently like coaching a boys' tennis team, coaching a girls' softball team is sufficiently like coaching a boys' hardball team, and, indeed, coaching a girls' volleyball or basketball team is sufficiently like coaching a boys' soccer team, to allow each pair of jobs to be described as involving equal work, as requiring equal skill, effort, and responsibility, and as being performed under similar working conditions. . . .

There are pitfalls in allowing any comparisons between different jobs, and they are illustrated by this case. One is a tendency to focus entirely on the measurable differences and ignore the equally or more important but less readily measurable ones. The witnesses in this case concentrated on the amount of skill and time required for coaching girls' and boys' teams and paid little attention to responsibility. It may be true that because the boys' teams tend to have more assistant coaches than the girls' teams, the head coaches of the boys' teams put in no more time than the head coaches of the girls' teams even when the boys' teams are larger and play more matches. But normally there is greater responsibility (one of the dimensions in which the statute requires equality between the jobs compared) if you have a staff than if you don't. That is one reason why the president of a company is paid more than a junior executive who, lacking staff assistance, may work longer hours. "Direction of others as well as value of commodity worked upon and overall importance of assignment may be considered as part of an [employee's] job responsibility." 109 Cong. Rec. 9209 (1963) (remarks of Congressman Goodell).

Another difference tends to be ignored when effort, which is hard to measure, is equated to time, which is easy to measure. Boys and girls differ on average in strength, speed, and perhaps other dimensions of athletic ability; there may also be important differences in their attitudes toward athletic competition. The differences between boys and girls in athletic aptitude and interest may make coaching a boys' team harder — or easier — than coaching a girls' team; there can be no confidence that the two jobs require equal effort. The district judge set aside this consideration by ruling that a difference in the sex of students, customers, etc., can't be used to justify a pay difference under the Equal Pay Act. But this is wrong. The reference to "factor other than sex" refers to the sex of the employee, not the sex of the employer's customers, clients, or suppliers. . . . Suppose that the school district happened to have just male, or just female, coaches and paid coaches more for coaching boys' teams than girls' teams. Men paid less than other men for coaching, or women paid less than other women, could not complain of a violation of the Equal Pay Act. . . . The Act did not seek to eliminate whatever differences between the sexes might make it harder to coach a boys' team than a girls' team. If it is harder (we are not saying it is harder — we are just discussing possibilities), the statutory requirement of equal effort is not met and the differential in pay is outside the scope of the Act.

Nevertheless, we are unwilling to hold that coaches of girls' and boys' teams can never be found to be doing equal work requiring equal skill, effort, and responsibility and performed under similar working conditions. Above the lowest rank of employee, every employee has a somewhat different job from every other one, even if the two employees being compared are in the same department. So if "equal work" and "equal skill, effort, and responsibility" were taken literally, the Act would have a minute domain. . . .

But the words "very much alike," "closely related," or, as the cases sometimes say, "substantially equal" — even the words "virtually identical" — are not synonymous with "identical." . . . There is a gray area, which we must be vigilant to police, between "very much alike," which is within the scope of the Act, and "comparable," which is outside; for it is plain that Congress did not want to enact comparable worth as part of the Equal Pay Act of 1964. . . .

The courts have thus had to steer a narrow course. The cases do not require an absolute identity between jobs, but do require substantial identity. The line is a fine, perhaps imperceptible, one. . . .

Whatever answer we might give, if we were the finders of fact, to the question whether coaching a girls' tennis team and coaching a boys' tennis team are sufficiently alike to be equal work within the meaning of the Act, we cannot, on the record compiled in this case (a potentially important qualification), deem the district court's determination clearly erroneous. . . .

Boys' teams might of course be greater revenue producers than girls' teams. Jacobs v. College of William & Mary, 517 F. Supp. 791, 797 (E.D. Va. 1980), aff'd without opinion, 661 F.2d 922 (4th Cir. 1981), relied on this factor. . . . But *Jacobs* involved college teams. Madison has only one revenue-producing team, the boys' high-school basketball team, and the plaintiffs do not complain about the higher wage that the head coach of that team received — they acknowledge that his job is not the same as that of any female coach. . . .

For those of us whose knowledge of athletic coaching is confined to newspaper and television accounts of the travails of professional and college coaches, the idea of homogenizing the coaching profession in the manner attempted by the plaintiffs and accepted by the district judge is discordant. But we must, by an effort of imagination, place ourselves in a different world, that of small-town high-school and junior-high-school athletics, where the coach's task is not to compete for money in a high-pressure environment but to impart elementary athletic skills and norms of sportsmanship to adolescents. Given these modest goals, a finding that the coaching of boys' and of girls' tennis involves inconsequential differences in skill, effort, responsibility, and working conditions is not so improbable that we can set it aside. . . .

Although we conclude that there is no objection in principle to comparing different coaching jobs, the record of the present case does require us to distinguish between coaching boys' and girls' teams of the same sport and coaching boys' and girls' teams of different sports. The judge equated coaching girls' basketball and girls' volleyball to coaching boys' soccer (and, in the assistant-coach comparisons, girls' basketball with boys' track), without regard for the fact that Madison treats coaching a different sport as a different coaching job irrespective of the sex of either the coach or the team. . . . We are willing to assume that hardball and fast-pitch softball — similar sports played under similar rules — are the same sport for purposes of the Equal Pay Act. See Brennan v. Woodbridge School District, 74 Labor Cases ¶33,121, at p. 46,627 (D. Del. 1974). But given the wage differentials among the male coaches, we cannot make this assumption for volleyball and soccer, or for basketball and soccer. Another consideration is the arbitrariness of the particular comparisons suggested by the plaintiffs. In 1980 Long, as girls' track coach, received the same wage as the male coach of the boys' soccer team. How was the school district to know that a court would think basketball and soccer or volleyball and soccer a closer pair than track and soccer? We vacate the findings of the district judge with respect to a violation of the Equal Pay Act in the comparison between boys' soccer and girls' volleyball, boys' soccer and girl's basketball, and boys' track and girls' basketball.

With this exception we conclude that the plaintiffs did establish a prima facie case of violation of the Equal Pay Act, and we move on to consider defenses, of which only one ("factor other than sex") is relevant. Madison argues that the sex of the teams is a factor other than sex, and though the district court thought this wrong, we disagree as we have said; the factor other than sex to which the Act refers is a factor other than the employee's sex. . . . If Madison, having decided for reasons unrelated to the sex of the coaches that coaches of male teams should be paid more than coaches of female teams, neither prohibited nor even discouraged women from coaching male teams, the difference in pay between male coaches of boys' teams and female coaches of girls' teams would be due to a decision unrelated to the sex of the coaches. But Madison discouraged women, including Cole and Long, from applying to coach boys' teams, which not only adds a reason related to the sex of the coaches for a difference in pay between men and women to a reason related solely to the sex of the team members, but also casts doubt on the bona fides of the school district's claim to have based the difference in the pay of coaches of male and of female teams solely on the sex of the team members. . . . There was contrary evidence: a woman once was hired to coach the boys' tennis team and was paid the same as her male predecessor; several times men were hired to coach girls' teams and paid the same as female coaches of those teams. But such job offers were very rare prior to the EEOC's investigation, and the district judge was entitled to find their evidentiary significance outweighed by the evidence that women were discouraged from applying to coach boys' teams.

The reason for discouraging women from coaching boys' teams was that the school authorities were concerned about the "locker room problem." This may or may not be a good reason . . . but it does suggest that women receive less pay than men for doing what the district court found was equal work within the meaning of the Equal Pay Act because they are women; their sex makes them ineligible to receive the higher wage that men receive for equal work. Even if the school district is entitled to insist that coaches and coached be of the same sex, if the work of each coach is the same and the reason for the difference in pay is the difference in the sex of the coach, the Equal Pay Act is violated. An employer cannot divide equal work into two job classifications that carry unequal pay, forbid women to compete for one of the classifications, and defend the resulting inequality in pay between men and women by reference to a "factor other than [the] sex" of the employees. . . . It would not be the sexual segregation that had caused the inequality in pay, but a decision to pay men more for doing the same work as women (albeit with a "clientele" of a different sex from the women's "clientele"). . . .

Hodgson v. Robert Hall Clothes, Inc.
473 F.2d 589 (3d Cir.), cert. denied sub nom.
Brennan v. Robert Hall Clothes, Inc., 414 U.S. 866
(1973)

James HUNTER, III, Circuit Judge.
. . . The Robert Hall store in question is located in Wilmington, Delaware. It sells clothing, and contains a department for men's and boys' clothing and another department for women's and girls' clothing. The store is a one-floor building, and the departments are in separate portions of it.

The merchandise in the men's department was, on the average, of higher price and better quality than the merchandise in the women's department; and Robert Hall's profit margin on the men's clothing was higher than its margin on the women's clothing. Consequently, the men's department at all times showed a larger dollar volume in gross sales, and a greater gross profit. Breaking this down, the salespeople in the men's department, on the average, sold more merchandise in terms of dollars and produced more gross profit than did the people in the women's department per hour of work.

The departments are staffed by full and part-time sales personnel. At all times, only men were permitted to work in the men's department and only women were permitted to work in the women's department. The complaint is not addressed to the propriety of such segregated employment.

The salespeople receive a base salary and can earn additional incentive payments. Various factors relating to the garment sold determine the amount of incentive payments. At all times, the salesmen received higher salaries than the saleswomen. Both starting salaries and periodic increases were higher for the males. The amount of incentive compensation was very slightly greater for the men. . . .

The initial question facing us is one raised by the Secretary [of Labor]. He contends that economic benefit to the employer cannot be used to justify a wage differential under [the Equal Pay Act].

He argues that "any other factor" does not mean any other factor. Instead he claims it means any other factor other than sex which "is related to job performance or is typically used in setting wage scales." He contends that economic benefits to an employer do not fall within this exception.

He recognizes that the men's department produces a greater profit for Robert Hall. His contention is that the salesmen have nothing to do with producing this benefit since the district court found that the salesmen and saleswomen performed equal work. Since the saleswomen cannot sell the higher-priced clothing sold in the men's department, this cannot be used as a factor on which to base a wage differential. Otherwise, "the exception could swallow the rule." Shultz v. First Victoria National Bank, 420 F.2d 648 (5th Cir. 1969). . . .

The Secretary's argument is incorrect for several reasons. It ignores the basic finding of the district court that Robert Hall's segregation of its work force was done for legitimate business purposes. It is also inconsistent with the wording of the statute. . . .

The Secretary recognizes this reasoning in §800.116(e) of his Wage-Hour Administrator's Interpretative Bulletin and §34d07 of his Field Office Handbook. In both of these the Secretary approves a commission system in which the amount of compensation is determined by the type of article sold. The stated hypothesis is that the salespeople are performing equal work. Since this is given, the only basis for approving such a system has to be that the economic benefit to the employer is greater. . . . That the salary in this case is a base salary rather than a commission is not a significant distinction. The principle remains the same: the compensation is based on economic benefit to the employer, and the work performed is equal.

This would make good business sense. The saleswomen are paid less because the commodities which they sell cannot bear the same selling costs that the commodities sold in the men's department can bear. Without a more definite indication from Congress, it would not seem wise to impose the economic burden of higher compensation on employers. It could serve to weaken their competitive position. . . .

The next question is whether Robert Hall proved that it received the economic benefits upon which it claimed it based its salary differentials. . . .

Robert Hall introduced evidence to show that for every year of the store's operation, the men's department was substantially more profitable than the women's department. . . .

. . . [I]t was not Robert Hall's practice to retain records of individual performance. . . .

. . . The question is whether the Equal Pay Act requires the employer to justify his base salary by correlating it to individual performance. . . .

While no business reason could justify a practice clearly prohibited by the act, the legislative history set forth above indicates a Congressional intent to allow reasonable business judgments to stand. It would be too great an economic and accounting hardship to impose upon Robert Hall the requirement that it correlate the wages of each individual with his or her performance. This could force it toward a system based totally upon commissions, and it seems unwise to read such a result into [the Equal Pay Act]. . . .

The Secretary contends that our decision in Shultz v. Wheaton Glass Company, [supra] . . . supports the district court's decision not to rely on group averages to justify the wage differential. . . . We do not agree that *Wheaton Glass* supports the district court. In that case the question, in part, was whether additional duties allegedly performed by certain males would justify paying males more than females. The courts held that the employers had failed to show that all of the males performed the additional duties. Here all of the salesmen perform the same duties. One could analogize to *Wheaton Glass* and say that as the alleged justification there was the additional duties, the alleged justification here is the economic benefits. And as the employer there did not prove that each individual performed the duties here Robert Hall did not prove that each individual provided economic benefits. However, the nature of the proof required distinguishes the two cases. It would not have been difficult in *Wheaton Glass* for the employer to have proved that each or most male workers performed the additional duties. That is not the case here.

Also, in *Wheaton Glass*, the court relied on the fact that there had been no finding that the women workers could not perform the additional duties allegedly performed by the men. Here there was a specific finding by the district court, unchallenged by the Secretary, that the women could not perform the work done by the men [i.e., "the frequent necessity for physical contact between the sales persons and the customers which would embarrass both and would inhibit sales unless they were of the same sex." 326 F. Supp. at 1269]. . . .

[The dissenting opinion of Van Dusen, Circuit Judge, is omitted.]

Notes

1. The Wage Gap. The wage gap between women's and men's earnings has been slowly eroding, although it is still significant. Adjusting for hours worked (but not for differences in education, experience or time in the workforce), women's median weekly earnings in 1979 were 63 percent those of men, while in 2000, the figure was 76 percent. U.S. Dep't of Labor, Bureau of Labor Statistics, Highlight of Women's Earnings in 2000, Report 952, at 1 (August 2001). The gap is less among African-Americans (85 percent) and Hispanics (88 percent). Id. Some women, of course, have benefitted more from the shrinking of the wage gap than others. Both women and men without a high school diploma have experienced a decline in inflation-adjusted earnings since 1979. Earnings for women with college degrees, however, have increased by over 30 percent since 1979 (again, adjusted for inflation) while those of male college graduates rose by just under 17 percent. Id. at 2. During this same period, women's share of employment in occupations typified by high earnings (executive, administrative and managerial positions) rose from 34.2 percent in 1983 to 47 percent in 2000, and women working in professional specialties rose from 47 percent to 52 percent. Id.

The disparity for older women is greater than for younger women. For example, in 2000 college-educated women in the 20-24 age bracket earned on average 91.9 percent of what men earn, while the figure for women in the 55-64 age range was only 68.5 percent. Id. at 1. It is unclear whether the higher wage percentages for younger women mean that conditions are improving for women generally or that wage differentials tend to widen as women age. The research is inconclusive but it would appear that while wage disparities are lessening over time, some slippage continues to occur in women's earnings in relation to men's as women progress through the life cycle. In the context of lawyer salaries, see further discussion on pages 163-165.

One phenomenon that correlates with the gap between men's and women's wages is the concentration of women in various lower-paying occupations. More than 75 percent of women are employed in two of six occupational categories: technical, sales, and administrative support; and managerial and professional specialties. However, according to Department of Labor figures, of the three subcategories within technical, sales, and administrative support, more than 63 percent of women work in the lowest paying area of administrative support. Additionally, women working in managerial and professional specialties are more likely to work in relatively lower paying professional occupations, such as teachers and registered nurses as opposed to engineers and mathematical and computer scientists. Id. at 2, 8-14.

In addition to the continuing gender gap in earnings for full-time employment, it should be noted that women are more likely to work part-time than men. Just under a quarter of women in wage and salary jobs are part-time employees, while only 10 percent of men are part-time workers. Id. at 2. Part-time workers are not only concentrated in wholesale and retail trade and service sectors in which even full-time workers tend to be poorly paid, but they are paid significantly less than full-time workers on a pro rata basis. They also receive fewer benefits. See Mary Ann Mason, Beyond Equal Opportunity: A New Vision for Women Workers, 6 Notre Dame J.L., Ethics & Pub. Pol'y 405-407 (1992). For frequently updated data on U.S. employment patterns by race, sex, and age, see the U.S. Bureau of Labor

Statistics Web site at http://www.bls.gov/data/home.htm. Further analysis of issues relating to part-time and contingent labor can be found at pages 360-364.

2. The Formal Equality Paradigm. The Equal Pay Act of 1963 is a paradigmatic application of formal equality principles in that it requires equal pay for equal work. The main interpretative task is defining what work is equal under the Act, taking into account the skill, effort, responsibility, and working conditions for each job. It obviously would be unfair to allow employers to circumvent the Act by minor variations in job titles or job descriptions. Thus, the Act has been applied to require the same wages for different job classifications entailing substantially equal duties and involving comparable skill, responsibility, and effort. Compare, e.g., Lawin-McEleney v. Marist College, 239 F.3d 476 (2d Cir. 2001) (work of male professor of biological sciences and female professor of criminal justice are substantially equivalent); Aldrich v. Randolph Central School Dist., 963 F.2d 520 (2d Cir.), cert. denied, 506 U.S. 965 (1992) (female "cleaners" and male "janitors" do essentially equal work, and the use of a civil service examination and classifications system for custodian's position not a "factor other than sex"); Usery v. Allegheny County Inst. Dist., 544 F.2d 148 (3d Cir. 1976), cert. denied, 430 U.S. 946 (1977) ("beautician" and "barber" positions equal); Brennan v. City Stores, Inc., 479 F.2d 235 (5th Cir. 1973) ("seamstress" and "tailor" jobs substantially equal), with Stopka v. Alliance of American Insurers, 141 F.3d 681 (7th Cir. 1998) (jobs of five male vice presidents required insurance skills that were substantially different from responsibilities of only female vice president whose job required administrative skills even though all division vice presidents were ranked equally under Alliance's Salary Administration Program); Spaulding v. University of Washington, 740 F.2d 686 (9th Cir.), cert. denied, 469 U.S. 1036 (1984) (largely female nursing faculty has responsibility, skill, and effort that is not substantially equal to that of predominantly male faculties of other university departments); Marshall v. Dallas Indep. School Dist., 605 F.2d 191 (5th Cir.), reh'g en banc denied, 608 F.2d 1373 (1979) (male "Helpers I" do heavier work than female "Helpers II").

When the challenge is to wages paid in the same job category, courts may require the plaintiff to identify a particular employee, or other employees, who are earning more for the same work. A composite of other employees in the job category is not sufficient. See, e.g., Houck v. Virginia Polytechnic Institute, 10 F.3d 204 (4th Cir. 1993) (affirming dismissal of suit by university professor who had used statistical evidence to establish a composite match of male professors to whom to compare herself, but failed to single out an actual individual with the same qualifications). However, once a suitable comparator proves the discrimination is not an isolated incident, an inequality claim can be established. See, e.g., Lawin-McEleney v. Marist College, supra (female professor's use of statistical averages from pool of entire college faculty was permitted to establish liability when there were only three other professors in her department); McMillan v. Massachusetts Society for the Prevention of Cruelty to Animals, 140 F.3d 288 (1st 1998) (statistical averages from sample of 46 veterinarians employed at the MSPCA over a period of ten years permissible to determine whether employer's conduct conformed to a general pattern of discrimination).

The Equal Pay Act addresses unjustified wage differentials based on sex but does not, itself, address any discrimination in hiring based on sex that may underlie the wage discrimination. It would not encompass, for example, discriminatory behavior that may have prevented women from becoming coaches of male sports teams at Madison Community Unit School, or salespeople in men's clothing departments at Robert Hall. These claims would be addressed under Title VII of the Civil Rights Act of 1964, discussed in the next section.

Wage discrimination claims may be brought under Title VII as well as the Equal Pay Act, but the Bennett Amendment to Title VII, 42 U.S.C. §§2000e-2(h), limits liability for wage discrimination claims to what is compelled by the Equal Pay Act. The relationship between the two Acts is explored in City of Los Angeles, Dept. of Water & Power v. Manhart, 435 U.S. 702, 711-714 (1978), set forth in Chapter 3, at page 364.

In addition to the affirmative defenses available under the Equal Pay Act, a number of public sector employers have sought protection from damages claims under the Eleventh Amendment, which provides states with immunity from federal claims unless Congress has specifically abrogated this immunity. See, e.g., City of Boerne v. Flores, 521 U.S. 507, 515 (1997). So far, the defense has not been successful in the Equal Pay Act context. See Varner v. Illinois State Univ., 226 F.3d 927 (7th Cir. 2000); Kovacevich v. Kent State Univ., 224 F.3d 806 (6th Cir. 2000); Hundertmark v. Florida Dep't of Transp., 205 F.3d 1272 (11th Cir. 2000); O'Sullivan v. Minnesota, 191 F.3d 965 (8th Cir. 1999); Anderson v. State Univ. of N.Y., 169 F.3d 117 (2d Cir. 1999), vacated and remanded, 528 U.S. 1111 (2000); Ussery v. Louisiana, 150 F.3d 431 (5th Cir. 1998), cert dismissed, 526 U.S. 1013 (1999).

3. Factors Justifying Differences in Pay. Should pay disparities based on the practice of matching an employee's salary at a previous position justify differences in salaries? This practice is, on the one hand, a practical response to competitive market conditions; on the other hand, it serves to immunize pay disparities that began elsewhere. The cases have not been uniform in their approaches to this issue. Compare, e.g., Brinkley v. Harbour Recreation Club, 180 F.3d 598 (4th Cir. 1999) (pay differential between plaintiff and male replacement hire reflected salary history and market demand and thus was not a factor related to sex), with Glenn v. General Motors Corp., 841 F.2d 1567 (11th Cir.), cert. denied, 488 U.S. 948 (1988) (rejecting employer justification for wage disparity that male clerks transferred from higher paying positions than female clerks); Futran v. RING Radio Co., 501 F. Supp. 734 (N.D. Ga. 1980) (wage differential not justified by fact that male talk show host with higher prior wage was in a stronger bargaining position than female talk show host). See also Smith v. Virginia Commonwealth University, 84 F.3d 672 (4th Cir. 1996) (in case brought by male faculty, reversing summary judgment against university that had raised female faculty salaries pursuant to a salary equity study that omitted consideration of, among other things, prior status as an administrator).

The Supreme Court in Corning Glass Works v. Brennan, 417 U.S. 188 (1974), faced with the employer's argument that it had to pay workers more money to work the night shift, concluded that some employer explanations for pay differences may be understandable as a matter of economics, but nonetheless illegal under the Equal Pay Act. 417 U.S. at 205. That case turned, however, on Corning Glass's prior history of failing to hire women for the night shift. 417 U.S. at 205-207. This approach would seem consistent with Judge Posner's approach in *Madison*, disallowing market or other employer explanations if women had been excluded from the higher-paying jobs. Is this an adequate qualification to the market factors allowance? In other words, should employers be limited in their market-based defenses only when they are directly responsible for the disadvantage women face in relation to those defenses?

What about a pay scheme with a greater benefit for workers who are a "head of household"? Some employer-subsidized fringe benefit features such as family medical insurance and tuition-benefit plans have such criteria. Could an employer reasonably assume that a head of household has a greater incentive to work and thus that he or she is likely to be more stable and productive? Or that heads of households have greater needs than other employees, and that providing the greatest amount of benefits to those with the greatest need maximizes employee satisfaction? Such rationales are quite familiar but, to the extent they have long justified paying women less than men, they should perhaps be viewed with some suspicion. See, e.g., Colby v. J.C. Penney Co., Inc., 811 F.2d 1119, 1127-1128 (7th Cir. 1987) (Judge Posner expressing skepticism about business justification for rule). Nonetheless, head-of-household fringe benefits have been upheld. See, e.g., Colby v. J.C. Penney Co., Inc. 926 F.2d 645 (7th Cir. 1991); EEOC v. J.C. Penney Co., Inc., 843 F.2d 249 (6th Cir. 1988).

What about the unchallenged practice in *Robert Hall* of using only sales*men* in its men's departments on the assumption that male customers would be uncomfortable trying on clothes in the presence of female sales personnel? Whether or not this is a violation of Title VII will be examined below. For present purposes, assume it is not. Assume also that men are not willing to work at the same low wages at which women are willing to work. Can the market "necessity" of paying men more to attract them to such jobs be justified under the "business reason" test or as a "factor other than sex"?

In 1998-1999, male coaches for Division I NCAA schools earned about twice what women's coaches earned. Welch Suggs, Uneven Progress for Women's Sports, Chron. Higher Educ., April 7, 2000, at A52, cited in Deborah Brake, The Struggle for Sex Equality in Sport and the Theory Behind Title IX, 34 U. Mich. J.L. Ref. 13, 80 (2001). Do you think that the kind of factors "other than sex" discussed above could justify this magnitude of differential?

Should differences in expected sports revenues justify differences in coach salaries, as Judge Posner suggests? According to Judge Posner, there is no problem as long as women are given access to the higher paid coaching jobs. If women have not been given equal access to the jobs, this is not only a violation of Title VII in itself, but it is relevant to the equal pay claim, in two ways: (1) it means the woman's sex is a reason for the difference in pay; and (2) it "casts doubt on the bona fides" of the district's explanations for the disparity in pay between male and female coaches. If women are not discriminated against in how these jobs are allocated, Judge Posner's view is that different revenue expectations may justify differences in the pay necessary to meet these expectations. What is to be made, then, of the fact that in college athletics, women hold only two percent of the coaching jobs in men's sports in all divisions? See Brake, supra, at 86 (citing unpublished 2000 study by Vivian Acosta and Linda Carpenter). In fact, women's share of coaching jobs for women's sports has *declined* in recent years. While prior to Title IX, women held over 90 percent of the jobs coaching female athletes, in 2000 women held only 45.6 percent of the head coaching jobs for women's intercollegiate women's teams, and this figure continues to decline. Id. at 85-86. Similarly, with respect to athletic administrative positions at the college and university level, only 17.4 percent of women's programs were headed by women in 2000, which represents a decrease from 19.4 percent in 1998. Women hold 34 percent of all intercollegiate athletic administrative positions, but of the 418 new jobs added at NCAA institutions since 1998, less than 11 percent went to women. Id.

In this context, one wonders whether rules designed to protect women's equal access to jobs are effective. And even if these rules are successful in preventing discrimination, does not reliance on revenues produced (or expected) reflect and perpetuate the gender bias of those from whom revenues are raised? Absolutely, according to the 1997 EEOC Enforcement Guidelines for interpreting Equal Pay Act claims brought by coaches. The new Guidelines insist on "equality in opportunity" and place greater burdens on defendant educational institutions in justifying pay disparities among opposite sex coaches. See Enforcement Guidance on Sex Discrimination in the Compensation for Sports Coaches in Educational Institutions, EEOC Notice No. 915.002, Empl. Prac. Guide (CCH) ¶ 5527 (Oct. 10, 1997), analyzed in Mel Narol & Joseph A. Martin, A New Defense to the Old Defenses? The EEOC Equal Pay Act Guidelines, 9 Marq. Sports L.J. 175 (1998). For example, prior to the Guidelines a defendant was able to defend a wage discrimination claim by establishing that jobs were not "significantly similar" through use of evidence of market-related forces. Now, the defendant must prove that the market-related forces are not themselves a result of discriminatory underpinnings. Under these Guidelines, in order to mount a revenue defense the institution must establish that the "revenue discrepancy in no way relates to: (1) institutional discrimination in opportunity, or (2) societal discrimination." In other words, under the Guidelines the revenue defense is not viable unless the school can show that (1) the female coach was provided the same opportunities as the male coach to become a revenue producer, and (2) the incongruity in revenue production is not related to lesser interest in female sports, lesser resources devoted to women's athletic programs, or historically discriminatory notions concerning women. The Guidelines also focus on traditional "factor other than sex" defenses, such as the "prior salary defense," the "marketplace defense," and the "additional duties," defense. In each case, the Guidelines make it more difficult for defendant institutions to escape liability by requiring that the "factor other than sex defense is not an element underlying the wage differential either expressly or by implication." Id. Other issues implicated by revenue-producing sports are raised in the discussion of Title IX, infra at pages 427-429.

Proposed legislation would take the EEOC's aggressive guidelines limiting the scope of affirmative defenses to the Equal Pay Act claims one step further, in an effort to eliminate job segregation on the basis of sex, race and national origin. The Fair Pay Act of 1999 (FPA) would eliminate the catchall, "factor other than sex" defense for all wage discrimination claims and eradicate wage differences based on seniority, merit, or quantity or quality wage systems. S. 702, 106th Cong. §3(a) (1999); H.R. 1271, 106th Cong. §3(a) (1999). In addition, the FPA would replace the "substantially equal work" standard of comparability with what the drafters intend to be a broader standard "equivalent work." Kimberly J. Houghton, The Equal Pay Act of 1963: Where Did We Go Wrong?, 15 The Labor Law. 155 (1999).

4. Equal Pay for Women Lawyers? Although some anecdotal evidence suggests that law firm interviewers are more concerned about the marital status and reproductive intentions of women than of men, women seem to fare about as well as men in the initial hiring process, and in initial salaries. Emily Campbell & Alan J. Tomkins, Gender, Race, Grades, and Law Review Membership as Factors in Law Firm Hiring Decision: An Empirical Study, 18 J. Contemp. L. 211, 241-242 (1992).

Soon, however, a gap develops that seems to widen over time. For example, a study of 1972-1975 graduates at the University of Michigan Law School found that although initial salaries of graduates were comparable, after fifteen years out of law school, men earned 40 percent more than women; this gap remained at 12.4 percent, after controlling for experience, family composition, and other factors. Robert G. Wood, et al., Pay

Differences Among the Highly Paid: The Male-Female Earnings Gap in Lawyers' Salaries, 11 J. Lab. Econ. 417 (1993). See also Kenneth G. Dau-Schmidt & Kavshik Mukhopadhaya, The Fruits of Our Labors: An Empirical Study of the Distribution of Income and Job Satisfaction Across the Legal Profession, 49 J. Legal Educ. 342, 349 (1999) (salaries of female Michigan law graduates from 1977-1981 graduating classes were 90.9 percent of their male counterparts five years out, and 73.9 percent of their male counterparts 15 years out). A study of Colorado lawyers similarly found that entry-level salaries for women in 1993 averaged $1,000 less than for men, and that the differences in pay persisted as the number of years of service increased, rising to an average of $12,000 at 10-20 years of experience. Cathleen Donnel, Joyce Sterling, and Nancy Richman, Gender Penalties: The Results of the Career and Compensation Study (Colorado Women's Bar Association, 1998). So too, a survey of 950 graduates from the law school classes of 1970, 1980, and 1985 of Harvard, the University of North Carolina at Chapel Hill, Brooklyn Law School, and the University of Missouri at Columbia showed an increasingly large gender wage gap over time, with neither the employment sector nor the specialty practiced significantly explaining the gap. Wynn R. Huang, Gender Differences in the Earnings of Lawyers, 30 Colum. J. L. & Soc. Probs. 267 (1997) (reporting gaps of 2 percent increasing to 35 percent after 17 years for the 1970 graduates, and 12 percent increasing to 28 percent after 7 years for 1980 graduates). Eighty percent of men, but only about 50 to 70 percent of women, achieved partnership within 10 years of graduation. Id. at 290. See also Virginia Valian, The Cognitive Basis of Gender Bias, 65 Brooklyn L. Rev. 1037, 1039 (1999) (despite rough equality in entry-level salaries, study of 500 corporate law departments found that income for male general counsel averaged $205,097, while females averaged $152,412).

The disparities in pay and promotion for lawyers of color are even greater. See Dau-Schmidt and Mukhopadhaya, supra, at 349 (Black Michigan law graduates earn 71.8 percent of their white counterparts 15 years out; Hispanics earn 67 percent of their non-Hispanic counterparts 15 years out).

Do these statistics show, necessarily, that discrimination exists? Some researchers attribute the gender disparity in earnings to women's different choices and the lower number of hours worked. See, e.g., Bernard F. Lentz & David N. Laband, Sex Discrimination in the Legal Profession 32 (1995). See also Kingsley R. Browne, Sex and Temperament in Modern Society: A Darwinian View of the Glass Ceiling and the Gender Gap, 37 Ariz. L. Rev. 971 (1995) (arguing that evolutionary factors lead women to make different career choices) (excerpt set forth on page 819 of this book). Others conclude that controlling for various personal characteristics such as education and experience, or employment context, such as sector, specialty, or firm size, consistently leave some portion of the disparity unexplained. Researchers also generally find significant differences in the returns to men and women for factors influencing income, like education and family status. For example, Huang found that in both small and large firms, men received large income premiums from attaining partnership while the impact of partnership on women's incomes was statistically insignificant. Huang, supra, at 302. Similarly, marriage is associated with a rise in income for men but a drop in income for women, and men receive higher income premiums from attending prestigious law schools. Id. at 304-05; see also Deborah J. Merritt et al., Family, Place, and Career: The Gender Paradox in Law School Hiring, 1993 Wis. L. Rev. 395, 397 (concluding that family ties and geographic constraints have negative impact for women law professors but not for white men in their job searches for tenure-track law school appointments).

Although part of the gender disparity in earning reflects women's over-representation in lower-earning specialties such as family law, public interest law, and government service, most research finds that occupational segregation is not the primary cause of the gender wage gap. Huang, supra, at 301, 308, 309; Donnel, Sterling and Richman, supra. Cf. Jo Dixon and Caroll Seron, Stratification in the Legal Profession: Sex, Sector, and Salary, 29 L. & Soc'y Rev. 381 (1995) (finding gender differences in returns to human and social capital but noting that disparities are less pronounced in government, which employs a greater percentage of women than the private sector and does not tie compensation to billable hours or business development).

Further discussion of factors affecting opportunities for women at high level jobs and the so-called glass ceiling appears on pages 181-212. Further analysis of human capital theories of the gender wage gaps begins on pages 309-315. The sociobiological explanation for the wage gap begins on page 819.

Putting Theory Into Practice

2-4. As head coach of the University of Southern California women's basketball team, Marianne Stanley led her team to four national women's basketball championships. In 1993, she sought a salary increase from $60,000 to $150,000, to match that paid to George Raveling, the head coach of the men's basketball team. At that time, she had brought her team to the previous three NCAA Tournaments where it advanced to the round of 16 in 1993 and the final eight in 1992. She was named PAC-10 Coach-of-the-Year in 1993. Raveling's team had never won a national championship and did not have as good an NCAA Tournament record.

Both head coaches recruited student athletes, coached basketball, provided academic guidance to team members and supervised their coaching staffs. Coach Raveling was under more pressure to increase the number of spectators in order to help alleviate the million-and-a-half dollar deficit in the athletic department. The pressure was created by the media, public and the school's administration and donors, which made the men's basketball team a potential source of funds, while the women's basketball team was not viewed as such. The average number of spectators for a men's basketball game was 4,103; for a women's game the average was 762. Stanley made herself available for public appearances but was not required to make any specific number of them, while Raveling's contract required participation in at least twelve outside speaking engagements per year and availability to the media for interviews.

While Stanley was head coach the USC women's basketball program produced just under $60,000 in revenue while, during the same period, the men's basketball program produced revenue of over $4.5 million. The revenue was derived from ticket sales, broadcast right fees, cable television right fees, PAC-10 conference revenue sharing, guarantees from away games, post season revenue sharing, and endowment income. Supporters donated close to $100,000 in gifts, as compared to under $13,000 in donations and endowment for the women's basketball team.

Stanley had 17 years of coaching experience, as compared to Raveling's 31 years coaching experience and nine years of marketing and promotional experience outside of coaching.

Does the Equal Pay Act require that USC pay Stanley as much as it pays Raveling? See Stanley v. Univ. of Southern California, 13 F.3d 1313 (9th Cir. 1994), aff'd 178 F.3d 1069 (9th Cir. 1999), cert. denied, 528 U.S. 1022 (1999) ("*Stanley II*") (no). Despite the EEOC's 1997 Enforcement Guidelines directing all equal-skill analyses to focus only on those abilities necessary to perform coaching-related duties, the *Stanley II* decision did not reveal how Raveling's worth as an author or media figure related to his coaching ability, nor did the court look at USC's history of resource allocation in areas like public relations. See Andrea M. Giampetro-Meyer, Recognizing and Remedying Individual and Institutional Gender-based Wage Discrimination In Sport, 37 Am. Bus. L.J. 343 (2000). See also Ira Berkow, NCAA Tournament: Sports of The Times; Auriemma Helps Pave The Way at UConn, N.Y. Times, April 2, 1995, sec. 8, p. 2 (male coach of national championship women's basketball team paid $80,000, compared with $150,000 for male coach of national championship men's basketball team).

Stanley has since become head women's basketball coach at the University of California at Berkeley, where she is paid a base salary comparable to that of the men's basketball coach. See Diane Heckman, On the Eve of Title IX's 25th Anniversary: Sex Discrimination in the Gym and Classroom, 21 Nova L. Rev. 545, 600 n. 321 (1997). Is this proof of discrimination, or of a well functioning market?

2. Title VII: Finding the Limits of Formal Equality

The linchpin of employment discrimination law is Title VII of the Civil Rights Act of 1964, §701 et seq., as amended, 42 U.S.C. §2000e et seq. (1994). The primary purpose of this legislation was to end employment discrimination based on race, and the customary story told is that sex was added by opponents of the bill hoping to defeat it. Note, Developments in the Law — Employment Discrimination and Title VII of the Civil Rights Act of 1964, 84 Harv. L. Rev. 1109, 1167 (1971). This story is refuted by Katherine M. Franke, who argues that the addition of sex to Title VII was the culmination of a "rich congressional legislative history concerning the equal rights of women." See Franke, The Central Mistake of Sex Discrimination Law: The Dissaggregation of Sex from Gender, 144 U. Pa. L. Rev. 1, 16 (1995).

Two theories of employment discrimination have emerged under Title VII. The *disparate treatment* theory addresses employment rules or decisions that treat an employee less favorably than others explicitly because of the employee's race, sex, religion, or national origin. To establish a prima facie case of disparate treatment based on sex, a woman must prove that (1) she was qualified for the position under dispute, or was performing her job at a level that rules out the possibility of firing for inadequate job performance; (2) she was not hired, or suffered some other adverse job action by the employer; and (3) someone with roughly equivalent qualifications was hired instead of her, or replaced her. See McDonnell Douglas Corp. v. Green, 411 U.S. 792, 802 (1973) (race discrimination); Texas Dep't of Community Affairs v. Burdine, 450 U.S. 248, 252-254 (1981) (sex discrimination). If the case is based on a charge of retaliatory action, she must prove (1) she engaged in a protected activity known to the employer; (2) thereafter she was subjected to an adverse employment decision by the employer; and (3) there was a causal link between the two. See Mattern v. Eastman Kodak Co., 104 F.3d 702, 705 (5th Cir. 1997), cert. denied, 522 U.S. 932 (1997). A prima facie case creates a rebuttable presumption that the employer's actions were discriminatory, shifting the burden of producing evidence to the employer to articulate some legitimate, non-discriminatory (or non-retaliatory) reason for the adverse action. The presumption does not shift the burden of persuasion, which remains on the plaintiff. Once rebutted, the presumption simply drops out of the case. The burden of production then shifts back to the plaintiff to show that the employer's explanation is pretextual by producing evidence from which a factfinder could reasonably disbelieve the employer's articulated legitimate reason, or believe that an invidious discriminatory reason was more likely than not a motivating or determinative cause of the employer's action. If the factfinder finds that the employer's explanation is pretextual, it may infer that discrimination occurred. It is not required to do so, however; the burden of persuasion on that issue remains with the plaintiff. See St. Mary's Honor Center v. Hicks, 509 U.S. 502, 511 (1993); Sheridan v. E.I. DuPont de Nemours & Co., 100 F.3d 1061, 1066 (3d Cir. 1996), cert. denied 521 U.S. 1129 (1997); Reeves v. Sanderson Plumbing Prods, Inc., 530 U.S. 133 (2000) (holding that factfinder is permitted, although not required, to infer discrimination from combination of prima facie case and proof that employer's articulated justification is pretextual).

Disparate treatment cases may be brought not only as an individual claim, but also as a "pattern and practice" claim of systematic disparate treatment against women. In a pattern and practice case, the plaintiff has the initial burden of demonstrating that unlawful discrimination has been the regular policy of the employer. A prima facie pattern and practice case shifts the burden to the employer to show that the employee's proof is inaccurate or insignificant, or to provide a nondiscriminatory explanation for the apparently discriminatory result. An often raised and fairly successful defense to pattern and practice claims backed up by statistical data demonstrating gross underhiring of females is that women have a "lack of interest" in the employment in question. See, e.g., EEOC v. Sears, Roebuck & Co., 628 F. Supp. 1264 (N.D. Ill. 1986), aff'd, 839 F.2d 302 (7th Cir. 1988). This case is further discussed in Chapter 3, pages 288-289.

If the plaintiff meets her burden of proving that the employer has discriminated against her based on her sex, the employer's only defense in a disparate treatment case is to prove that a sex-based requirement or restriction is a bona fide occupational qualification (BFOQ), which is reasonably necessary to the normal operation of its business. While a number of different tests for the BFOQ defense exist, basically the defense requires the employer to show that "the essence of the business operation would be undermined" by hiring employees without the qualification in question. See Diaz v. Pan American World Airways, Inc., 442 F.2d 385 (5th Cir.) (1971), cert. denied, 404 U.S. 950 (1971). See also UAW v. Johnson Controls, Inc., 499 U.S. 187 (1991), set forth on page 236, infra.

The second theory under Title VII is the *disparate impact* theory. Under this theory the plaintiff must show that a facially neutral job requirement or policy impacts disproportionately on women and that this requirement or policy is not related to job performance. See, e.g., Dothard v. Rawlinson, 433 U.S. 321 (1977), set forth on page 212. Unlike discriminatory impact cases brought under the United States Constitution, see *Feeney*, set forth on page 140, the plaintiff need not show discriminatory *intent*. Once disparate impact is shown, the burden shifts to the employer to either refute the elements of the plaintiff's case, or demonstrate that the facially neutral job requirement is justified by a business necessity. See Griggs v. Duke Power Co., 401 U.S. 424 (1971). The *Griggs* standard, though undermined by subsequent cases, was essentially reinstated by the Civil Rights Act of 1991, set forth in the Appendix.

In moving beyond explicitly sex-based discriminations to the effects of particular, facially neutral policies or practices, the disparate impact theory is a significant step beyond the disparate treatment theory, potentially reaching a large number of cases in which it is the consequences of rules and not their formal structure that is objectionable. To the extent the approach focuses on the results of a rule rather than its form, it more closely fits the model of substantive, rather than formal, equality. See Chapter 3.

Title VII has been a significant tool in helping women gain access to areas of employment previously closed to them. Title VII has eliminated explicit exclusions of women from employment (see, e.g., Laffey v. Northwest Airlines, Inc., 567 F.2d 429 (D.C. Cir. 1976), cert. denied, 434 U.S. 1086 (1978) (prohibiting exclusion of women applicants from positions as "pursers")); restrictions that imposed additional requirements on women that were not imposed on men (see, e.g., Phillips v. Martin Marietta Corp., 400 U.S. 542 (1971) (employer could not hire men with pre-school-age children and exclude women in the same category)); and job requirements assuming male qualifications that were not necessary for successful job performance (see, e.g., Dothard v. Rawlinson, 433 U.S. 321 (1977) (invalidating height and weight requirements not sufficiently correlated to job requirements of prison guards)). Title VII has had greater difficulty, even under disparate impact analysis, with rules that are based on women's actual differences from men. Such questions tend to divide into two separate phases of Title VII analysis: (1) the definitional question of whether the claimed discrimination constitutes "discrimination on the basis of sex"; and (2) the question whether, even if it is sex discrimination, the classification is nonetheless justified because of its relationship to legitimate business concerns of the employer. While these questions take different forms depending on their position in the proof process, in an important sense they amount to the same thing: in formal equality parlance, are women being treated differently from similarly situated men? Do the analyses provided in the cases that follow satisfactorily answer this question?

a. What Is Discrimination "Based on Sex"?

Craft v. Metromedia, Inc.

572 F. Supp. 868 (W.D. Mo. 1983), aff'd in part, rev'd in part, 766 F.2d 1205 (8th Cir. 1985), cert. denied, 475 U.S. 1058 (1986)

STEVENS, District Judge.

Plaintiff Christine Craft filed her four-count complaint against defendant Metromedia, Inc. on January 5, 1983. Count I alleges that defendant discriminated against plaintiff on the basis of sex in violation of Title VII of the Civil Rights Act of 1964. . . . [Separate counts for violations of the Equal

Pay Act, for fraudulent misrepresentations to induce plaintiff to accept employment, and for an action in tort were also filed but are omitted here.]
. . .

. . . Plaintiff Christine Craft was employed at KMBC [in Kansas City, Missouri] as a staff announcer and performed duties as a co-anchor and reporter from December, 1980, to August 14, 1981. At all times here relevant, R. Kent Replogle was vice president and general manager of KMBC and Ridge Shannon was news director. Replogle was the highest ranking station employee, and Shannon reported directly to him. . . .

[Craft was hired after the station determined it could "soften its image" by adding a female co-anchor for its news presentation.]. . .

Plaintiff began working at the station in late December, 1980. . . . She began as co-anchor on January 5, 1981 . . .

Soon after plaintiff began her duties as co-anchor, it became apparent to Shannon and Replogle that on several occasions plaintiff's on-air makeup and clothing were inappropriate. Shannon commented to plaintiff several times early in her employment that she should dress more conservatively and use makeup properly. He arranged for Lynn Wilford to come to Kansas City on January 14, 1981, to assist plaintiff in improving her appearance. During this visit, Wilford worked on plaintiff's wardrobe and makeup. In subsequent periodic visits to the station, Wilford continued these efforts, achieving only modest success.

During her initial months of employment, plaintiff had considerable discretion in the selection of her on-air clothing. Although Shannon made occasional suggestions or criticisms as to the appropriateness of certain pieces of clothing, neither he nor any other representative of defendant mandated that plaintiff observe any strict dress code during her first months at the station. Beginning in April, 1981, KMBC arranged for Macy's Department Store to provide clothing for plaintiff in exchange for advertising time. Maureen Shawver, a clothing consultant from Macy's, assisted plaintiff in making clothing selections. In addition, Wilford reviewed videotapes of plaintiff in various outfits. Plaintiff was not ordered to wear any of the clothes selected, and in fact she rejected several items suggested by Shawver.

On May 19 and 20, 1981, Steven Meacham of the Media Associates conducted four focus group discussions to learn how television viewers perceived KMBC's news program. A focus group is an accepted research technique whereby a small group of individuals with similar demographic characteristics meet to discuss a given subject, in this instance television news in Kansas City. A focus group does not produce scientifically reliable results because of the small statistical sample; however, it may suggest possible trends and areas for further research.

Meacham acted as moderator of the focus group discussions. Many topics were discussed, and the participants reviewed sample videotapes of local news programs. The response to plaintiff, and in particular to her appearance, was overwhelmingly negative. During the course of these discussions, and after the participants' attitude toward plaintiff had become apparent, Meacham on more than one occasion made derogatory remarks about plaintiff. Although his comments may have been indecorous and ill-advised, it is clear from listening to the tapes that they were made after the attitude of the group had been made very clear and they did not influence the opinions held by focus group participants.

Station management observed the focus groups from behind a one-way mirror. Shannon and Replogle met with plaintiff on May 21, 1981, to discuss the results and possible responses. Replogle advised plaintiff that there seemed to be some problems with her acceptance by the Kansas City viewing audience, but he indicated that management was ready to work with her to overcome those problems. Plaintiff eventually agreed to cooperate with defendant in that endeavor. Replogle stated that defendant would be instituting a clothing calendar for plaintiff. She agreed to follow the calendar when she received it. Thereafter, plaintiff's wardrobe was more closely supervised, but the clothing calendar was not formally instituted until late July or early August, a few weeks before plaintiff was removed as co-anchor.

As a follow-up to the focus groups, Media Associates conducted a telephone survey in late June, 1981, of the attitudes of four hundred randomly selected individuals residing in the greater Kansas City viewing area. All persons and organizations involved in the construction, administration, and analysis of the survey were experienced in market and broadcasting research. The survey measured the attitudes of Kansas City television viewers toward a wide range of selected aspects of television news in Kansas City . . . including plaintiff's dress and appearance. The questionnaire asked questions from both sides of the appearance and dress issues for plaintiff, in an attempt to see if persons surveyed perceived as strengths those qualities which the focus groups perceived as drawbacks. . . . The survey was conducted in accordance with generally accepted principles of survey research, and its results are trustworthy; moreover, defendant's reliance on those results was reasonable and appropriate. . . .

Shannon and Replogle received the final results of the June telephone survey on about August 3, 1981. The report concluded that plaintiff was having an extremely adverse impact on defendant's acceptance among Kansas City viewers. In the survey, plaintiff was compared to the female co-anchors at WDAF and KCMO and was found to be the least popular and least accepted of the three in almost every category. Comparisons were made primarily to Anne Peterson, who co-anchored at KMBC's primary competitor, KCMO. In virtually every comparison with Peterson, plaintiff trailed. On August 13, 1981, Shannon and Replogle met with consultants from Media Associates, who recommended that plaintiff be replaced immediately. Shannon and Replogle initially resisted the suggestion, but after discussing the matter in Replogle's office the next morning, Friday, August 14, they agreed to remove plaintiff as co-anchor and to reassign her to the position of

general assignment reporter at no loss in pay or other contractual benefits.
. . .

KMBC management was concerned about the appearance of all its on-air personnel, both male and female. Management expected grooming and dress to be consistent with community standards; on-air personnel understood the need to maintain a professional and business-like appearance. Whenever an appearance problem was detected, management responded with measures appropriate to the individual situation. Plaintiff received counseling in clothing and makeup, areas in which she acknowledged her lack of expertise.

Defendant also gave individualized attention to the appearance of male on-air personnel. The appearance of co-anchor Scott Feldman was generally satisfactory; however, on at least two occasions, he received specific directives regarding his choice of shirts. Shannon and Wilford told Mike Placke, the weekend weatherman, to lose weight and improve his wardrobe; he followed those suggestions. Wilford suggested that Bob Werley, a reporter, blow dry his hair, try contact lenses, and change his on-air makeup. Werley took the advice although he discovered that he could not wear contact lenses, so he changed his makeup to improve his appearance with glasses. Michael Mahoney, a reporter, was told that he needed to lose weight and improve his wardrobe; he did so. In addition, Mahoney occasionally experienced a nervous twitch in his mouth, which resembled a sneer. Management attempted to assist him in overcoming this problem. Shannon told Tim Richardson, a noon newscaster and reporter, to change his hairstyle; Richardson complied. . . .

Ratings, or measurements of the size of the viewing audience, are very important in the television industry because they have a direct effect on a station's advertising revenue. Two private companies, Arbitron and Nielsen, issue ratings several times a year. Ratings measure audience behavior by ascertaining the number of persons actually tuned to a given station. In contrast, audience research, such as that conducted by Media Associates, measures attitudes in an attempt to explain and forecast the ratings. Audience research enables station management to adjust its programming to increase, or at least to maintain, its share of the audience. . . .

. . . To the extent that plaintiff might argue that Title VII absolutely prohibits an employer from imposing reasonable but different standards of appearance for males and females, such a position must be rejected as contrary to the overwhelming weight of authority. Title VII "was never intended to interfere in the promulgation and enforcement of personal appearance regulations by private employers." Knott v. Missouri Pacific Railroad Co., 527 F.2d 1249, 1251-52 (8th Cir. 1975). . . .

The courts which have considered this issue have taken a realistic and commonsense approach. For instance, in Fagan v. National Cash Register Co., 481 F.2d 1115 (D.C. Cir. 1973), the court stated:

Perhaps no facet of business life is more important than a company's place in public estimation. That the image created by its employees dealing with the public when on company assignment affects its relations is so well known that we may take judicial notice of an employer's proper desire to achieve favorable acceptance. Good grooming regulations reflect a company's policy in our highly competitive business environment. Reasonable requirements in further-ance of that policy are an aspect of managerial responsibility.

Id. at 1124-25. Judge Collinson of this district has taken a similar approach:

Employment decisions . . . based on either dress codes or policies regarding hair length are more closely related to the company's choice of how to run its business rather than to its obligation to provide equal employment opportuni-ties. The decision to project a certain image as one aspect of company policy is the employer's prerogative which employees may accept or reject. If they choose to reject the policy, they are subject to such sanctions as deemed appropriate by the company. An employer is simply not required to account for personal preferences with respect to dress and grooming standards.

Lanigan v. Bartlett & Co. Grain, 466 F. Supp. 1388, 1392 (W.D. Mo. 1979). . . . Thus, defendant's standards of appearance for its on-air personnel can in no way be considered discriminatory per se. Both men and women were required to maintain a professional, business-like appearance consistent with community standards. Since television is a visual medium, as plaintiff admitted in her testimony, such a reasonable requirement is obviously critical to defendant's economic well-being.

Plaintiff's claim of sex discrimination is also based on defendant's standards of appearance as applied. She contends that defendant routinely and rigorously enforced dress and makeup requirements for women but not for men. This court recognizes that otherwise permissible appearance and grooming standards could be unlawful if invidiously applied. See *Knott*, 527 F.2d at 1252 (upholding validity of reasonable grooming and appearance standards when "imposed in an evenhanded manner on all employees"). Ultimately the issue is a matter of proof, and the evidence fails to sustain plaintiff's position. . . .

. . . Plaintiff was an employee of atypical aptitudes and attitudes, and defendant merely acted to correct appearance problems which plaintiff was unable or unwilling to remedy. The actions taken by defendant in regard to plaintiff's appearance were not the result of any general animus toward women or of any specific animus toward plaintiff as a woman. . . .

Plaintiff's second claim of sex discrimination concerns her removal as co-anchor. Insofar as this claim is based on the much-publicized litany — "too old, too unattractive, and not deferential enough to men" — allegedly uttered by Shannon on August 14, 1981, it is rejected since this court has concluded as a matter of fact that Shannon said no such thing. . . .

In summary, defendant's actions toward plaintiff during her employ-ment at KMBC were not based on her sex — with one notable and ironic exception: but for the fact that she is a female, plaintiff would not have been hired as a co-anchor in December, 1980, regardless of her other abilities. Thereafter, defendant's treatment of plaintiff was the result of the factors other than sex. . . . Her affinity for the casual beach life and her apparent indifference to matters of appearance required defendant to formulate and implement corrective measures appropriate to her unique circumstances. Defendant reassigned plaintiff because properly conducted audience research demonstrated unprecedented negative viewer response toward her. . . .

Notes

1. "Sex-Plus" Analysis. Employment criteria that impose "neutral requirements" on a sex-specific basis are often referred to as "sex-plus" requirements. The first sex-plus case decided by the United States Supreme Court was Phillips v. Martin Marietta, 400 U.S. 542 (1971). The *Phillips* Court held that an employment policy precluding women with pre-school-age children from certain jobs, but not men, violated Title VII. Workplace rules that impose sex-specific hair length, makeup, or dress codes are also examples of "sex plus" requirements, but they have uniformly upheld. Setting the stage was Willingham v. Macon Telegraph Pub. Co., 507 F.2d 1084 (5th Cir. 1975), in which the Fifth Circuit Court of Appeals held that employers may impose different hair length standards on male and female employees as long as "both sexes are being screened with respect to a neutral fact, i.e., grooming in accordance with generally accepted community standards of dress and appearance." 507 F.2d at 1092. Reasoning that the addition of "sex" to the categories of discrimination prohibited by Title VII appeared to have been an afterthought, the court concluded that "Congress in all probability did not intend for its proscription of sexual discrimination to have significant and sweeping implications," 507 F.2d at 1090, and, accordingly, narrowed the scope of Title VII to the limitation of opportunities based on "immutable characteristics": "[A] hiring policy that distinguishes on some other ground, such as grooming codes or length of hair, is related more closely to the employer's choice of how to run his business than to equality of employment opportunity." 507 F.2d at 1091.

The *Willingham* court distinguished *Phillips* by concluding that Congress' intent was to guarantee equal job opportunity for males and females, not the ability to dress or wear one's hair alike. 507 F.2d at 1091. It also noted that the decision whether to have children, implicated in *Phillips*, is a fundamental right, while the right to wear one's hair a certain length is not. See 507 F.2d at 1091. Is this a satisfactory distinction?

2. Discrimination Based on Appearance. Appearance matters. One study found that attractive attorneys earned more than their less attractive counterparts, and that the disparity increases over time. See Jeff E. Biddle &

Daniel S. Hamermesh, Beauty, Productivity and Discrimination: Lawyers' Looks and Lucre, 16 J. Lab. Econ. 172, 185-90 (1998). The wage differential between attractive and ugly people is about 10 percent for both sexes. Robert J. Barro, So You Want to Hire the Beautiful. Well, Why Not?, Bus. Week, Mar. 16, 1998, at 18.

Different aspects of appearance discrimination can pose different legal conundrums, explored in the notes below. But first, as a general matter, is a person's appearance something, like intelligence, that produces different opportunities that, as a society, we must simply accept? Or is it an unfair basis for discrimination that we should attempt to eliminate, as a matter of law? Does it matter that appearance standards are gendered, and may be harder on women than on men? Does it matter that research shows that beauty standards appear to be innate? See Nancy Etcoff, Survival of the Prettiest: The Science of Beauty 31-32 (1999) (describing study of babies who responded consistently to features based on faces rated for attractiveness by symmetry, balance and other standard measures).

3. Weight. Weight limits have been a common appearance requirement in some occupations. Notorious until recently were weight restrictions imposed on flight attendants. These weight restrictions were uniformly upheld in the courts, even though the standards for men took into account large frame sizes while the standards for women presupposed women of small or medium build. See, e.g., Jarrell v. Eastern Airlines, Inc., 430 F. Supp.884, 889 (E.D. Va. 1977), aff'd mem., 577 F.2d 869 (4th Cir. 1978); see also Delta v. New York State Division of Human Rights, 652 N.Y.S.2d 253, 259 (App. Div. 1996), aff'd, 689 N.E.2d 898 (N.Y. 1997) (employer, "particularly those whose business involves contact with the public[,] should be free to express and act upon a concern with the image which their employees communicate by their appearance and demeanor (citation omitted)"). However, in Frank v. United Airlines, Inc., 216 F.3d 845 (9th Cir. 2000), cert. denied, 121 S. Ct. 1247 (2001), the Ninth Circuit Court of Appeals seized upon the discrepancy in frame sizes as the grounds for holding weight standards for flight attendants to be facially discriminatory under a disparate treatment theory. The Court reasoned that United's weight policy was a violation of Title VII because the inconsistent frame categories imposed different "and more burdensome" weight standards on female employees without justifying those standards as a BFOQ. Id. at 845-55.

The court in *Jarrell* relied on the "fact" that the weight restrictions for women at issue in that case did not concern an "immutable characteristic":

Weight gain, unlike height, is a characteristic subject to the reasonable control of most individuals. . . . [T]here is nothing inherent in womanhood which makes Eastern's weight standards more difficult for women to satisfy than men. To be sure weight control is not as simple as cutting one's hair. Nonetheless,

. . . "discrimination based on factors of personal preference does not necessarily restrict employment opportunities and thus is not forbidden." [citation omitted].

430 F. Supp. at 892. This reasoning raises a number of issues. As a threshold matter, should the degree of control an individual can exercise over various job criteria be relevant to a Title VII analysis of "sex-plus" job requirements? Was it relevant in *Phillips*? For a comprehensive argument that the use of the immutability criterion to uphold employment requirements based on sex-based stereotypes violates the language and purpose of Title VII, see Peter Brandon Bayer, Mutable Characteristics and the Definition of Discrimination Under Title VII, 20 U.C. Davis L. Rev. 769 (1987). Further discussion of the immutability criterion in the context of constitutional analysis appears at pages 783-786 of Chapter 4.

Even if mutability should be relevant to Title VII analysis, how immutable should the characteristic have to be? There is some medical evidence that body weight is more or less fixed, either in childhood when the body produces the fat cells that the person carries for life (the "fat-cell theory"), or even earlier in the individual's genetic programming (the "set point theory"). For a nontechnical account, see Gina Kolata, Where Fat Is Problem, Heredity Is the Answer, Studies Find, N.Y. Times, May 24, 1990, at B9, col. 1. It is clear both that women's bodies require a higher proportion of body fat than men's, see T.M. Caro & D.W. Sellen, The Reproductive Advantages of Fat in Women, 11 Etiology and Sociobiology 51-66 (1990), and that as women age, their weight tends to increase at a more significant rate than men. Robert Pollack Seid, Never Too Thin: Why Women Are At War With Their Bodies 175 (1989).

Of what relevance to this issue is the problem of eating disorders for women? The research indicates that one out of every 200 to 250 women between the ages of 13 and 22 suffers from anorexia and that 12 to 33 percent of female college students struggle with induced vomiting, diuretics, and laxatives. See Susan Bordo, Unbearable Weight: Feminism, Western Culture, and the Body 140 (1993); Lynn S. Chancer, Reconcilable Differences: Confronting Beauty, Pornography, and the Future of Feminism 84-85 (1998). Ninety percent of anorectics are women, as are 80 percent of those who have their intestines partially removed to help control their weight. Id. Assume that this disparity arises from the social reality that women's physical appearance is more important, and more limiting, than men's. Is formal equality useful in challenging this reality? What are its limitations?

The cases have split on whether obesity is covered by the Americans with Disabilities Act. See Elizabeth M. Adamitis, Note, Appearance Matters: A Proposal to Prohibit Appearance Discrimination in Employment, 75 Wash. L. Rev. 195, 200-03 (2000). Some recent writing has argued that discrimination based on obesity should be prohibited. See,. e.g., Jane Byeff

Korn, Fat, 77 B.U.L. Rev. 25, 66-67 (1997) (arguing that discrimination based on obesity should be viewed as a form of discrimination based on disability, and often discrimination based on sex as well); Adamitis, supra (urging separate legislation prohibiting discrimination based on appearance). The state of Michigan, and the cities of Madison, Wisconsin, and Santa Cruz, California, specifically prohibit discrimination on the basis of weight. See Maureen J. Arrigo-Ward, No Trifling Matter: How the Legal System Supports Persecution of the Obese, 10 Wis. Women's L.J. 27, 35 (1995).

4. Dress and Grooming Standards. Do employee dress codes and appearance standards pose any different sex discrimination issues? At one end of the spectrum, some courts have shown considerable tolerance for dress code policies, reasoning, as the *Craft* court did, that such policies fall within the employer's prerogatives about how to run a business.

In analyzing dress codes and appearance standards, some courts have sought comparisons between how males and females are treated, finding violations of Title VII only where females appear to be held to stricter, or more demeaning, standards than men. See, e.g., Carrol v. Talman Fed. Sav. & Loan Ass'n, 604 F.2d 1028 (7th Cir. 1979), cert. denied, 445 U.S. 929 (1980) (dress code requiring men to wear "customary business attire" but women to wear uniforms demeaned professionalism of female employees and thus violated Title VII); O'Donnell v. Burlington Coat Factory, 656 F. Supp. 263 (S.D. Ohio 1987) (requirement that female sales clerks wear smocks and males wear business attire violates Title VII); Wislocki-Goin v. Mears, 831 F.2d 1374 (7th Cir. 1987), cert. denied, 485 U.S. 936 (1988) (upholding dress and grooming code violated by female employee, in the absence of evidence that similarly situated male employees were treated differently); Bellissimo v. Westinghouse Elec. Corp., 764 F.2d 175 (3d Cir. 1985), cert. denied, 475 U.S. 1035 (1986) (employer who told female attorney to "tone down" her attire did not violate Title VII where it also required male attorneys to dress conservatively).

When the dress standard for men is professional attire and women are asked to wear clothes that undermine their professionalism, there is a recognizable equality problem. But does the existence of harm depend on the way men are treated? See, e.g., EEOC v. Sage Realty Corp., 507 F. Supp. 599 (S.D.N.Y. 1981) (finding objectionable a requirement that women lobby attendants wear a very revealing and sexually provocative uniform, subjecting them to sexual harassment, not by making comparisons to the uniforms worn by male attendants but by the negative effect of the employment condition on women).

What about dress codes requiring women to wear high-heeled shoes? High-heeled shoes have been offered as the explanation for the fact that ninety percent of all forefoot surgery is performed on women, and that "seventy-five percent of the problems eventuating in the more than 600,000 bunionectomies, hammer toe repairs, neuroma excisions, and bunionette corrections performed annually in the United States 'either result from or are greatly aggravated by the use of high-fashion footwear.'" See Marc Linder, Smart Women, Stupid Shoes, and Cynical Employers: The Unlawfulness and Adverse Health Consequences of Sexually Discriminatory Workplace Footwear Requirements for Female Employees, J. Corp. L. 295, 296 (Winter 1997). Is the problem that women, and not men, are expected to wear clothing with this kind of impact, or is it that *no one* should be required to endure this kind of abuse?

In addition to the adverse health consequences, high heels have long been used as a symbol of idleness or, in Thorstein Veblen's words, of "the wearer's abstinence from productive employment." Id. at 329, citing Veblen, The Theory of the Leisure Class: An Economic Study of Institutions 121 (1899). Should the symbolic significance be enough, even without the health consequences, to prohibit employers from requiring women to wear high heels? To reach this result, the non-subordination principles examined in Chapter 4 would be very helpful. To see in more detail how these principles are applied, see Karl E. Klare, Power/Dressing: Regulation of Employee Appearance, 26 New Eng. L. Rev. 1395, 1417-1418 (1992) ("In using [phrases like *commonly accepted social norms* or *generally accepted community standards of dress and appearance*], the courts are of course referring to mainstream or conventional norms, which in our society are thoroughly sexist and patriarchal.").

Should all sex-specific dress and appearance codes be invalid? Most would agree that employers have a right to make reasonable business decisions about the tone they wish to set in their businesses, which dress and appearance codes may help them to achieve. The problem is not that employees face some constraints when they take a job, but that the constraints may be unfair in some unacceptable way. Under formal equality analysis, what is unacceptable has been determined largely through comparative analyses: women may be constrained by a certain set of community norms if men are also constrained by a parallel set of norms. Recognizing that the norms can themselves be discriminatory, non-subordination analysis stretches the inquiry a bit further: do the requirements, or the messages those requirements convey, disadvantage women in the workplace? For further elaboration of this line of analysis, see Katharine T. Bartlett, Only Girls Wear Barrettes: Dress and Appearance Standards, Community Norms, and Workplace Equality, 92 Mich. L. Rev. 2541 (1994).

Robert Post takes a more cautious view. Responding to the impulse that laws against discrimination based on appearance might "somehow [be] a *reductio ad absurdum* of the basic logic of American antidiscrimination law," Post offers a "sociological account" that attempts to describe how courts address appearance regulations less from some abstract determination of what is discriminatory and what is not, than from some practical sense of what social practices it is desirable for the law to help transform. See Post, Prejudicial Appearances: The Logic of American Antidiscrimination Law, 88

Cal. L. Rev. 1 (2000). This account adds a pragmatism to both formal equality analysis and to nonsubordination theory. Is it helpful?

Within the formal equality model, what should have been the focus of Christine Craft's case? What if it were shown in *Craft* that the critical audience surveys resulted from social stereotypes and prejudices that allowed a much narrower range of behavior and appearance for women than for men? For an excellent critique of use of viewer surveys on the grounds that they incorporate, and thus perpetuate, viewer prejudices and stereotypes, see Leslie S. Gielow, Note, Sex Discrimination in Newscasting, 84 Mich. L. Rev. 443 (1985). Further discussion of the role of customer preferences in establishing employer defenses for employment decisions that discriminate on the basis of sex follows the *Wilson* case, infra.

Christine Craft's complaint also included a count for fraud on the grounds that the station fraudulently represented to Craft that her appearance was fine and that it did not intend to make over or substantially change her appearance. The jury found in her favor, awarding her $375,000 in actual damages and $125,000 in punitive damages. The jury verdict was set aside by the judge on the grounds that it was "excessive and . . . the result of passion, prejudice, confusion, or mistake on the part of the jury." 572 F. Supp. at 881. On appeal, the court of appeals dismissed the fraud claim for failure to establish the station's intent to defraud her. Craft v. Metromedia, Inc., 766 F.2d 1205, 1218-1219 (8th Cir. 1985). For the whole story, from Craft's point of view, see Craft, Too Old, Too Ugly, and Not Deferential to Men (1988).

5. Age and Appearance. Just as weight standards become more burdensome as women age, see note 3, supra, so do the kinds of factors found deficient in Christine Craft. Sex and age can be a devastating combination. One survey, while perhaps now dated, showed that of 1,200 local news anchors around the country, 48 percent of the men were over forty years old and 16 percent were over fifty; only 3 percent of the women were over forty and none were over fifty. See Sally Bedell Smith, Television Newswoman's Suit Stirs a Debate on Values in Hiring, N.Y. Times, Aug. 6, 1983, at 44, col. 1. Should age be treated as an "immutable characteristic"? See Patti Buchman, Note, Title VII Limits on Discrimination Against Television Anchorwomen on the Basis of Age-Related Appearance, 85 Colum. L. Rev. 190, 190 (1985) (age-related appearance is analogous to the "immutable characteristics" of race and physical stature).

The sex-plus framework may have more promise. Many have argued that being an "older woman" renders one susceptible to a unique brand of mixed discrimination, whereby the effects of sex and age are masked by the combination of the two. A detailed study of 335 claims on behalf of older women under Title VII (sex) and the Age Discrimination in Employment Act (ADEA), 29 U.S.C. §621 (1994), brought between 1975 and 1995 revealed the difficulty faced by these litigants as their claims often fall between the cracks of the two statutes. See Women's Legal Defense Fund & A.A.R.P., Employment Discrimination Against Midlife and Older Women (A.A.R.P. 1996). Problems arise because the majority of courts treat sex and age discrimination claims as completely distinct from one another and thus analyze each individually under the relevant statue. Id. at 15. This means that if any other woman was hired or treated favorably, regardless of age, then the sex discrimination fails. Likewise, if any other older person was hired or treated favorably, regardless of sex, the age discrimination claim fails. As a result, any *combined* effect of sex and age is ignored. Less than 10 percent of the courts in the study recognized "older women" as a subclass of women protected under Title VII. Id. For the argument that older women should be treated as a subset of a protected class and receive the protection of sex-plus analysis under Title VII, see Sabina Crocette, Comment, Considering Hybrid Sex and Age Discrimination Claims by Women: Examining Approaches to Pleading and Analysis — A Pragmatic Approach, 28 Golden Gate U.L. Rev. 115 (1998).

Even if appearance-based discrimination constitutes discrimination based on sex, an employer may argue that the discrimination is justified by business considerations. Section b, below, beginning on page 212, discusses standards an employer must meet to show that a sex-related job requirement is justified as a "bona fide occupational qualification" (BFOQ) or a business necessity.

Putting Theory into Practice

2-5. A state court judge requires his male law clerks to wear neckties. He imposes no such requirement on his female law clerks. Applying Title VII principles, does this requirement violate the anti-discrimination principle? Is there anything else you need to know?

2-6. Pussycat Lounge is a bar that hires waitresses whom it deems to be physically attractive and sexually alluring in order to attract male customers willing to pay a handsome cover charge and buy drinks in search of relaxation in a sexually charged setting. Waitresses take orders for and serve drinks. Pussycat does not hire male waiters (although it hires both male and female bartenders). Among other physical requirements for the waitress positions, women must weigh less than 115 pounds and have large breasts ("C" cup size or larger). Do either of these physical requirements violate Title VII?

Is it relevant to the legality of the breast-size requirement that through surgical breast implants women can change their breasts to whatever size they want? Twenty-five percent of those receiving breast implants reportedly suffer sufficient complications to warrant reoperation within five years. These complications are said to include hardening or deformation of the breasts, chronic pain, necrosis (tissue death), and rupture of the implants causing migration of the silicone gel elsewhere in the body. Thomas M. Burton, Breast-Implant Reoperation Rate Is Put at 25%, Wall St. J., March 6, 1997, at B6. For further discussion of the health risks of silicone breast implants, see Chapter 6, pages 1048-1050.

2-7. The Houston Bar Association has issued a dress code which requires women to wear skirts to work. Association president Amy Taylor, a trial lawyer, reportedly endorses the skirts-only policy: "There are people in our bar who would be very offended by seeing women in slacks. . . . Frankly, we try to err on the side of being more conservative and hopefully not offending too many people." Twenty-seven percent of the Houston Bar Association is female. Tim Fleck, The Bar: Still Skirting the Past, www.houstonpress.com, News & Features, May 10, 2001. Is there an equality issue here?

2-8. Members of the City Council of the City of Santa Cruz, California wish to ban discrimination based against persons based on their personal appearance. Help them draft the ordinance.

For a discussion of the Santa Cruz ordinance, see Robert Post, Prejudicial Appearances: The Logic of American Antidiscrimination Law, 88 Cal. L. Rev. 1, 2-8, 40 (2000).

2-9. Plaintiff engineer wore feminine attire to work as part of a standard treatment in preparation for gender-reassignment surgery, which involves living full-time in the social role of the opposite sex for at least 12 months prior to surgery. After numerous warnings, he was fired one day when he wore a strand of pink pearls to work. Is this sex discrimination? Cf. Doe v. Boeing Co., 846 P.2d 531 (Wash. 1993) (gender dysphoria is not a handicap under a state statute banning discrimination against the handicapped).

2-10. Continental Airlines requires all women flight attendants (and no men) to wear make-up. The American Civil Liberties Union threatens suit. Is the suit likely to succeed under Title VII?

Price Waterhouse v. Hopkins
490 U.S. 228 (1989)

Justice BRENNAN announced the judgment of the Court and delivered an opinion, in which Justice MARSHALL, Justice BLACKMUN, and Justice STEVENS join.

Ann Hopkins was a senior manager in an office of Price Waterhouse when she was proposed for partnership in 1982. She was neither offered nor denied admission to the partnership; instead, her candidacy was held for reconsideration the following year. When the partners in her office later refused to repropose her for partnership, she sued Price Waterhouse under Title VII . . . charging that the firm had discriminated against her on the basis of sex in its decisions regarding partnership. Judge Gesell in the Federal District Court for the District of Columbia ruled in her favor on the question of liability . . . and the Court of Appeals for the District of Columbia Circuit affirmed. . . . We granted certiorari to resolve a conflict among the Courts of Appeals concerning the respective burdens of proof of a defendant and plaintiff in a suit under Title VII when it has been shown that an employment decision resulted from a mixture of legitimate and illegitimate motives. . . .

Ann Hopkins had worked at Price Waterhouse's Office of Government Services in Washington, D.C., for five years when the partners in that office proposed her as a candidate for partnership. Of the 662 partners at the firm at that time, 7 were women. Of the 88 persons proposed for partnership that year, only 1 — Hopkins — was a woman. Forty-seven of these candidates were admitted to the partnership, 21 were rejected, and 20 — including Hopkins — were "held" for reconsideration the following year. Thirteen of the 32 partners who had submitted comments on Hopkins supported her bid for partnership. Three partners recommended that her candidacy be placed on hold, eight stated that they did not have an informed opinion about her, and eight recommended that she be denied partnership.

In a jointly prepared statement supporting her candidacy, the partners in Hopkins' office showcased her successful 2-year effort to secure a $25 million contract with the Department of State, labeling it "an outstanding performance" and one that Hopkins carried out "virtually at the partner level." Despite Price Waterhouse's attempt at trial to minimize her contribution to this project, Judge Gesell specifically found that Hopkins had "played a key role in Price Waterhouse's successful effort to win a multi-million dollar contract with the Department of State." Indeed, he went on, "[n]one of the other partnership candidates at Price Waterhouse that year had a comparable record in terms of successfully securing major contracts for the partnership."

The partners in Hopkins' office praised her character as well as her accomplishments, describing her in their joint statement as "an outstanding professional" who had a "deft touch," a "strong character, independence and integrity." Clients appear to have agreed with these assessments. At trial, one official from the State Department described her as "extremely competent, intelligent," "strong and forthright, very productive, energetic and creative." Another high-ranking official praised Hopkins' decisiveness, broadmindedness, and "intellectual clarity"; she was, in his words, "a stimulating conversationalist." Evaluations such as these led Judge Gesell to conclude that Hopkins "had no difficulty dealing with clients and her clients appear to have been very pleased with her work" and that she "was generally viewed as a highly competent project leader who worked long hours, pushed vigorously to meet deadlines and demanded much from the multidisciplinary staffs with which she worked."

On too many occasions, however, Hopkins' aggressiveness apparently spilled over into abrasiveness. Staff members seem to have borne the brunt of Hopkins' brusqueness. Long before her bid for partnership, partners evaluating her work had counseled her to improve her relations with staff members. Although later evaluations indicate an improvement, Hopkins' perceived shortcomings in this important area eventually doomed her bid for partnership. Virtually all of the partners' negative remarks about Hopkins — even those of partners supporting her — had to do with her "interpersonal skills." Both "[s]upporters and opponents of her candidacy," stressed Judge Gesell, "indicated that she was sometimes overly aggressive, unduly harsh, difficult to work with and impatient with staff."

There were clear signs, though, that some of the partners reacted negatively to Hopkins' personality because she was a woman. One partner described her as "macho"; another suggested that she "overcompensated for being a woman"; a third advised her to take "a course at charm school." Several partners criticized her use of profanity; in response, one partner suggested that those partners objected to her swearing only "because it's a lady using foul language." Another supporter explained that Hopkins "ha[d] matured from a tough-talking somewhat masculine hard-nosed mgr to an authoritative, formidable, but much more appealing lady ptr candidate." But it was the man who, as Judge Gesell found, bore responsibility for explaining to Hopkins the reasons for the Policy Board's decision to place her candidacy on hold who delivered the coup de grace: in order to improve her chances for partnership, Thomas Beyer advised, Hopkins should "walk more femininely, talk more femininely, dress more femininely, wear make-up, have her hair styled, and wear jewelry."

Dr. Susan Fiske, a social psychologist and Associate Professor of Psychology at Carnegie-Mellon University, testified at trial that the partnership selection process at Price Waterhouse was likely influenced by sex stereotyping. Her testimony focused not only on the overtly sex-based comments of partners but also on gender-neutral remarks, made by partners who knew Hopkins only slightly, that were intensely critical of her. One partner, for example, baldly stated that Hopkins was "universally disliked" by staff, and another described her as "consistently annoying and irritating"; yet these were people who had had very little contact with Hopkins. According to Fiske, Hopkins' uniqueness (as the only woman in the pool of candidates) and the subjectivity of the evaluations made it likely that sharply critical remarks such as these were the product of sex stereotyping — although Fiske admitted that she could not say with certainty whether any particular comment was the result of stereotyping. Fiske based her opinion on a review of the submitted comments, explaining that it was commonly accepted practice for social psychologists to reach this kind of conclusion without having met any of the people involved in the decisionmaking process.

In previous years, other female candidates for partnership also had been evaluated in sex-based terms. As a general matter, Judge Gesell concluded, "[c]andidates were viewed favorably if partners believed they maintained their femin[in]ity while becoming effective professional managers"; in this environment, "[t]o be identified as a 'women's lib[b]er' was regarded as [a] negative comment." In fact, the judge found that in previous years "[o]ne partner repeatedly commented that he could not consider any woman seriously as a partnership candidate and believed that women were not even capable of functioning as senior managers — yet the firm took no action to discourage his comments and recorded his vote in the overall summary of the evaluations."

Judge Gesell found that Price Waterhouse legitimately emphasized interpersonal skills in its partnership decisions, and also found that the firm had not fabricated its complaints about Hopkins' interpersonal skills as a pretext for discrimination. Moreover, he concluded, the firm did not give decisive emphasis to such traits only because Hopkins was a woman; although there were male candidates who lacked these skills but who were admitted to partnership, the judge found that these candidates possessed other, positive traits that Hopkins lacked.

The judge went on to decide, however, that some of the partners' remarks about Hopkins stemmed from an impermissibly cabined view of the proper behavior of women, and that Price Waterhouse had done nothing to disavow reliance on such comments. He held that Price Waterhouse had unlawfully discriminated against Hopkins on the basis of sex by consciously giving credence and effect to partners' comments that resulted from sex stereotyping. Noting that Price Waterhouse could avoid equitable relief by proving by clear and convincing evidence that it would have placed Hopkins' candidacy on hold even absent this discrimination, the judge decided that the firm had not carried this heavy burden.

The Court of Appeals affirmed the District Court's ultimate conclusion, but departed from its analysis in one particular: it held that even if a plaintiff proves that discrimination played a role in an employment decision, the defendant will not be found liable if it proves, by clear and convincing evidence, that it would have made the same decision in the absence of discrimination. Under this approach, an employer is not deemed to have violated Title VII if it proves that it would have made the same decision in the absence of an impermissible motive, whereas under the District Court's approach, the employer's proof in that respect only avoids equitable relief. We decide today that the Court of Appeals had the better approach, but that both courts erred in requiring the employer to make its proof by clear and convincing evidence. . . .

[The separate concurring opinions of Justice O'Connor and Justice White are omitted.]

Justice KENNEDY, with whom THE CHIEF JUSTICE and Justice SCALIA join, dissenting. . . .

The ultimate question in every individual disparate-treatment case is whether discrimination caused the particular decision at issue. Some of the plurality's comments with respect to the District Court's findings in this case, however, are potentially misleading. As the plurality notes, the District Court based its liability determination on expert evidence that some evaluations of respondent Hopkins were based on unconscious sex stereo-types,[5] and on the fact that Price Waterhouse failed to disclaim reliance on these comments when it conducted the partnership review. The District Court also based liability on Price Waterhouse's failure to "make partners sensitive to the dangers [of stereotyping], to discourage comments tainted by sexism, or to investigate comments to determine whether they were influenced by stereotypes."

Although the District Court's version of Title VII liability is improper under any of today's opinions, I think it important to stress that Title VII creates no independent cause of action for sex stereotyping. Evidence of use by decisionmakers of sex stereotypes is, of course, quite relevant to the question of discriminatory intent. The ultimate question, however, is whether discrimination caused the plaintiff's harm. Our cases do not support the suggestion that failure to "disclaim reliance" on stereotypical comments itself violates Title VII. Neither do they support creation of a "duty to sensitize." As the dissenting judge in the Court of Appeals observed, acceptance of such theories would turn Title VII "from a prohibition of discriminatory conduct into an engine for rooting out sexist thoughts." [825 F.2d 458, 477 (1987) (Williams, J., dissenting).]

Employment discrimination claims require factfinders to make difficult and sensitive decisions. Sometimes this may mean that no finding of discrimination is justified even though a qualified employee is passed over by a less than admirable employer. In other cases, Title VII's protections properly extend to plaintiffs who are by no means model employees. As

---

5. The plaintiff who engages the services of Dr. Susan Fiske should have no trouble showing that sex discrimination played a part in any decision. Price Waterhouse chose not to object to Fiske's testimony, and at this late stage we are constrained to accept it, but I think the plurality's enthusiasm for Fiske's conclusions unwarranted. Fiske purported to discern stereotyping in comments that were gender neutral — e.g., "overbearing and abrasive" — without any knowledge of the comments' basis in reality and without having met the speaker or subject. "To an expert of Dr. Fiske's qualifications, it seems plain that no woman could be overbearing, arrogant, or abrasive: any observations to that effect would necessarily be discounted as the product of stereotyping. If analysis like this is to prevail in federal courts, no employer can base any adverse action as to a woman on such attributes." [825 F.2d 458, 477 (D.C. Cir. 1987)] (Williams, J., dissenting). Today's opinions cannot be read as requiring factfinders to credit testimony based on this type of analysis. . . .

Justice Brennan notes, courts do not sit to determine whether litigants are nice. . . .

The language of Title VII and our well-considered precedents require this plaintiff to establish that the decision to place her candidacy on hold was made "because of" sex. Here the District Court found that the "comments of the individual partners and the expert evidence of Dr. Fiske do not prove an intentional discriminatory motive or purpose," and that "[b]ecause plaintiff has considerable problems dealing with staff and peers, the Court cannot say that she would have been elected to partnership if the Policy Board's decision had not been tainted by sexually based evaluations." Hopkins thus failed to meet the requisite standard of proof after a full trial. I would remand the case for entry of judgment in favor of Price Waterhouse.

≣ *Ezold v. Wolf, Block, Schorr & Solis-Cohen*
983 F.2d 509 (3d Cir. 1992), cert. denied, 510 U.S. 826 (1993)

HUTCHINSON, Circuit Judge.

Wolf, Block, Schorr and Solis-Cohen (Wolf) appeals from a judgment of the United States District Court for the Eastern District of Pennsylvania granting relief in favor of Nancy O'Mara Ezold (Ezold) on her claim that Wolf intentionally discriminated against her on the basis of her sex in violation of Title VII . . . when it decided not to admit her to the firm's partnership effective February 1, 1989. . . .

I

Ezold sued Wolf under Title VII alleging that Wolf intentionally discriminated against her because of her sex when it decided not to admit her to the firm's partnership. . . .

The district court held that the nondiscriminatory reason articulated by Wolf for its rejection of Ezold's candidacy — that her legal analytical ability failed to meet the firm's partnership standard — was a pretext. . . .

. . . The court . . . awarded Ezold back pay in the amount of $131,784.00 for the period from her resignation on June 7, 1989 to January 31, 1991. The parties agreed that if the court's November 27, 1990 and March 15, 1991 orders were affirmed on appeal, Ezold would be instated as a partner. . . .

II

Ezold was hired by Wolf as an associate on a partnership track in July 1983. She had graduated in the top third of her class from the Villanova University School of Law in 1980 and then worked at two small law firms in Philadelphia. . . .

Ezold was hired at Wolf by Seymour Kurland, then chairman of the litigation department. The district court found that Kurland told Ezold during an interview that it would not be easy for her at Wolf because "she was a woman, had not attended an Ivy League law school, and had not been on law review." . . .

Ezold was assigned to the firm's litigation department. From 1983-87, Kurland was responsible for the assignment of work to associates in the department. He often delegated this responsibility to partner Steven Arbittier. . . . The district court found that Arbittier assigned Ezold to actions that were "small" by Wolf standards. . . .

Senior associates within two years of partnership consideration are evaluated annually; non-senior associates are evaluated semi-annually. The firm's partners are asked to submit written evaluations on standardized forms. . . . Ten criteria of legal performance are listed on the forms in the following order: legal analysis, legal writing and drafting, research skills, formal speech, informal speech, judgment, creativity, negotiating and advocacy, promptness and efficiency. Ten personal characteristics are also listed: reliability, taking and managing responsibility, flexibility, growth potential, attitude, client relationship, client servicing and development, ability under pressure, ability to work independently, and dedication. As stated by Ian Strogatz, Chairman of the Associates Committee: "The normal standards for partnership include as factors for consideration all of the ones . . . that are contained [on] our evaluation forms." . . .

[A lengthy discussion of the firm's evaluation procedures is omitted.]

The firm's partners evaluated Ezold twice a year as an associate and once a year as a senior associate from October 1983 until the Associates Committee determined that it would not recommend her for partnership in September 1988. The district court found that "in the period up to and including 1988, Ms. Ezold received strongly positive evaluations from almost all of the partners for whom she had done any substantial work." . . . Ezold's overall score in legal skills in the 1988 bottom line memorandum before the Associates Committee was a "G" for good [the second highest rating on a 5-part scale ranging from exceptional to unacceptable]. . . .

Evaluations in Ezold's file not mentioned by the district court show that concerns over Ezold's legal analytical ability arose early during her tenure at the firm. In an evaluation covering the period from November 1984 through April 1985, Arbittier wrote:

> I have discussed legal issues with Nancy in connection with [two cases]. I found her analysis to be rather superficial and unfocused. I am beginning to doubt that she has sufficient legal analytical ability to make it with the firm. . . . She makes a good impression with people, has common sense, and can handle routine matters well. However these traits will take you just so far in our firm. I think that due to the nature of our practice Nancy's future here is limited. . . .

That same year Schwartz wrote:

> I have worked a great deal with Nancy since my last evaluation. . . . Both cases are complex, multifaceted matters that have presented novel issues to us. While her enthusiasm never wanes and she keeps plugging away — I'm often left with a product that demonstrates uncertainty in the analysis of a problem. After extensive discussions with me, the analysis becomes a little more focused, although sometimes I get the sense that Nancy feels adrift and is just marching as best she can to my analytical tune. . . . In my view her energy, enthusiasm and fearlessness make her a valuable asset to us. While she may not be as bright as some of our best associates, her talents will continue to serve us well.

. . . Also in 1985, partner Donald Joseph rated Ezold's legal analytical ability as marginal and wrote "its [sic] too early to tell but I have been disappointed on her grasp of the problem, let alone performance." . . .

During her next evaluation period from April through November 1985, Ezold received similar negative evaluations. Arbittier, Robert Fiebach and Joseph rated her legal analytical abilities as marginal. Arbittier wrote:

> She took a long time getting [a summary judgment brief] done and I found it to be stilted and unimaginative. One of the main issues — dealing with the issue of notice — she missed completely and did not grasp our position. . . . Also, in considering whether to file a defensive motion . . . she failed to cite me to a clause in the agreement that was highly relevant leaving me with the impression that the motion could not succeed. I think Nancy tries hard and can handle relatively straight-forward matters with a degree of maturity and judgment, but when she gets into more complicated areas she lacks real analytical skill and just does what she is told in a mechanical way. She is not up to our minimal Wolf, Block standards. . . .

Boote made the following report on his performance review with Ezold after this evaluation period:

> Nancy appeared to accept the judgment, albeit a little grudgingly, that her analytical, research and writing ability was not up to our standards and that she should focus on the types of matters that she can handle effectively. . . . We made it very clear to Nancy that if she pursues general civil litigation work she is not on track toward partnership and that her only realistic chance for partnership in our opinion is to develop a good reputation for herself in one of the specialized areas of practice. . . .

In the evaluation period covering November 1985 to April 1986, Boote wrote the following to the Associates Committee:

> Nancy continues to get mixed reviews. Her pluses are that she is mature, courageous, pretty good on her feet and has the capacity to inspire confidence in clients. Her minuses are that there is doubt about her analytic and writing ability. . . . In considering Nancy's prospects for the long range, I think we should bear in mind that we have made mistakes in the past in letting people

go to other firms who really could have filled a valuable niche here. Whether Nancy is such a person, of course, remains to be seen. . . .

A summary of Ezold's performance review from October 1986 prepared by Schwartz stated:

Nancy was advised that several of the lawyers feel she has made very positive progress as a lawyer, Sy [Kurland] being one of them. However, he told her that other lawyers had strong negative sentiments about her capabilities and they feel she has a number of shortcomings in the way of complicated analysis of legal problems and in being able to handle the big complicated corporate litigation, and therefore, does not meet the standard for partnership at Wolf, Block. . . . Both Sy and I urged Nancy to seriously consider looking for employment elsewhere as she may not be able to turn the tide. . . .

Although several partners saw improvement in Ezold's work, negative comments about her analytical ability continued up until, and through, her 1988 senior associate evaluation, the year she was considered for partnership. . . .

. . . [In the 1988 review,] the Associates Committee voted 9-1 not to recommend Ezold for Category VI partnership.

. . . It did vote, however, to recommend her for the status of "Group VII" special partner that the firm had heretofore made available to associates who are valuable but fall below the firm's high standards for full partnership. The continuing existence of that category was, however, then under review by the firm's Executive Committee. It was in fact later eliminated.

Out of a total of eight candidates in Ezold's class, five male associates and one female associate were recommended for regular partnership. One male associate, Associate X, was not recommended for either regular or special partnership. . . .

. . . Ezold resigned from the firm on June 7, 1989. . . .

IV

Ezold claims Wolf intentionally discriminated against her because of her sex. Intentional discrimination in employment cases falls within one of two categories: "pretext" cases and "mixed-motives" cases. See Price Waterhouse v. Hopkins, 490 U.S. 228, 247 n.12 (1989) (plurality). . . .

[Ezold litigated this case as a pretext case, which is governed by] McDonnell Douglas Corp. v. Green, 411 U.S. 792, 802 (1973) and Texas Dep't of Community Affairs v. Burdine, 450 U.S. 248, 252-56 (1981). . . . The plaintiff must first establish by a preponderance of the evidence a prima facie case of discrimination. *Burdine*, 450 U.S. at 252. . . . The plaintiff can establish a prima facie case by showing that she is a member of a protected class; that she was qualified for and rejected for the position; and that non-members of the protected class were treated more favorably. . . . After the plaintiff has established a prima facie case, the burden shifts to the defendant to produce evidence of a legitimate, nondiscriminatory reason for the employee's rejection. *Burdine*, 450 U.S. at 252. . . . If the defendant's evidence creates a genuine issue of fact, the presumption of discrimination drops from the case. *Burdine*, 450 U.S. at 254-55. . . . Then, the plaintiff, since she retains the ultimate burden of persuasion, must prove, by a preponderance of the evidence, that the defendant's proffered reasons were a pretext for discrimination. *Burdine*, 450 U.S. at 257. . . .

The parties do not dispute the district court's conclusion of law that Ezold demonstrated a prima facie case, in particular that she was "qualified" for admission to the partnership. . . . In Title VII cases involving a dispute over "subjective" qualifications, we have recognized that the qualification issue should often be resolved in the second and third stages of the *McDonnell Douglas/Burdine* analysis, to avoid putting too onerous a burden on the plaintiff in establishing a prima facie case. . . . We agree with the district court's conclusion that favorable evaluations from partners with whom Ezold worked, and a score of "G" on her 1988 bottom line memo, demonstrate that she was qualified for partnership consideration. . . .

The defendant may rebut the presumption of discrimination arising out of the plaintiff's prima facie case by producing evidence that there was a "legitimate, nondiscriminatory reason" why the plaintiff was rejected. *Burdine*, 450 U.S. at 254; *McDonnell Douglas*, 411 U.S. at 802. . . .

The burden then shifts to the plaintiff to show that the defendant's articulated reasons are pretextual. Id. at 256. This burden merges into the plaintiff's ultimate burden of persuading the court that she has been the victim of intentional discrimination. Id. The plaintiff must demonstrate "by competent evidence that the presumptively valid reason[] for [the alleged unlawful employment action was] in fact a coverup for a . . . discriminatory decision." *McDonnell Douglas*, 411 U.S. at 805. Explicit evidence of discrimination — i.e., the "smoking gun" — is not required. . . . A plaintiff can establish pretext in one of two ways: "either directly by persuading the court that a discriminatory reason more likely motivated the employer or indirectly by showing that the employer's proffered reason is unworthy of credence." *Burdine*, 480 U.S. at 256.

In proving that the employer's motive was more likely than not the product of a discriminatory reason instead of the articulated legitimate reason, sufficiently strong evidence of an employer's past treatment of the plaintiff may suffice. . . . The employer's "general policy and practice with respect to minority employment" may also be relevant. . . . Alternately, if a plaintiff produces credible evidence that it is more likely than not that "the employer did not act for its proffered reason, then the employer's decision remains unexplained and the inferences from the evidence produced by the plaintiff may be sufficient to prove the ultimate fact of discriminatory intent.". . .

Wolf's articulated nondiscriminatory reason for denying Ezold's admission to the partnership was that she did not possess sufficient legal analytical skills to handle the responsibilities of partner in the firm's complex litigation practice. Ezold attempted to prove that Wolf's proffered explanation was "unworthy of credence" by showing she was at least equal to, if not more qualified than, similarly situated males promoted to partnership. She also contended that her past treatment at the firm showed Wolf's decision was based on a discriminatory motive rather than the legitimate reason of deficiency in legal analytical ability that the firm had articulated.

V

. . . The district court compared Ezold to eight successful male partnership candidates. . . . It found:

> The test that was put to the plaintiff by the Associates Committee that she have outstanding academic credentials and that before she could be admitted to the most junior of partnerships, she must demonstrate that she had the analytical ability to handle the most complex litigation was not the test required of male associates. . . .

The district court then concluded:

> Ms. Ezold has established that the defendant's purported reasons for its conduct are pretextual. The defendant promoted to partnership men having evaluations substantially the same or inferior to the plaintiff's, and indeed promoted male associates who the defendant claimed had precisely the lack of analytical or writing ability upon which Wolf, Block purportedly based its decision concerning the plaintiff. The defendant is not entitled to apply its standards in a more "severe" fashion to female associates. . . . Such differential treatment establishes that the defendant's reasons were a pretext for discrimination. . . .

Wolf says this finding of pretext is wrong. Analyzing its contentions, we perceive two reasons why this is so. First, the . . . only evidence in the record that Wolf considered Ezold's academic record is limited to the original decision to hire Ezold and to assignments given to Ezold early in her employment with Wolf, issues we consider in Part IX, infra. Second, in its analysis, the district court did not focus on Wolf's articulated reason for denying Ezold partnership — lack of analytic ability to handle complex litigation. Instead, the district court first substituted its own general standard for the qualities Wolf believed were essential to law firm partnership. Then, applying its own incorrect standard of comparison, the district court did not realize that a comparison of Ezold's legal analytic ability with that of the successful males could not support a finding of pretext. Overall, Ezold's evaluations in that category were not as good as that of even the least capable male associate who was offered a partnership position. . . .

VII . . .

The record does not show that anyone was taken into the partnership without serious consideration of their strength in the category of legal analytic ability. . . .

Wolf reserves for itself the power to decide, by consensus, whether an associate possesses sufficient analytical ability to handle complex matters independently after becoming a partner. It is Wolf's prerogative to utilize such a standard. . . .

. . . The partnership evaluation process at Wolf, though formalized, is based on judgment, like most decisions in human institutions. A consensus as to that judgment is the end result of Wolf's formal process. In that process, the Associates Committee has the role of collecting and weighing hundreds of evaluations by partners with diverse views before reaching its consensus as to a particular associate's abilities. . . .

The differing evaluations the partners first submit to the Associates Committee are often based on hearsay or reputation. No precise theorem or specific objective criterion is employed. . . .

Were the factors Wolf considered in deciding which associates should be admitted to the partnership objective, as opposed to subjective, the conflicts in various partners' views about Ezold's legal analytical ability that this record shows might amount to no more than a conflict in the evidence that the district court as factfinder had full power to resolve. . . . [The difficulty in this case] is the lack of an objective qualification or factor that a plaintiff can use as a yardstick to compare herself with similarly situated employees. . . .

. . . When an employer relies on its subjective evaluation of the plaintiff's qualifications as the reason for denying promotion, the plaintiff can prove the articulated reason is unworthy of credence by presenting persuasive comparative evidence that non-members of the protected class were evaluated more favorably, i.e., their deficiencies in the same qualification category as the plaintiff's were overlooked for no apparent reason when they were promoted to partner.

A plaintiff does not establish pretext, however, by pointing to criticisms of members of the non-protected class, or commendation of the plaintiff, in categories the defendant says it did not rely upon in denying promotion to a member of the protected class. Such comments may raise doubts about the fairness of the employer's decision. "The fact that a court may think that the employer misjudged the qualifications of the applicant does not in itself expose him to Title VII liability, although this may be probative of whether the employer's reasons are pretexts for discrimination." *Burdine*, 450 U.S. at 259. . . . Evidence establishing such incredibility must show that the standard or criterion the employer relied on was "obviously weak or implausible." . . . Ezold's evidence does not make this showing. . . .

The district court's failure to consider the negative evaluations of Ezold's legal analytic ability because the partners making them had little contact with Ezold cannot be excused in the face of the credence the district court gave to positive comments about Ezold's ability from those who likewise had little or no contact with her. While a factfinder can accept some evidence and reject other evidence on the basis of credibility, it should not base its credibility determination on a conflicting double standard.

Moreover, . . . [t]here is no evidence that Wolf's practice of giving weight to negative votes and comments of partners who had little contact and perhaps knew nothing about an associate beyond the associate's general reputation was not applied equally to female and male associates. . . .

VIII

[The court next reviews the evaluations of other associates selected for partnership, including negative comments about their analytical abilities. It concludes that the district court erred in not crediting the many favorable evaluations of these associates, and in not giving adequate weight to the negative comments about Ezold.]

. . . Because the evaluation files contain insufficient evidence to show that Ezold was evaluated more severely than the male associates, Ezold has not shown that Wolf's proffered reason for failing to promote her was "unworthy of credence." We therefore hold that the district court's ultimate finding of pretext cannot be sustained on this basis.

IX

We must, however, still consider certain additional evidence which Ezold says directly establishes that Wolf's articulated reason was a pretext by showing that a discriminatory reason more likely motivated its decision not to admit her to the partnership. . . .

This Court has recognized that when an employer discriminatorily denies training and support, the employer may not then disfavor the plaintiff because her performance is affected by the lack of opportunity. . . . Even if we assume that Ezold received "small" cases at the beginning of her tenure at Wolf, however, there is no evidence this was the result of sex discrimination. Her evaluations indicate, rather, that it may have been her academic credentials that contributed to her receipt of less complex assignments. For example, Davis stated that "the Home Unity case was the first really fair test for Nancy. I believe that her background relegated her to . . . matters (where she got virtually no testing by Wolf, Block standards) and small matters." . . . It is undisputed that Arbittier opposed hiring Ezold because of her academic history and lack of law review experience. In one of Ezold's early evaluations, Kurland wrote: "She has not, in my view, been getting sufficiently difficult matters to handle because she is not the Harvard

Law Review type. . . . We must make an effort to give her more difficult matters to handle." . . . He also stated: "I envisioned . . . her when I hired her as a "good, stand-up, effective courtroom lawyer.' " . . . In urging the Executive Committee to reconsider Ezold's candidacy Magarity wrote:

> [The] perception [that she is not able to handle complex cases] appears to be a product of how Sy Kurland viewed Nancy's role when she was initially hired. For the first few years Sy would only assign Nancy to non-complex matters, yet, at evaluation time, Sy, and some other partners, would qualify their evaluations by saying that Nancy does not work on complex matters. . . .

Nancy was literally trapped in a Catch 22. The Chairman of the Litigation Department would not assign her to complex cases, yet she received negative evaluations for not working on complex matters. . . .

While it would be unfortunate if these academic and intellectual biases were perpetuated after the decision was made to hire Ezold, academic or intellectual bias is not evidence of sex discrimination. The district court made no finding that Ezold was given small assignments because of her sex. . . .

The district court found that when Ezold suggested to Schwartz in her early years at Wolf that an unfairness in case assignments may have occurred because she was a woman, Schwartz replied: "Nancy, don't say that around here. They don't want to hear it. Just do your job and do well." . . . This statement, made years before the 1988 decision to deny Ezold partnership, does not show that Wolf's evaluation of her legal ability was pretextual. . . .

Ezold also points to a preliminary injunction matter early in her career that was reassigned to a man after she had been the sole volunteer. The district court found that Arbittier reassigned the injunction to a man "without explanation." . . . Arbittier, however, testified that he realized the case needed a more senior associate and so reassigned it. This too occurred early in Ezold's employment at Wolf and there is nothing in the record to show that it had any connection with Ezold's failure to attain partnership. . . .

The district court also found that when Ezold first got to the firm in 1983, she and a male associate not on partnership track were assigned to sort out a large group of minor cases previously handled by an associate who had left the firm. This finding fails to support the district court's ultimate finding of pretext. The assignment was made on an as-needed basis to fill the void created when the associate working on the matters had left. Additionally, the district court failed to recognize that Arbittier gave Ezold full authority to reassign the matters to other male associates and administer the whole affair. The small bankruptcy matters to which the district court refers were later reassigned by Kurland at Ezold's request. Kurland testified that he did this "both to free Nancy up a little and to give some demonstration that we [were] making an effort to change the nature of her assignments." . . .

Finally, the district court found that by allowing partners to bypass the formal assignment system, Kurland and Arbittier "prevented the plaintiff from securing improved assignments . . . [and] impaired her opportunity to be fairly evaluated for partnership." . . . The fact that Wolf's formal assignment process was often bypassed does not support the district court's finding of pretext. Title VII requires employers to avoid certain prohibited types of invidious discrimination, including sex discrimination. It does not require employers to treat all employees fairly, closely monitor their progress and insure them every opportunity for advancement. "Our task is not to assess the overall fairness of [Wolf's] actions.". . . It is a sad fact of life in the working world that employees of ability are sometimes overlooked for promotion. Large law firms are not immune from unfairness in this imperfect world. The law limits its protection against that unfairness to cases of invidious illegal discrimination. This record contains no evidence that Wolf's assignment process was tainted by a discriminatory motive. . . .

[T]he district court held that the four specific instances of conduct . . . evidenced a discriminatory animus and supported its finding of pretext. . . . It did not hold that these instances of conduct provided an independent or alternative basis for its finding, but viewed them only as support therefor.

The first instance of conduct on which the district court relied was that Ezold "was evaluated negatively for being too involved with women's issues . . . specifically her concern about the [firm's] treatment of paralegals," while Fiebach [a male partner] was not reproached for raising the "women's issue" of part-time employment. . . . Ezold's perception was that the firm mistreated its paralegals by overworking and underpaying them and that treatment would not have occurred but for the fact that they were predominantly women. The court's finding on this matter refers to a 1986 evaluation submitted by Schwartz, one of Ezold's partnership supporters, in which he wrote: "Judgment is better, although it still can be clouded by over-sensitivity to what she misperceives as "womens' [sic] issues." . . . Schwartz testified, however, that he was not criticizing Ezold for raising the issue of the firm's treatment of paralegals, but for her misperception that this was a "women's issue." Moreover, the fact that Fiebach . . . was not criticized for encouraging discussion of part-time employment is not probative of whether the partnership decision concerning Ezold was gender-based. This evidence is of marginal value. . . .

The second instance of conduct on which the district court relied was "the fact that a male associate['s] sexual harassment of female employees at the Firm was seen as insignificant and not worthy of mention to the Associates Committee in its consideration of that male associate for partnership." . . . While it is undisputed that the male associate, Associate X, engaged in some form of harassment of female employees, the district court's finding about Wolf's attitude towards it is unsupported by the evidence and thus clearly erroneous. The record shows that Strogatz, then Chairman of the Associates Committee, met with Associate X concerning these incidents, and that a memorandum was placed in his personnel file. There was testimony that the incident was reported to the associate's department chairman and to the Associates Committee. The record also indicates that the incident occurred after the Associates Committee decided it was unlikely to recommend Associate X for partnership in any event. There is no evidence Wolf viewed the incident as "insignificant." This incident is not evidence that the firm harbored a discriminatory animus against either women generally or Ezold specifically. It lends no support to the district court's finding of pretext.

The district court found that Ezold was "evaluated negatively for being 'very demanding,' while several male associates who were made partners were evaluated negatively for lacking sufficient assertiveness in their demeanors." . . . The criticisms of Ezold's assertiveness related to the way in which she handled administrative matters such as office and secretarial space, and not legal matters. . . . In particular, David Hofstein's evaluation of Ezold in 1984 stated:

> My one negative experience did not involve legal work. When my group moved to the south end of the 21st floor, Nancy had a fit because she had to move. As I. Strogatz and our [Office Manager] know, Nancy's behavior was inappropriate and I think affected everyone's perception of her. Dealing with administrative matters professionally is almost as important as dealing with legal matters competently, and at least in that instance, Nancy blew it. . . .

The district court refers to criticisms of male associates for lacking assertiveness, but in connection with their handling of legal matters. The district court was comparing apples and oranges. The record shows that male associates were also criticized for their improper handling of administrative problems. . . . The district court also quotes an evaluation of Ezold as a "prima donna" on administrative matters, but leaves out the full context of the statement which compares her to a male associate: "Reminds me of [a male associate] — very demanding, prima donna-ish, not a team player." . . .

The district court's finding that this evidence supports its conclusion that Ezold was treated differently because of her gender is clearly erroneous. An "unfortunate and destructive conflict of personalities does not establish sexual discrimination." Bellissimo [v. Westinghouse Elec. Corp.], 764 F.2d 175, 182 (3d Cir. 1985). Further, by the time of Ezold's final evaluation in 1988, there was no mention of her attitude on administrative matters. Rosoff testified that in independently reviewing the Associate Committee's decision not to recommend Ezold for partnership, he disregarded the criticisms of her handling of administrative matters from earlier years as "ancient history." . . . There is again no evidence that this incident played any role in Wolf's decision to deny Ezold's admission to the partnership.

Finally, the district court found that Ezold was the target of several comments demonstrating the firm's differential treatment of women. The district court found the following:

During the selection process . . . Mr. Kurland told Ms. Ezold that it would not be easy for her at Wolf, Block because she did not fit the Wolf, Block mold since she was a woman, had not attended an Ivy League law school, and had not been on law review. Mr. Kurland and Ms. Ezold stated that at one of the meetings with Ms. Ezold, only Ms. Ezold and he were present.

. . . Ezold did not raise this reference at a subsequent lunch with associate Liebenberg, a woman, and Schwartz, nor did she express concern over Wolf's treatment of women. Although Kurland denied making the statement, the district court resolved this credibility issue in Ezold's favor and we will not disturb it.

Wolf argues that this comment made in 1983 before Ezold accepted the job is not probative on whether its partnership decision five years later was gender-based. In Roebuck v. Drexel University, 852 F.2d at 733, the plaintiff alleged racial discrimination in the denial of tenure and we considered the probative value of evidence of a discriminatory attitude on the part of a key decisionmaker. There, the president of the university exercised a significant influence on the decisionmakers and had made the final tenure decision. He had also made two statements reflecting racial bias. Id. We held, although the "statements standing alone, occurring as they did over five years before the final denial of tenure, could not suffice to uphold a finding [of discrimination], they do add support, in combination with the other evidence, to the ultimate conclusion." Id. . . . Here, however, as we have painstakingly pointed out, other evidence of sex discrimination is lacking. In any event, Kurland made this comment before Ezold began her employment at Wolf, five years before the partnership decision. The comment's temporal distance from the decision Ezold says was discriminatory convinces us it is too remote and isolated to show independently that unlawful discrimination, rather than Wolf's asserted reason, more likely caused the firm to deny Ezold the partnership she sought in 1988.

Kurland himself had left the firm in January 1988, before Ezold's 1988 evaluation and before the Associates Committee and the Executive Committee denied her admission to the partnership. Thus, he did not take part in the final decision to deny Ezold's admission to the partnership, although he had consistently supported her candidacy despite his recognition of other partners' perceptions about her legal analytical ability. Stray remarks by non-decisionmakers or by decisionmakers unrelated to the decision process are rarely given great weight, particularly if they were made temporally remote from the date of decision. . . .

X

We have reviewed the evidence carefully and hold that it is insufficient to show pretext. Despite Ezold's disagreement with the firm's evaluations of her abilities, and her perception that she was treated unfairly, there is no evidence of sex discrimination here. The district court's finding that Wolf's legitimate non-discriminatory reason was incredible because Ezold was evaluated more severely than male associates because of her gender, as well as its finding that Wolf's requirement that she possess analytical skills sufficient to handle complex litigation was a pretext for discrimination, are clearly erroneous and find no support in the evidence. Finally, this record also lacks sufficient direct evidence of discriminatory animus to sustain a finding that Wolf more likely had a discriminatory motive in denying Ezold's admission to the partnership.

XI

Accordingly, we will reverse the judgment of the district court in favor of Ezold and remand for entry of judgment in favor of Wolf.

Notes

1. The "Glass Ceiling," Title VII, and Professional Partnerships. The gap between equality in principle and equality in practice is most apparent at the highest levels of business and professional employment. Although women have made enormous progress in the workplace over the last quarter century, they remain underrepresented at the top and overrepresented at the bottom. Women now account for about half of managerial and professional positions, but only 12 percent of corporate officers, four percent of top corporate earners, and under one percent of the Fortune 500 CEOs. Catalyst, Catalyst Facts: Women in Business (2000) and 2000 Census of Women Corporate Officials and Top Earners (2000). (See www.catalystwomen.org). As the materials in Chapter 5, Section D indicate, almost 30 percent of lawyers are women but they account for only about 15 percent of law firm partners and federal judges, 10 percent of law school deans and general counsel positions at Fortune 500 companies, and five percent of managing partners at major law firms. Commission on Women in the Profession, The Unfinished Agenda: Women in the Profession 5, 14, 23-27 (2001). The underrepresentation of women of color is still greater. They account for only about one percent of corporate officers and under one percent of law firm partners and general counsel. Id. at 14, 23-27; Catalyst, 2000 Census of Women Corporate Officers, *supra*; Catalyst, Minority Women in Management (1999); ABA Commission on Opportunities for Minorities in the Profession, Miles to Go: Progress of Women and Minorities in the Legal Profession (2000). For a discussion of the disparities in wage levels among male and female lawyers, see note 4 in Section B(1) of this Chapter, beginning on page 163.

Price Waterhouse and *Ezold* illustrate the difficulties in applying an equal opportunity principle to subjective job criteria that are especially prevalent in upper-level employment. Should the underrepresentation of women in these positions be of concern under a formal equality approach? Or should the law be indifferent to gender disparities in results, so long as the same criteria are applied to each individual? Reconsider these questions in light of the materials on substantive equality in Chapter 3; the market explanations for gender disparities, at pages 309-311; the sociobiological debate about gender differences, at pages 813-829; and the barriers confronting women in the legal profession, at pages 855-857 and 862-865.

A threshold question in *Price Waterhouse* and *Ezold* is the extent to which the law regulates employment practices by partnerships. As noted earlier, Title VII by its terms prohibits employers from depriving individuals of employment opportunities based on race, color, religion, sex, or national origin. The United States Supreme Court, in Hishon v. King and Spalding, 467 U.S. 69 (1984), held that the decision by a private law firm whether to offer partnership to a law associate falls under Title VII because opportunities for partnership constituted a term or privilege "linked directly with an [associate's] status as an employee." Id. at 76. It is not clear, however, whether the statute covers relations among partners or an employment package which, from the outset, decouples partnership consideration from performance as an associate. Justice Powell, in a concurring opinion in *Hishon*, stated his view that absent a claim based on the law firm's promise of partnership consideration, Title VII would not apply to such decisions.

> The relationship among law partners differs markedly from that between employer and employee — including that between the partnership and its associates. The judgmental and sensitive decisions that must be made among the partners embrace a wide range of subjects [including participation in profits, work assignments, approval of commitments in bar association, civil and political activities, questions of billing, and acceptance of new clients]. The essence of the law partnership is the common conduct of a shared enterprise.

476 U.S. at 79-80 & n.3 (Powell, J., concurring).

Even if Title VII covers the partnership decision, it may not cover treatment of partners by the partnership. Some cases have held that partners are not employees within the meaning of federal anti-discrimination statutes. See, e.g., Wheeler v. Main Hurdman, 825 F.2d 257 (10th Cir. 1987), cert. denied, 484 U.S. 986 (1987). The EEOC issued guidelines in 2000, however, that would bring those statutes into play when "the individual is subject to the organization's control," although they would not apply when "the individual acts independently and participates in managing the organization." See Covered Parties: Covered Individuals, EEOC Notice No. 915,003, EEOC Compliance Manual, (CCH) ¶ 7110 (May 5, 2000). For the theory that partners should be protected vis-à-vis one another by an implied contractual duty not to discriminate against one another, see Mark

S. Kende, Shattering the Glass Ceiling: A Legal Theory for Attacking Discrimination Against Women Partners, 46 Hast. L.J. 17 (1994).

To what extent should a partnership's First Amendment associational rights take precedence over equal opportunity guarantees? See part C at page 250 and problem 2-18 at page 262.

2. Proving Intent in Disparate Treatment Cases. Note that establishing discrimination in disparate treatment cases under Title VII requires proof of discriminatory intent or motive. When an employment rule or practice is facially discriminatory, this is not a problem, just as there is no problem with facially discriminatory rules challenged under the Equal Protection Clause. See Section A, starting on page 119. In some disparate treatment cases, however, the issue is whether the employment action was, in fact, discrimination based on sex, in which case discriminatory intent must be shown. It is this discriminatory motive or intent that was missing in the *Ezold* case.

While discriminatory intent must be proved in disparate treatment case, no intent to discriminate must be shown under Title VII in disparate impact cases. By way of contrast, recall that in disparate impact cases brought under the Equal Protection Clause, discriminatory intent must be proved. See Personnel Administrator of Massachusetts v. Feeney, 442 U.S. 256 (1979), set forth on page 140, supra. In recognition of the fact that discriminatory intent is not part of a disparate impact case under Title VII, the remedies available for disparate impact violations are limited to injunctive relief and legal costs and fees, while for disparate treatment violations, plaintiffs also may recover compensatory and punitive damages.

As noted in the introduction to this section, proof of discriminatory intent in disparate treatment cases takes two main forms: "mixed motives," and "pretext" discrimination. *Price Waterhouse* is an example of a mixed motives claim. *Ezold* is an example of a pretext claim. Which type of claim would you expect to be harder to establish?

3. Proving "Mixed Motives" under the Civil Rights Act of 1991. The *Price Waterhouse* rule, which gives employers a defense to a discrimination claim if they show a nondiscriminatory motive for reaching the same employment decision, has been modified by the Civil Rights Act of 1991. Under the Act, the defendant in a mixed-motives case will be liable if the plaintiff shows by direct evidence that sex was a "motivating factor for any employment practice, even though other factors also motivated the practice," although if an employer demonstrates that it "would have taken the same action in the absence of the impermissible motivating factor" remedies are limited to declaratory relief, injunctive relief, and attorney's fees. Financial damages, reinstatement, hiring, or promotion are not available. See 42 U.S.C. §2000e-2(m), 2000e-5(g)(2)(B) (1994), set forth in the Statutory Appendix.

The direct evidence requirement to trigger the application of a mixed-motives framework is a source of some confusion among the circuits. For a useful summary of the burden of proof requirements, see Wynn v. Mass. Commission on Discrimination, 729 N.E.2d 1068 (Mass. 2000) (affirming a finding of discrimination based on a law firm's failure to hire a woman as an attorney who had previously worked for the firm as a law clerk and whom it told it had no entry-level positions, based on fact that one of the partners said he would not have hired her as a law clerk had he known she was pregnant because it showed that her priorities were elsewhere than with the firm). See also Christopher Y. Chen, Note, Rethinking the Direct Evidence Requirement: A Suggested Approach in Analyzing Mixed-Motives Discrimination Claims, 86 Cornell L. Rev. 899 (2001) (analyzing the direct evidence requirement and its varying interpretations).

Sometimes information that would justify an adverse employment action is not known by the employer at the time the action is taken, but is discovered in the course of the litigation. This "after-acquired evidence" obviously could not have constituted the actual motivation for the decision. However, to the extent that the evidence would justify the employer's decision, it operates in much the same fashion as the permissible motive in a mixed motives case. In effect, the after-acquired evidence does not prevent liability, but can influence damages. See McKennon v. Nashville Banner Publishing Co., 513 U.S. 352, 360-361 (1995) (applying Age Discrimination in Employment Act). There is, however, one significant difference. While a plaintiff can receive no damages in a case establishing mixed motives, in an after-acquired evidence case a plaintiff may get back pay from the date of the unlawful practice to the date that the new information was discovered. Id. at 362. See Mardell v. Harleysville Life Ins. Co., 65 F.3d 1072 (3d Cir. 1995).

Is the Civil Rights Act's liability-but-no-damages rule an appropriate response when an employer has both discriminatory and nondiscriminatory motives? On the one hand, it would seem desirable to discourage employers from acting on discriminatory impulses. See Susan Bisom-Rapp, Of Motives and Maleness: A Critical View of Mixed Motive Doctrine in the Title VII Sex Discrimination Cases, 1995 Utah l. Rev. 1029, 1040 (plaintiff should be entitled both to a finding of liability and the full range of damages available under Title VII, regardless of the fact that there happens to be a non-discriminatory justification for the employment action). On the other hand, liability seems unreasonable in a case in which an employer's action was otherwise justified, the employee has not been injured and no damages can be established. See Paul N. Cox, A Defense of "Necessary Cause" in Individual Disparate Treatment Theory Under Title VII, 11 St. Louis U. Pub. L. Rev. 29 (1992) (employee should have to prove that the discriminatory motive was the "necessary cause" of the adverse employment action, or else Title VII would be inappropriately converted from an equal treatment statute into a model of "presumed discrimination"). Is the current approach a good compromise?

4. Unconscious Discrimination and Intent Under Title VII. While the existence of a discriminatory motive will trigger the approach offered by *Price Waterhouse*, proving discriminatory motive may be an overwhelming task, even when discrimination has actually occurred. One reason is that discrimination may be less a result of discriminatory motivation than of unintentional, cognitive errors in how individuals categorize and understand. Consider the following:

> . . . [T]he characteristics traditionally associated with women are at odds with many characteristics traditionally associated with professional success such as assertiveness, competitiveness, and business judgment. Some lawyers and clients still assume that women lack sufficient aptitude for complex financial transactions or sufficient combativeness for major litigation. Particularly in high stakes matters, risk averse managers are often reluctant to gamble on female practitioners.
>
> Yet professional women also tend to be rated lower when they depart from traditional stereotypes and adopt "masculine," authoritative styles. Negative evaluations are particularly likely when the evaluators are men, or the role is one typically occupied by men.
>
> As a consequence, female lawyers often face a double standard and a double bind. They risk appearing too "soft" or too "strident," too "aggressive" or "not aggressive enough." And what appears assertive in a man often appears abrasive in a woman. . . .
>
> The force of traditional stereotypes is compounded by the subjectivity of performance evaluations and by other biases in decision-making processes. People are more likely to notice and recall information that confirms prior assumptions than information that contradicts them. Attorneys who assume that working mothers are less committed tend to remember the times they left early, not the nights they stayed late.
>
> A related problem is that people share what psychologists label a "just world" bias. They want to believe that, in the absence of special treatment, individuals generally get what they deserve and deserve what they get. Perceptions of performance are frequently adjusted to match observed outcomes. Individuals are also motivated to interpret information in ways that maintain their own status and self-esteem.

ABA Commission on Women in the Profession, The Unfinished Agenda: A Report on the Status of Women in the Legal Profession 15-16 (2001). See also Virginia Valian, Why So Slow: The Advancement of Women 133 (1998). Does equal opportunity doctrine adequately address such biases? Could it?

As *Ezold* might illustrate, when employers act on stereotypes they hold and fail to give challenging assignments to a woman, the stereotypes become self-perpetuating. In this way, employers may apply discriminatory criteria to women, and yet honestly believe that the employee's performance is sub-par. Particularly in cases involving upper-level positions and subjective criteria, plaintiffs who claim discrimination in such cases may will generally have great difficulty establishing that nothing in their records could justify an employer's adverse decision. On cognitive bias, see Linda Hamilton Krieger, The Content of Our Categories: A Cognitive Bias Approach to Discrimination and Equal Employment Opportunity, 47 Stan. L. Rev. 1161, 1164, 1167. 1170, 1217 (1995); Charles R. Lawrence III, The Id, the Ego, and Equal Protection: Reckoning with Unconscious Racism, 39 Stan. L. Rev. 317 (1987). See also Susan Sturm, Second Generation Employment Discrimination: A Structural Approach, 101 Colum. L. Rev. 458, 460 (2001) (noting that unconscious cognitive bias and patterns of interaction have largely replaced deliberate intentional discrimination as the foundations of contemporary discriminatory employment practices).

Could these patterns of unconscious discrimination have been operating in the *Ezold* case? Would it be possible to know or prove whether partners' assessments of Nancy Ezold's abilities were affected by their early views of her credentials, compounded by the unchallenging assignments she received, or by her complaints about the way female staff were treated in the firm? Does this help explain why Ezold would not want to litigate her claim as a mixed-motive case?

Can we be sure that stereotypes were operating in *Price Waterhouse*?

> Glass ceiling cases are rarely stronger than this. At the time when Price Waterhouse withheld her promotion, all but 7 of the firm's 662 partners were male. Hopkins billed more hours and brought in more business than any other person nominated for partnership in the year of her rejection, and clients generally had given her high ratings. . . . Several men who obtained partnerships [in the year that Hopkins did not] were characterized as "abrasive," "overbearing," or "cocky." No one mentioned charm school for them. Although Hopkins eventually prevailed, it took seven years and five levels of judicial decision-making, with two trial and three appellate court rulings. And most of these judges found it a "close" case.

Deborah Rhode, Speaking of Sex 161 (1997). Do you accept this analysis?

It is often noted that the likelihood of gender bias in performance evaluations is greater in settings where women constitute a minority of the workforce, the applicant pool, and the senior management. When women constitute a substantial percentage of the work force, their performance ratings are consistently higher. See Valian, supra, at 139-40 (reviewing studies); Robin J. Ely, The Power in Demography; Women's Social Construction of Gender Identity at Work, 38 Acad. Management J. 589 (1995). The expert testimony of Dr. Susan Fiske in the *Price Waterhouse* case, introduced to explain the influence of gender stereotypes in Price Waterhouse's decision, was built in part on the influential work of Rosabeth Moss Kanter, Men and Women of the Corporation (1977), which established that groups constituting 15 percent or less of an organization are particularly vulnerable to stereotyping.

. . . Fiske stated that when there is dramatic underrepresentation of a group, the token individuals are much more likely to be thought about in terms of their social category. People expect token individuals to fit preconceived views about the traits of the group. . . . When a token person behaves in a way that is counterstereotypical — for example, when a woman acts in an aggressive, competitive, ambitious, independent, or active way — she is more likely to be regarded as uncaring or lacking in understanding. This does not mean that women can play safe by conforming to conventional stereotypes. The Catch 22 or double bind of the powerless group is that stereotypes associated with nondominant groups are also traits that are not highly valued in the organization. A woman who acts womanly acts in a way that may cast doubt on her competence and effectiveness; a woman who is thought to be too masculine may be regarded as deviant.

In describing how persons respond to an individual whose behavior is incongruent with prevailing stereotypes, Fiske referred to Kanter's four "role traps." Under this scheme, the dominant male group perceives token women as mothers, seductresses, iron maidens, or pets. . . . The role trap most applicable to Hopkins was that of the "iron maiden." . . . Under Fiske's theory, the explicitly sex-based comments describing Hopkins were a predictable response to her status as a token woman who did not fit the conventional feminine mold. . . .

An additional cue Fiske found which indicated that stereotyping was influencing decisionmaking was the intensity of the negative reaction toward Hopkins. . . . Claims were made, for example, that Hopkins was universally disliked, potentially dangerous, and likely to abuse authority. Fiske contrasted these extremely negative comments with positive comments by others in the organization who seemed to describe the same behavior. Supporters found Hopkins as "outspoken, sells her own ability, independent, [has] the courage of her convictions." Detractors found her "overbearing, arrogant, abrasive, runs over people, implies she knows more than anyone in the world about anything and is not afraid to let anybody know it." Fiske's testimony on this phenomenon of "selective perception" suggested that the differing reactions to Hopkins were not simply a function of the slice of Hopkins' behavior that each individual evaluator had witnessed. Instead, when all the evidence was in, the "real" Ann Hopkins might still not clearly emerge from putting all the pieces together. Fiske's use of Kanter's role traps also demonstrated how other people can contribute to the social construction of the personality of an individual. This made it more difficult to separate Hopkins' "real" personality from the environment in which she worked.

Martha Chamallas, Listening to Dr. Fiske: The Easy Case of Price Waterhouse v. Hopkins, 15 Vt. L. Rev. 89, 91 (1990).

Is this testimony persuasive? Of what? If it is accepted, would employers safely be able to make suggestions for improvement as to "weaknesses" that are rooted in traditional gender roles? Can't a woman be too assertive? Or not assertive enough? In the face of Dr. Fiske's testimony, what kind of evidence could ever counteract it? Does such evidence prove too much?

Yet without testimony of this sort, it is difficult to imagine how most employees could refute an employer's non-discriminatory justifications for an adverse decision. Smoking guns like the charm school comment are increasingly rare. As one court put it, employers of even "minimal sophistication" will "neither admit discriminatory . . . [conduct] nor leave a paper trail demonstrating it." Riordan v. Kempiners, 831 F. 2d 690, 697 (7th Cir. 1987). Managers who appear lacking in such sophistication are often counseled by human resources personnel to ensure that written performance reviews include concrete examples of employee weaknesses and avoid stereotypical characterizations.

In evaluating claims of sex discrimination, what significance should be given to "stray remarks" like those alleged in *Ezold*? Courts have reached inconsistent results. Compare Santiago-Ramos v. Centennial P.R. Wireless Corp., 217 F.3d 46 (1st Cir. 2000) (evidence of several remarks that questioned the ability of women to have children and still remain committed to work as well as blatant statements that the employer preferred hiring unmarried, childless women because they were more committed to their work is sufficient to prove pretext in a sex discrimination case contesting termination of a woman who expressed the desire to have another child in the near future) with Sreeram v. La. State Univ. Med. Ctr., 188 F.3d 314 (5th Cir. 1999) (in upholding decision against a terminated surgical resident claiming discrimination on the basis of sex and national origin, the court found irrelevant remarks by her evaluators such as that "her difficulties in the program were 'cultural;' " a concern by one superior about why women would put themselves through surgical residency particularly if they plan on having children because, "they're constantly tired, and they don't have time to put on their makeup and put on clothes and do a lot of things girls need to do. . . ."; and the observation of one superior that "she is not accepted well by the 'good old boys' "); Heim v. State of Utah 8 F. 3d 1541, 1546 (10th Cir. 1993) (holding comment by supervisor, "Fucking women, I hate having fucking women in the office," insufficient to show discrimination because it appeared directed at "women in general," rather than at plaintiff).

It has been argued that members of outsider groups, such as women and minorities, perceive themselves as subject to negative stereotypes and thus are "likely to feel the need to do significant amounts of 'extra' identity work to counter those stereotypes." Devon W. Carbado & Mitu Gulati, Working Identity, 85 Cornell L. Rev. 1259, 1262 (2000). Carbado and Gulati note that engaging in "signaling strategies" or "identity work" is common, such as when one acts harried and tired to overcome the impression that one is not busy, or sends an e-mail late at night to indicate that one has worked late. Id. at 1260. Additional strategies that members of outsider groups may engage — strategies that may actually compromise their own identities and have other psychic costs — include heterosexual "performances" to avoid suspicion of homosexuality, passing up lunches with outsiders of the same kind to avoid creating the impression of racial "cliquishness," and laughing at racist or sexist jokes directed against members of the outsider group to show that one can take a joke, is not obsessed with his or her outsider status, and can make others feel comfortable. Id. at 1277, 1286, 1290, 1302. Should engagement in these behaviors be evidence of discrimination? When discrimination is proved, should these behaviors count as evidence of damages?

How different are the pretext and mixed-motives approaches to proving discrimination? Would Nancy Ezold have been better off if she had tried her claim as a mixed-motives case? Note that the approaches are different in structure, but the ultimate question under each is whether improper discrimination influenced the adverse employment decision. Would an expert like Fiske have identified gender stereotypes and impermissible bias in *Ezold*? Given the appellate court's interpretation of the facts, is it likely that such testimony would have led to a finding of sex-based motivation? In reaching its conclusion and reversing the district court, the court of appeals was obligated to apply the "clearly erroneous" standard of review. Did it do exactly what it accused the district court of doing, i.e., "substitut[e] its own subjective judgment" for that of the appropriate fact-finder?

The original "mandatory presumption" proof mechanisms under Title VII as established in *McDonnell Douglas/Burdine* lessened the burden on the plaintiff to prove *intentional* discrimination. Under this plaintiff-friendly analysis, if the plaintiff showed that the defendant's proffered non-discriminatory reason was a pretext, a mandatory presumption of discrimination came into effect that required the fact finder to find in favor of the plaintiff. No showing of actual and intentional discriminatory motive was required. Ann McGinley suggests that this "mandatory presumption" analysis allowed for the application of Title VII to incidents of *unconscious* discrimination as well as intentional. See Ann C. McGinley, ¡Viva La Evolucion! Recognizing Unconscious Motive in Title VII, 9 Cornell J.L. & Pub. Pol'y 415 (2000). More recent law, as noted in the introduction to this section, merely permits a finding of discriminatory motive based on pretext but does not require it. See pages 166-167.

5. What Works to Eliminate Discrimination?   What mechanisms are most effective in eliminating job bias against women? Opinions on this subject are diverse. Conservative legal scholar Richard Epstein has argued that employer self-interest is a sufficient check against gender bias. A free market rewards efficiency, he argues, and since it is inefficient for employers to discriminate against qualified workers, women do not need law to guarantee equal opportunity. If they are not advancing at the same rate as men, the reason must be sex-based differences in female employees' choices and capabilities. Epstein, Forbidden Grounds: The Case Against Employment Discrimination Laws (1992). For comparable arguments in the wage context, see Chapter 3, Section A(3), note 1.

At the other end of the spectrum, many feminists have argued that law needs to be more proactive in addressing subtle but pervasive barriers. For example, one possibility would be to create two-tiered remedies similar to those applicable for personal injuries. Under such a framework, proof of intentional discrimination in disparate treatment cases would entitle a plaintiff to full compensation, including punitive damages where appropriate. Proof of unintentional discrimination would result in more restricted remedies such as legal costs, back pay and reinstatement. Krieger, supra, at 1243; David Benjamin Oppenheimer, Negligent Discrimination, 141 U. Penn. L. Rev. 899 (1993). In this latter category of unintended bias, a variation of the current mixed-motives standard would apply. The test would be whether an employee's group status in fact made a difference, not whether the employer intended that it make a difference in the adverse decision. Krieger, supra, at 1243. Employers would have a defense to such claims of discrimination if that could establish that they were not negligent — i.e., that they had taken affirmative steps to identify, remedy, and prevent bias. Under such a limited liability option, plaintiffs would no longer face the evidentiary difficulties and expense of proving invidious intent, and defendants would no longer suffer the stigma and remedial costs that attach to such a judgment. Employers would also have incentives to take proactive steps to prevent bias in order to refute claims of negligence.

Other commentators believe that the most promising approach to reducing gender inequality in the workforce is to shift emphasis away from after-the-fact enforcement of antidiscrimination prohibitions and to rely more on improving an employers' capacities to identify, prevent, and redress unconscious bias and exclusionary practices. Consider the following:

> Second generation claims frequently involve patterns of interaction among groups within the workplace that, over time, exclude nondominant groups. This exclusion is difficult to trace directly to intentional, discrete actions of particular actors. . . .
>
> [Take the example of a large law firm that] aggressively recruits women at the entry level and [yet] fails to track patterns in work assignment and promotion so that] the firm's management [was] largely unaware of any problem until [the following] complaints arose: . . . differences in patterns of work assignment and training opportunities among men and women; tolerance of a sexualized work environment by partners who are otherwise significant "rainmakers"; routine comments by male lawyers, particularly in the predominantly male departments, on the appearance, sexuality, and competence of women; harsh assessments of women's capacities and work styles based on gender stereotypes; avoidance of work-related contact with women by members of particular departments; and hyper-scrutiny of women's performance by some, and the invisibility of women's contributions to others. These complaints coincide with a concern about low morale and productivity among

diverse work teams. Upon examination, the firm discovers dramatic differences in the retention and promotion rates of men and women in the firm.

The problems of bias described in this scenario result from ongoing patterns of interaction shaped by organizational culture. These interactions influence workplace conditions, access, and opportunities for advancement over time, and thus constitute the structure for inclusion or exclusion. They cannot be traced solely to the sexism of a single "bad actor." Nor can they be addressed by disaggregating the problem into discrete legal claims. The overall gender impact of this conduct may be discernible only if examined in context and in relation to broader patterns of conduct and access. The absence of systematic institutional reflection about these patterns and their impact on workplace conditions, access, and opportunity for advancement contributes to their cumulative effect. The overall organizational culture affects the extent to which particular acts produce bias in a given workplace. Comments or behavior occurring in conjunction with sex segregation and marginalization may be discriminatory, while the same statements may produce little gender exclusion in a more integrated context. . . .

. . . [These] second generation problems cannot be reduced to a fixed code of specific rules or commands that establishes clear boundaries governing conduct. Instead, their resolution requires a different process, namely problem solving. That process identifies the legal and organizational dimensions of the problem, encourages organizations to gather and share relevant information, builds individual and institutional capacity to respond, and helps design and evaluate solutions that involve employees who participate in the day-to-day patterns that produce bias and exclusion. An effective system of external accountability, including judicial involvement as a catalyst, would encourage organizations to identify and correct these problems without creating increased exposure to liability, and to learn from other organizations that have engaged in similar efforts.

A rule-enforcement approach to regulating second generation problems discourages this type of proactive problem solving. That approach treats regulation as punishing violations of predefined legal rules and compliance as the absence of identifiable conduct violating those rules. Rules developed externally and imposed unilaterally, whether by courts or other regulatory bodies, cannot adequately govern the range of circumstances implicated by the general principle of nondiscrimination, or account for how those circumstances will shape the law's meaning in context. Any rule specific enough to guide behavior will inadequately account for the variability, change, and complexity characteristic of second generation problems. General rules, unless linked to local structures for their elaboration in context, provide inadequate direction to shape behavior. This is particularly true for more subtle and less familiar problems, such as second generation discrimination. Externally-imposed solutions also founder because they cannot be sufficiently sensitive to context or integrated into the day-to-day practice that shapes their implementation. Yet, internally-generated solutions are often insufficiently attentive to their normative implications, or to the connection between those local practices and the general antidiscrimination norm.

In a rule-enforcement process, problems tend to be redefined as discrete legal violations with sanctions attached. Fear of liability for violation of ambiguous legal norms induces firms to adopt strategies that reduce the short-term risk of legal exposure rather than strategies that address the underlying problem. They accomplish this in significant part by discouraging the production of information that will reveal problems, except in the context of preparation for litigation. Under the current system, employers producing information that reveals problems or patterns of exclusion increase the likelihood that they will be sued. Thus, lawyers counsel clients not to collect data that could reveal racial or gender problems or to engage in self-evaluation, because that information could be used to establish a plaintiff's case. Similarly, the rule-enforcement approach to compliance induces plaintiffs' lawyers and advocates to view information about institutional problems and failures as a potential basis for establishing liability. It thus encourages these important legal actors to overlook ways of using that information proactively to develop accountability systems and promote constructive structural change.

Fundamentally, the rule-enforcement model encourages lawyers to see issues as potential legal claims, rather than as problems in need of systemic resolution. This narrow focus on avoiding liability diverts attention from the structural dimensions underlying the legal violations, as well as the organizational patterns revealed through aggregating claims. . . .

Susan Sturm, Second Generation Employment Discrimination: A Structural Approach, 101 Colum. L. Rev. 458, 468, 470-71, 475-76 (2001).

Professor Sturm proposes that employers should be obligated to establish systems to collect information on recruitment, hiring, promotion, retention, and quality of life issues; monitor evaluation, assignment, and mentoring practices; provide adequate diversity training, family leave, and alternative schedule policies; and hold managers accountable for their performance in achieving diversity-related goals. See Sturm, supra, at 462-65, 493-568. Could such measures have made a difference to Nancy Ezold?

6. Alternative Dispute Resolution. An increasing number of employment contracts now include mandatory arbitration clauses. According to a federal General Accounting Office survey, some 300 corporations impose such regulations on some three million employees. Their use is increasing in professional partnerships as well, despite growing concerns about their unfairness. However, organizations such as the Equal Employment Opportunity Commission, the American Arbitration Association, and the National Academy of Arbitration all oppose compelling parties to arbitrate based on employment agreements predating the dispute. The reason is straightforward. The process permits little judicial oversight and reflects structural biases favoring employers.

Ordinarily, arbitration awards can be set aside only upon a showing of fraud, corruption, or misconduct. Yet the procedures that give rise to such awards are systematically skewed. According to the EEOC:

. . . As a "repeat player," the employer has an advantage over the employee, who is less able to make an informed selection of an arbitrator or be savvy regarding other aspects of the system.

The arbitrator also is likely to be influenced by the fact that it is the employer who is the potential source of future business. . . . [A survey] of non-union, employment law cases . . . found the more frequently an employer used arbitration, the better it fared in the outcome. . . .

"Unlike voluntary post-dispute arbitration — which must be fair enough to be attractive to the employee — the employer imposing mandatory arbitration is free to manipulate the arbitral mechanism to its benefit," the [EEOC concluded in a July 10, 1997 statement]. "The terms of the private agreement defining the arbitrator's authority and the arbitral process are characteristically set by the more powerful party, the very party that the public law seeks to regulate."

"When employees are forced into private, employer-designed arbitration systems to resolve their discrimination claims, there is no public accountability or decisions that are made up for employers who violate the law," [EEOC Chairman Gilbert Casellas said in the July 1997 statement].

Nancy Montwieler, EEOC Policy Guidance Reaffirms Opposition to Mandatory Arbitration, 66 U.S. Law Week (BNA) 2055-2056, July 22, 1997.

The problems are said to be compounded by the frequent lack of procedural safeguards in the appointment and oversight of arbitrators. Most of the arbitrators selected by the industry are white men who have specialized in employment law and who are not required to issue written opinions or to follow Title VII. Richard C. Reuben, The Lawyer as Peacemaker, ABA J. Aug. 1996, at 59-61. Significant recoveries are so infrequent that plaintiff lawyers seldom find it worthwhile to take such claims, and employers may lack significant incentives to prevent workplace bias.

The growing use of mandatory arbitration has generated a growing body of legal challenges. The U.S. Court of Appeals for the Ninth Circuit has refused to uphold mandatory arbitration clauses in the Title VII context because of their potential to interfere with congressionally authorized protections. See Duffield v. Robertson Stephens & Co., 144 F.3d 1182 (1998). See also Hooters of America v. Phillips, 173 F.3d 933 (4th Cir. 1999) (employee not required to arbitrate sex harassment claim because rules so "one sided as to undermine the neutrality of the proceeding"); Rosenberg v. Merrill Lynch, 170 F. 2d 3d 1 (1st Cir. 1999) (employee not required to arbitrate where employer failed to communicate arbitration rules). The EEOC Commission also has declined to view compulsory arbitration agreements as precluding EEOC claims. For review of court decisions both enforcing and refusing to enforce arbitration claims, see Alexandra Varner MacDonald, Escape from Arbitration, ABA J. Aug. 1999, at 32-33.

How should the law respond to compulsory arbitration clauses? Should Congress ban them entirely? Or should courts insist on compliance with standards developed by independent organizations like the American Arbitration Association, which provide for protections such as written decisions, adequate discovery, enforcement of applicable laws and selection of neutral arbitrators? According to some commentators, "ADR procedures that are fair in form as well as fact will not need to be compulsory. And procedures that fail to meet that standard do not belong in a system that implicates fundamental human rights." Deborah L. Rhode, Arbitration Pitfalls for Women, National L. J., Jan 31, 2000, at A21. Do you agree?

The circuits are split as to whether the EEOC is bound by a private arbitration agreement when bringing a suit in its own name to prosecute discriminatory behavior suffered by an employee who signed an arbitration agreement. Compare EEOC v. Kidder, Peabody & Co, 156 F.3d 298 (2nd Cir. 1998)(precluding the EEOC from seeking purely monetary relief in federal court on behalf of an employee who signed an arbitration agreement) with EEOC v. Frank's Nursery & Crafts, Inc., 177 F.3d 448 (6th Cir. 1999) (holding that the EEOC is not barred from bringing a federal suit even when the employee signed an arbitration agreement) and EEOC v. Waffle House, Inc., 193 F.3d 805 (4th Cir. 1999), cert. granted 121 S. Ct. 1401 (2001) (refusing to compel arbitration of EEOC claims involving injunctive relief in the public interest on behalf of an employee who signed an arbitration agreement, but also precluding the EEOC from seeking "make-whole" relief for the charging party in court due to the arbitration agreement).

7. Remedies for Title VII Sex Discrimination Claims. Prior to the Civil Rights Act of 1991, compensatory and punitive damages were available for victims of racial discrimination but not discrimination based on sex. The 1991 Act provides for compensatory and punitive damages for victims of intentional, disparate treatment sex discrimination, but with caps, ranging from $50,000 if the employer has between 15 and 100 employees, to $300,000 for employers who have more than 500 employees. 42 U.S.C. §1981(b) (1994), set forth in Statutory Appendix. These damages are still not available in disparate impact cases of sex discrimination. The caps do not apply to race discrimination awards.

Back pay is not subject to the damage caps because, like reinstatement and injunctive relief, it is considered equitable relief. After much confusion, the Supreme Court has recently decided that *front pay* — money awarded for lost compensation during the period between judgment and reinstatement or in lieu or reinstatement — is not subject to the damages cap of the 1991 Act. See Pollard v. E.I. duPont de Nemours, 532 U.S. 843 (2001).

Higher damages may, of course, be available under state non-discrimination statutes. Cf. Rush v. Scott Specialty Gases Inc., 930 F. Supp. 194 (E.D. Pa. 1996) (finding $3 million punitive damages in sexual harassment suit to be excessive and remitting for $2.7 million, noting that Title VII limit would be $300,000).

Attorney's fees and costs are also available to the prevailing party at the court's discretion. See 42 U.S.C. §2000e-5(k) (1994). This rule has been interpreted to mean that a prevailing plaintiff will be awarded attorney's fees in all but "special circumstances." Attorney's fees are awarded to successful defendants only if the court finds the claim was frivolous, unreasonable, or groundless, or that "the plaintiff continued to litigate after it clearly became so." Christiansburg Garment Co. v. EEOC, 434 U.S. 412, 422 (1978). Costs are available as a matter of course to the prevailing party, although they need not be awarded if it would be inequitable. In *Ezold*, the clerk taxed costs in favor of the law firm of over $24,000, in addition to appeal costs of over $36,000. On challenge by Ezold to the trial costs, the trial court ordered that given the fact that she had prevailed at the trial level (i.e., it was not a frivolous case) and that the issues of the case were complex and difficult, the firm's costs should be apportioned equally between the parties. See Ezold v. Wolf, Block, Schorr, and Solis-Cohen, 157 F.R.D. 13 (E.D. Pa. 1994).

On remand in *Price Waterhouse*, among other things, Judge Gesell ordered that Ann Hopkins be instated as a partner, 737 F. Supp. 1202 (D.D.C. 1990), aff'd, 920 F.3d 967 (D.C. Cir. 1990). A year into her partnership, her marriage had broken up due to the stresses of fighting the case, but Hopkins reported that the situation at work is "fine," and that she has enjoyed her work. See Stacey B. Chervin, Employment Discrimination: Breaking Through the Partnership Barrier in Hopkins v. Price Waterhouse, 1992/1993 Ann. Surv. Am. L. 203, 221 (1994) (based on telephone interview with Ann Hopkins, Jan. 28, 1992). Elizabeth Hishon (see note 1, at page 199) did not seek injunctive relief and settled her case against King and Spalding out of court. See Julie Tamminen, Law Firms Face New Challenges in Their Role as Employers: Hishon Opened the Door to Civil Rights Litigation Against Partnerships, 17 Legal Economics 41 (March 1991).

b. When Is Discrimination a "Bona Fide Occupational Qualification"?

≡ *Dothard v. Rawlinson*
≡ 433 U.S. 321 (1977)

Mr. Justice STEWART delivered the opinion of the Court.

Appellee Dianne Rawlinson sought employment with the Alabama Board of Corrections as a prison guard, called in Alabama a "correctional counselor." After her application was rejected, she brought this class suit under Title VII of the Civil Rights Act of 1964 . . . , and under 42 U.S.C.

§1983, alleging that she had been denied employment because of her sex in violation of federal law. . . .

I

At the time she applied for a position as correctional counselor trainee, Rawlinson was a 22-year-old college graduate whose major course of study had been correctional psychology. She was refused employment because she failed to meet the minimum 120-pound weight requirement established by an Alabama statute. The statute also establishes a height minimum of 5 feet 2 inches.

After her application was rejected because of her weight, Rawlinson filed a charge with the Equal Employment Opportunity Commission, and ultimately received a right-to-sue letter. She then filed a complaint in the District Court on behalf of herself and other similarly situated women, challenging the statutory height and weight minima as violative of Title VII and the Equal Protection Clause of the Fourteenth Amendment. A three-judge court was convened. While the suit was pending, the Alabama Board of Corrections adopted Administrative Regulation 204, establishing gender criteria for assigning correctional counselors to maximum-security institutions for "contact positions," that is, positions requiring continual close physical proximity to inmates of the institution. Rawlinson amended her class-action complaint by adding a challenge to Regulation 204 as also violative of Title VII and the Fourteenth Amendment.

Like most correctional facilities in the United States, Alabama's prisons are segregated on the basis of sex. . . .

A correctional counselor's primary duty within these institutions is to maintain security and control of the inmates by continually supervising and observing their activities. To be eligible for consideration as a correctional counselor, an applicant must possess a valid Alabama driver's license, have a high school education or its equivalent, be free from physical defects, be between the ages of 20½ years and 45 years at the time of appointment, and fall between the minimum height and weight requirements of 5 feet 2 inches, and 120 pounds, and the maximum of 6 feet 10 inches, and 300 pounds. Appointment is by merit, with a grade assigned each applicant based on experience and education. No written examination is given.

At the time this litigation was in the District Court, the Board of Corrections employed a total of 435 people in various correctional counselor positions, 56 of whom were women. Of those 56 women, 21 were employed at the Julia Tutwiler Prison for Women, 13 were employed in noncontact positions at the four male maximum-security institutions, and the remaining 22 were employed at the other institutions operated by the Alabama Board of Corrections. Because most of Alabama's prisoners are held at the four maximum-security male penitentiaries, 336 of the 435 correctional counselor jobs were in those institutions, a majority of them concededly in the "contact" classification. Thus, even though meeting the statutory height and weight requirements, women applicants could under Regulation 204 compete equally with men for only about 25% of the correctional counselor jobs available in the Alabama prison system. . . .

A

The gist of the claim that the statutory height and weight requirements discriminate against women does not involve an assertion of purposeful discriminatory motive. It is asserted, rather, that these facially neutral qualifications standards work in fact disproportionately to exclude women from eligibility for employment by the Alabama Board of Corrections. We dealt in Griggs v. Duke Power Co., [401 U.S. 424 (1971)], and Albemarle Paper Co. v. Moody, [422 U.S. 405 (1975)], with similar allegations that facially neutral employment standards disproportionately excluded Negroes from employment, and those cases guide our approach here.

Those cases make clear that to establish a prima facie case of discrimination, a plaintiff need only show that the facially neutral standards in question select applicants for hire in a significantly discriminatory pattern. Once it is thus shown that the employment standards are discriminatory in effect, the employer must meet "the burden of showing that any given requirement (has) . . . a manifest relationship to the employment in question." Griggs v. Duke Power Co., supra, [at 432]. If the employer proves that the challenged requirements are job related, the plaintiff may then show that other selection devices without a similar discriminatory effect would also "serve the employer's legitimate interest in "efficient and trustworthy workmanship.'" Albemarle Paper Co. v. Moody, supra, [at 425], quoting McDonnell Douglas Corp. v. Green, [411 U.S. 792, 801 (1973)].

Although women 14 years of age or older compose 52.75% of the Alabama population and 36.89% of its total labor force, they hold only 12.9% of its correctional counselor positions. In considering the effect of the minimum height and weight standards on this disparity in rate of hiring between the sexes, the District Court found that the 5'2"-requirement would operate to exclude 33.29% of the women in the United States between the ages of 18-79, while excluding only 1.28% of men between the same ages. The 120-pound weight restriction would exclude 22.29% of the women and 2.35% of the men in this age group. When the height and weight restrictions are combined, Alabama's statutory standards would exclude 41.13% of the female population while excluding less than 1% of the male population. Accordingly, the District Court found that Rawlinson had made out a prima facie case of unlawful sex discrimination.

The appellants argue that a showing of disproportionate impact on women based on generalized national statistics should not suffice to establish a prima facie case. They point in particular to Rawlinson's failure to adduce comparative statistics concerning actual applicants for correctional counselor positions in Alabama. There is no requirement, however, that a statistical showing of disproportionate impact must always be based on analysis of the characteristics of actual applicants. . . . The application process might itself not adequately reflect the actual potential applicant pool, since otherwise qualified people might be discouraged from applying because of a self-recognized inability to meet the very standards challenged as being discriminatory. See International Brotherhood of Teamsters v. United States, [431 U.S. 324, 365-367 (1977)]. A potential applicant could easily determine her height and weight and conclude that to make an application would be futile. Moreover, reliance on general population demographic data was not misplaced where there was no reason to suppose that physical height and weight characteristics of Alabama men and women differ markedly from those of the national population.

For these reasons, we cannot say that the District Court was wrong in holding that the statutory height and weight standards had a discriminatory impact on women applicants. . . .

B

We turn, therefore, to the appellants' argument that they have rebutted the prima facie case of discrimination by showing that the height and weight requirements are job related. These requirements, they say, have a relationship to strength, a sufficient but unspecified amount of which is essential to effective job performance as a correctional counselor. In the District Court, however, the appellants produced no evidence correlating the height and weight requirements with the requisite amount of strength thought essential to good job performance. Indeed, they failed to offer evidence of any kind in specific justification of the statutory standards.

If the job-related quality that the appellants identify is bona fide, their purpose could be achieved by adopting and validating a test for applicants that measures strength directly. Such a test, fairly administered, would fully satisfy the standards of Title VII because it would be one that "measure(s) the person for the job and not the person in the abstract." Griggs v. Duke Power Co., [401 U.S. at 436]. But nothing in the present record even approaches such a measurement.

For the reasons we have discussed, the District Court was not in error in holding that Title VII . . . prohibits application of the statutory height and weight requirements to Rawlinson and the class she represents.

III

Unlike the statutory height and weight requirements, Regulation 204 [excluding women from maximum security "contact positions"] explicitly discriminates against women on the basis of their sex. In defense of this overt discrimination, the appellants rely on §703(e) of Title VII, 42 U.S.C. §2000e-2(e), which permits sex-based discrimination "in those certain instances where . . . sex . . . is a bona fide occupational qualification reasonably necessary to the normal operation of that particular business or enterprise."

The District Court rejected the bona-fide-occupational-qualification (bfoq) defense. . . .

We are persuaded by the restrictive language of §703(e), the relevant legislative history, and the consistent interpretation of the Equal Employment Opportunity Commission that the BFOQ exception was in fact meant to be an extremely narrow exception to the general prohibition of discrimination on the basis of sex. In the particular factual circumstances of this case, however, we conclude that the District Court erred in rejecting the State's contention that Regulation 204 falls within the narrow ambit of the BFOQ exception.

The environment in Alabama's penitentiaries is a peculiarly inhospitable one for human beings of whatever sex. Indeed, a Federal District Court has held that the conditions of confinement in the prisons of the State, characterized by "rampant violence" and a "jungle atmosphere," are constitutionally intolerable. Pugh v. Locke, 406 F. Supp. 318, 325 (M.D. Ala. (1976)). The record in the present case shows that because of inadequate staff and facilities, no attempt is made in the four maximum-security male penitentiaries to classify or segregate inmates according to their offense or level of dangerousness — a procedure that, according to expert testimony, is essential to effective penological administration. Consequently, the estimated 20% of the male prisoners who are sex offenders are scattered throughout the penitentiaries' dormitory facilities.

In this environment of violence and disorganization, it would be an oversimplification to characterize Regulation 204 as an exercise in "romantic paternalism." Cf. Frontiero v. Richardson, [411 U.S. 677, 684 (1973)]. In the usual case, the argument that a particular job is too dangerous for women may appropriately be met by the rejoinder that it is the purpose of Title VII to allow the individual woman to make that choice for herself. More is at stake in this case, however, than an individual woman's decision to weigh and accept the risks of employment in a "contact" position in a maximum-security male prison.

The essence of a correctional counselor's job is to maintain prison security. A woman's relative ability to maintain order in a male, maximum-security, unclassified penitentiary of the type Alabama now runs could be directly reduced by her womanhood. There is a basis in fact for expecting that sex offenders who have criminally assaulted women in the past would be moved to do so again if access to women were established within the prison. There would also be a real risk that other inmates, deprived of a normal heterosexual environment, would assault women guards because they were women.[22] In a prison system where violence is the order of the day, where inmate access to guards is facilitated by dormitory living arrangements, where every institution is understaffed, and where a substantial portion of the inmate population is composed of sex offenders mixed at random with other prisoners, there are few visible deterrents to inmate assaults on women custodians.

Appellee Rawlinson's own expert testified that dormitory housing for aggressive inmates poses a greater security problem than single-cell lockups, and further testified that it would be unwise to use women as guards in a prison where even 10% of the inmates had been convicted of sex crimes and were not segregated from the other prisoners.[23] The likelihood that inmates would assault a woman because she was a woman would pose a real threat not only to the victim of the assault but also to the basic control of the penitentiary and protection of its inmates and the other security personnel. The employee's very womanhood would thus directly undermine her capacity to provide the security that is the essence of a correctional counselor's responsibility. . . .

The judgment is accordingly affirmed in part and reversed in part, and the case is remanded to the District Court for further proceedings consistent with this opinion. . . .

[The opinion of Mr. Justice Rehnquist, with whom The Chief Justice and Mr. Justice Blackmun joined, concurring in the result and concurring in part, is omitted.]

Mr. Justice MARSHALL, with whom Mr. Justice BRENNAN joins, concurring in part and dissenting in part. . . .

The Court properly rejects two proffered justifications for denying women jobs as prison guards. It is simply irrelevant here that a guard's occupation is dangerous and that some women might be unable to protect themselves adequately. Those themes permeate the testimony of the state officials below, but as the Court holds, "the argument that a particular job is too dangerous for women" is refuted by the "purpose of Title VII to allow the individual woman to make that choice for herself." . . . Some women, like some men, undoubtedly are not qualified and do not wish to serve as prison guards, but that does not justify the exclusion of all women from this employment opportunity. Thus, "[i]n the usual case," . . . the Court's

22. The record contains evidence of an attack on a female clerical worker in an Alabama prison, and of an incident involving a woman student who was taken hostage during a visit to one of the maximum-security institutions.

23. Alabama's penitentiaries are evidently not typical. Appellee Rawlinson's two experts testified that in a normal, relatively stable maximum-security prison characterized by control over the inmates, reasonable living conditions, and segregation of dangerous offenders women guards could be used effectively and beneficially. Similarly, an amicus brief filed by the State of California attests to that State's success in using women guards in all-male penitentiaries.

interpretation of the bfoq exception would mandate hiring qualified women for guard jobs in maximum-security institutions. The highly successful experiences of other States allowing such job opportunities, see briefs for the States of California and Washington, as amici curiae, confirm that absolute disqualification of women is not, in the words of Title VII, "reasonably necessary to the normal operation" of a maximum security prison.

What would otherwise be considered unlawful discrimination against women is justified by the Court, however, on the basis of the "barbaric and inhumane" conditions in Alabama prisons, conditions so bad that state officials have conceded that they violate the Constitution. . . . To me, this analysis sounds distressingly like saying two wrongs make a right. It is refuted by the plain words of §703(e). The statute requires that a BFOQ be "reasonably necessary to the normal operation of that particular business or enterprise." But no governmental "business" may operate "normally" in violation of the Constitution. Every action of government is constrained by constitutional limitations. While those limits may be violated more frequently than we would wish, no one disputes that the "normal operation" of all government functions takes place within them. A prison system operating in blatant violation of the Eighth Amendment is an exception that should be remedied with all possible speed, as Judge Johnson's comprehensive order in Pugh v. Locke, [406 F. Supp. 318 (M.D. Ala. 1976)], is designed to do. In the meantime, the existence of such violations should not be legitimatized by calling them "normal." Nor should the Court accept them as justifying conduct that would otherwise violate a statute intended to remedy age-old discrimination.

The Court's error in statutory construction is less objectionable, however, than the attitude it displays toward women. Though the Court recognizes that possible harm to women guards is an unacceptable reason for disqualifying women, it relies instead on an equally speculative threat to prison discipline supposedly generated by the sexuality of female guards. There is simply no evidence in the record to show that women guards would create any danger to security in Alabama prisons significantly greater than that which already exists. All of the dangers with one exception discussed below are inherent in a prison setting, whatever the gender of the guards.

The Court first sees women guards as a threat to security because "there are few visible deterrents to inmate assaults on women custodians." . . . In fact, any prison guard is constantly subject to the threat of attack by inmates, and "invisible" deterrents are the guard's only real protection. No prison guard relies primarily on his or her ability to ward off an inmate attack to maintain order. Guards are typically unarmed and sheer numbers of inmates could overcome the normal complement. Rather, like all other law enforcement officers, prison guards must rely primarily on the moral authority of their office and the threat of future punishment for miscreants. As one expert testified below, common sense, fairness, and mental and emotional stability are the qualities a guard needs to cope with the dangers of the job. . . . Well qualified and properly trained women, no less than men, have these psychological weapons at their disposal.

The particular severity of discipline problems in the Alabama maximum-security prisons is also no justification for the discrimination sanctioned by the Court. The District Court found in Pugh v. Locke, supra, that guards "must spend all their time attempting to maintain control or to protect themselves." 406 F. Supp., at 325. If male guards face an impossible situation, it is difficult to see how women could make the problem worse, unless one relies on precisely the type of generalized bias against women that the Court agrees Title VII was intended to outlaw. For example, much of the testimony of appellants' witnesses ignores individual differences among members of each sex and reads like "ancient canards about the proper role of women." Phillips v. Martin Marietta Corp., [400 U.S. 542, 545 (1971) (Marshall, J., concurring)]. The witnesses claimed that women guards are not strict disciplinarians; that they are physically less capable of protecting themselves and subduing unruly inmates; that inmates take advantage of them as they did their mothers, while male guards are strong father figures who easily maintain discipline, and so on. Yet the record shows that the presence of women guards has not led to a single incident amounting to a serious breach of security in any Alabama institution.[3] And, in any event, "[g]uards rarely enter the cell blocks and dormitories," Pugh v. Locke, 406 F. Supp., at 325, where the danger of inmate attacks is the greatest.

It appears that the real disqualifying factor in the Court's view is "[t]he employee's very womanhood." . . . The Court refers to the large number of sex offenders in Alabama prisons, and to "[t]he likelihood that inmates would assault a woman because she was a woman." . . . In short, the fundamental justification for the decision is that women as guards will generate sexual assaults. With all respect, this rationale regrettably perpetuates one of the most insidious of the old myths about women that women, wittingly or not, are seductive sexual objects. The effect of the decision, made I am sure with the best of intentions, is to punish women because their very presence might provoke sexual assaults. It is women who are made to pay the price in lost job opportunities for the threat of depraved conduct by prison inmates. Once again, "[t]he pedestal upon which women have been placed has . . . , upon closer inspection, been revealed as a cage." Sail'er Inn, Inc. v. Kirby, [485 P.2d 529, 541 (1971)]. It is particularly ironic that the cage is erected here in response to feared misbehavior by imprisoned criminals.[4]

---

3. The Court refers to two incidents involving potentially dangerous attacks on women in prisons. . . . But these did not involve trained corrections officers; one victim was a clerical worker and the other a student visiting on a tour.

4. The irony is multiplied by the fact that enormous staff increases are required by the District Court's order in Pugh v. Locke, 406 F. Supp. 318 (M.D. Ala. 1976). This necessary hiring would be a perfect opportunity for appellants to remedy their past discrimination against women, but instead the Court's decision permits that policy to continue. Moreover, once

The proper response to inevitable attacks on both female and male guards is not to limit the employment opportunities of law-abiding women who wish to contribute to their community, but to take swift and sure punitive action against the inmate offenders. Presumably, one of the goals of the Alabama prison system is the eradication of inmates' antisocial behavior patterns so that prisoners will be able to live one day in free society. Sex offenders can begin this process by learning to relate to women guards in a socially acceptable manner. To deprive women of job opportunities because of the threatened behavior of convicted criminals is to turn our social priorities upside down.[5] . . .

Wilson v. Southwest Airlines Co.
517 F. Supp. 292 (N.D. Tex. 1981)

HIGGINBOTHAM, District Judge.

This case presents the important question whether femininity, or more accurately female sex appeal, is a bona fide occupational qualification ("BFOQ") for the jobs of flight attendant and ticket agent with Southwest Airlines. Plaintiff Gregory Wilson and the class of over 100 male job applicants he represents have challenged Southwest's open refusal to hire males as a violation of Title VII. . . .

At the phase one trial on liability, Southwest conceded that its refusal to hire males was intentional. . . . Southwest contends, however, that the BFOQ exception to Title VII's ban on sex discrimination, 42 U.S.C. §703(e), justifies its hiring only females for the public contact positions of flight attendant and ticket agent. The BFOQ window through which Southwest attempts to fly permits sex discrimination in situations where the employer can prove that sex is a "bona fide occupational qualification reasonably necessary to the normal operation of that particular business or enterprise." Id. Southwest reasons it may discriminate against males because

---

conditions are improved in accordance with the *Pugh* order, the problems that the Court perceives with women guards will be substantially alleviated.

5. The appellants argue that restrictions on employment of women are also justified by consideration of inmates' privacy. It is strange indeed to hear state officials who have for years been violating the most basic principles of human decency in the operation of their prisons suddenly become concerned about inmate privacy. It is stranger still that these same officials allow women guards in contact positions in a number of nonmaximum-security institutions, but strive to protect inmates' privacy in the prisons where personal freedom is most severely restricted. I have no doubt on this record that appellants' professed concern is nothing but a feeble excuse for discrimination.

As the District Court suggested, it may well be possible, once a constitutionally adequate staff is available, to rearrange work assignments so that legitimate inmate privacy concerns are respected without denying jobs to women. Finally, if women guards behave in a professional manner at all times, they will engender reciprocal respect from inmates, who will recognize that their privacy is being invaded no more than if a woman doctor examines them. The suggestion implicit in the privacy argument that such behavior is unlikely on either side is an insult to the professionalism of guards and the dignity of inmates.

its attractive female flight attendants and ticket agents personify the airline's sexy image and fulfill its public promise to take passengers skyward with "love." Defendant claims maintenance of its females-only hiring policy is crucial to the airline's continued financial success. . . .

Factual Background

. . . Southwest was incorporated in March of 1967 and filed its initial application with the Texas Aeronautics Commission ("TAC") in November of 1967 to serve the intrastate markets of Dallas, Houston and San Antonio. Southwest's proposed entry as an intrastate commuter carrier sparked a hostile reaction from the incumbent air carriers serving the Texas market. . . . [A]s a result of the defensive tactics of Southwest's competitors . . . [i]n December of 1970, Southwest had $143 in the bank and was over $100,000 in debt, though no aircraft had ever left the ground.

Barely intact, Southwest, in early 1971, called upon a Dallas advertising agency, the Bloom Agency, to develop a winning marketing strategy. Planning to initiate service quickly, Southwest needed instant recognition and a "catchy" image to distinguish it from its competitors.

The Bloom Agency evaluated both the images of the incumbent competitor airlines as well as the characteristics of passengers to be served by a commuter airline. Bloom determined that the other carriers serving the Texas market tended to project an image of conservatism. The agency also determined that the relatively short haul commuter market which Southwest hoped to serve was comprised of predominantly male businessmen. Based on these factors, Bloom suggested that Southwest break away from the conservative image of other airlines and project to the traveling public an airline personification of feminine youth and vitality. A specific female personality description was recommended and adopted by Southwest for its corporate image: This lady is young and vital . . . she is charming and goes through life with great flair and exuberance . . . you notice first her exciting smile, friendly air, her wit . . . yet she is quite efficient and approaches all her tasks with care and attention. . . .

From the personality description suggested by The Bloom Agency, Southwest developed its now famous "Love" personality. Southwest projects an image of feminine spirit, fun, and sex appeal. Its ads promise to provide "tender loving care" to its predominantly male, business passengers. The first advertisements run by the airline featured the slogan, "AT LAST THERE IS SOMEBODY ELSE UP THERE WHO LOVES YOU." Variations on this theme have continued through newspaper, billboard, magazine and television advertisements during the past ten years.[4]

---

4. Unabashed allusions to love and sex pervade all aspects of Southwest's public image. Its T.V. commercials feature attractive attendants in fitted outfits, catering to male passengers while an alluring feminine voice promises in-flight love. On board, attendants in hot-pants (skirts are now optional) serve "love bites" (toasted almonds) and "love potions" (cocktails).

Bloom's "Love" campaign was given a boost in 1974-1975 when the last of Southwest's competitors moved its operations to the new Dallas/Fort Worth Regional Airport, leaving Southwest as the only heavy carrier flying out of Dallas' convenient and fortuitously named, Love Field.

Over the years, Southwest gained national and international attention as the "love airline." Southwest Airlines' stock is traded on the New York Stock Exchange under the ticker symbol "LUV." During 1977 when Southwest opened five additional markets in Texas, the love theme was expanded to "WE'RE SPREADING LOVE ALL OVER TEXAS."

As an integral part of its youthful, feminine image, Southwest has employed only females in the high customer contact positions of ticket agent and flight attendant. From the start, Southwest's attractive personnel, dressed in high boots and hot-pants, generated public interest and "free ink." Their sex appeal has been used to attract male customers to the airline. Southwest's flight attendants, and to a lesser degree its ticket agents, have been featured in newspaper, magazine, billboard and television advertisements during the past ten years. Some attendants assist in promotional events for other businesses and civic organizations. Southwest flight attendants and ticket agents are featured in the company's in-flight magazine and have received notice in numerous other national and international publications. The airline also encourages its attendants to entertain the passengers and maintain an atmosphere of informality and "fun" during flights. According to Southwest, its female flight attendants have come to "personify" Southwest's public image.

Southwest has enjoyed enormous success in recent years.[6] This is in no small part due to its marketing image. Though Southwest now enjoys a distinct advantage by operating its commuter flights out of "convenient" Love and Hobby Fields, the airline achieved a commanding position in the regional commuter market while flying "wing tip to wing tip" with national carriers who utilized the same airport, fares, schedules, and aircraft. The evidence was undisputed that Southwest's unique, feminized image played and continues to play an important role in the airline's success.

Less certain, however, is Southwest's assertion that its females-only hiring policy is necessary for the continued success of its image and its business. Based on two on-board surveys, one conducted in October, 1979, before this suit was filed, and another in August, 1980, when the suit was pending, Southwest contends its attractive flight attendants are the "largest single component" of its success. In the 1979 survey, however, of the attributes considered most important by passengers, the category "courte-

---

Even Southwest's ticketing system features a "quickie machine" to provide "instant gratification."

6. From 1979 to 1980, the company's earnings rose from $17 million to $28 million when most other airlines suffered heavy losses. As a percentage of revenues, Southwest's return is considered to be one of the highest in the industry.

ous and attentive hostesses" ranked fifth in importance behind (1) on time departures, (2) frequently scheduled departures, (3) friendly and helpful reservations and ground personnel, and (4) convenient departure times. . . . Apparently, one of the remaining eight alternative categories, "attractive hostesses," was not selected with sufficient frequency to warrant being included in the reported survey results. . . .

. . . [R]ather than Southwest's female personnel being the "sole factor" distinguishing the airline from its competitors, as Defendant contends, the 1980 survey lists Southwest's "personnel" as only one among five characteristics contributing to Southwest's public image. . . . Accordingly, there is no persuasive proof that Southwest's passengers prefer female over male flight attendants and ticket agents, or, of greater importance, that they would be less likely to fly Southwest if males were hired.

In evaluating Southwest's BFOQ defense, therefore, the Court proceeds on the basis that "love," while important, is not everything in the relationship between Defendant and its passengers. Still, it is proper to infer from the airline's competitive successes that Southwest's overall "love image" has enhanced its ability to attract passengers. To the extent the airline has successfully feminized its image and made attractive females an integral part of its public face, it also follows that femininity and sex appeal are qualities related to successful job performance by Southwest's flight attendants and ticket agents. The strength of this relationship has not been proved. It is with this factual orientation that the Court turns to examine Southwest's BFOQ defense.

Interpretations of the Bona Fide Occupational Qualification

. . . Early on, the Equal Employment Opportunity Commission ("EEOC"), created by Congress to administer Title VII, pronounced that "the bona fide occupational qualification as to sex should be interpreted narrowly." See EEOC Guidelines on Discrimination Because of Sex, 29 C.F.R. §1604.2(a) (1965). The agency Guidelines further stated that the BFOQ exception did not justify "the refusal to hire an individual because of the preferences of . . . the employer, clients or customers," except where necessary for authenticity as provided in §1604.2(a)(2). Id. at §1604.2(a)(1)(iii). . . .

To date, the Commission has steadfastly adhered to its position that customer preference gives rise to a bona fide occupational qualification for sex in one instance only, "(w)here it is necessary for the purpose of authenticity or genuineness . . . e.g. an actor or actress." Id. at §1604.2(a)(2) as amended by 45 Fed. Reg. 74676 (Nov. 10, 1980). . . .

Those courts which have analyzed Title VII's BFOQ exception, however, have broadened its sweep. Consistent with the language of §703(e), courts have held, or stated, that customer preference for one sex may be taken into account in those limited instances where satisfying customer preference is "reasonably necessary to the normal operation of the particular business or enterprise." . . .

This Circuit's decisions in Weeks v. Southern Bell Tel. & Tel. Co., 408 F.2d 228 (5th Cir. 1969) ("*Weeks*") and Diaz v. Pan American World Airways, Inc., 442 F.2d 385 (5th Cir.), cert. denied [404 U.S. 950 (1971)] ("*Diaz*") have given rise to a two step BFOQ test: (1) does the particular job under consideration require that the worker be of one sex only; and if so, (2) is that requirement reasonably necessary to the "essence" of the employer's business. . . . The first level of inquiry is designed to test whether sex is so essential to job performance that a member of the opposite sex simply could not do the same job. . . . As stated in *Weeks*, 408 F.2d at 235: (T)o rely on a bona fide occupational qualification exception, an employer has the burden of proving that he had reasonable cause to believe, that is a factual basis for believing, that all or substantially all women would be unable to perform safely and efficiently the duties of the job involved. The second level is designed to assure that the qualification being scrutinized is one so important to the operation of the business that the business would be undermined if employees of the "wrong" sex were hired. . . . *Diaz*'s "essence of the business" rule has now been adopted by every Circuit that has considered the matter. As the court there explained:

> . . . (T)he use of the word "necessary" in Section 703(e) requires that we apply a business necessity test, not a business *convenience* test. That is to say, discrimination based on sex is valid only when the *essence* of the business operation would be undermined by not hiring members of one sex exclusively.

Diaz, 442 F.2d at 388 (original emphasis).

Southwest concedes with respect to the *Weeks* test that males are able to perform safely and efficiently all the basic, mechanical functions required of flight attendants and ticket agents . . . Southwest's position, however, is that females are required to fulfill certain non-mechanical aspects of these jobs: to attract those male customers who prefer female attendants and ticket agents, and to preserve the authenticity and genuineness of Southwest's unique, female corporate personality.

A similar, though not identical, argument that females could better perform certain non-mechanical functions required of flight attendants was rejected in *Diaz*. There, the airline argued and the trial court found that being female was a BFOQ because women were superior in "providing reassurance to anxious passengers, giving courteous personalized service and, in general, making flights as pleasurable as possible within the limitations imposed by aircraft operations." 442 F.2d at 387; 311 F. Supp. 559, 563 (S.D. Fla. 1970). Although it accepted the trial court findings, the Court of Appeals reversed, holding that femininity was not a BFOQ, because catering to passengers' psychological needs was only "tangential" to what was "reasonably *necessary*" for the business involved (original emphasis). [442

F.2d at 388.] Characterizing the "essence" or "primary function" of Pan American's business as the safe transportation of passengers from one point to another, the court explained:

> While a pleasant environment, enhanced by the obvious cosmetic effect that female stewardesses provide as well as, according to the findings of the trial court, their apparent ability to perform the non-mechanical functions of the job in a more effective manner than most men, may all be important, they are tangential to the essence of the business involved. No one has suggested that having male stewards will so seriously affect the operation of the airline as to jeopardize or even minimize its ability to provide safe transportation from one place to another.

[442 F.2d at 388.]

Similar reasoning underlay the appellate court's rejection of Pan American's claim that its customers' preference for female attendants justified its refusal to hire males. Because the non-mechanical functions that passengers preferred females to perform were tangential to the airline's business, the court held, "the fact that customers prefer (females) cannot justify sex discrimination." [442 F.2d at 389.] The Fifth Circuit in *Diaz* did not hold that customer preference could never give rise to a sex BFOQ. Rather, consistent with the EEOC's exception for authenticity and genuineness, the Court allowed that customer preference could "be taken into account only when it is based on the company's inability to perform the primary function or service it offers," that is, where sex or sex appeal is itself the dominant service provided.

Diaz and its progeny establish that to recognize a BFOQ for jobs requiring multiple abilities, some sex-linked and some sex-neutral, the sex-linked aspects of the job must predominate. Only then will an employer have satisfied *Weeks'* requirement that sex be so essential to successful job performance that a member of the opposite sex could not perform the job. An illustration of such dominance in sex cases is the exception recognized by the EEOC for authenticity and genuineness. In the example given in [29 C.F.R.] §1604.2(a)(2), that of an actor or actress, the primary function of the position, its essence, is to fulfill the audience's expectation and desire for a particular role, characterized by particular physical or emotional traits. Generally, a male could not supply the authenticity required to perform a female role. Similarly, in jobs where sex or vicarious sexual recreation is the primary service provided, e.g. a social escort or topless dancer, the job automatically calls for one sex exclusively; the employee's sex and the service provided are inseparable. Thus, being female has been deemed a BFOQ for the position of a Playboy Bunny, female sexuality being reasonably necessary to perform the dominant purpose of the job which is forthrightly to titillate and entice male customers. See St. Cross v. Playboy Club, Appeal No. 773, Case No. CFS 22618-70 (New York Human Rights Appeal Board, 1971) (dicta); Weber v. Playboy Club, Appeal No. 774, Case No. CFS 22619-70 (New York Human Rights Appeal Board, 1971) (dicta). One court has also suggested, without holding, that the authenticity exception would give rise to a BFOQ for Chinese nationality where necessary to maintain the authentic atmosphere of an ethnic Chinese restaurant, Utility Workers v. Southern California Edison, 320 F. Supp. 1262, 1265 (C.D. Cal. 1970).

Application of the Bona Fide Occupational Qualification to Southwest Airlines

Applying the first level test for a BFOQ, with its legal gloss, to Southwest's particular operations results in the conclusion that being female is not a qualification required to perform successfully the jobs of flight attendant and ticket agent with Southwest. Like any other airline, Southwest's primary function is to transport passengers safely and quickly from one point to another.[24] To do this, Southwest employs ticket agents whose primary job duties are to ticket passengers and check baggage, and flight attendants, whose primary duties are to assist passengers during boarding and deboarding, to instruct passengers in the location and use of aircraft safety equipment, and to serve passengers cocktails and snacks during the airline's short commuter flights. Mechanical, non-sex-linked duties dominate both these occupations. Indeed, on Southwest's short-haul commuter flights there is time for little else. That Southwest's female personnel may perform their mechanical duties "with love" does not change the result. "Love" is the manner of job performance, not the job performed.

While possession of female allure and sex appeal have been made qualifications for Southwest's contact personnel by virtue of the "love" campaign, the functions served by employee sexuality in Southwest's operations are not dominant ones. According to Southwest, female sex appeal serves two purposes: (1) attracting and entertaining male passengers and (2) fulfilling customer expectations for female service engendered by Southwest's advertising which features female personnel. As in *Diaz*, these non-mechanical, sex-linked job functions are only "tangential" to the essence of the occupations and business involved. Southwest is not a business where vicarious sex entertainment is the primary service provided. Accordingly, the ability of the airline to perform its primary business function, the transportation of passengers, would not be jeopardized by hiring males.

---

24. Southwest's argument that its primary function is "to make a profit," not to transport passengers, must be rejected. Without doubt the goal of every business is to make a profit. For purposes of BFOQ analysis, however, the business "essence" inquiry focuses on the particular service provided and the job tasks and functions involved, not the business goal. If an employer could justify employment discrimination merely on the grounds that it is necessary to make a profit, Title VII would be nullified in short order.

Southwest does not face the situation . . . where an established customer preference for one sex is so strong that the business would be undermined if employees of the opposite sex were hired. Southwest's claim that its customers prefer females rests primarily upon inferences drawn from the airline's success after adopting its female personality. But according to Southwest's own surveys, that success is attributable to many factors. There is no competent proof that Southwest's popularity derives directly from its females-only policy to the exclusion of other factors like dissatisfaction with rival airlines and Southwest's use of convenient Love and Hobby Fields. Nor is there competent proof that the customer preference for females is so strong that Defendant's male passengers would cease doing business with Southwest as was the case in [Fernandez v. Wynn Oil Co., 20 Fair Empl. Prac. Cases (BNA) 1162 (C.D. Cal. 1979)]. In short, Southwest has failed in its proof to satisfy Diaz's business necessity requirement, without which customer preference may not give rise to a BFOQ for sex. . . .

It is also relevant that Southwest's female image was adopted at its discretion, to promote a business unrelated to sex. Contrary to the unyielding South American preference for males encountered by the Defendant company in *Fernandez*, Southwest exploited, indeed nurtured, the very customer preference for females it now cites to justify discriminating against males. . . . Moreover, the fact that a vibrant marketing campaign was necessary to distinguish Southwest in its early years does not lead to the conclusion that sex discrimination was then, or is now, a business necessity. Southwest's claim that its female image will be tarnished by hiring males is, in any case, speculative at best.

. . . [S]ex does not become a BFOQ merely because an employer chooses to exploit female sexuality as a marketing tool, or to better insure profitability. . . .

Conclusion

. . . Rejecting a wider BFOQ for sex does not eliminate the commercial exploitation of sex appeal. It only requires, consistent with the purposes of Title VII, that employers exploit the attractiveness and allure of a sexually integrated workforce. Neither Southwest, nor the traveling public, will suffer from such a rule. More to the point, it is my judgment that this is what Congress intended. . . .

Notes

1. The Business Necessity Defense. The height and weight job criteria challenged in *Dothard* did not exclude women based directly on their sex; rather, by excluding over 40 percent of the female population while excluding only 1 percent of males, it had a disparate impact on women. It thus required a business necessity, which the state could not show. The

Supreme Court's reasoning is that these criteria were proxies for strength, which could have been more directly measured. How likely do you think it is that substantially more women could qualify under a strength test? See Problem 2-13, infra. Of course if a disproportionate impact remained, that rule, too, would need to be justified under the business necessity test.

In light of the Court's recognition of prison security concerns that led it to uphold the male-only rule in maximum-security areas, what if the defendant had shown that the height and weight restrictions were necessary to create the *appearance* of strength, as vital to prison security as strength itself? Justice Rehnquist, concurring, raises this possibility. See 433 U.S. at 339-341.

The business necessity test is viewed by many courts as being somewhat more lenient on the employer than the BFOQ test. See, e.g., Yuhas v. Libby-Owens-Ford Co., 562 F.2d 496 (7th Cir. 1977), cert. denied, 435 U.S. 934 (1978) (anti-nepotism rule having a disproportionate effect on women was justified by employer concerns that were "far from frivolous" and "plausible"). Other courts treat the two tests as essentially the same. See, e.g., Chambers v. Omaha Girls Club, Inc., 834 F.2d 697 (8th Cir. 1987).

2. BFOQ and Sexual Authenticity. As facially discriminatory exclusions based on sex, the prison regulation excluding women as prison guards in maximum-security areas in *Dothard* and the exclusion of men as flight attendants in *Wilson* were examples of disparate treatment discrimination, which could be justified under Title VII only if the sex of the employee in each case was shown to be a bona fide occupational qualification or BFOQ. There are a few "easy" cases where it seems clear that sex is a necessary qualification for a particular job. Only a woman can be a wet nurse, for example, and only a man can be a semen donor. See Developments in the Law — Employment Discrimination and Title VII of the Civil Rights Act of 1964, 84 Harv. L. Rev. 1109, 1178-1179 (1971). Most other cases are more difficult. Under one recognized category of cases, sex is a BFOQ if the job requires sexual authenticity. 29 C.F.R. §1604.2(a)(2) (2000). The most common application arises in the entertainment industry, in circumstances in which an actor's or actress's plausibility depends on sexual identity with the character portrayed. See also Button v. Rockefeller, 351 N.Y.S.2d 488 (Sup. Ct. 1973) (sex a BFOQ for female undercover agents).

According to *Wilson*, sex may be used to establish a climate of female sex appeal only when the "essence" of the business relates to that sex appeal. While the cases are rare, it is generally taken for granted that a topless dancing bar or a Playboy Bunny Club may hire only women dancers, and may discharge an employee for failure to meet the employer's criteria relating to sexual image:

The "Bunny image" apparently depends upon the physique, attractiveness and beauty of the girl-employee who wears on the job a rabbit-like costume of scanty dimensions, quite unlike the fulsome attire (white gloves and formal dress) worn by the White Rabbit in Lewis Carroll's Alice in Wonderland. A particular employee's "Bunny image" has been rated by [Playboy Clubs International] on a numerical scale as follows: (1) "a flawless beauty"; (2) "exceptionally pretty, perhaps some minor flaw"; (3) "marginal or having some correctible deficiency, which might be weight [or] a cosmetic problem; something that is not of a more lasting, enduring, permanent nature"; (4) "loss of or the absence of the image requirements to be employed as a bunny."

Playboy Clubs Int'l, Inc. v. Hotel & Restaurant Employees & B.I.U., 321 F. Supp. 704 (1971) (discharge of 13 women for "lack of bunny image" not arbitrable under union agreement). A few unreported cases directly upholding sex as a BFOQ for Playboy Bunnies are cited in Guardian Capital Corp. v. New York State Div. of Human Rights, 360 N.Y.S.2d 937 (App. Div. 1974), appeal dismissed, 396 N.Y.S.2d 1027 (N.Y. 1975). *Guardian Capital* itself, however, holds that the replacement by a restaurant of male waiters with waitresses dressed in alluring costumes violates Title VII even if evidence demonstrates that restaurant sales increased slightly after doing so. Ironically perhaps, it would seem that the more explicitly the employer's business exploits sex for money — which is arguably more harmful to women than formal inequality, see Chapter 4, infra — the more easily it will satisfy the standard and permit the employer to discriminate on the basis of sex. See Rachel L. Cantor, Comment, Consumer Preferences for Sex and Title VII: Employing Market Definition Analysis for Evaluating BFOQ Defenses, 1999 U. Chi. Legal F. 493 (1999).

Is it clear that the case for "authentic" sex roles in films and plays or as Playboy "Bunnies" is more compelling that the role of female flight attendants in the "Luv" airline?

3. BFOQ and Customer Preferences. How strong a proposition do *Diaz* and *Wilson* present that customer preference based on sexual stereotypes cannot justify discriminatory conduct? In the lower court decision in *Diaz*, 311 F. Supp. 559 (S.D. Fla. 1970), the airline introduced evidence of a survey indicating that 79 percent of all passengers, male and female, preferred being served by female flight attendants. Expert psychological evidence was also introduced to explain the general preference of airline passengers for female attendants. It posited that the unique experience of being levitated off the ground and transported through the air at high speeds creates feelings of apprehension, boredom, and excitement; that females were psychologically better equipped to cope with these conflicting states and especially adept at relieving passenger apprehension; and that passengers of both sexes responded better to the presence of females. Id. at 565. This and other evidence persuaded the district court that sex was a BFOQ for flight attendants. The Fifth Circuit Court of Appeals took a harder line on the question of customer preferences, however, holding that the airline could take the interpersonal skills of flight attendant applicants into account, but that it could not do so by categorically excluding all men. 442 F.2d 385, 388 (5th Cir.), cert. denied, 404 U.S. 950 (1971). Is the rejection of the survey evidence in *Diaz* and *Wilson* consistent with its use in defending the employer's decision to reassign Christine Craft?

Fernandez v. Wynn Oil Co., 20 Fair Empl. Prac. Cas. (BNA) 1162 (C.D. Cal. 1979), distinguished with some difficulty in *Wilson*, was overturned by the Ninth Circuit Court of Appeals, 653 F.2d 1273 (9th Cir. 1981), in an opinion holding that an oil company could not refuse to hire female executives because its South American clients would refuse to deal with them. While the factual basis for this claim was not established in *Fernandez*, the court held that even if it had been, stereotyped customer preference cannot justify a sexually discriminatory practice. 653 F.2d at 1276-1277. Can this rule be reconciled with a BFOQ rule permitting female-only Playboy Bunnies? With KMBC's decision to reassign Christine Craft?

4. BFOQ and Privacy Considerations. Courts have also found the BFOQ test satisfied in some cases in which sex-specific hiring accommodates the concern of third parties for privacy or other related interests. In Fesel v. Masonic Home of Delaware, Inc., 447 F. Supp. 1346 (D. Del. 1978), aff'd mem., 591 F.2d 1334 (3d Cir. 1979), for example, nine of the nursing home's female residents signed an affidavit objecting "most strenuously" to male nurses or nurses' aides. The court accepted the employer's defense that female sex was a BFOQ for the nursing positions. Quite a number of cases in the context of hospitals and nursing homes have reached the same conclusion. See, e.g., Healey v. Southwood Psychiatric Hospital, 78 F.3d 128 (3d Cir. 1996) (sex is a BFOQ for purposes of scheduling assignments in psychiatric hospital for emotionally disturbed and sexually abused children, because matching of staff and patients is important for parental role modeling and because children who have been sexually abused will disclose their problems more easily to a member of a certain sex, depending on their sex and sex of the abuser); Jennings v. New York State Office of Mental Health, 786 F. Supp. 376 (S.D.N.Y.), aff'd, 977 F.2d 731 (2d Cir. 1992) (sex is a BFOQ at a state psychiatric hospital for "security hospital treatment assistant" whose duties included feeding, clothing, and cleaning patients, assisting in personal hygiene, and observing patients in bathrooms and bedrooms); Jones v. Hinds General Hospital, 666 F. Supp. 933 (S.D. Miss. 1987) (sex is a BFOQ for hospital orderlies where a significant number of male patients objected to having their private parts viewed or touched by female personnel); EEOC v. Mercy Health Center, 29 Fair Empl. Prac. Cas. (BNA) 159 (W.D. Okla. 1982) (in medical facility for high-risk pregnancies, complaints by male physicians and survey results indicating objections by prenatal patients to use of male nurses in labor and delivery area justified exclusion of male nurses to avoid "medically undesired tension").

Assume that in these nursing home and hospital cases patients *are* quite comfortable with male doctors, though the procedures they perform are equally invasive of their privacy. Doesn't the BFOQ exception applied to nurses in this context perpetuate age-old stereotypes about woman's proper role, i.e., washing up and cleaning up after people, and about man's proper role, i.e., as the skilled professional? In fact, isn't the "privacy" claim in this context simply another way of expressing "customer preference"? Recall Robert Hall's privacy concerns in maintaining a sex-segregated sales force (see page 157). Should these outweigh the interests of women in equal employment opportunities?

The problem posed by these cases is that employers are permitted "to exclude males from jobs requiring intimate contact with female patients while at the same time . . . [permitted] to hire females for positions requiring intimate contact with male patients." Deborah A. Calloway, Equal Employment and Third Party Privacy Interests: An Analytical Framework for Reconciling Competing Rights, 54 Fordham L. Rev. 327 (1985). Would the problem be resolved with a neutral rule that allowed employers to hire nurses so that all male patients would be served by male nurses, and female patients by female nurses? Under a formal equality approach, this rule would be no more objectionable than the practice, assumed to be legal in *Robert Hall*, of hiring men only for men's clothing departments and women only for women's departments. But should Title VII permit all men and women to be equally trapped by roles defined by their sex? The proposed rule is totally hypothetical in the hospital setting, since no hospital would want to operate with sex-segregated staffs and wards; and, as it turns out, male patients, as well as female patients, prefer female nurses. Could even these male patients have a legitimate complaint that their privacy interests were offended by having their genitals washed by male nurses, thus justifying the employer in hiring no male nurses whatsoever?

Most commentators have been highly critical of the broad BFOQ defense courts have defined in the privacy area. Nonetheless, hints in UAW v. Johnson Controls, 499 U.S. 187, 206 n.4 (1991) (Blackmun, J.) and 499 U.S. at 219 n.8 (White, J., concurring), set forth below at pages 240-241 and 243-244, suggest that the United States Supreme Court is inclined to endorse a privacy application of the BFOQ defense.

When the privacy claim is by a prisoner, rather than a patient or customer, it is likely to get short shrift. See, e.g., Michenfelder v. Sumner, 860 F.2d 328 (9th Cir. 1988); Gunther v. Iowa State Men's Reformatory, 612 F.2d 1079 (8th Cir.), cert. denied, 446 U.S. 966 (1980). When courts do recognize a right to privacy for inmates, it seems that women's privacy concerns are more likely to be given effect than men's. Compare Johnson v. Phelan, 69 F.3d 144 (7th Cir. 1995), cert. denied, 519 U.S. 1006 (1996) (upholding a monitoring policy that allowed female guards to observe male prisoners in various states of undress and noting that such a policy reduces hiring practices in conflict with Title VII), with Forts v. Ward, 621 F.2d 1210 (2nd Cir. 1980) (accommodating the privacy claims of females prisoners being viewed by male guards by ordering screens to be installed in the showers and allowing female inmates to cover their cell door for 15 minutes in the evening while they changed into pajamas) and Torres v. Wisconsin Dep't of Health & Soc. Servs., 859 F.2d 1523 (7th Cir. 1988), cert. denied, 489 U.S. 1017, cert. denied, 489 U.S. 1082 (1989) (holding that the exclusion of male prison guards from a female prison could be justified as a BFOQ to achieve the prison's stated goal of rehabilitating inmates). These cases and others are discussed in Rebecca Jurado, The Essence of Her Womanhood: Defining the Privacy Rights of Women Prisoners and the Employment Rights of Women Guards, 7 Am. U. J. Gender, Soc. Pol'y & L. 1 (1999). Is the "favoritism" to women appropriate?

5. **Sex as a BFOQ in Counseling Positions.** Should the BFOQ defense be recognized in cases in which it is shown that the effect of counseling for children may be affected by the sex of the counselor? Early cases thought so. See, e.g., City of Philadelphia v. Pennsylvania Human Relations Comm'n, 300 A.2d 97 (Pa. Commw. Ct. 1973) ("the biological differences between men and women which in turn produce psychological differences" justify counseling jobs using sex as a criterion). More recent cases have not. See, e.g., Scott v. Parkview Memorial Hospital, 175 F.3d 523 (7th Cir. 1999) (rejecting a male social worker's sex discrimination claim due to subjective interview techniques that he claimed were biased in favor of women because they emphasized such traits as warmth and helpfulness); EEOC v. Physicians Weight Loss Centers, 953 F. Supp. 301 (W.D. Mo. 1996) (although 95 percent of customers at a weight loss center were women and some objected to having their measurements taken by a man and did not feel comfortable discussing emotional and physiological issues associated with weight loss with a man, sex was not a BFOQ for center's counselors). Has the law improved? Or have changes in perception of gender made the case for a BFOQ less compelling in this context?

6. **Vulnerability to Rape as a BFOQ.** *Dothard* upholds a sex-based discrimination precluding women from taking positions as prison guards in maximum-security prisons on the grounds that the likelihood of assault, which is a direct consequence of the "employee's very womanhood," would pose a threat to "basic control of the penitentiary." Justice Marshall's dissenting opinion exhausts virtually every tool of traditional equality analysis: it disputes the factual premises of the rule — for example, that woman guards would create a danger to the prison's basic security; it identifies the stereotypes about women as "seductive sexual objects" that are reinforced through the exclusion; and it insists that some women will be able

to protect themselves and should be given the chance, as individuals, to prove that ability rather than be foreclosed from an opportunity on the basis of the average characteristics of their sex. It also challenges the quality of the justification offered by the state: inadequate staffing. If you think that this issue in *Dothard* is wrongly decided, is it because the Court failed to apply standard formal equality principles correctly? Because formal equality does not provide the tools necessary to analyze an exclusion based on factors "unique" to women? Or some other reason?

Is *Dothard* consistent with the other principles set forth in this section? In an important sense, of course, excluding women where they might present temptation for the prisoners is just a version of "consumer preference." Is the concern for prison safety and security sufficiently distinguishable from the kinds of business justifications rejected in other cases? Isn't it just a question of economics? Why should Southwest Airlines be required to forego the income attributable to being the "LUV" airline, while the state of Alabama may defend the limits it places on women's employment opportunities on the grounds that prison conditions are, under present staffing arrangements, insufficient?

Dothard presents a strong contrast to the main thread of Title VII law, some of which was discussed in the *Wilson* case, which prohibits rules that restrict women, for their own protection, from jobs considered dangerous or too strenuous. See UAW v. Johnson Controls, Inc., set forth below. Can *Dothard* be viewed as a holdover from the protective legislation cases like Muller v. Oregon, set forth in Chapter 1?

Putting Theory into Practice

2-11. (a) A 50-lawyer law firm handles, among other things, insurance and employment discrimination defense. A number of the firm's oldest and best clients prefer to work with male attorneys, because they have more confidence in their abilities. Most recently, an insurance client threatened to take his business elsewhere if Paula Smith, who was assigned to handle a personal injury defense case for his company, was not removed from the case in favor of one of the firms's "bright, new" (male) attorneys. The reassignment is made. Does Paula Smith have a Title VII claim?

(b) The firm also has a practice of assigning women attorneys to employment discrimination cases brought by women claiming sex discrimination, and assigning minority attorneys to employment discrimination cases in which race is an issue. Paul Smith, a white male attorney with the firm, believes that this policy in assigning cases reduces his opportunities to excel at the firm. Does he have a Title VII claim?

2-12. (a) Although male and female guards are used in men's prisons in State X, in women's prisons only female guards are hired in positions involving strip searches and surveillance of female inmates while undressed, using toilet facilities, showering and sleeping. In support of the policy, the superintendent of the women's prison testified as follows:

> [W]omen . . . when they come in have a history of being very influenced, if not dominated by men in their lives and one of our major goals is to teach them . . . self-respect and . . . dignity [and that they] have the capability of making their own decisions and living their lives based on their own perceptions of what they want and what their options are. And [if] we established atmospheres where men are playing the primary dominant force . . . that's just going to perpetuate that, that's just going to further compound what she's lived with in the past and she will probably defer to the male and that's not something we want her to do.

Torres v. Wis. Dep't of Health & Soc. Servs., 838 F.2d 944 (7th Cir. 1986) (dissenting opinion by Ripple, J.), rev'd en banc, 859 F.2d 1523 (7th Cir. 1988), cert. denied, 489 U.S. 1017, cert. denied, 489 U.S. 1082 (1989). Is sex a BFOQ in this case?

(b) A female prison guard in a small county jail was employed on the first shift for a few years. A state regulation required a female guard to be on duty whenever a female prisoner was present. The majority of all female inmates were brought in during the third shift. The lack of a female guard on duty during that time was a huge expense and inconvenience to the County as they had to call in a female deputy and pay her overtime to transport the female prisoner to a neighboring county where a female guard was on duty. The County decided to solve this problem by reassigning the female prison guard to the third shift. The guard sues claiming sex discrimination since her reassignment to the third shift occurred solely on the basis of her sex. Does she have a Title VII claim? See Reed v. County of Casey, 184 F.3d 597 (6th Cir. 1999) (holding that sex was a permissible BFOQ in this instance).

2-13. A transportation agency requires all foot patrol officers to be able to run 1.5 miles in under 12 minutes and maintain a 42.5 ml/kg/min aerobic capacity. The Agency claims that the qualification is necessary to deter crime. In the years 1991, 1993, and 1996, an average of only 12% of women applicants passed the 1.5 mile run compared to 60% of male applicants. Is this job qualification a BFOQ? See Lanning v. SEPTA, 2000 U.S. Dist. LEXIS 17612 (E.D. Pa. 2000), 84 Fair Empl. Prac. Cas. (BNA) 1012 (holding requirements valid as a business necessity).

2-14. The management of a new, expensive French restaurant intends to hire only male waiters, in line with the tradition of the "classiest" Continental establishments. If it tries to do so, will it be violating Title VII?

2-15. Professor V. works for a state university and conducts many research projects through grants obtained through the university. One of these projects is a study of women who have rejected settlement offers by a trust fund set up to satisfy the claims of women injured by the Dalkon Shield inter-uterine birth-control device and who must pursue their claims through non-judicial adjudicatory hearings set up under the terms of the trust. The purpose of the project is to study the effectiveness of those hearings and the surrounding process. The research plan requires the lengthy interviews of women claimants both before and after the hearings, with questions that probe, among other things, the intimate details of their sex lives, their sex partners, their contraception histories, and other matters relating to their experiences with the Dalkon Shield. Most of these women have suffered substantial distress and harm as a result of these experiences and many find it understandably difficult to discuss these experiences with strangers.

Professor V. wants to hire only white women, ages 35 to 45, to conduct these interviews. His reason is that the validity of his research requires the interviewer to create a neutral, nonjudgmental atmosphere in which the interviewees feel comfortable talking about one of the most private aspects of their lives. Research has shown that people of virtually every race, sex, and background, including blacks, Hispanics, men, and women, feel most comfortable talking about the intimate details of their lives with middle-aged white women between the ages of 35 and 45.

He asks your advice. May he hire only white women ages 35 to 45 as interviewers, without violating any laws? Should the law allow him to do so?

2-16. Hooters is an Atlanta-based restaurant chain that hires only female food servers, bartenders, and hosts. These women wear tight short-shorts and tank tops or half-tees with a large-eyed owl on the front. Some shirt backs read "More than a Mouthful." Hooters sells food, drink, posters, T-shirts, calendars, and other products. It also offers an atmosphere of what a spokeswoman described as "good-humored, wholesome sex appeal that the Hooters girls embody." Although it welcomes children, the sexy cheerleader image of the Hooters' girls is designed to attract its target audience of adult males. Does Hooters have a BFOQ defense to a sex discrimination suit brought by male applicants who were rejected for jobs because of their sex?

2-17. Upon her return from a medical leave, Joan was transferred by her employer from a day to an evening shift, whereupon she quit. She sues the employer, claiming she was discriminated against based on her sex in that the employer "preyed upon [her] wifely instincts" by transferring her to the second shift knowing that she would quit to take care of her husband. What does she have to show to prove her case? What problems will she have? For a related set of facts, see Grube v. Lau Industries Inc., 257 F.3d 723 (7th Cir. 2001).

≣ *UAW v. Johnson Controls, Inc.*
≣ 499 U.S. 187 (1991)

Justice BLACKMUN delivered the opinion of the Court.

In this case we are concerned with an employer's gender-based fetal-protection policy. May an employer exclude a fertile female employee from certain jobs because of its concern for the health of the fetus the woman might conceive?

I

Respondent Johnson Controls, Inc., manufactures batteries. In the manufacturing process, the element lead is a primary ingredient. Occupational exposure to lead entails health risks, including the risk of harm to any fetus carried by a female employee.

Before [Title VII] became law, Johnson Controls did not employ any woman in a battery-manufacturing job. In June 1977, however, it announced its first official policy concerning its employment of women in lead-exposure work:

> [P]rotection of the health of the unborn child is the immediate and direct responsibility of the prospective parents. While the medical profession and the company can support them in the exercise of this responsibility, it cannot assume it for them without simultaneously infringing their rights as persons. . . . Since not all women who can become mothers wish to become mothers (or will become mothers), it would appear to be illegal discrimination to treat all who are capable of pregnancy as though they will become pregnant. . . .

Consistent with that view, Johnson Controls "stopped short of excluding women capable of bearing children from lead exposure," . . . but emphasized that a woman who expected to have a child should not choose a job in which she would have such exposure. The company also required a woman who wished to be considered for employment to sign a statement that she had been advised of the risk of having a child while she was exposed to lead. The statement informed the woman that although there was evidence "that women exposed to lead have a higher rate of abortion," this evidence was "not as clear . . . as the relationship between cigarette smoking and cancer," but that it was, "medically speaking, just good sense not to run that risk if you want children and do not want to expose the unborn child to risk, however small. . . ."

Five years later, in 1982, Johnson Controls shifted from a policy of warning to a policy of exclusion. Between 1979 and 1983, eight employees became pregnant while maintaining blood lead levels in excess of 30 micrograms per deciliter. . . . This appeared to be the critical level noted by the Occupational Health and Safety Administration (OSHA) for a worker who was planning to have a family. See 29 C.F.R. §1910.1025 (1989). The company responded by announcing a broad exclusion of women from jobs that exposed them to lead:

> . . . [I]t is [Johnson Controls'] policy that women who are pregnant or who are capable of bearing children will not be placed into jobs involving lead exposure or which could expose them to lead through the exercise of job bidding, bumping, transfer or promotion rights. . . .

The policy defined "women . . . capable of bearing children" as "[a]ll women except those whose inability to bear children is medically documented." . . . It further stated that an unacceptable work station was one where, "over the past year," an employee had recorded a blood lead level of more than 30 micrograms per deciliter or the work site had yielded an air sample containing a lead level in excess of 30 micrograms per cubic meter. . . .

II

In April 1984, petitioners filed in the United States District Court for the Eastern District of Wisconsin a class action challenging Johnson Controls' fetal-protection policy as sex discrimination that violated Title VII. . . . Among the individual plaintiffs were petitioners Mary Craig, who had chosen to be sterilized in order to avoid losing her job, Elsie Nason, a 50-year-old divorcee, who had suffered a loss in compensation when she was transferred out of a job where she was exposed to lead, and Donald Penney, who had been denied a request for a leave of absence for the purpose of lowering his lead level because he intended to become a father. . . .

The District Court granted summary judgment for defendant-respondent Johnson Controls, 680 F. Supp. 309 (1988), having concluded that while "there is a disagreement among the experts regarding the effect of lead on the fetus," the hazard to the fetus through exposure to lead was established by "a considerable body of opinion"; that although "[e]xpert opinion has been provided which holds that lead also affects the reproductive abilities of men and women . . . [and] that these effects are as great as the effects of exposure of the fetus . . . a great body of experts are of the opinion that the fetus is more vulnerable to levels of lead that would not affect adults"; and that petitioners had "failed to establish that there is an acceptable alternative policy which would protect the fetus." . . . The court stated that, in view of this disposition of the business necessity defense, it did not "have to undertake a bona fide occupational qualification's (BFOQ) analysis." . . .

The Court of Appeals for the Seventh Circuit, sitting en banc, affirmed the summary judgment by a 7-to-4 vote. 886 F.2d 871 (1989). . . .

. . . We granted certiorari. . . .

III

The bias in Johnson Controls' policy is obvious. Fertile men, but not fertile women, are given a choice as to whether they wish to risk their reproductive health for a particular job. Section 703(a) of the Civil Rights Act of 1964 [Title VII] prohibits sex-based classifications in terms and conditions of employment, in hiring and discharging decisions, and in other employment decisions that adversely affect an employee's status. Respondent's fetal-protection policy explicitly discriminates against women on the basis of their sex. The policy excludes women with childbearing capacity from lead-exposed jobs and so creates a facial classification based on gender. . . .

Nevertheless, the Court of Appeals assumed, as did the two appellate courts who already had confronted the issue, that sex-specific fetal-protection policies do not involve facial discrimination [and thus could be justified under the more lenient business necessity test.] . . . That assumption, however, was incorrect.

First, Johnson Controls' policy classifies on the basis of gender and childbearing capacity, rather than fertility alone. Respondent does not seek to protect the unconceived children of all its employees. Despite evidence in the record about the debilitating effect of lead exposure on the male reproductive system, Johnson Controls is concerned only with the harms that may befall the unborn offspring of its female employees. . . . This Court faced a conceptually similar situation in Phillips v. Martin Marietta Corp., [400 U.S. 542 (1971)], and found sex discrimination because the policy established "one hiring policy for women and another for men — each having pre-school-age children." [Id. at 544.] Johnson Controls' policy is facially discriminatory because it requires only a female employee to produce proof that she is not capable of reproducing.

Our conclusion is bolstered by the Pregnancy Discrimination Act of 1978 (PDA), 92 Stat. 2076, 42 U.S.C. §2000e(k), in which Congress explicitly provided that, for purposes of Title VII, discrimination "on the basis of sex" includes discrimination "because of or on the basis of pregnancy, childbirth, or related medical conditions.". . . . In its use of the words "capable of bearing children" in the 1982 policy statement as the criterion for exclusion, Johnson Controls explicitly classifies on the basis of potential for pregnancy. Under the PDA, such a classification must be regarded, for Title VII purposes, in the same light as explicit sex discrimination. Respondent has chosen to treat all its female employees as potentially pregnant; that choice evinces discrimination on the basis of sex.

[T]he absence of a malevolent motive does not convert a facially discriminatory policy into a neutral policy with a discriminatory effect. Whether an employment practice involves disparate treatment through explicit facial discrimination does not depend on why the employer discriminates but rather on the explicit terms of the discrimination. . . .

. . . We hold that Johnson Controls' fetal-protection policy is sex discrimination forbidden under Title VII unless respondent can establish that sex is a "bona fide occupational qualification."

IV . . .

The wording of the BFOQ defense contains several terms of restriction that indicate that the exception reaches only special situations. The statute thus limits the situations in which discrimination is permissible to "certain instances" where sex discrimination is "reasonably necessary" to the "normal operation" of the "particular" business. Each one of these terms — certain, normal, particular — prevents the use of general subjective standards and favors an objective, verifiable requirement. But the most telling term is "occupational"; this indicates that these objective, verifiable requirements must concern job-related skills and aptitudes.

The concurrence defines "occupational" as meaning related to a job. . . . According to the concurrence, any discriminatory requirement imposed by an employer is "job-related" simply because the employer has chosen to make the requirement a condition of employment. . . . This reading of "occupational" renders the word mere surplusage. . . . By modifying "qualification" with "occupational," Congress narrowed the term to qualifications that affect an employee's ability to do the job.

Johnson Controls argues that its fetal-protection policy falls within the so-called safety exception to the BFOQ. Our cases have stressed that discrimination on the basis of sex because of safety concerns is allowed only in narrow circumstances. In Dothard v. Rawlinson, [433 U.S. 321 (1977)] this Court indicated that danger to a woman herself does not justify discrimination. [433 U.S. at 335.] We there allowed the employer to hire only male guards in contact areas of maximum-security male penitentiaries only because more was at stake than the "individual woman's decision to weigh and accept the risks of employment.". . . We also required in *Dothard* a high correlation between sex and ability to perform job functions and refused to allow employers to use sex as a proxy for strength although it might be a fairly accurate one.

Similarly, some courts have approved airlines' layoffs of pregnant flight attendants at different points during the first five months of pregnancy on the ground that the employer's policy was necessary to ensure the safety of passengers. . . . In two of these cases, the courts pointedly indicated that fetal, as opposed to passenger, safety was best left to the mother. . . .

We considered safety to third parties in Western Airlines, Inc. v. Criswell, [472 U.S. 400 (1985)], in the context of the [Age Discrimination in Employment Act]. We focused upon "the nature of the flight engineer's tasks," and the "actual capabilities of persons over age 60" in relation to those tasks. [472 U.S. at 406.] Our safety concerns were not independent of the individual's ability to perform the assigned tasks, but rather involved the possibility that, because of age-connected debility, a flight engineer might not properly assist the pilot, and might thereby cause a safety emergency. Furthermore, although we considered the safety of third parties in *Dothard* and *Criswell*, those third parties were indispensable to the particular business at issue. In *Dothard*, the third parties were the inmates; in *Criswell*, the third parties were the passengers on the plane. We stressed that in order to qualify as a BFOQ, a job qualification must relate to the "essence," *Dothard*, [433 U.S. at 333] or to the "central mission of the employer's business," *Criswell*, [472 U.S. at 413].

. . . Third-party safety considerations properly entered into the BFOQ analysis in *Dothard* and *Criswell* because they went to the core of the employee's job performance. Moreover, that performance involved the central purpose of the enterprise. . . . The concurrence attempts to transform this case into one of customer safety. The unconceived fetuses of Johnson Controls' female employees, however, are neither customers nor third parties whose safety is essential to the business of battery manufacturing. No one can disregard the possibility of injury to future children; the BFOQ, however, is not so broad that it transforms this deep social concern into an essential aspect of batterymaking. . . .

The PDA's amendment to Title VII contains a BFOQ standard of its own: unless pregnant employees differ from others "in their ability or inability to work," they must be "treated the same" as other employees "for all employment-related purposes." 42 U.S.C. §2000e(k). This language clearly sets forth Congress' remedy for discrimination on the basis of pregnancy and potential pregnancy. Women who are either pregnant or potentially pregnant must be treated like others "similar in their ability . . . to work." [Id.] In other words, women as capable of doing their jobs as their male counterparts may not be forced to choose between having a child and having a job. . . .

We conclude that the language of both the BFOQ provision and the PDA which amended it, as well as the legislative history and the case law, prohibit an employer from discriminating against a woman because of her capacity to become pregnant unless her reproductive potential prevents her from performing the duties of her job. We reiterate our holdings in *Criswell* and *Dothard* that an employer must direct its concerns about a woman's ability to perform her job safely and efficiently to those aspects of the woman's job-related activities that fall within the "essence" of the particular business.[4]

---

4. The concurrence predicts that our reaffirmation of the narrowness of the BFOQ defense will preclude considerations of privacy as a basis for sex-based discrimination. . . . We have never addressed privacy-based sex discrimination and shall not do so here because the sex-based discrimination at issue today does not involve the privacy interests of Johnson Control's customers. Nothing in our discussion of the "essence of the business test," however, suggests that sex could not constitute a BFOQ when privacy interest are implicated. See, e.g., Backus v. Baptist Medical Center, 510 F. Supp. 1191 (E.D. Ark. 1981), vacated as moot, 671 F.2d 1100

V

We have no difficulty concluding that Johnson Controls cannot establish a BFOQ. Fertile women, as far as appears in the record, participate in the manufacture of batteries as efficiently as anyone else. . . .

VI

A word about tort liability and the increased cost of fertile women in the workplace is perhaps necessary. . . . It is correct to say that Title VII does not prevent the employer from having a conscience. The statute, however, does prevent sex-specific fetal-protection policies. These two aspects of Title VII do not conflict.

More than 40 States currently recognize a right to recover for a prenatal injury based either on negligence or on wrongful death. . . . According to Johnson Controls, however, the company complies with the lead standard developed by OSHA and warns its female employees about the damaging effects of lead. It is worth noting that OSHA gave the problem of lead lengthy consideration and concluded that "there is no basis whatsoever for the claim that women of childbearing age should be excluded from the workplace in order to protect the fetus or the course of pregnancy." 43 Fed. Reg. 52952, 52966 (1978). See also id. at 54354, 54398. Instead, OSHA established a series of mandatory protections which, taken together, "should effectively minimize any risk to the fetus and newborn child." Id., at 52966. See 29 C.F.R. §1910.125(k)(ii) (1989). Without negligence, it would be difficult for a court to find liability on the part of the employer. If, under general tort principles, Title VII bans sex-specific fetal-protection policies, the employer fully informs the woman of the risk, and the employer has not acted negligently, the basis for holding an employer liable seems remote at best.

Although the issue is not before us . . . [w]hen it is impossible for an employer to comply with both state and federal requirements, this Court has ruled that federal law pre-empts that of the States. . . .

. . . [Moreover, t]he extra cost of employing members of one sex . . . does not provide an affirmative Title VII defense for a discriminatory refusal to hire members of that gender. See [City of Los Angeles, Dept. of Water & Power v. Manhart, 435 U.S. 702, 716-718, and n.32 (1978)]. Indeed, in passing the PDA, Congress considered at length the considerable cost of providing equal treatment of pregnancy and related conditions, but made the "decision to forbid special treatment of pregnancy despite the social costs associated therewith.". . .

(8th Cir. 1982) (essence of obstetrics nurse's business is to provide sensitive care for patient's intimate and private concerns).

We, of course, are not presented with, nor do we decide, a case in which costs would be so prohibitive as to threaten the survival of the employer's business. We merely reiterate our prior holdings that the incremental cost of hiring women cannot justify discriminating against them.

VII

Our holding today that Title VII . . . forbids sex-specific fetal-protection policies is neither remarkable nor unprecedented. Concern for a woman's existing or potential offspring historically has been the excuse for denying women equal employment opportunities. See, e.g., Muller v. Oregon, [208 U.S. 412 (1908)]. Congress in the PDA prohibited discrimination on the basis of a woman's ability to become pregnant. We do no more than hold that the Pregnancy Discrimination Act means what it says. . . .

The judgment of the Court of Appeals is reversed and the case is remanded for further proceedings consistent with this opinion.

Justice WHITE, with whom THE CHIEF JUSTICE and Justice KENNEDY join, concurring in part and concurring in the judgment. . . .

I . . .

. . . Common sense tells us that it is part of the normal operation of business concerns to avoid causing injury to third parties, as well as to employees, if for no other reason than to avoid tort liability and its substantial costs. This possibility of tort liability is not hypothetical; every State currently allows children born alive to recover in tort for prenatal injuries caused by third parties . . . and an increasing number of courts have recognized a right to recover even for prenatal injuries caused by torts committed prior to conception. . . .

The Court dismisses the possibility of tort liability by no more than speculating that if "Title VII bans sex-specific fetal-protection policies, the employer fully informs the woman of the risk, and the employer has not acted negligently, the basis for holding an employer liable seems remote at best." . . . Such speculation will be small comfort to employers. First, it is far from clear that compliance with Title VII will pre-empt state tort liability, and the Court offers no support for that proposition. Second, although warnings may preclude claims by injured employees, they will not preclude claims by injured children because the general rule is that parents cannot waive causes of action on behalf of their children, and the parents' negligence will not be imputed to the children. Finally, although state tort liability for prenatal injuries generally requires negligence, it will be difficult for employers to determine in advance what will constitute negligence. Compliance with OSHA standards, for example, has been held not to be a defense to state tort or criminal liability. . . . Moreover, it is possible that employers will be held strictly liable, if, for example, their manufacturing process is considered "abnormally dangerous." See Restatement (Second) of Torts §869, comment b (1979).

Dothard and *Criswell* make clear that avoidance of substantial safety risks to third parties is inherently part of both an employee's ability to perform a job and an employer's "normal operation" of its business. . . . On the facts of this case . . . protecting fetal safety while carrying out the duties of battery manufacturing is as much a legitimate concern as is safety to third parties in guarding prisons (*Dothard*) or flying airplanes (*Criswell*).[5]

Dothard and *Criswell* also confirm that costs are relevant in determining whether a discriminatory policy is reasonably necessary for the normal operation of a business. In *Dothard*, the safety problem that justified exclusion of women from the prison guard positions was largely a result of inadequate staff and facilities. See [433 U.S. at 335]. If the cost of employing women could not be considered, the employer there should have been required to hire more staff and restructure the prison environment rather than exclude women. Similarly, in *Criswell* the airline could have been required to hire more pilots and install expensive monitoring devices rather than discriminate against older employees. . . .

The Pregnancy Discrimination Act (PDA), 42 U.S.C. §2000e(k), contrary to the Court's assertion . . . did not restrict the scope of the BFOQ defense. The PDA was only an amendment to the "Definitions" section of Title VII, 42 U.S.C. §2000e, and did not purport to eliminate or alter the BFOQ defense. Rather, it merely clarified Title VII to make it clear that pregnancy and related conditions are included within Title VII's antidiscrimination provisions. . . .

. . . The Court's narrow interpretation of the BFOQ defense in this case . . . means that an employer cannot exclude even pregnant women from an environment highly toxic to their fetuses. It is foolish to think that Congress intended such a result, and neither the language of the BFOQ exception nor our cases require it.[8]

---

5. I do not, as the Court asserts, . . . reject the "essence of the business" test. Rather, I merely reaffirm the obvious — that safety to third parties is part of the "essence" of most if not all businesses. Of course, the BFOQ inquiry " 'adjusts to the safety factor.' " *Criswell,* [472 U.S. at 413]. . . . As a result, more stringent occupational qualifications may be justified for jobs involving higher safety risks, such as flying airplanes. But a recognition that the importance of safety varies among businesses does not mean that safety is completely irrelevant to the essence of a job such as battery manufacturing.

8. The Court's cramped reading of the BFOQ defense is also belied by the legislative history of Title VII, in which three examples of permissible sex discrimination were mentioned — a female nurse hired to care for an elderly woman, an all-male professional baseball team, and a masseur. . . . In none of those situations would gender "actually interfer[e] with the employee's ability to perform the job," as required today by the Court. . . . The Court's interpretation of the BFOQ standard also would seem to preclude considerations of privacy as a basis for sex-based discrimination, since those considerations do not relate directly to an employee's physical ability to perfom the duties of the job. The lower federal courts,

II

Despite my disagreement with the Court concerning the scope of the BFOQ defense, I concur in reversing the Court of Appeals because that court erred in affirming the District Court's grant of summary judgment in favor of Johnson Controls. First, the Court of Appeals erred in failing to consider the level of risk-avoidance that was part of Johnson Controls' "normal operation.". . . If the fetal protection policy insists on a risk-avoidance level substantially higher than other risk levels tolerated by Johnson Controls such as risks to employees and consumers, the policy should not constitute a BFOQ.

Second, even without more information about the normal level of risk at Johnson Controls, the fetal protection policy at issue here reaches too far. This is evident both in its presumption that, absent medical documentation to the contrary, all women are fertile regardless of their age . . . and in its exclusion of presumptively fertile women from positions that might result in a promotion to a position involving high lead exposure. . . .

Third, it should be recalled that until 1982 Johnson Controls operated without an exclusionary policy, and it has not identified any grounds for believing that its current policy is reasonably necessary to its normal operations. . . .

Finally, the Court of Appeals failed to consider properly petitioners' evidence of harm to offspring caused by lead exposure in males. . . . It seems clear that if the Court of Appeals had properly analyzed that evidence, it would have concluded that summary judgment against petitioners was not appropriate because there was a dispute over a material issue of fact.

Justice SCALIA, concurring in the judgment.

I generally agree with the Court's analysis, but have some reservations, several of which bear mention.

First, I think it irrelevant that there was "evidence in the record about the debilitating effect of lead exposure on the male reproductive system." . . . Even without such evidence, treating women differently "on the basis of pregnancy" constitutes discrimination "on the basis of sex," because Congress has unequivocally said so. . . .

Second . . . it would not matter if all pregnant women placed their children at risk in taking these jobs, just as it does not matter if no men do so. . . .

Third . . . [i]t is perfectly reasonable to believe that Title VII has accommodated state tort law through the BFOQ exception. However, all that need be said in the present case is that Johnson has not demonstrated a

---

however, have consistently recognized that privacy interests may justify sex-based requirements for certain jobs. . . .

substantial risk of tort liability — which is alone enough to defeat a tort-based assertion of the BFOQ exception.

Last, the Court goes far afield, it seems to me, in suggesting that increased cost alone — short of "costs . . . so prohibitive as to threaten survival of the employer's business" . . . — cannot support a BFOQ defense . . . I think, for example, that a shipping company may refuse to hire pregnant women as crew members on long voyages because the on-board facilities for foreseeable emergencies, though quite feasible, would be inordinately expensive. In the present case, however, Johnson has not asserted a cost-based BFOQ. . . .

Notes

1. Defining the Groups to be Compared under Formal Equality Analysis. In *Johnson Controls*, how should the groups to be compared under Title VII equality analysis be defined? Justice Blackmun insisted on comparing fertile women to fertile men, concluding that the fetal protection policy violates Title VII because it treats these two groups differently. Justice Blackmun referred in his opinion to evidence that lead exposure may damage sperm as well as ova to strengthen his analysis that men and women are similarly situated and thus the relevant groups for comparison. Would Blackmun's analysis remain intact if the evidence was clear that men did *not* face the same — or did not face any — reproductive risks? See Wendy W. Williams, Firing the Woman to Protect the Fetus: The Reconciliation of Fetal Protection with Employment Opportunity Goals Under Title VII, 69 Geo. L.J. 641, 663 (1981) (advocating that fetal protection policies be gender-neutral because of "uncertainties and ambiguities about harm to fetuses through both sexes," but conceding that if the workplace exposure was not harmful to men, sex-based restrictions might be permissible).

Justice Scalia did not need to define specifically the groups to be compared, finding that whether or not the Court thought the policy in question was a form of sex discrimination, in prohibiting the treatment of women differently "on the basis of pregnancy" Congress unequivocally had determined by legislative fiat (the Pregnancy Discrimination Act) that it was. For the same reason, Justice Scalia's analysis is not affected by whether or not there are any comparable fetal risks to be passed through male employees.

The Seventh Circuit Court of Appeals, in effect, compared employees who could bear children against employees who could not. As such, the policy was facially sex-neutral and thus could be justified by the "benign" purpose of protecting women's unconceived offspring. See 886 F.2d at 886-887. This approach is similar to the one used by the Supreme Court when it concluded in 1974 that discrimination on the basis of pregnancy (even though only women were thereby affected) was not discrimination between women and men but rather discrimination between pregnant and non-pregnant persons. See Geduldig v. Aiello, 417 U.S. 484 (1974), discussed in Chapter 3. The Pregnancy Discrimination Act reversed *Geduldig* as to whether discrimination on the basis of pregnancy is sex discrimination under Title VII, but left intact the reasoning of the case with respect to constitutional challenges.

As for other doctrinal components of the Court's analysis, Justice Blackmun identifies as crucial whether the discrimination is "reasonably necessary" to the "normal operation" of the "particular" business and — especially — whether the restriction is an "occupational" requirement related to the "essence" of the employer's business. Each one of these terms, he states, "prevents the use of general subjective standards and favors an objective, verifiable requirement." Is this assessment correct? As to any of these legal determinations, is there any discernible/determinate basis upon which to prefer one conclusion over another? Justice Blackmun implicitly accuses *Johnson Controls* of "word play." Does he avoid the game?

2. Women Workers and "Choice." The issue of women's choice with respect to fetal protection policies can be posed in different ways. Fetal protection policies do give women one kind of choice — between sterilization and losing their jobs. See David Kirp, Fetal Hazards, Gender Justice and the Justices: The Limits of Equality, 34 Wm. & Mary L. Rev. 101, 129 (1992) (quoting Judge Robert Bork in defense of his decision upholding American Cyanamid's fetal protection policy in Oil, Chem. and Atomic Workers Int'l. Union v. American Cyanamid Co., 741 F.2d 444 (D.C. Cir. 1984), at his 1987 Supreme Court confirmation hearings: "I suppose the five women who *chose* to stay on that job with higher pay and *chose* sterilization — I suppose that they were glad to have the *choice*"). Professor Kirp reports on the circumstances under which many women have made such choices, including one woman, Betty Riggs, who submitted to sterilization although she wanted more children, because her marriage was breaking up and she needed the money. Not long after Betty Riggs and four other women were sterilized, the company shut down its pigments department and their jobs were eliminated. Id. at 104-106.

The Court in *Johnson Controls*, seeming to recognize the problems with the nature of the choice fetal protection policies hand to women, invalidates those policies, concluding that women workers should make their own decisions about whether to assume the risks of the workplace for themselves and their potential offspring. In doing so, has the Court, finally, maximized women's choices? Consider the following:

> The Court's decision in *Johnson Controls* is . . . caught within the double bind of the sameness and difference dilemma. . . . The Court's equal treatment analysis affords women workers a "choice" to share the same burdens of men with respect to workplace hazards but that choice must be exercised within a

social and economic regime that disadvantages women. On the other hand, the court's BFOQ analysis affords employers the right to exclude women from the workplace if their physical characteristics prevent them performing their assigned job duties. "Difference" becomes an excuse to exclude women, and "sameness" becomes a veil to cover structural disadvantages.

In this sense, the *Johnson Controls* decision is coherent to the extent that its logic "coheres" with the dominant social conception of gender that posits a male standard as an "ideal workers" standard for judging claims of sex discrimination. This form of coherence is "bad," however, because it reinforces the very gender disadvantages that the law of sex discrimination was designed to change. The freedom to choose upheld in *Johnson Controls* conforms to gender hierarchy much in the same way Plessy v. Ferguson conformed to the system of racial hierarchy at the time it was decided. Both cases can be seen as advancing principles of formal equality which cohere with their own contemporary institutional legal, moral and political environments. . . .

Gary Minda, Title VII at the Crossroads of Employment Discrimination Law and Postmodern Feminist Theory: *United Auto Workers v. Johnson Controls, Inc.* and Its Implications for the Women's Rights Movement, 11 St. Louis U. Pub. L. Rev. 89, 127 (1992).

Is there a solution to the *Johnson Controls* problem that would give women greater meaningful choice? David Kirp suggests that there are steps Johnson Controls could have taken to both minimize the possibility of fetal damage and preserve greater autonomy for women. For example, it could have lowered the levels of airborne lead in its plants (it had already spent $15 million to lower lead levels but with considerable more money, levels might have been decreased still further); it could have narrowed the number of women subjected to the policy, for example, by lowering the age range (Johnson Controls' policy affected all women between the ages of 17 and 70 unless they could prove their sterility) and by offering the option of regular pregnancy tests with transfer to women who tested positive; and it could have delivered clearer information to women about their risks of lead exposure and measures they might take to reduce it. Kirp, supra, at 109-111. Deborah Stone suggests, in addition, the possibility of job rotation to reduce reproductive risks for both men and women when they wish to begin their families, and the provision of comprehensive health coverage to employees, including routine monitoring. See Stone, Fetal Risks, Women's Rights: Showdown at *Johnson Controls*, Am. Prospect 43, 52 (Fall 1990). Should the Court have compelled any of these alternatives? Should Congress?

The industry's early responses to the Court's decision in *Johnson Controls* was not to change anything substantive in the workplace, but to revert to their old "voluntary" plans and seek waivers of liability from their workers. See Laura Oren, Protection, Patriarchy, and Capitalism: The Politics and Theory of Gender-Specific Regulation in the Workplace, 6 UCLA Women's L.J. 321, 371 n.290 (1996).

3. Fetal Protection Policies vs. Women's Rights. What assumptions does the construction of the issue in *Johnson Controls* as a conflict between fetal protection and women's employment rights reveal? Several commentators, along with Justice Blackmun himself, have drawn parallels between fetal protection policies and protective legislation of the nineteenth century (discussed in Chapter 1), which was also backed by "scientific" data (most notably the "Brandeis Brief" submitted in *Muller v. Oregon*). See, e.g., Williams, supra, at 653-655; Mary E. Becker, From *Muller v. Oregon* to Fetal Vulnerability Policies, 53 U. Chi. L. Rev. 1219, 1221-1243 (1986). Professor Becker finds many similarities. In both cases, she argues, the risks against which women were protected were not weighed against the harm to women of exclusion; women were viewed solely in terms of their reproductive functions; the evidence upon which exclusion was based was weak or uncertain; the possibility that women might be in the best position to make their own decisions about their own safety or that of their potential children was ignored; and, perhaps most tellingly, women were protected only in areas where their employment was seen as marginal, i.e., in male-dominated job classifications:

> The electronics industry, for example, employs mostly women, and many of these women frequently come into contact with six of the seven substances [the presence of which was used to exclude women from traditionally male jobs in companies such as *Johnson Controls*]: lead, benzene, vinyl chloride, carbon tetrachloride, carbon monoxide, and carbon disulfide. Yet fetal vulnerability policies have not been instituted in this industry. Many women laundry workers and dry cleaners are exposed to carbon disulfide and benzene. Women laboratory technicians are often exposed to benzene and other dangerous chemicals. Infectious agents and chemicals create risks of fetal harm to health care workers and hospital laundry workers. Dental offices are often contaminated by mercury. Pottery painting, a traditionally female job, involves exposure to lead. Yet with the exception of hospitals that fire pregnant x-ray technicians or otherwise restrict their exposure, women are generally allowed to work in women's jobs without restrictions based on fetal safety.

Becker, supra, at 1238-1239. What conclusions is it fair to draw from this history? See Kirp, supra, at 115 ("Expressions of corporate concern for the plight of fetuses . . . have been highly selective. Businesses that depend heavily on women workers have been much less scrupulous about the dangers they impose on the unborn."). Some research suggests significant risks to women's reproductive health from extensive exposure to the electromagnetic fields produced by video display terminals. See Cheryl L. Meyer, Video Display Terminals and Reproductive Complications: Regulatory Issues Concerning Health Care in the Workplace, 9 Wis. Women's L.J. 1 (1994). Why do you suppose employers have not attempted to place restrictions on women's working 8-hour days in front of computer screens? Is this selective "protection" pattern relevant to formal equality analysis?

Should fetal risks, to which the company in *Johnson Controls* said it was responding, be totally irrelevant to the legal validity of the kind of policy at issue in the case? At what point should the interests served by antidiscrimination law give way to the interests of third parties? Should fetuses whom the mother does not intend to abort be considered third parties? How do you respond to this commentary:

> . . . [T]he Supreme Court's decision looks decidedly less heroic when regarded, not as a set of principles abstracted from the commonplace but rather as a statement about how to make real — and literally toxic — choices. *Johnson Controls* may have invested nondiscrimination with all the meaning it can be made to carry, but the opinions of the Justices speak more to the inadequacy of equal rights reasoning than to its potential to address the matter at hand. As Judge Easterbrook noted in his dissent: "How much risk is too much is a moral or economic or political question, one ill suited to the processes of litigation and not the sort of question Title VII puts to a judge." (886 F.2d 871, 917 (7th Cir. 1989) (Easterbrook, J., dissenting).) A less formally constrained conception of justice requires a language that honors claims about the public good deeper than merely the right to be treated no worse — or no better — than someone else because of reproductive capacity.

Kirp, supra, at 103.

4. Potential Tort Liability. The Court notes that some right to recover for prenatal injuries is recognized in at least 40 states. Does the Court give employers any reassurance that they will be protected from subsequent tort claims in the event of fetal injury? To the extent it does not, are women being given *too much* choice by being allowed to have it both ways: they may keep their jobs but also sue later if they miscarry or if their babies are born with birth defects attributable to the risks of their employment? Or is this simply a cost to the employer of being engaged in a risky business, which is best dealt with by ordinary business means, such as insurance, or passing the risks of business along to the consumer? Should mothers themselves be subject to tort liability for harm suffered by a child due to the mother's voluntary exposure to harmful substances during pregnancy?

C. STATE PUBLIC ACCOMMODATIONS LAWS AND FIRST AMENDMENT ASSOCIATIONAL FREEDOMS

Board of Directors of Rotary International v. Rotary Club of Duarte
481 U.S. 537 (1987)

Mr. Justice POWELL delivered the opinion of the Court.

We must decide whether a California statute that requires California Rotary Clubs to admit women members violates the First Amendment.

I

Rotary International (International) is a nonprofit corporation founded in 1905, with headquarters in Evanston, Illinois. It is "an organization of business and professional men united worldwide who provide humanitarian service, encourage high ethical standards in all vocations, and help build goodwill and peace in the world." . . . Individual members belong to a local Rotary Club rather than to International. In turn, each local Rotary Club is a member of International. . . . In August 1982, shortly before the trial in this case, International comprised 19,788 Rotary Clubs in 157 countries, with a total membership of about 907,750. . . .

Individuals are admitted to membership in a Rotary Club according to a "classification system." The purpose of this system is to ensure "that each Rotary Club includes a representative of every worthy and recognized business, professional, or institutional activity in the community." . . . Each active member must work in a leadership capacity in his business or profession. The general rule is that "one active member is admitted for each classification, but he, in turn, may propose an additional active member, who must be in the same business or professional classification." Thus, each classification may be represented by two active members. In addition, "senior active" and "past service" members may represent the same classifications as active members. . . . There is no limit to the number of clergymen, journalists, or diplomats who may be admitted to membership. . . .

Subject to these requirements, each local Rotary Club is free to adopt its own rules and procedures for admitting new members. . . .

Membership in Rotary Clubs is open only to men. . . . Herbert A. Pigman, the General Secretary of Rotary International, testified that the exclusion of women results in an "aspect of fellowship . . . that is enjoyed by the present male membership," . . . and also allows Rotary to operate effectively in foreign countries with varied cultures and social mores. Although women are not admitted to membership, they are permitted to attend meetings, give speeches, and receive awards. Women relatives of Rotary members may form their own associations, and are authorized to wear the Rotary lapel pin. Young women between 14 and 28 years of age may joint Interact or Rotaract, organizations sponsored by Rotary International. . . .

In 1977 the Rotary Club of Duarte, California, admitted Donna Bogart, Mary Lou Elliott, and Rosemary Freitag to active membership. International notified the Duarte Club that admitting women members is contrary to the Rotary constitution. After an internal hearing, International's board of directors revoked the charter of the Duarte Club and terminated its membership in Rotary International. The Duarte Club's appeal to the International Convention was unsuccessful.

The Duarte Club and two of its women members filed a complaint in the California Superior Court for the County of Los Angeles. The complaint alleged, inter alia, that appellants' actions violated the Unruh Civil Rights Act, Cal. Civ. Code Ann. §51 (West 1982).[2] . . .

II

In Roberts v. United States Jaycees, [468 U.S. 609 (1984)], we upheld against First Amendment challenge a Minnesota statute that required the Jaycees to admit women as full voting members. *Roberts* provides the framework for analyzing appellants' constitutional claims. As we observed in *Roberts*, our cases have afforded constitutional protection to freedom of association in two distinct senses. First, the Court has held that the Constitution protects against unjustified government interference with an individual's choice to enter into and maintain certain intimate or private relationships. Second, the Court has upheld the freedom of individuals to associate for the purpose of engaging in protected speech or religious activities. In many cases, government interference with one form of protected association will also burden the other form of association. In *Roberts* we determined the nature and degree of constitutional protection by considering separately the effect of the challenged state action on individuals' freedom of private association and their freedom of expressive association. We follow the same course in this case. . . .

A

The Court has recognized that the freedom to enter into and carry on certain intimate or private relationships is a fundamental element of liberty protected by the Bill of Rights. Such relationships may take various forms,

---

2. The Unruh Civil Rights Act provides, in part: "All persons within the jurisdiction of this state are free and equal, and no matter what their sex, race, color, religion, ancestry, or national origin are entitled to the full and equal accommodations, advantages, facilities, privileges, or services in all business establishments of every kind whatsoever." Cal. Civ. Code Ann. §51 (West 1982).

including the most intimate. . . . We have not attempted to mark the precise boundaries of this type of constitutional protection. The intimate relationships to which we have accorded constitutional protection include marriage . . . the begetting and bearing of children . . . child rearing and education . . . and cohabitation with relatives. . . . In determining whether a particular association is sufficiently personal or private to warrant constitutional protection, we consider factors such as size, purpose, selectivity, and whether others are excluded from critical aspects of the relationship. [468 U.S. at 620.]

The evidence in this case indicates that the relationship among Rotary Club members is not the kind of intimate or private relation that warrants constitutional protection. The size of the local Rotary Clubs ranges from fewer than 20 to more than 900. . . . There is no upper limit on the membership of any local Rotary Club. About 10 percent of the membership of a typical club moves away or drops out during a typical year. . . . The clubs therefore are instructed to "keep a flow of prospects coming" to make up for the attrition and gradually to enlarge the membership. . . . The purpose of Rotary "is to produce an inclusive, not exclusive, membership, making possible the recognition of all useful local occupations, and enabling the club to be a true cross section of the business and professional life of the community." . . . The membership undertakes a variety of service projects designed to aid the community, to raise the standards of the members' businesses and professions, and to improve international relations. Such an inclusive "fellowship for service based on diversity of interest," . . . however beneficial to the members and to those they serve, does not suggest the kind of private or personal relationship to which we have accorded protection under the First Amendment. To be sure, membership in Rotary Clubs is not open to the general public. But each club is instructed to include in its membership "all fully qualified prospective members located within its territory," to avoid "arbitrary limits on the number of members in the club," and to "establish and maintain a membership growth pattern."

Many of the Rotary Clubs' central activities are carried on in the presence of strangers. Rotary Clubs are required to admit any member of any other Rotary Club to their meetings. Members are encouraged to invite business associates and competitors to meetings. At some Rotary Clubs, the visitors number "in the tens and twenties each week." . . . Joint meetings with the members of other organizations, and other joint activities, are permitted. The clubs are encouraged to seek coverage of their meetings and activities in local newspapers. In sum, Rotary Clubs, rather than carrying on their activities in an atmosphere of privacy, seek to keep their "windows and doors open to the whole world." . . . We therefore conclude that application of the Unruh Act to local Rotary Clubs does not interfere unduly with the members' freedom of private association.

B

The Court also has recognized that the right to engage in activities protected by the First Amendment implies "a corresponding right to associate with others in pursuit of a wide variety of political, social, economic, educational, religious, and cultural ends." Roberts v. United States Jaycees, [468 U.S. at 622]. . . . For this reason, "[i]mpediments to the exercise of one's right to choose one's associates can violate the right of association protected by the First Amendment. . . . " Hishon v. King & Spalding, [467 U.S. 69, 80, n.4 (1984)] (Powell, J., concurring) (citing NAACP v. Button, [371 U.S. 415 (1963)]; NAACP v. Alabama ex rel. Patterson, [357 U.S. 449 (1958)]). In this case, however, the evidence fails to demonstrate that admitting women to Rotary Clubs will affect in any significant way the existing members' ability to carry out their various purposes.

As a matter of policy, Rotary Clubs do not take positions on "public questions," including political or international issues. . . . To be sure, Rotary Clubs engage in a variety of commendable service activities that are protected by the First Amendment. But the Unruh Act does not require the clubs to abandon or alter any of these activities. It does not require them to abandon their basic goals of humanitarian service, high ethical standards in all vocations, good will, and peace. Nor does it require them to abandon their classification system or admit members who do not reflect a cross section of the community. Indeed, by opening membership to leading business and professional women in the community, Rotary Clubs are likely to obtain a more representative cross section of community leaders with a broadened capacity for service.

Even if the Unruh Act does work some slight infringement on Rotary members' right of expressive association, that infringement is justified because it serves the State's compelling interest in eliminating discrimination against women. See Buckley v. Valeo, [424 U.S. 1, 25 (1976)] (per curiam) (right of association may be limited by state regulations necessary to serve a compelling interest unrelated to the suppression of ideas). On its face the Unruh Act, like the Minnesota public accommodations law we considered in *Roberts*, makes no distinctions on the basis of the organization's viewpoint. Moreover, public accommodations laws "plainly serv[e] compelling state interests of the highest order." [468 U.S. at 624.] In *Roberts* we recognized that the State's compelling interest in assuring equal access to women extends to the acquisition of leadership skills and business contacts as well as tangible goods and services. [Id. at 626.] The Unruh Act plainly serves this interest. We therefore hold that application of the Unruh Act to California Rotary Clubs does not violate the right of expressive association afforded by the First Amendment. . . .

Justice SCALIA concurs in the judgment.

Justice BLACKMUN and Justice O'CONNOR took no part in the consideration or decision of this case.

≡ *Isbister v. Boys' Club of Santa Cruz, Inc.*
≡ 707 P.2d 212 (Cal. 1985)

GRODIN, Justice. . . .

Facts

The Boys' Club of Santa Cruz, Inc., a private nonprofit California corporation, owns and operates a building which includes such recreational facilities as a gymnasium, an indoor competition-size swimming pool, a snack bar, and craft and game areas. The local Club is affiliated with the Boys' Clubs of America, Inc., a congressionally chartered organization. . . .

Only members may use the Club's programs and facilities, but membership is open to all Santa Cruz children between eight and eighteen, so long as they are male. Members pay only a $3.25 annual membership fee. The principal source of funding for the Club — providing approximately 50 percent of its annual budget — is a gift in trust from John T. and Ruth M. Mallery (the Mallery Trust). The Mallerys also donated the money for the Club building. The trial court found that the Mallery Trust was "unrestricted" as to gender. In 1978, after this suit began, the Mallerys made a $200,000 donation which was expressly conditioned on restriction of membership to boys. Remaining funds come from the United Way campaign, an annual golf event, and miscellaneous private donations.

The Club is run by an adult board of directors, officers of the corporation, and a paid staff headed by an executive director. Club members have no power over Club affairs or membership policies.

The Club is unique in northern Santa Cruz County in the range and low cost of the recreational facilities and programs it provides under one roof. No single program or facility open to girls offers a similar range of activities at similar cost.

In 1977, plaintiff girls were denied access to the Boys' Club's membership and facilities solely on the basis of their sex. This action for injunctive and declaratory relief [under the Unruh Act] followed. . . .

Analysis

1. The Boys' Club is a "business establishment" covered by the Unruh Act. . . .

2. The Boys' Club male-only membership policy is prohibited by the Unruh Act. . . .

The Club contends that its primary purpose — to combat delinquency — is an important social interest best served by concentrating on male youth. It introduced juvenile hall statistics suggesting that Santa Cruz boys are four times more likely than their female counterparts to get into trouble with the law. By extending service to girls, the Club urges, it will have to dilute its efforts with boys, who present the greater social problem.

It was conceded, however, that delinquency affects substantial numbers of girls. There was no evidence that boys need the recreation offered by the Club more than girls, that a sex-segregated "drop-in" recreational facility is more effective in combating juvenile delinquency than one open to both sexes, or that extension of membership to girls would cause an impractical net increase (or decrease) in membership. . . .

The Club suggests that its funding is in jeopardy if its membership policies change. But the trial court found on substantial evidence that the original Mallery Trust, the Club's major financial source, is unrestricted on that score. We recognize with concern that the Mallerys' 1978 gift of $200,000 is conditioned on continuation of the male-only policy. But admission of girls may well produce offsetting new revenue sources. There is no evidence of severe, permanent financial danger should the Club be forced to comply with the Act. In sum, this record provides no basis for an exception to the Act's rule against arbitrary discrimination by "business establishments." . . .

The judgment is affirmed.

BROUSSARD, REYNOSO and CHESNEY, JJ., concur.

[The concurring opinion of Chief Justice Bird is omitted.]

MOSK, Justice, dissenting.
I dissent.

The incredible concept that a private, charitably funded recreational club for boys cannot be allowed to exist as such because it is a "business establishment" would be an irresistible subject for ridicule and humor if it were not so serious in its impact. The majority opinion conjures up visions of young boys, who have been skinny-dipping in their club pool, donning three-piece suits to attend the board meeting of their "business establishment" where they may discuss such matters as the antitrust implications of a proposed takeover of girl scout cookies. Precocious indeed these teen and preteen youngsters must be.

Growing up into a world of sex equality is inevitable for all children, but the court-ordered elimination of traditional childhood activity is an exorbitant price to pay for accelerating the process.

The majority purport to be blithely oblivious to the extended reach of their decision, and disingenuously attempt to restrict their opinion to this one case, involving only this one Boys' Club in this one city. At the same time they appear to implore the Legislature to rescue society from this judicial folly and its consequences. . . . That is a plea I can enthusiastically endorse.

That the ultimate result of this case will strain our social fabric and send shock waves throughout the realm of children's organizations is made clear by the appearance of numerous apprehensive amici curiae representing both girls and boys. Girls' organizations throughout California are no more eager for an invasion by boys than are boys' groups for dilution of their programs by compulsory inclusion of girls. Briefs on behalf of the Santa Cruz club have been filed by the Boy Scouts of America, Girl Scout Councils of California, United Way of America, the Girls' Club of Vista, and the Boys' Clubs of Tustin, Vista, Oceanside, Chula Vista, Buena Park, Rio Hondo, Pasadena, Whittier, San Francisco, National City, Santa Clara County, Oakland, Santa Ana, and the San Dieguito Boys' and Girls' Clubs and Fallbrook Boys' and Girls' Clubs.

The majority's insouciance is disturbing. No girl's parents who are inclined to be litigious will fail to use this case as authority to demand their daughter's admission to other boys' clubs, the Boy Scouts, Cub Scouts, Young Men's Christian Association, and similar organizations that maintain camps or physical facilities. Conversely, boys could rely on this case to insist on their right to join girls' clubs, the Girl Scouts, Campfire Girls, Young Women's Christian Association, and like groups. There is no rational way to distinguish those situations.

In addition, the majority strike a death knell for fraternities and sororities as they exist on every college campus in California. There is no way any court can read the rationale of the majority opinion and yet deny the right of a male student to join a sorority, or a female student to become a fraternity member. If the Boys' Club of Santa Cruz is a business because it operates a gymnasium and swimming pool, a fortiori sororities and fraternities, which provide and charge for housing accommodations and eating facilities, are business establishments. Similar considerations will probably also affect separate college dormitories.

The natural extension of the majority opinion to women's colleges is even more potentially devastating. If a qualified male student seeks admission to Mills, Mount St. Mary's or Scripps — California's renowned educational institutions for women — there is no rational way in which a court could distinguish his demand from that of the plaintiff herein. Colleges that provide not only classes but living accommodations and food service are arguably more akin to a business establishment than is a recreational boys' club. . . .

. . . Services and facilities are provided by the Boys' Club for a nominal nonprofit fee of $3.25 per year; the relationship between the Boys' Club and its members is essentially gratuitous. The purpose of the Boys' Club — to help boys develop citizenship, leadership, values, health and fitness, personal adjustment and individual growth, and inter-group understanding — is primarily to provide services of a personal and social nature, and the relationship between the Boys' Club and its members is clearly noncommercial. Finally, boys may remain members for years; the relationship is thus continuous. . . .

The effects, tangible and intangible, of the majority opinion in this case are devastating.

First, the club will be required to compel joint use of facilities by boys and girls — swimming, basketball, handball, etc. In the alternative, the club will be required to cut the boys' recreational time in half and restrict their hours in order to accommodate girls: e.g., not a full day on Saturday but only a half day; not two hours after school but only one hour.

Second, the club will be compelled to build an additional locker room, showers, toilets, and other physical facilities. This, of course, will require a considerable expenditure of charitable funds.

Third, while being thus obligated to expand, the club will simultaneously lose a $200,000 gift that is conditioned on a male-only policy. The majority gratuitously declare that the admission of girls "may well produce offsetting new revenue sources." I doubt that my colleagues would enjoy serving on a fund-raising committee seeking to raise a $200,000 "offset" for this purpose in the Santa Cruz community.

Fourth, the majority effectively stifle any community incentive to create and construct a girls' club comparable to the Boys' Club.

Fifth, the Boys' Club may very well lose its national charter. By act of Congress, the Boys' Clubs of America are authorized "to promote the health, social, educational, vocational, and character development of boys throughout the United States of America. . . ." Parenthetically, it may be observed that Congress has chartered other sex-exclusive organizations, e.g., Daughters of the American Revolution . . . , Sons of the American Revolution . . . , and Veterans of Foreign Wars of the United States. . . .

Amicus Boy Scouts of America points out other significant policy considerations overlooked by the majority. By protecting the freedom to base sexual associations on personal affinities, society promotes its pluralism, with all the values that connotes — values such as a diversity of views, a variety of ideas, and preservation of traditions. Here, the plaintiff and her supporters believe that their community will benefit by making certain private facilities with limited capacity and with limited adult supervision available either to children of both sexes or to none at all. Other citizens — those who charitably donated the property and those who charitably maintain it — believe their community will benefit by more narrowly focusing the use of that property on boys, many of whom are disadvantaged.

The value of a pluralistic, democratic society is that it permits members of each group to join with others sharing their views, to pool their resources as they wish, to seek the resources of new members, and to experiment to try to prove the validity of their respective concepts. The charitable donors of the Boys' Club property and funds, and the volunteers who charitably organize and operate the club, have done just that. No law or policy bars plaintiff and others from seeking out charitable contributors who share their views. . . .

Another important factor that the majority have ignored is the policy favoring private charitable contributions, a policy manifested in tax laws and laws authorizing charitable contributions. . . . The more the state arbitrarily dictates the permissible goals and practices of charitable organizations, the tighter the pursestrings of potential donors are likely to be drawn.

For all of the foregoing reasons I would reverse the judgment.

KAUS, Justice, dissenting. . . .

. . . I feel compelled to express puzzlement at the majority's repeated mention of the fact that there is no comparable facility for girls in the Santa Cruz area. If there were a Girls' Club in Santa Cruz, would the majority be satisfied with "separate but equal" facilities? If there were two boys' clubs, would each have to admit girls? Two boys' clubs and one girls' club? Unless the majority is prepared to suggest that the existence of additional facilities might affect its conclusions, I respectfully submit that the references to the Club's monopoly are of no legal significance. . . .

To establish that the Club is a facility that is generally open to the public, the majority states that it "offers basic recreational facilities to a *broad segment* of the population, *excluding* only a *particular* group expressly recognized by the Act as a traditional target of discrimination." [707 P.2d at 220 (quoting the majority opinion).] Sounds good, but what are the facts? The "broad segment" of the population consists of boys between the ages of eight and eighteen. On the other hand, the "particular" group which is excluded is the rest of humanity. I submit that the only way to reach the conclusion that the Club is "generally open to the public" is to look at the included and excluded groups through different ends of a telescope.

Further, I believe that the Club has demonstrated "a compelling need to maintain single-sex facilities." The majority quite properly holds that section 51 only forbids arbitrary sex discrimination. One would think, then, that if one of the main goals of the Club is the control of juvenile delinquency and those who guide its affairs have made a reasoned decision that this goal is best advanced by a prophylactic application of the Club's limited resources to that group of youngsters from which the majority of serious delinquents seems to come — boys — that is surely not arbitrary. . . . No reason was given why it is arbitrary to spend the delinquency prevention dollar where it is thought to do the most good. . . .[3]

The majority seeks to improve on the trial court's *ipse dixit* by asserting that because some delinquents are girls, the Club should have proved that "a

---

3. I do not claim that the same considerations would be valid if, for example, statistics showed that members of a particular racial group or religion were more prone to turn delinquent. Some suspect classifications are simply more suspect than others and demand greater degrees of justification. . . .

sex-segregated . . . facility is more effective in combating juvenile delinquency than one open to both sexes. . . ." Why did the Club have a burden in that respect? If it acted in good faith — and no one claims that it did not — why should it have to prove that a perfectly defensible decision on how to spend its resources has actually proved to be the most effective one? . . .

. . . Evidently those responsible for the Club's policy have decided that it is beneficial for boys to have some time when they do not have to adjust their behavior to the presence of girls. There is, of course, a vast professional literature on the subject. Who are we to say that it is unreasonable for the Club's management to believe that there is a rational basis for giving boys a few hours a day when they do not have to carry their machismo on their sleeves? Whether or not we share these views is immaterial. What matters is that we have no right to force contrary theories on those who have devoted considerable time, energy, devotion and financial resources to the problem.

If I may suggest, the basic mistake of the majority opinion is that it views the Club's policies as being pointed toward the exclusion of girls. With that chip on the majority's shoulder, pejoratives come easily. If the court looked at the Club's activities more benignly as providing a service for boys — a service tailored to their needs — it would not find it necessary to reach such a wondrous result.

I therefore dissent.

Notes

1. State and Local Public Accommodations Laws.   Since no federal legislation reaches private clubs or associations, challenges to sex-based exclusions from these associations, like *Rotary Club* and *Isbister*, have been brought under state civil rights acts. These acts vary. Some prohibit discrimination only as to *places* of public accommodation, construed to mean entities that exist at a particular place and thereby excluding organizations that may meet in different locations, such as the Jaycees, Rotary Clubs, and some scouting organizations. Others apply to private clubs only in areas or at functions where nonmembers are present. Some apply only to businesses, although business may be quite broadly construed, as it was in *Isbister*. Some statutes specifically exempt "private" or "distinctly private" clubs. Examples of each of these types of statutes are discussed in Sally Frank, The Key to Unlocking the Clubhouse Door: The Application of Antidiscrimination Laws to Quasi-Private Clubs, 2 Mich. J. Gender & L. 27 (1994).

The federal constitutional issue raised by the application of these statutes is the extent to which the First Amendment protects the rights of individuals to associate in private clubs that discriminate on grounds prohibited by the statutes and to express themselves through these associations. The rights of free association and free expression have long been invoked to protect the activities and privacy of politically unpopular groups, including those involved in the civil rights movement. See, e.g., NAACP v. Alabama ex rel. Patterson, 357 U.S. 449 (1958); NAACP v. Button, 371 U.S. 415 (1963). The question is how far this protection extends, and to whom. In determining the answers to this question, the only limit formal equality would seem to impose is that the criteria applied be neutral, that is, that they do not unfairly privilege one group over another because of the content of their beliefs.

In light of this constraint, the effects of the criteria that have been developed may seem paradoxical. For example, the emphasis in *Rotary Club* on size, inclusiveness, openness to the public, and the failure to take positions on public questions means that the more exclusive and "discriminating" an association is, the more likely it will be allowed to discriminate. Similarly, the more connection there is between the exclusion and the expressive purpose of the association, the greater protection the association will likely be given. Thus, a white supremacy organization may be allowed to exclude blacks (but perhaps not women?), and a neo-Nazi group to exclude Jews, but a Rotary Club or Little League organization will not be allowed to so discriminate. Religious organizations, as well, will be given wide range to discriminate in carrying out their rituals, selecting their members, and employing people. See Frank, supra at 60, 79. The topic of how notions of privacy shield discriminatory behavior is further explored in Chapters 4 and 6.

Another factor likely to make a difference is the connection between the private organization and the organizations on which they are dependent to whom anti-discrimination laws may clearly apply. A New Jersey court held that the highly selective eating clubs at Princeton University were subject to the state anti-discrimination laws, because of their symbiotic interdependent relationship to the University. Frank v. Ivy Club, 576 A.2d 241 (N.J. 1990). This case may suggest that the more self-sufficient a group is, the more likely it will be to be left alone. Cf. *Isbister*, 707 P.2d at 92 (Bird, C.J., concurring) (stating that fact that Boys' Club charged only a nominal fee did not mean it was not a "business," because if it did, a wealthy organization that can afford to discriminate will be allowed to do so whereas a poor group could not).

Obtaining the benefits of a successful discrimination suit against a "private" association may pose greater challenges for the plaintiff than in the employment context. Social and recreational benefits are more difficult to secure, in a meaningful sense, than the economic benefits of a job. While shunning and stigmatization can also be a problem on the job, Title VII specifically addresses those practices, and makes them a further violation of the Act; state and local non-discrimination rules typically do not address the issue. For an account of the costs to the plaintiffs of one lawsuit to end gender-discriminatory practices at a Massachusetts country club to women, see Marcia Chambers, The High Price of Victory, N.Y. Times, April 2, 2001, at D1 (describing the ostracism and frustration of plaintiffs in lawsuit to challenge sex discrimination at the Haverhill County Club that led, among other things, to the divorce of one plaintiff, loss of clients and business to another who was a real-estate agent, and decision by another plaintiff to abandon the club altogether). The lawsuit is Borne v. The Haverhill Golf & Country Club, 1999 Mass. Super. LEXIS 523 (Nov. 19, 1999).

2. The End of Single-Sex Organizations? Each of the opinions written in *Isbister* seems to assume that the desegregation of organizations such as the Boy Scouts would be regrettable. In California, the exclusion of girls from the Boy Scouts was upheld from challenge under the Unruh Act (under which *Isbister* was decided) on grounds the Boy Scouts was not a business protected by the Act. See Yeaw v. Boy Scouts of America, 64 Cal. Rptr.2d 85 (Ct. App. 1997). See also Schwenk v. Boy Scouts of America, 551 P.2d 465 (Or. 1976) (state public accommodation act not intended to apply to Boy Scouts). The Boy Scouts still exclude girls, although since 1969 the Explorers have permitted boys and girls, ages 14 through 20, to join. Michael McCabe, Boy Scouts Under Attack in Court, The San Francisco Chronicle, July 1, 1991, at A1. Moreover, since 1988, adult women have been allowed to become Boy Scout troop leaders. Fred Tasker, Two Miami Girls Challenge the Boy Scouts, The Atlanta Constitution, July 8, 1991, at E5. The Boy Scouts also exclude homosexuals, a policy which the United States Supreme Court has held is protected by the organization's First Amendment right of expressive association. See Boy Scouts of America v. Dale, 530 U.S. 640 (2000). As to whether this case constitutes an issue of sex discrimination, see Chapter 4, page 787-790.

Financial as well as legal pressures have led a number of formerly all-male membership associations to expand their membership to women. See The Joy of Two Sexes, Fortune, Aug. 1, 1988, at 8, and Alan Franham, Girls in the Club, The Economist, April 1, 1989, at 54, both cited in Rosanne Calbo, The YWCA as a Single Sex Organization — Would It Survive a Legal Challenge? 22 Golden Gate L. Rev. 715, 717 nn.16-18 (1992). The Boy Scouts have experienced considerable financial consequences of their decision to exclude gays after that exclusion was upheld in *Dale*. See Continuing Boy Scouts Saga Unfold, Lesbian/Gay Law Notes, October 2000, at 179-80 (reporting on numerous cities, counties, and United Way and other non-profit funding agencies who have terminated financial support of the Boy Scouts as a result of its policy against gay members); David France, Scouts Divided, Newsweek, Aug. 6, 2001 at 44, 47 (describing loss backing of Boy Scouts by many United Way chapters and withdrawal by some cities of public parks and schools for Scout troop meetings, as well as 4.5 percent drop in Boy Scout membership in year folllowing *Dale* decision). The Girl Scouts have avoided these consequences by adopting a national guideline against discrimination based on sexual orientation, along with a policy against " 'sexual displays' or advocacy of personal lifestyles." Peg Tyre, Where the Girls Are: The Girl Scouts Try a Version of 'Don't Ask, Don't Tell,' Newsweek, Aug. 6, 2001, at 51. Local Girl Scout councils apparently are not dechartered if they violate the national policy. Id.

3. Special Needs of Boys. According to Ruth Mallery, the private donor who funded the Santa Cruz Boys' Club, boys need their own club because they get into more trouble than girls. "The problem . . . dates back to the days when farms were falling apart and families moved to the cities. While girls still had housework to occupy their time, boys no longer had milking and planting chores to keep them off the streets. Girls also mature faster. . . . Young men need to be around other young men without female pressure." Jill Wolfson, Santa Cruz Boys' Club Does the Unthinkable: The Invasion of the Girls, San Jose Mercury News, Feb. 27, 1986, at 1D. In addition to withdrawing a $200,000 contribution, Mrs. Mallery attempted to cancel the $15 million trust fund that brought in 75 percent of the club's annual budget, but was not able to do so because there had been no girl exclusion in her original gift. Id. By 1987, 30 percent of the members of the Boys' Club in Santa Cruz were girls, involved in all aspects of the club, including football and baseball. According to one report, there were "no signs of tension between boys and girls." Jill Zuckman, Boys' Club Finds Sugar and Spice, San Jose Mercury News, Aug. 14, 1987, at 1B.

Should *Isbister* apply, in reverse, to private girls' organizations, like the Girl Scouts? Does it matter whether the purpose of the Girl Scouts is to remedy past discrimination or to provide for girls' "special needs"? Which case would be the stronger one? The problems set forth below should be considered again in the context of Chapter 3, which addresses both of these rationales for all-female associations.

Putting Theory into Practice

2-18. Should a private law firm specializing in women's rights litigation be allowed to hire only women associates and partners? Can it decide to take only women clients? Hire only women who fit in with its own female tone and atmosphere? Contribute only to pro-women's political organizations and pro bono activities?

If so, should a private law firm specializing in men's rights litigation be able to make comparable choices that are compatible with their political and social goals?

2-19. The Young Women's Christian Association of the United States of America (YWCA) is an all-women's membership movement that, according to its mission statement, is "nourished by its roots in Christian faith and sustained by the richness of many beliefs and values. . . . Strengthened by diversity, the Association draws together members who strive to create opportunities for women's growth, leadership and power in order to attain a common vision: Peace, justice, freedom and dignity for all people." The YWCA's "One Imperative" is "to thrust our collective power toward the elimination of racism wherever it exists and by any means necessary." The organization was founded in 1866 to address the needs of women concerned about shifting family structures, safe housing, companionship, recreation, and religious and ethical beliefs and values in the ever-changing "machine age." The organization is founded on the belief that women and girls face discrimination in society and need special training, skills, and self-assurance to meet the challenges before them. It is also committed to the view that an autonomous women's organization can best manage the resources and focus the energies of the organization on its founding purposes. The YWCA offers a variety of programs, as various as health and fitness classes, career counseling for women re-entering the workforce, youth mentor programs, mastectomy support groups, counseling for battered women, art exhibits showcasing women's work, and self-defense classes. The organization is also a national advocacy group on behalf of women's interests.

Men can be staff members, financial donors, volunteers, program participants, and non-voting associates of the YWCA, but they cannot be voting members, executive directors, or board members. In a recent survey, 40 percent of the responding members believed that men should be able to become members; 53 percent thought the all-female membership policy should not be changed, with 56 percent of those opposing male membership fearing the loss of the YWCA's identity as a women's organization focused on women's issues, 31 percent fearing the loss of an environment free from male domination, and 15 percent expressing concern for the loss of opportunities for women in leadership roles in the organization. See Rosanne Calbo, The YWCA as a Single Sex Organization — Would It Survive a Legal Challenge? 22 Golden Gate U.L. Rev. 715, 715, 720-723 (1992) (including cites and sources).

Could the YWCA survive a legal challenge to its exclusion of men as voting members, executive directors, or board members, based on a public accommodations anti-discrimination statute such as those applied in *Rotary Club* or *Isbister*?

2-20. The National Black Women's Health Project (NBWHP) is an organization that provides a forum for speaking and organizing around such issues as racism, sexism, incest, domestic violence, homophobia, class, and color that are diluted in mainstream, largely white, women's organizations. While telephone inquiry to the Project yields the information that anyone may pay membership dues, NBWHP's written literature makes clear that the self-help groups that are the centerpiece of the organization's mission are for African-American women only. In defense of the right of the organization to discriminate on race and sex grounds, one commentator writes:

> If African-American women do not exclude white women from their associations, their sharing will be chilled by the presence of white women. African-American women will spend valuable time listening to white women defend their actions. In essence, African-American women will spend time concentrating on white women instead of focusing on themselves. Their communications will become stilted until they are effectively silenced in their own associations.

Pamela J. Smith, We Are Not Sisters: African-American Women and the Freedom to Associate and Disassociate, 66 Tul. L. Rev. 1467, 1511 (1992).

Could the NBWHP survive a legal challenge based on the anti-discrimination statute applied in *Rotary Club* or *Isbister?* Is there any advice you might give such an organization that would increase the chances that its policies would be legal?

3

Substantive Equality

While formal sex equality judges the *form* of a rule, requiring that it treat women and men on the same terms without special barriers or favors on account of their sex, substantive equality looks to a rule's *results* or *effects*. Formal equality does not always produce equal outcomes for men and women because of significant differences in their characteristics and circumstances. Advocates of substantive equality demand that rules take account of these differences to avoid differential impacts that are considered unfair. Determining what differences should be taken into account and in what ways — in short, what is fair — is not always an easy matter. Substantive equality is not one theory, but several theories, reflecting multiple types and sources of difference and a number of alternative or overlapping substantive ideals.

One formulation of substantive equality focuses on remedying the effects of past discrimination. Women historically have been excluded either by law or by gender role norms from having certain jobs or earning wages comparable to those earned by men. "Affirmative action" plans designed to boost women into occupational fields dominated historically by men and "comparable worth" schemes designed to restructure wage scales to eliminate the effects of past patterns of gender-based job segregation are examples of remedial measures designed to reverse the effects of past discrimination.

Another type of substantive equality focuses on biological differences between women and men. Only women become pregnant, for example, and pregnancy may disadvantage a woman worker with respect to job opportunities, seniority, and job security. Maternity leave provisions and flexible work schedules for parents are examples of measures within a substantive equality framework that are designed to neutralize this disadvantage. More radical substantive equality approaches look beyond biological difference and try to change the social expectations and practices that steer women into lower-paying occupational categories, encourage their economic dependence on men, and accept a disproportionate share of caretaking responsibilities.

Many differences between men and women are matters of *averages*, rather than definitional or across-the-board differences. Formal rule equality principles will be sufficient to achieve fair and equal outcomes for the exceptional or "non-average" woman who can compete successfully for an opportunity on the same basis as the average man. Other more result-oriented approaches may be required, however, to protect the interests of women as a whole, whose average characteristics or circumstances would otherwise disadvantage them in relation to men. For example, women-only sports teams in public education might be necessary to ensure equal opportunities for women, even where men-only teams might be constitutionally suspect. Likewise, substantive equality might support rules for child custody and spousal support at divorce that appear to favor women in order to prevent men from exploiting women's greater (average) economic vulnerability and their stronger (average) preference for custody of their children.

As you study the various examples of substantive equality in this chapter, notice the similarities and differences in approaches taken with respect to (1) which differences in circumstances or characteristics between men and women are, or should be, significant, (2) which outcomes are just, and (3) which strategies are most likely to lead to those outcomes. Compare and contrast also the reasoning in these examples with that in the formal equality approach. To what extent is it necessary to choose between approaches? Is there any one approach that would seem satisfactory in all situations surveyed in the chapter?

A. REMEDYING THE EFFECTS OF PAST DISCRIMINATION

1. Sex-Specific Public Benefits to Remedy Past Societal Discrimination

≡ *Kahn v. Shevin*
≡ 416 U.S. 351 (1974)

Mr. Justice DOUGLAS delivered the opinion of the Court.

Since at least 1885, Florida has provided for some form of property tax exemption for widows. The current law granting all widows an annual $500 exemption . . . has been essentially unchanged since 1941. Appellant Kahn is a widower who lives in Florida and applied for the exemption to the Dade County Tax Assessor's Office. It was denied because the statute offers no analogous benefit for widowers. [T]he Circuit Court for Dade County,

Florida, held the statute violative of the Equal Protection Clause of the Fourteenth Amendment. . . . The Florida Supreme Court reversed. . . .

There can be no dispute that the financial difficulties confronting the lone woman in Florida or in any other State exceed those facing the man. Whether from overt discrimination or from the socialization process of a male-dominated culture, the job market is inhospitable to the woman seeking any but the lowest paid jobs.[4] There are, of course, efforts under way to remedy this situation. . . . But firmly entrenched practices are resistant to such pressures, and, indeed, data compiled by the Women's Bureau of the United States Department of Labor show that in 1972 a woman working full time had a median income which was only 57.9% of the median for males — a figure actually six points lower than had been achieved in 1955. Other data point in the same direction.[6] The disparity is likely to be exacerbated for the widow. While the widower can usually continue in the occupation which preceded his spouse's death, in many cases the widow will find herself suddenly forced into a job market with which she is unfamiliar, and in which, because of her former economic dependency, she will have fewer skills to offer.

There can be no doubt, therefore, that Florida's differing treatment of widows and widowers "rest[s] upon some ground of difference having a fair and substantial relation to the object of the legislation." [Reed v. Reed, 404 U.S. 71, 76 (1971).]

This is not a case like Frontiero v. Richardson, [411 U.S. 677 (1973)], where the Government denied its female employees both substantive and procedural benefits granted males "solely . . . for administrative convenience." Id. at 690. We deal here with a state tax law reasonably designed to further the state policy of cushioning the financial impact of spousal loss upon the sex for which that loss imposes a disproportionately heavy burden. . . .

Affirmed.

Mr. Justice BRENNAN, with whom Mr. Justice MARSHALL joins, dissenting.

. . . In my view . . . a legislative classification that distinguishes potential beneficiaries solely by reference to their gender-based status as widows or widowers, like classifications based upon race, alienage, and national origin,

---

4. In 1970 while 40% of males in the work force earned over $10,000, and 70% over $7,000, 45% of women working full time earned less than $5,000, and 73.9% earned less than $7,000. U.S. Bureau of the Census: Current Population Reports, Series P-60, No. 80.

6. For example, in 1972 the median income of women with four years of college was $8,736 — exactly $100 more than the median income of men who had never even completed one year of high school. Of those employed as managers or administrators, the women's median income was only 53.2% of the men's, and in the professional and technical occupations the figure was 67.5%. Thus the disparity extends even to women occupying jobs usually thought of as well paid. Tables prepared by the Women's Bureau, Employment Standards Administration, U.S. Department of Labor.

must be subjected to close judicial scrutiny, because it focuses upon generally immutable characteristics over which individuals have little or no control, and also because gender-based classifications too often have been inexcusably utilized to stereotype and stigmatize politically powerless segments of society. See Frontiero v. Richardson, [411 U.S. 677 (1973)]. . . .

I agree that, in providing special benefits for a needy segment of society long the victim of purposeful discrimination and neglect, the statute serves the compelling state interest of achieving equality for such groups. No one familiar with this country's history of pervasive sex discrimination against women can doubt the need for remedial measures to correct the resulting economic imbalances. . . . [T]he purpose and effect of the suspect classification are ameliorative; the statute neither stigmatizes nor denigrates widowers not also benefited by the legislation. Moreover, inclusion of needy widowers within the class of beneficiaries would not further the State's overriding interest in remedying the economic effects of past sex discrimination for needy victims of that discrimination. While doubtless some widowers are in financial need, no one suggests that such need results from sex discrimination as in the case of widows.

The statute nevertheless fails to satisfy the requirements of equal protection, since the State has not borne its burden of proving that its compelling interest could not be achieved by a more precisely tailored statute or by use of feasible, less drastic means. [The statute] is plainly overinclusive, for the $500 property tax exemption may be obtained by a financially independent heiress as well as by an unemployed widow with dependent children. The State has offered nothing to explain why inclusion of widows of substantial economic means was necessary to advance the State's interest in ameliorating the effects of past economic discrimination against women.

. . . By merely redrafting that form to exclude widows who earn annual incomes, or possess assets, in excess of specified amounts, the State could readily narrow the class of beneficiaries to those widows for whom the effects of past economic discrimination against women have been a practical reality.

Mr. Justice WHITE, dissenting.

The Florida tax exemption at issue here is available to all widows but not to widowers. The presumption is that all widows are financially more needy and less trained or less ready for the job market than men. It may be that most widows have been occupied as housewife, mother, and home-maker and are not immediately prepared for employment. But there are many rich widows who need no largess from the State; many others are highly trained and have held lucrative positions long before the death of their husbands. At the same time, there are many widowers who are needy and who are in more desperate financial straits and have less access to the job market than many widows. Yet none of them qualifies for the exemption.

I find the discrimination invidious and violative of the Equal Protection Clause. There is merit in giving poor widows a tax break, but gender-based classifications are suspect and require more justification than the State has offered. . . .

It may be suggested that the State is entitled to prefer widows over widowers because their assumed need is rooted in past and present economic discrimination against women. But this is not a credible explanation of Florida's tax exemption; for if the State's purpose was to compensate for past discrimination against females, surely it would not have limited the exemption to women who are widows. Moreover, even if past discrimination is considered to be the criterion for current tax exemption, the State nevertheless ignores all those widowers who have felt the effects of economic discrimination, whether as a member of a racial group or as one of the many who cannot escape the cycle of poverty. It seems to me that the State in this case is merely conferring an economic benefit in the form of a tax exemption and has not adequately explained why women should be treated differently from men.

I dissent.

NOTE ON "BENIGN" SEX-BASED CLASSIFICATIONS TO REMEDY PAST DISCRIMINATION

As a result of the statute upheld in Kahn v. Shevin, a wealthy widow could receive a $500 property tax exemption while an impoverished widower could not. Can this result be justified under equal treatment principles?

Recall the government benefits cases discussed in Chapter 2, such as Frontiero v. Richardson, set forth on page 121, and Weinberger v. Wiesenfeld and Califano v. Goldfarb, described on pages 137-139. Can Kahn v. Shevin be reconciled with these cases?

Kahn v. Shevin is one of a few benefits cases that upheld group-based treatment more favorable to women than to men. In another example, Schlesinger v. Ballard, 419 U.S. 498 (1975), the Court upheld the Navy's "up or out" termination policy under which male officers were terminated when passed over for promotion a second time after nine years, while female officers were discharged for non-promotion only after thirteen years. The rationale was a compensatory one: since women could only be assigned to hospital ships and transports and not to vessels involved in combat, they did not have the same opportunities for compiling records warranting promotion as men did. Giving them a longer period for proving themselves was said to be simply a measure to counter the greater opportunities men had for career enhancement. 419 U.S. at 508.

The other principal case along this line was Califano v. Webster, 430 U.S. 313 (1977), a case that upheld a Social Security provision applied to retirements before 1972 that computed old-age benefits under a formula more favorable to women than to men. The benefits for both were determined according to an average monthly wage earned during certain years, but women were given the opportunity of excluding three additional lower earning years than men. In a per curiam opinion, the Court writes:

> . . . The statutory scheme involved here is more analogous to those upheld in *Kahn* [and Schlesinger v. Ballard] than to those struck down in [Weinberger v. Wiesenfeld, 430 U.S. 636 (1975), and Califano v. Goldfarb, 430 U.S. 199 (1977)]. The more favorable treatment of the female wage earner enacted here was not a result of "archaic and overbroad generalizations" about women . . . or of "the role typing society has long imposed" upon women . . . such as casual assumptions that women are "the weaker sex" or are more likely to be child-rearers or dependents. . . . Rather, "the only discernible purpose of [the statute's more favorable treatment is] the permissible one of redressing our society's longstanding disparate treatment of women." [*Goldfarb*, 430 U.S. at 209 n.8.]
>
> The challenged statute operated directly to compensate women for past economic discrimination. Retirement benefits under the Act are based on past earnings. But as we have recognized: "Whether from overt discrimination or from the socialization process of a male-dominated culture, the job market is inhospitable to the woman seeking any but the lowest paid jobs." [*Kahn*, 416 U.S. at 353.] Thus, allowing women, who as such have been unfairly hindered from earning as much as men, to eliminate additional low-earning years from the calculation of their retirement benefits works directly to remedy some part of the effect of past discrimination. . . .
>
> That Congress changed its mind in 1972 and equalized the treatment of men and women does not . . . constitute an admission by Congress that its previous policy was invidiously discriminatory. . . . Congress has in recent years legislated directly upon the subject of unequal treatment of women in the job market. Congress may well have decided that "[t]hese congressional reforms . . . have lessened the economic justification for the more favorable benefit computation formula. . . ." Moreover, elimination of the more favorable benefit computation for women wage earners, even in the remedial context, is wholly consistent with those reforms, which require equal treatment of men and women in preference to the attitudes of "romantic paternalism" that have contributed to the "long and unfortunate history of sex discrimination." [*Frontiero*, 411 U.S. at 684.]

430 U.S. at 317-318, 320. Are the Court's efforts to distinguish *Frontiero*, *Goldfarb* (decided in the same year as *Webster*), and *Wiesenfeld* persuasive? Should efforts to remedy the effects of past discrimination be judged under the same standards as efforts to take account of differences that cannot be linked to past discrimination?

Are the "benign" classifications upheld in *Kahn* and *Webster* good for women? How good? Consider the following, by a feminist who is sharply critical of both equal treatment and "special benefits" approaches to equality:

> The special benefits side of the difference approach has not compensated for the differential of being second class. The special benefits rule is the only place in mainstream equality doctrine where you get to identify as a woman and not have that mean giving up all claim to equal treatment — but it comes close. Under its double standard, women who stand to inherit something when their husbands die have gotten the exclusion of a small percentage of the inheritance tax to the tune of Justice Douglas waxing eloquent about the difficulties of all women's economic situation. If we're going to be stigmatized as different, it would be nice if the compensation would fit the disparity.

Catharine A. MacKinnon, Feminism Unmodified: Discourses on Life and Law 38 (1987). What are the costs of the kind of "benign" discrimination represented in Kahn v. Shevin? Are they worth it?

2. "Affirmative Action" in Hiring

Johnson v. Transportation Agency
480 U.S. 616 (1987)

Justice BRENNAN delivered the opinion of the Court.

Respondent, Transportation Agency of Santa Clara County, California, unilaterally promulgated an Affirmative Action Plan applicable, *inter alia*, to promotions of employees. In selecting applicants for the promotional position of road dispatcher, the Agency, pursuant to the Plan, passed over petitioner Paul Johnson, a male employee, and promoted a female employee applicant, Diane Joyce. The question for decision is whether in making the promotion the Agency impermissibly took into account the sex of the applicants in violation of Title VII of the Civil Rights Act of 1964. . . . The District Court for the Northern District of California . . . held that respondent had violated Title VII. The Court of Appeals for the Ninth Circuit reversed. . . . We affirm.[2]

I

A

In December 1978, the Santa Clara County Transit District Board of Supervisors adopted an Affirmative Action Plan (Plan) for the County Transportation Agency. The Plan implemented a County Affirmative Action Plan, which had been adopted, declared the County, because "mere

---

2. No constitutional issue was either raised or addressed in the litigation below. . . . We therefore decide in this case only the issue of the prohibitory scope of Title VII. . . .

prohibition of discriminatory practices is not enough to remedy the effects of past practices and to permit attainment of an equitable representation of minorities, women and handicapped persons." . . . Relevant to this case, the Agency Plan provides that, in making promotions to positions within a traditionally segregated job classification in which women have been significantly underrepresented, the Agency is authorized to consider as one factor the sex of a qualified applicant.

In reviewing the composition of its work force, the Agency noted in its Plan that women were represented in numbers far less than their proportion of the County labor force in both the Agency as a whole and in five of seven job categories. Specifically, while women constituted 36.4% of the area labor market, they composed only 22.4% of Agency employees. Furthermore, women working at the Agency were concentrated largely in EEOC job categories traditionally held by women: women made up 76% of Office and Clerical Workers, but only 7.1% of Agency Officials and Administrators, 8.6% of Professionals, 9.7% of Technicians, and 22% of Service and Maintenance Workers. As for the job classification relevant to this case, none of the 238 Skilled Craft Worker positions was held by a woman. . . . The Plan noted that this underrepresentation of women in part reflected the fact that women had not traditionally been employed in these positions, and that they had not been strongly motivated to seek training or employment in them "because of the limited opportunities that have existed in the past for them to work in such classifications." . . . The Plan also observed that, while the proportion of ethnic minorities in the Agency as a whole exceeded the proportion of such minorities in the County work force, a smaller percentage of minority employees held management, professional, and technical positions.

The Agency stated that its Plan was intended to achieve "a statistically measurable yearly improvement in hiring, training, and promotion of minorities and women throughout the Agency in all major job classifications where they are underrepresented." . . . As a benchmark by which to evaluate progress, the Agency stated that its long-term goal was to attain a work force whose composition reflected the proportion of minorities and women in the area labor force. . . . Thus, for the Skilled Craft category in which the road dispatcher position at issue here was classified, the Agency's aspiration was that eventually about 36% of the jobs would be occupied by women. . . .

The Agency's Plan . . . set aside no specific number of positions for minorities or women, but authorized the consideration of ethnicity or sex as a factor when evaluating qualified candidates for jobs in which members of such groups were poorly represented. One such job was the road dispatcher position that is the subject of the dispute in this case.

B

On December 12, 1979, the Agency announced a vacancy for the promotional position of road dispatcher in the Agency's Roads Division.

Dispatchers assign road crews, equipment, and materials, and maintain records pertaining to road maintenance jobs. . . . The position requires at minimum four years of dispatch or road maintenance work experience for Santa Clara County. The EEOC job classification scheme designates a road dispatcher as a Skilled Craft Worker.

Twelve County employees applied for the promotion, including Joyce and Johnson. Joyce had worked for the County since 1970, serving as an account clerk until 1975. She had applied for a road dispatcher position in 1974, but was deemed ineligible because she had not served as a road maintenance worker. In 1975, Joyce transferred from a senior account clerk position to a road maintenance worker position, becoming the first woman to fill such a job. . . . During her four years in that position, she occasionally worked out of class as a road dispatcher.

Petitioner Johnson began with the County in 1967 as a road yard clerk, after private employment that included working as a supervisor and dispatcher. He had also unsuccessfully applied for the road dispatcher opening in 1974. In 1977, his clerical position was downgraded, and he sought and received a transfer to the position of road maintenance worker. . . . He also occasionally worked out of class as a dispatcher while performing that job.

Nine of the applicants, including Joyce and Johnson, were deemed qualified for the job, and were interviewed by a two-person board. Seven of the applicants scored above 70 on this interview, which meant that they were certified as eligible for selection by the appointing authority. The scores awarded ranged from 70 to 80. Johnson was tied for second with a score of 75, while Joyce ranked next with a score of 73. A second interview was conducted by three Agency supervisors, who ultimately recommended that Johnson be promoted. Prior to the second interview, Joyce had contacted the County's Affirmative Action Office because she feared that her application might not receive disinterested review.[5] The Office in turn contacted the Agency's Affirmative Action Coordinator, whom the Agency's Plan makes responsible for, *inter alia*, keeping the Director informed of

---

5. Joyce testified that she had had disagreements with two of the three members of the second interview panel. One had been her first supervisor when she began work as a road maintenance worker. In performing arduous work in this job, she had not been issued coveralls, although her male co-workers had received them. After ruining her pants, she complained to her supervisor, to no avail. After three other similar incidents, ruining clothes on each occasion, she filed a grievance, and was issued four pairs of coveralls the next day. . . . Joyce had dealt with a second member of the panel for a year and a half in her capacity as chair of the Roads Operation Safety Committee, where she and he "had several differences of opinion on how safety should be implemented." . . . In addition, Joyce testified that she had informed the person responsible for arranging her second interview that she had a disaster preparedness class on a certain day the following week. By this time about 10 days had passed since she had notified this person of her availability, and no date had yet been set for the interview. Within a day or two after this conversation, however, she received a notice setting her interview at a time directly in the middle of her disaster preparedness class. . . . This same panel member had earlier described Joyce as a "rebel-rousing, skirt-wearing person." . . .

opportunities for the Agency to accomplish its objectives under the Plan. At the time, the Agency employed no women in any Skilled Craft position, and had never employed a woman as a road dispatcher. The Coordinator recommended to the Director of the Agency, James Graebner, that Joyce be promoted.

Graebner, authorized to choose any of the seven persons deemed eligible, thus had the benefit of suggestions by the second interview panel and by the Agency Coordinator in arriving at his decision. After deliberation, Graebner concluded that the promotion should be given to Joyce. As he testified: "I tried to look at the whole picture, the combination of her qualifications and Mr. Johnson's qualifications, their test scores, their expertise, their background, affirmative action matters, things like that. . . . I believe it was a combination of all those." . . .

The certification form naming Joyce as the person promoted to the dispatcher position stated that both she and Johnson were rated as well qualified for the job. The evaluation of Joyce read: "Well qualified by virtue of 18 years of past clerical experience including 3 1/2 years at West Yard plus almost 5 years as a [road maintenance worker]." . . . The evaluation of Johnson was as follows: "Well qualified applicant; two years of [road maintenance worker] experience plus 11 years of Road Yard Clerk. Has had previous outside Dispatch experience but was 13 years ago." . . . Graebner testified that he did not regard as significant the fact that Johnson scored 75 and Joyce 73 when interviewed by the two-person board. . . .

Petitioner Johnson filed a complaint with the EEOC alleging that he had been denied promotion on the basis of sex in violation of Title VII. . . .

II

As a preliminary matter, we note that petitioner bears the burden of establishing the invalidity of the Agency's Plan. . . .

The assessment of the legality of the Agency Plan must be guided by our decision in Steelworkers v. Weber, [443 U.S. 193 (1979)]. In that case, the Court addressed the question whether the employer violated Title VII by adopting a voluntary affirmative action plan designed to "eliminate manifest racial imbalances in traditionally segregated job categories." [Id. at 197.] The respondent employee in that case challenged the employer's denial of his application for a position in a newly established craft training program, contending that the employer's selection process impermissibly took into account the race of the applicants. The selection process was guided by an affirmative action plan, which provided that 50% of the new trainees were to be black until the percentage of black skilled craftworkers in the employer's plant approximated the percentage of blacks in the local labor force. Adoption of the plan had been prompted by the fact that only 5 of 273, or 1.83%, of skilled craftworkers at the plant were black, even though the work force in the area was approximately 39% black. Because of the historical exclusion of blacks from craft positions, the employer regarded its former policy of hiring trained outsiders as inadequate to redress the imbalance in its work force.

We upheld the employer's decision to select less senior black applicants over the white respondent, for we found that taking race into account was consistent with Title VII's objective of "break[ing] down old patterns of racial segregation and hierarchy." Id. at 208. As we stated:

> It would be ironic indeed if a law triggered by a Nation's concern over centuries of racial injustice and intended to improve the lot of those who had "been excluded from the American dream for so long" constituted the first legislative prohibition of all voluntary, private, race-conscious efforts to abolish traditional patterns of racial segregation and hierarchy.

Id. at 204 (quoting remarks of Sen. Humphrey, 110 Cong. Rec. 6552 (1964)).

We noted that the plan did not "unnecessarily trammel the interests of the white employees," since it did not require "the discharge of white workers and their replacement with new black hirees." [443 U.S. at 208.] Nor did the plan create "an absolute bar to the advancement of white employees," since half of those trained in the new program were to be white. . . . Finally, we observed that the plan was a temporary measure, not designed to maintain racial balance, but to "eliminate a manifest racial imbalance." . . . As Justice Blackmun's concurrence made clear, *Weber* held that an employer seeking to justify the adoption of a plan need not point to its own prior discriminatory practices, nor even to evidence of an "arguable violation" on its part. Id. at 212. Rather, it need point only to a "conspicuous . . . imbalance in traditionally segregated job categories." Id. at 209. Our decision was grounded in the recognition that voluntary employer action can play a crucial role in furthering Title VII's purpose of eliminating the effects of discrimination in the workplace, and that Title VII should not be read to thwart such efforts. Id. at 204.

In reviewing the employment decision at issue in this case, we must first examine whether that decision was made pursuant to a plan prompted by concerns similar to those of the employer in *Weber*. Next, we must determine whether the effect of the Plan on males and nonminorities is comparable to the effect of the Plan in that case.

The first issue is therefore whether consideration of the sex of applicants for Skilled Craft jobs was justified by the existence of a "manifest imbalance" that reflected underrepresentation of women in "traditionally segregated job categories." Id. at 197. In determining whether an imbalance exists that would justify taking sex or race into account, a comparison of the percentage of minorities or women in the employer's work force with the percentage in the area labor market or general population is appropriate in analyzing jobs that require no special expertise. . . . Where a job requires special training, however, the comparison should be with those in the labor force who possess the relevant qualifications. . . .

A manifest imbalance need not be such that it would support a prima facie case against the employer . . . since we do not regard as identical the constraints of Title VII and the Federal Constitution on voluntarily adopted affirmative action plans. Application of the "prima facie" standard in Title VII cases would be inconsistent with *Weber*'s focus on statistical imbalance, and could inappropriately create a significant disincentive for employers to adopt an affirmative action plan. . . .

As the Agency Plan recognized, women were most egregiously underrepresented in the Skilled Craft job category, since none of the 238 positions was occupied by a woman. . . .

[H]ad the Plan simply calculated imbalances in all categories according to the proportion of women in the area labor pool, and then directed that hiring be governed solely by those figures, its validity fairly could be called into question. This is because analysis of a more specialized labor pool normally is necessary in determining underrepresentation in some positions. If a plan failed to take distinctions in qualifications into account in providing guidance for actual employment decisions, it would dictate mere blind hiring by the numbers. . . .

The Agency's plan emphatically did not authorize such blind hiring. It expressly directed that numerous factors be taken into account. . . .

We next consider whether the Agency Plan unnecessarily trammeled the rights of male employees or created an absolute bar to their advancement. In contrast to the plan in *Weber*, which provided that 50% of the positions in the craft training program were exclusively for blacks, . . . the Plan sets aside no positions for women. The Plan expressly states that "[t]he 'goals' established for each Division should not be construed as 'quotas' that must be met." . . . Rather, the Plan merely authorizes that consideration be given to affirmative action concerns when evaluating qualified applicants. As the Agency Director testified, the sex of Joyce was but one of numerous factors he took into account in arriving at his decision. . . . The Plan thus resembles the "Harvard Plan" approvingly noted by Justice Powell in Regents of University of California v. Bakke, [438 U.S. 265, 316-319 (1978)], which considers race along with other criteria in determining admission to the college. As Justice Powell observed: "In such an admissions program, race or ethnic background may be deemed a 'plus' in a particular applicant's file, yet it does not insulate the individual from comparison with all other candidates for the available seats." Id. at 317. Similarly, the Agency Plan requires women to compete with all other qualified applicants. No persons are automatically excluded from consideration; all are able to have their qualifications weighed against those of other applicants.

In addition, petitioner had no absolute entitlement to the road dispatcher position. Seven of the applicants were classified as qualified and eligible, and the Agency Director was authorized to promote any of the seven. Thus, denial of the promotion unsettled no legitimate, firmly rooted expectation on the part of petitioner. . . .

Finally, the Agency's Plan was intended to attain a balanced work force, not to maintain one. The Plan contains 10 references to the Agency's desire to "attain" such a balance, but no reference whatsoever to a goal of maintaining it. . . .

. . . Express assurance that a program is only temporary may be necessary if the program actually sets aside positions according to specific numbers. . . . In this case, however, substantial evidence shows that the Agency has sought to take a moderate, gradual approach to eliminating the imbalance in its work force, one which establishes realistic guidance for employment decisions, and which visits minimal intrusion on the legitimate expectations of other employees. . . .

Justice STEVENS, concurring.

While I join the Court's opinion, I write separately to explain my view of this case's position in our evolving antidiscrimination law and to emphasize that the opinion does not establish the permissible outer limits of voluntary programs undertaken by employers to benefit disadvantaged groups.

I

Antidiscrimination measures may benefit protected groups in two distinct ways. As a sword, such measures may confer benefits by specifying that a person's membership in a disadvantaged group must be a neutral, irrelevant factor in governmental or private decisionmaking or, alternatively, by compelling decisionmakers to give favorable consideration to disadvantaged group status. As a shield, an antidiscrimination statute can also help a member of a protected class by assuring decisionmakers in some instances that, when they elect for good reasons of their own to grant a preference of some sort to a minority citizen, they will not violate the law. The Court properly holds that the statutory shield allowed respondent to take Diane Joyce's sex into account in promoting her to the road dispatcher position.

Prior to 1978 the Court construed the Civil Rights Act of 1964 as an absolute blanket prohibition against discrimination which neither required nor permitted discriminatory preferences for any group, minority or majority. The Court unambiguously endorsed the neutral approach, first in the context of gender discrimination[1] and then in the context of racial

---

1. "Discriminatory preference for any group, minority or majority, is precisely and only what Congress has proscribed. What is required by Congress is the removal of artificial, arbitrary, and unnecessary barriers to employment when the barriers operate invidiously to discriminate on the basis of racial or other impermissible classification." Griggs v. Duke Power Co., [401 U.S. 424, 431 (1971)].

discrimination against a white person. . . . If the Court had adhered to that construction of the Act, petitioner would unquestionably prevail in this case. But it has not done so.

In the *Bakke* case in 1978 and again in [*Weber* in 1979], a majority of the Court interpreted the antidiscriminatory strategy of the statute in a fundamentally different way. . . . It remains clear that the Act does not require any employer to grant preferential treatment on the basis of race or gender, but since 1978 the Court has unambiguously interpreted the statute to permit the voluntary adoption of special programs to benefit members of the minority groups for whose protection the statute was enacted. . . .

II

. . . Given the interpretation of the statute the Court adopted in *Weber*, I see no reason why the employer has any duty, prior to granting a preference to a qualified minority employee, to determine whether his past conduct might constitute an arguable violation of Title VII. Indeed, in some instances the employer may find it more helpful to focus on the future. Instead of retroactively scrutinizing his own or society's possible exclusions of minorities in the past to determine the outer limits of a valid affirmative-action program — or indeed, any particular affirmative-action decision — in many cases the employer will find it more appropriate to consider other legitimate reasons to give preferences to members of under-represented groups. Statutes enacted for the benefit of minority groups should not block these forward-looking considerations.

> Public and private employers might choose to implement affirmative action for many reasons other than to purge their own past sins of discrimination. The Jackson school board, for example, said it had done so in part to improve the quality of education in Jackson — whether by improving black students' performance or by dispelling for black and white students alike any idea that white supremacy governs our social institutions. Other employers might advance different forward-looking reasons for affirmative action: improving their services to black constituencies, averting racial tension over the allocation of jobs in a community, or increasing the diversity of a work force, to name but a few examples. Or they might adopt affirmative action simply to eliminate from their operations all de facto embodiment of a system of racial caste. All of these reasons aspire to a racially integrated future, but none reduces to "racial balancing for its own sake."

Sullivan, The Supreme Court — Comment, Sins of Discrimination: Last Term's Affirmative Action Cases, 100 Harv. L. Rev. 78, 96 (1986).

The Court today does not foreclose other voluntary decisions based in part on a qualified employee's membership in a disadvantaged group. Accordingly, I concur.

Justice O'CONNOR, concurring in the judgment. . . .

In my view, the proper initial inquiry in evaluating the legality of an affirmative action plan by a public employer under Title VII is no different from that required by the Equal Protection Clause. In either case, consistent with the congressional intent to provide some measure of protection to the interests of the employer's nonminority employees, the employer must have had a firm basis for believing that remedial action was required. An employer would have such a firm basis if it can point to a statistical disparity sufficient to support a prima facie claim under Title VII by the employee beneficiaries of the affirmative action plan of a pattern or practice claim of discrimination.

. . . As I read *Weber* . . . the Court . . . determined that Congress had balanced [its intent to root out invidious discrimination against any person on the basis of race or gender, and its goal of eliminating the lasting effects of discrimination against minorities] by permitting affirmative action only as a remedial device to eliminate actual or apparent discrimination or the lingering effects of this discrimination.

Contrary to the intimations in Justice Stevens' concurrence, this Court did not approve preferences for minorities "for any reason that might seem sensible from a business or a social point of view." . . .

. . . I concur in the judgment of the Court.

Justice WHITE, dissenting.

I agree with Parts I and II of Justice Scalia's dissenting opinion. Although I do not join Part III, I also would overrule *Weber*. . . .

Justice SCALIA, with whom THE CHIEF JUSTICE joins, and with whom Justice WHITE joins in Parts I and II, dissenting.

. . . The Court today completes the process of converting [Title VII] from a guarantee that race or sex will *not* be the basis for employment determinations, to a guarantee that it often *will*. Ever so subtly, without even alluding to the last obstacles preserved by earlier opinions that we now push out of our path, we effectively replace the goal of a discrimination-free society with the quite incompatible goal of proportionate representation by race and by sex in the workplace. . . .

I

Several salient features of the plan [at issue in this case] should be noted. Most importantly, the plan's purpose was assuredly not to remedy prior sex discrimination by the Agency. It could not have been, because there was no prior sex discrimination to remedy. The majority, in cataloging the Agency's alleged misdeeds . . . neglects to mention the District Court's finding that the Agency "has not discriminated in the past, and does not discriminate in the present against women in regard to employment opportunities in general and promotions in particular." . . . This finding was not disturbed by the Ninth Circuit.

Not only was the plan not directed at the results of past sex discrimination by the Agency, but its objective was not to achieve the state of affairs that this Court has dubiously assumed would result from an absence of discrimination — an overall work force "more or less representative of the racial and ethnic composition of the population in the community." Teamsters v. United States, [431 U.S. 324, 340, n.20 (1977)]. Rather, the oft-stated goal was to mirror the racial and sexual composition of the entire county labor force, not merely in the Agency work force as a whole, but in each and every individual job category at the Agency. In a discrimination-free world, it would obviously be a statistical oddity for every job category to match the racial and sexual composition of even that portion of the county work force *qualified* for that job; it would be utterly miraculous for each of them to match, as the plan expected, the composition of the entire work force. Quite obviously, the plan did not seek to replicate what a lack of discrimination would produce, but rather imposed racial and sexual tailoring that would, in defiance of normal expectations and laws of probability, give each protected racial and sexual group a governmentally determined "proper" proportion of each job category.

That the plan was not directed at remedying or eliminating the effects of past discrimination is most clearly illustrated by its description of what it regarded as the "Factors Hindering Goal Attainment" — i.e., the existing impediments to the racially and sexually representative work force that it pursued. The plan noted that it would be "difficult" . . . to attain its objective of across-the-board statistical parity in at least some job categories, because:

> a. Most of the positions require specialized training and experience. Until recently, relatively few minorities, women and handicapped persons sought entry into these positions. Consequently, the number of persons from these groups in the area labor force who possess the qualifications required for entry into such job classifications is limited. . . .
> c. Many of the Agency positions where women are underrepresented involve heavy labor; e.g., Road Maintenance Worker. Consequently, few women seek entry into these positions. . . .
> f. Many women are not strongly motivated to seek employment in job classifications where they have not been traditionally employed because of the limited opportunities that have existed in the past for them to work in such classifications. . . .

That is, the qualifications and desires of women may fail to match the Agency's Platonic ideal of a work force. The plan concluded from this, of course, not that the ideal should be reconsidered, but that its attainment could not be immediate. . . .

Finally, the one message that the plan unmistakably communicated was that concrete results were expected, and supervisory personnel would be evaluated on the basis of the affirmative-action numbers they produced. . . . [S]upervisors were reminded of the need to give attention to affirmative action in every employment decision, and to explain their reasons for failing to hire women and minorities whenever there was an opportunity to do so. . . .

The fact of discrimination against Johnson is much clearer, and its degree more shocking, than the majority and Justice O'Connor's concurrence opinion would suggest — largely because neither of them recites a single one of the District Court findings that govern this appeal. . . . Worth mentioning, for example, is the trier of fact's determination that, if the Affirmative Action Coordinator had not intervened, "the decision as to whom to promote . . . would have been made by [the Road Operations Division Director]," . . . who had recommended that Johnson be appointed to the position. . . . Likewise, the even more extraordinary findings that James Graebner, the Agency Director who made the appointment, "did not inspect the applications and related examination records of either [Paul Johnson] or Diane Joyce before making his decision," . . . and indeed "did little or nothing to inquire into the results of the interview process and conclusions which [were] described as of critical importance to the selection process." . . . In light of these determinations, it is impossible to believe (or to think that the District Court believed) Graebner's self-serving statements relied upon by the majority and Justice O'Connor's concurrence, such as the assertion that he "tried to look at the whole picture, the combination of [Joyce's] qualifications and Mr. Johnson's qualifications, their test scores, their expertise, their background, affirmative action matters, things like that." . . . It was evidently enough for Graebner to know that both candidates (in the words of Johnson's counsel, to which Graebner assented) "met the M.Q.'s, the minimum. Both were minimally qualified." . . . When asked whether he had "any basis" for determining whether one of the candidates was more qualified than the other, Graebner candidly answered, "No. . . . As I've said, they both appeared, and my conversations with people tended to corroborate, that they were both capable of performing the work." . . .

After a 2-day trial, the District Court concluded that Diane Joyce's gender was "*the determining factor*" . . . in her selection for the position. Specifically, it found that "[b]ased upon the examination results and the departmental interview, [Mr. Johnson] was more qualified for the position of Road Dispatcher than Diane Joyce," . . . that "[b]ut for [Mr. Johnson's] sex, male, he would have been promoted to the position of Road Dispatcher," . . . and that "[b]ut for Diane Joyce's sex, female, she would not have been appointed to the position. . . ." The Ninth Circuit did not reject these factual findings as clearly erroneous. . . .

II

The most significant proposition of law established by today's decision is that racial or sexual discrimination is permitted under Title VII when it is intended to overcome the effect, not of the employer's own discrimination, but of societal attitudes that have limited the entry of certain races, or of a particular sex, into certain jobs. . . .

In fact, . . . today's decision goes well beyond merely allowing racial or sexual discrimination in order to eliminate the effects of prior societal discrimination. The majority opinion often uses the phrase "traditionally segregated job category" to describe the evil against which the plan is legitimately (according to the majority) directed. As originally used in *Weber*, supra, that phrase described skilled jobs from which employers and unions had systematically and intentionally excluded black workers — traditionally segregated jobs, that is, in the sense of conscious, exclusionary discrimination. [See 443 U.S. at 197-198.] But that is assuredly not the sense in which the phrase is used here. It is absurd to think that the nationwide failure of road maintenance crews, for example, to achieve the Agency's ambition of 36.4% female representation is attributable primarily, if even substantially, to systematic exclusion of women eager to shoulder pick and shovel. It is a "traditionally segregated job category" not in the *Weber* sense, but in the sense that, because of longstanding social attitudes, it has not been regarded by women themselves as desirable work. Or as the majority opinion puts the point, quoting approvingly the Court of Appeals: " 'A plethora of proof is hardly necessary to show that women are generally underrepresented in such positions and that strong social pressures weigh against their participation.' " . . . Given this meaning of the phrase, it is patently false to say that "[t]he requirement that the 'manifest imbalance' relate to a 'traditionally segregated job category' provides assurance . . . that sex or race will be taken into account in a manner consistent with Title VII's purpose of eliminating the effects of employment discrimination." . . . There are, of course, those who believe that the social attitudes which cause women themselves to avoid certain jobs and to favor others are as nefarious as conscious, exclusionary discrimination. Whether or not that is so (and there is assuredly no consensus on the point equivalent to our national consensus against intentional discrimination), the two phenomena are certainly distinct. And it is the alteration of social attitudes, rather than the elimination of discrimination, which today's decision approves as justification for state-enforced discrimination. This is an enormous expansion, undertaken without the slightest justification or analysis.

III

. . . In *Weber* itself . . . and in later decisions . . . this Court has repeatedly emphasized that *Weber* involved only a private employer. . . .

[S]tate agencies, unlike private actors, are subject to the Fourteenth Amendment. . . . [I]t would be strange to construe Title VII to permit discrimination by public actors that the Constitution forbids.

In truth, however, the language of [Title VII] draws no distinction between private and public employers, and the only good reason for creating such a distinction would be to limit the damage of *Weber*. It would be better, in my view, to acknowledge that case as fully applicable precedent, and to use the Fourteenth Amendment ramifications — which *Weber* did not address and which are implicated for the first time here — as the occasion for reconsidering and overruling it. . . .

[H]ollow is the Court's assurance that we would strike this plan down if it "failed to take distinctions in qualifications into account," because that "would dictate mere blind hiring by the numbers." . . . For what the Court means by "taking distinctions in qualifications into account" consists of no more than eliminating from the applicant pool those who are not even minimally qualified for the job. Once that has been done, once the promoting officer assures himself that all the candidates before him are "M.Q.'s" (minimally qualifieds), he can then ignore, as the Agency Director did here, how much better than minimally qualified some of the candidates may be, and can proceed to appoint from the pool solely on the basis of race or sex, until the affirmative action "goals" have been reached. The requirement that the employer "take distinctions in qualifications into account" thus turns out to be an assurance, not that candidates' comparative merits will always be considered, but only that none of the successful candidates selected over the others solely on the basis of their race or sex will be utterly unqualified. That may be of great comfort to those concerned with American productivity; and it is undoubtedly effective in reducing the effect of affirmative-action discrimination upon those in the upper strata of society, who (unlike road maintenance workers, for example) compete for employment in professional and semiprofessional fields where, for many reasons, including most notably the effects of past discrimination, the numbers of "M.Q." applicants from the favored groups are substantially less. But I fail to see how it has any relevance to whether selecting among final candidates solely on the basis of race or sex is permissible under Title VII. . . .

. . . It is impossible not to be aware that the practical effect of our holding is . . . effectively [to require] employers, public as well as private, to engage in intentional discrimination on the basis of race or sex. This Court's prior interpretations of Title VII, especially the decision in Griggs v. Duke Power Co., [401 U.S. 424 (1971)], subject employers to a potential Title VII suit whenever there is a noticeable imbalance in the representation of minorities or women in the employer's work force. Even the employer who is confident of ultimately prevailing in such a suit must contemplate the expense and adverse publicity of a trial. . . . If, however, employers are free to discriminate through affirmative action, without fear of "reverse discrimination" suits by their nonminority or male victims, they are offered a threshold defense against Title VII liability premised on numerical disparities. Thus, after today's decision the failure to engage in reverse discrimination is economic folly, and arguably a breach of duty to shareholders or taxpayers, wherever the cost of anticipated Title VII litigation exceeds the cost of hiring less capable (though still minimally capable) workers. (This situation is more likely to obtain, of course, with respect to the least skilled jobs — perversely creating an incentive to discriminate against precisely those members of the nonfavored groups least likely to have profited from societal discrimination in the past.) It is predictable, moreover, that this incentive will be greatly magnified by economic pressures brought to bear by government contracting agencies upon employers who refuse to discriminate in the fashion we have now approved. A statute designed to establish a color-blind and gender-blind workplace has thus been converted into a powerful engine of racism and sexism, not merely permitting intentional race- and sex-based discrimination, but often making it, through operation of the legal system, practically compelled.

It is unlikely that today's result will be displeasing to politically elected officials, to whom it provides the means of quickly accommodating the demands of organized groups to achieve concrete, numerical improvement in the economic status of particular constituencies. Nor will it displease the world of corporate and governmental employers (many of whom have filed briefs as amici in the present case, all on the side of Santa Clara) for whom the cost of hiring less qualified workers is often substantially less — and infinitely more predictable — than the cost of litigating Title VII cases and of seeking to convince federal agencies by nonnumerical means that no discrimination exists. In fact, the only losers in the process are the Johnsons of the country, for whom Title VII has been not merely repealed but actually inverted. The irony is that these individuals — predominantly unknown, unaffluent, unorganized — suffer this injustice at the hands of a Court fond of thinking itself the champion of the politically impotent. I dissent.

Notes

1. **Affirmative Action: A Shifting Tide.** The different opinions in *Johnson* represent the range of judicial perspectives taken in affirmative action cases. A shift in the balance of the power on the Court, however, as well as changes in public attitudes about affirmative action, have created considerable uncertainty about the continued authority of *Johnson*. The most significant developments have been in the Supreme Court's approach to race-based minority set-aside programs. In a turn from its prior precedents, the Supreme Court in City of Richmond v. J.A. Croson, Co., 488 U.S. 469 (1989), invalidated under a "strict scrutiny" standard a city ordinance setting aside thirty percent of its contracting work for minority-owned

businesses. In so doing, the Court made it clear that the strict standard could be satisfied only by a showing of past discrimination by the city itself. In Adarand Constructors, Inc. v. Pena, 515 U.S. 200 (1995), the Court applied the same standard to a federal government set-asides, reversing its prior deference to Congress in determining how to effectuate equal protection guarantees. Compare, e.g., Fullilove v. Klutznick, 448 U.S. 448 (1980) (upholding federal set-aside preferences in award of public construction contracts).

Activities at the state level are also reversing government-sponsored affirmative action plans in some jurisdictions. For example, in 1996, California voters passed the California Civil Rights Initiative (Proposition 209) which prohibited "discrimination against, or . . . preferential treatment to, any individual on the basis of race, sex, color, ethnicity, or national origin in the operation of public employment, public education, or public contracting." Initially, a federal district court struck down the amendment, on the grounds that it imposed a special political burden on minorities and women to redress racial and gender problems, and that it contravened Congressional intent regarding the use of affirmative action as a method of achieving the goals of Title VII. See Coalition for Economic Equity v. Wilson, 946 F. Supp. 1480 (N.D. Cal. 1996). The court's decision, however, was reversed by the Ninth Circuit Court of Appeals, which concluded that Proposition 209 merely bans what the Equal Protection Clause, in rare cases, permits. It also found, without reference to the *Johnson* case, that the ban on "preferential" treatment on the basis of race and sex was entirely consistent with Title VII. Coalition for Economic Equity, 110 F.3d 1445-1448 (9th Cir. 1997), cert. denied, 522 U.S. 963 (1997). The state court decisions in California have run consistently in favor of enforcing Proposition 209, as if a prohibition of affirmative action was not only constitutionally permitted, but required by the U.S. constitution or, at least, "anathema to the very process of democracy." See, e.g., Hi-Voltage Wire Works, Inc. v. City of San Jose, 12 P.3d 1068, 1083 (Cal. 2000) (upholding application of Proposition 209 to invalidate a city outreach program toward minority and women subcontractors). A symposium on Proposition 209 can be found at 23 Hast. Const. L.Q., No. 4 (1996). Other examples of the rollback of affirmative action follow in the notes below.

2. Affirmative Action and Gender: A Separate Standard? After *Adarand*, the pivotal question is whether affirmative action plans on behalf of women should be reviewed under the same standard as race-based plans. On the one hand, the standard of review for sex-based classifications is well established: a sex-based classification must serve important governmental objectives and be substantially related to those objectives or, more recently, they must be supported "by an exceedingly persuasive justification." See United States v. Virginia, 518 U.S. 515 (1996), set forth below. This is intermediate, not strict, scrutiny. On the other hand, given the purpose(s) of affirmative action — to reverse the effects of past discrimination and/or to enhance diversity — there is no obvious reason why gender-based affirmative action should be treated more leniently than race-based plans. Indeed, having acknowledged that race is the more suspect category, it seems perverse to impose greater barriers to ending past race discrimination than are imposed to reverse the effects of past sex discrimination.

Courts have not been entirely consistent in responding to this conundrum. The Sixth Circuit Court of Appeals has applied the same strict scrutiny to female preferences as the law requires in reviewing race-based preferences. See, e.g., Brunet v. City of Columbus, 1 F.3d 390 (6th Cir. 1993), cert. denied, 510 U.S. 1164 (1994) (striking down preferences to female applicants in the city's fire department, under strict scrutiny test). See also Long v. City of Saginaw, 911 F.2d 1192, 1196 (6th Cir. 1990) ("The strict scrutiny standard was adopted by a majority of the Court in [*Croson*] as the standard by which 'affirmative action' cases are to be reviewed"). Other Circuit Courts of Appeal, in examining affirmative action plans favoring both minorities and women, have applied only intermediate scrutiny to the sex-based preferences of a affirmative action plan. See, e.g., Dallas Fire Fighters Association v. City of Dallas, 150 F.3d 438 (5th Cir. 1998), cert. denied, 526 U.S. 1038 (1999) (upholding summary judgment in favor of plaintiff challenging constitutionality of a promotion system that favored women and minorities, applying strict scrutiny to race and intermediate review to gender components of the system); Engineering Contractors Association v. Metropolitan Dade County, 122 F.3d 895 (11th Cir. 1997), cert. denied, 523 U.S. 1004 (1998) (invalidating race- and gender-based preferences in the awarding of county construction contracts, applying strict scrutiny to race preference and heightened intermediate scrutiny to gender preference); Concrete Works, Inc. v. City & County of Denver, 36 F.3d 1513 (10th Cir. 1994), cert. denied, 514 U.S. 1004 (1995) (applying strict scrutiny to racial preference in city contracting policy, and intermediate scrutiny to gender preference, and remanding summary judgment order to resolve certain issues of fact); Contractors Association of Eastern Pennsylvania v. City of Philadelphia, 6 F.3d 990 (3d Cir. 1993), cert. denied, 519 U.S. 1113 (1997) (invalidating construction contract affirmative action policy favoring both minorities and women, applying strict scrutiny to aspects of plan relating to race an ethnicity, and intermediate scrutiny to gender; and upholding preference for the handicapped under the rational basis test); Coral Construction Co. v. King County, 941 F.2d 910, 930 (9th Cir. 1991), cert. denied, 502 U.S. 1033 (1992) (upholding set-aside program for minority-and women-owned businesses, applying strict review to race aspects of program and intermediate review to gender).

Most of these courts have noted that in establishing an important governmental interest, past discrimination must be shown, but not necessarily discrimination by the governmental entity whose affirmative action plan is in dispute. See, e.g., Ensley Branch, N.A.A.C.P. v. City of Birmingham, 31

F.3d 1548, 1580 (11th Cir. 1994) (gender-conscious affirmative action requires demonstration of "some past discrimination against women, but not necessarily discrimination by the government itself"); Coral Construction, 941 F.2d at 932 ("some degree of discrimination must have occurred in a particular field before a gender-specific remedy may be instituted" but intermediate scrutiny "does not require any showing of governmental involvement . . . in the discrimination it seeks to remedy"). To an extent not seen in judicial analysis of race-based affirmative action plans, the courts emphasize that the purpose for reviewing gender-based discrimination is to make sure that sex-based rules are not based on archaic stereotypes. See, e.g., *Contractors Association*, 6 F.3d 990, 1010 (3d Cir. 1993) (affirmative action plans favoring women will pass intermediate scrutiny if it is shown to be "a product of analysis rather than a stereotyped reaction based on habit") (internal citation omitted).

A number of other decisions that have examined affirmative action plans giving special consideration to both minorities and women have articulated the strict scrutiny standard with respect to race-based classifications and then swept the gender-based aspects of the plan into the analysis without specific discussion of the appropriate test. See, e.g., Vogel v. City of Cincinnati, 959 F.2d 594 (6th Cir. 1992), cert. denied, 506 U.S. 827 (1992) (upholding affirmative action plan adopted pursuant to a consent decree, that set hiring goals with respect to minorities and women); Mallory v. Harkness, 895 F. Supp. 1556 (S.D. Fla. 1995), aff'd, 109 F.3d 771 (11th Cir. 1997) (invalidating the Florida Bar Board's quota system for filling vacancies on the judicial Nominating Commission to guarantee seats for minorities or women); American Subcontractors Ass'n v. City of Atlanta, 376 S.E.2d 662, 664 (Ga. 1989) (striking down preference for minority- and women-owned businesses).

A decade of survey data shows that there is between 10 to 20 percent greater support for affirmative action programs on behalf of women than for programs on behalf of blacks. See Dara Z. Strolovitch, Playing Favorites: Public Attitudes Toward Race- and Gender-Targeted Anti-Discrimination Policy, 10 Nat'l Women's Stud. Ass'n J. 27 (Fall 1998). Interestingly, the gap is less when questions on preferences for women immediately precede questions on preferences for men, suggesting a "reciprocity" effect. Charlotte Steeh & Maria Krysan, The Polls-Trends: Affirmative Action and the Public, 1970-1995, 60 Public Opinion Q. 128,137 (1996). Is this gap relevant to the question of what standard for reviewing sex-based affirmative action is appropriate? Strolovitch interprets the data as showing that opposition to affirmative action is more a product of self-interest and racism than it is a philosophical opposition to governmental activism and support for individual initiative. See Strolovitch, supra.

3. Women's "Choices": Explanation for a Segregated Workforce, or The Problem To Be Fixed? Justice Scalia offers an alternative explanation for the sex-segregated work categories that the county felt obliged to eliminate: Women do not choose to enter traditionally all-male jobs in significant numbers. Justice Scalia counts it as "absurd" to think that women could be "eager to shoulder pick and shovel." Could he be right? What lies behind this observation?

The significance of women's lack of interest in traditionally male occupations was the subject of a suit brought by the Equal Employment Opportunity Commission (EEOC) against Sears, Roebuck & Co. in the late 1980s. This suit alleged a nationwide pattern and practice of sex discrimination by Sears for failing to hire and promote females in commission sales positions. It was based on statistical evidence showing that a disproportionate number of men engaged in commission selling of "big ticket" items, such as major appliances, furnaces, roofing, tires, and sewing machines, and a disproportionate number of women in noncommission (and thus lower paying) sales jobs in apparel, linen, toys, paint, and cosmetics. Sears' defense was that female applicants were hard to attract to commission selling, and preferred selling clothing, jewelry, and cosmetics. The district court accepted the Sears defense, based on testimony from Dr. Rosalind Rosenberg that women viewed noncommission sales as more attractive than commission sales "because they can enter and leave the job more easily and because there is more social contact and friendship, and less stress in noncommission selling," and rejected testimony by other historians who asserted that women are influenced by the opportunities presented to them, not by their preferences. EEOC v. Sears, Roebuck & Co., 628 F. Supp. 1264, 1307 (N.D. Ill. 1986), aff'd, 839 F.2d 302 (7th Cir. 1988). The judgment for Sears was affirmed on appealed, over the dissent of Judge Cudahy who bemoaned the stereotypes implicit in the court's analysis that "women are by nature happier cooking, doing the laundry and chauffeuring the children to softball games than arguing appeals or selling stocks," and criticized the court's lack of recognition of the employer's role in shaping the interests of applicants. 839 F.2d at 361 (Cudahy, J., dissenting).

Vicki Schultz faults the "liberal" anti-stereotyping line of analysis for letting Sears off the hook.

> Because the liberal story assumes that women form their job preferences through pre-work socialization, it accepts the notion that only women who are socialized the same as men desire such work. To secure legal victory under the liberal approach, women must present themselves as ungendered subjects without a distinctive history, experience, culture or identity. But this approach only validates the conservative notion that women who are "different" ("feminine") in nonwork aspects automatically have "different" ("feminine") work preferences, as well.

Vicki Schultz, Telling Stories About Women and Work: Judicial Interpretations of Sex Segregation in the Workplace in Title VII Cases Raising the

Lack of Interest Argument, 103 Harv. L. Rev. 1749, 1808 (1990). The EEOC and even Judge Cudahy accepted the premise that women's job preferences pre-dated their contact with Sears, Schultz argues, by comparing to male applicants only those female applicants who had similar background experiences that might suggest an equal interest in commission sales work. "Once this assumption was accepted, it was impossible to analyze seriously the extent to which Sears had shaped the women's preferences." Schultz, supra, at 1809. This liberal approach has two problems, according to Schultz. First, insofar as it appears to deny women's different job preferences, it is less credible than the conservative story, which acknowledges clearly that gender and work are related. Second,

> [b]ecause it denies gender difference, the liberal approach misses the ways in which employers draw upon societal gender relations to produce sex segregation at work. The liberal prohibition against stereotyping assumes that the problem is that the employer has inaccurately identified the job interests of (at least some exceptional) women who have already formed preferences for nontraditional work. By stopping at this level of analysis, however, liberal courts fail to inquire into or discover the deeper process through which employers actively shape women's work aspirations along gendered lines. . . .
> [For example, through] their recruiting strategies, employers do more than simply publicize job vacancies to those who are already interested: They actually stimulate interest among those they hope to attract to the jobs. . . .

Id. at 1811. To what extent does the affirmative action plan at issue in *Johnson* address Schultz's point?

The lack of interest defense has been more successful in sex discrimination cases than in race discrimination cases, at least before 1977. Vicki Schultz & Stephen Petterson, Race, Gender, Work, and Choice: An Empirical Study of the Lack of Interest Defense in Title VII Cases Challenging Job Segregation, 59 U. Chi. L. Rev. 1073, 1081, 1097 (1992) (in cases between 1967 and 1977 addressing lack of interest defense, plaintiffs prevailed in 86 percent of race discrimination cases and 54.5 percent of sex discrimination cases; disparity eliminated after Supreme Court cases, starting in 1977, began to curtail the methods of proving statistical cases of discrimination). Based on empirical analysis of the cases studied, Schultz and Petterson reject explanations based on the different strengths of cases and conclude that judges view women's job preferences as more fixed and impervious to employer influence than job preferences of racial minorities. Id. at 1100-1135. Cf. Robert J. Gregory, You Can Call Me A "Bitch" Just Don't Use the "N-Word": Some Thoughts on Galloway v. General Motors Service Parts Operations and Rodgers v. Western-Southern Life Insurance Co., 46 DePaul L. Rev. 741 (1997) (arguing that courts are more likely to find other explanations for sexually harassing behavior and speech than for race-based harassment). Is this surprising?

4. Whose Discrimination May the State Attempt to Remedy? The debate over the validity of voluntary affirmative action plans may be viewed as a debate about whose discrimination an employer may attempt voluntarily to remedy. The *Johnson* case reveals the entire spread of options. To Justice Scalia, past discrimination by the employer itself is all that will justify such voluntary efforts. Justice O'Connor's opinion in *Johnson* does not require actual past discrimination, but the employer must have had some "firm basis for believing that remedial action is required," e.g., a statistical disparity sufficient to support a prima facie claim of discrimination under Title VII. Justice O'Connor's opinion shifted in *Croson*, where she stated that an "amorphous claim that there has been past discrimination in a particular industry cannot justify use of an unyielding racial quota," 488 U.S. at 499, and in *Adarand* she essentially came over to Justice Scalia's position, having concluded that "all racial classifications . . . must be analyzed by a reviewing court under strict scrutiny." 515 U.S. at 227. For Justice Brennan, the important factor in *Johnson* is that the Agency had identified a substantial underrepresentation of women in "traditionally segregated job categories" — whatever the cause of that underrepresentation. To Justice Stevens, the past is even less important; it is enough that the employer concludes, on the basis of "forward-looking" considerations, that it would be beneficial to have a more balanced work force.

Note that in Kahn v. Shevin, set forth on page 266, the Court seemed satisfied that Florida was attempting to address societal discrimination rather than any past acts by the state itself. A difference in *Johnson*, besides the applicability of Title VII, would seem to be the existence of a specific "victim" who, according to the district court, would have gotten the job at issue were it not for Santa Clara's "affirmative action" plan. Even Justice Brennan's opinion seems to require that the interests of the nonminority employees not be "unnecessarily trammelled." Should this difference in the specificity of the victim matter?

Under what theory of equality should the source of past patterns of significant underrepresentation matter? It matters from the point of view of formal equality, because opportunity is all that is guaranteed. If women chose not to take advantage of an opportunity to enter a particular male-dominated occupation, no violation has occurred. Justice Scalia emphasizes the district court's finding that the county had no history of discrimination against women. Some commentators have charged that this finding was "incredible" and evidences the Court's greater difficulty in seeing sex-based discrimination than in seeing discrimination based on race:

> Prior to the affirmative action plan at issue in [Steelworkers v. Weber, 443 U.S. 193 (1979)], 1.83 percent (five out of 275) of the skilled craft workers were blacks in Kaiser's plan. . . . (Compare zero women out of approximately 238 at the Agency prior to the affirmative action plan at issue in *Johnson*.) In *Weber*, the Court reversed the two lower court decisions holding Kaiser's plan illegal

and noted that "[j]udicial findings of exclusion from crafts on racial grounds are so numerous as to make such exclusion a proper subject for judicial notice." Women, too, have been traditionally, explicitly, and routinely excluded from crafts, but — unlike the exclusion of blacks which was judicially noticed in *Weber* — women's exclusion was apparently invisible to all the judges deciding *Johnson.*

Mary Becker, Prince Charming: Abstract Equality, 1987 Sup. Ct. Rev. 201, 210. Is this a question of what counts as discrimination or of the capacity to see it?

5. Diversity as an Alternative Rationale for Affirmative Action. Would the goal of greater diversity in the workplace offer a better theory for affirmative action than the elimination of past discrimination? The diversity rationale may have special resonance in workforces such as police departments, where diversity affects the effective functioning of the force, or in higher education where diversity may serve a pedagogical function. When the Supreme Court invalidated a state university affirmative action admissions program in Regents of the University of California v. Bakke, 438 U.S. 265 (1978), the pivotal vote came from Justice Powell, who took the position that while race may not be used as a decisive criterion, it might be considered as one element in a range of factors. Almost two decades later, however, the Fifth Circuit Court of Appeals in Hopwood v. Texas, 78 F.3d 932 (5th Cir. 1996) invalidated a race-based affirmative action plan at the University of Texas Law School, concluding that neither achieving a diverse student body nor eliminating any present effects of past discrimination by the university or by the public education system as a whole could justify use of race as an admissions factor. The Supreme Court denied certiorari. Texas v. Hopwood, 518 U.S. 1033 (1996).

Decisions by other courts have been mixed. Diversity was also held to be not sufficiently compelling to justify an admissions policy at the University of Georgia that awarded extra points for being non-white and extra points for being male. See Johnson v. Board of Regents of the University of Georgia, 263 F.3d 1234 (11th Cir. 2001). In Michigan, a federal district court held that neither diversity considerations nor the goal of ending historic discrimination justified giving significant weight to race in the admissions process at the University of Michigan Law School which had an unwritten goal of achieving 10-12 percent minority enrollment. See Grutter v. Bollinger, 137 F. Supp.2d 821 (E.D. Mich. 2001), stay granted by 247 F.3d 631 (6th Cir. 2001). A challenge to the undergraduate affirmative action plan at the University of Michigan, however, was dismissed on summary judgment, the court holding that the diversity rationale was plainly sufficient. Likewise, an affirmative action plan at the University of Washington Law School was upheld under an educational diversity rationale. See Smith v. University of Washington Law School, 233 F.3d 1188 (9th Cir. 2000), cert. denied, 121 S. Ct. 2192 (2001).

In another context, in 1978, the Federal Communications Commission decided to give preferences to women in granting construction permits and operation licenses for radio and television stations. The rationale was that women

> are a general population group which has suffered from a discriminatory attitude in various fields of activity, and one which, partly as a consequence, has certain separate needs and interests with respect to which the inclusion of women in broadcast ownership and operation can be of value.

In re Application of Mid-Florida Television Corp., 70 F.C.C.2d 281, 326 (Rev. Bd. 1978), set aside on other grounds, 87 F.C.C.2d 203 (1981). A similar preference for certain racial minorities had been upheld by the United States Supreme Court in Metro Broadcasting, Inc. v. FCC, 497 U.S. 547 (1990), on the grounds that enhancing broadcast diversity was a sufficiently important governmental goal to justify the race-based policy. 497 U.S. at 567-568. Nonetheless, holding that the FCC had not established with statistically meaningful evidence that women who own radio or television stations are more likely than white men to broadcast "women's programming," one federal appeals court found that the sex-based preference violated equal protection. Lamprecht v. FCC, 958 F.2d 382 (D.C. Cir. 1992). Distinguishing *Metro Broadcasting*, Judge Clarence Thomas cited data showing that while stations with majority black ownership broadcast 79 percent black programming (in contrast to 20 percent for non-black-owned stations), stations with majority women ownership broadcast only 35 percent women's programming (compared to 28 percent for male-owned stations). 958 F.2d at 399, Appendix Table 1. In dissent, Chief Judge Abner Mikva noted that even while the figures were not as high as for minority-owned stations, women-owned stations nonetheless are 20 percent more likely than other stations to broadcast women's programming, and about 30 percent more likely than stations owned by non-minorities to broadcast "minority programming." 958 F.2d at 404 (Mikva, C.J., dissenting). *Metro Broadcast* was eventually overruled by *Adarand*, discussed in note 1, supra.

What do you suppose constitutes "women's programming"? In your experience, what messages does programming that is directed toward women tend to send? Assume that women-owned radio and television stations do broadcast more programming directed toward women. Is this likely to help change the attitudes that cause women to be underrepresented in male job categories? Will "women's programming" perpetuate "archaic stereotypes" about separate women's interests and points of views? Judge Mikva was not concerned:

[Congress] has not relied on stereotypes of any kind. It has not assumed that women "share some cohesive, collective viewpoint," Metro, [497 U.S. at 582], or that female journalists will approach stories about the federal budget, school prayer, voting rights, or foreign relations any differently than male journalists would. . . . Nor has Congress endorsed the similarly controversial proposition that men and women think differently about most questions. (If it had, the constitutional issue might be closer: the Fourteenth Amendment does not enact Ms. Betty Friedan's The Second Stage.) It has merely assumed that some female programmers will choose to emphasize different subjects — breast cancer, say, or glass ceilings in the workplace — than male programmers will. The assumption strikes me as innocuous to the point of being obvious.

Lamprecht, 958 F.2d at 411 (dissenting opinion). Is Judge Mikva right that some female programmers will emphasize "different" subjects? Is that assumption "innocuous"? Realistic? Should it justify a sex-based preference?

6. What's at Stake? How much difference does affirmative action make? That depends on the context. In the skilled trades, women appear to have made little progress.

Despite myriad affirmative action programs and significant legal gains for women through the enforcement of antidiscrimination laws, U.S. workplaces remain grossly sex-segregated. Figures from the 1990 census reveal that one in fifty-three auto mechanics is a woman, one in fifty-eight carpenters is a woman, one in thirty-nine electricians is a woman, one in sixty-three roofers is a woman, one in twenty-four construction laborers is a woman, one in twenty welders is a woman, and one in thirty-three loggers is a woman. . . .

In contrast, . . . [w]omen . . . make up 98% of kindergarten and pre-kindergarten teachers, 98.5% of family child-care providers, and 93% of dressmakers. . . .

Katherine M. Franke, The Central Mistake of Sex Discrimination Law: The Disaggregation of Sex from Gender, 144 U. Pa. L. Rev. 1, 87-88 (1995). Does this mean Justice Scalia is right about women's job preferences?

Women have been more successful in integrating the professions. Law schools are a case in point. In the 1970s, only three law schools had ever had a woman dean and few had more than one or two women faculty. Today, as a result of deliberate attempts to increase the number of women and minorities in law school teaching and administration, 20 percent of full professors and 10 percent of law school deans are women, although only 5 percent of those in either position are women of color. ABA Commission on Women in the Profession, The Unfinished Agenda: A Report on the Status of Women in the Legal Profession 27 (2001). It is hard to say to what extent women and minorities have been "advantaged" by affirmative action and to what extent the slow, steady progress has been just a matter of removing barriers to their entry. One study shows that even with affirmative action, white women and men of color have only a slightly better chance of getting a teaching job at prestigious schools than white men with comparable credentials, and that minority women have no advantage at all. See Deborah Jones Merritt & Barbara F. Reskin, Sex, Race, and Credentials: The Truth About Affirmative Action in Law Faculty Hiring, 97 Colum. L. Rev. 199 (1997). Moreover, men are more likely than women of comparable ages, credentials, and work experience to receive initial offers at a higher professorial rank. Id. at 252-258. The strongest positive factors relating to initial rank of appointment is the presence of a nonemployed spouse. Id. at 256. White men also are hired to teach more prestigious courses, like constitutional law; women are more likely to be hired to teach trusts and estates, family law, and clinical courses. Id. at 258-267.

The impact of affirmative action in law school admissions is shown dramatically, in reverse, with the elimination of affirmative action programs in Texas and California. The entering class to the University of Texas School of Law in 1997, after *Hopwood*, had only 3 black students, in comparison to 31 students in the prior entering class. After the passage of Proposition 209 in California, the 1997 entering class at the University of California at Berkeley School of Law (Boalt Hall) went from 20 black students to one black student who was a holdover from the prior year's admitted class. See Peter Applebome, Minority Law School Enrollment Plunges in California and Texas, N.Y. Times, June 28, 1997, at A1, col. 5. Fourteen Latino students were admitted and half of these were deferred admits. See Rachel F. Moran, Diversity and its Discontents: The End of Affirmative Action at Boalt Hall, 88 Cal. L. Rev. 2241, 2247-48 (2000). As a result of Proposition 209, the percentage of blacks, Hispanics, and Native Americans more generally among state law schools in California fell from 18.4 percent in 1996, to 9.4 percent in 2000. See Law School Admission Council Aims to Quash Overreliance on LSAT, The Wall Street Journal, March 29, 2001, at B1. After these effects became clear, some adjustments were made in the admissions policies that reduced the weight attached to the LSAT and grade point averages and gave more weight to various discretionary criteria. A special experimental program giving special consideration to socioeconomically disadvantaged students benefitted primarily white and Asian American students, and was discontinued after one year. See Rachel F. Moran, Diversity and its Discontents, supra. What one makes of this impact of Proposition 209 depends, at least in part, on how one views the validity of admission factors without "affirmative action." Particularly, on use of the LSAT, see discussion on pages 297-298 and 302-303, infra.

7. A Comparative European Perspective. The evolution of affirmative action law with respect to gender in Europe has not been tied to affirmative action law with respect to race in the way it has been in the United States. In Europe, "positive action" applies only to women, not to blacks or other minorities. Nonetheless, some of the same conceptual dilemmas faced by U.S. courts have plagued the European courts in attempting to balance the desire to eliminate inequality in the opportunities available to women against the basic principle of equal treatment. In Kalanke v. Freie Hansestadt Bremen, Case C-450/93, 1995 E.C.R. I-3051, the European Court of Justice invalidated a provision of a Bremen policy that required that women who were equally qualified to male co-applicants be preferred in hiring and promotions in public sector positions in which they were underrepresented on the grounds that the preference violated the European Council's 1976 Equal Treatment Directive, stating that "there shall be no discrimination whatsoever on grounds of sex either directly or indirectly." Council Directive of 9 February 1976, 76/207/EEC, 1976 O.J. (L39/40), art. 2. The subsequent decision of Marschall v. Land Nordrhein-Westfalen, Case C-409/95, 1997 E.C.R. I-6363, however, upheld a rule of priority similar to the one invalidated in *Kalanke* except that the rule had an exception when "reasons specific to an individual [male] candidate . . . [tilted] the balance in his favour." See *Marschall*, 1997 E.C.R. I-6363, at para. 3. These cases are analyzed and compared to U.S. decisions in Kendall Thomas, The Political Economy of Recognition: Affirmative Action Discourse and Constitutional Equality in Germany and the U.S.A., 5 Colum. J. Eur. L. 329 (1999). For further discussion of positive action in the European Union in the context of women's pregnancy and childbearing, see pages 338-339.

8. Affirmative Action and the Merit Principle. One's views of affirmative action are likely to be affected by one's views of the underlying system to which an affirmative action plan is affixed. If the system is viewed as neutral and objective, the question is only whether the benefits of affirmative action justify a departure from neutrality and objectivity. If it is not, affirmative action may be viewed as a corrective to a biased, non-objective system. In each question, the goal is neutrality and objectivity: the question is the contribution affirmative action makes toward these goals.

One debate within the court in *Johnson* reflects the contrary positions on this central question. Justice Brennan, citing an Amicus Curiae brief from the American Society for Personnel Administration, responds to the implicit charge that affirmative action leads to a flood of less qualified women and minority hires:

> It is a standard tenet of personnel administration that there is rarely a single, "best qualified" person for a job. An effective personnel system will bring before the selecting official several fully-qualified candidates who each may possess different attributes which recommend them for selection. Especially where the job is an unexceptional, middle-level craft position, without the need for unique work experience or educational attainment and for which several well-qualified candidates are available, final determinations as to which candidate is "best qualified" are at best subjective.

480 U.S. at 641 n.17.

Justice Scalia rejects this view entirely:

> [Acceptance of the brief's contention] effectively constitutes appellate reversal of a finding of fact by the District Court in the present case ("[P]laintiff was more qualified for the position of Road Dispatcher than Diane Joyce. . . ."). More importantly, it has staggering implications for future Title VII litigation, since the most common reason advanced for failing to hire a member of a protected group is the superior qualification of the hired individual.

480 U.S. at 675 n.5 (Scalia, J., dissenting).

What is at stake here? The merit selection system itself? Consider Justice Scalia's point in light of the following: (1) A study published in 1986, in which forty-eight mid-level managers, 25% of whom were female, were asked to evaluate four fictitious employees as part of their participation in an MBA class. The resumes of the fictitious employees were identical in terms of the level of work success and causes thereof, but two of them bore women's names and two bore men's names. The managers were asked to assess each candidate's level of work success, evaluate each candidate for promotion and salary increase purposes, and rank order the four resumes. The resumes with the male names were consistently ranked higher than the females, by the female managers as well as by the males. See Asya Pazy, The Persistence of Pro-Male Bias Despite Identical Information Regarding Causes of Success, 38 Organizational Behavior & Human Decision Processes 366, 369 (1986). (2) The veteran's preference scheme upheld in Massachusetts v. Feeney, 442 U.S. 256 (1979), set forth on page 140. (3) The "legacy" preference given in many college and university admissions procedures to the offspring of former graduates. (4) The critique of employment criteria discussed below.

Susan Sturm & Lani Guinier, The Future of Affirmative Action: Reclaiming the Innovative Ideal
84 Cal. L. Rev. 953, 956-957, 970-971, 974-977, 988, 993, 1000, 1002, 1010, 1014 (1996)

[A]ffirmative action, as it is currently practiced, supplements an underlying framework of selection that is implicitly arbitrary and exclusionary. It does not challenge the overall operation of a conventional and static selection process; instead, it creates exceptions to that process. Those exceptions play into existing racial stereotypes, predictably generating backlash. By implicitly legitimizing a selection process that operates in the name of merit, affirmative action programs reinforce that backlash. Programs perceived as racial preferences also enable employers to cast issues of economic retrenchment in terms of racial conflict. Many white workers who acknowledge the lack of corporate responsibility for the economic well-being of workers still focus their wrath and blame on the workers perceived as beneficiaries of affirmative action. . . .

. . . The experience of women and people of color offers insights beyond showing how and why those particular people have been excluded. . . . [T]he current one-size-fits-all ranking system of predicting "merit" is no longer justified or productive for anyone.

. . . It denies opportunity for advancement to many poor and working-class Americans of all colors and genders who could otherwise obtain educational competence. It is underinclusive of those who can actually do the job. It is deeply problematic as a predictor of actual job performance. Across-the-board, it does violence to fundamental principles of equity and "functional merit" in its distribution of opportunities for admission to higher education, entry-level hiring, and job promotion.

Typical among the existing criteria and selection methods are paper-and-pencil tests, such as the Scholastic Assessment Test (SAT), the Law School Admissions Test (LSAT), and civil service exams. These tests, which are used to predict future performance based on existing capacity or ability, do not correlate with future performance for most applicants, at least not as a method of ranking those "most qualified." These tests and informal criteria making up our "meritocracy" tell us more about past opportunity than about future accomplishments on the job or in the classroom.

. . . [These tests] have been used as "wealth preferences" or poll taxes to determine who gets to participate as full citizens in our democracy. . . .

Even if we accept the inadequate definitions of success used in conjunction with standardized tests, research shows a tenuous connection between test scores and successful performance. Recent studies show that the measured relationship between a test and predicted job performance, referred to as the correlation coefficient, is weak. The best employment tests have correlations of approximately .3. Using the widely accepted statistical methodology for determining how much explanatory information a test provides, a correlation of .3 means that "the test explains only 9% of the variation in predicted performance. In other words, the test leaves unexplained 91% of the variance reflected in the performance measure."

Validity studies of aptitude tests used to predict performance as measured only by first-year grades show correlations similar to those in the employment context. A recent study of the correlation of SAT scores with freshman grades showed correlations ranging from .32 to .36. As David Owens notes, the correlation between "SAT scores and college grades . . . is lower than the correlation between weight and height; in other words, you would have a better chance of predicting a person's height by looking only at his weight than you would of predicting his freshman grades by looking only at his SAT scores." A recent study of the University of Pennsylvania Law School found that LSAT scores were weak predictors of performance in law school. LSAT explained 21% of the differences in third-year grades. For first- and second-year students, it explained even less: 14% and 15% respectively. . . .

. . . Many tests exclude applicants who could in fact perform successfully. A vivid example arose from an error in the scoring of the 1976 version of the Armed Services Vocational Aptitude Battery. A calibration error resulted in the admission to the military of over 300,000 recruits who actually failed the screening test used by the armed services. Studies examining the subsequent performance of those "potentially ineligibles" ("PIs") found that performance differentials were "not large and in several cases the PIs performed as well as or even better than the controls." The PIs "completed training; their attrition rates weren't unusually high; they were promoted at rates only slightly lower than their higher-scoring peers; and they reenlisted."

It is widely recognized that high school grades are more predictive of college freshman-year grades than the SAT. Perhaps even more significant is the extremely small increase in predictiveness gained by using the SAT in conjunction with high school grades. . . .

It is also difficult to justify the use of rankings to distinguish at the margins among people whose performance falls within a relatively narrow band. Our yardsticks of merit can be used to differentiate yards, perhaps, but not inches or half-inches. The statistical concept of the standard error of measurement suggests that any particular test score is only indicative of an individual's "scoring range." Although tests may offer useful information about people at the very top and very bottom of the pool, they cannot reliably differentiate among candidates at the margins or in narrow bands of test scores. Yet many "reverse discrimination" cases involve candidates whose scores fall within relatively narrow bands that cannot reliably be distinguished.

An additional problem in establishing correlations between test scores and performance stems from the possibility that some people who may perform well in an educational or work environment perform poorly under the unique circumstances of most testing conditions. Moreover, most test instruments measure a wide range of skills and abilities through the narrow lens of the linguistic and logical-mathematical domains; if test-takers "are not strong in those two areas, their abilities in other areas may be obscured." There is developing evidence that attributes that cannot easily be measured through standardized paper-and-pencil tests, such as discipline, emotional intelligence, commitment, drive to succeed, and reliability, may be more important to successful work or school performance than marginally better performance on tests of general intelligence or analytical ability. Emotional qualities, what Daniel Goldman calls "emotional intelligence," may be just as important a predictor of academic success as test-taking ability. Standardized tests "do not measure motivation, perseverance or teamwork skills." . . .

. . . Researchers are becoming increasingly aware that privileging the aspects of performance rewarded by standardized tests may well screen out the contributions of people who would bring important and different skills to the workplace or educational institution. . . .

. . . Standardized tests may reward qualities such as willingness to guess, conformity, and docility. If this is so, then test performance may not relate significantly to the capacity to function well in jobs that require creativity, judgment, and leadership. In a service economy, creativity and interpersonal skills are important, though hard to measure. In the stock scenario of civil service exams for police and fire departments, traits such as honesty, courage, and ability to manage anger are left out. In other words, people who rely heavily on numbers to make employment decisions "are being misled." . . .

The linkage between test performance and parental income is consistent and striking. "Average family income rises with each 100-point increase in SAT scores, except for the highest SAT category where the number of cases is small." . . . [T]his correlation between income level and test performance persists within every racial and ethnic group and across gender. . . .

There is also evidence that certain tests are less predictive for some groups than others. For example, although women as a group perform less well than males on the SAT, they equal or outperform men in first-year college grade point average, the most common measure of successful performance. . . .

This heightened visibility of race- and gender-driven exceptions to "objectively derived" test-score-based selection plays into existing biases and stereotypes, particularly about race. Studies and public opinion polls show that dominant group members often evaluate women and people of color more harshly than they do dominant group members, and that they continue to hold stereotypes that reinforce the perception that people of color are less qualified and thus would not be selected if merit standards were used. These views are particularly strong in situations where prevailing stereotypes tend to be more simplistic and linked to concerns about performance. . . .

[M]ost affirmative action programs in place do not respond to the bias and invalidity of selection practices by posing a direct and systemic challenge to those practices. Instead, they attempt to compensate for those inadequacies as they affect women and people of color by roughly approximating an outcome that might be achieved in a fair, unbiased world. They do not offer an alternative approach to defining or identifying qualified candidates. They have not suggested new ways of determining whether affirmative action programs have in fact leveled the playing field, as opposed to creating a new and more favorable set of rules for their beneficiaries. . . .

This approach maintains the dichotomy between diversity and merit. . . .

We are proposing a shift in the model of selection from prediction to performance. This model builds on the insight that the opportunity to participate creates the capacity to perform, and that actual performance offers the best evidence of capacity to perform. There simply is no substitute for experience, both in equipping people to perform and in producing informed judgments about the functional capacity of candidates. This approach shifts the emphasis away from the design of an instrument that is separate from the performance of the job, but that can be correlated with success in that job. Instead, the emphasis is on thinking creatively about how evaluation can proceed through the observation of applicants engaged in the work of those positions. The model also emphasizes the importance of creating opportunities to succeed and of structuring fair, inclusive, and participatory mechanisms to define and assess successful performance. This approach thus embeds performance and inclusion in the design of the selection process. . . .

For this model to work, institutions would . . . need to change the relationship of race, gender, and other categories of exclusion to the overall decisionmaking process. Institutions would continue to assess the impact of various selection processes on traditionally excluded groups. However, . . . [r]ather than operating as an add-on, after-the-fact response to failures of the overall process, race and gender would serve as both a signal of organizational failure and a catalyst of organizational innovation. . . .

NOTE ON GENDER AND STANDARDIZED TESTING

The appeal of standardized tests, used so often as a qualification for education advancement, tracking, admissions, scholarships, hiring, and promotion, is that they are apparently objective. Although the ACT scores for male and female high school seniors narrowed to "within a whisker" in 1996 (see Richard Whitmire, ACT Test Scores Up Third Straight Time: Gender Gap Narrow, Gannett News Service, Aug. 14, 1996), as of 1997 there was a 35-point gap still existing on the mathematics portion of SAT. Diane Ravitch, Showdown at Gender Gap, Forbes, April 7, 1997, at 68. According to a 1989 report from the Center for Women Policy Studies, some questions on the SAT favored boys because of the subject matter involved. For example, the following question from a 1989 test produced a 27 percent gap in favor of boys:

> A high school basketball team has won 40 percent of its first 15 games. Beginning with the sixteenth game, how many games in a row does the team now have to win in order to have a 50 percent winning record? (A) 3; (B) 5; (C) 6; (D) 11; (E) 15.

The following question produced a 13 percent gender gap in favor of boys:

> If 2/3 of n is 4, then 1/2 of n is: (A) 1/6; (B) 1/3; (C) 4/3; (D) 2; (E) 3.

The following question produced a 12 percent gender gap in favor of boys:

Pat made a total of 48 pottery plates and cups. If she made twice as many plates as cups, how many plates did she make? (A) 32; (B) 24; (C) 18; (D) 16; (E) 8.

Ravitch, supra.

What conclusion do you draw from these results? Are they evidence of sex discrimination?

In 1996 the Educational Testing Service decided to add a writing component to the PSAT to help boost women's scores, after women's success in receiving National Merit Scholarships based on these tests stalled at about 40 percent. See Rigging the Test Scores Justifiably, N.Y. Times, Oct. 14, 1996, at A16. Is such a measure "affirmative action"? See Katherine Connor & Ellen J. Vargyas, The Legal Implications of Gender Bias in Standardized Testing, 7 Berkeley Women's L.J. 13 (1992); Lora Silverman, Comment, Unnatural Selection: A Legal Analysis of the Impact of Standardized Test Use on Higher Education Resource Allocation, 23 Loy. L.A.L. Rev. 1433 (1990).

One federal court held that the exclusive use of the SAT to select recipients of the New York State Regents Scholarships violates Title IX of the Education Amendments of 1972 and possibly also the federal equal protection clause, because of its disparate impact against females. See Sharif v. New York State Educ. Dept., 709 F. Supp. 345 (S.D.N.Y. 1989); cf. United States v. Fordice, 505 U.S. 717 (1992) (automatic entrance standard based on American College Testing Program standardized test scores and minimum test scores requirement that failed to take into account high school grades — both of which perpetuated past de jure segregated university system — are "constitutionally problematic"). On this general subject, see N. Median & D. Neill, Fallout from the Testing Explosion: How 100 Million Standardized Exams Undermine Equity and Excellence in America's Public Schools (National Center for Fair & Open Testing (FAIRTEST) Oct. 1988); Andrea L. Silverstein, Standardized Tests: The Continuation of Gender Bias in Higher Education, 29 Hofstra L. Rev. 669 (2000).

The gender gap in math has been closing. One study based on 1988 data shows that eighth- and tenth-grade females of White, African-American, and Latino backgrounds all take, on average in their racial or ethnic group, more advanced math classes and perform, on average, better than males. See Sophia Catsambis, The Path to Math: Gender and Racial-Ethnic Differences in Mathematics Participation from Middle School to High School, 67 Soc. Educ. 199 (July 1994). Even in the twelfth grade, females perform slightly better on tests for math computation and abstract reasoning, although they trail slightly in math concepts and spatial skills, and do substantially less well when tested on mechanical and electronic subjects. See Nancy S. Cole (from the Educational Testing Service), The ETS Gender Study: How Females and Males Perform in Educational Settings (May 1997). But women report a lower level of interest and participation even in the grades at which they are out-performing males in math. Catsambis, supra. The problem of lowering self-esteem among girls as they progress through middle school, which is correlated with interest in math and science, is discussed infra, at pages 402-404.

A cross-national study showed a correlation between women's access to higher education and the labor market and the disparity between boys and girls in math performance; the disparity disappears, or even reverses, where there is less occupational stratification by gender. See David P. Baker & Deborah Perkins Jones, Creating Gender Equality: Cross-national Gender Stratification and Mathematical Performance, 66 Soc. Educ. 91 (April 1993).

The LSAT also has been criticized for working to the disadvantage of women and minorities. Women trail men by an average of almost two points on the test. See William C. Kidder, Portia Denied: Unmasking Gender Bias on the LSAT and Its Relationship to Racial Diversity in Legal Education, 12 Yale J.L. & Feminism 1, 7 (2000). Researchers disagree about whether this means that there is gender bias in the test. Compare id. at 2 (LSAT decreases women's, and especially minorities', opportunities to enter law school), with Linda F. Wightman, An Examination of Sex Differences in LSAT Scores From the Perspective of Social Consequences, 11 Applied Measurement in Educ. 255, 274 (1998) (no gender bias exists in the LSAT). For those who claim that bias exists, the explanations offered are that women and minorities expect to do worse, and thus do; women and minorities respond less well to time pressure and are less likely to guess on answers; the subject matter of the questions is more likely to favor men; and some questions are insensitive and thus distract members of offended groups, including women and minorities. Kidder, supra, at 25-34. Which of these explanations, if proved, would constitute gender bias? For related critiques of the LSAT, see William C. Kidder, The Rise of Testocracy: An Essay on the LSAT, Conventional Wisdom, and the Dismantling of Diversity, 9 Tex. J. Women & L. 167 (2000); Leslie G. Espinoza, The LSAT: Narratives and Bias, 1 Am. U. J. Gender & L. 121 (1993).

Whether or not there is gender bias in the LSAT, it is claimed that even if the test predicts success as a law student, it does not predict success as a lawyer. The Law School Admission Council is funding a project at the University of California at Berkeley to develop a test to complement or replace the LSAT that will evaluate criteria that will predict lawyering competence. The project's designer, Professor Marjorie Shultz, suggests as one possibility "multiday projects in which a group of applicants would be assigned a specific task. They would then be graded on how much they contributed to the group's success." See Law School Admission Council Aims to Quash Overreliance on LSAT, The Wall Street Journal, March 29, 2001, at 1. Does this sound promising? Is it likely to better identify lawyering potential? Will it help women? Professor David B. Wilkins states that the research shows that "the higher your LSAT score, the lower your likelihood to do community service." Id. See also David L. Chambers et al., Doing Well and Doing Good: The Careers of Minority and White Graduates of the University of Michigan Law School, 1970-1996, Law Quadrangle Notes, Summer 1999, at 60, 61 (although LSAT scores and undergraduate grade-point averages correlate well with law school grades, they do not correlate with achievement after law school, as measured by earned income, career satisfaction, or service to the profession and community). Is this a good reason to downplay the LSAT in the admissions process?

Putting Theory into Practice

3-1. The University of Georgia is concerned about the fact that an increasingly disproportionate number of its students are female. Its admissions director testifies that the Georgia is "49th in the country in the percentage of baccalaureate degrees going to males. It's a major problem in this state." See Johnson v. Board of Regents of the University of Georgia, 106 F. Supp.2d 1362, 1375 (S.D. Ga. 2000). Its research shows that women are finishing high school in larger percentages than men, are college bound at a higher percentage, and are finishing college at a faster rate. Id. Since 1997, the University has attempted to improve its gender balance by giving male applicants extra points in the admissions process. Even with this preference, only 39 percent of students are men, and it is expected that without the preference, the figure will decline to less than 35 percent. See Dan Carnevale, Lawsuit Prompts U. of Georgia to End Admissions Preferences for Male Applicants, The Chronicle of Higher Education, September 3, 1999, at A68.

What advice would you give the University about its admissions plan?

3-2. Assume that your law school has no female African-American faculty, and that it would like to have one or more. What steps might you urge your school to take? Under what standard would the school's "plan" for recruiting more female African-American faculty be reviewed, if challenged in court? Can you successfully defend the plan?

3. "Comparable Worth": Challenging the Economic Structure

≡ *American Nurses' Association v. Illinois*
783 F.2d 716 (7th Cir. 1986)

POSNER, Circuit Judge.

This class action charges the State of Illinois with sex discrimination in employment, in violation of Title VII of the Civil Rights Act of 1964 . . . and the equal protection clause of the Fourteenth Amendment. The named plaintiffs are two associations of nurses plus 21 individuals, mostly but not entirely female, who work for the state in jobs such as nursing and typing that are filled primarily by women. The suit is on behalf of all state employees in these job classifications . . . [and claims] that the state pays workers in predominantly male job classifications a higher wage not justified by any difference in the relative worth of the predominantly male and the predominantly female jobs in the state's roster.

. . . In April 1985 the district judge dismissed the complaint [on grounds] that the complaint pleaded a comparable worth case and that a failure to pay employees in accordance with comparable worth does not violate federal antidiscrimination law. The plaintiffs appeal. They argue that their case is not (or perhaps not just) a comparable worth case and that in characterizing the complaint as he did the district judge terminated the lawsuit by a semantic manipulation. . . .

Comparable worth is not a legal concept, but a shorthand expression for the movement to raise the ratio of wages in traditionally women's jobs to wages in traditionally men's jobs. Its premises are both historical and cognitive. The historical premise is that a society politically and culturally dominated by men steered women into certain jobs and kept the wages in those jobs below what the jobs were worth, precisely because most of the holders were women. The cognitive premise is that analytical techniques exist for determining the relative worth of jobs that involve different levels of skill, effort, risk, responsibility, etc. These premises are vigorously disputed on both theoretical and empirical grounds. Economists point out that unless employers forbid women to compete for the higher-paying, traditionally men's jobs — which would violate federal law — women will switch into those jobs until the only difference in wages between traditionally women's jobs and traditionally men's jobs will be that necessary to equate the supply of workers in each type of job to the demand. Economists have conducted studies which show that virtually the entire difference in the average hourly wage of men and women, including that due to the fact that men and women tend to be concentrated in different types of job, can be explained by the fact that most women take considerable time out of the labor force in order to take care of their children. As a result they tend to invest less in their "human capital" (earning capacity); and since part of any wage is a return on human capital, they tend therefore to be found in jobs that pay less. Consistently with this hypothesis, the studies find that women who have never married earn as much as men who have never married. To all this the advocates of comparable worth reply that although there are no longer explicit barriers to women's entering traditionally men's jobs, cultural and psychological barriers remain as a result of which many though not all women internalize men's expectations regarding jobs appropriate for women and therefore invest less in their human capital.

On the cognitive question economists point out that the ratio of wages in different jobs is determined by the market rather than by any a priori conception of relative merit, in just the same way that the ratio of the price of caviar to the price of cabbage is determined by relative scarcity rather than relative importance to human welfare. Upsetting the market equilibrium by imposing such a conception would have costly consequences, some of which might undercut the ultimate goals of the comparable worth movement. If the movement should cause wages in traditionally men's jobs to be depressed below their market level and wages in traditionally women's jobs to be jacked above their market level, women will have less incentive to enter traditionally men's fields and more to enter traditionally women's fields. Analysis cannot stop there, because the change in relative wages will send men in the same direction: fewer men will enter the traditionally men's jobs, more the traditionally women's jobs. As a result there will be more room for women in traditionally men's jobs and at the same time fewer opportunities for women in traditionally women's jobs — especially since the number of those jobs will shrink as employers are induced by the higher wage to substitute capital for labor inputs (e.g., more word processors, fewer secretaries). Labor will be allocated less efficiently; men and women alike may be made worse off.

Against this the advocates of comparable worth urge that collective bargaining, public regulation of wages and hours, and the lack of information and mobility of some workers make the market model an inaccurate description of how relative wages are determined and how they influence the choice of jobs. The point has particular force when applied to a public employer such as the State of Illinois, which does not have the same incentives that a private firm would have to use labor efficiently.

It should be clear from this brief summary that the issue of comparable worth . . . is not of the sort that judges are well equipped to resolve intelligently or that we should lightly assume has been given to us to resolve by Title VII or the Constitution. An employer (private or public) that simply pays the going wage in each of the different types of job in its establishment, and makes no effort to discourage women from applying for particular jobs or to steer them toward particular jobs, would be justifiably surprised to discover that it may be violating federal law because each wage rate and therefore the ratio between them have been found to be determined by cultural or psychological factors attributable to the history of male domination of society; that it has to hire a consultant to find out how it must, regardless of market conditions, change the wages it pays in order to achieve equity between traditionally male and traditionally female jobs; and that it must pay backpay, to boot. We need not tarry over the question of law presented by this example because as we understand the plaintiffs' position it is not that a mere failure to rectify traditional wage disparities between predominantly male and predominantly female jobs violates federal law. The circuits that have considered this contention have rejected it. . . .

The next question is whether a failure to achieve comparable worth — granted that it would not itself be a violation of law — might permit an inference of deliberate and therefore unlawful discrimination, as distinct from passive acceptance of a market-determined disparity in wages. The starting point for analyzing this question must be County of Washington v. Gunther, [452 U.S. 161 (1981)]. Women employed to guard female prisoners were paid less than men employed to guard male prisoners. Since male prison inmates are more dangerous than female ones and since each male guard on average guarded ten times as many prisoners as each female guard, the jobs were not the same. Therefore, paying the male guards more could not violate the Equal Pay Act of 1963, 29 U.S.C. §206(d), which requires equal pay only for equal work. The issue was whether it could violate Title VII, and the Court held that it could. A comparable worth study figured in this conclusion. The plaintiffs had alleged . . . that the county had conducted a comparable worth study and had determined that female guards should be paid 95 percent of what male guards were paid; that it had then decided to pay them only 70 percent; "and that the failure of the county to pay [the plaintiffs] the full evaluated worth of their jobs can be proved to be attributable to intentional sex discrimination. Thus, [the plaintiffs'] suit does not require a court to make its own subjective assessment of the value of the male and female guard jobs, or to attempt by statistical technique or other method to quantify the effects of sex discrimination on the wage rates." [452 U.S. at 181.]

All that this seems to mean, as the dissenting Justices pointed out, is "that even absent a showing of equal work, there is a cause of action under Title VII when there is direct evidence that an employer has intentionally depressed a woman's salary because she is a woman. The decision today does not approve a cause of action based on a comparison of the wage rates of dissimilar jobs." Id. at 204. The relevance of a comparable worth study in proving sex discrimination is that it may provide the occasion on which the employer is forced to declare his intentions toward his female employees. In *Gunther* the county accepted (it was alleged) the recommendation of its comparable worth consultant regarding the male guards — decided to pay them "the full evaluated worth of their jobs" — but then rejected the recommendation regarding the female guards and did so because of "intentional sex discrimination," that is, because they were female, not because they had easier jobs or jobs that, for any reason, the market valued below the guarding of male prisoners (however a comparable worth consultant might value them).

The State of Illinois asks us to limit the teaching of *Gunther* to cases where the employer has accepted the recommendation of the comparable worth consultant with respect to the male job classifications. . . . So limited, [as the majority of the Supreme Court in *Gunther* suggests,] its only effect would be to discourage employers from commissioning comparable worth studies.

Gunther suggests the type of evidence that is sufficient but perhaps not necessary to establish sex discrimination in wages for different work. A more recent case out of the State of Washington, American Federation of State, County & Municipal Employees (AFSCME) v. Washington, 770 F.2d 1401 (9th Cir. 1985), suggests the type of evidence that is insufficient. The state's traditional policy had been to pay state employees the prevailing market rates of pay. Beginning in 1974, however, the state commissioned a series of comparable worth studies, each of which found that employees in predominantly female job classifications were paid about 20 percent less than employees in predominantly male job classifications judged to be of comparable worth. Eventually the state passed legislation providing for the phasing in over a decade of a wage system based on comparable worth. The suit charged that the state's failure to act sooner was a form of discrimination. The case was tried and the plaintiffs won in the district court, but the Ninth Circuit reversed. It held that a decision to pay market wages is not discriminatory, that "comparable worth statistics alone are insufficient to establish the requisite inference of discriminatory motive," . . . and that "isolated incidents" of intentional discrimination in the form of help-wanted ads specifying the sex of the applicant were not enough to convert the case into one of wage discrimination across different jobs.

The *AFSCME* case resembles our hypothetical case of the firm accused of sex discrimination merely because it pays market wages. *AFSCME* shows that such a case is not actionable under Title VII even if the employer is made aware that its pattern of wages departs from the principle of comparable worth to the disadvantage of women (plus the occasional male occupant of a traditionally woman's job) and even if the employer is not so much a prisoner of the market that it cannot alter its wages in the direction of comparable worth, as eventually the State of Washington did. The critical thing lacking in *AFSCME* was evidence that the state decided not to raise the wages of particular workers because most of those workers were female. Without such evidence, to infer a violation of Title VII from the fact that the state had conducted a comparable worth study would, again, just discourage such studies.

The plaintiffs can get no mileage out of casting a comparable worth case as an equal protection case. The Supreme Court held in Washington v. Davis, [426 U.S. 229 (1976)], that the equal protection clause is violated only by intentional discrimination; the fact that a law or official practice adopted for a lawful purpose has a racially differential impact is not enough. [Personnel Administrator v. Feeney, 442 U.S. 256 (1979)]. . . .

. . . Knowledge of a disparity is not the same thing as an intent to cause or maintain it; if for example the state's intention was to pay market wages, its knowledge that the consequence would be that men got higher wages on average than women and that the difference might exceed any premium attributable to a difference in relative worth would not make it guilty of intentionally discriminating against women. Similarly, even if the failure to act on the comparable worth study could be regarded as "reaffirming" the state's commitment to pay market wages, this would not be enough to demonstrate discriminatory purpose. To demonstrate such a purpose the failure to act would have to be motivated at least in part by a desire to benefit men at the expense of women.

Neither *Davis* nor *Feeney* were Title VII cases, a point emphasized in Davis. [See 426 U.S. at 238-239.] But when intentional discrimination is charged under Title VII the inquiry is the same as in an equal protection case. The difference between the statutory and constitutional prohibitions becomes important only when a practice is challenged not because it is intended to hurt women (say), but because it hurts them inadvertently and is not justified by the employer's needs—when, in short, the challenge is based on a theory of "disparate impact," as distinct from "disparate treatment" (= intentional discrimination). The plaintiffs in this case, however, have said that they are proceeding on the basis of disparate treatment rather than disparate impact. . . .

So if all that the plaintiffs in this case are complaining about is the State of Illinois' failure to implement a comparable worth study, they have no case and it was properly dismissed. . . .

. . . But the [plaintiffs' mention of] "sex-segregated" [job classifications] blurs the picture. If the state has deliberately segregated jobs by sex, it has violated Title VII. . . .

. . . Paragraph 10 [of the complaint], after summarizing the comparable worth study, says, "Defendants knew or should have known of the historical and continuing existence of patterns and practices of discrimination in compensation and classification, as documented at least in part by the State of Illinois Study." All that the study "documents," however, is that 28 percent of the employees subject to the state's personnel code are employed in 24 job classifications, in each of which at least 80 percent of the employees are of the same sex, and that based on the principles of comparable worth the 12 predominantly female job classifications are underpaid by between 29 and 56 percent. For example, an electrician whose job is rated in the study at only 274 points in skill, responsibility, etc. has an average monthly salary of $2,826, compared to $2,104 for a nurse whose job is rated at 480 points. These disparities are consistent, however, with the state's paying market wages, and of course the fact that the state knew that market wages do not always comport with the principles of comparable worth would not make a refusal to abandon the market actionable under Title VII. But at the very end of paragraph 10 we read, "Moreover, defendants have knowingly and *willfully* failed to take any action to correct such discrimination" (emphasis added), and in the word "willfully" can perhaps be seen the glimmerings of another theory of violation that could survive a motion to dismiss. Suppose the state has declined to act on the results of the comparable worth study not because it prefers to pay (perhaps is forced by labor-market or fiscal constraints to pay) market wages but because it thinks men deserve to be paid more than women. Cf. Crawford v. Board of Education, [458 U.S. 527, 539 n.21 (1982)]. This would be the kind of deliberate sex discrimination that Title VII forbids. . . .

"Willfully" is, however, a classic legal weasel word. Sometimes it means with wrongful intent but often it just means with knowledge of something or other. . . . After reading the comparable worth study the responsible state officials knew that the state's compensation system might not be consistent with the principles of comparable worth ("might" because there has been no determination that the comparable worth study is valid even on its own terms — maybe it's a lousy comparable worth study). But it would not follow that their failure to implement the study was willful in a sense relevant to liability under Title VII. They may have decided not to implement it because implementation would cost too much or lead to excess demand for some jobs and insufficient demand for others. The only thing that would make the failure a form of intentional and therefore actionable sex discrimination would be if the motivation for not implementing the study was the sex of the employees — if for example the officials thought that men ought to be paid more than women even if there is no difference in skill or effort or in the conditions of work. . . .

Reversed and remanded.

Notes

1. Market Explanations for Job Segregation by Sex. Comparable worth is designed not to address wage differentials between male and female workers doing the same job — which is covered by the Equal Pay Act, addressed in Chapter 2 at pages 149-168 — but the segregation of male and female workers into different occupations, with "women's jobs" earning lower wages. For statistics on the extent of job segregation in the United States, see discussion in Chapter 2 on pages 248-249 and pages 287-291.

Conventional explanations of job segregation by sex focus on the different occupational and lifestyle choices men and women make — rational choices that then have pay consequences determined by the market. One model posits that women anticipate working fewer years than men with more interruptions, and therefore "self-select" into occupations that require lower levels of skill and less educational investment, thereby maximizing their earnings potential over time. See Solomon W. Polachek, Occupational Self-Selection: A Human Capital Approach to Sex Differences in Occupational Structure, 63 Rev. Econ. & Stat. 60 (1981). Women are also said to choose occupations that offer flexible hours and schedules to accommodate domestic responsibilities, flexibility that is offset by lower pay. See Jane Friesen, Alternative Economic Perspectives on the Use of Labor Market Remedies to Explain the Gender Gap in Compensation, 82 Geo. L.J. 31, 37 (1993). Specifically on part-time and contingent employment, see pages

360-364. Some also say women are more likely to choose jobs with better working conditions.

> Suppose two employees each have the same level of education, experience, and tenure, yet one works in a pleasant office environment within walking distance of home while the other labors in a remote location under unpleasant and hazardous conditions. The second job will have to pay a "compensating wage differential" if the employer is to be able to recruit and retain employees prepared to work under such unattractive conditions.

Paul Weiler, The Wages of Sex: The Uses and Limits of Comparable Worth. 99 Harv. L. Rev. 1728, 1783 (1986).

The empirical data in support of these theories are mixed. Economist Jane Friesen notes that evidence of compensating differentials for jobs with less favorable working conditions is "weak," except where risk of fatality is involved. See Friesen, supra, at 38. One study, however, found that including fringe benefits like insurance coverage, training/education subsidies, profit sharing, maternity/paternity leave, flexible hours, employer-subsidized child care, and retirement benefits as a measure of earnings reduced the gender gap from 87.4 percent to 96.4 percent for 24-36 year-olds across seven different occupations. See Eric Solberg & Teresa Laughlin, 48 Indus. & Lab. Rel. Rev. 692, 706-707 (1995). This study suggests that women may choose, at a higher rate than men, non-wage compensation in the form of security and working conditions that are compatible with household responsibilities.

Under a human capital or market model, comparable worth is a cure without a disease, and a dangerous one at that. The argument is that setting artificially high (i.e., non-market) wages in female-dominated occupations will increase the workers attracted to those occupations, thereby making them more competitive, and possibly also reducing the number of those jobs (since employers will be "overpaying" employees in these categories). Either way, women's access to the jobs they prefer will be reduced.

An alternative perspective, also grounded in economic theory, is that women do not choose at all, but are "sorted" into lower-paying occupations by the hiring barriers erected by profit-maximizing firms. The wage efficiency model posits that firms use gender (or other observable characteristics) as an indicator of productivity, when it is too costly or difficult to obtain perfect information from each applicant about willingness to work and commitment to the labor force. See Friesen, supra, at 47-50 for a review of the literature and alternative models. This model views the segregation of women into lower-paying jobs as a point of equilibrium in a market where wage rate corresponds to anticipated productivity; firms screen women out of high paying jobs where the cost of turnover or employee "monitoring" is relatively more expensive since women are expected to leave the workforce more often, and to experience lower penalties if fired for "shirking." See id. at 45-47.

The evidence, here, is also mixed. One study found that women still leave the labor force at a rate approximately three times that of men. See June O'Neill & Solomon Polachek, Why the Gender Gap in Wages Narrowed in the 1980s, 11 J. Lab. Econ. 205, 219 (1993). The implications are hard to determine, however, given the "simultaneity" between turnover and wage rates. "Women's wage rates may be lower because they have higher exogenously determined quit rates, or their quit rates may be higher due to the fact that women earn lower wages because of discrimination or other factors." Friesen, supra, at 47. The difference in men's and women's quit rates is "eliminated or reversed," Friesen writes, "when characteristics, including wages, are controlled for in the regression model." Id. A detailed study of departures from a large New York insurance firm over a ten-year period from 1971-1980 found that "[a]lthough women's quit rates are higher than men's at early tenure, the rates become similar to, and even lower than, men's rates once the analysis controls for standard individual and job characteristics." Nachum Sicherman, Gender Differences in Departures from a Large Firm, 49 Indus. & Lab. Rel. Rev. 484, 501 (1996). The fact that women were generally younger, less educated, less trained and, most importantly, in lower-level jobs, explained about half of the gender gap in departure rates. Id. at 493. After five years of tenure, women were less likely than men to leave the firm. Id. at 501. Consistent with general perceptions, the study found that women left for very different reasons than men; for example, 7 percent of women left for household considerations, a reason rarely cited by men; 6 percent of women cited personal health problems or family illness compared with 2.6% of men who cited personal health problems, but almost never family illness; and 5% of women left for pregnancy. Id. at 488. Specifically in regard to women lawyers, see discussion at pages 163-165.

As *American Nurses* illustrates, the law assumes these nondiscriminatory explanations for the job segregation by sex. Should it?

One set of explanations not explored in this section are the sociobiological ones. These are developed in Chapter 5, at section B.

2. Feminist Critiques. The main criticism of the human capital or market model is that it incorporates the very bias it is offered to refute. According to the feminist critiques, societal gender bias, the uneven distribution of household labor, and wage discrimination lie at the root of the choices women make, including how they develop their human capital. The human capital theory implicitly endorses differences in men's and women's investments in their job potential and other factors that sort women into lower-paying jobs, when what is needed are tough challenges to those differences. Gillian Hadfield argues, accordingly, that strategies to reduce the wage gap must address the organization of the household, which plays a large part in determining women's "choices" in the labor market and firms' perceptions of women workers. Hadfield, Households at Work: Beyond Labor Market Policies to Remedy the Gender Gap, 83 Geo. L.J. 89, 95-107 (1993).

Rosemary Hunter also emphasizes the historical socialization factors that are overlooked by the economic theories:

> Economic theories are notably ahistorical, and thus they fail to perceive that the phenomenon of gender segregation in the labor market is produced by particular social and historical forces. The majority of women in the labor market today were channeled into certain industries and occupations by social expectations (imposed and conditioned) about what was appropriate work for women (of their color). This channeling process is something far more pervasive and systemic than individual employers' "tastes for discrimination," or even statistical discrimination by employers. Indeed, to the extent that these forms of employer discrimination actually exist, they too arise out of the same social conditions.
>
> In Western societies, labor market work deemed appropriate for women has been, by and large, work that closely resembles women's domestic labor: cleaning, washing, cooking, garment making, socializing young children, nurturing, caring, and serving. There is nothing innate in women that makes them especially suited to these occupations. Gender definitions of work are not biologically based but are culturally constructed, as demonstrated by the fact that notions of appropriate work for women and men vary across different societies. . . . Gender definitions of work also vary historically. The occupation of secretary was originally a male occupation, and only became "feminized" after the Civil War. Even in new industries, such as computing, gender definitions soon assert themselves — men become programmers and women become operators.
>
> Moreover, a great many women in the labor market today were, as girls, educated to perform "women's work. . . ." Families did not invest in girls' education to the same extent as boys'. Schools taught boys a range of useful market skills, while girls were taught sewing and domestic science. Girls' aspirations to careers were actively dampened and deflected. To label all of this as women's rational "choices" about investment in human capital is repugnant. Indeed, the attractive-sounding concept of "choice" and "preference" in economic models obscure the operations of a patriarchal and racist social system. . . . Human capital and individual choice theories allow white males to ignore the fact that they are the beneficiaries of the most thorough and effective affirmative-action program ever known.

Hunter, Afterword: A Feminist Response to the Gender Gap in Compensation Symposium, 82 Geo. L.J. 147, 149-151 (1993).

Mary Becker, using similar analysis, argues that wage disparities cannot be eliminated by simple nondiscrimination remedies because, to a significant extent, discrimination is an indirect reflection of existing distributions of wealth, entitlements, and preferences, of gender socialization, and of unconscious bias and stereotypes. One cannot expect, Becker contends, that the problem of job segregation can be solved through economic efficiency principles, which themselves accept these circumstances as givens rather than the problem. See Becker, Barriers Facing Women in the Wage-Labor Market and the Need for Additional Remedies: A Reply to Fischel and Lazear, 53 U. Chi. L. Rev. 934 (1986).

Carol M. Rose uses the "prisoner's dilemma" model found in game theory to offer still another explanation for why the market does not prevent the systematic undervaluing of women's work. She argues that *perceptions* about what choices women make in comparison to men are as important in women's ability to obtain their share of economic goods as any *actual* differences between women and men.

> [T]he employment agreement is [a] positive-sum game: the employer values labor more than the wages he or she pays for it, whereas the employee puts a higher value on wage dollars than on the leisure he or she would enjoy otherwise. . . .
>
> . . . How do they split the gains they jointly make from the positive-sum game? In general, the employer might offer Sam a greater portion of those gains. Sam has less taste for cooperation than Louise does, and more tolerance for confrontation, so he can make a more credible threat that he will walk away from a potential job or quit an actual one.
>
> On the other hand, the employer might offer Louise a relatively small share of the collective gains from a labor-wage trade. The employer can rely on her taste for cooperation — her willingness to give up something to be sure that the cooperative relationship will take place or (perhaps a more likely scenario) to be sure that she can take care of others for whom she feels responsible. If Louise is skittish, the employer might offer her the same wage he offers Sam at the outset, in order to bring her into a relationship, but then give her relatively few promotions and pay raises over time. He can rely on the attachments she makes during the course of her employment to weaken her bargaining power over these issues. . . .
>
> It may not matter very much that any difference actually exists between Sam's and Louise's respective tastes. . . . What may matter is that people think such a difference exists. . . . Suppose, [in the employment example] that [Louise] has no such taste and refuses to take such a low cut. Given a sufficiently widespread cultural presumption that women have a greater taste for cooperation than men, the employer will continue to make low bids for women for some time before he changes his mind. Moreover, he may never change his mind at all because at least some Louises will take his low offer, and this will make him think he was right about Louises all along.
>
> Indeed, in a sense the employer may be right, because Louise may be unable to challenge this set of beliefs. If he thinks that she will only face another low bid from Employer B, she may well just accept Employer A's offer. The Louise who insists on something better may well not get a job at all, given a widespread set of beliefs about what her wage demands should be. In other words, it costs her something to try to break the stereotype that affects all the Louises in the labor market. Why, then, should she be the first to stick her neck out to break the pattern, particularly when the effort looks hopeless? This set of

beliefs, in short, presents Louise with a collective action problem; her failure to solve that problem only reinforces the belief system.

See Carol M. Rose, Women and Property: Gaining and Losing Ground, 78 Va. L. Rev. 421 (1992). Is the phenomenon Rose is describing a "market failure"? If so, how might it be corrected?

Paul Milgrom and Sharon Oster developed another, similar model of discrimination in which the skills of women workers are initially "invisible," and even when an employer "discovers" the worker's productivity, it is to its advantage to "hide" that insight in order to keep the workers in their lower level jobs. This obfuscation protects the excess rents earned off workers more productive than the *average* marginal product of all workers at that level, and prevents sending a signal (by a promotion, for example) to other potential employers of a woman worker's true "value." See Paul Milgrom & Sharon Oster, Job Discrimination, Market Forces, and the Invisibility Hypothesis, 102 Q.J. Econ. 453, 471 (1987). Oster argues that this form of discrimination, while perhaps beneficial to the employer in the long run, is inefficient because it discourages women from investing in human capital and thereby lowers overall productivity. See Oster, Is There a Policy Problem?: The Gender Wage Gap, 82 Geo. L.J. 109, 116-118 (1993). She argues that measures like affirmative action, in the long run, could eliminate wage disparities caused by this inefficient result of sex discrimination. See id. at 117.

Comparable worth theories challenge the free market model (which explains the gender pay gap as the efficient and rational pursuit of profits by employers, by insisting that discrimination in wage-setting is the real cause. Another model, the organizational inequality model, focuses more specifically on organizational practices that keep wages relatively low in female occupations relative to male-dominated job categories. These practices, according to sociologists Robert Nelson and William Bridges, include better political mobilization of male workers, better advocacy by male managers for male workers, historical pay practices, systems that benchmark female jobs to other female jobs, and other forms of bias in job evaluation schemes. See Nelson & Bridges, Legalizing Gender Inequality (1999), reviewed in Paula England, The Pay Gap between Male and Female Jobs: Organization and Legal Realities, 25 L. & Soc. Inquiry 913, 925-27 (2000). Both comparative worth and organizational inequality focus on results or outcomes, and are thus "substantive" not "formal." The organizational inequality model, however, focuses on variations across organizations that might be specifically addressed, while the comparative worth model identifies a common, pervasive condition of wage bias requiring systematic intervention in the wage structure.

Is the debate over comparable worth primarily an empirical debate or a normative one? Can it be resolved through economic principles, or is it a matter of determining the appropriate definition of discrimination?

Does most of the earnings gap result from discrimination? In one sense the answer is surely yes. In another sense, no. So much depends on the meaning of the word "discrimination." What kind? By whom? When? Where? With what motive?

A hypothetical experiment may help clarify the issue. Suppose a large, random sample of baby girls were, from the moment of birth, perceived by everyone (including themselves) as boys. They would, on average, be shorter than other boys, and probably not as strong, but at home, in school, and in the workplace, they would be regarded as males. What would they earn as adults? Most likely their wages would be close to the average wages of men; it strains credulity to believe that they would be one-third less. But this means that the present large gap could be said to result from discrimination — that is, from the *response* that gender *evokes* — rather than from any inherent difference between women and men. This discrimination begins in the nursery and is carried forward in families, schools, churches, and every other social institution.

Victor R. Fuchs, Women's Quest for Economic Equality 53 (1988).

3. Equalizing Job Classifications. While existing job evaluation studies are criticized by both advocates and critics of comparable worth, it would seem that any serious reform of the wage structure will require some evaluation tools by which to compare different jobs. Some tools have been in use and widely accepted in the public and private sectors since World War II. See Michele Andrisin Wittig & Gillian Turner, Implementing Comparable Worth: Some Measurement and Conceptual Issues in Job Evaluation, in Comparable Worth, Pay Equity, and Public Policy 143-144 (Rita Mae Kelly & Jane Bayes, eds., 1988).

Heidi I. Hartmann and other researchers have cautioned that the results of pay evaluations may be misleading in that they incorporate existing societal biases and thus *underreport* wage inequities.

> Job evaluation systems depend on the ability of raters to describe adequately and fairly the tasks required for incumbents in jobs. . . . Given the inherently subjective nature of the process, . . . job descriptions are vulnerable to systematic errors and biases resulting from stereotyping. Thus, to the extent that women's jobs are undervalued or seen as less responsible as a result of cultural stereotyping, job descriptions of women's jobs may be affected by expectancy bias and may not adequately reflect the abilities required to perform necessary job tasks. . . .
>
> Although existing quantitative job evaluations systems vary in their details, they tend to share certain basic features. A set of attributes of jobs, called compensable factors, is designated and points are assigned to defined levels of each factor. . . .
>
> . . . [T]he relative ranking of jobs is heavily dependent on which attributes of jobs are designated as compensable factors and how much weight each factor is assigned. . . . Historically, factors and factor weights have been chosen to maximize the prediction of existing pay rates, by capturing the implicit

policy underlying a firm's existing pay structure. The difficulty with this approach, however, is that it has the effect of incorporating any existing gender bias in wages and salaries. . . . Even when factors and factor weights are chosen de novo, there is the possibility that traditional cultural stereotypes as to what is valued enter into the choice of compensable factors or relative weight accorded various factors or both. For example, are coordinating activities, which tend to be characteristic of jobs performed mainly by women, identified as a comparable factor, and, if so, what is its weight relative to that of direct supervision, which tends to be characteristic of jobs performed mainly by men? Is being subjected to consistent interruptions identified as an "unfavorable working condition" comparable to working under noisy conditions? . . .

Evaluating the worth of jobs with respect to compensable factors is the final stage of the job evaluation process, and it too is subject to social judgment biases. There is preliminary evidence that, other things being equal, prestigious jobs or those with high salaries are rated more highly on compensable factors than lower-prestige and lower-paying jobs. . . . This labeling bias is thus likely to result in overestimation of the worth of traditionally male jobs relative to those jobs held mainly by women.

Heidi I. Hartmann, Patricia A. Roos & Donald J. Treiman, An Agenda for Basic Research on Comparable Worth, in Comparable Worth: New Directions for Research 9-12 (Heidi I. Hartmann ed., 1985).

How might these job evaluation tools be improved as more is understood about gender bias? Deborah L. Rhode examines two different conceptual approaches to job evaluation:

The most common job system involves a "policy-capturing" approach. This system focuses on the *relative worth* of particular positions under existing wage scales, either the employer's own rates or those of similarly situated employers. Through this approach, decisionmakers identify factors relevant to compensation and score jobs in terms of those factors, such as skill, responsibility, and working conditions. Then, statistical regression techniques are used to assess the relative importance of such factors in predicting current wages and to establish a weight for each factor. Each job receives a rating based on its weighted characteristics. This rating can serve as the basis for adjusting pay scales or for setting salaries for new jobs, although decisionmakers may make further modifications in response to market forces.

To pay equity advocates, such a policy-capturing approach is primarily useful for identifying racial or gender biases in an employer's own evaluation system. For example, statistical analysis can indicate the importance an employer attaches to particular factors in male-dominated or gender integrated jobs and determine whether the same factors command the same financial reward in female-dominated positions. . . .

. . . [T]he strengths of this system are also the source of its limitation. . . . Such a framework takes no position on what weight specific employment characteristics *should* assume. It only demands that employers consistently apply their own weighting system across job categories. . . . Although this approach is consistent with antidiscrimination principles reflected in existing legislation . . . it does not accomplish one central objective of pay equity advocates — to challenge societal devaluations of women's work. . . .

A more fundamental challenge to current norms is possible with techniques that focus on *intrinsic worth*. Under such an approach, decision-makers generally define a priori a set of factors *and* the factor weights that should serve as the basis for salary differentials. Typically, this system will rank job characteristics such as skill effort, responsibility, and working conditions, and then assign points to particular jobs based on their weighted characteristics. Compensation levels can then be adjusted to ensure parity between jobs with similar ratings. By valuing job characteristics without explicit reference to employers' existing salaries or market rates, such techniques often expose underpayment of predominantly female occupations. . . .

Rhode, Occupational Inequality, 1988 Duke L.J. 1207, 1228-1230. Is the "relative worth" concept compatible with market principles? What about "intrinsic worth"? Do you see any conceptual problems with this approach? How would one implement it?

4. Comparable Worth and Liberal Theory. Is comparable worth compatible with the principles of liberal theory assumed in the version of equality explored in Chapter 2? Consider the following:

> A liberal discourse on equality centers on the ideal of meritocracy. Liberal political thought accepts the notion of inequality and hierarchy: some will have more, some less; some will command, others follow; some will create, others only implement. Equality is defined as equal opportunity, and thus, from a liberal perspective, fairness exists when the distribution of individuals within unequal positions reflects their individual qualities — their differential motivation, talent, intelligence, and effort — and not their gender, race, religion, or family background. . . .
>
> [Advanced capitalist society assumes] that there are large and significant differences among individuals in talent and potential; that a complex industrial society requires hierarchies; that competition and differential rewards for various positions within the hierarchies will motivate the most talented people to fill the most central and important positions.

Johanna Brenner, Feminist Political Discourses: Radical Versus Liberal Approaches to the Feminization of Poverty and Comparable Worth, 1 Gender and Soc'y 447, 448-449 (1987).

Does comparable worth move beyond the hierarchies of a meritocratic society, and thus beyond liberalism and the hierarchies on which markets are based? Brenner argues not:

> As a political discourse, comparable worth's fundamental claim to legitimacy reinforces an existing ideology: the necessity and validity of meritocratic hierarchy. Rather than questioning the market as an arbiter of wages, comparable worth . . . aims primarily to rationalize the existing sorting

and selecting of individuals into unequal places and does not eliminate market criteria from job evaluation.

Id. at 457.

Others, comparing comparable worth to its realistic alternatives, find a more radical potential in the concept:

> Comparable worth does depart less from a liberal vision of the labor market than I and many others would prefer. However, [b]y demonstrating that the value of work can be an object of struggle, comparable worth reveals that the recognition of skill is itself an inherently political process. In other words, acknowledging the connection between skill and gender may open the wage relationship to greater scrutiny, revealing that what society deems valuable is in fact part of a field of social conflict, determined not by intrinsic value, "natural" merit, or abstract market forces but by power relations. This discovery places comparable worth substantially beyond the meritocratic view of the labor market. . . .
>
> . . . If affirmative action exemplifies the mainstream vision of the labor market, comparable worth . . . may move toward a more radical vision of class transformation. . . . . Affirmative action attempts to push women into male fields, and in so doing it implicitly accepts the devaluation of women's work and reinforces the greater social esteem accorded male activity. In contrast, comparable worth contests women's devaluation, extending the focus of radical (or cultural) feminism on rescuing female spheres from the denigration of misogynist culture.

Linda M. Blum, Between Feminism and Labor: The Significance of the Comparable Worth Movement 15, 16-19 (1991). How significant a challenge does the rescue of "female spheres" from the "denigration of misogynist culture" pose to the liberal, free-market premises of this society?

5. Comparable Worth after *American Nurses*. Did Judge Posner in *American Nurses* successfully distinguish *Gunther*? *Gunther* involved allegations by women prison guards that they were underpaid in relation to male guards stated a cause of action under Title VII. The jobs of female and male guards were admittedly not equal jobs, insofar as male guards supervised more than ten times as many prisoners per guard as did the female guards, and the females devoted much of their time to "less valuable" clerical duties. Notwithstanding these differences, and emphasizing that the Court was not upholding plaintiffs' claim on the basis of "the controversial concept of 'comparable worth,'" Justice Brennan, writing for the majority, relied on the fact that the county had itself undertaken to eliminate pay inequities, but then, after receiving the results of its own study that the female guards should be paid approximately 95 percent as much as the male guards, it paid them only about 70 percent as much: under these circumstances, "the failure of the county to pay [the female guards] the full evaluated worth of their jobs can be proven to be attributable to intentional sex discrimination." 452 U.S. at 181.

After *Gunther*, a public entity might well be hesitant to commissionn a comparable worth study, even though a voluntary approach might be thought superior to litigation. See Paul Weiler, The Wages of Sex: The Uses and Limits of Comparable Worth, 99 Harv. L. Rev. 1728, 1805-1806 (1986) (urging voluntary, but not judicial, strategies to correct market wage inequities). But after *AFSCME* and *American Nurses*, it is difficult to imagine plaintiffs satisfying their burden of demonstrating intent to discriminate without the kind of ignored studies present in *Gunther*. In *American Nurses*, is there more than a slim theoretical possibility that plaintiffs will ever be able to present sufficient evidence that the state deliberately maintained pay disparities between job categories because of an intent to discriminate against female employees? See California State Employees' Ass'n v. State of California, 724 F. Supp. 717 (N.D. Cal. 1989) (in a California case brought by state workers for wage discrimination, plaintiffs have to show not only discriminatory intent in wage-setting in the early 1930's, but also carry-over of this discriminatory intent into a 1938 wage restructuring upon which current wages were built).

At least 20 states have adjusted their payrolls to correct for sex or race bias, and others have launched studies to determine if gender affects pay. Cindy Richards, Maine Becomes First State Requiring Pay Equity, Women's eNews, http://www.womensenews.com/article.cfm/dyn/aid/500/context/archive (Sept. 17, 2001). Initial research supports the view that systematic market intervention produces results. A four-year study by the Institute for Women's Policy Research of comparable worth measures implemented found that "all twenty states were successful in closing the female/male wage gap without substantial negative side effects such as increased unemployment." Heidi I. Hartmann & Stephanie Aaronsen, Pay Equity and Women's Wage Increases: Success in the States, a Model for the Nation, 1 Duke J. Gender L. & Pol'y 69 (1994). Wage ratios rose to between 74 and 88 percent, compared to the national average of 71 percent in 1992. See id. at 80. The study revealed that the targeting method, whereby wages in predominantly female undervalued sectors were raised, was more successful than the programs that effected comparable worth through widespread systemic changes in job classification, evaluation, and compensation in that it achieved a greater reduction in the wage gap with less expenditures. See id. at 83. Employment losses were generally minimal (Minnesota experienced a .3 percent decrease in rate of employment growth), and tended to correlate with the rate at which the pay increases were implemented, with gradual phasing being a more successful strategy. See id. at 85. Hartmann concludes that the "substantial negative effects" predicted by critics of comparable worth did not come to pass. See id.

A more recent study by Deborah Figart and Jane Lapidus projects that if nationwide comparable worth wage adjustments were made in predominantly female undervalued sectors, women's median level of wages would rise 13.2 percent and the percentage of female to male wages would rise from 72.2 percent in 1995 to 81.9 percent. The number of working women living below the poverty level for a family of three would decline by almost 25 percent. See Figart & Lapidus, A Gender Analysis of U.S. Labor Market Policies for the Working Poor, 1 Feminist Economics 60, 65 (1995).

Equal pay legislation has been introduced in 30 states, with Maine apparently being the first to enact rules that will require comparable worth on the state level. The rules provide for gradual implementation, and the state is offering technical assistance to employers to help with compliance. Richards, supra.

B. ELIMINATING THE DISADVANTAGES OF WOMEN'S DIFFERENCES

1. Pregnancy

California Federal Savings & Loan Association v. Guerra
479 U.S. 272 (1987)

Justice MARSHALL delivered the opinion of the Court.

The question presented is whether Title VII of the Civil Rights Act of 1964, as amended by the Pregnancy Discrimination Act of 1978, pre-empts a state statute that requires employers to provide leave and reinstatement to employees disabled by pregnancy.

I

California's Fair Employment and Housing Act (FEHA), Cal. Govt. Code Ann. §12900 et seq. (West 1980 and Supp. 1986), is a comprehensive statute that prohibits discrimination in employment and housing. In September 1978, California amended the FEHA to proscribe certain forms of employment discrimination on the basis of pregnancy . . . now codified at Cal. Govt. Code Ann. §12945(b)(2) (West 1980). Subdivision (b)(2) . . . requires these employers to provide female employees an unpaid pregnancy disability leave of up to four months. [It has been construed] to require California employers to reinstate an employee returning from such pregnancy leave to the job she previously held, unless it is no longer available due to business necessity. In the latter case, the employer must make a reasonable, good-faith effort to place the employee in a substantially similar job. The statute does not compel employers to provide paid leave to pregnant employees. Accordingly, the only benefit pregnant workers actually derive . . . is a qualified right to reinstatement.

Title VII of the Civil Rights Act of 1964 . . . also prohibits various forms of employment discrimination, including discrimination on the basis of sex. However, in General Electric Co. v. Gilbert, [429 U.S. 125 (1976)], this Court ruled that discrimination on the basis of pregnancy was not sex discrimination under Title VII. In response to the *Gilbert* decision, Congress passed the Pregnancy Discrimination Act of 1978 (PDA), 42 U.S.C. §2000e(k). The PDA specifies that sex discrimination includes discrimination on the basis of pregnancy.[6]

II

Petitioner California Federal Savings & Loan Association (Cal Fed) is a federally chartered savings and loan association based in Los Angeles; it is an employer covered by both Title VII and §12945(b)(2). Cal Fed has a facially neutral leave policy that permits employees who have completed three months of service to take unpaid leaves of absence for a variety of reasons, including disability and pregnancy. Although it is Cal Fed's policy to try to provide an employee taking unpaid leave with a similar position upon returning, Cal Fed expressly reserves the right to terminate an employee who has taken a leave of absence if a similar position is not available.

Lillian Garland was employed by Cal Fed as a receptionist for several years. In January 1982, she took a pregnancy disability leave. When she was able to return to work in April of that year, Garland notified Cal Fed, but was informed that her job had been filled and that there were no receptionist or similar positions available. Garland filed a complaint with respondent Department of Fair Employment and Housing, which issued an administrative accusation against Cal Fed on her behalf.[7] Respondent charged Cal Fed with violating §12945(b)(2) of the FEHA. Prior to the scheduled hearing before respondent Fair Employment and Housing Commission, Cal Fed, joined by petitioners Merchants and Manufacturers Association and the California Chamber of Commerce, brought this action in the United States District Court for the Central District of California. They sought a declaration that §12945(b)(2) is inconsistent with and pre-empted by Title

---

6. . . . Subsection (k) provides, in relevant part: The terms "because of sex" or "on the basis of sex" include, but are not limited to, because of or on the basis of pregnancy, childbirth, or related medical conditions; and women affected by pregnancy, childbirth, or related medical conditions shall be treated the same for all employment-related purposes, including receipt of benefits under fringe benefit programs, as other persons not so affected but similar in their ability or inability to work, and nothing in section 703(h) of this title shall be interpreted to permit otherwise.

7. Cal Fed reinstated Garland in a receptionist position in November 1982, seven months after she first notified it that she was able to return to work.

VII and an injunction against enforcement of the section. The District Court granted petitioners' motion for summary judgment. . . .

The United States Court of Appeals for the Ninth Circuit reversed. . . . We granted certiorari . . . and we now affirm. . . .

III . . .

Petitioners argue that the language of the federal statute itself ambiguously rejects California's "special treatment" approach to pregnancy discrimination. . . . They contend that the PDA forbids an employer to treat pregnant employees any differently from other disabled employees. . . .

. . . [S]ubject to certain limitations, we agree with the Court of Appeals' conclusion that Congress intended the PDA to be "a floor beneath which related purposes, including receipt of benefits under fringe benefit programs, as other persons not so affected but similar in their ability or inability to work, and nothing in section 703(h) of this title shall be interpreted to permit otherwise. . . . pregnancy disability benefits may not drop — not a ceiling above which they may not rise." 758 F.2d at 396.

The context in which Congress considered the issue of pregnancy discrimination supports this view of the PDA. Congress had before it extensive evidence of discrimination against pregnancy, particularly in disability and health insurance programs like those challenged in *Gilbert*. . . . Opposition to the PDA came from those concerned with the cost of including pregnancy in health and disability-benefit plans and the application of the bill to abortion, not from those who favored special accommodation of pregnancy. . . .

We . . . find it significant that Congress was aware of state laws similar to California's but apparently did not consider them inconsistent with the PDA. In the debates and Reports on the bill, Congress repeatedly acknowledged the existence of state antidiscrimination laws that prohibit sex discrimination on the basis of pregnancy. Two of the States mentioned [Connecticut and Montana] then required employers to provide reasonable leave to pregnant workers. . . . [B]oth the House and Senate Reports suggest that these laws would continue to have effect under the PDA.

Title VII, as amended by the PDA, and California's pregnancy disability leave statute share a common goal. The purpose of Title VII is "to achieve equality of employment opportunities and remove barriers that have operated in the past to favor an identifiable group of . . . employees over other employees." . . . Rather than limiting existing Title VII principles and objectives, the PDA extends them to cover pregnancy. As Senator Williams, a sponsor of the Act, stated: "The entire thrust . . . behind this legislation is to guarantee women the basic right to participate fully and equally in the workforce, without denying them the fundamental right to full participation in family life." 123 Cong. Rec. 29658 (1977).

Section 12945(b)(2) also promotes equal employment opportunity. By requiring employers to reinstate women after a reasonable pregnancy disability leave, §12945(b)(2) ensures that they will not lose their jobs on account of pregnancy disability. California's approach is consistent with the dissenting opinion of Justice Brennan in General Electric Co. v. Gilbert, which Congress adopted in enacting the PDA. Referring to Lau v. Nichols, [414 U.S. 563 (1974)], a Title VI decision, Justice Brennan stated:

> [D]iscrimination is a social phenomenon encased in a social context and, therefore, unavoidably takes its meaning from the desired end products of the relevant legislative enactment, end products that may demand due consideration of the uniqueness of the "disadvantaged" individuals. A realistic understanding of conditions found in today's labor environment warrants taking pregnancy into account in fashioning disability policies. [429 U.S. at 159] (footnote omitted).

By "taking pregnancy into account," California's pregnancy disability-leave statute allows women, as well as men, to have families without losing their jobs.

We emphasize the limited nature of the benefits §12945(b)(2) provides. The statute is narrowly drawn to cover only the period of *actual physical disability* on account of pregnancy, childbirth, or related medical conditions. Accordingly, unlike the protective labor legislation prevalent earlier in this century, §12945(b)(2) does not reflect archaic or stereotypical notions about pregnancy and the abilities of pregnant workers. A statute based on such stereotypical assumptions would, of course, be inconsistent with Title VII's goal of equal employment opportunity. . . .

Moreover, even if we agreed with petitioners' construction of the PDA, we would nonetheless reject their argument that the California statute requires employers to violate Title VII. Section 12945(b)(2) does not prevent employers from complying with both the federal law (as petitioners construe it) and the state law. This is not a case where "compliance with both federal and state regulations is a physical impossibility," . . . or where there is an "inevitable collision between the two schemes of regulation." . . . Section 12945(b)(2) does not compel California employers to treat pregnant workers better than other disabled employees; it merely establishes benefits that employers must, at a minimum, provide to pregnant workers. Employers are free to give comparable benefits to other disabled employees, thereby treating "women affected by pregnancy" no better than "other persons not so affected but similar in their ability or inability to work." Indeed, at oral argument, petitioners conceded that compliance with both statutes "is theoretically possible." . . .

IV

Thus, petitioners' facial challenge to §12945(b)(2) fails. . . .

[The opinions of Justices Stevens and Scalia, concurring in the judgment, are omitted.]

Justice WHITE, with whom THE CHIEF JUSTICE and Justice POWELL join, dissenting.

I disagree with the Court. . . .

. . . [The PDA] mandates that pregnant employees "shall be treated the same for all employment-related purposes" as nonpregnant employees similarly situated with respect to their ability or inability to work. This language leaves no room for preferential treatment of pregnant workers. . . .

Contrary to the mandate of the PDA, California law requires every employer to have a disability leave policy for pregnancy even if it has none for any other disability. An employer complies with California law if it has a leave policy for pregnancy but denies it for every other disability. On its face, §12945(b)(2) is in square conflict with the PDA and is therefore preempted. . . .

The majority nevertheless would save the California law on two grounds. First, it holds that the PDA does not require disability from pregnancy to be treated the same as other disabilities; instead, it forbids less favorable, but permits more favorable, benefits for pregnancy disability. The express command of the PDA is unambiguously to the contrary, and the legislative history casts no doubt on that mandate.

The legislative materials reveal Congress' plain intent not to put pregnancy in a class by itself within Title VII, as the majority does with its "floor . . . not a ceiling" approach. . . . The Senate Report clearly stated:

> By defining sex discrimination to include discrimination against pregnant women, the bill rejects the view that employers may treat pregnancy and its incidents as *sui generis*, without regard to its functional comparability to other conditions. Under this bill, the treatment of pregnant women in covered employment must focus not on their condition alone but on the actual effects of that condition on their ability to work. Pregnant women who are able to work must be permitted to work on the same conditions as other employees; and when they are not able to work for medical reasons, they must be accorded the same rights, leave privileges and other benefits, as other workers who are disabled from working [citation omitted].

The House Report similarly stressed that the legislation did not mark a departure from Title VII principles:

> It must be emphasized that this legislation, *operating as part of Title VII*, prohibits only discriminatory treatment. Therefore, it does not require employers to treat pregnant employees in any particular manner with respect to hiring, permitting them to continue working, providing sick leave, furnishing medical and hospital benefits, providing disability benefits, or any other matter. H.R. 6075 in no way requires the institution of any new programs where none

currently exist. The bill would simply require that pregnant women be treated the same as other employees on the basis of their ability or inability to work [citation omitted].

. . . There is only one direct reference in the legislative history to preferential treatment. Senator Brooke stated during the Senate debate: "I would emphasize most strongly that S. 995 in no way provides special disability benefits for working women. They have not demanded, nor asked, for such benefits. They have asked only to be treated with fairness, to be accorded the same employment rights as men" [citation omitted]. Given the evidence before Congress of the wide-spread discrimination against pregnant workers, it is probable that most Members of Congress did not seriously consider the possibility that someone would want to afford preferential treatment to pregnant workers. The parties and their *amici* argued vigorously to this Court the policy implications of preferential treatment of pregnant workers. In favor of preferential treatment it was urged with conviction that preferential treatment merely enables women, like men, to have children without losing their jobs. In opposition to preferential treatment it was urged with equal conviction that preferential treatment represents a resurgence of the 19th-century protective legislation which perpetuated sex-role stereotypes and which impeded women in their efforts to take their rightful place in the workplace. . . . It is not the place of this Court, however, to resolve this policy dispute. Our task is to interpret Congress' intent in enacting the PDA. Congress' silence in its consideration of the PDA with respect to preferential treatment of pregnant workers cannot fairly be interpreted to abrogate the plain statements in the legislative history, not to mention the language of the statute, that equality of treatment was to be the guiding principle of the PDA. . . .

Nor does anything in the legislative history from the Senate side indicate that it carefully considered the state statutes, including those of Connecticut and Montana, and expressly endorsed their provisions. . . . Passing reference to state statutes without express recognition of their content and without express endorsement is insufficient in my view to override the PDA's clear equal-treatment mandate, expressed both in the statute and its legislative history.

The Court's second, and equally strange, ground is that even if the PDA does prohibit special benefits for pregnant women, an employer may still comply with both the California law and the PDA: it can adopt the specified leave policies for pregnancy and at the same time afford similar benefits for all other disabilities. This is untenable. California surely had no intent to require employers to provide general disability leave benefits. It intended to prefer pregnancy and went no further. Extension of these benefits to the entire work force would be a dramatic increase in the scope of the state law and would impose a significantly greater burden on California employers. That is the province of the California Legislature. . . .

Troupe v. May Department Stores Co.
20 F.3d 734 (7th Cir. 1994)

POSNER, Chief Judge.

The plaintiff, Kimberly Hern Troupe, was employed by the Lord & Taylor department store in Chicago as a saleswoman in the women's accessories department. . . . Until the end of 1990 her work was entirely satisfactory. In December of that year, in the first trimester of a pregnancy, she began experiencing morning sickness of unusual severity. The following month she requested and was granted a return to part-time status, working from noon to 5:00 p.m. Partly it seems because she slept later under the new schedule, so that noon was "morning" for her, she continued to experience severe morning sickness at work, causing what her lawyer describes with understatement as "slight" or "occasional" tardiness. In the month that ended with a warning from her immediate supervisor, Jennifer Rauch, on February 18, she reported late to work, or left early, on nine out of the 21 working days. The day after the warning she was late again and this time received a written warning. After she was tardy three days in a row late in March, the company on March 29 placed her on probation for 60 days. During the probationary period Troupe was late eleven more days; and she was fired on June 7, shortly after the end of the probationary period. She testified at her deposition that on the way to the meeting with the defendant's human resources manager at which she was fired, Rauch told her that "I [Troupe] was going to be terminated because she [Rauch] didn't think I was coming back to work after I had my baby." Troupe was due to begin her maternity leave the next day. . . . [A]t argument Lord & Taylor's counsel said that employees of Lord & Taylor are entitled to maternity leave with half pay. . . .

. . . The great, the undeniable fact is the plaintiff's tardiness. Her lawyer argues with great vigor that she should not be blamed — that she was genuinely ill, had a doctor's excuse, etc. That would be pertinent if Troupe were arguing that the Pregnancy Discrimination Act requires an employer to treat an employee afflicted by morning sickness better than the employer would treat an employee who was equally tardy for some other health reason. This is rightly not argued. If an employee who (like Troupe) does not have an employment contract cannot work because of illness, nothing in Title VII requires the employer to keep the employee on the payroll. . . .

Against the inference that Troupe was fired because she was chronically late to arrive at work and chronically early to leave, she has only two facts to offer. The first is the timing of her discharge: she was fired the day before her matenity leave was to begin. . . . Thus, her employer fired her one day before the problem that the employer says caused her to be fired was certain to end. If the discharge of an unsatisfactory worker were a purely remedial measure rather than also, or instead, a deterrent one, the inference that Troupe wasn't really fired because of her tardiness would therefore be a powerful one. But that is a big "if." We must remember that after two warnings Troupe had been placed on probation for sixty days and that she had violated the implicit terms of probation by being as tardy during the probationary period as she had been before. If the company did not fire her, its warnings and threats would seem empty. Employees would be encouraged to flout work rules knowing that the only sanction would be a toothless warning or a meaningless period of probation.

. . . [I]t might appear to be an issue for trial whether it is superior to Troupe's interpretation. But what is Troupe's interpretation? Not (as we understand it) that Lord & Taylor wanted to get back at her for becoming pregnant or having morning sickness. The only significance she asks us to attach to the timing of her discharge is as reinforcement for the inference that she asks us to draw from Rauch's statement about the reason for her termination: that she was terminated because her employer did not expect her to return to work after her maternity leave was up. We must decide whether a termination so motivated is discrimination within the meaning of the pregnancy amendment to Title VII.

Standing alone, it is not. (It could be a breach of contract, but that is not alleged.) . . . We must imagine a hypothetical Mr. Troupe, who is as tardy as Ms. Troupe was, also because of health problems, and who is about to take a protracted sick leave growing out of those problems at an expense to Lord & Taylor equal to that of Ms. Troupe's maternity leave. If Lord & Taylor would have fired our hypothetical Mr. Troupe, this implies that it fired Ms. Troupe not because she was pregnant but because she cost the company more than she was worth to it.

The Pregnancy Discrimination Act does not, despite the urgings of feminist scholars . . . require employers to offer maternity leave or take other steps to make it easier for pregnant women to work . . . — to make it as easy, say as it is for their spouses to continue working during pregnancy. Employers can treat pregnant women as badly as they treat similarly affected but nonpregnant employees. . . .

The plaintiff has made no effort to show that if all the pertinent facts were as they are except for the fact of her pregnancy, she would not have been fired. So in the end she has no evidence from which a rational trier of fact could infer that she was a victim of pregnancy discrimination. . . . The Pregnancy Discrimination Act requires the employer to ignore an employee's pregnancy, but . . . not her absence from work, unless the employer overlooks the comparable absences of nonpregnant employees. . . . Of course there may be no comparable absences . . . ; but we do not understand Troupe to be arguing that the reason she did not present evidence that nonpregnant employees were treated more favorably than she is that . . . there is no comparison group of Lord & Taylor employees. . . . We doubt that finding a comparison group would be that difficult. Troupe would be halfway home if she could find one nonpregnant employee of Lord & Taylor who had not been fired when about to begin a leave similar in length to hers.

She either did not look, or did not find. Given the absence of other evidence, her failure to present any comparison evidence doomed her case.

Herma Hill Kay, Equality and Difference: The Case of Pregnancy
1 Berkeley Women's L.J. 1, 26-31 (1985)

Philosophers recognize that, just as the concept of equality requires that equals be treated equally, so it requires that unequals be treated differently. To treat persons who are different alike is to treat them unequally. The concept of formal equality, however, contains no independent justification for making unequals equal. A different concept, that of equality of opportunity, offers a theoretical basis for making unequals equal in the limited sense of removing barriers which prevent individuals from performing according to their abilities. The notion is that the perceived inequality does not stem from an innate difference in ability, but rather from a condition or circumstance that prevents certain uses or developments of that ability. As applied to reproductive behavior, the suggestion would be that women in general are not different from men in innate ability. During the temporary episode of a woman's pregnancy, however, she may become unable to utilize her abilities in the same way she had done prior to her reproductive conduct. Since a man's abilities are not similarly impaired as a result of his reproductive behavior, equality of opportunity implies that the woman should not be disadvantaged as a result of that sex-specific variation.

As applied to the employment context, the concept of equality of opportunity takes on the following form. Let us postulate two workers, one female, the other male, who respectively engage in reproductive conduct. Assume as well that prior to this activity, both were roughly equal in their ability to perform their similar jobs. The consequence of their having engaged in reproductive behavior will be vastly different. The man's ability to perform on the job will be largely unaffected. The woman's ability to work, measured against her prior performance, may vary with the physical and emotional changes she experiences during pregnancy. At times, her ability to work may be unaffected by the pregnancy; at other times, she may be temporarily incapacitated by it. Ultimately, she may require medical care to recover from miscarriage, or to complete her pregnancy by delivery, or to terminate it earlier by induced abortion. In order to maintain the woman's equality of opportunity during her pregnancy, we should modify as far as reasonably possible those aspects of her work where her job performance is adversely affected by the pregnancy. Unless we do so, she will experience employment disadvantages arising from her reproductive activity that are not encountered by her male co-worker. . . .

. . . [P]regnancy differs from sex . . . in that pregnancy is an episodic occurrence, rather than an immutable trait. The category of pregnant persons is a sub-class within the larger category of women. . . . Employers must take those measures that may be reasonably necessary to permit pregnant workers to continue working until delivery, in order to avoid discrimination against them. Women returning from pregnancy leave must be allowed to resume their former status as workers. An episodic view of pregnancy requires that any benefits extended to pregnant workers or restrictions imposed on them be tailored to actual medical need resulting from the pregnancy, and not be triggered by stereotypical notions of what pregnant women should or should not do.

This interpretation of Title VII based on an episodic analysis of biological reproductive differences will permit pregnancy to be recognized as the normal consequence of reproductive behavior that can and should be accommodated in the workplace. Pregnancy is not itself a disability, although an individual pregnant woman may experience disabling symptoms and may require medical care. If she is temporarily impaired from performing at work up to her normal level of ability, the concept of equal employment opportunity embodied in Title VII requires not only that she remain free of resulting job reprisals, but also that she secure compensatory benefits to offset any potential work-related disadvantage. Under this analysis, women will be equal to men in their ability to work and to make reproductive choices. . . .

It follows from this analysis that, for constitutional purposes as well as statutory coverage under Title VII, a discrimination against a woman based on pregnancy is a facial discrimination against her because of her sex. The same intermediate standard of judicial review developed for equal protection sex discrimination cases can be adapted for use in pregnancy discrimination cases. The analysis will, however, be different . . . because there is no matching group of pregnant males to use for purposes of comparison. Instead, the constitutional test must be applied so as to assure pregnant women equality of opportunity to the same extent as that available to males who have engaged in reproductive conduct. Thus, pregnant women may be treated differently from such males if the result is to prevent a disadvantage that might otherwise follow from their condition. . . . [A] reasonable leave provided by a state employer to pregnant workers is not only constitutional, it is constitutionally compelled to avoid discrimination by the state against pregnant workers.

≡ ### *Richard A. Posner, Conservative Feminism*
≡ 1989 U. Chi. Legal F. 191, 195-198

Where the libertarian is apt to part company with the liberal or radical feminist in the field of employment is over the question whether employers should be forced to subsidize female employees, as by being compelled to offer maternity leave or pregnancy benefits, or to disregard women's greater longevity than men when fixing pension benefits. To the extent that women workers incur higher medical expenses than men (mainly but not entirely due to pregnancy), or live longer in retirement on a company pension, they cost the employer more than male workers do. So the employer should not be required to pay the same wage *and* provide the same package of fringe benefits. (Of course, to the extent that women impose lower costs — for example, women appear to be more careful about safety than men, and therefore less likely to be injured on the job — they are entitled to a correspondingly higher wage or more extensive fringe benefits.) This is not to suggest — which would be absurd — that women are blameworthy for getting pregnant or for living longer than men. It is to suggest merely that they may be more costly workers and that, if so, the disparity in cost should be reflected in their net compensation. If this disparity is not reflected, then male workers are being discriminated against in the same sense in which women would be discriminated against if they received a lower wage than equally productive (and no less costly) male workers. What is sauce for the goose should be sauce for the gander. More than symmetry is involved; we shall see in a moment that laws designed to improve the welfare of women may boomerang, partly though not wholly because of the economic interdependence of men and women.

I anticipate three objections to my analysis. The first is that in speaking of employers' subsidizing women I am taking as an arbitrary benchmark the costs and performance of male workers. I am not. Consider an employer who is female in a hypothetical female-dominated society and whose entire labor force is also female, so that for her the benchmark in setting terms of employment is female. A man applies for a job. He asks for a higher wage on the ground that experience shows that the average male employee's medical costs are lower than the average female employee's medical costs. If the employer refuses to pay him the higher wage, then, assuming that this worker is just as good as the employer's average female worker, the employer is discriminating against him. This should answer the second objection — that nature should not be allowed to determine social outcomes. I agree that natural law does not compel the conclusion that women should be penalized in the marketplace or anywhere else for living longer or for incurring greater medical costs on average than men. But neither is there any reason why men should be penalized for not living as long as women by being forced to pay for women's longer years of retirement. The matter should be left to the market.

The third objection to my analysis is that, in suggesting that the employer be allowed to make cost-justified differentiations based on sex, I am necessarily implying that he should be permitted to treat employees as members of groups whose average characteristics the particular employee may not share, rather than as individuals. That is true. Some women die before some men, just as some women are taller than some men. The difference is that while it is obvious on inspection whether a given woman is taller than a given man — and therefore it would be absurd for an employer to implement a (let us assume valid) minimum-height requirement of 5 feet 8 inches by refusing to accept job applications from women, it is not obvious which women employees will not live as long as which men employees or will not take as much leave or incur as high medical expenses. Any cost-based differentiation in these areas must be based on probabilistic consider-ations, of which sex may be the most powerful in the sense of having the greatest predictive power. The average differences between men and women are not invidious, and many cut in favor of women — they are safer drivers, and they live longer, and in a free insurance market would therefore be able to buy liability insurance and life insurance at lower rates than men. Women would not be stigmatized if the market were allowed to register these differences.

It is not even clear, moreover, that women benefit, on balance, from laws that forbid employers to take into account the extra costs that female employees can impose. Such laws discourage employers from hiring, promoting, and retaining women, and there are many ways in which they can discriminate in these respects without committing detectable violations of the employment-discrimination laws.[9] Sometimes there is no question of violation, as when an employer accelerates the substitution of computers for secretaries in response to an increase in the costs of his female employees.

There is an additional point. Most women are married — and many who are not currently married are divorced or widowed and continue to derive a benefit from their husband's earnings. The consumption of a married woman is, as I have noted, a function of her husband's income as well as of her own (in the divorce and widowhood cases as well, for the reason just noted). Therefore a reduction in men's incomes as a result of laws that interfere with profit-maximizing and cost-minimizing decisions by employers will reduce women's welfare as well as men's. Moreover, women who are not married are less likely to have children than women who are married; and where employer benefits are child-related — such as pregnancy benefits and maternity leave — their effect is not merely to transfer wealth from men to women but from women to women. The effect could be

---

9. Suits for employment discrimination are not a terribly effective remedy. They are rarely worth bringing even when the prospects for winning are good, because, in general, the successful plaintiff can obtain only back pay and reinstatement, not common law damages, and because the filing of an employment discrimination suit identifies the plaintiff as a "troublemaker," thereby making him or her unattractive to future employers. (Many women, I have been told, regard filing a sex-discrimination suit as tantamount to committing professional suicide.) In addition, most discrimination cases are difficult to win, because the plaintiff, unless irrationally willing to invest resources in investigation and proof that are disproportionate to the modest stakes in most such cases, will be hard-pressed to establish the counterfactual proposition essential to victory: for example, that she would not have been fired if she had been male. I am speaking here primarily of disparate-treatment (intentional discrimination) rather than disparate-impact litigation, but the latter will not eliminate most forms of sex discrimination.

dramatic. Compare the situation of a married woman with many children and an unmarried woman with no children. Generous pregnancy benefits and a generous policy on maternity leave will raise the economic welfare of the married woman. Her and her husband's wages will be lower, because all wages will fall in order to finance the benefit, but the reduction will probably be smaller than the benefits to her — in part because the unmarried female worker will experience the same reduction in wages but with no offsetting benefit. Feminists who support rules requiring employers to grant pregnancy benefits and maternity leave may therefore, and I assume unknowingly, be discouraging women from remaining single or childless. Feminists of all persuasions would think it outrageous if the government required fertile women to have children, yet many feminists support an oblique form of such a policy — a subsidy to motherhood. They do this, I suspect, because they have not considered the economic consequences of proposals that *appear* to help women.

Notes

1. When Is Pregnancy Discrimination "Based on Sex"? As noted by the Court in *Cal Fed*, Congress enacted the Pregnancy Discrimination Act (PDA) in response to the Supreme Court decision in General Electric Co. v. Gilbert, which held that discrimination on the basis of pregnancy did not amount to discrimination on the basis of sex under Title VII. *Gilbert* followed Geduldig v. Aiello, 417 U.S. 484 (1974), which had challenged the exclusion of pregnancy from an otherwise comprehensive list of disabilities covered by a state disability insurance plan under the equal protection clause. In *Geduldig*, the Court began by taking, as givens, the fundamental principles of the then-existing insurance system and the means by which the costs of the system were spread among workers:

> . . . California intended to establish this benefit system as an insurance program that was to function essentially in accordance with insurance concepts. . . . Since the program was instituted in 1946, it has been totally self-supporting, never drawing on general state revenues. . . . The Disability Fund is wholly supported by the one percent of wages annually contributed by participating employees. At oral argument, counsel for the appellant informed us that in recent years between 90% and 103% of the revenue . . . has been paid out in disability and hospital benefits. . . .
>
> Over the years California has demonstrated a strong commitment not to increase the contribution rate above the one-percent level [and] to provide the broadest possible disability protection that would be affordable by all employees, including those with very low incomes. Because any larger percentage or any flat dollar-amount rate of contribution would impose an increasingly regressive levy bearing most heavily upon those with the lowest

incomes, the State has resisted any attempt to change the required contribution from the one-percent level.

417 U.S. at 492-493. Compare this deference to the status quo, and to insurance concepts to the Court's decision in City of Los Angeles, Dept. of Water and Power v. Manhart, 435 U.S. 702 (1978), set forth at page 304.

The heart of the Court's analysis in *Geduldig* appears in the now-famous footnote 20 in Justice Stewart's majority opinion:

> . . . [T]his case is . . . a far cry from cases like [*Reed*] and [*Frontiero*], involving discrimination based upon gender as such. The California insurance program does not exclude anyone from benefit eligibility because of gender but merely removed one physical condition — pregnancy — from the list of compensable disabilities. While it is true that only women can become pregnant, it does not follow that every legislative classification concerning pregnancy is a sex-based classification. . . . Normal pregnancy is an objectively identifiable physical condition with unique characteristics. Absent a showing that distinctions involving pregnancy are mere pretexts designed to effect an invidious discrimination against the members of one sex or the other, lawmakers are constitutionally free to include or exclude pregnancy from the coverage of legislation such as this on any reasonable basis, just as with respect to any other physical condition.
>
> The lack of identity between the excluded disability and gender as such under this insurance program becomes clear upon the most cursory analysis. The program divides potential recipients into two groups — pregnant women and nonpregnant persons. While the first group is exclusively female, the second includes members of both sexes. The fiscal and actuarial benefits of the program thus accrue to members of both sexes.

417 U.S. at 496-497 n.20.

The fact that pregnancy is "unique" means, for the *Geduldig* Court at least, that pregnant women are not similarly situated to other, "nonpregnant persons" and thereby excuses explicitly different treatment. This view of uniqueness is consistent with the most formalistic (and content-less) version of the equal treatment model of equality that likes be treated alike. But in ignoring both the link between pregnancy and sex and the similarities between pregnancy and other disabilities with respect to the purposes of disability insurance, the Court seems blind to the reasons for giving classifications based on sex special scrutiny.

Pregnancy, to be sure, is a *real* difference, and unique. But is this a reason to give classifications based on pregnancy less scrutiny? Consider the following:

> Paradoxically, the uniqueness of pregnancy is probably the most important reason why it warrants special protection, for pregnancy's unique identifiability facilitates [the drafting of] laws and regulations based on exactly those generalizations, stereotypes, and assumptions that constitutional doctrine in

the area of sex discrimination was intended to curb. . . . [In particular the notion in *Geduldig* that pregnancy is unique reinforces assumptions] that women belong in the home raising children; that once women leave work to have babies, they do not return to the labor force; that pregnancy, though it keeps women from working, is not a "disability" but a blessing which fulfills every woman's deepest wish; that women are and should be supported by their husband, not themselves or the state.

Katharine T. Bartlett, Comment, Pregnancy and the Constitution: The Uniqueness Trap, 62 Cal. L. Rev. 1532, 1536, 1563 (1974). Does this reasoning support the result in Cal Fed? Compel it? For a recent application of *Geduldig*, see Bray v. Alexandria Women's Health Clinic, 506 U.S. 263, 271-272 (1993) (applying *Geduldig* in §1985 challenge to anti-abortion demonstrations and concluding that discrimination against women who seek abortions is not discrimination based on sex).

Shortly after winning the *Geduldig* case, California amended its disability benefits plan, first to include "abnormal and involuntary" complications of pregnancy, 1973 Cal. Stats. ch. 1163, and later to eliminate the pregnancy exclusion outright. 1979 Cal. Stats., ch. 663, 3.

Notwithstanding *Geduldig*, the Supreme Court has invalidated on constitutional grounds some rules that discriminate against pregnant women. In the same year *Geduldig* was decided, the Supreme Court held in Cleveland Bd. of Educ. v. LaFleur, 414 U.S. 632 (1974), that a school system could not conclusively presume that school teachers become physically incapable of being classroom teachers after the fourth month of pregnancy and require them to take (unpaid) maternity leave. The Court's analysis turned on the importance of women's right to bear children and the freedom of personal choice in matters of marriage and family life established in the Court's earlier privacy decisions, such as Roe v. Wade, 410 U.S. 113 (1973), and Griswold v. Connecticut, 381 U.S. 479 (1965). See *La Fleur*, 414 U.S. at 639-640, 650. The next year the court invalidated a Utah law that made pregnant women ineligible for unemployment benefits during any time from 12 weeks before the expected date of delivery to 6 weeks after the child's birth on the assumption that a woman during that period was not able, and thus not available, to work. Turner v. Dep't of Employment Sec., 423 U.S. 44 (1975). The Court in *Turner*, as in *LaFleur*, reasoned that a state rule constitutionally could not burden a woman's childbearing choices by irrebuttably presuming unfitness to work when she was pregnant. Are these decisions consistent with *Geduldig*?

A third case, Nashville Gas Co. v. Satty, 434 U.S. 136 (1977), held that it was a violation of Title VII for an employer to refuse to permit a woman who left work to bear a child to retain the seniority benefits accrued before leaving work. Justice Rehnquist, writing for the Court, explained that while the policy, like the policies at issue in *Geduldig* and *Gilbert*, was facially neutral, it was unlike the policies in those previous cases because it actually favored men over women.

Why was the Court able to see sex discrimination in *Satty* and not in *Geduldig* and *Gilbert?* Could it be that in the one case, women sought benefits for a condition not experienced by men, while in the other, they sought to preserve benefits earned "like a man"?

> Roughly translated, *Gilbert* and *Satty* read together seemed to stand for the proposition that insofar as a rule deprives a woman of benefits for actual pregnancy, that rule is lawful under Title VII. If, on the other hand, it denies her benefits she had earned while not pregnant (and hence like a man) and now seeks to use upon return to her non-pregnant (male-like) status, it has a disproportionate effect on women and is not lawful.

Wendy Williams, The Equality Crisis: Some Reflections on Culture, Courts, and Feminism, 7 Women's Rts. L. Rep. 175, 192-193 (1982). Can *LaFleur* and *Turner* be explained along similar lines?

Are *Cal Fed* and *Johnson Controls* (set forth on pages 320 and 236, respectively) consistent cases? It would seem that *Cal Fed* permits special legislation that gives pregnant women employees protection that other disabled employees may not get, while *Johnson Controls* prohibits any special protection. Is the rule that employers may give (may be even required by the state to give) special accommodations that favor pregnant women — accommodations they are free to accept or decline — but they may not protect them in a way that limits the choices available to them? In other words, protections that favor them are fine; protections that may hinder their work opportunities are not? Is this distinction satisfactory?

2. The Feminist Debate over "Equal" vs. "Special" Treatment. While a broad coalition of feminist groups advocated the passage of the PDA, once it was passed the feminist community split over the issue of what the new law meant. Feminists agreed that discrimination *against* pregnant women is sex discrimination, and bad, but disagreed profoundly over the legality and desirability of rules that attempt to eliminate some of the disadvantages experienced by women, and not by men, as a consequence of pregnancy and childbirth. Filing amicus curiae briefs in favor of upholding the statute were such organizations as the International Ladies Garment Worker's Union, AFL-CIO; the American Federation of State, County and Municipal Employees, District Council 36; California Federation of Teachers; 9 to 5; the California Women Lawyers; and the National Conference of State Legislatures. Principal opponents of the legislation included the American Civil Liberties Union, the Chamber of Commerce of the United States, and the National Organization for Women.

What is the case for "special treatment"? Simply put, it is that neutral rules do not take adequate account of the extent to which the material realities of women's lives are different from those of men's lives; same treatment cannot effectuate equality between men and women when their circumstances are so different. See Linda J. Krieger & Patricia N. Cooney, The Miller-Wohl Controversy: Equal Treatment, Positive Action and the Meaning of Women's Equality, 13 Golden Gate U.L. Rev. 513, 537 (1983).

The case against "special treatment" in favor of "equal treatment" can also be simply stated.

> Pregnancy [is] the centerpiece, the linchpin, the essential feature of women's separate sphere. The stereotypes, the generalizations, the role expectations [are] at their zenith when a woman [becomes] pregnant. . . .
>
> . . . [F]eminists who seek special recognition for pregnancy are starting from the same basic assumption, namely, that women have a special place in the scheme of human existence when it comes to maternity. . . .
>
> . . . The special treatment model has great costs. . . . [T]he reality [is] that conceptualizing pregnancy as a special case permits unfavorable as well as favorable treatment of pregnancy. Our history provides too many illustrations of the former. . . .

Wendy W. Williams, The Equality Crisis: Some Reflections on Culture, Courts, and Feminism, 7 Women's Rts. L. Rep. 175, 191, 195-196 (1982).

Judge Posner's analysis offers an alternative, market-based rationale against "special treatment." Does his analysis have the same consequences as Williams' rationale? To what extent is Judge Posner correct that maternity leave policies "subsidize" women? Are there ordinary employment policies that subsidize men?

What is the effect of formulating the pregnancy issue as a choice between "equal" and "special" treatment? Is there an alternative? Many have tried to focus the attention directly on the relevant policy issues, and away from the choice of gender theories. See, e.g., Lucinda Finley, Transcending Equality Theory: A Way Out of the Maternity and the Workplace Debate, 86 Colum. L. Rev. 1118 (1986) (emphasizing obligation of employers to structure workplace to accommodate an ideal worker who has family responsibilities); Joan Williams, Do Women Need Special Treatment? Do Feminists Need Equality?, 9 J. Contemp. Legal Issues 279, 285-296 (1998) (arguing that focus should be on three axes of policy choices: (1) the extent to which household work and resulting entitlements should be redistributed within the household; (2) the extent to which the costs of childrearing should be shifted from the private to the public arena; and (3) the extent to which employees should be pressured or required to restructure market work to better accommodate childrearing parents). Professor Williams' analysis is more fully developed in Unbending Gender: Why Family and Work Conflict and What To Do About It (2000).

3. From "Special Treatment" to Full Accommodation. Professor Herma Hill Kay uses the sex-based uniqueness rationale of her theory to limit, as well as justify, workplace accommodations on behalf of pregnant women. Only during the episode of pregnancy when the women's body functions in a unique way, she states, should the law be allowed to treat women differently from men. Kay, supra, 1 Berkeley Women's L.J. at 34.

Professor Kay's approach is consistent with *Cal Fed*, which permits leaves for pregnant and childbearing women even when leaves are not available for other disabilities, but only as to the sex-unique disability of pregnancy. In cases since *Cal Fed*, courts have overturned women-only childrearing leaves that go beyond the medical aspects of pregnancy- and childbirth-related conditions. See, e.g., Schafer v. Board of Public Educ., 903 F.2d 243 (3d Cir. 1990).

Should Kimberly Troupe have been accommodated? Can you write the law that would have required it? Is it a good rule? Without such a law, *Troupe* makes clear that the PDA requires that pregnant women be treated like other similarly-situated non-pregnant employees, not that pregnancy be accommodated. Is it realistic to expect Ms. Troupe could meet this standard, even if she was the victim of pregnancy discrimination? See Ruth Colker, Pregnancy, Parenting, and Capitalism, 58 Ohio St. L.J. 61, 80 (1997) ("[w]hat was she supposed to find — a nonpregnant employee with a sudden record of tardiness after a nearly spotless work record who also had scheduled a lengthy leave?"). See also Judith G. Greenberg, The Pregnancy Discrimination Act: Legitimating Discrimination Against Pregnant Women in the Workforce, 50 Me. L. Rev. 225, 241 (1998) (arguing that due to the unique condition of pregnancy it is frequently difficult for employees to either locate a comparable group of nonpregnant employees or to construct a comparison without relying on traditional stereotypes of pregnancy).

Another theory under existing law is that the failure to accommodate pregnancy has a disparate impact against women. While recognized in some cases as a possible theory, see Maganuco v. Leyden Community High School Dist. 212, 939 F.2d 440 (7th Cir. 1991), few plaintiffs have succeeded under it, especially in recent years. Compare, e.g., EEOC v. Warshawski & Co., 768 F. Supp. 647 (N.D. Ill. 1991) (employer's policy of discharging all first-year employees who requested long-term sick leave disproportionately impacted pregnant women, in violation of PDA), with Urbano v. Continental Airlines, Inc. 138 F.3d 204 (5th Cir. 1998), cert. denied, 525 U.S. 1000 (1998) (evidence of forty-eight nonpregnant employees who received transfers to light-duty positions was insufficient to support plaintiff's claim that employer's policy of allowing employees with occupational injuries to transfer to light duty has a disparate impact on pregnant employees); Ilhardt v. Sara Lee Corp., 118 F.3d 1151 (7th Cir. 1997) (part-time attorney failed to show discriminatory impact based on sex using "decades-old" studies showing that the majority of part-time workers are women with child care responsibilities); Lang v. Star Herald, 107 F.3d 1308 (8th Cir. 1997), cert.

denied, 522 U.S. 839 (1997) (plaintiff failed to show statistical support for her claim that unpaid leave policy of small employer disproportionately impacted pregnant women); *Maganuco*, supra (upholding terms of collective bargaining agreement that did not allow employees to combine paid sick leave and unpaid maternity leave). In *Cal Fed*, the Court specifically declined to address the disparate impact issue. 479 U.S. 272, 292 n.32. For the argument that the disparate impact approach blurs the distinction between antidiscrimination and accomodation principles, see Christine Jolls, Antidiscrimination and Accommodation, 115 Harv. L. Rev. 643 (2001).

European Community law prohibiting discrimination based on pregnancy has developed in a direction far more favorable to the claims of pregnant women. In one case, the nondiscrimination provisions of a Council Directive of the European Community Union was found to be violated when a pregnant woman was discharged, even though the only reason she had been hired was to replace another employee on maternity leave. See Case 32/93, Webb v. Emo Cargo (UK) Ltd., 1994 E.C.R. I-3567. See also Case 394/96, Brown v. Rentokil, Ltd., 1998 E.C.R. I-4185 (holding that under European Union law, it is direct discrimination for an employer to dismiss an employee at any time during pregnancy or maternity leave for any reason connected to pregnancy, including the inability to do the job because of pregnancy-related illness); Case 177/88, Dekker v. VJV-Centrum, 1990 E.C.R. I-3941 (nondiscrimination provisions violated when employer did not hire pregnant women because the foreseeability of her incapacity meant employer could not have obtained reimbursement from government under Dutch law). These cases go well beyond *Troupe* and the Pregnancy Discrimination Act by eliminating the necessity for comparison to other disabilities; pregnancy is protected regardless of whether other disabilities are protected. As one commentator explains, the European "no comparison necessary" approach places a "badge of protection" on pregnant women, protecting them from employment-based consequences as a result of the pregnancy, whether or not those consequences would flow from other disabilities. See Claire Kilpatrick, How Long Is a Piece of String? European Regulation of the Post-Birth Period, in Sex Equality Law in the European Union, 81, 82-83 (Tamara K. Hervey & David O'Keeffe, eds. 1996). Would this be a better approach to pregnancy than the one reflected in *Troupe*? Would it violate the PDA? European Union law is also more accommodating of family caretaking. See pages 355-357, 360-361, infra.

Among those noting the limitations of the PDA, especially insofar as it only attacks invidious discrimination against pregnant women and not the absence of accommodations to their needs, see, e.g., Samuel Issacharoff & Elyse Rosenblum, Women and the Workplace: Accommodating the Demands of Pregnancy, 94 Colum. L. Rev. 2154, 2157 (1994); Maxine Eichner, Square Peg in a Round Hole: Parenting Policies and Liberal Theory, 59 Ohio St. L.J. 133, 141 (1998) (PDA takes too narrow of a view of women's inequality by concentrating only on employment interests of pregnant employees and medical aspects of pregnancy and fails to recognize the value of childbearing and parenting to parents, children, and the community).

A few states (New York, New Jersey, Rhode Island, Hawaii, and California) now require partial wage replacement to workers who are temporarily disabled for non-work-related reasons, including pregnancy and childbirth. See Mike Meyers, Taking Pregnancy Leave, Star Tribune, (Minneapolis-St. Paul) Feb. 6, 1995, at 1D.

Some have argued that the next step on a nation-wide level is the extension to pregnancy of the Americans With Disabilities Act of 1990, 42 U.S.C. 12101-12213 (1995) ("ADA"), which requires "reasonable accommodations" for a worker's disability.

> . . . The equal treatment model is male-centered because it accepts maleness as the norm and forces women, especially pregnant workers, to compare themselves to men to get any rights. Similarly, the special treatment model is male-centered and reminiscent of protective legislation that has always worked against women's interests.
>
> The reasonable accommodation approach applied to pregnancy avoids these problems. First, [it] is not male-centered, because it requires an individualized, case-by-case assessment — determining what each pregnant woman needs in the circumstances and the reasonableness of accommodating that need. How an employer treats men, or other disabled employees, does not determine a pregnant worker's entitlements. This case-by-case approach eludes strained analogies because each covered person is deserving in her own right, without comparisons to other groups or individuals.
>
> Finally, the reasonable accommodation standard is unlike past protective labor legislation that has worked against women's interests. Under this standard, an employer cannot implement, for example, a blanket policy excluding women from certain jobs, because the need for accommodation must be determined case-by-case. An employer could not force a woman into some "protective" accommodation because the accommodation must be reasonable and the woman must be willing to accept the accommodation.

D'Andra Millsap, Comment, Reasonable Accommodation of Pregnancy in the Workplace: A Proposal to Amend the Pregnancy Discrimination Act, 32 Hous. L. Rev. 1411, 1434-1435 (1996). See also Colette G. Matzzie, Note, Substantive Equality and Antidiscrimination: Accommodating Pregnancy Under the Americans with Disabilities Act, 82 Geo. L.J. 193 (1993).

At present, the ADA is being interpreted to exclude pregnancy. EEOC regulations specifically state that pregnancy is a condition that is "not the result of a physiological disorder" and thus not an "impairment" under the ADA. See 29 C.F.R. Pt. 1630, Appendix, Interpretive Guidelines, Section 1630.2(h), Physical or Mental Impairment (1996). Moreover, pregnancy does not appear to meet the criteria of a disability that "substantially limits" a "major life activity," in terms of nature and severity, duration, and long-term impact. See 29 C.F.R. 1630.2(j)(2) (1996). See Laura Schlichtmann, Accommodation of Pregnancy-Related Disabilities on the Job, 15 Berkeley J. Emp. & Lab. L. 335, 392 (1994). Although pregnancy is not a *per se* disability under the ADA, courts are split as to whether pregnancy-related problems can be disabilities recognized by the Act. Compare Gabriel v. City of Chicago, 9 F. Supp.2d 274 (N.D. Ill. 1998) (back and stomach pain are disabilities of an abnormal pregnancy); Darian v. University of Mass., 980 F. Supp. 77 (D. Mass. 1997) (severe pelvic bone pain, back pain, and premature uterine contractions are conditions constituting disabilities under the ADA), with Gudenkauf v. Stauffer Communications, Inc., 922 F. Supp. 465 (D. Kan. 1996) (morning sickness, stress, nausea, back pain, swelling, and headaches are physiological conditions of a normal pregnancy not disabilities); Martinez v. NBC, Inc., 49 F. Supp.2d. 305 (S.D.N.Y. 1999) (affirming that pregnancy and related medical conditions are not disabilities under the ADA absent unusual circumstances).

4. Breastfeeding and the PDA. Should discrimination based on a woman's breastfeeding be protected by the PDA? Would it be protected within Professor Kay's "episodic approach" to equality? See Kay, supra, at 22, 24 (lactation covered).

Recall that the language of the PDA provides:

> The terms "because of sex" or "on the basis of sex" include, but are not limited to, because of or on the basis of pregnancy, childbirth, or related medical conditions; and women affected by pregnancy, childbirth, or related medical conditions shall be treated the same for all employment-related purposes . . . as other persons not so affected in their ability or inability to work.

42 U.S.C. §2000e(k) (1994).

To date, the small number of discrimination claims relating to breastfeeding in the workplace have been unsuccessful. In considering whether one claim alleging the failure of a cable television network to accommodate a woman's breastfeeding schedule was actionable under the PDA, the court reasoned:

> . . . there is and could be no allegation that [plaintiff] was treated differently than similarly situated men. . . . As there were and could be no men with the same characteristic, all that is left . . . is a work environment hostile to breast pumping, not a work environment that subjected women to treatment less favorable than was meted out to men.

Martinez v. NBC Inc., 49 F. Supp.2d 305, 310 (S.D.N.Y. 1999). Is this reasoning familiar? Is it a sound application of the PDA? See Henry Wyatt Christrup, Litigating a Breastfeeding and Employment Case in the New Millennium, 12 Yale L.J. & Feminism 263, 279-282 (2000) (use of

Geduldig/Gilbert reasoning in breastfeeding discrimination cases ignores congressional intent behind the PDA to change the definition of sex discrimination and protect working women from all forms of employment discrimination based on sex).

Why isn't breastfeeding a "related medical condition" within the definition of the PDA? Because, say courts, breastfeeding is a "choice" related to parenting and the PDA should be limited to "incapacitating medical conditions for which medical care or treatment is usual and normal." Wallace v. Pyro Mining Co., 789 F. Supp. 867, 869 (W.D. Ky. 1990), aff'd, 951 F.2d 351 (6th Cir. 1991); see also Fejes v. Gilpin Ventures, Inc., 960 F. Supp. 1487, 1491 (D. Colo. 1997) (employer's unwillingness to provide a part-time work schedule while employee weaned her newborn was permissible because breastfeeding and childbearing are not conditions related to pregnancy or childbirth within the meaning of the PDA, although they may be "natural 'concomitants' of pregnancy and childbirth").

Is the following argument likely to convince judges to the contrary?

> . . . [B]reast milk is by far the healthiest form of nourishment for newborns, conferring immunities against many diseases. Breast feeding also lowers the woman's risk of breast and ovarian cancers, diabetes, and post-menopausal bone loss, and helps reduce unhealthy pregnancy-related weight gain. Thus the law could, but currently does not, view breastfeeding as the final stage of the pregnancy cycle, readjusting the hormonal balance of the woman's body and continuing the developmentally crucial process of nourishment and bonding that began in the womb.

Jendi B. Reiter, Accommodating Pregnancy and Breastfeeding in the Workplace: Beyond the Civil Right Paradigm, 9 Tex. J. Women & L. 1, 2 (1999). Along similar lines, see Judith G. Greenberg, The Pregnancy Discrimination Act: Legitimating Discrimination Against Pregnant Women in the Workforce, 50 Me. L. Rev. 225, 230-231 (1998) ("the line between 'biological' and 'non-biological' effects of pregnancy is not self-evident in the way the court would have us believe"). Is the failure of courts to include breastfeeding discrimination within the PDA another example of courts' reasoning that child-related decisions are private choices as to which the individual woman or family should bear the full consequences? See Reiter, supra; see also Diana Kasdan, Reclaiming Title VII and the PDA: Prohibiting Workplace Discrimination Against Breastfeeding Women, 76 N.Y.U. L. Rev. 309, 333-336 (2001) (arguing that interpretations that focus on whether or not breastfeeding could be a related medical condition improperly ignore the possibility that breastfeeding might fall under "additional bases for sex discrimination" and is inconsistent with the broader goal of the PDA to "prevent all forms of sex discrimination against women").

Even if discrimination against a breastfeeding woman was actionable under the PDA, what would constitute discrimination? Wouldn't there still be the problem for plaintiff women, discussed in the notes above, that Title VII prohibits discrimination, but does not require accommodation?

For a review of the cases and a recommended set of proposals for accommodating breastfeeding women in the workplace, see Shana M. Christrup, Breastfeeding in the American Workplace, 9 Am. U. J. Gender Soc. Pol'y & L. 471 (2001). For a comprehensive set of legislative proposals, see Elizabeth N. Baldwin & Kenneth A. Friedman, A Current Summary of Breastfeeding Legislation in the U.S., available at http://www.lalecheleague.org/LawBills.html.

2. Work and Family

State v. Bachmann
521 N.W.2d 886 (Minn. Ct. App. 1994)

SCHUMACHER, Judge.

Appellant Suzanne Margie Bachmann claims that the district court erred by denying her motion for postconviction relief on the basis that she was not eligible for work-release privileges. We affirm.

In November 1993, Bachmann pleaded guilty to one count of burglary in the second degree and one count of check forgery. As part of her sentence, she was ordered to spend 90 days in the county jail.

Following her sentencing, Bachmann requested that she be granted work-release privileges while serving her 90-day jail term. Bachmann is not presently employed outside the home. Instead, she wished to be released from jail on weekdays in order to care for her four children and perform other homemaking services for her husband and children, for which her husband agreed to pay her $1.50 per hour. The district court concluded that Bachmann was not eligible for work-release and denied her motion.

Is a homemaker eligible for work-release? . . . Minn.Stat. §631.425, subd. 3 (1992) provides:

> If the person committed under [the work-release statute] has been regularly employed, the sheriff shall arrange for a continuation of the employment insofar as possible without interruption. If the person is not employed, the court may designate a suitable person or agency to make reasonable efforts to secure some suitable employment for that person. An inmate employed under this section must be paid a fair and reasonable wage for work performed and must work at fair and reasonable hours per day and per week.

Bachmann argues that homemaking is employment within the meaning of this statutory language. We disagree.

Bachmann's homemaking services clearly have economic value. Never-theless, homemaking is generally not considered employment. For example, in the context of workers' compensation:

> The upkeep and care of a home for one's self and family are not in the category of a trade, business, profession or occupation, as generally under-stood. A home is not established and maintained in the expectation of pecuniary gain. Such a venture is solely an expense. . . .
>
> Persons engage in a trade, business, profession or occupation for profit, or as a means to gain a livelihood, but not so in establishing and maintaining a home. . . .
>
> . . . But we think a housewife is not an occupation within the meaning of the compensation act, since that work pertains exclusively to the management of the home. Furthermore, in the maintenance of the home the husband and wife are one. The one acts for the other. No matter who is the legal owner of the home, the running thereof is not an industry nor a business, trade, profession or occupation within the purview of the Workmen's Compensation Act.

Eichholz v. Shaft [208 N.W. 18, 19-20 (Minn. 1926)].

Similarly, in holding that a domestic servant could not picket the home in which he had been employed, the supreme court reasoned:

> The validity of defendant's argument depends upon whether a home, exclusively used as such, may be said to be a place for the carrying on of an industrial or a business enterprise. Obviously the home cannot be so classified.
>
> "The home is an institution, not an industry." . . .

[Barres v. Watterson Hotel Co., 244 S.W. 308, 309, 310 (Ky. Ct. App. 1922).] . . .

And the same result was reached in Anderson v. Ueland, [267 N.W. 517, 518, 927] where we said:

> . . . the home is a sacred place for people to go and be quiet and at rest and not be bothered with the turmoil of industry," and that as such it is "a sanctuary of the individual and should not be interfered with by industrial disputes." We think [this] conception of "home" as "a sanctuary of the individual" is sound. The word is defined as, "the abiding place of the affections, esp. domestic affections'; as "the social unit formed by a family residing together in one dwelling," and as "an organized center of family life."

[State v. Cooper, 285 N.W. 903, 904-05 (Minn. 1939).]

The fact that Bachmann's husband has offered to pay an hourly wage to her does not change our conclusion. First, Bachmann has an obligation to care for her children regardless of whether she is paid to do so. . . . Second, income received by Bachmann is marital property. Thus, Bachmann's husband has a common ownership interest in her income. . . . The

Bachmanns have not shown that their proposed wage agreement results in either gain or loss to either person; unlike the typical employment relationship, the economic exchange between the Bachmanns would be purely illusory. . . .

The district court properly concluded that Bachmann was not eligible for work-release to perform homemaking responsibilities for her family.

Katharine Silbaugh, Turning Labor into Love: Housework and the Law
91 Nw. U. L. Rev. 1, 80-84 (1996)

By failing to enforce contracts between spouses providing wages for housework, the law explicitly prohibits attempts to obtain security for labor on the grounds that bargains in families are inappropriate to the affections of family life. When love motivates work at home, nothing but love should be its reward.

By providing no opportunity for houseworkers to make contributions to the social security system on their own behalf and to combine those contributions with contributions from wage labor, the law denies the houseworker the opportunity to gain a stake in the nation's old-age financial safety net. In social security law, financial security for houseworkers is ensured only through the maintenance of intimate relationships, not through a history of work in the home. By tying full-time houseworkers' social security payments to the length of a marriage, the emotions themselves become the measure of desert within the system.

At the time of divorce, wages are discussed as a part of the contribution to family wealth in dollar amounts, while housework is discussed in any number of ways, but almost never in terms of concrete dollar contributions. Housework can warrant property awards because a houseworker is financial-ly needy, but it is less common for courts to make financial awards because a houseworker is considered to have contributed as much to the material wealth of a family as a wage-earner. If a person contributes both wages and housework, only one of those contributions can be weighed at divorce. Because need and not desert sets the stage for alimony awards at divorce, any surplus wage, beyond the needs of a houseworker spouse, is retained by the wage-earner at the time of divorce, while the houseworker spouse is left without skills that translate into liquidity. When the affections of a marriage have died, the houseworker's stake in the wealth generated by her labor is also lost, including marketable human capital.

Mothers of very young children who receive AFDC are castigated in the welfare reform debate for lacking a desire to work, as though caring for children were not work. Disapproval of these mothers stems from their "chosen" marital status, but is expressed as disapproval of their "chosen" work status. Women who are married and performing identical work receive concrete approval within the welfare debate because the work is performed within a relationship and thus wrapped in the appropriate emotions.

The productive nature of housework is implicitly rejected in the failure to tax it as income. By treating the family, rather than the individuals within it, as the taxable unit, we assume a sharing of wealth that is not compelled by law. In tax, divorce, and contract law, we allow one spouse to earn cash and keep it away from the other spouse, but houseworkers have only a limited similar ability to withhold the benefits of their labor from a spouse. The sharing presumed by tax law and upon which benefits can be delivered to a wage-earning tax-payer must result from the emotional bond within a marriage because legal compulsion to share does not exist. . . .

Paid domestic workers, a field populated by immigrant women and women of color, do not receive the protection of basic labor laws in part because they work where expression takes the form of affections rather than of market dealings. Moreover, the wage of a paid domestic worker is driven down by competition with a tax-subsidized unpaid houseworker — the competition, the unpaid houseworker, can do the work for less because there are no taxes.

All other attempts to monetize housework depend on the paid domestic worker's substitution cost. For example, in loss of consortium and wrongful death cases, courts will often accept direct testimony on the costs of hiring a housekeeper, nurse, or child care worker. If those workers' wages are already deflated by tax subsidies to their competition, the low monetary value of housework will be perpetuated throughout the law. At divorce, housework is often understood to have lower economic value than the wage contribution of paid workers, particularly when the paid worker is middle class or richer. The courts' understanding of the value of housework, however, is influenced by a market for paid domestic labor that is itself a product of law.

In all of these ways, the affectionate characterizations of housework are used to justify treatment of the houseworker that leaves her without financial security. Given these consequences of a conception of housework as exclusively an expression of affection, houseworkers would benefit from a fuller conception of housework, one that shows its significant similarities to wage labor.

. . . It should not be surprising that the Minnesota Court of Appeals rejected Suzanne Bachmann's claim that housework and child care could be employment for work-release purposes. There is no discussion in the opinion of a purpose of the work-release statute that would be undermined by recognizing housework as employment. Instead, the court referred directly to the following other areas of law to support its contention that housework is not employment: that homemakers are not covered under workers' compensation; that the promise of payment from her spouse is illusory since she already had a duty to perform the work; and that because the home is not the site of industry, a paid domestic worker is not an employee for labor law purposes. The work-release statute did not speak to the status of houseworkers one way or the other, but the court found ample support in the law for its understanding that housework is so different from paid work that it cannot be covered by the same statute. This interpretation undoubtedly flies in the face of Suzanne Bachmann's understanding of her position: one suspects that from her first day in jail, the family took on new expenses either from her husband's lost wages or in the form of child care expenses. Bachmann certainly would understand that the money lost was a result of work that she could no longer do.

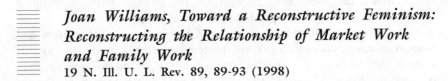

Joan Williams, Toward a Reconstructive Feminism: Reconstructing the Relationship of Market Work and Family Work
19 N. Ill. U. L. Rev. 89, 89-93 (1998)

"I decided to quit my job and stay home. But it was my choice; I have no regrets. I am going to start a part-time quilt business."

"Wouldn't you really rather be able to continue in your career, earning at your current salary rate, while being able to give your children the time you feel they need?"

"Well of course, that's what I really want."

The common assumption is that we live in the era of "the demise of domesticity in America." Domesticity is a gender system comprised most centrally of the organization of market work and family work that arose around 1780, and the gender norms that justify, sustain, and reproduce that organization. Before then, market work and family work were not sharply separated in space or time. By the turn of the nineteenth century this way of life was changing, as domesticity set up the system of men working in factories and offices, while women (in theory) stayed behind to rear the children and tend the "home sweet home."

Domesticity remains the entrenched, almost unquestioned, American norm and practice. As a gender system it has two defining characteristics. The first is its organization of market work around the ideal of a worker who works full-time and overtime and takes little or no time off for childbearing or childrearing. Though this ideal-worker norm does not define all jobs today, it defines the good ones: full-time blue-collar jobs in the working-class context, and high level executive and professional jobs for the middle-class and above. When work is structured in this way, caregivers often cannot perform as ideal workers. Their inability to do so gives rise to domesticity's second defining characteristic: its system of providing for caregiving by marginalizing the caregivers, thereby cutting them off from most of the social roles that offer responsibility and authority.

Domesticity introduced not only a new structuring of market work and family work but also a new description of men and women. The ideology of domesticity held that men "naturally" belong in the market because they are competitive and aggressive; women belong in the home because of their "natural" focus on relationships, children, and an ethic of care. In its original context, domesticity's descriptions of men and women served to justify and reproduce its breadwinner/housewife roles by establishing norms that identified successful gender performance with character traits suitable for those roles.

Both the ideology and the practice of domesticity retain their hold. A recent survey found that fully two-thirds of Americans believe it would be best for women to stay home and care for family and children. Domesticity's descriptions of men and women persist in vernacular gender talk such as John Gray's Men Are From Mars, Women Are From Venus, as well as in the strain of feminist theory that associates women with an ethic of care. [For more on this theory, see Chapter 5].

Even more important, market work continues to be structured in ways that perpetuate the economic vulnerability of caregivers. Their vulnerability stems from the way we define the ideal worker, as someone who works at least forty hours a week year round. This ideal worker norm, framed around the traditional life patterns of men, excludes most mothers. Nearly two-thirds of mothers of child-bearing age are not ideal workers even in the minimal sense of working full-time full year. One quarter of mothers of child-bearing age still are homemakers. Single, as well as married mothers are affected: never married mothers are the group of women most likely to be at home.

Moreover, full-time work is no guarantee of avoiding economic vulnerability: even mothers who work full-time often find themselves on the "mommy track." In addition, full-time workers who cannot work overtime often suffer economically because many of the best jobs now require substantial overtime. A rarely recognized, but extraordinarily important fact is that jobs requiring extensive overtime exclude virtually all mothers (93 percent).

Our economy is divided into mothers and others. Having children has a very strong negative effect on women's income, an effect that actually increased in the 1980s despite the fact that women have become better educated. . . . As a result, in an era when women's wages are catching up with men's, mothers' wages lag behind. Given that nearly 90% of women become mothers during their working lives, this pattern is inconsistent with gender equality.

If mothers have failed to achieve equality in market work, equality in the family has proved equally elusive. Buying and cooking food, doing dishes and laundry, caring for children: on average mothers spend thirty-one hours a week on these tasks. Many commentators have noted the contradiction:

despite our self-image of gender equality, American women still do 80% of child care and two-thirds of core housework.

In short, the basic elements of domesticity's organization of market work and family work remain intact. . . . Women still specialize in family work. Men still specialize in market work. Market work continues to be framed around the assumption that ideal workers have access to a flow of family work few mothers enjoy. Social and cultural norms still sustain and reproduce this organization of (market and family) work.

Domesticity did not die; it mutated. In the nineteenth century most married women were marginalized outside of the economy. Although women have reentered market work, most remain marginalized today. This is not equality.

Dorothy Roberts, *Spiritual and Menial Housework*
9 Yale J.L. & Feminism 51, 55-59 (1997)

. . . The "cult of domesticity" legitimized the confinement of women to the private sphere by defining women as suited for motherhood (and unsuited for public life) because of their moral or spiritual nature. Thus, the very idealization of women's spirituality bolstered the opposition between maternal nurturing in the home and masculine work in the cutthroat marketplace.

Household labor, however, is not all spiritual. It involves nasty, tedious physical tasks — standing over a hot stove, cleaning toilets, scrubbing stains off of floors and out of shirts, changing diapers and bedpans. The notion of a purely spiritual domesticity could only be maintained by cleansing housework of its menial parts. The ideological separation of home from market, then, dictated the separation of spiritual and menial housework. Housework's undesirable tasks had to be separated physically and ideologically from the moral aspects of family life.

This dichotomy has two important consequences. First, women may delegate housework's menial tasks to others while retaining their more valuable spiritual duties. Second, this fragmentation fosters a hierarchy among women because the menial aspects of housework are typically delegated by more privileged women to less privileged ones. At the same time, the availability of a class of menial workers, sustained by race and class subordination, makes this division of women's housework possible. Although women's participation in the market is now widely accepted, the assignment of household work to women and the distinction between spiritual and menial housework both persist. In the hit movie *The First Wives' Club*, the character played by Diane Keaton complains to her friends about the work she did for her ex-husband: "I washed his shorts, I ironed them, and I starched them." "You did?" her friends respond in amazement. "Well, I supervised," Keaton clarifies. This scene conveys the spiritual housewife's relationship to menial housework: she supervises the labor of less privileged women.

An early example of the distinction between spiritual and menial housework is embodied in the relationship between Mammy and her mistress. The image of Mammy was that of a rotund, handkerchiefed house servant who humbly nursed her master's children. Mammy was both the perfect mother and the perfect slave; whites saw her as a "passive nurturer, a mother figure who gave all without expectation of return, who not only acknowledged her inferiority to whites but who loved them." It is important to recognize, however, that Mammy did not reflect any virtue in Black motherhood. The ideology of Mammy placed no value in Black women as the mothers of their own children. Rather, whites claimed Mammy's total devotion to the master's children, without regard to the fate of Mammy's own offspring. Moreover, Mammy, while caring for the master's children, remained under the constant supervision of her white mistress. She had no real authority over either the white children she raised or the Black children she bore. Mammy's domestic labor is the perfect illustration of menial housework; her mistress, on the other hand, performed the spiritual work in the house.

One of Mammy's chores was to serve as a wetnurse for her mistress's babies. Delegating breastfeeding to a servant shows how housework's menial features can be detached from even the most intimate of maternal tasks. Today breastfeeding seems emblematic of the spiritual bond between mother and infant, the closest possible connection between two human beings. It is the epitome of maternal nurturing. Yet in the past the physical labor of breastfeeding was disengaged from its spiritual features to permit its performance by a morally inferior slave. When the servant nursed the mistress's baby, this act was not expected to create the sacred bond that existed between the white mother and her child. Thus, the servant could conveniently do the mistress's work without appropriating the mistress's spiritual attributes. In other words, the nature of the work — whether spiritual or menial — depended on the status of the woman performing it.

Today, the spiritual/menial split enables many professional women to go to work without disturbing the sexual division of housework or relinquishing their role as spiritual housekeepers. In her study of domestics and the women who employ them, Judith Rollins found that middle-class women's entry in the workplace did not change their attitudes toward their role in the home. According to Rollins, "The middle-class women I interviewed were not demanding that their husbands play a greater role in housekeeping; they accepted the fact that responsibility for domestic maintenance was theirs, and they solved the problem of their dual responsibilities by hiring other women to assist."[25] Female employers usually view their maids as an extension of the more menial part of themselves rather than as autonomous employees. Hiring a domestic worker leaves the employer free both to work outside the home and to devote herself to the spiritual aspects of being a wife and mother.

The modern household worker's job is defined in a way that prevents its interference with the female employer's spiritual prerogatives. Even if a child spends the entire day with her nanny while her mother is at work, the hour of "quality time" mother and child share at bedtime is considered most important. Of course, the mother expects the nanny to develop a warm and caring relationship with the child. She wants the nanny to treat the child as a special person, and not as a chore. But the mother nevertheless desires her own relationship with her child to be superior to — closer, healthier, and more influential than — the relationship the child has with the nanny.

In her study of working mothers who hire in-home nannies, Cameron Macdonald identified the employers' contradictory impulses:

> [T]he mother's expectation that her nanny care for and love her children as she would herself frequently collides with her own desire to be the primary care giver and with her belief in the ideology of mother-intensive child rearing; it also conflicts with the assumption that the quality of the mother-child relationship should be the same as if she were at home full-time and someone else were not doing the bulk of the actual care.[26]

Macdonald found that the mothers she studied wanted the nanny to operate as a "shadow mother," acting like a mother during the day and then vanishing as soon as the real mother returned, "leaving no trace of her presence in the psychic lives of the children they shared."

These incompatible motives parallel another dilemma mothers face in delegating child care to a less privileged employee. In another study of private child care arrangements, Julia Wrigley discovered that parents were torn between their desire to hire a high-status substitute mother and their preference for a manageable subordinate. "They would like caregivers who share their child-rearing values and who operate independently," Wrigley explains, "but they also want inexpensive, reliable, controllable employees."[29] Parents often resolve this dilemma by relying on their spiritual supervision of the low-status employees' menial work. For example, one employer commented that "sometimes it was better to accept 'dumb'

---

25. Judith Rollins, Between Women: Domestics and Their Employers 104 (1985), reprinted in Working in the Service Society (Cameron Lynne Macdonald & Carmen Sirianni eds., 1996).

26. [Cameron Lynne Macdonald, Shadow Mothers: Nannies, Au Pairs, and Invisible Work, in Working in the Service Society 250 (Cameron Lynne Macdonald & Carmen Sirianni eds., 1996).]

29. [Julia Wrigley, Other People's Children 5 (1995).]

employees who are under the parents' control rather than deal with cocky ones." In both studies, employers resolved their contradictory desires by distinguishing between their own spiritual and the employees' menial housework.

Thus, the mother's spiritual moments with her child are far more valuable than the long hours the nanny spends caring for the child. Moreover, the working mother might not be able to devote quality time to her child at all if she came home to face the chores that the nanny took care of during the day. Some working mothers also hire another woman, who has even lower status, to clean the house and run errands. By delegating work to a nanny and/or maid, affluent women can fulfill their spiritual calling as mother despite their career in the market.

What is wrong with distinguishing between the roles played by the mother and by the woman she hires to care for her children? Would we not expect to find a difference between a child's relationship with her parents and with the paid household help? My point is not that we should eradicate all distinctions among people who perform housework, but to demonstrate how the distinction made between spiritual and menial housework fosters both a gendered and racialized devaluation of this type of labor. By separating spiritual from menial housework, both the mother and the nanny continue to be under-compensated for their work in the home despite working women's supposed liberation from domestic confinement.

Notes

1. Women's Disproportionate Housework Burdens. Studies have consistently found that women spend more time on household chores than men, both on workdays and days off work. See Suzanne M. Bianchi et al., Is Anyone Doing the Housework? Trends in the Gender Division of Household Labor, 79(1) Soc. Forces 191, 196 (2000); Scott Coltrane, Research on Household Labor: Modeling and Measuring the Social Embeddedness of Routine Family Work, 62 J. Marriage & Fam. 1208 (2000) (reviewing more than 200 scholarly articles and books on household labor showing that women still do at least twice as much housework as men); see also Beth Anne Shelton, Women, Men and Time (1992). For example, data drawn from the National Survey of Families and Households, involving a nationwide sample of 13,007 households interviewed between 1987 and 1988 and again between 1992 and 1994, indicate that women spend a mean of 28.1 hours per week on housework, while men report a mean of 18.3 hours. See Joni Hersch and Leslie S. Stratton, "Housework and Wages," Discussion Paper No. 300, Harvard John M. Olin Discussion Paper Series, http://www.law.harvard.edu/programs/olin_center/ (visited September 3, 2001); see also John P. Robinson and Geoffrey Godbey, Time for Life: The Surprising Ways Americans Use Their Time 100, 334 (1997) (reporting time-diary data from 1985 showing that employed women spend 25.6 hours per week on family care activities, including housework, shopping, and child care, as compared to 14.5 hours for employed men). Sociologist Arlie Hochschild has coined the term "second shift" to describe the social norm under which women who work for wages are also expected to take care of the house and the children when they return home. See Hochschild, The Second Shift: Working Parents and the Revolution at Home (1989).

The 1997 National Study of the Changing Workforce, produced by the Families and Work Institute, found that the housework gender gap has narrowed somewhat: Over the past 20 years, employed married women's workday time on chores has decreased by 36 minutes per day, while men's time has increased by one hour. National Study of the Changing Workforce, Executive Summary, Families and Work Institute (1997), http://www.familiesandwork.org/announce/workforce.html (visited September 3, 2001). Nevertheless, the gap remains significant, and a substantial literature in economics attempts to account for it. See Naomi R. Cahn, Gendered Identities: Women and Household Work, 44 Vill. L. Rev. 525, 531-32 (1999) (summarizing various theories).

Most of the literature on housework sharing has focused on married couples. A 1993 study found that compared to both married and gay couples, lesbian couples tended to share tasks. In contrast with lesbian couples, gay couples and married couples were likely to have one or the other partner perform the tasks. Compared to married couples, gay couples and lesbian couples were more likely to split tasks so that each partner performed an equal number of different tasks. Lawrence A. Kurdek, The Allocation of Household Labor in Gay, Lesbian, and Heterosexual Married Couples, 49 J. of Social Issues 127 (1993).

2. Women's Disproportionate Childrearing Burdens. Although there is widespread agreement as a theoretical matter that apart from the tasks of pregnancy, labor, and breastfeeding, childrearing need not be an exclusively female activity, women continue to bear a substantially disproportionate share of the load. In a 1992 study based on hour-long telephone interviews, 67.6 percent of mothers and 61.4 percent of fathers reported that the mother assumed primary responsibility for minor children in the household. Ellen Galinsky & James T. Bond, Work and Family: The Experience of Mothers and Fathers in the Labor Force, in American Woman, 1996-1997, Where We Stand: Women and Work 79, 94 (Cynthia Costello & Barbara Kivimae Krimgold eds., 1996). Other researchers report that mothers are "available" to their children about twice as much as fathers, and spend about three times as much time as fathers in face-to-face interaction with children. Mothers also spend much more time taking responsibility for children in the sense of arranging child care, making medical appointments, deciding on the child's clothing, staying home with the child when he or she is ill, and other such matters. See Michael E. Lamb, et al., A Biosocial Perspective on Paternal Behavior and Involvement, in Parenting Across the Lifespan: Biosocial Dimensions 111, 127, 129 (eds. Jane B. Lancaster et al., 1987); Laura Sanchez & Elizabeth Thomson, Becoming Mothers and Fathers: Parenthood, Gender, and the Division of Labor, 11 Gender & Soc'y 747, 765 Table 4 (1997) (showing that when housework, childcare, and wage work are all considered, women with young children work, on average, twenty more hours a week than men).

Moreover, studies show that although working women do twice as much family work as working men, only one-quarter to one-third see this arrangement as unfair. See Mary Clare Lennon & Sarah Rosenfield, Relative Fairness and the Division of Housework: The Importance of Options, 100 Am. J. Soc. 506, 507 (1994). What might explain this fact? See id. (women who have fewer alternatives to marriage and less economic resources are more likely to view uneven division of housework as fair).

Why do wives do so much more housework and childcare than husbands? Some writers have suggested that young women often make educational and career choices based on the assumption, conscious or not, that they will some day drop out of the job market to take care of children. Their initial lower investment in their education and training then creates a self-fulfilling prophecy: it only "makes sense" that they should leave paid work, because their husbands (who have assumed they will always have to work) have more prestigious, highly-paid and demanding jobs. See Rhona Mahony, Kidding Ourselves: Breadwinning, Babies, and Bargaining Power (1995) (using economic game theory to show how negotiations within marriage can produce a traditional division of childcare labor even when both partners are consciously committed to equality); see also Peggy Orenstein, Flux: Women on Sex, Work, Love, Kids, and Life in a Half-Changed World (2000) (interviewing young career women who reported that they expected to some day marry a man with a high-paying job and leave the workforce to raise children).

Drawing on sociological theory, Naomi Cahn suggests that wives take responsibility for a disproportionate share of housework and child care as a way of "performing gender": since women are expected to mother and to take care of the house, doing so gives wives both social approval and interpersonal power. Naomi Cahn, Gendered Identities: Women and Household Work, 44 Vill. L. Rev. 525, 532 (1999); Naomi Cahn, The Power of Caretaking, 12 Yale J.L. & Feminism 177 (2000).

3. Family Work and Capitalism. Work-family conflicts are generally perceived as a "private" issue between couples, not a "public" issue to be resolved through law. Joan Williams attacks this premise, arguing that primary caregivers provide the flow of family work that allows "ideal workers" to take on heavy loads at the workplace. See Joan Williams, Unbending Gender: Why Family and Work Conflict and What To Do

About It 274 (2000); see also Nancy Folbre, The Invisible Heart: Economics and Family Values (2001) (arguing that family life and family values are integral to capitalist markets across a number of domains); Laura T. Kessler, The Attachment Gap: Employment Discrimination Law, Women's Cultural Caregiving, and the Limits of Economic and Liberal Legal Theory, 34 U. Mich. J.L. Ref. 371 (2001) (arguing that existing Title VII law relies on a view of women's nurturing work as the result of impaired agency growing out of gender socialization, rather than important and valuable to all of society).

How should the law respond to this insight? Williams argues that workplaces structured around male norms violate Title VII and that the wages of both spouses in a "traditional" marriage should be considered joint property. Williams, supra. Christine Littleton, focusing on more public responses, proposes mothers' preferences in employment, like those given veterans in military service during the draft, and social security credits in women's own names for labor performed in childrearing. Christine A. Littleton, Reconstructing Sexual Equality, 75 Cal. L. Rev. 1279, 1330 (1987); see also Mary Becker, Prince Charming: Abstract Equality, 1987 Sup. Ct. Rev. 201, 208-209 (suggesting a similar list of proposals); Kessler, supra, at 461-462 (proposing government-subsidized wage-replacement for caregiving, in the form of unemployment or disability insurance coverage, vouchers, welfare, or refundable tax credits; universally available, high-quality day-care, implemented through subsidies to private providers, vouchers for families, the expansion of Head Start, the public education system, or other innovative mechanisms; and a shortened work week); Silbaugh, supra (proposing full recognition of housework through changes in the law of social security, torts, tax, welfare, labor, and marital contracts). Do such proposals follow from Kay's "equal opportunity" model or do they require another paradigm? Do they strengthen capitalism or weaken it?

For further development of models of reform emphasizing the affirmative revaluing of women's nurturing work, rather than the alleviation of burdens resulting from women's differences, see Chapter 5, section C(2).

4. Lawyers and the Work/Family Conflict. Lawyers, of course, do not escape the work/family conflict.

> . . . . About two-thirds of surveyed lawyers report experiencing work/family conflict and most believe that it is the greatest barrier to women's advancement. Only a fifth of surveyed lawyers are very satisfied with the allocation of time between work and personal needs, or with their opportunities to pursue the social good.
>
> The most obvious failures in workplace structures are excessive hours and resistance to reduced or flexible schedules. Client expectations of instant responsiveness and total availability, coupled with lawyers' expectations of spiraling salaries, have pushed working hours to new and often excessive levels. Hourly requirements have increased dramatically over the last two decades,

and what has not changed is the number of hours in the day. Unpredictable deadlines, uneven workloads, or frequent travel pose further difficulties for those with substantial family obligations.

Unsurprisingly, most female attorneys feel that they do not have sufficient time for themselves or their families, and half report high levels of stress in juggling their responsibilities. Moreover, women who do not have families often have difficulty finding time for relationships that might lead to them. Unmarried associates frequently report ending up with disproportionate work because they have no acceptable reason for refusing it. Yet many lawyers who would like to adjust or reduce their hours bump up against considerable resistance. A wide gap persists between formal policies and accepted practices. Although over 90 percent of surveyed law firms allow part time schedules, only about three to four percent of lawyers actually use them. Most women surveyed believe that any reduction in hours or availability would jeopardize their prospects for advancement.

ABA Commission on Women in the Profession, The Unfinished Agenda: A Report on the Status of Women in the Legal Profession 6 (2001). To what extent are the pressures of contemporary law practice increasing the conflict? Do cell phones, e-mails, faxes, and beepers help or hurt?

How do you plan to cope with the challenges involved in balancing personal and professional commitments? Do you expect to work full-time after you graduate? If so, who will clean your house? Do you plan to have children? If so, who will take care of them? What accommodations do you think are fair to expect from your employer?

Further materials on women in law practice are provided in Chapter 5, section D.

5. Parenting Leave Laws: An International Perspective. Since *Cal Fed*, Congress passed the federal Family and Medical Leave Act ("FMLA"), 29 U.S.C. §§2601-2654 (1999), mandating that employers of more than 50 workers allow up to a three-month, unpaid leave for the care of a new infant or ill family member, with the right to be restored to the same or an equivalent position without loss of pre-leave employee benefits. The Act covers employees who have worked for the employer for at least 12 months and for 1,250 hours during the year preceding the start of the leave. At the time of the passage of the FMLA, South Africa was the only other industrialized state without a federal family leave policy.

From 1993 to 1995, approximately 20 million workers took advantage of the leave programs prescribed by the FMLA, and a 1996 report to Congress found that more than 90 percent of employers said most aspects of the law were "very easy" or "somewhat easy" to administer, more than 89 percent found they incurred "no cost" or "small costs," and more than 86 percent reported "no noticeable effect" on productivity, profitability, and growth. Marc Mory & Lia Pistilli, Note, The Failure of the Family and Medical Leave Act: Alternative Proposals for Contemporary Working

Families, 18 Hofstra Lab. & Employment L.J. 689, 697 (2001). As of 1998, however, "more than seventy-five percent of working mothers who were eligible to take advantage of rights afforded under the FMLA were unable to do so. 'In fact, a recent study by the U.S. Department of Labor found that 88 percent of eligible employees who need time off do not take it because they cannot afford to go without a paycheck.'" Id. at 689 (quoting 147 Cong. Rec. H188-89 (daily ed. Feb. 6, 2001) (statement of Rep. Woolsey)).

Meanwhile, in 1996, three years after the passage of the FMLA, the European Council adopted the European Union Directive on Parental Leave, which provides minimum standards with which the member states must comply. These minimum standards include a right to parental leave for at least three months, protection against dismissal, and the right to return to the same or similar position. Most of the Member States of the European Union apply standards that exceed European Union standards for parental leave. Cara A. McCaffrey and Austin Graff, Note, European Union Directive on Parental Leave: Will the European Union Face the Same Problems as Those Faced by the United States Under the 1993 Family and Medical Leave Act?, 17 Hofstra Lab. & Employment L.J. 229, 232 (1999). Mory and Pistilli observe:

> [United States supporters of mandatory paid leave] look to other countries, such as Sweden and Finland, which are among the most benevolent, allowing as much as thirty-eight weeks and thirty-five weeks paid leave, respectively. Moreover, according to the International Labour Organization in Geneva, of the countries that guarantee paid maternity leave for working women "many pay new mothers from a social security fund rather than have women assume the cost of leaving the workplace temporarily[.]" For instance, utilizing its social security fund, Hungary provides a minimum of six months paid leave. Similarly, Brazil offers up to four months maternity leave completely covered by social security. Even third world nations, such as Ghana and Haiti, have implemented paid leave programs.

Mory and Pistilli, supra, at 709.

The comparative generosity of other countries' family leave policies, however, obscures complex issues about implementation and equity. In some countries, liberal leave policies foster employer hostility against women workers. In Mexico, for example, where women are guaranteed twelve weeks' paid maternity leave, many employers believe they have the right to deny employment if women state an intention to take a leave; others administer illegal pregnancy tests. These infractions are only weakly sanctioned. Id. at 711. Similarly, Japan's Equal Employment Opportunity Law, effective in 1986, provided for equal opportunity and treatment in the job market for men and women. "Unfortunately, the provisions of the law were not mandatory and no enforcement provisions were provided, resulting in minimal effectiveness." Id. at 713.

Moreover, even where family leave policies are both generous and realized in practice as well as theory, problems of gender equality arise. Janet Gornick and Marcia Meyers observe:

> Although generous leave policies have economic and social benefits for families with very young children, they can create new forms of gender inequality. The total percentage of paid parental leave days taken by fathers amounts to less than 10 percent across the European welfare states. . . . Because leaves are taken overwhelmingly by mothers, many women pay a price for their long absences from the labor market in the form of lost human capital and career advancement.

Janet C. Gornick & Marcia K. Meyers, Support for Working Families, 12 Am. Prospect, Jan. 1-15, 2001, at 3. Mindful of similar issues in the United States, Michael Selmi argues that the FLMA should be amended to reward employers for establishing leave policies that succeed in getting men to take more parental leave. Michael Selmi, Family Leave and the Gender Wage Gap, 78 N.C. L.Rev. 707 (2000).

The problem of achieving workplace reform in ways that recognize that women and men face very different family realities but do not themselves perpetuate those realities by reinforcing women's differences has plagued all efforts to use law to transform the workplace. A new wave of analysis on this question is gathering under the heading of "reconstructive feminism," a term coined by Joan Williams. See Williams, Unbending Gender, supra, at 198; see also Nancy Dowd, Work and Family: The Gender Paradox and the Limitations of Discrimination Analysis in Restructuring the Workplace, 24 Harv. C.R.-C.L. L. Rev. 79 (1989). For a look at some of the theoretical issues involved in reconstructing law and social life around mothering and care work, see Chapter 5.

6. Child Care and the Market in Domestic Workers. The primary approach to child care in the United States has been to treat it as a "private" issue to be negotiated by individual women. Government involvement has largely been limited to providing mothers with resources to track down "deadbeat dads." See Ann Laquer Estin, Moving Beyond the Child Support Revolution, 26 Law & Soc. Inquiry 505 (2001). Women who must work but cannot afford nannies or high-quality day care centers look to their own relatives, to babysitters, or to low-cost, frequently unlicensed family day care centers that feature high turnover and poorly trained workers. See Lucie White, Quality Child Care for Low-Income Families: Despair, Impasse, Improvisation, in Joel F. Handler and Lucie White (eds.), Hard Labor: Women and Work in the Post-Welfare Era 116, 124-25 (1999).

Those women who can afford it turn to the market in domestic workers for help. Dorothy Roberts argues that the convergence of gender norms, racial norms, and market forces has meant that those who do child care work for wages — nannies, babysitters, au pairs, and housekeepers — are often nonwhite. Certainly they are poorly paid; in 1996, full-time child care workers in private households earned, on average, $198 per week. U.S. Department of Labor, Women's Bureau, Facts on Working Women: Child Care Workers (1997), http://www.dol.gov/dol/wb/public/wb_pubs/childc.htm (visited September 3, 2001). Child care workers are also overwhelmingly female: in 1996, 98.5 percent of family child care providers were women. Id.

Domestic workers are not only poorly paid; they are also unusually lacking in effective legal protections at work. Domestic work is explicitly excluded from coverage under the National Labor Relations Act (guaranteeing the right to organize and engage in collective bargaining); the Occupational Health and Safety Act; Title VII; and from most state workers compensation acts. The Fair Labor Standards Act, enacted in 1938, originally did not apply to domestic workers; although it was amended in 1974 to provide such coverage, babysitters are explicitly exempted. Domestic workers typically have only limited eligibility for unemployment benefits and are exempted from coverage under civil rights laws in eight states. See generally Peggie R. Smith, Regulating Paid Household Work: Class, Gender, Race, and Agendas of Reform, 48 Am. U. L. Rev. 851 (1999). Collective action is difficult for domestic workers because they are spatially isolated from one another, and enforcement of applicable laws and regulations is a serious problem, particularly when workers are undocumented. But see Peggie R. Smith, Organizing the Unorganizable: Private Paid Household Workers and Approaches to Employee Representation, 79 N.C. L. Rev. 45 (2000) (arguing that worker-run cooperatives represent a promising strategy for collective action).

7. Immigration and Domestic Work. In December 1992, Zoe Baird became the first woman nominated to the position of United States Attorney General. She subsequently withdrew her nomination, however, when it was discovered that she had failed to pay Social Security taxes for her undocumented live-in childcare worker, a woman named Lillian Cordero. The resulting controversy, known as "Nannygate," brought to the surface painful divisions among women: some working women lambasted Baird as a selfish, "yuppie" mom, while others pointed out that while many were quick to condemn Baird, few reproved Baird's law-professor husband for failing to stay at home with their child. See Taunya Lovell Banks, Toward a Global Critical Feminist Vision: Domestic Work and the Nanny Tax Debate, 3 J. Gender Race & Just. 1 (1999). In response to Zoe Baird's plight, Congress enacted the Social Security Domestic Employment Reform Act of 1994, popularly known as the Nanny Tax law. The new law increases the threshold amount of employee wages required to trigger the tax from $50 quarterly to $1000 annually and requires annual instead of quarterly payments of the tax to ease the reporting burden on employers like Baird. Id. at 3. Banks notes that this reform made it easier for households to hire women like Cordero, but failed to address the problems domestic workers face.

Cordero's undocumented status was not unusual. Domestic workers from outside the United States can enter the country in one of three ways. First, an American employer can sponsor a foreign worker for temporary employment through the H-2B visa application procedure. However, these visas are limited in number, the application process is long and cumbersome, and domestic workers are classified as "unskilled" labor, the lowest preference category for employment-based visas. Second, the Exchange Visitor Program provides participants with a J-1 visa for becoming an "au pair." Au pairs are typically young Western European women who enter the United States for one year for the purpose of international cultural exchange. The primary responsibility of an au pair is expected to be childcare and not other domestic work; au pairs are required to be paid only the minimum wage. See Linda Kelly, The Fantastic Adventure of Supermom and the Alien: Educating Immigration Policy on the Facts of Life, 31 Conn. L. Rev. 1045, 1059-60 (1999). Finally, a domestic worker may enter the United States through illegal means. Thousands of households resort to undocumented workers to meet their childcare needs; these workers are paid lower wages and work longer hours than their legal counterparts. See Melanie Ryan, Swept Under the Carpet: Lack of Legal Protection for Household Workers — A Call for Justice, 20 Women's L.Rep. 159 (1999). They also lack entitlement to overtime or health benefits, and "will be unable to receive social security benefits upon retirement, unemployment benefits if they are suddenly discharged, or disability benefits in case of illness or accident." Debra Cohen-Whelan, Protecting the Hand That Rocks the Cradle: Ensuring the Delivery of Work-Related Benefits to Child Care Workers, 32 Ind. L. Rev. 1187 (1999). Moreover, because of their undocumented status, these domestic workers are especially vulnerable to abuse. See Mary Romero, Immigration, the Servant Problem, and the Legacy of the Domestic Labor Debate: "Where Can You Find Good Help These Days!" 53 U. Miami. L.Rev. 1045 (1999) (describing the exploitation of undocumented child care workers).

8. Child Care Assistance. One form that greater public commitment to childrearing could take is child care assistance. Current law provides federal funds for various child care assistance programs, including Head Start. The Personal Responsibility and Work Opportunity Reconciliation Act of 1996, offsetting some of the losses to poor families achieved through "welfare reform," provides a four-billion-dollar increase in child care funding. This Act is discussed in Chapter 6, section C. In addition, federal tax laws allow a tax credit for a percentage of money certain taxpayers spend on child care under the Child and Dependent Care Tax Credit. In dollar terms, the CDCTC is the largest federal government program in the United States aimed at helping families with child care; an alternative tax relief program, the Dependent Care Assistance Plan (DCAP), is estimated to have cost the federal government $890 million in forgone tax revenues in fiscal year 1998. Alison P. Hagy, Child Care and Federal Tax Policy, 16 N.Y.L. Sch. J. Hum. Rts. 205 (1999). These measures are all discussed in Meghan M. Thomsen, The Role of Business and Government in the Provision of Child Care Assistance: A Comparative Analysis of the United States and Canada, 17 U. Pa. J. Int'l. Econ. L. 1209, 1215-1223 (1996). See also Sharon C. Nantell, The Tax Paradigm of Child Care: Shifting Attitudes Toward a Private/Parental/Public Alliance, 80 Marq. L. Rev. 879 (1997) (proposing tax reforms that would better support child care in the United States).

Most Western countries have gone considerably further in providing government assistance to families with children. Sweden, considered a model for advocates of more aggressive public family supports, provides numerous benefits without regard to need, including comprehensive pregnancy benefits, a basic child allowance for all families, increased allowances for families with three or more children, and additional allowances to replace support that a non-custodial parent is unable or unwilling to pay. There are additional income supports for post-childbirth leave and for the caretaker parents of handicapped children, as well as an extensive publicly-financed child care system. Preferences for child care and housing are available to single parents. The tax system encourages the entry of women into the workforce by taxing the second earner separately, rather than at the marginal rate of the primary wage earner. See Nancy E. Dowd, Envisioning Work and Family: A Critical Perspective on International Models, 26 Harv. J. Legis. 311, 319-323 (1989). France, like Sweden, has a family allowance system, one that is particularly generous to large families. France also has a nearly universally available child care and preschool education system, regardless of whether the parent or parents are in the paid work force. Id. at 331-335.

Nevertheless, it is not clear that a policy like Sweden's automatically produces gender equality. In 1986, "43 percent of Swedish working women were employed part time. Women continued to do a disproportionate share of family work and took fifty-two days of leave for every day taken by a man." Joan Williams, Unbending Gender: Why Family and Work Conflict and What To Do About It 51 (2000). Indeed, Sweden's level of sex segregation in the workforce is greater than that of the United States. Id.

In this country, some large employers have played a role in helping families balance work and family commitments. Approximately 3500 corporations in the United States and Canada provide some type of child care assistance to U.S. workers, including referral services, vouchers, and on-site day care centers. See Thomsen, supra, at 1237-1243.

9. Women and Contingent Work. A significant sector of the United States work force is made up of "contingent workers": all those workers employed other than on a full-time, permanent basis, including part-time workers, temporary workers, independent contractors, day laborers, and home-based workers. See generally Kathleen Barker and Kathleen Christensen, Contingent Work: American Employment Relations in Transition (1998); Toward a Disposable Workforce: The Increasing Use of "Contingent" Labor: Hearing before the Subcomm. of Labor of the Senate Comm. of Labor and Human Resources, 103rd Cong., 1st Sess. 23, 1 (1993). Data compiled by the Bureau of Labor Statistics shows that in 1997, 28.7% of American workers — about one out of three women (33.7%) and one out of four men (24.3%) — worked in nonstandard jobs, down slightly from 29.4% in 1995. Ken Hudson, No Shortage of "Nonstandard" Jobs: Nearly 30% of Workers Employed in Part-Time, Temping, and Other Arrangements, http://epinet.org/briefingpapers/hudson/hudson.html (visited August 2, 2001). Contingent work has thrived despite the recent boom in the United States economy; indeed, some researchers argue that heavy reliance on contingent labor is increasingly necessary to provide businesses with necessary flexibility in a global environment characterized by cheap overseas labor and "just in time" production methods. See Note, Marionettes of Globalization: A Comparative Analysis of Legal Protections for Contingent Workers in the International Community, 27 Syracuse J. Int'l L. & Com. 431, 438 (2000); Katherine M. Forster, Note, Strategic Reform of Contingent Work, 74 S. Cal. L. Rev. 541, 551 (2001); see also Ann Bookman, Flexibility at What Price? The Costs of Part-Time Work for Women Workers, 52 Wash. & Lee L. Rev. 799, 814 (1995) (arguing that the overall effects of contingent work on the economy are negative).

The wages, benefits, and conditions of contingent work vary greatly: some categories of contingent workers are paid at rates far higher than standard full-time workers, while others are paid much less. Hudson, supra. Women, however, are "concentrated in the nonstandard work arrangements that have the poorest-quality jobs. For example, regular part-time employees and temps — work arrangements with the largest pay penalties and the lowest likelihood of providing health insurance and pensions — are disproportionately female. In contrast, independent contractors — the best-paid type of nonstandard work — are disproportionately male." Id. Women constitute approximately two-thirds of the part-time workforce. See Chris Tilly, Short Hours, Short Shrift: The Causes and Consequences of Part-Time Employment, in New Policies for the Part-Time and Contingent Workforce 15, 42 (Virginia L. du Rivage ed. 1992) (hereinafter "New Policies"). Women are also two-thirds of the temporary workforce. See Francois Carre, Temporary Employment in the Eighties, in New Policies, supra, at 58.

Contingent workers, like domestic workers, receive minimal protection from social welfare schemes and federal labor regulations. See Forster, supra, at 558. Economists do not agree, however, on whether contingent work represents a market failure necessitating government action. See Gillian

Lester, Careers and Contingency, 51 Stan. L. Rev. 73 (1998) (arguing that contingent work is a symptom of "underemployment").

Beyond the tangible drawbacks of contingent work is a change in the "psychological contract" between employer and full-time employee.

> It has been widely reported that large corporations no longer offer their employees implicit contracts for lifetime employment. Work has become contingent, not in the sense that it is formally defined as short-term or episodic, but in the sense that the attachment between the firm and the worker has been reduced. The recasualization of work has reportedly become a fact of life both for blue-collar workers and for high-end professionals and managers.

Katherine V.W. Stone, The New Psychological Contract: Implications of the Changing Workplace for Labor and Employment Law, 48 UCLA L.Rev. 519 (2001); but see Sanford M. Jacoby, Melting Into Air? Downsizing, Job Stability, and the Future of Work, 76 Chi.-Kent L.Rev. 1195 (2000) (arguing that reports of the death of career-type jobs are greatly exaggerated). Stone notes that the disappearance of "internal labor markets" within corporate firms may help women and minorities, who have traditionally met with barriers to internal advancement. Stone, supra, at 605. However, new barriers to the advancement of women and people of color in the new "casual" workplace may arise. Stone identifies four such potential problems: (1) women and people of color may continue to be given less access to training; (2) the disappearance of formal hierarchies of authority and identifiable "corporate ladders" may make identifying, preventing, and redressing unlawful discrimination more difficult; (3) as employment decisions are increasingly ceded to peers, discrimination may flourish; and (4) as unionization with its proliferation of rules and regulations decreases, nepotism and favoritism may flourish as well. Id. at 606-609.

10. Work, Marriage, and Tax Policy. Edward McCaffery identifies the absence of a range of part-time employment options to accommodate dual-career families as one symptom of market failure and proposes tax-based government intervention to eliminate the inefficiency of current work patterns. His proposal would increase taxes on the primary wage-earner, the man in most two-earner families, and lighten the tax load of secondary workers, primarily women. Edward J. McCaffery, Slouching Towards Equality: Gender Discrimination, Market Efficiency, and Social Change, 103 Yale L.J. 595 (1993). McCaffery argues that this would simultaneously "[throw] some barriers in the way of men's ultra-commitment to the market" and increase women's clout in making the market more accepting of their choices "without having to contort their behavior to fit historically male labor-market participation patterns." McCaffery, supra, at 671. McCaffery also recommends dropping the regulatory prohibition against unequal pay to improve the rational decisionmaking processes of firms by allowing them to take into account the marginal productivity of workers in light of their expected longevity on the job: "[I]f markets work better with women getting paid less, at least in the present, so be it." Id. at 655. Otherwise, McCaffery argues, we penalize firms who "do the right thing" by hiring women, and reward firms who successfully isolate women into certain lower-paying job categories. "In important regards, the means chosen by Title VII to address discrimination might be counterproductive vis-à-vis its own apparent ends." Id.

The McCaffery tax proposal pursues greater efficiency through heavier taxes on inelastic labor supplies (those workers who are least responsive to changes in the tax rate) and lighter taxes on elastic labor supplies (those workers who are most responsive to changes in the tax rate), to encourage women's market work. Anne Alstott identifies some basic conflicts between McCaffery's efficiency objectives and traditional feminist goals such as equal treatment and support to caregivers. See Alstott, Tax Policy and Feminism: Competing Goals and Institutional Choices, 96 Colum. L. Rev. 2001, 2034-2037 (1996). While married women are historically an extremely elastic (responsive) labor supply, Alstott notes that the greatest beneficial effect of McCaffery's proposals would be on nonworking women married to high-earning men, i.e., upper-class housewives who are those most likely to be able to afford child care already. Alstott favors direct assistance to caregivers, since increased incentives to work would not increase the compatibility of working conditions with child care. Id. Along similar lines, Nancy Staudt argues that to adequately value both market and nonmarket work without pushing women into the labor market, housework should be taxed. Nancy C. Staudt, Taxing Housework, 84 Geo. L.J. 1571 (1996). Staudt argues that the burden of the new tax would be shared by the entire household, and that women stand to benefit from it because it would increase their social security benefits and thus their economic security in retirement. Id. at 1640.

Congress has recently showed a great deal of interest in the "marriage penalty" — the additional income tax burden that most dual income couples bear when they are married. See June O'Neill, Marriage Penalties and Bonuses in the Federal Income Tax, 16 N.Y.L. Sch. J. Hum. Rts. 119 (1999). Because greater equality of earnings between husbands and wives makes marriage penalties more likely and larger, "the overall effect of those shifts in women's work participation and earnings has been to increase the number of couples incurring penalties and to boost the size of the average penalty." Id. at 122. The marriage penalty is a concern both for economists desiring greater productivity (who want women in the labor market) and for defenders of traditional marriage (who want women to stay home).

Finally, should law continue to treat "the household" as the taxable unit? Marjorie Kornhauser advocates tax law reforms that abandon the fiction of economic marital partnership and take better account of women's circumstances and priorities toward their children. See Kornhauser, Theory

Versus Reality: The Partnership Model of Marriage in Family and Income Tax Law, 69 Temp. L. Rev. 1449 (1996) (favoring treating husbands and wives as separate taxable units and allocating tax preferences according to the parents' likelihood of spending money on their children); Kornhauser, Deconstructing the Taxable Unit: Intrahousehold Allocations and the Dilemma of the Joint Return, 16 N.Y.L. Sch. J. Hum. Rts. 140 (1999) (arguing that a system that treats each person as a separate taxable unit is more equitable, efficient, and more consistent with basic income tax principles than the current system of treating households as a unit).

Putting Theory into Practice

3-3. What accommodations should a law firm make to a female associate in a law firm who decides, in her third year of employment, to begin a family? What responses by the law firm to her request for time off should be legally mandated? With what model of equality is your answer most compatible?

C. RECOGNIZING SEX-LINKED AVERAGE DIFFERENCES

1. Fringe Benefit Plans, Insurance, and Other Actuarially-Based Systems

≣≣≣ *City of Los Angeles, Department of Water & Power*
≣≣≣ *v. Manhart*
≣≣ 435 U.S. 702 (1978)

Mr. Justice STEVENS delivered the opinion of the Court.

As a class, women live longer than men. For this reason, the Los Angeles Department of Water and Power required its female employees to make larger contributions to its pension fund than its male employees. We granted certiorari to decide whether this practice discriminated against individual female employees because of their sex in violation of [Title VII].

For many years the Department has administered retirement, disability, and death-benefit programs for its employees. Upon retirement each employee is eligible for a monthly retirement benefit computed as a fraction of his or her salary multiplied by years of service.[3] The monthly benefits for

---

3. The plan . . . provides for several kinds of pension benefits at the employee's option. . . . [T]he most common is a formula pension equal to 2% of the average monthly salary paid during

men and women of the same age, seniority, and salary are equal. Benefits are funded entirely by contributions from the employees and the Department, augmented by the income earned on those contributions. No private insurance company is involved in the administration or payment of benefits.

Based on a study of mortality tables and its own experience, the Department determined that its 2,000 female employees, on the average, will live a few years longer than its 10,000 male employees. The cost of a pension for the average retired female is greater than for the average male retiree because more monthly payments must be made to the average woman. The Department therefore required female employees to make monthly contributions to the fund which were 14.84% higher than the contributions required of comparable male employees. Because employee contributions were withheld from paychecks a female employee took home less pay than a male employee earning the same salary.[5] . . .

While this action was pending, the California Legislature enacted a law prohibiting certain municipal agencies from requiring female employees to make higher pension fund contributions than males. The Department therefore amended its plan, effective January 1, 1975. The current plan draws no distinction, either in contributions or in benefits, on the basis of sex. On a motion for summary judgment, the District Court held that the contribution differential [in the old plan] violated [Title VII] and ordered a refund of all excess contributions made before the amendment of the plan. The United States Court of Appeals for the Ninth Circuit affirmed. . . .

I

There are both real and fictional differences between women and men. It is true that the average man is taller than the average woman; it is not true that the average woman driver is more accident prone than the average man. Before [Title VII] was enacted, an employer could fashion his personnel policies on the basis of assumptions about the differences between men and women, whether or not the assumptions were valid.

It is now well recognized that employment decisions cannot be predicated on mere "stereotyped" impressions about the characteristics of males or females. Myths and purely habitual assumptions about a woman's inability to perform certain kinds of work are no longer acceptable reasons for refusing to employ qualified individuals, or for paying them less. This case does not, however, involve a fictional difference between men and women. It involves a generalization that the parties accept as unquestionably

---

the last year of employment times the number of years of employment. The benefit is guaranteed for life.

5. The significance of the disparity is illustrated by the record of one woman whose contributions to the fund (including interest on the amount withheld each month) amounted to $18,171.40; a similarly situated male would have contributed only $12,843.53.

true: Women, as a class, do live longer than men. The Department treated its women employees differently from its men employees because the two classes are in fact different. It is equally true, however, that all individuals in the respective classes do not share the characteristic that differentiates the average class representatives. Many women do not live as long as the average man and many men outlive the average woman. The question, therefore, is whether the existence or nonexistence of "discrimination" is to be determined by comparison of class characteristics or individual characteristics. A "stereotyped" answer to that question may not be the same as the answer that the language and purpose of the statute command.

[Title VII] makes it unlawful "to discriminate against any *individual* with respect to his compensation, terms, conditions, or privileges of employment, because of such *individual's* race, color, religion, sex, or national origin.". . . The statute's focus on the individual is unambiguous. It precludes treatment of individuals as simply components of a racial, religious, sexual, or national class. If height is required for a job, a tall woman may not be refused employment merely because, on the average, women are too short. Even a true generalization about the class is an insufficient reason for disqualifying an individual to whom the generalization does not apply.

That proposition is of critical importance in this case because there is no assurance that any individual woman working for the Department will actually fit the generalization on which the Department's policy is based. Many of those individuals will not live as long as the average man. While they were working, those individuals received smaller paychecks because of their sex, but they will receive no compensating advantage when they retire.

It is true, of course, that while contributions are being collected from the employees, the Department cannot know which individuals will predecease the average woman. Therefore, unless women as a class are assessed an extra charge, they will be subsidized, to some extent, by the class of male employees. It follows, according to the Department, that fairness to its class of male employees justifies the extra assessment against all of its female employees.

But the question of fairness to various classes affected by the statute is essentially a matter of policy for the legislature to address. Congress has decided that classifications based on sex, like those based on national origin or race, are unlawful. Actuarial studies could unquestionably identify differences in life expectancy based on race or national origin, as well as sex.[15] But a statute that was designed to make race irrelevant in the employment market. . . . could not reasonably be construed to permit a take-home-pay differential based on a racial classification.

---

15. For example, the life expectancy of a white baby in 1973 was 72.2 years; a nonwhite baby could expect to live 65.9 years, a difference of 6.3 years. See Public Health Service, IIA Vital Statistics of the United States, 1973, Table 5-3.

Even if the statutory language were less clear, the basic policy of the statute requires that we focus on fairness to individuals rather than fairness to classes. Practices that classify employees in terms of religion, race, or sex tend to preserve traditional assumptions about groups rather than thoughtful scrutiny of individuals. The generalization involved in this case illustrates the point. Separate mortality tables are easily interpreted as reflecting innate differences between the sexes; but a significant part of the longevity differential may be explained by the social fact that men are heavier smokers than women.

Finally, there is no reason to believe that Congress intended a special definition of discrimination in the context of employee group insurance coverage. It is true that insurance is concerned with events that are individually unpredictable, but that is characteristic of many employment decisions. Individual risks, like individual performance, may not be predicted by resort to classifications proscribed by Title VII. Indeed, the fact that this case involves a group insurance program highlights a basic flaw in the Department's fairness argument. For when insurance risks are grouped, the better risks always subsidize the poorer risks. Healthy persons subsidize medical benefits for the less healthy; unmarried workers subsidize the pensions of married workers; persons who eat, drink, or smoke to excess may subsidize pension benefits for persons whose habits are more temperate. Treating different classes of risks as though they were the same for purposes of group insurance is a common practice that has never been considered inherently unfair. . . .

An employment practice that requires 2,000 individuals to contribute more money into a fund than 10,000 other employees simply because each of them is a woman, rather than a man, is in direct conflict with both the language and the policy of the Act. Such a practice does not pass the simple test of whether the evidence shows "treatment of a person in a manner which but for that person's sex would be different." It constitutes discrimination and is unlawful unless exempted by the Equal Pay Act of 1963 or some other affirmative justification.

II

. . . The Equal Pay Act requires employers to pay members of both sexes the same wages for equivalent work, except when the differential is pursuant to one of four specified exceptions. The Department contends that the fourth exception applies here. That exception authorizes a "differential based on any other factor other than sex."

The Department argues that the different contributions exacted from men and women were based on the factor of longevity rather than sex. It is plain, however, that any individual's life expectancy is based on a number of factors, of which sex is only one. The record contains no evidence that any factor other than the employee's sex was taken into account in calculating the 14.84% differential between the respective contributions by men and women. We agree with Judge Duniway's observation that one cannot "say that an actuarial distinction based entirely on sex is 'based on any other factor other than sex.' Sex is exactly what it is based on." 553 F.2d 581, 588 (9th Cir. 1976). . . .

III

. . . [T]he Department argues that the absence of a discriminatory effect on women as a class justifies an employment practice which, on its face, discriminated against individual employees because of their sex. But even if the Department's actuarial evidence is sufficient to prevent plaintiffs from establishing a prima facie case on the theory that the effect of the practice on women as a class was discriminatory, that evidence does not defeat the claim that the practice, on its face, discriminated against every individual woman employed by the Department.

In essence, the Department is arguing that the prima facie showing of discrimination based on evidence of different contributions for the respective sexes is rebutted by its demonstration that there is a like difference in the cost of providing benefits for the respective classes. That argument might prevail if Title VII contained a cost justification defense comparable to the affirmative defense. . . . But neither Congress nor the courts have recognized such a defense under Title VII.

Although we conclude that the Department's practice violated Title VII, we do not suggest that the statute was intended to revolutionize the insurance and pension industries. All that is at issue today is a requirement that men and women make unequal contributions to an employer-operated pension fund. Nothing in our holding implies that it would be unlawful for an employer to set aside equal retirement contributions for each employee and let each retiree purchase the largest benefit which his or her accumulated contributions could command in the open market. Nor does it call into question the insurance industry practice of considering the composition of an employer's work force in determining the probable cost of a retirement or death benefit plan. . . .

Mr. Justice BRENNAN took no part in the consideration or decision of this case.

[The opinion of Mr. Justice BLACKMUN, concurring in part and concurring in the judgment, is omitted.]

Mr. CHIEF JUSTICE BURGER, with whom Mr. Justice REHNQUIST joins, concurring in part and dissenting in part. . . .

Gender-based actuarial tables have been in use since at least 1843, and their statistical validity has been repeatedly verified. The vast life insurance, annuity, and pension plan industry is based on these tables. As the Court recognizes . . . it is a fact that "women, as a class, do live longer than men." It is equally true that employers cannot know in advance when individual members of the classes will die. . . . Yet, if they are to operate economically workable group pension programs, it is only rational to permit them to rely on statistically sound and proved disparities in longevity between men and women. Indeed, it seems to me irrational to assume Congress intended to outlaw use of the fact that, for whatever reasons or combination of reasons, women as a class outlive men.

. . . An effect upon pension plans so revolutionary and discriminatory — this time favorable to women at the expense of men — should not be read into the statute without either a clear statement of that intent in the statute, or some reliable indication in the legislative history that this was Congress' purpose. . . .

The reality of differences in human mortality is what mortality experience tables reflect. The difference is the added longevity of women. All the reasons why women statistically outlive men are not clear. But categorizing people on the basis of sex, the one acknowledged immutable difference between men and women, is to take into account all of the unknown reasons, whether biologically or culturally based, or both, which give women a significantly greater life expectancy than men. It is therefore true as the Court says, "that any individual's life expectancy is based on a number of factors, of which sex is only one." . . . But it is not true that by seizing upon the only constant, "measurable" factor, no others were taken into account. All other factors, whether known but variable — or un-known — are the elements which automatically account for the actuarial disparity. And all are accounted for when the constant factor is used as a basis for determining the costs and benefits of a group pension plan.

Here, of course, petitioners are discriminating in take-home pay between men and women. . . . The practice of petitioners, however, falls squarely under the exemption provided by the Equal Pay Act of 1963 . . . [for] a differential based on any other factor other than sex. . . ." The "other factor other than sex" is longevity; sex is the umbrella-constant under which all of the elements leading to differences in longevity are grouped and assimilated, and the only objective feature upon which an employer — or anyone else, including insurance companies — may reliably base a cost differential for the "risk" being insured.

This is in no sense a failure to treat women as "individuals" in violation of the statute, as the Court holds. It is to treat them as individually as it is possible to do in the face of the unknowable length of each individual life. Individually, every woman has the same statistical possibility of outliving men. This is the essence of basing decisions on reliable statistics when individual determinations are infeasible or, as here, impossible.

Of course, women cannot be disqualified from, for example, heavy labor just because the generality of women are thought not as strong as men — a proposition which perhaps may sometime be statistically demonstrable, but will remain individually refutable. When, however, it is impossible to tailor a program such as a pension plan to the individual, nothing should prevent application of reliable statistical facts to the individual, for whom the facts cannot be disproved until long after planning, funding, and operating the program have been undertaken. . . .

Mr. Justice Marshall's opinion, concurring in part and dissenting [to the court's holding that the opinion should not be retroactive, is omitted].

Notes

1. **Group-Based vs. Individual-Based Equality.** What view of equality is reflected in *Manhart*? In an important sense, the case chooses formal equality over a form of "reverse" substantive equality: women and men must be treated alike at the pay-in side, even though as a (substantive) result women, because on average they will live longer, will on average obtain greater pay-out benefits than men. Put another way, taking account of men's and women's average differences so that the outcomes (again, on average) are the same is not allowed. Formal equality in these circumstances means that each employee will be treated as an individual rather than as a member of a group, but it also means that women, on average, will obtain more benefits than men, on average. Is that "fair"? Reconsider Judge Posner's view that disregarding women's greater longevity when fixing pension benefits amounts to a subsidy to women. See supra, page 330. That view looks at women as a group, instead of the individual woman who may or may not live longer than the average. Is his focus on equalizing the effects of an employment practice on a group, rather than on individuals, consistent with his opinion in American Nurses' Association v. Illinois, set forth at page 303, in which he wrote that pay differences between men and women who work in sex-segregated job categories, which were otherwise of equal worth, did not state a claim for discrimination? Wasn't the claim in *American Nurses'* about unequal, group-based (or average) effects?

Despite the concern expressed by the defendant in *Manhart* that women as a group receive a disproportionate share of pension benefits, women as a group are less likely to be covered by a pension plan (39 percent, as compared to 46 percent for men), and the average pay out for female retirees is less than half the pension benefits paid out to male retirees. See Dana M. Muir, From *Yuppies* to *Guppies*: Unfunded Mandates and Benefit Plan Regulation, 34 Ga. L. Rev. 195, 1220-21 (1999). Are these facts relevant to the legal issues in *Manhart*?

2. **Efficiency vs. Nondiscrimination in Fringe Benefit and Insurance Plans.** Is formal equality compatible with insurance principles? Much has been written about the actuarial assumptions at issue in *Manhart*. The

correlation between sex and longevity is explained by the fact that men engage in more self-destructive behaviors than women. Critics of *Manhart* have argued that sex is the most efficient proxy for these behaviors and that monitoring these behaviors directly would be too expensive and inefficient. See, e.g., George J. Benston, The Economics of Gender Discrimination in Employee Fringe Benefits: *Manhart* Revisited, 49 U. Chi. L. Rev. 489, 517-519, 530-531 (1982). Those who favor the result in *Manhart* argue that critics have confused correlation with causation: sex is not the cause of the actuarial differences but only the most efficient correlate. Where efficiency is the only value to be served, pro-*Manhart* advocates argue that the nondiscrimination principles of Title VII should prevail. See, e.g., Lea Brilmayer, Douglas Laycock & Teresa A. Sullivan, The Efficient Use of Group Averages as Nondiscrimination: A Rejoinder to Professor Benston, 50 U. Chi. L. Rev. 222, 223-225 (1983). Is the result unfair to men? Consider the following:

> It is hard to understand why the use of merged-gender mortality tables is unfair to men. It has a disparate impact on men as a group because it disadvantages self-destructors, and more men than women are self-destructors. The total annuity payout to [men] is less than the total amount paid to [women] because the total number of years the men [live] would be less. But are men, especially non-self-destructors, entitled to cash in on the fact that many of their sex self-destruct, and is this "entitlement" one that rises to the level of a right protected by Title VII? There is no merit in Benston's sweeping claim that men are discriminated against whenever sex is an efficient predictor but is not used.
>
> When sex is used to calculate pension contributions or benefits, the woman's complaint is clear. It is false to claim, as Benston does, that a woman receives subjective value equal to that which a man receives. She knows subjectively that an identically situated man has an equal life expectancy but gets higher periodic benefits. The reason may be that the insurance company lacks inexpensive access to accurate information concerning its annuitants' habits, but her understanding of the company's perspective does not increase her subjective valuation of the periodic benefits.

Id. at 226-227.

Brilmayer, Laycock, and Sullivan argue that as long as sex is not the "cause" but only a correlate, using rates and benefits based on sex as a predictor is akin to using race or ethnicity as a selection criterion for credit, college admissions, or hiring. As in these cases, judgments about individuals based on such protected group characteristics are exactly the kind of unfairness civil rights statutes prohibit. Brilmayer et al., supra, at 227-231. For Benston's response to these arguments, see George J. Benston, Discrimination and Economic Efficiency in Employee Fringe Benefits: A Clarification of Issues and a Response to Professors Brilmayer, Laycock, and Sullivan, 50 U. Chi. L. Rev. 250 (1983). See also Richard A. Miller, How to

Discriminate by Sex: Federal Regulation of the Insurance Industry, 17 Conn. L. Rev. 567 (1985) (prohibiting use of sex-based insurance rates and benefits ignores "true differences" between men and women and hence enhances unequal, rather than equal, treatment).

Some have defended formal sex-based equality in employee fringe-benefit plans, as insisted upon in *Manhart*, on the grounds that the effort to achieve true substantive equality would be too inefficient and, ultimately, inaccurate. See George Rutherglen, Sexual Equality in Fringe-Benefit Plans, 65 Va. L. Rev. 199, 248-255 (1979); cf. Leah Wortham, The Economics of Insurance Classification: The Sound of One Invisible Hand Clapping, 47 Ohio St. L.J. 835 (1986) (approving regulation of private insurance plans because existing "free market" forces do not lead to "rational" insurance rate structures). Others advocate a radical abandonment of the goal of neutral accuracy in insurance rate structures, arguing that it is appropriate to regulate insurance classifications systems to achieve larger social goals. See, e.g., Regina Austin, The Insurance Classification Controversy, 131 U. Pa. L. Rev. 517 (1983). What social goals relating to gender should the regulation of insurance plans attempt to achieve?

3. Extensions of *Manhart*. Justice Stevens concedes that an employer could simply give a fixed benefit to employees from which they could purchase their own retirement plan on the open insurance market. Functionally equivalent would be a plan whereby the employer makes fixed contributions to a private insurance carrier, which then pays out different monthly amounts on retirement according to the employee's sex in recognition of the longer life expectancy of women. This alternative too, however, was found to be a violation of Title VII. See Arizona Governing Committee for Tax Deferred Annuity and Deferred Compensation Plans v. Norris, 463 U.S. 1073 (1983) (giving employees choice of carriers when all carriers used sex-segregated mortality tables violates Title VII). See also Probe v. State Teachers' Retirement Sys., 780 F.2d 776 (9th Cir.), cert. denied, 476 U.S. 1170 (1986) (joint life-survivor option that gives lower monthly payments to male employee who designates a female beneficiary violates Title VII).

4. State Regulation of Sex-Based Insurance Rates. Except in the employment context, Congress has not yet undertaken to regulate discrimination in insurance rates, notwithstanding some efforts to do so. Some of the proposed federal bills are described in Stephen R. Ryan, Note, The Elimination of Gender Discrimination in Insurance Pricing: Does Automobile Insurance Rate Without Sex?, 61 Notre Dame L. Rev. 748, 752-753 (1986); Karen A. McCluskey, Note, Ending Sex Discrimination in Insurance: The Nondiscrimination in Insurance Act, 11 J. Legis. 457 (1984). Thus far, insurance rates are entirely a matter of state regulation. States have prohibited race as a factor in insurance, but for the most part, they have not prohibited sex-based rates. See Jill Gaulding, Note, Race, Sex, and Genetic Discrimination in Insurance: What's Fair?, 80 Cornell L. Rev. 1646, 1655, 1660 (1995).

Only Montana flatly forbids sex discrimination in insurance. See Mont. Code Ann. 49-2-309 (1999). California requires sex-specific tables for life insurance and annuities. See Cal. Ins. Code §790.03(f) (West 1993). Hawaii, Massachusetts, Michigan, and North Carolina by statute forbid use of sex as a factor in automobile insurance but not in other insurance. Gaulding, supra, at 1662-1663. See also Bartholomew v. Foster, 541 A.2d 393 (Pa. Commw. Ct. 1988), aff'd by an equally divided court, 563 A.2d 1390 (Pa. 1989), reh'g denied, 570 A.2d 508 (Pa. 1990) (automobile insurance rates based in part on sex, although authorized by statute, violate state Equal Rights Amendment).

Putting Theory into Practice

3-4. U.S. Department of Transportation data show that men have almost twice as many automobile accidents as women. They also show that men drive on average many more miles per year than women (17,671, as compared to 7,211 miles for women), and that as the number of miles driven per year increases, the accident rate per mile driven decreases. See Karen A. McCluskey, Note, Ending Sex Discrimination in Insurance: The Nondiscrimination in Insurance Act, 11 J. Legis. 457, 470 n.98 (1984). While in recent years women's mileage has increased 135 percent (as compared to 48 percent for men), men still drive more and are still twice as likely to be involved in fatal automobile accidents. Joseph B. Treaster, Deaths of Women in Car Crashes Are Rising, N.Y. Times, Nov. 15, 2001, at C12.

In light of this data, should sex be an appropriate risk factor in setting automobile insurance rates? If so, what are the different ways it could be taken into account? Which is the most "fair"?

3-5. A 1988 survey of insurers indicated that about half of the nation's largest insurers instruct that health, life, and disability insurance be denied to victims of domestic abuse. Deborah S. Hellman, Is Actuarially Fair Insurance Pricing Actually Fair? A Case Study in Insuring Battered Women, 32 Harv. C.R.–C.L.L. Rev. 355, 355-356 (1997). Assume the policy is actuarially sound. Should it be legal?

2. Education

a. Eligibility for School Athletic Teams

≡ *Petrie v. Illinois High School Association*
394 N.E.2d 855 (Ill. Ct. App. 1979)

GREEN, Justice.

Plaintiff Trent Petrie by his mother and next friend, Pattsi Petrie challenges (1) a rule of Champaign Central High School (Central) . . . which restricts membership on the sole volleyball team sponsored by the school to girls, and (2) rules of defendant Illinois High School Association (IHSA), a voluntary association of public and private high schools of the state, which restrict membership on the teams participating in the only volleyball tournament sponsored by it to girls.

. . . [Plaintiff is] a 16-year-old junior, 5'11" in height and 170 lbs. in weight, who had reported for the team and had been practicing with it when informed by school officials that he could not play in games with other schools because of defendants' rules. . . .

[In other cases in which rules prohibiting capable girls from playing on boys' teams were struck down on state or federal equal protection grounds, the] exclusion of girls from boys' teams was generally sought on grounds that girls, as a group, were less capable than boys at the sports involved and, in the contact sports, that they were more prone to injury. The courts rejected these arguments reasoning that the blanket prohibition placed a stigma of inferiority on girls as an excluded class and that the obviously better way to determine whether they were capable of playing was to give them a try out and then let the coach make a subjective determination as to whether they were capable of playing. The argument as to the danger of injury was answered by noting that not all girls were of a physique making them excessively injury prone and that, in any event, no objective standards had been set forth to eliminate the more frail boys.

Here, boys were the excluded class and their exclusion was made not because they were not likely to be good enough but because they were likely to be too good to permit adequate opportunities for girls. . . .

The evidence in this case . . . showed that, in general, high school boys are substantially taller, heavier and stronger than their girl counterparts and have longer extremities. Although we recognize that high school girls have no general disadvantage as to balance, coordination, strategic acumen, or quickness (as distinguished from running speed), we agree that they are generally at a substantial physical disadvantage in playing volleyball. Illustrative of the consequences of such disadvantage as applied to other sports were (1) the indication in [Gomes v. R.I. Interscholastic League, 469 F. Supp. 659 (D.R.I. 1979)] that at the plaintiff's high school the "overwhelming majority" of the positions on teams open to both sexes were held by boys, and (2) testimony in the instant case that in the high school track season previous to the trial, none of the girls' state record holders in track and field "would have qualified in any event for the boys' state track and field meet." Evidence in the instant case of isolated instances of male participation upon girls' teams creating an advantage for those teams indicated the likelihood of similar results if any substantial number of males chose to participate in volleyball.

Classification of a high school volleyball team to limit its membership to girls is consistent with a long-standing tradition in sports of setting up classifications whereby persons having objectively measured characteristics likely to make them more proficient are eliminated from certain classes of competition. Heavier persons are prohibited from competing in lighter weight classes in wrestling and boxing. Persons over a certain age are often prohibited from participating in interscholastic athletics and those under a certain age from competing in events sponsored for senior citizens. Membership in certain interscholastic teams has been limited to those who have not completed their sophomore year. At one time, intercollegiate football between teams whose members weighed no more than 150 lbs. was popular and many high schools and elementary schools have had heavy-weight and lightweight football teams. There is no stigma attached to a person eliminated by this system from competing in a class in which that person might have undue advantage.

Suggestion is made that rather than using sex as a classifying factor, teams should be classified on the basis of characteristics mentioned in the last paragraph and done in such a way that in sports where females had a physical disadvantage, they would compete in a class, where the disadvantage would be eliminated. Of course, height might be such a measure for volleyball and a school could have a team whereby most girls would be with boys more nearly their size. However, this would not compensate for the strength differential and would cause great hardship to the taller girls, most of whom would not have the musculature to compete with taller boys. We conclude that a system of measurement to put girls into classes whereby they would be on a physical par with males who would compete in that class would be too difficult to devise. Although systems of handicapping based on measurable prior performance such as golf or bowling scores are used, in those sports and in other individual sports, ratings can be obtained on the basis of prior performance. In team sports, however, any rating of players could only be done on a very subjective basis and would not be practical. Furthermore, even in the individual sports, a system of rating and handicapping places a premium on poor prior performance and is inconsistent with a system of full competition which boys have had for years and which girls are seeking to achieve.

[The court also rejected a quota system for boys, because it would lead to such accommodations as changes in the height of the net, no-spiking rules for boys, or relegating girls to the back court, all changes that work to the detriment of girls.]

The classification of public high school athletic teams upon the basis of gender in sports such as volleyball is itself based on the innate physical differences between the sexes. It is not based on generalizations that are "archaic" (Schlesinger v. Ballard, [419 U.S. 498, 508 (1975)]), nor does it represent an attitude of "romantic paternalism" (Frontiero v. Richardson, [411 U.S. 677, 684 (1973)]. Like all systems of classifications for competition, it is overbroad and underbroad in that it includes females who are athletically superior to many males and excludes males who are less well-endowed athletically than most females. However, we are convinced that it is the only feasible classification to promote the legitimate and substantial state interest of providing for interscholastic athletic opportunity for girls.

Schools could have varsity, subvarsity and lesser levels of varsity squads and no doubt eventually provide the opportunity for a very substantial number of girls to compete in each sport. We must recognize, however, that public institutions have a limited amount of funds and it is common knowledge that many school districts are extremely pressed to maintain their present programs. The extra expense of having this number of squads is obvious. Moreover, to arrange the program in such a way that many girls are denied the chance to be on a team that is described as the school team although with a gender designation, would seem to be a very high price to pay for a complete equality of sexes.

We have no trouble in concluding that having a separate volleyball team and separate tournaments in that sport for girls is substantially related to and serves the achievement of the important governmental objective of maintaining, fostering and promoting athletic opportunities for girls. It, therefore, satisfies the due process requirements of the fourteenth amendment.

[The court also concludes that having separate teams for girls is justified under the "strict scrutiny" standard of the state constitution.]

When a governmental goal is to preserve, foster and promote the opportunities of those of a gender, an element of affirmative action is necessarily involved. . . .

. . . The girls' volleyball season overlaps that of football. In Schlesinger v. Ballard, [419 U.S. 498 (1975)], a statutory provision permitting female naval officers to remain longer in grade than certain male officers was upheld as meeting Federal due process requirements because the female officers had no opportunity to go into combat and thus could not get the promotion enhancements available to males who did so. As the female officers in Ballard were given longer in grade because they could not go into combat, girls here are given volleyball playing opportunities because they have little if any in football. . . .

. . . We conclude that to furnish exactly the same athletic opportunities to boys as to girls would be most difficult and would be detrimental to the compelling governmental interest of equalizing general athletic opportunities between the sexes. . . .

. . . We affirm.

CRAVEN, Justice, dissenting: . . .

The difficulty with the defendants' position is that they are attempting to achieve a laudable goal ensuring a chance for athletic competition to both large and small, strong and weak students by an impermissible means. While it may in fact be true that most boys are generally larger and stronger than most girls, due process bars classifications based upon such permanent presumptions where individual determinations may, and in fact do, rebut them. . . . Sex-based generalizations have been discarded in many cases where there was statistical support for the presumption upon which the classifications were based. In [Reed v. Reed, 404 U.S. 71 (1971)], for instance, the court was unwilling to tolerate a mandatory preference for males over females as estate administrators, even while acknowledging that men, as a class, may indeed be more conversant with business. . . .

Defendants here argue that boys must be excluded from the all-girl volleyball team in order to allow the girls a fair chance to compete. In support of their position, they cite statistics on the relative height, strength, and physical development of the average male and the average female of high school age. In short, their position is actually not that they are protecting girls from boys or vice versa, but rather that they are protecting weaker from stronger athletes. The fallacy in their position is revealed by the fact that, although the differences in size and strength within each sex are shown by the evidence to be greater than the differences between the averages for the two sexes, no provision has been made to protect smaller, weaker females from competition with larger, stronger females, or smaller, weaker males from competition with larger, stronger males. . . .

Surely, not even the majority here, nor society generally, would condone the exclusion of blacks from an all-white basketball team on the grounds that blacks generally are more skilled at the game than whites and might tend to dominate it. Nor would we tolerate an exclusion of Catholics from an all-Protestant high school soccer team on the grounds that Catholic elementary schools have traditionally emphasized that sport so as to give their graduates an unfair advantage. Yet the constitutional prohibition against sex discrimination in Illinois is more specific than that against either racial or religious discrimination. There are legally tolerable means of categorizing athletes by size, strength, and ability. To adopt sex as a proxy for more precisely defined means of leveling off competition is both illegal and irrational. It is simply foolish to perpetuate the fear of equality between sexes. It is more than foolish to justify discrimination upon the asserted basis of protection and allowing "catch up" time. . . .

O'Connor v. Board of Education of School District 23

645 F.2d 578 (7th Cir. 1981), cert. denied, 454 U.S. 1084 (1981)

BAUER, Circuit Judge.

In this equal protection case, the district court granted a preliminary injunction restraining the Board of Education of Prospect Heights School District No. 23, and other defendants, from refusing to permit plaintiff-appellee Karen O'Connor to try out for the boys' sixth grade basketball team. We stayed enforcement of the preliminary injunction pending appeal and now reverse.

I

Karen O'Connor is an 11-year-old sixth grade student at MacArthur Junior High School in suburban Cook County, Illinois. The school is a member of the Mid-Suburban Junior High School Conference, an association of six junior high schools engaged in interscholastic athletics. Conference rules require separate teams for boys and girls in contact sports, including basketball.

On August 27, 1980, Karen's father asked that she be permitted to try out for the boys' interscholastic basketball team. Karen is a good athlete; a professional basketball coach who observed her play rated her ability as equal to or better than a female high school sophomore and equal to that of a male eighth-grade player. Nonetheless, on October 10, 1980, the Board of Education denied the request, but invited Karen to try out for the girls' interscholastic team.

. . . The district court . . . found that the school's classification violated her fundamental "right to develop" and that "the right to education is a fundamental right and the rights to the constituent elements of an education is a fundamental right (sic)." The court further held that the MacArthur programs for boys' and girls' basketball were unequal because Karen's competition with girls of substantially lesser skill was not as valuable as competition with persons of equal or better skills in the boys' program. The district court also rejected defendants' argument that they would have to open both teams to both sexes and that the boys would dominate. Applying a strict scrutiny analysis, the court held simply that the Board had failed to show that the MacArthur program was the least restrictive alternative. . . .

II

. . . We conclude that the district court abused its discretion in issuing this preliminary injunction. . . .

Neither Judge Marshall nor plaintiff cite any authority to support the proposition that either education or the "right to develop" is a fundamental right. The Supreme Court has expressly rejected the notion that education is a fundamental right. San Antonio Independent School District v. Rodriguez, [411 U.S. 1, 29-39 (1972)].

. . . Viewed under the correct standard, the main issue here is whether Karen O'Connor has demonstrated a reasonable likelihood that the two team approach is not substantially related to the objective of maximizing participation in sports, the avowed objective of the school board. We think she has failed. Unlike some interscholastic athletic programs, the MacArthur program treats the two sexes identically — plaintiff concedes that the teams are equal in terms of funding, facilities, and other "objective" criteria. Both teams are interscholastic. "Separate but equal" teams have received endorsement in many circuits, including this one. . . .

. . . [D]efendants have demonstrated that their program substantially serves the objective of increasing girls' participation in sports.

. . . As Justice Stevens held, in denying the application for a stay,

> In my opinion, the question whether the discrimination is justified cannot depend entirely on whether the girls' program will offer Karen opportunities that are equal in all respects to the advantages she would gain from the higher level of competition in the boys' program. The answer must depend on whether it is permissible for the defendants to structure their athletic programs by using sex as one criterion for eligibility. If the classification is reasonable in substantially all of its applications, I do not believe that the general rule can be said to be unconstitutional simply because it appears arbitrary in an individual case.

O'Connor v. Board of Education, [499 U.S. 1301, 1306 (1980) (denying petition to vacate stay)]. . . .

Reversed and remanded.

Notes

1. When Team Offered for Members of Only One Sex. *Petrie* holds that a boy is not entitled to an opportunity to compete for a girls' sports team, even if there is no comparable boys' team, because of the effect that competition would have on girls' sports opportunities. Yet, *O'Connor* notwithstanding, girls have successfully challenged all-boys' teams when a girls' team was not available in that sport. Although Title IX, discussed at pages 409 ff., exempts contact sports from its nondiscrimination provisions, 34 C.F.R. §106.41(b) (2000), courts have held that the Equal Protection Clause prohibits the exclusion of girls from both contact and non-contact sports teams, if no girls' team is offered in the sport. See, e.g., Adams v. Baker, 919 F. Supp. 1496 (D. Kan. 1996) (wrestling); Brenden v.

Independent Sch. Dist. 742, 477 F.2d 1292 (8th Cir. 1973) (tennis, cross-country-skiing, and track); Lantz v. Ambach, 570 F. Supp. 1020 (W.D. Mich. 1983) (football); Reed v. Nebraska Sch. Activities Ass'n, 341 F. Supp. 258 (D. Neb. 1972) (golf). What problems do you see with co-ed teams in, say, wrestling?

On the one hand, these cases are quite consistent with formal equality principles. What they stand for is that each individual girl be given the opportunity to show that she has the strengths and abilities required of other individuals (boys) who make the team. No special consideration, or lowered standards, are required; only that girls have the same opportunity made available to boys.

On the other hand, the reciprocal opportunity is not made available to boys. Is the differential treatment justified? The dissenting opinion of Justice Craven provides a formal equality analysis. Is it a satisfactory one? For what substantive equality principle does the majority opinion stand?

2. When Separate Teams Are Offered for Members of Each Sex. When a school offers a separate team for members of each sex, formal equality is more easily achieved in the group sense, but not in the individualized opportunity sense. A separate girls' team protects the *average* athletically-talented girl from playing on a team that is not "run over" by boys. But Karen O'Connor — the *exceptional* athletically-talented girl — is worse off since now she can't benefit from the higher level of competition offered by the boys' team. In this way, Karen O'Connor is being limited by generalizations made about members of her sex that are not applicable to her — a harm formal equality ordinarily does not permit.

The court in *O'Connor* assumes that if Karen O'Connor is allowed to try out for the boys' basketball team, boys must be allowed to try out for the girls' team. Does this result necessarily follow? Can a ruling allowing girls to compete for slots on the boys' team but not boys to compete for slots on the girls' team be defended on substantive equality grounds?

What about the fact that if Karen O'Connor makes the boys' team, there will be one less spot for a boy? Does it matter that Karen O'Connor is unusual, and thus that a rule allowing her participation will not tend to compromise boy's sports as a whole, in the same way that boys' participation on girls' teams would?

Is "separate but equal" consistent with formal equality? Karen L. Tokarz argues, in agreement with Judge Craven in *Petrie*, that sex-based teams are highly problematic:

> In addition to depriving individual women of opportunities for physical development, sex segregation in sports adversely affects women economically, socially, and politically. It excludes women from power, fosters the myth of male supremacy, limits occupational choices for women, perpetuates the sex

role stereotype of women as passive and weak, and invalidates the expressive/feminine aspect of sports.

Tokarz, Separate but Unequal Educational Sports Programs: The Need for a New Theory of Equality, 1 Berkeley Women's L.J. 201, 239 (1985). Which version of formal equality is superior — the group-based, separate-but-equal model, or the individual-based model favored by Karen O'Connor?

Some have argued that separate teams are not justified even on biological terms. Katherine M. Franke, for example, questions the rationality of athletic sex segregation, offering studies showing that

> [b]etween 1964 and 1985 women marathon runners have knocked more than an hour-and-a-half off their running times, while men's times during the same period have decreased by only a few minutes. . . . If the gap between highly trained male and female athletes were to continue to close at the current rate, in thirty to forty years men and women would compete in these sports on an equal basis.

Franke, The Central Mistake of Sex Discrimination Law: The Disaggregation of Sex from Gender, 144 U. Pa. L. Rev. 1, 37-38 (1995), citing Anne Fausto-Sterling, Myths of Gender: Biological Theories About Women and Men 218-219 (1989). Franke and others have also put into question whether the biological dimorphism assumed by sex-segregated sports, and other things as well, is well-founded. This topic is discussed in Chapter 7.

3. Historical Discrimination. While the court in *Petrie* refers vaguely to "past disparity of opportunity," this factor does not play as prominent a role in its analysis as (average) biological differences do. In reaching the same conclusion as the court in *Petrie*, other courts have put greater emphasis on the governmental interest in redressing the effects of past discrimination. See, e.g., Clark v. Arizona Interscholastic Ass'n, 695 F.2d 1126, 1131 (9th Cir. 1982), cert. denied, 464 U.S. 818 (1983) (rejecting challenge to girls' volleyball team). Is this a realistic goal? The brother of the plaintiff in the 1982 *Clark* case, in a later challenge to the same school's girls' volleyball team, argued that since single-sex sports have failed to remedy the effects of past discrimination, and since these effects are due primarily to social attitudes that will not be changed by single-sex sports teams, continued pursuit of the goal through single-sex teams is unconstitutional. The argument was rejected. See Clark v. Arizona Interscholastic Ass'n, 886 F.2d 1191 (9th Cir. 1989). What effect on social attitudes do you think the exclusion of boys from girls' sports teams has?

4. Different Rules for Boys' and Girls' Sports? Would separate boys' and girls' rules for the same sport increase, or decrease, equality in sports? The answer, again, may depend on whether the question is addressed from the point of view of Karen O'Connor or from that of some hypothetical girl of "average" physical characteristics and capacities. The cases, in fact, are split. Dodson v. Arkansas Activities Ass'n, 468 F. Supp. 394 (E.D. Ark. 1979), addressing a challenge to the use of different rules for boys' and girls' basketball, held that separate half-court rules for girls' basketball deprives girls of equal protection. A contrary conclusion was reached in Cape v. Tennessee Secondary Sch. Athletic Ass'n, 563 F.2d 793 (6th Cir. 1977) (upholding different girls' basketball rules based on differences in physical characteristics and capabilities). See also Ridgeway v. Montana High Sch. Ass'n, 633 F. Supp. 1564 (D. Mont. 1986), aff'd, 858 F.2d 579 (9th Cir. 1988) (different seasonal placements for boys' and girls' teams of the same sport not a violation of equal protection where such a system helps with management of student participation, availability of coaching staff and practice, and team support).

b. Sex-Segregated Schools

≡ **United States v. Virginia**
≡ 518 U.S. 515 (1996)

GINSBURG, J., delivered the opinion of the court, in which STEVENS, O'CONNOR, KENNEDY, SOUTER, and BREYER, JJ., joined.

Virginia's public institutions of higher learning include an incomparable military college, Virginia Military Institute (VMI). The United States maintains that the Constitution's equal protection guarantee precludes Virginia from reserving exclusively to men the unique educational opportunities VMI affords. We agree. . . .

II

From its establishment in 1839 as one of the Nation's first state military colleges, VMI has remained financially supported by Virginia and "subject to the control of the [Virginia] General Assembly." . . .

VMI today enrolls about 1,300 men as cadets. Its academic offerings in the liberal arts, sciences, and engineering are also available at other public colleges and universities in Virginia. But VMI's mission is special. It is the mission of the school to produce educated and honorable men, prepared for the varied work of civil life, imbued with love of learning, confident in the functions and attitudes of leadership, possessing a high sense of public service, advocates of the American democracy and free enterprise system, and ready as citizen-soldiers to defend their country in time of national peril. . . .

In contrast to the federal service academies, institutions maintained "to prepare cadets for career service in the armed forces," VMI's program "is directed at preparation for both military and civilian life;" "[o]nly about 15% of VMI cadets enter career military service."

VMI produces its "citizen-soldiers" through "an adversative, or doubting, model of education" which features "[p]hysical rigor, mental stress, absolute equality of treatment, absence of privacy, minute regulation of behavior, and indoctrination in desirable values." . . .

VMI cadets live in spartan barracks where surveillance is constant and privacy nonexistent; they wear uniforms, eat together in the mess hall, and regularly participate in drills. Entering students are incessantly exposed to the rat line, "an extreme form of the adversative model," comparable in intensity to Marine Corps boot camp. Tormenting and punishing, the rat line bonds new cadets to their fellow sufferers and, when they have completed the 7-month experience, to their former tormentors.

VMI's "adversative model" is further characterized by a hierarchical "class system" of privileges and responsibilities, a "dyke system" for assigning a senior class mentor to each entering class "rat," and a stringently enforced "honor code," which prescribes that a cadet " 'does not lie, cheat, steal nor tolerate those who do.' "

VMI attracts some applicants because of its reputation as an extraordinarily challenging military school, and "because its alumni are exceptionally close to the school." "[W]omen have no opportunity anywhere to gain the benefits of [the system of education at VMI]." . . .

In 1990, prompted by a complaint filed with the Attorney General by a female high-school student seeking admission to VMI, the United States sued the Commonwealth of Virginia and VMI, alleging that VMI's exclusively male admission policy violated the Equal Protection Clause of the Fourteenth Amendment. . . .

In the two years preceding the lawsuit, the District Court noted, VMI had received inquiries from 347 women, but had responded to none of them. "[S]ome women, at least," the court said, "would want to attend the school if they had the opportunity." The court further recognized that, with recruitment, VMI could "achieve at least 10% female enrollment" — "a sufficient 'critical mass' to provide the female cadets with a positive educational experience." And it was also established that "some women are capable of all of the individual activities required of VMI cadets." In addition, experts agreed that if VMI admitted women, "the VMI ROTC experience would become a better training program from the perspective of the armed forces, because it would provide training in dealing with a mixed-gender army."

[The District Court, nonetheless, ruled in favor of VMI, because admission of women would require alterations of some of the distinctive and beneficial aspects of VMI (766 F. Supp. 1407 (1991)); the Fourth Circuit Court of Appeals reversed and remanded, holding that the state could not achieve its purposes by favoring one gender and that VMI had to either admit women, establish a parallel institution or program, or abandon state support (976 F.2d 890 (1992)). In response to the Fourth Circuit's ruling, Virginia proposed a parallel program at Mary Baldwin College, a private liberal arts school for women: Virginia Women's Institute for Leadership (VWIL). The program was to be open, initially, to 25 to 30 students. The District Court decided that the program plan met the requirements of the Equal Protection Clause, (852 F. Supp. 471 (1994)) and a divided Court of Appeals affirmed, at 44 F.3d 1229 (1995).]

III

The cross-petitions in this case present two ultimate issues. First, does Virginia's exclusion of women from the educational opportunities provided by VMI — extraordinary opportunities for military training and civilian leadership development — deny to women "capable of all of the individual activities required of VMI cadets," the equal protection of the laws guaranteed by the Fourteenth Amendment? Second, if VMI's "unique" situation, — as Virginia's sole single-sex public institution of higher educa-tion — offends the Constitution's equal protection principle, what is the remedial requirement?

IV...

. . . To summarize the Court's current directions for cases of official classification based on gender: Focusing on the differential treatment or denial of opportunity for which relief is sought, the reviewing court must determine whether the proffered justification is "exceedingly persuasive." The burden of justification is demanding and it rests entirely on the State. [See Mississippi Univ. for Women v. Hogan, 458 U.S. 718, 724 (1982).] The State must show "at least that the [challenged] classification serves 'important governmental objectives and that the discriminatory means employed' are 'substantially related to the achievement of those objec-tives.'" Id. The justification must be genuine, not hypothesized or invented post hoc in response to litigation. And it must not rely on overbroad generalizations about the different talents, capacities, or preferences of males and females. . . .

The heightened review standard our precedent establishes does not make sex a proscribed classification. Supposed "inherent differences" are no longer accepted as a ground for race or national origin classifications. See Loving v. Virginia, 388 U.S. 1, 87 (1967). Physical differences between men and women, however, are enduring: "[T]he two sexes are not fungible; a community made up exclusively of one [sex] is different from a community composed of both." Ballard v. United States, 329 U.S. 187, 193 (1946).

"Inherent differences" between men and women, we have come to appreciate, remain cause for celebration, but not for denigration of the members of either sex or for artificial constraints on an individual's opportunity. Sex classifications may be used to compensate women "for particular economic disabilities [they have] suffered," Califano v. Webster, 430 U.S. 313, 320 (1977), to "promot[e] equal employment opportunity," see California Federal Sav. & Loan Ass'n v. Guerra, 479 U.S. 272, 289 (1987), to advance full development of the talent and capacities of our Nation's people.[7] But such classifications may not be used, as they once were, . . . to create or perpetuate the legal, social, and economic inferiority of women.

Measuring the record in this case against the review standard just described, we conclude that Virginia has shown no "exceedingly persuasive justification" for excluding all women from the citizen-soldier training afforded by VMI. We therefore affirm the Fourth Circuit's initial judgment, which held that Virginia had violated the Fourteenth Amendment's Equal Protection Clause. Because the remedy proffered by Virginia — the Mary Baldwin VWIL program — does not cure the constitutional violation, i.e., it does not provide equal opportunity, we reverse the Fourth Circuit's final judgment in this case.

V . . .

Single-sex education affords pedagogical benefits to at least some students, Virginia emphasizes, and that reality is uncontested in this litigation.[8] Similarly, it is not disputed that diversity among public educational institutions can serve the public good. But Virginia has not shown that VMI was established, or has been maintained, with a view to diversifying, by its categorical exclusion of women, educational opportunities within the State. In cases of this genre, our precedent instructs that "benign" justifications proffered in defense of categorical exclusions will not be accepted automatically; a tenable justification must describe actual state purposes, not rationalizations for actions in fact differently grounded. . . .

---

7. . . . We do not question the State's prerogative evenhandedly to support diverse educational opportunities. We address specifically and only an educational opportunity recognized by the District Court and the Court of Appeals as "unique," an opportunity available only at Virginia's premier military institute, the State's sole single-sex public university or college. Cf. Mississippi Univ. for Women v. Hogan, 458 U.S. 718, 720, n.1 (1982) ("Mississippi maintains no other single-sex public university or college. Thus, we are not faced with the question of whether States can provide 'separate but equal' undergraduate institutions for males and females").

8. On this point, the dissent sees fire where there is no flame. "Both men and women can benefit from a single-sex education," the District Court recognized, although "the beneficial effects" of such education, the court added, apparently "are stronger among women than among men." The United States does not challenge that recognition. Cf. C. Jencks & D. Riesman, The Academic Revolution 297-298 (1968): "The pluralistic argument for preserving all-male colleges is uncomfortably similar to the pluralistic argument for preserving all-white colleges. . . . The all-male college would be relatively easy to defend if it emerged from a world in which women were established as fully equal to men. But it does not. It is therefore likely to be a witting or unwitting device for preserving tacit assumptions of male superiority — assumptions for which women must eventually pay."

Neither recent nor distant history bears out Virginia's alleged pursuit of diversity through single-sex educational options. In 1839, when the State established VMI, a range of educational opportunities for men and women was scarcely contemplated. Higher education at the time was considered dangerous for women;[9] reflecting widely held views about women's proper place, the Nation's first universities and colleges — for example, Harvard in Massachusetts, William and Mary in Virginia — admitted only men. . . . VMI was not at all novel in this respect: In admitting no women, VMI followed the lead of the State's flagship school, the University of Virginia, founded in 1819. . . .

Debate concerning women's admission as undergraduates at the main university continued well past the century's midpoint. . . . If women were admitted, it was feared, they "would encroach on the rights of men; there would be new problems of government, perhaps scandals; the old honor system would have to be changed; standards would be lowered to those of other coeducational schools; and the glorious reputation of the university, as a school for men, would be trailed in the dust." . . .

Ultimately, in 1970, "the most prestigious institution of higher education in Virginia," the University of Virginia, introduced coeducation and, in 1972 [by court order], began to admit women on an equal basis with men. . . .

Virginia describes the current absence of public single-sex higher education for women as "an historical anomaly." But the historical record indicates action more deliberate than anomalous: First, protection of women against higher education; next, schools for women far from equal in resources and stature to schools for men; finally, conversion of the separate schools to coeducation. . . .

. . . [I]t is uncontested that women's admission would require accommodations, primarily in arranging housing assignments and physical training programs for female cadets. It is also undisputed, however, that "the VMI methodology could be used to educate women." The District Court even allowed that some women may prefer it to the methodology a

9. Dr. Edward H. Clarke of Harvard Medical School, whose influential book, Sex in Education, went through 17 editions, was perhaps the most well-known speaker from the medical community opposing higher education for women. He maintained that the physiological effects of hard study and academic competition with boys would interfere with the development of girls' reproductive organs. See E. Clarke, Sex in Education 38-39, 62-63 (1873); id., at 127 ("identical education of the two sexes is a crime before God and humanity, that physiology protests against, and that experience weeps over"); see also H. Maudsley, Sex in Mind and in Education 17 (1874) ("It is not that girls have not ambition, nor that they fail generally to run the intellectual race [in coeducational settings], but it is asserted that they do it at a cost to their strength and health which entails life-long suffering, and even incapacitates them for the adequate performance of the natural functions of their sex."); C. Meigs, Females and Their Diseases 350 (1848) (after five or six weeks of "mental and educational discipline," a healthy woman would "lose . . . the habit of menstruation" and suffer numerous ills as a result of depriving her body for the sake of her mind).

women's college might pursue. "[S]ome women, at least, would want to attend [VMI] if they had the opportunity," the District Court recognized, and "some women," the expert testimony established, "are capable of all of the individual activities required of VMI cadets." The parties, furthermore, agree that "some women can meet the physical standards [VMI] now impose[s] on men." In sum, as the Court of Appeals stated, "neither the goal of producing citizen soldiers," VMI's *raison d'etre*, "nor VMI's implementing methodology is inherently unsuitable to women."

In support of its initial judgment for Virginia, a judgment rejecting all equal protection objections presented by the United States, the District Court made "findings" on "gender-based developmental differences." These "findings" restate the opinions of Virginia's expert witnesses, opinions about typically male or typically female tendencies." For example, "[m]ales tend to need an atmosphere of adversativeness," while "[f]emales tend to thrive in a cooperative atmosphere." "I'm not saying that some women don't do well under [the] adversative model," VMI's expert on educational institutions testified, "undoubtedly there are some [women] who do"; but educational experiences must be designed "around the rule," this expert maintained, and not "around the exception."

The United States does not challenge any expert witness estimation on average capacities or preferences of men and women. Instead, the United States emphasizes that time and again since this Court's turning point decision in Reed v. Reed, 404 U.S. 71 (1971), we have cautioned reviewing courts to take a "hard look" at generalizations or "tendencies" of the kind pressed by Virginia, and relied upon by the District Court. . . .

It may be assumed, for purposes of this decision, that most women would not choose VMI's adversative method. As Fourth Circuit Judge Motz observed, however, in her dissent from the Court of Appeals' denial of rehearing en banc, it is also probable that "many men would not want to be educated in such an environment." 52 F.3d, at 93. (On that point, even our dissenting colleague might agree.) Education, to be sure, is not a "one size fits all" business. The issue, however, is not whether "women — or men — should be forced to attend VMI"; rather, the question is whether the State can constitutionally deny to women who have the will and capacity, the training and attendant opportunities that VMI uniquely affords.

The notion that admission of women would downgrade VMI's stature, destroy the adversative system and, with it, even the school, is a judgment hardly proved, a prediction hardly different from other "self-fulfilling prophec[ies]," see [*Hogan*], 458 U.S., at 730, once routinely used to deny rights or opportunities. When women first sought admission to the bar and access to legal education, concerns of the same order were expressed. . . .

[Such] fear, according to a 1925 report, accounted for Columbia Law School's resistance to women's admission, although

[t]he faculty . . . never maintained that women could not master legal learning. . . . No, its argument has been . . . more practical. If women were admitted to the Columbia Law School, [the faculty] said, then the choicer, more manly and red-blooded graduates of our great universities would go to the Harvard Law School!

The Nation, Feb. 18, 1925, p. 173.

. . . More recently, women seeking careers in policing encountered resistance based on fears that their presence would "undermine male solidarity," . . . deprive male partners of adequate assistance, and lead to sexual misconduct. . . .

Women's successful entry into the federal military academies,[13] and their participation in the Nation's military forces, indicate that Virginia's fears for the future of VMI may not be solidly grounded. . . .[15]

The State's misunderstanding and, in turn, the District Court's, is apparent from VMI's mission: to produce "citizen-soldiers," individuals "imbued with love of learning, confident in the functions and attitudes of leadership, possessing a high sense of public service, advocates of the American democracy and free enterprise system, and ready . . . to defend their country in time of national peril." . . .

Surely that goal is great enough to accommodate women, who today count as citizens in our American democracy equal in stature to men. Just as surely, the State's great goal is not substantially advanced by women's categorical exclusion, in total disregard of their individual merit, from the State's premier "citizen-soldier" corps.[16] Virginia, in sum, "has fallen far short of establishing the "exceedingly persuasive justification," " [*Hogan*], 458 U.S., at 731, that must be the solid base for any gender-defined classification.

---

13. Women cadets have graduated at the top of their class at every federal military academy.

15. Inclusion of women in settings where, traditionally, they were not wanted inevitably entails a period of adjustment. As one West Point cadet squad leader recounted, "[T]he classes of '78 and '79 see the women as women, but the classes of '80 and '81 see them as classmates." . . .

16. VMI has successfully managed another notable change. The school admitted its first African-American cadets in 1968. See The VMI Story 347-349 (students no longer sing "Dixie," salute the Confederate flag or the tomb of General Robert E. Lee at ceremonies and sports events). As the District Court noted, VMI established a Program on "retention of black cadets" designed to offer academic and social-cultural support to "minority members of a dominantly white and tradition-oriented student body." The school maintains a "special recruitment program for blacks" which, the District Court found, "has had little, if any, effect on VMI's method of accomplishing its mission."

VI

In the second phase of the litigation, Virginia presented its remedial plan — maintain VMI as a male-only college and create VWIL as a separate program for women. . . .

. . . The constitutional violation in this case is the categorical exclusion of women from an extraordinary educational opportunity afforded men. A proper remedy for an unconstitutional exclusion, we have explained, aims to "eliminate [so far as possible] the discriminatory effects of the past" and to "bar like discrimination in the future." Louisiana v. United States, 380 U.S. 145, 154 (1965).

Virginia chose not to eliminate, but to leave untouched, VMI's exclusionary policy. For women only, however, Virginia proposed a separate program, different in kind from VMI and unequal in tangible and intangible facilities. . . .

VWIL affords women no opportunity to experience the rigorous military training for which VMI is famed. . . . Instead, the VWIL program "deemphasize[s]" military education, and uses a "cooperative method" of education "which reinforces self-esteem."

VWIL students participate in ROTC and a "largely ceremonial" Virginia Corps of Cadets, but Virginia deliberately did not make VWIL a military institute. The VWIL House is not a military-style residence and VWIL students need not live together throughout the four year program, eat meals together, or wear uniforms during the school day. VWIL students thus do not experience the "barracks" life "crucial to the VMI experience," the spartan living arrangements designed to foster an "egalitarian ethic." "[T]he most important aspects of the VMI educational experience occur in the barracks," the District Court found, yet Virginia deemed that core experience nonessential, indeed inappropriate, for training its female citizen-soldiers.

VWIL students receive their "leadership training" in seminars, externships, and speaker series, episodes and encounters lacking the "[p]hysical rigor, mental stress, . . . minute regulation of behavior, and indoctrination in desirable values" made hallmarks of VMI's citizen-soldier training. Kept away from the pressures, hazards, and psychological bonding characteristic of VMI's adversative training, VWIL students will not know the "feeling of tremendous accomplishment" commonly experienced by VMI's successful cadets.

Virginia maintains that these methodological differences are "justified pedagogically," based on "important differences between men and women in learning and developmental needs," "psychological and sociological differences" Virginia describes as "real" and "not stereotypes." The Task Force charged with developing the leadership program for women, drawn from the staff and faculty at Mary Baldwin College, "determined that a military model and, especially VMI's adversative method, would be wholly inappropriate for educating and training *most women*." . . . [and noted that] while some women would be suited to and interested in [a VMI-style experience]," VMI's adversative method "would not be effective for *women as a group*"). . . .

As earlier stated, generalizations about "the way women are," estimates of what is appropriate for *most women*, no longer justify denying opportunity to women whose talent and capacity place them outside the average description. Notably, Virginia never asserted that VMI's method of education suits *most men*. It is also revealing that Virginia accounted for its failure to make the VWIL experience "the entirely militaristic experience of VMI" on the ground that VWIL "is planned for women who do not necessarily expect to pursue military careers." By that reasoning, VMI's "entirely militaristic" program would be inappropriate for men in general or *as a group*, for "[o]nly about 15% of VMI cadets enter career military service."

In contrast to the generalizations about women on which Virginia rests, we note again these dispositive realities: VMI's "implementing methodology" is not "inherently unsuitable to women," "some women . . . do well under [the] adversative model," "some women, at least, would want to attend [VMI] if they had the opportunity," "some women are capable of all of the individual activities required of VMI cadets," and "can meet the physical standards [VMI] now impose[s] on men." . . .

In myriad respects other than military training, VWIL does not qualify as VMI's equal. VWIL's student body, faculty, course offerings, and facilities hardly match VMI's. Nor can the VWIL graduate anticipate the benefits associated with VMI's 157-year history, the school's prestige, and its influential alumni network.

Mary Baldwin College, whose degree VWIL students will gain, enrolls first-year women with an average combined SAT score about 100 points lower than the average score for VMI freshmen. The Mary Baldwin faculty holds "significantly fewer Ph.D.'s," and receives substantially lower salaries than the faculty at VMI.

Mary Baldwin does not offer a VWIL student the range of curricular choices available to a VMI cadet. VMI awards baccalaureate degrees in liberal arts, biology, chemistry, civil engineering, electrical and computer engineering, and mechanical engineering. . . . VWIL students attend a school that "does not have a math and science focus," they cannot take at Mary Baldwin any courses in engineering or the advanced math and physics courses VMI offers. . . .

For physical training, Mary Baldwin has "two multi-purpose fields" and "[o]ne gymnasium." VMI has "an NCAA competition level indoor track and field facility; a number of multi-purpose fields; baseball, soccer and lacrosse fields; an obstacle course; large boxing, wrestling and martial arts facilities; an 11-laps-to-the-mile indoor running course; an indoor pool;

indoor and outdoor rifle ranges; and a football stadium that also contains a practice field and outdoor track."

Although Virginia has represented that it will provide equal financial support for in-state VWIL students and VMI cadets, and the VMI Foundation has agreed to endow VWIL with $5.4625 million, the difference between the two schools' financial reserves is pronounced. Mary Baldwin's endowment, currently about $19 million, will gain an additional $35 million based on future commitments; VMI's current endowment, $131 million — the largest per-student endowment in the Nation — will gain $220 million.

The VWIL student does not graduate with the advantage of a VMI degree. Her diploma does not unite her with the legions of VMI "graduates [who] have distinguished themselves" in military and civilian life. . . . A VWIL graduate cannot assume that the "network of business owners, corporations, VMI graduates and non-graduate employers . . . interested in hiring VMI graduates," will be equally responsive to her search for employment. . . .

Virginia, in sum, while maintaining VMI for men only, has failed to provide any "comparable single-gender women's institution." Instead, the Commonwealth has created a VWIL program fairly appraised as a "pale shadow" of VMI in terms of the range of curricular choices and faculty stature, funding, prestige, alumni support, and influence.

Virginia's VWIL solution is reminiscent of the remedy Texas proposed 50 years ago, in response to a state trial court's 1946 ruling that, given the equal protection guarantee, African Americans could not be denied a legal education at a state facility. . . . Reluctant to admit African Americans to its flagship University of Texas Law School, the State set up a separate school for Herman Sweatt and other black law students. As originally opened, the new school had no independent faculty or library, and it lacked accreditation. Nevertheless, the state trial and appellate courts were satisfied that the new school offered Sweatt opportunities for the study of law "substantially equivalent to those offered by the State to white students at the University of Texas."

Before this Court considered the case, the new school had gained "a faculty of five full-time professors; a student body of 23; a library of some 16,500 volumes serviced by a full-time staff; a practice court and legal aid association; and one alumnus who ha[d] become a member of the Texas Bar." This Court contrasted resources at the new school with those at the school from which Sweatt had been excluded. The University of Texas Law School had a full-time faculty of 16, a student body of 850, a library containing over 65,000 volumes, scholarship funds, a law review, and moot court facilities. [Sweatt v. Painter, 339 U.S. 629, 632-633 (1950).]

More important than the tangible features, the Court emphasized, are "those qualities which are incapable of objective measurement but which make for greatness" in a school, including "reputation of the faculty, experience of the administration, position and influence of the alumni, standing in the community, traditions and prestige." Facing the marked differences reported in the *Sweatt* opinion, the Court unanimously ruled that Texas had not shown "substantial equality in the [separate] educational opportunities" the State offered. Accordingly, the Court held, the Equal Protection Clause required Texas to admit African Americans to the University of Texas Law School. In line with *Sweatt*, we rule here that Virginia has not shown substantial equality in the separate educational opportunities the State supports at VWIL and VMI.

[Reversed and remanded.]

Justice THOMAS took no part in the consideration or decision of this case.

CHIEF JUSTICE REHNQUIST concurring in judgment. . . .

[U]nlike the majority, I would consider only evidence that postdates our decision in *Hogan*, and would draw no negative inferences from the State's actions before that time. I think that after *Hogan*, the State was entitled to reconsider its policy with respect to VMI, and to not have earlier justifications, or lack thereof, held against it.

Even if diversity in educational opportunity were the State's actual objective, the State's position would still be problematic. The difficulty with its position is that the diversity benefited only one sex; there was single-sex public education available for men at VMI, but no corresponding single-sex public education available for women. . . .

Had Virginia made a genuine effort to devote comparable public resources to a facility for women, and followed through on such a plan, it might well have avoided an equal protection violation. . . .

Justice SCALIA, dissenting.

Today the Court shuts down an institution that has served the people of the Commonwealth of Virginia with pride and distinction for over a century and a half. To achieve that desired result, it rejects (contrary to our established practice) the factual findings of two courts below, sweeps aside the precedents of this Court, and ignores the history of our people. As to facts: it explicitly rejects the finding that there exist "gender-based developmental differences" supporting Virginia's restriction of the "adversative" method to only a men's institution, and the finding that the all-male composition of the Virginia Military Institute (VMI) is essential to that institution's character. As to precedent: it drastically revises our established standards for reviewing sex-based classifications. And as to history: it counts for nothing the long tradition, enduring down to the present, of men's military colleges supported by both States and the Federal Government.

Much of the Court's opinion is devoted to deprecating the closed-mindedness of our forebears with regard to women's education, and even with regard to the treatment of women in areas that have nothing to do with education. Closed-minded they were — as every age is, including our own, with regard to matters it cannot guess, because it simply does not consider them debatable. The virtue of a democratic system with a First Amendment is that it readily enables the people, over time, to be persuaded that what they took for granted is not so, and to change their laws accordingly. That system is destroyed if the smug assurances of each age are removed from the democratic process and written into the Constitution. So to counterbalance the Court's criticism of our ancestors, let me say a word in their praise: they left us free to change. The same cannot be said of this most illiberal Court, which has embarked on a course of inscribing one after another of the current preferences of the society (and in some cases only the counter-majoritarian preferences of the society's law-trained elite) into our Basic Law. Today it enshrines the notion that no substantial educational value is to be served by an all-men's military academy — so that the decision by the people of Virginia to maintain such an institution denies equal protection to women who cannot attend that institution but can attend others. Since it is entirely clear that the Constitution of the United States — the old one — takes no sides in this educational debate, I dissent.

I . . .

[I]n my view the function of this Court is to *preserve* our society's values regarding (among other things) equal protection, not to *revise* them; to prevent backsliding from the degree of restriction the Constitution imposed upon democratic government, not to prescribe, on our own authority, progressively higher degrees. For that reason it is my view that, whatever abstract tests we may choose to devise, they cannot supersede — and indeed ought to be crafted *so as to reflect* — those constant and unbroken national traditions that embody the people's understanding of ambiguous constitutional texts. More specifically, it is my view that "when a practice not expressly prohibited by the text of the Bill of Rights bears the endorsement of a long tradition of open, widespread, and unchallenged use that dates back to the beginning of the Republic, we have no proper basis for striking it down." Rutan v. Republican Party of Ill., [497 U.S. 62, 95,] (1990) (Scalia, J., dissenting). The same applies, *mutatis mutandis*, to a practice asserted to be in violation of the post-Civil War Fourteenth Amendment. . . .

The all-male constitution of VMI comes squarely within such a governing tradition. Founded by the Commonwealth of Virginia in 1839 and continuously maintained by it since, VMI has always admitted only men. And in that regard it has not been unusual. For almost all of VMI's more than a century and a half of existence, its single-sex status reflected the uniform practice for government-supported military colleges. Another famous Southern institution, The Citadel, has existed as a state-funded school of South Carolina since 1842. And all the federal military colleges — West Point, the Naval Academy at Annapolis, and even the Air Force

Academy, which was not established until 1954 — admitted only males for most of their history. Their admission of women in 1976 (upon which the Court today relies), came not by court decree, but because the people, through their elected representatives, decreed a change. . . . In other words, the tradition of having government-funded military schools for men is as well rooted in the traditions of this country as the tradition of sending only men into military combat. The people may decide to change the one tradition, like the other, through democratic processes; but the assertion that either tradition has been unconstitutional through the centuries is not law, but politics-smuggled-into-law.

And the same applies, more broadly, to single-sex education in general, which, as I shall discuss, is threatened by today's decision with the cut-off of all state and federal support. Government-run *non*military educational institutions for the two sexes have until very recently also been part of our national tradition. "[It is] [c]oeducation, historically, [that] is a novel educational theory. From grade school through high school, college, and graduate and professional training, much of the Nation's population during much of our history has been educated in sexually segregated classrooms." Mississippi Univ. for Women v. Hogan, 458 U.S. 718, 736 (1982) (Powell, J., dissenting). These traditions may of course be changed by the democratic decisions of the people, as they largely have been.

Today, however, change is forced upon Virginia, and reversion to single-sex education is prohibited nationwide, not by democratic processes but by order of this Court. Even while bemoaning the sorry, bygone days of "fixed notions" concerning women's education, the Court favors current notions so fixedly that it is willing to write them into the Constitution of the United States by application of custom-built "tests." This is not the interpretation of a Constitution, but the creation of one.

II

To reject the Court's disposition today, however, it is not necessary to accept my view that the Court's made-up tests cannot displace longstanding national traditions as the primary determinant of what the Constitution means. It is only necessary to apply honestly the test the Court has been applying to sex-based classifications for the past two decades. . . . We have denominated this standard "intermediate scrutiny" and under it have inquired whether the statutory classification is "substantially related to an important governmental objective." . . .

Only the amorphous "exceedingly persuasive justification" phrase, and not the standard elaboration of intermediate scrutiny, can be made to yield this conclusion that VMI's single-sex composition is unconstitutional because there exist several women (or, one would have to conclude under the Court's reasoning, a single woman) willing and able to undertake VMI's program. Intermediate scrutiny has never required a least-restrictive-means analysis, but only a "substantial relation" between the classification and the state interests that it serves. . . .

Not content to execute a *de facto* abandonment of the intermediate scrutiny that has been our standard for sex-based classifications for some two decades, the Court purports to reserve the question whether, even in principle, a higher standard (i.e., strict scrutiny) should apply. . . . [The Court's] statements are misleading, insofar as they suggest that we have not already categorically *held* strict scrutiny to be inapplicable to sex-based classifications. . . . And the statements are irresponsible, insofar as they are calculated to destabilize current law. Our task is to clarify the law — not to muddy the waters, and not to exact over-compliance by intimidation. The States and the Federal Government are entitled to know *before they act* the standard to which they will be held, rather than be compelled to guess about the outcome of Supreme Court peek-a-boo.

The Court's intimations are particularly out of place because it is perfectly clear that, if the question of the applicable standard of review for sex-based classifications were to be regarded as an appropriate subject for reconsideration, the stronger argument would be not for elevating the standard to strict scrutiny, but for reducing it to rational-basis review. The latter certainly has a firmer foundation in our past jurisprudence: Whereas no majority of the Court has ever applied strict scrutiny in a case involving sex-based classifications, we routinely applied rational-basis review until the 1970's. . . .

It is hard to consider women a "discrete and insular minorit[y]" unable to employ the "political processes ordinarily to be relied upon," when they constitute a majority of the electorate. And the suggestion that they are incapable of exerting that political power smacks of the same paternalism that the Court so roundly condemns. Moreover, a long list of legislation proves the proposition false. . . .

III . . .

There can be no serious dispute that, as the District Court found, single-sex education and a distinctive educational method "represent legitimate contributions to diversity in the Virginia higher education system." As a theoretical matter, Virginia's educational interest would have been best served (insofar as the two factors we have mentioned are concerned) by six different types of public colleges — an all-men's, an all-women's, and a coeducational college run in the "adversative method," and an all-men's, an all-women's, and a coeducational college run in the "traditional method." But as a practical matter, of course, Virginia's financial resources, like any State's, are not limitless, and the Commonwealth must select among the available options. Virginia thus has decided to fund, in addition to some 14 coeducational 4-year colleges, one college that is run as an all-male school on the adversative model: the Virginia Military Institute.

Virginia did not make this determination regarding the make-up of its public college system on the unrealistic assumption that no other colleges exist. Substantial evidence in the District Court demonstrated that the Commonwealth has long proceeded on the principle that " '[h]igher education resources should be viewed as a whole — public and private' " — because such an approach enhances diversity and because " 'it is academic and economic waste to permit unwarranted duplication.' " It is thus significant that, whereas there are "four all-female private [colleges] in Virginia," there is only "one private all-male college," which "indicates that the private sector is providing for th[e] [former] form of education to a much greater extent that it provides for all-male education." In these circumstances, Virginia's election to fund one public all-male institution and one on the adversative model — and to concentrate its resources in a single entity that serves both these interests in diversity — is substantially related to the State's important educational interests. . . .

IV . . .

. . . Under the constitutional principles announced and applied today, single-sex public education is unconstitutional. By going through the motions of applying a balancing test — asking whether the State has adduced an "exceedingly persuasive justification" for its sex-based classification — the Court creates the illusion that government officials in some future case will have a clear shot at justifying some sort of single-sex public education. . . .

. . . [R]egardless of whether the Court's rationale leaves some small amount of room for lawyers to argue, it ensures that single-sex public education is functionally dead. The costs of litigating the constitutionality of a single-sex education program, and the risks of ultimately losing that litigation, are simply too high to be embraced by public officials. . . .

There are few extant single-sex public educational programs. The potential of today's decision for widespread disruption of existing institutions lies in its application to private single-sex education. Government support is immensely important to private educational institutions. Mary Baldwin College — which designed and runs VWIL — notes that private institutions of higher education in the 1990-1991 school year derived approximately 19 percent of their budgets from federal, state, and local government funds, *not including financial aid to students*. . . . [I]t is certainly not beyond the Court that rendered today's decision to hold that a donation to a single-sex college should be deemed contrary to public policy and therefore not deductible if the college discriminates on the basis of sex. . . .

The issue will be not whether government assistance turns private colleges into state actors, but whether the government *itself* would be violating the Constitution by providing state support to single-sex colleges. For example, in Norwood v. Harrison, [413 U.S. 455] (1973), we saw no room to distinguish between state operation of racially segregated schools and state support of privately run segregated schools. . . .

The only hope for state-assisted single-sex private schools is that the Court will not apply in the future the principles of law it has applied today. That is a substantial hope, I am happy and ashamed to say. After all, did not the Court today abandon the principles of law it has applied in our earlier sex-classification cases? And does not the Court positively invite private colleges to rely upon our ad-hocery by assuring them this case is "unique"? I would not advise the foundation of any new single-sex college (especially an all-male one) with the expectation of being allowed to receive any government support; but it is too soon to abandon in despair those single-sex colleges already in existence. It will certainly be possible for this Court to write a future opinion that ignores the broad principles of law set forth today, and that characterizes as utterly dispositive the opinion's perceptions that VMI was a uniquely prestigious all-male institution, conceived in chauvinism, etc., etc. I will not join that opinion. . . .

In an odd sort of way, it is precisely VMI's attachment to such old-fashioned concepts as manly "honor" that has made it, and the system it represents, the target of those who today succeed in abolishing public single-sex education. The record contains a booklet that all first-year VMI students (the so-called "rats") were required to keep in their possession at all times. Near the end there appears the following period-piece, entitled "The Code of a Gentleman":

> Without a strict observance of the fundamental Code of Honor, no man, no matter how "polished," can be considered a gentleman. The honor of a gentleman demands the inviolability of his word, and the incorruptibility of his principles. He is the descendant of the knight, the crusader; he is the defender of the defenseless and the champion of justice . . . or he is not a Gentleman.
> A Gentleman . . .
> Does not discuss his family affairs in public or with acquaintances.
> Does not speak more than casually about his girl friend.
> Does not go to a lady's house if he is affected by alcohol. He is temperate in the use of alcohol.
> Does not lose his temper; nor exhibit anger, fear, hate, embarrassment, ardor or hilarity in public.
> Does not hail a lady from a club window.
> A gentleman never discusses the merits or demerits of a lady.
> Does not mention names exactly as he avoids the mention of what things cost.
> Does not borrow money from a friend, except in dire need. Money borrowed is a debt of honor, and must be repaid as promptly as possible. Debts incurred by a deceased parent, brother, sister or grown child are assumed by honorable men as a debt of honor.

Does not display his wealth, money or possessions.

Does not put his manners on and off, whether in the club or in a ballroom. He treats people with courtesy, no matter what their social position may be.

Does not slap strangers on the back nor so much as lay a finger on a lady.

Does not "lick the boots of those above" nor "kick the face of those below him on the social ladder."

Does not take advantage of another's helplessness or ignorance and assumes that no gentleman will take advantage of him.

A Gentleman respects the reserves of others, but demands that others respect those which are his.

A Gentleman can become what he wills to be. . . .

I do not know whether the men of VMI lived by this Code; perhaps not. But it is powerfully impressive that a public institution of higher education still in existence sought to have them do so. I do not think any of us, women included, will be better off for its destruction.

Notes

1. The End of Single-Sex Colleges? At about the same time that VMI was under constitutional challenge, another military college, The Citadel, which had developed a substitute program for women that was not nearly as well thought out as VWIL, was held to be unconstitutional by the Fourth Circuit Court of Appeals. See Faulkner v. Jones, 66 F.3d 661 (4th Cir. 1995); Valorie K. Vojdik, At War: Narrative Tactics in The Citadel and VMI Litigation, 19 Harv. Women's L.J. 1 (1996) (summarizing tactical choices made in the *Faulkner* and *VMI* cases). The expert testimony in the *VMI* case relating to sex differences in education is reviewed and analyzed in Diane Avery, Institutional Myths, Historical Narratives and Social Science Evidence: Reading the "Record" in the *Virginia Military Institute* Case, 5 S. Cal. Rev. L. & Women's Stud. 189 (1996).

Kimberly Schuld criticizes the *VMI* case for using a "microscopic" perspective, which focuses on the individual level and ignores real sex differences, rather than a "macroscopic" perspective that "would examine the whole of society and the conglomerate of its offerings to determine whether males as a group and females as a group are offered relatively similar opportunities to make individual choices." See Kimberly M. Schuld, Rethinking Educational Equity: Sometimes, Different Can Be an Acceptable Substite for Equal, 1999 U. Chi. Legal F. 461, 469. Why isn't the "separate but equal" model that is applied to school sports just as applicable to the institutions themselves? Can an all-male state school be justified under any circumstances after *VMI*?

Mary Anne Case visited both VMI and VWIL after the *VMI* decision. She found the "rats" at VMI "a sorry lot — terrified, sweating, shaking, and exhausted . . . they were unable to tell their left feet from their right." By contrast nULLS (the VWIL equivalent to rats) were working together, learning the same values of accountability and discipline in a more supporting, encouraging, and non-intimidating environment. See Case, Two Cheers for Cheerleading: The Noisy Integration of VMI and the Quiet Success of Virginia Women in Leadership, 1999 U. Chi. Legal F. 347, 378. She noted, however, that VMI was still the more prestigious, sought-after alternative, even by many women.

> The paradoxes are many: First, the dominant class, men, have selected what appears to be the less attractive standard for themselves. Second, in part because they have selected it, this standard is assumed unquestionably to be desirable; inquiry into it is generally limited only to how far it will be extended to women. Much less attention is paid to whether the separate standard sought to be applied to women might in fact make some sense for women and men alike.

Case, supra, at 349. What do you make of this analysis? Reconsider it after you have read Chapters 4 and 5.

What is the impact of *VMI* on the constitutionality of all-women's colleges? Mississippi University for Women v. Hogan, 458 U.S. 718 (1982), cited in *VMI*, held that a traditionally all-female nursing school could not exclude men. In an opinion by Justice O'Connor, the Court reserved "in limited circumstances" the possibility that a gender-based classification favoring one sex might be justified "if it intentionally and directly assists members of the sex that is disproportionately burdened." Id. at 728. It rejected the compensatory purpose offered by the state in *Hogan*, however, based on the fact that the original mission of the school was not compensatory but rather reflected the stereotyped view of nursing as an exclusively woman's job. An emotional dissent written by Justice Powell and joined by Justice Rehnquist (Chief Justice Burger and Justice Blackmun wrote separate dissents) emphasized the strong and "honored" tradition of single-sex schools in this country, their benefits especially to women, and their contributions to educational diversity. Id. at 744. Justice Powell quoted from the Brief for the MUW Alumnae Association:

> . . . [I]n the aspect of life known as courtship or mate-pairing, the American female remains in the role of the pursued sex, expected to adorn and groom herself to attract the male. . . .
>
> An institution of collegiate higher learning maintained exclusively for women is uniquely able to provide the education atmosphere in which some, but not all, women can best attain maximum learning potential. It can serve to overcome the historic repression of the past and can orient a woman to function and achieve in the still male-dominated economy. It can free its students of the burden of playing the mating game while attending classes, thus giving academic rather than sexual emphasis.

458 U.S. at 739 (Powell, J., dissenting).

What significance should be given to history and tradition in evaluating all-women's colleges? Histories of women's education tell a story of the development of collegiate education for women because their " 'gentle,' 'unaspiring', and 'compliant' natures and heightened moral sensibilities rendered them particularly suitable for working with children." See Deborah L. Rhode, Association and Assimilation, 81 Nw. U.L. Rev. 106, 129 (1986). The expansion of educational opportunities for women raised considerable opposition based on doubts about women's physical and mental capacities.

> Critics assembled an array of "scientific" data: women's brains were too light, their foreheads too small, their powers of reasoning too inadequate for rigorous academic programs.

Id. at 130. Damage to women's reproductive capacities from rigorous study, referred to in footnote 9 of the *VMI* opinion, was also felt to be a possibility, perhaps because college-educated women were substantially less likely to marry and had lower reproductive rates than women generally. Rhode, supra, at 130. Rhode reports that even the defenders of higher education for women seemed somewhat ambivalent about its purposes.

> To some advocates of expanded female instruction, such as Catherine Beecher, the primary objective should be "the preparation of woman for her distinctive profession as housekeeper, mother, nurse, and chief educator of infancy and childhood. . . . [D]efenders of academic rigor . . . emphasized that the point of women's instruction in traditional disciplines was both to "enlarge their spheres of thought" and to render them "more interesting companions to men. . . ." Chemistry might be significant in its own right, but its principles were also applicable in the kitchen. . . . [Smith's] first president and early administrators denied that the college would produce competitors with men or diminish the "innate capacities which have even been the glory and charm of true womanhood."

Id. at 131-132 [citations omitted].

On the other hand, there is also impressive evidence that all-women's schools can be highly beneficial to women. Frequently cited as evidence is the fact that 59 women's colleges in the decades from 1910 to 1950 graduated twice as many women cited in Who's Who of American Women as did 289 coeducational colleges. See M. Elizabeth Tidball, Women's Colleges and Women Achievers Revisited, 5 Signs 505 (1980). Graduates of women's colleges constitute one-third of female board members of Fortune 1,000 companies, over 43 percent of female math doctorates, and over 50 percent of engineering doctorates, even though those colleges contribute less than four percent of total graduates. See Susan Estrich, For Girls' Schools and Women's Colleges: Separate Is Better, N.Y. Times, May 22, 1994, sec. 6, p. 39.

Research also documents practices at the college level that may help to undermine the benefits of co-education to women:

- When faculty members ask questions in class, "they mak[e] eye contact with men more often than with women, so that individual men students are more likely to feel recognized and encouraged to participate in class"

- Faculty members use tones that communicate interest, and "assume[] a posture of attentiveness (for example, leaning forward) when men speak" but a patronizing tone and inattentive posture (such as looking at the clock) when talking with women

- Faculty members call directly on men students more often than on women students, and are more likely to probe a male student's response to help the student work toward a fuller answer or explanation

- Faculty members call men students by name more often than women students, and credit comments and ideas to men but not to women;

- Faculty members "wait[] longer for men than for women to answer a question before going on to another student," and are more likely to interrupt a woman student

- Faculty members "ask[] women students questions that require factual answers . . . while asking men ["higher order"] questions that demand personal evaluation and critical thinking"

- Faculty members give longer and more complete responses to the questions of men students than to those of women students

- Faculty members "spontaneously offer[] to write letters of reference for men students but not for equally competent women students," and invite men, but not women, students to share authorships, accompany them on professional trips, and meet recognized scholars outside the department.

Katharine T. Bartlett & Jean O'Barr, The Chilly Climate on College Campuses: An Expansion of the "Hate Speech" Debate, 1990 Duke L.J. 574, 575-576 (citing Roberta M. Hall & Bernice R. Sandler, The Classroom Climate: A Chilly One for Women? 7-9 (Project on the Status and Education of Women 1982)). Have you observed any of these behaviors? Do they justify all-women's schools?

Justice Scalia strongly suggests that *VMI* puts even private single-sex education into jeopardy, making it unconstitutional for the government to provide any support to them. Whether he is right may depend, in part, on how close the "exceedingly persuasive justification" standard applied in *VMI* approaches the strict scrutiny test applied to cases of race-based discrimination, since public support of racially discriminatory private schools has been found to be unconstitutional. See Norwood v. Harrison, 413 U.S. 455 (1973). Note that this same "exceedingly persuasive justification" standard was articulated in *Hogan*, a case generally held as holding fast to an intermediate standard of review in sex cases. Is Justice Scalia correct that only by the highest level of scrutiny could the Court have found the exclusion of women from *VMI* to be unconstitutional?

The number of all women's colleges have declined from 300 in 1960 to 77 in 2000. In the past decade, however, the number of women attending all-women's colleges has increased 15 percent. See Jocelyn Anderson, Single-Sex Success: College Women Value Equality in Separateness, Chicago Tribune, June 21, 2000 (Woman News), at 2.

2. Single-Sex Schools at the Elementary and Secondary Level. Research documenting the loss of self-esteem among girls in their middle school years has also been used to argue in favor of all-female schools or all-female school programs. A 1991 study commissioned by the American Association of University Women points to profound differences between boys and girls as they progress through educational institutions, with girls experiencing a much steeper decline than boys in self-image and in career aspirations, especially those related to math and science:

> Girls, aged eight and nine, are confident, assertive, and feel authoritative about themselves. They emerge from adolescence with a poor self-image, constrained views of their future and their place in society, and much less confidence about themselves and their abilities. Sixty percent of elementary school girls say they are "happy the way I am," a core measure of personal self-esteem. More boys, 67 percent of those surveyed, also strongly agreed with the statement. Over the next eight years, girls' self-esteem falls 31 percentage points, with only 29 percent of high school girls saying they are happy with themselves. Almost half of the high school boys (46 percent) retain their high self-esteem. By high school, this gender gap increases from 7 points to 17 points.

Survey, Greenberg-Lake Analysis Group, Inc. & American Ass'n of Univ. Women, Shortchanging Girls, Shortchanging America 4 (1991). The survey finds a strong relationship between math and science confidence and adolescent self-esteem: students with higher self-esteem like math and science more. Id. at 12, 16. Most elementary school students have confidence in their ability to do math, with boys having a higher level of confidence (81 percent of girls like math, as compared to 84 percent of boys). The interest of adolescents in math drops far more precipitously for girls (to 61 percent for girls and 74 percent for boys). Id. at 12. Interestingly, when adjusted for race, black girls and Hispanic girls have higher self-esteem measures in elementary school than white girls, and do not reach as low a level in high school (white girls move from 55 high self-esteem to 22 percent; black girls from 65 percent to 58 percent; and Hispanic girls move from 68 percent to 30 percent). Id. at 9.

Peer sexual harassment of girls in schools can also contribute to an environment that is said to undermine self esteem. This issue is discussed in Chapter 4.

Some experts dispute the research showing the relative decline of girls' performance and self-esteem in schools. Psychologist Judith Kleinfeld charges that the AAUW's conclusion that schools shortchange girls is based on "soft and slippery issues, like the 'silencing' of girls in the classroom," rather than on educational achievement tests, college entrance and graduation rates, and earning of advanced degrees. See Judith Kleinfeld, The Myth That Schools Shortchange Girls: Social Science in the Service of Deception (Women's Freedom Network 1998), reported in Kimberly M. Schuld, Rethinking Education Equity: Sometimes, Different Can Be an Acceptable Substitute for Equal, 1999 U. Chi. Legal F. 461, 472-475. Kleinfeld concludes that when these measures are analyzed, from elementary school through college, females receive higher grades, obtain higher class marks, and receive more honors in every field but schience and sports. On standardized tests, while boys do better in mathematics, science, and geopolitics, the margins are small; girls do better in reading achievement, and surpass boys in writing skills by a significant amount. Schuld, supra, at 475. Gender differences are most visible in the top 10 percent of self-selected populations taking standardized tests than in the student population as a whole. Boys are more likely to be at the bottom of their class in schools or assigned to special education classes. Id. Similar conclusions were reached in a large-scale quantitative 1997 study commissioned by the Metropolitan Life Insurance Company Foundation, which measured faculty perceptions as well as students', and linked perceptions to various academic measures, classroom interactions, intentions to complete advanced studies, and interest in extracurricular activities. The study found that girls come out ahead of boys in terms of various self-esteem measures, such as being listened to in class and receiving helpful feedback from their teachers. Like Kleinfeld, the MetLife study found larger gender differences for self-selected high-stakes test-takers than for national representative samples, and like the AAUW study, found that minority girls hold the most optimistic views of the future, while minority boys are the most discouraged about the future and the least interested in getting a good education. Schuld, supra, at 476-477. Further discussion of the closing of the gender gap with respect to math test scores is on pages 301-302.

For other critiques, see Christina Hoff Sommers, Capitol Hill's Girl Trouble, Wash. Post C1 (July 17, 1994), reported in Schuld, supra, at 473 (AAUW only counted as positive the response "always true" to the question "I am happy the way I am"; if it had counted also "sort of true" and "sometimes true/sometimes false," only 12 percent of girls would have self-identified as genuinely unhappy); Kingsley R. Brown, Sex and Temperament in Modern Society: A Darwinian View of the Glass Ceiling and the Gender Gap, 37 Ariz. L. Rev. 972, 1032 (1995) (with respect to the AAUW's conclusion about boys' higher self-esteem, a "plausible explanation . . . is that it was measuring self-deception and braggadocio (and perhaps immaturity) rather than self-esteem"). See also Nancy Levit, Separating Equals: Educational Research and the Long-Term Consequences of Sex Segregation, 67 Geo. Wash. L. Rev. 451, 485-492 (1999) (reviewing the literature, much of it conflicting, and concluding that while girls who attend all-girls schools develop, on average, higher self-esteem, they do not benefit from higher achievement levels.)

Single-sex experimentation in public middle- and high-school education is on the rise. In 1996, a public all-girls school, the Young Women's Leadership School, was established in East Harlem in New York City. In 1997, the U.S. Department of Education found that the school violated anti-discrimination laws, but it was allowed to remain open on the provision that it create similar opportunities for boys. Its counterpart, the John Cleveland Charter School, opened in the fall of 2001, and will eventually serve boys from grades 6-12. Alison Gendar, Levy Backs All-Boys School: Harlem Charter Site to Open in Fall for 100 6th-Graders, Daily News, April 28, 2001, at 12. Does *VMI* permit these two schools to exist? See Denise C. Morgan, Anti-Subordination Analysis after United States v. Virginia: Evaluating the Constitutionality of K-12 Single-Sex Public Schools, 1999 U. Chi. Legal F. 381, 458 (no). Another Young Women's Leadership School opened in Chicago in 2000, apparently without an all-male counterpart. See Lauren Cowen, A Class of Their Own: A Girls Charter School Leaves Boys Out of the Equation, Chicago Tribune, Oct. 1, 2000 (Magazine), at 12. Could this school pass muster under *VMI?* See Amy H. Nemko, Single-Sex Public Education After *VMI*: The Case for Women's Schools, 20 Harv. Women's L.J. 19 (1998) (yes).

Public schools in 15 states are experimenting with single-sex education, most often in separate math and science classes for girls. See Elizabeth Zwerling, California Study: Single-Sex Schools No Cure-all, Women's e-news, at http://www.womensnews.org/article.cfm. In California, six all-girls and six all-boys schools were begun as pilot projects, but within three years, all but two of them had closed, lacking sufficient constituencies. These schools were originally envisioned as specialized academies with all-male programs for at-risk boys and all-female schools that focused on math and science. But federal law was interpreted to require identical curricula, which researchers believed contributed to the lack of support for the schools. One report concluded that to be successful, all-girls schools must not only promote self-esteem, gender identity and enhanced achievement, but "the school must be driven by an agenda of gender-equitable education," one of the purposes of which is to "challeng[e] societal assumptions about gender." Id. What could this mean and is it a valid goal of public education?

Private all-girls' schools are also on the rise. See Doug Cummings, A School of Their Own: Atlanta Girls' School Plan to Open in August at an Undetermined Site Inside the Perimeter, The Atlanta Journal and Constitution, Oct. 15, 1999, at 1H.

Some claim that girls are now doing better in education than boys, being less likely to repeat a grade, have a learning disability, or have their parents called at home to report a problem, and more likely to get better grades and higher scores on standardized tests in reading and writing. Women now make up 56 percent of college enrollments, and as college freshmen they spend more time doing volunteer work and participating in student clubs. See Jodi Wilgoren, Girls Rule: Girls Outperform Boys in High School and in College Enrollment Rates, New York Times Upfront, March 5, 2001, vol. 133, No. 13, at 8. Is this a problem? Philosopher Christina Hoff Sommers thinks so. For her popular treatment of the subject, see Sommers, The War Against Boys: How Misguided Feminism is Harming Our Young Men (2000).

3. Reconsidering Sex-Segregated Sports.   If you think all-women's schools or academic programs are problematic, reconsider all-women's sports teams. Are either all-men's, or all-women's, sports teams valid after *VMI?* See Dana Robinson, A League of Their Own: Do Women Want Sex-Segregated Sports? 9 J. Contemp. Legal Issues 321, 354 (1998) (*VMI* requires that "a team must allow the excluded sex when that team offers tangible and intangible benefits that are far greater than those offered by the excluded sex's team").

4. The Race/Sex Analogy.   Justice Scalia's dissent provides the occasion, once again, to rethink the race-sex analogy. Is government support for single-sex private women's colleges distinguishable from government support for private colleges that discriminate based on race? Should it matter which race, and which sex, the school is meant to serve?

Over the past decade, schools designed to address the special problems of African American males have been planned in Baltimore, Chicago, Detroit, Milwaukee, New York, San Diego, and Washington, D.C.. Minneapolis and Milwaukee have established co-educational schools for African American children. See Pamela J. Smith, Comment, All-Male Black Schools and the Equal Protection Clause: A Step Forward Toward Education, 66 Tul. L. Rev. 2003, 2006 & n.7 (1992).

Proponents of the Detroit plan detail the following "host of ills plaguing Black male teenagers":

> . . . [I]n 1989, the unemployment rate for African American males living in Detroit was 18.3% compared with 7.1% for all males in the state of Michigan. The homicide rate for Black males between ages fifteen and twenty-four in Wayne County, Michigan is fourteen times the national rate for all

males, twice the rate for African American males in the State of Michigan, and forty-seven times the homicide rate for white males in Michigan.

. . . Fifty-four percent of Detroit boys eventually drop out of school and over 66% receive suspensions. Boys fall further behind the national average academically in almost every successive year of elementary and secondary school. In the first grade, boys perform at or above grade level on academic achievement tests. By the twelfth grade, boys' achievement is over two grades behind in reading and over three grades behind in mathematics. The report also shows a disparity in academic performance between girls and boys in the Detroit school system. The male dropout rate is approximately 10% higher than the female dropout rate. Boys are suspended three times as often as girls, and boys consistently score lower than girls on standardized reading and math tests. . . .

. . . [E]lementary and adolescent boys often need greater discipline than girls in the same age group. The high suspension rates in Detroit testify to the acute disciplinary problems of Black boys. Some educators argue that young boys misbehave in class to impress young girls and that gender separation might alleviate social pressures that distract both boys and girls from their studies. . . . In the end, this arrangement would provide a better education for both boys and girls. Many educators also maintain that single-sex schools should employ a high proportion of Black male teachers because Black boys — often abandoned by their fathers — need Black male role models.

. . . [P]rograms designed specifically to address Black male violence might prove more successful in an all-male environment than in a coeducational environment. [E]ducators argue that because it is Black males that are "killing each other," schools should target violence prevention programs at them. Similarly, if disrespect for Black women leads Black men to engage in irresponsible sexual behavior or to eschew family responsibilities, then the schools should implement programs specifically designed to change male behavior.

Note, Inner-City Single-Sex Schools: Educational Reform or Invidious Discrimination? 105 Harv. L. Rev. 1741, 1743-1744 (1992).

One of the supporters of these resegregated schools, Judge Robert Carter, is a former NAACP attorney who worked on Brown v. Board of Education. While Judge Carter helped to litigate the concept of equality pursued in *Brown* that depended on the presence of white children, he has since sought to shift the focus from who attends schools with blacks to the quality of education offered in those schools. Robert Carter, A Reassessment of *Brown v. Board*, in Shades of Brown: New Perspectives on School Desegregation 21 (Derrick Bell ed., 1980). See also Derrick Bell, A Model Alternative Desegregation Plan, in Shades of Brown, supra, at 125 (goal of equal educational opportunity should not be racial balance, but empowerment of black communities that comes with strong black leadership, parental involvement, reinforcement of children's feelings of self-worth, and equal funding and educational standards for schools in black communities).

Note that the defense of all-male, all-black schools, above, has both comparative and qualitative components. Much of the emphasis is on the extent to which the problems of African-American males are greater than those of any other groups. See also Smith, supra, 66 Tul. L. Rev. at 2039 (defending all-male, all-black schools on the grounds that the life expectancy for males is 14 years less than that for females, and that black men are over five times more likely than black females to be incarcerated). Recall that researchers seem to agree that black males rank far lower in self-esteem than black women. See pages 402-403, supra. The qualitative component emphasizes not the degree of crisis in which black males find themselves, but the uniqueness of their educational needs. Which of these components is most important in defending all-male schools under the equal protection clause?

In Garrett v. Board of Education of School District of Detroit, 775 F. Supp. 1004 (E.D. Mich. 1991), plaintiffs successfully challenged the exclusion of girls from the Detroit all-male academies, which were held to violate both the federal and the state constitutions, as well as Title IX. Critics of the academies focused both on the exclusion of females and on the programmatic, Afrocentric focus.

> . . . Such programs are often replete with African-style, sexist "rites of passage" to manhood. By placing an emphasis on racial identity, these programs, such as the one at an all black academy in Los Angeles, encourage black boys to "think black, act black, speak black, buy black, pray black, love black and live black." Such schools are dedicated not to free inquiry and critical thought, but to indoctrination and ideological programming. Some choose to focus on the seven principles of Kwanzaa, which indoctrinate students with such ideological concepts as racial identity and "faith in our [racial and political] leaders." [Michael Meyers, All-Male, Black Schools Unequal, Oregonian, Sept. 30, 1992, at C9.] If such repeat-after-me schooling were designed for white students, one doubts whether educational authorities would tolerate such drivel, much less allow such schools to be subsidized by taxpayers. . . .
>
> The all-male black school is also paternalistic. It stigmatizes boys, ignores girls, and brazenly discounts women as capable teachers of boys. In the minds of all-male black school advocates, only males can teach boys to become men. Shockingly, advocates of this segregation blame black boys' parents, their homelives, and their loose morals for their underachievement. These separatists overgeneralize black males' social problems, using these problems as a scapegoat.

Michael Meyers, The Non-Viability of Single-Race, Single-Sex Schools, 21 N.Y.U. Rev. L. & Soc. Change 663, 665-666 (1994-1995). Is this a fair critique? From the substantive equality viewpoint, what is the response to it?

Critics of male-only black schools also pointed to the fact that the overall school drop-out rates for African-American females (12%) is close to the rate for males (13.5%). Boys and girls both leave school because they feel unsuccessful and do not achieve; girls, however, are more likely to leave school to help take care of their families or as a result of early pregnancy. In fact, 40 percent of the 10.6% of African-American girls who drop out of school do so because of pregnancy. Michelle Fine, Framing Dropouts 20 n.9 (1991). The homicide rate for young African-American females is four to five times that for young white women, although not as high as the seven to eight times rate differential between African-American and white male youths. African-American girls, in comparison with other girls and African-American boys, have a heightened sensitivity about their bodies and an awareness of their expected participation in domestic and household work. Teachers tend to underestimate their abilities, and they have lower self-esteem than African-American males, despite higher actual performance. Why do you suppose there has not been an effort, of the sort directed at the problems of African-American male youths, to address the needs of African-American girls?

> Although the view persists that schools for pregnant and parenting students represent such an effort, schools for pregnant students are in fact modeled on educational programs for temporarily disabled students, and schools for parenting students were created to benefit students who have primary responsibility for raising their children. The perpetuated notion that these schools are intended only for girls illustrates the tenacity of sex-role stereotyping in this society.

Walteen Grady Truely and Martha F. Davis, Public Education Programs for African-American Males: A Gender Equity Perspective, 21 N.Y.U. Rev. L. & Soc. Change 725, 732-734 (1994-1995).

All-black academies certainly would not be sustainable under existing race discrimination law. Under City of Richmond v. J.A. Croson Co., 488 U.S. 469 (1989), educators who seek all-black as well as all-male schools would have the almost impossible task of showing that these schools are a narrowly tailored means to address specific prior intentional discrimination against the group receiving the preference or to achieve a compelling state purpose. General societal discrimination will not do. As a practical matter, however, the "reverse race discrimination" issue does not arise because given the almost nonexistent white population in the inner city, only the exclusion of females, not whites, appears to be necessary to meet the purposes of these programs.

No authority contradicts *Garrett*, and it would appear that all-male public educational opportunities are also unacceptable. Those programs that have proceeded, as did the program in Detroit, have had to accept girls. See Daniel Gardenswartz, Public Education: An Inner-City Crisis! Single-Sex Schools: An Inner City Answer?, 42 Emory L.J. 591, 644 (1993) (arguing that because of the "urban crisis in our inner-cities," single-sex schools should be allowed provided they don't serve as detriments to females who are not included). According to one source, however, the intention of such programs continues to be "to cater to the needs of males." See Helaine Greenfield, Note, Some Constitutional Problems with the Resegregation of Public Schools, 80 Geo. L.J. 363, 370, 373 (1991). On what theory, if any, are schools that are open to girls, but designed for the "special needs" of boys, objectionable?

Putting Theory into Practice

3-6. A female Women's Studies professor at a co-educational college does not let men enroll in her feminist ethics course, arguing that, in her experience, male students inhibit the participation of women. As an alternative for male students, she offers one-on-one tutorials, which about two dozen men have taken since she began teaching in 1966. She is sued by a male student under Title IX, and under the Fourteenth Amendment's Equal Protection Clause. Who should win? See *Mary Daly v. Boston College*: The Impermissibility of Single-Sex Classrooms Within a Private University, Maryam Ahranjani 9 J. Gender, Soc. Pol'y & L. 179 (2001).

3-7. A group of law faculty are considering the formation of a new, all-women's law school based on data about women's comparative performance disadvantage collected at the University of California at Berkeley School of Law (Boalt Hall), Stanford Law School, Yale Law School, and the University of Pennsylvania Law School. See pages 853-857. They seek your advice on whether such an institution would be legal. What do you tell them? Of what relevance is data from other co-educational law schools showing that women law students perform well in comparison to men? Compare Jennifer Gerarda Brown, "To Give Them Countenance": The Case for a Women's Law School, 22 Harv. Women's L.J. 1 (1999) (favoring all-women's law school), with Jennifer Gerarda Brown, Apostasy?, 75 Chi.-Kent L. Rev. 837 (2000) (citing growing empirical evidence leading her to question her early proposal for a woman's law school and exploring costs to men excluded from all-female schools); Shannan N. Ball, Note, Separate But Equal Is Unequal: The Argument Against an All-Women's Law School, 15 Notre Dame J.L. Ethics & Pub. Pol'y 171 (2001) (opposing all-women's law school).

c. Equality in School Athletic Programs

Cohen v. Brown University

101 F.3d 155 (1st Cir. 1996), cert. denied, 520 U.S. 1186 (1997)

BOWNES, Senior Circuit Judge.

This is a class action lawsuit charging Brown University, its president, and its athletics director (collectively "Brown") with discrimination against women in the operation of its intercollegiate athletics program, in violation of Title IX of the Education Amendments of 1972, 20 U.S.C. §§1681-1688 ("Title IX"), and its implementing regulations, 34 C.F.R. §§106.1-106.71. The plaintiff class comprises all present, future, and potential Brown University women students who participate, seek to participate, and/or are deterred from participating in intercollegiate athletics funded by Brown.

This suit was initiated in response to the demotion in May 1991 of Brown's women's gymnastics and volleyball teams from university-funded varsity status to donor-funded varsity status. Contemporaneously, Brown demoted two men's teams, water polo and golf, from university-funded to donor-funded varsity status. As a consequence of these demotions, all four teams lost, not only their university funding, but most of the support and privileges that accompany university-funded varsity status at Brown.

[The District Court granted plaintiffs' request for a preliminary injunction, reinstating the women's gymnastics and volleyball teams to university-funded varsity status and prohibiting Brown from eliminating or reducing the status of any women's varsity team pending the outcome of a trial on the merits. On appeal, a panel of the 1st Circuit affirmed, and remanded for a trial on the merits. Following a bench trial, the District Court found Brown to be in violation of Title IX, and ordered a comprehensive plan for compliance be submitted. The Court found the plan submitted was not comprehensive and did not comply with the opinion. The Court rejected the plan and ordered Brown to elevate and maintain at university-funded varsity status the women's teams.]

. . . Brown challenges on constitutional and statutory grounds the test employed by the district court in determining whether Brown's intercollegiate athletics program complies with Title IX. . . .

I . . .

As a Division I institution within the National Collegiate Athletic Association ("NCAA") with respect to all sports but football, Brown participates at the highest level of NCAA competition. Brown operates a two-tiered intercollegiate athletics program with respect to funding: although Brown provides the financial resources required to maintain its university-funded varsity teams, donor-funded varsity athletes must themselves raise the funds necessary to support their teams through private donations. The district court found . . . that it is difficult for donor-funded varsity athletes to maintain a level of competitiveness commensurate with their abilities and that these athletes operate at a competitive disadvantage in comparison to university-funded varsity athletes. . . .

Brown's decision to demote the women's volleyball and gymnastics teams and the men's water polo and golf teams from university-funded varsity status was apparently made in response to a university-wide cost-cutting directive. The district court found that Brown saved $62,028 by demoting the women's teams and $15,795 by demoting the men's teams, but that the demotions "did not appreciably affect the athletic participation gender ratio." . . .

Plaintiffs alleged that, at the time of the demotions, the men students at Brown already enjoyed the benefits of a disproportionately large share of both the university resources allocated to athletics and the intercollegiate participation opportunities afforded to student athletes. Thus, plaintiffs contended, what appeared to be the even-handed demotions of two men's and two women's teams, in fact, perpetuated Brown's discriminatory treatment of women in the administration of its intercollegiate athletics program.

. . . The district court . . . summarized the history of athletics at Brown, finding, *inter alia*, that, while nearly all of the men's varsity teams were established before 1927, virtually all of the women's varsity teams were created between 1971 and 1977, after Brown's merger with Pembroke College. The only women's varsity team created after this period was winter track, in 1982. . . .

. . . . [T]he district court found that, in 1993-94, there were 897 students participating in intercollegiate varsity athletics, of which 61.87% (555) were men and 38.13% (342) were women. During the same period, Brown's undergraduate enrollment comprised 5,722 students, of which 48.86% (2,796) were men and 51.14% (2,926) were women. . . . [I]n 1993-94, Brown's intercollegiate athletics program consisted of 32 teams, 16 men's teams and 16 women's teams. Of the university-funded teams, 12 were men's teams and 13 were women's teams; of the donor-funded teams, three were women's teams and four were men's teams. At the time of trial, Brown offered 479 university-funded varsity positions for men, as compared to 312 for women; and 76 donor-funded varsity positions for men, as compared to 30 for women. In 1993-94, then, Brown's varsity program — including both university- and donor-funded sports — afforded over 200 more positions for men than for women. Accordingly, the district court found that Brown maintained a 13.01% disparity between female participation in intercollegiate athletics and female student enrollment, and that "[a]lthough the number of varsity sports offered to men and women are equal, the selection of sports offered to each gender generates far more individual positions for male athletes than for female athletes." . . . .

The district court found from extensive testimony that the donor-funded women's gymnastics, women's fencing and women's ski teams, as well as at least one women's club team, the water polo team, had demonstrated the interest and ability to compete at the top varsity level and would benefit from university funding. . . .

The district court did not find that full and effective accommodation of the athletics interests and abilities of Brown's female students would disadvantage Brown's male students.

II

Title IX provides that "[n]o person in the United States shall, on the basis of sex, be excluded from participation in, be denied the benefits of, or be subjected to discrimination under any education program or activity receiving Federal financial assistance." 20 U.S.C.A. §1681(a) (West 1990). As a private institution that receives federal financial assistance, Brown is required to comply with Title IX.

Title IX also specifies that its prohibition against gender discrimination shall not "be interpreted to require any educational institution to grant preferential or disparate treatment to the members of one sex on account of an imbalance which may exist" between the total number or percentage of persons of that sex participating in any federally supported program or activity, and "the total number or percentage of persons of that sex in any community, State, section, or other area." 20 U.S.C.A. §1681(b) (West 1990). Subsection (b) also provides, however, that it "shall not be construed to prevent the consideration in any . . . proceeding under this chapter of statistical evidence tending to show that such an imbalance exists with respect to the participation in, or receipt of the benefits of, any such program or activity by the members of one sex." Id.

Applying §1681(b), the prior panel held that Title IX "does not mandate strict numerical equality between the gender balance of a college's athletic program and the gender balance of its student body." The panel explained that, while evidence of a gender-based disparity in an institution's athletics program is relevant to a determination of noncompliance, "a court assessing Title IX compliance may not find a violation solely because there is a disparity between the gender composition of an educational institution's student constituency, on the one hand, and its athletic programs, on the other hand." . . .

Congress enacted Title IX in response to its finding — after extensive hearings held in 1970 by the House Special Subcommittee on Education — of pervasive discrimination against women with respect to educational opportunities. 118 Cong. Rec. 5804 (1972) (remarks of Sen. Bayh). . . .

The agency responsible for administering Title IX is the United States Department of Education ("DED"), through its Office for Civil Rights ("OCR"). Congress expressly delegated to DED the authority to promulgate regulations for determining whether an athletics program complies with Title IX. Pub. L. No. 93-380, 88 Stat. 612 (1974). The regulations specifically address athletics at 34 C.F.R. §§106.37(c) and 106.41. The regulation at issue in this case, 34 C.F.R. §106.41 (1995), provides:

(a) *General.* No person shall, on the basis of sex, be excluded from participation in, be denied the benefits of, be treated differently from another person or otherwise be discriminated against in any interscholastic, intercollegiate, club or intramural athletics offered by a recipient, and no recipient shall provide any such athletics separately on such basis.

(b) *Separate teams.* Notwithstanding the requirements of paragraph (a) of this section, a recipient may operate or sponsor separate teams for members of each sex where selection of such teams is based upon competitive skill or the activity involved is a contact sport. However, where a recipient operates or sponsors a team in a particular sport for members of one sex but operates or sponsors no such team for members of the other sex, and athletic opportunities for members of that sex have previously been limited, members of the excluded sex must be allowed to try-out for the team offered unless the sport involved is a contact sport. For the purposes of this part, contact sports include boxing, wrestling, rugby, ice hockey, football, basketball and other sports the purpose or major activity of which involves bodily contact.

(c) *Equal Opportunity.* A recipient which operates or sponsors interscholastic, intercollegiate, club or intramural athletics shall provide equal athletic opportunity for members of both sexes. In determining whether equal opportunities are available the Director will consider, among other factors:

(1) Whether the selection of sports and levels of competition effectively accommodate the interests and abilities of members of both sexes;

(2) The provision of equipment and supplies;

(3) Scheduling of games and practice time;

(4) Travel and per diem allowance;

(5) Opportunity to receive coaching and academic tutoring;

(6) Assignment and compensation for coaches and tutors;

(7) Provision of locker rooms, practice and competitive facilities;

(8) Provision of medical and training facilities and services;

(9) Provision of housing and dining facilities and services;

(10) Publicity. . . .

In 1978, several years after the promulgation of the regulations, OCR published a proposed "Policy Interpretation," the purpose of which was to clarify the obligations of federal aid recipients under Title IX to provide equal opportunities in athletics programs. . . . At issue in this appeal is the proper interpretation of the . . . so-called three-part test,[7] which inquires as follows:

(1) Whether intercollegiate level participation opportunities for male and female students are provided in numbers substantially proportionate to their respective enrollments; or

(2) Where the members of one sex have been and are underrepresented among intercollegiate athletes, whether the institution can show a history and continuing practice of program expansion which is demonstrably responsive to the developing interest and abilities of the members of that sex; or

(3) Where the members of one sex are underrepresented among intercollegiate athletes, and the institution cannot show a continuing practice of program expansion such as that cited above, whether it can be demonstrated that the interests and abilities of the members of that sex have been fully and effectively accommodated by the present program.

44 Fed. Reg. at 71,418.

The district court held that, "because Brown maintains a 13.01% disparity between female participation in intercollegiate athletics and female student enrollment, it cannot gain the protection of prong one." Nor did Brown satisfy prong two. While acknowledging that Brown "has an impressive history of program expansion," the district court found that Brown failed to demonstrate that it has "maintained a *continuing practice* of intercollegiate program expansion for women, the underrepresented sex." The court noted further that, because merely reducing program offerings to the overrepresented gender does not constitute program expansion for the underrepresented gender, the fact that Brown has eliminated or demoted several men's teams does not amount to a continuing practice of program expansion for women. As to prong three, the district court found that Brown had not "fully and effectively accommodated the interest and ability of the underrepresented sex 'to the extent necessary to provide equal opportunity in the selection of sports and levels of competition available to members of both sexes.'" . . .

The district court found that Brown predetermines the approximate number of varsity positions available to men and women, and, thus, that "the concept of any measure of unfilled but available athletic slots does not comport with reality." The district court concluded that intercollegiate athletics opportunities "means real opportunities, not illusory ones, and therefore should be measured by counting *actual participants*." . . .

---

7. For clarification, we note that the cases refer to each part of this three-part test as a "prong" or a "benchmark." Prong one is also called the "substantial proportionality test."

IV

Brown contends that . . . the district court's interpretation and application of the test is irreconcilable with the statute, the regulation, and the agency's interpretation of the law, and effectively renders Title IX an "affirmative action statute" that mandates preferential treatment for women by imposing quotas in excess of women's relative interests and abilities in athletics. Brown asserts, in the alternative, that if the district court properly construed the test, then the test itself violates Title IX and the United States Constitution. . . .

Brown's talismanic incantation of "affirmative action" has no legal application to this case and is not helpful to Brown's cause. While "affirmative action" may have different connotations as a matter of politics, as a matter of law, its meaning is more circumscribed. True affirmative action cases have historically involved a voluntary undertaking to remedy discrimination (as in a program implemented by a governmental body, or by a private employer or institution), by means of specific group-based preferences or numerical goals, and a specific timetable for achieving those goals. See Adarand [Const., Inc. v. Pena], [115 S. Ct. 2097] (1995) (remanding for review under strict scrutiny a challenge to a federal statute establishing a government-wide goal for awarding to minority businesses not less than 5% of the total value of all prime contracts and subcontracts for each fiscal year); . . . Johnson v. Transportation Agency, [480 U.S. 616] (1986) (upholding a temporary program authorizing a county agency to consider sex and race as factors in making promotions in order to achieve a statistically measurable improvement in the representation of women and minorities in major job classifications in which they had been historically underrepresented). . . .

Title IX is not an affirmative action statute; it is an anti-discrimination statute, modeled explicitly after another anti-discrimination statute, Title VI [42 U.S.C. §2000d et seq.]. No aspect of the Title IX regime at issue in this case — inclusive of the statute, the relevant regulation, and the pertinent agency documents — mandates gender-based preferences or quotas, or specific timetables for implementing numerical goals.

Like other anti-discrimination statutory schemes, the Title IX regime *permits* affirmative action. In addition, Title IX, like other anti-discrimination schemes, permits an inference that a significant gender-based statistical disparity may indicate the existence of discrimination. Consistent with the school desegregation cases, the question of substantial proportionality under the Policy Interpretation's three-part test is merely the starting point for analysis, rather than the conclusion; a rebuttable presumption, rather than an inflexible requirement. . . . In short, the substantial proportionality test is but one aspect of the inquiry into whether an institution's athletics program complies with Title IX. . . .

Another important distinction between this case and affirmative action cases is that the district court's remedy requiring Brown to accommodate fully and effectively the athletics interests and abilities of its women students does not raise the concerns underlying the Supreme Court's requirement of a particularized factual predicate to justify voluntary affirmative action plans. In reviewing equal protection challenges to such plans, the Court is concerned that government bodies are reaching out to implement race- or gender-conscious remedial measures that are "ageless in their reach into the past, and timeless in their ability to affect the future," . . . on the basis of facts insufficient to support a prima facie case of a constitutional or statutory violation, . . . to the benefit of unidentified victims of past discrimination. . . .

From a constitutional standpoint, the case before us is altogether different. Here, gender-conscious relief was ordered by an Article III court, constitutionally compelled to have before it litigants with standing to raise the cause of action alleged; for the purpose of providing relief upon a duly adjudicated determination that specific defendants had discriminated against a certified class of women in violation of a federal anti-discrimination statute; based upon findings of fact that were subject to the Federal Rules of Evidence. . . .

From the mere fact that a remedy flowing from a judicial determination of discrimination is gender-conscious, it does not follow that the remedy constitutes "affirmative action." Nor does a "reverse discrimination" claim arise every time an anti-discrimination statute is enforced. While some gender-conscious relief may adversely impact one gender — a fact that has not been demonstrated in this case — that alone would not make the relief "affirmative action" or the consequence of that relief "reverse discrimination." . . .

Brown maintains that the district court's decision imposes upon universities the obligation to engage in preferential treatment for women by requiring quotas in excess of women's relative interests and abilities. With respect to prong three, Brown asserts that the district court's interpretation of the word "fully" "requires universities to favor women's teams and treat them better than men's [teams]. . . . forces them to eliminate or cap men's teams. . . . [and] forces universities to impose athletic quotas in excess of relative interests and abilities." . . .

Brown simply ignores the fact that it is required to accommodate fully the interests and abilities of the underrepresented gender, not because the three-part test mandates preferential treatment for women *ab initio*, but because Brown has been found (under prong one) to have allocated its athletics participation opportunities so as to create a significant gender-based disparity with respect to these opportunities, and has failed (under prong two) to show a history and continuing practice of expansion of opportunities for the underrepresented gender.

. . . To adopt [Brown's] relative interests approach would be . . . to . . . entrench and fix by law the significant gender-based disparity in athletics opportunities found by the district court to exist at Brown. . . . According to

Brown's relative interests interpretation of the equal accommodation principle, the gender-based disparity in athletics participation opportunities at Brown is due to a lack of interest on the part of its female students, rather than to discrimination, and any attempt to remedy the disparity is, by definition, an unlawful quota. This approach is entirely contrary to "Congress's unmistakably clear mandate that educational institutions not use federal monies to perpetuate gender-based discrimination" . . . and makes it virtually impossible to effectuate Congress's intent to eliminate sex discrimination in intercollegiate athletics.

Brown also claims error in the district court's failure to apply Title VII standards to its analysis of whether Brown's intercollegiate athletics program complies with Title IX. The district court rejected the analogy to Title VII, noting that, while Title VII "seeks to determine whether gender-neutral job openings have been filled without regard to gender[,] Title IX . . . was designed to address the reality that sports teams, unlike the vast majority of jobs, *do* have official gender requirements, and this statute accordingly approaches the concept of discrimination differently from Title VII." . . .

It is imperative to recognize that athletics presents a distinctly different situation from admissions and employment and requires a different analysis in order to determine the existence *vel non* of discrimination. . . . To the extent that Title IX allows institutions to maintain single-sex teams and gender-segregated athletics programs, men and women do not compete against each other for places on team rosters. Accordingly, and notwith-standing Brown's protestations to the contrary, the Title VII concept of the "qualified pool" has no place in a Title IX analysis of equal athletics opportunities for male and female athletes because women are not "qualified" to compete for positions on men's teams, and vice-versa. In addition, the concept of "preference" does not have the same meaning, or raise the same equality concerns, as it does in the employment and admissions contexts. . . .

Interest and ability rarely develop in a vacuum; they evolve as a function of opportunity and experience. The Policy Interpretation recognizes that women's lower rate of participation in athletics reflects women's historical lack of opportunities to participate in sports. . . .

. . . [T]here exists the danger that, rather than providing a true measure of women's interest in sports, statistical evidence purporting to reflect women's interest instead provides only a measure of the very discrimination that is and has been the basis for women's lack of opportunity to participate in sports. Prong three requires some kind of evidence of interest in athletics, and the Title IX framework permits the use of statistical evidence in assessing the level of interest in sports.[15] Nevertheless, to allow a numbers-based lack-

15. Under the Policy Interpretation,

Institutions may determine the athletic interests and abilities of students by nondiscriminatory methods of their choosing provided:

of-interest defense to become the instrument of further discrimination against the underrepresented gender would pervert the remedial purpose of Title IX. We conclude that, even if it can be empirically demonstrated that, at a particular time, women have less interest in sports than do men, such evidence, standing alone, cannot justify providing fewer athletics opportunities for women than for men. Furthermore, such evidence is completely irrelevant where, as here, viable and successful women's varsity teams have been demoted or eliminated. . . .

Finally, the tremendous growth in women's participation in sports since Title IX was enacted disproves Brown's argument that women are less interested in sports for reasons unrelated to lack of opportunity. . . .

. . . Had Congress intended to entrench, rather than change, the status quo — with its historical emphasis on men's participation opportunities to the detriment of women's opportunities — it need not have gone to all the trouble of enacting Title IX.

V . . .

To the extent that Brown challenges the constitutionality of the statutory scheme itself, the challenge rests upon [the assumption that] . . . *Adarand* . . . compels us . . . to apply strict scrutiny to the analysis. . . .

First, . . . *Adarand* [applies] to review of legislative affirmative action schemes. This case presents the issue of the legality of a federal district court's determination, based upon adjudicated findings of fact, that a federal anti-discrimination statute has been violated, and of the statutory and constitutional propriety of the judicial remedy ordered to provide redress to plaintiffs with standing who have been injured by the violation.

Second, *Adarand* does not even discuss gender discrimination, and its holding is limited to explicitly race-based classifications. 115 S. Ct. at 2113. . . .

Third, even if *Adarand* did apply, it does not dictate the level of scrutiny to be applied in this case, as Brown concedes. For the last twenty years, the Supreme Court has applied intermediate scrutiny to all cases raising equal protection challenges to gender-based classifications, including the Supreme Court's most recent gender discrimination case, United States v. Virginia, [518 U.S. 515] (1996). . . .

---

a. The processes take into account the nationally increasing levels of women's interests and abilities;

b. The methods of determining interest and ability do not disadvantage the members of an underrepresented sex;

c. The methods of determining ability take into account team performance records; and

d. The methods are responsive to the expressed interests of students capable of intercollegiate competition who are members of an underrepresented sex.

44 Fed. Reg. at 71,417. . . .

Under intermediate scrutiny, the burden of demonstrating an exceedingly persuasive justification for a government-imposed, gender-conscious classification is met by showing that the classification serves important governmental objectives, and that the means employed are substantially related to the achievement of those objectives. . . .

We find that the first part of the test is satisfied. The governmental objectives of "avoid[ing] the use of federal resources to support discriminatory practices," and "provid[ing] individual citizens effective protection against those practices," Cannon [v. University of Chicago], 441 U.S. [677] at 704 (1979), are clearly important objectives. . . .

Applying the second prong of the intermediate scrutiny test, we find that the means employed by the district court in fashioning relief for the statutory violation are clearly substantially related to these important objectives. Intermediate scrutiny does not require that there be no other way to accomplish the objectives, but even if that were the standard, it would be satisfied in the unique context presented by the application of Title IX to athletics. . . .

Of course, a remedy that requires an institution to cut, add, or elevate the status of athletes or entire teams may impact the genders differently, but this will be so only if there is a gender-based disparity with respect to athletics opportunities to begin with, which is the only circumstance in which prong three comes into play. Here, however, it has not been shown that Brown's men students will be disadvantaged by the full and effective accommodation of the athletics interests and abilities of its women students.

. . .

There can be no doubt that Title IX has changed the face of women's sports as well as our society's interest in and attitude toward women athletes and women's sports. . . . In addition, there is ample evidence that increased athletics participation opportunities for women and young girls, available as a result of Title IX enforcement, have had salutary effects in other areas of societal concern. . . .

One need look no further than the impressive performances of our country's women athletes in the 1996 Olympic Summer Games to see that Title IX has had a dramatic and positive impact on the capabilities of our women athletes, particularly in team sports. These Olympians represent the first full generation of women to grow up under the aegis of Title IX . . . What stimulated this remarkable change in the quality of women's athletic competition was not a sudden, anomalous upsurge in women's interest in sports, but the enforcement of Title IX's mandate of gender equity in sports.

. . .

Affirmed in part, reversed in part, and remanded for further proceedings. . . .

TORRUELLA, Chief Judge (Dissenting).

Because I am not persuaded that the majority's view represents the state of the law today, I respectfully dissent. . . .

It is not necessary to equate race and gender to see that the logic of *Adarand* — counseling that we focus on the categories and justifications proffered rather than the labels attached — applies in the context of gender. While cognizant of differences between race-focused and gender-focused Equal Protection precedent, I nevertheless think that *Adarand* compels us to view so-called benign gender-conscious governmental actions under the same lens as any other gender-conscious governmental actions. . . .

. . . In United States v. Virginia, [116 S. Ct. 2264] (1996), the Court faced an Equal Protection challenge to Virginia's practice of maintaining the Virginia Military Institute as an all male institution. Rather than simply apply the traditional test requiring that gender classifications be "substantially related to an important government objective,". . . the Supreme Court applied a more searching "skeptical scrutiny of official action denying rights or opportunities based on sex," [id. at 2274], which requires that "[p]arties who seek to defend gender-based government action must demonstrate an "exceedingly persuasive justification' for that action." Id. . . .

Virginia "drastically revise[s] our established standards for reviewing sex-based classifications." [116 S. Ct. at 2291] (Scalia, J. dissenting). . . .

I conclude, therefore, that *Adarand* and *Virginia* are irreconcilable with [this court's decision] . . . because it applies a lenient version of intermediate scrutiny that is impermissible following *Adarand* and because it did not apply the "exceedingly persuasive justification" test of *Virginia*. . . .

I believe that the three-prong test, as the district court interprets it, is a quota. I am in square disagreement with the majority, who believe that "[n]o aspect of the Title IX regime at issue in this case . . . mandates gender-based preferences or quotas." . . . Put another way, I agree that "Title IX is not an affirmative action statute" . . . , but I believe that is exactly what the district court has made of it. As interpreted by the district court, the test constitutes an affirmative action, quota-based scheme.

I am less interested in the actual term "quota" than the legally cognizable characteristics that render a quota scheme impermissible. And those characteristics are present here in spades. I am not persuaded by the majority's argument that the three-part test does not constitute a quota because it does not permit an agency or court to find a violation solely on the basis of prong one of the test; instead, an institution must also fail prongs two and three. As Brown rightly argues, the district court's application of the three-prong test requires Brown to allocate its athletic resources to meet the as-yet-unmet interest of a member of the underrepresented sex, women in this case, while simultaneously neglecting any unmet interest among individuals of the overrepresented sex. To the extent that the rate of interest in athletics diverges between men and women at any institution, the district court's interpretation would require that such an institution treat an individual male student's athletic interest and an individual female student's athletic interest completely differently: one student's reasonable interest would have to be met, by law, while meeting the other student's interest would only aggravate the lack of proportionality giving rise to the legal duty. "The injury in cases of this kind is that a 'discriminatory classification prevent[s] . . . competition on an equal footing.'" *Adarand*, [115 S. Ct. at 2104]. As a result, individual male and female students would be precluded from competing against each other for scarce resources; they would instead compete only against members of their own gender. . . .

A pragmatic overview of the effect of the three-prong test leads me to reject the majority's claim that the three-prong test does not amount to a quota because it involves multiple prongs. In my view it is the result of the test, and not the number of steps involved, that should determine if a quota system exists. Regardless of how many steps are involved, the fact remains that the test requires proportionate participation opportunities for both sexes (prong one) unless one sex is simply not interested in participating (prong three). It seems to me that a quota with an exception for situations in which there are insufficient interested students to allow the school to meet it remains a quota. All of the negative effects of a quota remain, and the school can escape the quota under prong three only by offering preferential treatment to the group that has demonstrated less interest in athletics. . . .

. . . The majority is unsympathetic to Brown's claim that the disparity between athletic opportunities for men and women reflect a gender-based difference in interest levels. . . .

. . . If statistical evidence of interest levels is not to be considered by courts, however, there is no way for schools to determine whether they are in compliance. Any studies or surveys they might conduct in order to assess their own compliance would, in the event of litigation, be deemed irrelevant. Regardless of the efforts made by the academic institution, the specter of a lawsuit would be ever-present.

In addition, the majority has put the power to control athletics and the provision of athletic resources in the hands of the underrepresented gender. Virtually every other aspect of college life is entrusted to the institution, but athletics has now been carved out as an exception and the university is no longer in full control of its program. Unless the two genders participate equally in athletics, members of the underrepresented sex would have the ability to demand a varsity level team at any time if they can show sufficient interest. Apparently no weight is given to the sustainability of the interest, the cost of the sport, the university's view on the desirability of the sport, and so on. . . .

Notes

1. Title IX. Title IX has many exemptions. It excludes participation in contact sports (see 34 C.F.R. §106.41(b)(2000)), for example, and thus does not give a cause of action for exclusion by members of one sex from a team established for members of the other sex; the successful cases in this area are all Equal Protection cases. See page 380. It also exempts any institution "that traditionally and continually from its establishments has had a policy of admitting only students of one sex," see 20 U.S.C. §1681(a)(5) (1994); schools whose primary purpose is to train students for the military services, see §1681(a)(4), and single-sex groups such as the Boy Scouts and Girl Scouts, YWCAs and YMCAs, sororities and fraternities, mother-daughter or father-son activities, and scholarships for beauty contest winners, see §1681(a)(6)-(9). Thus, *MUW* and *VMI*, explored at pages 382-400, were decided on constitutional grounds, not under Title IX.

Title IX got off to a slow start even as to those areas to which it applies. A long delay in its application to institutions as a whole occurred with the 1984 decision of the United States Supreme Court, Grove City College v. Bell, 465 U.S. 555 (1984), which limited the application of Title IX to the specific school program receiving federal funds. This decision was reversed by Congress in the Civil Rights Restoration Act of 1987, 20 U.S.C. §§1687-1688 (1994), which extended Title IX to all of the programs of an institution receiving federal funds for any program or activity. Another barrier came down in 1992 when it was first established that individuals could sue for money damages under Title IX, at least for intentional discrimination. See Franklin v. Gwinnett County Public Schools, 503 U.S. 60 (1992).

Despite its limitations and its stalled beginnings, Title IX is widely regarded as having opened many doors for women. Perhaps its biggest impact has been in the expansion of school athletics opportunities for women. At one time, strenuous physical activity was thought to be harmful to women's reproductive capacities and competition antithetical to their moral standards. See Cynthia J. Harris, Note, The Reform of Women's Intercollegiate Athletics: Title IX, Equal Protection, and Supplemental Methods, 20 Cap. U.L. Rev. 691, 692-693 (1991). Under Title IX, participation in high school sports went from approximately 290,000 girls in 1971 to 2.4 million by the 1995-1996 season. Carrie Muskat, The Chicago Tribune, February 23, 1997, at 1. By 1994, 38 percent of high school athletes were women, as compared to 7 percent in 1971. John C. Weistart, Can Gender Equity Find a Place in Commercialized College Sports? 3 Duke J.L. & Gender Pol'y 191, 227 & n.120 (1996) (citing National Fed. of State High Sch. Ass'n, 1993-1994 Sports Participation Survey (1995)). Participation in college sports went from 30,000 to 135,000. See Jere Longman, How the Women Won, N.Y. Times, June 23, 1996, §6 (Magazine), at 26; women's college soccer alone grew from 300 women to over 8,000 by

1992. Weistart, supra, at 228 (citing NCAA, The Sports and Recreational Programs of the Nation's Universities and Colleges, 1957-1992, Report No. 8, at 25 (1992)).

2. Measuring Equality under Title IX. In dollar terms, the expenditures for women's collegiate athletics remains far below that for men's athletics at most schools. Despite impressive gains for women, men's athletics still consume 62 percent of the scholarships, 60 percent of the head coaches' salaries, and 76 percent of the assistant coaches' salaries. Men, however, hold a 63 to 37 percent participation advantage over women. They also consume 77 percent of total operating budgets in comparison to 23 percent for women. See Amy Shipley, Most College Funding Going to Men's Sports, Wash. Post, April 29, 1997, at E1 (citing 1997 NCAA Gender Equity Study). Nearly twice as much is paid to recruit male athletes than to recruit female athletes. See Deborah Brake, The Struggle for Sex Equality in Sport and the Theory Behind Title IX, 34 U. Mich. J. L. Ref. 13, 76 (2001). The gap in overall expenditures is increasing. From 1992-1997, while overall operating expenditures for women's intercollegiate athletics grew 89 percent, the increase for men's intercollegiate athletics increased by 139 percent. Id. at 77. The gender disparity is greater, on average, at the larger schools. While women received an average of 38 percent of athletic budgets and 40 percent of athletic-related financial aid budgets at I-AAA schools, they get an average of 19% of the athletic budget and 33 percent of financial aid at I-A schools. Tanya Alvert, I-AAA Women Get Bigger Cut of Budget, USA Today, March 5, 1997, at 9C. Continuously updated figures on gender equity in sports is available at a website of the Chronicle of Higher Education found at http://chronicle.com/stats/genderequity.

Title IX regulations reviewed in *Cohen* make it clear that Title IX does not require that women's sports receive *equal expenditures*, which would have been one way to measure equality. Title IX regulations with respect to scholarships require only that women's share match their share of participation rates. See 34 C.F.R. §106.37(c) (1999). With respect to athletic programs more generally, equality must be measured by consideration of a variety of open-ended factors relating to the availability of teams and levels of competition, equipment, supplies, scheduling, travel, tutoring, locker rooms, practice facilities, housing, publicity, and the like. See 34 C.F.R. §106.41(c) (2000). Much of the litigation has been prompted, as in *Cohen*, by school decisions to eliminate or downgrade sports teams. See, e.g., Favia v. Indiana University of Pennsylvania, 7 F.3d 332 (3d Cir. 1993) (affirming reinstatement of women's teams); Roberts v. Colorado State Board of Agriculture, 998 F.2d 824 (10th Cir.), cert. denied, 510 U.S. 1004 (1993) (same). Each of these decisions, like *Cohen*, applies a numerical parity paradigm, setting proportionality of representation of males and females in relation to their enrollment in the school as the goal, or at least as a "safe harbor"; until that goal is met, a school must demonstrate either a history of expanding opportunities or that all the interests of the underrepresentation sex are met. Note that Brown University did not contest the numerical parity paradigm; rather, it insisted that proportionality should be established in relation to the relative interests of males and females in athletics, rather than their proportionality in the total student body.

Is the problem that women's interests should not be relevant, or that there is no way of reliably measuring them? Among the evidence submitted by Brown were:

> (i) admissions data showing greater athletic interest among male applicants than female applicants; (ii) college board data showing greater athletic interest and prior participation rates by prospective male applicants than female applicants; (iii) data from the Cooperative Institutional Research Program at UCLA indicating greater athletic interests among men than women; (iv) an independent telephone survey of 500 randomly selected Brown undergraduates that reveals that Brown offers women participation opportunities in excess of their representation in the pool of interested, qualified students; (v) intramural and club participation rates that demonstrate higher participation rates among men than women; (vi) walk-on and try-out numbers that reflect a greater interest among men than women; (vii) high school participation rates that show a much lower rate of participation among females than among males; (viii) the NCAA Gender Equity Committee data showing that women across the country participate in athletics at a lower rate than men.

Cohen v. Brown University, 101 F.3d 155, 198 n.30 (1st Cir. 1996) (Torruella, C.J., dissenting). See also Michael Straubel, Gender Equity, College Sports, Title IX and Group Rights: A Coach's View, 62 Brooklyn L. Rev. 1039, 1070 (1996) (arguing that Title IX should include "safe harbors" for colleges and universities when the opportunity available to each sex matches either the national or state high school participation rates of each sex). Why do you suppose Brown's evidence of women's lower level of interest was not given any direct consideration in the majority opinion?

In what sense is the proportionality test in relation to numbers in the student body "affirmative action," while proportionality in relation to student interests is not? The answer lies in the extent to which a school may be required to make affirmative efforts to change or develop student interest, rather than merely accept it as a given. The more one accepts student choice as a given, or as a neutral fact, the more "affirmative" appear to be requirements that link compliance with the gender breakdown of the student body.

Cohen finds inequality in the history of women's sports at Brown that lead it to reject the neutrality of Brown's measures of student interest. Deborah Brake sets forth a more broad-based critique of college and university sports, citing numerous ways in which educational institutions contribute to the subordination of women in athletics. Brake, supra. Among the institutional factors she identifies are the dominance of men in leadership positions in college athletics with most women only in token roles ("athletics [is] another arena where men exert control over women"), id. at 84-88, 90; disparities in pay between male and female coaches and in other expenditures for women's sports, id. at 74-82; and the linking of sport with masculinity, which is evidenced in training methods built on norms of masculinity ("you throw like a girl"), hostile talk about women, lesbian-baiting, and the objectification of women in sport (starting with the "quintessentially 'feminine' role" of cheerleaders who "[stand] at the periphery, offering unconditional support for the athletes who play the traditionally masculine role of competing in the primary athletic event"). Id. at 92-122. For a detailed discussion of the sex disparities in jobs held in athletic administration and coaching at the college and university level, and in salaries paid, see pages 162-163.

Catharine MacKinnon starts even further back: the problem is not just that women have not been encouraged in sports, she claims; they have been taught to be disinterested:

> Women have learned a lot all these years on the sidelines, watching. Not only have we been excluded from resources, excluded from participation, we have learned actual disability, enforced weakness, lack of spirit/body connection in being and in motion. . . . It's not *not* learned; it's very specifically learned. . . . [M]en, learning to be men, learn not only sports but learn those things that become elevated, extended, measured, valued, and organized in and as sport itself. Women, simply learning to be women, do not learn those things, do learn the opposite of those things. So . . . being female and being athletic have been socially contradictory and . . . being male and being athletic have been more or less socially synonymous. Femininity has contradicted, masculinity has been consistent with, being athletic.

Catharine A. MacKinnon, Feminism Unmodified: Discourses on Life and Law 120 (1987). What are the implications of this observation?

Some have charged the media with presenting women athletes as ladies first, and athletes second, if at all.

> An especially graphic example of this type of coverage involved the retirement of professional tennis star Chris Evert in the late 1980s. Acknowledging the importance of this event, Sports Illustrated placed her on its cover. However, of all the ways Sports Illustrated could have portrayed her glorious athletic career, they chose to picture Evert with the caption "I'm Going to Be A Full-time Wife." This characterization of her retirement . . . [suggests] that Evert has completed her career as a professional woman, and thus it is time for her to put all else aside and return to her "proper" sphere, the home. [It also suggests] that involvement in sport may make a woman "too masculine." The feature article that accompanied the cover photograph . . . portrayed [Evert] as "Chrissie," America's answer to the more "manly" Eastern European players, such as [Martina] Navratilova, who were beginning to take over women's tennis during this time period. In the same feature article is a pictorial

chronology of Evert's "career," where we see her pictured from left to right with her first boyfriend, Jimmy Conners, then with short-lived flame Burt Reynolds, followed by Steve Ford (son of former president Gerald Ford), then with first husband, John Lloyd, and, finally, with current husband Andy Mill. This chronology suggests that Evert's true career is about her advancement as a future wife, not as a professional tennis player who had an enormously successful career as a professional athlete . . . for seventeen years . . . during which Evert won 157 singles titles, was ranked number one eight times, and won eighteen grand slam championships. . . .

. . . In a lengthy tribute to Evert after she announced her retirement, sports columnist Tom Powers . . . began by lamenting how, with Evert gone from the scene, "Today's youngsters . . . will grow up thinking all women tennis players have thighs like Schwarzenegger and last names that end in the letters o-v-a. But those of us who grew up with Chrissie know better." "Knowing better" apparently means being able to identify who the real (i.e., "proper") female athletes are. During·Evert's heyday, we could "[f]lip on the tube and see Chris volleying demurely from the baseline. Her opponent, often a European with serious facial hair, would be lunging and twisting and grunting after the ball. Chris would take a couple of quick steps and pop! . . . advantage Evert." Powers then stated that . . . [Chrissie] "stayed in the backcourt and hit away instead of charging forward like some disgusting buffalo."

Mary Jo Kane, Media Coverage of the Post Title IX Female Athlete: A Feminist Analysis of Sport, Gender, and Power, 3 Duke J. Gender L. & Poly. 95, 119-120 (1996); see also Note, Cheering on Women and Girls in Sports: Using Title IX To Fight Gender Role Oppression, 110 Harv. L. Rev. 1627, 1632-1633 (1997) (describing self-sexualization of female athletes, to assure their audiences they are not lesbians by wearing their hair long and in ponytails and emphasizing their feminine looks and interests in their off-the-court appearances). Is this a fair critique? What role do you think these media images play in how women perceive of themselves in sports? Should Brown University be responsible for these?

Once the court determines that Brown's measurements of women's interests in sports are tainted, where does this leave Brown? Can it possibly refute the court's disbelief about the underlying reality? Perhaps not, but the court's reading of Title IX and the 3-part test it endorses makes the empirical debate somewhat academic: so long as there is some unmet interest, either this interest must be met, or opportunities expanded, or opportunities must be proportional to the sex ratio at the school.

While *Cohen* may have seemed like a radical decision at the time, other federal courts are following its rejection of women's lack of sufficient interest as a defense to unequal offerings in sports. In consolidated lawsuits brought by women against Louisiana State University for discrimination against women in the provision of facilities and teams for intercollegiate athletics, for example, the Fifth Circuit Court of Appeals dismissed LSU's defense that although the student population was 51 percent male and 49 percent female, its participation rate was 71 percent male and 29 percent female because fewer females were interested in athletics. Specifically in relation to fast-pitch softball, the court reasoned:

> The heart of [LSU's] contention is that an institution with no coach, no facilities, no varsity team, no scholarships, and no recruiting in a given sport must have on campus enough national-caliber athletes to field a competitive varsity team in that sport before a court can find sufficient interest and abilities to exist. It should go without saying that adopting this criteria would eliminate an effective accommodation claim by any plaintiff, at any time.

Pederson v. Louisiana State University, 213 F.3d 858, 878 (5th Cir. 2000). Challenges by men to the university's reduction of men's teams in order to address identified gender inequities have generally failed and the Supreme Court has turned down the opportunity to review those cases (including *Cohen*) for which certiorari was sought. See, e.g., Neal v. Board of Trustees of the California State Universities, 198 F.3d 763 (9th Cir. 1999); Boulahanis v. Board of Regents, Illinois State University, 198 F.3d 633 (7th Cir. 1999), cert. denied, 120 S. Ct. 2762 (2000); Kelley v. Board of Trustees, University of Illinois, 35 F.3d 265 (7th Cir. 1994), cert. denied 513 U.S. 1128 (1995).

3. Title IX and Revenue Sports. Should "revenue" sports should be treated differently from other sports? Recall that coaches for a revenue sport might be paid more than coaches for a non-revenue sport, since the pressures entailed in generating revenue provide a "factor other than sex" under the Equal Pay Act. See pages 160-163. Is it reasonable to say, further, that the unique function of revenue sports at some schools, in terms of media interest, alumni relations, and publicity, make revenue sports something incomparable to other sports, and thus out of the equation, for Title IX purposes?

Even if revenue sports were counted in the equation, should there be a set-off for revenue produced? 1991-1992 UCLA athletic budget figures showed that while football expenses were over $5.2 million and basketball over $1.6 million, revenue from football exceeded $7.6 million and revenue from basketball was $3.8 million. Mark Alesia, UCLA Sports Inc: A Look at the Books, L.A. Daily News, Sept. 27, 1992, at S1, cited in John C. Weistart, Can Gender Equity Find a Place in Commercialized College Sports, 3 Duke J. Gender L. & Pol'y 191, 205-206 (1996). Some have argued that revenue sports must be supported at a competitive level because the revenues from these sports provides the income stream upon which other sports, including women's sports, depend. See, e.g., Lou Tepper [University of Illinois-Champaign head football coach], Opinions: Title IX, NCAA News, May 17, 1995, at 4 ("If [a farmer] has a couple of cash crops and a lot of other crops that aren't bringing in any cash, he's not going to fertilize them 50-50."), cited in Weistart, supra, at 212 n.74.

John Weistart points out several flaws in this analysis. First, if scholarships, administration, support services, and other overhead items were properly allocated among the individual sports, the profitability figures for the revenue sports look quite different. By Weistart's calculation, proper allocation of otherwise centralized expense items would show that roughly $13 million of the $20 million UCLA athletic budget, rather than $6.8 million, was spent on football and basketball. Weistart states that there are only a "small number of schools in which these expensive sports are not subsidized. . . . [W]hen all costs are considered, including allocated costs of stadia, very few Big Time programs actually make money." Weistart, supra at 207-208. Second, he notes that because of the highly competitive nature of revenue sports, most of the revenues are poured back into those sports, with little diverted to fund non-revenue sports. One study shows that for every additional $1 spent on athletic programs, only between three and seven cents is spent on nonrevenue sports. Arthur Padilla & David Baumer, Big Time College Sports: Management and Economic Issues, J. Sport & Soc. Issues, May 1994, at 123, 139, cited in Weistart, supra, at 213. Third, Weistart argues that the high expenditures in revenue sports are unnecessary, except at schools that have been allowed to compete without financial restraint for a competitive edge. Weistart, supra, at 207-212. "The insight that is missing from the highly vocal attacks on Title IX by football advocates is any recognition that the high consumption financial appetites of football programs come from the pressures of unrestrained economic competition rather than from any serious concern about the quality or safety of the game. . . . [T]he real cause of discomfort is the fact that men's revenue-producing sports have set themselves on a course in which there is no foreseeable relief from the pressure for increased spending." Id. at 248-249. Weistart advocates "mutual disarmament," arguing that an effective uniform cap on expenditures "will not diminish on-the-field competition," but will inevitably improve athletics, as well as allowing more teams to be able to participate on an equal footing. Id. at 249, 253. Fourth, Weistart challenges the presumed inevitability that only men's football and basketball programs can be revenue-producing. He notes that the women's basketball teams at Stanford University and the University of Colorado have outdrawn their men's counterparts in attendance in recent years, and that television coverage of women's basketball has surged. Weistart, supra, at 226-227. While only ten women's college basketball teams average at least 5,000 fans per game, the growth in numbers is impressive. At the University of Wisconsin, season ticket-holders went from 121 in 1994-1995 to 5,486 two years later. See Carrie Muskat, After 25 Years: Women's Sports are Entitled, Chicago Tribune, February 23, 1997, at 1.

Some argue that the revenue-generating aspect of college sports be separated from the rest and treated as businesses, rather than as part of the educational mission, and therefore not subject to Title IX. See, e.g., Matthew L. Daniel, Title IX and Gender Equity in College Athletics: How Honesty Might Avert a Crisis, 2 Ann. Surv. Am. L. 255, 306-307 (1995). Would this advance the interests of gender equity?

It should be noted that even when revenue sports are extracted from expenditure comparisons, significant revenue differentials remain. In 14 sports (not including football) at the Division I level of NCAA sports, there are 1.45 male athletes for each woman, and for every dollar spent for operating expenses for women's programs, $1.80 is spent on men's programs. See Malcom Moran, Campus Changes Coming, Like It or Not, N.Y. Times, June 22, 1992, at B5, B7.

4. Title IX Compliance. Few universities comply with the threshold proportionality standard described in *Cohen*. Brooklyn College is one of them, where 57 percent of the student body, and 57 percent of the school's athletes, are women. See Warren Richey, How Some Colleges Score Parity for Women's Athletics, Christian Science Monitor, June 5, 1997, at p. 3. Parity was achieved at Brooklyn College only after the college initially threatened to eliminate the entire athletic department because of a finding of noncompliance by the Office of Civil Rights. See David Lennon, Brooklyn's Sports Officially Ended, Newsday, July 2, 1992, at 127.

One news report based on the 1997 NCAA Gender Equity Study concluded that only nine percent of Division I schools came within five percentage points of having female athletes in proportion to their number in the student body. A number of these schools (e.g., the military academies) have low female enrollment and thus face a somewhat easier task, but the female enrollment in some of the schools approaches 50 percent, including Washington State (47%), the University of Kansas (50%), and the University of Washington (50%). See Erik Brady, Title IX Improves Women's Participation, USA Today, March 3, 1997, at 4C. These schools, and others, have counterbalanced the large roster of football players by creating or expanding women's soccer teams and women's crew. See Richey, supra.

In 1997, the National Women's Law Center filed complaints with the Office for Civil Rights against 25 colleges and universities for sex discrimination in the awarding of athletic scholarships. Two and one-half years later, eight institutions were found to be in compliance and the other 17 schools agreed to increase scholarship aid to female athletes. See Deborah Brake, The Struggle for Sex Equality in Sport and the Theory Behind Title IX, 34 U. Mich. J. L. Ref. 13, 75-76 (2001).

Should the NCAA be subject to Title IX? The Third Circuit Court of Appeals concluded that the NCAA's receipt of dues from federally-funded member institutions was sufficient to bring the organization under the statute, Smith v. National Collegiate Athletic Association v. Smith, 139 F.3d 180 (3d Cir. 1998), but the United States Supreme Court disagreed. See National Collegiate Athletic Association v. Smith, 525 U.S. 459 (1999).

5. Re-Defining Sport.   Is equality too limited a concept in college sports? Two commentators suggest that the current configuration of sports itself should be rethought at the collegiate level:

> [Title IX] clearly legitimizes the present and continued institutional linkage of sports to educational institutions. It leaves unquestioned the education value of athletics, the proper role of sports in schools, and the values behind the allocation of education funds. . . .
> . . . [T]he emphasis in school sports itself is on revenue production by spectator sports rather than on the lifelong benefits of athletic participation. The vast majority of the budgetary disputes about collegiate athletic budgets have to do with allocation of resources to varsity, interscholastic, or intercollegiate competition, not to the greater participation in intramural programs. Benefits accrue to the elite athletes, male and female, and not to the massive student body. Their role remains a passive one. Sports generate prestige for the educational institution, financial contributions from alumni, vicarious pleasure for the spectators, and athletic prowess and a privileged status for the few. Title IX does not purport to change this. In fact, one of the most disturbing and unexamined consequences of Title IX has been its failure to help eliminate another form of discrimination, racism. . . .
> In one of the few studies of minority women in collegiate sports, Alpha Anderson [in a 1979 unpublished master thesis for Temple University] discovered from a survey of 218 AIAW affiliated institutions that 91.6% of the female athletes were white, while Black (5.8%), Chicano (1.0%), Indian (.5%), Oriental (.91%) and Puerto Rican (.14%) women accounted for the remaining 8.4% of the female athletes. [In contrast to the less than 6% of female athletes who were black,] 14% of the college undergraduate female population is black. . . .
> . . . [T]he effects of Title IX will be to reproduce in female sports the same structural inequities already found in male sports. The domination of certain education institutions in male sports is well known. . . . It perhaps comes as no surprise that the pre-Title IX powerhouse names in women's basketball (for example Immaculata, Queens, Delta State, Montclair State) are being replaced by the same big-name schools which dominate men's sports (UCLA, Maryland, etc.).
> Along with the replication of the elite sporting schools for women's sports will come the same pressures to replicate the male standards of success for athletic programs. Female programs will be measured and evaluated by such factors as the number of scholarships given out, the size of the athletic budget, the active recruitment of elite athletes, the size of the gate receipts, the interest generated by the media, and the number of victories and other external criteria of achievement. The abuses that such standards have generated in male sports have . . . been noted.

Mary A. Boutilier & Lucinda SanGiovanni, The Sporting Woman 173-176 (1983).

Boutilier and SanGiovanni refer to the AIAW, or the Association for Intercollegiate Athletics for Women, an organization that pursued a less competitive model of sport than the NCAA and that was dedicated to protecting the "welfare of the student above that of the institution or external interests such as alumni, commercial groups, and the like." Id. at 178. After passage of Title IX, against which the NCAA had first lobbied strongly, the NCAA moved successfully to swallow up the AIAW and take over women's sports. See Murray Sperber, College Sports Inc.: The Athletic Department vs. The University 322-332 (1990); Wendy Olson, Beyond Title IX: Toward an Agenda for Women and Sports in the 1990's, 3 Yale J.L. & Feminism 105, 112 (1990). This takeover, some have contended, imposed a corrupt commercial system on a program that had superior athlete-centered, educationally oriented values. Sperber, supra, at 322-332. Is the takeover of the AIAW by the NCAA a problem under formal equality principles? Is it compelled by these principles?

Many women's advocates have argued that improving athletic opportunities for women does not mean making men's opportunities available to women — the formal equality option — but producing a more process-oriented, cooperative competition mode of sport that better meets women's goals of better health, stress reduction, friendship, and sociability. See Olson, supra, at 145. Catharine MacKinnon associates women's sports not only with the redefinition of sport, but of femininity as well:

> . . . [A]thletics to men is a form of combat. It is a sphere in which one asserts oneself against an object, a person, or a standard. It is a form of coming against and subduing someone who is on the other side, vanquishing enemies. It's competitive. From women's point of view, some rather major elements of the experience appear to be left out. . . . These include things that men occasionally experience, but that on the whole are not allowed to be the central purpose of male athletics, such as kinesthesis, pleasure in motion, cooperation (and by this I do not mean the male bond), physical self-respect, self-possession, and fun. Because of the history of women's subjection, physicality for women has a different meaning from physicality for men. Physicality for men has meant male dominance; it has meant force, coercion, and the ability to subdue and subject the natural world, one central part of which has been us.
>
> For women, when we have engaged in sport, when we have been physical, it has meant claiming and possessing a physicality that is our own. We have had something to fight and therefore something to gain here, and that is a different relation to our bodies than women are allowed to have in this society. We have had to gain a relation to our bodies *as if they are our own.* This physical self-respect and physical presence that women can get from sport is antithetical to femininity. It is our bodies as acting rather than as acted upon. It is our bodies as being and presence, our bodies that *we* do things with, that we in fact are and identify with as ourselves, rather than our bodies as things to be looked at or for us to look at in preparation for the crucialness of how we will appear, or even to carry out heads around in the world. In other words, athletics can give us our bodies as a form of being rather than as a form of appearance, or death-likeness.

MacKinnon, Feminism Unmodified: Discourses on Life and Law 121 (1987). What implications does MacKinnon's analysis have for the law?

John Weistart observes that the easiest solutions to the sports equity dilemma are not necessarily the best:

> [J]udicial and administrative review will actually be more difficult if an effort is made to maximize the flexibility afforded the future development of women's sports. The male model is an easy test for compliance. It is a model that provides quick answers for questions such as what is an adequate level of support and what is an appropriate structure for competition. But the easy answer may not be the best answer.

Weistart, supra, at 244. Following the logic of Boutilier and SanGiovanni, one might have thought that a greater commitment to club sports or intramurals rather than varsity sports might have been a step in the right direction. See also Brian Snow & William E. Thro, Still On the Sidelines: Developing the Non-Discrimination Paradigm Under Title IX, 3 Duke J. Gender L. & Pol'y 1, 44 (1996) (greater emphasis should be placed on the vast majority of college students who do not play intercollegiate athletics). *Cohen* and other successful Title IX cases, however, were brought to prevent the demotion of women's teams from varsity to club status, see, e.g., Favia v. Indiana Univ. of Pa., 7 F.3d 332 (3d Cir. 1993); other suits have sought the elevation of club teams to varsity status. See Diane Heckman, On the Eve of Title IX's 25th Anniversary: Sex Discrimination in the Gym and Classroom, 21 Nova L. Rev. 545, 579-585 (1997) (describing many such suits). Are these suits misguided?

What other kinds of reforms of college sports can you imagine that would be responsive to the points made by MacKinnon and Boutilier and SanGiovanni? Can you think of activities not currently recognized as "sports" that should be cultivated?

D. SUBSTANTIVE EQUALITY IN THE FAMILY

1. The Gender Gap in Divorce Reform

Saff v. Saff
402 N.Y.S.2d 690 (App. Div. 1978), appeal dismissed, 415 N.Y.S.2d 829 (N.Y. 1979)

SIMONS, Justice.

Appellant has obtained a divorce from respondent because he abandoned her. She appeals from so much of the judgment as denied her alimony and failed to impose a constructive trust on one half of all respondent's separately owned property. . . .

Appellant and her husband were married in 1936. At the time appellant worked as a maid and respondent was unemployed. Over the next few years both worked at various jobs and gradually they accumulated a small reserve of funds which they held in their joint names. In 1946, after a few false starts, respondent went into partnership with Wallace Dahl and the two men founded Jamestown Fabricated Steel as equal partners. Each man invested $2000 but Dahl was short of cash and respondent loaned him $1000 (later repaid) to purchase his half interest. The money for these payments came from the Saffs' joint funds. In 1950 the company was incorporated and the capital stock was divided between respondent and Dahl. The company . . . is now estimated to have a net worth exceeding $500,000. In 1975 it grossed $590,000. Appellant has never had any legal interest in the business or in the corporate stock.

A minority of the court would grant appellant relief by imposing a constructive trust on one half of her husband's stock in Jamestown Fabricated Steel, Inc., upon one half of whatever business profits respondent receives from the corporation by way of profit sharing, and upon one half of the annual installments paid to respondent by the corporation to acquire real property formerly owned by him. . . .

Before the court may declare that respondent holds his separately owned property as a trustee for appellant's benefit, appellant must prove that there was (1) a promise by him — express or implied, (2) which caused her to transfer property to him relying on the promise, (3) that a confidential relationship existed between the parties and (4) that respondent has been unjustly enriched at her expense by his conduct.

Marriage is a confidential relationship, of course, and there was a transfer of funds and labor by appellant to respondent. The remedy of constructive trust, however, requires that more be shown. There must be proof that the transfer was made in reliance on a promise that the property transferred would be held for the benefit of appellant, and that respondent was enriched unjustly by retaining the fruits of the transfer.

We find no express promise by respondent. Appellant testified that from 1946 to 1960, apparently after the purchase of the business, respondent told her on various occasions, "Baby girl, what is mine is yours; you're my wife. It's always all half yours, you're my wife." Such representations undoubtedly reflected the emotions of a happier time but they most assuredly did not constitute a promise by respondent that he held one half of his corporate stock as trustee for appellant. The statements meant precisely what most people would interpret them to mean — not that appellant had a proprietary interest in every personal belonging of respondent, be it clothing or corporate stock, but rather that the parties would share their successes equally in raising their family and enjoying their life together.

Failing an express promise, appellant contends there was an implied promise. Unquestionably an implied promise may be sufficient if the evidence otherwise supports a finding that respondent holds property as trustee for another. Such promises may be inferred from the factual circumstances and setting of the parties and they frequently are when the conduct of the injured party is otherwise inexplicable. The fact of the marriage is an important consideration indicating a confidential relationship between the parties, but standing alone it does not provide the basis for an implied promise which will support a constructive trust. Furthermore before a court implies a promise between husband and wife for purposes of a constructive trust, it must be careful to separate those promises going to the marriage relationship and those going to a business relationship. The two may not be mixed together in some sort of salmagundi, as the minority has done, to find an implied promise that the wife will share in the ownership of a specific business because of such unrelated acts as her employment as a maid or drill press operator, her care of the children or her handling of the family finances. The remedy of constructive trust may not be applied randomly to adjust general equities between spouses or as a punitive measure to divvy up a husband's separately owned property because of his past indiscretion.

In this case the marriage relationship cuts against a finding of implied promise to hold one half of respondent's interest in the corporation for the benefit of appellant. Appellant's participation in the business is easily explainable as a normal incident of marriage which was manifestly given as such and for the generous salary she received and without any expectation on her part of any future ownership of the business.

Thus, appellant testified that she worked as a bookkeeper for the company, without pay, from 1946 until 1950. In the beginning the work was minimal for the simple reason that the company had little business. Appellant estimated that during those years the books for a whole month could be done in one day and respondent helped her with the tax returns. The work required more time by 1950, when the business was incorporated, but appellant has never worked more than 20-24 hours per week and she testified that she frequently took the bookkeeping home and completed it there rather than work at the plant. Also, in 1950 the corporation hired an accountant and additional other women employees to do the office work, although appellant continued to do some of the bookkeeping. She has received a salary from the company since 1950. At the time of the divorce her salary from Jamestown Steel was $12,500 per year for this part-time work. During the marriage appellant also worked part-time for a doctor for about two years and she did part-time office work for another two years at Jamestown Plastics, another company then owned by her husband.

If any rebuttal is needed to appellant's claim of implied promise, the proof establishes that respondent consistently refused to give his wife any of the company stock or permit her to be an officer or director of any of his corporations and his wishes were well known to her from the beginning. Appellant has never played a management role in respondent's companies, even in the broadest sense. Her work was always part-time and entirely clerical and she shared in neither the liability, ownership, nor management of the business.

Thus, while there was a transfer of jointly owned funds to acquire the business, the transfer was not induced by the marriage relationship and was not referable to any express or implied promise of ownership. The funds, or at least appellant's share of them, represented a gift, or at best, a loan by appellant, not an investment made as part of her participation in a joint venture.

Further than that, there was no unjust enrichment of respondent. Appellant has been more than adequately compensated for her efforts and in ways fully to be expected in a marriage. Respondent, by his efforts at developing and operating the business, has kept the couple happily circumstanced for 30 years. All of his earnings from the company were deposited in the couple's joint accounts and were used to support appellant. Generous purchases of property and investments were made from these funds for her. The income has been sufficient to enable her to travel, to enjoy the satisfying social and athletic life which she described in her testimony as the routine of "the most beautiful marriage in the world." Appellant will continue to enjoy the support available through respondent's efforts, by the separately owned property accumulated for her or, if her needs require it, by respondent's income for as long as he is able to do so. There is no need for a division of respondent's capital. . . .

[A]ppellant is not penniless. She came to this marriage with few material assets but she has lived a financially secure life for over 30 years since then. The Trial Court granted her exclusive, tax free use of the marital residence and the extensive furnishings in it. She has joint ownership in $100,000 in stocks, several thousand dollars of various stocks in her own name, $15,200 in savings and ownership of a sizeable insurance policy on her husband's life. In addition to this, she receives $12,500 a year income from her part-time employment at Jamestown Steel and she has dividend income of $3,600 per year. Neither the Trial Court nor the majority of this court find alimony justified on these facts. . . .

Judgment affirmed.

CARDAMONE, Justice, dissenting.

. . . From the beginning everything was shared. At the outset of their marriage while Mr. Saff looked unsuccessfully for employment, the Saffs resided in a home where Mrs. Saff worked without pay as a maid for their joint room and board. Before coming to Jamestown, New York the couple lived and worked in various parts of the country. Sometimes one or the other, occasionally both, would have employment. In those years Mrs. Saff worked at the Lionel Train Corp., General Instruments and Standard Oil

Company of New Jersey. She was able to do welding, worked on assembly lines and learned to operate all kinds of machinery, including drill presses. She worked a 58-hour week at sixty cents per hour. Regardless of whether one or both worked, however, the Saffs' savings were always jointly held. They did more than jointly share their earnings. The first home they purchased and their marital home were jointly owned. Most persuasive are the circumstances surrounding Jamestown Plastics. Jamestown Plastics was a business in which Mrs. Saff performed the same duties as she did at Jamestown Steel. Later, it was incorporated. At the time of its sale in 1970, however, the proceeds of this plastics business enterprise were invested by Mr. Saff in jointly owned stock. This act is consistent with his promise concededly made during their marriage that everything was to be shared equally between them despite the fact that Mr. Saff testified that he would never permit Mrs. Saff to hold any stock or serve as an officer or director of any corporation that he had anything to do with. This investment was made in a "happier time"; and, it is only as a result of their marital difficulties that the husband no longer wishes to share half and half with his wife assets held solely in his name. The facts and circumstances of the parties' life together flatly contradict the notion that Mr. Saff's promise was merely a representation made in a "happier time." Rather, this was a promise made by a husband to his wife which he consistently kept until he decided to abandon her.

Mrs. Saff transferred her share of jointly held savings to start Jamestown Steel and rendered valuable services in the early development of this business in reliance on the belief that she shared in the ownership of it. A significant portion of the funds used to launch Jamestown Steel in 1946 was derived from the joint earnings of Mr. and Mrs. Saff and held by them together in a joint account. The business was started in a small, rented garage. The two men spent much of their time selling while Mrs. Saff stayed in the garage next to the telephone. The first load of steel beams the company received were too large to fit into the garage, so Mrs. Saff painted them in order to prevent them from rusting. She ran the office, did the banking, bookkeeping, kept all the books and ledgers, talked to creditors, made out the payroll and other checks, paid the bills, filled out government forms, handled collections and did the tax accounting. She also acted as a secretary. In addition to this work in the family business, Mrs. Saff also worked for a period of time in a doctor's office without pay for three hours per week in order to compensate the doctor for the shots he gave to aid her in becoming pregnant. When the Saffs were unsuccessful in having their own children, they adopted two children. The first adopted child contracted polio and in order for Mrs. Saff to give him the constant care required, she was obliged to bring the company's book work home at night where, her husband concedes, she questioned him endlessly about all transactions in order to keep the business records accurate. Another enterprise called Jamestown Plastics was later launched by the Saffs. Mr. Saff testified that his wife performed full-time duty for this enterprise while also continuing her work for Jamestown Steel. Both parties agreed that Mrs. Saff also handled all of the personal family finances. In brief, it seems an inescapable conclusion that Mrs. Saff was the financial member of this husband-wife team, in business and at home. Mr. Saff himself testified that his wife has been associated with him in business from 1946 to the present. To this very day Mrs. Saff continues to be the steel business bookkeeper. Although the husband testified that she did not begin work until six or eight months after the business had commenced, his testimony is contradicted by the fact that all the business records reflect that the entries from the very first day of business were in Mrs. Saff's handwriting. . . .

Since appellant-wife seeks here an equitable remedy, it is important to note that in granting Mrs. Saff a divorce from her husband on the grounds of abandonment, the Trial Court found that Leonard Saff had left the marital residence in 1972 and has not returned. It further found that Clara Saff had made her husband welcome in their home and never interfered with him or subjected him to any public criticism or ridicule before the separation; and that her complaints, in private, about his drinking were prompted by reason of a warning given by a family doctor. It should also be noted that 12 years prior to this separation Mr. Saff had fathered a child by another woman and that Mrs. Saff forgave him for this and continued their marriage.

Michael v. Michael
791 S.W.2d 772 (Mo. Ct. App. 1990)

James A. PUDLOWSKI, Presiding Judge.

This is an appeal from a judgment and decree of dissolution which awarded respondent the majority of marital property and awarded appellant $500.00 in attorney's fees and no maintenance.

The evidence adduced at trial established that appellant and respondent were married in August 1972 and separated in April 1987. There were no children born of this marriage. Both appellant and respondent are well educated. Appellant holds a baccalaureate degree in political science and a master's degree in journalism. Respondent holds a baccalaureate degree in journalism and a master's degree in public administration.

In 1972, on the day following the parties' marriage, the couple moved to Little Rock, Arkansas where respondent was going to work for Southwestern Bell Corporation. While living in Little Rock, appellant was employed as a reporter for a local newspaper.

In June 1974, respondent received a promotion and was transferred back to St. Louis. In St. Louis, appellant worked for APC Skills Company and then for Maritz, Inc. In 1978, appellant was fired from Maritz, Inc. Upon appellant being fired, the couple agreed that appellant would not seek outside employment but instead would devote time to writing fiction. In that same year respondent received another transfer and the couple moved to Oklahoma City.

While living in Oklahoma, appellant continued to pursue a writing career, however, later abandoned this endeavor without ever having written a chapter in a book or a scene in a play. After giving up the attempt at writing, appellant worked briefly in a food store and spent 8-9 months working free-lance public relations. When appellant was not employed outside of the home, the couple agreed that appellant would be responsible for the general upkeep of the house and also for the preparation of the evening meal. Appellant spent several hours a day preparing the couple's dinner. Respondent claimed that appellant's other domestic chores were very lax. For two years while the couple was living in Oklahoma appellant drove respondent to and from work. However, for the rest of the mornings, appellant slept until 10 or 11:00 a.m.

In 1984 respondent was again transferred to St. Louis. After moving to St. Louis, appellant continued to cook the couple's dinner. He also periodically took the respondent to work but did not seek outside employment.

Throughout the marriage, the couple's lifestyle improved and they had a significant amount of disposable income. They were able to purchase homes whenever respondent accepted a job transfer and the couple took many trips including visits to Europe. In addition, respondent generously and gratuitously provided her mother annually with support funds in the sum of $5,000.

At the time of trial, respondent had been working for Southwestern Bell for more than 15 years and was earning over $70,000 per year. Respondent's additional benefits from Southwestern Bell included vested pension benefits through the Southwestern Bell Corporation Management Pension Plan equal to $1,169.58 monthly payable at age sixty-five (65), as of March 1, 1988. Appellant's statement of income and expenses provides that he receives no income from employment, however he receives $75 per month in interest, and his share of the gross income on the previous year's Federal Income Tax Return was $1200.

It is with some interest that we note the gender roles of the parties in this marriage are reversed from the more traditional roles of husband and wife. In the present case the wife is the party who earned the lion's share of the income by working outside of the home during the marriage. The appellant is the party who remained at home throughout the majority of the marriage and did not work outside of the home for several years. However, certainly the sex of the parties should have no bearing on the division of marital property or on the allowance or prohibition of maintenance.

The trial court allocated $51,347 or 75.5% of the parties' marital property to respondent and $14,128 or 21.5% to appellant. The court granted appellant no maintenance but allowed appellant $500 for attorney's fees.

Appellant raises three points on his appeal. Appellant claims that the trial court abused its discretion by its distribution of the parties' marital property, abused its discretion by awarding appellant no maintenance, and abused its discretion by awarding appellant only $500 in attorney's fees. . . .

Mo. Rev. Stat. §452.330 (1988) directs the trial court to divide the marital property in a just manner, after considering all relevant factors including the five factors set out in the statute, as follows:

(1) The economic circumstances of each spouse at the time the division of property is to become effective, including the desirability of awarding the family home or the right to live therein for any reasonable periods to the spouse having custody of any children.

(2) The contribution of each spouse to the acquisition of the marital property, including the contribution of a spouse as a homemaker;

(3) The value of the non-marital property set apart to each spouse;

(4) The conduct of the parties during the marriage; and

(5) Custodial arrangements for minor children.

There are two guiding principles inherent in §452.330: "[F]irst property division should reflect the concept of marriage as a shared enterprise similar to a partnership; and, second property division should be utilized as a means of providing future support for an economically dependent spouse." Krauskopf, A Theory for "Just" Division of Marital Property in Missouri, 41 Mo. L. Rev. 165 (1976).

When applying these guiding principles inherent in §452.330 to the present case we find that the trial court abused its discretion in its division of marital property. We first look at the economic circumstances of each spouse at the time the division of property is to become effective. Throughout the course of the marriage, appellant has become economically dependent on the respondent. At the time of the dissolution of marriage, appellant was unemployed, had not been employed in his chosen field of journalism for fifteen years, and had not been employed full-time since 1978. Conversely, at the time of dissolution of marriage, respondent had elevated herself within the Southwestern Bell organization to a position directing press relations and was earning in excess of $70,000 per year. Additionally, respondent was the recipient of extensive employment benefits including vested pension benefits which equalled $1,169.68 monthly (at age 65) as of March 1, 1988, and a savings plan which at the time of trial had a total vested account balance of $9,968.85.

With regard to the second statutory factor, the contribution of each spouse to the acquisition of marital property, including the contribution of a spouse as homemaker, the trial court found that the respondent, for the greater part of the marriage, had been the sole financial support of the parties and the funds used to acquire the marital property had been earned almost solely by her. Also, the court found that the appellant made no substantial contribution to the marriage as a homemaker because he showed a marked disinclination to undertake the normal domestic duties of a homemaker, engaging only in those duties, such as cooking the evening meal, which he found fulfilling, stimulating and interesting.

Although appellant did not work outside of the home for the majority of the years of the marriage, he did have outside employment for nearly one-third of the marriage. For two additional years appellant drove respondent to work and picked her up from work in the evening. While the appellant's performance of traditional domestic chores was often times lax, he did prepare dinner for himself and respondent throughout the duration of the marriage. We are not finding that appellant's contributions entitled him to an equal division of the marital property, however, we do hold that the trial court's division of property is against the weight of the evidence and therefore an abuse of discretion.

In his second point appellant claims that the trial court erred and abused its discretion in awarding no maintenance to appellant. Appellant argues that although he is educated and possesses a degree in journalism and public administration, the fact that he is 40 years old and has not held employment in either of these fields for the past fifteen (15) years will have a negative effect on his ability to find employment in order to support himself. Appellant does not claim that he is completely unable to support himself. However, due to the extended period of time that appellant has been out of the work force in his field, he requires a period of rehabilitative maintenance during which time he can obtain the necessary education and retraining to allow him to gain satisfactory employment in the field of journalism. Appellant argues that he would require an additional two and one half or three years of education to take course work that would enable him to be self-supporting as a journalist.

We have said that maintenance is awarded when one spouse has detrimentally relied on the other spouse to provide the monetary support during the marriage. If the relying spouse's withdrawal from the marketplace so injures his/her marketable skills that he/she is unable to provide for his/her reasonable needs maintenance may be awarded. . . . "Rehabilitative maintenance" should be awarded for a term reasonably sufficient to receive job training. . . . Rehabilitative maintenance is appropriate where there is substantial evidence that the party seeking maintenance will or should become self-supporting. . . .

We have reviewed the record before us and we find that the trial court did err and abuse its discretion in finding that the appellant failed to show that his ten year absence from the journalism field has injured his ability to secure employment therein at this time and earn a sum sufficient to meet his reasonable needs and that appellant wholly failed to establish his entitlement to maintenance under Mo. Rev. Stat. §452.335 (1986).

Section 452.335 sets out the factors which the court shall consider in ordering maintenance. The second stated factor the court is to consider is the time necessary to acquire sufficient education or training to enable the party seeking maintenance to find appropriate employment.

At trial appellant testified that he intended to enroll for a semester at the University of Texas in a program on Latin American Studies in order to enable him to re-enter journalism as a reporter in Latin America. He indicated that he wrote to several of the major newspapers in Florida and received a response from the Miami Herald which indicated that the appellant's plans for further education would be attractive credentials for a newspaper like the Miami Herald. Appellant further testified that because his most recent articles are fifteen years old, he needs to develop some fresh stories that have been written in the recent past to show editors that he is still able to write and report.

Appellant's need to acquire fresh skills in order to re-enter the field of journalism is reasonable. Journalism is a competitive field. Every year newly graduated students enter the job market with fine skills. If appellant is to be able to compete with these other graduates, it can certainly be expected that additional education would be beneficial. Appellant's plan to return to school in order to increase his marketability as a journalist would ensure that he become self-sufficient. Our disposition of the issues of marital property and maintenance is consistent with the generally accepted principals . . . that marriage is a shared enterprise and that maintenance should be utilized as a means of providing support for an economically dependent spouse until said spouse is self-reliant. . . .

This matter is remanded for further proceedings consistent with this opinion.

Judge Williams H. CRANDALL, Jr., dissenting. . . .

If we accept the concept of marriage as a shared enterprise similar to a partnership, husband had a negative impact on that partnership. Husband did not sacrifice his career for wife, rather he was a hindrance to her progress. On the issue of maintenance, husband has simply shown that he is unwilling, rather than unable, to support himself through appropriate employment.

For the foregoing reasons I would affirm the decree of dissolution.

Riehl v. Riehl
595 N.W.2d 10 (N.D. 1999)

Opinion by Justice MARING.

Deborah Riehl appeals from a district court judgment dated June 8, 1998, which granted the parties a divorce, divided their marital property, placed the parties' minor children in Deborah's custody, and ordered Andrew to pay rehabilitative spousal and child support. Deborah challenges the award of spousal support. We hold the trial court's decision to award rehabilitative spousal support for only the period of time commensurate with the recipient's period of rehabilitation is clearly erroneous. We reverse and remand the judgment of the district court.

I

At the time of trial, Deborah was age 43 and Andrew was age 45. They had been married for 24 years and had four children. Only the two youngest children were minors at the time of trial. Early in the marriage, Andrew worked as a farm laborer and construction worker. He then attended night school at Bismarck State College (BSC) and after completing a welding program became a boilermaker working both in state and out. Since 1987 Andrew has worked as a boilermaker with Minnkota Power Company in Center, North Dakota. At the time of trial, Andrew was earning $51,352 annually. He is provided with life, disability, health and dental insurance, deferred compensation savings, a medical flex program, and a pension.

Deborah's role during the marriage was primarily that of a homemaker. Over the years, she worked in positions of temporary employment, such as newspaper delivery, janitorial work, telemarketing, teacher's aide, and hotel maid. When the oldest two children entered school, Deborah was able to attend the University of Mary to work toward an elementary education degree. After one year of college, she again became pregnant and, after their fourth child was born, she became a full time homemaker.

In the twelve months from the time the parties separated and the trial was held, Deborah pursued her education and employment options. She worked with the North Dakota Job Service and a private vocational counselor and underwent testing of her aptitudes, interests, and academic proficiency. She also attended adult education classes through the spring and summer of 1997 to prepare for her return to college. At the time of trial, Deborah had almost completed a program at BSC that exposed displaced homemakers to a variety of career options.

The exploratory phase of her rehabilitation efforts directed her to the field of nursing. As a result, Deborah attended BSC in the fall of 1998 to complete basic science related courses which will allow her to enter a full-time college program to earn a bachelor degree in nursing. Deborah will begin the first two years of her nursing education by completing an LPN program through BSC. The program's cost of approximately $7,000 will be funded by a scholarship for which she qualified as a displaced homemaker. Upon completion of the LPN program, she will begin a bachelor of science in nursing (BSN) program at the University of Mary, which requires two to two and a half years to complete depending on course sequencing. The program's approximate cost will be between $18,800 and $23,500.

Deborah commenced this divorce action on February 28, 1997. Shortly before trial, the parties stipulated to the equal division of marital property, allocation of debts, and custody of the minor children to Deborah. The trial court adopted the parties' agreement. Because the parties could agree to neither the amount and duration of spousal support, nor the amount of child support, these issues were presented to the court in a trial held on March 31, 1998. The trial court established child support . . . Deborah requested spousal support in the amount of $1,000 a month for three years, reduced thereafter to $800 a month for six years and then $600 a month for the following six years. At that point, Andrew would be of retirement age and the support would cease. The trial court set spousal support at $800 per month for five years. Deborah appeals that award.

II . . .

Trial courts in our state must consider the *Ruff-Fischer* guidelines [based on Ruff v. Ruff, 52 N.W.2d 107 (N.D. 1952) and Fischer v. Fischer, 139 N.W.2d 845 (N.D. 1966)] in making a determination of spousal support, both as to amount and duration. The factors include:

> the respective ages of the parties, their earning ability, the duration of the marriage and conduct of the parties during the marriage, their station in life, the circumstances and necessities of each, their health and physical condition, their financial circumstances as shown by the property owned at the time, its value at the time, its income-producing capacity, if any, whether accumulated before or after the marriage, and such other matters as may be material.

Although a trial court need not make specific findings as to each factor, we must be able to discern a rationale for its determination. . . .

To be awarded spousal support, the trial court must find the spouse to be "disadvantaged." Wiege v. Wiege, 518 N.W.2d 708, 711 (N.D. 1994). A "disadvantaged" spouse is one who has "foregone opportunities or lost advantages as a consequence of the marriage and who has contributed during the marriage to the supporting spouse's increased earning capacity." [Van Klootwyk v. Van Klootwyk, 563 N.W.2d 377 (N.D. 1997)]. Here, the trial court found Deborah to be disadvantaged by the divorce because she "devoted her time and effort throughout the marriage of the parties to maintaining a marital residence and providing child care . . . [and her] responsibilities have caused her to forego any opportunity for career development, resulting in her present earning capacity at less than one-fourth [of Andrew's]." . . .

Spousal support is aimed at balancing the burdens and disadvantages created by the divorce. We recognize permanent and rehabilitative spousal support as two distinct remedies. Permanent support is appropriate when the economically disadvantaged spouse cannot be equitably rehabilitated to make up for the opportunities and development she lost during the course of the marriage. . . .

Rehabilitative spousal support, on the other hand, is appropriate when it is possible to restore an economically disadvantaged spouse to independent economic status, . . . or to equalize the burden of divorce by increasing the disadvantaged spouse's earning capacity. . . . There are two approaches to awarding rehabilitative spousal support. . . . One is the "minimalist doctrine" which has as its objective rehabilitating the recipient for minimal self-sufficiency. We have rejected this doctrine in favor of the more "equitable" approach to determining rehabilitative spousal support, which attempts to provide education, training, or experience that will enable the recipient to achieve "adequate" or "appropriate" self-support while improving her employment skills.

There is no ready formula to determine what amounts to "adequate" or "appropriate" rehabilitative support. In making that determination, however, a trial court should consider the duration of the marriage, the parties' earning capacities, the value of the marital property and other *Ruff-Fischer* factors. . . . We have also said in a long-term marriage it is important to consider "continuing a standard of living . . . [or] balancing the burdens created by the separation when it is impossible to maintain two households at the predivorce standard of living."

Andrew initially argues the award of spousal support was equitable because Deborah received half of the marital property. Typically, the trial court should consider the marital property division when setting the amount of spousal support. . . . Here, however, the parties stipulated to an equal division of the marital property. Each party received half the sale proceeds of their home and farmland, Deborah received half of Andrew's pension and 401(k), and the parties had no debt. Any income from these assets will presumably be the same for each party. Andrew's argument ignores the fact that the property division does not adjust the disparate earning capacities of the parties. Under these circumstances, the parties' property division had little bearing on the award of spousal support.

Andrew also argues the award of spousal support was equitable because five years of spousal support adequately rehabilitates Deborah. At the end of five years, he argues, Deborah will be educated, self-supporting and able to "meet her needs." The flaw in his argument is that it endorses the "minimalist doctrine," an approach we have clearly rejected. [*Van Klootwyk*, supra]. "Equitable" rehabilitative support goes further than minimal self-sufficiency; it aims to mitigate marital disadvantage caused by the impact at divorce of an economic role assumed during marriage.

Deborah's BSN program will cost between $18,800 and $23,500, or approximately $315 to $390 per month over the five year period she will be receiving spousal support. After paying for her education, Deborah's rehabilitative spousal support will effectively range from $410 to $485 per month. At the end of five years, assuming all goes as planned, Deborah will have just completed her education and entered the work force as an entry-level registered nurse. During these five years, Deborah will have no other income other than interest income earned on her one-half of the marital assets. She will not be accumulating retirement or pension benefits. She will also have custody of the two younger children during the first three years and custody of the youngest through the fourth year. Meanwhile, Andrew will be earning a salary of at least $52,000 and substantial vested benefits. When Deborah enters the work force at the entry-level she will be 48 years old and earn approximately $27,000, roughly half of Andrew's salary. After deferring meaningful work and education for 24 years to raise her family and support her husband's career, Deborah will be just starting the pursuit of her own career.

As we have said, rehabilitative spousal support aims to make up for the opportunities and development a disadvantaged spouse lost while assuming her economic role in the marriage. . . . While we have not endorsed the "equalization of income between divorcing spouses," . . . we conclude the period of spousal support in this case does not adequately address the burdens of the divorce. Under these facts we are convinced a mistake was made when the trial court awarded spousal support to a homemaker of 24 years for a period commensurate with the length of re-education or rehabilitation at which time the disadvantaged spouse will only be able to earn half of what the payor spouse earns.

III

Deborah argues the trial court's failure to consider permanent spousal support was clearly erroneous. As discussed, permanent spousal support is generally appropriate when the disadvantaged spouse cannot be equitably rehabilitated to make up for the opportunities she lost in the course of the marriage. . . . Even when the disadvantaged spouse is capable of rehabilitation we have recognized permanent spousal support may be appropriate to equitably share the overall reduction in the parties' separate standard of living. . . .

Because this case involves a long-term marriage and the respective earning capacities and standards of living of the parties will be greatly disparate even after Deborah receives her RN degree, the trial court should consider whether permanent spousal support would also be equitable to offset the permanent economic disadvantage suffered by Deborah as a consequence of the time she has spent as a homemaker.

IV

The judgment is reversed and remanded to the trial court for consideration of a longer period of spousal support, factoring in Deborah's job-entry process, the parties disparate earning capabilities and standards of living, and Andrew's ability to pay.

[The dissenting opinion by Justice Sandstrom is omitted.]

Martha Albertson Fineman, Societal Factors Affecting the Creation of Legal Rules for Distribution of Property at Divorce
At the Boundaries of Law: Feminism and Legal Theory 265, 272-273, 278 (Martha Albertson Fineman & Nancy Sweet Thomadsen eds., 1991)

One source of the controversy about property distribution rules [at divorce], I believe, is the existence of two competing and, perhaps incompatible and unrealistic, political visions of contemporary marriage. The first is the more modern view that marriage as an institution has been transformed so as to be consistent with formalistic notions of equality between the sexes. The second is the more traditional policy stance that the family is the appropriate, perhaps solitary, institution to resolve problems of dependency or need that inevitably arise in the context of families. . . .

Feminist reformers have adhered for the most part to the ideal of egalitarian marriage in addressing the economic questions in divorce. There may be several reasons why feminists haven't argued for the employment of concepts of affirmative (or protective) action in the area of divorce reform. First, such arguments would cast doubts on the ideal of family equality. Second, although the family is distinguishable from the market, result-oriented arguments that women should be treated differently in the family area because of their gender-related social characteristics might be transferred with very different symbolic connotations into the market. Third, generalized result equality rules may actually reinforce the idea that biology is destiny. And finally, to the extent that feminists' overriding objective is the affirmation of the ideal of equality, result equality rules which concede that equality does not in fact exist may create an impression that it cannot exist.

In some states the equality norm is formally embodied in provisions which establish an initial presumption that all property of the spouses is to be equally divided upon divorce. This rule equality presumption is consistent with the organizing concept of marriage as an equal partnership.

. . . Even without a specific mandate that the court presume that property is to be divided equally, judges and lawyers will tend to start at 50/50 because of the social and professional conditioning that presents modern marriage as an equal partnership. Alteration of the partnership model will probably be possible only if the spouse arguing for such a deviation can meet the burden of establishing that her circumstances (needs) clearly are exceptional. . . .

An equality view of marriage denies reality for many women who assume, during and after the marriage, more than a partner's share in the conduct and burdens associated with household and child care. The partnership metaphor slips easily into equal sharing for property, children, debts, and so on at divorce. The metaphor has symbolic content that is preserved only at significant cost to many women who must suffer equality in this one area while the rest of the society and culture continues to treat them unequally.

Milton C. Regan, Jr., Divorce Reform and the Legacy of Gender
90 Mich. L. Rev. 1453, 1459-1461, 1465-1471 (1992)
(Book Review)

Marriage is both a source of [economic disparities between men and women] and a buffer against their full force. On the one hand, marriage perpetrates disadvantage because most married couples have children, and women still overwhelmingly assume primary responsibility for the care of those children. . . .

At the same time marriage provides some insulation from the economic disparities associated with gender. Spouses typically pool resources for use by all members of the household, without imposing strict eligibility requirements based on market contributions. Indeed, the family is often regarded as the paradigm of a social arrangement that allocates resources on the basis of need rather than entitlement. . . .[43]

Divorce destroys this buffer against economic vulnerability. . . . Women and men must confront life within a market system in which individual "human capital" is a crucial determinant of their standard of living. At this point, the latent fault line of gender, suppressed and concealed during marriage, often erupts with a vengeance. . . .

. . . [Insofar as feminists promoted] an equal division standard in property law, there were considerable practical, rather than merely symbolic, concerns that underlay their support. There was much concern at the time property reforms were being considered that the broad discretion typically afforded judges tended to lead to allocations that disfavored women. In particular, many feared that the male-dominated courts would undervalue women's nonmarket domestic contributions to the household. . . .

These concerns continue to be relevant. . . .

---

43. . . . This is not to say that economic disparities do not matter within an ongoing marriage. As Susan Moller Okin has observed, "[I]t is still clearly the case that the possession by each spouse of resources valued by the *outside* world, especially income and work status, rather than resources valuable primarily within the family, has a significant effect on the distribution of power in the relationship." Susan M. Okin, Justice, Gender, and the Family 158 (1989). . . .

The primary economic asset of most households is the stream of future income that represents a return on career investment. Men tend to have better future earnings prospects than women. . . .

At the same time, divorce reform has significantly curtailed the availability of alimony, or "maintenance," payments, and has emphasized property division as the preferred means to provide for the economic needs of spouses at divorce. . . . The change in emphasis from alimony to property thus has blocked access to the marital asset that has the most potential to redress gendered economic disadvantage. To the extent that this change has hindered efforts to provide access to postdivorce income, it is a far more serious source of divorcing women's distress than the adoption of an equal division standard.

. . . Certainly a preference for property division over alimony is consistent with images of equality and economic independence. Alimony historically has reflected an acknowledgement of dependence, while property has powerful cultural appeal as a symbol of autonomy and self-reliance. Those concerned with promoting notions of equality thus might well prefer a one-time lump-sum distribution of assets rather than the perpetuation of contact between an ex-wife and the ex-husband on whom she must rely to make regular alimony payments.

Yet I think the story cannot be reduced simply to this. The image of equality is one strand in a more complex fabric of attitudes and understandings about marriage and its obligations, a fabric whose patterns have shifted dramatically over the past generation or so. . . . [O]ne way to characterize the general outline of this shift is as the continued advance of individualistic tenets that trace their roots at least as far back as the Enlightenment. In the current age, these tenets are reflected in heightened awareness of and attention to the "inner" psychological life of the individual, greater solicitude for "private" life as a vehicle for personal growth and self-development, and increasing influence of the view that choice and consent should be the sources of personal obligation. . . .

. . . No-fault divorce, for instance, proceeds on the assumption that the individuals involved are the only legitimate judges of whether a marriage should continue; unilateral no-fault divorce carries the logic of individualism to its conclusion, by proclaiming that either member of the marriage has the right to disavow the marriage as inimical to his or her personal interest. . . .

This . . . creates a crisis of legitimacy for alimony. Alimony traditionally rested on an analytical foundation of moral reciprocity, which posited that a woman was entitled to the support of her husband in return for her performance of domestic responsibilities. A husband deemed at fault in a divorce action for failure to fulfill his marital duties continued to be subject to his support obligation, for the law proclaimed that he could not unilaterally evade his responsibility by breaching the marital contract. Conversely, a wife's fault could relieve the husband of his duty of support and preclude receipt of alimony after divorce. . . .

Thus, precisely when the most important marital assets are more difficult to conceptualize as property, and when a claim on future income is increasingly important, we seem less and less able to offer a theory of postdivorce obligation. It is that we seem to be less willing to conclude that a former spouse should be the one to meet that need. Furthermore, this is not the result simply of equality rhetoric, but of a complex dialectic between individualism and equality. Greater emphasis on the individual as a sovereign apart from social relationships leads naturally to the embrace of formal equality, which posits the abstract similarity of all individuals. In turn, this formulation reinforces our understanding of persons as fundamentally asocial entities, for whom nonconsensual obligation based on the mere fact of a prior relationship seems unfair.

Jana B. Singer, Alimony and Efficiency: The Gendered Costs and Benefits of the Economic Justification for Alimony
82 Geo. L.J. 2423, 2428-2433, 2437-2441, 2454-2455 (1994)

Unlike traditional theories of alimony, which focus on achieving distributive justice between divorcing spouses, the economic rationale views alimony primarily as a means of encouraging efficient behavior during marriage. . . .

The efficiency argument in favor of alimony is premised upon three central assumptions. First, efficiency theorists assume that married persons, like other rational individuals, seek to maximize their individual welfare through the production and acquisition of commodities. Second, . . . efficiency theory conceptualizes marriage as a husband-wife partnership in which both parties desire to maximize joint production of commodities. These commodities include not only traditional measures of market wealth, such as income and material goods, but also so-called "household commodities" such as home-cooked meals and time spent with children. They also include personal assets — enhancements in the ability of one or both spouses to produce income or other commodities in the future — that economists refer to as investments in human capital.

Third, . . . efficiency theorists invoke the principle of comparative advantage to argue that specialization within marriage enables spouses to maximize their joint production of market and nonmarket commodities. This principle holds that, to maximize overall production, the members of a household (or of any organization) should allocate their resources to various activities according to the members' comparative or relative efficiencies in those activities. . . .

. . . Initially, economic theorists were quite comfortable discussing and defending the efficiency of such marital specialization along explicit gender lines. That is, theorists generally assumed that women, by virtue of their biology, possessed a "natural" comparative advantage over men in household, as opposed to market, production and that men enjoyed a correspondingly "natural" comparative advantage in market, as opposed to non-market work. The efficient household, under this model, was one in which the husband specialized in market production and the wife specialized in domestic work.

More modern efficiency theorists — perhaps recognizing the divisiveness of these biological assumptions — generally disclaim reliance on intrinsic gender differences. Instead, they link specialization to efficiency by emphasizing the unequal earning capacities of most husbands and wives, and by asserting that men and women tend to invest differentially prior to marriage in sector-specific human capital. . . .

What does the economist's endorsement of specialization have to do with the justification for alimony? The link is that specialization within marriage is beneficial for both spouses only so long as the marriage stays intact. Divorce changes the picture dramatically. In the absence of alimony or a similar transfer of assets, the spouse who has specialized in household production — who has invested in the marriage, rather than in the market — finds herself economically disadvantaged relative to the spouse who has specialized in market production. Not only has the domestic specialist forgone the opportunity to develop and maintain her own market-oriented human capital, but many of the domestic assets and capacities that she has produced or enhanced during the marriage are of extremely limited economic value . . . in the event of divorce.

A rational spouse . . . is likely to protect herself by investing more in the market and less in the production of marriage-specific goods and services. Alternatively, or perhaps in addition, such a rational, well-informed spouse may insist that her higher-earning partner forgo some of his market-oriented production in order to assume a larger share of childcare and other household responsibilities. But while these strategies are likely to reduce the disproportionate financial losses flowing from divorce, they also reduce the productivity of the intact marriage, because they decrease the degree of otherwise efficient marital specialization. . . .

Thus, the efficiency theorist argues, the possibility of financial losses resulting from divorce distorts the incentives that would otherwise lead to efficient, role-specialized behavior during marriage. Alimony is justified, under this view, to remove these distorting incentives and to encourage those spouses who are comparatively better suited for domestic work to "do the right thing" and invest in their marriages rather than in the market.

The economists' emphasis on specialization and efficiency does more than provide a theoretical justification for alimony; it also plays a major role in determining the availability and appropriate measure of any particular alimony award. Because the purpose of alimony, under this theory, is to avoid discouraging a lower earning spouse from engaging in efficient marital sharing behavior, an optimal award should neutralize the adverse financial consequences of such sharing behavior for any particular divorcing spouse.

The award should thus compensate each particular household specialist for the value of the market opportunities she has forgone as a result of the decision to invest primarily in the marriage. It should, however, do no more than this. Thus, to the extent that income differentials between divorcing spouses are not attributable to specialization during marriage, but instead result from investments and choices made prior to marriage, the efficiency justification is inapposite, and alimony is therefore unavailable. . . .

For feminists, perhaps the most troubling aspect of the dominant economic theory of alimony is the theory's reliance on the efficiency — and hence the desirability — of role specialization during marriage. Although modern efficiency theorists prefer to characterize alimony as compensation for decreases in human capital, or as a way of removing incentives that inhibit efficient sharing behavior, their arguments in favor of both concepts rest centrally on the desirability of role specialization within marriage and on the corresponding undesirability of marriages that deviate from such an optimal division of household labor. . . .

This attempt to justify alimony as a mechanism for promoting efficient specialization within marriage is problematic on grounds both internal and external to economics. Internally, economic theory itself casts doubt on the efficiency of role specialization during marriage. As Margaret Brinig and June Carbone have pointed out, the standard efficiency argument for marital specialization considers only specialization between husbands and wives; it does not consider the possibility of specialization among women.[72] . . . [F]rom a pure efficiency standpoint, the most productive household today may be one in which both spouses engage in full-time market work and the bulk of the domestic tasks, including childcare, are performed by a low-wage employee — almost certainly another woman, and quite likely a woman of color. This is hardly a solution that most feminists would be inclined to endorse.

Even if one focuses solely on specialization between husband and wife, the link between specialization and efficiency may be more problematic than that suggested by the relatively simplistic theory of comparative advantage that underlies the economic justification for alimony. Margaret Brinig, for example, has suggested that the standard economic account of marital specialization fails to consider important psychic costs associated with specialization, such as the cost to women who are not working outside the home, but who would like to be, and the cost to men who are working long hours, but who would like to spend more time with their children. Factoring in these psychic costs . . . suggests that, for many couples, the most "efficient" marriage is not one characterized by a high degree of specialization. Rather, an efficient union would entail both partners having significant

---

72. [Margaret F. Brinig, The Law and Economics of No-Fault Divorce, 26 Fam. L.Q. 453, 456-457 (1993)]; June Carbone, Economics, Feminism, & the Reinvention of Alimony: A Reply to Ira Ellman, 43 Vand. L. Rev. 1465, 1489-1490 (1990).

ties to the paid labor force and spending significant time with their children.[76] Encouraging such "nonspecialized," but child-centered, unions may have significant societal benefits as well, including encouraging all parents to invest more heavily in developing their children's human capital. Unfortunately, the strong commitment to specialization that underlies the economic efficiency justification for alimony may hinder the sort of workplace and other societal changes that are necessary to facilitate these nonspecialized, child-centered unions.

Arlie Hochschild's documentation of married women's "second shift" also casts doubt on the efficiency of the traditional division of household labor. In her detailed study of married couples, Hochschild found that women who earn less than their husbands and who assume primary responsibility for childcare and other domestic tasks often accomplish this juggling act not by limiting their market production (as the theory of comparative advantage would predict), but by reducing their already scarce leisure time.[78] This finding also suggests a potential inefficiency in the specialized household, as the cost of reducing a husband's relatively abundant leisure time should be less than the cost of reducing by an equivalent amount either the wife's paid employment or her relatively scarce leisure time. This, in turn, suggests that the tenacity of the gender-based division of labor within marriage may be less a reflection of efficiency and more a manifestation of men's continuing power over women — or, to put it in economic terms, of successful strategic and rent-seeking behavior on the part of husbands. . . .

. . . Focusing on the overall efficiency (or productivity) of the household unit renders invisible — and hence, unproblematic — these gender-based power differentials. . . .

. . . I have previously proposed a regime of post-divorce income-sharing, under which divorcing spouses would continue to share their joint incomes equally for a set number of years after divorce. . . .

. . . Treating post-divorce income as jointly, rather than individually, owned is . . . likely to induce a number of desirable ex ante effects. First, a regime of post-divorce income sharing is likely to diminish existing power disparities during marriage, by removing a primary wage earner's ability to threaten his spouse with economic abandonment in the event of divorce. Second, such an income-sharing requirement is likely to encourage husbands to increase their investment in family care, "since the financial consequences of such an investment strategy would not be so devastating in the event of a divorce, and the benefits of investing solely in one's own career would not be so complete." Persuading men to increase their involvement in domestic life is likely, in turn, to facilitate (rather than hinder) the sort of changes in

---

76. [Brinig, supra note 72, at 457-458.]

78. Arlie Hochschild, The Second Shift: Working Parents and the Revolution at Home (1989). . . .

workplace structure that feminists and others have identified as essential to achieving long term gender equity and to nurturing the next generation. . . .

Notes

1. The Economic Consequences of Divorce. Studies have consistently shown that women and children are worse off economically after divorce than are men, although the extent of the measured disparity varies by study. See, e.g., Barbara Baker, Family Equity at Issue: A Study of the Economic Consequences of Divorce on Women and Children i (1987) (showing 33 percent decline in per capital income for divorced women and children and a 17 percent increase for divorced men); Heather R. Wishik, Economics of Divorce: An Exploratory Study, 20 Fam. L.Q. 79, 97-98 (1986) (in Vermont survey, divorced wives experienced a 33 percent drop in per capita income, and children a 25 percent drop, while men experienced increase); Leslie J. Brett et al., Women and Children Beware: The Economic Consequences of Divorce in Connecticut 7 (1990) (in Connecticut survey, mean per capita income of divorced wives fell by an average of 16 percent while that of divorced husbands increased by 23 percent).

Some have suggested that the introduction of no-fault divorce worsened the economic circumstances of women and children, as judged by the declining alimony and child support awards. See, e.g., Lenore J. Weitzman, The Divorce Revolution: The Unexpected Economic Consequences for Women and Children in America xiv, 32-36; H. Elizabeth Peters, Marriage and Divorce: Informational Constraints and Private Contracting, 76 Am. Econ. Rev. 437, 449 (June 1986) (women who divorced in 1979 in no-fault divorce states received less alimony and child support than those who divorced in states requiring a showing of fault). The basic argument is that no-fault divorce reduces the bargaining power of the wife to exact economic concessions in exchange for agreeing to a divorce. See Allen M. Parkman, No-Fault Divorce: What Went Wrong? 1-2 (1992).

The more accepted view is that financial support for divorced women and their children has always been inadequate, and that no-fault divorce was not the cause of any worsening situation. See, e.g., Marygold S. Melli, Constructing a Social Problem: The Post-Divorce Plight of Women and Children, 1986 Am. B. Found. Res. J. 759, 768-772 (financial awards to women and children were inadequate both before and after no-fault divorce reform); Marsha Garrison, The Economics of Divorce: Changing Rules, Changing Results, in Divorce Reform at the Crossroads 75-101 (Stephen D. Sugarman & Herma Hill Kay, eds. 1990) (New York study comparing 900 divorces before and 900 divorces after 1980 reform of alimony rules demonstrates no-fault divorce not a necessary factor in decline in alimony awards); Herbert Jacob, Another Look at No-Fault Divorce and the Post-Divorce Finances of Women, 23 L. & Soc'y Rev. 95, 111 (1989) (longitudinal study of 587 divorced young women over 15-year period showed effects of no-fault divorce "either modestly benign or neutral"). Many commentators have explained the economic plight of post-divorce women to be attributable to wage differentials in the labor market rather than to marriage or divorce. See, e.g., Stephen D. Sugarman, Dividing Financial Interests at Divorce, in Divorce Reform at the Crossroads, supra, at 130-165; Herbert Jacob, Faulting No-Fault, 1986 Am. B. Found. Res. J. 773, 774-780.

Contemporary fault-based divorce reform may permit further study of the relationship between the permissible grounds for divorce and its economic consequences for women. Louisiana and Arizona laws now provide for "covenant marriage." In Louisiana, parties choosing a covenant marriage cannot divorce except on grounds of adultery, a felony leading to a death sentence or imprisonment at hard labor, abandonment for one year with a constant refusal to return, physical or sexual abuse, or a two-year continuous separation. A divorce from bed and board is also available on these grounds, and for "habitual intemperance of the other spouse, or excesses, cruel treatment, or outrages of the other spouse" if such behavior renders living together "insupportable." Once a bed and board divorce is obtained, a permanent divorce may follow within a year, or within 18 months if there are children. See La. Rev. Stat. Ann. §9:307 (West 2000). Arizona's law is similar, although not identical. See Ariz. Rev. Stat. §25-904 (Supp. 2000-2001). Covenant marriage is the first success in a growing movement to tighten marriage laws as a way of strengthening marriage, especially when there are children. See, e.g., William Galston, Divorce American Style, 124 The Public Interest 12 (1996); Elizabeth S. Scott, Rational Decisionmaking about Marriage and Divorce, 76 Va. L. Rev. 9 (1990). Bills similar to those adopted in Louisiana and Arizona have been considered in many other states, some that would create a "contract marriage" option, some providing for longer waiting periods, and some eliminating no-fault grounds altogether. These proposals are criticized in Ira Mark Ellman & Sharon Lohr, Marriage as Contract, Opportunistic Violence, and Other Bad Arguments for Fault Divorce, 1997 U. Ill. L. Rev. 719, 724-736; Laura Bradford, Note, The Counterrevolution: A Critique of Recent Proposals to Reform No-Fault Divorce Laws, 49 Stan. L. Rev. 607 (1997). What gender-based critiques of these proposals would you expect?

2. Equality and Property Distribution at Divorce. At one time, property was distributed at divorce in accordance with simple property law principles. In common law property states, as illustrated in the *Saff* case, whoever held title to a piece of property left the marriage with that property. The inequities of this approach are illustrated in the case. Community property states worked differently, since their laws were based on a theory of marital partnership and deemed the earnings of each of the marriage partners to be the property of both.

Equitable distribution reform swept the nation in the 1970s and 1980s, leading to statutes that attempted to inject greater fairness into property distribution at divorce. The principles these reforms attempted to enact, however, were not entirely consistent. Implicit in most equitable distribution statutes was the notion of a marriage partnership, similar to the partnership principle inherent in community property states. This notion assumed the fairness of the division of responsibility during the marriage, and thus the fairness of an equal division of the property at divorce. The strictest equal division rules are found in the community property states of California, Louisiana and New Mexico. See Cal. Fam. Code §2550 (West 1994); La. Rev. Stat. Ann. §9:2801(4)(b) (West Supp. 2001); Ruggles v. Ruggles, 860 P.2d 182, 188 (N.M. 1993). While the presumption is strong in favor of an equal division in other states as well, including some common law property states, the law in many jurisdictions, including North Dakota where *Michael* was decided, recites a number of factors to consider in dividing property "equitably," including principles of contribution and need.

The principle of contribution invites investigation of how the assets were acquired, and thus tends to favor the spouse whose earnings or efforts produced non-consumed property, although this principle is often modified by giving a wife's (or in *Michael*, the husband's) "homemaker contribution" some recognition. The principle of need emphasizes the spouses' comparative abilities to support themselves after the marriage, and thus favors the more financially dependent spouse. Typically, equitable distribution statutes blend partnership, contribution, and need factors. See, e.g., Uniform Marriage and Divorce Act 307, 9A U.L.A. (1973).

The presumption applied in some states that marital property should be split 50-50 is, in part, an effort to eliminate some of the gender bias that may be incorporated into notions of what is just, especially when the husband made all the money. This is the perspective from which Regan argues that a 50-50 presumption is generally advantageous to women. Fineman is thinking of the Mrs. Riehl's of the world, however, for whom a 50-50 split does not recognize the disparities in earning power and need with which men and women are likely to leave marriage. It is from this perspective that she attacks the "equality ideal" and offers in its place a "substantive" conception of equality based on need. Is need necessarily incompatible with formal equality principles? Clearly it is not, since need can be implemented in a gender-neutral way. Would it matter to Fineman that her needs approach would help Mr. Michael, as well as Mrs. Riehl? Is either of these plaintiffs more sympathetic than the other? If so, why?

3. Equality and Alimony. While the rules of equitable distribution address property existing at the time of the divorce, as to which the jurisdiction gives the spouses some claim as a result of the marriage, alimony (or spousal support) concerns continuing claims beyond the marriage, usually on the income of one spouse that has not yet been earned at the time the marriage has ended. Traditionally, as the Regan excerpt explains, alimony represented compensation to a dependent wife for her husband's breach of marital duties. With the advent of no-fault divorce, a needs rationale supplanted the fault-based rationale, but it has not been an entirely satisfactory one. Among other things, it begs the question why one spouse should be the insurer of the financial security of the other, when modern marriage law entitles (in most jurisdictions) either spouse to leave the marriage when he or she wants to. Need supplies a standard, but not an explanation for liability that might define the contours of that standard. The analytical confusion is reflected in current law, which (1) disfavors alimony, preferring to accomplish a "clean break" for the parties through property distribution alone, if possible; (2) if alimony is ordered, favors term or "rehabilitative" alimony designed, as in both *Michael* and *Riehl*, to get a dependent spouse back on her (or his) feet so that a "clean break" can be accomplished some time in the future; (3) when need comes into play, applies open-ended needs and standard-of-living criteria that produce wildly disparate results; and (4) in about half of American jurisdictions, allows or requires consideration of marital fault.

One way to break this analytical log-jam is to treat alimony as a pay-back of one spouse's non-economic investments in the marriage on behalf of the family, thereby encouraging such investments, some of which would otherwise be irrational or inefficient. In other words, alimony corrects what would otherwise be distorting financial incentives, assisting parties in making decisions that will be to the benefit of the joint undertaking of marriage. See Ira Ellman, The Theory of Alimony, 77 Cal. L. Rev. 1, 12 (1989). What are the implications of this rationale? The Principles of Family Dissolution adopted by the American Law Institute (ALI) in May 1996, which were written by Ira Ellman as Chief Reporter, provide for "compensatory spousal payments" to close the gap between the parties' earning capacities attributed to lost opportunities by one spouse as a result of investments in the marriage. See Proposed Final Draft Part 1, Principles of the Law of Family Dissolution: Analysis and Recommendations, February 14, 1997 at Chapter 5.

One criticism of compensation-based approaches is that they would require parties seeking alimony to prove lost opportunities, which would often be difficult, especially in the case of an individual who did not have career expectations. The ALI Principles obviate this difficulty by using the length of the marriage as a proxy for "lost opportunity," which is then used as the multiplier in the income-gap-closing formula. The rate of increase is also enhanced when the dependent spouse has assumed primary caretaking responsibilities for the couple's offspring. Id. at §5.05. For a more explicitly restitituion-based approach to alimony, see June Carbone, Economics, Feminism and the Reinvention of Alimony: A Reply to Ira Ellman, 43 Vand. L. Rev. 1463 (1990).

Is Singer's primary criticism of compensation-based theories of alimony that they are not really efficient? Or that they provide incentive for role specialization in marriage, which is bad for women? Or both? How compatible is her proposal for equal sharing of post-divorce income with Fineman's rejection of equal division of marital property in favor of a disproportionate division based on need? Are they working in the same direction, or in different ones? For further exploration of the "efficiency" considerations that are sometimes omitted from consideration of rationales for alimony and other family law rules, see Ann Laquer Estin, Can Families Be Efficient? A Feminist Appraisal, 4 Mich. J. Gender & L. 1 (1996).

A number of other commentators have also urged equal sharing of post-divorce income. See, e.g., Joan Williams, Is Coverture Dead? Beyond a New Theory of Alimony, 82 Geo. L.J. 2227, 2258 (1994); Cynthia Starnes, Divorce and the Displaced Homemaker: A Discourse on Playing with Dolls, Partnership Buyouts and Dissociation Under No-Fault, 60 U. Chi. L. Rev. 67 (1993); Susan Moller Okin, Justice, Gender, and the Family 180-183 (1990); Jane Rutherford, Duty in Divorce: Shared Income As a Path to Equality, 58 Fordham L. Rev. 539, 577-592 (1990). Is such an approach best justified under formal equality principles or as an application of substantive equality? Does it matter? What should alimony or spousal support be used to accomplish?

Would private, pre-commitment strategies work better? Martha Ertman proposes as one way to narrow the post-divorce inequity between home-maker and breadwinner that couples construct "Premarital Security Agreements" in which homemakers are granted a security interest in post-divorce income and marital property by virtue of their specialization in domestic labor. Ertman, Commercializing Marriage: A Proposal for Valuing Women's Work Through Premarital Security Agreement, 77 Tex. L. Rev. 17 (1998). The proposal takes advantage of the fact that before marriage, both parties might be able to think more clearly about equity in the event of divorce than they can at the time of the divorce. Does it sound workable?

The Canadian courts have moved away from the "clean-break" goal of alimony, putting greater value, especially in long-term marriages, on evenly distributing between the parties the long-term economic consequences of the divorce, including the consequences of disparities in their earning capacities. See, e.g., Moge v. Moge, 3 S.C.R. 813 (1992).

Which approach would seem to be most appropriate to apply to the fact in *Michael*? To the facts in *Riehl*? Assume that after her training is complete, Mrs. Riehl will start, at age 48, by being able to earn half the amount her husband, at age 50, can earn. The court finds this to be inadequate for her to support herself. What would be enough? How is this to be determined? Will the rule apply equally well to Mr. Michael?

Spouses seeking alimony after a short marriage are typically treated even less generously than spouses after a long-term marriage. See, e.g., Roginsky v. Blake-Roginsky, 740 A.2d 125 (Md. Ct. App. 1999), cert. denied, 747 A.2d 645 (Md. 2000) (affirming denial of indefinite alimony, even though husband was a nuclear physicist and wife had only worked occasionally as a housekeeper and restaurant server, because marriage had only lasted five years, and wife was only 28 years old at the time of trial).

4. Educational Degree as Marital Property?   Regan refers to the fact that the most important marital assets are difficult to conceptualize as property, thus making property distribution unsatisfactory as the only vehicle for achieving post-divorce justice. One asset he had in mind is the educational degree or professional license earned during the marriage. The most compelling situation for treating a degree or license earned as a marital asset is when one spouse — usually the wife — supported the other spouse during the marriage while he earned an undergraduate or professional degree, in anticipation of the higher standard of living that the degree would bring to the family unit. What happens when the marriage ends before she has obtained any of the benefits of that degree? Typically, such families have no appreciable property to distribute, and the supporting spouse is not entitled to alimony since she has demonstrated that she can support herself. See Uniform Marriage and Divorce Act 308 (award of "maintenance" requires showing that obligee is "unable to support himself or herself through appropriate employment"). Should the husband be able to "walk away" from the marriage with his degree and owe his ex-wife nothing for her investment in his degree or for her disappointed expectations?

Courts have developed a number of different approaches to deal with this issue. New York courts have gone the furthest, treating a professional degree as marital property, subject to division at divorce at an amount representing the enhanced standard of living that degree would allow which is attributable to the wife's contribution and efforts toward attainment of the degree. O'Brien v. O'Brien, 489 N.E.2d 712 (N.Y. 1985); see also Grunfeld v. Grunfeld, 731 N.E.2d 142 (N.Y. 2000) (to avoid double-counting, value of spouse's law license could not be distributed as a marital asset without some adjustment in maintenance award that had been based on spouse's future income stream as a lawyer).

Most courts have rejected the property theory, however, on the grounds that a degree has none of the transferability attributes of property and that its value depends entirely on the efforts of the degree holder. See, e.g., In re Marriage of Graham, 574 P.2d 75, 77 (Colo. 1978):

> An educational degree, such as an M.B.A., is simply not encompassed even by the broad views of the concepts of "property." It does not have an exchange value or any objective transferable value on an open market. It is personal to the holder. It terminates on death of the holder and is not inheritable. It cannot be assigned, sold, transferred, conveyed, or pledged. An advanced degree is a cumulative product of many years of previous education, combined with diligence and hard work. It may not be acquired by the mere expenditure of money. It is simply an intellectual achievement that may potentially assist in the future acquisition of property. In our view, it has none of the attributes of property in the usual sense of that term.

While the *Graham* case rejected any relief at divorce to the wife, who had contributed 70 percent of the financial support of the family, including educational expenses, during the period her husband was earning his degree, a subsequent case in Colorado extended alimony to the wife on the grounds that her ability to support herself through *appropriate employment* (see the UMDA 308 standard, supra) had to be interpreted in light of the parties' expectations that they would enjoy a higher standard of living after the husband attained his degree. In re Marriage of Alar, 747 P.2d 676 (Colo. 1987).

Other courts have applied theories of contract and equity or other strained theories of alimony to arrive at awards that often combine features of alimony and lump-sum property division. See, e.g., DeLa Rosa v. DeLa Rosa, 309 N.W.2d 755 (Minn. 1981) (applying restitution theory to award wife return of monies she had spent to support husband while he earned his degree); In re Marriage of Francis, 442 N.W.2d 59 (Iowa 1989) (awarding "reimbursement alimony" to recompense wife for economic sacrifices that directly enhanced the future earning capacity of the husband); Mahoney v. Mahoney, 453 A.2d 527 (N.J. 1982) ("reimbursement alimony" available for "contributions made with mutual and shared expectation that both parties" would benefit from degree); Pyeatte v. Pyeatte, 661 P.2d 196 (Ariz. Ct. App. 1983) (recognizing possibility of award based on express or implied contract between parties). See also Meyer v. Meyer, 620 N.W.2d 382 (Wis. 2000) (appropriate for trial court to consider pre-marital contributions of one spouse to the medical education of the other in determining spousal maintenance). Do you see any problems with these theories? Do they reduce marriage to a balance sheet in which the contributions of each spouse are quantified and netted out? See Martinez v. Martinez, 818 P.2d 538, 540-541 (Utah 1991) (disapproving award of "equitable restitution" in professional degree context). Is recovery under any of the equitable or contract theories suggested above consistent with Fineman's approach?

Does the theory for recognizing one spouse's contribution toward the license or degree of the other stop with degrees and licenses? More common than a spouse who earns a degree during the marriage is the spouse who enhances his or her earning capacity through work experience. Why should the spouse who has invested most heavily in his earning capacity walk away with the benefits of that increase, especially if the other spouse has sacrificed career opportunities in order to invest herself more heavily in home and family? It is this slippery slope, of course, that has discouraged greater recognition of professional degrees and licenses. The one state, New York, that explicitly treats degrees and licenses as marital property has begun the slide, recognizing increased earning capacity in other contexts as well. See, e.g., Martin v. Martin, 514 N.Y.S.2d 775 (App. Div. 1994) (value of husband's law license earned during marriage was enhanced after twelve-year Congressional career, and subject to equitable division as marital property); Elkus v. Elkus, 572 N.Y.S.2d 901 (App. Div. 1991) (husband's involvement in opera singer Frederica von Stade's career, as well as his caring for the children, contributed to career's increase in value, and that increase is marital property); Golub v. Golub, 527 N.Y.S.2d 946 (Sup. Ct. 1988) (increase in value of model/actress Marisa Berenson's career found to be marital property, and husband entitled to his share of increase, limited to the degree to which such increase is attributable to his efforts).

5. Equality and Child Support. Although the problem of child support is not limited to the divorce context, the difficulties in obtaining realistic child support awards and in enforcing child support orders further exacerbate the economic vulnerability of divorced custodial mothers. In 1997, only 59 percent of the 11.9 million mothers living with children under the age of 21 with the children's fathers had a court decree or agreement for child support. See U.S. Department of Commerce, Bureau of the Census, Child Support for Custodial Mothers and Fathers: 1997, Current Population Reports, Series P-60, No. 154, Table A, at 6 (October 2000). The figures were higher for divorced mothers — 70 percent — but only 47 percent of divorced custodial mothers received any child support, the average amounting to only $4,326 per year or $360 per month. See U.S. Department of Commerce, Bureau of the Census, Child Support for Custodial Mothers and Fathers: 1997, Current Population Reports, Series P-60, No. 154, Table B, at 7 (October 2000).

The Child Support Enforcement Amendments of 1984 and the Family Support Act of 1988 and subsequent federal laws condition receipt of considerable federal monies on changes in state child support systems designed to improve the quantity, quality, and enforceability of child support orders. Among other things, states must have statewide support guidelines, which act as rebuttable presumptions in all support proceedings. 42 U.S.C. §667 (1994). States must also implement automatic wage withholding, unless "good cause" exists or the parties have agreed otherwise. 42 U.S.C. §§666(a)(8), 666(b)(3) (1994 & Supp. V. 1999). Other measures provide for the interception of tax refunds (§666(a)(3)), garnishment of federal wages (§666(a)(1)(4)), and parent locater services (§663). The Federal Child Support Recovery Act of 1992 now makes it a federal crime to cross state lines to avoid payment of child support. 29 U.S.C. 2601-2654 (1994). A number of federal Courts of Appeal have upheld the Act from the constitutional challenge that it exceeded Congress' authority. See, e.g., U.S. v. Crawford, 115 F.3d 1397 (8th Cir. 1997), cert. denied, 522 U.S. 934 (1997) (child support payments or debts resulting from non-payment are things in, or substantially related to, interstate commerce).

Aggressive state laws have also been added to help improve child support collections. For example, at least 15 states provide for the suspension, revocation, or denial of occupational or business licenses of child support delinquents. See, e.g., Iowa Code §252J.1, et seq. (West 2000). Fifteen states provide for the suspension or revocation of a delinquent child support obligor's driver's license. See, e.g., N.C. Gen. Stat. §50-13.12

(1999). Other statutes provide for the suspension of permanent license plates or motor vehicle registrations, hunting or fishing licenses, and even marriage licenses. See, e.g., Tex. Fam. Code Ann. §232.001 et seq. (Vernon Supp. 2001). Other statutes are cited and discussed in National Conference on State Legislatures, 1995 State Legislative Summary: Children, Youth & Family Issues (1995).

Also important are the standards for determining the amount of child support liability. Most state guidelines use a formula based either on the percentage of the obligor's income ("percentage formula") or on the parents' relative incomes ("income shares"). Under both formulas, the level of support sought to be defined in a child support order is the marginal expenditure that parent would be expected to pay for the child if the child still lived with the parent. Policymakers aim for this amount so that, theoretically at least, the obligor is paying only the child's expenses and not those of the parent with whom the child primarily lives.

The perceived fairness of child support awards under existing child support formulas depends on the goals one thinks should be achieved and, among other things, the relative earning powers of the two parents. When the parties' incomes are substantially different and the party with whom the child primarily lives is the lower-earning parent (as is typical), the standard of living enjoyed by the child in his or her primary residence is lower, sometimes substantially so, than the standard of living enjoyed by the nonresidential parent. When the parties' incomes are equivalent, the standards of living in the two households are likely to be equivalent. And when the primary residential parent earns more, the child support order may require substantial sacrifice from the obligee parent in order to subsidize a household that is living quite comfortably. Current formulas are insensitive to such variations. They are also insensitive to various changes in circumstances that may occur, such as remarriage of one or both parties and the birth of subsequent children by either parent. The effort to tighten enforcement has also increased inflexibility; federal law prohibits, for example, the retroactive modification of child support arrearages, even if the arrearages are a result of loss of employment or other circumstances affecting the obligee's ability to pay.

These issues can have gender implications of the substantive equality sort — that is, formally neutral rules may produce effects that tend, given social realities, to leave women worse off than men. These unequal effects explain the impulse behind income-equalization proposals made by Singer and others. Is this the answer? Is it practical? For the development of an income-equalization proposal solely in the context of child support that purports to have no alimony component, see Judith Cassetty et al., The ELS (Equal Living Standards) Model for Child Support Awards, in Essentials of Child Support Guidelines: Economic Issues and Policy Considerations 329 (Proceedings of the Women's Legal Defense Fund's National Conference on the Development of Child Support Guidelines, Sept. 1986); see also Marianne Takas, Improving Child Support Guidelines: Can Simple Formulas Address Complex Families, 26 Fam. L.Q. 171 (1992) (advocating the Melson formula, in effect in Delaware and a couple of other states, which follows a three-step approach producing greater income equalization than either income shares or percentage formula methods).

The American Law Institute's Principles of Family Dissolution attempt to achieve the goals underlying the marginal expenditure concept with an approach it calls the "enhanced marginal expenditure model" that is more sensitive to income disparities between the parties. The formula begins with a base amount, such as one produced under the conventional income shares or percentage formula approaches. It then adds a supplement, representing the diminution in income in the residential household likely to be attributable to the circumstances of being a residential parent. This supplement diminishes as actual income in the residential household approaches the obligee's income. Special self-support reserve provisions attempt to guarantee a minimum income for each parent. Additional principles, including income imputation rules, attempt to insure that both parties have an incentive to engage in full-time, productive employment. See American Law Institute, Principles of the Law of Family Dissolution, Tentative Draft No. 3, Part II, April 8, 1998 (ALI, Child Support Principles).

Special problems are caused by very high-income and very low-income parents. The problems of poor fathers, who are capable of providing little or no support for their children regardless of how strict the child support system is, are explored in Irwin Garfinkel et al., Fathers Under Fire: The Revolution in Child Support Enforcement (1999). More recent studies are cited in Ann Laquer Estin, Moving Beyond the Child Support Revolution, 26 L. & Soc. Inquiry 505, 517-21 (2001). The self-support reserve included in some proposals, including the American Law Institute Principles described above, attempt to address this set of cases.

As for high-income parents, most jurisdictions set a limit over which child support formulas are not applied. See, e.g., Minn. Stat. Ann. §518.551, subd. 5(b) (West Supp. 2001) (capping income considered for determining child support at $5,000/month). The theory is that over and above a certain income, the formula that would otherwise be applied is simply too far beyond the economic needs of the child and beyond what would have been spent on the child if he or she lived with the obligee. Paying child support based on an extraordinarily high income, it is assumed, will simply be diverted to the support of the residential parent, to whom the obligee's financial obligations, if any, have already been defined. However, can't children of high income parents ordinarily expect extravagance? In many states, parents cannot be ordered to support a child beyond age 18, even for college expenses. Should the custodial parent be enabled to save money from earlier, unneeded support for future needs? Should a child whose expectation for a large inheritance is likely to be frustrated by the obligee's greater loyalty to subsequently-formed children in another family be entitled to receive, instead, a super-enhanced child support award?

Subsequent families pose especially difficult analytical challenges. Should child support be refigured with each new family obligation, so that the children of an obligee are being supported at an equal level? Or is it to be assumed, when an obligee undertakes new family responsibilities, that the obligee enters those responsibilities reduced by whatever prior obligations have been incurred?

Perhaps the most difficult problem of all is how to handle adjustments in child support in the case of equally shared residential responsibility. Should an obligee's responsibilities be reduced in accordance with the amount of visitation time he or she exercises? It is generally recognized that even when custody is equally split, the lower earning parent should receive some support to reflect his or her lower capacity to pay. But how much? And how much visitation, if any, should trigger a set-off? Depending on the answer to such questions, the child support system may create an incentive to seek primary custody of a child when one would not otherwise do so. Is this desirable?

Putting Theory into Practice

3-8. Judith and Edgar Brown were married 15 years ago. Shortly after the marriage, Judith gave up her job as a nurse and moved to another city so that Edgar, who had been unemployed, could accept a job in construction. Soon thereafter she became pregnant, and their first child was born; their second child was born 15 months later. The couple decided that Judith would not pursue her nursing career, but rather would devote her full-time energy to the rearing of the children. Edgar was periodically unemployed and, to follow job opportunities, sometimes had to take jobs requiring him to be away for six days a week. During that period, Judith attended to all the needs of the children and managed the home. Several times she moved with the children solely to be nearer to job opportunities for Edgar.

Edgar found it increasingly difficult to find employment and after about ten years of marriage, he began drinking heavily. During periods of unemployment, he made no contribution to the household, either financially or with respect to care of the children and the household. Eventually, because of the combination of his drinking problem and a depressed building market, Edgar virtually gave up looking for work. When their younger child was eight, Judith went back to work and, except for small jobs Edgar obtained here and there, she contributed the full financial support of the household as well as most child- and home-related tasks. While Edgar was wasteful with money, spending much of it on drinking with his friends, Judith did her best to manage well what she could hold on to, working overtime and even saving about $5,000 over the next five years.

The couple now has decided to divorce. The parties have equity in their current home of $30,000, savings secretly stored away by Judith of $5,000, Judith's pension benefits from her hospital job worth $9,000, and two cars, each worth about $5,000. Judith earns $30,000 per year, and last year she earned about $9,000 in overtime. Edgar is currently unemployed and last year earned $6,500, nearly all of which he spent on himself.

In an equitable distribution state that uses the "laundry list" of factors including those listed in *Michael*, how should the parties' assets be divided? Which theory described by Fineman seems most appropriate in this case? Do you see any difficulties with this theory? Is the rule you have applied consistent with formal equality principles? Substantive equality?

Assume that the state applies Uniform Marriage and Divorce Act §308, permitting an award for maintenance to a spouse who "(1) lacks sufficient property to provide for his reasonable needs; and (2) is unable to support himself through appropriate employment or is the custodian of a child whose condition or circumstances make it appropriate that the custodian not be required to seek employment outside the home." Should Edgar be entitled to maintenance?

3-9. Daryl, a well-known rock star, fathered a child as a result of a one-night-stand with Joyce, who is unemployed and on welfare. Daryl has a net *monthly* income of $43,000. The state child support guidelines contain a rebuttable $1,000 monthly child support limit. Make the arguments you think each party would make with respect to the rebuttable $1,000 guideline. Who should win? See State v. Hall, 418 N.W.2d 187 (Minn. Ct. App. 1988) (limit upheld).

3-10. State X is considering a proposal providing that a noncustodial parent who does not exercise his or her visitation rights would be required to compensate the custodial parent for the additional economic and psychic costs of the failure to do so. Is this a good proposal? Is it good for women? See Carol Bruch, Making Visitation Work: Dual Parenting Orders, 1 Fam. Advoc. 22 (Summer 1978); Karen Czapanskiy, Child Support and Visitation: Rethinking the Connections, 20 Rutgers L.J. 619 (1989).

3-11. The rule in virtually every state is that child support and visitation are independent rights and obligations: failure to pay child support is not a defense to denial of visitation, and frustration of visitation is not a defense to failure to pay child support. Is this a good rule?

2. Women's "Special Role" as Child-Rearers

≡ *Rena K. Uviller, Father's Rights and Feminism:*
≡ *The Maternal Presumption Revisited*
≡ 1 Harv. Women's L.J. 107, 108-110, 112-114 (1978)

Recognition that women have any claim whatever to custody of their children following divorce was, interestingly, a twentieth century feminist victory. Until this century, fathers had a virtually absolute right to the custody of all children of the marriage. This paternal presumption, essentially irrebuttable, stemmed from English common law which viewed children as the servants of their fathers; the father was entitled to the child's services in return for which the father owed the duty of maintenance and support. "It is a well settled doctrine of common law," wrote the New Hampshire Supreme Court in 1860, "that the father is entitled to the custody of his minor children . . . that he is bound for their maintenance and nurture, and he has the corresponding right to their obedience and services." [State v. Richardson, 40 N.H. 272, 273 (1860).] . . .

By the late nineteenth century, nascent theories about the importance of the mother-infant bond occasionally made an inroad on the father's rights. The so-called "tender years doctrine" for the first time gave mothers a slim chance against a fit father. Yet that inroad was tentative indeed, in light of the father's consequent relief from child support duties upon award of children to the mother and because the "tender years" preference was valid only during the child's infancy. Thus, in transferring to the father a four and one-half year old child who had been in its mother's care from birth, a New York court in 1842 observed that the child no longer had need of the mother's "expertise" and noted the father's "natural right" to custody as well as his superior financial resources for the child's education and training. [People ex rel. Barry v. Mercein, 3 Hill 399 (N.Y. 1842).]

Only when the duty was imposed upon fathers to support children not in their custody did the maternal preference, at least for very young children, acquire some force. A father's absolute financial responsibility irrespective of custody was not widely imposed until the 1920's which witnessed the burgeoning influence of psychological theory, particularly Freudian theory, concerning child development and maternal attachment.[16] These factors, together with the entrenched assumptions about woman's role in society, resulted in a marked shift in custodial preference to the mother. In a few states the maternal preference was codified. But for the most part it was judicially imposed. . . .

The maternal presumption in divorce proceedings is anathema to most feminists. The legal presumption that children belong with their mothers absent maternal unfitness reinforces the enduring stereotype of women as instinctive child rearers, inherently unsuited for worldly pursuits. Abjured by those who also reject sex-role assignments in family life, the maternal

---

16. Anna Freud expressed the child's need for the mother in terms which seem almost obsessive today: "So long as the mother is constant in her role as provider for the child, without undue interruptions through physical absence or undue emotional preoccupation with other persons or matters of interest in her life, there is every chance that the child's attachment to her will remain constant now and that there will be a secure basis for the growth and development of further, similar attachments. . . ." Freud, Some Remarks on Infant Observations, 8 The Psychoanalytic Study of the Child 17 (1953).

presumption presupposes a societal order of stay-at-home mothers with fathers as sole economic providers. . . .

Yet giving fathers an equal footing with mothers in custody disputes is a feminist goal that bears reconsideration. Discarding the maternal preference before women as a class have made any substantial headway in the non-domestic world may just be a case of the proverbial cart and horse; under the guise of sex-neutrality, women who want their children may be at a distinct disadvantage in custody disputes due to their inferior earning capacity and an enduring social bias against working mothers. In addition, despite their feminist and child welfare rhetoric, rapidly proliferating "fathers' rights" groups are ringing an unmistakable note of sexist backlash. . . .

Equal custody rights for fathers remains an unchallenged women's movement tenet because it is viewed as a satellite of that star in the feminist firmament — shared child rearing *during* marriage. Foregoing parenthood is simply not an acceptable destiny for most people, rhetoric to the contrary notwithstanding. Yet it is only women who are compelled to make the choice between having children and achieving occupational success. It is still the working mother, not the father, who forgoes vocational advancement in order to care for her children, especially when they are small. Feminists of both sexes correctly perceive that unless daily concerns of child rearing become the shared responsibility of both father and mother, there is little chance that women with children will achieve equality outside the home. . . .

Since countless individual needs of children cannot be accommodated by day care centers, assuming such centers exist, the only alternative for most women is a husband who does much more than "help out." He is not merely willing to spend Saturday buying Susie galoshes; he remembers, as well, that she needs them. He accepts equal responsibility for the daily, endless attentions that children require. Such parental mutuality makes it possible for women to enter or remain in the job market after they have children. More important, it can ultimately alter the structure and expectations of the working world itself. . . .

. . . Not until men regularly are willing to leave the office early to attend to their children's needs will it be regarded as legitimate for women to do so. Only when acceptance as a "serious" producer in the working world does not preclude concurrent child care duties, when "working father" takes on the same connotation as "working mother," will employed women not be penalized for bearing children. . . .

. . . A sex-neutral custody law which does not take into account the mother's disproportionate child rearing responsibilities in the early years, nor her economic disadvantage when the marriage ends, is likely to have a profoundly discriminatory effect on the vast majority of divorced women who want to keep their children. As for the children themselves, a sex-neutral custody standard such as the "child's best interest" may, ironically, be the worst possible means for resolving custody disputes. . . .

. . . [T]he maternal preference, resting on the assumption that it has been the woman who has committed herself to care for home and children, should yield only to a showing that in fact it has been the father who has assumed that role during marriage. If a father can prove that he and not the mother has devoted his time to domestic duties, that he and not she has compromised his work for the sake of the family, then indeed he should prevail. This is not the same as determining who has been the "better" parent. Indeed, a parent less obsessed with child rearing may often be "better" for a child, especially if the exclusive domesticity of one parent has been realized at the cost of frustration and resentment. Nonetheless, it is quantity and not quality that should govern, if custody proceedings are not to denigrate into the psychological experts' swearing contest. . . .

For those of us dedicated to the elimination of rigidly dehumanizing sex-role assignments, it is disquieting to conclude that the maternal presumption should be defended and preserved. But, in a society which continues to discriminate against women in every other aspect of life, a mother's preferred status regarding custody of her children is not unlike the "reverse discrimination" and preferred status urged on behalf of historically disadvantaged groups in a variety of other contexts. Many civil libertarians have had little difficulty defending and rationalizing such compensatory treatment. For all the law prompts social change as well as reflects it, at this point in history the law should recognize a woman's option to keep the children whose daily care she has so disproportionately assumed.

≡ *DeCamp v. Hein*
≡ **541 So.2d 708 (Fla. Ct. App. 1989)**

LETTS, Judge. . . .

[W]e do not believe that the [tender years] doctrine has been totally abolished. For example, a six-month baby being nursed by her mother should obviously be in her mother's custody, unless the judge found her unfit. In the case at bar, there is no mention of whether the one-year-old was being nursed by the mother. Nonetheless, our version of common sense suggests that, under the facts of this particular case, the one-year-old female infant and her three-year-old sister preferably should reside with the mother. In Brown v. Brown, 409 So. 2d 1133 (Fla. Ct. App. 1982), Judge Hurley quoted with approval the testimony of a psychiatrist who opined: "From zero until four and a half, . . . the essential person in that child's life is the mother. . . . I maintain it's extremely important for [a] three year old little girl to be with her mother." . . . [T]he psychiatrist's pronouncement in *Brown* would still, in our opinion, prove to be a relevant factor in deciding the primary residence of these two baby girls. . . .

Burchard v. Garay

42 Cal. 3d 531, 229 Cal. Rptr. 800, 724 P.2d 486 (Cal. 1986)

BROUSSARD, J.

This case concerns the custody of William Garay, Jr., age two and one-half at the date of trial. Ana Burchard, his mother, appeals from an order . . . awarding custody to the father, William Garay.

As a result of a brief liaison between Ana and William, Ana became pregnant. Early in her term she told William that she was pregnant with his child, but he refused to believe that he was the father. . . .

. . . Ana undertook the difficult task of caring for her child, with the help of her father and others, while working at two jobs and continuing her training to become a registered nurse. William continued to deny paternity, and did not visit the child or provide any support.

. . . Ana [subsequently] brought a paternity and support action. After court-ordered blood tests established that William was the father, he stipulated to paternity and to support in the amount of $200 a month. Judgment entered accordingly on November 24, 1980. In December . . . William visited his son for the first time. In the next month he moved in with Ana and the child in an attempt to live together as a family; the attempt failed and six weeks later he moved out.

William asked for visitation rights; Ana refused and [sought] exclusive custody. William responded, seeking exclusive custody himself. . . .

. . . Applying the "best interests" test, [the court] awarded custody to William. Its decision appears to be based upon three considerations. The first is that William is financially better off—he has greater job stability, owns his own home, and is "better equipped economically . . . to give constant care to the minor child and cope with his continuing needs." The second is that William has remarried, and he "and the stepmother can provide constant care for the minor child and keep him on a regular schedule without resorting to other caretakers"; Ana, on the other hand, must rely upon babysitters and day care centers while she works and studies. Finally, the court referred to William providing the mother with visitation, an indirect reference to Ana's unwillingness to permit William visitation.

Pursuant to the court order William took custody of the child on August 15, 1982. Ana appealed from the order . . . and William, Jr., remained in his father's custody pending this appeal. . . .

[W]e conclude that the trial court erred in applying [the best interests] standard. . . .

. . . [C]omparative income or economic advantage is not a permissible basis for a custody award. . . . If in fact the custodial parent's income is insufficient to provide a proper care for the child, the remedy is to award child support, not to take away custody.

The court also referred to the fact that Ana worked and had to place the child in day care, while William's new wife could care for the child in their home. But in an era when over 50 percent of mothers and almost 80 percent of divorced mothers work, the courts must not presume that a working mother is a less satisfactory parent or less fully committed to the care of her child. A custody determination must be based upon a true assessment of the emotional bonds between parent and child, upon an inquiry into "the heart of the parent-child relationship . . . the ethical, emotional, and intellectual guidance the parent gives to the child throughout his formative years, and often beyond.". . . It must also reflect a factual determination of how best to provide continuity of attention, nurturing, and care. It cannot be based on an assumption, unsupported by scientific evidence, that a working mother cannot provide such care — an assumption particularly unfair when, as here, the mother has in fact been the primary caregiver. . . .

The order is reversed.

BIRD, C.J., concurring. I write separately to underscore that the trial court's ruling was an abuse of discretion not only in its failure to give due weight to the importance of continuity and stability in custody arrangements but in its assumption that there is a negative relation between a woman's lack of wealth or her need or desire to work and the quality of her parenting. As this case so aptly demonstrates, outmoded notions such as these result in harsh judgments which unfairly penalize working mothers. . . .

When the record contains no evidence as to which parent does provide [the greatest] care, clearly the "working mother" factor operates as a negative presumption. Even more clearly, this factor operates unfairly when the record indicates that the mother has in fact been the primary caregiver. The use of such a presumption as a basis for a custody award is of dubious constitutionality.

Furthermore, the presumption is inappropriate because the relationship between maternal employment and the "presumed facts" about a child's best interests is not supported by reason or experience. Typically, it is the mother who provides most day-to-day care, whether or not she works outside the home. . . . A presumption which ignores this fact is likely to lead to erroneous and unfair decisions.

Moreover, there is no accepted body of expert opinion that maternal employment per se has a detrimental effect on a child. . . .

The burden of the trial court's reasoning would certainly fall most heavily on women. In those cases where the father contests custody, he is the parent likely to have superior economic resources. . . . This alone would give him an advantage under the trial court's reasoning. Further, such resources may well include the ability to support a nonworking spouse. Conversely, the mother is likely to have no choice about working, particularly if she does not remarry. . . . In the 25 to 44 age range, the remarriage rate of divorced men is almost double that of divorced women. . . .

Yet, under the trial court's rationale, it is the mother — and not the father — who would be penalized for working out of the home. She and she alone would be placed in this Catch-22 situation. If she did not work, she could not possibly hope to compete with the father in providing material advantages for the child. She would risk losing custody to a father who could provide a larger home, a better neighborhood, or other material goods and benefits.[5] . . .

If she did work, she would face the prejudicial view that a working mother is by definition inadequate, dissatisfied with her role, or more concerned with her own needs than with those of her child. This view rests on outmoded notions of a woman's role in our society. Again, this presumption is seldom, if ever, applied even-handedly to fathers.[6] The result — no one would take an unbiased look at the amount and quality of parental attention which the child was receiving from each parent.

The double standard appears again when, as here, the father is permitted to rely on the care which someone else will give to the child. It is not uncommon for courts to award custody to a father when care will actually be provided by a relative, second wife, or even a babysitter. . . . However, the implicit assumption that such care is the equivalent of that which a nonworking mother would provide "comes dangerously close to implying that mothers are fungible — that one woman will do just as well as

---

5. For example, in Porter v. Porter, 274 N.W.2d 235 (N.D. 1979), the reviewing court affirmed a custody award to a working father because "he is in a position to lend more stability and guidance to nurturing the development of the children during those periods of time in which he would not be actually pursuing his employment. . . ." As the wife had forsaken a career during marriage to care for the children, the husband's earning capacity was substantially greater than hers. It was this greater earning capacity which apparently was the source of his "stability and guidance." . . .

6. For example, in In re Marriage of Levin [162 Cal. Rptr. 757 (1980)] footnote 1, the Court of Appeal dismissed the notion that the father's performance as an "excellent custodial parent" was impaired by placing the child in nursery school at the minimum age of two years on a nearly full-time basis.

See also In re Marriage of Estelle, [592 S.W.2d 277 (Mo. Ct. App. 1979)], in which the court affirmed a custody award to a working father, not remarried, as against an equally fit working mother. The reviewing court made no negative comments about the child's placement in day care, but rather emphasized that the father often prepared the child's breakfast and dinner and picked her up from the day care center himself. It is difficult to imagine a mother's performance of these chores even attracting notice, much less commendable comment. . . .

In its award to the father, the trial court "repeatedly emphasized [the mother's] employment" and "noted that [the mother's] 'career and need for obtaining a better livelihood has diminished her manifested ability to care for the child other than in Day Care homes.' " The trial court "did not remark upon [the father's] inability personally to care for the child during his working hours." The court concluded that "the husband [was] more inclined to the old fashioned virtues," that "the mother of the child is an energetic and ambitious career woman . . . . and that the father of the child is perhaps less ambitious than the mother, but is more of a homebody." These moralizing conclusions, supported only by the facts recited above, were sufficient to support an award of custody to the father.

See also Masek v. Masek [228 N.W.2d 334 (N.D. 1975)], in which a mother who taught music part time lost custody to a father who worked full time. The trial court noted that the mother slept until 9 a.m. on Saturdays, failed to prepare breakfast for her husband who left for work at 7 a.m., and on occasion had run out of jam and cookies. It concluded from these facts that she was unfit for custody because her "primary interests are in her musical career and outside of the house and family."

another in rearing any particular children." (Polikoff, [Why Are Mothers Losing: A Brief Analysis of Criteria Used in Child Custody Determinations, 7 Women's Rts. L. Rep. 235, 241 (1982)].) This is scarcely consistent with any enlightened views of childrearing. . . .

To force women into the marketplace and then to penalize them for working would be cruel. It is time this outmoded practice was banished from our jurisprudence.

Patricia Ann S. v. James Daniel S.
435 S.E.2d 6 (W. Va. 1993)

PER CURIAM . . .

The parties were married [in] 1967. . . . Three children were born of the marriage, [who are now ages 14, 11, and 7]. The [mother] was a kindergarten school teacher but left her employment upon the birth of their first child. The [father] is an architect. . . .

The primary issue in this case is the [mother]'s contention that she should be awarded custody of the parties' children. . . . [S]he cites three points of error committed by the circuit court in granting custody to the [father]: (1) the circuit court erred in failing to find that the [mother] was the primary caretaker; (2) the circuit court erred in utilizing psychological experts prior to the circuit court's determination as to who was entitled to the status of primary caretaker; and, (3) the circuit court erred in granting custody of the children to the [father].

The parties agree that the guidelines for establishing custody are clearly set forth in Garska v. McCoy, [278 S.E.2d 357] (1981). We defined primary caretaker . . . in *Garska*, as "that natural or adoptive parent who, until the initiation of divorce proceedings, has been primarily responsible for the caring and nurturing of the child." The law presumes that it is in the best interests of young children to be placed in the custody of the primary caretaker. . . .

It is the circuit court's responsibility to determine which parent is the primary caretaker. . . . In *Garska*, we listed the factors to be considered by the circuit court in making this determination. However, . . . we pointed out, "[i]f the trial court is unable to establish that one parent has clearly taken primary responsibility for the caring and nurturing duties of a child neither party shall have the benefit of the primary caretaker presumption."

It is clear from the evidence that the parties shared the primary caretaker duties as discussed in *Garska*. While the evidence presented established the fact that the [mother] was the homemaker and the [father] was the wage earner, this Court has recognized that the length of time a parent has alone with a child is not determinative of whether the primary caretaker presumption should attach. . . . The [mother] was at home for the children when they would return from school while the [father] would work throughout the day. However, the [father] was also a substantial participant in the child care duties once he came home from work.

With respect to the child care duties, the [mother] testified that she was a night person, meaning she would stay up late at night and sleep later in the morning. As a result, both parties testified that the [father] would be responsible for getting the boys ready for school and fixing their breakfast. Both parties further testified that the [mother] would primarily plan and prepare the evening meals on the weekdays, but on the weekends the [father] would often prepare the evening meals. The parties also testified that they shared the responsibility for getting the children ready for bed each night.

In terms of school and social activities for the children, the evidence is indicative of the fact that both parties were active in their childrens' social lives. . . . [The mother] participated in PTO (Parent Teacher Organization) meetings and school activities. [A teacher] also testified that the [father] was involved with the childrens' school activities; and, the [father] testified that he was instrumental in helping the children with their homework in the evenings.

Furthermore, each parent organized and participated in social activities with the children. [The mother] would organize birthday parties for the children, and she would often host pool parties for the children and their friends at the parties' home. On the other hand, the [father] would arrange and participate in camping, hiking, and biking trips as well as other sporting events with the children. . . .

Finally, the evidence suggests that the parties shared in the responsibility of disciplining the children. The [father] admitted that he used a belt to whip the boys, but he stated that he used his hand to whip Jennifer. The [mother], however, stated that she no longer uses the belt to whip the children. Rather, the [mother] testified that she had attended parenting classes, and as a result, she employed a new method of discipline such as taking away the childrens' privileges and grounding them for their wrongdoings.

. . . [W]e agree . . . that neither party is entitled to the status of primary caretaker because the child care duties were shared equally by the parties. Therefore, the issue of custody properly rests on the best interests of the child. . . .

With this in mind, we turn to the [mother's] second argument. The [mother] contends that the circuit court erred in utilizing psychological expert witnesses prior to the circuit court's determination as to who was entitled to the status of primary caretaker.

. . . [The father] called psychologist, Mari Sullivan Walker, to testify before the family law master. Ms. Walker met with the [father] and the three children for approximately ninety minutes on September 22, 1990. Ms. Walker was of the opinion that the children perceive their father as the more nurturing person rather than their mother. Ms. Walker testified that all three children told her that the [mother] "beat" them. . . . Based upon the childrens' responses [to her question how they thought life would be with their father versus life with their mother,] Ms. Walker opined that the children have more faith in their father as opposed to their mother whom they were afraid of and with whom they were angry. . . .

. . . Dr. Charles Yeargan, a child psychologist, . . . was initially hired by the [mother], but later the parties agreed to use him as a neutral expert to give his opinion regarding the welfare of the children. In October of 1990, Dr. Yeargan interviewed the entire S. family.

In response to questions asked by [father]'s counsel, Dr. Yeargan stated that he didn't ask the children where and with whom they wanted to live; however, based upon the childrens' comments, it was Dr. Yeargan's opinion that the children feel emotionally safer with the [father and that they would prefer to live with him].

Dr. Yeargan stated that the children perceive the [father] as emotional and supportive, and the [mother] is perceived as angry. Further, Dr. Yeargan testified that Jennifer told him that if her brothers live with the [father], then that is where she wants to live. Dr. Yeargan also opined that both parents have behavioral traits that they need to work out in order for them to be able to better cope with and relate to their children.

Ultimately, it was Dr. Yeargan's opinion that it was in the best interests of the two boys, Jason and Justin, that they live with the [father]. With respect to Jennifer, Dr. Yeargan admitted he did not have a lot to go on, but he recommended that Jennifer live with her mother because of "the interests of the two different parties," "the activity levels," "the socialization issues" and "the involvements."

. . . Dr. Carl McGraw . . . interviewed all three children, the [father], and the [father]'s mother, because she had been helping care for the children. Dr. McGraw stressed the importance of keeping the children together in order to keep the family unit intact. Dr. McGraw noted that he had difficulty understanding Dr. Yeargan's reasoning for splitting the children between each parent. Dr. McGraw testified that the children told him they felt their mother was mean. Dr. McGraw stated he didn't ask the children who they wanted to live with, but he testified that they were adamant about wanting to live with their father. It was Dr. McGraw's opinion that the children would "have a better chance" if all three of them were to live with the [father], considering the rapport [he] has with [them]. . . .

The circuit court determined that the best interests of the children would be served by awarding custody to the [father]. There was an abundance of evidence presented in this case, which included the testimony of the parties, neighbors, teachers, family members, friends, and psychologists.

[In addition to the psychological testimony,] Jessica Halstead Sharp, a neighbor and friend of the parties, testified that she found the [father] to be loving and nurturing towards the children unlike the [mother] who, in Mrs. Sharp's opinion, had a problem dealing with the children. Mrs. Sharp also stated that, on more than one occasion, she overheard the [mother] calling the children vulgar names.

In addition, Nancy Jo S. and Reese and Ron Webb, Jr. testified that the children interact well with the [father]. However, they all felt the [mother] acted hostile with the children, and thus, the children did not respond well to her. All three witnesses further confirmed Mrs. Sharp's testimony that the [mother] called the children vulgar names, and they added, she used bad language around the children as well. . . .

Jason, the eldest son at fourteen years of age, is old enough to make a decision as to which parent he wants to live with, and the record clearly supports the circuit court's finding that Jason should live with his father. . . . Justin, on the other hand, is eleven years of age and not quite capable of making such a decision, but the evidence supports the circuit court's finding that he should live with his father. In addition, the [mother] admits that there is a lot of hostility between the boys and her, and because of this anger she might not be able to manage them. . . .

However, with respect to Jennifer, we do not believe that the record has been adequately developed. . . .

. . . [W]e hold that the circuit court judge did not abuse his discretion by concluding that the best interests of the two boys would be served by awarding custody to the [father]. With respect to Jennifer, we remand the case to the circuit court for further development of the record in order to determine what is in her best interests. . . .

WORKMAN, Chief Justice, dissenting.

The majority opinion marks a sharp departure from the primary caretaker rule which has been a viable and working concept in West Virginia for more than a decade. More disturbing, however, is the determination that it is in the best interests of children to place them in the custody of a parent who has abused both the wife and the children. In doing so, the majority implicitly places its stamp of approval on physical and emotional spousal abuse.

Deaths by domestic violence are increasing dramatically every year in West Virginia, and there is much discussion about the inefficacy of the judicial system in dealing with family violence. But until judicial officers on every level come to a better understanding of the phenomenon of family violence in its finer gradations, the response of the court system will continue to fall short. The majority demonstrates a tragic lack of understanding of the true nature of the dynamics that underlie family violence.

Erosion of Primary Caretaker Presumption

The primary caretaker rule as set forth in Garska v. McCoy, [278 S.E. 2d 357] (1981), has been an important part of domestic relations law . . . for more than twelve years. . . .

> . . . In setting the child custody law in domestic relations cases we are concerned with three practical considerations. First, we are concerned to prevent the issue of custody from being used in an abusive way as a coercive weapon to affect the level of support payments and the outcome of other issues in the underlying divorce proceeding. Where a custody fight emanates from this reprehensible motive the children inevitably become pawns to be sacrificed in what ultimately becomes a very cynical game. Second, in the average divorce proceeding intelligent determination of relative degrees of fitness requires a precision of measurement which is not possible given the tools available to judges. . . . Third, there is an urgent need in contemporary divorce law for a legal structure upon which a divorcing couple may rely in reaching a settlement.

[278 S.E. 2d at 361-362.] After stating the rationale for implementing the primary caretaker rule, this Court [in *Garska*] ruled that: "in any custody dispute involving children of tender years it is incumbent upon the circuit court to determine as a threshold question which parent was the primary caretaker parent before the domestic strife giving rise to the proceeding began." [278 S.E.2d at 363.]

In the instant case, it was clearly an abuse of discretion for the family law master and the circuit court to deny primary caretaker status to the mother. It is unfathomable that a woman who gives up her career (in this case, that of being a kindergarten teacher) to stay home to raise three children does not qualify as the primary caretaker, when as a full-time stay-at-home mother she breast-fed all three children; was so concerned about unnecessary additives and excess sugar that she processed her own baby food; was responsible for the majority of meal planning and preparation; was primarily responsible for laundering the family's clothing and housecleaning; was a Girl Scout troop leader; was a regular volunteer at her children's school and an active member of the parent-teacher organization; was responsible for scheduling and taking the children to their medical appointments; and was primarily responsible for managing the children's social activities. For some unarticulated reason, both the family law master and the circuit court appear to have been bowled over by the fact that the father helped in the evenings and weekends. Not unlike many modern fathers, the [father] did participate in some of the household and childrearing responsibilities. The mother and father jointly oversaw the bedtime routine of the children. Upon the birth of the third child, the father, by agreement of the parties, awoke the two oldest children and prepared their breakfasts, because the baby (Jennifer) was up a lot at night.

As Jennifer grew older and began sleeping all night, the parties continued this routine. Although the mother stayed up late, during those evening hours she cleaned up from dinner, prepared lunches for the children to take to school the next day, and did other household duties. The [father] planned recreational activities such as camping and hiking trips, primarily for the boys. Given the father's admitted ten to twelve-hour work days combined with frequent business trips which took him away from home, it is difficult to conceive how he could ever qualify as having equal caretaking responsibility. The family law master and circuit court's conclusions that neither individual qualified as the primary caretaker has the effect of somehow elevating the father's necessarily limited hours with the children, given his lengthy work days, to accord him the same caretaker status as the full-time stay-at-home mother. The majority in essence places a higher value on a father's time and contribution.

By upholding the circuit court's ruling, the majority begins an erosion of the primary caretaker rule, or at least sends a signal to domestic relations practitioners that it will be situationally ignored when expedient. . . . Sadly, . . . this case boils down to . . . one expert versus another [which the primary caretaker presumption was intended to avoid.] We explained the dangers of relying on expert testimony in custody cases in David M. v. Margaret M., [385 S.E.2d 912, 919] (W. Va. 1989):

> Expert witnesses are, after all, very much like lawyers: They are paid to take a set of facts from which different inferences may be drawn and to characterize those facts so that a particular conclusion follows. There are indeed cases in which a mother or father may appear competent on the surface, only to be exposed after perfunctory inquiry as a child abuser. . . . When both parents are good parents, the battle of the experts can result only in gibberish.

In this case, the testimony of three expert witnesses was admitted. Only one of the three, Dr. Charles Yeargan, was deemed by the court to be an independent expert. The [father] sought out Dr. Mari Walker, who has since been disciplined by the West Virginia Psychological Association for violation of the ethical principles of the American Psychological Association for her testimony in this case [that is, making a recommendation that the father receive temporary custody of the children on the basis of a single ninety-minute interview]. Later, the [father] sought out another expert, Dr. Carl McGraw, who concurred with the findings of Dr. Walker that custody should be placed with the father. Of primary interest to Dr. McGraw was his concern that the children not be split up among the parents. While this is certainly a laudable concern, it appears that this focus may have totally overshadowed Dr. McGraw's "objectivity" with regard to his ultimate recommendation. . . .

The family law master and circuit court . . . erred by permitting testimony on the issue of the relative fitness of the parties. Fitness, once it has properly been raised, does not involve a comparison of the parties, but instead requires a showing that the individual designated as the primary caretaker is unfit. . . . Because there was no showing of unfitness on the part of the mother, who clearly qualified as the primary caretaker, the majority opinion does great disservice to the primary caretaker rule in addition to exacerbating the pain of this family. . . .

Majority Okays Spousal Abuse

This father not only takes a belt to the three children[5] regularly, but he also has taken a belt to his wife. Phenomenally, the family law master did not permit the wife to testify in detail to the physical abuse she endured throughout the marriage, as he apparently concluded it had nothing to do with the children.

In fact, spousal abuse has a tremendous impact on children.

> Children learn several lessons in witnessing the abuse of one of their parents. First, they learn that such behavior appears to be approved by their most important role models and that the violence toward a loved one is acceptable. Children also fail to grasp the full range of negative consequences for the violent behavior and observe, instead, the short term reinforcements, namely compliance by the victim. Thus, they learn the use of coercive power and violence as a way to influence loved ones without being exposed to other more constructive alternatives.
>
> In addition to the effect of the destructive modeling, children who grow up in violent homes experience damaging psychological effects. There is substantial documentation that the spouse abuser's violence causes a variety of psychological problems for children. Children raised in a home in which spouse abuse occurs experience the same fear as do battered children. . . .
>
> Spouse abuse results not only in direct physical and psychological injuries to the children, but, of greatest long-term importance, it breeds a culture of violence in future generations. Up to 80 percent of men who abuse their wives witnessed or experienced abuse in their family of origin. Abused children are at great risk of becoming abusive parents. Thus, the ultimate question in assessing the relative fitness for custody of the abuser and victim is which parent is most likely to provide the children with a healthy, caring and *nonviolent* home.

L. Crites & D. Coker, What Therapists See That Judges May Miss, The Judges' Journal, 9, 11-12, (Spring 1988). . . .

There is yet another aspect of spousal abuse that judges and many others find difficult to understand. These relationships are characterized not

---

5. According to the mother's testimony, the father also regularly disciplined Jason (the oldest boy) by grabbing his shoulders and pushing him up against a wall or tree, on one occasion bruising his head. The father admitted overreacting and perhaps using excessive force, but denied it happened on a regular basis. The mother admitted that she, at one time, also used corporal punishment on the children, but had taken parenting classes in 1989 and learned that there were better ways to handle discipline. She testified that she used time-outs and withdrawal of privileges following her completion of the parenting classes.

only by physical abuse, but also by repeated humiliation and other psychological abuse that " 'reaches the level of a campaign to reduce the partner's sense of self-worth and to maintain control[;]' " and "a pattern on the part of the abusive partner to control the victim's daily actions. . . ." Crites & Coker, supra, at 9.

It is clear from Mr. S.'s testimony that he ran this family with an iron hand, a significant trait in abusive relationships being the total power and control of one party. The evidence reflects that for some period of time Mrs. S. was not allowed to have a cent, not even grocery money. She was permitted to write a grocery list, and if her husband was ever-so-gracious, he would include her requests. Once she attempted to take $20 from his wallet and wound up in the emergency room after he wrestled with her over it. Mr. S. testified that he actually found the whole episode rather humorous, likening his wife clinging desperately to the $20 bill by hiding it in her mouth as resembling a lizard with lettuce sticking out of its mouth.

One of the complaints made about this mother is that she lacked the ability to manage the boys, ages twelve and ten at the time of the hearings, and surely the record is clear that it was difficult for her to manage these boys, especially Jason, the older of the two. In her petition for review, she pointed out that for several years, her husband had been "mentally, emotionally, and physically cruel" to her. Studies demonstrate that after ages five or six, children show strong indications of identifying with the aggressor and losing respect for the mother. See Crites & Coker, supra, at 11.

In her personal petition for review to the circuit court, she [the mother] stated:

> My two boys in particular identify with their father. Unfortunately, their father has downgraded me for years in front of them and continues to do so. I would become angry in response. The children have seen their father hit me with a belt. My oldest son Jason has bit me and kicked me so hard to have left bruises on me. Jason repeats to me in arguments what his father tells him happens in court. Jason has attacked my mother and caused my father to get a lump on his head by slamming an attic door on his grandfather. Jason is the thirteen year old who has the added problems of puberty on top of this divorce. My second son Justin is ten years old and is having difficulty adjusting. Since he has been with his father, his grades have gone from "A's" and "B's" to some "C's," "D's," and one "F." My six year old daughter, Jennifer is a 4.0 student in first grade. She is also in the gifted program. She has done fine under my care alone this past year.

The evidence reflects that Mr. S. modelled for these children the behavior of demeaning, discrediting, and otherwise disempowering the mother. For example, the father devised a point system to reward good behavior and punish bad behavior. When the mother attempted to participate in the system as a method of encouraging good behavior and managing the children, the children were told that "mommy's points don't count" and "mommy is crazy." The mother testified that the children's response was that "you're not the boss, daddy's the boss. . . ." Furthermore, the father would tally the points and take the children to the toy store for the payoff, which the mother had no financial resources to do.

From Dr. Yeargan's report:

> Mr. S. reported that he can't see himself trying to tell the boys to be kinder and gentler to their mother for fear that he'll lose credibility with them. He said, "I'm not too interested in finding a way to help the enemy camp look good or better . . . until all three kids are together and this is resolved. My primary objective is to have the three kids."

Mrs. S. testified that she attended counselling, both in an effort to save the marriage and in an effort to get help in working with the children, and that she read a number of books on parenting and divorce. She admitted that she used bad language (as did the whole family) and that the husband's constant demeaning of her in front of the children made her angry. She acknowledged she had made mistakes and was working to correct them.

Mr. S., however, presents himself as the perfect father as demonstrated by his testimony that his rapport with the children was "exemplary," and "that it would be very difficult to improve upon." He described himself as "nurturing," "kind," "loving," "caring," "understanding," and "patient."

But a look at Dr. Yeargan's report presents a very different picture of this man:

> Some of the same parental behaviors that previously contributed to the children feeling torn between parents is continuing; those behaviors are (a) increasing the alienation between the children and their mother and (b) exacerbating the loneliness which the boys feel for their sister and vice versa. In this examiner's opinion the behaviors of Mr. [S.]. . . . are of primary importance in the creation of more alienation and loneliness in the children.

The same report details the control and manipulation of the children by Mr. S.:

> All three children report pain over being split but the two boys report it in a way that reflects their father's opinion. Jason, for example, reports the opinion that the children should not be separated and says that they shouldn't " . . . because we'll grow up to be total strangers." Justin reports that being " . . . sad over Jennifer" is his biggest concern. He then goes on to say, "That's really the only problem. Dad says to just tough it out and he's working on it. It's wrong to split up the children cause they'd not grow up together and they'd be total strangers." Two weeks after I talked with the boys Mr. [S] . . . reported to me virtually verbatim the same rationale for why the children should not be split. I infer that (a) the children would naturally express their discomfort in existential terms of the things that they are not now enjoying, (b) their expression of concern for future estrangement indicates how their father

is contributing to, not allaying, their fears and (c) the boys, and possibly Jennifer, have been led by their father to hope that he will eventually get the children together under one roof. . . .

All three children report knowledge of complaints which their father has with their mother which should not be told to them. The obvious effect that this knowledge has is to (a) divide their allegiance deeper and (b) alienate them further from their mother. Jennifeer [sic], for example, mentions that her mother does not want to pay the phone bill. Jason reports of his mother, "She'll run up his (father's) credit cards, get new glasses, run up his medical bills, buy vitamins and stuff like that that she doesn't need." When asked how he knew about all of that he replied, "Dad tells us cause there's really nothing he has to hide from us." Justin reports that they "sometimes" still see parents fussing during the times when the parents are picking up or dropping off the children to one another. He goes on to report that his father tells them about various arguments which occur between him and their mother (arguments which occur on the phone, at the office, etc.).

Mr. [S.]. . . . arranged for the boys to see a counselor (Michael Sheridan) after the separation and reported to Mrs. [S.]. . . . that it was because of their relationship to their mother. According to Mrs. [S.] . . . she was excluded by Mr. [S.]. . . . from any information or advice by that counselor. Mr. [S.]. . . . reported to me that Mr. Sheridan had helped the boys to accept that some of the sanctions being imposed by their mother during visitations were a direct result of their behavior (trashing their mother's Christmas decorations, etc.). However, Mr. [S.] . . . did not use that opinion of Mr. Sheridan to support the boys' mother in dealing with the destructive things the boys were doing; he declined to tell her anything about what transpired in Mr. Sheridan's office. Furthermore, in his discussion with me he missed the point that the boys should assume responsibility (i.e. feel some measure of reproach or make amends for misbehaving.) Instead, he assumed that the important lesson that the boys learned from Mr. Sheridan was that " . . . you can esteem yourselves for coping well with difficulty."

Mr. S. acknowledges that (although less frequently on five-year-old Jennifer), yes, he does use a belt on all three children, and according to unrefuted testimony he also has grabbed Jason by the shoulders and banged Jason's head against a tree. His own description of how he handles physical discipline shows best the kind of fear he uses to exert control over this family:

Normally, the punishment is a smack on the behind with a belt. And I tell them what will happen if they transgress or exceed certain limitations; and, when they, on occasion — not recently, but on occasion — test an adult's authority, which all children are want (sic) to do, I have no choice but to follow through consistently with what I told them would happen.

And when I do that, we discuss it, and I make sure they understand the nature of the discipline. We even negotiate sometimes about how many smacks they want. I will frequently ask them how many smacks that they think that the offense is worth, and frequently they will say four, and I had only planned, maybe, to give them one, maybe two at most, and we will discuss the issue.

Frequently, I will, at the last minute, decide that I can't even spank them anyway, after having gotten them ready to be spanked, decide that I — it's difficult to do, and will let the belt fall aside and smack the bed or the floor and say to them, I'm going to let you go this time, but don't do that again.

On the occasions when I do smack their behinds with a belt, I will always make sure, after I have done it in a controlled and unemotional way — never in anger — that they understand what the punishment was for and why I had to do it, and I will always check their little bottoms to make sure that there is not sufficient force to seriously damage them, say bruising or whatever.

With all of these circumstances, one may wonder why the children were taken from the mother. A close reading of the record reveals that the most damaging things that can be said about Mrs. S. are that 1) she uses bad language; 2) she is very angry; 3) the children told the psychologists that they wanted to live with their father; and 4) one of the psychologists concluded that they "feel safer with their father."

Anger

What judges and indeed many therapists usually fail to understand is the behavior manifestations battered women frequently demonstrate. For example, a battered woman

> may appear in court as unstable, nervous, inarticulate, or angry — a result of her ordeal. The batterer, on the other hand, may appear in command of himself, calm, well spoken, and so forth — and may appear in court as the more fit parent. This may operate to the disadvantage of the victim not only in the eyes of the judge, but also with counselors meeting with one or both of the parents and with psychologists hired to do a psychological evaluation.

Crites & Coker, supra, at 40. It has further been recognized that:

> many women do not present a tearful passive personality to the psychologist. . . . Anger and a new assertiveness are positive characteristics of the recovering abuse victim. She is angry at being abused, and angry at having been blamed by him and by unaware therapists for having caused it. And she is especially angry at his attempts to take the children away.

Crites & Coker, supra, at 41.

Psychologists unfamiliar with all the circumstances and with the unique dynamics of family abuse may make these mistakes:

> 1. They fail to see that the victim's anger is appropriate and normal. . . . 2. They look to the victim's behavior and personality problems to explain the abuse. . . . Such blaming of the victim tends to reinforce the abuser's position that . . . the victim is crazy. 3. They seem to identify with the seemingly sociable, "appropriate" male as a man who has been pushed beyond his limits

by an "angry woman." 4. They fail to see beneath the sincere, positive image of the abuser, but look instead for the "typical" abuser personality. . . . 7. Finally, they criticize [the woman] for focusing her anger on her husband. . . .

Crites & Coker, supra, at 42.

It does not appear that any of the psychologists had any information on the domestic abuse and none dealt with the physical abuse; only Dr. Yeargan seems to have had any information on the psychological abuse and domination. If family law masters and judges are to make decisions on the lives of troubled families, they must become sufficiently knowledgeable about physical and emotional domination to enable them to recognize that these factors are just as invidious, and probably more pervasive, than physical abuse alone. And we must begin to see anger on the part of the victim as healthy.

Children's Preference

The children of David Koresh felt safe with him. While this dissent does not seek to compare Mr. S. with David Koresh, it implores judges to see that family relationships wherein one person has all the power (frequently not only through the purse-strings, but also as a result of both learned and socially-imposed helplessness) are also abusive.

These children learned from their father that their mother did not have even sufficient authority to purchase a package of Oreo cookies for them, that it was okay to demean, disobey, and verbally abuse her, and that physical violence awaited those who did not do as he said. The mother reacted with anger, and the father by word, deed, and dollar delivered the message that mommy's crazy and mommy's contemptible.

Jason was twelve years old at the time of the hearings before the family law master and thirteen by the time of the divorce. Thus, he was only thirteen at the time he last expressed a preference on the record in this case (not fourteen, as the majority indicates). We have said that a child has a right to nominate his own guardian at age fourteen, and that his preference can be accorded deference even before fourteen, depending on his age and maturity. See *David M.*, 385 S.E.2d at 920. Consequently, even though the mother was the primary caretaker, the circuit court cannot be said to have abused its discretion in giving weight to Jason's preference and placing him in the custody of his father. In all likelihood, and by all the evidence, this young man has already demonstrated a propensity to act out anger with violence, and we can only hope we do not see him in court in another generation.

Justin was ten years old and Jennifer six years old at the time their preferences were expressed. Although it could be argued that a ten-year-old's preference could be given some weight, Jennifer at six was too young to express a meaningful preference. Furthermore, a reading of the record makes it quite clear that Jennifer was spirited off to see psychologists by her father and instructed rather specifically on the way by her father and older brother regarding what to say. She related to her mother after-the-fact that she told lies and even Dr. Yeargan discerned that she had been coached.

Justin and Jennifer should have been placed in the custody of their mother. The majority wreaks further havoc on this family (especially Jennifer) by a remand for further evidence. It appears that anxiety and manipulation will again be the order of the day for this little girl, and life's most basic uncertainties will resume as the family is figuratively killed with due process. . . .

 ### Ronald K. Henry, "Primary Caretaker": Is It a Ruse?
17 Fam. Advoc. 53, 53-56 (Summer 1994)

Purposeful Bias

"Primary caretaker" is a warm, fuzzy phrase with a superficial appeal. Like all legal terms, however, the substance is in the definition; every definition that has been put forward for this term has systematically counted and recounted the types of tasks mothers most often perform while systematically excluding the ways that fathers most often nurture their children. No effort has been made to hide this bias.

In fact, in some definitions, the very first credit on the list of factors to be considered goes to that parent, regardless of gender, "who has devoted significantly greater time and effort than the other to . . . breast-feeding." The duration of the credit extended to the parent who has performed such services is unlimited according to some definitions, despite the obvious fact that an historic role as breast-feeder has little relevance to the determination of custody of an adolescent who is contemplating the merits of rival street gangs. The more fundamental problem, of course, is the lack of any consideration for the father's efforts on behalf of the child and his involvement throughout the child's life. No one seriously disputes the role of father absence in street gang formation, teenage pregnancy, and other pathologies. Yet, the primary caretaker theory remains fixated on "mothering" and ignores "fathering."

The primary caretaker theory aggressively asserts that traditional "women's work" is irrelevant. The typical definition of the primary caretaker gives credit for shopping but not for earning the money that permits the shopping; for laundering the Little League uniform but not for developing the interest in baseball; for vacuuming the floors but not for cutting the grass; and for chauffeuring the children, but not for driving to work.

Arbitrary Tasks

Generally, the tasks that count in accumulating primary caretaker points do not involve great skill or invoke debates about hormonal determination.

For example, points are usually given for planning and preparing meals. In our house, the 8-year-old loves canned spaghetti in ABC shapes; the 6-year-old hates the ABCs and loves the Ninja Turtles; and the 3-year-old can finger paint equally well with either. To establish a custody preference on the basis of opened-can counts is an affront to all parents and hardly squares with our understanding that many women entered the paid work force precisely because they were stupefied by the mindless tasks of daily child care.

Most unreasonable is the contempt for paid work that is apparent in the primary caretaker theory. Although time spent shopping counts, time spent doing work for pay does not. Often, grocery shopping, clothes shopping, and other shopping are counted separately. A single afternoon of shopping may be counted several times over, yet the paid work that makes the shopping possible is not counted at all. Which parent is really providing for the child's needs?

Going to work requires a parent's devotion and sacrifice. It is obscene to say that spending is nurturing while earning is mere, heartless cash waiting to be transferred under a child support order. I don't know any parent who is incapable of earning. Which is the better care giver?

In any childless, two-adult household, there is a division of the tasks necessary to simply carry on with life. Cooking, cleaning, and shopping are not counted as child care in a childless home any more than paid work, yard maintenance, and home repairs are so counted. The nature of these tasks does not change with the introduction of a child. Instead, all of the tasks — specifically *including* paid work — collectively support the child's environment.

The gender bias that is inherent in the primary caretaker theory is its insistence that the types of tasks most often performed by women — regardless of the presence of children — are more worthy than those most often performed by men. A child may increase the "task burden" in the household, but it does not cause one adult or one subset of tasks to suddenly become more valuable than the other: For every mother who reduces her hours doing paid work because of a "devotion to the child," there is a father who must increase his. . . .

Additionally, with an ever-increasing number of two-career couples, the primary caretaker is likely to be a day-care center. Should the day-care center be awarded custody?

Changing Needs

Even if it were possible to remove the gender bias from the selection of "primary care" factors, the theory still suffers from the fact the its "freeze frame" analysis of who-did-what during the marriage ignores the reality that children's needs change. The best breastfeeder may be a lousy soccer coach, math tutor, or spaghetti-can opener.

The historical division of labor during a marriage also says nothing about the abilities of the parents and their actual behavior before or after the marriage. Just as mom and dad had to fend for themselves before the marriage, so also will they be compelled to fend for themselves after the divorce. The "primary caretaker" father will have to get a job. The "wage slave" mother will have to cook more meals and wash her own laundry. Similarly, each will have to provide for the needs of the children during their periods of residence. We know this is necessary and we know that it happens even in cases of the minimalist "standard" visitation order.

The allocation of tasks that existed during the marriage necessarily must change upon divorce. The agreed specialization of labor during the joint enterprise of marriage cannot continue after divorce. Each former spouse will have to perform the full range of tasks, and the difficulties encountered by the former full-time homemaker who must now learn to earn a wage have been a central concern of feminists. The primary caretaker theory, with its imposition of single parent burdens upon the spouse least able to cope with the need for earning a living is thus tangibly damaging to the very class that its bias aims to aid. As growing number of leading feminists have come to understand:

> Shared parenting is not only fair to men and to children, it is the best option for women. After observing women's rights and responsibilities for more than a quarter-century of feminist activism, I conclude that shared parenting is great for women, giving time and opportunity for female parents to pursue education, training, jobs, careers, professions and leisure.
>
> There is nothing scientific, logical or rational to excluding the men, and forever holding the women and children, as if in swaddling clothes themselves, in eternal loving bondage. Most of us have acknowledged that women can do everything that men can do. It is now time to acknowledge that men can do everything women can do.

Karen DeCrow, former president of the National Organization for Women, as reported in the Syracuse News Times, Jan. 5, 1994. . . .

. . . No one will argue that America suffers from an excess of good parenting. Why, then, do we focus on finding easier ways to place children in single parent custody? The focus, instead, should be on developing a structure that demilitarizes divorce, that gets past winner-loser dichotomies, and that encourages the maximum continued involvement of both parents.

Children are born with and need two parents. In all but the small number of cases that involve a pathological parent, courts should strive to strengthen the child's relationship with both. If distance or other factors prevent substantially equal relationships, preference should be given to the parent who shows the greater willingness and ability to cooperate and nurture the child's relationship with the other parent. . . .

Notes

1. Maternal Preference Rules. Custody rules favoring women, early on, purported to recognize women's superior childrearing capacities. See, e.g., Commonwealth v. Addicks, 5 Binn. 520 (Pa. 1813) ("considering [the children's] tender age, they stand in need of that kind of assistance, which can be afforded by none so well as a mother"); Hines v. Hines, 185 N.W. 91, 92 (Iowa 1921) ("other conditions being equal, the mother is God's own institution for the rearing and upbringing of the child. It puts a premium on child culture in the hands of an expert"); Krieger v. Krieger, 81 P.2d 1081, 1083 (Idaho 1938) (the maternal preference "needs no argument to support it because it arises out of the very nature and instincts of motherhood; nature has ordained it"); Ellis v. Johnson, 260 S.W. 1010, 1012 (Mo. Ct. App. 1926) ("[i]t is well known by all men that no other love is quite so tender, no other solicitude quite so deep, no other devotion quite so enduring as that of a mother"); Tuter v. Tuter, 120 S.W.2d 203, 205 (Mo. Ct. App. 1938) ("[t]here is but a twilight zone between a mother's love and the atmosphere of heaven"). See also Ramsay Laing Klaff, The Tender Years Doctrine: A Defense, 70 Cal. L. Rev. 335, 344-345 (1982) (citing "a vast body of psychological literature" supporting the proposition that "mother-infant 'bonding' begins at the child's birth" and that "the quality and strength of this original bond largely determines the child's later capacity to fulfill his individual potential and to form attachments to other individuals and to the human community"); David Chambers, Rethinking the Substantive Rules for Custody Disputes in Divorce, 83 Mich. L. Rev. 477, 515-524 (1984) (citing some studies supporting women's biological advantages when it comes to parenthood, and other studies disputing it).

This reasoning is not completely out of date, as *DeCamp* demonstrates. Tennessee applied a tender years presumption until recently. See Tenn. Code Ann. §36-6-101(d) (1996) (although the gender of a party does not give rise to a presumption of custody, "in the case of a child of tender years, the gender of the parent may be considered by the court as a factor in determining custody after an examination of the fitness of each party seeking custody"), replaced by Tenn Code Ann. §36-6-101(d) (Supp. 2000). A preference for the mother of a child born outside a marriage remains in a number of jurisdictions, and the Supreme Court recently upheld distinctions between mothers and fathers of children born out of wedlock. See Section 3, infra.

The rationale reluctantly offered by Rena Uviller in favor of a maternal presumption is quite different than the one offered in the early cases cited above. Her point is not that women's superior caretaking role is biologically determined but that the social order currently dictates maternal care of children, which puts women at an economic disadvantage to men. From that disadvantage, she argues, a sex-neutral custody law would have discriminatory effects; a rule favoring women is necessary to counterbalance those effects. This line of argument is one based on a notion of substantive equality.

Is Chief Justice Bird in her concurring opinion to *Burchard* also urging a maternal preference? She does not say so explicitly, but the rationale she gives would certainly seem to point in that direction. She writes that, typically, "it is the mother who provides most day-to-day care, whether or not she works outside the home," and it is the mother who is harmed by a double standard by which courts judge mothers, penalizing mothers who work outside the home or forget to lay in a supply of jam and cookies, and rewarding fathers who have more than the mimimal amount of day-to-day responsibility for their children that is generally expected of them. What would counteract the double standard Chief Justice Bird writes of, except a maternal preference?

A number of other commentators have also favored a return to a maternal custody preference. See, e.g., Mary Ann Mason, Motherhood v. Equal Treatment, 29 J. Fam. L. 1, 24-26 (1990-1991) (based on same factors, favoring maternal preference); Mary Becker, Maternal Feelings: Myth, Taboo, and Child Custody, 1 S. Cal. Rev. L. & Women's Stud. 133, 203-224 (1992) (favoring maternal preference because it recognizes women's greater emotional commitment to their children and better protects women's physical, emotional, and economic interests).

Most explicit sex-based custody preferences have been eliminated from the law. Quite a few courts have found them to be either unconstitutional, or incompatible with the best-interests-of-the-child test. See, e.g., Pusey v. Pusey, 728 P.2d 117 (Utah 1986) (tender years doctrine both anachronistic and unconstitutional); State ex rel. Watts v. Watts, 350 N.Y.S.2d 285 (Fam. Ct. 1973) (violates best interests principle and equal protection clause); Ex parte Devine, 398 So. 2d 686 (Ala. 1981) (unconstitutional); Bazemore v. Davis, 394 A.2d 1377 (D.C. Ct. App. 1978) (violates best interests principle).

2. Preference for Same-Sex Parent. Should the law permit courts to give a preference in custody cases to the parent who is the same sex as the child? The scientific literature suggests that while school-age boys sometimes do better in the custody of their fathers in terms of overall measures of psychological well-being, self-esteem, depression, anxiety, and behavior problems, those fathers who have custody are not representative, but tend to begin with a greater emotional investment in their children and be more effective parents. See Bennett Leventhal et al., Divorce, Custody, and Visitation in Mid-Childhood, in The Scientific Basis of Child Custody Decisions 205, 218-19 (Robert M. Galatzer-Levy & Louis Kraus, eds., 1999); K. Alison Clarke-Stewart & Craig Howard, Advantages of Father Custody and Contact for the Psychological Well-Being of School-Age Children, 17 J. App. Dev. Psychol. 239, 257, 264 (1996); see also Linda Whobrey Rohman et al., The Best Interests of the Child in Custody

Disputes, in Psychology and Child Custody Determinations 59, 68 (Lois A. Weithorn ed., 1987) ("data do not provide sufficient basis for adopting legal preference for same-sex custody"). Researchers have not found a causal connection between a child's psychological well-being and living with the parent of the same sex. See Clarke-Stewart & Hayward, supra, at 255-59. One of few significant differences found in a study of 187 school-age children was that girls in father custody reported more masculine attitudes and girls in mother custody more feminine ones. However, this difference was small, and did not appear for boys. Moreover, there was no indication that having more masculine attitudes was detrimental for girls. Id. at 262. Another important factor was that children in father custody were less negative toward the noncustodial mother than children in mother custody were to the noncustodial father; if the relationship with the noncustodial mother was negative, the children were more likely to have psychological problems. Id. at 257. In their longitudinal study of children of divorce in two California counties, Eleanor E. Maccoby and Robert H. Mnookin expected to explain shifts in residential patterns over time in part by the fact that children were shifting to spend more time with the same-sex parent. This hypothesis was not borne out by the data. See Maccoby & Mnookin, Dividing the Child: Social and Legal Dilemmas of Custody 199 (1992).

Even if data showed that children benefit from close contact with the parent of the same sex, would this support a rule favoring that parent to have primary custody? How likely is it that any such evidence would, itself, be based on gendered meanings of healthy "sex role identification"? From your own experience, would you expect that successful role modeling depends upon sharing a primary residence with the same-sex parent?

Alabama appears to allow a same-sex parent preference, by statute. See Ala. Code §30-3-1 (1998) ("court may give custody . . . having regard to . . . the age and sex of the children"). Others explicitly prohibit it. See, e.g., Ariz. Rev. Stat. Ann. §25-403(E) (West 2000) (court "shall not prefer a parent as custodian because of that parent's sex"); Me. Rev. Stat. Ann. tit. 19-A, §1653(4) (West 1998) ("court may not apply a preference for one parent over the other . . . because of the parent's gender or the child's age or gender"). Likewise, in a few jurisdictions, courts have allowed a preference for a parent of the same sex during or right before adolescence on various role-modeling hypotheses. See, e.g., In re Marriage of Arcaute, 632 N.E.2d 1082, 1085 (Ill. App. Ct. 1994) (approving trial court's reasoning that "other things being equal, pre-adolescent children and adolescent young people derive substantial benefits from the close personal relationship with the same sex parents, to whom they look for a model"); Warner v. Warner, 534 N.E.2d 752, 754 (Ind. Ct. App. 1989) ("as a child gets older, being able to identify with a parent of the same sex is important"); see also Dalin v. Dalin, 512 N.W.2d 685, 689 (N.D. 1994) (in upholding custody award of daughter to mother, appellate court concluded that trial court's questions about who would help teach the child "certain things that a girl should learn that [are] easiest to learn from a woman" were "not motivated by or evidence of gender bias"). The majority rule, however, is that courts may not prefer the same-sex parent. See, e.g., Hubbell v. Hubbell, 702 A.2d 129 (Vt. 1997); Seeley v. Jaramillo, 727 P.2d 91, 95 (N.M. 1986); Synakowski v. Synakowski, 594 N.Y.S.2d 852, 853 (App. Div. 1993).

3. The Best-Interests Test. The majority opinion in *Burchard* applies a conventional best interests of the child test, which is applied in almost every jurisdiction in the United States. The best-interests test encompasses a wide range of factors, and the factors considered in *Burchard* are typical: the quality of the "emotional bonds between parent and child," "the ethical, emotional, and intellectual guidance the parent gives to the child throughout his formative years," and how to best provide continuity of care. The difficulty with such factors is that they are so subjective and future-looking as to leave room for wide discretion for judges to decide what is best for the child in accordance with their own instincts and biases. These factors also beg the advice of experts, who are likely to have their own biases and who, in any event, are likely to disagree, especially in close cases in which judges are inclined to rely on them the most. Did the experts in *Patricia Ann S.* play a useful role?

The most recent available national statistics indicate that mothers obtain physical custody of children in approximately 72 percent of cases, fathers 9 percent, and both parents 16 percent. See National Center for Health Statistics, Advance Report of Final Divorce Statistics, 1989 and 1990. Most cases, however, are uncontested. In contested cases, various studies have produced a different picture about how much mothers are favored in custody cases. See, e.g., Nancy Polikoff, Why Are Mothers Losing? 7 Women's Rts. L. Rep. 235, 236 (1982) (citing various studies showing father success rates ranging from 38% to 63%); Jeff Atkinson, Criteria for Deciding Child Custody Cases, 18 Fam. L.Q. 1, 10-11 (1984) (fathers win custody in 51 percent of custody cases decided by appellate courts nationwide); Jessica Pearson & Maria A. Ring, Judicial Decisionmaking in Contested Custody Cases, 21 J. Fam. L. 713, 719 (1982-1983) (in three Colorado counties, fathers won custody in 32.3%, 15.5%, and 21.2% of cases, respectively); Lenore J. Weitzman & Ruth B. Dixon, Child Custody Awards: Legal Standards and Empirical Patterns for Child Custody, Support and Visitation After Divorce, 12 U.C. Davis L. Rev. 473, 503 (1979) (fathers won custody in 35% of cases in 1968, 37% in 1972, and 63% in 1977).

What conclusions do you draw from these figures? Is the best-interests test biased in favor of women? Or against them? To what extent does your answer depend upon the model of equality you apply?

4. The Primary Caretaker Presumption. Potential bias, and the difficulties with the battle of experts illustrated in *Patricia Ann S.*, have led a number of commentators to favor adoption of a primary caretaker presumption. See, e.g., Martha Albertson Fineman, The Illusion of Equality: The Rhetoric and Reality of Divorce Reform 180-185 (1991) (for all children); David L. Chambers, Rethinking the Substantive Rules for Custody Disputes in Divorce, 83 Mich. L. Rev. 477 (1985) (for children between six months and five years).

For some years, West Virginia used a primary caretaker presumption, requiring the court to award custody to the primary caretaker parents unless that parent was shown to be unfit. See Garska v. McCoy, 278 S.E.2d 357, 363 (W. Va. 1981). Under this presumption, primary caretaker status was determined by examining which parent provides the day-to-day care of the child, including (1) preparing and planning of meals; (2) bathing, grooming, and dressing; (3) purchasing, cleaning, and care of clothes; (4) medical care, including nursing and trips to physicians; (5) arranging for social interaction among peers after school; (6) arranging alternative care; (7) putting child to bed at night, attending to child in the middle of the night, and waking child in the morning; (8) disciplining, teaching general manners, and toilet training; (9) educating; and (10) teaching elementary skills. *Garska*, supra, 278 S.E.2d at 363. Is Ronald Henry correct that this list is too heavily weighted in favor of the functions usually performed by women? What functions are missing that ought to be on the list? Should wage-earning be a function that counts as "caretaking"?

There is much to be said for a primary caretaking presumption. It is a more determinate standard than the best interests test, thereby reducing the likelihood of experts and prolonged litigation. Insofar as it removes discretion from the judge, it also reduces the likelihood of gender stereotyping. In linking parental rights with parental involvement in childrearing, it encourages that involvement during the marriage. Is that a legitimate goal of the law? Recall the discussion of efficiency in role specialization in the previous section.

It is not clear, however, that the anticipated advantages of the presumption are realized. Based on her review of appellate cases involving the primary caretaker presumption in West Virginia, Mary Becker argues that the rule increases rather than decreases litigation over child custody, and incorporates the same kind of gender-based stereotypes that disadvantage women under a best-interests-of-the-child test. Becker, Maternal Feelings: Myth, Taboo, and Child Custody, 1 S. Cal. Rev. L. & Women's Stud. 133, 195-200 (1992). Does *Patricia Ann S.* support Becker's thesis? If there is a problem with *Patricia Ann S.*, is it with the primary caretaker presumption, or the way it is applied?

Other critics of the primary caretaker presumption, like Ronald Henry, charge that the presumption incorporates gender stereotypes that *favor* mothers. Note that Henry's charge takes the same form as claims made for affirmative action, for accommodations to pregnancy, for aggressive mea-sures to increase women's opportunities for sports, and other claims represented in this chapter as claims for substantive equality. Examine the analytical foundations of this critique. The primary caretaker presumption purports to be gender-neutral but in fact, he claims, incorporates and thereby perpetuates the bias in favor of mothers. Is Henry correct?

West Virginia replaced its primary caretaker presumption in 2000. See note 5, infra. Two other states experimented with a primary caretaker presumption, but neither retained it. A primary caretaker standard adopted in Minnesota in 1985 by the state's highest court, see Pikula v. Pikula, 374 N.W.2d 705, 712 (Minn. 1985), was overruled by statute four years later. See Minn. Stat. Ann. §518.17 (subd. 1)(a)(3) (West Supp. 2001) (primary caretaker status is one factor to be taken into account, but may not be given presumptive weight). See also Judge Gary Crippen in Stumbling Beyond Best Interests of the Child: Reexamining Child Custody Standard-Setting in the Wake of Minnesota's Four Year Experiment with the Primary Caretaker Preference, 75 Minn. L. Rev. 427, 452-86 (1990) (finding that, contrary to expectations, the primary caretaker preference in Minnesota did not reduce litigation because of broad exceptions carved out of the preference, inappropriate reliance on parental fault and virtue, and gender stereotyping, which the appellate courts failed to correct). Montana also dropped its presumption. See Mont. Code Ann. §40-4-212(3)(a)(1995) (creating rebuttable presumption that custody should be granted to "the parent who has provided most of the primary care during the child's life"), repealed by 1997 Mont. Laws ch. 15, §343.

5. Joint Custody. Henry argues in favor of a joint physical custody presumption, a legal trend fueled in the 1980s by fathers' rights groups seeking to obtain the same access to children obtained by mothers. Every state today permits some form of joint physical custody, but the statutory rules vary widely, both with respect to whether joint custody is ordered, and what it means.

Most commonly, joint custody is simply one among a number of custody alternatives, often joined with a stated policy preference in favor of encouraging parents to share in the rights and responsibilities of raising their children. See, e.g., Ga. Code Ann. §19-9-3(a)(5) and §19-9-3(d) (1999). A number of states contain some type of presumption or preference in favor of joint custody. In some of these, the presumption is a narrow one that operates only when parents jointly agree. See, e.g., Cal. Fam. Code §3080 (West 1994). Other states have a presumption in favor of joint custody which can be overcome upon a showing that the child's best interests would not be served by it. See, e.g., D.C. Code Ann. §16-911(a)(5) (Supp. 2001). Florida has a presumption in favor of shared parental responsibility, which can only be overcome by a showing that it would be detrimental to the child. Fla. Stat. Ann. §61.13(2)(b)(2) (West Supp. 2001). However, Florida law also contemplates that a primary residence be designated (61.13(2)(b)(2)(a) (West Supp. 2001), and Florida courts developed a presumption against awarding rotating or divided custody. See, e.g., Langford v. Ortiz, 654 So. 2d 1237 (Fla. Ct. App. 1995) ("[r]otating custody . . . is presumptively not in the best interests of a child"); but see §61.13(4)(c)(5) (West Supp. 1997) (amending statute to eliminate presumption against rotating custody). Similarly, Iowa requires the court to order joint custody if either parent requests it unless it cites clear and convincing evidence that it is unreasonable and not in the child's best interests, Iowa Code Ann. §598.41(2) (West Supp. 2001), but joint custody in Iowa does not necessary mean joint physical care. Id. at §598.41(5).

A few states disfavor joint custody awards. Oregon, for example, prohibits an order unless both parents agree. Or. Rev. Stat. §107.169(3) (1999); see also Vt. Stat. Ann. tit. 15, §665(a) (1989) (when parents cannot agree, court must order primary or sole custody to one parent).

Is joint custody "good for women"? Arguments in favor of joint custody emphasize the potential it has to express a more egalitarian ideal of parenthood and to break down detrimental gender stereotypes. Joint custody might also offer economic and emotional benefits to women, who would have greater flexibility to pursue their employment objectives and other personal interests than if they had sole custody. See Katharine T. Bartlett & Carol B. Stack, Joint Custody, Feminism and the Dependency Dilemma, 2 Berkeley Women's L.J. 9 (1986); Barbara Stark, Divorce Law, Feminism, and Psychoanalysis: In Dreams Begin Responsibilities, 38 UCLA L. Rev. 1483, 1525 (1991).

The feminist response to rules that favor joint custody, however, has been largely negative. One objection is that to the extent that joint custody exerts any pressure against familiar gender stereotypes, it does so by reducing the custodial rights of mothers who have acted as primary parents in order to give rights to fathers who have not earned them.

An even more frequent objection is that laws that favor joint custody give additional leverage to men at divorce, who use it to exact concessions from women during divorce or to manipulate or harass women after the divorce. See Joanne Schulman & Valerie Pitt, Second Thought on Joint Child Custody: Analysis of Legislation and Its Implications for Women and Children, 12 Golden Gate U.L. Rev. 538, 554-560 (1982); Martha Fineman & Ann Opie, The Uses of Social Science Data in Legal Policymaking: Custody Determinations at Divorce, 1987 Wis. L. Rev. 107, 116-117; A.M. Delorey, Joint Legal Custody: A Reversion to Patriarchal Power, 3 Can. J. Women & L. 33 (1989).

This same critique is leveled against what is known as a "friendly parent" custody provision, under which the willingness and ability of a parent to cooperate in contact between the child and the other parent is taken into account in determining custody. See, e.g., Iowa Code Ann. §598.41(1) (West Supp. 2001) ("court . . . shall order the custody award . . . which will assure the child the opportunity for the maximum continuing physical and emotional contact with both parents"); Colo. Rev. Stat. §14-

10-124(1.5)(VI) (2000) (in awarding custody, court required to consider "[t]he ability of the custodian to encourage the sharing of love, affection, and contact between the child and the noncustodial party"). Critics of these provisions argue, among other things, that they enhance the opportunities for batterers to abuse and manipulate their victims, and discourage well-intentioned parents — usually mothers — from opposing joint custody for fear that this opposition might be used to label them as a "non-friendly" parent and therefore an inappropriate candidate for primary custodian. See Schulman & Pitt, supra, at 554-555; Elizabeth Scott & Andre Derdeyn, Rethinking Joint Custody, 45 Ohio St. L.J. 455, 476 (1984); Joan Zorza, "Friendly Parent" Provisions in Custody Determinations, 26 Clearinghouse Rev. 921 (1992). On the problem of domestic abuse and child custody, see pages 646-650.

Some commentators have argued that the problem for women is not joint custody per se, but the way joint custody rules have interacted with other rules that disadvantage women. See Bartlett & Stack, supra, at 35-40. The potential for joint custody to be used to enhance the opportunities for an abusive man to continue to manipulate and abuse his former spouse, for example, can be addressed through rules that require consideration of past and potential future abuse in *all* custody cases. This subject is further examined on pages 646-648.

Another problem for women is that joint custody may impose greater limitations on their ability to relocate with their children. Some have noted that in considering requests of a parent involved in a joint custody arrangement to relocate, courts have tended to assume that the careers and educational opportunities of mothers are less important than those of fathers. See Bartlett & Stack, supra, at 38. This issue is explored in the materials beginning on page 496.

Joint custody may also unfairly disadvantage women if in awarding it, courts make unrealistic assumptions about child support. This issue is discussed in the prior section, at pages 460-464. Child support orders are less common in joint custody cases than in sole custody cases, in part because some courts assume that equal custody ought to mean equal financial responsibility, and in part because mothers in joint residential custody cases tend to have higher incomes than mothers with sole custody. See Jessica Pearson & Nancy Thoennes, Child Custody and Child Support After Divorce, in Joint Custody and Shared Parenting 185, 195 (Jay Folberg ed., 2d ed. 1991) (child support orders made in 93% of sole maternal custody cases in four combined studies, as compared to 44% when joint custody was ordered). Child support collection is higher, however, in joint custody cases. Id. at 199 (ignoring cases in which support was collected through automatic wage withholding, 46% of mothers with sole maternal custody received all child support ordered, as compared to 64% in joint legal custody cases and 75% in joint residential custody cases). The degree of the correlation, however, is complicated by other factors. In the Pearson & Thoennes study, regression analysis of possible indicators of child support compliance showed that visitation and parental participation variables are important, but not as important as the employment stability of the obligor and the level of parental cooperation. Id. at 200-201. Moreover, to date, no one has been able to demonstrate whether joint custody stimulates greater child support compliance or whether it is simply the case that the kinds of parents involved in joint custody arrangements are also the kinds of parents who take their child support obligations seriously.

Even if there were a causal connection between child support compliance and father access, would this support greater use of joint custody? What sort of efforts are appropriate to increase the role of fathers in their children's lives? Would such efforts take for granted the interest of mothers in caring for their children — assume, in other words, that mothers are volunteers — while providing earned bonuses to fathers who cannot otherwise be counted on to act as responsible parents — assume, in other words, that fathers are "draftees"? On this point, see Karen Czapanskiy, Volunteers and Draftees: The Struggle for Parental Equality, 38 UCLA L. Rev. 1415 (1991). In what sense would this be discriminatory? Can the interests of children be separated from those of their parents?

The psychological literature evaluating the effects of joint custody on children has been mixed. When parents are able to value each other on behalf of the child, and have good psychological functioning, high self-esteem, and a low level of anger, the child of divorcing parents seems to do well with joint custody; when parents have intense and unremitting anger and hostility, a strong wish to punish the other spouse, low self-esteem, and the tendency to project blame on the other spouse, the arrangement is unlikely to work well and the children suffer. See Muriel Brotsky, Susan Steinman & Steven Zemmelman, Joint Custody Through Mediation: A Longitudinal Assessment of the Children, in Joint Custody and Shared Parenting, supra, at 167. Does the type of custody arrangement affect the level of parental cooperation and hence the ability of children to do well after the divorce of their parents? Some researchers have concluded that the custodial arrangement has little bearing on the amount of cooperation or conflict after divorce; the level of parental hostility at the time of the break-up is a better predictor of the amount of hostility and dissatisfaction thereafter. See id.; Eleanor E. Maccoby & Robert H. Mnookin, Dividing the Child: Social and Legal Dilemmas of Custody 247 (1992).

There is reason to think that despite the dramatic increase in joint custody statutes and the public attention given to the issue, the number of actual equally-shared residential arrangements is modest. In a two-county California study, while joint legal custody was awarded in 76 percent of cases, joint physical custody was awarded only 20 percent of the time. Of the cases in which joint physical custody was awarded, de facto dual residence — where the child spends at least one-third of the time living with each parent — occurred less than half of the time, id. at 152, although 16 percent of families who had not planned to do so ended up with de facto dual residence arrangements. Id. at 168.

Recognizing the variety in circumstances in today's families and the importance of the actual custodial arrangements that parents make on their own, Elizabeth S. Scott suggests an alternative to both joint custody and the primary caretaker presumption: Courts should order the custody arrangement at divorce that best approximates parenting patterns while the family was intact. Such an approach, she argues, promotes continuity and stability for children, encourages cooperative rather than adversarial behavior by parents, and provides incentives for both parents to invest in parenting before as well as after divorce. See Scott, Pluralism, Parental Preference, and Child Custody, 80 Cal. L. Rev. 615 (1992).

This approach is reflected in the American Law Institute's draft family law principles, which create a presumption in favor of the division of caretaking responsibility after divorce that approximates the shares of caretaking responsibility each parent assumed before the divorce. See American Law Institute, Principles of the Law of Family Dissolution, Final Draft, §2.08, (forthcoming 2002). This approach is following by the new West Virginia statute. See W. Va. Code Ann. §48-11-206 (Michie 1999). See also Wash. Rev. Code Ann. §26.09.187(3)(a)(i) (West 1997) (requiring courts to give "greatest weight" to "[t]he relative strength, nature, and stability of the child's relationship with each parent, including whether a parent has taken greater responsibility for performing caretaking functions relating to the daily needs of the child").

6. Fairness and Custody. To what extent should fairness be a factor in custody rules? It appears to be of significance in both opinions in *Burchard*. Should it be relevant to whether remarriage may be considered in a custody case that men remarry twice as often as women? Or that men tend to be more secure economically than women? Is it obvious that these factors have no relevance to a child's welfare?

One way to look at this issue is that these factors, while perhaps marginally relevant in some cases, play into unconscious, difficult-to-control stereotypes. If these factors were legitimate considerations, judges would rely on them, rather than on more relevant, but often difficult-to-ascertain factors, such as the quality of the parent-child bond. Viewed this way, the problem is less one of unfairness to mothers than biased or incorrect fact-finding, which is contrary to the child's best interests. Still, some cases focus on what appears to be Chief Justice Bird's concern about penalizing working mothers. See, e.g., Linda R. v. Richard E., 561 N.Y.S.2d 29 (App. Div. 1990). Is this the most strategically sensible focus?

What about fairness in *Patricia Ann S.*? Assume that (1) the children are more comfortable with their father and want to live with him; (2) the reason for this is that the father has physically and emotionally abused the mother, eliminating her self esteem and making her a bad mother; and (3) it is a reasonable prediction that the mother will not be able to regain the confidence and trust of her children. How should fairness to the mother be taken into account, if at all?

In re Marriage of Elser
895 P.2d 619 (Mont. 1995)

Justice Karla M. GRAY delivered the opinion of the Court.

Cindy Ann Ansell . . . appeals from the findings, conclusions, and order . . . denying her motion for an order permitting her to remove her minor children to a permanent residence outside of Montana and granting Dan Roy Elser's (Dan) motion to appoint him primary residential custodian if Cindy proceeds with her relocation. We affirm.

The District Court dissolved Cindy's and Dan's marriage via a final decree of dissolution dated November 17, 1993. Pursuant to the terms of a separation agreement incorporated into the final decree, Cindy and Dan were awarded joint custody of Amber and Jaimie, their two minor daughters; Cindy was designated the children's primary residential custodian. Dan was granted visitation rights on alternating weekends and major holidays, residential custody for two months in the winter, and any other visitation agreed to by Cindy and Dan which would not interfere with the children's education and social activities. The separation agreement also provided that "neither party shall remove any of the minor children to a permanent residence outside the State of Montana without the other party's prior written consent or prior approval of a court having proper jurisdiction over the minor children. . . ."

Cindy resided in Hamilton with the children after the dissolution; Dan maintained a residence in Corvallis. Cindy, a radiology assistant, desired to continue her education and applied for admission to the radiology technician program at St. Patrick's Hospital in Missoula. After St. Patrick's denied her application, Cindy notified Dan of her intention to relocate with the children to Kansas and enroll in the University of Kansas' radiology technician program. Dan refused to consent to the relocation.

Cindy moved the District Court for an order permitting her to remove the children to a permanent residence outside of Montana. She included a proposed visitation modification whereby Dan would be allowed to have his two-month custody of the girls during the summer instead of the winter and visitation on alternating major holidays. Dan objected to the children's relocation and moved the court to designate him as their primary residential custodian in the event Cindy relocated out of state. The District Court denied Cindy's motion and ordered that Dan would become the children's primary residential custodian in the event Cindy left Montana. Cindy appeals. . . .

. . . [T]he District Court's ruling on both motions ultimately rested on application of the best interest of the children standard. . . .

[W]e need only review its findings that the move to Kansas is not in the children's best interests. Cindy argues that the record supports findings that spending time with the children was not a priority for Dan and that he could have spent much more time with the children. However, her argument ignores the applicable standards of review.

We review a district court's findings relating to custody modification to determine whether those findings are clearly erroneous. . . .

The District Court first found that the high cost of travel and the impossibility of scheduling a time which coordinated with the children's school schedule and Dan's work schedule would deprive Dan of meaningful custody and visitation. It also found that Dan was committed to being an active parent who was involved with his children as much as possible and that Cindy agreed with Dan that it was important for the children to visit with Dan. Based on these findings, the District Court ultimately found that moving to Kansas was not in the children's best interest.

Ample evidence supports the court's finding that the children's school schedule and Dan's work schedule would make scheduling Dan's two-month extended visitation during the summer impossible. Dan testified that he performs seasonal highway construction work from April through November in Montana and Idaho. He typically works twelve to eighteen hours a day, five or six days a week. He travels home to Corvallis on Friday, arriving sometime early Saturday morning. The remainder of his April through November week-ends are spent doing laundry, catching up on sleep and, on Sunday afternoon, traveling back to the work site. Moreover, although Cindy acknowledged the importance of the children spending time with Dan, she conceded that the right to an extended visitation during the summer months — as she proposed in conjunction with her motion to relocate the children to Kansas — would be meaningless to Dan because of his work schedule. She also acknowledged that extended visitation during the winter months would be impossible from the children's standpoint because of their school schedules and that the relocation effectively would limit Dan's visitation to one week at Christmas.

The court also found that the high cost of travel would contribute to the impact Cindy's proposed move would have on Dan's ability to spend time with his children. Dan and Cindy approximated the airfare between Montana and Kansas at $1,000 and testified that neither of them makes a great deal of money. Dan stated that he could only afford one trip a year for the children to Montana. Cindy speculated that she could purchase one ticket per child per year, but did not commit to paying for any of the children's transportation for visitation.

The evidence also supported the court's determination that Dan is committed to being an active parent. The record reflects both Dan's belief in the importance of spending as much time as possible with his children and that he visited them nearly every other weekend and as often as permitted by his work schedule. Furthermore, Dan's concern about the children's welfare was supported by the fact that, although he has experienced financial difficulty, he continued to make child support payments and, at Cindy's request, paid the entire amount owed to the children's day care and school so they could continue attending.

We conclude that substantial evidence supports the District Court's finding that the proposed relocation to Kansas was not in the children's best interest

Affirmed.

Burgess v. Burgess
913 P.2d 473 (Cal. 1996)

Justice MOSK delivered the Opinion of the Court. . .

I

Paul D. Burgess (hereafter the father) and Wendy A. Burgess (hereafter the mother) were married and had two children, Paul and Jessica. Both parents were employed by the State Department of Corrections at the state prison in Tehachapi and owned a home in a suburb. They separated in May 1992, when the children were four and three years old. The mother moved with the children to an apartment in Tehachapi; the father remained in their former home, pending sale of the property. The mother petitioned for dissolution shortly thereafter.

In July 1992, the trial court entered a "Stipulation and Order" dissolving the marriage and providing for temporary custody and visitation in accordance with a mediation agreement between the parties. The parents agreed that they "shall share joint legal custody of the children. The mother shall have sole physical custody of the children."[2]

The mediation agreement expressly identified as "[a]t [i]ssue" the visitation schedule for the father "if the mother leaves Kern County." The parents agreed to a detailed schedule for weekly visitation by the father, as well as an alternative schedule for biweekly weekend visitation, depending on his work schedule.

---

2. " 'Joint legal custody' means that both parents shall share the right and the responsibility to make the decisions relating to the health, education, and welfare of a child." (Fam. Code, §3003.) " 'Sole physical custody' means that a child shall reside with and be under the supervision of one parent, subject to the power of the court to order visitation." (§3007.) "In making an order for custody with respect to both parents, the court may grant joint legal custody without granting joint physical custody." (§3085.) "An order of joint legal custody shall not be construed to permit an action that is inconsistent with the physical custody order unless the action is expressly authorized by the court." (§3083.)

At a hearing concerning custody in February 1993, the mother testified that she had accepted a job transfer to Lancaster and planned to relocate after her son's graduation from preschool in June. She explained that the move was "career advancing" and would permit greater access for the children to medical care, extracurricular activities, and private schools and day-care facilities. The travel time between Lancaster and her home in Tehachapi was approximately 40 minutes. The father testified that he would not be able to maintain his current visitation schedule if the children moved to Lancaster; he wanted to be their primary caretaker if the mother relocated.

The trial court issued a ruling providing that the father and the mother would share joint legal custody, with the mother to have sole physical custody. It retained the present visitation schedule, but provided that after June 1993, "the father will have visitation with the children, assuming the wife moves to Lancaster, on alternate weekends . . . with at least one three hour midweek visitation. . . ."

The father moved for reconsideration and for a change in custody, alleging that the mother "has constantly used my contact with the children to harass me." The mother opposed a change in custody, alleging that the father "does not utilize all of the time with our children that is available to him now."

In July 1993, the trial court denied the motion for reconsideration, ruling that the father failed to file an affidavit stating any "new or different facts." Shortly thereafter, it held a hearing on the motion for change in custody. The father presented no testimony concerning alleged harassment. He again testified that if his children relocated with the mother he would not be able to maintain his current visitation schedule; he sought a custody arrangement under which each parent would have the children for "[a]bout a month and a half." He also testified that he regularly traveled to Lancaster on alternate weekends, to shop and visit friends; he characterized the trip to Lancaster from his home as "an easy commute."

The mother testified that she had been working in Lancaster for four months and planned to move there. She identified several advantages to the children to living in Lancaster, including proximity to medical care and increased opportunities to participate in extracurricular activities. She also testified that the father objected to her move, at least in part, in order to retain control of her and the children. To her understanding, he did not want to change his work shift "because it keeps me in Tehachapi." She expressed her willingness to accommodate weekend visitation with the father as well as extended visitation in the summers.

In August 1993, the trial court issued an order on custody and visitation to the following effect. "The court finds that it is in the best interest of the minor children that the minors be permitted to move to Lancaster with the petitioner and that respondent be afforded liberal visitation. Due to the complexity of the work schedules of both of the parties, who are employed by the California Department of Corrections, the court requests that a four-way meeting be held by the parties within ten days from the date of this order to work out a mutually agreed upon visitation schedule. . . . "

The father appealed. . . .

The Court of Appeal reversed. It formulated the following test for relocation cases. The trial court initially must determine whether the move "will impact significantly the existing pattern of care and adversely affect the nature and quality of the noncustodial parent's contact with the child. The burden is on the noncustodial non-moving parent to show this adverse impact." If the impact is shown, the trial court must determine whether the move is "reasonably necessary," with "the burden of showing such necessity fall[ing] on the moving parent." If it concludes that the move is "necessary" — either because not moving would impose an unreasonable hardship on custodial parent's career or other interests or because moving will result in a discernible benefit that it would be unreasonable to expect the parent to forgo — the trial court "must resolve whether the benefit to the child in going with the moving parent outweighs the loss or diminution of contact with the nonmoving parent."

On the facts before it, the Court of Appeal concluded that "no showing of necessity was made." "[T]he reality here is that in moving, [the mother] primarily gained convenience." It reversed the orders and remanded for further proceedings consistent with the opinion. We granted review. We now reverse.

I . . .

[I]n a matter involving immediate or eventual relocation by one or both parents, the trial court must take into account the presumptive right of a custodial parent to change the residence of the minor children, so long as the removal would not be prejudicial to their rights or welfare. (Fam. Code, §7501 ["A parent entitled to custody of a child has a right to change the residence of the child, subject to the power of the court to restrain a removal that would prejudice the rights or welfare of the child."].) Accordingly, in considering all the circumstances affecting the "best interest" of minor children, it may consider any effects of such relocation on their rights or welfare.

The standard of appellate review of custody and visitation orders is the deferential abuse of discretion test. . . .

No abuse of discretion appears. . . .

The trial court's order was supported by substantial evidence concerning the "best interest" of the minor children. First, and most important, although they had almost daily contact with both parents during the initial period after the separation, the minor children had been in the sole physical custody of the mother for over a year at the time the trial court issued its order concerning permanent custody. Although they saw their father regularly, their mother was, by parental stipulation and as a factual matter, their primary caretaker. As we have repeatedly emphasized, the paramount need for continuity and stability in custody arrangements — and the harm that may result from disruption of established patterns of care and emotional bonds with the primary caretaker — weigh heavily in favor of maintaining ongoing custody arrangements. . . .

From the outset, the mother had expressed her intention to relocate to Lancaster. The reason for the move was employment related; the mother evinced no intention to frustrate the father's contact with the minor children. Moreover, despite the fact that the move was, as the Court of Appeal observed, primarily for the mother's "convenience," her proximity to her place of employment and to the children during the workday would clearly benefit the children as well. A reduced commute would permit increased and more leisurely daily contact between the children and their primary caretaker. It would also facilitate the children's participation, with their mother, in extracurricular activities. In the event of illness or emergency, the children could more promptly be picked up and treated, if appropriate, at their regular medical facility, which was also located in Lancaster.

Although it would be more convenient for the father to maintain a daily visitation routine with the children if they remained in Tehachapi, he would still, even under his present work schedule, be able to visit them regularly and often. . . .

III . . . .

The Court of Appeal relied on Family Code §3020: "The Legislature finds and declares that it is the public policy of this state to assure minor children frequent and continuing contact with both parents after the parents have separated or dissolved their marriage, and to encourage parents to share the rights and responsibilities of child rearing in order to effect this policy, except where the contact would not be in the best interest of the child, as provided in [Family Code] §3011."

In substance, the Court of Appeal concluded that Family Code section 3020 establishes an implicit requirement, limiting the trial court's discretion under Family Code section 3011, that, after separation or dissolution of marriage, the trial court may not award sole physical custody of the minor children to a parent unless he or she remains in the same locality or establishes that relocation is "necessary."

We are unpersuaded. . . .

[C]onstruing Family Code §3020 *by implication* to impose an additional burden of proof on a parent seeking to relocate would abrogate the presumptive right of a custodial parent to change the residence of the minor child. (Fam. Code §7501.) It has long been established that, under Family

Code §7501, the "general rule [is that] a parent having child custody is entitled to change residence unless the move is detrimental to the child." . . .

As this case demonstrates, ours is an increasingly mobile society. Amici curiae point out that approximately one American in five changes residences each year. . . . Economic necessity and remarriage account for the bulk of relocations. . . . Because of the ordinary needs for *both* parents after a marital dissolution to secure or retain employment, pursue educational or career opportunities, or reside in the same location as a new spouse or other family or friends, it is unrealistic to assume that divorced parents will permanently remain in the same location after dissolution or to exert pressure on them to do so. It would also undermine the interest in minimizing costly litigation over custody and require the trial courts to "micromanage" family decisionmaking by second-guessing reasons for everyday decisions about career and family.[5] . . .

More fundamentally, the "necessity" of relocating frequently has little, if any, substantive bearing on the suitability of a parent to retain the role of a custodial parent. . . .[7]

IV . . .

Although this matter involved an initial order of custody and visitation, the same conclusion applies when a parent who has sole physical custody under an *existing* judicial custody order seeks to relocate: the custodial parent seeking to relocate, like the noncustodial parent doing the same, bears no burden of demonstrating that the move is "necessary." Ordinarily, after a judicial custody determination, the noncustodial parent seeking to alter the order for legal and physical custody can do so only on a showing that there has been a substantial change of circumstances so affecting the minor child that modification is essential to the child's welfare. . . .

We conclude that the same allocation of the burden of persuasion applies in the case of a custodial parent's relocation as in any other proceeding to alter existing custody arrangements. . . .[9]

---

5. In this matter, the parties continue to dispute whether the mother's change of employment was merely a "lateral" move or was "career enhancing." The point is immaterial. Once the trial court determined that the mother did not relocate in order to frustrate the father's contact with the minor children, but did so for sound "good faith" reasons, it was not required to inquire further into the wisdom of her inherently subjective decisionmaking.

7. The father argues that most custodial parents seeking to relocate are merely "bluffing"; they will not move if it will result in loss of custody. Even assuming his assumption is sound, the Family Code provides no ground for permitting the trial court to test parental attachments or to risk detriment to the "best interest" of the minor children, on that basis. Nor should either parent be confronted with Solomonic choices over custody of minor children.

9. In some cases, a custodial parent may be required to provide advance notice of a change in residence of the child: "In making an order for custody, if the court does not consider it inappropriate, the court may specify that a parent shall notify the other parent if the parent plans to change the residence of the child for more than 30 days, unless there is prior written agreement to the removal. . . . To the extent feasible, the notice shall be provided within a

Similarly, the same standard of proof applies in a motion for change in custody based on the custodial parent's decision to relocate with the minor children as in any other matter involving changed circumstances: "[O]nce it has been established [under a judicial custody decision] that a particular custodial arrangement is in the best interests of the child, the court need not reexamine that question. Instead, it should preserve the established mode of custody unless some significant change in circumstances indicates that a different arrangement would be in the child's best interest." (Burchard v. Garay, supra, 42 Cal. 3d at p. 535.)

The showing required is substantial. . . . In a "move-away" case, a change of custody is not justified simply because the custodial parent has chosen, for any sound good faith reason, to reside in a different location, but only if, as a result of relocation with that parent, the child will suffer detriment rendering it " 'essential or expedient for the welfare of the child that there be a change.' " Id.

This construction is consistent with the presumptive "right" of a parent entitled to custody to change the residence of his or her minor children, unless such removal would result in "prejudice" to their "rights or welfare." (Fam. Code §7501.) The dispositive issue is, accordingly, *not* whether *relocating* is itself "essential or expedient" either for the welfare of the custodial parent or the child, but whether a *change in custody* is " 'essential or expedient for the welfare of the child.' " . . .

For the reasons discussed, we reverse the judgment of the Court of Appeal.

Lucas, C. J., and Kennard, George, Werdegar, and Chin, JJ., concur.

[The opinion of Justice Baxter, Justice, concurring and dissenting, is omitted.]

NOTE ON PARENTAL RELOCATION AND GENDER EQUALITY

In the five-year period from 1990 to 1995, 54.7 percent of divorced U.S. families changed living quarters, with 60.4 percent of this population relocating within the same county, 21 percent to a different county within the same state, and 15.9 percent to a different state. See U.S. Census Bureau, Population Division, Current Population Survey, March 1995: Geographical Mobility: 1990-1995. A number of courts have noted the intractable dilemma posed when one parent's desire to make decisions as basic as where to live with the child conflicts with the other parent's desire to maintain an existing relationship with the child. See, e.g., Tropea v. Tropea, 665 N.E.2d 145, 148 (N.Y. 1996) (relocation cases "present some of the

---

minimum of 45 days before the proposed change of residence so as to allow time for mediation of a new agreement concerning custody." (Fam. Code §3024.) . . .

knottiest and most disturbing problems that our courts are called upon to resolve"); Taylor v. Taylor, 849 S.W.2d 319, 333 (Tenn. 1993) (cases require courts to make "difficult, Solomon-like decisions"); Hoos v. Hoos, 562 N.E.2d 1292, 1294 (Ind. Ct. App. 1990) (case "presents one of the critical social dilemmas of our time . . . [t]he mobility of our society, the requirements of employment and the frequency of divorce and remarriage confront us with a reality that forbids easy answer").

The issue of continued custody when the parent with primary custody relocates can arise in many different procedural contexts, the two most common being a petition by the noncustodial parent to modify custody in response to an impending relocation by the parent with primary physical custody, and a petition by the relocating parent in the face of a prior court order or state statute requiring permission to relocate with the child. The issue can also come up, as it did in *Burgess*, before a permanent custody order has been issued. While a modification of custody ordinarily requires a threshold showing of changed circumstances as well as an assessment of the best interests of the child, this additional factor is not ordinarily a significant barrier. Whether the focus is only on the child's best interests, or whether changed circumstances is also an issue, what makes the difference is how the jurisdiction balances the conflict between one parent's desire for geographic mobility and continuity primary custody of the child, and the other parent's desire to maintain his or her meaningful noncustodial relationship with the child.

The law in this area has been unstable, but the clear trend, illustrated in the *Burgess* decision, has been toward increasing deference to the parent with whom the child has been primarily living. Among many other examples, see Aaby v. Strange, 924 S.E.2d 623 (Tenn. 1996) (custodial parent allowed to relocate unless non-custodial parent demonstrates that relocation is "intended to defeat or deter the visitation rights of the non-custodial parent" or "clearly posits a danger to the physical, mental or emotional well-being of the child"); Holder v. Polanski, 544 A.2d 852 (N.J. 1988) (custodial parent may move with child so long as any sincere, good-faith reason given — in this case, to live closer to relatives and to make a fresh start in life). New York at one time had the strictest test of any American jurisdiction, requiring a relocating parent to show "exceptional circum-stances," which was often very strictly interpreted. See, e.g., Daghir v. Daghir, 439 N.E.2d 324 (N.Y. 1982) (mother could not relocate with children to follow husband who was transferred to another country). The exceptional circumstances test has been abandoned in New York in favor of a balancing test requiring consideration of the reasons for the move, the moving party's good faith, the child's ties to the community, and the impact of the relocation on the child's relationship with the other parent. See Tropea v. Tropea, 665 N.E.2d 145 (N.Y. 1996). A few states continue to place the burden of proof for justifying a move on the relocating parent. See, e.g., 750 Ill. Ann. Stat. para. 5/609 (Smith-Hurd 1999).

Is there an approach to relocation that is truly fair? On the one hand, depriving a custodial parent of the right to move with his or her children is a high price to pay for custody. See Trent v. Trent, 890 P.2d 1309, 1313 (Nev. 1995) ("We find it disturbing that despite our [prior] decision . . . many district courts are using [Nevada's prior notification statute] as a means to chain custodial parents, most often women, to the state of Nevada."). On the other hand, the non-custodial parent also faces geographic constraints, if he or she wants to move and continue to have a strong relationship to the child, or if the custodial parent is allowed to move and the only way the other parent can continue to have the same relationship with the child is to follow.

Insofar as most children of divorced families are in the custody of their mothers, the relocation standard a court applies will have a gender impact. Should that impact be taken into account? If so, how? Is it an appropriate objective of the law to encourage parenting by fathers? What would be the most effective standard to achieve this objective? The interest some women have expressed in more equal sharing of childrearing responsibilities might suggest more protections for the custodial/visitation rights of fathers. On the other hand, to the extent women continue to bear the primary responsibility for children, giving men what may amount to an unfair veto power over a mother's decision to move, which weakens the woman's ability to pursue her own life plans. Moreover, if the real objective is encouraging joint parenting, how effective is a rule giving noncustodial fathers an easy time in stopping relocations? Wouldn't it be better to hinge their post-divorce custodial rights on the amount of caretaking they performed *during* the marriage?

Whatever deference is given to the custodial parent by virtue of being the custodial parent disappears if the parents share physical custody equally. The *Burgess* court, in footnote 12, made an explicit exception to the rule when the parents were equally sharing custodial time. See also Hoover v. Hoover, 764 A.2d 1192 (Vt. 2000) (when childrearing was equally shared, with active involvement by both parents, the usual rule strongly favoring relocating custodial parent does not apply, and custodial arrangements should be reassessed); Jaramillo v. Jaramillo, 823 P.2d 299, 309 (N.M. 1991) (neither party has burden of proof when physical custody is shared). Recall in *Patricia Ann S.*, however, how gender bias may enter into the consideration of how caretaking time was shared. Post-*Burgess* decisions may illustrate the same difficulty. See, e.g., Brody v. Kroll, 53 Cal. Rptr.2d 280 (Ct. App. 1996), rev. denied, 1996 Cal. LEXIS 5153 (Sept. 4, 1996) (finding parties had joint physical custody on grounds that although the child stayed with his father only two nights per week, he "saw [the child] as frequently as four or five days a week"). Does *Elser* represent another example?

The ALI standards, which permit a parent with primary residential responsibility for a child to relocate with the child so long as it is for a legitimate purpose and to a location that is reasonable in light of the purpose, designates certain purposes as legitimate; the relocating parent can offer different reasons but bears the burden of demonstrating that the reason is legitimate under the circumstances. The designated legitimate purposes are: significant health reasons, to be close to family or other support networks, to protect the safety of the child or another member of the child's household, to pursue an employment or educational opportunity, or to be with one's spouse or spouse equivalent. American Law Institute, Principles of the Law of Family Dissolution, Final Draft, §2.17(4)(a) (Sept. 26, 1997). Jurisdictions that have adopted standards substantially similar to these Principles include Tennessee, Nevada and Connecticut. See Tenn. Code Ann. §36-6-108 (Supp. 2000), interpreted in Caudill v. Foley, 21 S.W.3d 203 (Tenn. Ct. App. 1999); Hayes v. Gallacher, 972 P.2d 1138 (Nev. 1999); Ireland v. Ireland, 717 A.2d 676 (Conn. 1998).

Assuming courts are able to determine accurately past caretaking shares, how equal should they be to avoid application of a relocation-favoring rule? The ALI rule applies only in favor of a parent who is exercising "the clear majority" of custodial responsibility. The ALI rule focuses on the actual exercise of custodial responsibility, not the amount allocated to each parent in the court order. Id. See also In re Marriage of Francis, 919 P.2d 776, 780 (Colo. 1996); Taylor v. Taylor, 849S.W.2d 319, 321 n.1 (Tenn. 1993). This could be important. A California study showed that only 52 percent of decrees for joint physical custody actually resulted in joint residential arrangements, with the bulk of the remainder involving primary residence with the mother; within a few years of the divorce, the percentage had slipped to 45 percent. See Eleanor E. Maccoby & Robert H. Mnookin, Dividing the Child: Social and Legal Dilemmas of Custody 166 (1992).

Is there a right to travel implicated in the relocation issue? Technically not, many courts say, since what is at stake is not a parent's right to relocate, but to relocate *with the child*. See Maeda v. Maeda, 794 P.2d 268, 270 (Haw. Ct. App. 1990). But see Wis. Stat. Ann. §767.327(3)(c)(1) (West Supp. 2000) (courts may prohibit a relocation, without changing the child's physical placement, if it finds that the prohibition is in the best interest of the child). Several commentators do believe that a constitutional right to travel is implicated. See, e.g., Anne L. Spitzer, Moving and Storage of Post-divorce Children: Relocation, the Constitution and the Courts, 1985 Ariz. St. L.J. 1.

One commentator argues that re-opening custody decisions on grounds of a mother's relocation has constitutional implications with respect to the mother's privacy interest in family decisionmaking. See Arthur B. LaFrance, Child Custody and Relocation: A Constitutional Perspective, 34 J. Fam. L. 1 (1995-1996).

Within a large literature on the legal standards for relocation, one of the best analyses in favor of liberal relocation rules for custodial parents is found in Carol S. Bruch & Janet M. Bowermaster, The Relocation of Children and

Custodial Parents: Public Policy, Past and Present, 30 Fam. L. Q. 245 (1996) (arguing that relocation rules should give priority to child's relationship with the custodial parent). On the importance to the child of the psychological and economic well-being of the custodial parent, see Judith Wallerstein & Tony J. Tanke, To Move or Not to Move: Psychological and Legal Considerations in the Relocation of Children Following Divorce, 30 Fam. L.Q. 305 (1996). For discussion of the specific issue of relocation in the context of domestic violence, see Chapter 4, pages 649-650.

Commentary favoring stricter burdens on the parent seeking to relocate with the child includes Merril Sobie, Whatever Happened to the "Best Interests" Analysis in New York Relocation Cases? A Response, 15 Pace L. Rev. 685 (1995) (favoring "exceptional circumstances" test); Frank G. Adams, Child Custody and Parent Relocations: Loving Your Children From a Distance, 33 Duq. L. Rev. 143 (1994) (arguing greater weight should be given to the importance of the noncustodial parent-child relationship); Paula M. Raines, Joint Custody and the Right to Travel: Legal and Psychological Implications, 24 J. Fam. L. 625, 656 (1986) (when both parents have been involved in decision-making for child, relocation test "must focus on the impact of the move on children and the remaining parent, and not on the benefits derived from the move by one parent"; relocation is rarely justified given "the psychological detriment to the children and the remaining parent").

Putting Theory into Practice

3-12. Since the birth of her son, David, two years ago, Rhonda quit her job as an assistant office manager to care for her son at home, supported economically by her husband Hugh, who is a high school teacher. They are divorcing. Since Hugh does not make enough money to support two households, Rhonda has agreed that she must return to full-time employment and that David will have to be placed in day care. Rhonda wants primary custody of David. Hugh argues that he should have primary custody because his mother has agreed to take care of David while he and Rhonda are working if he has custody. Alternatively, he seeks joint custody. By what rule should such a case be decided? What further information should the court have in deciding the case?

3-13. In the problem above, Hugh presents the testimony of two experts that Rhonda is a disorganized, distant parent who takes care of David's physical requirements but has not attended to his emotional and developmental needs. Both experts agree that David responds more positively to Hugh than to Rhonda. Should this evidence be relevant in the resolution of the custody dispute? How important should it be?

3-14. When Janet and Mark divorced after an eight-year marriage, Janet had no job skills or training. During the marriage, she stayed at home to care for her three children, the first of whom was born almost immediately upon Janet's graduation from high school. At the divorce, Janet decided to give up primary custody of the children, then ages 3, 5, and 8, to Mark, who was planning to remarry, so that Janet would have the time to attend the community college full-time. Still, Janet had custody of the children every weekend and during school vacations, talked to them every night on the telephone, and continued to take primary responsibility for such things as doctor's appointments, clothing, haircuts, birthday presents, and the like. Janet missed seeing the children every day, but felt the arrangement was the only way she would be able to make herself economically independent. The children were cared for during the day, when they weren't in school themselves, by their stepmother, who did not work outside the home.

The arrangement seemed to be working well, until Mark announced that he had received a very large promotion and was moving to another state, 1,500 miles away. He intends to take the children with him. Should Janet be able to stop him from moving with the children? Under what general rule?

3. Unmarried Parents

Caban v. Mohammed
441 U.S. 380 (1979)

Mr. Justice POWELL delivered the opinion of the Court.

The appellant, Abdiel Caban, challenges the constitutionality of §111 of the New York Domestic Relations Law (McKinney 1977), under which two of his natural children were adopted by their natural mother and stepfather without his consent. We find the statute to be unconstitutional, as the distinction it invariably makes between the rights of unmarried mothers and the rights of unmarried fathers has not been shown to be substantially related to an important state interest.

I

Abdiel Caban and appellee Maria Mohammed lived together in New York City from September 1968 until the end of 1973. During this time Caban and Mohammed represented themselves as being husband and wife, although they never legally married. Indeed, until 1974 Caban was married to another woman, from whom he was separated. While living with the appellant, Mohammed gave birth to two children [one born in July 1969 and the other in March 1971]. [Caban] was identified as the father on each child's birth certificate, and lived with the children as their father until the end of 1973. Together with Mohammed, he contributed to the support of the family.

In December 1973, Mohammed took the two children and left the appellant to take up residence with appellee Kazin Mohammed, whom she married on January 30, 1974. For the next nine months, she took [the children] each weekend to visit her mother, Delores Gonzales, who lived one floor above Caban. Because of his friendship with Gonzales, Caban was able to see the children each week when they came to visit their grandmother.

In September 1974, Gonzales left New York to take up residence in her native Puerto Rico. At the Mohammeds' request, the grandmother took [the children] with her. According to appellees, they planned to join the children in Puerto Rico as soon as they had saved enough money to start a business there. During the children's stay with their grandmother, Mrs. Mohammed kept in touch with David and Denise by mail; Caban communicated with the children through his parents, who also resided in Puerto Rico. In November 1975, he went to Puerto Rico, where Gonzales willingly surrendered the children to Caban with the understanding that they would be returned after a few days. Caban, however, returned to New York with the children. When Mrs. Mohammed learned that the children were in Caban's custody, she attempted to retrieve them with the aid of a police officer. After this attempt failed, the appellees instituted custody proceedings in the New York Family Court, which placed the children in the temporary custody of the Mohammeds and gave Caban and his new wife, Nina, visiting rights.

In January 1976, appellees filed a petition under §110 of the New York Domestic Relations Law to adopt [the children]. In March, the Cabans cross petitioned for adoption. . . .

The Surrogate granted the Mohammeds' petition to adopt the children, thereby cutting off all of appellant's parental rights and obligations. . . .

II

Section 111 of the N.Y. Dom. Rel. Law (McKinney 1977) provides in part that

> consent to adoption shall be required as follows: . . . (b) Of the parents or surviving parent . . . of a child born in wedlock; [and] (c) Of the mother . . . of a child born out of wedlock. . . .

[Absent a showing that a parent has abandoned or relinquished his or her rights in the child or has been adjudicated incompetent to care for the child,] an unwed mother has the authority under New York law to block the adoption of her child simply by withholding consent. The unwed father has no similar control over the fate of his child, even when his parental relationship is substantial — as in this case. He may prevent the termination of his parental rights only by showing that the best interests of the child would not permit the child's adoption by the petitioning couple. . . .

III

. . . The question before us . . . is whether the distinction in §111 between unmarried mothers and unmarried fathers bears a substantial relation to some important state interest. . . .

Contrary to appellees' argument and to the apparent presumption underlying §111, maternal and paternal roles are not invariably different in importance. Even if unwed mothers as a class were closer than unwed fathers to their newborn infants, this generalization concerning parent-child relations would become less acceptable as a basis for legislative distinctions as the age of the child increased. The present case demonstrates that an unwed father may have a relationship with his children fully comparable to that of the mother. [They] lived together as a natural family for several years. As members of this family, both mother and father participated in the care and support of their children. There is no reason to believe that the Caban children — aged 4 and 6 at the time of the adoption proceedings — had a relationship with their mother unrivaled by the affection and concern of their father. We reject, therefore, the claim that the broad, gender-based distinction of §111 is required by any universal difference between maternal and paternal relations at every phase of a child's development.

As an alternative justification for §111, appellees argue that the distinction between unwed fathers and unwed mothers is substantially related to the State's interest in promoting the adoption of illegitimate children. . . .

The State's interest in providing for the well-being of illegitimate children is an important one. . . . But the unquestioned right of the State to further these desirable ends by legislation is not in itself sufficient to justify the gender-based distinction of §111. . . .

. . . It may be that, given the opportunity, some unwed fathers would prevent the adoption of their illegitimate children. This impediment to adoption usually is the result of a natural parental interest by both genders alike; it is not a manifestation of any profound difference between the affection and concern of mothers and fathers for their children. Neither the State nor the appellees have argued that unwed fathers are more likely to object to the adoption of their children than are unwed mothers; nor is there any self-evident reason why as a class they would be.

. . . Even if the special difficulties attendant upon locating and identifying unwed fathers at birth would justify a legislative distinction between mothers and fathers of newborns,[11] these difficulties need not persist past infancy. . . . In those cases where the father never has come forward to participate in the rearing of his child, nothing in the Equal Protection Clause precludes the State from withholding from him the privilege of vetoing the adoption of that child. . . . But in cases such as this, where the father has established a substantial relationship with the child and has admitted his paternity, a State should have no difficulty in identifying the father even of children born out of wedlock. . . .

In sum, we believe that §111 is another example of "overbroad generalizations" in gender-based classifications. . . . The effect of New York's classification is to discriminate against unwed fathers even when their identity is known and they have manifested a significant paternal interest in the child. The facts of this case illustrate the harshness of classifying unwed fathers as being invariably less qualified and entitled than mothers to exercise a concerned judgment as to the fate of the children. Section 111 both excludes some loving fathers from full participation in the decision whether their children will be adopted and, at the same time, enables some alienated mothers arbitrarily to cut off the paternal rights of fathers. We conclude that this undifferentiated distinction between unwed mothers and unwed fathers, applicable in all circumstances where adoption of a child of theirs is at issue, does not bear a substantial relationship to the State's asserted interests.

The judgment of the New York Court of Appeals is reversed.

[The dissenting opinion of Mr. Justice Stewart is omitted.]

Mr. Justice STEVENS, with whom THE CHIEF JUSTICE and Mr. Justice REHNQUIST join, dissenting. . . .

I

This case concerns the validity of rules affecting the status of the thousands of children who are born out of wedlock every day. All of these children have an interest in acquiring the status of legitimacy; a great many of them have an interest in being adopted by parents who can give them opportunities that would otherwise be denied; for some the basic necessities of life are at stake. The state interest in facilitating adoption in appropriate cases is strong—perhaps even "compelling."

Nevertheless, it is also true that §111(1)(c) gives rights to natural mothers that it withholds from natural fathers. Because it draws this gender-based distinction between two classes of citizens who have an equal right to

---

11. Because the question is not before us, we express no view whether such difficulties would justify a statute addressed particularly to newborn adoptions, setting forth more stringent requirements concerning the acknowledgment of paternity or a stricter definition of abandonment.

fair and impartial treatment by their government, it is necessary to determine whether there are differences between the members of the two classes that provide a justification for treating them differently. . . .

Men and women are different, and the difference is relevant to the question whether the mother may be given the exclusive right to consent to the adoption of a child born out of wedlock. Because most adoptions involve newborn infants or very young children, it is appropriate at the outset to focus on the significance of the difference in such cases.

Both parents are equally responsible for the conception of the child out of wedlock. But from that point on through pregnancy and infancy, the differences between the male and the female have an important impact on the child's destiny. Only the mother carries the child; it is she who has the constitutional right to decide whether to bear it or not. In many cases, only the mother knows who sired the child, and it will often be within her power to withhold that fact, and even the fact of her pregnancy, from that person. If during pregnancy the mother should marry a different partner, the child will be legitimate when born, and the natural father may never even know that his "rights" have been affected. On the other hand, only if the natural mother agrees to marry the natural father during that period can the latter's actions have a positive impact on the status of the child; if he instead should marry a different partner during that time, the only effect on the child is negative, for the likelihood of legitimacy will be lessened.

These differences continue at birth and immediately thereafter. During that period, the mother and child are together;[10] the mother's identity is known with certainty. The father, on the other hand, may or may not be present; his identity may be unknown to the world and may even be uncertain to the mother. These natural differences between unmarried fathers and mothers make it probable that the mother, and not the father or both parents, will have custody of the newborn infant.

In short, it is virtually inevitable that from conception through infancy the mother will constantly be faced with decisions about how best to care for the child, whereas it is much less certain that the father will be confronted with comparable problems. There no doubt are cases in which the relationship of the parties at birth makes it appropriate for the State to give the father a voice of some sort in the adoption decision. But as a matter of equal protection analysis, it is perfectly obvious that at the time and immediately after a child is born out of wedlock, differences between men and women justify some differential treatment of the mother and father in the adoption process.

10. In fact, there is some sociological and anthropological research indicating that by virtue of the symbiotic relationship between mother and child during pregnancy and the initial contact between mother and child directly after birth a physical and psychological bond immediately develops between the two that is not then present between the infant and the father or any other person. E.g., 1 & 2 J. Bowlby, Attachment and Loss (1969, 1973); M. Mahler, The Psychological Birth of the Human Infant (1975).

Most particularly, these differences justify a rule that gives the mother of the newborn infant the exclusive right to consent to its adoption. Such a rule gives the mother, in whose sole charge the infant is often placed anyway, the maximum flexibility in deciding how best to care for the child. It also gives the loving father an incentive to marry the mother, and has no adverse impact on the disinterested father. Finally, it facilitates the interests of the adoptive parents, the child, and the public at large by streamlining the often traumatic adoption process and allowing the prompt, complete, and reliable integration of the child into a satisfactory new home at as young an age as is feasible. Put most simply, it permits the maximum participation of interested natural parents without so burdening the adoption process that its attractiveness to potential adoptive parents is destroyed.

This conclusion is borne out by considering the alternative rule proposed by appellant. If the State were to require the consent of both parents, or some kind of hearing to explain why either's consent is unnecessary or unobtainable, it would unquestionably complicate and delay the adoption process. Most importantly, such a rule would remove the mother's freedom of choice in her own and the child's behalf without also relieving her of the unshakable responsibility for the care of the child. Furthermore, questions relating to the adequacy of notice to absent fathers could invade the mother's privacy, cause the adopting parents to doubt the reliability of the new relationship, and add to the expense and time required to conclude what is now usually a simple and certain process. While it might not be irrational for a State to conclude that these costs should be incurred to protect the interest of natural fathers, it is nevertheless plain that those costs, which are largely the result of differences between the mother and the father, establish an imposing justification for some differential treatment of the two sexes in this type of situation. . . .

I have no way of knowing how often disputes between natural parents over adoption of their children arise after the father "has established a substantial relationship with the child and [is willing to admit] his paternity," . . . but has previously been unwilling to take steps to legitimate his relationship. I am inclined to believe that such cases are relatively rare. But whether or not this assumption is valid, the far surer assumption is that in the more common adoption situations, the mother will be the more, and often the only, responsible parent, and that a paternal consent requirement will constitute a hindrance to the adoption process. Because this general rule is amply justified in its normal application, I would therefore require the party challenging its constitutionality to make some demonstration of unfairness in a significant number of situations before concluding that it violates the Equal Protection Clause. That the Court has found a violation without requiring such a showing can only be attributed to its own "stereotyped reaction" to what is unquestionably, but in this case justifiably, a gender-based distinction. . . .

I respectfully dissent.

Nguyen v. Immigration and Naturalization Service
533 U.S. 53 (2001)

Justice KENNEDY delivered the opinion of the Court. . . .

I

Petitioner Tuan Ahn Nguyen was born in Saigon, Vietnam, on September 11, 1969, to copetitioner Joseph Boulais and a Vietnamese citizen. Boulais and Nguyen's mother were not married. Boulais always has been a citizen of the United States, and he was in Vietnam under the employ of a corporation. After he and Nguyen's mother ended their relationship, Nguyen lived for a time with the family of Boulais' new Vietnamese girlfriend. In June 1975, Nguyen, then almost six years of age, came to the United States. He became a lawful permanent resident and was raised in Texas by Boulais.

In 1992, when Nguyen was 22, he pleaded guilty in a Texas state court to two counts of sexual assault on a child. He was sentenced to eight years in prison on each count. Three years later, the United States Immigration and Naturalization Service (INS) initiated deportation proceedings against Nguyen as an alien who had been convicted of two crimes involving moral turpitude, as well as an aggravated felony. . . .

Nguyen appealed to the Board of Immigration of Appeals and, in 1998, while the matter was pending, his father obtained an order of parentage from a state court, based on DNA testing. By this time, Nguyen was 28 years old. The Board dismissed Nguyen's appeal, rejecting his claim to United States citizenship because he had failed to establish compliance with 8 U.S.C. §1409(a), which sets forth the requirements for one who was born out of wedlock and abroad to a citizen father and a noncitizen mother.

Nguyen and Boulais appealed to the Court of Appeals [which appeal was denied]. . . .

II

The general requirement for acquisition of citizenship by a child born outside the United States and its outlying possessions and to parents who are married, one of whom is a citizen and the other of whom is an alien, is set forth in 8 U.S.C. §1401(g). The statute provides that the child is also a citizen if, before the birth, the citizen parent had been physically present in the United States for a total of five years, at least two of which were after the parent turned 14 years of age.

As to an individual born under the same circumstances, save that the parents are unwed, §1409(a) sets forth the following requirements where the father is the citizen parent and the mother is an alien:

(1) a blood relationship between the person and the father is established by clear and convincing evidence,

(2) the father had the nationality of the United States at the time of the person's birth,

(3) the father (unless deceased) has agreed in writing to provide financial support for the person until the person reaches the age of 18 years, and

(4) while the person is under the age of 18 years —

(A) the person is legitimated under the law of the person's residence or domicile,

(B) the father acknowledges paternity of the person in writing under oath, or

(C) the paternity of the person is established by adjudication of a competent court.

In addition, §1409(a) incorporates by reference, as to the citizen parent, the residency requirement of §1401(g).

When the citizen parent of the child born abroad and out of wedlock is the child's mother, the requirements for the transmittal of citizenship are described in §1409(c):

> (c) Notwithstanding the provision of subsection (a) of this section, a person born, after December 23, 1952, outside the United States and out of wedlock shall be held to have acquired at birth the nationality status of his mother, if the mother had the nationality of the United States at the time of such person's birth, and if the mother had previously been physically present in the United States or one of its outlying possessions for a continuous period of one year.

Section 1409(a) thus imposes a set of requirements on the children of citizen fathers born abroad and out of wed-lock to a noncitizen mother that are not imposed under like circumstances when the citizen parent is the mother. All concede the requirements of §1409(a)(3) and (a)(4), relating to a citizen father's acknowledgment of a child while he is under 18, were not satisfied in this case. . . .

III

For a gender-based classification to withstand equal protection scrutiny, it must be established " 'at least that the [challenged] classification serves 'important governmental objectives and that the discriminatory means employed' are 'substantially related to the achievement of those objectives.' " United States v. Virginia, 518 U.S. 515, 533 (1996) [internal citation omitted]. For reasons to follow, we conclude §1409 satisfies this standard. . . .

Before considering the important governmental interests advanced by the statute, [it should be observed that] . . . a citizen mother expecting a child and living abroad has the right to re-enter the United States so the child can be born here and be a 14th Amendment citizen. From one perspective, then, the statute simply ensures equivalence between two expectant mothers who are citizens abroad if one chooses to reenter for the child's birth and the other chooses not to return, or does not have the means to do so. This equivalence is not a factor if the single citizen parent living abroad is the father. For, unlike the unmarried mother, the unmarried father as a general rule cannot control where the child will be born. . . .

. . . Congress' decision to impose requirements on unmarried fathers that differ from those on unmarried mothers is based on the significant difference between their respective relationships to the potential citizen at the time of birth. Specifically, the imposition of the requirement for a paternal relationship, but not a maternal one, is justified by two important governmental objectives. We discuss each in turn.

A

The first governmental interest to be served is the importance of assuring that a biological parent-child relationship exists. In the case of the mother, the relation is verifiable from the birth itself. The mother's status is documented in most instances by the birth certificate or hospital records and the witnesses who attest to her having given birth.

In the case of the father, the uncontestable fact is that he need not be present at the birth. If he is present, furthermore, that circumstance is not incontrovertible proof of fatherhood. See Lehr v. Robertson, 463 U.S. 248, 260, n.16 (1983) (" 'The mother carries and bears the child, and in this sense her parental relationship is clear. The validity of the father's parental claims must be gauged by other measures' " [internal citation omitted].) Fathers and mothers are not similarly situated with regard to the proof of biological parenthood. The imposition of a different set of rules for making that legal determination with respect to fathers and mothers is neither surprising nor troublesome from a constitutional perspective. . . . Section 1409(a)(4)'s provision of three options for a father seeking to establish paternity — legitimation, paternity oath, and court order of paternity — is designed to ensure an acceptable documentation of paternity.

Petitioners argue that the requirement of §1409(a)(1), that a father provide clear and convincing evidence of parentage, is sufficient to achieve the end of establishing paternity, given the sophistication of modern DNA tests.

. . . Section 1409(a)(1) does not actually mandate a DNA test, however. The Constitution, moreover, does not require that Congress elect one particular mechanism from among many possible methods of establishing paternity, even if that mechanism arguably might be the most scientifically advanced method. With respect to DNA testing, the expense, reliability, and availability of such testing in various parts of the world may have been of particular concern to Congress [Miller v. Albright, 523 U.S. 420, 437 (1998) (opinion of Stevens, J.)]. The requirement of §1409(a)(4) represents a reasonable conclusion by the legislature that the satisfaction of one of several alternatives will suffice to establish the blood link between father and child required as a predicate to the child's acquisition of citizenship. . . . Given the proof of motherhood that is inherent in birth itself, it is unremarkable that Congress did not require the same affirmative steps of mothers.

Finally, to require Congress to speak without reference to the gender of the parent with regard to its objective of ensuring a blood tie between parent and child would be to insist on a hollow neutrality. As Justice Stevens pointed out in *Miller*, Congress could have required both mothers and fathers to prove parenthood within 30 days or, for that matter, 18 years, of the child's birth. 523 U.S., at 436. Given that the mother is always present at birth, but that the father need not be, the facially neutral rule would sometimes require fathers to take additional affirmative steps which would not be required of mothers, whose names will appear on the birth certificate as a result of their presence at the birth, and who will have the benefit of witnesses to the birth to call upon. The issue is not the use of gender specific terms instead of neutral ones. Just as neutral terms can mask discrimination that is unlawful, gender specific terms can mark a permissible distinction. The equal protection question is whether the distinction is lawful. Here, the use of gender specific terms takes into account a biological difference between the parents. . . .

B

1

The second important governmental interest furthered in a substantial manner by §1409(a)(4) is the determination to ensure that the child and the citizen parent have some demonstrated opportunity or potential to develop not just a relationship that is recognized, as a formal matter, by the law, but one that consists of the real, everyday ties that provide a connection between child and citizen parent and, in turn, the United States. . . . In the case of a citizen mother and a child born overseas, the opportunity for a meaningful relationship between citizen parent and child inheres in the very event of birth, an event so often critical to our constitutional and statutory understandings of citizenship. The mother knows that the child is in being and is hers and has an initial point of contact with him. There is at least an opportunity for mother and child to develop a real, meaningful relationship.

The same opportunity does not result from the event of birth, as a matter of biological inevitability, in the case of the unwed father. Given the 9-month interval between conception and birth, it is not always certain that a father will know that a child was conceived, nor is it always clear that even the mother will be sure of the father's identity. This fact takes on particular significance in the case of a child born overseas and out of wedlock. One concern in this context has always been with young people, men for the most part, who are on duty with the Armed Forces in foreign countries. . . .

When we turn to the conditions which prevail today, we find that the passage of time has produced additional and even more substantial grounds to justify the statutory distinction. The ease of travel and the willingness of Americans to visit foreign countries have resulted in numbers of trips abroad that must be of real concern when we contemplate the prospect of accepting petitioners' argument, which would mandate, contrary to Congress' wishes, citizenship by male parentage subject to no condition save the father's previous length of residence in this country. In 1999 alone, Americans made almost 25 million trips abroad, excluding trips to Canada and Mexico. See U. S. Dept. of Commerce, 1999 Profile of U. S. Travelers to Overseas Destinations 1 (Oct. 2000). . . .

Principles of equal protection do not require Congress to ignore this reality. To the contrary, these facts demonstrate the critical importance of the Government's interest in ensuring some opportunity for a tie between citizen father and foreign born child which is a reasonable substitute for the opportunity manifest between mother and child at the time of birth. Indeed, especially in light of the number of Americans who take short sojourns abroad, the prospect that a father might not even know of the conception is a realistic possibility. See *Miller*, supra, at 439 (opinion of Stevens, J.). Even if a father knows of the fact of conception, moreover, it does not follow that he will be present at the birth of the child. Thus, unlike the case of the mother, there is no assurance that the father and his biological child will ever meet. Without an initial point of contact with the child by a father who knows the child is his own, there is no opportunity for father and child to begin a relationship. Section 1409 takes the unremarkable step of ensuring that such an opportunity, inherent in the event of birth as to the mother-child relationship, exists between father and child before citizenship is conferred upon the latter.

The importance of the governmental interest at issue here is too profound to be satisfied merely by conducting a DNA test. The fact of paternity can be established even without the father's knowledge, not to say his presence. Paternity can be established by taking DNA samples even from a few strands of hair, years after the birth. See Federal Judicial Center, Reference Manual on Scientific Evidence 497 (2d ed. 2000). Yet scientific proof of biological paternity does nothing, by itself, to ensure contact between father and child during the child's minority.

Congress is well within its authority in refusing, absent proof of at least the opportunity for the development of a relationship between citizen parent and child, to commit this country to embracing a child as a citizen entitled as of birth to the full protection of the United States, to the absolute right to enter its borders, and to full participation in the political process. If citizenship is to be conferred by the unwitting means petitioners urge, so that its acquisition abroad bears little relation to the realities of the child's own ties and allegiances, it is for Congress, not this Court, to make that determination. . . .

2

Having concluded that facilitation of a relationship between parent and child is an important governmental interest, the question remains whether the means Congress chose to further its objective — the imposition of certain additional requirements upon an unwed father — substantially relate to that end. Under this test, the means Congress adopted must be sustained.

First, it should be unsurprising that Congress decided to require that an opportunity for a parent-child relationship occur during the formative years of the child's minority. In furtherance of the desire to ensure some tie between this country and one who seeks citizenship, various other statutory provisions concerning citizenship and naturalization require some act linking the child to the United States to occur before the child reaches 18 years of age. See, e.g., 8 U.S.C. §1431 (child born abroad to one citizen parent and one noncitizen parent shall become a citizen if, *inter alia*, the noncitizen parent is naturalized before the child reaches 18 years of age and the child begins to reside in the United States before he or she turns 18); §1432 (imposing same conditions in the case of a child born abroad to two alien parents who are naturalized).

Second, petitioners argue that . . . although a mother will know of her child's birth, "knowledge that one is a parent, no matter how it is acquired, does not guarantee a relationship with one's child." . . . They thus maintain that the imposition of the additional requirements of §1409(a)(4) only on the children of citizen fathers must reflect a stereotype that women are more likely than men to actually establish a relationship with their children. . . .

This line of argument misconceives the nature of both the governmental interest at issue and the manner in which we examine statutes alleged to violate equal protection. As to the former, Congress would of course be entitled to advance the interest of ensuring an actual, meaningful relationship in every case before citizenship is conferred. Or Congress could excuse compliance with the formal requirements when an actual father-child relationship is proved. It did neither here, perhaps because of the subjectivity, intrusiveness, and difficulties of proof that might attend an inquiry into any particular bond or tie. Instead, Congress enacted an easily administered scheme to promote the different but still substantial interest of ensuring at least an opportunity for a parent-child relationship to develop. Petitioners' argument confuses the means and ends of the equal protection inquiry; §1409(a)(4) should not be invalidated because Congress elected to advance an interest that is less demanding to satisfy than some other alternative.

Even if one conceives of the interest Congress pursues as the establishment of a real, practical relationship of considerable substance between parent and child in every case, as opposed simply to ensuring the potential for the relationship to begin, petitioners' misconception of the nature of the equal protection inquiry is fatal to their argument. A statute meets the equal protection standard we here apply so long as it is " 'substantially related to the achievement of' " the governmental objective in question. [citations omitted] It is almost axiomatic that a policy which seeks to foster the opportunity for meaningful parent-child bonds to develop has a close and substantial bearing on the governmental interest in the actual formation of that bond. None of our gender-based classification equal protection cases have required that the statute under consideration must be capable of achieving its ultimate objective in every instance. . . .

V

To fail to acknowledge even our most basic biological differences — such as the fact that a mother must be present at birth but the father need not be — risks making the guarantee of equal protection superficial, and so disserving it. Mechanistic classification of all our differences as stereotypes would operate to obscure those misconceptions and prejudices that are real. The distinction embodied in the statutory scheme here at issue is not marked by misconception and prejudice, nor does it show disrespect for either class. The difference between men and women in relation to the birth process is a real one, and the principle of equal protection does not forbid Congress to address the problem at hand in a manner specific to each gender.

The judgment of the Court of Appeals is affirmed.

[The opinion of Justice Scalia, with whom Justice Thomas joins, concurring, is omitted.]

Justice O'CONNOR, with whom Justice SOUTER, Justice GINSBURG, and Justice BREYER join, dissenting. . . .

II . . .

A

According to the Court, "[t]he first governmental interest to be served is the importance of assuring that a biological parent-child relationship exists." . . . The majority does not elaborate on the importance of this interest, which presumably lies in preventing fraudulent conveyances of citizenship. Nor does the majority demonstrate that this is one of the actual purposes of §1409(a)(4). Assuming that Congress actually had this purpose in mind in enacting parts of §1409(a)(4), cf. Miller v. Albright, 523 U.S. 420, 435-436 (1998) (opinion of Stevens, J.), the INS does not appear to rely on this interest in its effort to sustain §1409(a)(4)'s sex-based classification. Cf. Brief for Respondent 11 (claiming that §1409 serves "at least two important interests: first, ensuring that children who are born abroad out of wedlock have, during their minority, attained a sufficiently recognized or formal relationship to their United States citizen parent — and thus to the United States — to justify the conferral of citizenship upon them; and second, preventing such children from being stateless"). In light of the reviewing court's duty to "determine whether the proffered justification is 'exceedingly persuasive,'" *Virginia*, 518 U.S., at 533, this disparity between the majority's defense of the statute and the INS' proffered justifications is striking, to say the least.

The gravest defect in the Court's reliance on this interest, however, is the insufficiency of the fit between §1409(a)(4)'s discriminatory means and the asserted end. . . . It is difficult to see what §1409(a)(4) accomplishes in furtherance of "assuring that a biological parent-child relationship exists," . . . that §1409(a)(1) does not achieve on its own. The virtual certainty of a biological link that modern DNA testing affords reinforces the sufficiency of §1409(a)(1). See *Miller*, supra, at 484-485 (Breyer, J., dissenting).

It is also difficult to see how §1409(a)(4)'s limitation of the time allowed for obtaining proof of paternity substantially furthers the assurance of a blood relationship. Modern DNA testing, in addition to providing accuracy unmatched by other methods of establishing a biological link, essentially negates the evidentiary significance of the passage of time. Moreover, the application of §1409(a)(1)'s "clear and convincing evidence" requirement can account for any effect that the passage of time has on the quality of the evidence. . . .

The majority concedes that Congress could achieve the goal of assuring a biological parent-child relationship in a sex-neutral fashion, but then, in a surprising turn, dismisses the availability of sex-neutral alternatives as irrelevant. As the Court suggests, "Congress could have required both mothers and fathers to prove parenthood within 30 days or, for that matter, 18 years, of the child's birth." . . .

In our prior cases, the existence of comparable or superior sex-neutral alternatives has been a powerful reason to reject a sex-based classification. . . . The majority, however, turns this principle on its head by denigrating as "hollow" the very neutrality that the law requires. . . . While the majority trumpets the availability of superior sex-neutral alternatives as confirmation of §1409(a)(4)'s validity, our precedents demonstrate that this fact is a decided strike *against* the law. Far from being "hollow," the avoidance of gratuitous sex-based distinctions is the hallmark of equal protection. . . .

B . . .

Assuming, as the majority does, that Congress was actually concerned about ensuring a "demonstrated opportunity" for a relationship, it is questionable whether such an opportunity qualifies as an "important" governmental interest apart from the existence of an actual relationship. By focusing on "opportunity" rather than reality, the majority presumably improves the chances of a sufficient means-end fit. But in doing so, it dilutes significantly the weight of the interest. It is difficult to see how, in this citizenship-conferral context, anyone profits from a "demonstrated opportunity" for a relationship in the absence of the fruition of an actual tie. Children who have an "opportunity" for such a tie with a parent, of course, may never develop an actual relationship with that parent. . . . If a child grows up in a foreign country without any postbirth contact with the citizen parent, then the child's never-realized "opportunity" for a relationship with the citizen seems singularly irrelevant to the appropriateness of granting citizenship to that child. Likewise, where there is an actual relationship, it is the actual relationship that does all the work in rendering appropriate a grant of citizenship, regardless of when and how the opportunity for that relationship arose. . . .

[A]vailable sex-neutral alternatives would at least replicate, and could easily exceed, whatever fit there is between §1409(a)(4)'s discriminatory means and the majority's asserted end. According to the Court, §1409(a)(4) is designed to ensure that fathers and children have the same "opportunity which the event of birth itself provides for the mother and child.". . . Even assuming that this is so, Congress could simply substitute for §1409(a)(4) a requirement that the parent be present at birth or have knowledge of birth. . . . Congress could at least allow proof of such presence or knowledge to be one way of demonstrating an opportunity for a relationship. . . .

Indeed, the idea that a mother's presence at birth supplies adequate assurance of an opportunity to develop a relationship while a father's presence at birth does not would appear to rest only on an overbroad sex-based generalization. . . . There is no reason, other than stereotype, to say that fathers who are present at birth lack an opportunity for a relationship on similar terms. The "[p]hysical differences between men and women," *Virginia*, 518 U.S., at 533, therefore do not justify §1409(a)(4)'s discrimination. . . .

. . . The Court admits that "Congress could excuse compliance with the formal requirements when an actual father-child relationship is proved," but speculates that Congress did not do so "perhaps because of the subjectivity, intrusiveness, and difficulties of proof that might attend an inquiry into any particular bond or tie." . . . We have repeatedly rejected efforts to justify sex-based classifications on the ground of administrative convenience. . . . There is no reason to think that this is a case where administrative convenience concerns are so powerful that they would justify the sex-based discrimination, . . . especially where the use of sex as a proxy is so ill fit to the purported ends as it is here. And to the extent Congress might seek simply to ensure an "opportunity" for a relationship, little administrative inconvenience would seem to accompany a sex-neutral requirement of presence at birth, knowledge of birth, or contact between parent and child prior to a certain age. . . .

In denying petitioner's claim that §1409(a)(4) rests on stereotypes, the majority articulates a misshapen notion of "stereotype" and its significance in our equal protection jurisprudence. The majority asserts that a "stereotype" is "defined as a frame of mind resulting from irrational or uncritical analysis." . . . This Court has long recognized, however, that an impermissible stereotype may enjoy empirical support and thus be in a sense "rational." See, e.g., *J.E.B.*, supra, at 139, n. 11 . . . Indeed, the stereotypes that underlie a sex-based classification "may hold true for many, even most, individuals." *Miller*, 523 U. S., at 460 (Ginsburg, J., dissenting). But in numerous cases where a measure of truth has inhered in the generalization, "the Court has rejected official actions that classify unnecessarily and overbroadly by gender when more accurate and impartial functional lines can be drawn." Id. . . .

Nor do stereotypes consist only of those overbroad generalizations that the reviewing court considers to "show disrespect" for a class. . . . The hallmark of a stereotypical sex-based classification under this Court's precedents is not whether the classification is insulting, but whether it "relie[s] upon the simplistic, outdated assumption that gender could be used as a 'proxy for other, more germane bases of classification.'" . . .

C

The Court has also failed even to acknowledge the "volumes of history" to which "[t]oday's skeptical scrutiny of official action denying rights or opportunities based on sex responds." [*Virginia*, 518 U.S. at 531]. . . .

Section 1409 was first enacted as §205 of the Nationality Act of 1940, 54 Stat. 1139-1140. The 1940 Act had been proposed by the President, forwarding a report by a specially convened Committee of Advisors, including the Attorney General. The Committee explained to Congress the rationale for §205, whose sex-based classification remains in effect today:

> [T]he Department of State has, at least since 1912, uniformly held that an illegitimate child born abroad of an American mother acquires at birth the nationality of the mother, in the absence of legitimation or adjudication establishing the paternity of the child. This ruling is based . . . on the ground that the mother in such case stands in the place of the father. . . . [U]nder American law the mother has a right to custody and control of such child as against the putative father, and *is bound* to maintain it as its *natural guardian*. This rule seems to be in accord with the old Roman law and with the laws of Spain and France." To Revise and Codify the Nationality Laws of the United States, Hearings on H. R. 6127 before the House Committee on Immigration and Naturalization, 76th Cong., 1st Sess., 431 (1945) (reprinting Message from the President, Nationality Laws of the United States (1938)) (emphasis added and internal quotation marks and citations omitted).

Section 1409(a)(4) is thus paradigmatic of a historic regime that left women with responsibility, and freed men from responsibility, for nonmarital children. . . .

It is, of course, true that the failure to recognize relevant differences is out of line with the command of equal protection. . . . But so too do we undermine the promise of equal protection when we try to make our differences carry weight they simply cannot bear. This promise informs the proper application of heightened scrutiny to sex-based classifications and demands our scrupulous adherence to that test.

III . . .

No one should mistake the majority's analysis for a careful application of this Court's equal protection jurisprudence concerning sex-based classifications. Today's decision instead represents a deviation from a line of cases in which we have vigilantly applied heightened scrutiny to such classifications to determine whether a constitutional violation has occurred. I trust that the depth and vitality of these precedents will ensure that today's error remains an aberration. I respectfully dissent.

Notes

1. Custodial Preference for Unmarried Mothers. Despite the clear trend in the law against explicit sex-based custody preferences, some states retain a statutory custodial preference for the mother when the parents are unmarried. See, e.g., Okla. Stat. Ann. tit. 10, §6 (West 1998), interpreted in In re Adoption of Baby Boy D., 742 P.2d 1059, 1068 (Okla. 1985), cert. denied, 484 U.S. 1072 (1988) ("The mother of an illegitimate minor is entitled to its custody"); Vt. Stat. Ann. tit. 14, §2644 (1989) (mother of illegitimate child is child's guardian), interpreted in In re S.A.M., 436 A.2d 736, 738 (Vt. 1981); Ark. Code Ann. §9-10-113 (Michie 1998) (legal custody shall be in woman giving birth to the child, unless father petitions and proves his fitness, the fact that he has assumed responsibilities toward the child, and that it is in the child's best interests for him to have custody); Ga. Code Ann. §29-4-2 (Michie 1997), interpreted in Brown v. King, 388 S.E.2d 400 (Ga. Ct. App. 1989) (mother of illegitimate child has prima facie right to custody); see also Rainer v. Feldman, 568 So. 2d 1226, 1227 (Ala. 1990) (mother of child born out of wedlock has superior custody rights). Is such a preference consistent with *Caban*? Is it defensible within formal equality principles? Or is it, as Justice O'Connor states, an "aberration'?

2. Evaluation of the "Substantial Relationship" Test in Step-Parent Adoption Cases. *Caban* extends an earlier case, Stanley v. Illinois, 405 U.S. 645 (1972), which held that the state could not conclusively presume the unfitness of an unmarried father, without notice and a hearing, by making his children wards of the state at the death of the mother. Mr. Stanley had lived with his children for all their lives and with their mother for eighteen years before her death. The pivotal importance of a significant parental relationship evolved further in a subsequent case, Quilloin v. Walcott, 434 U.S. 246 (1978), which upheld a stepparent adoption over the father's objection based on the best interests of the child standard because the father had never lived with the mother and child and had supported and visited the child only irregularly. Moving beyond the procedural rights to notice and a hearing at issue in *Stanley*, *Quilloin*, like *Caban*, concerned the substantive grounds for cutting off the father's rights, establishing that the best interests test was unconstitutional only as applied to fathers who had a significant relationship to their children.

The importance of a significant parental relationship between the unmarried father and the child was further affirmed in the subsequent case of Lehr v. Robertson, 463 U.S. 248 (1983). Mr. Lehr, an unmarried father, had lived with the mother before the child's birth and visited her in the hospital after the child was born, but after that time, according to Lehr, the mother concealed the child's whereabouts and prevented visitation and other contact. The mother married another man who, without Lehr's knowledge, initiated stepfather adoption proceedings. When the child was two years old, Lehr filed an action for paternity and visitation but before that action could be heard, the stepparent adoption was finalized. Lehr challenged the adoption on the grounds that he had never received advance notice.

In an opinion written by Justice Stevens, the Supreme Court rejected Lehr's challenge to the adoption, finding constitutional a New York statute that distinguished between unmarried mothers and fathers. The unmarried mother had a right to veto the adoption and the right to prior notice and an opportunity to be heard. An unmarried father was not even entitled to notice, however, unless he had been formally adjudicated to be the father, was named on the child's birth certificate as father, was openly acknowledged by the mother as the father, was living openly with the child and holding himself out as the child's father, had married the child's mother before the child was six months old, or had filed notice of his intent to establish paternity in a putative father registry. Note that all of these options required the cooperation of the mother except that of filing in the putative father registry, an option about which Lehr had no knowledge. The Court found the statute constitutional as applied to Lehr because he had "never established any custodial, personal, or financial relationship with [the child]," and thus his interests — unlike those of Mr. Caban — were merely "inchoate." 463 U.S. at 267.

The substantial relationship test has appealed to a number of courts in other countries who have also made distinctions in their adoption law between fathers who have been involved in the lives of their children and those who have not. Cases from Canada and the United Kingdom, and from the European Court of Human Rights are summarized in the leading case so holding from the Constitutional Court of South Africa. See Fraser v. The Children's Court, Pretoria North, Case CCT 31/96 (1997).

Does *Lehr* mean that a mother may cut off a biological father's rights without notice to him simply by preventing him from having anything to do with the child? Not exactly. *Lehr* is usually read to require that a state must provide some means through which a father may unilaterally protect his rights; New York did this through the putative father registry option. For a detailed discussion of putative father registries, see Rebeca Aizpuru, Note, Protecting the Unwed Father's Opportunity to Parent: A Survey of Paternity Registry Statutes, 18 Rev. Litig. 703 (1999). Under some circumstances, however, some courts have upheld adoptions even where the unmarried father had no opportunity to object. In In re Karen A.B., 513 A.2d 770 (Del. 1986), for example, an adoption without notice to the father was upheld even though the mother refused to disclose the identity of the father because she thought he might harass her if he learned of the child's existence and because he would not be a suitable custodian. Other states, however, have found in favor of the unwed father when the mother either concealed the identity of the true father or took other steps to prevent the father from learning of the baby's existence and thereby effectively precluding him from exercising his parental rights. See In re A.J.F., 764 So.2d 47 (La. 2000) (awarding custody of newborn child to the unwed father after the unwed mother fraudulently misrepresented the identity of the birth father during the adoption proceedings); In the Matter of Baby Boy W., 988 P.2d 1270 (Okla. 1999) (holding that the unmarried father's parental rights could not be terminated in an adoption proceeding because the mother lied about the identity and whereabouts of the father in court and the adoption agency unnecessarily delayed in finding and informing the father of the pending adoption).

Some of the difficulties raised by unmarried, nonresidential fathers seeking to block the adoption of a child by the man with whom the child and mother actually live might be alleviated if the law had the flexibility to recognize more than one father (and, in other circumstances, more than one mother) at a time. A limited model for legal recognition of multiple, "non-exclusive" parental rights is developed in Katharine T. Bartlett, Rethinking Parenthood as an Exclusive Status: The Need for Legal Alternatives When the Premise of the Nuclear Family Has Failed, 70 Val. L. Rev. 879 (1984); see also Mary L. Shanley, Unwed Fathers' Rights, Adoption, and Sex Equality: Gender-Neutrality and the Perpetuation of Patriarchy, 95 Colum. L. Rev. 60, 101 (1995) ("the possibility of such recognition might avoid some cases in which an unwed biological father . . . is motivated not so much by [his] desire to raise a child as by his fear of losing all opportunity to know a child he has sired").

Caban takes a formal equality approach to the rights of unmarried parents who object to the adoption of their children (at least their older children) by another. Is the Court in *Caban* blind to the gender-based realities involved? Can it really be assumed that unmarried fathers are as motivated to make sound decisions on behalf of their children as unmarried mothers? Does this ignore reality? Does it help improve reality?

Does the Stevens position in *Caban*, reinforced in *Lehr* and followed in *Nguyen*, successfully distinguish between mothers and fathers? Stevens' analysis in both cases turns on the differences between men and women. However, none of these differences — that the mother carries the child and has the constitutional right to decide whether to bear the child or not; that in "many cases" only the mother knows who fathered the child, a fact she may choose to hide; that the mother may take many steps, such as marrying a different partner before the child is born, that will affect the legal determination of paternity; that the mother is present at birth and only her identity is "known with certainty" — seem to bear on the "substantial relationship" test evolved in *Stanley*, *Quilloin*, *Caban*, and *Lehr*. Indeed, some of these factors turn on legal rules, including the rule presuming paternity by the husband of a married mother, the very validity of which is implicitly at issue. In fact, doesn't Justice Stevens' analysis build on precisely those sex-based stereotypes that *Reed*, *Frontiero*, *Stanton*, and other equal protection cases meant to preclude? See Kristin Collins, Note, When Fathers' Rights Are Mothers' Duties: The Failure of Equal Protection in Miller v. Albright, 109 Yale L.J. 1669 (2000) (arguing that §1409 perpetuates and reinforces the expectation that women voluntarily assume parental responsibilities while men do not, and that women are superior parents). Justice Stevens' answer in the *Caban* dissent is that women and men are simply not similarly situated, but this explanation would seem to beg the question: why not give the individual father an opportunity, as in *Stanley*, to prove that, whatever the average characteristics of unmarried fathers, he is as serious and responsible as the individual mother?

Does *Nguyen* effectively overrule *Caban*? If Justice Stevens' dissenting view in *Caban* were to become the new constitutional boundary, for how long should a mother be given the advantage in custodial matters? And what should be sufficient to overcome the presumption that the mother is better situated to make decisions with respect to the child?

New York subsequently adopted different rules for newborns (children under six months) than those upheld in *Lehr*, allowing an adoption without the consent of the unmarried father unless he openly lived with the child, acknowledged his paternity, and paid reasonable pregnancy and birth expenses. N.Y. Dom. Rel. L. §111(1)(e) (1988). In 1990 the state court of appeals held that the New York statute did not give the unmarried father adequate constitutional protection, concluding that "a father who has promptly taken every available avenue to demonstrate that he is willing and able to enter into the fullest possible relationship with his under-six-month old child should have an equally fully protected interest in preventing termination of the relationship by strangers, even if he has not as yet actually been able to form that relationship." Matter of Raquel Marie X., 559 N.Y.S.2d 855 (N.Y. 1990), cert. denied sub nom. Robert C. v. Miguel T., 498 U.S. 984 (1990). In lieu of an actual parental relationship, however, the court specified some criteria that should be applied to determine whether the father of a newborn was entitled to block an adoption. These factors include the father's willingness to assume custody of the child, his public acknowledgment of paternity, his payment of pregnancy and birth expenses, and prompt steps taken to establish legal responsibility for the child. 559 N.Y.S.2d at 865, on remand, 570 N.Y.S.2d 604 (A.D. 2d Dept. 1991) (father's involvement insufficient to require constitutional protection); see also Matter of Robert O. v. Russell K., 590 N.Y.S.2d 37 (N.Y. 1992) (unwed father who was unaware of pregnancy or birth of his child until almost 18 months after the child's birth was not entitled to notice of child's adoption to withhold his consent to it, because he failed to take any steps to discover the pregnancy or birth).

As an alternative to the tests discussed above for resolving the rights of unmarried parents to a newborn child, Karen Czapanskiy has attempted to develop an "ungendered" approach that applies two "responsibility" tests. The first test looks to whether the parent participated "to the fullest extent of his or her capacities in the rearing of the child" and the other test looks to whether the parent has been supportive of the child's other parent. Under these tests, the responsibility displayed toward the fetus by the mother would "count," but so would the father's support for the mother throughout her pregnancy, as well as each parent's willingness to take custody and provide for the child soon after the child's birth, and the father's ability to "enter into mutually respectful conversations with the mother about the future of the child before invoking a legal process." Czapanskiy, Volunteers and Draftees: The Struggle for Parental Equality, 38 UCLA L. Rev. 1415, 1477-1478 (1991). This approach aspires to the equal treatment model, while acknowledging the advantage that mothers may have:

> [T]he same tests of responsibility that apply to fathers should apply to mothers except that her physical contribution to the child's birth must be given recognition. If a mother delivers a child, she should be credited with having demonstrated sufficient commitment to be accorded the right to participate in deciding whether the child should be adopted at birth.

Id. at 1478. Czapanskiy argues that the mother should be required to identify the father and notify him of the birth, "except when the father has made threats or acted violently, or when he consistently has failed to respect her needs or feelings. In such a case, a judicial bypass may be necessary, similar to the judicial bypass available to minors seeking abortions." Id. at 1478-79. Is this really a gender-neutral standard? Some argue that the father's relationship with the mother should be irrelevant and instead the focus should be on his desire or demonstrated ability to form a supportive relationship with the child. See Scott A. Resnik, Seeking the Wisdom of Solomon: Defining the Rights of Unwed Fathers in Newborn Adoptions, 20 Seton Hall Legis. J. 363 (1996); Toni L. Craig, Comment, Establishing the Biological Rights Doctrine to Protect Unwed Fathers in Contested Adoptions, 25 Fla. St. U.L. Rev. 391 (1998).

3. Adoption by Third-Party Strangers. In determining the rights of unmarried fathers to block an adoption, should the law distinguish between stepparent adoptions and adoptions by third-party strangers? It is one thing when a mother seeks to have her husband who lives with her and her children obtain legal recognition as the children's father. But should a mother be able to give her child up to strangers over the objection of the biological father? In this situation, courts have tended to be more protective of the fathers' interests. See, e.g., In re Interest of B.G.C., 496 N.W.2d 239 (Iowa 1992) (denying adoption petition to third party when the unwed father asserted parental rights 30 days after the baby was placed with the prospective third-party adoptive parents); In re Petition of Doe, 638 N.E.2d 181 (Ill. 1994), cert. denied sub nom. Baby "Richard" by O'Connell v. Kirchner, 513 U.S. 994 (1994) (voiding third-party adoption of Baby Richard three years after placement with adoptive parents when father never consented to adoption and later asserted paternity); Adoption of Kelsey S., 4 Cal. Rptr. 2d 615 (Cal. 1992) (father who makes diligent attempts to obtain custody of child retains right to object to adoption by third parties).

Is this increased protection justified? From whose point of view? Compare Nancy Erickson, The Feminist Dilemma over Unwed Parents' Custody Rights: The Mother's Rights Must Take Priority, 2 L. & Ineq. J. 447, 466 (1984) (arguing that mother should be able to give child up for adoption to third-party strangers, over the objection of father, because she has endured the risks, inconvenience, and pain of pregnancy and childbirth), with Toni L. Craig, Comment, Establishing the Biological Rights Doctrine to Protect Unwed Fathers in Contested Adoptions, 25 Fla. St. U.L. Rev. 391 (1998) (arguing that an unwed father should be presumed fit to take custody of his newborn child when he withholds consent to a third-party adoption and that his parental rights should trump the prospective adoptive parents if he has made any effort to assume responsibility for the unborn or newborn child).

4. Non-Marital Motherhood-by-Choice. One justification for giving the unmarried mother wide berth to make adoption decisions that exclude the biological father is the state's asserted interest in promoting adoptions that would give the child the benefits of a two-parent home — whether that be through stepparent adoption or adoption by third-party strangers. The importance of this factor may help to account for why women who are not offering a two-parent home with both a mother and a father have been less successful in blocking all rights asserted by the father. Thus, for example, in a case in which a woman pursuing a plan to become a single mother became pregnant through artificial insemination, the biological father was later able to establish paternity and obtain visitation rights over her objection. Under the California artificial insemination statute, biological fathers (i.e., sperm donors) ordinarily have no rights, but the court held that the statute did not apply because the procedure was not done under the supervision of a doctor. See Jhordan C. v. Mary K., 179 Cal. App. 3d 386, 224 Cal. Rptr. 530 (Ct. App. 1986).

Is judicial preference for placement in a two-parent home a realistic or desirable societal goal? Is it relevant that almost a third of U.S. births now occur to unmarried mothers and more than a quarter of U.S. children grow up in single parent homes? See Jason Fields, Current Population Reports, Fall 1996: Living Arrangements of Children (2001); Marsha Garrison, Law Making for Baby Making: An Interpretive Approach to the Determination of Legal Parentage, 113 Harv. L. Rev. 835 (2000).

5. The Unmarried Father vs. the Married Mother. What if a child is born to an unmarried father and a mother who is married to someone else? If the father establishes a "substantial relationship" with the child, can the mother and her husband nonetheless cut off his involvement with the child, including visitation? Michael H. v. Gerald D., 491 U.S. 110 (1989), involved the constitutionality of a California statute, Cal. Evid. Code §621(a) (West Supp. 1989), that created, under some circumstances, an irrebuttable presumption that the father of a child born of a married woman is the woman's husband, precluding the exercise of paternal rights by any other man, including the biological father. Michael H. claimed to have lived off and on with the mother and the child and thus to have satisfied the "substantial relationship" test of *Stanley, Quilloin, Caban,* and *Lehr,* entitling him to visitation rights when the mother cut off contact. The state, however, denied him standing under the statute to assert his rights as father; the Supreme Court in *Michael H.* upheld the constitutionality of the statute.

Michael H. marked an important doctrinal shift, both for the rights of unmarried fathers and for the recognition of liberty interests under substantive due process analysis more generally. Justice Scalia, writing for the Court, reinterpreted the Court's past rulings in the substantive due process area by insisting "that the asserted liberty interest be rooted in history and tradition." 491 U.S. at 123. Characterizing the father's claim as that of an "adulterous natural father," 491 U.S. at 127 n.6, and construing the Court's previous precedents as ones that recognized the importance of "relationships that develop in the unitary family," 491 U.S. at 123, Justice Scalia reasoned that the father's claim arising from his biological connection to the child could not prevail in the face of an intact marital unit, which the state had chosen to protect.

Tradition had been used in previous cases to limit the state's ability to impose uniformity on families and to restrict their intimate practices. See, e.g., Moore v. City of East Cleveland, 431 U.S. 494, 503 (1977) (invalidating zoning ordinance that prohibited grandmother from living in single-family residence zone with her two grandchildren, based on deeply rooted institution of the extended family in this nation's history and tradition); Griswold v. Connecticut, 381 U.S. 479, 486 (1965) (invalidating ban on contraceptives based on importance of privacy in marital relationship that is "older than the Bill of Rights"). Along with Bowers v. Hardwick, 478 U.S. 186 (1986), discussed at pages 752-754, *Michael H.* signals the use of tradition to restrict, rather than to expand, constitutionally-recognized liberty interests. While the case itself denied the right of a biological father, not mother, the mother's interests were legally superior only because she was attached legally to a man; her victory thereby might be said to reinforce familiar, often oppressive, gender role norms.

Can an analysis that requires asserted liberty interests to be "deeply rooted" in this nation's traditions and history and that rejects liberty claims that run counter to any long-standing social traditions be sensitive to groups whose subordination is "deeply rooted" in this nation's traditions and history? In fact, recalling the materials from the beginning of this chapter relating to the elimination of past discrimination, shouldn't such traditions warrant special remedial steps?

Presumption of legitimacy statutes are prevalent in the United States, yet are far from uniform. Some states deny standing to the adulterous father to challenge the presumed paternity of the mother's husband. See, e.g., Dawn D. v. Superior Ct., 952 P.2d 1139 (Cal. 1998), cert. denied sub nom Jerry K. v. Dawn D., 525 U.S. 1055 (1998); Evans v. Steelman, 970 S.W.2d 431 (Tenn. 1998); Hauser v. Reilly, 536 N.W.2d 865 (Mich. Ct. App. 1995). Other states grant standing to the putative father to challenge the presumed paternity of the husband. See, e.g., Callender v. Skiles, 591 N.W.2d 182 (Iowa 1999); K.S. v. R.S., 669 N.E.2d 399 (Ind. 1996); Ivy v. Harrington, 644 So. 2d 1218 (Miss. 1994). Is one approach more equality-enhancing than the other?

Putting Theory into Practice

3-15. *O*, age 25, is a college graduate and is currently employed at a bank. He was hired in a management-training position at an annual salary of $34,500, and has the potential to achieve economic security as he moves his way up the bank management ladder. About 18 months ago, his girlfriend *A*, then age 18, abruptly broke off their two-year relationship, saying that *O*, who kept asking *A* to marry him and to settle down and have a family, had gotten too serious for her. *O* has just found out that a year ago, *A* had a baby who is his biological child, and that the real reason she broke up with him was because she knew *O* would want to get married and raise the child, whom *A* wanted to place up for adoption.

Although *A* had planned originally to put the child up for adoption immediately at birth, before the adoption was finalized she met another man, has married him, and now wants her new husband to adopt the child. *O* seeks to block the adoption, claiming that if he had known about the child, he would have manifested his interest in and commitment toward the child by offering financial support and by attempting to obtain custody or visitation. State law permits adoption without the consent of the unmarried biological father if he has not manifested an interest in the child within six months of the child's birth. Is this law constitutional? Is it wise? To which theory of equality does your answer most closely correspond?

How, if at all, would your answer be affected if the intended adoption was by a couple who is unrelated to either parent, rather than by *A*'s new husband?

3-16. Elise has obtained a child support order against Jude for support of her one-year-old, Thomas. The order, however, resulted in Jude insisting upon his rights to see Thomas. Elise objects to his visits because they require her to interact with Jude, whom she considers a despicable person and a bad influence on Thomas. Jude agrees to leave her and Thomas alone, if she will forego her rights to child support. Should such an agreement be enforceable?

3-17. Indiana law allows the changing of a child's name, upon petition of a parent, if the change is in the child's best interest. Stephen Warren petitioned the court seeking to change the surname of his four-year old child from his mother's surname to his own surname. The child has had his mother's surname since birth and he is known to family and friends by that name. Warren argues that it is in the child's best interests to have his surname because (1) he is a Potowami Indian and it is "relevant to the child's Indian heritage"; and (2) he pays child support, has visitation, and is involved in the child's life. The mother opposes the petition because (1) the child has had her surname since birth and would be confused by the change; (2) all of his records use her surname; and (3) he has siblings with the same surname. Should the court grant the petition? Explain. See In re Tibbitts, 668 N.E.2d 1266 (Ind. Ct. App. 1996) (petition granted). For a history of surnames and their gendered importance, see Lisa Kelly, Divining the Deep and Inscrutable: Toward a Gender-Neutral, Child-Centered Approach to Child Name Change Proceedings, 99 W. Va. L. Rev. 1 (1996); Merle H. Weiner, "We Are Family": Valuing Associationalism in Disputes Over Children's Surnames, 75 N.C. L. Rev. 1625 (1997).

4

Nonsubordination

The nonsubordination perspective on women and law shifts the focus of attention from gender-based difference to gender-based inequality and the imbalance of power between women and men. This perspective, sometimes referred to as dominance theory, makes the relevant inquiry not whether women are like, or unlike, men, but whether a rule or practice serves to subordinate women to men. Accordingly, similarities and differences between women and men are important not as givens that produce certain expected, rational consequences in the law, but as part of a larger conceptual system designed to make women's subordination seem natural and legitimate. Catharine MacKinnon calls this theory feminism "unmodified," because it analyzes the situation of all women *as women* and abandons the "gender-neutral absolutes, such as difference and sexuality and speech and the state" that are characteristic of qualified theories such as socialist feminism and liberal feminism. See Catharine A. MacKinnon, Feminism Unmodified: Discourses on Life and Law 16 (1987).

This chapter introduces nonsubordination theory by pairing John Stuart Mill's description of women's nineteenth-century "subjection" as a "solitary breach" in the fundamental laws of modern civilization with Catharine MacKinnon's characterization of women's legal subordination as the ability of those with power — men — to identify their own point of view as "point-of-viewlessness." The remainder of the chapter explores, primarily through legal materials relating to sexual harassment, pornography, domestic violence, and heterosexuality, nonsubordination theory's claim that the law defines sex and sexual difference in ways that mask the universality of men's point of view and naturalize women's relative powerlessness in this society.

It is no accident that most of the topics of this chapter relate to sexual behavior — inside families, workplaces, educational institutions, and elsewhere. This is largely because the sexual realm is where dominance theory has the most to offer in understanding the relationship between gender and

533

law. With respect to other forms of sex-based discrimination in access to employment, education, and other public benefits, traditional equality theory appears to have achieved significant improvements in the position of women. MacKinnon's complaint with equality theory, of whichever variety, is that while it is adequate to handle certain marginal exceptions — e.g., privileged women who fit the male profile — it is insufficient to address the central inequalities faced by women — sexual violence and abuse, poverty, deprivation of control over reproductive decisions, and so on. To get at these questions, MacKinnon argues that we must move beyond questions of sameness and difference to the construction of women's sexuality, which she finds to be at the core of the processes that underpin these more central inequalities. This construction of sexuality is reflected in pornography, sexual harassment, domestic violence, and other topics addressed in this chapter but, according to MacKinnon, it sustains all forms of gender subordination and devaluation. What does dominance theory add to, and how does it revise, the equality principles studied thus far? Which theoretical framework do you find the most satisfactory?

A. WOMEN'S RIGHTS AND POWER IN THE LIBERAL STATE

John Stuart Mill, The Subjection of Women
Three Essays by John Stuart Mill
427-428, 430, 433-434, 443-444, 449-450
(World's Classics edition 1912) (1869)

[T]he principle which regulates the existing social relations between the two sexes — the legal subordination of one sex to the other — is wrong in itself, and now one of the chief hindrances to human improvement; . . . it ought to be replaced by a principle of perfect equality, admitting no power or privilege on the one side, nor disability on the other.

The . . . difficulty of the case . . . is that which exists in all cases in which there is a mass of feeling to be contended against. So long as an opinion is strongly rooted in the feelings, it gains rather than loses in stability by having a preponderating weight of argument against it. For if it were accepted as a result of argument, the refutation of the argument might shake the solidity of the conviction; but when it rests solely on feeling, the worse it fares in argumentative contest, the more persuaded its adherents are that their feeling must have some deeper ground, which the arguments do not reach; and while the feeling remains, it is always throwing up fresh entrenchments of argument to repair any breach made in the old. And there are so many causes tending to make the feelings connected with this subject the most intense and most deeply-rooted of all those which gather round and protect old institutions and customs, that we need not wonder to find them as yet less undermined and loosened than any of the rest by the progress of the great modern spiritual and social transition; nor suppose that the barbarisms to which men cling longest must be less barbarisms than those which they earlier shake off. . . .

All causes, social and natural, combine to make it unlikely that women should be collectively rebellious to the power of men. They are so far in a position different from all other subject classes, that their masters require something more from them than actual service. Men do not want solely the obedience of women, they want their sentiments. All men, except the most brutish, desire to have, in the woman most nearly connected with them, not a forced slave but a willing one; not a slave merely, but a favorite. They have therefore put everything in practice to enslave their minds. The masters of all slaves rely, for maintaining obedience, on fear; either fear of themselves, or religious fears. The masters of women wanted more than simple obedience, and they turned the whole force of education to effect their purpose. All women are brought up from the very earliest years in the belief that their ideal of character is the very opposite to that of men; not self-will, and government by self-control, but submission, and yielding to the control of others. All the moralities tell them that it is their nature, to live for others; to make complete abnegation of themselves, and to have no life but in their affections. And by their affections are meant the only ones they are allowed to have — those to the men with whom they are connected, or to the children who constitute an additional and indefeasible tie between them and a man. When we put together three things — first, the natural attraction between opposite sexes; secondly, the wife's entire dependence on the husband, every privilege or pleasure she has being either his gift, or depending entirely on his will; and lastly, that the principal object of human pursuit, consideration, and all objects of social ambition, can in general be sought or obtained by her only through him — it would be a miracle if the object of being attractive to men had not become the polar star of feminine education and formation of character. And, this great means of influence over the minds of women having been acquired, an instinct of selfishness made men avail themselves of it to the utmost as a means of holding women in subjection, by representing to them meekness, submissiveness, and resignation of all individual will into the hands of a man, as an essential part of sexual attractiveness. . . .

The social subordination of women thus stands out an isolated fact in modern social institutions; a solitary breach of what has become their fundamental law; a single relic of an old world of thought and practice exploded in everything else, but retained in the one thing of most universal interest. . . .

Catharine A. MacKinnon, Feminism Unmodified: Discourses on Life and Law
32-37, 40-43 (1987)

What is a gender question a question of? What is an inequality question a question of? These two questions underlie applications of the equality principle to issues of gender, but they are seldom explicitly asked. I think it speaks to the way gender has structured thought and perception that mainstream legal and moral theory tacitly gives the same answer to them both: these are questions of sameness and difference. The mainstream doctrine of the law of sex discrimination that results is, in my view, largely responsible for the fact that sex equality law has been so utterly ineffective at getting women what we need and are socially prevented from having on the basis of a condition of birth: a chance at productive lives of reasonable physical security, self-expression, individuation, and minimal respect and dignity. . . .

Two alternate paths to equality for women emerge within [the] dominant approach. . . . The leading one is: be the same as men. This path is termed gender neutrality legally and the single standard philosophically. . . . To women who want equality yet find that you are different, the doctrine provides an alternate route: be different from men. This equal recognition of difference is termed the special benefit rule or the special protection rule legally, the double standard philosophically. . . .

My concern is not with which of these paths to sex equality is preferable . . . although most discourse on sex discrimination revolves about these questions as if that were all there is. My point is logically prior: to treat issues of sex equality as issues of sameness and difference *is to take a particular approach.* I call this the difference approach because it is obsessed with the sex difference. . . .

Under the sameness standard, women are measured according to our correspondence with man, our equality judged by our proximity to his measure. Under the difference standard, we are measured according to our lack of correspondence with him, our womanhood judged by our distance from his measure. Gender neutrality is thus simply the male standard, and the special protection rule is simply the female standard, but do not be deceived: masculinity, or maleness, is the referent for both. . . . As applied, the sameness standard has mostly gotten men the benefit of those few things women historically had — for all the good they did us. Almost every sex discrimination case that has been won at the Supreme Court level has been brought by a man. . . .

In reality, which this approach is not long on because it is liberal idealism talking to itself, virtually every quality that distinguishes men from women is already affirmatively compensated in this society. Men's physiology defines most sports, their needs define auto and health insurance coverage, their socially designed biographies define workplace expectations and successful career patterns, their perspectives and concerns define quality in scholarship, their experiences and obsessions define merit, their objectification of life defines art, their military service defines citizenship, their presence defines family, their inability to get along with each other — their wars and rulerships — defines history, their image defines god, and their genitals define sex. For each of their differences from women, what amounts to an affirmative action plan is in effect, otherwise known as the structure and values of American society. But whenever women are, by this standard, "different" from men and insist on not having it held against us, whenever a difference is used to keep us second class and we refuse to smile about it, equality law has a paradigm trauma and it's crisis time for the doctrine. . . .

The women that gender neutrality benefits, and there are some, show the suppositions of [the difference] approach in highest relief. They are mostly women who have been able to construct a biography that somewhat approximates the male norm, at least on paper. They are the qualified, the least of sex discrimination's victims. When they are denied a man's chance, it looks the most like sex bias. The more unequal society gets, the fewer such women are permitted to exist. Therefore, the more unequal society gets, the less likely the difference doctrine is to be able to do anything about it, because unequal power creates both the appearance and the reality of sex differences along the same lines as it creates its sex inequalities. . . .

There is an alternative approach, one that threads its way through existing law and expresses, I think, the reason equality law exists in the first place. It provides a second answer, a dissident answer in law and philosophy, to both the equality question and the gender question. In this approach, an equality question is a question of the distribution of power. Gender is also a question of power, specifically of male supremacy and female subordination. The question of equality, from the standpoint of what it is going to take to get it, is at root a question of hierarchy, which — as power succeeds in constructing social perception and social reality — derivatively becomes a categorical distinction, a difference. Here, on the first day that matters, dominance was achieved, probably by force. By the second day, division along the same lines had to be relatively firmly in place. On the third day, if not sooner, differences were demarcated, together with social systems to exaggerate them in perception and in fact, because the systematically differential delivery of benefits and deprivations required making no mistake about who was who. Comparatively speaking, man has been resting ever since. Gender might not even code as difference, might not mean distinction epistemologically, were it not for its consequences for social power.

I call this the dominance approach, and it is the ground I have been standing on in criticizing mainstream law. The goal of this dissident approach is not to make legal categories trace and trap the way things are. It is not to make rules that fit reality. It is critical of reality. Its task is not to formulate abstract standards that will produce determinate outcomes in particular cases. Its project is more substantive, more jurisprudential than formulaic, which is why it is difficult for the mainstream discourse to dignify it as an approach to doctrine or to imagine it as a rule of law at all. It proposes to expose that which women have had little choice but to be confined to, in order to change it.

The dominance approach centers on the most sex-differential abuses of women as a gender, abuses that sex equality law in its difference garb could not confront. It is based on a reality about which little of a systematic nature was known before 1970, a reality that calls for a new conception of the problem of sex inequality. This new information includes not only the extent and intractability of sex segregation into poverty, which has been known before, but the range of issues termed violence against women, which has not been. It combines women's material desperation, through being relegated to categories of jobs that pay nil, with the massive amount of rape and attempted rape — 44 percent of all women — about which virtually nothing is done; the sexual assault of children — 38 percent of girls and 10 percent of boys — which is apparently endemic to the patriarchal family; the battery of women that is systematic in one quarter to one third of our homes; prostitution, women's fundamental economic condition, what we do when all else fails, and for many women in this country, all else fails often; and pornography, an industry that traffics in female flesh, making sex inequality into sex to the tune of eight billion dollars a year in profits largely to organized crime.

These experiences have been silenced out of the difference definition of sex equality largely because they happen almost exclusively to women. Understand: for this reason, they are considered not to raise sex equality issues. Because this treatment is done almost uniquely to women, it is implicitly treated as a difference, the sex difference, when in fact it is the socially situated subjection of women. The whole point of women's social relegation to inferiority as a gender is that for the most part these things aren't done to men. . . .

The second approach — which is not abstract, which is at odds with socially imposed reality and therefore does not look like a standard according to the standard for standards — became the implicit model for racial justice applied by the courts during the sixties. It has since eroded with the erosion of judicial commitment to racial equality. It was based on the realization that the condition of Blacks in particular was not fundamentally a matter of rational or irrational differentiation on the basis of race but was fundamentally a matter of white supremacy, under which racial differences became invidious as a consequence. To consider gender in this way, observe again that men are as different from women as women are from men, but socially the sexes are not equally powerful. To be on the top of a hierarchy is certainly different from being on the bottom, but that is an obfuscatingly neutralized way of putting it, as a hierarchy is a great deal more than that. If gender were merely a question of difference, sex inequality would be a problem of mere sexism, of mistaken differentiation, of inaccurate categorization of individuals. This is what the difference approach thinks it is and is therefore sensitive to. But if gender is an inequality first, constructed as a socially relevant differentiation in order to keep that inequality in place, the sex inequality questions are questions of systematic dominance, of male supremacy, which is not at all abstract and is anything but a mistake.

If differentiation into classifications, in itself, is discrimination, as it is in difference doctrine, the use of law to change group-based social inequalities becomes problematic, even contradictory. This is because the group whose situation is to be changed must necessarily be legally identified and delineated, yet to do so is considered in fundamental tension with the guarantee against legally sanctioned inequality. If differentiation is discrimination, affirmative action, and any legal change in social inequality, is discrimination — but the existing social differentiations which constitute the inequality are not? This is only to say that, in the view that equates differentiation with discrimination, changing an unequal status quo is discrimination, but allowing it to exist is not.

Looking at the difference approach and the dominance approach from each other's point of view clarifies some otherwise confusing tensions in sex equality debates. From the point of view of the dominance approach, it becomes clear that the difference approach adopts the point of view of male supremacy on the status of the sexes. Simply by treating the status quo as "the standard," it invisibly and uncritically accepts the arrangements under male supremacy. In this sense, the difference approach is masculinist, although it can be expressed in a female voice. The dominance approach, in that it sees the inequalities of the social world from the standpoint of the subordination of women to men, is feminist.

NOTE ON DOMINANCE THEORY AND LIBERALISM

John Stuart Mill — the leading spokesman for nineteenth-century liberalism — finds the subordination of women an aberrational blind spot of liberalism. MacKinnon, on the other hand, finds the subordination of women a more or less inevitable consequence of liberalism's emphasis on the individual, its claim to objectivity, and its idealism. As you proceed through the materials in this chapter, try to determine whether this difference is significant. Try, also, to identify the areas of agreement and disagreement between liberal theory, represented best by the formal equality principles developed in Chapter 2, and the nonsubordination or dominance approach represented in these two readings. In addition to the points of tension MacKinnon identifies, consider the following:

> . . . MacKinnon's dominance approach is . . . inconsistent with liberalism's commitment to neutrality with respect to contested conceptions of the good. MacKinnon's approach assumes that equality is the dominant, lexically prior

political value. Thus, the fact that anti-pornography laws might result in the suppression of works of serious artistic or literary merit is shrugged off by MacKinnon with the remark, "[I]f a woman is subjected, why should it matter that the work has other value?" [Catharine A. MacKinnon, Feminism Unmodified: Discourses on Life and Law 152-153 (1987).] Similarly, the fact that sweeping judicially-ordered comparable worth reforms might have serious repercussions for the nation's economic health is not seen as a good reason why courts should refrain from treating market-driven pay inequities as actionable forms of sex discrimination. [Id. at 36.] By contrast, current sex discrimination law does not view equality as a sovereign good that invariably trumps such competing values as individual liberty, individual rights, or the common good. It recognizes that there may be "important governmental objectives" [Craig v. Boren, 429 U.S. 190, 199-200 n.7 (1976)] that on occasion override the state's interest in promoting gender equality.

Gregory Bassham, Feminist Legal Theory: A Liberal Response, 6 Notre Dame J.L. Ethics & Pub. Pol'y 293, 302 (1992). How might MacKinnon respond to this critique? How much of a challenge does MacKinnon's dominance approach raise to liberal theory? For other versions of nonsubordination theory that provide useful points of comparison, see Robin West, Caring for Justice (1997); Iris Marion Young, Justice and the Politics of Difference (1990); Carol Smart, Feminism and the Power of Law (1989).

B. SEXUAL HARASSMENT

1. Sexual Harassment in the Workplace

Catharine A. MacKinnon, The Sexual Harassment of Working Women
1, 9-10, 23 (1979)

Intimate violation of women by men is sufficiently pervasive in American society as to be nearly invisible. Contained by internalized and structural forms of power, it has been nearly inaudible. Conjoined with men's control over women's material survival, as in the home or on the job, or over women's learning and educational advancement in school, it has become institutionalized. . . .

Sexual harassment, most broadly defined, refers to the unwanted imposition of sexual requirements in the context of a relationship of unequal power. Central to the concept is the use of power derived from one social sphere to level benefits or impose deprivations in another. The major dynamic is best expressed as the reciprocal enforcement of two inequalities.

When one is sexual, the other material, the cumulative sanction is particularly potent. American society legitimizes male sexual dominance of women and employer's control of workers. . . .

[T]he sexual harassment of women can occur largely because women occupy inferior job positions and job roles; at the same time, sexual harassment works to keep women in such positions. Sexual harassment, then, uses and helps create women's structurally inferior status. . . .

Catharine A. MacKinnon, Feminism Unmodified: Discourses on Life and Law
105-106 (1987)

It is hard to unthink what you know, but there was a time when the facts that amount to sexual harassment did not amount to sexual harassment. . . . The facts amounting to the harm did not socially "exist," had no shape, no cognitive coherence; far less did they state a legal claim. It just happened to you. To the women to whom it happened, it wasn't part of anything, much less something big or shared like gender. It fit no known pattern. It was neither a regularity nor an irregularity. Even social scientists didn't study it, and they study anything that moves. When law recognized sexual harassment as a practice of sex discrimination, it moved it from the realm of "and then he . . . and then he . . . ," the primitive language in which sexual abuse lives inside a woman, into an experience with a form, an etiology, a cumulativeness — as well as a club.

[I]t is the very qualities which men find sexually attractive in the women they harass that are their real qualifications for the jobs for which they hire them. Women know this. They know that the appearance an employer finds gratifying, that image which is much of what he is really paying for, is, in substance, that "nice" provocativeness that she drops at her economic risk. It is this good-girl sexiness (in the case of black women, well-contained bad-girl sexiness) that qualifies a woman for her job that leaves her open to sexual harassment at any time and to the accusation that she invited it.

Kathryn Abrams, Gender Discrimination and the Transformation of Workplace Norms
42 Vand. L. Rev. 1183, 1207-1209 (1989)

[S]exually oriented behavior in the workplace produces at least two responses among women that contribute to their subordination. . . . One response is a fear of sexual coercion. Sexually oriented behavior brings into the workplace echoes of a context in which men and women often are radically unequal. A woman struggling to establish credibility in a setting in which she may not be, or may not feel, welcome, can be swept off balance by a reminder that she can be raped, fondled, or subjected to repeated sexual demands. Her employment setting, already precarious, can be transformed instantly into an unwanted sexual encounter in which she is likely to feel even less control, a transformation that can cast shadows even when demands are not being made. The feelings of anxiety, fear, or vulnerability produced by the spectre of sexual coercion prevent women from feeling, or being viewed as, the equals of their male counterparts in the workplace.

But a woman need not be threatened with sexual coercion to feel, and to be perceived as, unequal in the workplace. Sexual inquiries, jokes, remarks, or innuendoes sometimes can raise the spectre of coercion, but they more predictably have the effect of reminding a woman that she is viewed as an object of sexual derision rather than as a credible coworker. A woman who is continuously queried by male colleagues about her sexual preferences, referred to by coworkers as "the fucking flag girl," or depicted on the walls of men's restrooms in sexual poses is being told that she is not, first and foremost, a credible colleague and an equal. This message would be disturbing to any worker, even one who felt comfortable and secure in the workplace. For a woman worker, who may not have been socialized to feel comfortable in that role, and who may have faced numerous men who have difficulty viewing women as workers rather than wives or dates, this message can be devastating. Treatment that sexualizes women workers prevents them from feeling, and prevents others from perceiving them, as equal in the workplace.

L. Camille Hébert, *The Economic Implications of Sexual Harassment for Women*
3 Kan. J.L. & Pub. Pol'y 41, 47-50 (Spring 1994)

A common view is that sexual harassment . . . is motivated by sexual desire and that women are targets of sexual harassment because they are sexually attractive to their harasser. . . .

Existing patterns of sexual harassment in the workplace, however, are difficult to explain as caused by only sexual desire — even nonmutual, one-sided sexual desire.

One aspect of the pattern of sexual harassment in the workplace that suggests sexual harassment is motivated, or at least caused, by economic considerations is the profile of the women who are most often subjected to harassment. One characteristic common among women who report sexual harassment is economic vulnerability. . . .

[M]any women who report sexual harassment are very dependent on their jobs, which would make them economically vulnerable to sexual harassment. Women with low seniority and those in low-status and low-skill jobs are more frequently subjected to sexual harassment than women in higher status and higher skill jobs. Women in trainee positions and women on probation are also more frequently subjected to sexual harassment. There is no reason to expect that these women are more sexually attractive or desirable than women who are not in these jobs. . . .

[W]omen who are members of minority groups are more likely to be sexually harassed than nonminority women. . . .

. . . Highly educated women appear to be more likely to be sexually harassed than other women; similarly, women moving into nontraditional jobs — jobs traditionally dominated by men — frequently are subjected to sexual harassment. There is no reason to believe that such women are more sexually attractive than other women.

Nor, however, are these women necessarily more economically vulnerable than other women. In fact, the converse is likely to be true. . . . This does not mean, however, that sexual harassment against these women is not the result of economic factors. In these situations, economic factors other than economic vulnerability appear to be at work, such as the desire of men to ensure continued economic dominance over women in the workplace by discouraging women from entering jobs in which they would compete with men.

Some commentators have argued that sexual harassment is motivated by factors other than power imbalances by pointing to the fact that sexual harassment most often occurs among co-workers rather than between a supervisor and a subordinate. Such a contention, however, fails to recognize that forms of economic power other than supervisory power exist in the workplace. Males may be able to exert economic power over female co-workers by withholding information and training necessary to job performance, particularly when women are moving into jobs that traditionally have been held by men. Men may also be able to assert economic power over female co-workers by threatening to sabotage work or job performance. Finally, men, because of their longer job tenure (and because of their maleness), may simply have more authority with supervisors than newer female employees and thereby be able to influence the supervisor's perception of the women's job performance.

Sexual harassment in the workplace may even be motivated by the frustration some men feel over the loss of economic power in the workplace. . . . Some men feel threatened, both socially and economically, by the advancement of women; some of these men react to these women with hostility.

It is not surprising that this hostility would manifest itself in abusive sexual activity directed toward women. Because of both biological and social factors, men often have, or believe themselves to have, power over women in their sexual relationships. Some men may resort to sexual harassment in the workplace to assert power in a sexual context, in which they believe they have an advantage over women, and to express frustration over their loss or lack of relative power over women in the workplace context. . . .

A final reason to doubt the sexual attractiveness theory of sexual harassment is that women surveyed in sexual harassment studies report that their harassers also harass others at work. This finding suggests that sexual harassment is more a pattern of abusive behavior than the result of "isolated instances of personal sexual attraction."

Meritor Savings Bank v. Vinson
477 U.S. 57 (1986)

Justice REHNQUIST delivered the opinion of the court.

This case presents important questions concerning claims of workplace "sexual harassment" brought under Title VII of the Civil Rights Act of 1964. . . .

I

In 1974, respondent Mechelle Vinson met Sidney Taylor, a vice president of what is now petitioner Meritor Savings Bank (bank) and manager of one of its branch offices. . . . With Taylor as her supervisor, respondent started as a teller-trainee, and thereafter was promoted to teller, head teller, and assistant branch manager. She worked at the same branch for four years, and it is undisputed that her advancement there was based on merit alone. In September 1978, respondent notified Taylor that she was taking sick leave for an indefinite period. On November 1, 1978, the bank discharged her for excessive use of that leave.

Respondent brought this action against Taylor and the bank, claiming that during her four years at the bank she had "constantly been subjected to sexual harassment" by Taylor in violation of Title VII. She sought injunctive relief, compensatory and punitive damages against Taylor and the bank, and attorney's fees.

At the 11-day bench trial, the parties presented conflicting testimony about Taylor's behavior during respondent's employment. Respondent testified that during her probationary period as a teller-trainee, Taylor treated her in a fatherly way and made no sexual advances. Shortly thereafter, however, he invited her out to dinner and, during the course of the meal, suggested that they go to a motel to have sexual relations. At first she refused, but out of what she described as fear of losing her job she eventually agreed. According to respondent, Taylor thereafter made repeated demands upon her for sexual favors, usually at the branch, both during and after business hours; she estimated that over the next several years she had intercourse with him some 40 or 50 times. In addition, respondent testified that Taylor fondled her in front of other employees, followed her into the women's restroom when she went there alone, exposed himself to her, and even forcibly raped her on several occasions. These activities ceased after

1977, respondent stated, when she started going with a steady boyfriend.
. . .

Taylor denied respondent's allegations of sexual activity, testifying that he never fondled her, never made suggestive remarks to her, never engaged in sexual intercourse with her, and never asked her to do so. He contended instead that respondent made her accusations in response to a business-related dispute. The bank also denied respondent's allegations and asserted that any sexual harassment by Taylor was unknown to the bank and engaged in without its consent or approval.

The District Court denied relief. . . .

The Court of Appeals for the District of Columbia Circuit reversed. [753 F.2d 141 (D.C. Cir. 1985).] . . .

II . . .

Respondent argues . . . that unwelcome sexual advances that create an offensive or hostile working environment violate Title VII. Without question, when a supervisor sexually harasses a subordinate because of the subordinate's sex, that supervisor "discriminate[s]" on the basis of sex. Petitioner apparently does not challenge this proposition. It contends instead that in prohibiting discrimination with respect to "compensation, terms, conditions, or privileges" of employment, Congress was concerned with what petitioner describes as "tangible loss" of "an economic character," not "purely psychological aspects of the workplace environment." . . . In support of this claim petitioner observes that in both the legislative history of Title VII and this Court's Title VII decisions, the focus has been on tangible, economic barriers erected by discrimination.

We reject petitioner's view. First, the language of Title VII is not limited to "economic" or "tangible" discrimination. The phrase "terms, conditions, or privileges of employment" evinces a congressional intent "'to strike at the entire spectrum of disparate treatment of men and women'" in employment. . . .

Second, in 1980 the EEOC issued Guidelines specifying that "sexual harassment," as there defined, is a form of sex discrimination prohibited by Title VII. . . . The EEOC Guidelines fully support the view that harassment leading to noneconomic injury can violate Title VII.

In defining "sexual harassment," the Guidelines first describe the kinds of workplace conduct that may be actionable under Title VII. These include "[u]nwelcome sexual advances, requests for sexual favors, and other verbal or physical conduct of a sexual nature." 29 CFR §1604.11(a) (1985). Relevant to the charges at issue in this case, the Guidelines provide that such sexual misconduct constitutes prohibited "sexual harassment," whether or not it is directly linked to the grant or denial of an economic *quid pro quo*, where "such conduct has the purpose or effect of unreasonably interfering with an individual's work performance or creating an intimidating, hostile, or offensive working environment." §1604.11(a)(3).

In concluding that so-called "hostile environment" (i.e., non *quid pro quo*) harassment violates Title VII, the EEOC drew upon a substantial body of judicial decisions and EEOC precedent holding that Title VII affords employees the right to work in an environment free from discriminatory intimidation, ridicule, and insult. See generally 45 Fed. Reg. 74676 (1980). Rogers v. EEOC, 454 F.2d 234 (5th Cir. 1971), cert. denied, [406 U.S. 957 (1972)], was apparently the first case to recognize a cause of action based upon a discriminatory work environment. In *Rogers*, the Court of Appeals for the Fifth Circuit held that a Hispanic complainant could establish a Title VII violation by demonstrating that her employer created an offensive work environment for employees by giving discriminatory service to its Hispanic clientele. The court explained that an employee's protections under Title VII extend beyond the economic aspects of employment: "[T]he phrase 'terms, conditions or privileges of employment' in [Title VII] is an expansive concept which sweeps within its protective ambit the practice of creating a working environment heavily charged with ethnic or racial discrimination. . . . One can readily envision working environments so heavily polluted with discrimination as to destroy completely the emotional and psychological stability of minority group workers. . . ." 454 F.2d at 238. Courts applied this principle to harassment based on race, religion, and national origin. Nothing in Title VII suggests that a hostile environment based on discriminatory sexual harassment should not be likewise prohibited. The Guidelines thus appropriately drew from, and were fully consistent with, the existing case law.

Since the Guidelines were issued, courts have uniformly held, and we agree, that a plaintiff may establish a violation of Title VII by proving that discrimination based on sex has created a hostile or abusive work environment. As the Court of Appeals for the Eleventh Circuit wrote in Henson v. Dundee, 682 F.2d 897, 902 (1982): "Sexual harassment which creates a hostile or offensive environment for members of one sex is every bit the arbitrary barrier to sexual equality at the workplace that racial harassment is to racial equality. Surely, a requirement that a man or woman run a gauntlet of sexual abuse in return for the privilege of being allowed to work and make a living can be as demeaning and disconcerting as the harshest of racial epithets." . . .

Of course, as the courts in both *Rogers* and *Henson* recognized, not all workplace conduct that may be described as "harassment" affects a "term, condition, or privilege" of employment within the meaning of Title VII. See Rogers v. EEOC, [454 F.2d at 238] ("mere utterance of an ethnic or racial epithet which engenders offensive feelings in an employee" would not affect the conditions of employment to sufficiently significant degree to violate Title VII); *Henson*, 682 F.2d, at 904 (quoting same). For sexual harassment to be actionable, it must be sufficiently severe or pervasive "to alter the conditions of [the victim's] employment and create an abusive working environment." Id. Respondent's allegations in this case — which include not only pervasive harassment but also criminal conduct of the most serious nature — are plainly sufficient to state a claim for "hostile environment" sexual harassment. . . .

[T]he District court apparently believed that a claim for sexual harassment will not lie absent an economic effect on the complainant's employment. See id. "It is without question that sexual harassment of female employees in which they are asked or required to submit to sexual demands as a *condition to obtain employment or to maintain employment or to obtain promotions* falls within protection of Title VII") (emphasis added). Since it appears that the District Court made its findings without ever considering the "hostile environment" theory of sexual harassment, the Court of Appeals' decision to remand was correct.

[T]he District Court's conclusion that no actionable harassment occurred might have rested on its earlier "finding" that "[i]f [respondent] and Taylor did engage in an intimate or sexual relationship . . . , that relationship was a voluntary one." Id. at 42. But the fact that sex-related conduct was "voluntary," in the sense that the complainant was not forced to participate against her will, is not a defense to a sexual harassment suit brought under Title VII. The gravamen of any sexual harassment claim is that the alleged sexual advances were "unwelcome." 29 CFR §1604.11(a) (1985). While the question whether particular conduct was indeed unwelcome presents difficult problems of proof and turns largely on credibility determinations committed to the trier of fact, the District Court in this case erroneously focused on the "voluntariness" of respondent's participation in the claimed sexual episodes. The correct inquiry is whether respondent by her conduct indicated that the alleged sexual advances were unwelcome, not whether her actual participation in sexual intercourse was voluntary.

Petitioner contends that even if this case must be remanded to the District Court, the Court of Appeals erred in one of the terms of its remand. Specifically, the Court of Appeals stated that testimony about respondent's "dress and personal fantasies," [753 F.2d. at 146 n.36], which the District Court apparently admitted into evidence, "had no place in this litigation." Id. The apparent ground for this conclusion was that respondent's voluntariness vel non in submitting to Taylor's advances was immaterial to her sexual harassment claim. While "voluntariness" in the sense of consent is not a defense to such a claim, it does not follow that a complainant's sexually provocative speech or dress is irrelevant as a matter of law in determining whether he or she found particular sexual advances unwelcome. To the contrary, such evidence is obviously relevant. The EEOC Guidelines emphasize that the trier of fact must determine the existence of sexual harassment in light of "the record as a whole" and "the totality of circumstances, such as the nature of the sexual advances and the context in which the alleged incidents occurred." 29 CFR §1604.11(b) (1985).

Respondent's claim that any marginal relevance of the evidence in question was outweighed by the potential for unfair prejudice is the sort of argument properly addressed to the District Court. In this case the District Court concluded that the evidence should be admitted, and the Court of Appeal's contrary conclusion was based upon the erroneous, categorical view that testimony about provocative dress and publicly expressed sexual fantasies "had no place in this litigation." [753 F.2d at 146 n.36.] While the District Court must carefully weigh the applicable considerations in deciding whether to admit evidence of this kind, there is no *per se* rule against its admissibility. . . .

IV. . . .

Accordingly, the judgement of the Court of Appeals reversing the judgement of the District Court is affirmed, and the case is remanded for further proceedings consistent with this opinion.
It is so ordered.

≡ ***Harris v. Forklift Systems, Inc.***
≡ 510 U.S. 17 (1993)

Justice O'CONNOR delivered the opinion of the Court.

In this case we consider the definition of a discriminatorily "abusive work environment" (also known as a "hostile work environment") under Title VII. . . .

I

Teresa Harris worked as a manager at Forklift Systems, Inc., an equipment rental company, from April 1985 until October 1987. Charles Hardy was Forklift's president.

The Magistrate found that, throughout Harris' time at Forklift, Hardy often insulted her because of her gender and often made her the target of unwanted sexual innuendos. Hardy told Harris on several occasions, in the presence of other employees, "You're a woman, what do you know" and "We need a man as the rental manager"; at least once, he told her she was "a dumb ass woman." . . . Again in front of others, he suggested that the two of them "go to the Holiday Inn to negotiate [Harris'] raise." . . . Hardy occasionally asked Harris and other female employees to get coins from his front pants pocket. He threw objects on the ground in front of Harris and other women, and asked them to pick the objects up. . . . He made sexual innuendos about Harris' and other women's clothing.

In mid-August 1987, Harris complained to Hardy about his conduct. Hardy said he was surprised that Harris was offended, claimed he was only joking, and apologized. . . . He also promised he would stop, and based on this assurance Harris stayed on the job. But in early September, Hardy began anew: While Harris was arranging a deal with one of Forklift's customers, he asked her, again in front of other employees, "What did you do, promise the guy . . . some [sex] Saturday night?" . . . On October 1, Harris collected her paycheck and quit.

Harris then sued Forklift, claiming that Hardy's conduct had created an abusive work environment for her because of her gender. The United States District Court for the Middle District of Tennessee, adopting the report and recommendation of the Magistrate, found this to be "a close case," . . . but held that Hardy's conduct did not create an abusive environment. The court found that some of Hardy's comments "offended [Harris], and would offend the reasonable woman," . . . but that they were not "so severe as to be expected to seriously affect [Harris'] psychological well-being." A reasonable woman manager under like circumstances would have been offended by Hardy, but his conduct would not have risen to the level of interfering with that person's work performance. "Neither do I believe that [Harris] was subjectively so offended that she suffered injury. . . . Although Hardy may at times have genuinely offended [Harris], I do not believe that he created a working environment so poisoned as to be intimidating or abusive to [Harris]." . . .

In focusing on the employee's psychological well-being, the District Court was following Circuit precedent. See Rabidue v. Osceola Refining Co., 805 F.2d 611, 620 (6th Cir. 1986), cert. denied, 481 U.S. 1041 (1987). The United States Court of Appeals for the Sixth Circuit affirmed in a brief unpublished decision, 976 F.2d 733 (6th Cir. 1992). . . .

II

Title VII . . . makes it "an unlawful employment practice for an employer . . . to discriminate against any individual with respect to his compensation, terms, conditions, or privileges of employment, because of such individual's race, color, religion, sex, or national origin." 42 U.S.C. §2000e-2(a)(1). As we made clear in Meritor Savings Bank v. Vinson, 477 U.S. 57 (1986), this language "is not limited to 'economic' or 'tangible' discrimination. The phrase 'terms, conditions, or privileges of employment' evinces a congressional intent 'to strike at the entire spectrum of disparate treatment of men and women' in employment," which includes requiring people to work in a discriminatorily hostile or abusive environment. Id., at 64, quoting Los Angeles Dept. of Water & Power v. Manhart. . . . When the workplace is permeated with "discriminatory intimidation, ridicule, and insult," id., at 65, that is "sufficiently severe or pervasive to alter the condition of the victim's employment and create an abusive working environment," id., at 67, Title VII is violated.

This standard, which we reaffirm today, takes a middle path between making actionable any conduct that is merely offensive and requiring the conduct to cause a tangible psychological injury. As we pointed out in *Meritor*, "mere utterance of an . . . epithet which engenders offensive feelings in an employee," . . . does not sufficiently affect the conditions of employment to implicate Title VII. Conduct that is not severe or pervasive enough to create an objectively hostile or abusive work environment — an environment that a reasonable person would find hostile or abusive — is beyond Title VII's purview. Likewise, if the victim does not subjectively perceive the environment to be abusive, the conduct has not actually altered the conditions of the victim's employment, and there is no Title VII violation.

But Title VII comes into play before the harassing conduct leads to a nervous breakdown. A discriminatorily abusive work environment, even one that does not seriously affect employees' psychological well-being, can and often will detract from employees' job performance, discourage employees from remaining on the job, or keep them from advancing in their careers. Moreover, even without regard to these tangible effects, the very fact that the discriminatory conduct was so severe or pervasive that it created a work environment abusive to employees because of their race, gender, religion, or national origin offends Title VII's broad rule of workplace equality. The appalling conduct alleged in *Meritor*, and the reference in that case to environments "'so heavily polluted with discrimination as to destroy completely the emotional and psychological stability of minority group workers,'" [id.] at 66, quoting Rogers v. EEOC, 454 F.2d 234, 238 (5th Cir. 1971), cert. denied, 406 U.S. 957 (1972), merely present some especially egregious examples of harassment. They do not mark the boundary of what is actionable.

We therefore believe the District Court erred in relying on whether the conduct "seriously affect[ed] plaintiff's psychological well-being" or led her to "suffe[r] injury." Such an inquiry may needlessly focus the factfinder's attention on concrete psychological harm, an element Title VII does not require. Certainly Title VII bars conduct that would seriously affect a reasonable person's psychological well-being, but the statute is not limited to such conduct. So long as the environment would reasonably be perceived, and is perceived, as hostile or abusive, *Meritor*, supra, 477 U.S. at 67, there is no need for it also to be psychologically injurious.

This is not, and by its nature cannot be, a mathematically precise test. We need not answer today all the potential questions it raises. . . . But we can say that whether an environment is "hostile" or "abusive" can be determined only by looking at all the circumstances. These may include the frequency of the discriminatory conduct; its severity; whether it is physically threatening or humiliating, or a mere offensive utterance; and whether it unreasonably interferes with an employee's work performance. The effect on the employee's psychological well-being is, of course, relevant to determining whether the plaintiff actually found the environment abusive. But while psychological harm, like any other relevant factor, may be taken into account, no single factor is required. . . .

We therefore reverse the judgment of the Court of Appeals, and remand the case for further proceedings consistent with this opinion.

Justice SCALIA, concurring. . . .

"Abusive" (or "hostile," which in this context I take to mean the same thing) does not seem to me a very clear standard — and I do not think clarity is at all increased by adding the adverb "objectively" or by appealing to a "reasonable person's" notion of what the vague word means. Today's opinion does list a number of factors that contribute to abusiveness, . . . but since it neither says how much of each is necessary (an impossible task) nor identifies any single factor as determinative, it thereby adds little certitude. As a practical matter, today's holding lets virtually unguided juries decide whether sex-related conduct engaged in (or permitted by) an employer is egregious enough to warrant an award of damages. One might say that what constitutes "negligence" (a traditional jury question) is not much more clear and certain than what constitutes "abusiveness." Perhaps so. But the class of plaintiffs seeking to recover for negligence is limited to those who have suffered harm, whereas under this statute "abusiveness" is to be the test of whether legal harm has been suffered, opening more expansive vistas of litigation.

Be that as it may, I know of no alternative to the course the Court today has taken. One of the factors mentioned in the Court's nonexhaustive list — whether the conduct unreasonably interferes with an employee's work performance — would, if it were made an absolute test, provide greater guidance to juries and employers. But I see no basis for such a limitation in the language of the statute. Accepting *Meritor*'s interpretation of the term "conditions of employment" as the law, the test is not whether work has been impaired, but whether working conditions have been discriminatorily altered. I know of no test more faithful to the inherently vague statutory language than the one the Court today adopts. For these reasons, I join the opinion of the Court.

Justice GINSBURG, concurring.

Today the Court reaffirms the holding of Meritor Savings Bank v. Vinson . . . : "[A] plaintiff may establish a violation of Title VII by proving that discrimination based on sex has created a hostile or abusive work environment." The critical issue, Title VII's text indicates, is whether members of one sex are exposed to disadvantageous terms or conditions of employment to which members of the other sex are not exposed. . . . As the Equal Employment Opportunity Commission emphasized . . . the adjudicator's inquiry should center, dominantly, on whether the discriminatory conduct has unreasonably interfered with the plaintiff's work performance.

To show such interference, "the plaintiff need not prove that his or her tangible productivity has declined as a result of the harassment." Davis v. Monsanto Chemical Co., 858 F.2d 345, 349 (6th Cir. 1988). It suffices to prove that a reasonable person subjected to the discriminatory conduct would find, as the plaintiff did, that the harassment so altered working conditions as to "ma[k]e it more difficult to do the job." . . .

The Court's opinion, which I join, seems to me in harmony with the view expressed in this concurring statement.

Notes

1. The Problem of Sexual Harassment.   For centuries, women have been subject to behavior now understood to be sexual harassment, but the law offered neither a label nor a remedy for their experience. Slaves, domestic servants, factory workers, and clerical assistants all were frequently subject to sexual abuse and unwanted advances. See Chapter 1, pages 46-51, above; see also, e.g., Jacqueline Jones, Labor of Love, Labor of Sorrow: Black Women, Work, and the Family from Slavery to the Present 20, 28-38 (1988); Kerry Seagrave, The Sexual Harassment of Women in the Workplace, 1600-1993, at 23-39 (1994); Helen Cambell, Prisoners of Poverty: Women Wage-Workers, Their Trades, and Their Lives 234 (1887); Faye B. Dudden, Serving Women: Household Service in Nineteenth-Centry America 213-219 (1983). The term "sexual harassment" came into use in the mid-1970s. Its origins are generally traced to a consciousness-raising session held by Lin Farley as part of a Cornell University course on women and work. Lin Farley, Sexual Shakedown xi-xiii (1978). Catharine A. MacKinnon's pathbreaking Sexual Harassment of Working Women (1979) provided a theoretical framework for conceptualizing such harassment as a form of sex discrimination actionable under civil rights laws and the equal protection clause of the Fourteenth Amendment.

The frequency of sexual harassment is difficult to gauge with any precision because what constitutes actionable harassment is sometimes unclear and because relatively few individuals make formal complaints. The United States Merit Systems Protection Board conducted the earliest systematic studies of workplace harassment and found that about 40 percent of federal employees had experienced harassment in the two preceding years. Barbara A. Gutek, Understanding Sexual Harassment at Work, 6 Notre Dame J.L. Ethics & Pub. Pol'y, 335, 344 (1992) (citing studies). This figure is consistent with the 30-40 percent figure often reported in private business, although lower than in some other sectors such as the military. See Catalyst, Women in Financial Services: The Word on the Street (2001) (about a third of surveyed Wall Street women report experiencing harassment); Joanna L. Grossman, The First Bite Is Free: Employer Liability for Sexual Harassment, 61 U. Pitt. L. Rev. 671, 673-674 (2000) (citing studies and case histories); Kimberly T. Schneider et al., Job-Related and Psychological Effects of Sexual Harassment in the Workplace: Empirical Evidence from Two Organizations, 82 J. Applied Psychol. 401, 406 (1997); Department of Defense, Report of the 1995 Study on Sexual Harassment (1996); for notes on harassment in the military, see pages 790-804. The practice of law is no exception. Between one-half to two-thirds of female lawyers report experiencing sexual harassment, and almost three-quarters believe that it is a problem in their workplaces. See ABA Commission on Women in the Profession, The Unfinished Agenda: A Report on the Status of Women in the Legal Profession 19 (2001) (citing surveys). About 85 percent of formal sexual harassment complaints involve men harassing women; about 1 percent involve women harassing men, and the remainder involve same-sex harassment. Men account for about 14 percent of claims. Reed Abelson, Men Increasingly Are the Ones Claiming Sex-Harassment by Men, N.Y. Times, June 10, 2001, at A1; Catharine A. MacKinnon, Sex Equality 916 (2001) (citing surveys).

While many women report having experienced sexual harassment on the job, only about 5 to 10 percent report it, and fewer still can afford the financial and psychological costs of litigation. See Louise Fitzgerald, Suzanne Swan, & Karla Fisher, Why Didn't She Just Report Him? The Psychological and Legal Implications of Women's Responses to Sexual Harassment, 51 J. Soc. Issues 117 (1995); Mary P. Koss et al., No Safe Haven: Male Violence Against Women at Home, at Work, and in the Community 135 (1994). Major barriers to reporting include guilt, shame, fear of reprisal or blacklisting, unwillingness to jeopardize working relationships or be known as a humorless whiner, concerns about loss of privacy, and doubts that an effective response to a complaint would be forthcoming. See Fitzgerald, Swan, & Fisher, supra; Beth A. Quinn, The Paradox of Complaining: Law, Humor, and Harassment in the Everyday Work World, 25 Law & Soc. Inquiry 1151 (2000); Mary F. Radford, By Invitation Only: The Proof of Welcomeness in Sexual Harassment Cases, 72 N.C. L. Rev. 499, 523 (1994) (citing studies); Celia Morris, Bearing Witness: Sexual Harassment and Beyond — Everywoman's Story 114-144 (1994) (offering narrative accounts of threats and humiliation for complainants).

How the law responds, or fails to respond, to sexual harassment depends partly on how the phenomenon is explained. When the behaviors in question are viewed as a natural or biological consequence of physical attraction between the sexes, the law may be considered an unwelcome intruder, too "clumsy [a tool] for shaping human behavior." Alex Kozinski, The False Protection of a Gilded Cage, S.F. Recorder, May 27, 1992, at 10. Consider the following argument by defendant president of a company who rubbed his hands up and down plaintiff's sides, touched her breasts, pinched her, patted her buttocks, kissed her, and put his hands up her dress:

[I]t is important to point out that one of the traditional places where man meets woman is at the work place. Such meetings often result in dating, blossom into love, and eventually into marriage. . . . If civil liability is implanted on an employer for its employees['] natural interaction between the genders, either the collapse of our commercial system or the end of the human race can be foreseen. No employer could safely employ both males and females, and the number of marriages with children will be substantially decreased. There should be nothing wrong with a man, even a supervisor, telling a female that she looks nice. Nor can there be anything wrong with a man, even a supervisor, asking a female out [on] a date. In doing so the man should not have to gamble on civil liability on her "yes" response.

Jones v. Wesco Investments, Inc., 846 F.2d 1154, 1157 n.6 (8th Cir. 1988) (citing from defendant's brief). See also Barnes v. Costle, 561 F.2d 983, 1001 (D.C. Cir. 1977) (MacKinnon, J., concurring) (sexual advances need not be "intrinsically offensive" in that they may involve "normal and expectable" social behaviors).

Feminists generally define the function of sexual harassment differently. Consider the following accounts:

According to the theory I develop . . . , the sexual harassment of a woman by a man is an instance of sexism precisely because the act embodies fundamental gender stereotypes: men as sexual conquerors and women as sexually conquered, men as masculine sexual subjects and women as feminine sexual objects. . . . Sexual harassment is a technology of sexism. It is a disciplinary practice that inscribes, enforces, and polices the identities of both harasser and victim according to a system of gender norms that envisions women as feminine, (hetero)sexual objects, and men as masculine, (hetero)sexual subjects. . . .

On my account, sexual harassment — between any two people of whatever sex — is a form of sex discrimination when it reflects or perpetuates gender stereotypes in the workplace. I suggest a reconceptualization of sexual harassment as gender harassment. Understood in this way, sexual harassment is a kind of sex discrimination not because the conduct would not have been undertaken if the victim had been a different sex, not because it is sexual, and not because men do it to women, but precisely because it is a technology of sexism. That is, it perpetuates, enforces, and polices a set of gender norms that seek to feminize women and masculinize men. . . .

Similarly, sexual harassment operates as a means of policing traditional gender norms particularly in the same-sex context when men who fail to live up to a societal norm of masculinity are punished by their male coworkers through sexual means.

Katherine M. Franke, What's Wrong with Sexual Harassment, 49 Stan. L. Rev. 691, 693, 696 (1997).

In some cases, sexual harassment has emerged as a means of preserving male control over the workplace, particularly where the entry of women into a particular workforce appears to call that control into question. A prime example is sexual harassment directed at women who have entered predominantly male fields. Some types of harassment within this category are particularly flagrant, including physical or sexual aggression or persistent, targeted verbal abuse so severe as to serve unequivocal notice that women are not welcome. Women targeted in this way are often compelled to leave the workplace or transfer to a job with different coworkers or another supervisor. Even when they stay, it is clear that they remain at the sufferance of their male coworkers; they have no hope of getting sufficient purchase on the workplace to make it in any sense their own.

Other forms of harassment aimed at preserving male control are slightly subtler. Supervisors or coworkers may sexualize women employees by either propositioning them directly or treating them in a manner that highlights their sexuality, as opposed to other, work related characteristics. Supervisors may demand that women workers conform to dominant feminine stereotypes that operate outside the workplace by making repeated comments or suggestions regarding the employees' physical appearance, or through instructions to behave in a feminine manner. In some cases, it may be applied categorically to signal that women are not taken seriously: that they are considered sex objects or "pets" instead of competent workers. These latter forms of harassment may not be sufficient to compel all women to leave any particular workplace. Yet they make clear — to women and the men who work with them — that mere presence is not equal to influence or control. These forms of harassment suggest that whatever professional goals women pursue, they will continue to be viewed and judged by reference to more traditional female roles and whatever careers they enter, they still will occupy subordinate roles.

Kathryn Abrams, The New Jurisprudence of Sexual Harassment, 83 Cornell L. Rev. 1169, 1206-1208 (1998).

Hostile environment sexual harassment, I argue, is a type of incivility or — in the locution that I prefer — disrespect. For purposes of doctrine, accordingly, hostile environment complaints should refer to respect; the plaintiff should be required to prove that the defendant — a man, or a woman, or a business entity — did not conform to the standard of a respectful person. This respectful person standard would rightly supplant references to reason and reasonableness; respect is integral to the understanding and remedying of sexual harassment, whereas reason is not.

In giving content to the ideal of equality behind Title VII as well as the ideal of individual autonomy behind dignitary-tort law, this respectful person standard would fit within the two most important legal bases for redressing sexual harassment in the workplace. Focus on respect addresses the concerns of both those who identify with the imperfect humanity of the accused harasser and those who seek foremost to purge sexual coercion from the workplace.

Anita Bernstein, Treating Sexual Harassment with Respect, 111 Harv. L. Rev. 445, 450-451 (1997).

A man apparently can make sexual jokes and comments, use sexual obscenities, proposition women at work, dress to attract women, and still be considered a desirable worker: analytical, rational, tough, a good leader. The sexual aspect of the male sex role does not interfere with the perception of men as serious, professional workers. A woman cannot be an analytical, rational leader and a sex object at the same time. When she becomes a sex object, her status as a sex object overpowers other aspects of her sex role and completely overwhelms the work role she is trying to occupy. . . .

Barbara Gutek, Sex and the Workplace 166 (1985).

Contrary to the assumption of the cultural-radical feminist tradition that inspired the development of harassment law, men's desire to exploit or dominate women sexually may not be the exclusive, or even the primary, motivation for harassing women at work. Instead, a drive to maintain the most highly rewarded forms of work as domains of masculine competence underlies many, if not most, forms of sex-based harassment on the job. . . . Contrary to many prevailing assumptions, workplace harassment is not a mere reflection of unequal gender relations that have already been created elsewhere, such as in the domestic sphere. . . . The problem . . . is, instead, that by portraying women as less than equal at work, men can secure superior jobs, resources, and influence — all of which afford men leverage over women at home and everyplace else. . . . [The focus of legal inquiry should be whether the conduct at issue has] the purpose or effect of undermining women's "right to participate in the workplace on [an] equal footing."

Vicki Schultz, Reconceptualizing Sexual Harassment, 107 Yale L.J. 1683, 1755, 1760-1761, 1800-1801 (1998).

For further discussion of factors such as stereotyping, male socialization, paternalism, and desires to protect male power, status, and security, see Susan T. Fiske & Peter Glick, Ambivalence and Stereotypes Cause Sexual Harassment: A Theory with Implications for Organizational Change, 51 J. Soc. Issues, Spring 97 (1995); David E. Terpstra & Douglas D. Baker, Sexual Harassment at Work: The Psychosocial Issues, in Vulnerable Workers: Psychosocial and Legal Issues 179 (Marilyn J. Davidson & Jill Earnshaw eds., 1991).

Which of these accounts seems to best capture the dynamics described in the readings in this chapter? What implications would they have for how the law should define sexual harassment?

2. Defining Sexual Harassment. As *Meritor* indicates, Title VII prohibits two types of sexual harassment: (1) quid pro quo harassment, in which sexual contact or favor is required as a condition of employment or advancement and (2) environmental sexual harassment, based on conditions that create an "intimidating, hostile, or offensive" work environment. Cases of quid pro quo harassment are easy enough to define (if not to prove). A plaintiff establishes a case of quid pro quo harassment if she shows that "tangible job benefits are conditioned on an employee's submission to conduct of a sexual nature and that adverse job consequences result from the employee's refusal to submit to the conduct." Hicks v. Gates Rubber Co., 833 F.2d 1406, 1414 (10th Cir. 1987). Quid pro quo harassment is actionable whether or not the victim submits to the propositions. See Karibian v. Columbia University, 14 F.3d 773, 779 (2d Cir.), cert. denied, 512 U.S. 1213 (1994).

A somewhat more difficult issue is whether co-workers should have a claim where an employee acceded to requests for sexual favors and received job benefits that might have gone to other employees. EEOC Guidelines, under a heading diplomatically titled "other related practices," holds that "[w]here employment opportunities or benefits are granted because of an individual's submission to the employer's sexual advances or requests for sexual favors, the employer may be held liable for unlawful sex discrimination against other persons who were qualified for but denied that opportunity or benefit." 45 Fed. Reg. 74,676, 74,677 (1980). However, not all courts have imposed liability under such situations. According to one court, male employees who claimed that they were unfairly passed over for promotion did not have a sex discrimination claim because they were "not prejudiced because of their status as males; rather they were discriminated against because [the program] administrator preferred his [paramour]. Appellees faced exactly the same predicament as that faced by any woman applicant for the promotion." DeCintio v. Westchester County Medical Center, 807 F.2d 304, 308 (2d Cir. 1986), cert. denied, 484 U.S. 825 (1987); see also Candelore v. Clark County Sanitation District, 752 F. Supp. 956 (D. Nev. 1990), aff'd, 975 F.2d 588 (9th Cir. 1992). Which approach makes the most sense?

Defining a hostile work environment has also presented difficulties. The Court's opinion in *Harris* establishes that "mere utterance" of an "offensive epithet" is not enough, but that "tangible psychological injury" is not required. Justice Ginsburg finds the key in whether the conduct alters the working conditions so as to make it "more difficult to do the job." If Justice Scalia is correct that no basis for such a limitation is apparent in the text or legislative history of Title VII, what follows from that fact?

Consider the following case, in which a plaintiff introduced the following evidence of harassment: (1) her supervisor referred to her as a "pretty girl," as in "There's always a pretty girl giving me something to sign off on." (2) Once when she was wearing a leather skirt, he made a grunting sound like "um um um" as she turned to leave his office. (3) Once when she commented on how hot his office was, he raised his eyebrows and said, "Not until you stepped your foot in here." (4) Once when the announcement "May I have your attention, please" was broadcast over the public-address system, the supervisor stopped at her desk and said, "You know what that means, don't you? All pretty girls run around naked." (5) The supervisor once told her that his wife had told him "I had better clean up my act" and "better think of you as Ms. Anita Hill." (6) When she asked why he had left the office Christmas party early, the supervisor replied that there were so many pretty girls there that he "didn't want to lose control, so I thought I'd better leave." (7) Once when she complained that his office was "smokey" from cigarette smoke, the supervisor replied, "Oh really? Were we dancing, like in a nightclub?" (8) When she asked him whether he had gotten his wife a Valentine's Day card, he responded that he had not but he should because it was lonely in his hotel room, at which point he looked ostentatiously at his hand with a gesture suggesting masturbation. Is this sexual harassment?

Judge Richard Posner analyzed the conduct by considering each incident individually and by noting what it did not include:

> He never touched the plaintiff. He did not invite her, explicitly or by implication, to have sex with him, or to go out on a date with him. He made no threats. He did not expose himself, or show her dirty pictures. He never said anything to her that could not be repeated on prime time television. The comment about Anita Hill was the opposite of solicitation, the implication being that he would get into trouble if he didn't keep his distance. . . . Some of his repartee, such as "not until you stepped your foot in here," or, "Were we dancing, like in a nightclub?," has the sexual charge of an Abbott and Costello movie. The reference to masturbation completes the impression of a man whose sense of humor took final shape in adolescence. It is no doubt distasteful to a sensitive woman to have such a silly man one's boss, but only a woman of Victorian delicacy — a woman mysteriously aloof from contemporary American popular culture in all its sex-saturated vulgarity — would find [his] patter substantially more distressing than the heat and cigarette smoke of which the plaintiff does not complain.

Baskerville v. Culligan International Co., 50 F.3d 428, 431 (7th Cir. 1995). How would you evaluate this analysis?

3. The Reasonable Person Standard. One central issue in determining what constitutes a hostile work environment involves whether it should be judged from the perspective of a "reasonable person" or from that of a "reasonable woman." Advocates of the reasonable woman standard argue that a wide array of evidence has found that women are more likely to perceive certain behaviors, such as unsolicited invitations for sex, as harassing. See Jeremy A. Blumenthal, The Reasonable Woman Standard: A Meta-Analytic Review of Gender Differences in Perceptions of Sexual Harassment, 22 Law & Hum. Behav. 71 (1997); Richard L. Wiener et al., Perceptions of Sexual Harassment: The Effects of Gender, Legal Standard, and Ambivalent Sexism, 21 Law & Hum. Behav. 71 (1997). According to these commentators, a reasonable person standard that ignores the perspectives of women is, in effect, a reasonable man standard that will legitimate, rather than reduce, the incidence of sexual harassment. See, e.g., Caroline A. Forrell & Donna M. Mathews, A Law of Her Own: The Reasonable Woman as a Measure of Man 35-58 (2000); Deborah B. Goldberg, The Road to Equality: The Application of the Reasonable Woman Standard in Sexual Harassment Cases, 2 Cardozo Women's L.J. 195, 212 (1995); Caroline Forell, Essentialism, Empathy, and the Reasonable Woman, 1994 U. Ill. L. Rev. 769 (1994).

By contrast, some feminists have objected to the reasonable woman standard on the grounds that it fails to recognize the diversity in women's experience and fails to ensure that decisionmakers will in fact take that experience into account in applying the standard. For example, one district court denied a claim by a woman whose co-workers had used a flashlight to peer up her skirt as she walked up stairs. From that judge's perspective, a "reasonable woman" would find such conduct "childish," not harassing. Vermett v. Hough, 627 F. Supp. 587, 607 (W.D. Mich. 1986). See also Stephanie M. Wildman, Ending Male Privilege: Beyond the Reasonable Woman, 98 Mich. L. Rev. 1797, 1812 (2000) (noting that who is interpreting standards is more critical than formulation). Moreover, according to many feminists, it is counterproductive to impose a single, uniform standard on a group — women — whose subordination has been made possible by the attribution of uniform, usually condescending, characteristics. Women may be harmed more than they are helped by the assumption that they are all alike and are easily offended victims. See Radtke v. Everett, 501 N.W.2d 155, 167 (Mich. 1993) (gender-conscious standard "could entrench the very sexist attitudes it is attempting to counter"); see also Naomi R. Cahn, The Looseness of Legal Language: The Reasonable Woman Standard in Theory and in Practice, 77 Cornell L. Rev. 1398, 1403 (1992) ("reasonable woman" standard ignores the reality that women's experiences are diverse); Kathryn Abrams, Gender Discrimination and the Transformation of Workplace Norms, 42 Vand. L. Rev. 1183, 1209-1215 (1989) ("reasonable woman" standard must be coupled with a recognition that there is no one correct response among women to harassment); Lucinda Finley, A Break in the Silence: Including Women's Issues in a Torts Course, 1 Yale J.L. & Feminism 41, 63-64 (1989) (it is "counterproductive to replace one caricature with another"). The problems entailed in using woman as a single category of analysis (i.e., capable of being captured within a single standard of "reasonableness") are more fully explored in Chapter 7.

Harris refers to the reasonable person standard, which most courts subsequently followed. Only the Ninth Circuit Court of Appeals has applied a reasonable woman standard. See Ellison v. Brady, 924 F.2d 872 (9th Cir. 1991); Fuller v. City of Oakland, 47 F.3d 1522, 1527-1528 (9th Cir. 1995) (using interchangeably "the perspective of a reasonable person with the same fundamental characteristics" and "a reasonable woman"); Steiner v. Showboat Operating Co., 25 F.3d 1459, 1464 (9th Cir. 1994), cert. denied, 513 U.S. 1082 (1995) ("*Ellison* unequivocally directs us to consider what is offensive and hostile to a reasonable woman").

In Oncale v. Sundowner Offshore Services, Inc., 523 U.S. 75 (1998), infra, the Supreme Court, speaking through Justice Scalia, reaffirmed that the "objective severity of harassment should be judged from the perspective of a reasonable person in the plaintiff's position, considering 'all the circumstances.'" Id. at 81. Does that standard require focusing, as do Justices Ginsberg and Scalia, on how the allegedly harassing conduct in fact affects the performance or opportunities of the plaintiff? Or should courts also consider how the conduct would affect most individuals in the position of the plaintiff?

Consider the case of Paula Jones, who alleged that then-Governor William Clinton invited her to his hotel room while she was a state employee, stroked her leg, exposed himself, and invited her to perform oral sex. The district court held that even if the facts were as Jones stated them, they failed to meet the definition of harassment. Clinton had not promised job benefits, and Jones alleged no demonstrable job detriment apart from failure to receive flowers on Secretary's Day and a trivial change in job duties. Nor was this single incident sufficient to show an "abusive environment." Jones v. Clinton, 990 F. Supp. 657, 675 (E.D. Ark. 1998). Jones missed no work following the alleged encounter and made no attempt to avoid daily trips to the Governor's office. She received favorable job evaluations and all available raises. Her only evidence of emotional distress was a belated declaration, filed just before Clinton's summary judgment motion, by a "purported expert with a Ph.D. in education and counseling." After a single meeting with Jones nearly seven years after the alleged incident, he found her to suffer from "severe emotional distress and consequent sexual aversion." Id. at 678 (quoting Patrick Carnes, Jones's expert). According to the trial court, these "vague and conclusory" opinions were unsupported by other evidence. In the court's view, Clinton's alleged conduct, while "boorish and offensive," did not have a demonstrable effect on Jones's job performance, and Clinton was therefore entitled to summary judgement as a matter of law. Id. at 675.

Should the court have allowed the case to go to trial? If, as the district judge found, there was no credible evidence of job detriment or damages, could the lawyers for Jones have been subject to sanctions for bringing a frivolous lawsuit? See note 5, below. Feminists who did not condemn Clinton's conduct as sex harassment were accused of "tak[ing] a powder on Paula Jones." See Ellen Goodman, Feminists Retreat from Jones Case for Good Reason, Boston Globe, Jan. 16, 1997, at A21 (quoting Human Events magazine). Some feminists responded that Clinton's behavior was offensive, but not harassment, since it was neither pervasive nor severe. See id.; Susan Estrich, Clinton's Conduct Offensive, but Not Sexual Harassment, S.F. Recorder, Nov. 8, 1996, at 5. According to Goodman, "Even in this litigious country, there are still wrongs for which there are no legal remedies. Not every piece of piggish behavior is illegal. You can feel humiliated without being legally sexually harassed." Goodman, What Is

Sexual Harassment, Boston Globe, Feb. 23, 1997, at E7. Estrich agrees: "There's no law saying he can't ask. . . ." Estrich, supra. Should there be? Other commentators, citing Equal Employment Opportunity Commission (EEOC) policy, maintained that a jury could find one incident involving sexual touching sufficient to justify liability. In their view, male bosses should not be "entitled to one free hit." Gwendolyn Mink, Misreading Sexual Harassment Law, N.Y. Times, Mar. 30, 1998, at A19; Stuart Taylor, Abandoning One of Their Own, S.F. Recorder, Jan. 22, 1997, at 4.

How should courts determine what acts are sufficiently pervasive and abusive to justify liability? Consider the proposal of Gillian K. Hadfield, who would define sex-based harassment as "sex-based non-job-related workplace conduct that would lead a rational woman to alter her workplace behavior — such as by refusing overtime, projects, or travel that will put her in contact with a harasser, requesting a transfer, or quitting — if she could do so at little or no cost to her." Gillian K. Hadfield, Rational Women: A Test for Sex-Based Harassment, 83 Cal. L. Rev. 1151, 1157 (1995). Hadfield argues that when a woman rationally alters her workplace behavior to eliminate the risk of such conduct, the behavior is discriminatory. Id. at 1174-1181. This test "does not privilege women's evaluation of workplace practices over men's," nor require that environments be "non-abusive in the abstract." It requires only that "workplace environments be neutral in their effects on men's and women's employment decisions." Id. at 1181. Nor, Hadfield argues, does the test

> privilege one particular group of women's preferences about workplace practices over others'. . . . Because Title VII targets sex discrimination . . . the issue is whether a workplace practice has systematically negative consequences for women vis-à-vis men. Even if significant numbers of women enjoy an atmosphere in which sexual jokes abound, if systematically more women than men find this costly, then the practice is discriminatory. . . .

Id. at 1182. A focus on the rational-woman-seeking-to-avoid-costs-of-harassment would, according to Hadfield, eliminate the need for "the misguided inquiry into a plaintiff's subjective psychological reasons" and the actual employment costs to a given plaintiff. Id. It would also eliminate the need to show that the behavior was unwelcome, since "those behaviors that rational women would be willing to pay to avoid are by definition unwelcome." Id. at 1185. See note 4, below.

Hadfield's test also "places the onus on men, employers, and organizations to become educated about what behavior on their subordinates' part would prompt employment changes by a rational female employee. The test rejects the notion that men are entitled to the protection of their misimpressions about how such behavior is interpreted by women." Id. at 1186. Is Hadfield's approach consistent with equality analysis? Would Jones

v. Clinton have been decided differently under Hadfield's test? Should it have been?

Jane L. Dolkart also seeks legal standards that gauge the effect of the harasser's conduct on the employee's work environment. This concern leads her to focus, however, on harassers' conduct rather than its effect on real or potential victims. See Jane L. Dolkart, Hostile Environment Harassment: Equality, Objectivity, and the Shaping of Legal Standards, 43 Emory L.J. 151, 198 (1994). Dolkart advocates a "contextualized reasonable victim" standard in which the harasser's conduct is evaluated through the broader lens of gender subordination, with the burden of proof on the defendant to prove that the plaintiff's perception of abuse is unreasonable. Id. at 217.

Kathryn Abrams also would place the burden on the defendant to demonstrate that the behavior at issue "was not likely to create a fear of sexual coercion or a sense of devaluative sexualization among women." Abrams, Gender Discrimination and the Transformation of Workplace Norms, 42 Vand. L. Rev. 1183, 1211 (1989). In Abrams's view, it is "normatively desirable to assume that sexual behavior sufficiently offensive to drive a plaintiff to court is harassing and to put the burden on the defendant to show otherwise." Id. at 1248 n.116.

Which of these approaches would you favor? How much difference is the choice of standards likely to make in the outcome of litigation? Note that the trial court in *Harris* applied a reasonable woman standard and found the circumstances to be a "close case" that did not ultimately justify liability, while the Supreme Court, which used "reasonable person" language, concluded that the facts may have been sufficient to state a case of sexual harassment. According to some commentators, whether a court views conduct as "romantic," "childish," or "boorish" rather than harassing often depends on preconceptions that the choice of doctrinal language is unlikely to affect. For example, in Lipsett v. Rive-Mora, 669 F. Supp. 1188 (D.P.R. 1987), rev'd, 864 F.2d 881 (1st Cir. 1988), the trial court interpreted a pattern of repeated sexual insults concerning a woman medical student, including provocative comments about her appearance and frequent denigrating assertions about women's surgical abilities, as "flattering remarks" signifying "romantic attraction" rather than sex discrimination. From the court's perspective, the law should not be used as a tool of "judicial blackmail" or a "vehicle to vindicate the 'petty slights of the hypersensitive.'" See Kim Lane Scheppele, The Reasonable Woman, 1 The Responsive Community 36, 42 (Fall 1991) (discussing *Lipsett*).

Was the conclusion of the trial court in *Lipsett* reasonable? Do courts need to be concerned about preventing the harassing use of harassment procedures? Can harassment work both ways? See Deborah L. Rhode, Conflicts of Commitment: Legal Ethics in the Impeachment Context, 52 Stan. L. Rev. 269, 289-295 (2000) (citing observers who believed that the lawyers in *Jones* pursued the claims more out of a desire to humiliate and politically cripple the defendant than to remedy any injury to the plaintiff.)

Harris clearly imposes both an objective and a subjective standard: the plaintiff must have been offended, and it must have been reasonable for her to have been so. Is there really any other choice? Is there any doubt whether Teresa Harris's case satisfies all of the proposed standards? What about Jones's claim? On remand, Harris was awarded $151,435 in damages plus attorney's fees and costs. Harris v. Forklift Systems, Inc., 66 Fair Empl. Prac. Cas. (BNA) 1886 (M.D. Tenn. 1994). Clinton settled the *Jones* appeal for $850,000, an amount that fell short of covering the plaintiff's attorney's fees, which totaled over $2 million. Jones ultimately received $200,000 from the settlement. Chuck Bartels, Jones's Lawyers Agree on Settlement, AP Online, Mar. 5, 1999.

4. When Is Sexual Conduct "Unwelcome"? What is the purpose of the requirement that the plaintiff in a hostile environment sexual harassment case prove that the conduct was "unwelcome"? The EEOC argued for this standard out of concern that sexual harassment charges not become "a tool by which one party to a consensual sexual relationship may punish the other." Brief for EEOC in *Meritor*, quoted in Ann C. Juliano, Note, Did She Ask for It?: The "Unwelcome" Requirement in Sexual Harassment Cases, 77 Cornell L. Rev. 1558, 1575 (1992). The same rationale has been offered in the context of rape: a woman who acts and dresses like she is "asking for it" may be deemed, by a jury, if not by the law itself, to have consented to whatever follows. Susan Estrich, Sex at Work, 43 Stan L. Rev. 813, 827 (1991) (arguing that in sexual harassment cases, "[u]nwelcomeness has emerged as the doctrinal stepchild of the rape standards of consent and resistance and shares virtually all of their problems"). See also Jeanne Schroeder, Abduction from the Seraglio: Feminist Methodologies and the Logic of Imagination, 70 Tex. L. Rev. 109, 205 n.297 (1991). For a discussion of this issue in context of rape, see pages 964-970 and 974-975.

What determines whether sexual advances were "welcome" under the *Meritor* test? Justice Rehnquist finds "sexually provocative speech or dress . . . obviously relevant." How would you analyze this conclusion from a nonsubordination/dominance perspective? Compare the following:

> The concept of women dressing to please men is obsolete and incorrect. First, definitions of "sexually enticing" clothing are subjective. What a man views as "enticing" may not be considered so by the wearer of the garment. Sexual attraction and desire do not rule everyone's daily decisions. Second, a woman may dress nicely to bolster her own self-esteem, rather than to attract the attention of others. Society does not, nor should it, require women to dress like nuns in order to avoid sending unknown and unintended messages. Finally, a woman may dress in order to look attractive to someone. Because a woman is attempting to attract one individual, however, does not mean that she welcomes sexual attention from *all* men.

Juliano, supra, at 1585-1586.

> Like it or not, women attach value to their own sexual attractiveness to men. Using sexual harassment as a legal tool to close the market for sexual attractiveness is likely to be as effective as the Eighteenth Amendment was at eliminating the consumption of alcohol.

Marie T. Reilly, A Paradigm for Sexual Harassment: Toward the Optimal Level of Loss, 47 Vand. L. Rev. 427, 475 (1994). Does the relevance of sexually provocative speech or dress depend on what drives harassing conduct in a particular workplace context? For example, should it matter what signals Paula Jones sent about her sexual availability in going to the hotel room of a governor who was widely known as a "womanizer"? Her complaint alleged that she had accepted a state trooper's invitation to meet Clinton in the hope that it might lead to an "enhanced employment opportunity. . . ." Jones v. Clinton, 990 F. Supp. 657, 663 (E.D. Ark. 1998). Should it matter whether a judge or jury found that claim credible? Should Jones's conduct be relevant in assessing Clinton's?

Under Justice Rehnquist's test in *Meritor*, if an employee is required to act in a sexually alluring manner as part of the job description itself, has she consented to being treated as a sexual object? In one case, plaintiffs, while performing their duties as cocktail waitresses, "were required by [Ramada Inn] pursuant to a marketing scheme called the 'confetti concept' to project an air of sexual availability to customers through the use of provocative outfits. [T]hey were required to flirt with customers and to dance, in a sexually provocative and degrading fashion. . . . [P]ursuant to the confetti concept, [plaintiffs] were required to dress in revealing, thematic attire for events such as 'Bikini Night,' 'P.J.Night,' and 'Whips and Chains Night.'" Are the sexual proposals and verbal and physical abuse they then received "unwelcome"? Or when women market their ability to act in a sexual manner, are they in a sense "accept[ing] the risk of negative sexual conduct in exchange for money or other benefits"? See Reilly, supra, at 465; EEOC v. Newtown Inn Assocs., 647 F. Supp. 957, 958 (E.D. Va. 1986) (not resolving merits of charges); Kelly Ann Cahill, Hooters: Should There Be an Assumption of Risk Defense to Some Hostile Work Environment Sexual Harassment Claims?, 48 Vand. L. Rev. 1107 (1995). How should a court respond to the claim of a Minneapolis woman who brought a hostile environment claim against her employer, a sex-toy shop, on the basis of all the lewd conversations she had to listen to in the workplace? See Gerald D. Skoning, 2000's Ten Wackiest Employment Lawsuits, Nat'l L.J., Apr. 2, 2001, at A21.

Should a complainant's activities outside of work ever be relevant to her sexual harassment charges? In Burns v. McGregor Electronic Industries, Inc., 955 F.2d 559 (8th Cir. 1992), plaintiff filed charges of sexual harassment on the basis of repeated behavior by at least two employees and the owner of the company, which manufactured stereo speakers. In addition to repeated propositions for dates and oral sex, the owner "showed [plaintiff] advertisements for pornographic films in Penthouse magazine, talked about sex, asked her to watch pornographic movies with him, and made lewd gestures, such as ones imitating masturbation." The harassment escalated after the co-workers learned that the plaintiff had appeared in the nude in two motorcycle magazines.

Although the plaintiff did not herself take copies of the magazines to the plant, the district court concluded that the pictures were relevant to her claims. "[I]n view of [plaintiff's] willingness to display her nude body to the public in Easy Riders publications, crude magazines at best, her testimony that she was offended by sexually directed comments and Penthouse or Playboy pictures is not credible." Citing *Meritor*, the court stated that although it had no doubt that the owner had made unwelcome sexual advances toward the plaintiff, she had exaggerated their severity and pervasiveness and had failed to prove that they were sufficient to create an abusive work environment. Id. at 562-563. The Eighth Circuit Court of Appeals reversed and remanded on grounds that the trial court's conclusion that the sexual advances were unwelcome was inconsistent with its finding that the plaintiff was not credible and with its finding that the plaintiff had exaggerated the severity and pervasiveness of the harassment. The appellate court also concluded that "a reasonable person would consider the conduct of [defendants] to be sufficiently severe or pervasive to alter the conditions of employment and create an abusive work environment." Id. at 566. Nonetheless, on the basis of Justice Rehnquist's guidance in *Meritor*, the court held that "the nude photo evidence, though relating to an activity engaged in by [plaintiff] outside of the work place, may be relevant to explain the context of some of the comments and actions" and that on remand plaintiff would have to show that she was "at least as affected as the reasonable person under like circumstances." Id. at 565-566. On remand, the district court again found for the defendant because the plaintiff did not prove that she was "affected" as a reasonable person in her situation would be, which decision was reversed on appeal. 989 F.2d 959 (8th Cir. 1993). How likely is it that a plaintiff in her position would be able to meet this burden? Is this plaintiff fair game for unwanted sexual advances and innuendos at the workplace? For how long?

Should a plaintiff's participation in the sexual banter of a workplace preclude a claim of sexual harassment based in part on that banter? Courts have found evidence of such participation relevant as to whether the conduct was unwelcome and whether it created a hostile and intimidating environment. In one case, plaintiff admitted at trial that she cursed and used vulgar language while at work. Her co-workers also testified that she often made jokes about sex, including jokes about "screwing her boss," and that she participated in frequent discussions and bantering about sex. Faced with this evidence, the court concluded that "[a]ny harassment plaintiff received . . . was prompted by her own actions, including her tasteless joking. Considering plaintiff's contribution to and apparent enjoyment of the situation, it cannot be said that the defendants created 'an intimidating, hostile, or offensive working environment.'" Loftin-Boggs v. City of Meridian, 633 F. Supp. 1323, 1327 (S.D. Miss. 1986), aff'd, 824 F.2d 971 (5th Cir. 1987), cert. denied, 484 U.S. 1063 (1988). See also Barrett v. Omaha Nat'l Bank, 584 F. Supp. 22, 29 (D. Neb. 1983), aff'd, 426 F.2d 424 (8th Cir. 1984) ("It is clear that [plaintiff] was not, in every instance, a mere bystander when it came to talk of sexual activity. Indeed, on occasion she spoke . . . about her relationship with her boyfriend. Therefore, it is doubtful that the general sexual talk shocked plaintiff as much as she would have this Court believe"). But see Swentek v. USAIR, Inc., 830 F.2d 552 (4th Cir. 1987) (trial court held that plaintiff's foul language and conduct, including putting a dildo in her supervisor's mailbox and grabbing the genitals of a pilot with a "frank invitation to a sexual encounter," meant that defendant's conduct, which included reaching under plaintiff's skirt for her genitals, was not unwelcome, even though she asked him to leave her alone; appellate court reversed on grounds that use of foul language or sexual innuendo does not waive plaintiff's legal protections against sexual harassment); Spencer v. General Elec. Co., 697 F. Supp. 204 (E.D. Va. 1988), aff'd, 894 F.2d 651 (4th Cir. 1990) (joining in milder forms of sexual horseplay that occurred in the office did not waive plaintiff's protection against sexual harassment). For an analysis of several cases in this area, see Dawn D. Bennett-Alexander, Lower Court Interpretation of the *Meritor* Decision: Putting Flesh on the Supreme Court's Sexual Harassment Skeleton, 6 Wis. Women's L.J. 35 (1991).

What, besides consent to sexual advances, might explain an employee's participation in such conduct? Might such behavior sometimes serve as a survival technique, a way to achieve acceptance or defuse a potentially unpleasant situation? See Beth A. Quinn, The Paradox of Complaining: Law, Humor, and Harassment in the Everyday Work World, 25 Law & Soc. Inquiry 1151, 1179-1181 (2000). Indeed, if MacKinnon is right, is such playing along evidence of the (successful) "internalized and structural" coercion of sexual harassment?

A similar phenomenon may explain situations in which a plaintiff at some point makes a statement dismissing the significance of the harassment, such as it was "[not] that big of a deal." The Sixth Circuit Court of Appeals found in one case that such a statement should be viewed as a concession that the harassment was not offensive. See Highlander v. K.F.C. Nat'l Management Co., 805 F.2d 644 (6th Cir. 1986). Commenting on that conclusion, Kathryn Abrams writes: "[Plaintiff's] statements that she did not want to raise 'a big stink' may have expressed the discomfort that she felt as a new employee about complaining to management, or the anxiety produced by the entire incident." Abrams, supra, 42 Vand. L. Rev., at 1201.

One way a woman might signal that particular behavior is offensive and unwelcome is to complain about it. But when should she complain? At the first glimmer of discomfort? When conditions have become intolerable? Is there an in-between? Note, again, the potential catch-22 situation: if the woman complains too early, she is hypersensitive, unreasonable, someone who is "looking for trouble"; if she waits too long, she will be judged to have accepted, or at least to be ambivalent toward, the behavior. See Susan Estrich, Sex at Work, 43 Stan. L. Rev. 813, 826-834, 843-847 (1991); Reed v. Shepard, 939 F.2d 484, 492 (7th Cir. 1991) (female police officer's receptiveness to co-workers' sexually suggestive jokes and activities because she wanted to be accepted by others on the police force was fatal to her sexual harassment claim).

The continued friendly relations between a plaintiff and the alleged harasser also may serve as proof that the behavior in question did not constitute harassment. See, e.g., Scott v. Sears, Roebuck & Co., 798 F.2d 210, 212-214 (7th Cir. 1986). Does this possible outcome "ignore[ ] the reality of what women must do to make life bearable in an all-male workplace"? Wendy Pollack, Sexual Harassment: Women's Experience vs. Legal Definitions, 13 Harv. Women's L.J. 35, 72-73 (1990).

What alternative to the "unwelcome" test would better take account of the concerns of nonsubordination/dominance theory than the current case law? Consider the following two proposals:

[B]urdening the victim with proving that the conduct is unwelcome assumes that sexual advances by any man to any woman are by definition welcome until she proves otherwise. We submit that this is a very odd assumption. Indeed, it seems to us far more reasonable to suggest the opposite: that sexual attention in the workplace should be presumed to be unwelcome, unless the initiator determines otherwise. Thus, the burden falls on the defendant to demonstrate how he knew he was welcome. Shifting the burden of communication in this manner focuses the inquiry where it belongs — on the defendant's behavior, rather than the plaintiff's.

Louise Fitzgerald, Suzanne Swan, & Karla Fisher, Why Didn't She Just Report Him? The Psychological and Legal Implications of Women's Responses to Sexual Harassment, 51 J. Soc. Issues 117, 134 (1995).

The idea of welcomeness is wholly inapplicable in cases where the conduct is not specifically solicited. . . . In the case where the defendant has taken no steps to ascertain whether his attentions might be welcome, or where his initial overtures are explicitly sexual, there is no room for the operation of "welcomeness," even as a defense. . . .

There is no justification in a civil action for continuing to presume that a woman welcomes any and all sexual advances made by her coworkers. The element of unwelcomeness should be removed from the prima facie case, and the burden should be on the defendant to show that the plaintiff actually wanted the impugned conduct. An argument of welcomeness by the defendant should not be seriously entertained where the impugned conduct is outside the parameters of a potentially consensual relationship. Welcomeness would not be in issue, in other words, where the defendant's comments consist of sexual remarks or slurs, physical interference on the job, pornographic photos or objects, or sexual contact not preceded by a mutual expression of interest. Welcomeness should only be invoked in the unusual case in which a hostile environment sexual harassment claim is based on sexual intercourse or related behavior and where the defendant can establish that the impugned conduct was mutual, consensual, and unaffected by workplace hierarchies.

Janine Benedet, Hostile Environment Sexual Harassment Claims and Unwelcome Influence of Rape Law, 3 Mich. J. Gender & L. 125, 166, 173-174 (1995). Is this proposal realistic?

5. Employer Liability. The Supreme Court in *Meritor* addressed the issue of employer liability for harassment of one of its employees by another employee, but declined to issue "a definitive rule." 477 U.S. at 72. The Court rejected both the "strict liability" rule urged by plaintiff and the employer's position that the existence of a sex harassment policy and grievance procedure that the plaintiff failed to use precluded liability. Rather, *Meritor* interpreted congressional intent as requiring courts to look to general agency principles for guidance. Id. Lower courts divided as to what those principles required, and in 1998, the Supreme Court issued two companion opinions clarifying the issue, Faragher v. City of Boca Raton, 524 U.S. 775 (1998), and Burlington Industries v. Ellerth, 524 U.S. 742 (1998).

Faragher involved a claim by a college student who worked as a lifeguard for Boca Raton. She alleged that her supervisors had created a "sexually hostile atmosphere" by repeatedly subjecting female lifeguards to "'uninvited and offensive touching,' by making lewd remarks, and by speaking of women in offensive terms." 524 U.S. at 780. One lifeguard allegedly had told Faragher, "Date me or clean the toilets for a year." Id. Although the City had a sexual harassment policy, it was not distributed to her supervisors, and they were unaware of its requirements. While the plaintiff discussed the offensive behavior with a supervisor, she did not consider the discussions to constitute a formal complaint, and the supervisor did not report the problems to any City official. Later, after another female lifeguard made a written complaint to the City's Personnel Director, an investigation was conducted, and the supervisors were sanctioned. The trial court found the City liable under a theory of constructive knowledge, and the court of appeals reversed.

The Supreme Court, speaking through Justice Souter, held:

[In *Meritor*, w]e observed that the very definition of employer in Title VII, as including an "agent," expressed Congress's intent that courts look to traditional principles of the law of agency in devising standards of employer liability. . . .

[W]e . . . agree with Faragher that in implementing Title VII it makes sense to hold an employer vicariously liable for some tortious conduct of a supervisor made possible by abuse of his supervisory authority. . . .

In order to accommodate the principle of vicarious liability for harm caused by misuse of supervisory authority, as well as Title VII's equally basic policies of encouraging forethought by employers and saving action by objecting employees, we adopt the following holding. . . . An employer is subject to vicarious liability to a victimized employee for an actionable hostile environment created by a supervisor with immediate (or successively higher) authority over the employee. When no tangible employment action is taken, a defending employer may raise an affirmative defense to liability or damages, subject to proof by a preponderance of the evidence. The defense comprises two necessary elements: (a) that the employer exercised reasonable care to prevent and correct promptly any sexually harassing behavior, and (b) that the plaintiff employee unreasonably failed to take advantage of any preventive or corrective opportunities provided by the employer or to avoid harm otherwise. While proof that an employer had promulgated an antiharassment policy with complaint procedure is not necessary in every instance as a matter of law, the need for a stated policy suitable to the employment circumstances may appropriately be addressed in any case when litigating the first element of the defense. And while proof that an employee failed to fulfill the corresponding obligation of reasonable care to avoid harm is not limited to showing an unreasonable failure to use any complaint procedure provided by the employer, a demonstration of such failure will normally suffice to satisfy the employer's burden under the second element of the defense. No affirmative defense is available, however, when the supervisor's harassment culminates in a tangible employment action, such as discharge, demotion, or undesirable reassignment. . . .

. . . The City points to nothing that might justify a conclusion by the District Court on remand that the City had exercised reasonable care. Nor is there any reason to remand for consideration of Faragher's efforts to mitigate her own damages, since the award to her was solely nominal. . . .

[Reversed and remanded for entry of judgment for Faragher.]

524 U.S. at 792, 802, 807-809.

In Burlington Industries v. Ellereth, the plaintiff alleged that she had been subject to constant sexual harassment by one of her supervisors, who threatened to make her life difficult, but did not take any specific adverse employment actions against her. The plaintiff had not complained to anyone in authority. The Court reiterated principles set forth in *Faragher*, which impose liability for tangible employment actions by supervisors, but which provide an affirmative defense when no such actions are taken. Under the Court's definition, a "tangible employment action constitutes a significant change in employment status, such as hiring, firing, failing to promote, reassignment with significantly different responsibilities, or a decision causing a significant change in benefits." 524 U.S. at 761. Because a tangible employment decision requires an "official act of the enterprise . . .

[it] becomes for Title VII purposes, the act of the employer," which is sufficient to justify liability. The Court remanded the case to allow the plaintiff to amend her pleading or supplement her discovery, and to allow the employer to assert any affirmative defense.

Faragher and *Burlington* did not explicitly resolve all issues involving employer liability. One involves the basis for liability in cases of hostile environment. Lower courts have generally held that employers are account-able only if they are negligent: i.e., when they know or should know of the harassment and fail to make an appropriate response. Such an approach is consistent with the reasoning in *Faragher* and *Burlington*, since those cases limited vicarious liability to circumstances where a tangible action by a supervisor could be appropriately imputed to the employer. As the court noted in *Faragher*, those cases present greater justification for liability, since employees have more disincentives to report harassment when it involves a supervisor rather than a co-worker, and actions by a supervisor, unlike those of a co-worker, are imbued with the authority of the organization.

Another key issue involves whether employers will be liable if they make some response to a complaint of harassment, but fail to ensure that the misconduct ceases. Recent cases suggest that employers who wish to avoid accountability must make prompt and thorough investigations and take remedial actions reasonably calculated to prevent further harassment and to protect the complainant. However, failure to stop the abuse is not necessarily essential to an effective defense against liability. See cases cited in Joanna L. Grossman, The First Bite Is Free: Employer Liability for Sexual Harassment, 61 U. Pitt. L. Rev. 671, 699 (2000).

What constitutes a reasonable remedial action? Should employers be able to avoid liability if they transfer complainants out of range of the harasser? Suppose the complainants or their co-workers object to reassign-ment? Should innocent parties suffer if it is more convenient to transfer them than their harasser? Compare Sparks v. Regional Medical Center Bd., 792 F. Supp. 735 (N.D. Ala. 1992) (finding no liability for a hospital that transferred a lab technician away from a doctor even though changes in the technician's schedule "created resentment and anger among plaintiff's co-workers who had to carry plaintiff's workload whenever her activities involved direct contact with [the doctor]") with Saxton v. American Telephone & Telegraph Co., 10 F.3d 526, 535-536 (7th Cir. 1993) (after victim declined transfer, company transferred harasser).

How proactive should employers be in attempting to identify and remedy harassment? A survey of some 100 post-*Faragher* and -*Burlington* cases found that as long as the employer had a viable anti-harassment policy, an employee's failure to make a prompt complaint was fatal to any later claims. In effect, claims one observer, the message was that employers should have a good preventive program, but "it should not be so good as to encourage employee reporting." Peter Aronson, Silent Suffering Kills Sex Cases, Nat'l L.J., July 9, 2001, at B1. Accordingly, the survey concludes that in order to minimize liability, employers "should not engage in or should eliminate extensive preventive efforts such as expensive sexual harassment sensitivity training, or more particularly, harassment-reporting hotlines." David Sherwyn, Michael Heise, & Zev J. Eigen, Don't Train Your Employees and Cancel Your "1-800" Harassment Hotline: An Empirical Examination and Correction of the Flaws in the Affirmative Defense to Sexual Harassment Charges, 69 Fordham L. Rev. 1265, 1304 (2001). Is this a perverse result? Should the liability rules that create this incentive structure be reconsidered? Or do employers still have adequate reasons to encourage reporting that will prevent harassment from becoming severe and pervasive? See Susan Sturm, Second Generation Employment Discrimination: A Structural Approach, 101 Colum. L. Rev. 458, 483 (2001).

Should employers attempt to minimize liability by banning romantic involvement between individuals in direct supervisory relationships? Only about a third of surveyed companies have such policies. Most managers are concerned that they would be unenforceable or would simply drive relationships underground. See Deborah L. Rhode, Danger or Delight? Is Romance at Work All Bad?, Nat'l L.J., Nov. 23, 1998, at A21. Bureau of National Affairs studies note that over 7 million married couples met at work, and an American Management Association survey found that about half of workplace romances led to marriage or long-term relationships. Harvey R. Meyer, When Cupid Takes Aim in the Workplace, 86 Nation's Business 58 (July 1, 1998). Could a well-crafted policy on relations between supervisors and subordinates preserve opportunities for office romances, while minimizing risks of abuse of power, unfairness to co-workers, or backlash if a consensual relationship later sours?

If employers are found liable for sexual harassment, how should damages be assessed in class action contexts? Consider the case involving Astra USA, a drug manufacturer that paid nearly $10 million to settle charges by the EEOC that its top male managers had harassed scores of female sales representatives and subordinates. Rather than adjudicating each employee's claim individually, Astra and the EEOC agreed to a procedure in which a special master would divide claimants into categories, with awards for the categories ranging between $12,000 and $300,000. Individuals were assigned to categories based not only on the severity of the abuse, but also on the alleged harasser's position in the company. Women who complained of continual touching by lower-level supervisors received $150,000, while those who complained of similar behavior by senior managers received $250,000. Does this result make sense? Mark Maremont, A Case Puts a Value on Touching and Fondling, Wall St. J., May 25, 1999, at B1.

6. Sexual Harassment Remedies and the First Amendment. The potential remedies for sex discrimination under Title VII include injunctive relief as well as damages. In Robinson v. Jacksonville Shipyards, Inc., 760 F. Supp. 1486 (M.D. Fla. 1991), plaintiff established a "hostile environment" case of sexual harassment under Title VII based on the pervasive display at the overwhelmingly male workplace of pornographic pictures (many directed specifically to the plaintiff) and on repeated sexual and demeaning remarks and jokes directed against the plaintiff, all of which the court found to have been condoned and approved by the employer. The court ordered injunctive relief requiring, among other things, that the employer prohibit the display, reading, or viewing of pictures, posters, calendars, graffiti, and other materials that are "sexually suggestive, sexually demeaning, or pornographic." In determining what falls within the prohibition,

> [a] picture will be presumed to be sexually suggestive if it depicts a person of either sex who is not fully clothed or in clothes that are not suited to or ordinarily accepted for the accomplishment of routine work in and around the shipyard and who is posed for the obvious purpose of displaying or drawing attention to private portions of his or her body.

760 F. Supp. at 1542 (Appendix).

Does such an order raise a First Amendment issue? The court concluded it did not because (1) the employer had "no intention to express itself through the sexually-oriented pictures" and had limited other forms of speech (e.g., by banning political campaign literature and buttons); (2) pictures and verbal harassment "are not protected speech [when] they act as discriminatory conduct in the form of a hostile work environment"; (3) "regulation of discriminatory speech in the workplace constitutes nothing more than time, place, and manner regulation of speech"; (4) "female workers were a captive audience in relation to the speech that comprised the hostile work environment"; (5) even if the speech is "treated as fully protected by the First Amendment," the governmental interest in "cleansing the workplace of impediments to the equality of women is . . . a compelling interest that permits [a regulation] . . . narrowly drawn to serve this interest"; and (6) even a governmental employer has the power to enforce workplace rules impinging on free speech rights, in order to maintain discipline and order in the workplace. Id. at 1534-1536.

Can this decision be reconciled with American Booksellers Association v. Hudnut, 771 F.2d 323 (7th Cir. 1985), aff'd mem., 475 U.S. 1001 (1986), excerpted infra, at page 704? There, a federal appellate court held, and the Supreme Court summarily affirmed, that an anti-pornography ordinance was a content-based restriction on speech that violated the First Amendment. The court in Robinson held that Hudnut was distinguishable because the record involving Jacksonville Shipyards demonstrated a concrete harm for identifiable individuals and the remedy "went no further than to regulate the time, place, and manner of the offensive speech." 760 F. Supp. at 1536. Are you persuaded? The constitutionality of the Robinson order was raised on appeal, but the employer's bankruptcy precipitated a settlement before the case was decided.

On appeal, counsel for Jacksonville Shipyards argued that the lower court had erred in applying a reasonable woman standard, and that the case would have come out differently under a reasonable person standard. In support of that claim, counsel referred to testimony by a psychologist and a sociologist who were experts on the effects of sexual materials. Both testified that pornographic pinups and calendars do not create a serious or probable harm to the average woman worker. Jacksonville Shipyards also relied on trial testimony at trial by supervisors. One claimed that nudity and "cussing" were common occurrences in nautical workplaces; even boats often had nude women as figureheads. Others claimed that television, advertisements, and articles and pictures in women's magazines often included pictures that were just as explicit as those in Jacksonville Shipyards. The defendant had also introduced testimony by a woman craftsworker who stated that she was not offended by pictures of naked women and that the plaintiff was spending "too much time attending to the pictures and not enough time attending to her job." Barbara Dingle, quoted in Caroline A. Forell & Donna M. Matthews, A Law of Her Own: The Reasonable Woman as a Measure of Her Own 54 (2000).

If you had been counsel for the plaintiff, how would you have responded? If you had been one of the appellate judges, how would you have ruled?

Cases after *Robinson* have frequently found that the pervasive presence of pornography has either provided a context for, or been a form of, sexual harassment. See cases cited in Catharine A. MacKinnon, Sex Equality 1639-1641 (2001). A leading exception is Johnson v. County of Los Angeles Fire Department, 865 F. Supp. 1430 (C.D. Cal. 1994). There, a federal district court struck down a Los Angeles County ban on sexually oriented magazines, particularly those including nude pictures, such as Playboy, Penthouse, and Playgirl, in all fire station work locations, including dormitories, rest rooms, and lockers. Although acknowledging that the prevention of sexual harassment was a compelling government interest, the court held that there was insufficient evidence that the presence of the offending material "directly contributes to a sexually harassing environment. . . . " Id. at 1439. In defending the ordinance, the County introduced expert testimony to the effect that reading magazines such as Playboy may result in "sex-role stereotyping," which in turn may result in "inequitable treatment of women or even sexual harassment." Id. at 1441. Citing *Hudnut*, the trial court held that "it is a fundamental principle of First Amendment law that the government cannot regulate material in order to prevent the readers from developing certain ideas." Id. The court further concluded that the County had not carried its "burden of showing that reading Playboy actually leads to such 'stereotyping' [or] that the existence of 'sex-role stereotyping' leads to an harassing environment." Id. Unlike other cases involving workplace pornography, the women firefighters who were offended by the magazines were not captive audiences: by "averting their eyes," they could avoid exposure to objectionable contents. Id. at 1440.

Are *Robinson* and *Johnson* distinguishable? If not, which ruling do you find more persuasive? Some commentators have preferred *Johnson* and criticized the use of sexual harassment law to regulate workplace speech. Their primary concern is that because the boundaries of sexual harassment are often vague and because employers have no general interest in preserving employee speech, they may adopt overbroad restrictions to minimize their chances of liability for hostile environments. To prevent such restrictions, these commentators would limit the scope of harassment law as it applies to workplace expression. See Eugene Volokh, Comment, Freedom of Speech and Workplace Harassment, 39 UCLA L. Rev. 1791 (1992) (contending that harassment law should target only offensive speech directed at a particular employee); Kingsley R. Browne, Title VII as Censorship: Hostile-Environment Harassment and the First Amendment, 52 Ohio St. L.J. 481 (1991) (arguing that a broad definition of hostile work environment establishes a content- or viewpoint-based restriction of expression; only harassment involving touching or quid pro quo should be the basis of liability under Title VII); Nadine Strossen, Regulating Workplace Sexual Harassment and Upholding the First Amendment — Avoiding a Collision, 37 Vill. L. Rev. 757 (1992) (overly broad range of prohibited speech in the workplace undermines both free speech and gender equality).

By contrast, other commentators have argued that sex harassment law is no more vague than other laws implicating freedom of speech, such as prohibitions on defamation (i.e., speech that "lowers an individual in the estimation of the community") or intentional infliction of emotional distress (i.e., speech that is "so outrageous . . . as to go beyond all bounds of decency"). See J.M. Balkin, Free Speech and Hostile Environments, 99 Colum. L. Rev. 2295, 2307 (1999). These commentators also note that whatever incentives employers have to restrict potentially harassing speech are often trumped by their desire to avoid labor force disruption and to maintain morale and loyalty among valued male employees. Id. at 2305. From these commentators' perspective, courts should apply captive audience principles to circumstances in which individuals are unavoidably and unjustly coerced into exposure to harassing expression. Id. at 2310; Suzanne Sangree, Title VII Prohibitions Against Hostile Environment Sexual Harassment and the First Amendment: No Collision in Sight, 47 Rutgers L. Rev. 461, 539-540 (1995); Jessica M. Karner, Political Speech, Sexual Harassment, and a Captive Workforce, 83 Cal. L. Rev. 637, 689 (1995). For further discussion of First Amendment issues, see Section 4, below, on harassment in educational contexts.

7. Street Hassling. How serious an offense is "street hassling" — i.e., wolf whistles, leers, catcalls, grabs, pinches, crude sexual invitations, and other rude behaviors from strangers, directed at women in public places?

Several feminist scholars have argued that the law should reach this conduct. See, e.g., Cynthia Grant Bowman, Street Harassment and the Informal Ghettoization of Women, 106 Harv. L. Rev. 517 (1993) (advocating redefinition of torts of assault, intentional infliction of emotional distress, and invasion of privacy to encompass street harassment, and a criminal ordinance making street harassment punishable by a $250 fine); Deborah M. Thompson, "The Woman in the Street": Reclaiming the Public Space from Sexual Harassment, 6 Yale J.L. & Feminism 313 (1994) (advocating adoption of complaint procedures by companies that have workers in public places and anti-harassment codes applicable to everyone in public places).

Should street hassling be permitted? If so, how should it be defined? Cynthia Bowman proposes the following:

> Street harassment occurs when one or more unfamiliar men accost one or more women in a public place, on one or more occasions, and intrude or attempt to intrude upon the woman's attention in a manner that is unwelcome to the woman, with language that is explicitly or implicitly sexual. Such language includes, but is not limited to, references to male or female genitalia or to female body parts or to sexual activities, solicitation of sex, or reference by word or action to the target of the harassment as the object of sexual desire, or similar words that by their very utterance inflict injury or naturally tend to provoke violent resentment, even if the woman did not herself react with violence. The harasser's intent, except his intent to say the words or engage in the conduct, is not an element of this offense. This [definition] does not apply to any peaceable activity intended to express political views or provide public information to others.

Bowman, supra, at 575-576. See also Tiffanie Heben, A Radical Reshaping of the Law: Interpreting and Remedying Street Harassment, 4 S. Cal. Rev. L. & Women's Stud. 183, 213 (1994) (definition should also cover insults related to a person's racial or homosexual identity).

Do you see any problems with such definitions?

8. Legal Ethics Issues in Sexual Harassment Cases. Sexual harassment cases can often present ethical issues for lawyers on both sides of the litigation. For lawyers representing plaintiffs, the issues include how much evidence is necessary to justify bringing a lawsuit, what to do if the litigation seems motivated by a desire to punish or humiliate the defendant, and how extensively to probe the defendant's background for potentially embarrassing incidents. Consider, for example, the conduct of the lawyers for Paula Jones. By Jones's account, she initially consulted attorneys not because of adverse consequences at work, but because American Spectator magazine reported allegations that she had been involved in a sexual relationship with then-Governor Clinton. Jones frequently asserted that all she originally wanted was a retraction from the magazine and an apology from Clinton. When neither was forthcoming, she agreed to file suit. Paula Jones

Settlement, Wash. Post, Nov. 15, 1998, at C6; Michael Isikoff, Uncovering Clinton 50-51 (1999). Her legal expenses were subsidized by the Rutherford Institute, a foundation that had funded many right-wing political causes. The Institute also recommended different, more politically connected attorneys, who promptly amended Jones's original complaint to add a claim of sexual assault based on a new allegation: that Clinton had slid his hand up Jones's leg. Under the recently enacted Violence Against Women Act, this claim brought Clinton within the scope of a provision aimed at sexual predators, which entitled lawyers to introduce evidence of his prior sexual history and to obtain broad discovery into prior intimate relationships. Fed. R. Evid. 415(a).

Yet while Jones's lawyers sought information from over 150 individuals concerning Clinton's history, they made almost no effort to discover facts about their client's, such as whether she had suffered adverse job consequences following the hotel incident. They did not even review her employment records before or after she filed suit. See Deborah L. Rhode, Conflicts of Commitment: Legal Ethics in the Impeachment Context, 52 Stan. L. Rev. 269, 295, 313 (2000).

Was the lawyers' behavior unethical? Negligent? Rule 11 of the Federal Rules of Civil Procedure authorizes sanctions if a lawsuit is pursued for "any improper purpose such as to harass" and/or includes claims that lack "evidentiary support" or are unlikely to prove well grounded "after a reasonable opportunity for further investigations or discovery." The Model Rules of Professional Conduct similarly authorize ethical sanctions against lawyers who assert frivolous or harassing claims. Rules 3.1, 3.4. Could Jones's lawyers have been subject to sanctions? Was it ethical for them to seek extensive information about Clinton's prior consensual relationships, including his relationship with Monica Lewinsky, on the theory that such information might have revealed a pattern of rewarding employees for sexual favors? How should attorneys respond when a claim appears extremely unlikely to succeed at trial, but when threats of embarrassing pretrial discovery might serve some other purpose or prompt a substantial settlement? Are cases like *Jones* a harassing use of harassment law?

By the same token, lawyers for defendants often have comparable opportunities to harass their opponents in harassment cases. Rule 412(b)(2) of the Federal Rules of Evidence provides as follows:

> In a civil case, evidence offered to prove the sexual behavior or sexual predisposition of any alleged victim is admissible if . . . its probative value substantially outweighs the danger of harm to any victim and of unfair prejudice to any party. Evidence of an alleged victim's reputation is admissible only if it has been placed in controversy by the alleged victim.

The Rule also provides an in camera proceeding to determine admissibility. However, under Rule 11 of the Federal Rules of Civil Procedure, attorneys may seek not only evidence relevant to their clients' cases, but also information that might reasonably lead to such evidence. Many courts have interpreted this Rule to allow lawyers to ask complainants about intimate sexual matters that might shed light on whether a defendant's conduct was unwelcome or was in fact the cause of the damages alleged. Such questioning has focused on everything from closeted lesbian experiences and intimate marital difficulties or infidelities to mental health records, birth control practices, and bra sizes. See M.G. Sungaila, Heroine Chic, S.F. Daily J., Jan. 20, 1998, at 4; Jane Aiken, Sexual Character Evidence in Civil Actions: Refining the Propensity Rule, 1997 Wis. L. Rev. 1221, 1224; Andrea Bernstein, The Fight for Damages Gets Uglier, Ms., July-Aug. 1996, at 18; Rochelle Sharpe, Fighting Back: Mitsubishi U.S. Unit Is Taking a Hard Line in Harassment Battle, Wall St. J., Apr. 22, 1996, at A1; Ellen E. Schultz & Junda Woo, The Bedroom Ploy: Plaintiffs' Sex Lives Are Being Laid Bare in Harassment Cases, Wall St. J., Sept. 19, 1994, at A1. The fear of having their personal lives paraded in court proceedings often deters victims from bringing or pursuing harassment claims. See Schultz & Woo, supra, at A1; Miranda Oshige, What's Sex Got to Do with It?, 47 Stan. L. Rev. 565, 581 (1995). In the criminal context, see pages 956-970.

Whose responsibility is it to prevent intrusive questioning of parties in sexual harassment litigation? Trial judges have broad discretion under Rules 26(e) and 45(c) of the Federal Rules of Civil Procedure to limit disclosures to prevent "undue burden" or "embarrassment." As some courts and commentators have recognized, constitutional rights to privacy may be jeopardized by overbroad inquiries into intimate matters. See Barrenda L. v. Superior Court, 76 Cal. Rptr. 2d 727, 732 (1998) (holding that plaintiff's right to privacy outweighed defendant's need for information about sexual encounters); Boler v. Superior Court, 247 Cal. Rptr. 185, 189 (Ct. App. 1987) (holding that discovery order compelling defendant to answer questions about relationships with a woman not party to the suit was overbroad and an "impermissible intrusion into sexual privacy"); but see Holt v. Welch Allyn, Inc., 1997 WL 210420 (N.D.N.Y. April 15, 1997) (permitting defendant to subpoena photos of plaintiff attending party at which male stripper performed, but declining to determine whether they would be admissible at trial). To protect parties from needlessly intrusive discovery, should courts require a threshold showing that a plaintiff's claim is well grounded and that there is a clear and convincing need for such evidence? See Rhode, Conflicts of Commitment, supra, 52 Stan. L. Rev. at 305; Diane H. Mazur, Sex and Lies: Rules of Ethics, Rules of Evidence, and Our Conflicted Views of the Significance of Honesty, 14 Notre Dame J.L. Ethics & Pub. Pol'y 679, 720 (2000).

If courts do not limit discovery, do lawyers have an independent obligation to do so? Rule 4.4 of the Model Rules of Professional Conduct provides: "In representing a client, a lawyer shall not use means that have no substantial purpose other than to embarrass, delay, or burden a third person.

. . ." Model Rule 1.2 of the Model Rules of Professional Conduct provides that lawyers "shall abide by a client's decisions concerning the objectives of representation," but permits lawyers to forego actions that they consider "repugnant or imprudent." Withdrawal from representation is permissible if it can be accomplished without prejudice when the client insists on pursuing a matter that the lawyer considers "repugnant" or "imprudent." How would these Rules guide your conduct on the issues posed in Putting Theory into Practice?

Should bar associations sanction lawyers who engage in sexual harassment? Neither the ABA Code of Professional Responsibility nor the Model Rules of Professional Conduct expressly address sexual harassment, but a growing number of states have adopted some form of rules barring sex-based discrimination or sexual relations with clients. See ABA Commission on Women in the Profession, The Unfinished Agenda: Women and the Legal Profession 48 n.307 (2001). Some courts and ethical committees have also imposed sanctions based on general ethical rules prohibiting conduct that adversely reflects on fitness to practice law. See id.; Cincinnati Bar Ass'n v. Young, 731 N.E.2d 631 (Ohio 2000) (imposing two-year suspension for harassment of law student). Would you support rules or disciplinary opinions explicitly banning harassment or discriminatory conduct?

Putting Theory into Practice

4-1. If you had been the lawyer for the defendant in any of the cases discussed in note 4 involving claims that the plaintiff welcomed the conduct at issue, how would you have proceeded? Did the plaintiffs in those cases put their reputations in issue?

4-2. If you had been one of Clinton's lawyers, would you have advised questioning Paula Jones concerning her sexual history on the ground that it was relevant to whether she found Clinton's conduct unwelcome and whether she was likely to have suffered emotional distress? If courts are prepared to permit such questions, does it follow that attorneys are obligated to ask them? Would it matter whether you believed that Jones's claims were without merit and that her attorneys had committed ethical violations by seeking discovery to harass and politically disable the defendant?

4-3. Consider the case of an associate who sued her law firm and one of its partners for three years of harassing incidents. This partner's conduct included grabbing the associate's breasts, announcing wet t-shirt contests over the office intercom, and displaying sexual devices on his lap. The law firm defended the claim on the grounds that the conduct was not severe and pervasive and that the associate had worn "short skirts . . . so the conduct wasn't unwelcome." Catherine Brennan, Associate Wins 80K Sex Harassment Verdict, Daily Rec., Dec. 31, 1996, at 2. If you had been a lawyer for the firm, would you have made those arguments? Would you have questioned the associate about her apparel and her own sexual conduct if the client had insisted that you do so?

2. Same-Sex Harassment and Men as Victims

≡ *Oncale v. Sundowner Offshore Services, Inc.*
≡ 523 U.S. 75 (1998)

Justice SCALIA delivered the opinion for a unanimous Court.

This case presents the question whether workplace harassment can violate Title VII's prohibition against "discriminat[ion] . . . because of . . . sex," when the harasser and the harassed employee are of the same sex. . . .

. . . The precise details are irrelevant to the legal point we must decide, and in the interest of both brevity and dignity we shall describe them only generally. In late October 1991, Oncale was working for respondent Sundowner Offshore Services on a Chevron U.S.A., Inc., oil platform in the Gulf of Mexico. He was employed as a roustabout on an eight-man crew which included respondents John Lyons, Danny Pippen, and Brandon Johnson. Lyons, the crane operator, and Pippen, the driller, had supervisory authority. . . . On several occasions, Oncale was forcibly subjected to sex-related humiliating actions against him by Lyons, Pippen and Johnson in the presence of the rest of the crew. Pippen and Lyons also physically assaulted Oncale in a sexual manner, and Lyons threatened him with rape. [As described by the appellate court, the harassment included "the use of force by Lyons to push a bar of soap into Oncale's anus while Pippen restrained Oncale as he was showering on Sundowner premises." 83 F.3d 118, 118-119 (5th Cir. 1996).]

Oncale's complaints to supervisory personnel produced no remedial action; in fact, the company's Safety Compliance Clerk, Valent Hohen, told Oncale that Lyons and Pippen "picked [on] him all the time too," and called him a name suggesting homosexuality. . . . Oncale eventually quit—asking that his pink slip reflect that he "voluntarily left due to sexual harassment and verbal abuse." . . . When asked at his deposition why he left Sundowner, Oncale stated, "I felt that if I didn't leave my job, that I would be raped or forced to have sex." . . .

[T]he district court held that "Mr. Oncale, a male, has no cause of action under Title VII for harassment by male co-workers." [The Fifth Circuit affirmed.] . . .

Title VII's prohibition of discrimination "because of . . . sex" protects men as well as women, . . . and in the related context of racial discrimination in the workplace we have rejected any conclusive presumption that an employer will not discriminate against members of his own race. "Because of the many facts of human motivation, it would be unwise to presume as a matter of law that human beings of one definable group will not discriminate against other members of that group.". . . If our precedents leave any doubt on the question, we hold today that nothing in Title VII necessarily bars a claim of discrimination "because of . . . sex" merely because the plaintiff and the defendant (or the person charged with acting on behalf of the defendant) are of the same sex.

Courts have had little trouble with that principle in cases [in which] an employee claims to have been passed over for a job or promotion. But when the issue arises in the context of a "hostile environment" sexual harassment claim, the state and federal courts have taken a bewildering variety of stances. Some, like the Fifth Circuit in this case, have held that same-sex sexual harassment claims are never cognizable under Title VII. . . . Other decisions say that such claims are actionable only if the plaintiff can prove that the harasser is homosexual (and thus presumably motivated by sexual desire). . . . Still others suggest that workplace harassment that is sexual in content is always actionable, regardless of the harasser's sex, sexual orientation, or motivations. . . .

We see no justification in the statutory language or our precedents for a categorical rule excluding same-sex harassment claims from the coverage of Title VII. As some courts have observed, male-on-male sexual harassment in the workplace was assuredly not the principal evil Congress was concerned with when it enacted Title VII. But statutory prohibitions often go beyond the principal evil to cover reasonable comparable evils, and it is ultimately the provisions of our laws rather than the principal concerns of our legislations by which we are governed. Title VII prohibits "discriminat[ion] . . . because of . . . sex" in the "terms" or "conditions" of employment. Our holding that this includes sexual harassment must extend to sexual harassment of any kind that meets the statutory requirements. . . .

Courts and juries have found the inference of discrimination easy to draw in most male-female sexual harassment situations, because the challenged conduct typically involves explicit or implicit proposals of sexual activity; it is reasonable to assume those proposals would not have been made to someone of the same sex. The same chain of inference would be available to a plaintiff alleging same-sex harassment, if there were credible evidence that the harasser was homosexual. But harassing conduct need not be motivated by sexual desire to support an inference of discrimination on the basis of sex. A trier of fact might reasonably find such discrimination, for example, if a female victim is harassed in such sex-specific and derogatory terms by another woman as to make it clear that the harasser is motivated by general hostility to the presence of women in the workplace. A same-sex harassment plaintiff may also, of course, offer direct comparative evidence about how the alleged harasser treated members of both sexes in a mixed-sex workplace. Whatever evidentiary route the plaintiff chooses to follow, he or she must always prove that the conduct at issue was not merely tinged with offensive sexual connotations, but actually constituted "*discrimina[tion]* . . . because of . . . sex."

. . . The prohibition of harassment on the basis of sex requires neither asexuality nor androgyny in the workplace; it forbids only behavior so objectively offensive as to alter the "conditions" of the victim's employment. "Conduct that is not severe or pervasive enough to create an objectively hostile or abusive work environment — an environment that a reasonable person would find hostile or abusive — is beyond Title VII's purview." . . . We have always regarded that requirement as crucial, and as sufficient to ensure that courts and juries do not mistake ordinary socializing in the workplace — such as male-on-male horseplay or intersexual flirtation — for discriminatory "conditions of employment."

We have emphasized, moreover, that the objective severity of harassment should be judged from the perspective of a reasonable person in the plaintiff's position, considering "all the circumstances." . . . In same-sex (as in all) harassment cases, that inquiry requires careful consideration of the social context in which particular behavior occurs and is experienced by its target. A professional football player's working environment is not severely or pervasively abusive, for example, if the coach smacks him on the buttocks as he heads onto the field — even if the same behavior would reasonably be experienced as abusive by the coach's secretary (male or female) back at the office. The real social impact of workplace behavior often depends on a constellation of surrounding circumstances, expectations, and relationships which are not fully captured by a simple recitation of the words used or the physical acts performed. Common sense, and an appropriate sensitivity to social context, will enable courts and juries to distinguish between simple teasing or roughhousing among members of the same sex, and conduct which a reasonable person in the plaintiff's position would find severely hostile or abusive. . . .

Notes

1. Liability for Same-Sex Harassment. What was the motive for the harassment in *Oncale*? Should it matter? Neither Oncale nor the men who harassed him are gay. Oncale is married with two children and does not consider himself a "standard bearer for gay rights," although neither is he a "gay-basher." Joanna Weiss, Same Sex Harassing Illegal Too, Court Says, Times Picayune, Mar. 5, 1998, at A1. Consider the descriptions of harms of sexual harassment in note 1, supra. Which of these theories best accounts for cases in which men are victims?

According to some researchers, men often harass other men to enforce "the traditional heterosexual male gender role" by encouraging "stereotypical forms of 'masculine' behavior" and punishing "feminine" conduct:

"Such behavior can be interpreted as arising from the societal devaluation of femininity and the complementary valorization of male heterosexuality and masculinity." Craig R. Waldo, Jennifer L. Berdahl, & Louise F. Fitzgerald, Are Men Sexually Harassed? If So by Whom?, 22 Law & Hum. Behav. 59, 61 (1998). If this theory is right, what would Joseph Oncale need to show on remand to demonstrate that he was harassed "because of sex"? Are there risks that after *Oncale*, spurious claims of harassment may be used to "out" closeted gays and lesbians or to punish those who are open about their homosexual orientation? See Mary Coombs, Title VII and Homosexual Harassment After *Oncale*: Was It a Victory?, 6 Duke J. of Gender L. & Pol'y 113, 114 (1999).

2. Sexual Harassment: Just an Equality Issue? Is same-sex harassment properly viewed as an issue of sex equality? If so, what kind of equality? Mary Anne C. Case finds an identity between sexual harassment of homosexuals and harassment of women, an identity she establishes through an examination of the harassment of effeminate men:

> By examining the similarity of the taunts typically hurled at both women and gay or effeminate men in hostile environments, taunts that stress feminine sexual passivity of all three groups, [it is apparent] that the sexual harassment inflicted on all three groups may have in common the desire of certain "active" masculine males to drive out of the workplace those they see as contaminating it with the taint of feminine passivity. Such harassment is, therefore, a form of gender discrimination against the feminine, one with serious effects on the job performance and security of its victims, who should have a legal remedy against it regardless of their sex.

Case, Disaggregating Gender from Sex and Sexual Orientation: The Effeminate Man in the Law and Feminist Jurisprudence, 105 Yale L.J. 1, 7 (1995).

Is the disadvantaging of members of one sex in relation to the other the primary feature of sexual harassment that makes it objectionable? What if a boss treats every worker in exactly the same way — abusively, and as a sexual object? Is this sex discrimination? Should the conduct be illegal? In the European Union, a Recommendation on the Protection of Dignity of Women and Men at Work defines the issue in terms of workplace dignity, rather than sex discrimination. See 1992 O.J. (L 49) 1-2. Does this offer a way out of any of the pitfalls or anomalies discussed in this chapter?

3. Men Harassed by Women. If sexual harassment is viewed primarily as a means of reinforcing gender subordination in the workplace, what accounts for cases in which women harass male subordinates or co-workers? Although such cases have been rare, they have resulted in some of the largest verdicts in harassment litigation, and their numbers are increasing. See Reed Abelson, Men Increasingly Are the Ones Claiming Sex-

Harassment by Men, N.Y. Times, June 10, 2001, at A1; Man Wins Sex-Harassment Suit Against a Woman, N.Y. Times, May 21, 1993, at A12 (male manager of spa manufacturing company who sued his former female supervisor for sexual harassment obtained first $1 million verdict in a harassment case). Descriptions of some of these lawsuits can be found in Aimee L. Widor, Comment, Fact or Fiction?: Role-Reversal Sexual Harassment in the Modern Workplace, 58 U. Pitt. L. Rev. 225 (1996); Caroline A. Forell & Donna M. Matthews, A Law of Her Own: The Reasonable Woman as a Measure of Man 71-73 (2000).

Most of these cases involve quid pro quo harassment. See, e.g., Gardinella v. General Electric Co., 833 F. Supp. 617 (W.D. Ky. 1993) (upholding claim brought against supervisor who discriminated against male employee after he refused to continue a sexual relationship with her). Do these cases suggest that the romantic attraction view of harassment can sometimes have validity? Or do they indicate that women, no less than men, are capable of abusing power in the workplace? For a critique of the theory underlying role-reversal sexual harassment suits and the ways in which popular culture has reinforced portraits of (1) women who have stepped outside traditional gender roles as sexually manipulative and (2) white men as victims of anti-discrimination laws and unjust accusations, see Maria L. Ontiveros, Fictionalizing Harassment — Disclosing the Truth, 93 Mich. L. Rev. 1373 (1995) (book review).

4. Men as Victims of Unjust Accusations. Should men who are harmed by sexual harassment charges that are not adequately proved have a remedy against their employer or their accuser? Consider the case in which a Milwaukee County jury ordered the Miller Brewing Company and two employees to pay $26 million to an executive fired by the company after repeated charges of sexual harassment. One such charge included the executive's recounting to an offended female co-worker a racy episode of *Seinfeld*. The award included $1.5 million in punitive damages against the complaining co-worker. On appeal, the judgment was overturned on the ground that the fired executive had no legal cause of action. Mackenzie v. Miller Brewing Co., 623 N.W.2d 739 (Wis. 2001). At the time of the jury's verdict, the largest known judgment for a single plaintiff victim of sexual harassment was a $7 million punitive damages award against a law firm, Baker & McKenzie, based on its failure to prevent egregious and repeated harassment by a powerful senior partner. That verdict was later cut in half. See Odd Jobs, Wash. Post, Dec. 4, 1994, at H5. What accounts for jurors' willingness to punish an employer's overreaction to harassment charges far more severely than unresponsiveness? In cases where facts are murky, are employers in a no-win situation, at risk of liability for either imposing or not imposing sanctions?

5. The Bisexual "Equal Opportunity" Harasser. In a celebrated footnote in an early sexual harassment case, the District of Columbia Circuit Court of Appeals discussed a hypothetical case of a bisexual supervisor whose "insistence upon sexual favors would not constitute gender discrimination because it would apply to male and female employees alike." Barnes v. Costle, 561 F.2d 983, 990 n.55 (D.C. Cir. 1977). Most courts that have agreed have done so in cases where the bisexual defense was only hypothetical. See Catharine A. MacKinnon, Sex Equality 928 (2001). In cases where the harassment of both sexes is actually raised as a defense, courts sometimes have found that the abuse was not in fact equal. See Steiner v. Showboat Operating Co., 25 F.3d 1459, 1464 (9th Cir. 1994), cert. denied, 513 U.S. 1082 (1995) (defendant's abuse of men in no way related to their gender, [while] his abuse of female employees . . . centered on the fact that they were females"; Kopp v. Samaritan Health Sys. Inc., 13 F.3d 264, 269 (8th Cir. 1993) (a fact-finder could conclude that the defendant's "treatment of women is worse than his treatment of men").

However, in one recent case, the Seventh Circuit Court of Appeals squarely rejected claims by a man and wife who alleged that their supervisor had sexually harassed each of them individually. Holman v. Indiana, 211 F.3d 399 (7th Cir.), cert. denied, 531 U.S. 880 (2000). Under the court's analysis, "Title VII does not cover the 'equal opportunity' or 'bisexual' harasser, then, because such a person is not *discriminating* on the basis of sex. He is not treating one sex better (or worse) than the other; he is treating both sexes the same (albeit badly)." Id. at 403. Compare Judge Posner's observation in dicta in McDonnell v. Cisneros, 84 F.3d 256, 260 (7th Cir. 1996): "It would be exceedingly perverse if a male worker could buy his supervisors and his company immunity from Title VII liability by taking care to harass sexually an occasional male worker, although his preferred targets were female." Do such cases underscore the need for general workplace prohibitions or tort remedies against harassment whether or not it is based on sex? See generally Kenji Yoshino, The Epistemic Contract of Bisexual Erasure, 52 Stan. L. Rev. 353, 432-458 (2000).

Putting Theory into Practice

4-4. Analyze each of the following situations to determine whether it constitutes a case of "discrimination based on sex." What insight into these situations, if any, is gained when nonsubordination theory is added to conventional equality analysis?

a. An employee uses obscene language and tells sexually explicit jokes, which are offensive to many co-workers, both male and female.

b. A supervisor berates all of his subordinate staff, both men and women; he refers to male associates who are insufficiently combative as wimps and pussies, and he refers to assertive women as castrating bitches.

c. A bisexual employee harasses both male and female workers.

d. A male employee complains that his supervisor, over a two-year period, stood close to him, touched him with her hips and thighs, invited him to her apartment, pinched his nipple while supposedly looking for a cigarette in his pocket, and reached into the front pocket of his pants.

e. Antonio works at a restaurant, where he has been subjected to taunts by co-workers as "she" or "her," mocked for walking and carrying a tray "like a woman," and called "faggot" and other homophobic names.

f. Fred is bothered by a male co-worker, assumed by others to be a homosexual, who once stood next to him in the rest room and "peeped at his privates" and who another time stood behind him while he worked, causing them to bump into each other. At a Christmas party, the co-worker asked Fred to dance. In addition to these incidents, the co-worker "hangs around" Fred when he can.

g. Julie is highly offended by the sexualized atmosphere at her all-female office, a mortgage company, where the women make lewd jokes with one another, ask each other about their sexual experiences, discuss whose breasts are bigger, change clothes in front of one another, and otherwise engage in what seems to her overly candid dialogue about their own and each other's bodies.

h. (1) Two first-year associates complain to their law firm managing partner that one of their colleagues, an attractive single woman, has consistently received better assignments than they have from the supervising partner in the litigation section. That partner is in the midst of a messy divorce and has made a point of including their colleague in evening strategy sessions and out-of-town depositions on a major case.

(2) The managing partner raises the issue with the supervisor, who responds that he is not having an affair with the associate, although he is seeing her "socially." He has channeled assignments to her because she is more available in the evening and for travel than her married colleagues. As long as the relationship is consensual, he views it as "none of the firm's business."

i. A male construction worker, when he sees a mistake made by a female co-worker, often loudly shares his view that "they should never have allowed women in these jobs." See Kent Greenwalt, Fighting Words 90-91 (1995).

4-5. How would you handle each of the following situations?

a. You are the ombudsperson for sexual harassment claims at your law firm. You have received several complaints about an informal e-mail distribution list for attorneys and staff who wish to exchange X-rated humor. All members of the list have requested to be on it, and e-mails come with a warning that they should be viewed behind closed doors. The messages mainly involve sexually explicit jokes and graphics. Several female secretaries have walked in on male attorneys while they were viewing the e-mails, and they are now uncomfortable about continuing to work with these attorneys. How should you respond?

b. You own a grocery store. Several employees complain to you about their exposure to explicit drawings and conversation by male supervisors and co-workers concerning homosexual activities. No sexual overtures or homophobic comments are made.

c. You are the Human Relations Officer for the Minneapolis Public Library, against which 12 Minnesota librarians have lodged a complaint about male library patrons who leave sexually explicit images on computer screens and in printers. Litigating Librarians, Wall St. J., June 8, 2001, at 19.

4-6. The faculty of a medical school department were split between those who supported the department chairman and those who opposed him. When Dr. A, a woman faculty member who was a long-time friend of the chairman, came to work in the department, opponents of the chairman began circulating false rumors that Dr. A and the chairman were having an affair and that Dr. A was gaining favorable treatment as a result. The rumors eventually circulated within other departments in the university and in other institutions. Two male faculty members made sexually explicit comments suggesting that Dr. A was using her sex as a tool to better her position in the department and posted sexually suggestive cartoons of Dr. A and the chairman that could be seen by faculty and students in the department. Another faculty member called Dr. A a "slut" and a "whore" as she walked down a hall.

This conduct left Dr. A feeling hurt, humiliated, and ashamed, and it affected her reputation both in and out of the department and the university. Is it actionable as sexual harassment? See Jew v. University of Iowa, 749 F. Supp. 946 (S.D. Iowa 1990). See also Spain v. Gallegos, 26 F.3d 439 (3d Cir. 1994) (claiming sex harassment based on employer's failure to stop rumors that plaintiff was having an affair with her superior, which caused embarrassment and ostracism by co-workers); Chad W. King, Sex, Love Letters, and Vicious Rumors: Anticipating New Situations Creating Sexually Hostile Work Environments, 9 BYU J. Pub. L. 341 (1995).

4-7. A police officer works for the same police department as his wife, who is a dispatcher. The wife has had a number of extramarital affairs with other employees of the department, some of them involving open flirting, touching, frequent visits and breaks, and use of department phones for lengthy calls with sexual content. As a result of this behavior, other department employees have subjected the officer to sexually explicit jokes and comments. Some have questioned the paternity of his children. Others have challenged his masculinity. Such comments have caused extreme humiliation and embarrassment. He also claims that his continuation as a police officer was conditioned on his acquiescence to the behavior and on his continuing to act in a nonconfrontational manner toward the men who had

had affairs with his wife. Does this conduct amount to sexual harassment? See Mathews v. City of LaVerne, 1997 WL 351073 (C.D. Cal. 1997).

3. The Politics of Race and Sex in Workplace Harassment: The Hill-Thomas Hearings as a Case Study

In 1991, the Senate Judiciary Committee convened nationally televised hearings on the confirmation of Clarence Thomas for a seat on the United States Supreme Court. One of the witnesses called to testify before the Committee was Anita Hill, a young African-American woman lawyer who had worked under Thomas's supervision first at the Department of Education and then when he moved to head the EEOC. She testified that Thomas had made frequent sexual overtures and that he had described pornographic videos and his own sexual experiences in graphic detail. The Committee called numerous other witnesses in an effort to confirm or contradict this testimony, including other employees of Thomas, friends and acquaintances of Hill, and Thomas himself. The Senate confirmed Thomas by a narrow two-vote margin. The following article describes the dynamics and legacies of those hearings.

Emma Coleman Jordan, Race, Gender, and Social Class in the Thomas Sexual Harassment Hearings: The Hidden Fault Lines in Political Discourse
15 Harv. Women's L.J. 1, 7-23 (1992)

The cues to race, gender, and social class were oddly distorted in that super-heated weekend under the intensity of the klieg lights. Many pre-existing racial and sexual stereotypes undercut Professor Hill's credibility: a man does not commit sexual harassment unless the woman encouraged his sexual interests in some way; a charge of sexual harassment made against a man of high status by a woman of lesser status is to be viewed with suspicion because the woman has something to gain from publicity, no matter how unflattering; sexual harassment charges are frequently concocted and therefore there must be independent corroboration of the events alleged; black women are unchaste; black women who report sexual misconduct by black men are traitors to the race and do not deserve community support. Professor Hill found herself burdened by all of these stereotypes. . . .

Analyzing the social class variables that were at work during the hearings is difficult, because explicit discussions about socioeconomic status are virtually taboo in polite conversation in America. We all cherish the myth of our classless society. However, drawing subtle class distinctions between

Hill and other women was an apparent part of the Thomas strategy to search and destroy his accuser.

This strategy exploited a complicated irony of women's upward mobility — the undercurrent of competition between women in jobs traditionally reserved for women, such as secretaries and administrative assistants, and women who aspire to break the glass ceiling by joining the executive ranks. While virtually all women acknowledge that sexual harassment in the workplace exists, a sharp division among women regarding Professor Hill's allegations emerged based on socioeconomic status.

The first four "character" witnesses for Judge Thomas — all women of color — sought to separate Professor Hill from the national audience of middle and working class women. These Thomas witnesses attempted to strip Professor Hill of her racial and working class identity, to sever her from her black, Baptist farm-family origins. Her strengths were portrayed as faults. Her upward mobility from National Merit Scholar and class valedictorian in tiny, rural Morris, Oklahoma to Yale Law School and beyond became a basis for criticism.

J.C. Alvarez, a former Thomas special assistant, openly displayed her animosity toward Professor Hill's achievements. Alvarez's testimony is a classic example of the subtle warfare that takes place in many offices across the nation. Alvarez testified that Hill was a "relentless debater . . . [who] always acted as if she was a little bit superior to everyone, a little holier than thou . . . mostly kept to herself . . . [and] only occasionally participate[d] in some of the girl talk among the women at the office. . . ."

For some women, "Hill's ambitiousness was a liability that shifted the burden of proof to her." The fact that "she was using him, as he was using her" led some to diminish the importance of her complaint. From this perspective she did not need the job to "put food on the table" and therefore was expected to quit at the first sign of trouble. This provides one explanation for poll results that showed that women of lower socioeconomic status disbelieved Hill's allegations.

Hill's ten-year delay in reporting, and her decision to follow Thomas from the Department of Education to the EEOC, are understandable to a narrow band of women for whom ambition is a virtue, not a vice. The choices such women make are driven by recognition that in the highest levels of management and government service, a small group of highly influential mentors may enjoy a lifetime of input into one's career advancement. These "women who have ambition to get ahead, women who are not just looking for money, those who are looking for personal fulfillment, power, and influence in their line of work are especially vulnerable to a sexual harasser." Professor Hill guessed correctly that Clarence Thomas's star would continue to rise and that he would therefore be one of a painfully small number of influential blacks in the Reagan and Bush administrations whose opinion of her could undo her hard won academic and professional achievements. . . .

In the Hill-Thomas dispute, the fact that the central figures of this high-stakes dispute are both black was at once supremely important, and of no particular importance. For Judge Thomas, the process by which he had risen in the ranks of black conservatives required him to carve a deep ravine between his own views and the social and political preferences of a majority of black citizens.

Thomas was introduced to the American public by a President who was willing to assert boldly that Judge Thomas's race had nothing to do with his selection. Two profoundly contradictory messages soon became apparent. On the one hand, he was a black man from Pin Point, Georgia, whose dramatic rise from poverty and the crushing limitations of racial segregation made him an icon of neo-conservatism, whose success could be cited as proof of the viability of self-help economics and the racial fairness of white conservatives who supported him. On the other hand, it was argued that because Judge Thomas's successes were achieved despite traumatic incidents of racism, he would bring a deep personal sensitivity to the resolution of the racial conflicts that often form the basis of Supreme Court litigation.

Professor Hill's racial identity also rested on a foundation of ambiguous characterization. Thomas and his supporters sought to portray her as a "white" feminist who happened to be black, a tool of abortion-rights supporters who sought to bring down Thomas with a last-minute claim of sexual harassment.

This characterization was plausible because of the inflexibility of our models for race and gender debates. In the shorthand of public policy discourse about gender conflicts, we assume that all women are white and that all blacks are men. When a black woman appears to speak for herself, these unspoken assumptions force her to shed one identity or the other. Moreover, when there are conflicts between a black man and a black woman, racism "trumps" sexism. The hierarchy of interests within the black community assigns a priority to protecting the entire community against the assaultive forces of racism. This conceptualization of the relationship between the entire community and the interests of its female members creates a powerful dynamic in which black women must subordinate matters of vital concern in order to continue to participate in community life. Women who break the expectation of silence may be made to feel disloyal, shunned, or vilified.[64] . . .

Complex racial and cultural arguments are now being developed, in a series of highly publicized controversies, in defense of black men who use obscene, often violent language and imagery in communicating with and about black women. One such argument is that obscenity is part of the black

---

64. See Rosemary Bray, Taking Sides Against Ourselves, N.Y. Times, Nov. 17, 1991 (Magazine), at 56 ("Anita Hill put her private business in the street and she downgraded a black man to a room filled with white men who might alter his fate — surely a large enough betrayal for her to be read out of the race.").

vernacular and should be understood by both black men and women as harmless, situationally appropriate repartee between the sexes.

An important recent contributor to this post-modern cultural defense of language that enshrines a culture of degradation and violence against black women is Henry Louis Gates, Jr., Chairman of the Afro-American Studies Department at Harvard University. Gates offered a cultural defense to the obscenity charges brought against the 2-Live Crew rap group. Although the First Amendment is certainly broad enough to protect even the black-woman-hating lyrics of 2-Live Crew, the cultural acceptability of such language is a distinct question that cannot be answered solely with reference to black male subcultures.

Harvard sociologist Orlando Patterson extends Gates's argument, dismissing Hill's claim of sexual harassment as over-sensitivity to a black male's "down-home style of courting."[68] Patterson thus joins the debate with the implausible assertion that the pornographic descriptions attributed to Thomas were within the cultural tradition of conversation between black men and women, and therefore "immediately recognizable to Professor Hill and most women of Southern working-class backgrounds, white or black, especially the latter."

Patterson argues that since the language Hill accused Thomas of using is part of

> a verbal style that carries only minor sanction in [the black] subcultural context. . . . Judge Thomas was justified in denying making the remarks, even if he had in fact made them, not only because the deliberate displacement of his remarks made them something else but on the moral utilitarian grounds that any admission would have immediately incurred a self-destructive and grossly unfair punishment.[70]

This utilitarian argument, linked as it is with the black-culture defense, requires one to balance the damage to Professor Hill caused by Thomas's denial against the potential damage to Judge Thomas of telling the truth. In concluding that the balancing tips in favor of Judge Thomas's denial, Patterson demeans both the harm Professor Hill suffered from being forced

---

68. Orlando Patterson, Race, Gender and Liberal Fallacies, N.Y. Times, Oct. 20, 1991, 4 at 15.

This defense was also evident in the rape trial of former heavyweight boxing champion Mike Tyson. During the trial, Tyson's attorneys sought to portray him as a crude, unrefined "street dude" who courted women on the first meeting by asking them if they wanted to "f——." Tyson offered a curious perversion of black male sexual stereotypes — seeking to immunize his behavior by asserting that any woman who conducted ordinary conversation and dating relationships with him would understand his sexual "message" and would therefore be deemed to have impliedly consented to the full range of sexual contact with him. Tyson was convicted of one count of rape and two counts of deviate sexual conduct. See William Raspberry, The Real Victim in Indianapolis, Wash. Post., Feb. 14, 1992, at A25.

70. Patterson, supra note 68.

to listen to Thomas's "dirty words," and the harm she suffered in being portrayed as a delusional liar.

Patterson's relativistic approach is also misguided. Cultural relativism in the workplace will quickly become a slippery slope if workers are permitted to carve cultural exemptions to Title VII. Moreover, even if one might want to take cultural factors into account, surely neither Judge Thomas, nor Patterson on his behalf, would want to argue that the early childhood conventions of Pin Point and Savannah, Georgia should be the standards by which then-EEOC Chairman Thomas's conduct should be measured.

The single most intriguing aspect of the Hill-Thomas hearings was Thomas's complete abandonment of his earlier plea to be judged by the content of his character, not by the color of his skin. Like his fellow black conservative, author Shelby Steele, Thomas in his writings and speeches prior to nomination subscribed to the view that black people have developed a "victim-focused identity"[72] which leads "us . . . to claim more racial victimization than we have actually endured."[73] Judge Thomas frowned on this "whining" from civil rights leaders. Yet, in his opening statement he charged the Senate Judiciary Committee with conducting a "high-tech lynching."[74] He told the Committee that stereotypes existed in the "language about the sex organs of black men, . . . and these are charges that play into racist, bigoted, stereotypes, that these are the kind of charges that are impossible to wash off."[75] He went on to say that: "I wasn't harmed by the Klan. I wasn't harmed by the Knights of Camellia. I wasn't harmed by the Ar[y]an race. I wasn't harmed by a racist group. I was harmed by this process."[76]

Because no one on the Committee responded to his lynching charge, the country was left with a distorted image of a racial victim. No one pointed out that it was a black woman who claimed he had victimized her. No one pointed out the terrible harms and stereotypes to which black women have been subjected. Although the sexual stereotypes of all black people are damaging, "[t]he institutionalized rape of black women has never been as powerful a symbol of black oppression [within the black community] as the spectacle of lynching."[78] . . .

---

72. See Shelby Steele, The Content of Our Character, A New Vision of Race in America 172 (1990) ("To retrieve our individuality and find opportunity, blacks today must — consciously or unconsciously — disregard the prevailing victim-focused black identity.").

73. Id. at 67.

74. Hearings of the Senate Judiciary Committee [Fed. News Serv., Oct. 12, 1991]. See also Associated Press, Thomas Excerpts: "I'd Rather Die Than Withdraw My Bid," L.A. Times, Oct. 13, 1991, at A14.

75. Hearings of the Senate Judiciary Committee, [supra note 74].

76. Id.

78. Hazel V. Carby, Reconstructing Womanhood: The Emergence of the Afro-American Woman Novelist 39 (1987). See also Darlene Clark Hine, Rape and the Inner Lives of Black Women in the Middle West: Preliminary Thoughts on the Culture of Dissemblance, 14 Signs 912, 917 (1989).

Slave women were sexual property. The world they inhabited was bereft of legal protection for their sexual autonomy. Today, black women seek to claim that vital core of individual dignity, the right to determine one's sexual interactions. These efforts present complex challenges to the definitions of acceptable interaction between the genders. The slave legacy stands as a reminder that black women can successfully resist sexual imposition despite disabling legal doctrine. . . .

Judge Thomas's use of powerful racial imagery transformed him from sexual harasser to racial victim, perhaps the single most important element leading to his confirmation. His use of race worked to his advantage because "the critical segment of public opinion was the opinion of black voters in the black belt of the South. Thomas reminded black people that he was a black man who was in danger of being oppressed for being uppity, by going beyond his assigned station in life."[88]

This perception tapped the widely shared belief among large segments of the black community that black politicians and other prominent leaders are subject to a double standard of morality.[89] Judge Thomas, like former Washington D.C. Mayor Marion Barry, was able to tap a deep and "well-founded skepticism about the effort of the white power structure to embarrass prominent black men."[90] . . .

Those who sought to discredit Professor Hill made use of a treacherous combination of stereotypes and myths about black and white women. The Freudian notion of women's hysterical fabrication of claims of sexual abuse[96] merged with the politico-psychiatric diagnosis of erotomania,[97] to provide a formidable tool with which to shape public opinion and diminish Professor Hill's powerful presentation. . . .

This diagnosis was repeated and accepted by many, notwithstanding the absence of any scientific or medical support. Dr. Robert Spitzer, former Chair of the American Psychiatric Association Committee that developed the current diagnostic manual, asserts that while

88. Interview with Professor Patricia King, Georgetown University Law Center, in Washington, D.C. (Oct. 24, 1991).

89. See Alison Muscatine, Answering Credibility Question: Accuser's Testimony Proof Enough; Tyson Caught by Words, Image, Wash. Post, Feb. 12, 1992, at B3.

90. [Telephone interview with Professor Lani Guinier (a black Yale Law School class-mate of Justice Thomas), University of Pennsylvania Law School (Oct. 23, 1991).] One concrete example of disparate treatment is the F.B.I. wiretaps of the private sexual activity of Dr. Martin Luther King, Jr., and the threat to disclose his private life, compared with the treatment accorded President Kennedy, who slept with a movie star and the girlfriend of a Mafia boss during the same period. The suspicion that black men who engage in sexual misconduct are more likely to be subjected to public pillorying therefore has a firm foundation in reality.

96. See Sigmund Freud, Collected Papers 32-33 (Ernest Jones ed., 1959).

97. See American Psychiatric Association, Work Group to Revise D.S.M.-III, D.S.M.-III-R in Development, 2nd Draft (Aug. 1, 1986) (defining erotomania as "a delusional disorder in which the predominant theme of the delusion(s) is that another person of higher status is in love with him or her"). For a discussion of the political dimension of this diagnosis, see Alessandra Stanley, Erotomania: A Rare Disorder Runs Riot — in Men's Minds, N.Y. Times, Nov. 10, 1991, §4, at 2.

[i]t is inappropriate to make a psychiatric diagnosis without actually conducting a psychiatric interview of the person being examined . . . it is possible to render a judgment, based on information that is not disputed about Professor Hill. . . . The diagnosis of Erotomania has been suggested based on the hypothesis that Professor Hill has a delusion that Judge Thomas is, or has been, in love with her. Patients with Erotomania do have the delusion that someone, who may barely know them, is in love with them. However, they do not believe that the person who is in love with them is harming them in any way. . . . Therefore, this diagnosis is inconsistent with Professor Hill's charges of sexual harassment.

Because Professor Hill is a black woman, she was portrayed not only as delusional, but also as Sapphire: the black, gonad-grinding woman "out of control." The Sapphire image with all of its connotations of black male emasculation resonated within the black community. Hill's status as a black woman multiplied the possible lines of attack by making available additional stereotypes that could be used against her.

Hill's credibility was also challenged by the fact that she only revealed specific details of Thomas's pornographic references gradually. That such gradual revelation is the norm for women who have undergone traumatic experiences was a fact lost on both the Senators and the public.

The public also found it incredible that a woman lawyer would be the target of harassment, especially from another lawyer. Even if harassed, a woman lawyer is expected to be able to handle it herself. Contrary to this expectation, one survey found that of the 918 female attorneys in large law firms who responded, sixty percent had been the object of unwanted sexual attention. Only seven percent reported these incidents. Ironically, even women who have been the victims of sexual harassment expect a woman lawyer to be more assertive in handling a workplace harasser. Many members of the public view women lawyers as smarter and more aggressive than other women, and therefore able to take care of themselves. But even women lawyers have supervisors whose displeasure can affect their career advancement.

Notes

1. The Aftermath of the Hill-Thomas Hearings. The Hill-Thomas hearings were a defining moment in women's history in this country. Watching an all-male Judiciary Committee grill a woman with no motive to lie on humiliating sexual details mobilized many women who had never before identified with the "women's movement." For many viewers, the hearings called into question certain fundamental assumptions about women's sexuality and workplace opportunities, as well as the capacity of law to cope with sexual harassment.

During the hearings themselves, most Americans did not believe Anita Hill. A New York Times/CBS News poll at the time found that only about a quarter of viewers thought Hill was telling the truth; 58 percent believed Justice Thomas. See Elizabeth Kolbert, The Thomas Nomination: Most in National Survey Say Judge Is the More Believable, N.Y. Times, Oct. 15, 1991, at A1. One year later, however, according to a Wall Street Journal/NBC News poll, her credibility rating had risen to 44 percent, while his had slipped to 34 percent. See Jill Abramson, Reversal of Fortune: Image of Anita Hill, Brighter in Hindsight, Galvanizes Campaigns, Wall St. J., Oct. 5, 1992, at A1.

Strange Justice: The Selling of Clarence Thomas (1994), an account of the Thomas nomination by seasoned Wall Street Journal reporters Jane Mayer and Jill Abramson, concluded that the preponderance of the evidence suggested that Thomas had lied under oath in denying Hill's claims. And a decade after the confirmation process, David Brock, the author of a best-selling book that had attacked Hill, published another book acknowledging that he had previously lied in print in order to protect the reputation of Thomas. In the first book, The Real Anita Hill (1993), Brock repeated his earlier assertions that Hill was "a little bit nutty, a little bit slutty." David Brock, The Real Anita Hill, American Spectator, Mar. 1992, at 18. In Blinded by the Right: The Conscience of an Ex-Conservative (2001), Brock conceded that he had demonized Hill and her supporters without adequate factual basis and that he had falsely stated that there was no evidence that Thomas had rented pornographic videos. See Alex Kuczynski and William Glaberson, Book Author Says He Lied in His Attacks on Anita Hill, N.Y. Times, June 27, 2001, at A12.

One consequence of the Hill-Thomas hearings was the mobilization of women as a political force. Women voters accounted for 54 percent of the votes in the 1992 general election, supporting President Clinton over former President Bush by a 6 percent gender gap. The biggest political action committee in the election was EMILY's List (EMILY is an acronym for "early money is like yeast"), which had contributed over $6 million to Senate and House candidates. EMILY's List, Notes from Emily — Women Are Victorious in '92, at 1 (Dec. 1992). Women ran for political office in record numbers in the 1992 elections, some directly in reaction to these events. Four women gained seats in the U.S. Senate, raising the number of women senators from two to six. The number of women in the House of Representatives moved from 28 to 47, while women increased their share of elective offices at the state executive level to slightly more than 20 percent. AP, Female Ranks in Elected Jobs Get a Big Boost, N.Y. Times, Nov. 8, 1992, at A18. Many of the new successful candidates were women of color; as a result of the 1992 election, one-third of the Democratic women in the House were African American or Hispanic. EMILY's List, supra, at 6.

Moreover, while activists feared that the abuse experienced by Anita Hill would dampen women's willingness to report incidents of sexual harassment, exactly the opposite occurred. One year after the hearings, reports of sexual harassment to the Equal Employment Opportunity Commission were up by over 50 percent. See Jane Gross, Suffering in Silence No More: Fighting Sexual Harassment, N.Y. Times, July 13, 1992, at A1, A16. The Navy was forced to respond sharply to incidents of sexual harassment among members of the military. See John Lancaster, 24 Women Assaulted on Gulf Duty; Perpetrators Often Were Higher-Ranking Soldiers, Army Says, Wash. Post, July 21, 1992, at A1 (reporting on rapes and sexual assaults of U.S. Army servicewomen during Operations Desert Shield and Desert Storm); Eric Schmitt, Wall of Silence Impedes Inquiry into a Rowdy Navy Convention, N.Y. Times, June 14, 1992, at A1, col. 1 (reporting on Tailhook scandal). (Issues related to sexual harassment in the military are discussed at pages 790-804.) Although the number of formal complaints remains small, an unprecedented number of women, unknown and well known, came forth publicly to tell their own stories of sexual harassment. Average verdicts in harassment suits rose from just over $10,000 in 1991 to over $50,000 in 1995. Marianne Lavelle, Defiance Can Backfire in Sexual Harassment Cases, Nat'l L.J., June 17, 1996, at B1. A growing industry has emerged to train employers and employees how to end sexual harassment in the workplace. See Gross, supra.

Not everyone applauds the increased attention on the harms of sexual harassment. Sociologist Orlando Patterson, whose op-ed piece is discussed in Emma Coleman Jordan's essay, states that variations in gender, class, ethnicity, and region must be taken into account in determining "what constitutes proper and effective male-female relations." Patterson, Race, Gender and Liberal Fallacies, N.Y. Times, Oct. 10, 1991, at 4-15.

> With his mainstream cultural guard down, Judge Thomas on several misjudged occasions may have done something completely out of the cultural frame of his white, upper-middle-class work world, but immediately recognizable to Professor Hill and most women of Southern working-class backgrounds, white or black, especially the latter.

Id. Is this what it means to take into account differences in race and class?

Patterson also writes that "[i]f women are to break through the glass ceiling, they must escape the trap of neo-Puritan feminism with its reactionary sacralization of women's bodies." Id. Does he have a point? How would this judgment be characterized within anti-subordination theory?

Of the extensive writing on the Hill-Thomas hearings, four excellent collections focus specifically on the controversial issues of race and gender politics raised by these hearings. See Race, Gender, and Power in America (Anita Faye Hill & Emma Coleman Jordan eds., 1995); Symposium, Gender, Race, and the Politics of Supreme Court Appointments: The Import of the Anita Hill/Clarence Thomas Hearings, 65 S. Cal. L. Rev.

1279 (1992); Race-ing Justice, En-gendering Power: Essays on Anita Hill, Clarence Thomas, and the Construction of Social Reality (Toni Morrison ed., 1992); Court of Appeal: The Black Community Speaks Out on the Racial and Sexual Politics of Thomas v. Hill (Robert Chrisman & Robert L. Allen eds., 1992).

2. Women of Color as a Protected Group. When a woman of color is subject to abuse through terms like "black bitch," is it possible to separate harassment based on gender and harassment based on race? Many commentators have argued that it is not, and some courts have agreed. Andrea L. Dennis, Note, Because I Am Black, Because I Am Woman: Remedying the Sexual Harassment Experience of Black Women, 1996 Ann. Surv. Am. L. 555. For example, in Anthony v. County of Sacramento, 898 F. Supp. 1435 (E.D. Cal. 1995), an African-American woman who was a former sheriff's deputy alleged that she had been subject to "incidents which were offensive on racial grounds and others which targeted her as female, and still others in which she was mistreated as an African-American female." Id. at 1445. The district court agreed with the plaintiff that the incidents should be treated cumulatively and that the jury should also be entitled to consider physical abuse directed at African-American inmates, since such racial hostility created a climate in which the plaintiff "felt not only unwelcome but endangered. . . ." Id. at 1448-1449. If this analysis is correct, are there other groups besides women of color that should also be entitled to aggregate claims?

Consider the following concern:

> The combined racial and sexual stereotyping experienced by women of color makes insertion of race into the reasonable woman standard risky. Inserting sexual orientation or class creates similar risks. When a target is not white, middle-class, and heterosexual, decision makers are likely to harbor negative stereotypes about the *kind* of woman she is. Thus highlighting a woman's race, class, or sexual orientation as well as her gender increases the risk of stereotypes such as "hot" Chicana, "submissive" Asian, "loose" African American, "macho" Lesbian, "trashy" lower-class white. . . . When the harm suffered is *sexual* or *sexist*, it is pragmatic to focus solely on that aspect of a person that is the fulcrum of her injury: gender. Similarly, when the harm suffered is racial harassment, it makes practical sense to focus solely on her race.

Caroline A. Forell & Donna M. Matthews, A Law of Her Own: The Reasonable Woman As A Measure of Man 88 (2000).

For cases where the racial and sexual harassment appear inseparable, Forell and Matthews recommend allowing a plaintiff to bring either claim or a combined claim. To support a combined claim, a plaintiff would need to put forth sufficient facts to satisfy a prima facie finding for both forms of discrimination. Id. at 89. Intersecting sex and race discrimination is further discussed in Chapter 7, section A(1).

Would you support such an approach? Is there a preferable alternative?

4. Sexual Harassment in Educational Institutions

a. The Nature of the Problem

Deborah L. Rhode, Sex in Schools: Who's Minding the Adults?
Directions in Sexual Harassment Law (Catharine A. MacKinnon & Reva Siegel eds., expected publication 2002)

The prevalence of harassment in [educational settings] is difficult to gauge with precision. The sexes vary in their assessments of what is unwelcome or abusive behavior, and their perceptions depend partly on shifting cultural and legal standards. However, virtually all studies find significant levels of unwanted sexual conduct. In representative studies of college campuses, between 30 to 50% of female students report harassment by professors and 70-80% from peers; the incidents range from insulting comments and propositions to bribes, threats, and assaults. Research on elementary and secondary schools generally finds that between 75 to 85 percent of girls and 75 percent of boys experience harassing conduct ranging from sexual taunts to physical attacks. Over 95 percent of surveyed students observe repeated homophobic behavior.[2]

Such conduct remains common in part because many constituencies deny its significance. These denials take somewhat different form for elementary and secondary schools than for colleges and universities, but common themes emerge. Widespread assumptions are that much harassment is harmless, that victims often invite it, and that overreaction by courts and administrators is a greater problem than the abuse they target.

At the elementary and secondary level, many educators believe that harassment is seldom serious and largely inescapable. As one school principal put it, "children are going to bother each other, tease each other and make each other feel bad. But that is the story of man. That's part of growing up. I really think that calling it sexual harassment is too far out." A mother whose son was suspended for two days complained tearfully that the school was

---

2. For variations in perspectives and limitations of surveys, see Kingsley R. Browne, Evolutionary Perspective on Sexual Harassment: Seeking Roots in Biology Rather than Ideology, 8 J. of Contemp. Legal Issues 1, 8, 27, 40 (1997). For surveys, see Bernice Resnick Sandler, Student-to-Student Sexual Harassment, in Sexual Harassment on Campus, Bernice R. Sandler and Robert J. Shoop, eds., 50, 56 (1997); Judith Berman Brandenberg, Confronting Sexual Harassment (1997), 12-13; [Valerie E. Lee, Robert G. Croninger, Eleanor Linn, and Xianglei Chen, The Culture of Sexual Harassment in Secondary Schools, 33 Amer. Educ. Research J. 383, 397 (1996)]; American Association of University Women, America's Hostile Hallways (1993).

"robbing my boy of his childhood." His childhood included calling a classmate a dyke and shoving her face into a concrete wall.[3]

A related assumption is that victims are responsible either for provoking sexual abuse or for learning to cope with it. Parents and administrators often tell girls who complain about harassment that they "ask for it" by "inappropriate" clothing or conduct. A case in point involves the Los Angeles Spur Posse, a group of high school students who competed with each other for sexual conquests. When some of the teens faced disciplinary action and criminal prosecution for acts including harassment, molestation, and rape, many parents rose to their sons' defense. In their view, the conduct was simply part of any "red blooded American boy's" "testosterone thing." After all, "those girls were trash." Even more demurely behaved victims are told to accept the fact that the "story of man" includes the persecution of woman. As one teacher explained, people will call girls names all their lives and they "have to learn to deal with it."[4]

This willingness to trivialize harassment is encouraged by the media's fixation on trivial examples. Hard cases may make bad law, but bad cases make great press. The infrequent instances of administrative overreaction are grossly overreported. Journalists have a field day with the facts when six- or seven-year-olds are "suspended for a smooch." "Loose Lips," "Kiss and Yell," "Peck of Trouble," chortle the headlines.[5]

From these highly publicized cases, the public receives a highly distorted picture of what the problem is. Conservative critics appear correct in their descriptions of "PC paranoia": "hypersensitive," neopuritan "neurotics" seem to be swamping the system with frivolous complaints. To John Leo, the message of school harassment codes is that "chit-chat about sex can get you brought up on charges," and that the friends who might snitch to authorities should not be trusted. "Better to talk about the weather."[6]

In the equally puritanical environment that Katie Roiphe describes, baseless charges "materialize out of thin air" and even ogling will alert the feminist fanatics now patrolling school corridors. Columnist Debbie Price

3. Peter Kendall, quoted in Karen Mellencamp Davis, Reading, Writing, and Sexual Harassment: Finding a Constitutional Remedy When Schools Fail, 69 Ind. L. J. 1123, 1163 (1994); Parents for Title IX Newsletter, October 1995, 1.

4. For parents and administrators, see Myra Sadker and David Sadker, Failing at Fairness: How America's Schools Cheat Girls 9 (1994). For the Spur Posse, see Jill Smolowe, Sex With a Scorecard, Time, April 5, 1993, at 41; Emily Yoffe, Girls That Go Too Far, Newsweek, July 22, 1991, at 58. For the teacher's statement, see Tamar Lewin, Students Seeking Damages for Sex Bias, N.Y. Times, July 15, 1994, at B12.

5. Deborah L. Rhode, You Must Remember This . . ., Nat'l L. J., October 28, 1996, A21.

6. Stuart Taylor, Real Sexual Harassment, Legal Times, May 6, 1996, at 23 (paranoia); Katie Roiphe, The Morning After: Sex, Fear and Feminism on Campus 93 (1992) (hypersensitive); Lewin, Students Seeking Damages, (quoting Gwendolyn Gregory, hypersensitive); Camille Paglia, Vamps and Tramps 48 (1994) (neurotics); John Leo, Two Steps Ahead Of the Thought Police 236 (1994).

wonders whether we really should address restroom graffiti in federal lawsuits and turn girls "into sniveling emotional cripples . . . ?" Christina Hoff Sommers worries about the boys who are the real victims — those targeted by the "anti-male influence" of a flourishing "gender bias industry."[7]

Yet if the charge is exaggeration, critics, not complainants, are the worst offenders. Of course, borderline cases do exist, and recent changes in cultural norms have created some genuine confusion about boundaries. But the cases that now reach educational administrators and legal authorities do not involve idle chit-chat or corridor ogling. They generally feature serious repeated abuse. Girls are taunted, threatened, and mauled, and students of color are especially likely to experience physical abuse. Many victims experience fear, depression, insomnia, and loss of self esteem; the result is lower school performance, increased absenteeism, and, in extreme cases, even suicide.[8]

Few of these victims file complaints. Contrary to popular assumptions, the most serious problem with sexual harassment enforcement involves underreporting, not overreaction. The vast majority of students are silenced by humiliation, fear of retaliation, and skepticism about likely remedies. These concerns are well-founded. Formal complaints often yield ineffectual reprimands from administrators and severe retaliation by classmates. The much martyred six-year-old sex criminal received a one day "in school" suspension. He was separated from his class and missed coloring and an ice cream party. Even such minimal punishment for harassment is the exception; "boys will be boys" is still the rule.[9]

Beleaguered administrators are, of course, correct that kids can be cruel in many ways and that no sexual harassment policy is likely to transform educational institutions into Sunnybrook Farms. But we also need better strategies for increasing accountability among those who harass and those best able to prevent it.

---

7. Roiphe, The Morning After, supra at 99; Debbie M. Price, Victims of Their Gender?, San Francisco Daily J., 24 March 1992, at 4; Christina Hoff Sommers, The War Against Boys, Boston Globe, October 24, 1996, at A21.

8. For abuse and retaliation, see AAUW, Hostile Hallways; Leora Tanenbaum, "Sluts" and Suits, In These Times, May 13, 1996, at 23; Judy Mann, What's Harassment? Ask a Girl, Washington Post, June 23, 1993, at D26; Jane Gross, Schools Are Newest Arenas for Sex-Harassment Issues, N.Y. Times, March 11, 1992, at B8; Stephanie B. Goldberg, Classroom Distractions, American Bar Association Journal, May, 1997, 18.

9. AAUW, Hostile Hallways. Brandenburg, Confronting Sexual Harassment, supra, at 51; Mann, What's Harassment?, D26; Jane Gross, Schools Are Newest Arena For Sex Harassment Issues, at B8; Leora Tannenbaum, Sluts and Suits, 23. For the six year old's penalties, see Adam Nossiter, Six Year Old's Sex Crime: Innocent Peck on Cheek, N.Y. Times, September 27, 1996, at A9.

b. Legal Liability for Sexual Harassment in Educational Settings

The law with respect to sexual harassment in the educational setting is less developed than that relating to the workplace. Title IX of the Education Amendments of 1972, 20 U.S.C. §1681 et seq. (1994) (set forth in the Appendix and discussed more generally at pages 409-432) has been held to prohibit both quid pro quo harassment and hostile environment harassment. In Franklin v. Gwinnett County Public Schools, 503 U.S. 60 (1992), a case involving allegations that a teacher had coercive sexual intercourse with a high school student, the United States Supreme Court held that remedies for violations of this Act are not limited to injunctive relief, but can include damages as well. *Gwinnett*, however, left open the issue of standards of liability, and lower courts divided about the circumstances under which schools could be held accountable for harassment by peers or employees.

The Supreme Court ultimately spoke to those issues in two cases, Gebser v. Lago Vista Independent School District, 524 U.S. 274 (1998), and Davis v. Monroe County Board of Education, 526 U.S. 629 (1999). In *Gebser*, parents of a female student sued the school district after police found that their daughter was having a sexual affair with one of her teachers. By a 5-4 vote, the Court held that schools are not liable for harassment of a student by an employee unless officials had actual notice of the specific misconduct and responded with "deliberate indifference." Id. at 292-293. Under the majority's analysis, it does not matter if the school lacks adequate harassment policies. That decision stands in contrast to other decisions governing workplace harassment from the Court's same 1998 term, discussed at pages 568-571. In both Faragher v. City of Boca Raton, 524 U.S. 775 (1998), and Burlington Industries v. Ellerth, 524 U.S. 742 (1998), the majority held that employers could be liable for a supervisor's harassment even if they lacked specific knowledge of the abuse unless they had adequate policies and procedures that the worker unreasonably failed to use. In effect, the Court has provided more protection from harassment for school employees than for students.

What accounts for this difference in standards? In explaining this result, Justice O'Connor's majority opinion reasoned that any stricter standard would be at odds with the overall compliance scheme of Title IX, which requires federal enforcement agencies to provide notice of any violation of nondiscrimination requirements before initiating enforcement actions. The "central purpose" of this notice is to "avoid diverting education funding from beneficial uses where a recipient was unaware of discrimination in its programs and is willing to institute prompt corrective measures." 524 U.S. at 289. Justice Stevens's dissent noted that the Court's opinion creates incentives to avoid the knowledge that should trigger corrective action. Id. at 299, 300-301 (Stevens, J., dissenting). According to some commentators, the liability standard in *Gebser* may encourage the see-no-evil/hear-no-evil attitudes already in place in many education districts. "When ignorance is bliss, and a defense to legal judgments, why should schools establish effective complaint strategies?" Rhode, Sex in Schools, supra. Moreover, in some respects, this double standard for educational and employment settings seems perverse. "Students often have fewer options for avoiding an abusive situation than an adult employee, their capacities for resistance are less developed, and their values are more open to influence. Schools are powerful socializing institutions and their failure to address harassment perpetuates the attitudes that perpetuate problems." Id. See also Heather D. Redmond, Davis v. Monroe County Board of Education: Scant Protection for the Student Body, 18 Law & Ineq. 393 (2000).

Peer harassment in schools can cause special problems:

> Sexual harassment in coeducational schools occurs in many contexts. Often, coeducation stifles participation by girls in class discussion. Subtle oppression by boys, who act obviously bored, sighing, groaning and rolling their eyes, sends a powerful message when a girl contributes in class. . . .
>
> Boys verbally abuse girls in and outside the classroom. In addition to the constant attach on the intellectual and academic abilities of girls, boys degrade girls with language that is pejorative of women. . . .
>
> In addition to purposeful abuse, boys oppress girls by monopolizing physical space. In 1977, teachers in England conducted research on coeducational schools. They found that while boys occupy the total area surrounding schools by playing football, girls observe from benches or wander in the periphery of the "boys' space." . . .
>
> Seven years later, other teachers expanded upon the previous research using photographs of boys and girls in and around the school building. Their research showed that: (1) girls spend their lunch hour clustered in small groups of two to four in inconspicuous areas; (2) girls walk around paths which hug the buildings while boys walk directly across large, open areas; (3) girls often serve as spectators for boys' activities; (4) boys' activities are faster and more violent than girls' activities, and commonly involve large groups; (5) girls use less space than boys when they play active games; and finally, (6) boys regularly expand their dominion over certain areas by climbing on each other and on structures such as fences and walls.
>
> . . . Contempt for feminine characteristics among adolescent males causes them to emphasize their masculinity to prove that they are as unlike girls as possible. Boys use girls as their negative reference group. . . . [T]o survive — that is to escape sexual harassment themselves — boys must demonstrate at least an appreciation for sexually predatory heterosexual behavior.

Laurie LeClair, Note, Sexual Harassment Between Peers Under Title VII and Title IX: Why Girls Just Can't Wait to Be Working Women, 16 Vt. L. Rev. 303, 325-327 (1991).

In a 5-4 vote, the Supreme Court in Davis v. Monroe County Board of Education, 526 U.S. 629 (1999), clarified the standards for schools' liability for peer harassment. There, a female student alleged repeated acts of harassment by one of her male classmates, including verbal and physical assaults such as attempts to touch her genital area. Despite several complaints, the school failed to take adequate remedial action. The majority held that a school district's "deliberate indifference to known acts of harassment" by students could give rise to liability. Id. at 633. However, a school could be liable only where it "exercises substantial control over the harasser and the context in which the known harassment occurs" and where the conduct is so "severe, pervasive, and objectively offensive that it can be said to deprive the victims of access to the educational opportunities or benefits provided by the school." Id. In assessing the adequacy of remedial responses, courts should not expect that administrators can entirely "purg[e] their schools of actionable peer harassment" and "should refrain from second-guessing [administrators'] disciplinary decisions. Id. at 648.

Critics of the *Gebser* standard generally found *Davis* problematic on the same grounds. Although the decision clearly represents progress over the previous lower court rulings that had denied liability for peer harassment under any circumstances, it still creates an incentive for educators to avoid knowledge that might subject them to legal accountability. Could a plaintiff prove "reckless indifference" if she did not complain about harassment because there was no publicized complaint channel? The problem is compounded by lower court rulings that require notice to be given to a school board member or senior supervisor with authority to ensure Title IX compliance. Joan E. Schaffner, Davis v. Monroe County Board of Education: The Unresolved Questions, 21 Women's Rts. L. Rep., 79, 88-90 (2000). See, e.g., Floyd v. Walters, 171 F.3d 1264 (11th Cir. 1999); cf. Canutilla Independent School District v. Leija, 101 F.3d 393, 394-400 (5th Cir. 1996), cert. denied, 520 U.S. 1265 (1997). Given the reluctance of students to complain to anyone, such requirements often may create an unrealistic limitation on accountability where other, less senior school personnel had knowledge of a problem and failed to take reasonable remedial action. See AAUW, Hostile Hallways, supra, at 4, 7 (finding that only 7 percent of the 81 percent of students who had been sexually harassed had told a teacher).

On the other hand, argues Deborah L. Brake, the deliberate indifference test may be superior to an alternative, discriminatory intent standard insofar as it focuses on and acknowledges the role schools play in exacerbating the harm that results from sexual harassment instead of engaging in the elusive and difficult search for discriminatory intent. See Brake, School Liability for Peer Sexual Harassment After *Davis*: Shifting from Intent to Causation in Discrimination Law, 12 Hastings Women's L.J. 5 (2001).

Would a preferable approach be for state or federal legislation to hold schools to the same standards applicable to employment cases? Justice Ginsberg proposes such standards in her *Gebser* dissent. In essence, her approach would impose liability on school districts even if they lacked specific knowledge of harassment unless they had an effective policy for reporting and redressing such abuse that the complainant failed to use. 524 U.S. at 304 (Ginsberg, J., dissenting). See Doe v. Covington County School Board, 969 F. Supp. 1264 (M.D. Ala. 1997), aff'd, 233 F.3d 1367 (11th Cir. 2000), cert. denied sub nom. Davis v. DeKalb Sch. Dist., 121 S. Ct. 2217 (2001) (holding that if school fails to develop and publish an adequate grievance system, school officials cannot avoid liability by claiming lack of notice of harassment); Verna L. Williams & Deborah L. Brake, When a Kiss Isn't Just a Kiss: Title IX and Student-to-Student Harassment, 30 Creighton L. Rev. 423 (1997); Amy M. Rubin, Peer Sexual Harassment: Existing Harassment Doctrine and Its Application to School Children, 8 Hastings Women's L.J. 141 (1997); Jill Suzanne Miller, Title VI and Title VII: Happy Together as a Resolution of Title IX Peer Sexual Harassment Claims, 1995 U. Ill. L. Rev. 699.

Alternatively, would a better approach be the standards developed by the U.S. Department of Education's Office for Civil Rights (OCR) prior to the Court's decisions in *Gebser* and *Davis*? See Sexual Harassment Guidance: Harassment of Students by School Employees, Other Students, or Third Parties, 62 Fed. Reg. 12034 (March 13, 1997). Under the original Guidelines, a school could be liable for quid pro quo sexual harassment by an "employee in a position of authority, such as teacher or administrator, whether or not it knew or should have known . . . of the harassment at issue." Id. at 12039. In the case of elementary school students, the Guidelines treated any sexual relationship with an adult school employee as nonconsensual and also created a "strong presumption" that such a relationship with a secondary student is nonconsensual. With respect to postsecondary students, the Guidelines set forth a range of factors to determine whether sexual overtures were welcome, including the nature of the relationship, the degree of an employee's influence over the student, and the student's ability to consent. Id. at 12040. According to the Guidelines, strict liability for employee harassment reflects well-established agency law that makes institutions responsible for abuse of their authority. Id. at 12039. The rationale for that accountability in educational contexts is the same as in other workplace settings: employers should bear the costs of harassment because they are in the best position to prevent it.

The OCR Guidelines also authorized institutional liability for sexual harassment by students that creates a hostile environment under two circumstances: if schools lacked effective harassment policies and procedures or if administrators knew or should have known of the abusive conduct and failed to take "immediate and appropriate corrective action." Id. at 12039-12040. The rationale for a negligence rather than a strict liability standard is that students are not agents of a school and peer harassment is more common and more difficult to prevent in the absence of notice than employees' misconduct. However, unlike the Court's approach in *Davis*, this standard would have required school officials to take reasonable steps to investigate and respond to abusive conduct that is plainly visible, serious, and pervasive.

School officials have generally opposed a strict liability standard on the ground that they have limited control over abusive conduct. While other employers can dismiss workers who persist in harassment, administrators believe that they have fewer options in the face of recalcitrant students or faculty who have their own due process rights. Where facts are contested or ambiguous, officials feel "caught in the middle. . . . We weren't doing the harassing. We're the entity with the deep pockets." Guy W. Horsley, quoted in Robin Wilson, William and Mary Seeks to Shift Liability for Damages to Professor in Federal Sexual Harassment Case, Chronicle of Higher Education, June 9, 1995, at A20. The greater a school's responsibility to respond to severe and pervasive harassment, the greater the risk of expensive disputes over whether such harassment occurred and whether the response was adequate. As one school board attorney adds, "Schools are fighting for their financial survival, and every dollar in damages paid out in [sex harassment cases] is a dollar taken away from educational programs." Larry J. Frierson, quoted in Tamar Lewin, Students Seeking Damages for Sex Bias, N.Y. Times, July 15, 1994, at B12.

The proposed OCR Guidelines have been revised to conform to *Gebser* and *Davis*. See Revised Sexual Harassment Guidance: Harassment of Students by School Employees, Other Students, or Third Parties, 65 Fed. Reg. 66092 (Nov. 2, 2000).

Is it likely that judges and jurors would hold educational institutions liable if they had appropriate policies, procedures, and training and acted promptly to investigate and address complaints regardless of the standard? Recent research suggests that the vast majority of harassment victims do not seek substantial damages and that appropriate preventative and enforcement strategies reduce harassment and improve administrators' responses when complaints arise. Judith Berman Brandenberg, Confronting Sexual Harassment 1-13, 49-73 (1997); Bernice Resnick Sandler, Student-to-Student Sexual Harassment, in Sexual Harassment on Campus 55 (Bernice R. Sandler & Robert J. Shoop eds., 1997); Howard Gadlin, Mediating Sexual Harassment, in Sandler & Shoop, Sexual Harassment on Campus, supra, at 189; Elizabeth A. Williams et al., The Impact of a University Policy on the Sexual Harassment of Female Students, 63 U. Higher Educ. 50, 57-63 (1992). For examples of policies, see Sarah Diane Stevenson, The Revenge of the Hot Dog Slut: Peer Harassment After Davis v. Monroe, 10 S. Cal. Rev. L. & Women's Stud. 137 (2000). Such initiatives should include curricular and support programs, particularly for same-sex harassment where the frequency and severity of abuse is particularly pronounced. See Judy Mann, Where Homophobia Does the Most Harm, Wash. Post, Mar. 1, 2000, at C15.

Would another possibility be to impose §1983 liability when the harasser is a school agent? See Doe v. Taylor Independent School Dist., 15

F.3d 443 (5th Cir.) (en banc), cert. denied, 513 U.S. 815 (1994) (school district liable under §1983 for failure to take seriously warnings about teacher's predatory conduct toward female students, which eventually led to sexual intercourse with one student, when supervisory failures manifested a deliberate indifference to the constitutional rights of the student); Nabonzy v. Podelsny, 92 F.3d 446 (7th Cir. 1996) (concluding that reasonable fact-finder could find a §1983 violation based on harassment against gay male student). For the applicability of §1983 to sex abuse in schools, see Laura Oren, Section 1983 and Sex Abuse in Schools: Making a Federal Case Out of It, 72 Chi.-Kent L. Rev. 747 (1997).

c. Antiharassment Policies and Free Speech

One approach to addressing sexual and racial harassment in educational institutions, especially at the college and university level, has been speech codes that prohibit "verbal conduct" or "expression" that interferes with a student's ability to benefit from the educational environment. These codes have drawn fierce criticism from free speech advocates, who consider them a form of censorship and urge that the appropriate remedy for hurtful speech is not less, but more, speech. See, e.g., Nadine Strossen, Defending Pornography: Free Speech, Sex, and the Fight for Women's Rights (1995); Nadine Strossen, Regulating Racist Speech on Campus: A Modest Proposal?, 1990 Duke L.J. 484. Advocates of such regulation respond that in a sexist and racist society, "free speech" is available only to those with the power to exercise it, and anti-harassment codes are critical to protect the dignity and integrity of individuals who cannot effectively "fight back" with counterspeech. In the university setting, it is argued that official tolerance of racist and sexist speech prevents some students from participating fully in the university community and from developing their psychological and intellectual potential. See, e.g., Mari J. Matsuda, Charles R. Lawrence III, Richard Delgado, & Kimberlé Williams Crenshaw, Words That Wound: Critical Race Theory, Assaultive Speech, and the First Amendment (1993). Many commentators have identified the Internet as one of the sources of sexual harassment that should not be overlooked under university harassment codes. See, e.g., Evelyn Oldenkamp, Pornography, the Internet, and Student-to-Student Sexual Harassment: A Dilemma Resolved with Title VII and Title IX, 4 Duke J. Gender L. & Pol'y 159, 162 (1997) (arguing that openly viewing pornography in computer centers constitutes per se hostile environment sexual harassment that should be covered by university conduct codes); David K. McGraw, Note, Sexual Harassment in Cyberspace: The Problem of Unwelcome E-mail, 21 Rutgers Computer & Tech. L.J. 491 (1995) (proposing regulation analogous to current obscene phone call statutes to protect victims of unwanted, harassing e-mail).

For the most part, speech codes have not fared well in the courts. In general, the Supreme Court has permitted restrictions on expression that would substantially interfere with the "basic educational mission" or that would "impinge upon the rights of others." Bethel School District No. 403 v. Fraser, 478 U.S. 675 (1986); Tinker v. Des Moines Independent Community School District, 393 U.S. 503, 512-513 (1969). However, the Court also has viewed academic freedom as a "special concern of the First Amendment, which does not tolerate laws that cast a pall of orthodoxy over the classroom." Keyishian v. Board of Regents of the University of the State of New York, 385 U.S. 589, 590 (1967). The tension between schools' interests in both preventing harassment and protecting expression has provoked increasing disputes, but no Supreme Court decision and few lower court rulings. One decision concerned a Michigan regulation prohibiting "[a]ny behavior, verbal or physical, that stigmatizes or victimizes an individual on the basis of race, ethnicity, religion, sex, sexual orientation, creed, national origin, ancestry, age, marital status, handicap or Vietnam-era veteran status, and that . . . [i]nvolves an express or implied threat to . . . or has the purpose or reasonably foreseeable effect of interfering with an individual's academic efforts, employment, participation in University sponsored extra-curricular activities or personal safety." A psychology graduate student challenged the regulation, claiming that his discussion of "controversial theories positing biologically-based differences between sexes and races might be perceived as 'sexist' and 'racist' by some students" and would thus be "chilled" by the regulation. The regulation was invalidated as impermissibly overbroad and vague. Doe v. University of Michigan, 721 F. Supp. 852 (E.D. Mich. 1989). The Third Circuit Court of Appeals reached a similar result in Saxe v. State College Area School District, 240 F.3d 200 (3d Cir. 2001), with respect to a policy defining harassment as "verbal, written or physical conduct which offends, denigrates or belittles an individual . . . [including] unsolicited derogatory remarks, jokes, demeaning comments or behaviors, slurs, mimicking, name calling, graffiti, innuendo, gestures, physical conduct, stalking, [and]threatening [or] bullying [con-duct]." Id. at 202, 203. A University of Wisconsin code prohibiting speech and other expressive conduct that intentionally demeans individuals based on certain protected categories and "create[s] an intimidating, hostile, or demeaning environment for education . . . or other university-authorized activity" was also found unconstitutionally vague and overbroad. See UWM Post, Inc. v. Board of Regents of Univ. of Wisconsin, 774 F. Supp. 1163 (E.D. Wis. 1991).

When these codes have been used against classroom behavior by professors, courts have been similarly protective of First Amendment concerns. For example, one federal trial court held that a university could not impose sanctions for sexually related speech under a policy prohibiting "[u]nwelcome sexual advances, requests for sexual favors and other verbal or physical conduct of a sexual nature. " The case involved a university writing professor who was suspended without pay for a period of at least one year and required to complete counseling based on the following conduct.

On February 24, 1992, Silva made the following statement to his technical writing class,

> I will put focus in terms of sex, so you can better understand it. Focus is like sex. You seek a target. You zero in on your subject. You move from side to side. You close in on the subject. You bracket the subject and center on it. Focus connects experience and language. You and the subject become one. . . .

Two days later, during the second technical writing class session at issue, Silva employed the following pedagogical approach:

> I used Little Egypt's definition of belly dancing to illustrate how a good definition combines a general classification (belly dancing) with concrete specifics in a metaphor (like jello shimmying on a plate) to bring home clearly the meaning to one who wishes to learn this form of ethnic dancing.

Specifically, Silva stated to his class, "Belly dancing is like jello on a plate with a vibrator under the plate." . . . Silva explains,

> I used the definition to catch the attention of my class to gain their attention when they did not comprehend the explanation. . . .

> Little Egypt's definition of belly dancing is classic in its use of concrete differentia and simple metaphor, i.e., the trembling jello equates to the essential movements necessary to the dance. It is unlike the dance but also its very essence. . . .

> The intellectual task was to increase the student's understanding of definition and apply it in her own attempts to define concepts in her technical report, using the simple example as a model. . . .

Silva v. University of New Hampshire, 888 F. Supp. 293, 299 (D.N.H. 1994). Do you believe that these statements violate the policy? If so, are they protected by the First Amendment? Eight formal complaints were submitted to the university, including the following:

> I find Don Silva's constant referrals to sex offensive. He has yet to hold a class in which he did not make a sexually suggestive, or bluntly sexual statement. . . . I am not a prude, but this is not an appropriate way for a writing teacher to communicate with his students. I have three daughters. I would not want this man teaching them.

> I felt that [Professor Silva's comments] were disgusting & unnecessary — he assumed all kids present had experience with vibrators, which I find personally insulting, and I felt that the young women, right out of High School, were being seriously degraded.

Professor Silva responded:

> The comparison was on an intellectual plane and the purpose was to relate an abstract comment to everyday experiences most students are familiar with. . . . I used the definition [of belly dancing] to catch the attention of my class. . . .

The trial court was persuaded. The judge held that the school's harassment policy as applied to Silva's classroom speech "is not reasonably related to the legitimate pedagogical purpose of providing a congenial academic environment because it employs an impermissibly subjective standard that fails to take into account the nation's interest in academic freedom." Id. at 314.

A similar anti-harassment policy prohibiting verbal, written, or physical conduct that has the "effect of . . . creating an intimidating, hostile, or offensive learning environment" was found impermissibly vague in another case involving a university writing instructor who discussed subjects such as obscenity, cannibalism, and consensual sex with children in a "devil's advocate" style. Cohen v. San Bernardino Valley College, 92 F.3d 968 (9th Cir. 1996), cert. denied, 520 U.S. 1140 (1997). See also Levin v. Harleston, 770 F. Supp. 895 (S.D.N.Y. 1991), aff'd in part and vacated in part, 966 F.2d 85 (2d Cir. 1992) (absent evidence of harm to students in classroom, public university violated free speech rights of a tenured professor, who advanced views outside the classroom about the intellectual inferiority of blacks, by creating alternative "shadow classes" for his courses).

The law is developing in the other direction in Canada, where the Supreme Court of Canada upheld a statute penalizing the communication of statements that willfully promote hatred against any identifiable racial, religious, or ethnic group, in the context of a conviction of a high school teacher for instructing his students in various anti-Semitic views, including the view that the Holocaust was a myth. See Regina v. Keegstra, [1990] 3 S.C.R. 697.

Which approach would you favor? Should professors be sanctioned for sexually explicit discussion that is unrelated to the subject under consideration? Should they be subject to training workshops, public meetings, open forums, letters, course evaluations, or collective protests? How would you deal with complaints against a law professor who gave as a part of a first year criminal law exam a hypothetical titled "Revenge of the Big Monkey," consisting of a composite of actual cases involving a victim of a sexual assault who had unsuccessfully sought a late-term abortion? The defendant, following the mandates of a religious cult, attacked the woman and killed her fetus, for which she expressed gratitude. A critique and a defense of the way the complaints over this incident were handled are set forth in Harvey A. Silvergate, Teach at Your Own Risk, Nat'l L. J., Dec. 11, 2000, at A19, and David Leebron, Big Question on Columbia Exam, Nat'l L. J., Jan. 15, 2001, at A21.

d. Faculty-Student Relationships

Faculty-student dating has been another subject of campus concern. The limited available data suggest that such relationships are not uncommon. See Kimberly A. Mango, Comment, Students Versus Professors: Combating Sexual Harassment Under Title IX of the Education Amendments of 1972, 23 Conn. L. Rev. 355, 359-360 (1991) (citing survey findings that a quarter of male faculty at one University of California campus had sexual relationships with a student). Only a small minority of colleges and universities have rules banning sexual relationships between teachers and students under their supervision. See Sherry Young, Getting to Yes: The Case Against Banning Consensual Relationships in Higher Education, 4 Am. U. J. Gender & L., 269, 272-273 (1996); Jerome W.D. Stokes & D. Frank Vinik, Consensual Sexual Relations Between Faculty and Students in Higher Education, 96 Ed. Law Rptr. 899 (1995). The conventional assumption is that broad prohibitions are unnecessary, unenforceable, or unduly paternalistic. For example, opponents of categorical rules maintain:

> "Being sexually propositioned . . . is a normal and healthy part of life. (The real psychological and emotional tragedy probably befalls those who are not)." Edward Greer, What's Wrong with Faculty-Student Sex? Response I, 47 J. Legal Educ. 437, 438 (1997).
>
> "It is hardly self evident that the 'power imbalance' in such [relationships] favors the teacher. . . . If matters turn out badly, his career is finished." Id.
>
> "The urge to merge is a powerful one. . . . "Dan Sabotnik, What's Wrong with Faculty-Student Sex? Response II, 47 J. Legal Educ. 441, 443 (1997).
>
> "You can't legislate love." Dan Blatt, quoted in University of Virginia Considers Wide Ban on Intimate Teacher-Student Ties, N.Y. Times, Apr. 14, 1993, at A22.
>
> Consensual relationships "are none of the university's business." University of Texas at Arlington faculty, quoted in Elisabeth A. Keller, Consensual Amorous Relationships Between Faculty and Students: The Constitutional Right to Privacy, 15 J. College & Univ. L. 21, 22 (1988).

Some feminists raise other concerns. Literary critic Jane Gallop argues that women are at a "disadvantage" in a faculty-student relationship, but believes that "denying women the right to consent further infantilizes us." Jane Gallop, Feminism and Harassment Policy, Academe, Sept.-Oct. 1994, at 16, 22. See also Jane Gallop, Feminist Accused of Sexual Harassment 41-43 (1997). Law Professor Sherry Young similarly maintains that "[f]eminists should not be in the business of reducing the range of choice available to women, no matter how much they may question the wisdom of some of the choices that are made. . . . Feminists should not promote an image of women as helpless victims incapable of functioning under conditions of inequality of power. . . . The most pernicious idea to emerge from the debate on consensual relationship policies is the notion that feminists should be in the business of questioning the capacity of women, limiting the choices available to women, or urging institutions to disregard the testimony of women about their lives, their aspirations, and their emotional commitments." Young, supra, at 298, 302.

Compare Robin West's analysis:

Smart male students view themselves as all sorts of things, including young intellectuals. A good male student will often attach himself to a brilliant professor, and will aspire to *be like* him. . . . Unlike the male student, [the good female student] is more likely to be attracted to the brilliant professor, and aspire not to be like him, but to give herself *to* him. In her own way the "giving" female student will seek the recognition and praise which all students crave, by offering her sexuality. She may be intellectually gifted and she may perceive herself as such. But to the extent that the female student . . . tries to define herself as an intellectual, she does so at the cost of internal war. For the definition of "self" as a sexually giving self rather than an academically demanding self is always there, always in competition, always available. For the female student, the intellectual self must fight the giving self, both in external and internal reality. The women who lose this battle have lost far more than the women who lost the A to which they were entitled, and so has the world. . . .

. . . "Falling-in-love" with high school teachers, college professors, or research assistants really does destroy the productivity, the careers, the earning potential, and eventually the self respect of many gifted women. Smart women drop out of high school, college and graduate school (and pretty women are at the highest risk) to date, marry, to help, and to serve those they perceive as intellectual giants. Eventually they learn boredom, the weariness of inactivity, and the self-contempt of nonproductivity. But in spite of its incredible familiarity, most academic men and many academic women do not see this worth discussing. This ignorance must be ideological. My guess is that we cannot see the harm of these consensual relationships to precisely the degree to which we have adopted the blinders of liberalism. It is a harm caused not by coercive, occasional acts, but by the way we have defined the self that consents to the non-coercive relationship in which we engage. It is a harm that a liberal legal regime which resolutely regards the giving of consent as the infallible proxy of an increase in self-regarded and self-assessed value cannot possibly address.

Robin L. West, The Difference in Women's Hedonic Lives: A Phenomenological Critique of Feminist Legal Theory, 3 Wis. Women's L.J. 81, 109-111 (1987).

Other feminists agree. In part, their concerns are based on students' own accounts of sexual overtures by faculty. In one representative study, almost three-quarters of those who rejected a professor's advances considered them coercive and about half of those who had sexual relationships believed that some degree of coercion was involved. See surveys discussed in Caroline Forell, What's Wrong with Faculty-Student Sex? The Law School

Context, 47 J. Legal Educ. 1, 49 n.11, 57 n.39, 41 (1997). Moreover, "faculty whose self-image and self-interest are at stake may underestimate the pressures that students experience. Regardless of the teacher's own intentions, students may believe that their acceptance or rejection of sexual overtures will have academic consequences. Given the power disparities involved, even relationships that appear consensual at the outset may become less so over time." Rhode, Sex in Schools, supra.

Many feminists also doubt that power differentials can be offset by students' theoretical remedies for harassment. Except in egregious cases, few students have been willing to file complaints, and few institutions have been willing to impose serious sanctions. Some campus codes lack adequate authorization for such sanctions, and even where the rules are clear, the evidence often is not. Moreover, most campus enforcement structures address only those faculty-student sexual relationships that meet conventional definitions of sexual harassment. But many feminists believe that the harms to both individuals and institutions can be significant even in the absence of an explicit quid pro quo or a pervasive hostile environment. In relationships where the professor has any advisory or supervisory authority over the student, both the fact and the appearance of academic integrity are at risk. Even when the relationship is fully consensual, the potential for unconscious bias in evaluation, recommendations, and mentoring is inescapable. And even if the professor does not in fact offer or deliver special advantages, others may suspect favoritism, and the reputation of both parties to the relationship may be compromised. Neither the student nor others whose opinions matter can trust the objectivity of the professor's assessment. Forell, supra; see also Carol Sanger, The Erotics of Torts, 96 Mich. L. Rev. 1852 (1998) (reviewing Jane Gallop, Feminist Accused of Sexual Harassment, supra).

A few schools attempt to discourage faculty-student relationships through prohibitions, warnings and aspirational standards. William and Mary bans "amorous relations between faculty and undergraduates," or between graduate students and their supervisors. Diana Jean Schemo, William & Mary: Not if She's His Student, N.Y. Times, Dec. 2, 2001, at A34. The University of Minnesota Policy on Consensual Relationships states that faculty-student relationships, "while not expressly forbidden, are generally deemed very unwise" and warns professors that it considers their power "to greatly diminish the student's actual freedom of choice," which will make it "exceedingly difficult" for the professor to prove consent if a charge of harassment is brought. See Young, supra, at 273 (citing Minnesota policy from The Educator's Guide, app. V, at 275). The University of Michigan, the University of California at Santa Cruz, and New York University Law School have similar precatory policies or presumptions. Policies at Yale, Harvard, Temple, Tufts, the University of Iowa, and the University of Virginia forbid faculty-student relationships where the professor has direct academic responsibility for the student. Id. at 273-275; Patrick

Dilger, Putting an End to Risky Romance, Yale Alumni Mag., Apr. 1998, at 30.

Do policies that attempt to discourage student-faculty dating stereotype or infantilize female students? Why do you suppose more campuses have not adopted rules requiring students in a dating relationship with a supervising faculty member to transfer or to obtain other arrangements for assessment of their work?

Putting Theory into Practice

4-8. For each of the following problems, state (1) whether the conduct constitutes sexual harassment; (2) whether it would be appropriate for a university to attempt to prohibit the conduct through rules and regulations; and (3) if the conduct is undesirable, what types of nonregulatory strategies a university might wisely engage in.

a. A male college student pursues a female student for a date. He calls her frequently on the phone, and when he sees her on campus, he approaches her and asks her to go out with him. She repeatedly refuses and tells him that she does not want him to keep calling her or approaching her for dates or for any other reason. He persists. He has never touched her.

b. One fraternity on campus has an annual "red light district" party. All female students who attend are required to dress as prostitutes. At the party, the male students simulate "pick-ups" of the prostitutes. Invariably, some "mock" solicitations develop during that evening into actual seductions. Another fraternity invites a stripper to perform on campus the routine she offers at a local club.

c. A university professor finds himself attracted to one of his students, whom he feels is also attracted to him. Aware of the problems that can arise with faculty-student dating, he attempts to put his feelings of attraction aside. After picking up more and more "signals" that the student would welcome some initiative on his part, however, he finally asks her out for coffee one afternoon. This leads to an invitation to attend university events such as lectures and to come as his guest to dinners for visiting professors.

d. Students post anatomically explicit and derogatory remarks on a male-only computer bulletin board. Other students circulate a poster with a nude caricature of a woman candidate for office of a student organization and send to an e-mail list of 20 friends a parody titled "Top 75 Reasons Why Women [Bitches] Should Not Have Freedom of Speech."

e. Male students claim that an openly gay male professor has come on to them sexually by leering at them after class and by including favorable references to same-sex relationships in his lectures on ancient Greece. One student claims that the professor brushed his buttocks when leaving class in a crowded corridor.

C. DOMINANCE THEORY AND DOMESTIC VIOLENCE

1. Domestic Violence: The Problem

State v. Norman
378 S.E.2d 8 (N.C. 1989)

MITCHELL, Justice.

. . . At trial, the State presented the testimony of Deputy Sheriff R.H. Epley of the Rutherford County Sheriff's Department, who was called to the Norman residence on the night of 12 June 1985. Inside the home, Epley found the defendant's husband, John Thomas Norman, lying on a bed in a rear bedroom with his face toward the wall and his back toward the middle of the room. He was dead. . . . A later autopsy revealed three gunshot wounds to the head, two of which caused fatal brain injury. The autopsy also revealed a .12 percent blood alcohol level in the victim's body.

Later that night, the defendant related an account of the events leading to the killing. . . . The defendant told Epley that her husband had been beating her all day and had made her lie down on the floor while he slept on the bed. After her husband fell asleep, the defendant carried her grandchild to the defendant's mother's house. The defendant took a pistol from her mother's purse and walked the short distance back to her home. She pointed the pistol at the back of her sleeping husband's head, but it jammed the first time she tried to shoot him. She fixed the gun and then shot her husband in the back of the head as he lay sleeping. After one shot, she felt her husband's chest and determined that he was still breathing and making sounds. She then shot him twice more in the back of the head. The defendant told Epley that she killed her husband because "she took all she was going to take from him so she shot him."

The defendant presented evidence tending to show a long history of physical and mental abuse by her husband due to his alcoholism. At the time of the killing, the thirty-nine-year-old defendant and her husband had been married almost twenty-five years and had several children. The defendant testified that her husband had started drinking and abusing her about five years after they were married. His physical abuse of her consisted of frequent assaults that included slapping, punching and kicking her, striking her with various objects, and throwing glasses, beer bottles and other objects at her. The defendant described other specific incidents of abuse, such as her husband putting her cigarettes out on her, throwing hot coffee on her, breaking glass against her face and crushing food on her face. Although the defendant did not present evidence of ever having received medical treatment for any physical injuries inflicted by her husband, she displayed several scars about her face which she attributed to her husband's assaults.

The defendant's evidence also tended to show other indignities inflicted upon her by her husband. Her evidence tended to show that her husband did not work and forced her to make money by prostitution, and that he made humor of that fact to family and friends. He would beat her if she resisted going out to prostitute herself or if he was unsatisfied with the amounts of money she made. He routinely called the defendant "dog," "bitch" and "whore," and on a few occasions made her eat pet food out of the pets' bowls and bark like a dog. He often made her sleep on the floor. At times, he deprived her of food and refused to let her get food for the family. During those years of abuse, the defendant's husband threatened numerous times to kill her and to maim her in various ways.

The defendant said her husband's abuse occurred only when he was intoxicated, but that he would not give up drinking. She said she and her husband "got along very well when he was sober," and that he was "a good guy" when he was not drunk. She had accompanied her husband to the local mental health center for sporadic counseling sessions for his problem, but he continued to drink.

In the early morning hours on the day before his death, the defendant's husband, who was intoxicated, went to a rest area off I-85 near Kings Mountain where the defendant was engaging in prostitution and assaulted her. While driving home, he was stopped by a patrolman and jailed on a charge of driving while impaired. After the defendant's mother got him out of jail at the defendant's request later that morning, he resumed his drinking and abuse of the defendant.

The defendant's evidence also tended to show that her husband seemed angrier than ever after he was released from jail and that his abuse of the defendant was more frequent. That evening, sheriff's deputies were called to the Norman residence, and the defendant complained that her husband had been beating her all day and she could not take it anymore. The defendant was advised to file a complaint, but she said she was afraid her husband would kill her if she had him arrested. The deputies told her they needed a warrant before they could arrest her husband, and they left the scene.

The deputies were called back less than an hour later after the defendant had taken a bottle of pills. The defendant's husband cursed her and called her names as she was attended by paramedics, and he told them to let her die. A sheriff's deputy finally chased him back into his house as the defendant was put into an ambulance. The defendant's stomach was pumped at the local hospital, and she was sent home with her mother.

While in the hospital, the defendant was visited by a therapist with whom she discussed filing charges against her husband and having him committed for treatment. Before the therapist left, the defendant agreed to go to the mental health center the next day to discuss those possibilities. The therapist testified at trial that the defendant seemed depressed in the hospital, and that she expressed considerable anger toward her husband. He testified that the defendant threatened a number of times that night to kill her husband and that she said she should kill him "because of the things he had done to her."

The next day, the day she shot her husband, the defendant went to the mental health center to talk about charges and possible commitment, and she confronted her husband with that possibility. She testified that she told her husband later that day: "J.T., straighten up. Quit drinking. I'm going to have you committed to help you." She said her husband then told her he would "see them coming" and would cut her throat before they got to him.

The defendant also went to the social services office that day to seek welfare benefits, but her husband followed her there, interrupted her interview and made her go home with him. He continued his abuse of her, threatening to kill and to maim her, slapping her, kicking her, and throwing objects at her. At one point, he took her cigarette and put it out on her, causing a small burn on her upper torso. He would not let her eat or bring food into the house for their children.

That evening, the defendant and her husband went into their bedroom to lie down, and he called her a "dog" and made her lie on the floor when he lay down on the bed. Their daughter brought in her baby to leave with the defendant, and the defendant's husband agreed to let her baby-sit. After the defendant's husband fell asleep, the baby started crying and the defendant took it to her mother's house so it would not wake up her husband. She returned shortly with the pistol and killed her husband.

The defendant testified at trial that she was too afraid of her husband to press charges against him or to leave him. She said that she had temporarily left their home on several previous occasions, but he had always found her, brought her home and beaten her. Asked why she killed her husband, the defendant replied: "Because I was scared of him and I knowed when he woke up, it was going to be the same thing, and I was scared when he took me to the truck stop that night it was going to be worse then he had ever been. I just couldn't take it no more. There ain't no way, even if it means going to prison. It's better than living in that. That's worse hell than anything."

The defendant and other witnesses testified that for years her husband had frequently threatened to kill her and to maim her. When asked if she believed those threats, the defendant replied: "Yes. I believed him; he would, he would kill me if he got a chance. If he thought he wouldn't a had to went to jail, he would a done it."

[The Norman case is continued on page 660.]

Karla Fischer, Neil Vidmar, and René Ellis, *The Culture of Battering and the Role of Mediation in Domestic Violence Cases*
46 SMU L. Rev. 2117, 2141, 2121-2122, 2126-2130, 2133, 2135-2138 (1993)

The culture of battering refers to the relationship context of an abusive relationship. The first of the three elements of the culture of battering is the abuse, which includes at least one of the following types: physical, emotional, sexual, familial, and property. Professionals have increasingly recognized non-physical forms of abuse as harmful to domestic violence victims. The second element is the systematic pattern of domination and control that the batterer exerts over his victim. This pattern may be initiated by the batterer's gradual imposition of a series of rules that his victim must follow or be punished for violating. Over time, victims may censor their own behavior in anticipation of yet-unexpressed rules. The abuser's rein on the members of the household is enhanced by the use of emotional abuse and financial and social isolation, all of which help keep the victim in fear of impending abuse. Victims may engage in episodes of rebellion or resistance to the rules, which are nearly always met with more serious violence. Even separating from the abuser, an act of rebellion by itself, does not secure the end of the abuse; rather, it frequently escalates it. The third element, hiding, denying, and minimizing the abuse, refers to typical coping strategies that battered women use to reduce the psychological impact of the abuse. Each of these elements to some degree must be present in order for a culture of battering to be established. . . .

As sociologist Liz Kelly has noted, the prevailing stereotype about domestic violence is that assaults are "physical, frequent, and life threatening." Yet, the reality of battered women's lives does not conform solely to this image. Advocates for battered women have long noted that financial abuse and property abuse are forms of emotional abuse inflicted upon women. Abusers frequently restrict women's access to money and destroy their personal property in an effort to gain control over them or keep them in a state of fear. Emotional and sexual abuse may be even more common. Forms of emotional abuse include acts that do not constitute overt threats of injury or violence, such as constant humiliation, insults, degradation, and ridicule. Of course, explicit threats to harm or kill, including those attached to vivid descriptions of the method the abuser would use to carry it out, also have emotional consequences. The abuser may extend threats of harm to the victim's extended family or her children. . . .

Battered women have frequently reported that abusers are extremely controlling of the everyday activities of the family. This domination can be all encompassing: as one of the batterers from Angela Browne's study was fond of stating, "[y]ou're going to dance to my music . . . be the kind of wife I want you to be." Charlotte Fedders' account of the escalating rules imposed by her husband over the course of their seventeen year, extremely violent marriage is particularly illuminating about the range of control that abusers can exert. Her husband insisted that no one (including guests and their toddler children) wear shoes in the house, that the furniture be in the same indentations in the carpet, that the vacuum marks in the carpet be parallel, and that any sand spilled from the children's sandbox during their play be removed from the surrounding grass. Charlotte was not allowed to write checks from their joint checking account. Any real or perceived infraction of these rules could result in her husband beating her, or at the very least, the expression of his irritation that was frequently a harbinger to a beating.

Typically, battered women talk to the men about the abuse, partly as an attempt to concretize the rules that are connected to the absence of abuse. In turn, many abusers promise to stop the abuse. One abuser in Browne's study formalized such discussions into a written document, where he set forth a list of conditions that his victim was to agree to in exchange for cessation of his violence. These conditions were: (1) the children were to keep their rooms clean without being told; (2) the children could not argue with each other; (3) he was to have absolute freedom to come and go as he wished, and could have a girlfriend if he wanted one; (4) she would perform oral sex on him anytime he requested; and (5) she would have anal sex with him. He enforced this document shortly after she "agreed" to it and continued to sexually assault her until his death. This abuser simply made explicit the rules in the relationship and made it obvious that abuse was the punishment for violating the rules.

In many abusive relationships, however, the rules do not need to be verbally expressed to create a family atmosphere controlled by the batterer. Charlotte Fedders' story is a prototype of a battered woman who becomes very good at reading nonverbal messages from her abuser. She writes of how she restricted the play of her four young boys in order to avoid her husband's increasingly subtle signs of displeasure:

> Eventually . . . we just stopped using the living room and the family room because little things out of place would make him angry. . . . If [the boys'] rooms were a mess, he'd complain to me, so I was reluctant to let them play there. So they pretty much played in the basement. . . . I'd let them play only in the backyard, not the front, because John was so proud and particular about it. He wanted it perfectly green, and orderly. . . . He didn't like my putting a swing set up for the kids in the backyard, so it had to go all the way in the back, where no one would see it.

[Charlotte Fedders & Laura Eliott, Shattered Dreams 140-141 (1987).]

The characteristics of the Fedders' marriage are consistent with accounts reported by other battered women indicating that the violence does not need to be a constant presence for the victims to feel threatened that it could erupt at any point, nor does the explosion always have to be physical. Violence need only symbolize the threat of future abuse in order to keep the victim in fear and control her behavior. . . .

As time goes on in a battering relationship, as in the Fedders' case, specific rules and their attached consequences give way to a general climate of increasingly subtle control, where the batterer needs to do less and less to structure his family's behavior. Caught up in the day to day fight for survival, the victims may not even be aware of this censorship process. . . .

What fuels this self censorship process is the responsibility the victim feels, both as a woman socialized into believing that making relationships work is her job, and the responsibility added by the abuser, who blames her for the "failure" of the relationship, as evidenced by the occurrence of abuse. Women are taught in our society to care for others, to make decisions around what is best for other people, even if it denigrates their own needs. Batterers reinforce this societal message by consistently blaming women for everything that goes awry in their lives. The end result is manifested in frantic attempts by the woman to be the perfect wife, mother, and homemaker. . . .

The pattern of rule-making and rule-enforcing, nested within the control and domination exerted by the batterer over his family, is frequently interspersed with episodes of rebellion by the victims. . . . These resistance incidents are not initiated with ignorance on the part of victims, and they are very much aware that any type of challenge to the batterer is likely to result in further, perhaps escalating, violence. . . .

. . . Fischer specifically asked the battered women in her study who had obtained court protective orders about the methods they had employed in attempting to stop the violence. Of the thirty-one strategies described, the women in her sample had tried an average of thirteen different strategies, including talking to the abuser about the abuse, consulting family and friends, calling the police, leaving him, and seeking counseling or legal advice. Fischer concluded that the number and variety of strategies tried suggests that battered women continue over time to increase their helpseeking rather than to decrease it and become passive. . . .

Our argument that abuse occurs within a relationship context of control and domination is an explicit rejection of the popular belief that abuse is simply a logical extension of a heated argument or disagreement. . . .

Battered women's narratives of the context of abuse suggests quite the opposite of conflict. Women are typically beaten in a variety of situations that could hardly be classified as conflict: while sleeping, while using the toilet, and while in another room that the batterer suddenly entered to begin his beating. The usual scenario women describe is that at one moment all is calm and in the next, there is a major, seemingly untriggered explosion:

> I remember walking in, got undressed, and put my robe on, and I was going to
> get a glass of milk. At one moment we were laying together and kissing and

everything seemed fine. And, it was like a second later, he was saying that I stayed out too late, and asked who was there and stuff, and then just . . . everything blew up. I know he threw me off the bed. And he told me he was going to beat me to death. And, then he said, "I'm going to set the trailer on fire with you and your daughter in it." And then he goes, "well, first, bitch, you are going to get me a glass of ice water."

In addition to the information about context, batterers' behavior during abusive incidents does not support an image that these men are out of control with anger. Women have reported deliberate, calculating behavior, ranging from searching for and destroying a treasured object of hers to striking her in areas of her body that do not show bruises (e.g. her scalp) or in areas where she would be embarrassed to show others her bruises.

Anger and conflict may be frequently confused with violence because both can be a proxy for abuse. The abuser may in fact be angry when he beats his victim or a conflict over what she has served for dinner may have developed before the incident of violence. But this simple coexistence in time does not mean that the anger or conflict has caused the violence. Lurking underneath the surface anger or conflict is the batterer's need to express his power over his victim. Even if the anger is controlled and all sources of conflict are removed from the relationship, violence still occurs. After all, batterers are usually involved in other social relationships, at work or elsewhere, where they become angry or have conflicts with others that they do not abuse. Their ability to cope with anger in some situations but not at home suggests that conflict and anger are not at the root of domestic violence. Perhaps the best evidence, however, that abuse is not about anger or conflict is that violence continues to occur, frequently escalating, after women leave their abusers.

≡≡≡ *Martha R. Mahoney, Legal Images of Battered*
≡≡≡ *Women: Redefining the Issue of Separation*
≡≡≡ 90 Mich. L. Rev. 1, 2-3, 5-7 (1991)

The courtroom is the theater in which the dramas of battered women have been brought to public attention. Trials like that of Francine Hughes, whose story became the book and movie The Burning Bed, create a cultural and legal spotlight that has in some ways benefited women by increasing public knowledge of the existence of domestic violence. However, the press has emphasized sensational cases that have a high level of terrorism against women and a grotesque quality of abuse. These cases come to define a cultural image of domestic violence, and the women in these cases define an image of battered women.

These images disguise the commonality of violence against women. Up to one half of all American women — and approximately two thirds of women who are separated or divorced — report having experienced physical assault in their relationships. However, litigation and judicial decisionmaking in cases of severe violence reflect implicit or explicit assumptions that domestic violence is rare or exceptional.

For actors in the courtroom drama, the fiction that such violence is exceptional allows denial of the ways in which domestic violence has touched their own lives. Perhaps most damagingly, the fiction of exceptionality also increases the capacity of women to deny that the stories told in the publicized courtroom dramas have anything to do with our own lives. Therefore, it limits the help we may seek when we encounter trouble, the charges we are willing to file, our votes as jurors when charges have been filed by or against others, and our consciousness of the meaning of the struggles and dangers of our own experience. . . .

. . . The question "why didn't she leave?" shapes both social and legal inquiry on battering; much of the legal reliance on academic expertise on battered women has developed in order to address this question. At the moment of separation or attempted separation — for many women, the first encounter with the authority of law — the batterer's quest for control often becomes most acutely violent and potentially lethal. Ironically, although the proliferation of shelters and the elaboration of statutory structures facilitating the grant of protective orders vividly demonstrate both socially and legally the dangers attendant on separation, a woman's "failure" to permanently separate from a violent relationship is still widely held to be mysterious and in need of explanation, an indicator of her pathology rather than her batterer's. We have had neither cultural names nor legal doctrines specifically tailored to the particular assault on a woman's body and volition that seeks to block her from leaving, retaliate for her departure, or forcibly end the separation. I propose that we name this attack "separation assault."

Separation assault is the common though invisible thread that unites the equal protection suits on enforcement of temporary restraining orders, the cases with dead women that appear in many doctrinal categories, and the cases with dead men — the self-defense cases. As with other assaults on women that were not cognizable until the feminist movement named and explained them, separation assault must be identified before women can recognize our own experience and before we can develop legal rules to deal with this particular sort of violence. Naming one particular aspect of the violence then illuminates the rest: for example, the very concept of "acquaintance rape" moves consciousness away from the stereotype of rape (assault by a stranger) and toward a focus on the woman's volition (violation of her will, "consent"). Similarly, by emphasizing the urgent control moves that seek to prevent the woman from ending the relationship, the concept of separation assault raises questions that inevitably focus additional attention on the ongoing struggle for power and control in the relationship. . . .

Notes

1. Defining Domestic Violence. The language used to describe physical and verbal attacks against intimate partners is evolving rapidly. Battered women's advocates initially introduced the term "domestic violence" to replace more colloquial terms such as "wife beating." More recently, some individuals and organizations have begun to use the terms "intimate violence" or "intimate partner violence," rather than "domestic violence," as a way of encompassing not only the abuse of women, but also the abuse of elders, children, and siblings. Mahoney's proposed term "separation assault" highlights the heightened danger the victims of intimate violence face when they attempt to leave the relationship.

Another moving target is the best way to describe the core of intimate partner violence. Domestic violence workers introduced the word "battering" to replace "beating." The popular meaning of "battering" is physical abuse, however, and many researchers (such as Fischer, Vidmar, and Ellis) now argue that the quest for control, and not physical violence per se, best characterizes a battering relationship. Thus, "battering" can be a problematic term to the extent that it leads investigators to look for broken bones rather than the sometimes subtle forms of self-censorship that Fischer, Vidmar, and Ellis describe. Incidents of stalking, death threats, isolation, and control over material necessities, for example, may not appear in studies of "battering" at all. Evan Stark, Re-Presenting Woman Battering: From Battered Woman Syndrome to Coercive Control, 58 Alb. L. Rev. 973, 983 (1995).

As the concept of "intimate partner violence" expands, is there a danger that all relationships marked by control issues will come to fall under its umbrella? Are Fischer, Vidmar, and Ellis persuasive in their attempt to clearly distinguish the relationships they consider pathological from ordinary conflict between intimates?

2. Incidence of Domestic Violence. Determining the frequency and severity of intimate violence is difficult both because varying criteria are used to define it and because intimate violence is an underreported phenomenon. Moreover, few studies have been done on violence against women as a whole. The National Research Council reports, "Most surveys have focused on single aspects of women's experiences of violence, such as rape or physical violence. For example, studies of intimate partner violence that neglect to ask about sexual violence may miss information on and understanding of marital rape." National Research Council, Understanding Violence Against Women 40-41 (1996).

One source of suggestive statistics is the National Violence Against Women Survey (NVAWS), conducted by the Center for Policy Research and co-sponsored by the National Institute of Justice and the Centers for Disease Control and Prevention. The survey consisted of telephone interviews with a nationally representative sample of 8,000 U.S. men and 8,000 U.S. women; the participants were asked about their experiences as victims of various kinds of violence, including intimate partner violence. Patricia Tjaden & Nancy Thoennes, Full Report of the Prevalence, Incidence, and Consequences of Violence Against Women, Findings from the National Violence Against Women Survey (NCJ 183781), Nov. 2000, available at http://www.ncjrs.org; see also Patricia Tjaden & Nancy Thoennes, Extent, Nature, and Consequences of Intimate Partner Violence, Findings from the National Violence Against Women Survey (NCJ 181867), July 2000. The July 2000 report analyzing survey results concluded:

> Intimate partner violence is pervasive in U.S. society. Nearly 25 percent of surveyed women and 7.6 percent of surveyed men said they were raped and/or physically assaulted by a current or former spouse, cohabiting partner, or date at some time in their lifetime; 1.5 percent of surveyed women and 0.9 percent of surveyed men said they were raped and/or physically assaulted by a partner in the previous 12 months. According to these estimates, approximately 1.5 million women and 834,732 men are raped and/or physically assaulted by an intimate partner annually in the United States. Because many victims are victimized more than once, the number of intimate partner victimizations exceeds the number of intimate partner victims annually. Thus, approximately 4.8 million intimate partner rapes and physical assaults are perpetrated against U.S. women annually, and approximately 2.9 million intimate partner physical assaults are committed against U.S. men annually.

Id. at iii.

Researchers have come to no consensus about whether women or men are more likely to be victimized by domestic violence. The NVAWS concluded that women are significantly more likely to be the victim of intimate violence than men. This conclusion is consistent with the finding of the Bureau of Justice Statistics' National Crime Victimization Survey that intimate violence is primarily a crime against women. See U.S. Department of Justice, Bureau of Justice Statistics, Summary Findings: Intimate Violence, available at http://www.ojp.usdoj.gov.bjs/cvict_c.htm#relate (in 1998, females were the victims in 72 percent of intimate murders and the victims in about 85 percent of the nonlethal intimate violence). However, the National Family Violence Survey found that men and women are equally likely to be physically assaulted by an intimate partner. See Murray A. Straus & Richard J. Gelles, Societal Change in Family Violence from 1975 to 1985 as Revealed by Two National Surveys, in Physical Violence in American Families: Risk Factors and Adaptations to Violence in 8,145 Families 119-120 (Murray A. Straus & Richard J. Gelles eds., 1990); Murray A. Straus, Physical Violence in American Families: Incidence Rates, Causes, and Trends, in Abused and Battered: Social and Legal Responses to Family Violence 17 (Dean D. Knudsen & Jo Ann L. Miller eds., 1990).

The conclusion that men are as likely to be victimized by intimate partner violence as women is strongly contested by researchers who argue that the studies reaching this conclusion fail to take account of the context of battering relationships.

> [T]he greater average size and strength of men, and their greater aggressiveness, mean that the same act (for example, a punch) is likely to be very different in the amount of pain or injury inflicted. Even more important, a great deal of violence by women against their husbands is retaliation or self-defense. One of the most fundamental reasons why some women are violent within the family, but not outside the family, is that the risk of assault for a typical American woman is greatest in her own home.

Straus & Gelles, in Physical Violence, supra, at 120. See also Elizabeth M. Schneider, Particularity and Generality: Challenges of Feminist Theory and Practice in Work on Woman-Abuse, 67 N.Y.U. L. Rev. 520, 540 n.80 (1992) (citing studies and literature critical of studies). Issues raised by battered women who strike back and assault or kill their abusers are considered in Section 3, beginning on page 652.

3. Characteristics of Domestic Violence. The physical assaults that characterize domestic violence may take many forms. While women are almost twice as likely to throw something at their husbands, husbands are more likely to beat up their wives, hit them with a fist, or engage in other, more violent acts. Richard J. Gelles & Murray A. Straus, Intimate Violence: The Causes and Consequences of Abuse in the American Family 250-251 (1988). The NVAWS report found that 39 percent of female intimate violence victims, compared with 24.8 percent of male intimate violence victims, reported being injured during their most recent physical assault. Tjaden & Thoennes, Full Report, supra, at iv; see also Tjaden & Thoennes, Extent, Nature, and Consequences, supra, at iv (finding that women experience more chronic and more injurious physical assaults at the hands of intimate partners than men).

The NVAWS data reveal a strong association between physical assault and control-seeking behavior. Women whose partners were jealous, controlling, or verbally abusive were significantly more likely to report being raped, physically assaulted, and/or stalked by their partners; indeed, having a verbally abusive partner was the variable most likely to predict victimization. Tjaden & Thoennes, Extent, Nature, and Consequences, supra, at iv.

The study also supported the conclusion that stalking is a serious problem in the United States. Almost 5 percent of surveyed women and 0.6 percent of surveyed men reported being stalked by a current or former spouse, cohabiting partner, or date during their lifetime, and 0.5 percent of surveyed women and 0.2 percent of surveyed men reported having been stalked within the past 12 months. Id. at iii. If these numbers are representative, 503,485 women and 185,496 men are stalked by an intimate partner annually in the United States. Id.

As Mahoney's excerpt above suggests, it is commonly believed that women are most likely to be injured by an intimate in the course of trying to end the relationship. The NVAWS report found that married women who lived apart from their husbands were nearly four times more likely to report that their husbands had raped, physically assaulted, and/or stalked them than women who lived with their husbands (20 percent and 5.4 percent, respectively). Tjaden & Thoennes, Extent, Nature, and Consequences, supra, at 37. Another study found that up to three-fourths of reported domestic assaults occur after the victim has left the batterer. See Barbara J. Hart, Gentle Jeopardy: The Further Endangerment of Battered Women and Children in Custody Mediation, 7 Mediation Q. 317, 324 (1990). It is not always clear in such studies, however, whether the violence triggered the separation or the separation triggered the violence.

Since domestic violence characteristically takes place in the home, children in the family are likely to be affected as well. An estimated minimum of 3.3 million children witness domestic violence each year. See Lee H. Bowker, Michelle Arbitell, & J. Richard McFerron, On the Relationship Between Wife Beating and Child Abuse, in Perspectives on Wife Abuse 158, 162 (Kersti Yllo & Michele Bograd eds., 1988). Effects that researchers have traced to witnessing abuse include "internalizing" effects such as depression, anxiety, and withdrawal, as well as "externalizing" effects such as aggression, "acting out" behaviors, and delinquency. See Stephen Doyne et al., Custody Disputes Involving Domestic Violence: Making Children's Needs a Priority, 50 Juv. & Fam. Ct. J. 1 (Spring 1999); Amy B. Levin, Comment, Child Witnesses of Domestic Violence: How Should Judges Apply the Best Interests of the Child Standard in Custody and Visitation Cases Involving Domestic Violence?, 47 UCLA L. Rev. 813, 833 (2000). Children of battered women also run the risk of being abused themselves. One study estimates that 70 percent of men who abuse their female partners also abuse their children. Bowker, Arbitell, & McFerron, supra; see also Developments in the Law — Legal Responses to Domestic Violence, 106 Harv. L. Rev. 1597, 1608-1609 (1993) (children who witness domestic violence are abused at a rate 15 times higher than the national average).

4. Domestic Violence in Population Subgroups. Although advocates commonly assert that domestic violence occurs across lines of class, race, and sexual orientation, relatively little research has attempted to directly measure and compare the incidence of domestic violence among various ethnic and sexual minority communities. The NVAWS survey begins to fill this gap. With respect to race, the survey found that when data on African-American, Asian/Pacific-Islander, American-Indian/Alaska-Native, and mixed-race women were combined, the differences in incidence of domestic violence between white and nonwhite women were insignificant.

See Tjaden & Thoennes, Full Report, supra, at 21. However, when the category of "women of color" was broken down into subgroups, significant differences emerged. Mixed race women were significantly more likely than white women to report they had been raped. Id. at 22. American Indian/Alaska Native women were significantly more likely to report being raped than white women or African-American women; they were also significantly more likely than white women or African-American women to report being stalked. Id. The findings about American Indian women were in accordance with other statistics on the victimization of American Indians generally; for example, the Bureau of Justice Statistics has reported that the rate of violent victimization for American Indians was more than twice the rate for the nation. Id at 23 (citing studies). Compare Gloria Valencia-Weber & Christine Zuni, Domestic Violence and Tribal Protection of Indigenous Women in the United States, 69 St. John's L. Rev. 69 (1995); Donna Coker, Enhancing Autonomy for Battered Women: Lessons from Navajo Peacemaking, 47 UCLA L. Rev. 1, 16-32 (1999) (describing the causes of battering in the Navajo nation).

Studies investigating the incidence of domestic violence among persons who identify themselves as Hispanic have come to contradictory conclusions: some studies have found no significant difference from other populations, and others have reported higher or lower incidences. A study of Los Angeles households found that the rates of intimate partner violence were similar between Mexican Americans born in Mexico and non-Hispanic whites born in the United States (20 percent and 21.6 percent, respectively), while the rate for United States-born Mexican Americans was higher (30.9 percent). See Sana Loue, Intimate Partner Violence: Bridging the Gap Between Law and Science, 21 J. Legal Med. 1, 3 (2000). A national U.S. study found similar rates of wife assaults among Anglo and Hispanic Americans, but detected an increased risk of wife assault among Mexican-American and Puerto Rican husbands born in the United States. Id. The NVAWS study found that Hispanic women were significantly less likely to report that they had been raped than women who identified themselves as non-Hispanic; however, Hispanic women and non-Hispanic women were equally likely to report having been physically assaulted or stalked. Tjaden & Thoennes, Full Report, supra, at 23; see generally Jenny Rivera, Domestic Violence Against Latinas by Latino Males: An Analysis of Race, National Origin, and Gender Differentials, 14 B.C. Third World L.J. 231 (1994); Murray A. Straus & Christine Smith, Violence in Hispanic Families in the United States: Incidence Rates and Structural Interpretations, in Physical Violence in American Families: Risk Factors and Adaptations to Violence in 8,145 Families 341 (Murray A. Straus & Richard J. Gelles eds., 1990) (physical violence).

Studies investigating the incidence of domestic violence across social class are few. Some research indicates that when the data are controlled for class-related variables, such as family income and occupation, violence rates are lower for African Americans than whites, and equivalent for Hispanics. See Noel A. Caznave & Murray A. Straus, Race, Class, Network Embeddedness, and Family Violence: A Search for Potent Support Systems, in Physical Violence, supra, at 321, 336; Murray A. Straus & Christine Smith, Violence in Hispanic Families in the United States: Incidence Rates and Structural Interpretations, in Physical Violence, supra, at 341, 364. A study of all women killed in New York City from 1990 through 1994 found that two-thirds of the domestic violence killings were in the poorest boroughs, the Bronx and Brooklyn. See Pam Belluck, Women's Killers Are Very Often Their Partners, A Study Finds, N.Y. Times, Mar. 31, 1997, at B1.

Research on the incidence of domestic violence in different Asian-American and Pacific Islander groups also remains scant and inadequate. For example, the NVAWS sample of Asian/Pacific Islander women who reported some experience with intimate partner violence was too small to produce statistically significant results. Tjaden & Thoennes, supra, at 22. See generally Karen Wang, Battered Asian American Women: Community Responses from the Battered Women's Movement and the Asian American Community, 3 Asian L.J. 151 (1996); Nilda Rimonte, Domestic Violence Among Pacific Asians, in Asian Women United of California, Making Waves: An Anthology of Writings by and About Asian American Women 327 (1989). Additionally, no national data are kept on the incidence of domestic violence among immigrants to the United States, although data provided by organizations working with battered immigrants suggest that the problem is not rare. See Felicia E. Franco, Unconditional Safety for Conditional Immigrant Women, 11 Berkeley Women's L.J. 99, 102 (1996); Maurice Goldman, The Violence Against Women Act: Meeting Its Goal in Protecting Battered Immigrant Women?, 37 Fam. & Conciliation Cts. Rev. 375, 377 n.14 (1999) (reporting that, according to one survey conducted by a Washington, D.C., organization that assists battered immigrants, 77 percent of Latina immigrants reported being subject to abuse).

There is also inadequate research being done on battering in lesbian and gay communities, in part because of reluctance within those communities to discuss intimate partner violence. See Nancy J. Knauer, Same-Sex Domestic Violence: Claiming a Domestic Sphere While Risking Negative Stereotypes, 8 Temp. Pol. & Civ. Rts. L. Rev. 325, 325 (1999); Kathleen Finley Duthu, Why Doesn't Anyone Talk About Gay and Lesbian Domestic Violence?, 18 Thomas Jefferson L. Rev. 23, 23-24 (1996). It is often said that same-sex intimate partner violence occurs at the same rate as cross-sex intimate partner violence; this was the conclusion, for example, of a report released in 1997 by the National Coalition of Anti-Violence Programs. See Knauer, Same-Sex Domestic Violence, supra, at 330. However, the research to support the conclusion that the incidences of same-sex and cross-sex intimate partner violence are the same is methodologically flawed, and many scholars have overgeneralized from the available evidence. See Ryiah Lilith, Reconsidering the Abuse That Dare Not Speak Its Name: A Criticism of

Recent Legal Scholarship Regarding Same-Gender Domestic Violence, 7 Mich. J. Gender & L. 181, 188-189 (2001). There is some indication that the incidence of domestic violence among lesbians is lower than the incidence among gay men. The NVAWS study, for example, found that among same-sex cohabiting couples (who were not asked their sexual orientation), same-sex cohabiting women were nearly three times more likely to report being victimized by a male partner than by a female partner (30.4 percent versus 11.4 percent). Tjaden & Thoennes, Extent, Nature, and Consequences, supra, at 30. Similarly, opposite-sex cohabiting women were nearly twice as likely to report victimization by their male partners as were same-sex cohabiting women by their female partners (20.3 percent versus 11.4 percent). Same-sex cohabiting men were nearly twice as likely to report being victimized by their male partners as were opposite-sex cohabiting men by their female partners (15.4 percent and 7.7 percent). Id. at 31. The authors of the NVAWS report conclude that intimate partner violence is perpetrated primarily by men, whether against male or female partners. Id.

5. Barriers Unique to Battered Immigrant Women. Lack of language ability, cultural differences, unfamiliarity with the U.S. legal system and local social services, and economic dependence on the abuser are all factors that may combine to trap battered immigrant women in violent relationships. See Linda Kelly, Stories from the Front: Seeking Refuge for Battered Immigrants in the Violence Against Women Act, 92 Nw. U. L. Rev. 665 (1998). In addition to these social barriers, immigrant women may face a maze of complex legal problems arising from their immigration status; their ability to seek protection against intimate violence is compromised by the possibility of their deportation. See Tien-li Loke, Note, Trapped in Domestic Violence: The Impact of United States Immigration Laws on Battered Immigrant Women, 6 B.U. Pub. Int. L.J. 589 (1997); Catherine K. Klein & Leslye E. Orloff, Providing Legal Protection for Battered Women: An Analysis of State Statutes and Case Law, 21 Hofstra L. 801 (1993).

The 1994 Violence Against Women Act (VAWA) was adopted by Congress in part to aid immigrant women seeking to escape from intimate partner abuse. However, VAWA has its limitations, as Cecelia Espenoza explains:

> The VAWA provides relief to immigrant victims by empowering them to obtain immigration status independent of their abusers. In order to qualify for this relief as a VAWA applicant, however, the applicant must meet statutory requirements that include proof that they have good moral character, a requirement that may not be met if the immigrant women are prosecuted as perpetrators of domestic violence. At the present time, no mechanism exists in

either criminal or immigration law to evaluate whether a domestic violence conviction should lead to a loss of VAWA eligibility.

Furthermore, there is no guidance in either body of law to evaluate the woman's motivation. In addition, a further complication emerges because under the new immigration law's definition many domestic violence crimes constitute aggravated felonies.

Cecelia M. Espenoza, No Relief for the Weary: VAWA Relief Denied for Battered Immigrants Lost in the Intersections, 83 Marq. L. Rev. 163 (1999); see also Lee J. Teran, Barriers to Protection at Home and Abroad: Mexican Victims of Domestic Violence and the Violence Against Women Act, 17 B.U. Int'l L.J. 1 (1999) (discussing the situation of undocumented women who flee from intimate partner abuse in Mexico, only to face deportation by the Immigration and Naturalization Service).

6. Do Gender Roles Cause Domestic Violence? Some empirical studies have identified a connection between domestic violence and traditionally patriarchal heterosexual families. For example, in a national survey of 2,143 families in the late 1970s, less than 3 percent of wives in couples that followed an "egalitarian" pattern of decisionmaking had been violently attacked in the preceding year. The corresponding figures were 7 percent of wives in "wife-dominant" couples and over 20 percent for wives in "husband-dominant" couples. Murray A. Straus, R. Gelles, & Suzanne Steinmetz, Behind Closed Doors: Violence in the American Family 194 (1980). Husband-beating was also most frequent in husband-dominant households (15 percent) as compared to wife-dominant households (6 to 10 percent) and egalitarian ones (under 5 percent). Id. Child abuse is also more frequent in husband-dominated households. Lee H. Bowker, Michelle Arbitell, & J. Richard McFerron, On the Relationship Between Wife Beating and Child Abuse, in Perspectives on Wife Abuse, supra, at 164-165 (child abuse twice as likely in husband-dominated household as in wife-dominated household, and abuse tends to be more severe as well). Some researchers cite evidence that family violence rates are highest in states where women have the lowest economic and educational status as support for the patriarchy theory. See Kersti A. Yllo & Murray A. Straus, Patriarchy and Violence Against Wives: The Impact of Structural and Normative Factors, in Physical Violence, supra, at 383, 397 ("[t]he greatest force is needed to keep wives 'in their place' in states where women have the lowest status"). What explains this association? Researchers R. Emerson Dobash and Russell P. Dobash "see violence used by men against women in the family as attempts to establish and maintain a patriarchal social order. Violence is used by men to chastise their wives for real or perceived transgressions of his authority and as attempts to reaffirm and maintain a hierarchical and moral order within the family." R. Emerson Dobash & Russell P. Dobash, Wives: The "Appropriate" Victims of Marital Violence, 2 Victimology 426, 438 (1978).

What are the implications of this asserted connection between domestic violence and patriarchal family structure for battering in same-sex relationships? Ryiah Lilith argues that "the gendered model of domestic violence as resulting from male supremacy does not adequately account for same-gender abuse. For example, female partners have never possessed any legal proprietary interest in one another; on the contrary, courts have often refused to recognize the ties between same-gender partners. Likewise, same-gender couples are neither afforded the 'sanctity of marriage' nor the State's protection of their private, domestic sphere." Lilith, Reconsidering the Abuse That Dare Not Speak Its Name, supra, at 188-189.

Some theorists have hazarded that social masculinity, rather than biological masculinity, is a risk factor for battering; thus, lesbians who take on "butch" roles may experience themselves as socially male and may be more likely to batter their female partners. See Christine A. Littleton, Women's Experience and the Problem of Transition: Perspectives on Male Battering of Women, 1989 U. Chi. Legal F. 23, 28 n.20 ("it is not that battering is non-sexual, but rather that sexual roles are non-biological"). Others have dismissed this theory as "heteronormative." See Mary Eaton, Abuse by Any Other Name: Feminism, Difference, and Intralesbian Violence, in The Public Nature of Private Violence: The Discovery of Domestic Abuse 195, 207 (Martha Albertson Fineman & Roxanne Mykitiuk eds., 1994); see also Elizabeth Schneider, Particularity and Generality: Challenges of Feminist Theory and Practice in Work on Woman-Abuse, 67 N.Y.U. L. Rev. 520, 543, 544 (1992); Phyllis Goldfarb, Describing Without Circumscribing: Questioning the Construction of Gender in the Discourse of Intimate Violence, 64 Geo. Wash. L. Rev. 582, 600-602 (1996). In an effort to include same-sex and opposite-sex intimate partner violence in the same analysis, some theorists have backed away from the "patriarchy" model of domestic violence and adopted a "nongendered" model that stresses psychological rather than sociological explanations. See Lilith, supra, at 189.

Does the problem of gay and lesbian domestic violence point us away from dominance theory as an explanation for battering? Nancy Knauer calls for "domestic violence activists and feminists to uncouple their concepts of power and dominance from the frame of gender difference and consider the role of other identifications, such as race, age, sexual orientation, and disability, in the deployment of power and violence." Knauer, supra, at 350.

7. Contemporary Social Responses to Domestic Violence. The contemporary women's rights movement renewed interest in, and responses to, domestic violence as a social issue with severe consequences for many women. Still, much of the response depended on gathering private resources to meet the needs of battered women rather than changing the legal and social climate within which wife abuse flourished. Among the most positive of these private-sector responses was an astounding growth in facilities for battered women. In 1970, there were no shelters for battered women; by 1987, there were more than 700. Naomi R. Cahn, Civil Images of Battered Women: The Impact of Domestic Violence on Child Custody Decisions, 44 Vand. L. Rev. 1041, 1048 (1991) (citing NOW Legal Defense and Legal Education Fund, and R. Cherow-O'Leary, The State-by-State Guide to Women's Legal Rights 33 (1987)). For a history of the battered women's movement, see Linda Gordon, Heroes of Their Own Lives: The Politics and History of Family Violence, Boston 1880-1960 (1988); Susan Schechter, Women and Male Violence: The Visions of the Battered Women's Movement (1982). Still, it is sometimes asserted that there are fewer shelters for battered women than there are animal shelters. See, e.g., Comment, Stalking Stuffers: A Revolutionary Law to Keep Predators Behind Bars, 35 Santa Clara L. Rev. 1027, 1034 (1995). Moreover, lesbians, women of color, and immigrants do not always have full access to, or feel comfortable in, battered women's shelters, which are traditionally geared toward heterosexual, white, and English-speaking women. See, e.g., Linda Geraci, Making Shelters Safe for Lesbians, in Naming the Violence: Speaking Out About Lesbian Battering 77 (Kerry Lobel ed., 1986) (shelter staff may be homophobic); Nomi Porat, Support Groups for Battered Lesbians, in Naming the Violence, supra, at 80 (lesbians are rejected from social services and labeled "divisive"); Nancy Hammond, Lesbian Victims and the Reluctance to Identify Abuse, in Naming the Violence, supra, at 196 (battered women's service providers do not reach out to gay and lesbian communities because of homophobia); Kimberlé Crenshaw, Mapping the Margins: Intersectionality, Identity Politics, and Violence Against Women of Color, 43 Stan. L. Rev. 1241, 1245 (1991) (black battered women face unique problems); Soraya M. Coley & Joyce O. Beckett, Black Battered Women: Practice Issues, 69(8) Soc. Casework, 483, 484, 486-488 (1988) (African-American women often feel that "shelters are for white women" or that shelter personnel do not respect their cultural differences); Jenny Rivera, Domestic Violence Against Latinas by Latino Males: An Analysis of Race, National Origin, and Gender Differentials, 14 B.C. Third World L.J. 231 (1994), reprinted in Nancy K.D. Lemon, Domestic Violence Law 155, 167 (2001) (shelters seldom employ bilingual and bicultural personnel who could aid Latinas); Catherine E. Klein & Leslye Orloff, Providing Legal Protection for Battered Women: An Analysis of State Statutes and Case Law, 21 Hofstra L.Rev. 801, 1021-1022 (1993) (few shelters provide bilingual services for immigrant women).

2. Legal Responses to Domestic Violence

Re-read State v. Rhodes and the excerpt from Blackstone in Chapter 1, at pages 51-54.

≣ *Elizabeth M. Schneider, The Violence of Privacy*
≣ 23 Conn. L. Rev. 973, 983-985 (1991)

Battering is deeply threatening. It goes to our most fundamental assumptions about the nature of intimate relations and the safeness of family life. The concept of male battering of women as a "private" issue exerts a powerful ideological pull on our consciousness because, in some sense, it is something that we would like to believe. By seeing woman-abuse as "private," we affirm it as a problem that is individual, that only involves a particular male-female relationship, and for which there is no social responsibility to remedy. . . . Focusing on the woman, not the man, perpetuates the power of patriarchy. Denial supports and legitimates this power; the concept of privacy is a key aspect of this denial.

Denial takes many forms and operates on many levels. Men deny battering in order to protect their own privilege. Women need to deny the pervasiveness of the problem so as not to link it to their own life situations. Individual women who are battered tend to minimize the violence in order to distance themselves from some internalized negative concept of "battered woman." I see denial in the attitudes of jurors, who try to remove themselves and say that it could never happen to me; if it did, I would handle it differently. . . . The findings of many state task force reports on gender bias in the courts have painstakingly recorded judicial attitudes of denial. Clearly, there is serious denial on the part of state legislators, members of Congress and the Executive Branch who never mention battering as an important public issue. In battering, we see both the power of denial and the denial of power. The concept of privacy is an ideological rationale for this denial and serves to maintain it. . . .

[A]s Martha Minow has suggested, [the] social failure to intervene in male battering of women on grounds of privacy should not be seen as separate from violence, but as a part of the violence.

> When clerks in a local court harass a woman who applies for a restraining order against the violence in her home, they are part of the violence. Society is organized to permit violence in the home; it is organized through images in mass media and through broadly based social attitudes that condone violence. Society permits such violence to go unchallenged through the isolation of families and the failures of police to respond. Public, rather than private patterns of conduct and morals are implicated. Some police officers refuse to respond to domestic violence; some officers themselves abuse their spouses. Some clerks and judges think domestic violence matters do not belong in court. These failures to respond to domestic violence are public, not private, actions.

[Martha Minow, Words and the Door to the Land of Change: Law, Language, and Family Violence, 43 Vand. L. Rev. 1665, 1671-1672 (1990)]. Although social failure to respond to problems of battered women has been justified on grounds of privacy, this failure to respond is an affirmative political decision that has serious public consequences. The rationale of privacy masks the political nature of the decision. Privacy thus plays a particularly subtle and pernicious ideological role in supporting, encouraging, and legitimating violence against women. . . .

Stevenson v. Stevenson
714 A.2d 986 (N.J. Super. Ct. 1998)

COOK, J.S.C. . . .

In what appears as a matter of first impression in New Jersey, this case presents the question whether a final restraining order issued under the Prevention of Domestic Violence Act, N.J.S.A. §2C:25-17-33, must be dissolved in all cases where the plaintiff so requests. For the reasons expressed below, this court determines that dissolution of a final restraining order at the request of plaintiff is not mandatory. Rather, dissolution in such cases is at the court's discretion, and should depend upon a showing of good cause, with an independent finding by the court based upon the facts presented in each case. . . .

On November 6, 1997, the parties appeared before this court for a hearing on plaintiff's complaint charging defendant with numerous violations of the Prevention of Domestic Violence Act (the Act). The testimony of plaintiff, the photographic exhibits offered by her counsel, and the graphic appearance at the hearing of the residual effects of the severe physical injuries she suffered, established by a clear preponderance of the evidence that defendant was guilty of attempted criminal homicide, aggravated assault, terroristic threats, criminal restraint and burglary, all in violation of the Act. These violations arose from a brutal, sadistic and prolonged attack by defendant on his wife during the late evening and early morning hours of October 29-30, 1997.

Plaintiff, who appeared at the hearing with two black and severely swollen eyes, testified that on the late evening of October 29, 1997, defendant came into the marital bedroom, went into a total rage, punched plaintiff with both fists, held her down with his knees, kicked her in the back and ribs, and continued beating her there for approximately 25 minutes. Defendant then dragged her by her hair down the stairs and out of the house, and shoved her into his van, saying that they were going to go to a friend's house. Plaintiff was bleeding from her ears, nose and mouth. She got out of the van, ran to a neighbor's house and banged on the door. Defendant chased her, screaming he would kill her, and that he should have killed her before. She was "petrified". He caught up to her outside the neighbor's house, and choked her with both hands around her throat. He then dragged her down the street and pushed her back into the van. She escaped again and ran to another neighbor's house. At that point, defendant's vicious attack on his wife had been going on for 45 minutes. She went inside the neighbor's house and asked her neighbor to call the police, while she went into a powder room, closed the door, and tried to hide from defendant. Defendant went into the neighbor's house and proceeded to rip the powder room door off its hinges. The door landed on plaintiff. He dragged her out of the house, and back towards their house. Plaintiff grabbed onto trees along the way, trying to resist. He was furious because she had asked her neighbor to call the police. Finally, he let go of her, got into the van and left. She was badly injured and very scared. A neighbor came with a blanket and rendered first aid. She was rushed by ambulance to the Emergency Room of West Jersey Hospital. She had three large lumps on her head, two black eyes, blood running from her ears, and abrasions and lacerations all over her body. She also had trouble breathing. At the West Jersey Hospital Emergency Room, she was diagnosed as having head and lung injuries, and was in such critical condition that she had to be medevac'd by helicopter to the Cooper Hospital Trauma Center. She had a fractured skull, a concussion, four broken ribs, and a punctured lung (pneumothorax), in addition to the injuries noted above. She remained hospitalized at Cooper for several days, and was still under medical care at the time of the hearing on November 6, 1997.

At the hearing, the court had the opportunity not only to hear the testimony of plaintiff, but to observe her injuries and review the photographic exhibits submitted by her counsel as well. Plaintiff's eyes were severely swollen, black and blue, and almost closed. She was in obvious physical pain and distress. The photographic exhibits submitted by plaintiff's counsel depicted her injuries, as well as the powder room door that defendant ripped off its hinges in the neighbor's home where plaintiff sought refuge. The photos, including those of plaintiff's facial and head injuries, and the hole in her chest where a tube was inserted to re-inflate her punctured lung, depicted a severally beaten and battered woman.

Plaintiff testified she was in fear of defendant. She related a prior history of domestic violence on his part, including previous assaults. She was afraid he would take their ten year-old son and leave the area, noting that he would do anything and everything to get physical custody and keep their son away from her. She added that their ten year-old son was in the house throughout the forty-five minute period that the beating of his mother took place.

Defendant, who was represented by counsel at the hearing, did not testify. No evidence was presented to controvert plaintiff's testimony, or the domestic violence charges she made against him. . . .

Because of (1) the barbaric conduct of the defendant during the nightmarish incident of October 29-30, 1997; (2) the evidence of his drunkenness that night and in the past; (3) his prior history of domestic violence; and (4) plaintiff's clearly expressed fear that defendant would take her son away if not restrained, a final restraining order was entered. The order prohibited any further acts of domestic violence, and barred him from having any contact or communication with the plaintiff and from harassing or stalking her. The order also required defendant to undergo substance abuse and psychological evaluations, and restricted him to supervised visitation only. He was also ordered to pay plaintiff's attorneys' fees of $2,400 by December 12, 1997; child and spousal support; all household expenses; and other expenses enumerated in the order. The deadline for payment of plaintiff's counsel fees was modified by an order of December 23, 1997 [to allow for monthly payments]. . . .

At the hearing on plaintiff's request that the court dissolve the final restraining order, several violations of the order came to light. For example, it appeared that the defendant has engaged in *unsupervised visitation* with the child, including trips out-of-state. He has continually attempted to contact plaintiff. He has not abided by the psychotherapy recommendations of the Steininger Center, nor with the substance abuse recommendations of Segaloff. Both of those reports are discussed below. He has not paid any of the attorney's fees he was ordered to pay. In short, the defendant has flouted and violated the final restraining order. . . .

At the hearing on March 13, 1998, plaintiff asked the court to dissolve the final restraining order. She claimed she had reconsidered her relationship with the defendant and wanted him to be involved with their son's life. She requested that the restraints be dissolved, but only on the condition that he commit no future violence.

The final restraining order permitted *supervised visitation only,* pending a risk assessment and further order of the court. Risk assessment evaluations, substance abuse evaluations, and psychological evaluations of defendant were received by the court. At the request of and by agreement of both parties, through their counsel, copies of those evaluation reports were provided to the parties and their counsel. Plaintiff testified she had read the reports. . . .

Those reports include (1) a psychological evaluation of defendant by Dr. Stuart Kurlansik, Chief Psychologist, The Steininger Center; and (2) a drug and alcohol abuse evaluation of defendant by Patricia Thurman, a substance abuse counsellor at the Substance Abuse Center in Southern New Jersey, Inc., t/a Segaloff Counseling and Treatment Center. . . .

The report of Dr. Kurlansik of The Steininger Center is extensive, and covers eight pages. Dr. Kurlansik conducted two testing and interview sessions with defendant, each a week apart. Dr. Karlansik reported inter alia that:

> When asked to describe the events which resulted in his referral to this office, Mr. Stevenson reported that "I assaulted my wife. *I beat her up very badly."* . . .
> He reported prior fights with his wife, but "nothing to this degree." He claimed that *every time they fought, he was drunk.* He stated that she never had to go to the hospital in previous fights. He stated that the previous fights involved punching, although not to the face. He stated that he bruised her in

prior fights, but then claimed that she bruises easily. He reported that he had been in fights with other people during the period of his marriage as well. He stated that he boxes and plays hockey, and fought during the course of a game. He stated that he has had a few fights outside of the sport events, however. He then said there had been a handful, the most recent occurring [a year ago] at a roller rink [when] the other coach had been a poor sport, and "we ended up in a physical confrontation." . . . Another time, four years ago, he stated that he was a spectator at an ice hockey [game] in which his son was playing. He stated that a parent of one of his teams' children became involved in a fight with three of the opposing team's parents, and he "intervened." *He reported having a fight five years ago in a bar, and stated that he was intoxicated at the time.* He stated that he had played a game of pool for twenty dollars and the other person lost the game, and did not want to pay, "so I hit him." . . .

He denied any arrests as a result of fighting as an adult. As a juvenile, he stated that he was incarcerated at Glen Mills for a total of three years, and stated that "we could go on for hours" regarding juvenile incidents. He stated that he was at Glen Mills twice — once at age thirteen for assault, and the second time at age fourteen for robbery.

His current marriage has been his only marriage. He married on December 28, 1986. The most recent separation occurred October 29, 1997. He reported one other separation, two years ago. He stated that "things just weren't working well." This separation lasted about three months.

Mr. Stevenson reported no [Dept. of Youth and Family Services] involvement in his family of origin, but stated that he left home when he was about twelve years old. He stated that he ran away to California, and knew no one there. He was arrested for trying to rob a restaurant, was held for sixty days, and was sent to Glen Mills. . . . He was later arrested for fighting, and was again sent to Glen Mills for fourteen months. . . . He left Glen Mills when he turned seventeen. . . .

He reported that he has a *short temper*, although "not now." He claimed that the experience which brought him here has changed his life and a short temper is "not gonna be a trait for me anymore." . . .

An objective measure of personality functioning, the Million Clinical Multiaxial Inventory — III, was administered. . . . [T]he interpretive report stated that "on the basis of the test data (assuming denial is not present), it may be reasonable to assume that the patient is exhibiting psychological dysfunction of mild to moderate severity." An Axis I (an "acute" disorder) diagnosis of Generalized Anxiety Disorder is suggested, while Axis II (enduring features of an individual's personality, and therefore more "chronic") diagnosis of: "*Antisocial Personality Traits*," "*Passive-Aggressive Personality Traits*," "*Avoidant Personality Traits*," and "*Sadistic Personality Features*" are suggested. The NCS report hypothesizes . . . that he may manifest (among other things) a lack of empathy, intolerance, and display "impulsive and quixotic emotionality." It goes on to state that *individuals with his profile can "be easily provoked into sudden and unpredictable reactions*," which "*may be punctuated periodically by angry outbursts.*"

Recommendations:

> *It is strongly urged that Mr. Stevenson participate in psychotherapy, to help him learn to control his anger* (and to find more appropriate ways of expressing it), as well as to reduce his anxiety. Psychotherapy might also address what appears to be an issue with *excessive use of alcohol at times.*

In her substance abuse evaluation of defendant, Ms. Thurman, a substance abuse counsellor at the Substance Abuse Center of Southern New Jersey, t/a Segaloff Counseling and Treatment Center, reported that: . . .

Robert, a 34 year-old white male, was interviewed on November 29, 1997, at 8:30 A.M. Eye contact was fair, affect closed, guarded and *very accusatory toward his estranged wife, Melody.*

When asked about his use of drugs and alcoholic beverages, Mr. Stevenson states he's never used drugs of any kind and attempts to portray himself as a modest drinker, however, says the *day he was charged "I had a little too much to drink"*. . . . But, Robert was quick to defend his actions by blaming the problem on "I caught my wife trying to buy drugs on the phone" and sees no relationship between his drinking and his current family problems. . . .

Concluding, based upon the limited information available to us, *we strongly suspect Mr. Stevenson is drinking more than he reports and we feel he would greatly benefit from outpatient counseling to enable him to cease drinking and evaluate his family problems in a drug free state. The fact the client admits he was under the influence at the time of the altercation with his wife prompts us to question the severity of his drinking and its relationship to his family problems.* . . . If Mr. Stevenson is not already in treatment for substance abuse, *we would then recommend he be mandated to complete at least 3 months in substance abuse treatment.* . . .

At a risk assessment conference with a Family Court staff therapist, plaintiff expressed concern over defendant's *"need for control,"* and again said she feared he would flee with their son, perhaps to Arizona. . . . She also said that on more than one occasion, defendant has threatened that he "will do anything and everything he has to" in order to gain custody of his son. Plaintiff requested that supervised visitation continue.

There remain several criminal charges pending against defendant as a result of his sadistic attack on his wife, including criminal attempt — murder; aggravated assault; burglary; criminal mischief; threatened violence; and criminal restraint. He is reportedly free on $75,000 cash bail, and is awaiting further proceedings in the criminal case.

When considering a plaintiff's request to dissolve the Final Restraining Order, a court must not forget that it is the public policy of the State of New Jersey, expressed by the Legislature in the Act, N.J.S.A. §2C:25-18, *that victims of domestic violence must be assured the maximum protection from abuse the law can provide; that the official response to domestic violence, including that of the courts, shall communicate the attitude that domestic violent behavior will not be excused or tolerated; and that it is the responsibility of the courts to protect victims of domestic violence* by ordering those remedies and sanctions that are *available to assure the safety of the victims* and the public. Addressing the problem of domestic violence and its prevention, the preamble to the Act states: . . .

> Further, it is the responsibility of the courts to protect victims of violence that occurs in a family or family-like setting by providing access to both emergent and long-term civil and criminal remedies and sanctions, and by ordering those remedies and sanctions, that are available to assure the safety of the victims and the public. To that end, the Legislature encourages the training of all police and judicial personnel in the procedures and enforcement of this act, and about the social and psychological contest in which domestic violence occurs; and it further encourages the broad application of the remedies available under this act in the civil and criminal courts of this State. It is further intended that the official response to domestic violence shall communicate the attitude that violent behavior will not be excused or tolerated, and shall make clear the fact that the existing criminal laws and civil remedies created under this act will be enforced without regard to the fact that the violence grows out of a domestic situation.

N.J.S.A. §2C:25-18; see also, Torres v. Lancellotti, [607 A.2d 1375 (N.J. CH. Div. 1992)].

In addition, the Legislature has mandated that a final restraining order cannot be dissolved [or modified], *unless good cause is shown.* . . . Even where good cause is shown, the language of the statute, N.J.S.A. §2C:25-29d., expressly makes dissolution *discretionary,* not mandatory (". . . final order *may* be dissolved").

Plaintiff's dissolution request, made despite the latest brutal beating she suffered at the hands of a drunken husband who has a past history of wife-beating and an alcohol abuse problem, is consistent with phase three of "the battered woman's syndrome." That phase of the battering cycle is characterized by a period of loving behavior by the batterer, during which pleas for forgiveness and protestations of devotion are often mixed with promises to seek counselling, stop drinking and refrain from further violence. A period of relative calm may last as long as several months, but in a battering relationship the affection and contrition of the batterer will eventually fade, and phases one and two, the "tension-building" phase and the "acute battering incident" phase, will start anew. State v. Kelly, [478 A.2d 364 (N.J. 1984)]. Plaintiff has gone through the battering cycle with defendant at least twice. Through this dissolution request she seeks to remain in the situation. She thus meets the definition of a "battered woman." Id., quoting from L. Walker, The Battered Woman at xv (1979). The New Jersey Legislature recognized the plight of battered women when it enacted the Act and provided battered women with the remedy of *permanent* restraining orders against wife-beaters and other batterers of women. Id. . . .

. . . Obviously, if there were no basis at all for plaintiff to fear further violence — as most certainly there is, given the nature and extent of this attack and defendant's past history of violence, including domestic violence against plaintiff; then there would be no need to condition dissolution on the absence of further violence. But there is that inherent fear, a fear that this court and any reasonable person viewing this situation would certainly share.

. . . [Because fear is vital to the continuance of power and control in a domestic violence relationship, and this fear can impact the victim's ability to act in the best interests of her child, it is important to consider the victim's fear of the defendant. Carfagno v. Carfagno, 672 A.2d 751 (N.J. Ch. Civ. 1995).] When considering the question of fear of defendant, *Carfagno* notes that the test should not be the victim's subjective fear. Rather, the test is one of objective fear, i.e., that fear which a reasonable victim similarly situated would have under the circumstances. . . .

When considering a victim's application to dissolve, and whether there is good cause to do so, a court must determine whether objective fear can be said to continue to exist, and also whether there is a real danger of domestic violence recurring, in the event the restraining order is dissolved. . . . Whether or not this plaintiff would agree, it is clear that *from the standpoint of objective fear,* that a reasonable victim of such a brutal beating by a husband, who has assaulted her in the past and has a history of other violent behavior, and is the subject of experts' findings of uncontrolled anger and excessive use of alcohol, would have a reasonable fear that future violence by her husband would occur, were the restraining order dissolved.

Even in cases of reconciliation, the court must still make *an independent finding* that continued protection is unnecessary before vacating a restraining order. Torres v. Lancelloti, [607 A.2d 1375 (N.J. Ch. Div. 1992)]. The "good cause" proviso of N.J.S.A. §2C:25-29d requires no less. Without making an independent finding based on the objective evidence, a court does not meet the public policy dictates of the Act . . . N.J.S.A. §2C:25-18. . . .

In this case, given the uncontroverted evidence of defendant's brutality against his wife, his history of violence both within and without the domestic arena, his alcohol abuse and uncontrolled assaultive behavior when under the influence, and the reports before the court, including those of The Steininger Center and Segaloff, a reasonable, objective and independent determination of the facts leads to the inescapable conclusion that a real threat of recurrence of domestic violence by defendant upon his battered wife will exist, if the Final Restraining Order is dissolved. This court will not be an accomplice to further violence by this defendant, by wholly dissolving at this point the restraints that have been entered against him. Accordingly, and for lack of good cause shown, plaintiff's application to dissolve the Final Restraining Order is denied.

The court does find cause to modify the Final Restraining Order with respect to certain matters concerning the child of the parties, as follows. The final restraining order shall remain in full force and effect, except that contact or communication between plaintiff and defendant relating to supervised visitation, and to the safety, health, education, welfare, status or activities of the minor child of the parties, shall be permitted. There shall be no further modification of the final restraining order, without application to and with the express approval of the court.

Defendant shall promptly undergo psychotherapy as recommended in the report of Dr. Kurlansik of The Steininger Center. He shall also promptly undergo at least three months of substance abuse treatment at the Camden County Division of Alcoholism and Substance Abuse, as recommended by Patricia Thurman of the Segaloff Counseling and Treatment Center. Upon completion of psychotherapy and substance abuse treatment, the court will consider unsupervised visitation.

Notes

1. Legal Responses to Domestic Violence: An Historical Perspective. As Reva Siegel reports, "The Anglo-American common law originally provided that a husband, as master of his household, could subject his wife to corporal punishment or 'chastisement' so long as he did not inflict permanent injury upon her." Reva B. Siegel, "The Rule of Love": Wife Beating as Prerogative and Privacy, 105 Yale L.J. 2117, 2118 (1996). Although as early as 1641 the Massachusetts Bay Colony had moved away from this rule — proclaiming in its "Body of Liberties" that "[e]verie marryied woeman shall be free from bodilie correction or stripes by her husband, unless it be in his owwn defence upon her assault" — it was not until the nineteenth century that feminist agitation successfully brought "wife beating" to the attention of law reformers in the United States and Britain. See Evan Stark, Re-Presenting Woman Battering: From Battered Woman Syndrome to Coercive Control, 58 Alb. L. Rev. 973, 987-988 (1995).

By the end of the Civil War, the American legal system had repudiated the doctrine of chastisement. However, during the Reconstruction Era, a new body of common law emerged under which judges, instead of declaring that a husband had the right to beat his wife, asserted that "the legal system should not interfere in cases of wife beating, in order to protect the privacy of the marriage relationship and to promote domestic harmony." Siegel, supra, at 2120. Siegel continues:

These changes in the rule structure of marital status law were justified in a distinctive rhetoric: one that diverged from the traditional idiom of chastisement doctrine. Instead of reasoning about marriage in the older, hierarchy-based norms of the common law, jurists began to justify the regulation of domestic violence in the language of privacy and love associated with companionate marriage in the industrial era.

Id.

Meanwhile, wife beating was quickly transformed from a women's rights issue to a "law and order" issue. Siegel reports that by the end of the nineteenth century, wife beating was increasingly characterized as solely the practice of "lawless or unruly men of the 'dangerous classes,'" particularly African-American men and men from low-status immigrant ethnic groups such as German and Irish Americans. Id. at 2139. A particularly popular punishment for such men in the imagination of law reformers was the whipping post: between 1876 and 1906, 12 states and the District of Columbia considered legislation that would enable wife beaters to be flogged, and several prominent members of the American Bar Association campaigned for such legislation. Id. at 2137. Thus, wife beating was used as an excuse for stigmatizing and disciplining racially "other" men; as a corollary, domestic violence among the economically and racially privileged classes disappeared from view.

Legal reformers made significant distinctions among the victims of domestic violence as well as the perpetrators. For example, English reformers were careful to distinguish between "good women," who should be protected from domestic violence, and "the naggy harpy" or "virago," who brought beatings upon herself. See Stark, supra, at 989.

By the 1920s, the victims of child abuse and woman battering had been transferred from "protection societies," which saw themselves as providing women and children a safe haven from abusive men, to "child welfare agencies," which attempted to regulate domestic life more broadly. In the process, mothers were increasingly seen as part of the problem. For example, Stark notes that "[i]n 1899, the new Illinois juvenile courts replaced the term 'child abuse' with the term 'neglect,' while 'family' or 'domestic relations' courts sought to decriminalize woman battering by taking 'domestic trouble cases' as an occasion to help the wives master the habits of cleanliness, nutrition, and child care." Id. at 991. By the New Deal, child abuse was being defined as the fault of mothers who were overly "domineering," and male violence against women faded from public view. Id. at 992. The goal of the new family court system was to keep the family intact; accordingly, judges encouraged battered women to accept responsibility for their role in provoking the violence and discouraged them from filing criminal charges. Siegel, supra, at 2170. The view that domestic violence simply represented a private conflict that had gotten out of hand lasted well into the 1970s.

Throughout the 1960s and 1970s, the underenforcement of crimes involving family members was notorious. A study of thousands of incidents in Boston, Chicago, and Washington, D.C., found that in cases where both victim and offender were present when police arrived, only 45 percent of all felonies involving family members resulted in arrest (55 percent if the victim asked police to make an arrest). See Lawrence W. Sherman, The Influence of Criminology on Criminal Law: Evaluating Arrests for Misdemeanor Domestic Violence, 83 J. Crim. L. & Criminology 1, 11 (1992) (citing Donald J. Black, The Manners and Customs of the Police 94 (1980)). In one Ohio county, a study of cases involving current or former spouses or lovers found that arrests were made in only 12 percent of the cases. Id. (citing Edna Erez, Intimacy, Violence and the Police, 39 Hum. Rel. 265 (1986)). See also Sarah Mausolff Buel, Note, Mandatory Arrest for Domestic Violence, 11 Harv. Women's L.J. 213, 217 (1988) (citing surveys showing arrest rates from 3 to 10 percent).

For further historical accounts of violence against women in Anglo-American social life and efforts to control it, see A. James Hammerton, Cruelty and Companionship: Conflict in Nineteenth-Century Married Life (1992); Linda Gordon, Heroes of Their Own Lives: The Politics and History of Family Violence (1988); Elizabeth Pleck, Domestic Tyranny: The Making of Social Policy Against Family Violence from Colonial Times to the Present (1987).

2. Contemporary Legal Responses to Domestic Violence: Mandatory Arrest, Prosecution, and Reporting Policies. Beginning in the 1960s, second-wave feminists sought to make "private" violence a public issue. Feminists created shelters to help protect the safety and mental health of battered women and children. Feminists also undertook public education campaigns to call the public's attention to male violence and state inaction and to change attitudes about the victims of abuse. See Bernadette Dunn Sewell, Note, History of Abuse: Societal, Judicial, and Legislative Responses to the Problem of Wife Beating, 23 Suffolk U. L. Rev. 983, 997 (1989). Finally, advocates began to use legal means "to reform how the police officers, prosecutors, health workers, and judges who compose the front line of the criminal justice system respond to cases of intimate abuse." Linda G. Mills, Killing Her Softly: Intimate Abuse and the Violence of State Intervention, 113 Harv. L. Rev. 550, 557 (1999). Toward this end, reformers have pursued mandatory arrest, mandatory prosecution, and mandatory reporting policies to force domestic violence cases into the criminal justice system.

Mandatory or pro-arrest policies require police officers to arrest a suspect if there is probable cause to believe that an assault or battery has occurred, without regard to the victim's consent or objection. Id. at 558. At least 15 states and Washington, D.C., have adopted such policies. Id.; see Miriam H. Ruttenberg, A Feminist Critique of Mandatory Arrest: An Analysis of Race and Gender in Domestic Violence Policy, 2 Am. U. J. Gender & L. 171, 180 n.44 (1994) (listing statutes). These policies began to appear in the wake of a landmark Minneapolis study of the relationship between arrest and recidivism in domestic violence cases, published in 1984 by Lawrence W. Sherman and Richard A. Berk. Sherman & Berk, The Specific Deterrent Effects of Arrest for Domestic Assault, 49 Am. Soc. Rev. 261 (1984). The Minneapolis experiment — along with several high-profile lawsuits against police departments — stimulated a wave of mandatory arrest statutes. By 1996, a survey of U.S. police departments indicated that one-third had changed their arrest policies in domestic violence cases. Mills, supra, at 559.

Mandatory or no-drop prosecution policies require prosecutors to prosecute domestic violence cases regardless of the victim's wishes. By 1995, nine jurisdictions had adopted mandatory prosecution policies. See Cheryl Hanna, No Right to Choose: Mandated Victim Participation in Domestic Violence Prosecutions, 109 Harv. L. Rev. 1850 (1996). Do you see any problem with these policies? Do they seem realistic? See Mills, supra at 561 (when battered women are reluctant to testify against their batterers, prosecutors may use strategies similar to those used in murder cases: introducing spontaneous statements made by the victim at the time of arrest, police officers' testimony, and videos or photographs taken at the time of the injury in lieu of the victim's testimony).

Mandatory reporting laws are another form of intervention. These laws require physicians to file a domestic violence report with the police when they suspect that a patient's injuries are the result of intimate partner violence. Mills, Killing Her Softly, supra, at 562. As of 1998, most states had some mandatory reporting laws governing cases in which medical personnel suspected domestic violence, while five states had adopted broader reporting requirements. Id.; see Linda G. Mills, The Heart of Intimate Abuse: New Interventions in Child Welfare, Criminal Justice, and Health Settings 85-87 (1998). For a discussion of mandatory sentencing in the context of the Violence Against Women Act, see page 690, infra.

Mandatory intervention policies are controversial among legal reformers. Most concerns have focused on their effectiveness. Defenders argue that mandatory policies are the best way to force domestic violence to be taken seriously and that these policies, because of their mandatory nature, minimize the possibility of invidious discrimination. See, e.g., Hanna, supra, at 1886; Forum: Mandatory Prosecution in Domestic Violence Cases, 7 UCLA Women's L.J. 169-199 (1997); Jeffrey Fagan, National Institute of Justice Research Report, The Criminalization of Domestic Violence: Promises and Limits 1, 6-11 (1996). Critics are skeptical that mandatory interventions have any long-term positive effect. A 1992 study by Lawrence Sherman and others found that over the long term, violence increased in cases where the perpetrator was arrested and that the frequency of repeat violence increased when the persons arrested were unemployed, unmarried, high school dropouts, or African American. Lawrence W. Sherman et al., The Variable Effects of Arrest on Criminal Careers: The Milwaukee Domestic Violence Experiment, 83 J. Crim. L. & Criminology 137, 158-163 (1992); see also Robert C. Davis et al., The Deterrent Effect of

Prosecuting Domestic Violence Misdemeanors, 44 Crime & Delinq. 434, 441 (1998) (finding no effect of mandatory prosecution on re-arrest); Mia M. McFarlane, Mandatory Reporting of Domestic Violence: An Inappropriate Response for New York Health Care Professionals, 17 Buff. Pub. Int. L.J. 1 (1998-1999). Eleven articles debating the methodologies and interpretations of the mandatory arrest studies, including feminist critiques by Cynthia Grant Bowman, Lisa A. Frisch, and Lisa G. Lerman, can be found in Symposium on Domestic Violence, 83 J. Crim. L. & Criminology 1 (1992); see also Nancy James, Domestic Violence: A History of Arrest Policies and a Survey of Modern Laws, 28 Fam. L.Q. 509 (1994); Joan Zorza & Laurie Woods, Mandatory Arrest: Problems and Possibilities (1994); Joan Zorza, Must We Stop Arresting Batterers?: Analysis and Policy Implications of New Police Domestic Violence Studies, 28 New Eng. L. Rev. 929 (1994) (arguing that the published studies, correctly interpreted, show that arrest is generally the superior method of deterring future violence).

While some favor mandatory arrest and prosecution strategies because they minimize the likelihood of discrimination, others underline the fact that arrest and prosecution will be more frequent in African-American and Latino communities because they are already disproportionately targeted, given racial stereotypes about the violent nature of African-American and Latino men. See, e.g., Miriam H. Ruttenberg, A Feminist Critique of Mandatory Arrest: An Analysis of Race and Gender in Domestic Violence Policy, 2 Am. U. J. Gender & L. 171, 182 (1994); see also Barbara Fedders, Lobbying for Mandatory-Arrest Policies: Race, Class, and the Politics of the Battered Women's Movement, 23 N.Y.U. Rev. L. & Soc. Change 281 (1997) (arguing that mandatory arrest policies disserve women of color). Donna Coker concludes that a focus on domestic violence policies that provide women with material resources such as housing, food, clothing, or money should take priority over policies that merely seek greater punishment for batterers. Donna Coker, Shifting Power for Battered Women: Law, Material Resources, and Poor Women of Color, 33 U.C. Davis L. Rev. 1009 (2000).

Finally, some feminists also worry that mandatory interventions, because of their disregard for the victims' wishes, are harmful to the trauma recovery process. Linda Mills argues that mandatory policies "visit upon these victims an entirely distinct violent interaction, one that contains many of the emotionally abusive elements of the victim's relationship with the batterer." Mills, Killing Her Softly, supra, at 568. In Mills's view, feminist support of such policies "may be a product of [a] patriarchal influence on feminist perspective." Id. at 569. To what extent are these critiques also applicable to the *Stephenson* case? See note 4, infra. Can you think of additional difficulties?

3. Contemporary Legal Responses to Intimate Violence: New Crimes. In addition to efforts to secure greater compliance with existing laws, some new crimes have been created to address specifically the circumstances of domestic abuse. Some states, for example, have separate domestic abuse statutes. See Minn. Stat. Ann. §518B.01 (West 1990 & Supp. 1997). In 1990, California was the first state to enact an anti-stalking law, after actress Rebecca Schaeffer was killed there by an obsessed fan in 1989. Within two years of the passage of the California statute, over half the states had passed laws to criminalize stalking; by 1998, all 50 states had stalking laws. Carol E. Jordan, Karen Quinn, Bradley Jordan, & Celia R. Daileader, Stalking: Cultural, Clinical and Legal Considerations, 38 Brandeis L.J. 513, 516 (2000); see also Kristin J. Bouchard, Note, Can Civil Damage Suits Stop Stalkers?, 6 B.U. Pub. Int. L.J. 551 (1997); Heather M. Stearns, Comment, Stalking Stuffers: A Revolutionary Law to Keep Predators Behind Bars, 35 Santa Clara L. Rev. 1027 (1995). The first wave of such statutes was plagued with constitutional problems of vagueness and overbreadth, but later statutes were more narrowly written, tracking the model code developed by the Justice Department in conjunction with the National Criminal Justice Administration and the National Institute of Justice and released in October 1993. See National Institute of Justice Research Report, Domestic Violence, Stalking, and Antistalking Legislation: An Annual Report to Congress Under the Violence Against Women Act 4 (1996). For an overview of the statutes and case law, see Jordan et al., supra.

The federal Violence Against Women Act, enacted in 1994, extends funding to states to address problems of stalking and domestic violence. See 42 U.S.C. §§14031-14042 (1995). The Act is discussed in more detail at pages 690-692.

4. Contemporary Legal Responses to Intimate Violence: Civil Enforcement. All 50 states plus the District of Columbia and Puerto Rico now have procedures for civil restraining orders, which can enjoin an abuser from harassing, threatening, or abusing a victim. The varying requirements and procedures for obtaining these orders are discussed in Catherine F. Klein & Leslye E. Orloff, Providing Legal Protection for Battered Women: An Analysis of State Statutes and Case Law, 21 Hofstra L. Rev. 801 (1993); see also Kit Kinports & Karla Fischer, Orders of Protection in Domestic Violence Cases: An Empirical Assessment of the Impact of the Reform Statutes, 2 Tex. J. Women & the Law 163 (1993). As a practical matter, these orders are only as effective as the willingness of the abuser to obey them and the ability of the state to enforce them. See David M. Zlotnick, Empowering the Battered Woman: The Use of Criminal Contempt Sanctions to Enforce Civil Protection Orders, 56 Ohio St. L.J. 1153 (1995); Karla Fischer & Mary Rose, When "Enough Is Enough": Battered Women's Decision Making Around Court Orders of Protection, 41 Crime & Delinq. 414 (1995). The effectiveness of these legal avenues depends as well on the resources and stamina of victims for whose use they are intended, and how well these victims stand up to real or potential escalation of violence or other retaliation that use of the legal process may stimulate. See Walter W. Steele, Jr. & Christine W. Sigman, Reexamining the Doctrine of Self Defense to Accommodate Battered Women, 18 Am. J. Crim. L. 169, 172-174 (1991). Thirty-four states have adopted criminal contempt laws to help enforce protection orders, and forty-five jurisdictions have made violating a protection order a statutory crime. Deborah Epstein, Effective Intervention in Domestic Violence Cases: Rethinking the Roles of Prosecutors, Judges, and the Court System, 11 Yale J.L. & Feminism 3, 12 (1999).

What about the approach of the court in *Stephenson*: keeping a protective order in effect, even over the objection of the victim? Review the criticisms of mandatory arrest, prosecution and reporting laws in note 2, supra. Are the mandatory policies the natural consequence of viewing domestic violence as a public problem rather than a private one? What are the costs? See Cathleen A. Booth, No-Drop Policies: Effective Legislation or Protectionist Attitude? 30 U. Tol. L. Rev. 621, 644-645 (1999) (*Stephenson* is an admirable decision, but it may have some costs for battered women, including the loss of leverage in divorce settlements and the potential diminution in safety); see also Ruth Jones, Guardianship for Coercively Battered Women: Breaking the Control of the Abuser, 88 Geo. L.J. 605 (2000) (advocating guardianship as a tool to assist battered women).

Another legal resource for survivors of intimate violence is the civil damages suit. Tort claims brought by women against their spouses face the barrier of interspousal immunity, a holdover from the days of coverture. See Clare Dalton, Domestic Violence, Domestic Torts and Divorce: Constraints and Possibilities, 31 New Eng. L. Rev. 319 (1997). Nonetheless one commentator advocates the use of the tort of intentional infliction of emotional distress for domestic violence victims. Merle H. Weiner, Domestic Violence and the Per Se Standard of Outrage, 54 Md. L. Rev. 183 (1995). The various legal issues raised by such tort actions are examined in Douglas D. Scherer, Tort Remedies for Victims of Domestic Abuse, 43 S.C. L. Rev. 543 (1992); Rhonda L. Kohler, Comment, The Battered Woman and Tort Law: A New Approach to Fighting Domestic Violence, 25 Loy. L.A. L. Rev. 1025 (1992).

Survivors of domestic violence have also sought to hold the state itself accountable for its failure to protect them. Some courts have allowed federal civil rights actions under §1983 against municipalities whose police failed to respond to domestic violence complaints or who applied special arrest policies that discriminated against the victims of domestic violence. See, e.g., Hynson v. City of Chester, 864 F.2d 1026 (3d Cir. 1988) (mother and children of woman killed by her abusive boyfriend allowed to sue police who refused to arrest the boyfriend the day before the murder because the woman's restraining order had expired); Watson v. Kansas City, 857 F.2d 690 (10th Cir. 1988) (wife whose abusive husband was a police officer was told when reporting incidents never to call the police again or they would have her arrested and take away her children; the police department took no disciplinary action against the husband, whose behavior culminated in a brutal rape of his wife and attack on his children); Thurman v. City of Torrington, 595 F. Supp. 1521 (D. Conn. 1984) (police repeatedly ignored woman's complaints about estranged husband and even stood by as abusive incidents occurred). The *Thurman* case led to a consent judgment against the city for $2.3 million. See George P. Choundas, Neither Equal nor Protected: The Invisible Law of Equal Protection, the Legal Invisibility of Its Gender-Based Victims, 44 Emory L.J. 1069 (1995); Amy Eppler, Battered Women and the Equal Protection Clause: Will the Constitution Help Them When the Police Won't?, 95 Yale L.J. 788, 795 n.31 (1986).

After the Supreme Court's decision in DeShaney v. Winnebago County Department of Social Services, 489 U.S. 189 (1989), holding that §1983 damages actions will not lie for injuries sustained because the state did not protect a victim from violence by private parties over which it has no control, such actions cannot be based solely on the failure of the police to protect women against "private violence" by their husbands or boyfriends. However, a §1983 claim for discriminatory enforcement of laws protecting victims of domestic violence under the equal protection clause — the theory pursued in *Thurman*, *Watson*, and *Hynson* — remains a viable legal avenue. See, e.g., Culbertson v. Doan, 65 F. Supp. 2d 702 (S.D. Ohio 1999) (denying motion to dismiss for failure to state a claim when the chief of police failed to act on the decedent's reports of her boyfriend's abuse and beatings, asking, "Why does she keep going back to it?"; the decedent was eventually murdered by the boyfriend). Some courts have held that a "special relationship" imposing on the police a duty to act may arise under certain situations. See, e.g., Mastroianni v. County of Suffolk, 668 N.Y.S.2d 542 (N.Y. 1997) (special relationship arose when the police failed to arrest a husband despite their knowledge of his violent history and their knowledge that he had violated an order of protection; minutes after the police left, the husband stabbed the wife to death); Joan Zorza, Suing the Police After Deshaney (National Center for Women & Family Law, unpublished manuscript 1995), printed in Nancy K.D. Lemon, Domestic Violence Law 548 (2001).

5. Domestic Violence and Child Custody. Battered women often have young children. Indeed, women's role in the care of children is a factor nonsubordination theorists often point to as an effective control mechanism by which men can dominate women. A battered mother is all the more reluctant to leave her batterer if by doing so she jeopardizes the economic support of her children. Moreover, custody and visitation law was not developed with intimate violence in mind: a battered mother's psychological profile or her reluctance to cooperate with the batterer may work against her in her efforts to secure permanent custody of the children, and she may even be blamed for her failure to protect them from abuse. Visitation rights and joint custody arrangements may also give batterers the ability to continue their abuse. Finally, battered mothers who escape the relationship and leave the children behind may jeopardize their safety and their own future ability to regain custody.

At least in theory, custody and visitation law has recognized the problem of domestic violence. "At least 39 states, the District of Columbia, and the Virgin Islands have statutes requiring courts to consider domestic violence in custody determinations; every state has case law allowing courts to consider domestic violence in custody disputes; and the Congress unanimously passed a resolution calling on every state to enact a presumption that batterers not obtain sole or joint legal or physical custody but that they receive at most supervised visitation. Both the National Council of Juvenile and Family Court Judges and the American Bar Association's report to its president recommend passage of similar legislation." Joan Zorza, Protecting the Children in Custody Disputes When One Parent Abuses the Other, Clearinghouse Rev. 1113 (April 1996), reprinted in Lemon, Domestic Violence Law supra, at 334; see generally Family Violence Project of The National Council of Juvenile and Family Court Judges, Family Violence in Child Custody Statutes: An Analysis of State Codes, 29 Fam. L.Q. 197 (1995); Pauline Quirion et al., Protecting Children Exposed to Domestic Violence in Contested Custody and Visitation Litigation, 6 B.U. Pub. Int. L.J. 501 (1997). At least 11 states have a rebuttable presumption or mandate against an award of joint custody upon a finding of domestic violence, and about 10 states have rebuttable presumptions against an award of custody to a parent who has perpetrated domestic violence. Nancy K.D. Lemon, Statutes Creating Rebuttable Presumptions Against Custody to Batterers: How Effective Are They?, 28 William Mitchell L. Rev. (forthcoming 2002); Lynne R. Kurtz, Comment, Protecting New York's Children: An Argument for the Creation of a Rebuttable Presumption Against Awarding a Spouse Abuser Custody of a Child, 60 Alb. L. Rev. 1345, 1367 (1997).

Although states have been slower to act in placing limitations on visitation than on custody in disputes involving domestic violence, by 1998 eight states had passed supervised visitation legislation patterned after the Model Code on Domestic and Family Violence. The Model Code permits a court to grant visitation by a parent who has committed domestic violence only if adequate provision for the safety of the child and the abused parent can be made. Maureen Sheeran & Scott Hampton, Supervised Visitation in Cases of Domestic Violence, 50 Juv. & Fam. Ct. J. 13 (1999), reprinted in Lemon, Domestic Violence Law, supra, at 353-354. Another 17 states had legislation specifically permitting visitation in proceedings involving domestic violence under various conditions. Id. at 354. Finally, "visitation centers" have begun to emerge in some states, providing security procedures and confidentiality policies that can help prevent further harm. Id. at 355-356.

Despite these laws and programs, however, research indicates that custody evaluators — usually psychologists — seldom consider domestic violence when they make child custody recommendations. Stephen E.

Doyne et al., Custody Disputes Involving Domestic Violence: Making Children's Needs a Priority, 50 Juv. & Fam. Ct. J. 1 (1999). Indeed, one survey found that over three-quarters of custody evaluators recommended denying sole or joint custody to a parent who "alienates the child from the other parent by negatively interpreting the other parent's behavior." Lemon, supra, at 346. Joan Zorza reports that because of evaluators' negative reactions to women who raise the issue of abuse, "[b]atterers who physically or sexually abuse their children are more likely to win full or joint custody than abusive fathers who have never physically or sexually abused a child." Zorza, Protecting the Children, in Lemon, Domestic Violence Law, supra, at 335. Moreover, family court judges are often unaware of or incorrectly interpret the presumption statutes, or lack guidance about how much weight to accord to domestic violence; indeed, many family court judges are uneducated about the effects of domestic violence on families. Amy Levin, Comment, Child Witnesses of Domestic Violence: How Should Judges Apply the Best Interests of the Child Standard in Custody and Visitation Cases Involving Domestic Violence?, 47 UCLA L. Rev. 813, 817 (2000).

The realities of domestic violence are frequently at odds with the underlying policy of custody and visitation law, which seeks to preserve and foster family relationships. Thus, for example, battered women seeking custody of their children are made vulnerable by so-called friendly parent provisions that favor awarding custody to the parent who will foster the better relationship between the child and the other parent. Zorza, Protecting the Children, in Lemon, Domestic Violence Law, supra, at 335. The assumption that joint custody is ordinarily in the best interest of the children becomes similarly problematic when battering has taken place. Id. at 337.

Another difficult issue concerning the children in battering relationships is allocating culpability when the children themselves are being abused. Courts have held that a parent who allows another to abuse her children is guilty of criminal child abuse or neglect as well. Indeed, some courts have employed a strict liability standard in abuse or neglect cases, holding that any parent whose child becomes caught up in intimate violence is unfit without regard to fault. See, e.g., In re Glenn G., 154 Misc. 2d 677 (N.Y. Fam. Ct. 1992) (rejecting strict liability as the standard for abuse proceedings, but adopting it for neglect; thus, mother who was a battered woman neglected children by providing inadequate protection from father's sexual abuse); State v. Williquette, 385 N.W.2d 145 (Wis. 1986) (criminal conviction for child abuse based on mother's failure to protect her children from father's physical and sexual abuse). See also People v. Stanciel, 606 N.E.2d 1201 (Ill. 1992) (upholding murder convictions of two women for failing to stop their boyfriends from beating the women's children to death). Do such holdings ignore the state's own responsibility for its failure to protect the woman? Do they reveal the fantasy that a "good mother" can perform the impossible on behalf of her children? See G. Kristian Miccio, A Reasonable Battered Mother? Redefining, Reconstructing, and Recreating the Battered Mother in Child Protective Proceedings, 22 Harv. Women's L.J. 89 (1999) (arguing for a "reasonable battered mother test"); Lesley E. Daigle, Empowering Women to Protect: Improving Intervention with Victims of Domestic Violence in Cases of Child Abuse and Neglect; A Study of Travis County, Texas, 7 Tex. J. Women & L. 287, 313 (1998) (exploring programmatic initiatives to protect children in dangerous situations); see also V. Pualani Enos, Prosecuting Battered Mothers: State Laws' Failure to Protect Battered Women and Abused Children, 19 Harv. Women's L.J. 229 (1996) (arguing that too many battered mothers are losing custody of their children under the theory that they have "failed to protect" their children from the abuser).

Deborah Epstein suggests that "children's rights advocates, in their fight to protect young children from injury and death, too often fail to consider the dynamics of spousal abuse. However, domestic violence activists, desperate to bring the problem of woman abuse into public awareness and engender concern, have felt compelled to insist that all battered women are completely innocent victims. They have resisted recognizing that some victims belong to families where each member relates to one another through violence and threats of violence." Deborah Epstein, Effective Intervention in Domestic Violence Cases: Rethinking the Roles of Prosecutors, Judges, and the Court System, 11 Yale J.L. & Feminism 3, 36-37 (1999). For a thoughtful exploration of the difficulty of avoiding either demonizing or sentimentalizing mothers of abused children, see Dorothy E. Roberts, Mothers Who Fail to Protect Their Children: Accounting for Private and Public Responsibility, in Mother Troubles: Rethinking Contemporary Maternal Dilemmas 31 (Julia E. Hanigsberg & Sara Ruddick eds., 1999).

Finally, how should the law respond when a battered woman flees with the children — or when an abuser does? See Janet M. Bowermaster, Relocation Custody Disputes Involving Domestic Violence, 46 U. Kan. L. Rev. 433 (1998) (describing the possible scenarios and legal responses). The Uniform Child Custody Jurisdiction and Enforcement Act (UCCJEA) was recently promulgated to promote communication and cooperation among courts in various jurisdictions and to protect victims of intimate violence. See Billie Lee Dunford-Jackson, The Uniform Child Custody Jurisdiction and Enforcement Act: Affording Enhanced Protection for Victims of Domestic Violence and Their Children, 50 Juv. & Fam. Ct. J. 55 (1999), reprinted in Lemon, Domestic Violence Law, supra, at 366. Other relevant statutes are the Parental Kidnapping Prevention Act (PKPA), 28 U.S.C. §1738A, and the full faith and credit requirements of the Violence Against Women Act (VAWA), 18 U.S.C. §2265. When parent abductors flee the United States altogether, the Hague Convention mandates the return of children to their place of "habitual residence" to restore the status quo so that a custody determination can be made. The drafters of the Convention created an exception for cases where there is a grave risk of danger to the child if he or she is returned; however, American courts have not interpreted this exception to include victims of domestic violence. See Regan Fordice Grilli, Domestic Violence: Is It Being Sanctioned by the Hague Convention?, 4 Sw. J.L. & Trade Am. 71 (1997), reprinted in Lemon, Domestic Violence Law, supra, at 372.

6. Alternative Fora for Domestic Violence Cases: Mediation, Domestic Violence Courts, and "Peacemaking." The preference in many states for mediation or conciliation procedures in domestic cases also creates tension between the aims of family law — in this case, to reduce judicial backlogs and resolve family law disputes without unnecessary hostility — and the realities of intimate partner violence. Many states mandate mediation for custody and visitation issues. See, e.g., Cal. Fam. Code §3170 (West 1998); Holly Joyce, Mediation and Domestic Violence: Legislative Responses, 14 J. Am. Acad. Matrim. Law. 447 (1997) (describing various state provisions). Even in jurisdictions with mandatory mediation, however, parties usually are not required to mediate where domestic violence has occurred. Some states prohibit mediation in domestic violence cases; others leave the decision to judicial discretion. California alone does not provide a complete exemption, but rather permits the mediator to meet separately with the parties where there has been a history of domestic violence. See Cal. Fam. Code §3181 (West 1998); Kerry Loomis, Domestic Violence and Mediation: A Tragic Combination for Victims in California Family Court, 35 Cal. W. L. Rev. 355 (1999).

Should mediation be favored in the resolution of divorce cases where domestic violence has been present in the marriage? Some think so. Mediation supporters argue that "mediation can provide a supportive, empowering environment for women who in many cases have been stripped of their identity, dignity, and self-esteem." Joyce, supra, at 458. Mediation is less adversarial than the judicial system; it also encourages the parties to take responsibility themselves rather than depending on a lawyer's counsel. Mediation procedures can be structured to minimize contact between the spouses, and a trained mediator can possibly even help "break the cycle of abuse." Finally, not all domestic violence cases are alike; while mediation will be inappropriate in some situations, it may be suited to others. Id. at 456-458.

Many battered women's advocates, however, emphatically reject mediation as an acceptable approach to domestic disputes involving intimate partner violence. As Donna Coker describes some of the objections:

> The normative problem that exists in mediation stems from the ideology of mediator neutrality coupled with the hidden or informal rules that disadvantage women, enact gendered understandings of appropriate mediating behavior, and largely ignore claims of past injustice between parties. In family court

mediation, the ideal mediator is supposed to be neutral, with the sole purpose of effectuating the desires of the parties. As Trina Grillo writes, this ideal of neutrality frequently masks mediation's informal rules of behavior: Focus on the future and not the past, do not be too emotional, and especially do not be too angry. Sara Cobb similarly notes the manner in which mediation "domesticates" stories of violence by moving the focus from the victim's rights to the victim's needs. In part, this is a result of a mediation methodology that eschews fact finding and blame. For battered women, this creates the risk that mediation will reinforce the batterer's belief in the rightness of his behavior, minimize the harm of his violence and control, and undermine the victim's belief in her right not to be beaten. The insistence on a purportedly neutral mediator fails to identify the immorality of the batterer's (past, present, ongoing) behavior and limits the support a mediator can give a battered woman.

Donna Coker, Enhancing Autonomy for Battered Women: Lessons from Navajo Peacemaking, 47 UCLA L. Rev. 1, 88-89 (1999) (citing Trina Grillo, The Mediation Alternative: Process Dangers for Women, 100 Yale L.J. 1545 (1991), and Sara Cobb, The Domestication of Violence in Mediation, 31 Law & Soc'y Rev. 397, 410 (1997)); see also Penelope E. Bryan, Killing Us Softly: Divorce Mediation and the Politics of Power, 40 Buff. L. Rev. 441 (1992); Karla Fischer, Neil Vidmar, & René Ellis, The Culture of Battering and the Role of Mediation in Domestic Violence Cases, 46 SMU L. Rev. 2117 (1993). Is it odd, given the criticisms dominance theorists have levied against the formal legal system as a tool of male control of women, that some women's advocates nevertheless prefer formal, legalized mechanisms for responding to domestic violence over less formal, nonadversarial alternatives? Consider this question again after you have read Chapter 5.

As advocates for battered women point out, the process of ending an abusive relationship, particularly when marriage and/or children are involved, is extraordinarily complex, often requiring multiple lawsuits in both criminal and civil courts. One solution might be the development of specialized domestic violence courts. As of 1999, three jurisdictions — the District of Columbia, Florida, and Hawaii — had created such unified courts. Deborah Epstein, Effective Intervention in Domestic Violence Cases: Rethinking the Roles of Prosecutors, Judges, and the Court System, 11 Yale J.L. & Feminism 3, 28 (1999). As Epstein notes:

> Integrated domestic violence courts typically aim to achieve at least three fundamental goals. First, they try to provide victims with a "one-stop shopping" intake center that provides comprehensive assistance with the full range of intimate violence litigation and related social services. Second, they try to coordinate civil protection order, family law, and criminal dockets so that the court can handle cases, to the greatest extent possible, on a "one family, one judge" basis. Finally, they ensure that the court itself is located in a place that provides victims with security and protection from physical assault.

Id. at 29.

Donna Coker argues that the Navajo practice of Peacemaking may be autonomy enhancing for some battered women. "In Peacemaking, parties meet with a peacemaker and others who have either a special relationship to the parties (e.g., family and friends) or relevant expertise (e.g., alcohol treatment counselors and hospital social workers). Each participant is given a chance to describe the problem that the petitioner has identified as the reason for the session. The peacemaker then leads the group in developing recommendations and agreements designed to ameliorate or solve the problem." Coker, Enhancing Autonomy, supra, at 34-35. In the Navajo legal system, criminal cases may be referred to Peacemaking by the court as the result of diversion or as a condition of probation; civil courts also have the authority to refer cases to Peacemaking. Peacemaking may also be initiated by a petitioner. Id. at 37. How does the Peacemaking model seem to differ from mediation? Do you agree with Coker that it may be useful in some intimate partner abuse cases?

3. Domestic Violence and Substantive Criminal Law

Martha Mahoney, *Legal Images of Battered Women: Redefining the Issue of Separation*
90 Mich. L. Rev. 1, 71-75, 82 (1991)

There is a two-layered problem in seeing through the criminal cases involving abuse of women. First, these cases appear in various doctrinal guises, and few explicitly acknowledge that they concern domestic violence at all. Second, on closer examination, many of the "wife-murder" cases turn out to be "ex-wife murder," the most extreme violence turned against women at separation. Many of the women killed by their husbands are killed after they have separated. Ironically, since those women are not alive to tell their stories, their voices disappear into the narrative voices of the courts, where the women are not usually identified as battered:

> On a day in early September in 1977, the petitioner and his wife of 28 years had a heated argument in their home. During the course of this altercation, the petitioner, who had consumed several cans of beer, threatened his wife with a knife and damaged some of her clothing. At this point, the petitioner's wife declared that she was going to leave him, and departed to stay with relatives. [This was not the first time that he and his wife had been separated as a result of his violent behavior.] That afternoon she went to a Justice of the Peace and secured a warrant charging the petitioner with aggravated assault. A few days later, while still living away from home, she filed suit for divorce. [A court hearing date was set, and several efforts to persuade the wife to return home were rebuffed.] At some point during this period, his wife moved in with her

mother. . . . [Several angry phone calls were exchanged, while she refused to reconcile.]

At this juncture, the petitioner got out his shotgun and walked with it down the hill from his home to the trailer where his mother-in-law lived. Peering through a window, he observed his wife, his mother-in-law, and his 11-year-old daughter playing a card game. He pointed the shotgun at his wife through the window and pulled the trigger. The charge from the gun struck his wife in the forehead and killed her instantly. He proceeded into the trailer, striking and injuring his fleeing daughter with the barrel of the gun. He then fired the gun at his mother-in-law, striking her in the head and killing her instantly.

[Godfrey v. Georgia, 446 U.S. 420, 424-425 (1980).]

Godfrey v. Georgia presents an almost perfect picture of the dangers for women at separation: Mrs. Godfrey had resolutely separated from her husband and energetically sought the protection of the law. However, her story does not enter the criminal law casebook as a domestic violence case. Rather, Godfrey is a death penalty case presenting the issue of whether this murder was unambiguously "outrageously or wantonly vile, horrible or inhuman," or whether the case revealed ambiguity and vagueness in the death penalty statute. The Supreme Court essentially found Mrs. Godfrey's death to be quite an ordinary murder. I believe the majority was correct — this was an ordinary murder — but the facts were even more ordinary than the majority realized.

Mary McNeill has shown that several torts cases on duty are actually domestic violence cases in disguise. However, once the domestic violence is perceived, separation assault appears to be a further hidden issue in at least one of the cases. In Jablonski by Pahls v. United States, [712 F.2d 391 (9th Cir. 1983)], Melinda Kimball had repeatedly approached the psychologists who examined the man she lived with, telling his doctors that she was afraid of him. They failed to commit him or to seek his medical records, which would have revealed that he had ten years earlier been diagnosed as schizophrenic and had then had homicidal ideas about his wife. One doctor told Kimball that she should avoid Jablonski if she heard him. Kimball left after a priest also urged her to separate from Jablonski. She was murdered when she returned to the apartment to pick up some baby diapers. Since there is no record of any attempt to kill her before she left, separation appears to be at least a precipitating factor in Kimball's death.

In Garcia v. Superior Court, [789 P.2d 960, 961-962 (Cal. 1990)], Grace Morales was killed by Napoleon Johnson, Jr., the man from whom she had recently separated. According to the complaint, Johnson's parole officer was aware that Johnson had killed his first wife after she left him. Although he was notified Johnson had threatened to kill Morales and that Morales was filing a temporary restraining order, the parole officer advised Morales that Johnson would not come looking for her. Johnson kidnapped Morales and killed her; her children sued. The court distinguished the parole officer's "negligent representations" from a failure to warn for which the officer might have been liable under Tarasoff v. Regents of the University of California, [551 P.2d 334 (Cal. 1976),] and held that the plaintiffs must allege that Morales reasonably relied on the parole officer's advice. . . .

Even feminist literature on battering may overlook the particularity of attacks on women's autonomy. For example, the feminist newsletter Response cites the 1988 case of Balistreri v. Pacifica Police Department, [855 F.2d 1421 (9th Cir. 1988), amended on other grounds, 901 F.2d 696 (9th Cir. 1990)], in a short article entitled "Court Rules in Favor of Abused Wife." The one-paragraph article describes Balistreri as

> an abused wife who sued police for not protecting her. . . . Police had refused to arrest the batterer when summoned following a beating, failed to offer medical assistance, and did not protect the woman over a 3-year period during which she reported incidents to police and obtained a restraining order.

Most of the facts of *Balistreri* concern attacks after separation. When Balistreri's husband beat her severely in February 1982, officers failed to help her. She divorced her husband — apparently promptly, because "throughout 1982" she complained to police of vandalism and harassing phone calls by the husband "from whom she was now divorced." In November that year, her "former husband" crashed his car into her garage, and in March 1983, a firebomb was thrown through the window of her house. From 1983 to 1985, telephone harassment and vandalism continued. Balistreri emerges as a woman of great strength — resisting her ex-husband's repeated attacks and pursuing her complaint within the legal system when her lawyer would go no further. "Abused wife," the term used by Response, captures neither her determined resistance nor her separation as the keys to the repeated violence she suffered. . . .

. . . Collectively, the jury can only "know" what it is possible for them to discuss. Women will still find it impossible to incorporate our own experience in the jury room unless the lens through which we perceive battered women has been entirely transformed. Men will also remain unable to discuss their experience as witnesses to violence against women or their capacity to seek control violently. As long as we have no way to discuss or understand the violence many of us have experienced — or to sort out what we have heard from others — there remains a critical need for expert testimony to explain to the jury things beyond their capacity for collective knowledge and discussion, even if these things are within their individual personal experience.

≣ **People v. Berry**
556 P.2d 777 (Cal. 1976)

SULLIVAN, Justice.

Defendant Albert Joseph Berry was charged by indictment with one count of murder and one count of assault by means of force likely to produce great bodily injury. . . . The assault was allegedly committed on July 23, 1974, and the murder on July 26, 1974. In each count, the alleged victim was defendant's wife, Rachel Pessah Berry. A jury found defendant guilty as charged and determined that the murder was of the first degree. Defendant was sentenced to state prison for the term prescribed by law. He appeals from the judgment of conviction.

Defendant contends that there is sufficient evidence in the record to show that he committed the homicide while in a state of uncontrollable rage caused by provocation and flowing from a condition of diminished capacity and therefore that it was error for the trial court to fail to instruct the injury on voluntary manslaughter as indeed he had requested. . . .

Defendant, a cook, 46 years old, and Rachel Pessah, a 20-year-old girl from Israel, were married on May 27, 1974. Three days later Rachel went to Israel by herself, returning on July 13, 1974. On July 23, 1974, defendant choked Rachel into unconsciousness. She was treated at a hospital where she reported her strangulation by defendant to an officer of the San Francisco Police Department. On July 25, Inspector Sammon, who had been assigned to the case, met with Rachel and as a result of the interview a warrant was issued for defendant's arrest.

While Rachel was at the hospital, defendant removed his clothes from their apartment and stored them in a Greyhound Bus Depot locker. He stayed overnight at the home of a friend, Mrs. Jean Berk, admitting to her that he had choked his wife. On July 26, he telephoned Mrs. Berk and informed her that he had killed Rachel with a telephone cord on that morning at their apartment. . . .

At trial defendant did not deny strangling his wife, but claimed through his own testimony and the testimony of a psychiatrist, Dr. Martin Blinder, that he was provoked into killing her because of a sudden and uncontrollable rage so as to reduce the offense to one of voluntary manslaughter. He testified that upon her return from Israel, Rachel announced to him that while there she had fallen in love with another man, one Yako, and had enjoyed his sexual favors, that he was coming to this country to claim her and that she wished a divorce. Thus commenced a tormenting two weeks in which Rachel alternately taunted defendant with her involvement with Yako and at the same time sexually excited defendant, indicating her desire to remain with him. Defendant's detailed testimony, summarized below, chronicles this strange course of events.

After their marriage, Rachel lived with defendant for only three days and then left for Israel. Immediately upon her return to San Francisco she told defendant about her relationship with and love for Yako. This brought about further argument and a brawl that evening in which defendant choked Rachel and she responded by scratching him deeply many times. Nonetheless they continued to live together. Rachel kept taunting defendant with

Yako and demanding a divorce. She claimed she thought she might be pregnant by Yako. She showed defendant pictures of herself with Yako. Nevertheless, during a return trip from Santa Rosa, Rachel demanded immediate sexual intercourse with defendant in the car, which was achieved; however upon reaching their apartment, she again stated that she loved Yako and that she would not have intercourse with defendant in the future.

On the evening of July 22d defendant and Rachel went to a movie where they engaged in heavy petting. When they returned home and got into bed, Rachel announced that she had intended to make love with defendant, "But I am saving myself for this man Yako, so I don't think I will." Defendant got out of bed and prepared to leave the apartment, whereupon Rachel screamed and yelled at him. Defendant choked her into unconsciousness.

Two hours later defendant called a taxi for his wife to take her to the hospital. He put his clothes in the Greyhound bus station and went to the home of his friend Mrs. Berk for the night. The next day he went to Reno and returned the day after. Rachel informed him by telephone that there was a warrant for his arrest as a result of her report to the police about the choking incident. On July 25th defendant returned to the apartment to talk to Rachel, but she was out. He slept there overnight. Rachel returned around 11 a.m. the next day. Upon seeing defendant there, she said, "I suppose you have come here to kill me." Defendant responded, "yes," changed his response to "no," and then again to "yes," and finally stated "I have really come to talk to you." Rachel began screaming. Defendant grabbed her by the shoulder and tried to stop her screaming. She continued. They struggled and finally defendant strangled her with a telephone cord.

Dr. Martin Blinder, a physician and psychiatrist, called by the defense, testified that Rachel was a depressed, suicidally inclined girl and that this suicidal impulse led her to involve herself ever more deeply in a dangerous situation with defendant. She did this by sexually arousing him and taunting him into jealous rages in an unconscious desire to provoke him into killing her and thus consummating her desire for suicide. Throughout the period commencing with her return from Israel until her death, that is from July 13 to July 26, Rachel continually provoked defendant with sexual taunts and incitements, alternating acceptance and rejection of him. This conduct was accompanied by repeated references to her involvement with another man; it led defendant to choke her on two occasions, until finally she achieved her unconscious desire and was strangled. Dr. Blinder testified that as a result of this cumulative series of provocations, defendant at the time he fatally strangled Rachel, was in a state of uncontrollable rage, completely under the sway of passion.

We first take up defendant's claim that on the basis of the foregoing evidence he was entitled to an instruction on voluntary manslaughter as defined by statute which is "the unlawful killing of a human being, without malice . . . upon a sudden quarrel or heat of passion." [In an earlier case the court approved the following quotation of the law:] "[T]he fundamental of the inquiry is whether or not the defendant's reason was, at the time of his act, so disturbed or obscured by some passion — not necessarily fear and never, of course, the passion for revenge — to such an extent as would render ordinary men of average disposition liable to act rashly or without due deliberation and reflection, and from this passion rather than judgment."

We further held . . . that there is no specific type of provocation required by section 192 and that verbal provocation may be sufficient. [In a previous case] in the course of explaining the phrase "heat of passion" used in the statute defining manslaughter we pointed out that "'passion' need not mean 'rage' or 'anger'" but may be any "[v]iolent, intense, high-wrought or enthusiastic emotion" and concluded there "that defendant was aroused to a heat of 'passion' by a series of events over a considerable period of time. . . ." Accordingly we there declared that evidence of admissions of infidelity by the defendant's paramour, taunts directed to him and other conduct, "supports a finding that defendant killed in wild desperation induced by [the woman's] long continued provocatory conduct." We find this reasoning persuasive in the case now before us. Defendant's testimony chronicles a two-week period of provocatory conduct by his wife Rachel that could arouse a passion of jealousy, pain and sexual rage in an ordinary man of average disposition such as to cause him to act rashly from this passion. It is significant that both defendant and Dr. Blinder testified that the former was in the heat of passion under an uncontrollable rage when he killed Rachel.

The Attorney General contends that the killing could not have been done in the heat of passion because there was a cooling period, defendant having waited in the apartment for 20 hours. However, the long course of provocatory conduct, which had resulted in intermittent outbreaks of rage under specific provocation in the past, reached its final culmination in the apartment when Rachel began screaming. . . .

. . . There was no clear direction to the jury to consider the evidence of Rachel's course of provocatory conduct so as to determine whether defendant, as an ordinary man of average disposition, having been exposed to such conduct, was provoked into committing the homicide under a heat of passion. Therefore we conclude that the jury's determination that defendant was guilty of murder of the first degree under the instructions given did not necessarily indicate that "the factual question posed by the omitted instruction was necessarily resolved adversely to the defendant under other, properly given instructions" — in other words that the jury had found that defendant had not killed Rachel under a heat of passion. Since this theory of provocation constituted defendant's entire defense to the first count, we have no difficulty concluding that the failure to give such instruction was prejudicial error and requires us to reverse the conviction of murder of the first degree.

Donna K. Coker, Heat of Passion and Wife Killing: Men Who Batter/Men Who Kill
2 S. Cal. Rev. L. & Women's Stud. 71 93-94, 116, 117-120, 123, 128 (1992)

[H]omicide law divides sane individuals who intentionally kill into two major categories: those who premeditate murder and those who act in the heat of passion. Social stereotypes of wife-killing that characterize the killer as a previously non-violent man who "snapped" under pressure, roughly parallel the understandings which underlie heat-of-passion doctrine. However, this social stereotype is grossly inaccurate when applied to men who are identified as "batterers" and when applied to the general category of husband-wife killings. Violence perpetrated by abusive men is purposeful, not spontaneous; the majority of men who kill their wives have a documented history of violent assaults. Furthermore, one would expect to find empirical evidence of wife-killers who fit the stereotype of the heat-of-passion killer in those reports of forensic psychiatrists whose job it is to aid defense counsel, yet these reports seem to confirm that men who kill and men who batter have remarkably similar personality traits and similar motivations. While further research is needed before we can determine whether or not the "impassioned" wife-killer exists, if he does exist, he is apparently part of a very small group of wife-killers. . . .

. . . The case of People v. Berry appears in many criminal law textbooks as well as legal treatises, generally for the proposition that the question of "cooling off" is a jury question. . . .

[Coker reviews the facts of the case and Dr. Blinder's testimony.]

The defense needed Blinder's testimony for two different, but equally critical, reasons. First, the fact that Berry had a prior conviction for stabbing and injuring his second wife had already been ruled admissible. Blinder's testimony was required to neutralize this damaging fact, but, in fact, Blinder went one step better by explaining that Berry's past violence resulted from his repeated emotional victimization at the hands of women. Second, Blinder's testimony was needed most obviously in order to cast the killing as a heat of passion killing and, in particular, to explain the 20-hour wait in Rachel's apartment as a result of cumulative passion and not premeditation and lying-in-wait. The result was psychiatric testimony that brilliantly — if tautologically — turned facts about Berry that suggested the antithesis of a "heat of passion killer" — i.e., a proclivity for violence, a history of serious prior assaults on the victim identical in kind to the fatal assault, Berry's stabbing of his ex-wife under remarkably similar circumstances, and a psychological profile fitting that of an abuser — into evidence of Berry's increasing provocation as the result of Rachel's relentless "taunting." . . .

In essence, Berry's defense was that he was the sort of man who abused women — but the twist was Blinder's psychiatric explanation that Berry's violence was a result of his choosing women who enraged him and provoked him to violence. The fact that Berry had a prior conviction for assaulting his ex-wife with a butcher knife, that in past relationships with other women he had destroyed their property, forcing former girlfriends to "put him out of the house, locking the door," indicated to Blinder the personality of the women with whom Berry involved himself, more than it demonstrated Berry's dangerous and abusive nature. Blinder testified that these women "offer[ed] him the promise of comfort but ultimately deliver[ed] emotional pain." Yet Blinder's testimony provides a classic portrait of an abuser. Berry was most dangerous when women threatened to leave him. Berry was "emotionally dependent" on wives and girlfriends; he threatened physical violence in order to control women; he destroyed women's property; and he had a history of violent relationships with wives and lovers. The Supreme Court's opinion read Dr. Blinder's testimony to focus narrowly on the effect of Rachel's "provocative" behavior on Berry's mental state. Dr. Blinder's testimony, however, refers to a cumulative rage resulting from the provocation of all the women in Berry's entire life:

Q: . . . How would you characterize [Berry's] state of mind . . . [at the time of the homicide]?

A: . . . I would say that he was in a state of uncontrollable rage which was a product of having to contend with what seems to me an incredibly provacative [sic] situation, an incredibly provacative [sic] young woman, and that this immediate situation was superimposed upon Mr. Berry having encountered the situation time and time again. So that we have a cumulative effect dating back to the way his mother dealt with him. . . .

Q: . . . [Y]ou say that the situation involving Rachel Berry and Albert Berry . . . was the product of . . . cumulative . . . provocations. Now, specifically, what would you base your opinion as to provocations on? . . .

A: . . . We have two factors here. . . . The past history, that is, the history of this man well in advance of his meeting the deceased. And then the history of his relationship with her. And I think the two go together. . . . After 15 years [of marriage to his second wife] and five children, his wife leaves him for . . . another man. . . . They continued to live together, during which time his wife taunted him about her boyfriend. . . .

One night while they were having sex, his wife [called him by the name of her boyfriend.] Despondent and enraged at the same time, he went into the kitchen, obtained a knife, and stabbed his wife in the abdomen. And she was not serious [sic]. He only got to spend a year in jail for that. . . .

So we have this pattern of enormous dependency on these women and then rupture of the relationship with tremendous rage, almost uncontrollable. I think in one instance he put his foot through the stereo . . . he had purchased for one of these girls [sic]. . . .

So we see a succession of women, beginning with his mother, who offer the promise of comfort but ultimately deliver indifference and emotional pain.

The irony of this defense testimony is found in its confirmation that Berry had a propensity to assault wives and lovers under circumstances in which he claimed the woman's infidelity provoked him. Rachel, then, became the recipient of Berry's cumulative rage against all the past women in his life. In a tautological way, Berry's past abuse of other women was used to strengthen his claim of Rachel's provocative nature: Berry had a pattern of involvement with emotionally abusive women; his violence was in response to their "abuse" — never the other way around. Rachel was involved with Berry; therefore, it is more than likely that Rachel emotionally abused Berry and that his violence was the result of provocation occasioned by her abuse. . . .

. . . The California Supreme Court opinion repeatedly echoes the tenor of Blinder's words — using terms such as "the result" or "culmination" — terms that diffuse responsibility and make Berry's violence seem inevitable and uncontrollable. . . .

Though Blinder's testimony focused on Rachel's "provocative" sexual behavior, the truth is that Berry didn't kill Rachel until it appeared that she might make good on her threat to leave him. . . . Blinder's testimony completely ignores this fact. Not surprisingly, perhaps, Blinder's testimony is completely from Berry's perspective: the relationship dynamics continue, even though Rachel has rejected attempts at reconciliation and has filed a police report. Of course, a defense witness tells it from the perspective of the accused, but in this circumstance, the defendant's perspective is largely that of the Court and that of the Law, as well. That perspective, as identified in this article, suggests that a woman's "abandonment" of a husband is provocative — and that a woman's preference of another lover is provocation of the worst sort.

State v. Norman
378 S.E.2d 8 (N.C. 1989)

[The facts of the case are given at pages 613-615, above.]

Two expert witnesses in forensic psychology and psychiatry who examined the defendant after the shooting, Dr. William Tyson and Dr. Robert Rollins, testified that the defendant fit the profile of battered wife syndrome. This condition, they testified, is characterized by such abuse and degradation that the battered wife comes to believe she is unable to help herself and cannot expect help from anyone else. She believes that she cannot escape the complete control of her husband and that he is invulnerable to law enforcement and other sources of help.

Dr. Tyson, a psychologist, was asked his opinion as to whether, on 12 June 1985, "it appeared reasonably necessary for Judy Norman to shoot J.T. Norman?" He replied: "I believe that . . . Mrs. Norman believed herself to be doomed . . . to a life of the worst kind of torture and abuse, degradation that she had experienced over the years in a progressive way; that it would only get worse, and that death was inevitable. . . ." Dr. Tyson later added: "I think Judy Norman felt that she had no choice, both in the protection of herself and her family, but to engage, exhibit deadly force against Mr. Norman, and that in so doing, she was sacrificing herself, both for herself and for her family."

Dr. Rollins, who was the defendant's attending physician at Dorothea Dix Hospital when she was sent there for evaluation, testified that in his opinion the defendant was a typical abused spouse and that "[s]he saw herself as powerless to deal with the situation, that there was no alternative, no way she could escape it." Dr. Rollins was asked his opinion as to whether "on June 12th, 1985, it appeared reasonably necessary that Judy Norman would take the life of J.T. Norman?" Dr. Rollins replied that in his opinion, "that course of action did appear necessary to Mrs. Norman."

Based on the evidence that the defendant exhibited battered wife syndrome, that she believed she could not escape her husband nor expect help from others, that her husband had threatened her, and that her husband's abuse of her had worsened in the two days preceding his death, the Court of Appeals concluded that a jury reasonably could have found that her killing of her husband was justified as an act of perfect self-defense. The Court of Appeals reasoned that the nature of battered wife syndrome is such that a jury could not be precluded from finding the defendant killed her husband lawfully in perfect self-defense, even though he was asleep when she killed him. We disagree.

The right to kill in self-defense is based on the necessity, real or reasonably apparent, of killing an unlawful aggressor to save oneself from *imminent* death or great bodily harm at his hands. . . . Our law has recognized that self-preservation under such circumstances springs from a primal impulse and is an inherent right of natural law. . . .

The killing of another human being is the most extreme recourse to our inherent right of self-preservation and can be justified in law only by the utmost real or apparent necessity brought about by the decedent. For that reason, our law of self-defense has required that a defendant claiming that a homicide was justified and, as a result, inherently lawful by reason of perfect self-defense must establish that she reasonably believed at the time of the killing she otherwise would have immediately suffered death or great bodily harm. Only if defendants are required to show that they killed due to a reasonable belief that death or great bodily harm was imminent can the justification for homicide remain clearly and firmly rooted in necessity. The imminence requirement ensures that deadly force will be used only where it is necessary as a last resort in the exercise of the inherent right of self-preservation. . . .

The term "imminent," as used to describe such perceived threats of death or great bodily harm as will justify a homicide by reason of perfect self-defense, has been defined as "immediate danger, such as must be instantly met, such as cannot be guarded against by calling for the assistance of others or the protection of the law." Black's Law Dictionary 676 (5th ed. 1979). . . .

The evidence in this case did not tend to show that the defendant reasonably believed that she was confronted by a threat of imminent death or great bodily harm. The evidence tended to show that no harm was "imminent" or about to happen to the defendant when she shot her husband. The uncontroverted evidence was that her husband had been asleep for some time when she walked to her mother's house, returned with the pistol, fixed the pistol after it jammed and then shot her husband three times in the back of the head. The defendant was not faced with an instantaneous choice between killing her husband or being killed or seriously injured. Instead, *all* of the evidence tended to show that the defendant had ample time and opportunity to resort to other means of preventing further abuse by her husband. . . .

Dr. Tyson . . . testified that the defendant "believed herself to be doomed . . . to a life of the worst kind of torture and abuse, degradation that she had experienced over the years in a progressive way; that it would only get worse, and that death was inevitable." Such evidence of the defendant's speculative beliefs concerning her remote and indefinite future, while indicating she had felt generally threatened, did not tend to show that she killed in the belief — reasonable or otherwise — that her husband presented a threat of imminent death or great bodily harm. . . .

The reasoning of our Court of Appeals in this case . . . proposes justifying the taking of human life not upon the reasonable belief it is necessary to prevent death or great bodily harm — which the imminence requirement ensures — but upon purely subjective speculation that the decedent probably would present a threat to life at a future time and that the defendant would not be able to avoid the predicted threat. . . .

. . . The relaxed requirements for perfect self-defense proposed by our Court of Appeals would tend to categorically legalize the opportune killing of abusive husbands by their wives solely on the basis of the wives' testimony concerning their subjective speculation as to the probability of future felonious assaults by their husbands. Homicidal self-help would then become a lawful solution, and perhaps the easiest and most effective solution, to this problem. . . . It has even been suggested that the relaxed requirements of self-defense found in what is often called the "battered woman's defense" could be extended in principle to *any type of case* in which a defendant testified that he or she subjectively believed that killing was necessary and proportionate to any perceived threat. . . .

In conclusion, we decline to expand our law of self-defense beyond the limits of immediacy and necessity which have heretofore provided an appropriately narrow but firm basis upon which homicide may be justified. . . .

Reversed.

MARTIN, Justice, dissenting.

At the outset it is to be noted that the peril of fabricated evidence is not unique to the trials of battered wives who kill. The possibility of invented evidence arises in all cases in which a party is seeking the benefit of self-defense. Moreover, in this case there were a number of witnesses other than defendant who testified as to the actual presence of circumstances supporting a claim of self-defense. This record contains no reasonable basis to attack the credibility of evidence for the defendant. . . .

Evidence presented by defendant described a twenty-year history of beatings and other dehumanizing and degrading treatment by her husband. In his expert testimony a clinical psychologist concluded that defendant fit "and exceed[ed]" the profile of an abused or battered spouse, analogizing this treatment to the dehumanization process suffered by prisoners of war under the Nazis during the Second World War and the brainwashing techniques of the Korean War. The psychologist described the defendant as a woman incarcerated by abuse, by fear, and by her conviction that her husband was invincible and inescapable:

Mrs. Norman didn't leave because she believed, fully believed that escape was totally impossible. There was no place to go. He, she had left before; he had come and gotten her. She had gone to the Department of Social Services. He had come and gotten her. The law, she believed the law could not protect her; no one could protect her, and I must admit, looking over the records, that there was nothing done that would contradict that belief. . . .

. . . For the battered wife, if there is no escape, if there is no window of relief or momentary sense of safety, then the next attack, which could be the fatal one, is imminent. In the context of the doctrine of self-defense, "imminent" is a term the meaning of which must be grasped from the defendant's point of view. Properly stated, the second prong of the question is not whether the threat was *in fact* imminent, but whether defendant's belief in the impending nature of the threat, given the circumstances as she saw them, was reasonable in the mind of a person of ordinary firmness.

Defendant's intense fear, based on her belief that her husband intended not only to maim or deface her, as he had in the past, but to kill her, was evident in the testimony of witnesses who recounted events of the last three days of the decedent's life. This testimony could have led a juror to conclude that defendant reasonably perceived a threat to her life as "imminent," even while her husband slept. . . .

From this evidence of the exacerbated nature of the last three days of twenty years of provocation, a juror could conclude that defendant believed that her husband's threats to her life were viable, that serious bodily harm was imminent, and that it was necessary to kill her husband to escape that harm. And from this evidence a juror could find defendant's belief in the necessity to kill her husband not merely reasonable but compelling. . . .

Notes

1. **"Heat of Passion" Manslaughter and the Reasonable "Man."** A feature of Anglo-American law since the early English common law has been that a killing in the "sudden heat of passion" is not murder, but rather the lesser crime of voluntary manslaughter, and that "adequate provocation" by the victim may cause a reasonable man to lose his reason and act in the heat of passion. See Joshua Dressler, Understanding Criminal Law §31.07[A], at 490 (2d ed. 1995, reprinted 2000). Catching one's spouse in the act of adultery is frequently described in the literature as the quintessential adequate provocation. See id. at §131.07[C] at 497 (adultery is "the highest invasion of [a husband's] property," quoting Regina v. Mawdridge, Kel. J. 119, 137, 84 Eng. Rep. 1107, 1115 (1707), and Rex v. Greening, 3 K.B. 846, 849, 23 Cox. Crim. Cas. 601, 603 (1913)). Sexual taunting, as in People v. Berry, perhaps provides a contemporary equivalent.

The heat of passion doctrine is not the only means by which killings out of male sexual jealousy have been legally condoned. In some southern and western states in the early twentieth century, juries recognized an "unwritten law" of "honor defense" that allowed a defendant to be acquitted entirely when he killed his wife or his wife's lover out of sexual jealousy. See Laurie J. Taylor, Comment, Provoked Reason in Men and Women: Heat-of-Passion Manslaughter and Imperfect Self Defense, 33 UCLA L. Rev. 1679, 1694 (1986). Indeed, until the 1960s and 1970s, statutes in four states — Georgia, New Mexico, Texas, and Utah — made it justifiable homicide for a husband to kill his wife's lover. Id.

In several contemporary American jurisdictions that have codified the common law doctrine of heat of passion, many of the more stringent conditions on which a voluntary manslaughter instruction may be granted have been relaxed. For example, the judge no longer decides which behaviors are or are not adequate provocation as a matter of law. Rather, the question of whether a "reasonable man" would be put into the heat of passion by the victim's behavior is given to the jury. In addition, the traditional requirement of "cooling time" has been relaxed, as in *Berry*. Instead, courts have begun to reason that provocation and passion may build up over a long period of time.

The Model Penal Code (MPC) represents the furthest edge of this liberalizing trend. Under the MPC, a homicide that would otherwise be murder may be reduced to manslaughter if the defendant can show that he acted under the influence of "extreme mental or emotional disturbance for which there is reasonable explanation or excuse." Whether there is a reasonable explanation or excuse for the disturbance is to be judged from the point of view of "a person in the actor's situation under the circumstances as he believes them to be." MPC §210.3(1)(b). The intention of the MPC drafters was to focus on the defendant's disturbed state of mind, rather than the existence of justifying circumstances, and to eliminate the older categorical approach to finding "adequate provocation." See MPC §210(3) comment at 61.

Which version of the law — the older common law approach, the newer common law approach, or the MPC approach — best serves women? Victoria Nourse compiled heat of passion cases from each of these three types of jurisdictions and reported two interesting findings. First, she found that a woman's attempt to leave the relationship, or the man's belief in her infidelity, was the most common "provocation" when men killed women and sought reduction of their crime to manslaughter. Nourse also found that the behavior identified as "infidelity" was quite various in MPC jurisdictions:

> Claims of "discovered infidelity" appear quite rarely in my MPC data set, whether the claim arises in the context of a former or a current relationship. Far more frequent are claims based on confessions or allegations of infidelity. Less frequent, but also present, are cases involving lesser breaches, such as "dancing with [an]other man," "receiv[ing] a phone call from a former boyfriend," or seeing the victim with another.

Victoria Nourse, Passion's Progress: Modern Law Reform and the Provocation Defense, 106 Yale L.J. 1331, 1363-1364 (1997).

Second, Nourse's study demonstrated that claims of infidelity in which the relationship had ended were much more likely to go to the jury in MPC states than in states following the common law:

> In MPC jurisdictions, unlike traditional ones, I found three times as many infidelity cases reporting separation (thirty-seven percent) as cases of infidelity in a continuing relationship (twelve percent). Indeed, cases of "separation and infidelity" are the single largest category in reform jurisdictions. In all of these cases, the relationship was ending or was over. Consider, for example, [a case in which the] victim moved, sought to end her marriage, filed for divorce, notified the police, and obtained a restraining order. Testimony at trial suggested that the victim told the defendant that she would not return and may have "mentioned another man," or told the defendant that "he could believe what he wanted to believe about the rumors" about another man. Clearly, this case is not simply about a rival (even if we assume that there is another man, as my methodology requires). One party has sought to end the relationship, and the other refuses to accede to that choice, killing the party who seeks to leave.

Id. at 1359-1360. Nourse asks: "If intimate homicide frequently involves separated couples why does our canonical legal image still revolve around sexual infidelity?" Id. at 1345.

The result of doctrines such as "heat of passion" is, frequently, a lesser sentence for wife killers. Myrna Raeder cites statistics published by the Bureau of Justice Statistics of the Department of Justice in a 1995 study:

[W]hile sixty-eight percent of husbands had been charged with first degree murder for killing their wives, only thirty-seven percent were convicted of that offense. Indeed thirty-two percent were convicted of some type of manslaughter, although only two percent had originally been charged at that level. Ultimately, forty-seven percent of husbands were convicted of a less serious offense. Of those who pled guilty, the results were even more stark: the plea was to a reduced charge seventy-six percent of the time. In all, only twenty-one percent of female spousal murders resulted in a conviction of first degree murder. Only thirteen percent of the husbands convicted received life imprisonment and two percent were sentenced to death.

Myrna S. Raeder, The Admissibility of Prior Acts of Domestic Violence: Simpson and Beyond, 69 S. Cal. L. Rev. 1463, 1477 (1996) (citing Patrick A. Langan & John M. Dawson, Spouse Murder Defendants in Large Urban Counties (U.S. Dept. of Justice 1995)).

Has the modernization of the law in this area had a paradoxical effect of reinforcing rather than confronting male dominance? Should law reform move back in the direction of the traditional common law approach, under which "words alone" are never adequate provocation and infidelity must be witnessed? See Emily L. Miller, Comment, (Wo)manslaughter: Voluntary Manslaughter, Gender, and the Model Penal Code, 50 Emory L.J. 665, 666 (2001) (arguing that "the MPC formulation of voluntary manslaughter has rendered an untenable expansion of the doctrine," one that has been "particularly disastrous for women").

Should "hot-blooded" separation murders and assaults be seen as deserving of more punishment than cold-blooded killings rather than less? For example, Minnesota authorizes a finding of first-degree murder based on repeated abuse. See Minn. Stat. Ann §609.185(6) (West 1995) (defining murder in the first degree as, among other things, causing "the death of a human being . . . while committing domestic abuse, when the perpetrator has engaged in a past pattern of domestic abuse upon the victim and the death occurs under circumstances manifesting an extreme indifference to human life"). Or is the law correct to treat people who act in the extremes of emotion as less culpable and to acknowledge the unfortunate, but inescapable, truth that threats to end a relationship, particularly when entwined with sexual jealousy, in fact enrage men? Is equality to be reached by restricting the heat of passion doctrine or by enlarging it to mitigate the kinds of intimate killings women commit? Consider this question again after you have read the next note.

2. The Battered Woman's Syndrome. Battered woman's syndrome (BWS) is considered a subcategory of post-traumatic stress disorder and consists of a "collection of thoughts, feelings, and actions that logically follow a frightening experience that one expects could be repeated." Lenore E.A. Walker, Battered Women Syndrome and Self-Defense, 6 Notre Dame J.L. Ethics & Pub. Pol'y 321, 327 (1992). The syndrome is associated with three major symptom clusters, each of which can be accompanied by neurochemical and other physical changes. These clusters are (1) cognitive disturbances, including repetitive intrusive memories and flashbacks that cause battered women to reexperience fragments of previous abusive incidents and that increase their perception of danger; (2) high arousal symptoms that cause battered women to be nervous, jumpy, and hypervigilant to cues of potential danger; and (3) avoidance symptoms, including depression, denial, minimization, and repression, often leading to isolation as the batterer exerts his power and control needs over the woman. Id. at 327-328.

BWS researchers offer two psychological theories to help juries understand the syndrome: learned helplessness and the cycle theory of violence. The theory of learned helplessness is an effort to explain how a woman in an abusive relationship, evidenced by some combination of these symptoms, might lose the ability to respond to various situations rationally — which is to say, to respond as others viewing the situation from the outside think they would have acted. The theory was first developed by experimental psychologist Marvin Seligman to explain the fact that dogs and other animals subjected to electric shocks that they are powerless to control will soon cease to try to control the shocks. See Cynthia K. Gillespie, Justifiable Homicide: Battered Women, Self-Defense, and the Law 153-154 (1989). In the context of battered women, the theory of learned helplessness puts a woman's failure to leave an abusive relationship in the context of a recognizable cycle, characterized by a tension-building phase, an acute battering incident, and a period of loving-contrition or absence of tension, which leads the battered woman to believe that she is unable to help herself and that others cannot help her either. Walker, supra, at 330.

In this state of learned helplessness, what causes a battered woman to turn on her batterer? Many battered women do not, but others at some point "experience a turning point when the violence or abuse done to them comes to be felt as a basic threat, whether to their physical or social self, or both." See John M. Johnson & Kathleen J. Ferraro, The Victimized Self: The Case of the Battered Woman, in The Existential Self in Society 118 (J. Kotarba & A. Fontana eds., 1984), cited in Charles Patrick Ewing, Battered Women Who Kill: Psychological Self-Defense as Legal Justification 65 (1987). The turning point may come when there is a marked increase in the severity of the abuse, when the abuse becomes visible to others who question the woman's denial or rationalizations, or when the "loving-contrition" phase becomes increasingly short or disappears altogether. Ewing, supra, at 65. At that point, the victim moves from the state of learned helplessness to a state of the "victimized self," who concludes that she must either assert herself or be killed. Id. at 65-66. For some victims, this means finally being able to leave their batterers; others stay and suffer various forms of "psychological death"; a few kill their batterers. Id. at 66; see also

According to the cycle theory of violence proposed by Lenore Walker, three distinct phases typify the battering relationship.

> [V]iolence does not constantly occur in most battering relationships, nor does it occur randomly. Rather, there are three predictable phases: a phase of tension building, leading up to a second phase which is the acute battering incident, followed by a third phase, which is a period of loving contrition or at least a cessation of the violent behavior.
>
> The third phase provides positive reinforcement for women to remain in the relationship. This periodic reinforcement provides a powerful incentive to remain in a battering relationship: the woman hopes that the undesirable behavior of phases I and II will not recur and that the phase III behavior will continue. Unfortunately, according to our results, the tension building period actually becomes more pronounced, and the periods of loving contrition shorten and become less reinforcing over time. Many of the battered women we interviewed terminated the relationship when the ratio between abusive and loving behavior changed in this manner.

Lenore E. Walker, Roberta K. Thyfault, & Angela Browne, Beyond the Juror's Ken: Battered Women, 7 Vt. L. Rev. 1, 9 (1982).

3. The Battered Woman in Self-Defense Law: Substantive and Procedural Proposals. The most common criticism of the law of self-defense in the battered woman context is that it reflects male notions of a face-to-face "fair fight" between physical equals meeting in a one-time, time-bound confrontation and fails to take into account the realities of battered women who may kill their abusers in settings that do not have these characteristics. Specifically, it is charged that the "objective standard" of reasonableness in the law of self-defense ignores any special or unique circumstances on the part of a woman caught in an abusive relationship that a man would feel he could leave. See Walter Steele & Christine Sigman, Reexamining the Doctrine of Self Defense to Accommodate Battered Women, 18 Am. J. Crim. L. 169, 175-176 (1991). In addition, words are considered an inadequate provocation, a fact that may fail to account for the genuine risk of threats, acted on in the past, that have gotten progressively more severe over time. Id. at 177-178. The "imminence" standard, in assuming that "a threat of attack may be withdrawn at the last minute, implicitly adopts bluff and counterbluff as a norm of social interaction between two equal aggressors." Id. at 178. The rule that only proportionate force be used in self-defense also assumes a "confrontation . . . between two equal males." Id. at 180. For criticisms of the law along these lines, see Laura E. Reece, Women's Defenses to Criminal Homicide and the Right to Effective Assistance of Counsel: The Need for Relocation of Difference, 1 UCLA Women's L.J. 53, 55 (1991); Stephen J. Schulhofer, The Gender Question in Criminal Law, 7 Soc. Phil. & Pol'y 105, 127 (1990); M.J. Willoughby, Rendering Each Woman Her Due: Can a Battered Woman

Claim Self-Defense When She Kills Her Sleeping Batterer?, 38 Kan. L. Rev. 169, 183-184 (1989); Victoria M. Mather, The Skeleton in the Closet: The Battered Woman Syndrome, Self-Defense, and Expert Testimony, 39 Mercer L. Rev. 545, 569 (1988); Phyllis L. Crocker, The Meaning of Equality for Battered Women Who Kill Men in Self-Defense, 8 Harv. Women's L.J. 121, 123, 126 (1985). For a book-length treatment of these themes, see Cynthia K. Gillespie, Justifiable Homicide: Battered Women, Self-Defense, and the Law (1989). Do these criticisms seem justified in the context of *Norman?*

Proposals for reform, corresponding to the criticisms described above, call for the substitution of a "reasonable woman" standard, see Crocker, supra, at 152; Mather, supra, at 573 or even a "reasonable battered woman" standard, see Kit Kinports, Comment, Defending Battered Women's Self-Defense Claims, 67 Or. L. Rev. 393, 416 (1988); for a modification of the "imminence" requirement to shift to the jury the determination whether the use of deadly force was "necessary", see Richard A. Rosen, On Self-Defense, Imminence, and Women Who Kill Their Batterers, 71 N.C. L. Rev. 371 (1993); for the elimination of the duty to retreat in one's own home that still exists in a few jurisdictions, see Gillespie, supra, at 187-188); and for evidentiary rules that make more liberal allowance for admission of expert testimony about battered woman's syndrome, see Christine A. Littleton, Women's Experience and the Problem of Transition: Perspectives of Male Battering of Women, 1989 U. Chi. Legal F. 23, 37; Kinports, supra, at 451-453.

Some commentators have argued that the problem is not so much the law, but how it is applied. Kit Kinports, for example, argues that when properly understood, the law of self-defense should accommodate the situations of many battered women who strike back and kill their abusers. See Kinports, supra, at 396. Holly Maguigan takes an even stronger stance, arguing against some reform proposals on the grounds that they are based on mistaken assumptions about both battered women who kill and the law. After surveying appellate cases involving battered women who killed their abusers, Maguigan concludes that the "real problem" in homicide cases in which battered women are the defendants is not the existing law, but the fact that judges in these cases do not interpret the law fairly and thus that self-defense instructions too seldom get to the jury. Maguigan, Battered Women and Self-Defense: Myths and Misconceptions in Current Reform Proposals, 140 U. Pa. L. Rev. 379, 382-387, 457-458 (1991).

Assuming that expert testimony on battered woman's syndrome should have gone to the jury in *Norman*, should the defendant's circumstances (once understood in that light) constitute a justification, exonerating her from guilt, or merely an excuse or mitigating factor affecting the degree of crime or the sentence? Most reformers have assumed the former. For the argument that excuse or mitigation is the better approach, see Cathryn J. Rosen, The Excuse of Self-Defense: Correcting a Historical Accident on

Behalf of Battered Women Who Kill, 36 Am. U. L. Rev. 11 (1986). See also State v. Koss, 551 N.E.2d 970 (Ohio 1990) (Holmes, J., concurring opinion) (battered woman syndrome is excuse rather than justification); State v. Torres, 393 S.E.2d 535 (N.C. Ct. App. 1990) (battered woman's syndrome may be a mitigating factor affecting sentence, but failure to find it a mitigating factor in this case not an error); Chapman v. State, 386 S.E.2d 129 (Ga. 1989) (syndrome affects mens rea and thus the degree of crime).

4. The Opportunistic Battered Woman? Uneasiness about use of the battered woman's syndrome is based on various types of concerns. The *Norman* court's objection was that the syndrome evidence could be too easily manipulated, thus encouraging opportunistic killing by scheming, premeditating wives. In an effort to test the validity of this concern, one scholar collected the data from numerous studies comparing battered women who killed their husbands to those who did not. He concluded that women who kill their husbands suffer from far more frequent, more severe, and more prolonged abuse than other battered women; they have less ability to support themselves and thus to escape from their situations; they are more likely to have children who are also being abused by the batterer; and they are more likely to live in an environment where a gun is present and where the batterer abuses alcohol or other drugs. See Charles Patrick Ewing, Battered Women Who Kill: Psychological Self-Defense as Legal Justification 23-40 (1987). See also Lenore E. Walker, Terrifying Love: Why Battered Women Kill and How Society Responds 101-169 (1989) (reaching similar conclusions, and emphasizing that the behavior of battered women who kill needs to be understood as normal rather than crazy); Angela Browne, When Battered Women Kill 127-130 (1987) (identifying same predictive factors and explaining how act or words by abuser can constitute a "turning point" beyond which the battered woman can no longer endure abuse). What are the reform implications of these conclusions?

It should be noted that testimony about battered woman's syndrome does not ensure that battered women who kill their batterers will succeed in avoiding criminal liability. Of the 28 cases studied by Lenore Walker and her associates, 14 went to trial, and expert testimony was admitted in 11 of them. Seven of these 11 were acquitted, and 4 were convicted, receiving sentences ranging from 10 years' probation to a 25-year prison term. Of the others, some were still waiting trial, charges against one woman had been dropped, and in 7 cases, women had pleaded guilty to reduced homicide charges. Lenore E. Walker et al., Beyond the Juror's Ken: Battered Women, 7 Vt. L. Rev. 1, 14 (1982). See also Elizabeth M. Schneider & Susan B. Jordan, Representation of Women Who Defend Themselves in Response to Physical or Sexual Assault, 4 Women's Rights L. Rep. 149, 149-150 n.3 (1978) (of 16 cases, 7 were acquitted on grounds of self-defense, 1 was found not guilty by reason of insanity, and 8 were convicted of murder or manslaughter); Browne, supra, at 12, 163 (of 42 women charged with a crime in the death or serious injury of their mates, only 9 were acquitted, and in only 1 case were the charges dropped before trial).

5. Social Scientific Objections to the Battered Woman's Syndrome. David L. Faigman and Amy J. Wright assert that "[t]he battered woman syndrome illustrates all that is wrong with the law's use of science." David L. Faigman & Amy J. Wright, The Battered Woman's Syndrome in the Age of Science, 39 Ariz. L. Rev. 67, 68 (1997). With respect to the "cycle theory" of violence, Faigman and Wright point out several flaws in Walker's original method. For example, her interview technique allowed the subjects to guess what answer the researchers were looking for and relied on the interviewers' interpretation of the subjects' answers rather than their actual responses. In addition, Walker did not offer any data as to the duration of the "cycle of violence," and Walker's own data failed to substantiate that all or even most subjects experienced all three stages of the cycle. Id. at 77-78.

With respect to the theory of learned helplessness, Faigman and Wright join other social scientists in doubting its applicability to battered women. The data originally generated from dog experiments suggest that battered women suffering from learned helplessness will become completely passive and make no attempt to assert control over their environment. Research, however, suggests that battered women continue to resist in myriad ways. Most glaringly, learned helplessness fails to explain cases in which women fight back by killing their batters. Id. at 79.

As to the use of BWS evidence in the courts, Faigman and Wright point out that BWS implies an excuse theory of mitigation based on the woman's helplessness and the lasting effects of psychological trauma; yet self-defense is a justification theory based on the reasonableness of the defendant's behavior. They note that the strong undercurrents of excuse theory in BWS testimony have encouraged courts to require women who kill their batterers to undergo psychiatric examinations. Id. at 90. Finally, they argue that as a practical matter BWS evidence, though often proffered in court, seldom produces an acquittal, citing numbers similar to those cited in the previous note. Id. at 113.

6. Women's Advocates' Objections to the Battered Woman's Syndrome. Some of the concerns about use of the battered woman's syndrome are raised by women's advocates themselves. While these advocates maintain that the battered woman's syndrome is an improvement on the traditional view that battered women who kill their husbands are crazy or irrational (see Schneider & Jordan, supra, at 150), they fear some negative consequences of "syndrome" evidence. One is that its widespread use will create a standard for battered women that all battered women might then be expected to meet: if a woman acts differently from the profile contained in the syndrome, she may be assumed (by herself as well as others) to be not really battered, her assailant not really criminal, her act of defense not really justified:

> An ironic twist to the increased public awareness [of battered woman's syndrome] is that it has informed the ignorant as well as the enlightened. Those who previously responded to the case of a battered woman with prejudice now pretend to accept the legitimacy of a true battered woman's self-defense, as well as the accompanying expert testimony, but structure their opposition to the defense by asserting that the woman in question "does not fit the mold." This skewed perception has given rise to distinctions between "good" and "bad" battered women.
>
> . . . "Good" battered women are passive, loyal housewives, acting as loving companions to their abusers. These women must have flawless characters and continually appeal to the police and courts for help, regardless of the futility of their efforts. By contrast, the "bad" battered woman is one who fails to possess any of the virtues of the "good" woman, and who may have even obtained an education and pursued a career. This demonstration of control often operates to disqualify the "bad" battered woman from the group. Infidelity or abuse of drugs is equally discrediting.

Michael Dowd, Dispelling the Myths About the "Battered Woman's Defense": Towards a New Understanding, 19 Fordham Urb. L.J. 567, 581 (1992). Along the same lines, see Phyllis L. Crocker, The Meaning of Equality for Battered Women Who Kill Men in Self-Defense, 8 Harv. Women's L.J. 121, 144-150 (1985).

The risk Dowd describes may be highest for black women, one notewriter argues, because they are subject to the stereotype that all black women are angry, and thus more likely to be seen as acting out of revenge and anger rather than fear. See Sharon Angella Allard, Rethinking Battered Woman Syndrome: A Black Feminist Perspective, 1 UCLA Women's L.J. 191, 197 (1991). Compare this general problem to that of using the rape trauma syndrome to defend against a rape charge, explored in Chapter 6, at pages 970-971. Lesbian and gay victims of battering, too, may fail to fit the profile of a "battered woman." See Phyllis Goldfarb, Describing Without Circumscribing: Questioning the Construction of Gender in the Discourse of Intimate Violence, 64 Geo. Wash. L. Rev. 582 (1996) (describing how, in a group of eight women who had killed their batterers and were petitioning for commutation of their sentences, the lesbian who had killed her female partner "faced the longest odds in her struggle to be seen and heard").

Another risk, and the one to which Mahoney seems most sensitive, is that the syndrome will reinforce the view of woman as passive, sick, powerless, and victimized, a view from which so many negative conse-quences flow. See Anne M. Coughlin, Excusing Women, 82 Cal. L. Rev. 1 (1994); Elizabeth M. Schneider, Describing and Changing: Women's Self-Defense Work and the Problem of Expert Testimony on Battering, 9

Women's Rts. L. Rep. 195, 214-215 (1986). One of these consequences is loss of child custody, discussed above at pages 646 to 650, In an important sense, this dilemma reflects a chronic issue in the effort to achieve gender equality: rules developed to respond to women's special circumstances and needs must be applied in gendered contexts in which other forms of disadvantage are produced or reinforced.

Several women's rights advocates would shift the focus of domestic violence evidence from the particular violent acts of the batterer and the psychology of the victim to the overall pattern of coercion and control that characterizes a battering relationship. See, e.g., Evan Stark, Re-presenting Woman Battering: From Battered Woman Syndrome to Coercive Control, 58 Alb. L. Rev. 973 (1995); Karla Fischer, Neil Vidmar, & René Ellis, The Culture of Battering and the Role of Mediation in Domestic Violence Cases, 46 SMU L. Rev. 2117 (1993). Myrna Raeder suggests that the problem of stereotyping that arises from BWS evidence as currently used in courtrooms stems from overreliance on "syndromes" and "profiles" as the only way to introduce expert testimony, and she argues that experts should be permitted to give more general "social framework" testimony about domestic violence. Myrna S. Raeder, The Better Way: The Role of Batterers' Profiles and Expert "Social Framework" Background in Cases Implicating Domestic Violence, 68 U. Colo. L. Rev. 147, 151-152 (1997). More broadly, Elizabeth Schneider sees the problem as the tendency to see battered women simplistically, as either victims or agents, without grappling with the more complex notion of "situated agency," which better characterizes their lives. Elizabeth Schneider, Resistance to Equality, 57 U. Pitt. L. Rev. 477, 499 (1996). Seeking real gender equality, she suggests, necessitates an understanding of how people can be both agents and victims, acting and acted upon.

One strength of nonsubordination theory may be that it helps to frame women's victimization not simply as an individual problem, but also in terms of the overall institutional context of oppression. Keeping that institutional context in focus, as well as pointing out the extent to which, even in battering situations, women are often agents — survivors — as well as victims, may help to avoid the unfair disadvantages of theories that rely on the notion of victimization. See Elizabeth M. Schneider, Particularity and Generality: Challenges of Feminist Theory and Practice in Work on Woman-Abuse, 67 N.Y.U. L. Rev. 520, 548-550 (1992). Joyce McConnell's conceptualization of battered women's cases as instances of involuntary servitude, protected by the Thirteenth Amendment, might be seen as one effort in this direction. See McConnell, Beyond Metaphor: Battered Women, Involuntary Servitude, and the Thirteenth Amendment, 4 Yale J.L. & Feminism 207, 253 (1992) (involuntary servitude theory may help to prevent the battered woman label from being used "to describe the whole woman, thereby swallowing the ways in which she is not a victim at all").

Jane Cohen defines a regime of "private tyranny" as a condition in which "the life of at least one person who lives or formerly lived in the same household with the tyrant [is] subject to his domination and control in respect to such objectively important elements of everyday life that a reasonable member of society would not ordinarily consent to live under the same terms and conditions and would not view the consent of any other person to live under such circumstances as a rational exercise of choice." Jane Maslow Cohen, Regimes of Private Tyranny: What Do They Mean to Morality and for the Criminal Law? 57 U. Pitt. L. Rev. 757, 763 (1996). She argues that the killing of a private tyrant can be a morally justified act and that such killings should further be treated legally as justified homicide under some circumstances. Cohen, like McConnell, makes an analogy between such situations and slavery. Id.

7. Post-Conviction Strategies for Battered Women. After serving four years of her six-year sentence, Judy Norman's sentence was commuted to time served by Governor James Martin. No reasons were given. See Elizabeth Leland, Abused Wife's Sentence Commuted, Charlotte Observer, July 8, 1989, at B1. Systematic efforts for clemency on behalf of convicted women in over 20 other states have yielded some results. Ohio Governor Richard F. Celeste granted clemency to 25 battered women in December 1990, and in 1991, Governor William D. Schaefer of Maryland commuted the sentences of eight women convicted of killing or assaulting abusive men. Elizabeth Schneider reports:

> By 1993, governors in seven states, including Jim Edgar of Illinois, Lawton Chiles of Florida, and Pete Wilson of California, had granted clemency to thirty-eight formerly battered women convicted of killing or assaulting their batterers. At least twenty-six states have since set up committees to review the cases of incarcerated battered women. In recent years, however, the trend toward granting clemency to battered women appears to have slowed. Most of the clemency petitions that have been granted were granted in the 1980s and early 1990s. Since 1978, a total of 88 battered women from 21 states have received clemency.

Schneider, Particularity and Generality, supra, at 519.

What criteria would you advise governors to apply in considering clemency requests by battered women convicted of killing their abusers? See Jennifer S. Bales, Equal Protection and the Use of Protest Letters in Parole Proceedings: A Particular Dilemma for Battered Women Inmates, 27 Seton Hall L. Rev. 33 (1997); Christine Noelle Becker, Note, Clemency for Killers? Pardoning Battered Women Who Strike Back, 29 Loy. L.A. L. Rev. 297 (1995); Joan H. Krause, Of Merciful Justice and Justified Mercy: Commuting the Sentences of Battered Women Who Kill, 46 Fla. L. Rev. 699 (1994); Linda L. Ammons, Discretionary Justice: A Legal and Policy

Analysis of a Governor's Use of the Clemency Power in the Cases of Incarcerated Battered Women, 3 J.L. & Pol'y 1 (1994).

4. Domestic Violence, Feminism, and the Patriarchal State

United States v. Morrison
529 U.S. 598 (2000)

Chief Justice REHNQUIST delivered the opinion of the Court.

In these cases we consider the constitutionality of 42 U.S.C. §13981, which provides a federal civil remedy for the victims of gender-motivated violence. The United States Court of Appeals for the Fourth Circuit, sitting en banc, struck down §13981 because it concluded that Congress lacked constitutional authority to enact the section's civil remedy. Believing that these cases are controlled by our decisions in United States v. Lopez, 514 U.S. 549 (1995), United States v. Harris, 106 U.S. 629 (1883), and the In re Civil Rights Cases, 109 U.S. 3 (1883), we affirm.

I

Petitioner Christy Brzonkala enrolled at Virginia Polytechnic Institute (Virginia Tech) in the fall of 1994. In September of that year, Brzonkala met respondents Antonio Morrison and James Crawford, who were both students at Virginia Tech and members of its varsity football team. Brzonkala alleges that, within 30 minutes of meeting Morrison and Crawford, they assaulted and repeatedly raped her. After the attack, Morrison allegedly told Brzonkala, "You better not have any . . . diseases." In the months following the rape, Morrison also allegedly announced in the dormitory's dining room that he "like[d] to get girls drunk and. . . ." The omitted portions, quoted verbatim in the briefs on file with this Court, consist of boasting, debased remarks about what Morrison would do to women, vulgar remarks that cannot fail to shock and offend.[1]

Brzonkala alleges that this attack caused her to become severely emotionally disturbed and depressed. She sought assistance from a university psychiatrist, who prescribed antidepressant medication. Shortly after the rape Brzonkala stopped attending classes and withdrew from the university.

In early 1995, Brzonkala filed a complaint against respondents under Virginia Tech's Sexual Assault Policy. During the school-conducted hearing

---

1. [The comments to which Justice Rehnquist alludes include Morrison's remark, immediately after raping Brzonkala, that "You better not have any fucking diseases"; his public announcement some months later that "I like to get girls drunk and fuck the shit out of them"; and a remark made later to Crawford by another male student athlete that he "should have killed the bitch."]

on her complaint, Morrison admitted having sexual contact with her despite the fact that she had twice told him "no." [The school initially found Morrison guilty of sexual assault and suspended him. However, Morrison subsequently challenged the conviction in court, alleging the policy under which he was convicted had not been widely circulated to students. But Morrison again was convicted under a separate policy and suspended for "using abusive language." Morrison then appealed and his sentence was set aside; the university senior vice president and provost found it excessive when compared to similar cases.]

. . . After learning from a newspaper that Morrison would be returning to Virginia Tech for the fall 1995 semester, she dropped out of the university.

In December 1995, Brzonkala sued Morrison, Crawford, and Virginia Tech in the United States District Court for the Western District of Virginia. Her complaint alleged that Morrison's and Crawford's attack violated §13981 and that Virginia Tech's handling of her complaint violated Title IX of the Education Amendments of 1972. . . .

The District Court dismissed Brzonkala's Title IX claims against Virginia Tech for failure to state a claim upon which relief can be granted. It then held that Brzonkala's complaint stated a claim against Morrison and Crawford under §13981, but dismissed the complaint because it concluded that Congress lacked authority to enact the section under either the Commerce Clause or §5 of the Fourteenth Amendment. . . .

A divided panel of the Court of Appeals reversed the District Court, reinstating Brzonkala's §13981 claim and her Title IX hostile environment claim. The full Court of Appeals vacated the panel's opinion and reheard the case en banc. The en banc court then issued an opinion affirming the District Court's conclusion that Brzonkala stated a claim under §13981. . . . Nevertheless, the court by a divided vote affirmed the District Court's conclusion that Congress lacked constitutional authority to enact §13981's civil remedy. Because the Court of Appeals invalidated a federal statute on constitutional grounds, we granted certiorari. . . .

Section 13981 was part of the Violence Against Women Act of 1994, §40302, 108 Stat. 1941-1942. It states that "[a]ll persons within the United States shall have the right to be free from crimes of violence motivated by gender." 42 U.S.C. §13981(b). To enforce that right, subsection (c) declares:

> A person (including a person who acts under color of any statute, ordinance, regulation, custom, or usage of any State) who commits a crime of violence motivated by gender and thus deprives another of the right declared in subsection (b) of this section shall be liable to the party injured, in an action for the recovery of compensatory and punitive damages, injunctive and declaratory relief, and such other relief as a court may deem appropriate.

Section 13981 defines a "crim[e] of violence motivated by gender" as "a crime of violence committed because of gender or on the basis of gender, and due, at least in part, to an animus based on the victim's gender." §13981(d)(1). It also provides that the term "crime of violence" includes any

> (A) . . . act or series of acts that would constitute a felony against the person or that would constitute a felony against property if the conduct presents a serious risk of physical injury to another, and that would come within the meaning of State or Federal offenses described in section 16 of Title 18, whether or not those acts have actually resulted in criminal charges, prosecution, or conviction and whether or not those acts were committed in the special maritime, territorial, or prison jurisdiction of the United States;" and "(B) includes an act or series of acts that would constitute a felony described in subparagraph (A) but for the relationship between the person who takes such action and the individual against whom such action is taken." §13981(d)(2).

Further clarifying the broad scope of §13981's civil remedy, subsection (e)(2) states that "[n]othing in this section requires a prior criminal complaint, prosecution, or conviction to establish the elements of a cause of action under subsection (c) of this section." And subsection (e)(3) provides a §13981 litigant with a choice of forums: Federal and state courts "shall have concurrent jurisdiction" over complaints brought under the section.

Although the foregoing language of §13981 covers a wide swath of criminal conduct, Congress placed some limitations on the section's federal civil remedy. Subsection (e)(1) states that "[n]othing in this section entitles a person to a cause of action under subsection (c) of this section for random acts of violence unrelated to gender or for acts that cannot be demonstrated, by a preponderance of the evidence, to be motivated by gender." Subsection (e)(4) further states that §13981 shall not be construed "to confer on the courts of the United States jurisdiction over any State law claim seeking the establishment of a divorce, alimony, equitable distribution of marital property, or child custody decree."

Every law enacted by Congress must be based on one or more of its powers enumerated in the Constitution. "The powers of the legislature are defined and limited; and that those limits may not be mistaken or forgotten, the constitution is written." Marbury v. Madison, 1 Cranch 137, 176 (1803) (Marshall, C. J.). Congress explicitly identified the sources of federal authority on which it relied in enacting §13981. It said that a "federal civil rights cause of action" is established "[p]ursuant to the affirmative power of Congress . . . under section 5 of the Fourteenth Amendment to the Constitution, as well as under section 8 of Article I of the Constitution." 42 U.S.C. §13981(a). We address Congress' authority to enact this remedy under each of these constitutional provisions in turn.

II . . .

As we observed in *Lopez*, modern Commerce Clause jurisprudence has "identified three broad categories of activity that Congress may regulate under its commerce power." . . .

Petitioners do not contend that these cases fall within either of the first two of these categories of Commerce Clause regulation. They seek to sustain §13981 as a regulation of activity that substantially affects interstate commerce. Given §13981's focus on gender-motivated violence wherever it occurs . . . we agree that this is the proper inquiry. . . .

. . . [A] fair reading of *Lopez* shows that the noneconomic, criminal nature of the conduct at issue was central to our decision in that case. . . . *Lopez*'s review of Commerce Clause case law demonstrates that in those cases where we have sustained federal regulation of intrastate activity based upon the activity's substantial effects on interstate commerce, the activity in question has been some sort of economic endeavor.

The second consideration that we found important in analyzing §922(q) was that the statute contained "no express jurisdictional element which might limit its reach to a discrete set of firearm possessions that additionally have an explicit connection with or effect on interstate commerce." Such a jurisdictional element may establish that the enactment is in pursuance of Congress' regulation of interstate commerce.

Third, we noted that neither §922(q) "'nor its legislative history contain[s] express congressional findings regarding the effects upon interstate commerce of gun possession in a school zone.'" While "Congress normally is not required to make formal findings as to the substantial burdens that an activity has on interstate commerce," the existence of such findings may "enable us to evaluate the legislative judgment that the activity in question substantially affect[s] interstate commerce, even though no such substantial effect [is] visible to the naked eye." . . .

Finally, our decision in *Lopez* rested in part on the fact that the link between gun possession and a substantial effect on interstate commerce was attenuated. . . .

We rejected these "costs of crime" and "national productivity" arguments because they would permit Congress to "regulate not only all violent crime, but all activities that might lead to violent crime, regardless of how tenuously they relate to interstate commerce." . . .

With these principles underlying our Commerce Clause jurisprudence as reference points, the proper resolution of the present cases is clear. Gender-motivated crimes of violence are not, in any sense of the phrase, economic activity. While we need not adopt a categorical rule against aggregating the effects of any noneconomic activity in order to decide these cases, thus far in our Nation's history our cases have upheld Commerce Clause regulation of intrastate activity only where that activity is economic in nature. . . .

In contrast with the lack of congressional findings that we faced in *Lopez*, §13981 is supported by numerous findings regarding the serious impact that gender-motivated violence has on victims and their families. But the existence of congressional findings is not sufficient, by itself, to sustain the constitutionality of Commerce Clause legislation. . . . Rather, "[w]hether particular operations affect interstate commerce sufficiently to come under the constitutional power of Congress to regulate them is ultimately a judicial rather than a legislative question, and can be settled finally only by this Court." . . .

In these cases, Congress' findings are substantially weakened by the fact that they rely so heavily on a method of reasoning that we have already rejected as unworkable if we are to maintain the Constitution's enumeration of powers. Congress found that gender-motivated violence affects interstate commerce

> "by deterring potential victims from traveling interstate, from engaging in employment in interstate business, and from transacting with business, and in places involved in interstate commerce; . . . by diminishing national productivity, increasing medical and other costs, and decreasing the supply of and the demand for interstate products." . . .

Given these findings and petitioners' arguments, the concern that we expressed in *Lopez* that Congress might use the Commerce Clause to completely obliterate the Constitution's distinction between national and local authority seems well founded. The reasoning that petitioners advance seeks to follow the but-for causal chain from the initial occurrence of violent crime (the suppression of which has always been the prime object of the States' police power) to every attenuated effect upon interstate commerce. If accepted, petitioners' reasoning would allow Congress to regulate any crime as long as the nationwide, aggregated impact of that crime has substantial effects on employment, production, transit, or consumption. Indeed, if Congress may regulate gender-motivated violence, it would be able to regulate murder or any other type of violence since gender-motivated violence, as a subset of all violent crime, is certain to have lesser economic impacts than the larger class of which it is a part.

Petitioners' reasoning, moreover, will not limit Congress to regulating violence but may, as we suggested in *Lopez*, be applied equally as well to family law and other areas of traditional state regulation since the aggregate effect of marriage, divorce, and childrearing on the national economy is undoubtedly significant. Congress may have recognized this specter when it expressly precluded §13981 from being used in the family law context. See 42 U.S.C. §13981(e)(4). Under our written Constitution, however, the limitation of congressional authority is not solely a matter of legislative grace. . . .

We accordingly reject the argument that Congress may regulate noneconomic, violent criminal conduct based solely on that conduct's aggregate effect on interstate commerce. The Constitution requires a distinction between what is truly national and what is truly local. . . . The regulation and punishment of intrastate violence that is not directed at the instrumentalities, channels, or goods involved in interstate commerce has always been the province of the States. . . .

III

Because we conclude that the Commerce Clause does not provide Congress with authority to enact §13981, we address petitioners' alternative argument that the section's civil remedy should be upheld as an exercise of Congress' remedial power under §5 of the Fourteenth Amendment. . . .

Petitioners' §5 argument is founded on an assertion that there is pervasive bias in various state justice systems against victims of gender-motivated violence. This assertion is supported by a voluminous congressional record. Specifically, Congress received evidence that many participants in state justice systems are perpetuating an array of erroneous stereotypes and assumptions. Congress concluded that these discriminatory stereotypes often result in insufficient investigation and prosecution of gender-motivated crime, inappropriate focus on the behavior and credibility of the victims of that crime, and unacceptably lenient punishments for those who are actually convicted of gender-motivated violence. . . . Petitioners contend that this bias denies victims of gender-motivated violence the equal protection of the laws and that Congress therefore acted appropriately in enacting a private civil remedy against the perpetrators of gender-motivated violence to both remedy the States' bias and deter future instances of discrimination in the state courts.

As our cases have established, state-sponsored gender discrimination violates equal protection unless it "'serves "important governmental objectives and . . . the discriminatory means employed" are "substantially related to the achievement of those objectives."'" United States v. Virginia, 518 U.S. 515, 533 (1996). . . . However, the language and purpose of the Fourteenth Amendment place certain limitations on the manner in which Congress may attack discriminatory conduct. These limitations are necessary to prevent the Fourteenth Amendment from obliterating the Framers' carefully crafted balance of power between the States and the National Government. . . . Foremost among these limitations is the time-honored principle that the Fourteenth Amendment, by its very terms, prohibits only state action. . . .

[The Court elucidates its view that the Fourteenth Amendment prohibits only discriminatory state action, not discriminatory private conduct — and that the statute at hand deals with private conduct, not state action. The Court further states that the statute's remedy also fails to offend the Amendment, as it visits no consequences on state actors.]

Section 13981 is also different from these previously upheld remedies in that it applies uniformly throughout the Nation. Congress' findings indicate that the problem of discrimination against the victims of gender-motivated crimes does not exist in all States, or even most States. . . .

For these reasons, we conclude that Congress' power under §5 does not extend to the enactment of §13981.

IV

. . . If the allegations here are true, no civilized system of justice could fail to provide her a remedy for the conduct of respondent Morrison. But under our federal system that remedy must be provided by the Commonwealth of Virginia, and not by the United States. The judgment of the Court of Appeals is Affirmed.

[The concurring opinion of Justice THOMAS is omitted.]

Justice SOUTER, with whom Justice STEVENS, Justice GINSBURG, and Justice BREYER join, dissenting. . . .

I . . .

One obvious difference from United States v. Lopez is the mountain of data assembled by Congress, here showing the effects of violence against women on interstate commerce. Passage of the Act in 1994 was preceded by four years of hearings, which included testimony from physicians and law professors; from survivors of rape and domestic violence; and from representatives of state law enforcement and private business. The record includes reports on gender bias from task forces in 21 States, and we have the benefit of specific factual findings in the eight separate Reports issued by Congress and its committees over the long course leading to enactment. . . .

With respect to domestic violence, Congress received evidence for the following findings:

> "Three out of four American women will be victims of violent crimes sometime during their life." H.R. Rep. No. 103-395, p. 25 (1993) (citing U.S. Dept. of Justice, Report to the Nation on Crime and Justice 29 (2d ed.1988)).
> "Violence is the leading cause of injuries to women ages 15 to 44. . . ." S. Rep. No. 103-138, p. 38 (1993) (citing Surgeon General Antonia Novello, From the Surgeon General, U.S. Public Health Services, 267 JAMA 3132 (1992)).
> "[A]s many as 50 percent of homeless women and children are fleeing domestic violence." S. Rep. No. 101-545, p. 37 (1990) (citing E. Schneider,

Legal Reform Efforts for Battered Women: Past, Present, and Future (July 1990)).

"Since 1974, the assault rate against women has outstripped the rate for men by at least twice for some age groups and far more for others." S. Rep. No. 101-545, at 30 (citing Bureau of Justice Statistics, Criminal Victimization in the United States (1974) (Table 5)).

"[B]attering 'is the single largest cause of injury to women in the United States.'" S. Rep. No. 101-545, at 37 (quoting Van Hightower & McManus, Limits of State Constitutional Guarantees: Lessons from Efforts to Implement Domestic Violence Policies, 49 Pub. Admin. Rev. 269 (May/June 1989)). "An estimated 4 million American women are battered each year by their husbands or partners." H.R. Rep. No. 103-395, at 26 (citing Council on Scientific Affairs, American Medical Assn., Violence Against Women: Relevance for Medical Practitioners, 267 JAMA 3184, 3185 (1992)).

"Over 1 million women in the United States seek medical assistance each year for injuries sustained [from] their husbands or other partners." S. Rep. No. 101-545, at 37 (citing Stark & Flitcraft, Medical Therapy as Repression: The Case of the Battered Woman, Health & Medicine (Summer/Fall 1982)).

"Between 2,000 and 4,000 women die every year from [domestic] abuse." S. Rep. No. 101-545, at 36 (citing Schneider, supra).

"[A]rrest rates may be as low as 1 for every 100 domestic assaults." S. Rep. No. 101-545, at 38 (citing Dutton, Profiling of Wife Assaulters: Preliminary Evidence for Trimodal Analysis, 3 Violence and Victims 5-30 (1988)).

"Partial estimates show that violent crime against women costs this country at least 3 billion — not million, but billion — dollars a year." S. Rep. No. 101-545, at 33 (citing Schneider, supra, at 4).

"[E]stimates suggest that we spend $5 to $10 billion a year on health care, criminal justice, and other social costs of domestic violence." S. Rep. No. 103-138, at 41 (citing Biden, Domestic Violence: A Crime, Not a Quarrel, Trial 56 (June 1993)).

The evidence as to rape was similarly extensive, supporting these conclusions:

"[The incidence of] rape rose four times as fast as the total national crime rate over the past 10 years." S. Rep. No. 101-545, at 30 (citing Federal Bureau of Investigation Uniform Crime Reports (1988)).

"According to one study, close to half a million girls now in high school will be raped before they graduate." S. Rep. No. 101-545, at 31 (citing R. Warshaw, I Never Called It Rape 117 (1988)).

"[One hundred twenty-five thousand] college women can expect to be raped during this — or any — year." S. Rep. No. 101-545, at 43 (citing testimony of Dr. Mary Koss before the Senate Judiciary Committee, Aug. 29, 1990).

"[T]hree-quarters of women never go to the movies alone after dark because of the fear of rape and nearly 50 percent do not use public transit alone after dark for the same reason." S. Rep. No. 102-197, p. 38 (1991) (citing M. Gordon & S. Riger, The Female Fear 15 (1989)).

"[Forty-one] percent of judges surveyed believed that juries give sexual assault victims less credibility than other crime victims." S. Rep. No. 102-197, at 47 (citing Colorado Supreme Court Task Force on Gender Bias in the Courts, Gender Justice in the Colorado Courts 91 (1990)).

"Less than 1 percent of all [rape] victims have collected damages." S. Rep. No. 102-197, at 44 (citing report by Jury Verdict Research, Inc.).

"'[A]n individual who commits rape has only about 4 chances in 100 of being arrested, prosecuted, and found guilty of any offense.'" S. Rep. No. 101-545, at 33, n.30 (quoting H. Feild & L. Bienen, Jurors and Rape: A Study in Psychology and Law 95 (1980)).

"Almost one-quarter of convicted rapists never go to prison and another quarter received sentences in local jails where the average sentence is 11 months." S. Rep. No. 103-138, at 38 (citing Majority Staff Report of Senate Committee on the Judiciary, The Response to Rape: Detours on the Road to Equal Justice, 103d Cong., 1st Sess., 2 (Comm. Print 1993)).

"[A]lmost 50 percent of rape victims lose their jobs or are forced to quit because of the crime's severity." S. Rep. No. 102-197, at 53 (citing Ellis, Atkeson, & Calhoun, An Assessment of Long-Term Reaction to Rape, 90 J. Abnormal Psych., No. 3, p.264 (1981)).

Based on the data thus partially summarized, Congress found that

"crimes of violence motivated by gender have a substantial adverse effect on interstate commerce, by deterring potential victims from traveling interstate, from engaging in employment in interstate business, and from transacting with business, and in places involved, in interstate commerce . . . [,] by diminishing national productivity, increasing medical and other costs, and decreasing the supply of and the demand for interstate products. . . ." H.R. Conf. Rep. No. 103-711, p. 385 (1994), U.S. Code Cong. & Admin. News 1994, pp. 1803, 1853.

Congress thereby explicitly stated the predicate for the exercise of its Commerce Clause power. Is its conclusion irrational in view of the data amassed? True, the methodology of particular studies may be challenged, and some of the figures arrived at may be disputed. But the sufficiency of the evidence before Congress to provide a rational basis for the finding cannot seriously be questioned. . . .

Indeed, the legislative record here is far more voluminous than the record compiled by Congress and found sufficient in two prior cases upholding Title II of the Civil Rights Act of 1964 against Commerce Clause challenges. . . .

II . . .

The premise that the enumeration of powers implies that other powers are withheld is sound; the conclusion that some particular categories of subject matter are therefore presumptively beyond the reach of the commerce power is, however, a non sequitur. From the fact that Art. I, §8, cl. 3 grants an authority limited to regulating commerce, it follows only that Congress may claim no authority under that section to address any subject that does not affect commerce. It does not at all follow that an activity affecting commerce nonetheless falls outside the commerce power, depending on the specific character of the activity, or the authority of a State to regulate it along with Congress. My disagreement with the majority is not, however, confined to logic, for history has shown that categorical exclusions have proven as unworkable in practice as they are unsupportable in theory. . . .

III

All of this convinces me that today's ebb of the commerce power rests on error, and at the same time leads me to doubt that the majority's view will prove to be enduring law. There is yet one more reason for doubt. . . . As our predecessors learned then, the practice of such ad hoc review cannot preserve the distinction between the judicial and the legislative, and this Court, in any event, lacks the institutional capacity to maintain such a regime for very long. This one will end when the majority realizes that the conception of the commerce power for which it entertains hopes would inevitably fail the test expressed in Justice Holmes's statement that "[t]he first call of a theory of law is that it should fit the facts." O. Holmes, The Common Law 167 (Howe ed.1963). The facts that cannot be ignored today are the facts of integrated national commerce and a political relationship between States and Nation much affected by their respective treasuries and constitutional modifications adopted by the people. The federalism of some earlier time is no more adequate to account for those facts today than the theory of laissez-faire was able to govern the national economy 70 years ago.

Justice BREYER, with whom Justice STEVENS joins, and with whom Justice SOUTER and Justice GINSBURG join as to Part I-A, dissenting. . . .

[Justice Breyer reasons that the economic/non-economic distinction is difficult to apply, that it requires awkward exceptions, and that "[n]othing in the Constitution's language, or that of earlier cases prior to *Lopez*, explains why the Court should ignore one highly relevant characteristic of an interstate-commerce-affecting cause (how "local" it is), while placing critical constitutional weight upon a different, less obviously relevant, feature (how "economic" it is)."]

. . . To determine the lawfulness of statutes simply by asking whether Congress could reasonably have found that aggregated local instances significantly affect interstate commerce will allow Congress to regulate almost anything. . . .

This consideration, however, while serious, does not reflect a jurisprudential defect, so much as it reflects a practical reality. We live in a Nation knit together by two centuries of scientific, technological, commercial and environmental change. Those changes, taken together, mean that virtually every kind of activity, no matter how local, genuinely can affect commerce, or its conditions, outside the State . . . at least when considered in the aggregate. . . .

Since judges cannot change the world, the "defect" means that, within the bounds of the rational, Congress, not the courts, must remain primarily responsible for striking the appropriate state/federal balance. . . .

Moreover, as Justice SOUTER has pointed out, Congress compiled a "mountain of data" explicitly documenting the interstate commercial effects of gender-motivated crimes of violence. . . . After considering alternatives, it focused the federal law upon documented deficiencies in state legal systems. And it tailored the law to prevent its use in certain areas of traditional state concern, such as divorce, alimony, or child custody. 42 U.S.C. §13981(e)(4). Consequently, the law before us seems to represent an instance, not of state/federal conflict, but of state/federal efforts to cooperate in order to help solve a mutually acknowledged national problem. Cf. §§300w-10, 3796gg, 3796hh, 10409, 13931 (providing federal moneys to encourage state and local initiatives to combat gender-motivated violence). . . .

II

Given my conclusion on the Commerce Clause question, I need not consider Congress' authority under §5 of the Fourteenth Amendment. Nonetheless, I doubt the Court's reasoning rejecting that source of authority. . . .

. . . [W]hy can Congress not provide a remedy against private actors? Those private actors, of course, did not themselves violate the Constitution. But this Court has held that Congress at least sometimes can enact remedial "[l]egislation . . . [that] prohibits conduct which is not itself unconstitutional." The statutory remedy does not in any sense purport to "determine what constitutes a constitutional violation." It intrudes little upon either States or private parties. It may lead state actors to improve their own remedial systems, primarily through example. It restricts private actors only by imposing liability for private conduct that is, in the main, already forbidden by state law. Why is the remedy "disproportionate"? And given the relation between remedy and violation — the creation of a federal remedy to substitute for constitutionally inadequate state remedies — where is the lack of "congruence"?

The majority adds that Congress found that the problem of inadequacy of state remedies "does not exist in all States, or even most States." But Congress had before it the task force reports of at least 21 States documenting constitutional violations. And it made its own findings about pervasive gender-based stereotypes hampering many state legal systems, sometimes unconstitutionally so. . . . The record nowhere reveals a congressional finding that the problem "does not exist" elsewhere. Why can Congress not take the evidence before it as evidence of a national problem? This Court has not previously held that Congress must document the existence of a problem in every State prior to proposing a national solution. And the deference this Court gives to Congress' chosen remedy under §5, . . . suggests that any such requirement would be inappropriate.

Despite my doubts about the majority's §5 reasoning, I need not, and do not, answer the §5 question, which I would leave for more thorough analysis if necessary on another occasion. Rather, in my view, the Commerce Clause provides an adequate basis for the statute before us. And I would uphold its constitutionality as the "necessary and proper" exercise of legislative power granted to Congress by that Clause.

Catharine A. MacKinnon, Disputing Male Sovereignty: On United States v. Morrison
114 Harv. L. Rev. 135, 168-172 (2000)

The controversy over the scope of the §5 power to legislate equality is as much about where the line between public and private is drawn as about which part of the government will draw it. Historically, those forces who wanted to prevent racial equality and maintain white supremacy opposed laws against racial discrimination in society, so they opposed the recognition of the power to pass laws that would guarantee equality by those bodies that would pass them. Transparently, states keeping the power to legislate citizen-to-citizen equality in their hands, rather than permitting the federal government to give that power to harmed individuals to enforce themselves, was the formal vehicle through which equality rights could continue to be denied. White supremacy may be more visible behind the precedents of the past, federalism their foil, than male supremacy is behind the same fig leaf today. Whatever the reason, none of the *Morrison* opinions considers the impact on the possibilities for addressing women's inequality by law of the majority's choice of where to draw the public/private line — or exhibits any awareness that they are creating, not just retracing, that line.

The Fourth Circuit drew the same line between public and private domains as the *Morrison* majority, although in more ideological and less temperate terms. With deep historical resonance, the Fourth Circuit began its ruling sonorously:

> We the People, distrustful of power, and believing that government limited and dispersed protects freedom best, provided that our federal government

would be one of enumerated powers, and that all power unenumerated would be reserved to the several States and to ourselves.[198]

Strikingly, these judges, writing in their judicial capacity, felt it appropriate to identify themselves as speaking in their personal capacity: as "we the People" and "ourselves," those to whom power is reserved that is not otherwise granted to others over them. One senses that it was not Christy Brzonkala with whom they were identifying. To state the obvious, women were not "we the People" who decided to arrange the government along the lines described. Women had no voice in designing the doctrines or institutions that the Court wielded in *Morrison* to exclude them from access to court. Women never configured the geography of federalism so the "private" was a subprovince of the "local," for instance. These arrangements were made before women were even permitted to vote. Women, too, distrust power, but the power they have learned to distrust includes that of men being states and men like "ourselves," along with the other forms that dominance takes. The Fourth Circuit's preamble speaks in the voice of men who trust their own power but not the power of other men over them. But it is principally men's power over women that the VAWA addresses.

The experience of subordinated groups has not necessarily taught that government "limited and dispersed protects freedom best." This system has protected their inequality, hence their lack of freedom. The experience of African Americans has been that states protect their freedom least; only the federal government has been any match for the power of the states. It has been the freedom of those with power in society whose power is protected in the name of freedom by the federal system the Fourth Circuit evoked and, in so doing, enforced. This is not to say that states are the sole source of the maldistribution of power in society, only that they have not effectively changed it and have often obstructed changing it. As a result, making the states the sole avenue for seeking equality can be, and has been, a means of preventing equality from being effectively achieved. Actually, because the state is not the exclusive fountainhead of male power, confining constitutional sex equality initiatives to a narrow conception of state action guarantees that sex inequality will continue.

Violence against women, the Fourth Circuit decided, is wholly within state authority yet not embraced by state action, just as "family law [is] an area of law that clearly rests at the heart of the traditional authority of the States," yet what goes on in the family is "purely private." The Fourth Circuit wanted to have it both ways: this sphere is for the states when the federal legislative power is invoked but not of the states when the equality

---

198. [Brzonkala v. Va. Polytechnic Inst. & State Univ., 169 F.3d 820, 825-826 (4th Cir. 1999) (en banc) (holding that the challenged section of the VAWA could not be upheld under the Commerce Clause and that the section was not a constitutionally legitimate exercise of Congress's power under the enforcement section of the Fourteenth Amendment).]

clause is invoked. What states do, on the VAWA record showing, in the vision of the federal system that the Fourth Circuit and the *Morrison* majority defended, is monopolize the power to address violence against women in order to do little about it. It would seem that states must exclusively occupy this territory so that inequality within it will continue. But the Constitution is already involved in family law in the interest of equality. The *Morrison* and *Brzonkala* courts' conception of family law as an inviolable preserve blinkers rulings like Loving v. Virginia [388 U.S. 1 (1967)] and Palmore v. Sidoti [466 U.S. 409 (1984)], not to mention Orr v. Orr [440 U.S. 268 (1979)] and Kirchberg v. Feenstra [450 U.S. 455 (1981)], all of which assert the preeminence of constitutional equality over state family statutory and case law. These decisions, although not per se providing precedent for the VAWA under §5, undermine the affirmative nature of the decision in *Morrison* to permit unredressed violence against women in the name of what is called the private. The VAWA would hardly have been the first invasion by the Constitution in the name of equality into a state legal regime denominated private. The public, the law, the federal Constitution, the Fourteenth Amendment, are already there.

The *Morrison* majority does not simply respect a preexisting line between what is private and what is public. It draws that line by abandoning women wherever violence against them takes place. *Morrison* effectively defines the private as the location where effective redress for sex-based violence is unavailable, ignoring the destruction of women's freedom and equality in private by the lack of public limits on male violence. The private is thus constructed of public impunity. The jealous guarding of this specific line between public and private acts, under which exercise of state power is accountable to public authority but exercise of so-called private power is not, thus becomes one of the central public means of maintaining a system in which male power over women remains effectively without limit. Christy Brzonkala was away at school when she was raped, paying to attend a public educational institution. She was gang-raped by men she had barely met in a room not her own. Public officials effectively condoned her violation through public legal processes. In what sense was her rape private?

At this juncture, one might well ask: why limit equality rights to the narrowest of official violations if not to ensure that the private remains unequal? *Morrison* is an official national decision that what men do to women in private will be beyond the reach of a public authority. Officially limiting equality rights to state acts while defining state acts extremely narrowly, thus keeping the so-called private a sphere of impunity for violence against women, is a public act. In dividing public from private along its chosen line — the identical line chosen by the Fourth Circuit, if with less overt venom — the Supreme Court failed to recognize the extent of the public's complicity in promoting violence against women in private by creating, and in constitutionally entrenching, a public standard of impunity for it. . . .

Practices of inequality occupy various positions in relation to state action, calling for flexible approaches if equality is to be achieved. The *Morrison* Court quoted Shelley v. Kraemer for the proposition that the Constitution does not cover purely private acts. But racially restrictive housing covenants are ineffective pieces of paper if they are not enforceable at law. Withdrawing legal backing from them eliminates their ability to enforce inequality. Violence against women, by contrast, is self-enforcing. It is effective unless addressed by law. In defining freedom from sex-based violence as a federal civil right, Congress recognized what the Supreme Court denied: the problem pervades the nation's civil society and state inseparably, so could only be effectively addressed by an instrument that distinguished neither between one state and another nor between official and other acts in determining what creates an inequality problem and what does not.

Congress recognized that an effective remedy to the inequality problem of violence against women, a problem primarily of aggression by one sex against the other, called for an approach that fit the contours of the problem. Most violence against women is engaged in by non-state actors, people who are not public officials or acting with what is recognized as state authority. But they do act with the virtually total assurance that, as statistics confirm, their acts will be officially tolerated, they themselves will be officially invisible, and their victims will be officially silenced. That is, their acts will be kept private by exclusion from public recognition or public redress. They are state-exempt acts. Sex discrimination through sexual violence, so long as it is publicly unredressed, will be a fact of public life that is no less of public concern when committed in so-called private — quite the contrary. Violated women are abandoned alone there. Discriminatory abdication by public authority makes private acts public.

Government is constructed to be sensitive to the dominance of some men over other men by formal institutional means. It is not created to be wary of the dominance of men over women by means seen as informal or noninstitutionalized. In this light, the Fourth Circuit's opening formulation presents the question: whose freedom is protected by the structural distribution of institutional power that court defends, and whose power does that court distrust? To put not too fine a point on it, one wonders why the Fourth Circuit and Supreme Court majorities, not doctrinally required to reach this result, made sure that women do not have equal rights against unofficial gender-based aggression. What was at stake? In connection with the Fourth Circuit's opinion, it is also worth pondering why ensuring that nothing effective is done about violence against women is a systemic value worthy of rhetorically refighting the Civil War. Presumably, inflicting violence against women with official impunity was not one of "our fundamental liberties" that the division between state and federal government-mental powers was originally adopted to protect. Or was it?

Notes

1. The Violence Against Women Act. The Violence Against Women Act (VAWA) committed the federal government to fighting domestic violence through a number of different mechanisms. Passed as part of the Violent Crime Control and Law Enforcement Act of 1994, Pub. L. No. 103-322, 108 Stat. 1796 (codified as amended in scattered sections of 8 U.S.C., 16 U.S.C., 18 U.S.C., 28 U.S.C., and 42 U.S.C.), a massive omnibus crime bill, VAWA links child abuse with violence against women and focuses on the criminal justice system as the key to addressing both. See generally George B. Stevenson, Federal Antiviolence and Abuse Legislation: Toward Elimination of Disparate Justice for Women and Children, 33 Willamette L. Rev. 855 (1997).

The larger crime bill of which VAWA was a part, for example, tightens the controls over offenders in probation or post-prison status and limits offenders' opportunities for probation. Courts are required to sentence all first-time domestic violence offenders to prison or probation, rather than deferred or diverted prosecution as under previous practice. One condition of first-time offender probation is participation in a nonprofit rehabilitation program approved by the court in consultation with a State Coalition Against Domestic Violence. Stevenson, supra, at 860. Assault with intent to rape, sexual abuse, and attempt, conspiracy, or solicitation to commit these offenses qualify as "serious violent felonies" under the federal "three strikes and you're out" sentencing program requiring life imprisonment for persons convicted in federal court of a serious violent felony after prior conviction in a state or federal court of two serious felonies or a serious violent offense and a serious drug offense. Id. at 859.

The Safe Homes for Women Act, created under VAWA, provides law enforcement personnel with the authority to enforce civil protection orders from other states. Id. at 872. It also requires every state or Indian tribe to give full faith and credit to protection orders issued by any other state or tribe. Id. VAWA authorizes funding for entering data on stalking and domestic violence into local, state, and national databases and authorizes technical assistance to state and tribal judges handling stalking and domestic violence cases. Id. at 873.

VAWA also expanded the State Justice Institute's authority and mission to study and eliminate gender bias in all criminal justice and court systems, requiring each federal circuit judicial council to form gender bias task forces to study gender bias and implement reforms. "The Institute has the authority to award grants to develop model programs to be used in training state and Indian tribal judges and court personnel on dealing with rape, sexual assault, domestic violence, and other crimes of gender-motivated violence." Id. at 881-882.

Feminist commentators hailed VAWA as a historic moment in the struggle to have the law recognize the unique experiences of women of color. Jenny Rivera notes:

> The VAWA recognizes that within communities of color there are different issues and discrete culturally-based concerns. For example, law enforcement and prosecution federal grants are available for, inter alia, purposes of "developing or improving delivery of victim services to racial, cultural, ethnic, and language minorities. . . ." Further, states must set forth in their grant applications the demographics of the service population, including information on "race, ethnicity and language background . . ." in order to qualify for a grant. Applicants for the National Domestic Violence Hotline grant had to provide a plan for servicing "non-English speaking callers," such as by employing Spanish-speaking hotline personnel, and had to demonstrate a commitment to "diversity, and to the provision of services to ethnic, racial, and non-English speaking minorities. . . ."

Jenny Rivera, The Violence Against Women Act and the Construction of Multiple Consciousness in the Civil Rights and Feminist Movements, 4 J.L. & Pol'y 464, 494-495 (1996). The Act also expanded remedies available to battered immigrant women: battered immigrant wives with conditional resident status can now self-petition to adjust their status without the cooperation of their sponsor-husbands, and VAWA also allows suspension of deportation proceedings for undocumented battered spouses and children of U.S. citizens or residents. See 8 U.S.C. §1154a(1)(A)(iii)(I) (Supp. 2001).

Finally, VAWA created new substantive law. The Act makes it a federal crime to cross state lines for the purpose of or in the course of "harassing, intimidating, or injuring a spouse or intimate partner." Most controversially, the Act created a civil rights remedy for "crimes of violence motivated by gender." Under this provision, any person, including a person who acts under color of state law, who commits a crime of violence "because of gender or on the basis of gender and due, at least in part, to an animus based on the victim's gender" shall be liable for "compensatory and punitive damages, injunctive and declaratory relief, and such other relief as a court may deem appropriate." 42 U.S.C. §13981 (1994). See generally Victoria Nourse, The Violence Against Women Act: A Legislative History, in Violence Against Women: Law and Practice (David Frazee & Ann Noel eds., 1996); Symposium, The Violence Against Women Act of 1994: A Promise Waiting to Be Fulfilled, 4 J.L. & Pol'y 371 (1996). It was this aspect of the VAWA that was held to be without constitutional foundation in *Morrison*.

2. Domestic Violence and the Public/Private Dichotomy. As the readings in Chapter 1 explore, Anglo-American legal doctrine has historically treated husbands, fathers, and slaveowners as miniature heads of state, responsible for governing those in their households. Commentators' analogies between "family government" and state government explicitly elevate the male head of household to giver of the Law. Later, judges turned to concepts of privacy rather than status to explain why women could not look to the law for protection from intimate partner violence and marital rape; but, as feminists like Elizabeth Schneider argue at page 631 above, the effect is the same: separating a legally unregulated (woman's) private realm from a (man's) public realm leaves women vulnerable to forms of "private" exploitation the law is deemed unsuitable to reach. In addition, the Violence Against Women Act imposes mandatory prison or probation for domestic violence offenders. See page 690 infra.

Viewing domestic violence in terms of the public/private dichotomy has helped feminists to explain how even the experience of domestic violence, which is very personal, is politically structured: in short, how "the personal is political." Abuse is experienced on the personal level, as are one's options — whether leaving one's spouse would betray one's marital vows or upset family expectations, whether one can afford to live without one's spouse, whether one has the psychological resources to withstand the pressure to return, and so on. Treatment for the batterer, too, is seen as an individual or family matter, on which objective or scientific expertise may be brought to bear. See Carolyn Puzella, Social Scientists' Perspectives on the Causes of Spousal Abuse, 11 J. Contemp. Legal Issues 37 (2000) (reviewing the gamut of social science explanations for intimate partner violence, which run from the purely psychiatric to the purely sociocultural). Yet much conduct that would be considered criminal if done between strangers — pushing, slapping, and shoving, for example — is still considered by many to be generally acceptable within the privacy of the family as long as it does not lead to serious injury. What resources are made available to the battered woman and how others expect her, and her batterer, to act are also factors structured by larger social and political forces within which the individual must operate. Even the fact that abuse is experienced as personal, as Schneider points out in the reading above, is not a "given," but a choice structured by the larger society.

What is the role of the government in such a society? MacKinnon argues that the government's failure to enforce its own laws is attributable to the government, and when that failure is on the basis of sex, it is sex discrimination. Consider, as well, Isabel Marcus's analysis of domestic violence:

> What are we to make of a situation in which specific formal structures of subordination and control articulated in legal doctrine are eliminated by legislative enactment and/or judicial construction, but the coercive practices of violence, or the threat of it, which support and maintain such subordination and control, are tacitly endorsed? Surely the coercion is critical to the maintenance of the subordination; surely the practitioners of that coercion are aware of the utility of their strategy. Can it be said that contemporary practitioners of such coercion actually reenact coverture by denying a separated

identity to their spouse or partner? I am prepared to say that we can make such a connection and, thereby, explore the possibility that coverture has not yet been abolished in the United States.

I argue that such contemporary violence and the response of our legal system to it does constitute a current manifestation of what we conventionally consider the discarded and archaic American domestic relations common-law doctrine and practice, coverture, or the erasure of a specific legal identity for married women. More specifically, I suggest that a legal system which "naturalizes" violence against women in the home, by allowing perpetrators to act without fear of punishment by the state, is a legal system devoted to maintaining control over women. For violence against women in the home was and is premised on beliefs regarding the "rightness" of male power and the "entitlement" of men to exercise control over women's behavior and actions.

Isabel Marcus, Reframing "Domestic Violence": Terrorism in the Home, in Martha Albertson Fineman & Roxanne Mykitiuk, The Public Nature of Private Violence: The Discovery of Domestic Abuse 11, 18 (1994).

Does the Court's opinion in *Morrison* reaffirm that coverture still exists in the United States?

3. Domestic Violence as an International Human Rights Issue. Marcus goes on to argue that the very term "domestic violence" plays into the public/private distinction and suggests that international law is not applicable. Instead, Marcus proposes that domestic violence be viewed as an international human rights issue.

I am persuaded that the value of this broader perspective lies in its inclusive "bottom line." As international human rights theory and practice move beyond the limitations and constraints of traditional, Western, liberal, political theory, they articulate an expansive vision which substitutes a global "our" for a narrower "my" rights. We know that family violence, especially wife abuse, is a widespread phenomenon; the global "our" is clearly applicable to it, despite the fact that "some acts of violation are not crimes in law, others are legitimized in custom or court opinion, and most are blamed on the victims themselves."

Marcus, supra, at 28. See also Dorothy Q. Thomas & Michele E. Beasley, Domestic Violence as a Human Rights Issue, 58 Alb. L. Rev. 1119 (1995); Rhonda Copelon, Recognizing the Egregious in the Everyday: Domestic Violence as Torture, 25 Colum. Hum. Rts. L. Rev. 291 (1994).

The issue was brought to the fore in June 1999, when a federal immigration appeals panel overturned a grant of asylum to Rodi Alvarado Pena, a Guatemalan woman seeking refuge in the United States because the Guatemalan legal system had failed to protect her from her abusive husband. In re R-A, Int. Dec. 3403, 1999 WL 424364 (B.I.A. June 11, 1999). The decision created a public outcry and seemingly flew in the face of Immigration and Naturalization Service guidelines promulgated in 1995 that recognized rape, domestic abuse, and other forms of violence against women as possible grounds for asylum. See Karen Musalo, Matter of R-A: An Analysis of the Decision and Its Implications, 76 Interpreter Releases 1177 (Aug. 9, 1999); Amanda Blanck, Domestic Violence as a Basis for Asylum Status: A Human Rights Based Approach, 22 Women's Rts. L. Rep. 47 (2000). The opinion was later vacated by Attorney General Janet Reno. See http://www.usdoj.gov/graphics/lawsregs/biadec.htm (January 19, 2001). A different result was reached in Aguirre-Cervantes v. INS, 242 F.3d 1169 (9th Cir. 2001), in which the Ninth Circuit overturned the Bureau of Immigration Appeals and granted asylum to a woman who, along with other members of her immediate family, had been abused by her father. This opinion, too, was subsequently vacated on a rehearing en banc. Aguirre-Cervantes v. INS, 273 F3d 1220 (9th Cir. 2001).

Canada and Australia, as well as the United States, have adopted nonbinding guidelines for asylum inspectors that call on them to consider claims of domestic violence in assessing asylum claims. See Andrew N. Langham, Comment, The Erosion of Refugee Rights in Australia: Two Proposed Amendments to the Migration Act, 8 Pac. Rim L. & Pol'y J. 651, 662 (1999) (describing the process for reviewing asylum applications in Australia).

In the United States, the right to asylum is tied to the petitioner's status as a refugee. The United Nations Convention Relating to the Status of Refugees defines a refugee in part as any person who "owing to a well-founded fear of being persecuted for reasons of race, religion, national origin, membership in a particular social group or political opinion, is outside the country of his nationality and is unable or, owing to such fear, is unwilling to avail himself of the protection of that country." 1951 Convention relating to the Status of Refugees, July 28, 1951, 19 U.S.T. 6259, 189 U.N.T.S. 137. Victims of domestic violence have generally based their claims for asylum on the "membership in a particular social group [or political opinion]" category. For an analysis of this requirement and discussion of many of the relevant cases, see Andrea Binder, Gender and the "Membership in a Particular Social Group" Category of the 1951 Refugee Convention, 10 Colum. J. Gender & L. 167 (2001). The British House of Lords and the Canadian Supreme Court have interpreted the Convention to allow gender to be the defining characteristic of a particular social group where a pattern of discriminatory treatment existed. See Ex parte Shah v. Secretary of State for the Home Department, [1999] 2 All E.R. 545; Canada v. Ward, [1993] 2 S.C.R. 689. These cases are analyzed in Deborah Anker, Refugee Status and Violence Against Women in the "Domestic" Sphere: The Non-State Actor Question, 15 Geo. Immigr. L.J. 391 (2001); see also Mattie L. Stevens, Comment, Recognizing Gender-Specific Persecution: A Proposal to Add Gender as a Sixth Refugee Category, 3 Cornell J.L. & Pub. Pol'y 179 (1993).

There is some support in other international documents for treating domestic violence as a human rights issue. The Declaration on the Elimination of Violence Against Women and the UNHCR Guidelines on the Protection of Refugee Women recognize domestic violence as a form of gender discrimination, and thus a human rights violation. Blanck, supra, at 47-48. The UN Convention Against Torture is another possible foundation for asylum claims when women flee domestic violence; Blanck reports that "the United Nations Special Rapporteur on Violence Against Women has recommended that bodies that report on human rights abuses and violence against women and treaty bodies consider treating domestic violence as an internationally proscribed form of torture." Id. at 72; see Barbara Cochrane Alexander, Note, Convention Against Torture: A Viable Alternative Legal Remedy for Domestic Violence Victims, 15 Am. U. Int'l L. Rev. 895 (2000).

Should women fleeing domestic violence in their home countries be entitled to claim asylum in the United States? Many feminist scholars argue that they should. See, e.g., Joan Fitzpatrick, The Gender Dimension of U.S. Immigration Policy, 9 Yale J.L. & Feminism 23, 47 (1997); Pamela Goldberg, Anyplace but Home: Asylum in the United States for Women Fleeing Intimate Violence, 26 Cornell Int'l L.J. 565, 569 (1993).

4. Feminist Critiques of the Public/Private Dichotomy. What flows from the argument, outlined in note 2 above, that the line separating a "private" domestic sphere from a "public" state and market sphere leaves women unprotected against intimate violence? Is any conception of a "private" sphere where the law may not reach illegitimate? In her comprehensive study of the different forms the critique of the public/private dichotomy has taken, Ruth Gavison distinguishes internal criticisms, which question where the line between public and private is drawn, from external criticisms, which challenge the distinction between public and private itself. See Ruth Gavison, Feminism and the Public/Private Distinction, 45 Stan. L. Rev. 1 (1992). Gavison argues that the real question is not whether there is to be a division between public and private; the division is inevitable and necessary to women as well as to men. The question is, rather, whether or not the line between the two, in particular concrete circumstances, is drawn in ways that subordinate women. Id. at 36-37. See also Tracy E. Higgins, Reviving the Public/Private Distinction in Feminist Theorizing, 75 Chi.-Kent L. Rev. 847 (2000) (arguing that feminists have much to gain in preserving the public/private line and the right of privacy). As you consider the various contexts in which the distinction between the public and the private has operated in law, including pornography (examined in section D of this chapter) and abortion and reproductive rights (explored in Chapter 6), evaluate whether Gavison's formulation of the issue is a satisfactory one.

How should the state's refusal to acknowledge lesbian relationships at all influence feminist analyses of the public/private divide? See Nancy J.

Knauer, Same-Sex Domestic Violence: Claiming a Domestic Sphere While Risking Negative Stereotypes, 8 Temp. Pol. & Civ. Rts. L. Rev. 325, 340 (1999) ("[s]ame-sex couples exist outside of a state recognized private or domestic sphere"). Should the gay and lesbian effort be to establish a private sphere or to abolish it?

5. The Nonsubordination Approach and the Dilemma of Criminalization. Nonsubordination theorists have pointed out that the state is not neutral, but rather amplifies and protects male power over women. If this analysis is correct, does it make sense for feminist advocates to expect the law, particularly the criminal justice system, to adequately challenge domestic violence? Consider Naomi Cahn's analysis:

> Because not all criminal laws are equally enforced, the mere legal conclusion of criminality does not mean that society's power is brought to bear on the crime. Thus people quite frequently engage in various forms of criminal behavior. Indeed, it is the failure of the criminal justice system to address domestic violence crimes that lead, in large part, to the development of civil protection orders. While the criminal justice system continues to establish certain baseline moral judgments, it is a crude means for recognizing women's needs. To the extent that the law is based on community and public norms developed through public consensus, it does not and cannot reflect the needs of outsider groups. Where social groups are unequal, regardless of the existence of legal discrimination, it is difficult for those groups to influence policy.
>
> The criminal route also serves to give control to the state. Where sensitivity to women is not a real priority, women can sacrifice control, getting little support in return. Finally, many of the assumptions underlying criminal law are "nonneutral." Thus, instead of the criminal justice system alone, we need to use more affirmative and civil supports for women.

Naomi Cahn, Policing Women: Moral Arguments and the Dilemmas of Criminalization, 49 DePaul L. Rev. 817, 820-821 (2000). What are the implications for the *Stephenson* case, set forth at page 632?

The dilemma is particularly acute if the state is non-neutral with respect not only to gender, but also to race. If domestic violence activists turn to the criminal justice system for protection, the result may be further criminalization of people of color generally, and men in particular. Angela Davis frames the problem this way:

> We need an analysis that furthers neither the conservative project of sequestering millions of men of color in accordance with the contemporary dictates of globalized capital and its prison industrial complex, nor the equally conservative project of abandoning poor women of color to a continuum of violence that extends from the sweatshops through the prisons, to shelters, and into bedrooms at home. How do we develop analyses and organizing strategies

against violence against women that acknowledge the race of gender and the gender of race?

Angela Davis, Keynote Address to Color of Violence Conference, recorded in Charles Brown, The Color of Violence Against Women (Oct. 25, 2000) printed in 3 (3) Color Lines (Fall 2000), available at http:// www.arc.org./C_Lines/CLArchive/story3_3_02.html; see also Jenny Rivera, Domestic Violence Against Latinas by Latino Males: An Analysis of Race, National Origin, and Gender Differentials, 14 B.C. Third World L.J. 231, 248 (1994) (noting that for women of color, using the criminal justice state to combat domestic violence will only intensify the racist criminalization of men of color); Machaela M. Hoctor, Comment, Domestic Violence as a Crime Against the State: The Need for Mandatory Arrest in California, 85 Cal. L. Rev. 643, 691 (1997) (questioning the use of the criminal justice system to challenge domestic violence, given the already outlaw status of gay men and lesbians); Donna Coker, Crime Control and Feminist Law Reform in Domestic Violence Law: A Critical Review, 4 Buff. Crim. L. Rev. 801, 805 (2000) ("Not only does a focus on crime control deflect attention from other anti-domestic violence strategies, crime control policies result in greater state control of women, particularly poor women.").

The dilemma may be an inescapable one for feminists living under a legal system that simultaneously acknowledges sex equality as a norm and preserves status-based inequality. See generally Feminists Negotiate the State: The Politics of Domestic Violence (Cynthia R. Daniels ed., 1997).

What is to be done? Donna Coker suggests a way forward:

> How might we diminish the risk that increasing state intervention against domestic violence will increase state control of women? First, we must organize for more material assistance for battered women. Crime control policies are costly, but lawmakers continue to be willing to allocate funds for purpose that sound like "fighting crime." We must begin to articulate that economic justice for women and children is part of domestic violence prevention. Bundling services within crime control programs does not adequately address this need. This is true both because of the limitations of the programs and because many battered women do not come to the attention of the criminal justice system. A focus on economic justice requires that battered women's advocates work to strengthen coalitions with activists and organizations that attend to the broader picture of violence against women in inner cities and the broader picture of women's economic status.
>
> Second, we must recognize that universal policies are unlikely to be successful. Rather, effective policies must derive from local struggles and local organizing efforts.
>
> Third, we must explore alternatives to mandatory policies for establishing control of the state's response to domestic violence. . . .
>
> Finally, in developing anti-domestic violence strategies, we must attend to the coercive power of the state, as well as the coercive power of battering men.

Coker, supra, at 859-860. What do you think?

Putting Theory into Practice

4-8. Sharon's three children were removed from her home when her husband, who is the father of two of the children, was found to have repeatedly abused the children by beating them with a stick, throwing things at them, and swearing at them and calling them names like "stupid." A mental health evaluation of Sharon showed that she did not always put the needs of the children first, that her parenting skills were weak, and that she was a battered wife who had a history of relationships with men who abused her and a social profile and personality type that made her very vulnerable to abuse. Child Protective Services seeks to terminate Sharon's parental rights to her children on the theory that even if she leaves her dangerous husband, she is likely to enter into another relationship that will be dangerous to the children.

Parental rights can be terminated in the jurisdiction if the state can show that a parent has failed to prevent another person from abusing her child and that it is reasonably likely that the child will be abused if returned to the parent.

You are Sharon's advocate. What arguments can you make to help her prevent the termination of her parental rights? Should you win?

4-9. Debra and Terrance are cocaine addicts, arrested for the commission of several armed robberies. Debra admits the crimes, but claims a defense of duress, on the grounds that she participated in the robberies out of fear that Terrance would kill her if she did not do as he told her. In support of her defense, Debra seeks to present expert testimony explaining that she suffers from battered woman's syndrome, based on a history of physical and emotional abuse that escalated every time she tried to leave Terrance. Evidence of battered woman's syndrome has been admitted in the jurisdiction in cases in which a battered woman has killed her batterer and claims self-defense. What arguments do you anticipate in opposition to Debra's offer to produce expert testimony on battered woman's syndrome in support of her duress defense? As Debra's lawyer, how will you answer those arguments? This issue is later addressed at pages 915-917.

D. PORNOGRAPHY

1. The Background of Pornography Controversies

Sex sells. That has always been true, but increased technological innovations have created increased opportunities for private consumption of pornography. Adult theatres, rental videos, pay-per-view movies on cable and world-sites, phone sex, and Internet Web sites are estimated to generate somewhere between $10 billion and $14 billion annually. Americans spend more on pornography than on all other movies, performing arts, and professional football, basketball, and baseball combined. Frank Rich, Naked Capitalists, N.Y. Times Magazine, May 20, 2001, at 51; Hearings on Protecting Children from Inappropriate Materials on the Internet, Before the Subcomm. on Telecommunications, Trade, and Consumer Protection of the House Comm. on Commerce, 105th Cong. 1, 22 (Sept. 11, 1998) [hereinafter Hearings] (testimony of Congressman Ernest J. Istook, Jr.).

≡≡≡ *Deborah L. Rhode*
≡≡ **Speaking of Sex 130-132 (1997)**

Our current controversy [over pornography] builds on longstanding difficulties in legal doctrine. Until quite recently, "pornography" was not a term that figured in American law. Legal standards have referred to "obscenity," and they have been vaguely defined and idiosyncratically enforced. At the height of censorship, government authorities prosecuted everything from nudity on playing cards to classics by Tolstoy. Contemporary Supreme Court doctrine holds that the government can ban material if, under contemporary community standards, the work as a whole appeals to the "prurient interest," depicts sex in a "patently offensive" way, and lacks serious literary, artistic, political, or scientific value.

This obscenity standard is problematic both in theory and in practice. A threshold difficulty is the odd psychological state that judges and juries must reach in order to find a work legally obscene. They must admit that the material is both sexually arousing *and* patently offensive. . . . Since this is a state that few individuals are happy to admit, the threshold standard for censorship is rarely met. Even when it is, the material often is exempt from regulation based on its socially redeeming value.

Moreover, the cost of item-by-item enforcement is far too great to contain a mushrooming industry. Once sexually degrading materials begin to saturate a local market, it becomes increasingly difficult to prove that they are offensive under contemporary community standards. As a consequence, American pornography suppliers have become solidly entrenched, with estimated annual profits exceeding $10 billion. Consumers rent more than

400 million X-rated videos each year, and computer technology is expanding opportunities for interactive sadism. . . . Bulletin board systems on the Internet also are competing to be "the nastiest place on earth," complete with images of parents forcing children to have sex with animals.

Not only is current obscenity law unable to stem industry growth; it also cannot prevent harassing prosecutions. Law enforcement officials often bring charges that have little chance of prevailing, particularly against works by gay, lesbian, and minority artists. Among the most highly publicized examples have been the prosecutions of Two Live Crew for offensive song lyrics and of the Cleveland Art Museum for showing homoerotic photographs by Robert Mapplethorpe. Many schools, libraries, and arts organizations also have banned or denied funding for "dirty" materials. Frequently suppressed "smut" includes books by William Faulkner, J.D. Salinger, and Alice Walker.

Yet obscenity law misses what many feminists see as the main harm of pornography: the way that it portrays women. These feminists focus on misogyny rather than morality. . . .

2. Pornography and Dominance Theory

≡≡≡ *Catharine A. MacKinnon, Feminism Unmodified:*
≡≡≡ *Discourses on Life and Law*
≡≡ 171-172 (1987)

. . . Pornography sexualizes rape, battery, sexual harassment, prostitution, and child sexual abuse; it thereby celebrates, promotes, authorizes and legitimizes them. More generally, it eroticizes the dominance and submission that is the dynamic common to them all. It makes hierarchy sexy and calls that "the truth about sex" or just a mirror of reality. Through this process pornography constructs what a woman is as what men want from sex. . . .

Pornography constructs what a woman is in terms of its view of what men want sexually, such that acts of rape, battery, sexual harassment, prostitution, and sexual abuse of children become acts of sexual equality. Pornography's world of equality is a harmonious and balanced place. Men and women are perfectly complementary and perfectly bipolar. Women's desire to be fucked by men is equal to men's desire to fuck women. All the ways men love to take and violate women, women love to be taken and violated. The women who most love this are most men's equals, the most liberated; the most participatory child is the most grown-up, the most equal to an adult. Their consent merely expresses or ratifies these preexisting facts.

The content of pornography is one thing. There, women substantively desire dispossession and cruelty. We desperately want to be bound, battered, tortured, humiliated, and killed. . . . What pornography does goes beyond its

content: it eroticizes hierarchy, it sexualizes inequality. It makes dominance and submission into sex. Inequality is its central dynamic; the illusion of freedom coming together with the reality of force is central to its working
. . . .

From this perspective, pornography is neither harmless fantasy nor a corrupt and confused misrepresentation of an otherwise natural and healthy sexual situation. It institutionalizes the sexuality of male supremacy, fusing the erotization of dominance and submission with the social construction of male and female. To the extent that gender is sexual, pornography is part of constituting the meaning of that sexuality.

Catharine A. MacKinnon, Pornography as Defamation and Discrimination
71 B.U. L. Rev. 793, 799-803, 809-810 (1991)

Pornography has a central role in actualizing . . . [a] system of subordination in the contemporary West, beginning with the conditions of its production. Women in pornography are bound, battered, tortured, harassed, raped, and sometimes killed; or in the glossy men's entertainment magazines, "merely" humiliated, molested, objectified, and used. In all pornography, women are prostituted. This is done because it means sexual pleasure to pornography's consumers and profits to its providers, largely organized crime. But to those who are exploited, it means being bound, battered, tortured, harassed, raped, and sometimes killed, or merely humiliated, molested, objectified, and used. It is done because someone who has more power than they do, someone who matters, someone with rights, a full human being and a full citizen, gets pleasure from seeing it, or doing it, or seeing it as a form of doing it. In order to produce what the consumer wants to see, it must first be done to someone, usually a woman, a woman with few real choices. Because he wants to see it done, it is done to her. . . .

Over time, the evidence on the harm of pornography has only become stronger. When explicit sex and express violence against women are combined, particularly when rape is portrayed as pleasurable or positive for the victim, the risk of violence against women increases as a result of exposure. It is uncontroversial that exposure to such materials increases aggression against women in laboratory settings, increases attitudes which are related to violence against women in the real world, and increases self-reported likelihood to rape. As a result of exposure, a significant percentage of men, many not otherwise predisposed, as well as the twenty-five to thirty-five percent who report some proclivity to rape a woman, come to believe that violence against women is acceptable. Materials which combine sex with aggression also have perceptual effects which desensitize consumers to rape trauma and to sexual violence. In one study, simulated juries who had been exposed to such material were less able than real juries to perceive that an account of a rape was an account of a rape, through which the victim was harmed.

The most advanced research in this area studies the effects of materials which degrade and dehumanize women without showing violence, as that term is defined in the research. Such material has been shown to lower inhibitions on aggression by men against women, increase acceptance on women's sexual servitude, increase sexual callousness toward women, decrease the desire of both sexes to have female children, increase reported willingness to rape, and increase the belief in male dominance in intimate relationships. For high-frequency consumers, these materials also increase self-reported sexually aggressive behavior.

Men who use pornography often believe that they do not think or do these things. But the evidence shows that the use of pornography makes it impossible for men to tell when sex is forced, that women are human, and that rape is rape. Pornography makes men hostile and aggressive toward women, and it makes women silent. While these effects are not invariant or always immediate, and do not affect all men to the same degree, there is no reason to think they are not acted upon and every reason and overwhelming evidence to think that they are — if not right then, then sometime, if not violently, then through some other kind of discrimination. . . .

[P]ornography, through its production, is revealed as a traffic in sexual slavery. Through its consumption, it further institutionalizes a subhuman, victimized, second class status for women by conditioning men's orgasm to sexual inequality. When men use pornography, they experience in their bodies, not just their minds, that one-sided sex — sex between a person (them) and a thing (it) — is sex, that sexual use is sex, sexual abuse is sex, sexual domination is sex. This is the sexuality that they then demand, practice, purchase, and live out in their everyday social relations with others. Pornography works by making sexism sexy. As a primal experience of gender hierarchy, pornography is a major way in which sexism is enjoyed and practiced, as well as learned. It is one way that male supremacy is spread and made socially real. Through the use of pornography for masturbation . . . power and powerlessness are experienced and inculcated as sexual excitement and release. Inequality between women and men is what is sexy about pornography — the more unequal the sexier. In other words, pornography makes sexuality into a key dynamic in gender inequality by viscerally defining gender through the experience of hierarchical sexuality. On the way, it exploits inequalities of race, class, age, religion, sexual identity, and disability by sexualizing them through gender.

Seen in this way, pornography is at once a concrete practice and an ideological statement. The concrete practices are discriminatory; the ideological statements are defamatory. Construed as defamation in the conventional sense, pornography says that women are a lower form of human life defined by their availability for sexual use. Women are dehumanized through the conditioning of male sexuality to their use and abuse, which sexualizes, hence lowers, women across the culture, not only in express sexual interactions. . . .

. . . A discrimination theory of defamation would center on its harm to subordinate groups. Group libel is an equality issue when its promotion undermines the social equality of a target group that is traditionally and systematically disadvantaged. Group defamation promotes the disadvantage of disadvantaged groups. Group-based enmity, ill-will, intolerance, and prejudice are the attitudinal engines of the exclusion, denigration, and subordination that comprise social inequality. Without bigotry, social systems of enforced separation and apartheid would be unnecessary, impossible, and unthinkable. Stereotyping and stigmatization of historically disadvantaged groups through group hate propaganda shape their social image and reputation, arguably controlling the opportunities of individual members more powerfully than their individual abilities do. It is impossible for an individual to receive equality of opportunity when surrounded by an atmosphere of group hatred or contempt.

In this light, group defamation can be seen as a specific kind of discriminatory practice, a verbal form inequality takes. Anti-Semitism promotes the inequality of Jews on the basis of religion and ethnicity. White supremacy promotes inequality on the basis of race, color, and sometimes ethnic origin. Group defamation in this sense is not the mere expression of anti-Semitic or white supremacist opinion but a practice of discrimination similar to sexual harassment and other discriminatory acts that take verbal form. It is arguably an integral link in systemic discrimination which keeps target groups in subordinated positions through the promotion of terror, intolerance, degradation, segregation, exclusion, vilification, violence, and genocide. The nature of the practice can be seen and proven from the damage it does, from immediate psychic wounding to consequent physical aggression. Where advocacy of genocide is part of group defamation, an equality approach to its regulation would observe that to be liquidated because of the group you belong to is the ultimate inequality.

3. Efforts to Define Pornography as Sex-Based Discrimination: The Legal Response

American Booksellers Association, Inc. v. Hudnut
771 F.2d 323 (7th Cir. 1985), aff'd mem., 475 U.S. 1001, reh'g denied, 475 U.S. 1132 (1986)

EASTERBROOK, Circuit Judge.

Indianapolis enacted an ordinance defining "pornography" as a practice that discriminates against women. "Pornography" is to be redressed through the administrative and judicial methods used for other discrimination. The City's definition of "pornography" is considerably different from "obscenity," which the Supreme Court has held is not protected by the First Amendment.

To be "obscene" under Miller v. California, [413 U.S. 15 (1973)], "a publication must, taken as a whole, appeal to the prurient interest, must contain patently offensive depictions or descriptions of specified sexual conduct, and on the whole have no serious literary, artistic, political, or scientific value." Brockett v. Spokane Arcades, Inc., [472 U.S. 491, 501 (1985)]. Offensiveness must be assessed under the standards of the community. Both offensiveness and an appeal to something other than "normal, healthy sexual desires" (Brockett, supra, 472 U.S. at 498) are essential elements of "obscenity."

"Pornography" under the ordinance is "the graphic sexually explicit subordination of women, whether in pictures or in words, that also includes one or more of the following: (1) Women are presented as sexual objects who enjoy pain or humiliation; or (2) Women are presented as sexual objects who experience sexual pleasure in being raped; or (3) Women are presented as sexual objects tied up or cut up or mutilated or bruised or physically hurt, or as dismembered or truncated or fragmented or severed into body parts; or (4) Women are presented as being penetrated by objects or animals; or (5) Women are presented in scenarios of degradation, injury, abasement, torture, shown as filthy or inferior, bleeding, bruised, or hurt in a context that makes these conditions sexual; or (6) Women are presented as sexual objects for domination, conquest, violation, exploitation, possession, or use, or through postures or positions of servility or submission or display." Indianapolis Code §16-3(q). The statute provides that the "use of men, children, or transsexuals in the place of women in paragraphs (1) through (6) above shall also constitute pornography under this section." The ordinance as passed in April 1984 defined "sexually explicit" to mean actual or simulated intercourse or the uncovered exhibition of the genitals, buttocks or anus. An amendment in June 1984 deleted this provision, leaving the term undefined.

The Indianapolis ordinance does not refer to the prurient interest, to offensiveness, or to the standards of the community. It demands attention to particular depictions, not to the work judged as a whole. It is irrelevant under the ordinance whether the work has literary, artistic, political, or scientific value. The City and many amici point to these omissions as virtues. They maintain that pornography influences attitudes, and the statute is a way to alter the socialization of men and women rather than to vindicate community standards of offensiveness. And as one of the principal drafters of the ordinance has asserted, "if a woman is subjected, why should it matter that the work has other value?" Catharine A. MacKinnon, Pornography, Civil Rights, and Speech, 20 Harv. C.R.-C.L. L. Rev. 1, 21 (1985).

Civil rights groups and feminists have entered this case as amici on both sides. Those supporting the ordinance say that it will play an important role in reducing the tendency of men to view women as sexual objects, a tendency that leads to both unacceptable attitudes and discrimination in the workplace and violence away from it. Those opposing the ordinance point out that much radical feminist literature is explicit and depicts women in ways forbidden by the ordinance and that the ordinance would reopen old battles. It is unclear how Indianapolis would treat works from James Joyce's Ulysses to Homer's Iliad; both depict women as submissive objects for conquest and domination.

We do not try to balance the arguments for and against an ordinance such as this. The ordinance discriminates on the ground of the content of the speech. Speech treating women in the approved way — in sexual encounters "premised on equality" (MacKinnon, supra, at 22) — is lawful no matter how sexually explicit. Speech treating women in the disapproved way — as submissive in matters sexual or as enjoying humiliation — is unlawful no matter how significant the literary, artistic, or political qualities of the work taken as a whole. The state may not ordain preferred viewpoints in this way. The Constitution forbids the state to declare one perspective right and silence opponents.

I

The ordinance contains four prohibitions. People may not "traffic" in pornography, "coerce" others into performing in pornographic works, or "force" pornography on anyone. Anyone injured by someone who has seen or read pornography has a right of action against the maker or seller.

Trafficking is defined in §16-3(g)(4) as the "production, sale, exhibition, or distribution of pornography." The offense excludes exhibition in a public or educational library, but a "special display" in a library may be sex discrimination. Section 16-3(g)(4)(C) provides that the trafficking paragraph "shall not be construed to make isolated passages or isolated parts actionable."

"Coercion into pornographic performance" is defined in §16-3(g)(5) as "[c]oercing, intimidating or fraudulently inducing any person . . . into performing for pornography. . . ." The ordinance specifies that proof of any of the following "shall not constitute a defense: I. That the person is a woman; . . . VI. That the person has previously posed for sexually explicit pictures . . . with anyone . . . ; . . . VIII. That the person actually consented to a use of the performance that is changed into pornography; . . . IX. That the person knew that the purpose of the acts or events in question was to make pornography; . . . XI. That the person signed a contract, or made statements affirming a willingness to cooperate in the production of pornography; XII. That no physical force, threats, or weapons were used in the making of the pornography; or XIII. That the person was paid or otherwise compensated."

"Forcing pornography on a person," according to §16-3(g)(5), is the "forcing of pornography on any woman, man, child, or transsexual in any place of employment, in education, in a home, or in any public place." The statute does not define forcing, but one of its authors states that the definition reaches pornography shown to medical students as part of their education or given to language students for translation. MacKinnon, supra, at 40-41.

Section 16-3(g)(7) defines as a prohibited practice the "assault, physical attack, or injury of any woman, man, child, or transsexual in a way that is directly caused by specific pornography."

For purposes of all four offenses, it is generally "not . . . a defense that the respondent did not know or intend that the materials were pornography . . . ." Section 16-3(g)(8). But the ordinance provides that damages are unavailable in trafficking cases unless the complainant proves "that the respondent knew or had reason to know that the materials were pornography." It is a complete defense to a trafficking case that all of the materials in question were pornography only by virtue of category (6) of the definition of pornography. In cases of assault caused by pornography, those who seek damages from "a seller, exhibitor or distributor" must show that the defendant knew or had reason to know of the material's status as pornography. By implication, those who seek damages from an author need not show this. A woman aggrieved by trafficking in pornography may file a complaint "as a woman acting against the subordination of women" with the office of equal opportunity. Section 16-17(b). A man, child, or transsexual also may protest trafficking "but must prove injury in the same way that a woman is injured. . . ." Id. Subsection (a) also provides, however, that "any person claiming to be aggrieved" by trafficking, coercion, forcing, or assault may complain against the "perpetrators." . . .

The office investigates and within 30 days makes a recommendation to a panel of the equal opportunity advisory board. The panel then decides whether there is reasonable cause to proceed (§16-24(2)) and may refer the dispute to a conciliation conference or to a complaint adjudication committee for a hearing (§§16-24(3), 16-26(a)). The committee uses the same procedures ordinarily associated with civil rights litigation. It may make findings and enter orders, including both orders to cease and desist and orders "to take further affirmative action . . . including but not limited to the power to restore complainant's losses. . . ." Section 16-26(d). Either party may appeal the committee's decision to the board, which reviews the record before the committee and may modify its decision. . . . The board's decisions are subject to review in the ordinary course. Ind. Stat. 4-22-1-14. . . .

The district court held the ordinance unconstitutional. 598 F. Supp. 1316 (S.D. Ind. 1984). . . .

II

The plaintiffs are a congeries of distributors and readers of books, magazines, and films. The American Booksellers Association comprises about 5,200 bookstores and chains. The Association for American Publishers includes most of the country's publishers. Video Shack, Inc., sells and rents video cassettes in Indianapolis. Kelly Bentley, a resident of Indianapolis, reads books and watches films. There are many more plaintiffs. Collectively the plaintiffs (or their members, whose interests they represent) make, sell, or read just about every kind of material that could be affected by the ordinance, from hard-core films to W.B. Yeats's poem "Leda and the Swan" (from the myth of Zeus in the form of a swan impregnating an apparently subordinate Leda), to the collected works of James Joyce, D.H. Lawrence, and John Cleland. . . .

III

"If there is any fixed star in our constitutional constellation, it is that no official, high or petty, can prescribe what shall be orthodox in politics, nationalism, religion, or other matters of opinion or force citizens to confess by word or act their faith therein." West Virginia State Board of Education v. Barnette, [319 U.S. 624, 642 (1943)]. Under the First Amendment the government must leave to the people the evaluation of ideas. Bald or subtle, an idea is as powerful as the audience allows it to be. A belief may be pernicious—the beliefs of Nazis led to the death of millions, those of the Klan to the repression of millions. A pernicious belief may prevail. Totalitarian governments today rule much of the planet, practicing suppression of billions and spreading dogma that may enslave others. One of the things that separates our society from theirs is our absolute right to propagate opinions that the government finds wrong or even hateful. . . .

Under the ordinance graphic sexually explicit speech is "pornography" or not depending on the perspective the author adopts. Speech that "subordinates" women and also, for example, presents women as enjoying pain, humiliation, or rape, or even simply presents women in "positions of servility or submission or display" is forbidden, no matter how great the literary or political value of the work taken as a whole. Speech that portrays women in positions of equality is lawful, no matter how graphic the sexual content. This is thought control. It establishes an "approved" view of women, of how they may react to sexual encounters, of how the sexes may relate to each other. Those who espouse the approved view may use sexual images; those who do not, may not.

Indianapolis justifies the ordinance on the ground that pornography affects thoughts. Men who see women depicted as subordinate are more likely to treat them so. Pornography is an aspect of dominance. It does not persuade people so much as change them. It works by socializing, by establishing the expected and the permissible. In this view pornography is not an idea; pornography is the injury.

There is much to this perspective. Beliefs are also facts. People often act in accordance with the images and patterns they find around them. People raised in a religion tend to accept the tenets of that religion, often without independent examination. People taught from birth that black people are fit only for slavery rarely rebelled against that creed; beliefs coupled with the self-interest of the masters established a social structure that inflicted great harm while enduring for centuries. Words and images act at the level of the subconscious before they persuade at the level of the conscious. Even the truth has little chance unless a statement fits within the framework of beliefs that may never have been subjected to rational study.

Therefore we accept the premises of this legislation. Depictions of subordination tend to perpetuate subordination. The subordinate status of women in turn leads to affront and lower pay at work, insult and injury at home, battery and rape on the streets.[2] In the language of the legislature, "[p]ornography is central in creating and maintaining sex as a basis of discrimination. Pornography is a systematic practice of exploitation and subordination based on sex which differentially harms women. The bigotry and contempt it produces, with the acts of aggression it fosters, harm women's opportunities for equality and rights [of all kinds]." Indianapolis Code §16-1(a)(2).

Yet this simply demonstrates the power of pornography as speech. All of these unhappy effects depend on mental intermediation. Pornography affects how people see the world, their fellows, and social relations. If pornography is what pornography does, so is other speech. Hitler's orations affected how some Germans saw Jews. Communism is a world view, not simply a Manifesto by Marx and Engels or a set of speeches. Efforts to suppress communist speech in the United States were based on the belief that the public acceptability of such ideas would increase the likelihood of totalitarian government. Religions affect socialization in the most pervasive way. The opinion in Wisconsin v. Yoder, [406 U.S. 205 (1972)], shows how a religion can dominate an entire approach to life, governing much more than the relation between the sexes. Many people believe that the existence of television, apart from the content of specific programs, leads to intellectual laziness, to a penchant for violence, to many other ills. The Alien and Sedition Acts passed during the administration of John Adams rested on a sincerely held belief that disrespect for the government leads to social collapse and revolution — a belief with support in the history of many nations. Most governments of the world act on this empirical regularity,

2. MacKinnon's article collects empirical work that supports this proposition. The social science studies are very difficult to interpret, however, and they conflict. Because much of the effect of speech comes through a process of socialization, it is difficult to measure incremental benefits and injuries caused by particular speech. Several psychologists have found, for example, that those who see violent, sexually explicit films tend to have more violent thoughts. But how often does this lead to actual violence? National commissions on obscenity here, in the United Kingdom, and in Canada have found that it is not possible to demonstrate a direct link between obscenity and rape or exhibitionism. . . . The several opinions in Miller v. California discuss the U.S. commission.

suppressing critical speech. In the United States, however, the strength of the support for this belief is irrelevant. Seditious libel is protected speech unless the danger is not only grave but also imminent. See New York Times Co. v. Sullivan, [376 U.S. 254 (1964)]; cf. Brandenburg v. Ohio, supra; New York Times Co. v. United States, [403 U.S. 713 (1971)].

Racial bigotry, anti-semitism, violence on television, reporters' biases — these and many more influence the culture and shape our socialization. None is directly answerable by more speech, unless that speech too finds its place in the popular culture. Yet all is protected as speech, however insidious. Any other answer leaves the government in control of all of the institutions of culture, the great censor and director of which thoughts are good for us.

Sexual responses often are unthinking responses, and the association of sexual arousal with the subordination of women therefore may have a substantial effect. But almost all cultural stimuli provoke unconscious responses. Religious ceremonies condition their participants. Teachers convey messages by selecting what not to cover; the implicit message about what is off limits or unthinkable may be more powerful than the messages for which they present rational argument. Television scripts contain unarticulated assumptions. People may be conditioned in subtle ways. If the fact that speech plays a role in a process of conditioning were enough to permit governmental regulation, that would be the end of freedom of speech. . . .

The more immediate point, however, is that the image of pain is not necessarily pain. In Body Double, a suspense film directed by Brian DePalma, a woman who has disrobed and presented a sexually explicit display is murdered by an intruder with a drill. The drill runs through the woman's body. The film is sexually explicit and a murder occurs — yet no one believes that the actress suffered pain or died. . . . In Carnal Knowledge a woman grovels to please the sexual whims of a character played by Jack Nicholson; no one believes that there was a real sexual submission, and the Supreme Court held the film protected by the First Amendment. Jenkins v. Georgia, [418 U.S. 153 (1974)]. And this works both ways. The description of women's sexual domination of men in Lysistrata was not real dominance. Depictions may affect slavery, war, or sexual roles, but a book about slavery is not itself slavery, or a book about death by poison a murder.

Much of Indianapolis's argument rests on the belief that when speech is "unanswerable," and the metaphor that there is a "marketplace of ideas" does not apply, the First Amendment does not apply either. The metaphor is honored; Milton's Areopagitica and John Stewart Mill's On Liberty defend freedom of speech on the ground that the truth will prevail, and many of the most important cases under the First Amendment recite this position. The Framers undoubtedly believed it. As a general matter it is true. But the Constitution does not make the dominance of truth a necessary condition of freedom of speech. To say that it does would be to confuse an outcome of free speech with a necessary condition for the application of the amendment.

A power to limit speech on the ground that truth has not yet prevailed and is not likely to prevail implies the power to declare truth. At some point the government must be able to say (as Indianapolis has said): "We know what the truth is, yet a free exchange of speech has not driven out falsity, so that we must now prohibit falsity." If the government may declare the truth, why wait for the failure of speech? Under the First Amendment, however, there is no such thing as a false idea, Gertz v. Robert Welch, Inc., [418 U.S. 323, 339 (1974)], so the government may not restrict speech on the ground that in a free exchange truth is not yet dominant.

At any time, some speech is ahead in the game; the more numerous speakers prevail. Supporters of minority candidates may be forever "excluded" from the political process because their candidates never win, because few people believe their positions. This does not mean that freedom of speech has failed. . . .

We come, finally, to the argument that pornography is "low value" speech, that it is enough like obscenity that Indianapolis may prohibit it. Some cases hold that speech far removed from politics and other subjects at the core of the Framers' concerns may be subjected to special regulation. E.g., FCC v. Pacifica Foundation, [438 U.S. 726 (1978)]; Young v. American Mini Theatres, Inc., [427 U.S. 50, 67-70 (1976)] (plurality opinion); Chaplinsky v. New Hampshire, [315 U.S. 568, 571-572 (1942)]. These cases do not sustain statutes that select among viewpoints, however. In Pacifica the FCC sought to keep vile language off the air during certain times. The Court held that it may; but the Court would not have sustained a regulation prohibiting scatological descriptions of Republicans but not scatological descriptions of Democrats, or any other form of selection among viewpoints. See Planned Parenthood Ass'n v. Chicago Transit Authority, 767 F.2d 1225, 1232-33 (7th Cir. 1985).

At all events, "pornography" is not low value speech within the meaning of these cases. Indianapolis seeks to prohibit certain speech because it believes this speech influences social relations and politics on a grand scale, that it controls attitudes at home and in the legislature. This precludes a characterization of the speech as low value. True, pornography and obscenity have sex in common. But Indianapolis left out of its definition any reference to literary, artistic, political, or scientific value. The ordinance applies to graphic sexually explicit subordination in works great and small. The Court sometimes balances the value of speech against the costs of its restriction, but it does this by category of speech and not by the content of particular works. . . . Indianapolis has created an approved point of view and so loses the support of these cases.

Any rationale we could imagine in support of this ordinance could not be limited to sex discrimination. Free speech has been on balance an ally of those seeking change. Governments that want stasis start by restricting speech. Culture is a powerful force of continuity; Indianapolis paints pornography as part of the culture of power. Change in any complex system ultimately depends on the ability of outsiders to challenge accepted views and the reigning institutions. Without a strong guarantee of freedom of speech, there is no effective right to challenge what is.

IV

. . . The offense of coercion to engage in a pornographic performance . . . has elements that might be constitutional. Without question a state may prohibit fraud, trickery, or the use of force to induce people to perform — in pornographic films or in any other films. Such a statute may be written without regard to the viewpoint depicted in the work. New York v. Ferber, [458 U.S. 747 (1982)], suggests that when a state has a strong interest in forbidding the conduct that makes up a film (in *Ferber* sexual acts involving minors), it may restrict or forbid dissemination of the film in order to reinforce the prohibition of the conduct. A state may apply such a rule to non-sexual coercion (although it need not). . . .

But the Indianapolis ordinance, unlike our hypothetical statute, is not neutral with respect to viewpoint. The ban on distribution of works containing coerced performances is limited to pornography; coercion is irrelevant if the work is not "pornography," and we have held the definition of "pornography" to be defective root and branch. A legislature might replace "pornography" in §16-3(g)(4) with "any film containing explicit sex" or some similar expression, but even the broadest severability clause does not permit a federal court to rewrite as opposed to excise. Rewriting is work for the legislature of Indianapolis. . . .

Much speech is dangerous. Chemists whose work might help someone build a bomb, political theorists whose papers might start political movements that lead to riots, speakers whose ideas attract violent protesters, all these and more leave loss in their wake. Unless the remedy is very closely confined, it could be more dangerous to speech than all the libel judgments in history. The constitutional requirements for a valid recovery for assault caused by speech might turn out to be too rigorous for any plaintiff to meet. But the Indianapolis ordinance requires the complainant to show that the attack was "directly caused by specific pornography" (§16-3(g)(7)), and it is not beyond the realm of possibility that a state court could construe this limitation in a way that would make the statute constitutional. We are not authorized to prevent the state from trying.

Again, however, the assault statute is tied to "pornography," and we cannot find a sensible way to repair the defect without seizing power that belongs elsewhere. Indianapolis might choose to have no ordinance if it cannot be limited to viewpoint-specific harms, or it might choose to extend the scope to all speech, just as the law of libel applies to all speech. An attempt to repair this ordinance would be nothing but a blind guess.

No amount of struggle with particular words and phrases in this ordinance can leave anything in effect. The district court came to the same conclusion. Its judgment is therefore Affirmed.

[A concurring opinion by Swygert, Senior Circuit Judge, is omitted.]

4. Feminist Responses to Feminist Anti-Pornography Initiatives

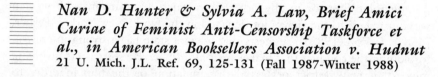

Nan D. Hunter & Sylvia A. Law, Brief Amici Curiae of Feminist Anti-Censorship Taskforce et al., in American Booksellers Association v. Hudnut
21 U. Mich. J.L. Ref. 69, 125-131 (Fall 1987-Winter 1988)

The [Indianapolis] ordinance defines pornography in gender specific terms as "the graphic sexually explicit subordination of women" that also presents "women" in particular ways proscribed by the law. . . . The heart of the ordinance is the suppression of sexually explicit images of women, based on a finding of "subordination," a term which is not defined. The ordinance implies that sexually explicit images of women necessarily subordinate and degrade women and perpetuates stereotypes of women as helpless victims and people who could not seek or enjoy sex.

The ordinance also reinforces sexist stereotypes of men. It denies the possibility that graphic sexually explicit images of a man could ever subordinate or degrade him. It provides no remedy for sexually explicit images showing men as "dismembered, truncated or fragmented" or "shown as filthy or inferior, bleeding, bruised or hurt." . . .

The ordinance reinforces yet another sexist stereotype of men as aggressive beasts. Appellants assert:

> By conditioning the male orgasm to female subordination, pornography . . . makes the subordination of women pleasurable and seemingly legitimate. Each time men are sexually aroused by pornography, they learn to connect a woman's sexual pleasure to abuse and a woman's sexual nature to inferiority. They learn this in their bodies, not just their minds, so that it becomes a natural physiological response. At this point pornography leaves no more room for further debate than does shouting "kill" to an attack dog.

Men are not attack dogs, but morally responsible human beings. The ordinance reinforces a destructive sexist stereotype of men as irresponsible beasts, with "natural physiological responses" which can be triggered by sexually explicit images of women, and for which the men cannot be held accountable. Thus, men are conditioned into violent acts or negative beliefs by sexual images; women are not. Further, the ordinance is wholly blind to the possibility that men could be hurt and degraded by images presenting them as violent or sadistic.

The ordinance also reinforces sexist images of woman as incapable of consent. It creates a remedy for people "coerced" to participate in the production of pornography. . . .

In effect, the ordinance creates a strong presumption that women who participate in the creation of sexually explicit material are coerced. A woman's manifestation of consent — no matter how plain, informed, or even self-initiated — does not constitute a defense to her subsequent claim of coercion. Women are judged incompetent to consent to participate in the creation of sexually explicit material and condemned as "bad" if they do so. . . .

This provision does far more than simply provide a remedy to women who are pressured into the creation of pornography which they subsequently seek to suppress. It functions to make all women incompetent to enter into legally binding contracts for the production of sexually explicit material. When women are legally disabled from making binding agreements, they are denied power to negotiate for fair treatment and decent pay. Enforcement of the ordinance would drive production of sexually explicit material even further into an underground economy, where the working conditions of women in the sex industry would worsen, not improve. . . .

The ordinance damages individuals who do not fit the stereotypes it embodies. It delegitimates and makes socially invisible women who find sexually explicit images of women "in positions of display" or "penetrated by objects" to be erotic, liberating, or educational. These women are told that their perceptions are a product of "false consciousness" and that such images are so inherently degrading that they may be suppressed by the state. At the same time, it stamps the imprimatur of state approval on the belief that men are attack dogs triggered to violence by the sight of a sexually explicit image of a woman. It delegitimates and makes socially invisible those men who consider themselves gentle, respectful of women, or inhibited about expressing their sexuality.

Even worse, the stereotypes of the ordinance perpetuate traditional social views of sex-based difference. By defining sexually explicit images of women as subordinating and degrading to them, the ordinance reinforces the stereotypical view that "good" women do not seek and enjoy sex. As applied, it would deny women access to sexually explicit material at a time in our history when women have just begun to acquire the social and economic power to develop our own images of sexuality. Stereotypes of hair-trigger male susceptibility to violent imagery can be invoked as an excuse to avoid directly blaming the men who commit violent acts.

Finally, the ordinance perpetuates a stereotype of women as helpless victims, incapable of consent, and in need of protection. . . . We have learned through hard experience that gender-based classifications protecting women from their own presumed innate vulnerability reflect "an attitude of 'romantic paternalism' which, in practical effect, puts women not on a pedestal but in a cage." Frontiero v. Richardson, 411 U.S. 677, 684 (1973). . . .

Women were, and continue to be, in a position of social and economic vulnerability that inhibits their ability to negotiate fair terms and conditions of wage labor. Further, the pervasive sexism and violence of our culture make women vulnerable to exploitation and inhibit their ability to enter into sexual or other relationships on a free and voluntary basis. . . .

. . . But even accurate generalizations about women's need for help do not justify sex-based classifications such as those in this ordinance. It is also true that women generally are still the ones who nurture young children. Yet we understand that laws giving mothers an irrebuttable "tender years" presumption for custody, or offering child rearing leaves only to mothers but not to fathers, ultimately hurt women and are unconstitutional. . . .

Carlin Meyer, Sex, Sin, and Women's Liberation: Against Porn-Suppression
72 Tex. L. Rev. 1097, 1136, 1138-1141, 1155-1156, 1184-1185, 1187-1189, 1192-1193 (1994)

The subject matters of much porn are complex and contradictory and may, depending on the manner in which they are presented, absorbed, or understood, contribute to feminist goals. Pornography breaks the boundaries of traditionally confined sex and sexual depiction. . . . Precisely because pornography is so outrageous, it can be explosively subversive, challenging social strictures that keep women oppressed. . . .

Women who dare to admit that they enjoy porn note that its images are "many and varied" — some "fragmented and idealized," others "crude and unflattering," others "dreamy, psychedelic," and still others "violent, reptilian." They emphasize that their responses to it are "layered and complex and multiple." For young women, porn not only offers otherwise unavailable information about sex, but by providing imaginary transgressions of traditionally restrictive sexual parameters, it provides reassurance and permission to be sexual. And the same porn imagery that shows women on display often also portrays them as sexually powerful. The very power of sexual imagery to objectify women may be — and often is — subversively employed to reverse or at least question the process or basis of objectification.

Moreover, literal subject matter does not capture meaning or import. Contemporary scholarship in fields ranging from semiotics to cultural critique have taught us that within the "language" of depiction, images vary according to subtle, cloaked signs and symbols; references, pre-conceptions, "understood" vocabulary, gaze, and perspective all affect meaning. . . .

Indeed, it is not content alone, but also context and audience reception that determine whether a portrayal degrades women. Porn gains its meaning because of sexual "taboos" that confine viewing to secrecy; because of the predispositions of its largely male audience concerning what it ought to mean and how they ought to react to it; because it is shown in "stag" contexts — often in association with military and sports conquest; and because it is used as a ritual of male bonding, of Oedipal rebellion against the authority of mothers, of growth towards manhood, and hence is linked to exclusion and vanquishment of the female. Disassociated from some or all of these contexts and meanings, its import may change.

By treating "subordination" as residing in the image itself rather than in the engagement between image and audience, anti-porn advocates ignore the "play" between the two. Point of view, presentation, medium, and, most importantly, the pre-existing understandings, beliefs, cultural discourses, and language of the audience invest an image with meaning. Significance arises not from the images alone, but from their place within the artistic, cultural, moral, and sexual discourse that changes over time and according to the audience and the particular context. . . .

Some, like Barbara Omolade, bell hooks, and Angela Harris argue that the lens of race is at least as important as that of sex in understanding patriarchal sexuality. Omolade points to European men's "cultural definitions of sex, nudity, and blackness as base, foul and bestial,"[260] and hooks describes the contemporary commodification of "race and ethnicity" as "resources for pleasure" such that "the culture of specific groups, as well as the bodies of individuals, can be seen as constituting an alternative playground where members of dominating races, genders, [and] sexual practices affirm their power-over in intimate relations with the Other."[261] Harris notes that "[f]or black women, rape is . . . an experience as deeply rooted in color as in gender."[262] Still other writers point to the importance of class, noting the sexual stigmatization of lower classes — such as prostitutes, "foreigners," slaves, and minorities — and arguing that the creation of the category "pornography" may itself be a product of dominant groups' desire to maintain power. To require that debate over these issues eschew evocative sexual depiction and take place only in arid scholarly form is to deny feminism one of the most powerful tools of exploration and change. . . .

Most pornography, because of its exaggerated and unrealistic portrayal, invites the viewer or reader to suspend belief rather than to take its portrayals as "true." The manner in which it is typically "consumed" — in secret, "stag" arenas, or specially zoned theaters — heightens its unreal quality.

260. [Barbara Omolade, Hearts of Darkness in Powers of Desire, supra, at 350, 351.]
261. [bell hooks, Black Looks: Race and Representation 23 (1992).]
262. [Angela P. Harris, Race and Essentialism in Feminist Legal Theory, 42 Stan. L. Rev. 581, 598 (1990).]

Unlike television's serials, soaps, and even, sometimes, advertisements, which purport to portray "real life" by situating themselves in "real" time and space and wrestling with true life problems, porn is suspended in time and space, presenting a fantasy world of endless sex uninterrupted by daily tasks and unmarred by mundane detail or real-life responsibilities. Thus, although it may be "at the pinnacle of the sexist iconography of insatiable male sexual activity and ubiquitous female sexual availability," and may even be "the 'truest' form of patriarchal ideology," it represents a fantasy world that neither creates nor expresses men's "straightforwardly conscious wishes and intentions."[419]

. . . Porn's shallow world of insatiable women and unflaggingly erect men is hardly the stuff from which the complex web of Western sexuality could be woven. Rather, contrasting notions of "acceptable male emotions associated with the approved discourses on male sexuality" — for example "[s]ex restrained by love and marriage, sex which is 'protective,' 'respectable' and 'faithful'" — are essential to and give meaning to porn's contrary world of "sex greedy for immediate, unlimited, self-centered gratification." Empedestaled, chaste, and virtuous women are central to constituting other women as sexually "debased" and therefore available for sexual domination or abuse. Men are induced to find pleasure in fantasies of sexual domination not only by treating women as sex objects, but also by treating them as too pure to touch, or too stupid, flutter-brained, or frigid to be sexual at all. Aggression is "eroticized" not simply by treating women as objects of male lust, but by placing them in the contradictory roles of virgins and whores; of mothers, wives, servants, and lovers; of guardians of morality who impel men to sin and then punish them for their "Fall." Male domination is sexualized not merely when women are pictured as enjoying rape, but also when a boy's growth towards manhood is associated with conquest and vanquishment — of nature, of enemies, and of women.

To reduce Western erotica to a pornographic picture is to understate the power and depth of patriarchal conditioning, which could not be captured within porn's one-sided, shallow, and repetitive imagery. Porn is meant, like the popular mystery genre, to allow escape into shallow plots and fantasies of quick and easy satisfaction, not to foster conversion. . . .

Nor is it likely that porn's blatant show of force against women increases its effectiveness in persuading its audience to view women as objects or to use force against them. . . . In other words, porn's graphic display of male sexual power over and violence toward women, as well as the similar portrayals in mainstream advertising, television, and film, are the likely symptoms of and reactions to weakening male power, rather than indications of porn's centrality to establishing male power in the first instance. . . .

419. [Lynne Segal, Slow Motion: Changing Masculinities, Changing Men 222 (1990).]

[E]ven were it the case that bodily arousal or the repeat viewing that porn seems to spawn enhances audience absorption of an ideological subtext, suppression would not be a viable strategy. For it would be impossible to suppress all imagery that is arousing at the expense of women. One would have to get rid of depictions ranging from Alfred Hitchcock's *Psycho*, in which the protagonist's unnatural attachment to his own mother drives him to murder women to whom he is attracted, to slasher and other horror films, to large segments of popular music and music videos. Indeed, one might even have to suppress advertising imagery, for much of it aims to persuade by arousal, and expresses the same views of women as are found in porn. . . .

[W]omen do not seem to be as silenced as anti-porn advocates claim: Across class, race, occupation, ethnicity, and geographic locale, women are speaking out and being listened to as never before. Advocates of suppression answer that porn is proliferating precisely because women's voices have begun to emerge, and porn is part of society's way of shutting women back up. Though the evidence of backlash against women's changing roles and newly emergent power is plentiful, and though porn proliferation is very likely part of it, it is but a minor part and has not, so far, seemed to silence women. Indeed, "it is precisely since the 1970s, and the explosion of pornography in the West, that women have been most vociferously — and successfully — objecting to men's violence against them."[464]

In sum, porn simply is not the powerful force that anti-porn advocates imagine. It may often be sexist, vulgar, violent, and horrific. The wish to be rid of it is surely understandable. But there are no easy ways to be rid of imagery that portrays women in ways we might wish women not be portrayed — nor, especially, be treated — and suppressionist quick-fix strategies do more harm than good.

Mary C. Dunlap, Sexual Speech and the State: Putting Pornography in Its Place
17 Golden Gate U. L. Rev. 359, 365-369 (1987)

The need for "sexually explicit" expression, and for more and clearer communication about sexual matters, seems to multiply with every day's revelations of new relationships, possibilities between people, and phenomena. . . . [B]efore any further restrictions on sexual speech are urged, the proponents of such restrictions [should] consider the following list of priorities of the feminist and human rights movements, and the concrete implications of restrictions upon "sexually explicit" expression upon each priority:

---

464. [Lynne Segal, Slow Motion, supra note 419, at 227.]

1. The effort to give children better, more effective tools to combat sexual abuse, including familial sexual abuse and incest;

2. Enablement/empowerment of both minors and adults to know more about their own developing sexualities (including the pro's and con's of being gay, lesbian, bisexual, heterosexual, celibate or otherwise); the methods and effects of particular forms of contraception; pregnancy in and out of marriage; surrogate motherhood; venereal disease; abortion choice; AIDS/ARC causes, modes of prevention and treatment; rape and sexual assault; the sex industry (including prostitution, pornography, commercialization of sex);

3. Improvement of intimate relationships, by people learning to say what they do and do not like, want or need in the way of sex;

4. Breaking down sex-stereotyping and sex-role stereotyping in all realms of life, in work, play, economics, sexual activity;

5. Expanding the possibilities of aesthetic and artistic adventuring about sex (viewing sexual activity as a frontier, in which fantasy, imagination and art need to be free to develop, alongside "safe sex" and auto-erotic practices) and developing rich and satisfying sources of erotica (that is, non-violent and egalitarian sexual media);

6. Working to overcome the dichotomization and polarization of "women" versus "ladies," and of sexually active women including "promiscuous" women, prostitutes, single mothers and teenage females versus virtuous females, virgins, and monogamous, virtuous wives;

7. Elevating and enriching the level of public media about sexual activity (from the "dirty secrets" approach common in current media to something at once loftier and deeper) with attention to preserving fun as well as dignity and to respecting the need for privacy as well as public education in sexual matters;

8. Getting the government out of the bedroom where the activities occurring there are both "victimless" and essentially private while getting the government to act to prevent and remedy forms of serious and damaging violence against women that have been historically legally neglected or insulated from legal scrutiny by assertions of male, paternal privilege and authority (e.g. marital rape; child abuse and incest; sexual harassment);

9. Distinguishing between sex and violence.

[E]ach of the above listed items cuts against the approach of the "anti-pornography" ordinance, literally (in terms of a conflict between serving that priority and enforcing the ordinance), in policy terms, and in terms of constitutional and political development of "free speech."

NOTE ON PORNOGRAPHY, DOMINANCE THEORY, AND THE FIRST AMENDMENT

Hudnut reflects the conventional First Amendment response to legal restrictions on pornography. Nadine Strossen, president of the ACLU, presents a fuller statement of objections to pornography regulation based on the First Amendment, which she believes is fully consistent with women's interests in free speech, in Defending Pornography: Free Speech, Sex, and the Fight for Women's Rights (1995).

Some defenses of pornography regulation have focused on reconciling such regulation with existing First Amendment doctrine. They note that

> . . . free expression is not the only value that we value, and courts have long tolerated many content-based restrictions on speech. Obvious examples include prohibitions on libel, bribery, fraud, workplace harassment, and employers' threats concerning unions. The harms associated with some of this restricted speech are not self-evidently greater than those traceable to certain pornography, such as sexually violent material.

Rhode, Speaking of Sex, supra, at 53. See Cass Sunstein, Pornography and the First Amendment, 1986 Duke L.J. 589 (arguing that pornography is "low value" expression, which produces sufficient harm to justify regulation). Other commentators argue that anti-pornography statutes like the Indianapolis ordinance are no more vague than existing obscenity law and may in fact be less subject to inconsistent, idiosyncratic enforcement. See, e.g., James Lindgren, Defining Pornography 141 U. Pa. L. Rev. 1153, 1214-1215 (1993) (finding that law students were better able to apply the ordinance's concept of subordination than the *Miller* obscenity standard).

With respect to the harms of pornography, MacKinnon maintains:

> Laissez-faire might be an adequate theory . . . in a nonhierarchical society. In a society of gender inequality, the speech of the powerful impresses its view upon the world, concealing the truth of powerlessness under a despairing acquiescence that provides the appearance of consent and makes protest inaudible as well as rare. Pornography can invent women because it has the power to make its vision into reality, which then passes, objectively, for truth. So while the First Amendment supports pornography on the belief that consensus and progress are facilitated by allowing all views, however divergent and unorthodox, it fails to notice that pornography . . . is not at all divergent or unorthodox. It is the ruling ideology. Feminism, the dissenting view, is suppressed by pornography. Thus, while defenders of pornography argue that allowing all speech, including pornography, frees the mind to fulfill itself, pornography freely enslaves women's minds and bodies inseparably, normalizing the terror that enforces silence on women's point of view.

Catharine A. MacKinnon, Toward a Feminist Theory of the State 205 (1989). See also In Harm's Way: The Pornography Civil Rights Hearings

(Catharine A. MacKinnon & Andrea Dworkin eds., 1997); Catharine A. MacKinnon, Only Words (1993); Catharine A. MacKinnon, Feminism Unmodified: Discourses on Life and Law 127-138 (1987); Andrea Dworkin, Against the Male Flood: Censorship, Pornography, and Equality, 8 Harv. Women's L.J. 1 (1985). Did you find this view persuasive?

A somewhat different way of characterizing the pornography debate is as a conflict between individualism, which the First Amendment values highly, and pluralism or group rights. See Robert C. Post, Cultural Heterogeneity and Law: Pornography, Blasphemy, and the First Amendment, 76 Cal. L. Rev. 297 (1988); Censorship and Silencing: Practices of Cultural Regulation (Robert Post ed., 1998). Seen this way, protecting pornography represents a choice in favor of individual freedom over group rights. As the reading above suggests, however, MacKinnon sees it the other way around: protecting pornography protects socially prevalent group norms, while pornography regulation protects those individuals who are oppressed by those norms. Which is it?

Legislation somewhat similar to the Indianapolis ordinance has been upheld by the Canadian Supreme Court. In Regina v. Butler, 89 D.L.R.4th 449 (S.C.C. 1992), the court sustained a statute that criminalizes "any publication a dominant characteristic of which is the undue exploitation of sex, or of sex and any one or more of the following subjects, namely crime, horror, cruelty and violence," interpreting the statute to prohibit any "materials that subordinate, degrade or dehumanize women." Cf. Regina v. Keegstra, [1990] 3 S.C.R. 697 (upholding statute penalizing communication of statements that willfully promote hatred against any identifiable racial, religious, or ethnic group). Whether *Butler* has been effective in challenging pornography and whether it has been selectively applied to gay and lesbian publications remain a matter of controversy. See Brenda Cossman, Feminist Fashion or Morality in Drag? The Sexual Subject of the *Butler* Decision, in Bad Attitudes on Trial: Pornography, Feminism and the *Butler* Decision (Lisa Botell & Becki L. Ross eds., 1997); Joan Kennedy Taylor, Does Sexual Speech Harm Women? The Split Within Feminism, 5 Stan. L. & Pol'y Rev. 49, 52 (1994) (discussing selective enforcement). But see Ann Scales, Avoiding Constitutional Depression: Bad Attitudes and the Fate of *Butler*, 7 Can. J. of Women & Law 349 (1994) (defending *Butler* and arguing that it was misapplied in the high-profile case against lesbian literature, which critics use as an example of the dangers of anti-pornography regulation).

5. The Harms of Pornography

≡≡≡ *Deborah L. Rhode*
Speaking of Sex 133-135 (1997)

The harms that feminists associate with pornography are not the ones that lawmakers traditionally associate with obscenity: the corruption of morals, the offense to public sensibilities, and the erosion of family values. Rather, what many feminists stress are injuries to women both as individuals and as a group. According to these feminists, pornography eroticizes inequality. It degrades, dehumanizes, and objectifies women, legitimates men's brutality, and perpetrates racist stereotypes.

The most obvious harms involve models who are coerced and abused in the creation of pornographic material. In theory, these individuals have remedies under existing criminal and civil law; in practice, such remedies are almost never available. Rarely do women want to compound their injuries by initiating litigation that usually involves considerable financial costs, personal humiliation, fear of retaliation, and difficulties of proof. Yet while it is clear that some models have experienced barbaric treatment, it is less clear how often this happens, and what would effectively prevent it. We lack any systematic research on the frequency of exploitation, and many sex workers claim that it is not a widespread problem. Nor is it obvious that bans on pornography would lessen the risk. As America's history with alcohol prohibition indicates, forcing a highly profitable industry underground is unlikely to protect participants. Even with laws like the Indianapolis ordinance, [which provides a civil rights remedy against those who traffic in pornography] victims would confront most of the same deterrents to reporting abuse that make current legal provisions so ineffectual.

A second category of harms involves the use of pornography as a blueprint for sexual violence and degradation. The testimony of injured victims, particularly when coupled with police reports and psychiatric records, leaves no doubt about the brutality that pornographic materials sometimes inspire. But again, the difficulty is that we have no gauge of frequency. Nor do we know whether pornography actually *causes* abuse, or only influences its form. Even if we could link sexual violence to certain pornographic works, suppression would not necessarily be an appropriate response. "Copycat" crimes are common, and pornography is by no means the only or even the most common source of inspiration. Dramatizations of *The Brothers Karamazov, Roots, The Ten Commandments,* and *The Burning Bed* (a feminist account of domestic violence) are among the culprits. Comprehensive research also finds that no literary work equals the Bible as a reported factor in inspiring and justifying sexual abuse.

A more indirect harm, but in many feminists' view the most pervasive one, involves pornography's effects on attitudes toward sexual violence and sexual subordination. Most boys first learn about sex through pornography, and the messages it sends scarcely encourage relationships of mutual respect, caring, and intimacy. Selections like "Cheerleader Gang Bang," "Black Bitch," "Teen Twits and Twats," and "Jap Sadists' Virgin Slave" link sexual pleasure with female degradation and racial domination. Because such messages work at the noncognitive level, the usual remedy for offensive speech — more speech — may not be effective. . . .

Two decades of laboratory research provide concrete evidence of harmful effects. Studies have consistently found that exposure to sexually violent material increases viewers' expressed willingness to commit rape and decreases their sensitivity to its damage. Yet such research cannot adequately demonstrate the duration or degree of pornography's effect on behavior in the outside world. Most experts believe that the change in viewers' attitudes following laboratory experience with pornography reflects the violence more than the sex. Although this distinction can be difficult to draw, many experts estimate that violent materials account for well under 10 percent of the pornography market. Sex offenders do not differ significantly from other individuals in their exposure or response to pornography. These offenders are more likely to be readers of *Field and Stream* than of sexually explicit material.

Other efforts to measure the harms of pornography by comparing changes over time or across cultures have been even more inconclusive. Although reported rapes have increased in some countries when pornography laws have grown more liberal, reported crimes are a highly imperfect index of sexual violence. Moreover, correlation does not prove causation. Other factors may account for the increase both in pornography and in reported assaults, and not all studies even find such correlations. Cross-cultural research also raises doubts about direct causal relationships. Some countries with high pornography consumption have low rates of reported violence against women. Other countries that heavily censor sexual expression are scarcely feminist meccas; middle-eastern Muslim societies have little pornography *or* gender equality.

Yet it is a mistake to conclude, as do many civil libertarians, that there is *no* demonstrable link between sexual expression, sexual attitudes, and sexual violence. In a nation that spends some $130 billion each year in advertising, it should not be necessary to belabor the point that images matter. A quarter-century's research leaves no doubt that aggression is in large part learned behavior, and that at least part of the learning process involves words and images. In short, the real question is not whether there is *some* link between pornography and social harms, but whether it is strong enough to justify the risks of regulation.

[One risk is that the vagueness of terms like "subordination" and "degradation" will lead to overbroad or biased enforcement.] Experience in Canada bears this out. There, recently modified prohibitions authorize the suppression of sexually explicit material that is violent, degrading, or dehumanizing. Prominent targets of Canadian censorship have not been brutal misogynist works . . . but gay and lesbian publications. These feminist-inspired changes may not have created the problem, but neither have they prevented it. Ironically enough, border patrols have seized two books by antipornography crusader Andrea Dworkin. . . .

A related concern is the absence of any logical limiting principle for legislation targeting subordination. Women are not the only, or necessarily the most, subordinate group in American society — and sexually explicit images are not necessarily the most harmful ones. As social science experts like Edward Donnerstein and Daniel Linz note, materials "outside of the pornographic or the X-rated market may in fact be of more concern, since they are imbued with a certain legitimacy, and tend to have much wider acceptance." So too, if the government can suppress sexually explicit expression that degrades women, what about hate speech that contributes to racial violence, or homophobic parodies that encourage gay-bashing? Though some restrictions may be justifiable, the risks of overly broad control are substantial. Once regulation starts down this road, logical stopping points might be hard to find.

A further concern is that provisions distinguishing between "good" and "bad" forms of sexual pleasure will reinforce sexist stereotypes. Some recent studies suggest that women rent 40 percent of hard-core videos, and almost half of surveyed women report watching pornographic films regularly. Many of these viewers find some images of female subordination arousing, as is obvious from any stroll into the world of [paperback romance novels]. Even if such enjoyment is the product of sexist conditioning, it does not follow that women need more "sexual shame, guilt, and hypocrisy — this time served up as feminism." . . . For many individuals, nonviolent erotica can provide a safe outlet for channeling sexual domination, treating sexual dysfunctions, and fantasizing about practices that they would not attempt in real life. In that sense, pornography provides some of the "safest sex" available.

Even if our society's ultimate goal is to reduce the prevalence of pornographic material, censorship has never been adequate to the task. Suppression generally increases the appeal of sexually arousing materials. . . .

Yet it does not follow that all the line drawing is futile, or that all antipornography regulation would carry the same risks as recent initiatives. For example, some First Amendment scholars propose banning only sexually explicit visual portrayals of force or violence that lack redeeming literary, artistic, political, or scientific value. Such a standard would sweep far less broadly than either prevailing obscenity laws or alternatives focused on subordination, and would target only material that is most clearly harmful. While such narrow prohibitions will be difficult to enforce, our experience with child pornography legislation suggests that limited restrictions can somewhat reduce the availability and acceptability of targeted material. At the very least, a narrowly drawn prohibition would make an important symbolic statement with relatively little cost to core First Amendment values.

Films like "Dorothy: Slave to Pain" and "Pussy on a Stick" are not cornerstones of democratic discourse.

Yet neither should we overstate the importance of such pornography prohibitions or place them at the top of women's agenda. Given the limited reach and barriers to enforcement of proposed legislation, any effect on cultural norms is likely to be quite small. Moreover, while censorship strategies may look like the "cheapest items on [women's] shopping list," they carry hidden costs. Suppression requires political coalitions that strengthen antifeminist organizations and deflect energy from strategies that are less sexy but ultimately more critical.

Notes

1. Evaluating the Harm of Pornography. The premise of an Indianapolis-style ordinance is that violent pornography is more harmful and therefore more appropriate for regulation than nonviolent pornography. By contrast, some feminists, including Carlin Meyer, contend that the most damage to women's self-image comes from nonviolent mainstream images that are seen as more acceptable and normal. In one sense, Meyer's point is fully consistent with one principle of dominance theory, which is that legal rules proscribing only the most severe forms of certain behaviors thereby legitimize the remainder. See Katharine T. Bartlett, Porno-Symbolism: A Response to Professor McConahay, 51 Law & Contemp. Probs. 71, 73 (Winter 1988). Wouldn't MacKinnon's own dominance theory also suggest that tighter controls on violent pornography would further eroticize violence against women? Is the answer to regulate more, or less?

Meyer argues for less regulation, both because she does not believe that violent pornography causes the harms for which MacKinnon holds it responsible and because, even if it did, trying to prevent it through legal regulation would be counterproductive. On the latter point, David Cole agrees.

> Sexual expression . . . inevitably confounds society's attempts to regulate it. It subverts every taboo by making it a fetish. The forbidden is simultaneously eroticized. As a result, attempts to regulate sexual expression are doomed to failure; by creating taboos to transgress, regulation only adds to sexual expression's appeal.

David Cole, Playing by Pornography's Rules: The Regulation of Sexual Expression, 143 U. Pa. L. Rev. 111, 116 (1994). See also Jeffrey G. Sherman, Love Speech: The Social Utility of Pornography, 47 Stan. L. Rev. 661 (1995) (arguing that gay male pornography is valuable both because it affirms the sexual lives of gay men and because it undercuts homophobia, the eradication of which means the eradication of misogyny); Amy Adler,

What's Left?: Hate Speech, Pornography, and the Problem for Artistic Expression, 84 Cal. L. Rev. 1499 (1997) (restrictions on pornography and hate speech sacrifice vital interests of protest and criticism from within the left).

Should feminist energy focus on challenging the ordinary commercial images of mass culture? See Cheryl B. Preston, Consuming Sexism: Pornography Suppression in the Larger Context of Commercial Images, 31 Ga. L. Rev. 771 (1997). Or are the harms of at least some forms of pornography sufficiently serious to justify targeted efforts at restriction? To what extent is the feminist campaign against pornography itself an appropriate and effective strategy for addressing, among other things, ordinary commercial images of mass culture?

2. Pornography and Agency. At the heart of the debate over pornography regulation is the extent to which women, or men, are capable of defining their own sexuality. Those favoring regulation of pornography assume that its proliferation prevents women from being independent agents in their own sexuality. From this perspective, women's choices appear constrained by the ways in which sex has been defined in *men's* interests. Those opposing regulation assume that women have the capacity to think and act for themselves, and to know what they want. For a thorough examination of the history of this battle within feminism and of the tension between agency and coercion views of women, see Kathryn Abrams, Sex Wars Redux: Agency and Coercion in Feminist Legal Theory, 95 Colum. L. Rev. 304 (1995). Abrams argues that neither extreme view is convincing and that a more adequate theory would recognize both women's capacity for self-direction and the constraints within which this capacity must often be exercised. Id. at 350-376. See also Mary Joe Frug, Postmodern Legal Feminism 151-152 (1992) (arguing that opponents of pornography should attempt to deconstruct rather than repress it and should focus their efforts on exploring alternative visions of sexuality); Meyer, supra, at 1194-1199 (arguing for largely nonlegal strategies to create alternative media images — in a word, counterspeech.)

Is pornography similarly damaging to men's sexual agency? Consider Harry Brod's argument:

> I shall be claiming that pornography has a negative impact on men's own sexuality. This is a claim that an aspect of an oppressive system, patriarchy, operates, at least in part, to the disadvantage of the group it privileges, men. This claim does not deny that the overall effect of the system is to operate in men's advantage, nor does it deny that the same aspect of the system under consideration, that is, male sexuality and pornography under patriarchy, might not also contribute to the expansion and maintenance of male power even as it also works to men's disadvantage. . . . I view raising consciousness of the prices of male power as part of a strategy through which we could at least potentially

mobilize men against pornography's destructive effects on both women and men. . . .

In terms of both its manifest image of and its effects on male sexuality, that is, in both intrinsic and consequentialist terms, pornography restricts male sensuality in favor of a genital, performance oriented male sexuality. Men become sexual acrobats endowed with oversized and overused organs. . . . The predominant image of women in pornography presents women as always sexually ready, willing, able, and eager. The necessary corollary to pornography's myth of female perpetual availability is its myth of male perpetual readiness. Just as the former fuels male misogyny when real-life women fail to perform to pornographic standards, so do men's failures to similarly perform fuel male insecurities. . . . Men [feel] needs for intimacy, but are trained to deny them, and are encouraged further to see physical affection and intimacy primarily if not exclusively in sexual terms. This leads to the familiar syndrome wherein, as one man put it:

> Although what most men want is physical affection, what they end up thinking they want is to be laid by a Playboy bunny.

This puts a strain on male sexuality. Looking to sex to fulfill what are really non-sexual needs, men end up disappointed and frustrated. Sometimes they feel an unfilled void, and blame it on their or their partner's sexual inadequacy.

Harry Brod, Pornography and the Alienation of Male Sexuality, in Rethinking Masculinity: Philosophical Explorations in Light of Feminism 149, 151-154 (Larry May & Robert A. Strikwerda eds., 1992).

If Brod is right, why has it been so difficult to enlist men in efforts to restrict pornography or to challenge mainstream portrayals of male sexuality?

Compare Brod's analysis with Brad Armstrong's autobiographical account of his work as a porn star:

> I'm just very happy with what I've done. On a social level, I think these movies are helping people's lives. A lot of our crowd, our audience, is made up of guys who maybe aren't the best-looking dudes in town. Maybe they're dorks or disabled or something like that, and there's no chance they're ever going to get laid. And I think the adult business definitely gives those guys an outlet. Otherwise, they'll explode.
>
> And lately, a lot of couples are benefitting from our films as well. . . . There are so many people who are so unhappy sexually. But now, because of the way sex has become so important in the media and so open, and people are finally talking about stuff and showing stuff sexually, people are realizing how unhappy they are and doing something about it. For the guys to bring these movies home to their spouses or girlfriends, sometimes it can really stimulate their relationship. Sometimes it works, sometimes it doesn't. But at least if a guy is unhappy with the way his wife is performing, he can watch porno and jerk off maybe, rather than have an affair. Everyone can disagree, but I think it's definitely at least an outlet for guys.

Brad Armstrong, Porn Star, in Gig: Americans Talk About Their Jobs at the Turn of the Millenium 359, 364 (John Bowe et al. eds., 2000).

Are you persuaded? If Armstrong is right, does it follow that pornography will serve men's sexual interests?

If pornography, advertising, law, and other social influences do not define sexuality and sex-based roles, what does? Is there some "natural" set of sexual drives and desires that these other influences distort? Or is it a question of which forces should be allowed to influence the formation of choice and intent and which ones should not?

First Amendment doctrine strives for "neutrality" on this issue, but as Cass Sunstein argues, prevailing views of neutrality assume as baselines the naturalness and justice of existing sexual practices, including ones that subordinate women to men. See Sunstein, Neutrality in Constitutional Law (with Special Reference to Pornography, Abortion, and Surrogacy), 92 Colum. L. Rev. 1, 49 (1992) (arguing that a better view of neutrality would seek to identify and prohibit practices that make women's sexuality into an object to be controlled and used by others). Drucilla Cornell argues that the best way to think about autonomy in this context is as an "imaginary domain" that the law should protect, but not interfere with. In her view, "no woman should be forced to see her 'sex' as it is stereotypically presented in hardcore porn." This view leads her to support zoning ordinances to channel pornography's possible encroachment, but no more. See Cornell, The Imaginary Domain; Abortion, Pornography and Sexual Harassment 103 (1995). For further explanation of the meaning of autonomy and choice in sexual matters, see Chapter 6.

Is there a danger that the feminist campaign against pornography will "strengthen[ ] the political power of the Right to censor sexual and oppressive discourse and to pass measures aimed at controlling women's bodies and sexuality"? Meyer, supra, at 1101. Some have accused MacKinnon of making alliances with "traditional political and religious conservatives who staunchly oppose women's rights, but who also seek to suppress pornography." Strossen, supra, at 13. MacKinnon has refuted such charges, pointing out in detail the misrepresentations giving rise to them, as well as the lack of conservative advocates or politicians supporting the feminist civil rights ordinance. See Catharine A. MacKinnon, The Roar on the Other Side of Silence, in In Harm's Way: The Pornography Civil Rights Hearings 3, 10 (Catharine A. MacKinnon & Andrea Dworkin eds., 1997). What about the fact that those opposing the feminist anti-pornography civil rights ordinance range from conservative judges such as Judge Frank Easterbrook (author of *Hudnut*) and liberal members of the ACLU such as Nadine Strossen? See Catharine A. MacKinnon, Pornography Left and Right, 30 Harv. C.R.-C.L. L. Rev. 143, 147-148 (1995) (questioning why convergence of the left and right against feminist civil rights ordinance is not viewed as an "unholy alliance").

3. Pornography, the Internet, and Children. The increasingly accessible Internet has expanded opportunities for the creation and distribution of pornography. See generally Steven E. Miller, Civilizing Cyberspace (1996): Marty Rimm, Marketing Pornography on the Information Superhighway: A Survey of 917,410 Images, Descriptions, Short Stories, and Animations Downloaded 8.5 Million Times by Consumers in Over 2000 Cities in Forty Countries, Provinces, and Territories, 83 Geo. L.J. 1849 (1995).

The Internet poses special challenges for regulation. The first problem is detection. The sheer size of cyberspace makes it difficult to police. A second problem is accountability. Even if illegal content is discovered online, the responsible party may be impossible to track. Both of these difficulties are exacerbated by encryption technology, which allows parties to disguise their identities. A third problem is jurisdictional. If pornographers are located outside the state's territory, the state cannot enforce an action against them. Within the United States, this may be partially resolved by recent decisions finding personal jurisdiction anywhere that individuals can foresee their Web content being viewed. See, e.g., Inset Systems, Inc. v. Instruction Set, Inc., 937 F. Supp. 161 (D. Conn. 1996). However, no such jurisdiction is available for pornography originating outside the United States, and efforts to deal with the problems posed by the international nature of cyberspace have yielded inadequate results. See, e.g., The International Convention of Crime by the Council of Europe (1999), at http://conventions.coe.int/treaty/en/projecs/cybercrime.htm [hereinafter Treaty] (including provisions aimed at creating greater uniformity in cyberjurisdiction).

There are, moreover, other problems in applying existing obscenity law to cyberporn. Which community's "community standards" are to be imposed when on-line materials can be downloaded anywhere? The Internet's decentralized structure resists regulation by permitting users to reroute access around "blocks." Further, users can post messages anonymously through the use of remailers, making it difficult to suspend privileges or identify senders. There are also costs of overly broad efforts to restrict sexual expression. As Meyer notes, "[c]ybersex offers us a chance to oust the dominant masculinist and misogynist pornographers from their control over sexual territory and to begin reclaiming and reconstructing sexuality in the relative safety of cyberspace." Carlin Meyer, Reclaiming Sex from the Pornographers: Cybersexual Possibilities, 83 Geo. L.J. 1969, 1979-1994 (1995) (discussing enforcement barriers and risks). See Keth A. Ditthavong, Note, Paving the Way for Women on the Information Superhighway: Curbing Sexism Not Freedoms, 4 Am. U. J. Gender & L. 455 (1996).

A related problem involves enforcement of laws attempting to restrict minors' access to pornography. The same technologies that make it easy for individuals to disguise their identity make it equally easy to disguise their age. The first congressional attempt to cope with this problem borrowed from dial-a-porn, criminalized transmissions of "obscene or indecent" and "patently offensive" messages to a minor. See Communications Decency Act, 47 U.S.C. §223(a), (d) (Supp. 1997) (also known as the "Exon Bill"). In reviewing the constitutionality of the Act, the Supreme Court rejected the analogy to the heavily regulated broadcast media, on grounds that the Internet is neither a "scarce" resource nor an "invasive" medium, and invalidated the "indecent" and "patently offensive" sections as overly broad restrictions on speech. See Reno v. ACLU, 521 U.S. 844 (1997). An anti-obscenity portion of the statute remains intact, but the application of local "community standards" in determining whether speech is obscene is problematic in the increasingly interconnected on-line world. See Sean J. Petrie, Note, Indecent Proposals: How Each Branch of the Federal Government Overstepped Its Institutional Authority in the Development of Internet Obscenity Law, 49 Stan. L. Rev. 637 (1997).

A subsequent act, the Child Online Protection Act, 47 U.S.C. §§231a-e (Supp. IV 1998) (COPA), imposes criminal penalties on those who knowingly make available to minors through the World Wide Web commercial materials "harmful to minors." Harm is defined in terms modeled on the *Miller* obscenity standard. The Third Circuit enjoined the statute. In its view, COPA had not remedied problems with the "community standard" that the Supreme Court had identified in *Reno*: that any communication available to a nationwide audience will be judged by the community most likely to be offended by the message." ACLU v. Reno, 217 F.3d 162, 174 (3rd Cir. 2000), cert. granted sub nom. Ashcroft v. American Civil Liberties Union, 121 S. Ct. 1997 (2001). The circuit court also raised without resolving other potential problems that may be addressed by the Supreme Court, which has agreed to hear the case, such as "whether the statute's failure to distinguish between material that is harmful to a 6 year old versus a 16 year old is problematic." Id. at 174 n.19.

Following passage of COPA, Congress enacted the Children's Internet Protection Act (CHIPA) (codified as 20 U.S.C. §7001). It requires publicly funded elementary schools, secondary schools, and libraries that provide Internet access to (1) block or filter adults' access to visual depictions of obscenity or child pornography and (2) block or filter children's access to obscenity, child pornography, or other material that is "harmful to minors."

Constitutional challenges are already under way. Critics claim that current filtering systems are overly subjective, that they are ineffective in blocking all access to harmful materials, and that they pose undue risks of censoring because users are unaware that content is restricted. See, e.g., Lawrence Lessig, Code and Other Laws of Cyberspace 154, 180 (1999). However, similar difficulties arise with other potential strategies to restrict minors' access to pornography, such as zoning systems requiring adult identification. Lessig, supra, at 177; see also Reno v. ACLU, 521 U.S. 844 (1997) (invalidating provisions of Communications Decency Act seeking to protect minors from obsenity on the Internet). For a general discussion of the problem and the need for better technological responses, see Lillian Edwards, Pornography and the Internet, in Law and the Internet: A Framework for Electronic Commerce 275, 280 (Lillian Edwards & Charlotte Waelde eds., 2000); Blake T. Bilstad, Obscenity and Indecency in a Digital Age: The Legal and Political Implications of Cybersmut, Virtual Pornography, and the Communications Decency Act of 1996, 13 Santa Clara Computer & High Tech L.J. 321, 335 (1997).

The Child Pornography Prevention Act, 18 U.S.C. §2251 et seq. (CPPA), marks the latest congressional effort to deal with the proliferation of pornography featuring children. A March 2000 report of President Clinton's working group on Internet crime summarizes this legislation:

> Child pornography offenses are covered by 18 U.S.C. §2251 et seq. These laws specifically include computers within the proscribed means of distribution and possession of child pornography. They specifically prohibit the production, transportation, receipt, or distribution of visual depictions that involve the use of a minor (any person under the age of 18) engaged in sexually explicit conduct, where the producer or distributor knows or has reason to know, that the depiction was or will be transported in interstate commerce or was created using a camera (or the like) that had traveled in interstate commerce. Computer graphic images — including computer or computer-generated images or pictures of a minor engaged in sexually explicit conduct; "morphed" images that appear to be (through computer manipulation) of a minor engaged in sexually explicit conduct; and images that are adults promoted as children engaged in sexually explicit conduct — are included within the definition of "visual depictions." 18 U.S.C. §2256(5) and (8).

The Electronic Frontier: The Challenge of Unlawful Conduct Involving the Use of the Internet, Report of the President's Working Group (2000), at http://www.usdoj.gov/criminal/cybercrime/unlawful.htm.

The CPPA has come under attack for its provisions criminalizing visual depictions where no actual child is involved. Critics of these provisions claim that they reach too far — especially in those situations where the child is a digitally simulated creation. By contrast, supporters argue that these images are flooding the market and, when seen by children, present just as great a risk of harm as pornography using live models. The circuits have divided on the constitutionality of the legislation and the Supreme Court has granted certiorari to resolve the conflict. See Free Speech Coalition v. Reno, 198 F.3d 1083 (9th Cir. 1999), cert granted sub nom. Ashcroft v. Free Speech Coalition, 1215 S. Ct. 876 (2001); George Ivezaj, Child Pornography on the Internet: An Examination of the International Communities' Proposed Solutions for a Global Problem, 8 MSU-DCL J. Int'l L. 819 (1999).

At oral argument on the statute, a central issue involved the adequacy of the statute's affirmative defense for movies produced using adult actors for scenes that appear to involve sexual conduct by minors. Films like Lolita, Traffic, and Titanic all involve such scenes. Justice Scalia questioned whether there would in fact be "radical tragic consequences" for First Amendment jurisprudence if such scenes could not be shown. "What great works could be taken away from us if we were unable to show minors copulating?" When counsel for the plaintiffs mentioned Traffic, the Tin Drum, and several films with Brooke Shields, Justice Scalia responded, "This is not, you know, the Mona Lisa or Venus De Milo or anything that has lasted more than thirty years." When Justice Stevens smilingly interjected a reference to Romeo and Juliet, Justice Scalia responded, "you've seen a different version of that play than I have." Tony Mauro, Virtual Reality Check, American Lawyer, Dec. 2001, at 70 (quoting Justice Scalia).

If you had been counsel for the plaintiff, how would you have responded? If you were on the Court, how would you weigh the free speech interests of the public against the harms to children? According to Congressional findings, even where minors are not involved in making scenes involving sexual activity, the resulting images may desensitize the viewer to the sexual exploitation of children. Is this risk sufficient to sustain the statute?

Putting Theory into Practice

4-10. Suppose that you are a staff attorney for a local women students' organization. Your organization is approached by both sides in the *Hudnut* case and asked to file an amicus brief. What would you do, and how would you make your decision?

4-11. Your organization is contacted by a women students' organization of a nearby state university. The group is offended by the practices of several fraternities, which show porn films and invite strippers to perform on campus at all-male parties. The students believe that these practices encourage date rape. When they approached the university administration, they were advised that the male students were entitled to exercise their First Amendment rights. How would you respond? What strategies would you propose?

E. HETEROSEXISM: SUBORDINATION BY LEGAL DEFINITION

The term "homosexual" emerged in the nineteenth century to describe same-sex orientation activity. The term "gay," which has been traced to medieval Europe, came into broader use in the 1960s, as a reference for both individuals and a political movement. Although the term historically was gender neutral, in contemporary usage gay often refers to men, and lesbians is the preferred term for women.

Estimates of the number of individuals who are gay or lesbian are difficult to come by, especially given that an individual's sexual preference for members of one sex or the other is best understood as a continuous rather than a binary variable. See Richard A. Posner, Sex and Reason 294 (1992). Most studies, depending on methodology and definitions used, place the figures between 6 and 13 percent of men and 2 and 6 percent of women. Id. (estimating that 6 percent of adult men and 2 percent of adult women are more or less exclusively homosexual in their sexual preferences); Richard Schneider, "The People Gay" and the 10% Debate, 7 Harv. Gay & Lesbian Rev. 4 (March 22, 2000, available at 2000 WL 25098410) (estimating that 6 percent of men and 4 percent of women "self-identify" as gay or lesbian); Gay and Lesbian Stats: A Pocket Guide of Facts and Figures 10-12 (Bennet L. Singer & David Deschamps eds. 1994).

In the United States, gays and lesbians have long been the subject of pervasive discrimination in many aspects of their lives. This discrimination remains largely exempt from legislative or constitutional prohibitions.

1. Gay Marriage Is Not Marriage

Jones v. Hallahan
501 S.W.2d 588 (Ky. 1973)

VANCE, Commissioner.

The appellants, each of whom is a female person, seek review of a judgment of the Jefferson Circuit Court which held that they were not entitled to have issued to them a license to marry each other.

Appellants contend that the failure of the clerk to issue the license deprived them of three basic constitutional rights, namely, the right to marry; the right of association; and the right to free exercise of religion. They also contend that the refusal subjects them to cruel and unusual punishment.

The sections of Kentucky statutes relating to marriage do not include a definition of that term. It must therefore be defined according to common usage.

Webster's New International Dictionary, Second Edition, defines marriage as follows:

> A state of being married, or being united to a person or persons of the opposite sex as husband or wife; also, the mutual relation of husband and wife; wedlock; abstractly, the institution whereby men and women are joined in a special kind of social and legal dependence, for the purpose of founding and maintaining a family.

The Century Dictionary and Encyclopedia defines marriage as:

The legal union of a man with a woman for life; the state or condition of being married; the legal relation of spouses to each other; wedlock; the formal declaration or contract by which a man and a woman join in wedlock.

Black's Law Dictionary, Fourth Edition, defines marriage as:

The civil status, condition or relation of one man and one woman united in law for life, for the discharge to each other and the community of the duties legally incumbent upon those whose association is founded on the distinction of sex.

Kentucky statutes do not specifically prohibit marriage between persons of the same sex nor do they authorize the issuance of a marriage license to such persons.

Marriage was a custom long before the state commenced to issue licenses for that purpose. For a time the records of marriage were kept by the church. Some states even now recognize a common-law marriage which has neither the benefit of license nor clergy. In all cases, however, marriage has always been considered as the union of a man and a woman and we have been presented with no authority to the contrary.

It appears to us that appellants are prevented from marrying, not by the statutes of Kentucky or the refusal of the County Court Clerk of Jefferson County to issue them a license, but rather by their own incapability of entering into a marriage as that term is defined.

A license to enter into a status or a relationship which the parties are incapable of achieving is a nullity. If the appellants had concealed from the clerk the fact that they were of the same sex and he had issued a license to them and a ceremony had been performed, the resulting relationship would not constitute a marriage.

This is a case of first impression in Kentucky. To our knowledge, only two other states have considered the question and both of them have reached the same result that we reach in this opinion. Baker v. Nelson, [191 N.W.2d 185 (Minn. 1971), appeal dismissed for want of a substantial federal question, 409 U.S. 810 (1972)]; Anonymous v. Anonymous, [325 N.Y.S.2d 499 (Sup. Ct., Queens Co. 1971)].

Baker v. Nelson considered many of the constitutional issues raised by the appellants here and decided them adversely to appellants. In our view, however, no constitutional issue is involved. We find no constitutional sanction or protection of the right of marriage between persons of the same sex.

The claim of religious freedom cannot be extended to make the professed doctrines superior to the law of the land and in effect to permit every citizen to become a law unto himself. Reynolds v. United States, [98

U.S. 145 (1878)]. We do not consider the refusal to issue the license a punishment.

In substance, the relationship proposed by the appellants does not authorize the issuance of a marriage license because what they propose is not a marriage.

The judgment is affirmed.

All concur.

Baehr v. Lewin
852 P.2d 44 (Haw. 1993)

LEVINSON, J. . . .

On May 1, 1991, the plaintiffs filed a complaint for injunctive and declaratory relief in the Circuit Court of the First Circuit, State of Hawaii, seeking, inter alia: (1) a declaration that Hawaii Revised Statutes §572-1 (1985) — the section of the Hawaii Marriage Law enumerating the [r]equisites of [a] valid marriage contract" — is unconstitutional insofar as it is construed and applied by the Department of Health [DOH] to justify refusing to issue a marriage license on the sole basis that the applicant couple is of the same sex; and (2) preliminary and permanent injunctions prohibiting the future withholding of marriage licenses on that sole basis. . . .

In addition to the necessary jurisdictional and venue-related averments, the plaintiffs' complaint alleges the following facts: (1) on or about December 17, 1990, ["the applicant couples"] filed applications for marriage licenses with the DOH, pursuant to Haw. Rev. Stat. §572-6; (2) the DOH denied the applicant couples' marriage license applications solely on the ground that the applicant couples were of the same sex; (3) the applicant couples have complied with all marriage contract requirements and provisions under Haw. Rev. Stat. ch. 572, except that each applicant couple is of the same sex; (4) the applicant couples are otherwise eligible to secure marriage licenses. . . .

[T]he plaintiffs' complaint avers that: (1) the DOH's interpretation and application of Haw. Rev. Stat §572-1 to deny same-sex couples access to marriage licenses violates the plaintiffs' right to privacy, as guaranteed by article I, section 6 of the Hawaii Constitution, as well as to the equal protection of the laws and due process of law, as guaranteed by article I, section 5 of the Hawaii Constitution. . . .

On July 9, 1991, Lewin [the Director of DOH] filed his motion for judgment on the pleadings. . . .

The circuit court . . . [granted Lewin's motion]. . . .

It is now well established that "'a right to personal privacy, or a guarantee of certain areas or zones of privacy,'" is implicit in the United States Constitution. . . . And article I, section 6 of the Hawaii Constitution expressly states that "[t]he right of the people to privacy is recognized and shall not be infringed without the showing of a compelling state interest." . . . The framers of the Hawaii Constitution declared that the "privacy concept" embodied in article I, section 6 is to be "treated as a fundamental right[.]" . . .

The . . . case law demonstrates that the federal construct of the fundamental right to marry — subsumed within the right to privacy implicitly protected by the United States Constitution — presently contemplates unions between men and women. (Once again, this is hardly surprising inasmuch as such unions are the only state-sanctioned marriages currently acknowledged in this country.) . . .

[W]e do not believe that a right to same-sex marriage is so rooted in the traditions and collective conscience of our people that failure to recognize it would violate the fundamental principles of liberty and justice that lie at the base of all our civil and political institutions. Neither do we believe that a right to same-sex marriage is implicit in the concept of ordered liberty, such that neither liberty nor justice would exist if it were sacrificed. Accordingly, we hold that the applicant couples do not have a fundamental constitutional right to same-sex marriage arising out of the right to privacy or otherwise . . . .

In addition to the alleged violation of their constitutional rights to privacy and due process of law, the applicant couples contend that they have been denied the equal protection of the laws as guaranteed by article I, section 5 of the Hawaii Constitution. . . . [W]e agree that the circuit court erred when it concluded, as a matter of law, that: (1) homosexuals do not constitute a "suspect class" for purposes of equal protection analysis under article I, section 5 of the Hawaii Constitution; (2) the classification created by Haw. Rev. Stat. §572-1 is not subject to "strict scrutiny," but must satisfy only the "rational relationship" test; and (3) Haw. Rev. Stat. §572-1 satisfies the rational relationship test because the legislature "obviously designed [it] to promote the general welfare interests of the community by sanctioning traditional man-woman family units and procreation." . . .

The applicant couples correctly contend that the DOH's refusal to allow them to marry on the basis that they are members of the same sex deprives them of access to a multiplicity of rights and benefits that are contingent upon that status. Although it is unnecessary in this opinion to engage in an encyclopedic recitation of all of them, a number of the most salient marital rights and benefits are worthy of note. They include: (1) a variety of state income tax advantages, including deductions, credits, rates, exemptions, and estimates . . . (2) public assistance from and exemptions relating to the Department of Human Services . . . (3) control, division, acquisition, and disposition of community property . . . (4) rights relating to dower, curtesy, and inheritance . . . (5) rights to notice, protection, benefits, and inheritance . . . (6) award of child custody and support payments in divorce proceedings . . . (7) the right to spousal support . . . (8) the right to enter into premarital agreements . . . (9) the right to change of name . . . (10) the right to file a nonsupport action . . . (11) post-divorce rights relating to support and property division under HRS chapter 580 (1985 and Supp. 1992) . . . (12) the benefit of the spousal privilege and confidential marital communications . . . (13) the benefit of the exemption of real property from attachment or execution . . . and (14) the right to bring a wrongful death action. . . .

Relying primarily on four decisions construing the law of other jurisdictions, Lewin contends that "the fact that homosexual [sic — actually, same-sex] partners cannot form a state-licensed marriage is not the product of impermissible discrimination" implicating equal protection considerations, but rather "a function of their biologic inability as a couple to satisfy the definition of the status to which they aspire." Put differently, Lewin proposes that "the right of persons of the same sex to marry one another does not exist because marriage, by definition and usage, means a special relationship between a man and a woman." We believe Lewin's argument to be circular and unpersuasive. . . .

. . . Loving [v. Virginia, 388 U.S. 1 (1967),] involved the appeal of a black woman and a caucasian man (the Lovings) who were married in the District of Columbia and thereafter returned to their home state of Virginia to establish their marital abode. [388 U.S. at 2.] The Lovings were duly indicted for and convicted of violating Virginia's miscegenation laws, which banned interracial marriages. . . .

In a landmark decision, the United States Supreme Court, through Chief Justice Warren, struck down the Virginia miscegenation laws on both equal protection and due process grounds. The Court's holding as to the former is pertinent for present purposes:

> There can be no question but that Virginia's miscegenation statutes rest solely upon distinctions drawn according to race. *The statutes proscribe generally accepted conduct* if engaged in by members of different races. . . . At the very least, the Equal Protection Clause demands that racial classifications . . . be subjected to the "most rigid scrutiny," . . . and, if they are ever to be upheld, *they must be shown to be necessary to the accomplishment of some permissible state objective, independent of the racial discrimination which it was the object of the Fourteenth Amendment to eliminate.* . . .
>
> There is patently no legitimate overriding purpose independent of invidious discrimination which justifies this classification. . . . We have consistently denied the constitutionality of measures which restrict the rights of citizens on account of race. There can be no doubt that restricting the freedom to marry solely because of racial classifications violates the central meaning of the Equal Protection Clause.

Id. at 10-12 (emphasis added and citation omitted).

The facts in *Loving* and the respective reasoning of the Virginia courts, on the one hand, and the United States Supreme Court, on the other, both

. . . unmask the tautological and circular nature of Lewin's argument that Haw. Rev. Stat. §572-1 does not implicate article I, section 5 of the Hawaii Constitution because same sex marriage is an innate impossibility. Analogously to Lewin's argument and the rationale of the *Jones* court, the Virginia courts declared that interracial marriage simply could not exist because the Deity had deemed such a union intrinsically unnatural, 388 U.S. at 3, and, in effect, because it had theretofore never been the "custom" of the state to recognize mixed marriages, marriage "always" having been construed to presuppose a different configuration. With all due respect to the Virginia courts of a bygone era, we do not believe that trial judges are the ultimate authorities on the subject of Divine Will, and, as *Loving* amply demonstrates, constitutional law may mandate, like it or not, that customs change with an evolving social order. . . .

. . . This court has applied "strict scrutiny" analysis to "'laws classifying on the basis of suspect categories or impinging upon fundamental rights expressly or impliedly granted by the [c]onstitution,'" in which case the laws are "'presumed to be unconstitutional unless the state shows compelling state interests which justify such classifications'" . . . .

[W]e hold that sex is a "suspect category" for purposes of equal protection analysis under article I, section 5 of the Hawaii Constitution and that Haw. Rev. Stat. §572-1 is subject to the "strict scrutiny" test. It therefore follows, and we so hold, that (1) Haw. Rev. Stat. §572-1 is presumed to be unconstitutional (2) unless Lewin, as an agent of the State of Hawaii, can show that (a) the statute's sex-based classification is justified by compelling state interests and (b) the statute is narrowly drawn to avoid unnecessary abridgements of the applicant couples' constitutional rights. . . .

Concurring Opinion by BURNS, J. . . .

As used in the Hawaii constitution, to what does the word "sex" refer? In my view, the Hawaii constitution's reference to "sex" includes all aspects of each person's "sex" that are "biologically fated." The decision whether a person when born will be a male or a female is "biologically fated." Thus, the word "sex" includes the male-female difference. Is there any other aspect of a person's "sex" that is "biologically fated"?

In March 1993, the Cox News Service reported in relevant part as follows:

> The issue of whether people become homosexuals because of "nature or nurture" is one of the most controversial subjects scientists have confronted in recent years. . . .
>
> Until the middle 1980s, the prevailing view among most scientists was that homosexual "tendencies" were mostly the result of upbringing. . . .
>
> Later, researchers at the Salk Institute in San Diego found anatomical differences between homosexual and heterosexual men in parts of the brain noted for differences between men and women.
>
> Theories gravitate to the role of male sex hormones. . . .

The Honolulu Advertiser, March 9, 1993, at A8, col. 1.

In March 1993, the Associated Press reported in relevant part as follows:

> CHICAGO — Genes appear to play an important role in determining whether women are lesbians, said a researcher who found similar results among gay men. . . .
>
> "I think we're dealing with something very complex, perhaps the interaction between hormones, the environment and genetic components," [Roger] Gorski [an expert in biological theories of homosexuality] said yesterday. . . .

The Honolulu Advertiser, March 12, 1993, at A-24, col. 1.

On the other hand, columnist Charles Krauthammer reports as follows:

> It is natural, therefore, that just as parents have the inclination and right to wish to influence the development of a child's character, they have the inclination and right to try to influence a child's sexual orientation. Gay advocates argue, however, that such influence is an illusion. Sexual orientation, they claim, is biologically fated and thus entirely impervious to environmental influence.
>
> Unfortunately, as E.L. Pattullo, former director of Harvard's Center for the Behavioral Sciences, recently pointed out in Commentary magazine, the scientific evidence does not support such a claim. . . .

The Honolulu Advertiser, May 2, 1993, at B2, cols. 3, 4 and 5.

If heterosexuality, homosexuality, bisexuality, and asexuality are "biologically fated[,]" then the word "sex" also includes those differences. Therefore, the questions whether heterosexuality, homosexuality, bisexuality, and asexuality are "biologically fated" are relevant questions of fact which must be determined before the issue presented in this case can be answered. If the answers are yes, then each person's "sex" includes both the "biologically fated" male-female difference and the "biologically fated" sexual orientation difference, and the Hawaii constitution probably bars the State from discriminating against the sexual orientation difference by permitting opposite-sex Hawaii Civil Law Marriages and not permitting same-sex Hawaii Civil Law Marriages. If the answers are no, then each person's "sex" does not include the sexual orientation difference, and the Hawaii constitution may permit the State to encourage heterosexuality and discourage homosexuality, bisexuality, and asexuality by permitting opposite-sex Hawaii Civil Law Marriages and not permitting same-sex Hawaii Civil Law Marriages.

[The opinion of Heen, J., dissenting, is omitted.]

Baker v. State
744 A.2d 864 (Vt. 1999)

AMESTOY, C.J.

May the State of Vermont exclude same-sex couples from the benefits and protections that its laws provide to opposite-sex married couples? . . .

We conclude that under the Common Benefits Clause of the Vermont Constitution, . . . plaintiffs may not be deprived of the statutory benefits and protections afforded persons of the opposite sex who choose to marry. We hold that the State is constitutionally required to extend to same-sex couples the common benefits and protections that flow from marriage under Vermont law. Whether this ultimately takes the form of inclusion within the marriage laws themselves or a parallel "domestic partnership" system or some equivalent statutory alternative, rests with the Legislature. Whatever system is chosen, however, must conform with the constitutional imperative to afford all Vermonters the common benefit, protection, and security of the law.

Plaintiffs are three same-sex couples who have lived together in committed relationships for periods ranging from four to twenty-five years. Two of the couples have raised children together. Each couple applied for a marriage license from their respective town clerk, and each was refused a license as ineligible under the applicable state marriage laws. Plaintiffs thereupon filed this lawsuit against defendants — the State of Vermont, the Towns of Milton and Shelburne, and the City of South Burlington — seeking a declaratory judgment that the refusal to issue them a license violated the marriage statutes and the Vermont Constitution.

[The trial court dismissed the complaint, ruling] that the marriage statutes could not be construed to permit the issuance of a license to same-sex couples. The court further ruled that the marriage statutes were constitutional because they rationally furthered the State's interest in promoting "the link between procreation and child rearing." This appeal followed.

I. The Statutory Claim

[The court holds that same-sex couples do not qualify to be married under the state's marriage statutes.]

II. The Constitutional Claim

Assuming that the marriage statutes preclude their eligibility for a marriage license, plaintiffs contend that the exclusion violates their right to the common benefit and protection of the law guaranteed by Chapter I, Article 7 of the Vermont Constitution. They note that in denying them access to a civil marriage license, the law effectively excludes them from a broad array of legal benefits and protections incident to the marital relation, including access to a spouse's medical, life, and disability insurance, hospital visitation and other medical decisionmaking privileges, spousal support, intestate succession, homestead protections, and many other statutory protections. . . .

B. Text . . .

We first focus on the words of the Constitution themselves. . . . One of the fundamental rights included in Chapter I of the Vermont Constitution of 1777, entitled "A Declaration of Rights of the Inhabitants of the State of Vermont," the Common Benefits Clause as originally written provided:

> That government is, or ought to be, instituted for the common benefit, protection, and security of the people, nation or community; and not for the particular emolument or advantage of any single man, family or set of men, who are a part only of that community; and that the community hath an indubitable, unalienable and indefeasible right, to reform, alter or abolish government, in such manner as shall be, by that community, judged most conducive to the public weal.

Vt. Const. of 1777, ch. I, art. VI. [The only change that has been made to this original version has been the substitution of "person" and "persons" for "man" and "men." See Vt. Const., ch. I, art. 7.]

. . . Unlike the Fourteenth Amendment, . . . the Common Benefits Clause mirrors the confidence of a homogeneous, eighteenth- century group of men aggressively laying claim to the same rights as their peers in Great Britain or, for that matter, New York, New Hampshire, or the Upper Connecticut River Valley. . . . The same assumption that all the people should be afforded all the benefits and protections bestowed by government is also reflected in the second section, which prohibits not the denial of rights to the oppressed, but rather the conferral of advantages or emoluments upon the privileged.

The words of the Common Benefits Clause are revealing. While they do not, to be sure, set forth a fully-formed standard of analysis for determining the constitutionality of a given statute, they do express broad principles which usefully inform that analysis. Chief among these is the principle of inclusion. As explained more fully in the discussion that follows, the specific proscription against governmental favoritism toward not only groups or "set[s] of men," but also toward any particular "family" or "single man," underscores the framers' resentment of political preference of any kind. The affirmative right to the "common benefits and protections" of government and the corollary proscription of favoritism in the distribution of public "emoluments and advantages" reflect the framers' overarching objective "not only that everyone enjoy equality before the law or have an equal voice in government but also that everyone have an equal share in the fruits of the common enterprise." W. Adams, The First American Constitutions 188 (1980) (emphasis added). Thus, at its core the Common Benefits Clause expressed a vision of government that afforded every Vermonter its benefit and protection and provided no Vermonter particular advantage.

C. Historical Context . . .

. . . The historical origins of the Vermont Constitution . . . reveal that the framers, although enlightened for their day, were not principally concerned with civil rights for African-Americans and other minorities, but with equal access to public benefits and protections for the community as a whole. The concept of equality at the core of the Common Benefits Clause was not the eradication of racial or class distinctions, but rather the elimination of artificial governmental preferments and advantages. The Vermont Constitution would ensure that the law uniformly afforded every Vermonter its benefit, protection, and security so that social and political preeminence would reflect differences of capacity, disposition, and virtue, rather than governmental favor and privilege.

D. Analysis Under Article 7 . . .

We must ultimately ascertain whether the omission of a part of the community from the benefit, protection and security of the challenged law bears a reasonable and just relation to the governmental purpose. Consistent with the core presumption of inclusion, factors to be considered in this determination may include: (1) the significance of the benefits and protections of the challenged law; (2) whether the omission of members of the community from the benefits and protections of the challenged law promotes the government's stated goals; and (3) whether the classification is significantly underinclusive or overinclusive. As Justice Souter has observed in a different context, this approach necessarily "calls for a court to assess the relative 'weights' or dignities of the contending interests." Washington v. Glucksberg, 521 U.S. 702 (1997) (Souter, J., concurring). What keeps that assessment grounded and objective, and not based upon the private sensitivities or values of individual judges, is that in assessing the relative weights of competing interests courts must look to the history and "traditions from which [the State] developed" as well as those "from which it broke," id. at 767 (quoting Poe v. Ullman, 367 U.S. 497, 542 (1961) (Harlan, J., dissenting)), and not to merely personal notions. Moreover, the process of review is necessarily "one of close criticism going to the *details* of the opposing interests and to their relationships with the historically recognized principles that lend them weight or value." Id. at 769 (emphasis added).

Ultimately, the answers to these questions, however useful, cannot substitute for "[t]he inescapable fact . . . that adjudication of . . . claims may call upon the Court in interpreting the Constitution to exercise that same capacity which by tradition courts always have exercised: reasoned judgment." Id. (quoting Planned Parenthood of Southeastern Pa. v. Casey, 505 U.S. 833, 849 (1992)). The balance between individual liberty and organized society which courts are continually called upon to weigh does not lend itself to the precision of a scale. It is, indeed, a recognition of the imprecision of "reasoned judgment" that compels both judicial restraint and respect for tradition in constitutional interpretation.

E. The Standard Applied

. . . The first step in our analysis is to identify the nature of the statutory classification. As noted, the marriage statutes apply expressly to opposite-sex couples. Thus, the statutes exclude anyone who wishes to marry someone of the same sex.

Next, we must identify the governmental purpose or purposes to be served by the statutory classification. The principal purpose the State advances in support of excluding same-sex couples from the legal benefits of marriage is the government's interest in "furthering the link between procreation and child rearing." . . . The State contends, further, that the Legislature could reasonably believe that sanctioning same-sex unions "would diminish society's perception of the link between procreation and child rearing . . . [and] advance the notion that fathers or mothers . . . are mere surplusage to the functions of procreation and child rearing." The State argues that since same-sex couples cannot conceive a child on their own, state-sanctioned same-sex unions "could be seen by the Legislature to separate further the connection between procreation and parental responsibilities for raising children." Hence, the Legislature is justified, the State concludes, "in using the marriage statutes to send a public message that procreation and child rearing are intertwined."

. . . It is beyond dispute that the State has a legitimate and long-standing interest in promoting a permanent commitment between couples for the security of their children. It is equally undeniable that the State's interest has been advanced by extending formal public sanction and protection to the union, or marriage, of those couples considered capable of having children, i.e., men and women. And there is no doubt that the overwhelming majority of births today continue to result from natural conception between one man and one woman. . . .

It is equally undisputed that many opposite-sex couples marry for reasons unrelated to procreation, that some of these couples never intend to have children, and that others are incapable of having children. Therefore, if the purpose of the statutory exclusion of same-sex couples is to "further [ ] the link between procreation and child rearing," it is significantly underinclusive. The law extends the benefits and protections of marriage to many persons with no logical connection to the stated governmental goal.

Furthermore, while accurate statistics are difficult to obtain, there is no dispute that a significant number of children today are actually being raised by same-sex parents, and that increasing numbers of children are being conceived by such parents through a variety of assisted-reproductive techniques. . . .

Thus, with or without the marriage sanction, the reality today is that increasing numbers of same-sex couples are employing increasingly efficient assisted-reproductive techniques to conceive and raise children. See [Lisa] Ikemoto, The In/Fertile, the Too Fertile, and the Dysfertile, 47 Hastings L.J. 1007, 1056 & n.170 (1996). The Vermont Legislature has not only recognized this reality, but has acted affirmatively to remove legal barriers so that same-sex couples may legally adopt and rear the children conceived through such efforts. See 15A V.S.A. §1-102(b) (allowing partner of biological parent to adopt if in child's best interest without reference to sex). The state has also acted to expand the domestic relations laws to safeguard the interests of same-sex parents and their children when such couples terminate their domestic relationship. See 15A V.S.A. §1-112 (vesting family court with jurisdiction over parental rights and responsibilities, parent-child contact, and child support when unmarried persons who have adopted minor child "terminate their domestic relationship").

Therefore, to the extent that the state's purpose in licensing civil marriage was, and is, to legitimize children and provide for their security, the statutes plainly exclude many same-sex couples who are no different from opposite-sex couples with respect to these objectives. If anything, the exclusion of same-sex couples from the legal protections incident to marriage exposes their children to the precise risks that the State argues the marriage laws are designed to secure against. In short, the marital exclusion treats persons who are similarly situated for purposes of the law, differently.

The State also argues that because same-sex couples cannot conceive a child on their own, their exclusion promotes a "perception of the link between procreation and child rearing," and that to discard it would "advance the notion that mothers and fathers . . . are mere surplusage to the functions of procreation and child rearing." Apart from the bare assertion, the State offers no persuasive reasoning to support these claims. Indeed, it is undisputed that most of those who utilize nontraditional means of conception are infertile married couples . . . and that many assisted-reproductive techniques involve only one of the married partner's genetic material, the other being supplied by a third party through sperm, egg, or embryo donation. . . . The State does not suggest that the use of these technologies undermines a married couple's sense of parental responsibility, or fosters the perception that they are "mere surplusage" to the conception and parenting of the child so conceived. Nor does it even remotely suggest that access to such techniques ought to be restricted as a matter of public policy to "send a public message that procreation and child rearing are intertwined." Accordingly, there is no reasonable basis to conclude that a same-sex couple's use of the same technologies would undermine the bonds of parenthood, or society's perception of parenthood. . . .

. . . The legal benefits and protections flowing from a marriage license are of such significance that any statutory exclusion must necessarily be grounded on public concerns of sufficient weight, cogency, and authority that the justice of the deprivation cannot seriously be questioned. . . . [T]he exclusion falls substantially short of this standard. The laudable governmental goal of promoting a commitment between married couples to promote the security of their children and the community as a whole provides no reasonable basis for denying the legal benefits and protections of marriage to same-sex couples, who are no differently situated with respect to this goal than their opposite-sex counterparts. Promoting a link between procreation and childrearing similarly fails to support the exclusion. . . .

The State asserts that a number of additional rationales could support a legislative decision to exclude same-sex partners from the statutory benefits and protections of marriage. Among these are the State's purported interests in "promoting both male and female role models," minimizing the legal complications of surrogacy contracts and sperm donors, "bridging differences" between the sexes, discouraging marriages of convenience for tax, housing or other benefits, maintaining uniformity with marriage laws in other states, and generally protecting marriage from "destabilizing changes." The most substantive of the State's remaining claims relates to the issue of childrearing. It is conceivable that the Legislature could conclude that opposite-sex partners offer advantages in this area, although we note that child-development experts disagree and the answer is decidedly uncertain. The argument, however, contains a more fundamental flaw, and that is the Legislature's endorsement of a policy diametrically at odds with the State's claim. In 1996, the Vermont General Assembly enacted, and the Governor signed, a law removing all prior legal barriers to the adoption of children by same-sex couples. . . . At the same time, the Legislature provided additional legal protections in the form of court-ordered child support and parent-child contact in the event that same-sex parents dissolved their "domestic relationship." . . . In light of these express policy choices, the State's arguments that Vermont public policy favors opposite-sex over same-sex parents or disfavors the use of artificial reproductive technologies are patently without substance.

Similarly, the State's argument that Vermont's marriage laws serve a substantial governmental interest in maintaining uniformity with other jurisdictions cannot be reconciled with Vermont's recognition of unions, such as first-cousin marriages, not uniformly sanctioned in other states. . . . In an analogous context, Vermont has sanctioned adoptions by same-sex partners . . . notwithstanding the fact that many states have not. . . . Thus, the State's claim that Vermont's marriage laws were adopted because the Legislature sought to conform to those of the other forty-nine states is not only speculative, but refuted by two relevant legislative choices which demonstrate that uniformity with other jurisdictions has not been a governmental purpose.

The State's remaining claims (e.g., recognition of same-sex unions might foster marriages of convenience or otherwise affect the institution in "unpredictable" ways) may be plausible forecasts as to what the future may hold, but cannot reasonably be construed to provide a reasonable and just basis for the statutory exclusion. The State's conjectures are not, in any event, susceptible to empirical proof before they occur.

Finally, it is suggested that the long history of official intolerance of intimate same-sex relationships cannot be reconciled with an interpretation of Article 7 that would give state-sanctioned benefits and protection to individuals of the same sex who commit to a permanent domestic relationship. We find the argument to be unpersuasive for several reasons. First, to the extent that state action historically has been motivated by an animus against a class, that history cannot provide a legitimate basis for continued unequal application of the law. See [MacCallum v. Philip Seymour's Adm'r., 686 A.2d 935, 939 (Vt. 1996)] (holding that although adopted persons had "historically been a target of discrimination," social prejudices failed to support their continued exclusion from intestacy law). As we observed recently in [Brigham v. State, 692 A.2d 384, 396 (Vt. 1997),] "[E]qual protection of the laws cannot be limited by eighteenth-century standards." Second, whatever claim may be made in light of the undeniable fact that federal and state statutes — including those in Vermont — have historically disfavored same-sex relationships, more recent legislation plainly undermines the contention. . . .

Thus, viewed in the light of history, logic, and experience, we conclude that none of the interests asserted by the State provides a reasonable and just basis for the continued exclusion of same-sex couples from the benefits incident to a civil marriage license under Vermont law. Accordingly, in the faith that a case beyond the imagining of the framers of our Constitution may, nevertheless, be safely anchored in the values that infused it, we find a constitutional obligation to extend to plaintiffs the common benefit, protection, and security that Vermont law provides opposite-sex married couples. It remains only to determine the appropriate means and scope of relief compelled by this constitutional mandate.

F. Remedy

. . . Although plaintiffs sought injunctive and declaratory relief designed to secure a marriage license, their claims and arguments here have focused primarily upon the consequences of official exclusion from the statutory benefits, protections, and security incident to marriage under Vermont law. While some future case may attempt to establish that — notwithstanding equal benefits and protections under Vermont law — the denial of a marriage license operates per se to deny constitutionally-protected rights, that is not the claim we address today.

We hold only that plaintiffs are entitled under Chapter I, Article 7, of the Vermont Constitution to obtain the same benefits and protections afforded by Vermont law to married opposite-sex couples. We do not purport to infringe upon the prerogatives of the Legislature to craft an appropriate means of addressing this constitutional mandate, other than to note that the record here refers to a number of potentially constitutional statutory schemes from other jurisdictions. These include what are typically referred to as "domestic partnership" or "registered partnership" acts, which generally establish an alternative legal status to marriage for same-sex couples, impose similar formal requirements and limitations, create a parallel licensing or registration scheme, and extend all or most of the same rights and obligations provided by the law to married partners. See Report, Hawaii Commission on Sexual Orientation and the Law (Appendix D-1B) (1995) (recommending enactment of "Universal Comprehensive Domestic Partnership Act" to establish equivalent licensing and eligibility scheme and confer upon domestic partners "the *same* rights and obligations under the law that are conferred on spouses in a marriage relationship") (emphasis added). . . . We do not intend specifically to endorse any one or all of the referenced acts, particularly in view of the significant benefits omitted from several of the laws.

Further, while the State's prediction of "destabilization" cannot be a ground for denying relief, it is not altogether irrelevant. A sudden change in the marriage laws or the statutory benefits traditionally incidental to marriage may have disruptive and unforeseen consequences. Absent legislative guidelines defining the status and rights of same-sex couples, consistent with constitutional requirements, uncertainty and confusion could result. Therefore, we hold that the current statutory scheme shall remain in effect for a reasonable period of time to enable the Legislature to consider and enact implementing legislation in an orderly and expeditious fashion. . . . In the event that the benefits and protections in question are not statutorily granted, plaintiffs may petition this Court to order the remedy they originally sought. . . .

III. Conclusion

While many have noted the symbolic or spiritual significance of the marital relation, it is plaintiffs' claim to the secular benefits and protections of a singularly human relationship that, in our view, characterizes this case. The State's interest in extending official recognition and legal protection to the professed commitment of two individuals to a lasting relationship of mutual affection is predicated on the belief that legal support of a couple's commitment provides stability for the individuals, their family, and the broader community. Although plaintiffs' interest in seeking state recognition and protection of their mutual commitment may — in view of divorce statistics — represent "the triumph of hope over experience," the essential aspect of their claim is simply and fundamentally for inclusion in the family of state-sanctioned human relations.

The past provides many instances where the law refused to see a human being when it should have. See, e.g., Dred Scott, 60 U.S. at 407 (concluding that African slaves and their descendants had "no rights which the white man was bound to respect"). The future may provide instances where the law will be asked to see a human when it should not. . . . The challenge for future generations will be to define what is most essentially human. The extension of the Common Benefits Clause to acknowledge plaintiffs as Vermonters who seek nothing more, nor less, than legal protection and security for their avowed commitment to an intimate and lasting human relationship is simply, when all is said and done, a recognition of our common humanity.

The judgment of the superior court upholding the constitutionality of the Vermont marriage statutes under Chapter I, Article 7 of the Vermont Constitution is reversed. The effect of the Court's decision is suspended, and jurisdiction is retained in this Court, to permit the Legislature to consider and enact legislation consistent with the constitutional mandate described herein.

[The concurring opinion of DOOLEY, J., is omitted.]

JOHNSON, J., concurring in part and dissenting in part. . . .

I concur with the majority's holding, but I respectfully dissent from its novel and truncated remedy, which in my view abdicates this Court's constitutional duty to redress violations of constitutional rights. I would grant the requested relief and enjoin defendants from denying plaintiffs a marriage license based solely on the sex of the applicants. . . .

Notes

1. **Follow-Up to Baehr v. Lewin.** In December 1996, the circuit court to which Baehr v. Lewin was remanded ruled that the state of Hawaii had failed to show any compelling reason for the state's ban on same-sex marriage. Baehr v. Miike, No. 91-1394 (Haw. 1st Cir., Dec. 3, 1996). As anticipated, voters in Hawaii passed a constitutional amendment authorizing the legislature to restrict marriage to opposite-sex couples. Haw. Const. art. I, §23 (Michie Supp. 2000). The legislature had previously found that the people of Hawaii had chosen "to preserve the tradition of marriage as a unique social institution based upon the committed union of one man and one woman." Haw. Rev. Stat. Ann. §572C-1 (Michie 1999). In limiting marriage to opposite-sex couples, the legislature created a "reciprocal beneficiaries" status, permitting unmarried couples, including same-sex couples, to qualify for health benefits, family leave, joint auto insurance, survivorship benefits, property rights, and other benefits. Id. As to some of these benefits, the reciprocal beneficiaries status legislation has been allowed

to expire. See Haw. Rev. Stat. Ann. §87-25.5 (Michie 2000) (repealing entitlement to health benefits for reciprocal beneficiaries after legislature failed to renew prior legislation). Others remain. See, e.g., Haw. Rev. Stat. Ann. §323-2 (Michie 2000) (visitation and health care decision privileges); §327-3 (Michie 2000) (right to execute anatomical gift); §431:10-234 (Michie 1998) (right in life insurance policy); §431:10H-402 (Michie Supp. 2000) (long-term care insurance); §509-2 (Michie 2000) (creation of joint tenancy, tenancy by entirety, and tenancy in common); §560:2-102 (Michie 1999) (right of intestate succession); §560:2-202 (Michie 1999) (right to elective share of decedent's estate); §560:2-402 (Michie 1999) (homestead allowance); §560-2-403 (Michie 1999) (exempt property from decedent's estate); §560:2-404 (Michie 1999) (family allowance).

The Hawaii Supreme Court subsequently dismissed the *Baehr* case. See Baehr v. Miike, 994 P.2d 566 (Haw. 1999).

Litigation in Alaska went much the same way as the Baehr v. Lewin litigation in Hawaii. A trial court in Alaska found a a fundamental right to "choose a life partner" under the Alaska state constitution. Brause v. Bureau of Vital Statistics, 1998 No. 3AN-95-6562 Cl., 1998 WL 88743 (Alaska Super. Ct. 1998). In response, the Alaska legislature approved a constitutional amendment defining marriage as the union of a man and a woman, which the voters also approved. Alaska Const. art. I, §25 (Lexis 2000). The original case was then dismissed. See David Orgon Coolidge & William C. Duncan, Reaffirming Marriage: A Presidential Priority, 24 Harv. J.L. & Pub. Pol'y 623, 628-629 (2001). A subsequent case by the same parties challenging the denial of benefits that were by law available only to married people was dismissed on the grounds that plaintiffs did not show that any specific benefits were denied to them. Brause v. State, 21 P.3d 357 (Alaska 2001).

2. Follow-Up to Baker v. State. Also as anticipated, the Vermont legislature in response to Baker v. State did not extend marriage benefits to same-sex couples, but rather created a new "civil union" status entitling the parties to "all the same benefits, protections and responsibilities under law, whether they derive from statute, administrative or court rule, policy, common law or any other source of civil law, as are granted to spouses in a marriage." Vt. Stat. Ann. tit. 15, §1204 (2001). The requisites of a valid civil union are the same as those for marriage in Vermont, except that the persons do not need to be of the opposite sex. Id. at §§1202, 1203. Couples who do not qualify for either a marriage or a civil union may still qualify as reciprocal beneficiaries, which entitles the parties to make legal decisions for one another, such as those relating to hospital visitation and medical care, anatomical gifts, disposition of remains, and nursing home care. See Vt. Stat. Ann. tit. 15, §§1301-1306 (Supp. 2001).

In the first year after Vermont's recognition of same-sex civil unions, about 2,000 civil-union licenses were granted, with about 80 percent of these granted to out-of-state residents. In that same period, about 5,000 traditional marriage licenses were granted. Tammerlin Drummond, The Marrying King, Time, May 14, 2001, at 52.

3. Reinforcing Opposite-Sex Marriage. While courts and legislatures in Hawaii and Vermont have flirted with same-sex marriage, no state to date allows it and, in fact, the law in many jurisdictions has tightened in favor of allowing only opposite-sex marriage.

First, except for the courts in Hawaii and Vermont, all states that have considered the question have rejected challenges to the exclusion of same-sex couples from marriage. See, e.g., Adams v. Howerton, 486 F. Supp. 1119 (C.D. Cal. 1980), aff'd, 673 F.2d 1036 (9th Cir.), cert. denied, 458 U.S. 1111 (1982) (denying immigration status based on marriage of male couple; deportation of same-sex partner upheld in Sullivan v. Immigration and Naturalization Serv., 772 F.2d 609 (9th Cir. 1985)); Singer v. Hara, 522 P.2d 1187 (Wash. 1974) (same-sex marriages prohibited in Washington notwithstanding state Equal Rights Amendment); Baker v. Nelson, 191 N.W.2d 185 (Minn. 1971), appeal dismissed, 409 U.S. 810 (1972) (Minnesota does not recognize marriage between two men); Murphy v. State of Texas, 653 S.W.2d 567 (Tex. Ct. App. 1983) (same, in Texas). One case attempting to secure a marriage license for two men who wanted to marry (and who also sought $1.25 million in compensatory and punitive damages for the District of Columbia's refusal to grant them a license) was brought under one of the strongest anti-discrimination laws in the country, granting lesbians and gay men "equal opportunity in all aspects of life." D.C. Code §1-2511 (1987). The plaintiffs lost, in light of the contemporaneous enactment of the D.C. Marriage and Divorce Act, which referred only to marriages between "husband" and "wife." See Dean v. District of Columbia, 653 A.2d 307 (D.C. 1995).

Out of concern that the recognition of same-sex marriage in one state might be thought to require other states to recognize such marriages, in 1996 Congress passed the Defense of Marriage Act (DOMA), which permits states to choose not to recognize same-sex marriages performed in another state. See 28 U.S.C. §1738C (1996). At least 34 states have enacted laws pursuant to the DOMA that deny recognition to same-sex marriages regardless of their validity where performed. 1999 Supplement and 2000 Update, at 70-71, to William B. Rubenstein, Cases and Materials on Sexual Orientation and the Law (2d ed. 1997). Some of the state enactments are cited in Larry Kramer, Same-Sex Marriage, Conflict of Laws, and the Unconstitutional Public Policy Exception, 106 Yale L.J. 1965, 1966 n.3 (1997).

It is unclear how much DOMA adds to the law. Although there is not a "roving" public policy exception to the full faith and credit clause, see Baker v. General Motors Corp., 522 U.S. 222, 233 (1998), even without DOMA, if marriages are covered by the full faith and credit clause, the forum's "public policy" remains relevant to which state's law is found applicable to a particular controversy involving the validity of a marriage. See Brian H. Bix, State of the Union: The States' Interest in the Marital Status of Their Citizens, 55 U. Miami L. Rev. 1, 25 (2000); see also Restatement (Second) of Conflict of Laws, §283 (1971).

Several authorities have questioned the constitutionality of DOMA, and state laws passed pursuant to the Act. See, e.g., Diane M. Guillerman, The Defense of Marriage Act: The Latest Maneuver in the Continuing Battle to Legalize Same-Sex Marriage, 34 Hous. L. Rev. 425 (1997); Mark Strasser, *Loving* the *Romer* Out for *Baehr*: On Acts in Defense of Marriage and the Constitution, 58 U. Pitt. L. Rev. 279 (1997). One scholar argues that not only does DOMA violate the full faith and credit clause, but the public policy exception to the rule requiring recognition of out-of-state marriages does as well. See Kramer, supra.

As the next step to restricting same-sex marriage, in July 2001 a new constitutional amendment was proposed by conservative groups, which would be substantially more significant in its effects than DOMA. The federal marriage amendment would, as presently drafted, prohibit any state from enacting same-sex marriage and prevent arrangements that attempt to extend to same-sex couples legal benefits otherwise available only to married couples. The preliminary draft of the amendment provides as follows:

> Marriage in the United States shall consist only of the union of a man and a woman. Neither this Constitution or the constitution of any state, nor state or federal law, shall be construed to require that marital status or the legal incidents thereof be conferred upon unmarried couples or groups.

Jason Carr, Marriage Amendment Should Die a Quiet Death, Houston Chronicle, July 19, 2001, at A35.

4. The Comparative Context. Germany and Holland now recognize same-sex marriages. Belgium and Portugal have been debating legislation that would do the same. Kate Connolly Berlin, The Observer, July 22, 2001, at 19. Among Western countries, Denmark (1989), Norway (1993), Greenland (1994), Sweden (1995), Iceland (1996), and the Netherlands (1998) all recognize a limited form of marriage between same-sex couples, most of them called "registered partnerships." See Nancy G. Maxwell, Opening Civil Marriage to Same-Gender Couples: A Netherlands-United States Comparison, 18 Ariz. J. Int'l & Comp. L. 141 (2001); Barbara J. Cox, But Why Not Marriage: An Essay on Vermont's Civil Unions Law, Same-Sex Marriage, and Separate But (Un)Equal, 25 Vt. L. Rev. 113, 119 (2000). In France, as of 1999, same-sex couples may enter into a "civil solidarity pact," which entitles them to marriagelike rights in the areas of housing and social welfare. Suzanne Daley, France Gives Legal Status to Unmarried Couples, N.Y. Times, Oct. 14, 1999, at A3. In the Czech

Republic, the survivor of a same-sex relationship may inherit the deceased partner's property if they have lived together for three years. Cox, supra, at 119 n.31. See also Edward Brumby, Note, What Is in a Name: Why the European Same-Sex Partnership Acts Create a Valid Marital Relationship, 28 Ga. J. Int'l & Comp. L. 145 (1999).

Canada has liberal same-sex partner immigration regulations. Courts in Canada and Hungary have required that domestic partnership laws applicable to opposite-sex couples also be applied to same-sex couples. In Canada, a leading case is Attorney General v. M. & H., [1999] 2 S.C.R. 3 (exclusion of same-sex partners from the definition of spouse in the Family Law Act for purposes of spousal support violated the Canadian Charter of Rights and Freedoms). The federal Canadian Modernization of Benefits and Obligations Act extends to same-sex partners who have lived together for one year most of the rights and obligations already afforded to heterosexual unmarried partners. See Nicholas Bala, Alternatives for Extending Spousal Status in Canada, 17 Can. J. Fam. L. 169, 184 (2000). Since *M. & H.*, lawsuits have been filed in a number of provinces seeking to establish a right of same-sex couples to marry. Greg Johnson, Vermont Civil Unions: The New Language of Marriage, 25 Vt. L. Rev. 25, 48 (2000).

In Hungary, the Constitutional Court in 1995 ruled that same-sex couples had to be permitted to enter into common law marriage, but not civil marriage. Subsequent legislation in Hungary extended to same-sex couples many marital rights. See id. at 48-49.

Limited rights for same-sex couples have also been created in Spain, New South Wales, Argentina, Israel, and Brazil. Id. at 49. See also William N. Eskridge, Jr., Comparative Law and the Same-Sex Marriage Debate: A Step-by-Step Approach Toward State Recognition, 31 McGeorge L. Rev. 641 (2000) (listing laws and cases of other countries); Nancy D. Polikoff, Recognizing Partners but Not Parents/Recognizing Parents but Not Partners: Gay and Lesbian Family Law in Europe and the United States, 17 N.Y. L. Sch. J. Hum. Rts. 711 (2000) (comparing rights afforded by domestic partnership laws in different countries, including parental rights).

Apparently relatively few same-sex couples have taken advantage of registration procedures that allow them to receive available benefits. See Eskridge, supra, at 653-654, 661 (only 2,372 Danish couples after nine years of registered partnership law, 674 couples after four years of the Norwegian law, 749 after four years of the Swedish law, 45 after two years of the Icelandic law, and 5,217 after one year of the Dutch law). Male couples take advantage of partnership registration at much higher rates than female couples, "in some years at double or triple the rates," although the ratio falls off over time. Id. at 661. Can you think of an explanation for this disparity?

5. Does the U.S. Constitution Support a Right of Same-Sex Marriage? Many advocates argue that there is a constitutional right of same-sex couples to marry. See, e.g., David B. Cruz, "Just Don't Call It

Marriage": The First Amendment and Marriage as an Expressive Resource, 74 S. Cal. L. Rev. 925 (2001) (arguing in favor of a First Amendment right of same-sex couples to marry); Mark Strasser, Equal Protection at the Crossroads: On Baker, Common Benefits, and Facial Neutrality, 42 Ariz. L. Rev. 935 (2000) (arguing that prohibition of same-sex marriage violates federal equal protection guarantee, as well as Vermont constitution); Mark Strasser, Mission Impossible: On Baker, Equal Benefits, and the Imposition of Stigma, 9 Wm. & Mary Bill of Rts. J. 1 (2000) (arguing that "separate but equal" status of civil unions for same-sex couples does not solve constitutional difficulties of same-sex marriage ban).

The case for a constitutional privacy right to same-sex marriage would seem to be completely undermined by the United States Supreme Court's decision in Bowers v. Hardwick, 478 U.S. 186 (1986). In upholding Georgia's criminal statute against sodomy based on what the Court found to be a strong national tradition of prohibiting homosexual acts, *Hardwick* legitimates state laws, founded in traditions deemed at least as strong as those at issue in the case, that restrict state-endorsed marriage to heterosexual couples. Bruce C. Hafen, writing before *Hardwick*, defends the result:

> This society's normative and legal tradition of maintaining laws that . . . [confine sexuality to lawful marriage] is . . . in Justice Harlan's words, a very deliberate "pattern so deeply pressed into the substance of our social life that any Constitutional doctrine in this area must build upon that basis." [Poe v. Ullman, 367 U.S. 497, 546 (1961) (Harlan, J., dissenting).] To extend constitutionally sanctioned sexual privacy beyond marriage would not only depart from that pattern, it would seriously undermine it.

Hafen, The Constitutional Status of Marriage, Kinship, and Sexual Privacy: Balancing the Individual and Social Interests, 81 Mich. L. Rev. 463, 543 (1983). How do you respond to this point? The most complete set of arguments against the constitutionality claims for same-sex marriages is found in George W. Dent, Jr., The Defense of Traditional Marriage, 15 J.L. & Politics 581 (1999); Lynn Wardle, A Critical Analysis of Constitutional Claims for Same-Sex Marriage, 1996 B.Y.U. L. Rev. 1; see also Lynn D. Wardle, Legal Claims for Same-Sex Marriage: Efforts to Legitimize a Retreat from Marriage by Redefining Marriage, 39 Tex. L. Rev. 735 (1998) (recognition of same-sex marriage would represent devaluation of marriage, and thus compromise important goals that marriage serves in this society).

Given Loving v. Virginia, the claim to a right to same-sex marriage may seem stronger than the privacy claim, as the court in *Baehr* finds. But isn't the state entitled to define marriage as it wishes? The courts, by and large, have assumed so.

> [I]t is apparent that the state's refusal to grant a license allowing the appellants to marry . . . is based upon the state's recognition that our society as a whole views marriage as the appropriate and desirable form for procreation and the

rearing of children. This is true even though married couples are not required to become parents and even though some couples are incapable of becoming parents and even though not all couples who produce children are married. These, however, are exceptional situations. The fact remains that marriage exists as a protected legal institution primarily because of societal values associated with the propagation of the human race. Further, it is apparent that no same-sex couple offers the possibility of the birth of children by their union. Thus the refusal of the state to authorize same-sex marriage results from such impossibility of reproduction rather than from an invidious discrimination "on account of sex."

Singer v. Hara, 522 P.2d at 1195.

Is this reasoning strengthened or weakened by the fact that approximately 20 percent of married heterosexual couples will not have a child? U.S. Bureau of the Census, Fertility of American Women: Population Characteristics, June 1998, Current Population Reports Series P-20, No. 526, Table C, at 4 (2000). When an estimated 30 percent share of unmarried-partner households are same-sex couples? Alternative Family Lifestyles, Forecast, June 18, 2001, at 8-9. When about 9 percent of households with two unrelated adults and children are households in which the adult partners are of the same sex? See U.S. Census Bureau, Marital Status and Living Arrangements, Table 8, Households with Two Unrelated Adults, by Marital Status, Age, and Sex: 1998, at 71 (December 1998). When "there are as many as 3 million gay fathers and 5 million lesbian mothers in the United States who are parents to an estimated 14 million children"? See Devon Brooks & Sheryl Goldberg, Gay and Lesbian Adoptive and Foster Care Placements: Can They Meet the Needs of Waiting Children?, 46 Social Work 147, 148 (Apr. 2001); see also Mary Becker, Family Law in the Secular State and Restrictions on Same-Sex Marriage: Two Are Better than One, 2001 U. Ill. L. Rev. 1, 48 (reporting data that 32 percent of lesbians, as compared to 36 percent of heterosexual women, and 15 percent of gay men, as compared to 28 percent of heterosexual men, have children at home); Judith Stacey & Timothy J. Biblarz, (How) Does the Sexual Orientation of Parents Matter, 66 Am. Soc. Rev. 159, 164 (2001) (analyzing data and concluding that somewhere between 1 and 12 percent of all children have a gay or lesbian parent). See Jennifer Wriggins, Marriage Law and Family Law: Autonomy, Interdependence, and Couples of the Same Gender, 41 B.C. L. Rev. 265 (2000) (allowing same-sex marriage supports pro-family, communitarian values).

Does a nonsubordination rationale strengthen the analogy to *Loving* and help to support the result in *Baehr*? Consider the following:

[T]he taboo against homosexuality is not entirely irrational, but serves a function, and that function is similar to the function served by the taboo against miscegenation. Both taboos police the boundary that separates the dominant from the dominated in a social hierarchy that rests on a condition of birth. In the same way that the prohibition of miscegenation preserved the polarities of race on which white supremacy rested, the prohibition of homosexuality preserves the polarities of gender on which rests subordination of women.

Andrew Koppelman, Why Discrimination Against Lesbians and Gay Men Is Sex Discrimination, 69 N.Y.U. L. Rev. 197, 101 (1994). Is this a promising line of argument?

6. Domestic Partnership Benefits. As of August 22, 2001, 113 state and local governments, 155 colleges and universities, 145 Fortune 500 companies, and 3,872 other private companies, nonprofits, and unions offered domestic partner health benefits. For a continually updated count provided by the Human Rights Campaign, see http://www.hrc. org/worknet.; see also http://www.lambdalegal.org; Nancy Levit, A Different Kind of Sameness: Beyond Formal Equality and Antisubordination Strategies in Gay Legal Theory, 61 Ohio St. L.J. 867 (2000).

Local government employee benefit plans have been voided in some jurisdictions on the grounds that the plans exceeded local home rule authority. See Arlington County v. White, 528 S.E.2d 706 (Va. 2000) (invalidating extension of health insurance benefits to domestic partners of county employees); Connors v. City of Boston, 714 N.E.2d 335 (Mass. 1999) (invalidating Boston mayor's Executive Order extending group health benefits to domestic partners of city employees).

Without specific rules or policies extending benefits to same-sex couples, courts have not been friendly to claims that domestic partners should be entitled to the kinds of benefits afforded to legal spouses. See, e.g., Raum v. Restaurant Associates, Inc., 675 N.Y.S.2d 343 (App. Div. 1st Dept.), appeal dismissed, 704 N.E.2d 229 (N.Y. 1998) (denying same-sex partner right to bring wrongful death action following his lover's death from food poisoning); University of Alaska v. Tumeo, 933 P.2d 1147 (Alaska 1997) (denial of health insurance benefits to domestic partners of university employees not in violation of state human rights act); Rutgers Council of AAUP Chapters v. Rutgers, 689 A.2d 828 (N.J. Super. Ct. App. Div. 1997) (denial of health insurance benefits to same-sex domestic partners of employees did not violate state's law against discrimination, right to equal protection under state constitution, or order prohibiting executive branch agencies from discrimination on basis of sexual orientation); In re Estate of Cooper, 592 N.Y.S.2d 797 (App. Div. 1993) (surviving member of homosexual couple has no right of election against partner's will); Coon v. Joseph, 237 Cal. Rptr. 873 (Ct. App. 1987) (gay partner does not qualify as "close relationship" for purposes of recovery for tort of intentional infliction of emotional distress).

There are a few exceptions. In Tanner v. Oregon Health Sciences University, 971 P.2d 435 (Or. Ct. App. 1998), for example, a university's failure to extend eligibility for life and medical insurance benefits to domestic partners was held to violate the Oregon Constitution, which forbids granting privileges or immunities to one group of citizens without granting them equally to other groups. Under the decision, gay or lesbian employees could obtain benefits by swearing that they and their partners have "continuously lived together as a family and shared a close personal relationship, which is exclusive and loving, for an extended period of time, and they intend to maintain that family and relationship with each other for the rest of their lives." 971 P.2d at 439. See also Levin v. Yeshiva University, 730 N.Y.S.2d 15 (N.Y. 2001) (lesbian couple raised a question of fact about whether policy of excluding same-sex couples from Yeshiva University's family housing violated New York City human rights law because it created a disparate impact based on sexual orientation as a result of the fact that unmarried same-sex couples could not marry, whereas unmarried opposite-sex couples could; dismissal of claim against University reversed by unanimous court); Braschi v. Stahl Assocs., 543 N.E.2d 49 (N.Y. 1989) (construing rent control statute to include surviving partner of the leaseholder).

The cases in this area parallel decisions involving unmarried cohabitants, who are also generally unsuccessful in seeking some of the customary incidents of marriage. See, e.g., Norman v. Unemployment Ins. Appeals Bd., 663 P.2d 904 (Cal. 1983) (leaving work to follow unmarried cohabitant does not satisfy "good cause" requirement to obtain state unemployment insurance benefits).

As between parties, cases involving unmarried heterosexual couples and same-sex couples are receiving similar treatment. Compare, e.g., Marvin v. Marvin, 557 P.2d 106 (Cal. 1976) (express or implied contract between unmarried cohabitants is enforceable as to those aspects not involving "meretricious" services) with Crooke v. Gilden, 414 S.E.2d 645 (Ga. 1992) (enforcing lesbian cohabitation contract, without mentioning sexual orientation of either) and Posik v. Layton, 695 So. 2d 759 (Fla. Dist. Ct. App. 1997) (cohabitation agreement between unmarried homosexual adults enforceable on standard contract principles). Those promoting the contract route to rights for same-sex couples, at least as a second-best option, include Martha M. Ertman, Contractual Purgatory for Sexual Marginorities: Not Heaven, but Not Hell Either, 73 Denv. U. L. Rev. 1107 (1996) (arguing that contracts offer a medium ground (or "purgatory") for persons not legally allowed to marry); Raymond C. O'Brien, Domestic Partnership: Recognition and Responsibility, 32 San Diego L. Rev. 164 (1995) (promoting legally recognized domestic partnerships). But see Mary Becker, Problems with the Privatization of Heterosexuality, 73 Denv. U. L. Rev. 1169 (1996) (expressing reservations about contract approach, since in heterosexual couples, it facilitates the domination of one party by the other).

Are legal benefits the only thing, or even the main thing, at stake in the controversy over same-sex marriage? See Mary Becker, Family Law in the

Secular State and Restrictions on Same-Sex Marriage: Two Are Better than One, 2001 U. Ill. L. Rev. 1, 31-44 (stressing importance of availability of marriage as a source of emotional support to its participants, and describing research showing that, even controlling for differences between cohabitors and those who marry, cohabitors are less happy and more depressed than their married counterparts).

7. Gay and Lesbian Marriage: Dominance or Freedom? The gay and lesbian community is split over whether legal reform that permits marriage of same-sex couples would be beneficial to homosexuals. On the one hand, from an "equal treatment" perspective, gay and lesbian marriage would permit homosexual couples to obtain some of the legal benefits of marriage — many of these summarized in *Baehr* — on the same basis as heterosexual couples. In addition, recognition of same-sex marriage would help to "normalize" the status of gays and lesbians, thus both stabilizing those relationships themselves and potentially eliminating some of the fears and prejudice surrounding homosexuality in society at large. The fullest analyses of same-sex marriage from a positive perspective include William Eskridge, The Case for Same-Sex Marriage (1996); David L. Chambers, What If? The Legal Consequences of Marriage and the Legal Needs of Lesbian and Gay Male Couples, 95 Mich. L. Rev. 447 (1996). One of the classics on why gays and lesbians should work to make marriage legal for themselves and their partners is Thomas Stoddard, Why Gay People Should Seek the Right to Marry, 2 Out/Look, Nat'l Gay & Lesbian Q. 9 (Fall 1989).

On the other hand, some commentators have pointed out that gays should be suspicious of gaining access to social forms that have historically defined and controlled women in oppressive ways. Perhaps not surprisingly, this argument has been pursued less by gay men than by lesbians, who worry that importing the trappings of heterosexual relationships into lesbian relations ("hetero-relationizing") will weaken the broader, extended relationships within lesbian communities; encourage possessive, patriarchal-style patterns of submission and dominance; and cultivate unacceptable distinctions between married and unmarried lesbians. Consider the following:

> [M]arriage will not liberate us as lesbians and gay men. In fact, it will constrain us, make us more invisible, force our assimilation into the mainstream, and undermine the goals of gay liberation. [A]ttaining the right to marry will not transform our society from one that makes narrow, but dramatic, distinctions between those who are married and those who are not married to one that respects and encourages choice of relationships and family diversity. Marriage runs contrary to two of the primary goals of the lesbian and gay movement: the affirmation of gay identity and culture; and the validation of many forms of relationships. . . .
>
> . . . Justice for gay men and lesbians will be achieved only when we are accepted and supported in this society *despite* our differences from the

dominant culture and the choices we make regarding our relationships. Being queer is more than setting up house, sleeping with a person of the same gender, and seeking state approval for doing so. It is an identity, a culture with many variations. It is a way of dealing with the world by diminishing the constraints of gender roles which have for so long kept women and gay people oppressed and invisible. Being queer means pushing the parameters of sex, sexuality, and family, and in the process transforming the very fabric of society.
. . .

   The moment we argue, as some among us insist on doing, that we should be treated as equals because we are really just like married couples and hold the same values to be true, we undermine the very purpose of our movement and begin the dangerous process of silencing our different voices. As a lesbian, I am fundamentally different from non-lesbian women. That's the point. Marriage, as it exists today, is antithetical to my liberation as a lesbian and as a woman because it mainstreams my life and voice. I do not want [to] be known as "Mrs. Attached-To-Somebody-Else." Nor do I want to give the state the power to regulate my primary relationship.

Paula L. Ettelbrick, Since When Is Marriage a Path to Liberation, 2 Out/Look, Nat'l Gay & Lesbian Q. 9, 14 (Fall 1989). For related views, see Nancy D. Polikoff, We Will Get What We Ask For: Why Legalizing Gay and Lesbian Marriage Will Not "Dismantle the Legal Structure of Gender in Every Marriage," 79 Val. L. Rev. 1535 (1993); Paula L. Ettelbrick, Wedlock Alert: A Comment on Lesbian and Gay Family Recognition, 5 J.L. & Pol'y 107 (1996); Ruthann Robson & S.E. Valentine, Lov(h)ers: Lesbians as Intimate Partners and Lesbian Legal Theory, 63 Temp. L. Rev. 511 (1990); Mary C. Dunlap, The Lesbian and Gay Marriage Debate: A Microcosm of Our Hopes and Troubles in the Nineties, 1 Law & Sexuality 63 (1991). See also Katha Pollitt, Gay Marriage? Don't Say I Didn't Warn You, in Subject to Debate: Sense and Dissents on Women, Politics, and Culture 109 (Katha Pollitt ed. 2001) ("Marriage will not only open up to gay men and lesbians whole new vistas of guilt, frustration, claustrophobia, bewilderment, unfairness and sorrow, it will offer them the opportunity to prolong this misery by tormenting each other in court."). For further views, both for and against, see Same-Sex Marriage: Pro and Con, A Reader (Andrew Sullivan ed. 1997).
   Is it necessary to choose between these various perspectives?

Putting Theory Into Practice

   4-12. Roberta, who was born with male genitalia, has a successful operation to align his biological sex with his psychological sex, which is female. He then marries George. Ten years later, Roberta files for divorce and seeks spousal support against George. George challenges the validity of the marriage on the grounds that the state does not recognize marriage

between two men. Who should win? Compare In re Estate of Gardiner, 22
P.3d 1086 (Kan. Ct. App. 2001) and M.T. v. J.T., 355 A.2d 204 (N.J.
Super. Ct. App. Div. 1976) (transsexual marriage valid) with Littleton v.
Prange, 9 S.W.3d 223 (Tex. Ct. App. 1999) and In re Ladrach, 513 N.E.2d
828 (Ohio P. Ct. 1987) (transsexual marriage not valid). See also Chapter 7,
section A(3).

4-13. Assume the following two cases. The first involves a man and a
woman who were married for one year, during which time the man, a pro
basketball player, earned almost $3 million, $2 million of which he saved.
Under state law, at divorce the woman is entitled to half of that amount as
her share of the community property. The second involves the break-up of
two gay men who lived together for over 20 years, during which time one of
them encouraged the economic dependence of the other. At the time of the
break-up, the dependent partner sought a share of the $2 million in assets
held by the other partner that were accumulated during their relationship.
Because the parties are not married, he is not entitled to any of these assets.

Are these outcomes coherent? Can they be justified? See American Law
Institute, Principles of the Law of Family Dissolution: Analysis and
Recommendation, Proposed Final Draft, Part I, Chapter 5 (Feb. 14, 1997),
and American Law Institute, Principles of the Law of Family Dissolution:
Analysis and Recommendation, Tentative Draft No. 4, Chapter 6 (Apr. 10,
2000) (comprehensive recommendations for equalizing treatment of support issues at family dissolution between family relationships based on
marriage and domestic partnerships).

2. Lesbian Parent Is Not a Parent

In the Matter of Alison D. v. Virginia M.
569 N.Y.S.2d 586 (N.Y. 1991)

PER CURIAM.

At issue in this case is whether petitioner, a biological stranger to a child
who is properly in the custody of his biological mother, has standing to seek
visitation with the child under Domestic Relations Law §70. Petitioner relies
on both her established relationship with the child and her alleged
agreement with the biological mother to support her claim that she has
standing. We agree with the Appellate Division . . . that, although petitioner
apparently nurtured a close and loving relationship with the child, she is not
a parent within the meaning of Domestic Relations Law §70. Accordingly,
we affirm.

I

Petitioner Alison D. and respondent Virginia M. established a relationship in September 1977 and began living together in March 1978. In March 1980, they decided to have a child and agreed that respondent would be artificially inseminated. Together, they planned for the conception and birth of the child and agreed to share jointly all rights and responsibilities of childrearing. In July 1981, respondent gave birth to a baby boy, A.D.M., who was given petitioner's last name as his middle name and respondent's last name became his last name. Petitioner shared in all birthing expenses and, after A.D.M.'s birth, continued to provide for his support. During A.D.M.'s first two years, petitioner and respondent jointly cared for and made decisions regarding the child.

In November 1983, when the child was 2 years and 4 months old, petitioner and respondent terminated their relationship and petitioner moved out of the home they jointly owned. Petitioner and respondent agreed to a visitation schedule whereby petitioner continued to see the child a few times a week. Petitioner also agreed to continue to pay one half of the mortgage and major household expenses. By this time, the child had referred to both respondent and petitioner as "mommy." Petitioner's visitation with the child continued until 1986, at which time respondent bought out petitioner's interest in the house and then began to restrict petitioner's visitation with the child. In 1987 petitioner moved to Ireland to pursue career opportunities, but continued her attempts to communicate with the child. Thereafter, respondent terminated all contact between petitioner and the child, returning all of petitioner's gifts and letters. No dispute exists that respondent is a fit parent. Petitioner commenced this proceeding seeking visitation rights pursuant to Domestic Relations Law §70. . . .

II

Pursuant to Domestic Relations Law §70 "either parent may apply to the supreme court for a writ of habeas corpus to have such minor child brought before such court; and [the court] may award the natural guardianship, charge and custody of such child to either parent . . . as the case may require." Although the Court is mindful of petitioner's understandable concern for and interest in the child and of her expectation and desire that her contact with the child would continue, she has no right under Domestic Relations Law §70 to seek visitation and, thereby, limit or diminish the right of the concededly fit biological parent to choose with whom her child associates. She is not a "parent" within the meaning of §70.

Petitioner concedes that she is not the child's "parent"; that is, she is not the biological mother of the child nor is she a legal parent by virtue of an adoption. Rather she claims to have acted as a "de facto" parent or that she should be viewed as a parent "by estoppel." Therefore, she claims she has standing to seek visitation rights. These claims, however, are insufficient under §70. Traditionally, in this State it is the child's mother and father who, assuming fitness, have the right to the care and custody of their child, even in situations where the nonparent has exercised some control over the child with the parents' consent. . . . To allow the courts to award visitation — a limited form of custody — to a third person would necessarily impair the parents' right to custody and control. . . . Petitioner concedes that respondent is a fit parent. Therefore she has no right to petition the court to displace the choice made by this fit parent in deciding what is in the child's best interests.

Section 70 gives parents the right to bring proceedings to ensure their proper exercise of their care, custody and control. . . . Where the Legislature deemed it appropriate, it gave other categories of persons standing to seek visitation and it gave the courts the power to determine whether an award of visitation would be in the child's best interests (see, e.g., Domestic Relations Law §71 [special proceeding or habeas corpus to obtain visitation rights for siblings]; §72 [special proceeding or habeas corpus to obtain visitation rights for grandparents]. . . . We decline petitioner's invitation to read the term parent in §70 to include categories of nonparents who have developed a relationship with a child or who have had prior relationships with a child's parents and who wish to continue visitation with the child (accord, Nancy S. v. Michele G., 279 Cal. Rptr. 212 (Ct. App. 1991)). While one may dispute in an individual case whether it would be beneficial to a child to have continued contact with a nonparent, the Legislature did not in §70 give such nonparent the opportunity to compel a fit parent to allow them to do so. . . .

KAYE, Judge (dissenting).

The Court's decision, fixing biology as the key to visitation rights, has impact far beyond this particular controversy, one that may affect a wide spectrum of relationships — including those of longtime heterosexual stepparents, "common-law" and nonheterosexual partners such as involved here, and even participants in scientific reproduction procedures. Estimates that more than 15.5 million children do not live with two biological parents, and that as many as 8 to 10 million children are born into families with a gay or lesbian parent, suggest just how widespread the impact may be (see, Polikoff, This Child Does Have Two Mothers: Redefining Parenthood to Meet the Needs of Children in Lesbian-Mother and Other Nontraditional Families, 78 Geo. L.J. 459, 461, n.2 (1990); Bartlett, Rethinking Parenthood as an Exclusive Status: The Need for Legal Alternatives When the Premise of the Nuclear Family Has Failed, 70 Va. L. Rev. 879, 880-881 (1984) . . .).

But the impact of today's decision falls hardest on the children of those relationships, limiting their opportunity to maintain bonds that may be crucial to their development. The majority's retreat from the courts' proper role — its tightening of rules that should in visitation petitions, above all, retain the capacity to take the children's interests into account—compels this dissent.

In focusing the difference, it is perhaps helpful to begin with what is not at issue. This is not a custody case, but solely a visitation petition. The issue on this appeal is not whether petitioner should actually have visitation rights. Nor is the issue the relationship between Alison D. and Virginia M. Rather, the sole issue is the relationship between Alison D. and A.D.M., in particular whether Alison D.'s petition for visitation should even be considered on its merits. I would conclude that the trial court had jurisdiction to hear the merits of this petition.

The relevant facts are amply described in the Court's opinion. Most significantly, Virginia M. agrees that, after long cohabitation with Alison D. and before A.D.M.'s conception, it was "explicitly planned that the child would be theirs to raise together." It is also uncontested that the two shared "financial and emotional preparations" for the birth, and that for several years Alison D. actually filled the role of coparent to A.D.M., both tangibly and intangibly. In all, a parent-child relationship—encouraged or at least condoned by Virginia M.—apparently existed between A.D.M. and Alison D. during the first six years of the child's life.

While acknowledging that relationship, the Court nonetheless proclaims powerlessness to consider the child's interest at all, because the word "parent" in the statute imposes an absolute barrier to Alison D.'s petition for visitation. That same conclusion would follow, as the Appellate Division dissenter noted, were the coparenting relationship one of 10 or more years, and irrespective of how close or deep the emotional ties might be between petitioner and child, or how devastating isolation might be to the child. I cannot agree that such a result is mandated by §70, or any other law.

Domestic Relations Law §70 provides a mechanism for "either parent" to bring a habeas corpus proceeding to determine a child's custody. Other State Legislatures, in comparable statutes, have defined "parent" specifically (see, e.g., Cal. Civ. Code §7001 [defining parent-child relationship as between "a child and his natural or adoptive parents"]), and that definition has of course bound the courts (see Nancy S. v. Michele G., [279 Cal. Rptr. 212 (Cal. App. 1991) (applying the statutory definition)]). Significantly, the Domestic Relations Law contains no such limitation. Indeed, it does not define the term "parent" at all. That remains for the courts to do, as often happens when statutory terms are undefined.

The majority insists, however, that the word "parent" in this case can only be read to mean biological parent; the response "one fit parent" now forecloses all inquiry into the child's best interest, even in visitation proceedings. We have not previously taken such a hard line in these matters, but in the absence of express legislative direction have attempted to read otherwise undefined words of the statute so as to effectuate the legislative purposes. The Legislature has made plain an objective in §70 to promote "the best interest of the child" and the child's "welfare and happiness."

(Domestic Relations Law §70.) Those words should not be ignored by us in defining standing for visitation purposes — they have not been in prior case law. . . .

As the Court wrote in Matter of Bennett v. Jeffreys, [356 N.E.2d 277 (N.Y. 1976)] — even in recognizing the superior right of a biological parent to the custody of her child — "when there is a conflict, the best interest of the child has always been regarded as superior to the right of parental custody. Indeed, analysis of the cases reveals a shifting of emphasis rather than a remaking of substance. This shifting reflects more the modern principle that a child is a person, and not a subperson over whom the parent has an absolute possessory interest."

Apart from imposing upon itself an unnecessarily restrictive definition of "parent," and apart from turning its back on a tradition of reading §70 so as to promote the welfare of the children, in accord with the parens patriae power, the Court also overlooks the significant distinction between visitation and custody proceedings.

While both are of special concern to the State, custody and visitation are significantly different. . . . Custody disputes implicate a parent's right to rear a child — with the child's corresponding right to be raised by a parent. . . . Infringement of that right must be based on the fitness — more precisely the lack of fitness — of the custodial parent.

Visitation rights also implicate a right of the custodial parent, but it is the right to choose with whom the child associates. . . . Any burden on the exercise of that right must be based on the child's overriding need to maintain a particular relationship. . . . Logically, the fitness concern present in custody disputes is irrelevant in visitation petitions, where continuing contact with the child rather than severing of a parental tie is in issue. For that reason, we refused to extend the Bennett "extraordinary circumstances" doctrine — which relates to the fitness of the custodial parent — to visitation petitions (Matter of Ronald FF. v. Cindy GG., [511 N.E.2d 75 (N.Y. 1987)].

The Court now takes the law a step beyond *Ronald FF.* by establishing the Bennett "extraordinary circumstances" test as the only way to reach the child's best interest in a §70 proceeding. In that *Ronald FF.* determined that extraordinary circumstances are irrelevant in the visitation context, our holding today thus firmly closes the door on all consideration of the child's best interest in visitation proceedings such as the one before us, unless petitioner is a biological parent.

Of course there must be some limitation on who can petition for visitation. Domestic Relations Law §70 specifies that the person must be the child's "parent," and the law additionally recognizes certain rights of biological and legal parents. Arguments that every dedicated caretaker could sue for visitation if the term "parent" were broadened, or that such action would necessarily effect sweeping change throughout the law, overlook and misportray the Court's role in defining otherwise undefined statutory terms to effect particular statutory purposes, and to do so narrowly, for those purposes only.

Countless examples of that process may be found in our case law, the Court looking to modern-day realities in giving definition to statutory concepts. . . . Only recently, we defined the term "family" in the eviction provisions of the rent stabilization laws so as to advance the legislative objective, making abundantly clear that the definition was limited to the statute in issue and did not effect a wholesale change in the law (see Braschi v. Stahl Assocs. Co., [543 N.E.2d 49 (N.Y. 1989)]).

In discharging this responsibility, recent decisions from other jurisdictions, for the most part concerning visitation rights of stepparents, are instructive (see, e.g., Gribble v. Gribble, [583 P.2d 64 (Utah 1978)]; Spells v. Spells, [378 A.2d 879 (Pa. Super. 1977)]). For example in *Spells*, [378 A.2d at 881-882], the court fashioned a test for "parental status" or "in loco parentis" requiring that the petitioner demonstrate actual assumption of the parental role and discharge of parental responsibilities. It should be required that the relationship with the child came into being with the consent of the biological or legal parent, and that the petitioner at least have had joint custody of the child for a significant period of time (see, Rethinking Parenthood as an Exclusive Status, supra, 70 Va. L. Rev. at 945-946). Other factors likely should be added to constitute a test that protects all relevant interests — much as we did in *Braschi*. . . .

It is not my intention to spell out a definition but only to point out that it is surely within our competence to do so. It is indeed regrettable that we decline to exercise that authority in this visitation matter, given the explicit statutory objectives, the court's power, and the fact that all consideration of the child's interest is, for the future, otherwise absolutely foreclosed.

I would remand the case to Supreme Court for an exercise of its discretion in determining whether Alison D. stands *in loco parentis* to A.D.M. and, if so, whether it is in the child's best interest to allow her the visitation rights she claims.

Notes

1. **Custody by Homosexual Parents.** Even biological parents may face difficult custody issues if they are homosexual. The law has followed a number of different approaches. The most extreme approach is that homosexuality renders a parent per se unfit to have custody of a child. This approach was taken in Roe v. Roe, 324 S.E.2d 691, 694 (Va. 1985), but qualified a decade later in Bottoms v. Bottoms, 457 S.E.2d 102 (Va. 1995). In *Bottoms*, the Virginia Supreme Court stated that Virginia does not have a per se unfitness rule, but it upheld a custody award to a maternal grandmother over the objection of a lesbian mother whose "active lesbianism" would likely create social condemnation and disturb the child's

relationship with peers, who disappeared for a day without informing the grandmother of her absence, who moved about "from place to place," who relied on others for support, who used welfare funds to do her fingernails before buying food for the child, and who was previously promiscuous with numerous men in the home. Id. at 108.

More commonly, courts take a parent's homosexuality into account not under a per se unfitness rule, but under an approach that permits an inference that a parent's homosexual conduct is harmful to a child. See, e.g., Ex parte J.M.F., 730 So. 2d 1190, 1194-1196 (Ala. 1998) (upholding modification of custody from mother to father, based on court finding that a change in the mother's lesbian relationship from a discreet affair to one that was "openly homosexual" was a change of circumstances and that the trial court did not abuse its discretion in determining on the basis of "scientific studies" that a change in custody would materially promote the child's best interests); Pulliam v. Smith, 501 S.E.2d 898 (N.C. 1998) (affirming trial court's assumption that homosexual activity within the home, including kissing in the presence of the child and being in bed together, is detrimental to a child's best interests); Tucker v. Tucker, 910 P.2d 1209 (Utah 1996) (upholding trial court award of custody to father over bisexual mother who was involved in monogamous, cohabiting relationship with another woman, based in part on grounds that cohabitation with another person in the presence of the child before the divorce, whether homosexual or heterosexual, had a bearing on her moral fitness). See also Lynn D. Wardle, The Potential Impact of Homosexual Parenting on Children, 1997 U. Ill. L. Rev. 833, 894 (proposing rebuttable presumption that "ongoing homosexual relations by an adult seeking or exercising parental rights is not in the best interests of a child").

Increasingly, however, homosexual orientation or behavior, like heterosexual extramarital sexual conduct, is held to be irrelevant to a parent's fitness unless adverse effects on the children are demonstrated. See, e.g., J.A.D. v. F.J.D., 978 S.W.2d 336, 339 (Mo. 1998) (a homosexual parent is not ipso facto unfit for custody, but it is not error to consider the impact of homosexual or heterosexual misconduct on the children in making a custody determination); Fox v. Fox, 904 P.2d 66 (Okla. 1995) (modification request by father not proper as he had not shown that mother's lesbianism was harmful to the children); Hassenstab v. Hassenstab, 570 N.W.2d 368 (Neb. Ct. App. 1997) (affirming refusal to modify custody of 11-year-old child based on lesbian relationship of mother, in absence of showing that daughter was directly exposed to the sexual activity or that she was in any way harmed by her mother's relationship); In re Marriage of R.S. & S.S., 677 N.E.2d 1297 (Ill. App. Ct. 1996) (overturning trial court modification of custody based on mother's homosexual relationship because no showing made of harmful effect on children). See also American Law Institute, Principles of Family Dissolution: Analysis and Recommendations, Tentative Draft No. 3, Part I, §2.14(1)(d), (e) (subsequently re-numbered §2.12(1)(d), (e)) (Mar.

20, 1998) (prohibiting in custody cases consideration of sexual orientation and consideration of sexual conduct of a parent except when harm to the child is shown). (Much in these Notes is taken from the Commentary to these Principles.)

Generally under the demonstrated harm test, real or imagined stigma from having a homosexual parent is insufficient. In Blew v. Verta, 617 A.2d 31, 35-36 (Pa. Super. Ct. 1992), for example, an appellate court reversed a trial court's limitations on the ability of a lesbian mother to visit with her son in the presence of her lover on the grounds that the child had to learn to accept his parent's homosexuality.

> [O]ne of life's realities is that one of his parents is homosexual. In the absence of evidence that the homosexuality in some way harms the boy, limiting [his] relationship with that parent fails to permit him to confront his life situation, however unconventional it may be. . . . [The child's] best interest is served by exposing him to reality and not fostering in him shame or abhorrence for his mother's non-traditional commitment.

Id. at 36. See also S.N.E. v. R.L.B., 699 P.2d 875, 879 (Alaska 1985) (in affirming trial court award of custody to lesbian mother, court found it "impermissible to rely on any real or imagined social stigma"); Jacoby v. Jacoby, 763 So. 2d 410, 413 (Fla. Dist. Ct. App. 2000) (law cannot give effect to private biases, which in any event "flow not from the fact that the children were living with a homosexual mother, but from the fact that she is a homosexual"); Matter of Adoption of Evan, 583 N.Y.S.2d 997 (Sur. Ct. 1992) (court perpetuates stigma when it denies custody or visitation because of a parent's sexual identity); Conkel v. Conkel, 509 N.E.2d 983, 987 (Ohio Ct. App. 1987) (affirming overnight visitation to bisexual father after concluding that children will have to come to terms with the fact that their father is a homosexual and that the extension of visitation would not exacerbate that issue); M.P. v. S.P., 404 A.2d 1256, 1263 (N.J. Super. Ct. App. Div. 1979) (as a result of exposure to community intolerance, children might be "better equipped to search out their own standards of right and wrong, better able to perceive that the majority is not always correct in its moral judgments, and better able to understand the importance of conforming their beliefs to the requirements of reason and tested knowledge, not the constraints of currently popular sentiment or prejudice"). But see S. v. S., 608 S.W.2d 64, 66 (Ky. Ct. App. 1980), cert. denied, 451 U.S. 911 (1981) (possibility of teasing harassment or damage to the child's mental health as a result of parent's homosexuality may be determinative). For legal commentary on the stigma point, see David K. Flaks, Gay and Lesbian Families: Judicial Assumptions, Scientific Realities, 3 Wm. & Mary Bill of Rts. J. 345, 361-363 (1994); Julie Shapiro, Custody and Conduct: How the Law Fails Lesbian and Gay Parents and Their Children, 71 Ind. L.J. 623, 642-645, 650-654 (1996).

The harm standard can be tricky. A homosexual parent may run into trouble if she is too open about her lesbianism in front of her children. See, e.g., Hertzler v. Hertzler, 908 P.2d 946 (Wyo. 1995) (mother snuggled with children and her female companion in bed, had children march with her in a gay and lesbian rights parade, and had children participate in a "commitment ceremony" with her companion; children had "astonishing grasp of anatomical terminology"); Chicoine v. Chicoine, 479 N.W.2d 891 (S.D. 1992) (given evidence of open homosexual conduct by mother with lover, trial court abused its discretion in allowing unsupervised overnight visitation by mother without home study and enforcement measures to assure compliance with restrictions). On the other hand, if a parent lies about her relationship with her lover, that deception is a character flaw that may constitute an independent basis for concluding that the parent is unfit. See, e.g., T.C.H. v. K.M.H., 784 S.W.2d 281 (Mo. Ct. App. 1989) (mother's "lies" denying her homosexuality are evidence in support of trial court's award of custody to father, despite preference of children to live with mother).

Other cases in which the harm standard was satisfied include Marlow v. Marlow, 702 N.E.2d 733 (Ind. Ct. App. 1998) (upholding restrictions on visitation by gay father of three young sons who were being raised by their mother in a conservative Christian setting in which homosexuality was considered a sin and who had exhibited behavior consistent with emotional distress while visiting with their father, including bed-wetting, difficulty sleeping, and nightmares); Piatt v. Piatt, 499 S.E.2d 567, 570 (Va. Ct. App. 1998) (upholding award of primary physical custody to the father based on findings that the mother's post-separation sexual relationships with other women and her "experimentation" with her sexual orientation had manifested her inner "turmoil" and "lack of control," which had a direct bearing on her ability to provide a stable home environment); In re Marriage of Martins, 645 N.E.2d 567 (Ill. App. Ct. 1995) (mother failed to give adequate time and attention to the children after announcement that she was a lesbian and had multiple female roommates whose moving in and out of the home the children did not like; also, children had behavioral problems and emotional struggles, requiring counseling).

2. Lesbian De Facto Parents. Until recently, *Alison D.* represented the clear majority approach to lesbian co-parent cases. Almost all courts denied visitation and custody rights to lesbians who were de facto, nonbiological parents, either because they lacked standing or because they failed to meet the substantive criteria for parenthood under the state's custody statute. See also West v. Sacramento County, 69 Cal. Rptr. 2d 160 (Cal. Ct. App. 1997); Liston v. Pyles, No. 97APF01-137, 1997 WL 467327 (Ohio Ct. App. Aug. 12, 1997); McGuffin v. Overton, 542 N.W.2d 288 (Mich. Ct. App. 1995), appeal denied, 546 N.W.2d 256 (Mich. 1996).

In 1995, a Wisconsin case provided a framework for awarding custody to a lesbian co-parent. See In re Marriage of H.S.H.-K., 533 N.W.2d 419 (Wis. 1995) (court has equitable power to hear visitation petition by co-parent of lesbian mother upon the parties' separation). This case, like others that followed, applied equitable doctrines such as equitable parenthood, parent by estoppel, or *in loco parentis* to extend rights to visitation or, in some cases, custody, to lesbian co-parents. See, e.g., Rubano v. DiCenzo, 759 A.2d 959, 966 (R.I. 2000) (lesbian co-parent entitled to bring action to enforce visitation agreement); V.C. v. M.J.B., 748 A.2d 529 (N.J. 2000) (upholding standing of lesbian co-parent, who was child's psychological parent, to seek visitation or custody); E.N.O. v. L.M.M., 711 N.E.2d 886 (Mass. 1999), cert. denied, 528 U.S. 1005 (1999) (upholding visitation award to woman with whom biological mother had made a co-parenting agreement); LaChapelle v. Mitten, 607 N.W.2d 151 (Minn. Ct. App. 2000) (lesbian partner who undertook to raise child together with child's biological mother has standing in custody action after separation from mother); Fowler v. Jones, 949 S.W.2d 442 (Tex. Ct. App. 1997) (under Texas statute, lesbian co-parent has standing to seek "possessory conservatorship" if had actual care, control, and possession of child for not less than six months preceding filing of petition), rev'd on other grounds, 969 S.W.2d 429 (Tex. 1998); J.A.L. v. E.P.H., 682 A.2d 1314 (Pa. Super. Ct. 1996) (mother's former long-term partner has standing to seek partial custody of child).

In addition to the hostility to homosexual parents, which will be explored in the next note, the long and deep tradition that a child should have no more than one father and one mother presents a barrier to the recognition of same-sex co-parents. Legal proposals for securing parental status for lesbian co-parents have thus focused on how existing legal definitions of exclusive parenthood might be altered. See, e.g., Nancy D. Polikoff, This Child Does Have Two Mothers: Redefining Parenthood to Meet the Needs of Children in Lesbian-Mother and Other Nontraditional Families, 78 Geo. L.J. 459 (1990) (developing concept of equitable parenthood); Katharine T. Bartlett, Rethinking Parenthood as an Exclusive Status: The Need for Legal Alternatives When the Premise of the Nuclear Family Has Failed, 70 Va. L. Rev. 879 (1984) (advocating non-exclusive parenthood status for nonparents who have developed significant custodial relationships).

The most promising current avenue for lesbian co-parents seeking to establish a legal parental status is co-parent adoption, which is allowed in a growing number of jurisdictions, including the state in which *Alison D.* was decided. See Matter of Jacob, 660 N.E.2d 397 (N.Y. 1995); Galen v. Galen, 680 N.E.2d 70 (Mass. 1997); In re B.L.V.B., 628 A.2d 1271 (Vt. 1993); Adoption of Two Children by H.N.R., 666 A.2d 535 (N.J. Super. Ct. App. Div. 1995); Petition of K.M. & D.M., 653 N.E.2d 888 (Ill. Ct. App. 1995); In re M.M.D., 662 A.2d 837 (D.C. 1995). See also Nancy G. Maxwell et al., Legal Protection for All the Children: Dutch-United States Comparison of Lesbian and Gay Parent Adoptions, 17 Ariz. J. Int'l & Comp. L. 309, 315 n.27 (2000) (describing trial cases allowing adoptions to same-sex couples in Alaska, California, Indiana, Oregon, Texas, and Washington and describing conflicting authority in Pennsylvania).

Adoptions by homosexuals are expressly prohibited in Florida. Fla. Stat. Ann. §63.042(3) (West 1997). See Lofton v. Kearney, 157 F. Supp. 2d 1372 (S.D. Fla. 2001) (upholding statute from constitutional challenge). In addition, gay parent adoption may be unavailable to the partner of a gay or lesbian parent, even though it is not explicitly barred, in those jurisdictions that prevent second-parent adoption by a person of the same sex as the biological parent who wishes to retain parental rights. See, e.g., In the Interest of Adoption of Baby Z., 724 A.2d 1035 (Conn. 1999); Matter of Adoption of T.K.J., 931 P.2d 488 (Colo. App. Ct. 1996), cert. denied, 1997 Colo. LEXIS 70 (Colo. Jan. 21, 1997); In re Angel Lace M., 516 N.W.2d 678 (Wis. 1994).

3. The Resistance to Gay and Lesbian Parenting. What exactly is the nature of the opposition to lesbian and gay custody of children? Among the most deeply held rationales would seem to be that lesbian and gay parents are bad role models and that their children are not well adjusted. The studies seem to show, however, that children of homosexuals do not differ significantly in their psychosocial development from children in heterosexual families. A study by Richard Green and others, for example, comparing children raised by 50 lesbian mothers (30 daughters, 26 sons) with children raised by 40 single heterosexual mothers (28 daughters, 20 sons), found no differences on measures of intelligence, gender identity, wishes to be the other sex, popularity with peers, or social adjustment. See Richard Green et al., Lesbian Mothers and Their Children: A Comparison with Solo Parent Heterosexual Mothers and Their Children, 15 Archives Sexual Behav. 167 (1986). In the Green study, there were some differences in the daughters studied: daughters of lesbian mothers were more likely to dress in boys' clothes, aspire to traditional masculine occupations, and demonstrate interests in boy-type activities. Id. at 176-179. Should this be a cause for concern? See also Raymond W. Chan, Barbara Raboy, & Charlotte J. Patterson, Psychosocial Adjustment Among Children Conceived via Donor Insemination by Lesbian and Heterosexual Mothers, 69 Child Development 443, 453-455 (1998) (concluding, based on study of 80 families who had conceived children through artificial insemination, 55 headed by lesbians and 25 by heterosexual parents, that child's psychosocial adjustment was not affected by either sexual orientation of parents or number of parents in household); David K. Flaks et al., Lesbians Choosing Motherhood: A Comparative Study of Lesbian and Heterosexual Parents and Their Children, 31 Developmental Psychology 105, 111-112 (1995) (comparing 15 lesbian couples and 15 matched heterosexual-parent families and finding no significant differences between children's cognitive functioning and behavioral adjustment); Julie Schwartz Gottman, Children of Gay and Lesbian Parents, in Homosexuality and Family Relations 177, 190 (Frederick W. Bozett & Marvin B. Sussman eds., 1990) (daughters of lesbian mothers achieved scores for femininity and masculinity that closely resemble standard population norms; no evidence that they become homosexual themselves); Sharon L. Huggins, A Comparative Study of Self-Esteem of Adolescent Children of Divorced Lesbian Mothers and Divorced Heterosexual Mothers, in Homosexuality and the Family 123, 131-133 (Frederick W. Bozett ed., 1989) (no significant differences in self-esteem scores of adolescent children with divorced heterosexual mothers and those with divorced lesbian mothers; father's acceptance or nonacceptance of mother's lesbianism has important influence on child's acceptance, which correlates positively with high self-esteem).

Another concern is that homosexual adults, especially men, are likely to molest children to whom they have access. Examination of this fear is complicated by difficulties about whom to count as "homosexual," since many individuals have both homosexual and heterosexual experiences. Sex researcher Alfred Kinsey created a scale to measure the degree of heterosexual preference ranging from 0 to 6, with 0 representing an absolute heterosexual preference and 6 representing an absolute homosexual preference; according to this data, about 4 percent of males are exclusively homosexual, while about 37 percent have had at least one homosexual experience. See Richard A. Posner, Sex and Reason 294 (1992). Reviews of the literature produce no reliable support that homosexual men represent more of a threat to children than heterosexual men. See, e.g., Carole Jenny et al., Are Children at Risk for Sexual Abuse by Homosexuals?, 94 Pediatrics 41, 44 (July 1994) (reporting study showing that children are at no greater risk of being molested by identifiable homosexual adult than by heterosexual adult); Frederick W. Bozett, Children of Gay Fathers, in Gay and Lesbian Parents 39, 47 (Frederick W. Bozett ed., 1987); see also Susan J. Becker, Child Sexual Abuse Allegations Against a Lesbian or Gay Parent in a Custody or Visitation Dispute: Battling the Overt and Insidious Bias of Experts and Judges, 74 Denv. U. L. Rev. 75, 77 (1996) (describing studies).

The methodologies of the various studies concluding that being raised by a homosexual parent is not detrimental to a child are challenged in Lynn D. Wardle, The Potential Impact of Homosexual Parenting on Children, 1997 U. Ill. L. Rev. 833. Among the criticisms are small sample sizes; overreliance on convenience rather than random samples; inappropriate comparison groups; failure to control for such variables as income, education, employment, health, age, religion, and existence of family and other support systems; absence of longitudinal data; and "social desirability" bias in the analysis and collection of data. Id. at 844-852. See also Diana Baumrind, Commentary on Sexual Orientation: Research and Social Policy Implications, 31 Developmental Psychology 130 (1995) (reviewing literature and criticizing methodology of some of the studies); Paul Cameron &

Kirk Cameron, Did the APA Misrepresent the Scientific Literature to Courts in Support of Homosexual Custody?, 131 J. Psychology 313 (1997) (criticizing American Psychological Association and others for misreading studies and ignoring evidence of influence of homosexual parents on sexual orientation of children). For a response to Professor Wardle, see Carlos A. Ball & Janice Farrell Pea, Warring with Wardle: Morality, Social Science, and Gay and Lesbian Parents, 1998 U. Ill. L. Rev. 253, 279-308.

What if it *is* established that being raised by a homosexual parent makes a child more likely to be a homosexual? Should that be considered harm? What if it is established that being raised by a homosexual made a child more accepting of homosexual relationships? Susan Golombok and Fiona Tasker have concluded, from a comparative longitudinal study, that while there is no significant difference in sexual attraction to someone of the same gender between those raised by lesbian single mothers and those raised by heterosexual single mothers, children raised in lesbian families are more likely to consider, and to have, homosexual involvement than are their peers raised by heterosexual mothers. See Golombok & Tasker, Do Parents Influence the Sexual Orientation of Their Children? Findings from a Longitudinal Study of Lesbian Families, 32 Developmental Psychology 3, 7 (1996); Tasker & Golombok, Growing Up in a Lesbian Family: Effects on Child Development 102-114 (1997). Is this a benign factor or an indication of harm? What about evidence that young people from lesbian families report more positive relationships with their mother's female partner, both as adolescents and as adults, than children of heterosexual mothers report with their mother's male partners? See Golombok & Tasker, supra, at 53.

Putting Theory into Practice

4-14. In a dispute over the custody of their five-year-old daughter, Elizabeth, Sam introduces evidence that Robin adheres to the beliefs of some radical lesbians that "our children are the daughters of women who love women over men. Daughters of lesbians, like freedom fighters everywhere, need to be enlisted in infancy, and protected against heterofemininity by words and actions." See Baba Copper, The Radical Potential in Lesbian Parenting of Daughters, in Politics of Mothering: A Lesbian Parenting Anthology 233, 239 (Sandra Pollock & Jeanne Vaughn eds., 1987), cited in Richard A. Posner, Sex and Reason 419 (1992). If you represented Robin, how would you approach this case? What further information might you seek, and what advice would you give your client? If she insists on teaching her daughter, through both words and actions, that a lesbian life-style is preferable to a heterosexual one, what arguments will you use on her behalf? Do you think you should win?

4-15. Thomas orally agreed with a lesbian couple that his sperm would be used to inseminate one of them and that he would forego all parental rights to any child born as a result. They also agreed that Thomas would be available to meet the child if she became curious about her origins. A child was born and when she was about five years old, the couple contacted Thomas so that she could meet him. For the next five or six years, Thomas visited with the child several times and began developing a relationship with her, with the permission of the child's mothers. The parties eventually began to disagree, however, about the length and terms of the visits. Thomas files an action seeking court-ordered visitation. Should he succeed? See Thomas S. v. Robin Y., 618 N.Y.S.2d 356 (App. Div. 1st Dept. 1994) (father entitled to filiation proceeding so that he could pursue a visitation action).

Should advocates of the custodial rights of homosexual parents favor Thomas's claim or not? If so, what access to the child should Thomas be allowed? See Nancy D. Polikoff, Breaking the Link Between Biology and Parental Rights in Planned Lesbian Families: When Semen Donors Are Not Fathers, 2 Geo. J. Gender & L. 57 (2000) (rights of sperm donor should be defined, and limited, by the agreement between the donor and the mother, which should be enforceable); Fred A. Bernstein, This Child Does Have Two Mothers . . . and a Sperm Donor with Visitation, 22 N.Y.U. Rev. L. & Soc. Change 1 (1996) (advocating court-ordered maintenance of sperm donor-child relationship at approximate level permitted by mothers prior to litigation).

3. Employment Discrimination Based on Sexual Orientation

≡≡≡ *DeSantis v. Pacific Telephone & Telegraph Co., Inc.*
608 F.2d 327 (9th Cir. 1979)

CHOY, Circuit Judge. . . .

[Appellants,] all males, claimed that Pacific Telephone & Telegraph Co. (PT & T) impermissibly discriminated against them because of their homosexuality. . . . The district court dismissed their complaint. . . .

[W]e conclude that Title VII's prohibition of "sex" discrimination applies only to discrimination on the basis of gender and should not be judicially extended to include sexual preference such as homosexuality. . . .

Appellants argue . . . that in a trial they could establish that discrimination against homosexuals disproportionately effects men and that this disproportionate impact and correlation between discrimination on the basis of sexual preference and discrimination on the basis of "sex" requires that sexual preference be considered a subcategory of the "sex" category of Title VII. . . . Adoption of this bootstrap device . . . would achieve by judicial "construction" what Congress did not do. . . .

Appellants next contend that . . . an employer generally may not use different employment criteria for men and women. They claim that if a male employee prefers males as sexual partners, he will be treated differently from a female who prefers male partners. . . . We must again reject appellants' efforts to "bootstrap" Title VII protection for homosexuals. . . . [W]e note that whether dealing with men or women the employer is using the same criterion: it will not hire or promote a person who prefers sexual partners of the same sex. . . .

Appellants argue that the EEOC has held that discrimination against an employee because of the race of the employee's friends may constitute discrimination based on race in violation of Title VII. . . . They contend that analogously discrimination because of the sex of the employees' sexual partner should constitute discrimination based on sex.

Appellants, however, have not alleged that appellees have policies of discriminating against employees because of the gender of their friends. That is, they do not claim that the appellees will terminate anyone with a male (or female) friend. They claim instead that the appellees discriminate against employees who have a certain type of relationship, i.e., homosexual relationship with certain friends. As noted earlier, that relationship is not protected by Title VII. . . .

Affirmed.

[The opinion of Judge Sneed, concurring and dissenting, is omitted.]

≡≡≡ *Padula v. Webster*
≡≡≡ 822 F.2d 97 (D.C. Cir. 1987)

SILBERMAN, Circuit Judge.

Appellant Margaret A. Padula alleges that the Federal Bureau of Investigation ("FBI" or "Bureau") refused to employ her as a special agent because of her homosexuality, in violation of both Bureau policy and the equal protection guarantee of the Constitution. Ruling on a motion for summary judgment, the district court rejected both these challenges, concluding that the hiring decision was committed to the FBI's discretion by law and did not infringe upon appellant's constitutional rights. We affirm.

. . . Padula alleges that the FBI refused to hire her solely because of her homosexuality and that this action denied her the equal protection of the law guaranteed by the fourteenth amendment. She urges us to recognize homosexuality as a suspect or quasi-suspect classification. A suspect classification is subjected to strict scrutiny and will be sustained only if "suitably tailored to serve a compelling state interest" . . . whereas under heightened scrutiny given to a quasi-suspect class, the challenged classification must be "substantially related to a legitimate state interest." . . .

We perceive ostensible disagreement between the parties as to the description of the class in question. The government insists the FBI's hiring policy focuses only on homosexual conduct, not homosexual status. By that, we understand the government to be saying that it would not consider relevant for employment purposes homosexual orientation that did not result in homosexual conduct. Plaintiff rejects that distinction, suggesting that "homosexual status is accorded to people who engage in homosexual conduct, and people who engage in homosexual conduct are accorded homosexual status." But whether or not homosexual status attaches to someone who does not — for whatever reason — engage in homosexual conduct, appellant does not claim those circumstances apply to her. The parties' definitional disagreement is therefore irrelevant to this case. The issue presented us is only whether homosexuals, when defined as persons who engage in homosexual conduct, constitute a suspect or quasi-suspect classification and accordingly whether the FBI's hiring decision is subject to strict or heightened scrutiny.

The Supreme Court has used several explicit criteria to identify suspect and quasi-suspect classifications. In San Antonio School Dist. v. Rodriguez, [411 U.S. 1 (1973)], the Court stated that a suspect class is one "saddled with such disabilities, or subjected to such a history of purposeful unequal treatment, or relegated to such a position of political powerlessness as to command extraordinary protection from the majoritarian political process." [Id. at 28.] The immutability of the group's identifying trait is also a factor to be considered. See Frontiero v. Richardson, [411 U.S. 677, 686 (1973)]. However, the Supreme Court has recognized only three classifications as suspect: race . . . alienage . . . and national origin . . . and two others as quasi-suspect: gender . . . and illegitimacy. . . . Appellant, asserting that homosexuals meet all the requisite criteria, would have us add homosexuality to that list. Appellees, on the other hand, contend that two recent cases, Bowers v. Hardwick, [478 U.S. 186 (1986),] and Dronenburg v. Zech, 741 F.2d 1388 (D.C. Cir. 1984), are insurmountable barriers to appellant's claim. We agree.

In *Dronenburg*, a naval petty officer claimed violation of his constitutional rights to privacy and to equal protection of the laws because he was discharged from the Navy for engaging in homosexual conduct. A panel of this court rejected the claim, holding that "we can find no constitutional right to engage in homosexual conduct and, . . . as judges, we have no warrant to create one." Id. at 1397. . . .

Dronenburg anticipated by two years the Supreme Court's decision in *Hardwick*, in which the Court upheld a Georgia law criminalizing sodomy against a challenge that it violated the due process clause. In *Hardwick*, the Court explained that the right to privacy as defined in its previous decisions inheres only in family relationships, marriage and procreation and does not extend more broadly to all kinds of private sexual conduct between consenting adults. 478 U.S. at 191. Putting the privacy precedent aside, the

Court further concluded that a right to engage in consensual sodomy is not constitutionally protected as a fundamental right since it is neither "implicit in the concept of ordered liberty," id. at 191-192 (quoting Palko v. Connecticut, [302 U.S. 319, 325-326 (1937)]), nor "deeply rooted in this Nation's history and tradition." Id. at 192 (quoting Moore v. East Cleveland, [431 U.S. 494 (1977)] (opinion of Powell, J.)). Accordingly, the Court's review of the Georgia statute inquired only whether a rational basis for the law existed. And the Court determined that the presumed beliefs of the Georgia electorate that sodomy is immoral provide an adequate rationale for criminalizing such conduct. Id. at 196. . . .

. . . We . . . think the courts' reasoning in *Hardwick* and *Dronenburg* forecloses appellant's efforts to gain suspect class status for practicing homosexuals. It would be quite anomalous, on its face, to declare status defined by conduct that states may constitutionally criminalize as deserving of strict scrutiny under the equal protection clause. More importantly, in all those cases in which the Supreme Court has accorded suspect or quasi-suspect status to a class, the Court's holding was predicated on an unarticulated, but necessarily implicit, notion that it is plainly unjustifiable (in accordance with standards not altogether clear to us) to discriminate invidiously against the particular class. . . . If the Court was unwilling to object to state laws that criminalize the behavior that defines the class, it is hardly open to a lower court to conclude that state sponsored discrimination against the class is invidious. After all, there can hardly be more palpable discrimination against a class than making the conduct that defines the class criminal. . . .

That does not mean, however, that any kind of negative state action against homosexuals would be constitutionally authorized. Laws or government practices must still, if challenged, pass the rational basis test of the equal protection clause. A governmental agency that discriminates against homosexuals must justify that discrimination in terms of some government purpose. . . . In *Dronenburg*, the court held that it was rational for the Navy to conclude that homosexual conduct was detrimental to the maintenance of morale and discipline. 741 F.2d at 1398. The court observed that homosexuality "generate[s] dislike and disapproval among many . . . who find it morally offensive," and, moreover, is criminalized in many states. Id.

The FBI, as the Bureau points out, is a national law enforcement agency whose agents must be able to work in all the states of the nation. To have agents who engage in conduct criminalized in roughly one-half of the states would undermine the law enforcement credibility of the Bureau. Perhaps more important, FBI agents perform counterintelligence duties that involve highly classified matters relating to national security. It is not irrational for the Bureau to conclude that the criminalization of homosexual conduct coupled with the general public opprobrium toward homosexuality exposes many homosexuals, even "open" homosexuals, to the risk of possible blackmail to protect their partners, if not themselves. We therefore conclude the Bureau's specialized functions, like the Navy's in *Dronenburg*, rationally justify consideration of homosexual conduct that could adversely affect that agency's responsibilities. The judgment of the district court is hereby Affirmed.

Shahar v. Bowers
114 F.3d 1097 (11th Cir. 1997) (en banc), cert. denied, 522 U.S. 1049 (1998)

EDMONDSON, Circuit Judge.

. . . Plaintiff Robin Joy Shahar is a woman who has "married" another woman in a ceremony performed by a rabbi within the Reconstructionist Movement of Judaism. According to Shahar, though the State of Georgia does not recognize her "marriage" and she does not claim that the "marriage" has legal effect, she and her partner consider themselves to be "married."

Since August 1981, Defendant-Appellee Michael J. Bowers has been the Attorney General of the State of Georgia, a statewide elective office. He has been elected to the office four times. As the Attorney General, Bowers is the chief legal officer of the State of Georgia and head of the Georgia Department of Law (the "Department"). His responsibilities include enforcing the laws of the State by acting as a prosecutor in certain criminal actions. . . .

[After hearing of her "marriage," the Attorney General withdrew an employment offer to Shahar.]

Shahar brought the present action against the Attorney General, individually and in his official capacity, seeking both damages and injunctive relief (including "reinstatement"). She said revoking her offer violated her free exercise and free association rights and her rights to equal protection and substantive due process. Bowers moved for summary judgment on all causes of action. . . .

Even when we assume, for argument's sake, that either the right to intimate association or the right to expressive association or both are present, we know they are not absolute. . . . We conclude that the appropriate test for evaluating the constitutional implications of the State of Georgia's decision — as an employer — to withdraw Shahar's job offer based on her "marriage" is the same test as the test for evaluating the constitutional implications of a government employer's decision based on an employee's exercise of her right to free speech, that is, the balancing test [of Pickering v. Board of Educ., 391 U.S. 563 (1968)]. . . . [G]overnment employees who have access to their employer's confidences or who act as spokespersons for their employers, as well as those employees with some policy-making role, are in a special class of employees and . . . seldom prevail under the First Amendment in keeping their jobs when they conflict with their employers.

As both parties acknowledge, this case arises against the backdrop of an ongoing controversy in Georgia about homosexual sodomy, homosexual marriages, and other related issues, including a sodomy prosecution — in which the Attorney General's staff was engaged — resulting in the well-known Supreme Court decision in Bowers v. Hardwick, [478 U.S. 186] (1986) (criminal prosecution of homosexual sodomy does not violate substantive due process). When the Attorney General viewed Shahar's decision to "wed" openly — complete with changing her name — another woman (in a large "wedding") against this background of ongoing controversy, he saw her acts as having a realistic likelihood to affect her (and, therefore, the Department's) credibility, to interfere with the Department's ability to handle certain kinds of controversial matters (such as claims to same-sex marriage licenses, homosexual parental rights, employee benefits, insurance coverage of "domestic partners"), to interfere with the Department's efforts to enforce Georgia's laws against homosexual sodomy, and to create other difficulties within the Department which would be likely to harm the public perception of the Department. . . .

In addition, because of Shahar's decision to participate in such a controversial same-sex "wedding" and "marriage" and the fact that she seemingly did not appreciate the importance of appearances and the need to avoid bringing "controversy" to the Department, the Attorney General lost confidence in her ability to make good judgments for the Department. . . .

Shahar says that by taking into account . . . concerns about public reaction, the Attorney General impermissibly discriminated against homosexuals; and she refers us to the Supreme Court's recent decision in Romer v. Evans, [517 U.S. 620] (1996). In *Romer*, the Supreme Court struck down an amendment to a state constitution as irrational because the amendment's sole purpose was to disadvantage a particular class of people (to "den[y] them protection across the board," [id. at 1628]) and because the government engaged in "classification of persons undertaken for its own sake, something the Equal Protection Clause does not permit." [Id. at 1629.]

Romer is about people's condition; this case is about a person's conduct. And, *Romer* is no employment case. Considering (in deciding to revoke a job offer) public reaction to a future Staff Attorney's conduct in taking part in a same-sex "wedding" and subsequent "marriage" is not the same kind of decision as an across-the-board denial of legal protection to a group because of their condition, that is, sexual orientation or preference . . . .

We do not decide today that the Attorney General did or did not do the right thing when he withdrew the pertinent employment offer. That decision is properly not ours to make. What we decide is much different and less: . . . the Law Department's . . . Attorney General has made a personnel decision which none of the asserted federal constitutional provisions prohibited him from making.

Affirmed.

TJOFLAT, Circuit Judge, specially concurring, ...

[I]n order to find that Shahar's relationship is protected as an intimate association, we must find that homosexual relationships have "played a critical role in the culture and traditions of the Nation by cultivating and transmitting shared ideals and beliefs." I conclude that this simply is not the case. Shahar has pointed to nothing to suggest that homosexual relationships have played a critical role in our history and tradition. On the contrary, the Supreme Court's decision in Bowers v. Hardwick, [478 U.S. 186] (1986), suggests that homosexual relationships have not played such a role. . . . [A] court cannot engage in *Pickering* balancing without identifying the constitutional source of the employee's right and assigning the right a weight or constitutional value. . . .

GODBOLD, Senior Circuit Judge, joined by BARKETT, Circuit Judge, and KRAVITCH, Senior Circuit Judge, dissenting.

The court en banc has pretermitted decision of whether Shahar has constitutional rights of intimate association or expressive association. Instead it assumes that she enjoyed such rights and decides that these presumed rights have not been violated because the Attorney General acted reasonably in "revoking [Shahar's] employment offer."

I would grasp the nettle and hold that in the particular circumstances of this case Shahar enjoyed rights of intimate association and expressive association and that the Attorney General violated those rights because he did not act reasonably in revoking the agreement made with Shahar.

Shahar does not assert a right to be married as provided by the laws of Georgia (statutory or common law), or to be issued a marriage license, or to inherit from her spouse, or to be entitled to social security benefits through her spouse. She does not question the constitutionality of the Georgia marriage license statute or any provisions of Georgia law that speak in terms of marriage as a ceremony, or as a status, between persons of different sexes. Nor does she question the validity of Georgia principles of common law marriages. As the panel of this Court held in its now-vacated opinion:

> What Shahar claims is that she proposed to — and did — engage in a Jewish religious ceremony that is recognized as a marriage ceremony by the branch of Judaism to which she adheres; that this conferred upon her and her partner a religious-based status that is apart from and independent of civil marriage as provided by Georgia law; and that she can accept, describe, and hold out both the ceremonial event and the status created by it by using the term "marriage."

The religious and historical roots of the associational rights that Shahar defends were spelled out in the panel opinion. Because that opinion has now been vacated, they deserve to be repeated.

> The intimate association Shahar asserts is not based upon false or sham assertions of religious belief, or hasty decision, of overnight conversion. She and her partner grew up in traditional Jewish families. Shahar attended Hebrew school from the third grade. She was bat mitzvahed at age 13 and continued in Hebrew school until she was confirmed at age 16. Greenfield grew up in a conservative, kosher, Jewish home. She went through Jewish training through high school, attended Jewish summer camps, and was involved in Jewish youth groups.
>
> Shahar and Greenfield have been significant participants in the life of their synagogue, located in Atlanta. It is affiliated with the Reconstructionist Movement, one of several movements within Judaism. . . .

The evidence demonstrates without dispute that same-sex marriage is accepted within the Reconstructionist Movement of Judaism, that Shahar and her partner are committed to that belief, and that, in keeping with their Jewish principles, they carefully and thoughtfully prepared for marriage. The Attorney General did not act reasonably. . . . Respectfully, I dissent.

BIRCH, Circuit Judge, joined by BARKETT, Circuit Judge, GODBOLD and KRAVITCH, Senior Circuit Judges, dissenting. . . .

The inferences from Shahar's acknowledged homosexuality that she is likely to violate Georgia's sodomy law, or would be unable or unwilling to enforce Georgia's sodomy or marriage laws, is no more justified on behalf of Bowers or his employees than it is on behalf of the public. Moreover, it is important to note that Bowers' speculation regarding Shahar's ability to handle certain types of cases is just that: speculation. Bowers has emphatically refused to meet with Shahar to discuss any of his concerns. Compounding this deficiency in Bowers' assertion that his prediction is "reasonable" is the fact that Bowers does not make the same assumption with respect to any of his other employees: He does not assume, for instance, that an unmarried employee who is openly dating an individual of the opposite sex has likely committed fornication. . . .

In short, Bowers' asserted interests in taking adverse action against Shahar are based on inferences from her status as a homosexual which Bowers claims that he, the public, and department staff are entitled to make. In light of the Supreme Court's decision in *Romer*, these status-based inferences, unsupported by any facts in the record and explained only by animosity toward and stereotyping of homosexuals, do not constitute a legitimate interest that outweighs Shahar's First Amendment right of intimate association. . . .

[The separate dissenting opinions of Judge Kravitch and Judge Barkett are omitted.]

Toni M. Massaro, Gay Rights, Thick and Thin
49 Stan. L. Rev. 45, 47, 54-56, 92, 95-96 (1996)

[W]hen advancing arguments for gay rights, advocates should avoid thick doctrinal arguments that alter existing legal categories, extend the upper echelon tiers of review, or construct gay rights as such. Rather, they should emphasize thin doctrinal arguments that merely say that homosexuality cannot and should not be a basis for official discrimination. Such a nondiscrimination policy involves only minimal modification of existing legal doctrine. Specifically, litigants should focus attention on the ways in which such discrimination violates minimal — "thin" — principles of neutrality, conventionally understood, and avoid arguments that require the courts to define, or appear to endorse, homosexual or bisexual identities. In short, litigants should address the following question: "What is wrong with homosexuality?", not "What is homosexuality?"

. . . Thick doctrinal arguments appeal to principles such as freedom of speech, privacy, association, and equal protection. Although these arguments present the possibility of achieving success for gay rights advocates, they also heighten the risks of losing the litigation and of provoking a political backlash against these same groups. I suggest that gay rights advocates focus on the thin doctrinal arguments that militate for rationality review and appeal to the reason and empathy of judges and lawmakers. The thin doctrinal approach both appears more moderate, and hence less dangerous . . . and is best suited to deal with the most critical obstacle to gay rights — intolerance. . . . Every litigation strategy that gay advocates have deployed or might deploy leads to a double-bind or boomerang that may constrain gay people more than it liberates them. . . .

Janet Halley's work . . . shows how short-term legal victories may become long-term losses if courts define sexuality in ways that those being defined may later wish to escape. [See Janet E. Halley, The Politics of the Closet: Towards Equal Protection for Gay, Lesbian, and Bisexual Identity, 36 UCLA L. Rev. 915, 972-973 (1989).] Her well-known illustration of this peril is about lawyers who pursue "suspect class" status for gay men and lesbians. In order to secure the judicial review advantages of suspect classes, the lawyers inevitably impose an essentialist framework onto sexuality that later denies the possibility of choice in sexual identity and suppresses the experimental zones that people otherwise might enter or already inhabit. These advocates might unwittingly trade the destructive "sodomy = homosexual" assumption that drove the majority opinion in *Hardwick* for the equally reductive and potentially destructive one that "homosexuality = immutable characteristic." It is unlikely that courts will make a defining move that captures the myriad historical, social, ethnic, religious, economic, familial, and maturational aspects of the desires and behaviors that properly fall under the umbrella of "sexuality." Nuance here is crucial, yet almost impossible to achieve. The available legal compartments are simply too crude. . . .

Even lawyers who are aware of the perils of merging sexual conduct with sexual identity may confront problems in pursuing their litigation strategies. Disaggregating homosexual status and homosexual conduct might secure for gay people the dubious right to say "I am a homosexual," but *not* the right to engage in conduct that might give evidence of that identity, such as holding hands in public, marrying, or engaging in sexual acts with a same-sex partner. These attempts to litigate around judges' tendencies to conflate sexual conduct and homosexual identity may bifurcate the gay or lesbian individual in strange and undesirable ways.

Likewise, arguments that challenge regulation of expressive gay conduct on free speech grounds — that is, recasting conduct between same-sex couples as speech — might be unwise. This approach might assist in getting parade permits, demonstrating on the Mall, or otherwise expressing sexual difference in quintessentially public fora. But it hardly paves the way to inclusion in the curriculum, or admission to other, more discriminating aspects of public life. Indeed, it could well do the opposite: Invoking the "one man's vulgarity" mentality of free speech doctrine could formally relegate gay identity to the same political/moral plane as neo-Nazi or white supremacist expressive conduct, which government cannot suppress but likewise does not condone. More fundamentally, pursuing such a strongly libertarian legal strategy could make it extremely difficult to curtail antigay expression and conduct.

In fact, all of the approaches to gay constitutional rights proposed thus far produce comparable double-binds. One reason for this is quite basic: Legal categories, like other kinds of discourses, tend to repress or problematize nuances. These sophisticated shadings are the underpinnings of the more complex constitutional framework that Halley and many others deem critical to any gay rights worth the candle. The very nature of legal reasoning, especially its reliance on analogical reasoning, demands that lawyers hew to heterosexual norms when arguing for gay rights. However, this strategy, in flattening crucial nuances, produces marginality instead of equality.

Another risk . . . is that courts may analogize gay men and lesbians to other groups with whom they do not want to be linked. Sunstein has phrased this analogical choice posed by gay rights as follows: "Is a ban on homosexual sodomy like a ban on the use of contraceptives in marriage, or like a ban on incest?" [Cass R. Sunstein, On Legal Theory and Legal Practice, in Theory and Practice: NOMOS XXXVII 267, 282 (Ian Shapiro & Judith Wagner DeCew eds., 1995).] Such binarisms foreclose the option of saying, "Homosexual 'sodomy' is nothing like incest or any other activity banned by law, and thus requires a new vocabulary, a new conceptual framework, and a new reference point." . . .

[T]he best doctrinal cover may be rational basis analysis — the thin constitutional rights approach. Unlike strict scrutiny, privacy, free speech, or other doctrinally thick rivals, the thin rights approach minimizes doctrinal props. It forces to the foreground the central issue — whether homosexuality is wrong — and enables judges to hear, free of jargon, the nondoctrinal material that is so crucial to influencing judges on matters of sexuality. . . .

The primary usefulness of . . . empirical arguments is that they . . . tend to show that many of the arguments commonly advanced in support of the regnant accounts of homosexuality are just too flimsy to support government regulation that interferes with such basic, essentially private, decisions as whom to love and marry, with whom to have sexual relations, or which religious account of sexuality to embrace. For example, they help to demonstrate that the state's only justification for sodomy laws is a blanket . . . assertion that the state can enforce whatever laws "the majority" might pass. This argument simply extends too far to make sense in a secular constitutional culture, which has always anticipated that at least some restrictions on popular will can, and must be, enforced by the courts. The arguments thus are best deployed not as calls to reason, but as calls for closer scrutiny of the unreason evident in much judicial and popular thinking on sexuality. . . .

Our constitutional practices also make clear that certain arguments, taken alone, cannot suffice to support antigay legislation. For example, the fact that homosexuals have often been subject to discrimination and prejudice cannot alone justify continued discrimination. . . . The Court's claim in *Hardwick* that proscriptions of homosexuality have "ancient roots" is, by itself, insufficient to continue these prohibitions, particularly when one comes to recognize their steep, cruel cost to many human lives.

Notes

1. Discrimination Based on Sexual Orientation Is Not Discrimination Based on Sex. *DeSantis* states what remains the standard view of Title VII with respect to discrimination against homosexuals: it does not constitute discrimination based on sex. Efforts to enact legislation prohibiting discrimination based on sexual orientation have been largely unsuccessful. A federal law, the Employment Non-Discrimination Act (ENDA), has been proposed in different forms on multiple occasions since 1993. In its most common version, ENDA would "forbid[ ] employers from discriminating on the basis of sexual orientation with regard to hiring, firing, or terms of employment; [and] forbid[ ] retaliatory conduct." Although similar to Title VII, the statute would not apply to military and religious organizations or disparate impact claims. It would not permit affirmative action based on sexual orientation and would not require benefits for domestic partners. Twelve states — California, Connecticut, Hawaii, Maryland, Massachusetts, Minnesota, Nevada, New Hampshire, New Jersey, Rhode Island, Vermont, and Wisconsin — and the District of Columbia have general laws protecting homosexual employees, and only 204 municipalities have such laws. See http://www.lambdalegal.org, last visited November 29, 2001. About 20 other countries have national anti-discrimination laws protecting homosexuals. See www.gayrightsinfo.com. For discussion of domestic partnership laws, see pages 750-752, 754-756, supra.

Why do you suppose that legislation prohibiting employment discrimination based on sexual orientation has been so difficult to enact? Despite the absence of legislative requirements, a growing number of businesses have begun to add sexual orientation to their anti-discrimination policies. Half of Fortune 500 companies now prohibit such discrimination. See Kristin Choo, Some Countries Welcoming Gay, Lesbian Employers at www.womensnews.org, Oct. 6, 2000. What accounts for the greater receptivity of large corporations than legislators?

2. Sexual Orientation and Strict Scrutiny. If discrimination based on sexual orientation is not discrimination based on sex, should it be a specially protected status, like sex or race? Without such a status, any claims of bias would be tested under the rationality standard of review rather than the strict scrutiny standard. Gay rights advocates have frequently attempted to establish that homosexuals as a class have the characteristics required for special constitutional protection: (1) a history of discrimination; (2) exhibition of obvious, immutable, or distinguishing characteristics that define them as members of a discrete group; and (3) political powerlessness, or the burdening of a fundamental right. See Bowen v. Gilliard, 483 U.S. 587 (1987). Do gays and lesbians meet these criteria?

a. History of Discrimination. Many judges, including those in Ben-Shalom v. Marsh, 881 F.2d 454 (7th Cir. 1989), cert. denied, 494 U.S. 1004 (1990), have reasoned that while gays and lesbians have suffered a history of discrimination, they seem to have enough political power today such that discrimination against them is not "invidious." Id. at 465-466. Is this reasoning persuasive? On this reasoning, how would you account for the persistence of discrimination and the lack of legal remedies in areas such as employment, housing, and family law? See note c below.

In upholding a Georgia sodomy statute, the Supreme Court in Bowers v. Hardwick, 478 U.S. 186 (1986), reasoned that the extended history of criminal prohibitions of homosexual conduct was inconsistent with any fundamental right to engage in same-sex practices, even in the privacy of the home.

. . . Proscriptions against that conduct have ancient roots. . . . Sodomy was a criminal offense at common law and was forbidden by the laws of the original thirteen States when they ratified the Bill of Rights. In 1868 when the Fourteenth Amendment was ratified, all but 5 of the 37 States in the Union had criminal sodomy laws. In fact, until 1961, all 50 States outlawed sodomy, and today, 24 States and the District of Columbia continue to provide criminal penalties for sodomy performed in private and between consenting adults.

Id. at 192-194. Is *Hardwick*'s use of history and tradition consistent with the *Ben-Shalom* court's analysis of historical discrimination? Does *Hardwick* allow a history of prior prejudice to serve as justification for perpetuating it?

Consider an alternative view of historical discrimination in a case involving exclusionary policies by the military: "In all probability, homosexuality is not considered a deeply-rooted part of our traditions *precisely because* homosexuals have historically been subjected to invidious discrimination." Watkins v. United States Army, 875 F.2d 699, 719 (9th Cir. 1989) (Norris, J., concurring), cert. denied, 498 U.S. 957 (1990). Which view of history do you find most persuasive? For a history of persecution of homosexuals dating from the third century, see Able v. United States, 968 F. Supp. 850, 852-855 (E.D.N.Y. 1997). For a focus on the criminalization of lesbian conduct, see Ruthann Robson, Lesbianism in Anglo-American Legal History, 5 Wis. Women's L.J. 1, 21-41 (1990).

b. "Exhibition" of "Obvious" or "Immutable" Characteristics. For gays and lesbians, a standard requiring "exhibition" of "obvious" characteristics often poses a no-win situation. Individuals who do not "exhibit" their homosexuality are not entitled to special constitutional review. See Steffan v. Cheney, 780 F. Supp. 1, 5-6 (D.D.C. 1991), aff'd sub nom. Steffan v. Perry, 41 F.3d 677 (D.C. Cir. 1994). On the other hand, the more overt the "exhibition" of sexual orientation, the stronger the argument that gays or lesbians threaten legitimate concerns of order and morale in the workplace. See Steffan v. Perry, 41 F.3d 677 (D.C. Cir. 1994) (en banc); see also Doe v. Gates, 981 F.2d 1316 (D.C. Cir.), cert. denied, 510 U.S. 928 (1993) (upholding discharge of CIA employee not because he was gay, but because he had hidden information about his involvement in same-sex activity that the agency viewed as relevant for security reasons).

The issue of "immutability" poses a related dilemma for gays and lesbians. On the one hand, part of the harm of discrimination is the pressure it creates to suppress, and thereby alter, same-sex orientation. On the other hand, if sexual orientation is alterable, gays and lesbians have the ability to avoid discrimination. The costs of such alteration might be clearer to heterosexuals if they imagined the tables turned:

Would heterosexuals living in a city that passed an ordinance banning those who engaged in or desired to engage in sex with persons of the *opposite* sex find it easy not only to abstain from heterosexual activity but also to shift the object of their sexual desires to persons of the same sex?

Watkins v. United States Army, 847 F.2d 1329, 1347-1348 (9th Cir. 1988), after reh'g, 875 F.2d 699 (9th Cir.), cert. denied, 498 U.S. 957 (1990).

Should the immutability requirement be redefined? Consider Judge Norris's observation in a case involving military policy:

> It is clear that by "immutability" the Court has never meant strict immutability in the sense that members of the class must be physically unable to change or mask the trait defining their class. People can have operations to change their sex. Aliens can ordinarily become naturalized citizens. The status of illegitimate children can be changed. People can frequently hide their national origin by changing their customs, their names, or their associations. Lighter skinned blacks can sometimes "pass" for white, as can Latinos for Anglos, and some people can even change their racial appearance with pigment injections. See J. Griffin, Black Like Me (1977). At a minimum, then, the Supreme Court is willing to treat a trait as effectively immutable if changing it would involve great difficulty, such as requiring a major physical change or a traumatic change of identity. Reading the case law in a more capacious manner, "immutability" may describe those traits that are so central to a person's identity that it would be abhorrent for government to penalize a person for refusing to change them, regardless of how easy that change might be physically. Racial discrimination, for example, would not suddenly become constitutional if medical science developed an easy, cheap, and painless method of changing one's skin pigment.

Watkins, 875 F.2d at 726 (Norris, J., concurring). See also Able v. United States, 968 F. Supp. 850, 863-864 (E.D.N.Y. 1997) (whether or not homosexuality is genetic and immutable, it forms a significant part of a person's identity justifying heightened scrutiny).

Should the criterion of immutability be eliminated altogether? Recall the discussion of the issue of immutability as it related to appearance and weight requirements in Chapter 2 at pages 175-177. Weight is mutable in one sense and immutable in another, but in either case, weight restrictions systematically subordinate women. Janet E. Halley, whose work is discussed in the Massaro reading, has developed an extended critique of immutability analysis. According to Halley, this analysis misrepresents the complex way in which sexual identity develops and the harmful effects of discrimination on that identity. The invidiousness of discrimination does not depend on the immutability of homosexuality. Rather,

> [a]ntihomosexuality discrimination encourages people to manipulate the identity they attach to themselves, both in the secrecy of their own minds and on the public stage, in . . . their subjective and their public identities. It ensures that personal desires, sexual behavior, subjective identity and public identity will frequently get out of sync with each other. However carefully an individual

disposes these elements, they are all subject to sudden, either joyous or catastrophic, rearrangement. That is to say, they are mutable. . . .

Janet E. Halley, The Politics of the Closet: Towards Equal Protection for Gay, Lesbian, and Bisexual Identity, 36 UCLA L. Rev. 915, 933 (1989). See also Janet E. Halley, Sexual Orientation and the Politics of Biology: A Critique of the Argument from Immutability, 46 Stan. L. Rev. 503 (1994).

Halley argues that it is a group's "acute vulnerability in the political process" rather than the immutability of any trait uniting or defining the group that gives rise to the need for stringent constitutional review:

> [I]mmutability is not required by the Court's equal protection precedents, which focus instead on process implications often associated with apparently immutable traits. A proper reading of these precedents demonstrates that the equal protection clause vigilantly protects not monolithic groups but rather the dialogue that generates group identity and suggests that gay rights advocates and courts attend not to product but to process, not to the class but to the classification of homosexuals. . . .

Halley, Politics of the Closet, supra, at 923, 926-927.

Halley's analysis leads to a distinction between discrimination that interferes with public debate and disclosure of sexual orientation, which deserves constitutional protection, and other legislative decisions to deter homosexuality, which do not warrant special constitutional scrutiny. Id. at 923. She finds an analogy to this distinction in First Amendment law that protects speech, but not conduct. Id. at 967. Yet Halley is also critical of the way the speech/conduct distinction has been invoked in contexts such as discrimination by the military. See Section 4 below.

The focus on political vulnerability received some indirect support from the Supreme Court's decision in Romer v. Evans, 517 U.S. 620 (1996). There, for the first time, the Court found that a law penalizing same-sex orientation was unconstitutional. At issue was a Colorado constitutional amendment (Proposition 2) repealing and prohibiting all state and local anti-discrimination policies with respect to homosexuals. In the majority's view, this amendment failed to meet the rational relationship standard under the equal protection clause because it arbitrarily prevented a group from protecting its interests through the normal political process. This discrimination, the Court stated, could not be justified by a "bare desire to harm a politically unpopular group" (quoting Dept. of Agriculture v. Moreno, 413 U.S. 528, 534 (1973)). For discussion of the *Romer* case, see symposia at 68 U. Colo. L. Rev. 285 (1997), and at 50 Vand. L. Rev. 361 (1997); see also Andrew M. Jacobs, *Romer* Wasn't Built in a Day: The Subtle Transformation in Judicial Argument over Gay Rights, 1996 Wis. L. Rev. 893 (1996) (tracing the shift of the gay rights debate from questions about the morality of homosexuality to questions about the consequences and wisdom of penalizing it.)

Legal theories emphasizing the importance of both mutable and immutable forces in the formation of gay identity draw on a wide array of social science research. Most recent work suggests that sexuality is not solely a result of physiological or cultural influences, but rather is shaped through "a complex interaction of biological, psychological, and social forces." See, e.g., Gregory M. Herek, Myths About Sexual Orientation: A Lawyer's Guide to Social Science Research, 1 Law & Sexuality 133, 151 (1991). Such work reinforces concerns about the usefulness of the immutability standard in cases involving sexual orientation. Steffan v. Cheney, 780 F. Supp. at 6-7.

c. Political Powerlessness. The issue of political powerlessness is equally problematic. In Steffan v. Cheney, 780 F. Supp. at 7-9, the court observed:

> . . . Even *if* it were proven that homosexual orientation was immutable, or indeed, not subject to individual choice, it is still very clear that homosexuals as a class enjoy a good deal of political power in our society, not only with respect to themselves, but also with respect to issues of the day that affect them.
>
> It is beyond doubt that the homosexual community has been able to reach out and gain the attention of politicians of all sorts. One need only remember St. Patrick's Day 1991 in New York City to see Mayor David Dinkins marching in the traditionally Irish-Catholic parade with homosexual groups and activists who were important supporters during his tough mayoral campaign. There are many other important and high visibility issues which have brought the homosexual community into the political landscape in this country and in the states, not the least of which is the AIDS epidemic and the related issues of funding for research and drugs, school attendance for children who are HIV-positive, and insurance coverage for victims.
>
> Assuming arguendo that there is continuing antipathy and prejudice exhibited towards the plaintiff's class, it cannot successfully be maintained that the political branches are not paying attention to homosexuals or to those who advocate legislation favorable to them. Just because there are only a few members of Congress who are openly homosexual does not mean that homosexuals are a class without influence. There are not many medical doctors in Congress either, and yet that profession is exceptionally well represented on Capitol Hill. It is far more important to notice that references to sexual orientation, sexual preference and AIDS show up from time to time in the law of the various states, localities, and in the federal law.

How would you try to measure the political influence of gays and lesbians? How does it compare with the influence of other groups that enjoy special constitutional protection? Would it strengthen the argument for stricter scrutiny of sexual orientation cases if Mayor Dinkins had not marched with homosexuals in the St. Patrick's Day parade, if the AIDS epidemic had never occurred, or if references to sexual orientation did not "show up from time to time in the law"?

3. The "Rational Basis" for Discrimination Based on Sexual Orientation. As the court in *Padula* concedes, even if gays and lesbians are not entitled to special protection under the equal protection clause, discrimination against them must be "rational." A growing number of commentators, along with Massaro, claim that challenging the rationality of such discrimination is legally and politically the best line of attack for gay rights advocates. Do you agree? A few courts have found exclusion of homosexuals from the military irrational, only to be reversed on appeal. See, e.g., Steffan v. Aspin, 8 F.3d 57 (D.C. App. 1993), rev'd en banc, Steffan v. Perry, 41 F.3d 677 (D.C. Cir. 1994); Meinhold v. United States Dep't of Defense, 808 F. Supp. 1455 (C.D. Cal. 1993), rev'd, 34 F.3d 1469 (9th Cir. 1994).

How sound are the rationales in support of the exclusion of Margaret Padula from the FBI? In what sense is law enforcement credibility undermined? How about the "possible blackmail" issue? Is this rational in a case in which the plaintiff "is unembarrassed and open about [her sexual orientation] and it is a fact well known to her family, friends and co-workers"? How significant is the concern that even if the plaintiff does not need to protect herself from exposure as a homosexual, she may need to "protect [her] partners"? Padula v. Webster, supra, at 99, 104.

4. Discrimination on the Basis of Sexual Orientation by "Private" Associations. A divided United States Supreme Court in Boy Scouts of America v. Dale, 530 U.S. 640 (2000), upheld the right of the Boy Scouts to exclude members based on sexual orientation. The case involved James Dale, who joined the Scouts at age eight and for the next 12 years was an exemplary member. He earned 25 merit badges and the honored status of Eagle Scout. Shortly after being appointed an assistant troop leader, Dale enrolled at Rutgers University, where he became co-president of the Lesbian and Gay Alliance. His membership in the Scouts was revoked after a Newark newspaper identified him as president and quoted comments that he made in connection with a seminar on health needs of gay and lesbian teens.

Dale then filed a complaint under New Jersey public accommodation law, which bars discrimination based on characteristics such as race, ethnicity, and sexual orientation. The New Jersey Supreme Court upheld his claim, and in a 5-4 decision, the United States Supreme Court reversed. Writing for the majority, Chief Justice Rehnquist concluded that the New Jersey law violated the Boy Scouts' rights of speech and association. Under the Court's analysis, "the presence of a gay rights activist would force the organization to send a message that the Boy Scouts accepts homosexual conduct." According to Scout leadership, such a message would be inconsistent with its oath and laws requiring Scouts to be "morally straight" and "clean" in body and mind.

In upholding the Scouts' policy, the majority relied heavily on its prior decision in Hurley v. Irish-American Gay, Lesbian and Bisexual Group of

Boston, Inc., 515 U.S. 557 (1995). In *Hurley*, the Court ruled that organizers of a St. Patrick's Day parade could not be compelled by Massachusetts public accommodation law to let gays and lesbians march behind a GLBG banner. Just as those parade organizers had the right "not to propound a particular point of view," the Boy Scouts had a right not to convey the message of legitimacy that Dale's membership would imply.

> The Boy Scouts asserts that it "teach[es] that homosexual conduct is not morally straight" . . . and that it does "not want to promote homosexual conduct as a legitimate form of behavior. . . ." We need not inquire further to determine the nature of the Boy Scouts' expression with respect to homosexuality. . . .
>
> . . . As we give deference to an association's assertions regarding the nature of its expression, we must also give deference to an association's view of what would impair its expression. . . .
>
> . . . The Boy Scouts takes an official position with respect to homosexual conduct, and that is sufficient for First Amendment purposes. In this same vein, Dale makes much of the claim that the Boy Scouts does not revoke the membership of heterosexual Scout leaders that openly disagree with the Boy Scouts' policy on sexual orientation. But if this is true, it is irrelevant. The presence of an avowed homosexual and gay rights activist in an assistant scoutmaster's uniform sends a distinctly different message from the presence of a heterosexual assistant scoutmaster who is on record as disagreeing with Boy Scouts policy.

530 U.S. at 651, 653, 655-656.

Justice Stevens, writing for himself and three other Justices, took issue with the majority's analysis of both the facts and the law.

> [N]either one of [the Scouts' guiding] principles — "morally straight" and "clean" — says the slightest thing about homosexuality. Indeed, neither term in the Boy Scouts' Law and Oath expresses any position whatsoever on sexual matters.
>
> BSA's published guidance on that topic underscores this point. Scouts, for example, are directed to receive their sex education at home or in school, but not from the organization. . . .
>
> Several principles are made perfectly clear by [the Court's past cases in this area]. First, to prevail on a claim of expressive association in the face of a State's antidiscrimination law, it is not enough simply to engage in *some kind* of expressive activity. . . . Second, it is not enough to adopt an openly avowed exclusionary membership policy. . . . Third, it is not sufficient merely to articulate *some* connection between the group's expressive activities and its exclusionary policy. . . .
>
> Rather, [the question is whether an anti-discrimination law] "impose[s] any *serious burdens?*" on the group's "collective effort on behalf of [its] *shared goals*. . . ."

The evidence before this Court makes it exceptionally clear that BSA has, at most, simply adopted an exclusionary membership policy and has no shared goal of disapproving of homosexuality.

530 U.S. at 668-669, 682-684.

The *Dale* holding has been controversial among constitutional scholars, policymakers, and the general public. Some commentators have viewed the decision as inconsistent with prior cases involving discrimination by private associations. In upholding state bans on exclusion of women from groups like the Rotary Club and Jaycees, the Court has concluded that any incidental burden on expression is more than outweighed by compelling government interests in minimizing prejudice. By contrast, other commentators have defended the decision as a reaffirmation of the "sovereignty of the individual, enshrined in the First Amendment's freedom of speech, thought, and association." Fred Chou, Good Cases Make Bad Law, N.Y. Times, Apr. 27, 2000, at A31.

What is at stake for the Boy Scouts? Are their reasons for discrimination on the basis of sexual orientation constitutionally justified? Is it relevant that the Girl Scouts has no comparable policy? Nor does Boy Scouts Canada, which has the world's first official gay and lesbian Scout troop. James Brook, In Canada Gay Pride Can Be Part of Scout's Honor, N.Y. Times, July 3, 2000, at A8.

Following the *Dale* decision, related disputes have also surfaced about whether public entities like schools and police departments should eliminate their support of Boy Scout activities. According to gay rights advocates, taxpayer funds should not assist an organization that claims in its recruiting material that "any boy is welcome," but decides otherwise in practice. Given the high incidence of physical violence, harassment, isolation, depression, and school-related difficulties suffered by gay youths, many child development experts similarly argue that public support should go only to organizations that inculcate values of tolerance and mutual respect. See Brief of Amicus Curiae American Psychological Association in Boy Scouts v. Dale, 199 U.S. Briefs 699 (2000)

Supporters of Boy Scouts respond that public funds for Scout activities primarily target poor communities. And as one commentator maintains,

> Defunding the Scouts would be a tragic loss for inner-city youths and for the country. Gay pride that comes at the expense of poor children is bought at too high a price. If gay activists are so convinced that boys need gay role models, they can start alternative organizations with just that goal. But they should leave the Scouts alone.

Heather MacDonald, Boy Scout Battle Pits Gay Activists vs. Minority Kids, Wall St. J., July 6, 2000, at A26. If you were a member of a school board or city council in a poor community, would you favor cutting all ties with the Boy Scouts? Would your answer be affected by how local troop leaders deal with the sexual orientation issue or on how many privately supported charitable programs would be lost by eliminating public ties?

5. Sexual Orientation and Military Policy. Much of the law concerning discrimination on the basis of sexual orientation has developed in the context of military policy. The military has long excluded or discharged individuals who are found to be homosexual or who have engaged in homosexual acts. What began as an effort by the Clinton administration to eliminate such discrimination led rather to the enactment of congressional legislation codifying a "Don't Ask, Don't Tell," policy. Under the National Defense Authorization Act of 1994, military authorities may not expressly ask service members if they are homosexual, but may exclude or discharge them from the military if they acknowledge being a homosexual or if they have engaged, or have a "propensity to engage," in homosexual acts. Although the statute appears to focus on conduct rather than status, identification as a homosexual gives rise to a presumption of propensity to engage in homosexual acts. Once service members acknowledge being homosexual, they can remain in military service only upon disproving the propensity to engage in homosexual conduct. 10 U.S.C. §654(b)(1), (2) (1994). Service members who have engaged in homosexual conduct may avoid discharge only by showing such conduct is a departure from their usual behavior or unlikely to recur. Id. The statute is set forth in the Appendix.

Section 654(a) of the Act sets forth congressional findings that combat effectiveness requires "high morale, good order and discipline, and unit cohesion"; that the ban on open homosexuals continues to be imperative because of "the unique circumstances of military service"; and that open homosexuals would pose an unacceptable threat to the necessary "high morale, good order and discipline." 10 U.S.C. §654(a)(6), (13)-(15) (1998). Those claims have been largely accepted by courts in challenges brought to the military's exclusion of gays and lesbians. However, according to many experts, the evidence supporting such claims is strikingly thin. For example, with respect to concerns about security, "the military has been unable to provide any evidence to show that any homosexual soldier has been a security risk with the exception of one Austrian 'closet' case in World War I. The military's own reports . . . suggest that security is not an issue except for the fact that, as one scholar notes, 'Sanctions make rule-utilitarian justifications self-fulfilling prophecies.'" Judith Hicks Stiehm, Managing the Military's Homosexual Exclusion Policy: Text and Subtext, 46 U. Miami L. Rev. 685, 692 (1992). Individuals who can afford to be open about their sexuality are not likely to be blackmailed, while those who face such consequences as the loss of a job might be at risk. Richard D. Mohr, Gays/Justice: A Study of Ethics, Society, and Laws 198 (1988).

With respect to military order and morale, a representative conclusion is this:

Homosexuality is incompatible with military service. The presence in the military environment of persons who engage in homosexual conduct or who, by their statements, demonstrate a propensity to engage in homosexual conduct, seriously impairs the accomplishment of the military mission. The presence of such members adversely affects the ability of the Military Services to maintain discipline, good order, and morale; to foster mutual trust and confidence among service members[;] to ensure the integrity of the system of rank and command; to facilitate assignment and worldwide deployment of service members who frequently must live and work under close conditions affording minimal privacy; to recruit and retain members of the Military Services; to maintain the public acceptability of military service; and to prevent breaches of security. . . .

Steffan v. Cheney, 780 F. Supp. at 10. Is this a frivolous concern? A self-fulfilling prophecy? Can it be proved?

The court in Dronenberg v. Zech, 741 F.2d 1388 (D.C. Cir. 1984), reasons:

The Navy is not required to produce social science data or the results of controlled experiments to prove what common sense and common experience demonstrate. This very case illustrates dangers of the sort the Navy is entitled to consider. A 27-year-old petty officer had repeated sexual relations with a 19-year-old seaman recruit. The latter then chose to break off the relationship. Episodes of this sort are certain to be deleterious to morale and discipline, to call into question the even-handedness of superiors' dealings with lower ranks, to make personal dealings uncomfortable where the relationship is sexually ambiguous, to generate dislike and disapproval among many who find homosexuality morally offensive, and it must be said, given the powers of military superiors over their inferiors, to enhance the possibility of homosexual seduction.

Id. at 1398.

Is the court describing something unique to same-sex relationships? Is there something about these relationships that increases the risks of sexual misconduct? Is it appropriate for the court to rest its decision on "common sense and common experience" rather than evidence? If the problem is that gay or lesbian members of the armed services cannot command the respect of others, should the military permit discriminatory attitudes to justify continued discrimination? Is this constitutionally acceptable? Consider Judge Abner Mikva's observation in Steffan v. Aspin:

[A] cardinal principle of equal protection law holds that the government cannot discriminate against a certain class in order to give effect to the prejudice of others. Even if the government does not itself act out of prejudice, it cannot discriminate in an effort to avoid the effects of others' prejudice. Such discrimination plays directly into the hands of the bigots; it intensifies and encourages their prejudice. . . .

8 F.3d, 57, 68 (D.C. Cir. 1993), rev'd en banc sub nom. Steffan v. Perry, 41 F.3d 677 (D.C. Cir. 1994) (en banc).

Prior to the announcement of the 1993 "Don't Ask, Don't Tell" policy, Secretary of Defense Les Aspin requested from the National Defense Research Institute (NDRI) information and analysis that would be useful in helping to formulate a policy. The NDRI reviewed analogous institutions and experiences, finding that in countries that allow homosexuals to serve in the military, including Canada, France, Germany, Israel, the Netherlands, and Norway, (1) the number of openly homosexual service members is small and is believed to represent only a minority of homosexuals actually serving, (2) service members who acknowledge their homosexuality were "appropriately circumspect" in their behavior and did not call attention to themselves, and (3) few problems were reported that were caused by the presence of homosexual service members, and those that did arise were resolved satisfactorily on a case-by-case basis. NDRI, Sexual Orientation and U.S. Military Personnel Policy: Options and Assessment 11-15 (1993). The NDRI study made similar findings with respect to fire and police departments in the United States that have policies of nondiscrimination, including Chicago, Houston, Los Angeles, New York, San Diego, and Seattle. Acknowledged homosexuals are sensitive to the overall norms and customs of their organizations and try to avoid causing trouble. Anti-gay prejudice does not disappear, but negative behavior is more moderate than commonly predicted. With respect to the unit cohesion rationale, the study concluded that many factors work to promote the norms of cohesion and performance, even in the face of hostility based on sexual orientation. As a result, the inability of some individuals to accept the presence of an acknowledged gay or lesbian generally results in a degree of ostracism rather than a breakdown of the unit. Id. at 28-31.

The study further found that implementation of nondiscrimination policies is most successful where the message is unambiguous, consistently delivered, and uniformly enforced. Id. at 15-20. These findings correspond to the lessons learned from the history of racial integration in the U.S. military in the late 1940s. Id. at 20-22. How significant is this kind of information under a rationality standard of review? Consider General Colin Powell's response to analogies based on racial integration:

> [O]pen homosexuality . . . is something quite different than the acceptance of benign characteristics such as color or race or background. . . . It involves matters of privacy and human sexuality that, in our judgment, if allowed to openly exist within the force, will create serious issues having to do with cohesion and having to do with the well-being of the force.

Assessment of the Plan to Lift the Ban on Homosexuals in the Military: Hearings Before the Military Forces and Personnel Subcomm. of the Comm. on Armed Servs., House of Representatives, 103d Cong. 32 (1994) (testimony of Gen. Colin Powell, Chairman, Joint Chiefs of Staff). How would you respond?

In Smith & Grady v. United Kingdom, 29 Eur. Ct. H.R. 493 (1999), the European Court of Human Rights struck down the United Kingdom's prohibition on homosexuals in the military. Under the court's analysis, the prohibition violated service members' right to privacy guaranteed by Article 8(1) of the European Convention for the Protection of Human Rights and Fundamental Freedoms, Nov. 4 1950, 312 U.N.T.S. 221. In so ruling, the court rejected the UK's claim that "negative attitudes" toward homosexual service members made the policy necessary for military morale and "fighting power," and therefore "necessary in a democratic society" under Article 8(2), which authorizes exceptions to individual privacy rights. According to the court, the existence of prejudice should not justify its perpetuation. Negative attitudes toward gays and lesbians were no more acceptable than "similar negative attitudes toward those of a different race, origin, or color." Id. ¶97. By all accounts, implementation of the *Grady* decision is proceeding without significant difficulty. Raymond A. Psonak, Don't Ask, Don't Tell, Don't Discharge, At Least in Europe: A Comparison of the Policies on Homosexuals in the Military in the United States and Europe After *Grady v. United Kingdom*, 33 Conn. L. Rev. 337, 346 (2000); Scott Morris, Europe Enters a New Millennium while the United States Drowns in Don't Ask, Don't Tell: Twin Decisions by the European Court of Human Rights, 9 Am. U. J. Gender Soc. Pol'y & L. 423 (2001). The *Grady* ruling leaves the United States with the most restrictive military policy toward sexual orientation among Western industrialized countries. Id. Should the experience of other nations be relevant in assessing the rationality of U.S. policy?

Although sponsors of the "Don't Ask, Don't Tell" policy intended it to reduce harassment and exclusion of gay and lesbian soldiers, the results have been otherwise. About twice as many service members have been discharged under the Don't Ask policy as under its predecessor. Jim Garamone, DOD Clarifies Don't Ask, Don't Tell Policy, American Forces Information Service, www.defenselink.mil/news/Aug1999 (Aug. 1999); Servicemembers Legal Defense Network, Conduct Unbecoming: Annual Report on "Don't Ask, Don't Tell, Don't Pursue" 1 (2000). Of those discharged due to sexual orientation in 1997, 29 percent were women, although women make up only 14 percent of the active force. See Michael I. Spak, Don't Ask (and) Don't Tell Don't Work: Now What?, 10 Transnat'l L. & Contemp. Probs. 105, 115 (2000). What do you think accounts for the increased discharge rate and for this harsher treatment of lesbian than gay soldiers?

6. First Amendment Challenges to Discrimination in the Military: Distinguishing Conduct from Status. In rejecting First Amendment challenges to military policies on sexual orientation, courts have distinguished between homosexual status, which is protected by the First

Amendment, and homosexual conduct, which is not. See, e.g., Ben-Shalom v. Marsh, 881 F.2d 454, 464 (7th Cir. 1989), cert. denied, 494 U.S. 1004 (1990). Janet Halley criticizes this distinction on the ground that status is penalized when homosexual conduct or propensity is presumed from homosexual status and when individuals who have engaged in homosexual conduct can disprove propensity by establishing their status as a heterosexual. See Janet E. Halley, Don't: A Readers' Guide to the Military's Anti-Gay Policy (1999); Janet E. Halley, The Status/Conduct Distinction in the 1993 Revisions to Military Anti-Gay Policy: A Legal Archaeology, 3 GLQ: J. Lesbian & Gay Stud. 159, 183-188 (1996). In Halley's view, this "actuarial model of propensity" is even worse for gays and lesbians than an outright exclusion based on homosexual identity, since conduct seems more related to military order than status and more justifiable as a basis for exclusion. As Halley notes, "Every moving part of the new policy is designed to *look like* conduct regulation in order to *hide* the fact that it turns decisively on status. At least the old policy was as bad as it looked; problems of deceptive appearance, ruse, tautology, and outright misrepresentation make the new policy a regulatory Trojan Horse." Halley, Don't, supra, at 2 (emphasis in original).

How should gay rights advocates respond to the current military policy? Should they continue to challenge its rationality, on the grounds that legitimation of homophobic attitudes does not serve military objectives? See Cass Sunstein, Homosexuality and the Constitution, 70 Ind. L.J. 1 (1994) (under contemporary conditions, there is more to gain from incremental rationality review and from legislative activity than from more ambitious claims). Cf. Diane H. Mazur, The Unknown Soldier: A Critique of "Gays in the Military" Scholarship and Litigation, 29 U.C. Davis L. Rev. 223 (1996) (arguing that both sides in debate could more rationally discuss pros and cons of military policy); Francisco Valdes, Queers, Sissies, Dykes, and Tomboys: Deconstructing the Conflation of "Sex," "Gender," and "Sexual Orientation" in Euro-American Law and Society, 83 Cal. L. Rev. 1, 22-23 (1995) (arguing that gays and lesbians should resist the "conflation" between homosexual identity and conduct).

For consideration of the special issues relating to lesbians in the military, see Section F, below.

Putting Theory into Practice

4-16. The Federal Sentencing Guideline §3A1.1 permits increased penalties if the victim of the crime was "unusually vulnerable due to age, physical or mental condition, or . . . otherwise particularly susceptible to the criminal conduct." A defendant is convicted of extortion after having attempted to blackmail a married man who had had a homosexual affair. Under the Guidelines, should the victim's homosexuality be a factor in considering whether he was unusually vulnerable to blackmail? See U.S. v. Lallemand, 989 F.2d 936 (7th Cir. 1993).

F. WOMEN IN THE MILITARY

Throughout the nation's history, cultural expectations and legal restrictions have severely limited female involvement in the armed forces. Until the early 1970s, women constituted less than two percent of the American military and discrimination in placement and promotion was widespread, particularly for women of color. Enrollment was limited through quotas on female applicants; exclusion from combat positions, military academies, and training programs; and disqualification of women who became pregnant or had minor children. After most of these restrictions were modified or withdrawn during the mid-1970s, female participation in the armed forces substantially increased, reaching 10 percent by the late 1980s and 13 percent by the turn of the century. Deborah L. Rhode, Justice and Gender 98 (1989); Report of the Federal Advisory Committee on Gender-Integrated Training and Related Issues 2 (1998). However, such changes occurred largely without judicial intervention. The prevailing view was apparent in one 1968 federal district court opinion: "In providing for involuntary service for men and voluntary service for women, Congress followed the teachings of history that if a nation is to survive, men must provide the first line of defense while women keep the home fires burning." United States v. St. Clair, 291 F. Supp. 122, 125 (S.D.N.Y. 1968).

The first case to reach the Supreme Court concerning sex discrimination in the military was Rostker v. Golberg, 453 U.S. 57 (1981). At issue was a claim by a male plaintiff that the military's compulsory draft registration system, which included only men, constituted a violation of the equal protection clause. Speaking for the majority, Justice Rehnquist rejected that claim.

> No one could deny that under Craig [v. Boren], the Government's interest in raising and supporting armies is an "important governmental interest." Congress and its Committees carefully considered and debated . . . alternative means of furthering that interest. . .
>
> . . . Congress was fully aware not merely of the many facts and figures presented to it by witnesses who testified before its Committees, but [also] of the current thinking as to the place of women in the Armed Services. . . .
>
> This case is quite different from several of the gender-based discrimination cases we have considered in that, despite appellees' assertions, Congress did not act "unthinkingly" or "reflexively and not for any considered reason." . . .
> The question of registering women for the draft not only received considerable national attention and was the subject of wide-ranging public debate, but also

was extensively considered by Congress in hearings, floor debate, and in committee. . . .

[T]he decision to exempt women from registration was not the "'accidental by-product of a traditional way of thinking about females.'" . . .

. . . The purpose of registration [historically], therefore was to prepare for a draft *of combat troops.*

Women as a group, however, unlike men as a group, are not eligible for combat. . . . Congress specifically recognized and endorsed the exclusion of women from combat in exempting women from registration. In the words of the Senate Report:

> The principle that women should not intentionally and routinely engage in combat is fundamental, and enjoys wide support among our people. It is universally supported by military leaders who have testified before the Committee. . . . Current law and policy exclude women from being assigned to combat in our military forces, and the Committee reaffirms this policy. . . .

The Senate Report specifically found that "[w]omen should not be intentionally or routinely placed in combat positions in our military services." . . . The President expressed his intent to continue the current military policy precluding women from combat. . . .

The existence of combat restrictions clearly indicates the basis for Congress' decision to exempt women from registration. The purpose of registration was to prepare for a draft of combat troops. Since women are excluded from combat, Congress concluded that they would not be needed in the event of a draft, and therefore decided not to register them.

453 U.S. at 70-72, 74, 76-77.

Since the plaintiff had not challenged the constitutionality of the combat exemption, the Court found it unnecessary to resolve that issue, although the tenor of the decision left little doubt that a majority of Justices were prepared to defer to congressional judgment. Justice Marshall, joined by Justice Brennan, dissented. As they read the record, the government had not sustained the burden of showing that a gender-based classification substantially furthered the goal of military preparedness. Even assuming the legitimacy of excluding women from combat, their exclusion from registration did not follow. According to government estimates, about a third of those drafted during a national mobilization would not need combat skills. The registration system at issue included non-combat-eligible males, and the Joint Chiefs of Staff had been united in their desire to include females as well. Although some cost would be involved in registering more women than necessary in a system that precluded their combat service, the dissent noted that Supreme Court decisions had often rejected administrative expense as a rationale for gender classifications. 453 U.S. at 85 (Marshall, J., dissenting).

Justice Rehnquist's opinion emphasizes that the exclusion of women was not an accidental byproduct "of a traditional way of thinking about females." What if it was a deliberate byproduct of traditional gender stereotypes? See discussion in Chapter 2, pages 147-148.

Legislative debates about women's participation in the military, particularly in combat positions, reflect an extended array of stereotypes about women's physical and psychological unfitness for fighting and the cultural costs of seeing the nation's nurturers as "cannon fodder." Many military and congressional leaders remain convinced that actual "fighting is a man's job" and that most female soldiers lack sufficient strength, endurance, aggressiveness, or ability to "kill impersonally" in combat. See sources quoted in Deborah L. Rhode, Speaking of Sex 30 (1998); Linda Bird Francke, Ground Zero: The Gender Wars in the Military 130-151 (1997). Recent popular commentary echoes similar themes and warns that American national security has been threatened by the "feminization" of the military. See Stephanie Gutman, The Kinder, Gentler Military: Can America's Gender-Neutral Fighting Force Still Win Wars? (2000); Brian Mitchell, Women in the Military: Flirting with Disaster (1998).

Rush Limbaugh summarizes a widespread view:

What will feminists seek in the military, first and foremost? Equality. Fairness. Gender quotas. Well, the military's chief goal is excellence. We shouldn't emasculate (pun intended) by shackling it with the demands of every silly social movement that is currently fashionable in society. The military has a job to do. . . . Its success will always be measured by its ability to destroy and decimate; not by whether it has a requisite percentage of women in foxholes, in daycare centers, or flying F-16s. I know this sounds harsh, but that's the way war is. Frankly, I don't believe that women should be in combat roles even if they can do the job. Why? You ask. Simple. Women have a civilizing role in society. War is that cruel last option in human relations. It isn't about career opportunities. Women have definite societal roles that are crucial to the continuation of mankind. They establish enduring values that are handed down from generation to generation. Women are the ones who give birth, without which the propagation of the species would not be perpetuated.

I just don't believe that we have to subject women to the horrors and rigors of war. . . . [I]t's bad enough that men come home in body bags. Why do we need to put women in them as well?

Rush Limbaugh III, The Way Things Ought to Be 200-201 (1992).

Opponents of women in combat raise a host of concerns about pregnancy, promiscuity, and "gender-norming," the practice of adjusting strength and fitness standards to reflect sex-based differences. According to these commentators, the military's effort to accommodate women is fostering resentment, diluting performance requirements, creating double standards, inspiring inappropriate chivalry, compromising morale, impairing recruitment, and diverting attention from more central goals of combat preparedness. Underlying these concerns were a host of symbolic issues about masculinity, manhood, and dominance. General William Westmoreland expressed a common attitude with uncommon candor. "No man with any gumption wants a woman to fight his nation's battles." William

Westmoreland, quoted in Judith Wagner Decrew, The Combat Exclusion and the Role of Women in the Military, Hypatia, Winter 1995, at 62. See generally Kenneth Karst, The Pursuit of Motherhood and the Desegregation of the Armed Forces, 38 UCLA L. Rev. 499 (1991).

Supporters of equal opportunity in the military have responded on several levels. First, with respect to physical capabilities, the most recent comprehensive studies, sponsored by the Army Research Institute and the British Ministry of Defense, conclude that with appropriate training the vast majority of women can meet the physical demands of combat. J. Michael Brower, Undermining Old Taboos: U.S. Studies Say Women Can Meet Physical Demands of Combat, Armed Forces J. Int'l, May 1996, at 13. Such findings are consistent with a wide range of other studies about women's performance in combat, simulated combat, and related police and military contexts here and abroad. See Rhode, Justice and Gender 100 (1989); Francke, supra, at 248; Mark Hagar, GI Jane and the Limits of Liberalism, 10 Transnat'l J.L. & Contemp. Probs. 219 (2000).

As in civilian contexts, military positions requiring particular levels of strength, endurance, or agility can be allocated under gender-neutral guidelines that match individual capabilities with job requirements. Moreover, as many experts have noted, technological changes in warfare have reduced the relevance of physical strength in combat and eroded the distinctions between combat and combat-related positions. Federal judge Richard Posner puts it this way: "We live in an age of push-button warfare. Women can push buttons as well as men." Richard Posner, Overcoming Law 55 (1995).

Definitions of combat have changed over time, and many combat exclusions have been recently lifted, including the exclusion from flying combat missions and the proscription against serving on combatant naval vessels. Michael J. Frevola, Damn the Torpedoes, Full Speed Ahead: The Argument for Total Sex Integration in the Armed Services, 28 Conn. L. Rev. 621, 626 (1996). However, the general ban on women participating in direct ground combat remains, with combat defined as follows: "Engaging an enemy on the ground with individual or crew-served weapons while being exposed to direct enemy fire, a high possibility of direct physical contact with the enemy, and a substantial risk of capture. Direct combat takes place while repelling assault by fire, maneuver, or shock effect in order to destroy or capture, or while repelling assault by fire, close combat, or counterattack." James D. Milko, Comment, Beyond the Persian Gulf Crisis: Expanding the Role of Servicewomen in the United States Military, 41 Am. U. L. Rev. 1307 (1992).

As soldiers have become more efficient at causing injury and death at substantial distances from the enemy, the distinctions between combat and noncombat positions have blurred. Over 90 percent of Air Force and Navy positions are now open to women, as are about two-thirds of Army and Marine Corps. positions. Madeline Morris, By Force of Arms: Rape, War, and Military Culture, 45 Duke L.J. 651, 736-737 (1996). Moreover, many women who are not officially in combat, such as nurses, are at risk of death and capture because of their support services. As the Persian Gulf War again demonstrated, combat exclusion does not prevent women from being killed. It prevents them from killing or being trained to kill. As Kenneth Karst puts it: "The exclusion of women from combat positions does not keep women out of harm's way; it keeps women in their place. [Exclusion of women, like exclusion of gays, serves] to maintain the gender line, and thus to maintain for the services a traditionally masculine image: power and weapons in the hands of 'real men.'" Karst, supra, at 579.

A further justification for restricting women's role in the military involves the costs associated with pregnancy and childrearing. Hagar, supra, at 239-241. However, in assessing these costs, it bears note that women also have fewer discipline and substance-related problems than men, so their overall absenteeism rates are lower despite their risks of pregnancy. Id. at 240 n.88. Moreover, many of the costs associated with childrearing, such as daycare and subsidized family health insurance, are increasingly important to men as well as women and have large payoffs in recruitment and retention of talented service members. Id.

Whether to challenge sex-based policies, particularly those that exclude women from combat and draft registration systems, has been a matter of long-standing dispute within the feminist community. Advocates of equal treatment argue that protective policies disserve women's interests by protecting women out of positions of greatest power, status, and reward. Lack of combat eligibility restricts women's job opportunities, credibility, and career advancement in the military and limits their ability to capitalize on wartime service in other political and employment contexts. Double standards in the military also carry other costs in reinforcing traditional gender roles and stereotypes. In this vein, Mary Becker notes:

> Exclusion of women from militia service in combat denies women the obligations of full citizenship. This denial inevitably translates into disadvantaging women as citizens by depriving them of power they would otherwise share more equally with men. . . .
>
> [K]eeping women out of combat maintains the image of the male warrior, who is superior to physically passive women who need his protection and cannot resist his violence. . . . The military trains men to operate within a macho culture with the belief that they are superior to women. . . .
>
> [K]eeping women out of combat positions . . . supports the taboo against women using force, especially lethal force. . . . Maintaining male control of lethal force clearly preserves male interests both with respect to control of the military itself (a powerful institution in its own right) and with respect to men's power over women through physical intimidation throughout society. . . .

Mary E. Becker, The Politics of Women's Wrongs and the Bill of "Rights": A Bicentennial Perspective, 59 U. Chi. L. Rev. 453, 496-498 (1992). If service in the military is an incidence of citizenship, is it simply a matter of whether women should be allowed to participate in the military? Shouldn't they feel obligated to do so? See Diane H. Mazur, A Call to Arms, 22 Harv. Women's L.J. 39 (1999) (arguing that feminists are not in a position to criticize the military's treatment of servicewomen until they accept responsibility of participation in the military).

By contrast, other feminists argue that women should seek to challenge military culture, not to assimilate within it. Following President Carter's 1980 proposal for gender-neutral draft registration, a New Haven women's group issued the following response:

— Women have traditionally fought for peace, and there is no reason for us to abandon that position now.

— Our quest for equality must not lead us to embrace blindly all the standards and values of male institutions.

— We reject the war reflex as an instance of male hysteria; in its essence, feminism is opposed to violence.

Women's experience leads us firmly to reject the claim that might makes right. . . . Anything that legitimates violence is inherently a threat to women, who are disproportionately the victims of violent acts. It is impossible to separate America's use of violence abroad from the use of violence against women in the American home and on American streets. . . .

. . . The conscription of women will not change the structure of power in the military or in this country. Why should we bide by a decision over which we have had no say? Once we are drafted, who will decide where we will serve? . . . These decisions will be made as they have always been made, by the *men* in the Pentagon and the White House, men who have refused to fight for equal rights for women, men who have on countless occasions demonstrated their disregard for the legitimate grievances and sovereign rights of oppressed people all over the world. . . .

Feminist Opposition to the Draft, quoted in Catharine A. Mac Kinnon, Sex Equality 270-271 (2001).

Similar issues resurfaced during the Gulf War as media coverage focused on images of mothers being sent to areas within range of enemy fire. Columnist Ellen Goodman responded to widespread concerns from feminists about whether women had gotten "more equality than we bargained for."

War does not respect motherhood, whether military or civilian. In all the wars of the 1980s, three out of every four people killed were civilians. Women and their children were not "protected" in Kuwait. Nor will they be protected in Baghdad or Riyadh if war comes.

A truly just war, I argue, a war of self-defense, of survival, is worthy of sacrifice. A war any less moral, a war confused in its purpose, is unworthy of any lost life. To say a conflict is worth the sacrifice of men but not women, fathers but not mothers, is to plea-bargain with the gods.

But this does not counter [my feminist friend's] second thoughts. Remember, she says, when women first supported the idea that mothers were like fathers? Most of us assumed that working beside men, fighting beside them, was part of a trade-off. In return, men would father more and women would become decision makers. It was a deal we were making.

Now, in the lopsidedness of change, fewer women have made it to the top than have filled in the bottom. More women are on the front lines than in the inner circle. What happened to the deal?

My friend draws a border around the photograph in the paper of George Bush. . . . She says in a word, "Suits." The men in suits are still making the policy moves. Only now they have military pawns of both genders. . . .

So these images — "suits" drawing lines in the sand and babies waving to "mommy" soldiers — become second thoughts. If this is what equality looks like, were we better off before? Only, of course, this is not what equality looks like. This is what it looks like in the middle of lopsided change, in the uneven, unsettling process, on a path that looks more rugged and more circuitous than we knew at the beginning.

In the desert, the mother-soldiers waving to their children are not a reminder that women have gotten more than we bargained for. But that we have gotten so much less.

Ellen Goodman, Value Judgments 158-159 (1993).

Who speaks for women on these issues? How relevant are the preferences of female members of the armed forces? In one representative survey, about 10 percent of servicewomen indicated that they would volunteer for combat duty, about a third believed that women should be subject to combat requirements on the same terms as men, and about four-fifths thought women should be able to volunteer. Women in Combat: Hearings Before the Subcomm. on Military Forces and Personnel of the House Comm. on Armed Services, 103rd Cong. 47 (1993). Can women have it both ways—that is, have the right to serve in combat without the obligation? If not, which way should they try to have it?

Another long-standing concern involving women and the military is sexual abuse. Certain characteristics of military life increase the risks of sexual misconduct: a highly masculine culture that reinforces aggression; strict hierarchies and limited opportunities for subordinates to escape abusive circumstances; stresses caused by lack of privacy and dangerous or onerous living conditions; separation from spouses or partners; and traditions of hazing for new or "deviant" recruits. The result has been a high level of domestic violence, sexual harassment, and rape during wartime.

Although the reluctance of victims to report abuse makes the full extent of these problems difficult to gauge, the military's own studies give ample grounds for concern. For example, an Army survey of some 55,000 soldiers at 47 bases found that one in three families suffered some form of domestic violence, which was twice the civilian sample that was used for comparison. DOD FY 86-FT-93, Child Abuse and Spouse Maltreatment: Causes and

Rates, Defense Department Report (May 27, 1994). Recent estimates indicate that active-duty service members and their spouses report 20,000 to 23,000 incidents of abuse each year and most experts believe that the number of unreported incidents is much higher. Lauren R. Taylor, Pentagon Says Domestic Violence Must End, www.womensenews.org, Dec. 4, 2000. Other studies have found that between about half and four-fifths of servicewomen report experiencing some form of sexual harassment, and about a fifth report being targets of sexual coercion or assault. Department of Defense, Results of the 1995 Sexual Harassment Study (1996); Philip Shenon, Army's Leadership Blamed in Report on Sexual Abuses, N.Y. Times, Sept. 12, 1997, at A1. Harassment of suspected lesbians is a particular problem. Christin M. Damiano, Lesbian Baiting in the Military: Institutionalized Sexual Harassment Under "Don't Ask, Don't Tell, Don't Pursue," 7 Am. J. U. Gender Soc. Pol'y & L. 499 (1999). Surveys on reported rapes by military personnel present a more complicated picture. Some studies suggest that military rates are lower than those among civilian populations in times of peace, but substantially higher in times of war. See Morris, supra, at 661-662, 664.

Women's increasing role in the military, as well as in the political and media institutions that oversee its performance, has brought increased attention to these issues. A series of notorious scandals have also fueled greater public concern. One involved a 1991 Tailhook Convention, in which over 200 Navy and Marine Corps officers engaged in sexual misconduct, including a gauntlet in which they stripped, mauled, and assaulted women. A majority of those officers received no sanctions, and only a few ended up with more than letters of caution. Rhode, Speaking of Sex, supra, at 101. Another, more recent scandal involved the Army's Aberdeen Proving Ground training installation, at which sexual misconduct between drill sergeants and subordinate trainees was pervasive. Follow-up investigations made clear that Aberdeen was not unique. Elaine Scolinina, Sergeant Convicted of 18 Counts of Raping Female Subordinates, N.Y. Times, Apr. 30, 1997, at A1; Martha Chamallas, The New Gender Panic: Reflections on Sex Scandals and the Military, 83 Minn. L. Rev. 305 (1998). The conduct of servicemen overseas became a focus of concern during the trial of three American soldiers for the rape of a 12-year-old Japanese school girl in Okinawa. Sheryl Wu Dunn, Rape Trial in Okinawa Is Suspended, N.Y. Times, Dec. 29, 1995, at A10.

Such examples reflect limitations less in formal policies than in daily enforcement. Since the early 1990s, the Uniform Code of Military Justice has declared zero tolerance for sexual harassment. Prohibitions on quid pro and hostile environmental harassment are similar to those developed under Title VII, explored earlier in this chapter. However, few women or men are willing to report violations of these prohibitions. In a recent representative Army survey, only 13 percent of those who identified themselves as recent victims of harassment had made a formal complaint; over half had preferred to ignore or put up with the abuse or find some other way of dealing with it. Shenon, supra, at A16.

The reasons were well illustrated by a recent case in which Lt. General Claudia Kennedy, the Army's highest-ranking woman, revealed that she had not complained of harassment occurring four years earlier by an officer chosen for the position of deputy inspector general. That position included investigating sexual harassment. His appointment was withdrawn, but coverage of the incident made clear that many other similar incidents were unlikely to be revealed because of women's reluctance to open their personal lives to investigation for fear of being blamed for inviting a sexual advance. Elizabeth Becker, Women in Military Say Silence on Harassment Protects Careers, N.Y. Times, May 12, 2000, at A1. In commenting on Lt. General Kennedy's dilemma, one female officer noted, "Now instead of being remembered as the first woman to earn three stars in the Army, she is going to be remembered as that woman with the sex complaint." Id.

Although such deterrents to reporting are not unique to miliary settings, the costs are compounded by the difficulties of quitting or transferring jobs and by the career-threatening consequences for soldiers who complain of homophobic incidents. Women who rebuff advances or report hostile environments may risk being labeled lesbians, which further discourages reporting. Damiano, supra, at 502. In addition, sweeping bans on "fraternization" between officers and enlisted members have proven impossible to enforce, and sanctions have been selectively imposed, often to women's disadvantage. Chamallas, supra, at 358 & n.206.

Strategies for improving the military's responsiveness to sexual abuse include more training and accountability of officers and service providers; more information and outreach to victims; greater representation of women, particularly in supervisory positions; more protection and remedies for soldiers who report misconduct; redefinition of rules prohibiting "fraternization" to focus on nonconsensual conduct and relationships presenting conflicts of interest. Taylor, supra; Michael F. Noone, Chimera or Jackalope? Department of Defense Efforts to Apply Civilian Harassment Criteria to the Military, 6 Duke J. Gender L. & Pol'y 151 (1999); Chamallas, supra, at 374-375. What strategies strike you as most promising? In the final analysis, Diane Mazur notes:

> The reason the chain of command has been ineffective in controlling sexual misconduct in the military is that no one, at any level, has truly considered it a priority. The "zero tolerance" slogan is just a slogan, unconnected to serious consequences for those who fail to change behavior. The military is quite talented at changing behavior; it has to want to change that behavior.

Diane Mazur, The Beginning of the End for Women in the Military, 48 Fla. L. Rev. 461, 469-470 (1996). How can the military become more motivated?

5

Women's Different Voice(s)

In this chapter, concern for women's equality is filtered through a commitment to revaluing rather than eliminating or overcoming certain characteristics that are historically associated with women. Within different voice theory (also referred to as cultural feminism, or relational feminism, or difference theory), women's differences are viewed less as problems to be overcome than as potentially valuable resources that might serve as a better model of social organization and law than existing "male" characteristics and values. These differences are said to include a greater sense of interconnectedness, a priority on relationships over rights, and a preference for more contextualized, less abstract forms of reasoning. This chapter investigates the nature of these claimed differences and their implications for our legal system.

Many advocates of the theories propounded in previous chapters of this book (and some of the authors included in this chapter) view different voice theory with suspicion because of the risk that the attribution of certain common values to women will reinforce the ideologies of subordination that those theories are intended to dispel. At the same time, almost everyone assumes that the increasing presence of women in law schools, in law practice, in elected office, on juries, and on the bench will affect how law is taught, practiced, applied, and made. Can this apparent contradiction be reconciled? Does it matter whether the purported differences between women and men are based in biology or are a result of social conditioning?

The tension between assertions of sameness and assumptions of difference present in much feminist theory provides the occasion for a general exploration in this chapter of the impact of women in all roles in the legal system. It also facilitates further examination of the relationship between theory and practice: is the insistence that women are like men a

805

truth upon which theory should be built or a strategy to achieve a form of justice that must be justified on other premises?

A. THE CONNECTION THESIS

≡ *Robin West, Jurisprudence and Gender*
≡ 55 U. Chi. L. Rev. 1, 1-3, 14-15, 58-60 (1988)

[V]irtually all modern American legal theorists, like most modern moral and political philosophers, either explicitly or implicitly embrace what I will call the "separation thesis" about what it means to be a human being: a "human being," whatever else he is, is physically separate from all other human beings. I am one human being and you are another, and that distinction between you and me is central to the meaning of the phrase "human being." . . .

. . . By virtue of their shared embrace of the separation thesis, all of our modern legal theory . . . is essentially and irretrievably masculine. . . . [T]he cluster of claims that jointly constitute the "separation thesis" — the claim that human beings are, definitionally, distinct from one another, the claim that the referent of "I" is singular and unambiguous, the claim that the word "individual" has an uncontested biological meaning, namely that we are each physically individuated from every other, the claim that we are individuals "first," and the claim that what separates us is epistemologically and morally prior to what connects us — while "trivially true" of men, [is] patently untrue of women. Women are not essentially, necessarily, inevitably, invariably, always, and forever separate from other human beings: women, distinctively, are quite clearly "connected" to another human life when pregnant. In fact, women are in some sense "connected" to life and to other human beings during at least four recurrent and critical material experiences: the experience of pregnancy itself; the invasive and "connecting" experience of heterosexual penetration, which may lead to pregnancy; the monthly experience of menstruation, which represents the potential for pregnancy; and the post-pregnancy experience of breast-feeding. Indeed, perhaps the central insight of feminist theory of the last decade has been that women are "essentially connected," not "essentially separate," from the rest of human life, both materially, through pregnancy, intercourse, and breast-feeding, and existentially, through the moral and practical life. . . .

The "connection thesis" is simply this: Women are actually or potentially materially connected to other human life. Men aren't. This material fact has existential consequences. While it may be true for men that the individual is "epistemologically and morally prior to the collectivity," it is not true for women. The potential for material connection with the other defines women's subjective, phenomenological and existential state, just as surely as the inevitability of material separation from the other defines men's existential state. Our potential for material connection engenders pleasures and pains, values and dangers, and attractions and fears, which are entirely different from those which follow, *for men*, from the necessity of separation. Indeed, it is the rediscovery of the multitude of implications from this material difference between men and women which has enlivened (and divided) both cultural and radical feminism in this decade. . . . As Carol Gilligan notes, this development is somewhat paradoxical: during the same decade that liberal feminist political activists and lawyers pressed for equal (meaning same) treatment by the law, feminist theorists in the non-legal disciplines rediscovered women's differences from men. . . .

If both cultural and radical feminists hold some version of the connection thesis, then one way of understanding the issues that divide [them] . . . [is to examine their] contrasting accounts of the subjective experience of the material and existential state of connection. According to cultural feminist accounts of women's subjectivity, women value intimacy, develop a capacity for nurturance, and an ethic of care for the "other" with which we are connected, just as we learn to dread and fear separation from the other. Radical feminists tell a very different story. According to radical feminism, women's connection with the "other" is above all else invasive and intrusive: women's potential for material "connection" invites invasion into the physical integrity of our bodies, and intrusion into the existential integrity of our lives. Although women may "officially" value the intimacy of connection, we "unofficially" dread the intrusion it inevitably entails, and long for the individuation and independence that deliverance from that state of connection would permit. . . .

By the claim that modern jurisprudence is "masculine," I mean two things. First, I mean that the values [and] the dangers that characterize women's lives are not reflected at any level whatsoever in contracts, torts, constitutional law, or any other field of legal doctrine. The values that flow from women's material potential for physical connection are not recognized as values by the Rule of Law, and the dangers attendant to that state are not recognized as dangers by the Rule of Law.

First, the Rule of Law does not value intimacy — its official value is autonomy. The material consequence of this theoretical undervaluation of women's values . . . is that women are economically *impoverished*. . . . Nurturant, intimate labor is neither valued by liberal legalism nor compensated by the market economy. It is not compensated in the home and it is not compensated in the workplace — wherever intimacy is, there is no compensation. Similarly, separation of the individual from his or her family, community, or children is not understood to be a harm, and we are not protected against it. . . .

Nor does the Rule of Law recognize . . . the contradiction which characterizes women's, but not men's, lives: while we value the intimacy we find so natural, we are endangered by the invasion and dread the intrusion in our lives which intimacy entails, and we long for individuation and independence. Neither sexual nor fetal invasion of the self by the other is recognized to be a harm worth bothering about. Sexual invasion through rape is understood to be a harm, and is criminalized as such, only when it involves some other harm: today, when it is accomplished by violence that appears in a form men understand (meaning a plausible threat of annihilation); in earlier times, when it was understood as theft of another man's property. But marital rape, date rape, acquaintance rape . . . are either not criminalized, or if they are, they are not punished — to do so would force a recognition of the concrete, experiential harm to identity formation that sexual invasion accomplishes.

Similarly, fetal invasion is not understood to be harmful. . . . [T]he danger an unwanted fetus poses is not to the body's security at all, but rather to the body's integrity. [T]he woman's fear is not that she will die, but that she will cease to be or never become a self. The danger of unwanted pregnancy is the danger of invasion by the other, not of annihilation by the other. In sum, the Rule of Law does not recognize the danger of invasion, nor does it recognize the individual's need for, much less entitlement to, individuation and independence from the intrusion which heterosexual penetration and fetal invasion entails. The material consequence of this lack of recognition in the real world is that women are *objectified* — regarded as creatures who can't be harmed.

Leslie Bender, From Gender Difference to Feminist Solidarity: Using Carol Gilligan and an Ethic of Care in Law
15 Vt. L. Rev. 1, 36-37, 39-42 (1990)

[Psychologist Carol] Gilligan noted two distinct, although not mutually exclusive, perspectives in her analysis of people's orientations in solving moral dilemmas. One perspective, which she denominated an ethic of justice, closely parallels the dominant rationality and methodology of Anglo-American law. This justice ethic is based on a rights model, where problem-solving consists of the application of abstract, generalized principles to arbitrate rights disputes between separate individuals (conflicting rights-holders) and to privilege one right over another. The justice-oriented problem-solver seeks a distanced stance from which to make objective decisions by applying formal rules of equality and other general principles of justice. Traditionally, this perspective was deemed the highest stage of moral development, and it has monopolized legal reasoning.

Gilligan observed, however, that some people solve moral dilemmas using a different, but equally adequate, methodology. This second distinctive perspective, which Gilligan called an ethic of care, focuses attention on the unique context of the dispute and the parties' on-going relationships and interdependencies. The care-oriented problem-solver examines the connections between and among people, looking at their interpersonal responsibilities and needs. Preventing hurt, preserving relationships, and developing cooperative solutions rooted in the concrete particulars of the conflict are objectives of a care-oriented ethical analysis. A care-based problem-solver often "questions the hypothetical" to gather more relevant information in order to better understand the full scope of the problem and the practical, material consequences of any decision. By considering the specific needs of all the parties, as articulated from those parties' own perspectives, and by attending to particularized contexts rather than abstract rights and universalizable rules, care-oriented problem-solvers frequently design creative, alternative solutions that may never occur to their justice-oriented counterparts.

Gilligan's thesis is that care concerns are a largely unacknowledged or unprivileged way of analyzing moral dilemmas, and that while they are used by both men and women, women focus on care and relationships considerably more than men do. . . .

Some feminist theories reject Gilligan's gender-linked analysis of ethical orientations because they fear that it will reinscribe women with characteristics that are a consequence of, or have been the fodder for, gender domination. This is a very serious concern. Carol Gilligan's work has been critiqued for burdening women with continuing tasks of caregiving, pleasing others, and self-sacrifice. . . .

A second, related criticism of Gilligan's ethic of care is that caregiving itself is draining and self-sacrificing. If women are expected to maintain our caregiving work, particularly in our workplaces, we will not have time and energy left to fulfill our own needs, to care for our families, or to promote our personal and political advancement. This is especially true, since women are still responsible for the majority of housekeeping, caregiving, and emotional work in the home. If we advertise ourselves as caregivers, we will be forced to continue our extra work at home and in the workplace.

Finally, there is an equally strong criticism that these caregiving traits do not apply to all women, that many women do not exhibit them, and that many women do not even want to be associated with them. The truth of this last criticism is self-evident. All of the above critiques are searing, and each has a strong ring of truth. Those of us who advocate that gender differences be acknowledged need to worry about them. . . .

Acknowledging the possible link between care and gender, [Catharine] MacKinnon and others suggest that care is a voice of oppression or subordination. If that is how this ethic of care and responsibility is created, she argues, we should not celebrate its link to women. . . .

. . . That the origins of an ethic of care are in part suspect advises especial caution, but not necessarily rejection. Caring and cooperation are quintessential values and should be promoted and nurtured in our society, even if historically their work has been unduly, unfairly, and disproportionately foisted upon women. Rather than reject caring as lesser because of its association with women and women's work, or its correlation with oppressed statuses, we can decide that care, cooperation and interpersonal responsibility are so vital to human progress and happiness that they ought to be done by everyone. If we truly value caregiving, we should reward the people who do it with our society's traditional indicia of respect — prestige and economic advantages. Society's positive reinforcement of its important values encourages more people to excel at those tasks, master those skills, and adopt those orientations.

Caregiving, cooperation and an orientation toward interpersonal responsibility can be socially and legally promoted as easily as economic efficiency, competitive hierarchies, and self-interest have been. If, in fact, these traits do correlate with being men or women, they are not sex-linked, but gender-linked. Because gender is a process of socialization, men can be socialized to be caregivers and to assume an orientation of interpersonal responsibility and cooperation, just as easily as women have been. Certainly some men are already extremely competent caregivers. Cooperation, caregiving, and interpersonal responsibility orientations need not be taught through subordination, exclusion, marginalization, and fear. If an ethic of care is an orientation that we want reproduced and promoted in everyone, we need to discover ways to inculcate it without oppression. . . .

Mary Becker, Patriarchy and Inequality: Toward a Substantive Feminism
1999 U. Chi. Legal F. 21, 21-22, 48-49

As we reach the turn of the century, feminism seems to be at an impasse. Young women agree that women should receive equal pay and equal treatment as workers, but many insist that they are not feminists. Women have made strides in educational institutions and as workers during the current wave of the feminist movement, yet progress now seems to be at a snail's pace. Most women continue to do most caretaking and domestic work at home and now also work for wages. Most men are aware of women's second shift and its unfairness, but are uninterested in change. Media treat women better in some ways, but continue to focus primarily on men and on women in relationship to men. Most heroines are thin and beautiful. Women, particularly young women, are more obsessed than in earlier eras with weight and physical appearance as measures of merit. Real equality appears to be an ever-receding chimera.

I suggest that part of the problem is the failure of feminists, particularly feminists working for legal change, to look at the big picture: a social structure that is male-centered, male-identified, male-dominated, and which valorizes qualities narrowly defined as masculine. Neither of the approaches to change dominant in legal circles — liberal feminism and dominance feminism — has the potential to seriously threaten this structure because both are empty at their core, offering no values inconsistent with patriarchal values. Cultural feminism does offer values inconsistent with patriarchal values, but has been widely discredited in legal circles.

In this essay, I outline a variation on cultural feminism I call "relational feminism." This approach offers benefits to all members of society, not just women. Human beings, whether men, women, or children, do not flourish when hyper-masculinity is glorified and traditionally feminine qualities (such as care, caretaking, and valuing relationships) are denigrated. Nor do human beings flourish when all males are pressured to adopt hyper-masculine attributes and repress feminine ones, and all females are pressured to adopt traditionally feminine attributes and repress masculine ones. Relational feminism has the potential to improve life for many people, not just women.

. . .

Relational feminism does not reject either the equal treatment of similarly-situated women and men (formal equality's focus) nor more power as it is currently defined (dominance feminism's focus). But relational equality has a different focus: working for human happiness and fulfillment for women (and men). Similar treatment of similarly-situated women and men is often appropriate from this perspective. And giving more power, as it is currently described, to women is often appropriate. All else being equal, it is good (conducive to human happiness and fulfillment) for similar individuals to be treated similarly regardless of sex and good for women to have as much power, as it is currently defined, as men.

Sometimes, however, all is not otherwise equal, and other goods may be more important for women than either of these. If, for example, individual decisionmakers unconsciously prefer men because of patriarchal biases, a rule mandating formally equal treatment of women and men may be inappropriate. Or there may be instances in which something may be more important than power for women's happiness and fulfillment.

More importantly, one's focuses determine one's agenda and priorities. A focus on formal equality will produce a quite different agenda with quite different priorities from an anti-subordination focus. Similarly, a relational feminism focus will produce a quite different agenda with quite different priorities from either of the others. For example, the need to value caretaking and relationships, particularly with dependents, will be high on a relational feminism agenda, and might not even appear on a formal equality or anti-subordination agenda.

To date, cultural feminism is the only strand of feminist theory with values that are incompatible with patriarchal values. Cultural feminism has, therefore, the potential to challenge patriarchy.

Notes

1. Gilligan's "Ethic of Care."   Lawrence Kohlberg's six-stage model of moral development associates progression in moral thinking with increasingly abstract levels of reasoning. In her 1982 work, In a Different Voice: Psychological Theory and Women's Development, Carol Gilligan demonstrated that this model reflected the stages through which boys typically progressed better than it did those for girls. In one of her most well known studies, Gilligan compared how boys and girls responded to "Heinz's dilemma," in which Heinz's wife is dying of cancer and requires a drug that Heinz cannot afford to purchase from the local pharmacist. The children are asked whether Heinz should steal the drug. Summarizing Gilligan's findings, Carrie Menkel-Meadow writes:

> Jake, an eleven-year-old boy, sees the problem as one of "balancing rights," like a judge who must make a decision or a mathematician who must solve an algebraic equation. Life is worth more than property, therefore Heinz should steal the drug. For Amy, an eleven-year-old girl, the problem is different. Like a "bad" law student who "fights the hypo" she wants to know more facts. Have Heinz and the druggist explored other possibilities, like a loan or credit transaction? Why couldn't Heinz and the druggist simply sit down and talk it out so that the druggist would come to see the importance of Heinz's wife's life? In Gilligan's terms, Jake explores the Heinz dilemma with the "logic of justice" while Amy uses the "ethic of care." Amy scores lower on the Kohlberg scale because she sees the problem rooted in the persons involved rather than in the larger universal issues posed by the dilemma.

Carrie Menkel-Meadow, Portia in a Different Voice: Speculations on a Women's Lawyering Process, 1 Berkeley Women's L.J. 39, 46 (1985). Is it clear that Jake's mode of analysis is closer to the legal paradigm of reasoning? What does it mean for problems to be "rooted in the persons involved rather than in the larger universal issues"?

Gilligan's work has been extended and revised in subsequent work, some of which appears in Mapping the Moral Domain: A Contribution of Women's Thinking to Psychological Theory and Education (Carol Gilligan, Janie Victoria Ward, & Jill McLean Taylor eds., 1988). See also Mary Field Belenky, Blythe McVicker Clinchy, Nancy Rule Goldberger, & Jill Mattuck Tarule, Women's Ways of Knowing: The Development of Self, Voice, and Mind (1986).

2. Implications of the Ethic of Care.   Theorists associated with cultural feminism concur that this voice has been wrongfully neglected in social life and that its inclusion has potentially revolutionary effects. Gilligan argues that Amy's "different voice" can make a legitimate contribution to moral reasoning and should not be seen as necessarily inferior to Jake's abstract logic. Philosopher Sara Ruddick argues that maternal commitments to preservation, nurturance, and training can provide a sound foundation for "peacemaking" — the process of resolving international and domestic political conflicts. Ruddick, Maternal Thinking: Toward a Politics of Peace (1989). Mary Becker, in the reading above, argues that only relational feminism offers a head-on challenge to patriarchy.

Those who are critical of cultural feminism tend, like MacKinnon, to see it as supporting rather than challenging patriarchy because it takes stereotypical gender associations as true. Sara Ruddick notes, for example, that the association of men with war, women with peace is romantic rather than realistic: many men abhor war, and many women are excited by it. Ruddick, supra, at 154-155. Moreover, images that stem from this association — such as the image of women "keeping the home fires burning" while their men go to war — can be used to perpetuate warrior culture rather than challenge it. Linking "war" to men and "peace" to women suggests that both war and maleness itself are part of the natural order. Id. at 156-157. In this way, the ethic of care can be understood as socially conservative rather than progressive. These and other critiques of cultural feminism are explored throughout the chapter.

B. THE CONNECTION THESIS: A BIOLOGICAL BASIS?

≣ *Richard A. Epstein, Gender Is for Nouns*
41 DePaul L. Rev. 981, 989-990 (1992)

[B]iological differences must be taken into account in dealing with all forms of human behavior, however far removed they may appear to be from biological roots.

[C]onsider the question of differences in spatial perception. Here, the traditional account of its origins is quite persuasive. So long as there is any division of labor between the two sexes, it must be decided who will stay with the newborn child and who will venture forth to explore, to fight, and to hunt. This is true because there are clear losses to the family unit if both parents have identical tasks. In economic terms, the potential gains from specialization and trade are too large to be ignored, especially under conditions of extreme scarcity. The mere fact that the mother carries with her a supply of milk makes it clear that she is the better candidate for staying with the child, consequently leaving the male of the species to engage in a broad class of explorative activities. The nurturing instincts usually attributable to women are a set of attitudinal adaptations that reduce the cost of doing activities that help promote the survival of both her and her offspring. Although modern women operate in settings far different from those of their ancient mothers, the initial tendency still remains: If nurturing brings greater pleasure or requires lower cost for women than for men, then we should expect to see women devote a greater percentage of their resources to it than men. This specialization will endure in the aggregate and should be accepted for what it is: a healthy adaptation that works for the benefit of all concerned, and not as a sign of inferiority or disrespect.

There are offsetting adjustments in the male, for the devotion of greater mental resources to spatial arrangements at the cost of other advantages carries with it a strong reproductive payoff. The ability to give this characteristic selectively to one sex to the exclusion of the other also carries with it a strong reproductive advantage in that it is possible to leave superior endowments in all offspring. The alternative strategy, which gives the same cognitive skills and basic attitudes to all offspring, will leave both males and females at a relative disadvantage for their biologically specialized tasks, especially since there is no gain from reversing the sex roles in parenting. The other gains from specialization are still too great to be overcome. This explanation involves the interaction of social function with biological fitness. Is there any purely social explanation that can account for these differences?

Kathryn Abrams, *Social Construction, Roving Biologism, and Reasonable Women: A Response to Professor Epstein*
41 DePaul L. Rev. 1021, 1024-1028 (1992)

[O]f all the possible influences over the division of labor within the family, Professor [Richard] Epstein begins from a biological capacity that is no longer inexorably linked to differentiation. Breast milk is not, nor has it in memory been, the only alternative for nourishing infants. . . . To enshrine this difference as central, at a time when we have the technological capacity to generate adequate substitutes is a bit like describing the structure of contemporary society as arising from the human inability to master air travel. However, Professor Epstein argues that despite the changes wrought by contemporary technology, the critical seeds of differentiation have already been sown: Once the adaptations described "become embedded in the brain, the glacial pace of evolutionary change means that they cannot be undone in an age when infant formula is a tolerable substitute for mother's milk." So it seems that these adaptations also require scrutiny.

The male adaptation is arguably more plausible, though it might still be challenged as insufficiently empirically grounded or as inadequately explained. . . . [I]t is not clear . . . why the initial division of labor arising from breastfeeding would necessarily reinforce [his explorative and spatial perception advantages]. Why should the male adventurer have more opportunity to develop these capacities than the female, who is constantly balancing and shifting her infants, or cannily judging the distance between her children and danger?

The female adaptation — the development of a gender-wide capacity for nurturance — is even more problematic. Nurturance is an attitude, an attribute of personality. Only the most extreme proponents of sociobiology — those who begin with Darwin and "extrapolate from the species to the individual and from physical characteristics to psychological ones"[19] — would assert that nurturance is or comes to be embodied in a particular portion of the brain. . . . [I]t may be useful to juxtapose a countervailing explanation offered by proponents of social construction, one that reflects not only greater plausibility but the analytic complexity of such efforts.

Nurturance is an attitudinal characteristic that arises in response to certain circumstances and is passed on — to the extent that it is not a function of continuing adaptation to changing circumstances — by women watching and mothering each other. It thus becomes important to ask: To what is nurturing a necessary adaptation? It seems plausible that it was a response, at one time, to the evidently restrictive need to feed an infant, from one's own body, every few hours. But to describe it simply, and contemporarily, in this way is to overlook the numerous social and attitudinal structures that grew up to reinforce women's restriction to these tasks. These include the convictions of husbands, which may have emerged originally to protect their access to the "broad class of explorative activities" that women's childrearing labor permitted them, but continued in response to solidifying social convictions that childcare is "women's work" or that it is a sign of a husband's weakness or failure to provide if a wife with children "has to work." Nurturance may also have been an adaptation to limited opportunities for women outside the home, which began with workplaces that excluded women entirely, excluded pregnant women as unseemly or unfit, or regulated the hours of working women in deference to their "first task" in the home. In more contemporary times, women's decision to develop this aspect of their personalities may have responded to employers' failure to accommodate workers who are also parents, or spouses' failure to share the domestic tasks that fall disproportionately to mothers who continue to work. This explanation should not be understood to undercut the value of nurturance, or to deny that there are many attributes of small children that are attractive, lovable, or inducing of nurturant impulses. It is intended simply to suggest that to describe nurturance as an adaptation to the capacity to breastfeed, passed on through some variant of Lamarckian evolution is to miss many features of the social world in which human beings have evolved.

[Another] point of controversy is Professor Epstein's conclusion that because nurturance brings more pleasure or lower cost to women than men,

---

19. Cynthia Fuchs Epstein, [Deceptive Distinctions: Sex, Gender and the Social Order 47 (1988)] (citing Carol Tavris & Carole Wade, The Longest War: Sex Differences in Perspective (2d ed. 1984)). Prominent among the sociobiologists thus described is entomologist Edward Wilson. See Edward O. Wilson, On Human Nature (1978).

it should be accepted as a "healthy adaptation that works to the benefit of all concerned." Setting aside the doubts previously raised about the origins of this development, this assertion makes the further error of confusing results that have some biological basis with results that are socially or normatively acceptable. . . . The lower cost of nurturance to women . . . is attributable largely to the fact that, given the rigidity of familial patterns and workplace structures, many men have never been given the opportunity to develop it. Moreover, lower cost (in relation to men) should not automatically be associated with greater pleasure in nurturing for women. The increasingly audible discontent of women with the current division of labor in the family belies this conclusion, as the low pay and low social valuation of those who perform childcare in place of biological mothers belies the conclusion that the current specialization is no "sign of inferiority or disrespect."

Amy L. Wax, Against Nature — On Robert Wright's The Moral Animal
63 U. Chi. L. Rev. 307, 314-316, 318-323, 330, 346-347, 354-356 (1996)

[Robert Wright in The Moral Animal: Evolutionary Psychology and Everyday Life (1994) asserts] that evolutionary forces have produced biologically programmed differences in the psychology of male and female. Sexual difference begins — but does not end — with the obvious specialization in reproductive capacity: anatomical sexual dimorphism. Evolutionary theory postulates that anatomical sexual dimorphism exerts selective pressures that produce wide-ranging average differences between the sexes in emotion, attitude, interest, and behavior. The anatomical fact most crucial to this process is that men produce sperm whereas women produce eggs and, eventually, babies. From this simple disparity of function flows a momentous consequence: a woman in a lifetime can produce at most twenty children. Moreover, the investment a woman was required to make in the ancestral environment to insure each baby's survival — including nine months of pregnancy, intensive and prolonged breast-feeding, and the day-to-day care of the very young child — virtually ruled out significant engagement in any other demanding activity for most of her adult life. In contrast, an ancestral man could produce hundreds or even thousands of offspring in a lifetime. A brief sexual encounter might be all that was required to get his genes into the next generation. . . .

. . . Because behavior influences survival, and psychology influences behavior, evolutionary theory predicts that the reproductive pressure exerted by these structural disparities will be felt in the personalities of the sexes. Thus, for example, evolution will select women who cherish each reproductive opportunity, and who exert a high level of care in the selection of sexual partners and the nurturing of offspring, whereas it will favor men who are somewhat less interested in providing intensive nurturing than in fathering more children.

A spinning out of this logic leads to the theory of "sexual selection" — the predominance of behaviors in each sex that represent "whatever each sex must do to get what it wants from the other" [Wright, supra, at 63-64]. For example, a woman will maximize her reproductive success by choosing men in the best position, and more willing, to help her care for her children. Since women favor men with resources and status (the better to nurture her offspring), men correspondingly develop a taste for wealth and status, and the capacity to compete with other men to maintain status. Since men favor women whose offspring they can identify as their own, they will tend to favor female sexual fidelity and reserve, and females will come to display those traits. In sum, evolution selects for men who are competitive, sexually jealous, and randy (that is, ready to jump at any sexual opportunity). It selects for women who are relatively coy (that is, picky about their mates' status, prowess, and devotion), nurturing (willing to care for their babies), and not particularly competitive (since fertile women get impregnated as a matter of course, and the exigencies of motherhood in the ancestral environment didn't leave much time for direct competition for resources). The genes for these traits will tend to multiply in the population both because these traits make for attractiveness to the opposite sex and because they directly foster reproductive success. These complex patterns are driven by the simple fact that unsuccessful strategies — whether the male failure to monopolize resources and females, or the female failure to harness the resources of a successful male for her children — spelled reproductive doom in the ancestral environment. . . .

[Wright also explains how man developed into a "moral animal."] His account takes as its starting point the evolution of reciprocal altruism. . . . [R]eciprocal altruism can proceed atomistically: each person decides how he will deal with every other on a case-by-case basis, depending on how he has been treated in the past and anticipates being treated in the future. But . . . man has not been content to proceed atomistically. . . . Persons not only react, they also judge . . . by developing a principled sense of how persons in general ought to behave. . . .

Evolutionary theory predicts that, once the tendency to cooperate has spread within a population, individuals who adhere to the conventions of "surplus maximizing" reciprocity will obtain an advantage over those who are less skilled at responding appropriately to others. . . .

In sum, certain social virtues are preserved by evolution because they enable individuals to enlist the aid of others in maximizing material advantage and attaining greater reproductive success. . . .

["S]tatus hunger" drives a desire not just to do, but more precisely, "to be seen doing [ ] whatever everyone says is good" [Wright, supra, at 212].
. . .

Within this framework, normative cultural conventions succeed not by opposing the "artificial" or the conventional to the natural, but by calling a truce in the war of conflicting natural impulses. The "natural" longing to be known as good, admirable, honorable, or worthy within a shared scheme of moral valuation is enlisted to fight the "natural" tendency to engage in short-term, egotistical, selfish, individualistic, domineering strategies. The need to be held in high esteem by one's fellows (and perhaps oneself) is as reliable a feature of man's evolved psychology as, for example, his need for sexual gratification. . . .

. . . Wright's discussion leads us to understand that successful moral systems achieve stability by harnessing one set of evolved psychological tendencies against others. Moral institutions are the methods by which desire fights desire. . . .

Lessons of sociobiology align with fundamental precepts of social conservatism for three reasons. First, although an evolutionary approach does not require denying the efficacy of concerted social intervention to influence behavior — indeed, it explains why such social intervention is a common feature of communal life — it identifies the main obstacles to radical social change as lying within the individual rather than outside of him. It posits unavoidable tradeoffs ultimately grounded in biological nature — between freedom and order, desire and well-being, and stability and equality — that confront every melioristic or utopian project. Second, sociobiology suggests that the observed superiority of some traditional institutions (such as the two-parent family) in performing certain functions (such as raising children) does not stem from the arbitrary decision to "privilege" those institutions (although they have indeed been privileged in law and custom). Rather, the functional superiority is the product of features inherent to the institutions as they respond to our biological endowments. Third, sociobiology points to the importance of moral climate and "cultural values" in fostering behaviors that make for a peaceful and prosperous society. . . .

The picture of human psychology that emerges from the study of evolution suggests that projects for social change have the greatest chance of success if framed as attempts to create norms of acceptable or commendable behavior. Changing norms will likely prove more important than effecting purely external or structural changes in institutions on the one hand, or transforming individual personality or fundamental preference structures on the other. Rather than justifying the ends to which the techniques of social control can be applied, these insights invite us to view the "moralization" of conduct as a method that can be put to many uses.

These observations are applicable to a range of social issues from drunk driving to parenting to teen pregnancy. They also have implications for the common feminist aspiration of greater equality for the sexes inside and outside of marriage. If conventional monogamy can be enforced "against nature," why not the feminist ideal? If civilization exists to frustrate natural preferences, it could as well be feminist civilization as any other. . . .

. . . [T]he most efficacious approach to the quest for greater sexual equality would not be one primarily directed at working a fundamental change in men's "primary" tastes and preferences. It would not necessarily have to await the emergence of a greater impulse for "nurturing" or a diminished attraction to competition in the male population. Rather than focusing on such transformations of feelings or attitudes, the focus should be on cultivating social expectations that play to the sense of moral duty and social obligation. . . . The most effective "nonsexist" upbringing may not consist of getting boys to play with dolls, but in defining proper conduct as fulfilling the duties of helpfulness, caring, and fairness, and in instilling egalitarian expectations concerning compliance with those duties.

Kingsley R. Browne, Sex and Temperament in Modern Society: A Darwinian View of the Glass Ceiling and the Gender Gap
37 Ariz. L. Rev. 971, 974, 976-977, 979-981, 983-984, 1016, 1065-1066, 1071, 1081-1082 (1995)

The idea of a fundamental "human nature" is resisted by many, apparently out of concern that recognition of biological roots of human nature would deny the autonomy and dignity of the individual. . . . Many also have political objections to the idea of a fundamental human nature, fearing that appeals to a biological human nature are merely a subterfuge to maintain the status quo. Nonetheless, an understanding of why we are the way we are is a precondition to our becoming the way that we hope to be. . . .

Although some people apparently believe that biological differences are unlikely because one can point to social reinforcements of these differences, the existence of social inputs does not imply the lack of a substantial biological contribution. After all, the fact that parents pressure their children to eat their dinners and not to run out into the middle of the street does not imply that children's hunger and drive for self-preservation are "socially constructed." . . .

If it is not the improbability of biological differences that causes people to reject them, then perhaps it is their implications. But what are these implications? The answer is that there are no necessary implications, since the existence of such differences does not in itself tell us what to do about them. We could decide that despite their biological basis we want to suppress these differences, or at least suppress any economic or other social consequences that they might cause, just as we suppress other kinds of behaviors that have some basis in biology, such as rape. On the other hand, we might decide that since these are "natural" differences, we are willing to live with them in a way that we would not if they were purely socially constructed. Moreover, no matter what our views about whether to accept these differences, knowledge of their causes may help in estimating the costs of social change and in formulating a strategy for effecting that change. At bottom, however, it seems the height of folly to base our public policies upon unexamined assumptions of behavioral identity that are so lacking in empirical support and, indeed, so strongly contradicted by a wealth of theoretical prediction and empirical data.

The current debate over the respective roles of the sexes in the workplace proceeds on the basis of usually unstated assumptions about the nature of man and woman. A concrete application of such assumptions can be found in the literature on the "glass ceiling." The "glass ceiling" is a metaphor that is meant to reflect the fact that women tend to be substantially underrepresented in the upper reaches of management. It is a clever metaphor for it not only captures an empirical observation — that women's progression up the hierarchy tends to "stall" at some point — but it also contains within it an assumption that the causes of this lack of progression are often-invisible forces that are external to women but internal to the organization. . . .

The assumption that men and women are substantially identical in respects relevant to the workplace leads to a reflexive suspicion whenever differences in outcome exist between the sexes, at least when the comparison is viewed as unfavorable to women. Thus, we speak of a gender gap in compensation to characterize the lower income of women, although one seldom hears about a gender gap in occupational deaths, despite the fact that thirteen men die on the job for every woman who dies. When viewed through the current lens of "gender equality," the former is a "problem" while the latter is merely a "fact."

If a major cause of these differential outcomes is the nature of men and women themselves, our attitudes toward them might change. Suppose, for example, that by nature men and women differ temperamentally and that these temperamental differences are substantial causes of the differences in outcome. How would we, or should we, respond? That is an important question to ponder even if one doubts the existence of such differences, since it helps illuminate one's conception of sexual equality.

The clarity of our definition of equality is not seriously challenged as long as we assume that the "second class" status of women in the workplace is due to unfair actions of employers or society that create artificial distinctions between effectively identical people. If unfair behavior has caused inequality, then fair behavior will presumably cause equality. However, if the differential status of men and women in the workplace is caused by true and fundamental sex differences, the response is not as obvious. One could argue that if differential outcomes are reflections of real differences, they are not arbitrary and require no correction. On the other hand, one might hold that even real sex differences cannot justify differential outcomes, either because differential outcomes are inherently unfair whatever their cause or because the differential outcomes are a consequence of employers' and society's arbitrarily and unfairly overvaluing male traits and undervaluing female ones.

In order to evaluate the validity of the argument that it is unfair to structure a reward system in a way that tends to favor men, one must understand the workings of the system. One should also examine the underlying premise itself—that men are favored by current arrangements. Assume that for some reason men are more competitive than women and more inclined to expend effort to climb hierarchies. Would it be unfair if a disproportionate number of men achieved the highest positions in the hierarchy? . . .

Suppose also that men are more inclined to take "career risks" than women. If men are more willing to put themselves into positions where there is substantial personal accountability and possibility of failure, one would expect more of the great successes — and great failures — to be men. Again, the question is whether it would be appropriate to structure workplace rewards in such a way as to equalize rewards between those who take risks for their success and those who do not.

Along the same lines, assume that men are more single-minded about acquiring resources than women. This is not to suggest that women are not interested in acquiring resources; almost everyone views resource acquisition positively and, all else being equal, would prefer more to less. The assumption that the reader is asked to indulge is that men place a higher priority on resource acquisition than women. Starting from this assumption, the question is whether it is arbitrary or unfair to have a system that leads to greater resource acquisition by those who are most willing to make sacrifices in other areas of their lives to obtain them.

Assume further that women are inclined to be more nurturant and oriented toward others, resulting in a greater attachment to their children and a lesser willingness to trade material resources for time spent with their children or in other activities. The psychic satisfaction they receive from devotion to family outweighs for them the reduced economic satisfaction that results from a lesser attachment to the workplace. If women work less because they have other forces in their lives that are as important as, or more important than, work, it is not obvious that social policy should be oriented toward ensuring that economic outcomes are nonetheless equivalent.

Consider also the "gender gap" in occupational deaths. The concentration of men in dangerous occupations has resulted in a substantial overrepresentation of men among those who die on the job. Should we be as concerned about this gender gap as we are about the gap in compensation? If not, why not? . . .

[T]he anthropological literature demonstrates a remarkable cross-cultural consistency in the sex differences under consideration, and the biological and psychological literatures are bulging with data tending to show that inherent differences exist between the sexes and explaining many of the biological mechanisms in both proximate and ultimate terms. These data suggest that we may have been confusing cause and effect; our patriarchal social structure — to the extent that we have one — may be more an effect of sex differences than their cause.

I should at this point say exactly what I am arguing. It is my central thesis that much of what we call the glass ceiling and gender gap is the product of basic biological sex differences in personality and temperament. These differences have resulted from differential reproductive strategies that have been adopted by the two sexes during human history and are every bit as much a product of natural selection as our bipedal locomotion and opposable thumbs. Although these temperamental traits evolved in our hunting-and-gathering ancestral environment, they remain with us today whether or not they remain adaptive.

I should similarly emphasize what I am not arguing. It is not my position that biology is the exclusive cause of the glass ceiling or the gender gap. Indeed, such a claim would be specious, since all behavior involves the organism's interaction with its environment. But even beyond this truism, I do not doubt that some portion of these two phenomena are produced by social attitudes, some of them arbitrary, as well as by outright sex discrimination that may be based upon false assumptions about the relative capacities of the sexes. I also do not argue that social reinforcement of these differences is insignificant. It would be very strange if social institutions were oblivious to these differences. . . .

Evolutionary theory predicts that men will tend to exhibit greater status-seeking, competitiveness, and risk-taking than women, and that women will exhibit more nurturance and affiliative behavior. These predictions are borne out in every known human society. With respect to all of these traits, the differences are statistical, in the sense that they are generalizations that do not hold true for all individuals. However, even relatively small between-group differences can have a dramatic effect on the sex ratio at the extremes. Moreover, since the glass ceiling and the gender gap in compensation are themselves both group-based phenomena, it seems appropriate to seek an explanation for them in terms of group-based traits. . . .

It is a common observation — sometimes a complaint — that in order for women to attain the highest levels of success in the working world they must "be like men." Prominent among the qualities of successful female executives are the "male" traits of aggressiveness, ambition and drive, strong career orientation ("a passion for success"), and risk-taking. Women are consistently perceived to have a lesser level of these traits than men. Even apart from commitment to children, women as a class differ in important temperamental ways from men. Combined with women's greater commitment to families these temperamental differences have a powerful effect. . . .

If a substantial contributor to the "glass ceiling" is the fact that women tend not to display, to the same degree that men do, the temperamental traits and accompanying behaviors that result in achieving the highest levels, then in order for women to achieve parity, something must change: either the job requirements or women themselves. Many students of the glass ceiling have advocated both changes: employers should stop rewarding driven and ambitious people, and girls should be socialized to manifest the same drive and ambition as males. For a whole host of reasons, both of these suggestions are unlikely to bear fruit.

It seems unlikely in the extreme that employers will cease rewarding employees who exhibit a high degree of commitment to the employer. All else being equal — and in the absence of some prohibition — an employer will generally prefer a worker who puts in more hours to one who puts in fewer; it will prefer a worker who will travel or relocate to one who will not; and it will prefer a worker whose career is not interrupted by lengthy absences from the labor market to one whose is. Those employees are simply more valuable. Moreover, it is a fact of life in modern America that men work more hours, are more willing to travel and relocate, and are less likely to leave the labor force for extended periods. . . .

[T]he simplistic observation that men and women have different average earnings tells one very little, but the fact that earnings are easier to quantify and compare than other important job attributes has led to an undue focus on wage disparities. To the extent that compensation differences are due to the kinds of differences described above, it is not clear why there should be societal intervention. The studies described above suggest that if women make the same kinds of human-capital investments and occupational choices as men, their compensation will be much more similar to men's than it is now. If they choose to work fewer hours, seek less job-related training, and select jobs that have advantages that for them outweigh the lower pay, it is difficult to see why there is any need for correction. Preventing employers from giving higher pay to employees who work more hours, have greater job-related training, or occupy riskier jobs seems foolish.

Notes

1. **Cultural Feminist Explanations for Women's Ethic of Care.** There are a number of sociological and psychological theories to explain the apparent association between women and an ethic of care, touching all points along the spectrum from purely biological to purely cultural explanations. In emphasizing the role of pregnancy and breast-feeding and the "invasive" aspects of sexual intercourse for women, Robin West seems to share Richard Epstein's reliance on biological foundations. Do these two theorists use "biology" in the same way?

Other feminist theorists combine socialization theories with psychological theories, surmising that women's ethic of care is deeply imprinted in their psyches by childhood experience. One version of this hypothesis is that because mothers raise children in this society, boys develop by separating from their differently gendered mothers, thus reinforcing values of separation and individual identity; girls, on the other hand, develop by identifying with their mothers to whom they remain connected, thus reinforcing values of relationship and communal identity. See Nancy Chodorow, The Reproduction of Mothering: Psychoanalysis and the Sociology of Gender (1978); see also Nancy Chodorow, Feminism and Psychoanalytic Theory (1989); Dorothy Dinnerstein, The Mermaid and the Minotaur: Sexual Arrangements and Human Malaise (1976).

Still other feminist theorists are reluctant to too closely associate an ethic of care with women. Philosopher Sara Ruddick acknowledges an identifiably "female" perspective on the world, but locates its source in the social practice of "mothering," which she argues is potentially gender-neutral. Sara Ruddick, Maternal Thinking: Toward a Politics of Peace (1989). In Ruddick's view, both men and women can be mothers, and not all women are mothers (although she recognizes that most women have at least considered mothering as a likely part of their lives). Joan Tronto goes further, arguing that "we need to stop talking about 'women's morality' and start talking instead about a care ethic that includes the values traditionally associated with women." Joan C. Tronto, Moral Boundaries: A Political Argument for an Ethic of Care 3 (1993).

Is this gender-neutral approach appealing? Consider the following:

> [S]ome who have been attracted by the advantages of an ethic of care have argued that it has non-gender-based sources and could be adopted as a "humanist" approach to law, that is, one that promotes the value of caring apart from any language of gender relations. Frankly, while I am sympathetic to feminists who make this argument, I believe it is politically, theoretically, and factually unsound to move women from center stage in this proposed reconstruction of legal and ethical discourse based on an ethic of care. Interpersonal caregiving is something that women have specialized in for years. We have special knowledge and insights to offer. After many, many years of being submerged, we have finally come above the surface and caught our long-awaited breath. The air tastes good. A change to "humanism," I fear, will ultimately press us under water again. While we clearly must be very cautious about perpetuating disempowering or disadvantaging stereotypes, the move from "women" to "human" seems to dupe us into an even worse co-optation of being reabsorbed, resilenced, and resubmerged into a newly invisible system of male dominance. Consequently, I reject critiques of a gender-based ethic of care that locate the ethic of care in a humanist approach.

Leslie Bender, From Gender Difference to Feminist Solidarity: Using Carol Gilligan and an Ethic of Care in Law, 15 Vt. L. Rev. 1, 40 (1990). For agreement on this point, see Linda J. Lacey, Mimicking the Words, but Missing the Message: The Misuse of Cultural Feminist Themes in Religion and Family Law Jurisprudence, 35 B.C. L. Rev. 1, 46 (1993). Is there middle ground? See Robin West, Caring for Justice 20 (1997) (arguing that it is true both that "the experiences that inform an ethic of care are largely the caregiving experiences of women" and that "men as well as women can and should employ such an ethic"). What is at stake here?

2. Biology and Feminist Legal Theories. The controversial question of whether and to what extent differences between men and women are rooted in biology has produced an extensive scientific literature — too extensive to permit even a representative sampling. Without the opportunity to fully explore the research, the question for this chapter will have to be not *whether* the premises of evolutionary biology (also called "developmental biology" and "sociobiology") are true, but rather *what follows* if they are true.

First, it is useful to review the possible role that each theory presented thus far in this book leaves for biology. Formal equality theorists tend to downplay differences, biological or otherwise, and to emphasize similarities and thus the need for equal treatment. Biological differences are harder to deny than other differences. Nevertheless, formal equality advocates conclude that many characteristics that appear as differences — even pregnancy — are similar enough to a common human condition not unique to women — like disability. Thus, even biological differences are not assumed to justify different treatment.

Substantive equality theorists highlight sex-based differences and use them to justify the social intervention necessary to achieve equal outcomes. What differences should be significant depends upon the version of substantive equality to which one subscribes. Some versions of substantive equality, such as Herma Hill Kay's episodic analysis set forth at pages 328-330, accommodate only biological differences. Other proposals, such as those summarized in Chapter 3, section B(2), note 3 on pages 337-342, 354-355, and 357, urge accommodations for differences, such as heavier caretaking roles for women, that are produced by social practice or design.

Dominance theorists, like substantive equality theorists, emphasize women's differences from men rather than their similarities. Their account of these differences, however, is one of social construction, not biological determinism. The point of dominance theory is not to "accommodate" women's differences, biological or otherwise, but to terminate the subordination that results when these differences are manipulated to legitimize and perpetuate male power over women. Difference is fundamentally man-made, not biological.

Relational feminists approach the issue of biology with some ambivalence. Unlike formal equality theorists, they highlight rather than minimize difference, even biological difference, as a source of strength and diversity. But while substantive equality theorists (along with dominance theorists) are concerned most about how ignoring difference perpetuates sexual subordination, relational feminists are concerned about the loss to society of devaluing perspectives that would improve community and its moral integrity and cohesion. That some of these perspectives may be biologically based helps relational theorists establish the actual existence of differences that formal equality advocates want to deny. But insofar as these theorists seek a blueprint for a less combative and more interconnected and caring world, proving that gender difference is biologically based can be, if anything, an impediment, since it would seem to require working — in Amy Wax's terms — "against nature."

3. The Normative Implications of the Evolutionary Thesis. Are there any necessary policy implications to be drawn from sociobiological premises? To Richard Epstein, different personality types and social roles are a matter of efficiency — nature's efficiency. Efforts to change the instincts that have emerged as adaptive behaviors are simply inefficient. Kingsley Browne, while he states that there are no "necessary" implications, makes it clear that once the "glass ceiling" or the gender gap in women's earnings is explained as a product of natural selection processes, there is no longer sex discrimination for which a legal remedy is necessary. Elsewhere he states that efforts to prohibit sexual harassment are doomed, insofar as they go "against the grain" of human psychology. See Browne, An Evolutionary Perspective of Sexual Harassment: Seeking Roots in Biology Rather than Ideology, 8 J. Contemp. Legal Issues 5 (1997); see also Kingsley R. Browne, Women at War: An Evolutionary Perspective, 49 Buff. L. Rev. 51, 56 (2001) (using evolutionary psychology and the literature of sex-linked cognitive and behavioral differences to challenge the assumption that "all it will take to integrate women into combat roles is educating men out of their ideology of masculinism").

Amy Wax draws different conclusions from evolutionary biology because she emphasizes not the characteristics directly produced (according to sociobiology) by the sexually dimorphic scramble to keep one's genes alive, but the moral principles that must evolve to harness the self-destructive aspects of these characteristics. One could differ, of course, about what those moral principles should be. To George Gilder, the traditional two-parent nuclear family is the answer, for it is the only way women can channel men's roving sexual impulses toward the good of the family and, by extension, the good of society as a whole.

A man without a woman has a deep inner sense of dispensability, perhaps evolved during the millennia of service in the front lines of tribal defense. He is sexually optional. Several dominant males could impregnate all the women and perpetuate the tribe. It is this sense of dispensability that makes young men good fighters, good crusaders, good martyrs. But it also weakens the male ability to care deeply and long and stunts young men's sense of the preciousness of human beings. Because the woman has always been directly responsible for infants and almost always exclusively responsible, she is dubious about the dying and killing that have surrounded male activities.

Once the man marries he can change. He has to change, for his wife will not long have him if he remains in spirit a single man. He must settle his life, and commit it to the needs of raising a family. He must exchange the moral and spiritual rhythms of the hunt for a higher, more extended mode of sexual life. He must submit, ethically and sexually, to the values of maternal morality and futurity.

Gilder, Men and Marriage 15-16 (1986). To Gilder, the problem with women pursuing employment outside the home is not only that children need their care but also that unless men's energies are directed toward the long-term goal of providing for their families, their sexual energies and aggressions will necessarily be turned against society. Id. at 153. In contrast to Gilder, Wax talks about implementing "the feminist ideal." What do you think she means? Do you see any dangers in the approach she suggests? For another sociobiological account that promises a "morally indifferent" approach to regulating sex and gender relations, see Richard A. Posner, Sex and Reason (1992).

4. Evolutionary Biology: The Feminist Critique. The feminist response to evolutionary biology, as exemplified by the Abrams reading, has been largely negative. Why do you suppose this would be? Consider the following:

> The point of human nature theories . . . is to attribute a fixed bottom line, an unchangeability that we must live within and keep in view, a baseline that no choice or policy can alter. These theories set limits, telling us that "there have always been" certain things, as if no further explanation is needed, certainly not a social one; as if the fact that "there have always been" certain things necessarily points to biology. This assumption, while not justified, does not in itself make such theories false, but the variability of sexual facts across and within cultures and times, as well as the fact that the particular limits thus asserted reinscribed the unequal gendered social status quo, tends to undermine their claim to being prior to society. In other words, theories that attempt to explain facts of women's inequality to men — say, rape or prostitution or sexual harassment or pornography — in terms of human nature are first and last theories of what women must put up with.

Catharine A. MacKinnon, Pornography Left and Right, 30 Harv. C.R.-C.L. L. Rev. 143, 151-152 (1995).

Do we have to choose between "the concept of biological potentiality, with a brain capable of the full range of human behaviors and predisposed toward none, [and] the idea of biological determinism with specific genes for specific behavioral traits"? This is the choice put by Steven Jay Gould, Biological Potential vs. Biological Determinism, in The Sociobiology Debate: Readings on Ethical and Scientific Issues 343, 349 (Arthur L.

Caplan ed., 1978), cited in Wax, supra, at 328. Katharine Baker suggests the choice is a false one:

> . . . For years feminists have been describing a world in which sexual violence is pervasive, marriage is a Faustian and dangerous bargain for women, and caretaking is a huge amount of usually unrewarded work. This is the world that the biologists describe also. If the biologist's description is more frightening than the feminist one, it is only because of the common but unnecessary presumption that, because the world is that way, it must stay that way. No biologist believes this. How we act is a complex function of both genetic composition and social environment. Indeed, prominent evolutionary biologist Timothy Goldsmith suggests that it is meaningless to try to determine the extent to which any given human action is genetically or culturally determined. [Timothy H. Goldsmith, The Biological Roots of Human Nature: Forging Links Between Evolution and Behavior 87 (1991).] Richard Dawkins, one of the most important figures in modern evolutionary theory, writes that
>
> > it is a fallacy — incidentally a very common one — to suppose that genetically inherited traits are by definition fixed and unmodifiable. Our genes may instruct us to be selfish, but we are not necessarily compelled to obey them all our lives. . . . Human society based simply on the gene's law of universal ruthless selfishness would be a very nasty society in which to live.
>
> [Richard Dawkins, The Selfish Gene 3 (1989).] Biologists do not tell us that genes necessarily determine our behavior; they tell us how genes can strongly influence our behavior. It is up to social constructions of morality, equality, and justice to provide a counterinfluence that makes the world a place in which we want to live.
>
> Therein lies biology's attraction to feminists. By laying bare the harsh reality of nature, it forces us to embrace our normative convictions. Biology, along with Catharine MacKinnon, belies the assumption that rape is totally different than sex. [MacKinnon, Toward a Feminist Theory of the State 174 (1989).] Biology, along with Mary Becker, refutes the naive presumption that men's and women's interests coincide, even in marriage. [Becker, Politics, Differences and Economic Rights, 1989 U. Chi. Legal F. 169, 169-190.] Biology, along with Martha Fineman, makes clear that mothering is work; it is work done predominantly by women, and fathering has remarkably little to do with parenting. [Fineman, The Neutered Mother, the Sexual Family and Other Twentieth Century Tragedies (1995).] What feminists call patriarchal culture, biologists call nature, but whatever it is called, anyone with any moral sensitivity can readily see that it is an altogether inferior, unjust, and undesirable place to be. And as biology makes plain, it is up to us to change it.

Katharine K. Baker, Biology for Feminists, 75 Chi.-Kent. L. Rev. 805 , 806-807 (2000). See also Wax, supra, at 329-330 ("[M]an does indeed have tendencies, some stronger, more pervasive, and more 'hard wired' than others. To say that, however, is not to say that the tendencies cannot be curbed or overcome by the forces of culture or morality.")

Can the confidence that Baker and Wax have that feminists can work within sociobiological premises be justified?

The connections between rape and biology are explored in a growing academic literature. See, e.g., Owen D. Jones, Law and the Biology of Rape: Reflections on Transitions, 11 Hastings L.J. 151 (2000); Owen D. Jones, Sex, Culture, and the Biology of Rape: Toward Explanation and Prevention, 87 Cal. L.Rev. 827 (1999); Deborah W. Denno, Evolutionary Biology and Rape, 39 Jurimetrics J. 243 (1999); and other articles in Symposium, Biology and Sexual Aggression, 39 Jurimetrics J. (Fall & Winter 1999).

5. Evolutionary Biology: What's at Stake for Feminists? Is there a specifically "female" experience of the world? If so, what is its source? Does it matter whether the source is biological, cultural, or a combination of the two? Robin West suggests that what matters more is that the difference between male and female experience, values, and commitments is real:

> It truly would be extremely odd, as [Gilligan] argued, if it turned out that the vastly greater amount of child raising and homekeeping, the world over and throughout history, in which women engage — a fact apparently conceded by all — has *no impact whatsoever* on the moral orientations of the two sexes. Similarly it really would be extremely odd if it turned out that our shared experience as infants and children under the protection and tutelage and love of *women* — our shared experiences derived from the fact that we are all *to woman* born — also has *no* differentiating effect or impact on the way the two sexes view relational ethics. It would be odd if it turned out that the experiences of pregnancy and childbirth, shared by the majority of all women everywhere, have no effect, and lend to women's perspectives no unifying and distinguishing threads. The null hypothesis, if we are questioning sameness or difference, might more defensibly be identified as the claim of difference, rather than the claim of sameness, in the face of these quite different early experiences of the world.

Robin West, Caring for Justice 18-19 (1997).

C. THE LEGAL IMPLICATIONS OF THE "ETHIC OF CARE"

1. Relational Values in Substantive Law

≡ *Leslie Bender, A Lawyer's Primer on Feminist*
≡ *Theory and Tort*
≡ 38 J. Legal Educ. 3, 31-36 (1988)

Negligence law could begin with Gilligan's articulation of the feminine voice's ethic of care — a premise that no one should be hurt. We could convert the present standard of "care of a reasonable person under the same or similar circumstances" to a standard of "conscious care and concern of a responsible neighbor or social acquaintance for another under the same or similar circumstances." . . .

The recognition that we are all interdependent and connected and that we are by nature social beings who must interact with one another should lead us to judge conduct as tortious when it does not evidence responsible care or concern for another's safety, welfare, or health. Tort law should begin with a premise of responsibility rather than rights, of interconnectedness rather than separation, and a priority of safety rather than profit or efficiency. The masculine voice of rights, autonomy, and abstraction has led to a standard that protects efficiency and profit; the feminine voice can design a tort system that encourages behavior that is caring about others' safety and responsive to others' needs or hurts, and that attends to human contexts and consequences. . . .

One of the most difficult areas in which questions of duty and the standard of care arise is the "no duty to rescue" case. The problem is traditionally illustrated by the drowning-stranger hypothetical and the infamous case of Yania v. Bigan.[117] . . .

Each year that I teach torts I watch again as a majority of my students initially find this legal "no duty" rule reprehensible. After the rationale is explained and the students become immersed in the "reasoned" analysis, and after they take a distanced, objective posture informed by liberalism's concerns for autonomy and liberty, many come to accept the legal rule that intuitively had seemed so wrong to them. They are taught to reject their emotions, instincts, and ethics, and to view accidents and tragedies

---

117. [155 A.2d 343 (1959)]. Yania was a business competitor of Bigan and had gone onto Bigan's land to speak with him. Both men were involved in strip-mining, and Bigan was working at a deep trench partially filled with water. Although the facts are ambiguous, there was testimony that Bigan dared or cajoled Yania to jump into the pit, in which he drowned as Bigan looked on. It is equally possible that Yania jumped into the pit to demonstrate to Bigan his expertise in solving the problem there. In either case, Yania drowned and Yania's widow sued Bigan. She lost. The Pennsylvania Supreme Court refused to impose an affirmative duty on one party to rescue or aid another.

abstractly, removed from their social and particularized contexts, and to apply instead rationally-derived universal principles and a vision of human nature as atomistic, self-interested, and as free from constraint as possible. They are also taught that there are legally relevant distinctions between acts and omissions.

How would this drowning-stranger hypothetical look from a new legal perspective informed by a feminist ethic based upon notions of caring, responsibility, interconnectedness, and cooperation? If we put abstract reasoning and autonomy aside momentarily, we can see what else matters. In defining duty, what matters is that someone, a human being, a part of us, is drowning and will die without some affirmative action. That seems more urgent, more imperative, more important than any possible infringement of individual autonomy by the imposition of an affirmative duty. If we think about the stranger as a human being for a moment, we may realize that much more is involved than balancing one person's interest in having his life saved and another's interest in not having affirmative duties imposed upon him in the absence of a special relationship, although even then the balance seems to me to weigh in favor of imposing a duty or standard of care that requires action. The drowning stranger is not the only person affected by the lack of care. He is not detached from everyone else. He no doubt has people who care about him — parents, spouse, children, friends, colleagues; groups he participates in — religious, social, athletic, artistic, political, educational, work-related; he may even have people who depend upon him for emotional or financial support. He is interconnected with others. If the stranger drowns, many will be harmed. It is not an isolated event with one person's interests balanced against another's. When our legal system trains us to understand the drowning-stranger story as a limited event between two people, both of whom have interests at least equally worth protecting, and when the social ramifications we credit most are the impositions on personal liberty of action, we take a human situation and translate it into a cold, dehumanized algebraic equation. We forget that we are talking about human death or grave physical harms and their reverberating consequences when we equate the consequences with such things as one person's momentary freedom not to act. People are decontextualized for the analysis, yet no one really lives an acontextual life. . . .

If instead we impose a duty of acting responsibly with the same self-conscious care for the safety of others that we would give our neighbors or people we know, we require the actor to consider the human consequences of her failure to rescue. . . .

. . . The duty to act with care for another's safety, which under appropriate circumstances would include an affirmative duty to act to protect or prevent harm to another, would be shaped by the particular context. One's ability to aid and one's proximity to the need would be relevant considerations. Whether one met that duty would not be determined by how a reasonable person would have acted under the circumstances but by whether one acted out of a conscious care and concern for the safety, health, and well-being of the victim in the way one would act out of care for a neighbor or friend. . . . This seemingly minor change would transform the core of negligence law to a human, responsive system.

Richard A. Posner, Conservative Feminism
1989 U. Chi. Legal F. 191, 214

[M]ost people are what they are; most neighbors are not caring, and most accident victims are not neighbors. Human nature will not be altered by holding injurers liable for having failed to take the care that a caring neighbor would have taken. The only effect of adopting Bender's proposal would be to shift negligence liability in the direction of strict liability. Her "caring neighbor" is an unnecessary step in the analysis. Bender might as well argue directly for strict liability on the ground that it is the more altruistic regime than negligence.

Is it? Strict liability is sometimes defended on the ground that it provides more compensation to more accident victims. This is a partial analysis. Strict liability can also result in higher prices, and the burden may be borne by consumers. The net distributive impact is unclear. If these complications are ignored, maybe a feminine outlook on law could be expected to stress compensation — obviously Bender associates altruism with women. On the other hand, strict liability is more rule-like, less standard-like, less contextualist, less sensitive to the particulars of the individual accident, than negligence is; in that respect it is the more masculine standard.

Notes

1. **"Mainstreaming" the Ethic of Care in the Law.** Feminist legal reformers concerned to recognize and affirm the values of connection, cooperation, and community have drawn on relational feminism to propose changes in virtually every area of substantive law. Much of this work integrates nonsubordinationist concerns about eliminating male dominance with the values associated with an ethic of care.

Some relational feminist critiques have examined procedural and evidentiary issues and argued that procedural rules often incorporate gendered priorities into the legal system. Judith Resnik, a pioneer in this area, examines judicial tasks denoted by the gendered term "housekeeping" (as in "mere housekeeping"), which are reassigned from Article III judges to Article I judges or to state courts, refused appellate review, and in other ways given less attention and status in the judicial system. Housekeeping matters tend to involve more fact-finding rather than abstract legal analysis, as well as "the complex and messy activity of interacting with litigants, witnesses, and lawyers." They also include a disproportionate number of cases such as prisoner petitions and social security cases that are tedious and mundane. See Resnik, Housekeeping: The Nature and Allocation of Work in Federal Trial Courts, 24 Ga. L. Rev. 909, 945, 960-961 (1990). Resnik advocates "[r]etrieving — without romanticizing — the importance of 'humble' activities, acknowledging the power in the work of maintenance and of the organization of daily structures, and reallocating obligations for caretaking," id. at 957, a process that entails "identifying, understanding, reassessing, and reallocating 'housekeeping' — the daily, sometimes powerful, poignant, and compelling, sometimes repetitive and non-engaging, activities that nourish oneself and others." Id. at 964. See also Resnik, "Naturally" Without Gender: Women, Jurisdiction, and the Federal Courts, 66 N.Y.U. L. Rev. 1682, 1698-1699 (1991) (arguing that many jurisdictional rules assumed (wrongly) to be "natural," including the "domestic relations" exception to federal jurisdiction in diversity cases, reflect an official hierarchy of legal issues in which women's concerns come last); Roy L. Brooks, Feminist Jurisdiction: Toward an Understanding of Feminist Procedure, 43 Kan. L. Rev. 317, 349 (1995) (arguing, among other things, that the Supreme Court's holding that the presence of a father's children in a state did not constitute a "minimum contact" between the state and the father for purposes of personal jurisdiction reflected the Court's inattention to feminist values of care and connection); Kit Kinports, Evidence Engendered, 1991 U. Ill. L. Rev. 413 (criticizing evidence law for characteristics, such as abstractness, formality, hierarchy, and adversarialness, that tend both to institutionalize female disadvantage in concrete cases and to reinforce values that are not congenial to many women); Rosemary C. Hunter, Gender in Evidence: Masculine Norms vs. Feminist Reforms, 19 Harv. Women's L.J. 127, 129 (1996) (criticizing rules of evidence for, among other things, privileging "fact over value, reason over emotion, presence over absence, physical over psychological, perception over intuition"). Related critiques concerning the practices of judging, dispute resolution, criminal sentencing, civil remedies, and legal reasoning itself are explored later in this chapter.

Other relational feminist critiques focus on particular subject matter areas. For example, feminists draw on relational feminism to criticize the "private law" of contracts and tort. See, e.g., Debora L. Threedy, Feminists and Contract Doctrine, 32 Ind. L. Rev. 1247 (1999) (noting similarities between relational feminism and the emerging theory of "relational contracts").

Public law has also been the subject of numerous relational feminist critiques. For example, tax law has been a particularly lively area for exploration of relational justice themes. Marjorie Kornhauser defends progressive income tax rules from a "female voice" perspective that emphasizes interdependence and altruism. See Kornhauser, The Rhetoric of the Anti-Progressive Income Tax Movement: A Typical Male Reaction, 86 Mich. L. Rev. 465 (1987); but see William J. Turnier et al., Redistributive Justice and Cultural Feminism, 45 Am. U. L. Rev. 1275 (1996) (reporting study based on 1992 national telephone poll showing that while women are more supportive of redistributive *spending* measures, men are more supportive of redistributive *taxation* measures). See also Gwen Thayer Handelman, Sisters in Law: Gender and the Interpretation of Tax Statutes, 3 ULCA Women's L.J. 39, 65 (1993) (advocating focus on tax system as a means of strengthening the community and methods of interpreting tax statutes that "[p]ersonify[ ] and situat[e] the drafters in their historical context and employ[ ] empathy to connect with them" to ascertain their intent). Kenneth Karst offers a relational feminist critique of constitutional law. Kenneth L. Karst, Woman's Constitution, 1984 Duke L.J. 447. Mary Becker argues for campaign finance reform and for cumulative voting procedures in order to allow women's political voices to be heard. Mary Becker, Patriarchy and Inequality: Toward a Substantive Feminism, 1999 U. Chi. Legal F. 21.

With respect to business and labor law, Marion Crain advocates "feminized" labor unions to achieve collective empowerment for working women based on values of connection and community rather than separation and autonomy. See Marion Crain, Feminizing Unions: Challenging the Gendered Structure of Wage Labor, 89 Mich. L. Rev. 1155, 1198 (1991); Marion Crain, Images of Power in Labor Law: A Feminist Deconstruction, 33 B.C. L. Rev. 481, 486 (1992). In a pioneering article, Kathleen A. Lahey and Sarah W. Salter challenged the "patriarchal nature of the dominations upon which corporate culture depends" and urged legal reforms in corporate law that reflect "'the ethics of care, responsibility, connection and sharing' and that are organized about 'the values of contextuality, continuity, and holistic participation.'" See Kathleen A. Lahey & Sarah W. Salter, Corporate Law in Legal Theory and Legal Scholarship: From Classicism to Feminism, 23 Osgoode Hall L.J. 543, 555-556, 570 (1985); see also Theresa A. Gabaldon, Feminism, Fairness, and Fiduciary Duty in Corporate and Securities Law, 5 Tex. J. Women & L. 1 (1995) (identifying a number of issues of corporate and securities laws as to which caring and compassion values suggest enlarged responsibilities by, and to, corporate officers and directors); see generally Barbara Ann White, Feminist Foundations for the Law of Business: One Law and Economics Scholar's Survey and (Re)View, 10 UCLA Women's L.J. 39 (1999).

Other proposals abound. Susan Stefan, for example, urges that the law of competence applied in cases involving such matters as guardianships, medical treatment decisions, and the validity of divorce separation agreements move beyond current assumptions about rational decisionmaking that better reflect men's concepts of rationality and positions of autonomy than women's. See Stefan, Silencing the Different Voice: Competence, Feminist Theory and Law, 47 U. Miami L. Rev. 763 (1993). Others use ethic of care principles to promote various agendas sometimes associated through the umbrella term of "ecofeminism," including environmental justice, animal rights, and international world peace. See, e.g., Robert R.M. Verchick, In a Greener Voice: Feminist Theory and Environmental Justice, 19 Harv. Women's L.J. 23 (1996); Beyond Animal Rights: A Feminist Caring Ethic for the Treatment of Animals (Josephine Donovan & Carol J. Adams eds., 1996); Bringing Peace Home: Feminism, Violence, and Nature (Karen J. Warren & Duane L. Cady eds., 1996). International law scholars attempt to bring women's values into the processes of international lawmaking and practice. See, e.g., Hilary Charlesworth, Christine Chinkin, & Shelley Wright, Feminist Approaches to International Law, 85 Am. J. Int'l L. 615 (1991); Karen Engle, International Human Rights and Feminism: When Discourses Meet, 13 Mich. J. Int'l L. 517 (1992); Gendered States: Feminist (Re)Visions of International Relations Theory (V. Spike Peterson ed., 1992).

2. The Feminist Critique of Relational Justice Theory. Linda C. McClain catalogs the major feminist objections to legal theories based on an ethic of care. Most of these criticisms fall into one of two categories: (1) an ethic of care is an impractical and unworkable foundation for law, and (2) an ethic of care is bad for women. See McClain, "Atomistic Man" Revisited: Liberalism, Connection, and Feminist Jurisprudence, 65 S. Cal. L. Rev. 1171, 1196-1202 (1992). A classic debate on these issues, especially the issue whether cultural feminism is bad for women, occurred at SUNY-Buffalo School of Law in 1985 between leading feminists. See Ellen C. DuBois, Mary C. Dunlap, Carol J. Gilligan, Catharine A. MacKinnon, & Carrie J. Menkel-Meadow, Feminist Discourse, Moral Values, and the Law, 34 Buff. L. Rev. 11 (1985).

Linda J. Lacey argues that the problem is not that cultural feminism is bad for women, but that it is often misapplied — for example, as a basis for opposing abortion rights or for reimposing fault standards in divorce law. See Lacey, Mimicking the Words, but Missing the Message: The Misuse of Cultural Feminist Themes in Religion and Family Law Jurisprudence, 35 B.C. L. Rev. 1 (1993). She concedes that some cultural feminist ideas may backfire, but not, as is sometimes claimed, because they are "the master's tools." Id. at 45-46.

McClain suggests another critique of the "ethic of care," one echoed by Joan Tronto: the voice of care is important, but is better attributed to liberal humanist values than specifically "female" values. Her point is that there is room within liberal theory for debate about these values and that rather than forcing a "stark pick between mothering and contract, or care and justice, or connection and separation," feminists should engage in dialogue about how their insights about interdependency, connection, and responsibility can be incorporated within the liberal legal system. "[P]rinciples of justice, equality, and autonomy can coexist with and inform care and responsibility, just as care and connection, for both liberals and feminists, aid in the pursuit of justice." McClain, supra, at 1263. Recall the other views on the subject on pages 824-825. Is it important that the ethic of care be seen as humanist rather than feminist?

2. Taking Women's Work Seriously

Martha Albertson Fineman, Cracking the Foundational Myths: Independence, Autonomy, and Self-Sufficiency
8 Am. U. J. Gender Soc. Pol'y & L. 13, 18-19 (1999)

It is puzzling, as well as paradoxical, that the term dependency has such negative connotations [in political discourse]. Its very existence prompts and justifies mean spirited and ill-conceived political responses, such as the recent welfare "reform." Far from being pathological, avoidable, and the result of individual failings, dependency is a universal and inevitable part of the human development. It is inherent in the human condition.

All of us were dependent as children, and many of us will be dependent as we age, become ill, or suffer disabilities. In this sense, dependency is "inevitable" and not deserving of condemnation or stigma. Note that the examples I have chosen to illustrate this category of inevitable dependency are biological or physical in nature. Biological dependencies, however, do not exhaust the potential range of situations of dependence. For example, in addition to biological dependence, one may be psychologically or emotionally dependent on others. In fact, these other forms of dependence may even accompany the physiological or biological dependence, which I have labeled inevitable. But economic, psychological, and emotional dependency are not generally understood to be universally experienced. As a result, assertions about their inevitability in each individual's life would be controversial. It is the characteristic of universality (which indisputably accompanies inevitable dependence) that is central to my argument for societal or collective responsibility. In other words, the realization that biological dependency is both inevitable and universal is theoretically important. Upon this foundational realization is built my claim for justice — the demand that society value and accommodate the labor done by the caretakers of inevitable dependants.

I argue that the caretaking work creates a collective or societal debt. Each and every member of society is obligated by this debt. Furthermore, this debt transcends individual circumstances. In other words, we need not be elderly, ill, or children any longer to be held individually responsible. Nor can we satisfy or discharge our collective responsibility within our individual, private families. Merely being financially generous with our own mothers or duly supporting our own wives will not suffice to satisfy our share of the societal debt generally owed to all caretakers.

My argument that the caretaking debt is a collective one is based on the fact that biological dependency is inherent to the human condition, and therefore, of necessity of collective or societal concern. Just as individual dependency needs must be met if an individual is to survive, collective dependency needs must be met if a society is to survive and perpetuate itself. The mandate that the state (collective society) respond to dependency, therefore, is not a matter of altruism or empathy (which are individual responses often resulting in charity), but one that is primary and essential because such a response is fundamentally society-preserving.

If infants or ill persons are not cared for, nurtured, nourished, and perhaps loved, they will perish. We can say, therefore, that they owe an individual debt to their individual caretakers. But the obligation is not theirs alone — nor is their obligation confined only to their own caretakers. A sense of social justice demands a broader sense of obligation. Without aggregate caretaking, there could be no society, so we might say that it is caretaking labor that produces and reproduces society. Caretaking labor provides the citizens, the workers, the voters, the consumers, the students, and others who populate society and its institutions. The uncompensated labor of caretakers is an unrecognized subsidy, not only to the individuals who directly receive it, but more significantly, to the entire society. . . .

The assignment of responsibility for the burdens of dependency to the family in the first instance, and within the family to women, operates in an unjust manner because this arrangement has significant negative material consequences for the caretaker. This obvious observation allows me to introduce an additional, but often overlooked, form of dependency into the argument — "derivative dependency." Derivative dependency arises on the part of the person who assumes responsibility for the care of the inevitable dependent person. I refer to this form of dependency as derivative to capture the very simple point that those who care for others are themselves dependent on resources in order to undertake that care. Caretakers have a need for monetary or material resources. They also need recourse to institutional supports and accommodation, a need for structural arrangements that facilitate caretaking.

Currently, neither the economic nor the structural supports for caretaking are adequate. Many caretakers and their dependents find themselves impoverished or severely economically compromised. Some of their economic problems stem from the fact that within families, caretaking work is unpaid and not considered worthy of social subsidies. There are also, however, direct costs associated with caretaking. Caretaking labor interferes with the pursuit and development of wage labor options. Caretaking labor saps energy and efforts from investment in career or market activities, those things that produce economic rewards. There are foregone opportunities and costs associated with caretaking, and even caretakers who work in the paid labor force typically have more tenuous ties to the public sphere because they must also accommodate caretaking demands in the private. These costs are not distributed among all beneficiaries of caretaking (institutional or individual). Unjustly, the major economic and career costs associated with caretaking are typically borne by the caretaker alone.

Further, most institutions in society remain relatively unresponsive to innovations that would lessen the costs of caretaking. Caretaking occurs in a larger context and caretakers often need accommodation in order to fulfill multiple responsibilities. For example, many caretakers also engage in market work. Far from structurally accommodating or facilitating caretaking, however, workplaces operate in modes incompatible with the idea that workers also have obligations for dependency. Workplace expectations compete with the demands of caretaking — we assume that workers are those independent and autonomous individuals who are free to work long and regimented hours.

In discussing the costs and impediments associated with undertaking the tasks of caretaking, it is important to emphasize that, unlike inevitable dependency, derivative dependency is not a universal experience. In fact, many people in our society totally escape the burdens and costs that arise from assuming a caretaking role, perhaps even freed for other pursuits by the caretaking labor of others. The status of derivative dependency is structured by and through existing societal institutions, culturally and socially assigned according to a script rooted in ideologies, particularly those of capitalism and patriarchy. These scripts function at an unconscious (and therefore, unexamined) level, and channel our beliefs and feelings about what is considered natural and what are appropriate institutional arrangements. When individuals act according to these scripts, consistent with prevailing ideology and institutional arrangements, we say they have chosen their path from the available options. The construction of this notion of individual choice allows us to avoid general responsibility for the inequity and justify the maintenance of the status quo. We ignore the fact that individual choice occurs within the constraints of social conditions. These constraints include ideology, history, and tradition, all of which funnel decisions into prescribed channels and often operate in a practical and symbolic manner to limit options.

As it now stands in this society, derivative dependents are expected to get both economic and structural resources within the family. The market is unresponsive and uninvolved, and the state is perceived as a last resort for financial resources, the refuge of the failed family. A caretaker who must resort to governmental assistance may do so only if she can demonstrate that she is needy in a highly stigmatized process. . . .

In order to move from our current situation to a more just resolution for the dilemma of caretaking and dependency, we will need more than a responsive state. The state will also have to be an active participant in shaping and monitoring other societal institutions. One fundamental task will be monitoring and preventing the exploitation and appropriation of the labor of some citizens through institutional and ideological arrangements. This must be prevented even when the justification for the labor's appropriation and exploitation is that it is used for the good of the majority. Further, it must be prevented even in contexts where social constraints and conventions coerce consent from the laborer.

In this endeavor, the state must use its regulatory and redistributive authority to ensure that those things that are not valued or are undervalued in market or marriage are, nonetheless, publicly and politically recognized as socially productive and given value. Conferral of value requires the transfer of some economic resources from the collective society to caretakers through the establishment of mechanisms that tax those who receive the benefits of caretaking in order to compensate those who do the caretaking. Other societies do this in a variety of ways, such as using tax revenues to provide childcare allowances and universal benefits that assist caretakers, or through a basic income guarantee. Money, however, is not enough. The active state must also structure accommodation of the needs of caretaking into society's institutions.

[Additional portions of this article are set forth at page 1160, infra.]

Vicki Schultz, Life's Work
100 Colum. L. Rev. 1881, 1883-1886, 1900-1905 (2000)

In this Essay, I elaborate on the concept of a "life's work" to describe some of the central elements of a utopian vision in which women and men from all walks of life can stand alongside each other as equals, pursuing our chosen projects and forging connected lives. In the process, we come to view each other as equal citizens and human beings, each entitled to equal respect and a claim on society's resources because of our shared commitments and contributions. As individuals, our work provides us with a forum to realize at least some of our aspirations, to form bonds with others, to serve society, and to project ourselves into the larger world beyond our own families and friends. It also provides us with the wherewithal to sustain ourselves, economically and socially, so that we may enter into intimate relationships with the security that permits us to love (and leave) freely, without need of recompense. This world of equal citizenship, stable community, and a strong, secure selfhood for everyone is the world I believe feminism was born to bring into being.

Recently, however, a number of feminists and liberals have begun to move away from such a vision; some even associate an emphasis on equal work with conservatism. Some feminist legal scholars now advocate paying women to care for their own families in their own households; many seem to have given up on achieving genuine gender integration of the work done in both households and workplaces. Some liberal thinkers urge that we provide everyone a guaranteed income or capital allotment; they believe tying the distribution of social goods to work interferes with individual freedom and choice. The presence of these discourses has moved me to articulate a feminist vision of the significance of paid work to the good life, to equality, and to women. I agree that it is vitally important to create society-wide mechanisms for allocating the costs of household labor and for allowing people to realize their preferences. But, unless we pay attention to the institutional contexts through which housework is valued and individual choice realized, stubborn patterns of gender inequality will continue to reassert themselves — including the gender-based distribution of work that is at the root of women's disadvantage. In the search for social justice, separatism simply won't suffice. . . .

In my view, a robust conception of equality can be best achieved through paid work, rather than despite it. Work is a site of deep self-formation that offers rich opportunities for human flourishing (or devastation). To a large extent, it is through our work — how it is defined, distributed, characterized, and controlled — that we develop into the "men" and "women" we see ourselves and others see us as being. Because law's domain includes work and its connection to other spheres of existence, the prospect of who we become as a society, and as individuals, is shaped profoundly by the laws that create and control the institutions that govern our experiences as workers. I believe that it is only by recognizing the formative power of such forces that we can imagine and invent ourselves as full human agents. . . .

. . . Paid work has the potential to become the universal platform for equal citizenship it has been imagined to be, but only if we ensure meaningful participation in the workforce by attending to the specific needs of various social groups and individuals. In the past, legal efforts to achieve equality focused on protecting people from identity-based discrimination; we have tended to take the number and quality of jobs, job-holding services, wages, and working conditions produced by the market as a neutral baseline to which no one is to be denied access because of group status. But in order to make paid work the basis for equal citizenship, we will have to take steps to ensure that what the market produces is both substantively adequate and universally available for everyone. This means that, in the future, we will have to supplement employment discrimination law with measures like job-creation programs, wage subsidies, universal child care and health care programs, enhanced employee representation, and a reduced workweek for everyone. To achieve such reforms, feminists must move beyond an identity politics that presses for cultural recognition and revaluation of "women's experience." We must join forces with a broad array of groups — including the labor movement — not simply to advance each other's interests, but to fashion a shared interest in creating a social order in which work is consistent with egalitarian conceptions of citizenship and care. . . .

. . . It is vitally important to acknowledge the hidden labor that is performed in households, and to create society-wide mechanisms for allocating its costs rather than continuing to impose them on individual family members (too often, women). One method of doing so is already being implemented on a massive scale: collectivizing housework by converting it into employment. A great deal of work once performed in private households has been handed over to day-care providers, cleaning services, home health aides, landscapers, and the like. Feminists could think creatively about how to capitalize on this trend by supporting efforts to upgrade the pay, promotional prospects, and working conditions associated with work once performed by at-home spouses. Compared to marriage and intimate relationships, labor markets and workplaces are spaces in which it is easier for workers to mobilize to obtain public accountability and protection. By transforming at least some forms of household work into paid employment, we could more easily protect those who do the work from discrimination, unfair labor practices, wage and hour violations, adverse working conditions, health and safety threats, and other problems on the job. We could also make it easier for those who perform household labor to engage in collective action to improve their situation. The recent victory of 70,000 California home health care workers in organizing a union, for example, holds promise for highlighting — and upgrading — the value of service work. Such victories continue the work started by the comparable worth campaigns of the 1980s.

Converting household work into paid employment not only provides jobs for many people who need them, it also frees those who provide unpaid family labor to pursue more fully for pay the work that suits them best. Countless middle- and working-class families buy time or convenience by purchasing such things as child care, cleaning services, dinners from McDonald's, lawn mowing, haircuts, car repair, and other services that should count as commercialized forms of household labor. There may, of course, be some forms of household labor that cannot or should not be commodified. There may also be some services that average- or low-income people cannot afford. But, there is no reason why a commercialization strategy must be limited to pure market forces. Some services could be subsidized for those who cannot afford them, or even made available for free to everyone (like public schooling, a now universal service that was once provided exclusively within the family setting).

Despite the fact that converting household labor into paid work collectivizes it and renders it more visible and publicly accountable, feminists in the movement to value housework tend to shun this approach. Instead, these feminists are proposing schemes to compensate women for performing household labor in private homes. Some legal feminists argue that (heterosexual) women's household labor provides their male partners with the time and resources to specialize in market work, and thus the men should compensate the women. These feminists propose marriage-based "joint property" schemes that redistribute income from husbands (or sometimes higher wage-earners, assumed to be husbands) to wives (or lower wage-earners, assumed to be wives) at divorce. Other feminists promote state-based "welfare" strategies in which the government pays caregiver stipends that are not tied to paid employment, but are instead intended to permit women to choose full-time or near full-time homemaking and child care. In joint property proposals the source of funding is the husband, while in welfare approaches it is the state. But both strategies channel funds through the family unit to pay women to keep house and care for our own kin.

Wittingly or unwittingly, advocates of these family-based approaches replicate some of the same conservative assumptions that have been used traditionally to justify women's disadvantage. Indeed, feminists in this movement tend to rely on the human capital literature to assert that it is women's disproportionate responsibility for housework and child care that accounts for our lower wages and our inferior position in the workforce. Unfortunately, many of these feminists seem unaware of (or uninformed about) the body of sociological work that casts doubt on the validity of human capital theory. Within the social sciences, the debate is between conventional economists — who pin women's plight on our family roles — and feminist sociologists (and sociologically-inclined economists) — who have produced evidence that discriminatory workplace dynamics are a more fundamental cause. The sociological literature points toward a more contextual approach that rejects static family-based conceptions of women's difference; it shows instead that socially-constructed features of the work-world help create the very gender differences (manifested in work aspirations, employment patterns, and familial divisions of labor) that human capital theory attributes to women themselves. Such an approach creates greater possibilities for change. If the sources of women's disadvantage lie not in sociobiological forces that commit women more heavily to child care and housework but instead in the political economy of paid work, we can challenge the sex bias in allegedly gender-neutral forces in labor markets and work places. We can create more empowering gender arrangements by demanding work and working conditions that will give women more economic security, more political clout, more household bargaining power, and perhaps even more personal strength with which to pursue our dreams.

[Additional portions of this article are set forth at page 1172, infra.]

≣ *Linda C. McClain, Families, Schools, and Sex*
Equality
69 Fordham L. Rev. 1617, 1620-23 (2001)

[T]he idea of families as "seedbeds of civic virtue" — as well as of virtues generally — helpfully connotes that families, in a good society, serve as places or sources of growth and development of capacities and virtues. But taking the rhetoric about families as seedbeds of civic virtue seriously invites careful attention to . . . questions . . . concerning how families foster capacities for self-government and under what circumstances families are able to do so. Too often, prescriptions for fortifying families as seedbeds of virtue focus primarily on shoring up one form of the family, the two-parent, marital (heterosexual) family, and fail to consider the possible relevance to the capacity of families to generate self-government of such matters as forms of family self-governance, what values parents teach their children, and how they socialize them. Should the norms of institutions of civil society, such as families, be "congruent" with public norms and institutions "all the way down," so that "the membership and internal organization of associations should be a matter of public policy, legally enforced"? If families are not congruent in this way, and do not explicitly mirror or generate democratic values, could they be said to be "seedbeds of virtue" if they play a "mediating" role in indirectly supporting those values by fostering in persons a "whole range of moral dispositions, presumptively supportive of political order"?

. . . I urge greater attention to sex equality as a core element in a conception of civic virtue in a good society and to the implications of taking sex equality seriously for a formative project. . . . Sex equality is not only a civic virtue — one that should guide how government treats female and male citizens and how citizens treat and regard each other — but also is (or should be) a virtue of everyday life, a principle of political morality that should inform and regulate forms of personal self-government. . . .

[The Constitution] precludes states from requiring or supporting a patriarchal form of family governance. But it does not rule out either families constituting themselves in ways that reinforce traditional gender roles or parents seeking to ingrain those roles in their children. The most acute form of such adherence to traditional roles may be religious fundamentalist households, which follow a form of family self-governance of male authority and female submission with supposed scriptural roots, but such role division also exists in the many households in which women continue to bear disproportionate responsibility for domestic and caretaking labor.

There are significant constitutional principles and prudential considerations that argue against an insistence that families organize themselves according to a robust vision of sex equality. But this does not rule out government carrying out a formative project to promote sex equality by a wide range of measures that fall short of coercion. Such forms of governmental action could encourage sex equality within families and also inculcate in children norms of sex equality in sites outside of the family. For example, I believe that schools have an appropriate role to play in inculcating sex equality, particularly if families fail to do so, even though some families perceive this as a threat to their ability to foster their own conceptions of virtue. I offer some preliminary thoughts about how fostering sex equality should be a proper component of already-existing curricular tasks such as civic education and character education and I advocate that schools should incorporate into their curriculum gender education (by which I mean education to counter sex role stereotyping and the harms it imposes on both girls and boys). The contemporary challenge is both to affirm and support the important role of families in fostering the capacities for self-government and in cultivating civic and personal virtues and to affirm and support principles of sex equality and liberty. This latter commitment requires the repudiation of a legally-supported model of family governance that denies or hinders women's responsible self-government and invites careful examination of how gender ideology prescribes family roles.

Notes

1. Is Caretaking a Public Good?   Fineman's assertion that caretaking is a public good, and therefore a collective social responsibility, accords with the arguments of other feminist thinkers. Economist Nancy Folbre, for example, argues that the "invisible hand" of the market cannot function without the "invisible heart" of care: "Markets cannot function effectively outside the framework of families and communities built on values of love, obligation, and reciprocity." Nancy Folbre, The Invisible Heart: Economics and Family Values xi (2001); see also Mona Harrington, Care and Equality: Inventing a New Family Politics (arguing for a public conversation on rethinking the family); Maxine Eichner, Square Peg in a Round Hole: Parenting Policies and Liberal Theory, 59 Ohio St. L.J. 133 (1998) (arguing for a "community-oriented treatment of parenting" that "actively promotes the welfare of parents, children, and the relationships between them as collective societal goals"). Fineman, Folbre, and Harrington all reason that because caretaking has traditionally been performed without pay by women, now that women are flooding into paid work societies must find some other equitable way to provide caretaking services. Do you agree that the care of children, the elderly, and the disabled is a public good? Or should the decision to bear and raise children, for example, be considered a private decision, and not an undertaking worthy of public concern? Should feminists worried about a care deficit focus on encouraging the men in their lives to stay home and care for children?

If caretaking is a public good, is there a reason why it should be singled out for coordinated social policy over other public goods such as the development of socially useful technology and socially uplifting art? Are babies more important than novels, paintings, cures for cancer?

2. Feminism and the "Delegation" Strategy.   Assuming that caretaking should be viewed as a public and not a wholly private issue, another question is whether, as a matter of sound social policy, the market or the state should take responsibility for picking up the slack left by women who have moved into paid employment. American theorists early in the second wave of feminism often argued that this work would or should be assumed by the state:

> When Betty Friedan wrote in the '60s [Friedan, The Feminine Mystique (1963)], she assumed that very soon there would be a national system of subsidized child care centers that would be as free, accessible, and high in quality as public libraries. She actually believed this. Not only did she believe this, it was not an implausible vision. After all, that is what has happened in Belgium. That's what happened in France. [Nancy E. Dowd, Envisioning Work, and Family: A Critical Perspective on International Models, 26 Harv. J. Legis. 311, 334 (1989) (explaining that child care for the very young in France is subsidized by municipalities).] Ninety-five percent of nursery school age children in those countries are in government-subsidized child care. [Barbara R. Bergmann, Saving Our Children from Poverty: What the United States Can Learn from France 27-79 (1996) (estimating that 95 percent of nursery-school-age children are in publicly subsidized child care programs).]

Symposium, Unbending Gender: Why Family and Work Conflict and What to Do About It, 49 Am. U. L. Rev. 901, 904 (2000).

Friedan's vision was not realized. Instead, as Joan Williams notes,

> In 1971, when Congress passed a Comprehensive Child Development Act, President Nixon vetoed it under pressure from an intense lobbying campaign that decried the proposal as "a radical piece of social legislation" designed to deliver children to "communal approaches to child-rearing over and against the family-centered approach." A 1975 proposal was also defeated, decried as an effort to "[s]ovietize the family." As a result, the U.S. offers less governmental support for child care than does any other industrialized nation.

Joan Williams, Toward a Reconstructive Feminism: Reconstructing the Relationship of Market Work and Family Work, 19 N. Ill. U. L. Rev. 89, 150-151 (1998). In the absence of government institutions and programs to support caretaking, American women turned to the market to purchase the caretaking services for which they were still considered ultimately responsible. Joan Williams refers to this strategy as "full commodification"; Adrienne Davis calls it "delegation." Symposium, supra, at 903. The full commodification strategy has its costs, however. As Dorothy Roberts suggests at pages 348-351, the delegation strategy relies on a labor force that is overwhelmingly female, poorly paid, and disproportionately populated by immigrant women and native-born women of color. Many policymakers also worry that delegation to the market produces either inferior care or no care for those without money to pay for it, as well as an across-the-board industry focus on cost-cutting and efficiency at the expense of quality. See, e.g., Folbre, The Invisible Heart, supra, at 60-64. For a critique of full commodification and a suggestion that "reconstructive feminism" provides a way forward, see Williams, Unbending Gender: Why Family and Work Conflict and What to Do About It (2000).

3. The State and "Family Values": Family or Workplace Reforms? What might greater state support for caretaking look like? One possibility is government programs such as income supplements for families with dependents, greater subsidies through the tax code for child care expenses, and mandatory paid leave. Some of these sorts of programs already exist in other countries. See Chapter 3 at page 342. These reforms leave existing employment and family patterns relatively intact. Other, more ambitious feminist reforms seek to capture more income for women performing housework and caretaking labor by changing marriage law or by using contract law principles as a supplement to marriage law. See, e.g., Joan Williams, Unbending Gender, supra, at 124-127 (advocating that wives receive a greater portion of husbands' income after divorce as a way of recognizing women's greater contributions to housework and child care); Martha M. Ertman, Commercializing Marriage: A Proposal for Valuing Women's Work Through Premarital Security Agreements, 77 Tex. L. Rev. 17, 41-46 (1998) (proposing premarital "security agreements" as a way of doing the same); Katharine B. Silbaugh, Marriage Contracts and the Family Economy, 93 Nw. U. L. Rev. 65, 67 (1998) (arguing that a homemaker's nonmonetary contributions should be seen as part of a marital exchange with the husband's monetary contributions and hence treated equally by judges in premarital contract cases); Katharine Silbaugh, Turning Labor into Love: Housework and the Law, 91 Nw. U. L. Rev. 1 (1996) (arguing that the legal system's failure to assign economic value to housework harms the women who do it and that therefore housework should be treated the same as paid work); see also Linda R. Hirshman & Jane E. Larson, Hard Bargains: The Politics of Sex 280-283 (1998) (proposing the creation of a "concubinage" contract that would compensate women for their unmarried sexual relationships with men, which would extend the economic valuation of women's household work to include sexual relations). These reforms seek to support women's caring work through family policy.

For other feminists, involving the government in subsidizing care work requires rethinking "the family" entirely. Martha Fineman, for example, argues that the state has a legitimate interest in caring for dependents, but no legitimate interest in the kinds of intimate relationships adults form with one another. Therefore, marriage should be abolished as a legal category, while state support should flow to "caregiving families," understood as dependents and the people who nurture them. Fineman also argues that the paradigm of the caregiving family should be the dyad of Mother/Child rather than Husband/Wife. Martha Albertson Fineman, The Neutered Mother, the Sexual Family, and Other Twentieth Century Tragedies 228-236 (1995).

Vicki Schultz argues against using family law and income transfers as the platform for equality; in her view, only participation in the paid work force can bring women full citizenship. Thus, feminist reform efforts should center on the workplace rather than the family, and feminists should make common cause with the labor movement to provide decent work for all. Does her argument adequately address the concerns of relational feminists? Is Schultz's argument necessarily at odds with that of Fineman?

4. The State and "Family Values": Should Families Be Regulated? Although Americans tend to uncritically laud the raising of children in individual families as the healthiest environment for young people, feminists have argued that in fact the family is often the site of the reproduction of various kinds of injustice. Philosopher Susan Moller Okin, for example, argues that the family is often a place where children learn about, and are expected to accept, sex inequality. Susan Moller Okin, Justice, Gender, and the Family (revised ed. 1991). Linda McClain, drawing on Okin's work, suggests that the physical care and basic socialization of dependents is not the only public good the family has traditionally provided. Democratic nations also rely on families to inculcate "civic virtues" in their citizens. McClain suggests that if this is true and if one of those virtues is a strong commitment to sex equality, then the state is justified either in intervening directly in education and family life to foster equality or in creating incentives for families and schools to foster sex equality.

McClain and Okin point out that families are often the site of sex inequality. Joan Williams similarly argues that the family is also a key site for the reproduction of class inequality:

Underlying domesticity's romantic description of mothers selflessly devoted to children's needs are class aspirations acknowledged today only in accepted codes (parents want their children to be "successful" and "productive"). To quote Lillian Rubin, "professional middle-class parents . . . assum[e] that their children are destined to do work like theirs — work that calls for innovation, initiative, flexibility, creativity, sensitivity to others, and a well-developed set of interpersonal skills. . . ." [Lillian Rubin, Worlds of Pain 128 (1976).] Mothers stay home to develop these skills in their children. Barbara Ehrenreich is one of the few writers who recognize the link between gender roles and class formation:

> The concern was expressed in various ways: "I don't want to miss the early years"; or "I don't want to leave my children with just anyone." But the real issue was the old middle-class dilemma of whether "anyone" such as a Jamaican housekeeper or a Hispanic day-care worker was equipped to instill such middle-class virtues as concentration and intellectual discipline. For many young middle-class couples the choice was stark: Have the mother work and risk retarding the child's intellectual development, or have the mother stay home, build up the child's I.Q., and risk being unable to pay for a pricey nursery school or, later, private college. [Barbara Ehrenreich, Fear of Falling 221 (1989).]

"It is one thing to have children," Ehrenreich notes, "and another thing . . . to have children who will be disciplined enough to devote the first twenty or thirty years of their lives to scaling the educational obstacles to a middle-class career." [Id. at 83.] Much of what mothers do is designed to preserve and pass on what has been called the family's social capital: their style of life, religious and ethnic rituals, and social position.

Joan Williams, Toward a Reconstructive Feminism: Reconstructing the Relationship of Market Work and Family Work, 19 N. Ill. U. L. Rev. 89, 131-132 (1998).

Indeed, some feminists have argued that Western society's focus on "the family" as the site of all nonmercenary values has prevented the development of other social institutions and practices that could promote caring:

> The world around the family is not a pre-existing harsh climate against which the family offers protection and warmth. It is as if the family had drawn comfort and security into itself and left the outside world bereft. As a bastion against a bleak society it has made that society bleak. It is indeed a major agency for caring, but in monopolizing care it has made it harder to undertake other forms of care. It is indeed a unit of sharing, but in demanding sharing within it has made other relations tend to become more mercenary. It is indeed a place of intimacy, but in privileging the intimacy of close kin it has made the outside world cold and friendless, and made it harder to sustain relations of security and trust except with kin. Caring, sharing and loving would be more widespread if the family did not claim them for its own.

Michele Barrett & Mary McIntosh, The Anti-Social Family 80 (1982).

Can "the family" as popularly imagined — that is, the heterosexual nuclear family memorialized in the United States in the 1950s — survive a feminist analysis? If not, are there other social practices and institutions that would do a better job of helping foster relationships of caring, love, and virtue?

5. Comparing Substantive Equality and Different Voice Theory as a Basis for Legal Reform. The program for workplace reform generated by relational theory overlaps considerably the agenda of those urging the "special treatment" substantive equality approach discussed in Chapter 3. Both include such items as greater public responsibility for children, family leave policies, and more expansive employer policies for flex-time and part-time work possibilities. The limited progress on these fronts is reported in Chapter 3 at pages 337-340 and 351-364.

Compare the justifications for these reforms offered by the different approaches. Within substantive equality models, measures to improve women's legal and economic status are woman-centered and justified as a means of eliminating some of the disadvantages women would otherwise experience — i.e., making the best of a bad world. In contrast, cultural feminism justifies such measures as part of the blueprint for a more ideal world for everyone. Is this a real difference?

Putting Theory into Practice

5-1. From among the courses in which you are currently enrolled, identify some law reform proposals that might better reflect "woman's voice" than current law does. Try to justify each of these proposals in terms of one of the approaches featured in the previous chapters of this book. Which is the better framework for advancing the proposal?

5-2. Consistent with her emphasis on connection and responsibility, Robin West proposes that women's reproductive freedoms rest on responsibility as well as rights:

> [S]upport for expanded reproductive freedom should rest on the claim that only by accepting the responsibility to make these judgments do women manifest their freedom to pursue their authentically chosen and desired life goals. . . . Women need the freedom to make reproductive decisions not merely to vindicate a right to be left alone but often to strengthen their ties to others: to plan responsibly and have a family for which they can provide, to pursue professional or work commitments made to the outside world, or to continue supporting their families or communities. At other times the decision to abort is necessitated not by a murderous urge to end life, but by the harsh reality of a financially irresponsible partner, a society indifferent to the care of children, and a workplace incapable of accommodating or supporting the needs of working parents. At many other times the need to abort follows directly from a violent sexual assault. When made for any of these reasons, the decision to abort is not one made in an egoistic private vacuum. Whatever the reason, the decision to abort is almost invariably made within a web of interlocking, competing, and often irreconcilable responsibilities and commitments.

Robin West, Foreword, Taking Freedom Seriously, 104 Harv. L. Rev. 43, 83-85 (1990) (further portions appear in Chapter 6, at page 1099). What are the consequences of tying the abortion right to the concept of responsibility? Does West's position have any implications, for example, with respect to what restrictions the law ought to impose on drug-abusing pregnant women? Does the concept of responsibility support the right to abortion, or undermine it?

5-3. In 1990, Harvard Law School had 61 tenured faculty members. Three were black and five were women. None was Hispanic. A group of students, the Harvard Law School Coalition for Civil Rights, sued the law school for discriminatory employment practices, claiming that they were denied the benefits of association with an integrated faculty that is guaranteed under the state's employment anti-discrimination laws and under their implied contract with the law school. Their suit was dismissed for lack of standing, on grounds that the anti-discrimination laws protected only the employer-employee relationship and that the school's affirmative action plan and other references in the school's catalog and literature did not create a contract with students obligating the law school to provide them an integrated faculty. Harvard Law School Coalition for Civil Rights v. President and Fellows of Harvard College, 595 N.E.2d 316 (Mass. 1992).

Should the law be changed to allow such a suit? If so, would the necessary changes be an application of different voice theory?

Considerable public attention was brought to the complaints raised in this lawsuit in 1990 when Derrick Bell, Harvard's first black law professor, took an unpaid leave of absence to protest the fact that Harvard had never had a tenured non-white woman on the faculty. Two years later, Harvard had still not hired a minority woman faculty member, and because of the university's two-year limit on leaves of absence, Bell's relationship with Harvard was terminated. See Harvard Law Notifies Bell of Dismissal for Absence, N.Y. Times, July 1, 1992, at A19. In what sense might Bell's actions be seen as an affirmation of connection theory, and in what sense a rejection of them? Robert Clark, dean of Harvard Law School, was quoted as saying that he was "saddened" by Bell's decision not to return to the school, but wrote to Bell, "I continue to believe that the path of protest you have chosen — withdrawal from the law school community — is an unfortunate one." Id. Which position is most consistent with relational values?

5-4. The following case is described in David Margolick, At the Bar, N.Y. Times, July 10, 1992, at B8. Michael Mattioli is a 66-year-old retired psychologist. For over 30 years, he lived in a Manhattan apartment complex owned by New York University. Four years ago, he moved "temporarily" to Rochester to care for his mother, age 95, and his father, age 99, so that they would be spared the "indignity of dying in a nursing home." His mother died last October, but his father, who has just had his 103rd birthday, lives on. New York University seeks to evict Mattioli from his Manhattan apartment on the basis of a statute allowing eviction of tenants who do not use the premises as their primary residence. Mattioli thinks he should be able to keep his apartment, since he intends to return there as soon as his father no longer needs him. "I'm sure that at N.Y.U.'s medical school and law school and nursing school, they're teaching about the problems of the elderly," he said. "I don't think they're teaching that people who are taking responsibility for their own parents should be driven out of their apartments."

Should the circumstances of Mattioli's departure from his apartment and his intention to return sometime in the indefinite future provide a defense to the eviction action? How, if at all, can different voice theory be used in this case? Is the theory helpful only to Mattioli, or can New York University appeal to it as well?

5-5. What are the implications of the ethic of care when a "surrogate mother" wants to change her mind once the child is born and, instead of giving the child up to the biological father, retain primary custody of the child herself? (This substantive issue is addressed in Chapter 6, at pages 1116-1137.)

D. THE TEACHING AND PRACTICE OF LAW

1. Historical Background

If it is true that women have a "different voice," one might expect that the participation of women in the legal system might have a distinctive impact on that system. As the materials in Chapter 1 indicated, women's place in eighteenth- and nineteenth-century America was confined to the domestic sphere, and women were not welcome in the law. In the colonial era, when labor was scarce and relatively few occupations required formal licenses, a few women did manage to participate in legal transactions either by acting as their husband's representative or by obtaining special authorization to proceed independently. During the late eighteenth century, however, the gradual formalization of bar admission criteria made it increasingly difficult for women to act as lawyers. The inability of married women to make contracts reinforced the barriers to any independent career. And, of course, African-American women under slavery had no capacity to assert legal rights.

After the Civil War, the rise in women's educational and political activism contributed to a growing stream of female applicants to the bar. In 1867, Iowa became the first state to license a woman attorney, Belle Babb Mansfield, and the following decades witnessed a gradual increase in female candidates from largely white middle- and upper-middle-class backgrounds. Women's initial reception as lawyers in most jurisdictions was less than enthusiastic. As is clear from the *Bradwell* and *Goodell* cases excerpted in Chapter 1, many nineteenth-century lawmakers invested the sexes' "separate spheres" with both spiritual and constitutional significance. According to the concurring Justices in *Bradwell*, "The family organization, which is founded in the divine ordinance, as well as in the nature of things, indicates the domestic sphere as that which properly belongs to the domain and functions of womanhood." Bradwell v. Illinois, 83 U.S. 130, 141 (1872) (Bradley, J., concurring). The precise method of divine communication was, however, never elaborated, and a growing number of aspiring female applicants remained unconvinced. By the turn of the century, various political, legal, and social forces had coalesced to secure women's rights to admission to the bar in about half the states, and by 1920, formal barriers were largely removed. Deborah L. Rhode, Justice and Gender 23 (1985). Informal obstacles, however, remained. "Bring on as many women lawyers as you choose," predicted one District of Columbia judge. "I do not believe they will be a success." Belva Lockwood, My Efforts to Become a Lawyer, in Women and the American Economy: A Documentary History 1675-1929, at 297-301 (W. Elliot Brownlee & Mary M. Brownlee eds., 1976).

Many bar associations and law schools denied female applicants or limited their admission. Almost no excuse was too trivial: law books were too heavy for women students; men would be distracted by their presence; or separate lavatory facilities were unavailable. Rhode, Justice and Gender, supra, at 24; Cynthia Fuchs Epstein, Women in the Legal Profession at the Turn of the Twenty-First Century: Assessing Glass Ceilings and Open Doors, 49 Kan. L. Rev. 733 (2001). The first woman was admitted into an American law school in 1868. Admission to the other elite law schools did not come until much later. Columbia did not enroll women law students until 1927, and Harvard remained all male until 1950. Not until 1972 did all accredited law schools eliminate explicit sex-based restrictions. Karen Berger Morello, The Invisible Bar: The Woman Lawyer in America 1638 to the Present 11, 44, 96, 100 (1986); Donna Fossum, Women in the Legal Profession: A Progress Report, 67 Women's L.J. 1 (1981). Until the 1960s, women constituted about 3 percent of enrollment in law schools and less than 3 percent of the profession. Carrie Menkel-Meadow, The Comparative Sociology of Women Lawyers: The "Feminization" of the Legal Profession, 24 Osgoode Hall L.J. 897, 902 (1989); Deborah L. Rhode, Perspectives on Professional Women, 40 Stan. L. Rev. 1163, 1173-1175 (1988); Cynthia Epstein, Women in Law 61-67 (1981).

Discrimination against racial, ethnic, and religious minorities was also pervasive. Throughout the nineteenth and early twentieth centuries, many employers, law schools, and bar associations excluded Jews, Eastern European immigrants, and applicants of color. Jerold Auerbach, Unequal Justice: Lawyers and Social Change in Modern America (1976). Not until the mid-1960s were all members of the Association of American Law Schools able to report that they did not officially discriminate on the basis of race or ethnicity. Lack of financial resources and educational preparation also restricted access to law school. Once admitted to the bar, minority lawyers faced continued resistance from potential employers and clients. Barriers to women of color were especially great because the few institutions that did not discriminate on the basis of race often did so on the basis of sex. Charlotte Ray, one of the first black women to graduate from law school (Howard, 1873), gained admittance by using her initials rather than her first name on application papers. After an unsuccessful struggle to obtain legal work, she returned to her earlier career of teaching in public schools. Between 1875 and 1925, no more than 25 black women were reported to be practicing law. By 1940, the number had only doubled. Geraldine Segal, Blacks in the Law 1, 4, 215, 240 (1983); Morello, supra, at 143-147.

During the 1960s and 1970s, the climate for both white women and women of color improved substantially. The women's rights and civil rights movements encouraged more women, including racial and ethnic minorities, to apply to law schools and to challenge discriminatory practices. During the Vietnam War, a reduction in the pool of qualified male law school applicants also helped to boost women's admission. By the mid-1980s, over a third of new entrants to law school were women. By the turn of the century, women constituted a majority of law students. The growth of affirmative action and financial aid programs also increased the representation of women of color.

2. Legal Education and Gender Issues

During this period, American law schools became the subject of a growing critique that their authoritarian, teacher-centered methods fostered alienation and hierarchy. See, e.g., Duncan Kennedy, Legal Education as Training for Hierarchy, in The Politics of Law: A Progressive Critique 38-58 (David Kairys ed., 2d ed. 1990) (orig. pub. 1982). To this critique was added the complaint that this process systematically disadvantaged women. Studies at the University of California at Berkeley School of Law (Boalt Hall), Stanford, and a number of other law schools in the 1980s and the early 1990s found that female students performed less well than their male classmates, given predictions based on test scores and college performance, and were less likely to graduate at the top of the class or to hold other key positions such as membership on law review. The gap was widest for women of color. The basic studies are Linda F. Wightman, Law School Admission Council Research Report Series, Women in Legal Education: A Comparison of the Law School Performance and Law School Experience of Women and Men 25 (1996); Lani Guinier, Michael Fine, & Jane Balin, Becoming Gentlemen 41 (1997); Lorraine Dutsky, Still Unequal: The Shameful Truth About Women and Justice in America 29 (1996); Suzanne Homer & Lois Schwartz, Admitted but Not Accepted: Outsiders Take an Inside Look at Law School, 5 Berkeley Women's Law (1989-1990). Many of these studies also found that women had higher levels of alienation and lower levels of self-esteem than men and that problems of harassment and devaluation were greatest for lesbian and gay students and students of color. Wightman, supra; Homer & Schwartz, supra, at 52; Catherine Weiss & Louise Melling, The Legal Education of Twenty Women, 40 Stan. L. Rev. 1299, 1300-1302, 1363 (1988); Janice L. Austin et al., Results from a Survey: Gay, Lesbian, and Bisexual Students' Attitudes About Law School, 48 J. Legal Educ. 157 (1998); Scott N. Ihrig, Sexual Orientation in Law School:

Experiences of Gay, Lesbian, and Bisexual Law Students, 14 Law & Ineq. 555 (1996).

In most studies, women had substantially lower rates of class participation than men. See research summarized in Wightman, supra, at 25, 36, 72-74; Nancy Levit, Keeping Feminism in Its Place: Sex Segregation and the Domestication of Female Academics, 49 Kan. L. Rev. 775, 780 (2001); Deborah L. Rhode, Whistling Vivaldi: Legal Education and the Politics of Progress, 23 N.Y.U. Rev. L. & Soc. Change 217, 219-223 (1997); Elizabeth Mertz et al., What Difference Does Difference Make: The Challenge for Legal Education, 48 J. Legal Educ. 1 (1998).

Other, more recent research paints a more complicated picture. Studies at some, but not all, schools find that women are performing academically at least as well as men and are overrepresented on law reviews. Shannan N. Ball, Separate but Equal Is Unequal: The Argument Against an All-Women's Law School, 15 Notre Dame J.L. Ethics & Pub. Pol'y 171 (2001); Jennifer Brown, To Give Them Countenance: The Case for a Women's Law School, 22 Harv. Women's L.J. 1 (1999). The most comprehensive study of classroom participation finds that gender differences are mediated by other factors such as the sex, race, and teaching style of the professor and the male/female class ratio. Mertz et al., supra, at 75-77.

So, too, some research indicates that gender may be less influential than other factors, such as preexisting ideological commitments and career goals, in explaining satisfaction with the educational experience. For example, in a study of Harvard students, women who entered law school primarily for reasons such as status, income, and job security were generally satisfied with their training, while women who entered with predominantly social justice motivations found the institution sexist and dehumanizing. Robert Granville, The Making of Elite Lawyers, 104-106 (1992).

What implications should be drawn from these findings? What do you think accounts for the differences across schools and subgroups of women? Which descriptions are most consistent with your experience? Which of the following strategies seem most likely to be effective in addressing gender-related problems:

- More participatory and less competitive learning techniques, such as cooperative problem-solving exercises, simulations, student-run discussions, narratives from film and literature, and experiential reflections in journals and short assignments;

- More curricular integration of materials involving gender, race, ethnicity, class, and sexual orientation;

- More efforts to promote tolerance and to curb harassing or demeaning conduct;

- More mentoring and feedback on student performance;

- More efforts to hold faculty accountable on diversity-related issues through student course evaluations and peer review.

See Rhode, Whistling Vivaldi, supra, at 223-224. For a broad range of critiques of legal education and proposals for reform, see Mary Jane Mossman, Gender Equality Education and the Legal Profession, 12 Sup. Ct. Rev. (2d) 187 (Spring 2000); Paula Gaber, Just Trying to Be Human in This Place: The Legal Education of Twenty Women, 10 Yale J.L. & Feminism 165 (1998); Judith D. Fischer, Portia Unbound: The Effects of a Supportive Law School Environment on Women and Minority Students, 7 UCLA Women's L.J. 81 (1996); Guinier, Fine, & Balin, supra; Judy Scales-Trent, Sameness and Difference in a Law School Classroom: Working at the Crossroads, 4 Yale J.L. & Feminism 415 (1992); Beverly Balos, Learning to Teach Gender, Race, Class, and Heterosexism: Challenge in the Classroom and Clinic, 3 Hastings Women's L.J. 161 (1992); Alice K. Dueker, Diversity and Learning; Imagining a Pedagogy of Difference, 19 N.Y.U. Rev. L. & Soc. Change 101 (1991-1992); Phyllis Goldfarb, A Theory-Practice Spiral: The Ethics of Clinical Teaching, 75 Minn. L. Rev. 1599 (1991); Ann E. Freedman, Feminist Legal Method in Action: Challenging Racism, Sexism and Homophobia in Law School, 24 Ga. L. Rev. 849 (1990); Morrison Torrey, Jackie Casey, & Karin Olson, Teaching Law in a Feminist Manner: A Commentary from Experience, 13 Harv. Women's L.J. 87 (1990); Black Women Law Professors: Building a Community at the Intersection of Race and Gender, A Symposium, 6 Berkeley Women's L.J. I (1990-1991). Stephanie M. Wildman, The Question of Silence: Techniques to Ensure Full Class Participation, 38 J. Legal Educ. 147 (1988); Patricia A. Cain, Teaching Feminist Legal Theory at Texas: Listening to Difference and Exploring Connections, 38 J. Legal Educ. 165 (1988).

The report of the ABA Commission on Women in the Profession notes that women faculty have made substantial progress in legal education, but remain substantially underrepresented in positions of greatest status, influence, and job security.

> . . . Only 20 percent of full professors and 10 percent of law school deans are female, and only about 5 percent of those in either position are women of color. Women faculty are still clustered in the least prestigious academic specialties and positions, such as librarians, research and writing instructors, and non-tenured clinicians. Gender inequalities persist within as well as across these specialties. For example, women account for two-thirds of legal writing instructors, but are only half as likely as their male counterparts to hold tenured positions or to direct writing programs. At many schools, women students are also underrepresented in the most prestigious positions such as law review editors, class officers, and members of academic honor societies. The limited research available finds that these gender and racial disparities cannot be entirely explained by objective factors such as academic credentials or experience. Some evidence also suggests that women of color are underrepre-

sented in student bodies relative to their undergraduate performance and academic potential.

ABA Commission on Women in the Profession, The Unfinished Agenda: A Report on the Status of Women in the Legal Profession 27 (2001).

What accounts for these disparities has been subject to dispute. The most comprehensive recent effort to explain women's underrepresentation is Deborah Merritt's study of some 1,100 faculty who began teaching between 1986 and 1991. Deborah Jones Merritt, Are Women Stuck on the Academic Ladder? An Empirical Perspective, 10 UCLA Women's L.J. 249 (2000). In essence, Merritt found that differences in experience, credentials, and geographic mobility explained some gender differences, but not others. For example, controlling for relevant variables accounted for women's greater likelihood to take non-tenure-track positions and men's greater likelihood to obtain positions at the most prestigious schools. Id. at 250-252. However, differences in credentials and geographic constraints did not explain why men were hired at higher ranks and ended up teaching more prestigious subjects (such as constitutional law rather than legal writing). Nor was it entirely clear why white men were considerably more likely to obtain tenure, hold chairs, or serve as deans. Id. at 252-253. Some of the difference may have been attributable to the fact that white men published more scholarly articles (particularly in prestigious journals) than white women and women of color. Id. White men also attached less value than women to public service and to addressing non-academic audiences. Women did, however, match men in serving as associate deans, and women of color were even more likely than white men (or women) to hold such positions. Id. For similar findings, see Richard K. Neumann, Jr., Women in Legal Education: What the Statistics Show, 60 J. Legal Educ. 1, 10 (2000); Levitt, supra, at 778-783. For a response to Neumann, arguing that women's different biological makeup and different choices concerning family and career priorities largely explain their underrepresentation on law faculties, see Dan Subotnik, Bah, Humbug to the Bleak Story of Women Law Faculty: A Response to Professor Newmann, 51 J. Legal Educ. 141, 143-148 (2001).

In analyzing her results, Merritt suggests that unconscious discrimination, unequal family commitments, and different career priorities are all at work. Women appear less willing to relocate in pursuit of the most prestigious jobs and clerkships, and less focused on obtaining deanships or publishing articles in the most elite academic journals. Merritt, supra, at 245-247. "If women want different career paths than men," Merritt concludes, "then we shouldn't measure their advancement along traditional lines." Id. at 247.

If Merritt is right, how should we measure women's achievement? Should we assume that women's different priorities are always freely chosen or that they are the primary explanation for different levels of advancement? For example, women's failure to achieve tenure at the same rate as men may reflect a broad variety of factors such as greater family responsibilities (i.e., the convergence of women's biological and tenure clocks); exclusion from networks of mentoring and support; disproportionate assumption of counseling, committee, and public service work; and devaluation of nontraditional subjects, skills education, or perspectives such as feminist or critical race theory. If these are the barriers that impede women's advance, how should law schools respond? See Marina Angel, The Glass Ceiling for Women in Legal Education: Contract Positions and the Death of Tenure, 50 J. Legal Educ. 1 (2000); Susan B. Apel, Gender and Invisible Work: Musings of a Woman Law Professor, 31 U.S.F. L. Rev. 993 (1997); Pamela J. Smith, The Tyrannies of Silence of the Untenured Professors of Color, 33 U.C. Davis L. Rev. 1105 (2000); Cheryl I. Harris, Law Professors of Color and the Academy of Poets and Kings, 68 Chi.-Kent L. Rev. 331 (1992). Alternatively, if Subotnik is correct that women's family commitments explain their underrepresentation in the most demanding academic positions, does it follow that they "lack the psychological makeup for success"? Subotnik, supra, at 147.

Putting Theory Into Practice

5-6. The ABA Commission on Women in the Profession, like many commentators in this field, has recommended that law schools establish committees to identify and address gender-related concerns. ABA Commission, Don't Just Hear It Through the Grapevine: Studying Gender Questions at Your Law School (1998). Does your school have such a committee? What might such a committee accomplish? What are its potential pitfalls?

5-7. Have there been any gender patterns in class participation in the course for which you have been reading this book? Analyze these patterns. How does one get called on in your class? What factors seem to affect who gets called on, who asks questions, and who stays after class to ask questions?

To the extent that female students participate less in class and feel more alienated from the educational process, what strategies, if any, should a law professor consider to address these disparities? Analyze each of these strategies in light of the frameworks of formal equality, substantive equality, and different voice theory.

3. A Different Voice in the Lawyering Process?

≡≡≡ *Carrie Menkel-Meadow, Portia in a Different*
Voice: Speculations on a Women's Lawyering
Process
1 Berkeley Women's L.J. 39, 55-60 (1985)

Does the female voice of relationship, care and connection lead to a different form of law practice? Although the present adversarial system may limit the ways in which concern for others may be expressed toward adversaries, the values of relationship and care may be expressed with one's work partners. In this area at least, we have some evidence that Portia's voice has had an influence. As [Cynthia] Epstein has documented [in Women in Law, ch. 9 (1981)] early attempts to form a separate feminist practice focused on establishing non-hierarchical organizations with participatory decision-making. This was a political expression of the psychological qualities observed by Gilligan in the relationships and connections that women lawyers sought to forge with each other while engaged in practices that pitted them against the traditional models. Some of these women lawyers were explicit in their rejection of male principles in the ordering of legal work. . . .

While hierarchy produces efficiency and individual achievement, as lawyers, Amy and Hilary [two of Gilligan's female subjects] might choose to emphasize other values such as collectivity and interpersonal connection. This attempt to work in a different way not only affects relationships within the working unit, but is also apparent in the work of feminists who seek to demystify law and the legal profession by working with clients on lay advocacy projects or self-representation.

To illustrate the issues involved in a woman's way of practicing law, consider the following example. My colleague Grace Blumberg, an expert in marital property law, was asked to write the first draft of an amicus brief in a case involving the legal treatment of a professional degree in a community property regime. She describes the work on this effort with a group of California women lawyers as follows:

> The effort to transform a generally literate coherent brief into "proper form" took some 100 person hours, more than eight times the amount of time it took the author to write the brief. . . . The participants, leaving the author aside, seemed to get some substantial psychic rewards from this 100 hours spent mostly in conferences of two and three persons. They created an atmosphere of social intimacy between relative strangers. Although at least 90 percent of the time was spent hard at work, the atmosphere was of a social event. Food was always served even though it was not any discernible meal time. . . . Personal information and confidences were exchanged in the interstices of work. I was struck by the incongruity of my product (female) and my process (male) and in contrast, their product (male) and process (female). My product was revealing, tentative and dialectic. In contrast my process was individualistic and

individual, highly concerned with the goal of efficiency and not at all interested in collaboration as an end in itself. In contrast, their product was extremely formal, authoritarian, concealing and impersonal. Their process was communitarian and communicative, full of feeling and interpersonal experience.

The story of this brief-writing exercise also reveals another aspect of the women's lawyering process — concern for the interconnection of personal and professional life. In the "interstices of work," the lawyers engaged in this project shared information about their personal lives and brought sustenance to each other (intellectually, emotionally and nutritionally). Virtually every report of women lawyers discusses the impact of personal lives on professional lives and vice versa, where one finds almost no such reports in the descriptions and ethnographies of male lawyers. The concern for the quality of life and the relation between one's work and one's personal life is consistent with the ethic of care and relationship exhibited by Gilligan's female subjects. To Jake, who can separate life and property, the division between work and the rest of one's life is easier. Indeed, the inability to individuate reported by Gilligan has been noted as sociologically dysfunctional for women lawyers who do not have enough "role virtuosity" to separate different aspects of themselves so that they can convert from adversarial courtroom conduct in one moment to a collegial meal with opposing counsel in the next moment.

Perhaps the most salient feature of Portia's different voice is in the lawyer-client relationship, where the values of care and responsibility for others seem most directly applicable. Amy and Hilary, with their ability to "take the part of the other and submerge the self," may be able to enter the world of the client, thereby understanding more fully what the client desires and why, without the domination of what the lawyer perceives to be "in the client's best interest." More fully developed sensitivities to empathy and altruism . . . may enable women lawyers to understand a fuller range of client needs and objectives. . . . Where the Jakes of this world may make assumptions about the primacy of economic and efficiency considerations of their cases, the Amys and Hilarys may see a greater number of issues in the social, psychological and moral aspects. Of course, in a fully mature and integrated vision of lawyering all of these aspects of the case would be considered important. . . .

[T]he tendency to personalize and contextualize problems may incline women lawyers to ask for more information on a broader range of subjects and thereby develop a fuller understanding of the context of the client's life. This, in turn, may make women better lawyers, especially in their relationships with clients and in their ability to see the human complexities of some legal problems.

. . . If Amy "fights the hypo" to learn more facts, might she not have a different conception of relevance and admissibility in deciding a dispute? If women are more concerned with the context in which the dispute is embedded, would they not search for more facts and be less concerned about creation of a precedent of universal applicability? . . .

If Amy and Hilary use different considerations in their moral reasoning, would they create different ethical codes for the profession based on their different ways of engaging in moral reasoning? . . . Would Amy and Hilary create rules about relationships between lawyers, based on mutual affiliation in the same profession, and requiring greater candor and fairness in dealing with each other? Would the conflict of interest rules or withdrawal from representation rules be different because of an ethic of care and affiliation that would lead to a different conception of client loyalty? Might a broader conception of the legal problem and its causes lead to less concern about the unauthorized practice of law and more toleration, if not encouragement, of work with other professionals and lay persons to solve those problems?

≡≡≡ **Katharine T. Bartlett, Feminist Legal Methods**
≡≡ 103 Harv. L. Rev. 829, 836-837, 843-847, 862-863 (1990)

When feminists "do law," they do what other lawyers do: they examine the facts of a legal issue or dispute, they identify the essential features of those facts, they determine what legal principles should guide the resolution of the dispute, and they apply those principles to the facts. This process unfolds not in a linear, sequential, or strictly logical manner, but rather in a pragmatic, interactive manner. Facts determine which rules are appropriate, and rules determine which facts are relevant. In doing law, feminists like other lawyers use a full range of methods of legal reasoning — deduction, induction, analogy, and use of hypotheticals, policy, and other general principles.

In addition to these conventional methods of doing law, however, feminists use other methods. These methods, though not all unique to feminists, attempt to reveal features of a legal issue which more traditional methods tend to overlook or suppress. One method, asking the woman question, is designed to expose how the substance of law may silently and without justification submerge the perspectives of women and other excluded groups. Another method, feminist practical reasoning, expands traditional notions of legal relevance to make legal decisionmaking more sensitive to the features of a case not already reflected in legal doctrine. A third method, consciousness-raising, offers a means of testing the validity of accepted legal principles through the lens of the personal experience of those directly affected by those principles. . . .

Is asking the woman question really a method at all, or it is a mask for something else, such as legal substance, or politics? The [United States] legal system has assumed that method and substance have different functions, and that method cannot serve its purpose unless it remains separate from, and independent of, substantive "bias." Rules of legal method, like rules of legal procedure, are supposed to insulate substantive rules from arbitrary application. . . . Within this conventional view, it might be charged that the method of asking the woman question fails to respect the necessary separation between method and substance. Indeed, asking the woman question seems to be a "loaded," overtly political activity, which reaches far beyond the "neutral" tasks of ascertaining law and facts and applying one to the other.

Of course, not only feminist legal methods but *all* legal methods shape substance; the difference is that feminists have been called on it. . . .

The real question is . . . [not] whether [a method has substantive consequences] but whether the relationship between method and substance is "proper." . . . A purely result-oriented method in which decisionmakers may decide every case in order to reach the result they think most desirable . . . improperly exerts no meaningful constraints on the decisionmaker. Also improper is a method that imposes arbitrary or unjustified constraints, such as one that requires a decisionmaker to decide in favor of all female claimants or against all employers.

In contrast, the method of asking the woman question . . . demands . . . special attention to a set of interests and concerns that otherwise may be, and historically have been, overlooked. The substance of asking the woman question lies in *what* it asks to uncover: disadvantage based upon gender. The political nature of this method arises only because it seeks information that is not supposed to exist. The claim that this information may exist — and that the woman question is therefore necessary — is political, but only to the extent that the stated or implied claim that it does not exist is *also* political.

Asking the woman question confronts the assumption of legal neutrality, and has substantive consequences only if the law is not gender-neutral. The bias of the method is the bias toward uncovering a certain kind of bias. The bias disadvantages those who are otherwise benefited by law and legal methods whose gender implications are *not* revealed. If this is "bias," feminists must insist that it is "good" (or "proper") bias, not "bad." . . .

[As for more contextualized methods of legal reasoning,] feminists' substantive analyses of legal decisionmaking have revealed to them that so-called neutral means of deciding cases tend to mask, not eliminate, political and social considerations from legal decisionmaking. Feminists have found that neutral rules and procedures tend to drive underground the ideologies of the decisionmaker, and that these ideologies do not serve women's interests well. Disadvantaged by hidden bias, feminists see the value of modes of legal reasoning that expose and open up debate concerning the underlying political and moral considerations. By forcing articulation and understanding of those considerations, practical reasoning forces justification of results based upon what interests are actually at stake.

The "substance" of feminist practical reasoning consists of an alertness to certain forms of injustice that otherwise go unnoticed and unaddressed. Feminists turn to contextualized methods of reasoning to allow greater understanding and exposure of that injustice. Reasoning from context can change perceptions about the world, which may then further expand the contexts within which such reasoning seems appropriate, which in turn may lead to still further changes in perceptions. The expansion of existing boundaries of relevance based upon changed perceptions of the world is familiar to the process of legal reform. The shift from Plessy v. Ferguson to Brown v. Board of Education, for example, rested upon the expansion of the "legally relevant" in race discrimination cases to include the actual experiences of black Americans and the inferiority implicit in segregation. Much of the judicial reform that has been beneficial to women, as well, has come about through expanding the lens of legal relevance to encompass the missing perspectives of women and to accommodate perceptions about the nature and role of women. Feminist practical reasoning compels continued expansion of such perceptions.

Notes

1. **A Profile of Women in the Legal Profession.** The statistical profile of women lawyers in the United States reflects both dramatic progress and continued constraints for women in the legal profession. Since the 1960s, women's representation in the American bar has increased from about 3 to 30 percent, and at the turn of the century, they constituted a majority of entering law students. Yet in the legal profession women remain underrepresented at the top and overrepresented at the bottom in terms of status, power, and financial reward. Women account for only 15 percent of federal judges and law firm partners, 10 percent of law school deans and general counsels, and 5 percent of managing partners of large firms. The gap widens for women of color, who account for only 3 percent of the profession, and their small numbers limit the information available about their experience. See ABA Commission on Women in the Profession, The Unfinished Agenda: A Report on the Status of Women in the Legal Profession 5, 13 (2001). See also ABA Commission on Opportunities for Minorities in the Profession, Miles to Go: Progress of Minorities in the Legal Profession (2000).

In summarizing recent trends, an American Bar Foundation (ABF) statistical report notes that "the most pervasive underrepresentation of female lawyers, although of lesser magnitude than in [previous decades exists] . . . among partners in law firms. In spite of improvements over time, only . . . 60 percent as many female lawyers [are] partners in law firms . . . as would have been expected had women been fully represented among partners." Kathleen E. Hull & Robert Nelson, Divergent Paths: Gender Differences in the Careers of Urban Lawyers, 10 Researching Law 1 (Summer 1999). The problem is not simply that women have not been in the pipeline long enough to achieve substantial representation among partners. Rather, the ABF report indicates that, when representation was controlled for age, women were persistently underrepresented in all age groups. In the New York Bar glass ceiling study, women were three times less likely to become partners as men, and in the ABF study, women's chances were less than half of men's. Cynthia Fuchs Epstein et al., Glass Ceilings and Open Doors: Women's Advancement in the Legal Profession, 64 Fordham L. Rev. 291; id. at 359 (finding women's chances to be about 5 percent and men's 17 percent); Hull & Nelson, supra, at 4 (finding men's chances to be 40 percent and women's 16 percent). The disparities are especially pronounced for equity and managing partners. Among large firm partners, only about 60 percent of female attorneys, compared with three-quarters of male attorneys, have equity status. Matt Fleischer, Women in Nat'l L.J. 250 Hit a Glass Plateau, Nat'l L.J., Dec. 11, 2000, at A1; Chris Klein, Women's Progress Slows at Top Firms, Nat'l L.J., May 6, 1998, at 1, 15. Only about 5 percent of managing partners in the surveyed firms are women. ABA Commission on Women in the Profession, The Unfinished Agenda: A Report on the Status of Women in the Legal Profession 14 (2001).

Underrepresentation is greatest for women of color. Their proportion of equity partners remains stuck at under 1 percent, and almost none remain at the firm at which they began. Arthur S. Hayes, Asians Increase at Big Firms, Nat'l L.J., Feb. 18, 2000, at A11 (noting that African Americans, Asians, and Hispanics each account for only about 1 percent of equity partners and that the percentages have not significantly increased since 1998); David B. Wilkins, Partners Without Power?: A Preliminary Look at Black Partners in Corporate Law Firms, 2 J. Inst. for Study of Leg. Ethics 15 (1999). For attrition rates, see National Association of Law Placement Foundation, Beyond the Bidding Wars: A Survey of Associate Attrition, Departure, Destinations, and Workplace Initiatives 23 (2000). Only 10 percent of general counsels of Fortune 500 companies were women, and only one of those was a woman of color. Terry Carter, Paths Need Paving, ABA J., Sept. 2000, at 37; Lawyers for One America, Affirmative Action: The Difference We Make 6 (2000).

There are sex-based differences in career paths that affect women's representation in particular practice settings. Female lawyers are more likely than male lawyers to work in private industry, government, legal aid, and public defender programs, and they are less likely to practice in law firms. ABA Commission on Women in the Profession, The Unfinished Agenda: A Report on the Status of Women in the Legal Profession 23 (2001). Do such differences prove discrimination against women by private law firms and corporate counsel positions? Are they even necessarily a concern? Consider Carrie Menkel-Meadow's observation:

> Achievement of high-status and lucrative positions in large law firms represents the liberal feminist achievement of the American Dream. But is it a dream or a

nightmare? Monetary and prestige measures of success, drawn from conventional male-constructed sociology, all too often are taken as the measure of women's progress in the profession, even where there is some evidence women themselves look to other measures, like doing socially useful work or having meaningful relationships at work with clients and co-workers. Both cultural and more radical feminist critiques remind us that becoming surrogate males is not the feminist-humanist transformative vision. Committing many hours to routinized tasks, within a highly stratified hierarchy, on cases and transactions with debatable social utility, while leaving one's children in the care of low-income women is hardly the feminist vision of a more humane world. . . . Women want to be in the workforce but may want to reconstruct what it means to be a productive worker.

Carrie Menkel-Meadow, Exploring a Research Agenda of the Feminization of the Legal Profession: Theories of Gender and Social Change 14 Law & Soc. Inquiry 289, 307-308 (1989). See also Deborah L. Rhode, Balanced Lives: Changing the Culture of Legal Practice (ABA Commission on Women in the Profession, 2002).

Studies of career change also show some gender disparities. In a study of 1976, 1977, and 1978 law graduates of prominent law schools, a larger proportion of men than women stated that they moved from one job to another for reasons such as "advancement and salary considerations," while women were more likely than men to change jobs because of dislike of the environment, discrimination, and "other" reasons. See Linda Liefland, Career Patterns of Male and Female Lawyers, 35 Buff. L. Rev. 601, 606, 626 (1986). In another study, women were more likely than men to report dissatisfaction with their first jobs (62 percent to 41 percent) and were less likely to give advancement-related reasons for changing jobs. See Paul W. Mattessich & Cheryl W. Heilman, The Career Paths of Minnesota Law School Graduates: Does Gender Make a Difference?, 9 Law & Ineq. J. 59, 85 (1990). A Wisconsin Bar Association study also found disparities in the reasons stated for a career change, with men more influenced by opportunities for professional growth (36 percent to 27 percent), career advancement (40 percent to 26 percent), and compensation (35 percent to 20 percent); family considerations were mentioned by the same percentage (12 percent) of women and men. See Christy Brooks, Research Survey Report of the State Bar's Special Committee on the Participation of Women in the Bar, Wis. Bar Bull., Mar. 1987, at 8. The Michigan study found that while 73 percent of men leaving a law firm job went to another law firm, only 37 percent of women did so. See David L. Chambers, Tough Enough: The Work and Family Experiences of Recent Women Graduates of the University of Michigan Law School 18-19 (1987), cited in American Bar Association Commission on Women in the Profession, Options and Obstacles: A Survey of the Studies of the Careers of Women Lawyers (July 1994).

Evaluate this analysis from the point of view of the other perspectives studied in this course. Is Kingsley Browne right: There is no glass ceiling, only different career paths? See supra, at page 819. What do women want from a career in law? What do feminists want? Is it possible to generalize about either group on the issues that matter most? What would success in the law look like in a "more humane world"? Reconsider Problem 3-3 on page 364 in light of these questions.

2. When Does Gender Difference Make a Difference? Do women bring special qualities to the practice of law? Matthew Hale Carpenter, in unsuccessfully defending the right of Myra Bradwell to become a member of the Illinois Bar (see Bradwell v. Illinois, 83 U.S. (16 Wall.) 130 (1872), excerpted in Chapter 1, at page 30, argued that while some cases may require the "rough qualities possessed by men, . . . [t]here are many causes in which the silver voice of a woman would accomplish more than the severity and sternness of man could achieve." Id. at 137.

Among contemporary lawyers, perceptions of gender differences are widely shared. In the recent ABA Journal poll, only 8 percent of women lawyers believed that male and female lawyers had the same strengths, and only 18 percent believed that they had the same weaknesses. Terry Carter, Paths Need Paving, ABA J., Sept. 2000, at 34. Slightly under half of male lawyers believed that men and women had the same strengths and weaknesses. Id. Women lawyers were thought to have greater empathy and "better people skills," but insufficient assertiveness and aggressiveness. Id.

What do you think of the claim that women lawyers practice in a "different voice," more sensitive to values of care, compassion, and cooperation than prevailing legal norms? See, e.g., Rand Jack & Dana Crowley Jack, Moral Vision and Professional Decisions: The Changing Values of Women and Men Lawyers (1989); Susan P. Sturm, From Gladiators to Problem-Solvers: Connecting Conversations About Women, the Academy, and the Legal Profession, 4 Duke J. Gender L. & Pol'y 119 (1997).

In law teaching, men are significantly more likely to teach constitutional law, while women are more likely to teach trusts and estates and skills courses; white women are significantly more likely to teach family law. See Deborah Jones Merritt & Barbara F. Reskin, Sex, Race, and Credentials: The Truth About Affirmative Action in Law Faculty Hiring, 97 Colum. L. Rev. 199, 258-259 (1997). Is there a plausible "different voice" explanation for these disparities?

The evidence for the many presumed gender differences between male and female lawyers is weaker than commonly supposed. None of the work on gender differences in the legal profession draws on large-scale, methodologically adequate empirical surveys. See, e.g., Jack & Jack, supra (relying on interviews with 36 attorneys in one county). And the most recent, comprehensive social science research finds few characteristics on which men and women consistently differ along gender lines. Even on these characteristics, gender typically accounts for only about 5 percent of the variation. See sources cited in Rhode, Speaking of Sex, supra, at 21-42. Contextual forces and other factors like race, ethnicity, and sexual orientation can be equally significant.

For example, surveys of leadership styles and decisionmaking behavior have reached mixed results that underscore the contextual variations in gender difference. Some research based on laboratory experiments and individuals' self-descriptions finds that women display greater interpersonal skills and adopt more participatory, democratic styles, while men rely on more directive and task-oriented approaches. Jeanette Cleveland, Margaret Stockdale, & Karen R. Murphy, Women and Men in Management 307 (1999); Alice H. Eagly & Blair T. Johnson, Gender and Leadership Style: A Meta-Analysis, 108 Psychol. Bull. 233, 233-256 (1990); Alice H. Eagly, Steven J. Karau, & Mona G. Makhijani, Gender and the Effectiveness of Leaders: A Meta-Analysis, 117 Psychol. Bull. 125, 125-145 (1995). Yet other large-scale studies based on self-reports find no such gender differences. Radcliffe Public Policy Institute and The Boston Club, Suiting Themselves: Women's Leadership Styles in Today's Workplace (1999). Nor do these differences emerge in most research involving evaluations of leaders by supervisors, subordinates, and peers in real-world settings. Gary N. Powell, Women and Men in Management 45-49, 105-109 (1988); Karin Klenke, Women and Leadership: A Contextual Perspective 160 (1996); Gary N. Powell, One More Time: Do Female and Male Managers Differ?, 4 Acad. Management Executive 68 (1990); Eagly & Johnson, supra, at 246-247; Cherryl Simrell King, Sex Role Identity and Decision Styles: How Gender Helps Explain the Paucity of Women at the Top, in Gender Power, Leadership and Governance 67, 71 (Georgia Duerst-Lahti & Rita Mae Kelly eds., 1995).

Sex stereotyping, of course, may help to explain these divergent results. Sex stereotypes are particularly likely to influence lab studies and self-descriptions. In experimental situations where participants have relatively little information about each other, they are more likely to fall back on conventional assumptions about appropriate masculine and feminine behavior. Such assumptions may also skew individuals' willingness to behave or to describe their behavior in ways that deviate from stereotypical norms. Klenke, supra, at 151; Cleveland, Stockdale, & Murphy, supra, at 307; Eagly, Makhijani, & Klonsky, supra, at 18. Since women do not enjoy the same presumption of competence, the same latitude for assertiveness, and the same access to power as their male colleagues, a less autocratic style may seem necessary. Eagly & Johnson, supra, at 247-248. By contrast, the force of conventional stereotypes is weaker in actual organizational settings than in lab studies or self-assessments. Women who have achieved decisionmaking positions in traditionally male-dominated professions generally have been socialized to follow prevailing practices. Joanne Martin & Debra Meyerson, Women and Power: Confronting Resistance and Disorganized Action, in Power and Influence in Organizations 311, 313 (Roderick M. Kramer &

Margaret A. Neale eds., 1998); Cynthia Fuchs Epstein, Deceptive Distinctions: Sex, Gender, and the Social Order 173-184 (1988); Cleveland, Stockdale, & Murphy, supra, at 293-299.

Efforts to determine whether women lawyers approach their work differently than men yield similarly mixed results. The bottom line appears to be "some women, some of the time." The most systematic research involves negotiating behavior. Over the past two decades, a large body of theoretical and empirical research has attempted to determine whether men and women have different negotiating styles and effectiveness. A recent summary of this work finds

> conflicting claims and widely disparate results — such as the most recent studies' conclusions that "men negotiate significantly better outcomes than women" . . . ; "women behave more cooperatively than men" . . .; "women may obtain lower joint outcomes in integrative bargaining because of a higher level of concern for the other" . . . , but also that "there are no statistically significant differences in negotiation outcomes and performance between men and women". . . .

Carrie Menkel-Meadow, Teaching About Gender and Negotiation: Sex, Truths, and Videotape, 16 Negotiation J. 357 (Oct. 2000).

In accounting for these conflicting results, it may be significant that gender is mediated by other aspects of the negotiating context that vary across research settings. These other aspects include the relative social status, perceived power, and attitudes toward conflict of the participants. Whether negotiators are the same sex, whether they have ongoing relationships, and whether they are acting for themselves or as representatives for someone else also matters. For reviews of multiple studies, see id.; Carol Watson, Gender vs. Power as a Predictor of Negotiation Behavior and Outcomes, 10 Negotiation J. 117 (1994); Sandra R. Farber & Monica Rickenberg, Under-Confident Women and Over-Confident Men: Gender and a Sense of Competence in a Simulated Negotiation, 11 Yale J.L. & Feminism 271, 286, 301 (1999).

One of the few findings of gender difference that holds up across multiple studies is that women seem to feel less confident than men even when there are no objective differences in outcome. Watson, supra, at 123-211; Farber & Rickenberg, supra, at 301. Another common finding is that male and female lawyers are expected to perform differently even where there is little actual difference in goals, orientation, or outcomes. See studies cited in Carrie Menkel-Meadow, Portia Redux: Another Look at Gender, Feminism and Legal Ethics, 2 Va. J. Soc. Pol'y & L. 75 (1994). What do you think explains the persistence of these different expectations and self-evaluations?

It is, of course, possible to argue for more caring and cooperative approaches to legal practice on the basis of feminist commitments, not feminine characteristics. Much recent work by feminists as well as other commentators concludes that non-adversarial collaborative and problem-solving techniques may be more effective than more conventional adversarial methods and that more participatory, less hierarchical lawyering styles can improve representation of clients. See Carrie Menkel-Meadow, The Limits of Adversarial Ethics, in Ethics in Practice: Lawyers' Roles, Responsibilities, and Regulation (Deborah L. Rhode ed., 2000); Deborah L. Rhode, In the Interests of Justice 49-115 (2001); Sturm, supra, at 127-128, 135-137; Peggy Davis, Contextual Legal Criticism: A Demonstration Exploring Hierarchy and "Feminine" Style, 66 N.Y.U. L. Rev. 1635 (1991).

3. Feminist Legal Method? The readings in this section suggest that feminist legal analysis is more contextualized than more traditional forms of analysis. Among the many scholars who have made this claim, see Ann Scales, Feminist Legal Method: Not So Scary, 2 UCLA Women's L.J. 1 (1992); Mary Jane Mossman, Feminism and Legal Method: The Difference It Makes, 3 Wis. Women's L.J. 147 (1987); Heather Wishik, To Question Everything: The Inquiries of Feminist Jurisprudence, 1 Berkeley Women's L.J. 64 (1986). Others have similarly advocated "pragmatic" or "situated" forms of decisionmaking, or "practical reasoning," not necessarily under the "feminist" label. See, e.g., Linda R. Hirshman, The Book of "A," 70 Tex. L. Rev. 971 (1992); Margaret Jane Radin, The Pragmatist and the Feminist, 63 S. Cal. L. Rev. 1699 (1990); Catharine Pierce Wells, Situated Decisionmaking, 63 S. Cal. L. Rev. 1727 (1990); Martha Minow, Foreword: Justice Engendered, 101 Harv. L. Rev. 10 (1987). Although contextualized forms of analysis are not uniquely "feminist," part of the appeal for feminism is their capacity to consider the consequences of abstract rules, together with facts and perspectives that rules may not have contemplated. In re Lamb, set forth at the end of this chapter at page 922, is an opportunity to see how the same facts appear at different degrees of contextualization. Its further appeal is that it might make the relationship between rules and power more transparent. See Lucinda M. Finley, Breaking Women's Silence in Law: The Dilemma of the Gendered Nature of Legal Reasoning, 64 Notre Dame L. Rev. 886, 896 (1989) (arguing that the rhetoric of law and legal reasoning make it difficult to articulate "the complex relationship between power, gender, and knowledge").

What difference does feminist method make? Will it help women? Is it biased? How does it compare, for example, to the law and economics method?

It is important to note that the feminist hypothesis that the law is not as neutral and objective as it claims to be when it comes to women is just that — a hypothesis. As a hypothesis, that judgment only kicks off the method. There is no impact (political or otherwise) from feminist method until it is proved. If the hypothesis is proved, this means that gender bias does (or did) exist, in which case it is not the scholar who has proved it that is partisan, but the law itself. . . .

[A]lthough feminist method looks to women's experiences for its evidence, it must establish what it purports to show. Factual assertions need to be proven, even if feminist inquiry results in altering what constitutes proof. Material must be relevant, even if feminists, applying feminist method, succeed in redrawing the boundaries of relevance. Normative claims must be persuasive, even if what is deemed persuasive is changed by feminist questioning of underlying assumptions and paradigms.

In important respects, feminist method has had much in common with the methods of law and economics scholarship. Law and economics scholars begin with a hypothesis — that individuals act in self-interested, profit-maximizing ways and that the law can best serve its goals if it takes account of these motivations. This hypothesis, based on prior discoveries that individuals act in self-interested, profit-maximizing ways, directs the inquiry of law and economics scholars in specific legal contexts to determine how the law operates, and how it might be improved to enhance desirable and efficient behavior. And like feminist scholarship, the hypothesis has no effect, other than to give direction to the research, until some proposition is shown through evidence and argument that is persuasive to those whom the scholars would like to persuade.

Katharine T. Bartlett, Cracking Foundations as Feminist Method, 8 Am. U. J. Gender Soc. Pol'y & L. 31, 39-41 (2000). Why does feminist method appear, to some, so political? Is it sometimes, simply put, unpersuasive (as law and economics analysis can also be unpersuasive)? Is it that its detractors are too interested (or "political") to accept it? Id. at 41-42. Are there additional explanations?

Some have argued that the law's need for stability, predictability, and impartiality "would be seriously undermined by a jurisprudence that strongly privileges responsibility over rights, relationships over fairness, and context-specific judgment over rule-based decision-making." Gregory Bassham, Feminist Legal Theory: A Liberal Response, 6 Notre Dame J.L. & Pub. Pol'y 293, 310 (1992). Is this a fair criticism of feminist practical reasoning? Or does it suggest too dichotomous a view of context-specific and rule-based analysis?

4. Women Judges

Judith Resnik, On the Bias: Feminist Reconsiderations of the Aspirations for Our Judges
61 S. Cal. L. Rev. 1877, 1879, 1885-1886, 1921-1927 (1988)

I have two central questions: First, what are the contemporary aspirations for those who judge? Second, how do feminist theories inform or challenge these aspirations?

At one level, the answer to the first question is so easy that some might suggest it is a "straw person." A vast body of legal literature addresses the question of what qualifies a person to be a judge. We speak about seeking individuals who will be "impartial," "disengaged," "independent," and who will hear both sides and judge fairly. . . .

One can also understand the impulse towards seeking judges who lack self-interest. Judges hold awesome powers in this society. Their judgments change lives, transfer assets, imprison individuals, and even determine life and death. How tremendously frightening it would be to think that judgments were motivated by personal gain, that the interests of others were routinely sacrificed to advance judges' self-serving goals. Statements of the requirement of disengagement assuage our anxiety about judicial promotion of self.

Two other aspects of disengagement might be understood from the differing vantage points of the judges and the judged. Disengagement may free judges to act. Psychologically, the distance between judges and their judgments may enable judges to render the decisions that so profoundly affect the lives of others. If freed from having to engage personally with what occurs subsequent to their judgments, judges may be enabled to impose rulings that would otherwise be too painful to pronounce. And, psychologically, those who are judged may wish for a judge who is, at some level, a mystical "Other," not like ourselves but endowed with special wisdom and insight.

The imagery of Justice is emblematic of many of these hopes. The judicial icon is a goddess-like figure, frequently shown with scales, sword, and, after the sixteenth century, with a blindfold. First a goddess within the Greek and Roman traditions, Justitia evolved into Justice, one of the cardinal virtues endorsed by Christianity. And the power to judge shifted from kings, in the name of gods, to kings in their own right, and then from kings to judges, governing bodies continued to adorn their buildings with scenes of the Last Judgment and with images of Justice. Not simply a relic of the past, Justice still appears in courthouses and other civic buildings throughout the country. How ironic, in a world in which all judges were men, that sovereigns continued to display Justitia as the paradigm judge. Yet, given the magnitude of the power that resides in judges, how appropriate to seek an Other, some mythical figure, quintessentially nonpartisan, who would have the wisdom of the divine.

Impartiality, freedom from bias or prejudgment, independence, disengagement. These are terms that are culturally dependent. Anthropologists remind us that other systems of justice do not require such attributes for their judges. But taken in the context of the exercise of judgment by state officials rather than by elders known to the community, in the context of the history of ongoing struggles between judges and sovereigns, and in the context of the immense power that judges possess, the quest for such qualities in judges can be readily appreciated. . . .

The language of the law of judges and the language of feminism have virtually no convergences. . . . A touchstone of feminism is connection; over and over again, feminist theories speak about our interrelatedness, our interdependencies, our selves and others as impossible of comprehension in isolation. . . .

The case law and commentary on the role of judges have none of these qualities. Instead one finds that fiat: "No man is permitted to try cases where he has an interest in the outcome." Such a statement is not accompanied by an acknowledgment that we are all interested, that not all interests are equal nor equally bad, and that the kind of interest intended to be banned is a particular form of self-aggrandizement. Rather, the traditional aspirations for judges assume a single kind of undesirable interest, a connection linked to corruption. The terms of the world of the judge — disinterest, disengagement, impartiality, independence — are words that are deeply suspicious of relationship. . . .

At one level, what is missing is evident: We do not, but we could, demand that those who hold power do so with attentive love, with care, with nurturance, with a responsible sense of one's self as connected to and dependent upon those who are being judged. . . . But there are (at least) three difficulties. The first is one of domination. Assuming that we could alter the aspirations for judging, what would happen if the list of judicial qualifications were simply enlarged by adding the qualities feminist theories have helped us learn to value? Here, we must heed Rosemary Ruether's warning to reject an androgynous Judg/ess because, under conditions of patriarchy, the addition of traits associated with the female only ratifies their second class status. . . . Ruether's point may also be echoed in legal doctrine about the relationship between the law and equity. Law is the starting place. Equity is the cabined, secondary response — appended, ad hoc, supplementary and suspect. Stirring a bit of connection and responsible nurturance in the pot of powerful disengagement of our judges is hardly the kind of transformative response that feminist insights demand. A revised, rather than an expanded, list of attributes, is required.

A second problem is one of enthusiasm. How sure can we be that connection and care are qualities we want for our judges? Women's experience of connection and care have not been uniformly uplifting. As Robin West so well summarizes, radical feminists remind us that with connection can come debasement, the experience of intimacy as paralysis, of interdependence as moments when one loses a sense of self, all accompanied by what Sara Ruddick describes as "cheery denial." Judges, like women, may well fear intimacy. Isolating judges by calls for distance and disengagement and by fragmentation of responsibility could, in one sense, have been understood as enabling. How, one might ask, could an empathic judge sentence another-in-whom-one-sees-oneself to years of incarceration? How could judges impose economic burdens on struggling individuals or entities? For those of us who might applaud a possible reduction in criminal penalties which such intimacy and empathy might foster, we must recognize that our empathic judges would not simply experience connection with defendants, but also with victims. Might such judges respond with too harsh condemnations? Or with paralysis from being torn in too many directions?

I think paralysis-by-connection to be no more likely than paralysis-by-intellectualization. In our current world, in which we do not ask judges to recognize their connectedness to those before them, some judges impose harsh sentences and some more lenient ones; some judges impose obligations upon litigants without much apparent stress while others appear reluctant to sanction. The length of judicial opinions and the energy of some dissents bear testimony to the tugs and pulls of contemporary judging, complete with its claims of dispassion and disinterest.

But then, one might ask if feminist revision is needed, and (not surprisingly), my answer is yes. Recognition of the tugs, the pulls, and the burdens of judging would be beneficial. . . . Perhaps if we learned to speak of judging as a terrible and terrifying job, as a burden of inflicting pain by virtue of judgment, we might develop modes of resolution different from those so readily accepted today. We might seek more communal modes of decision-making, insisting upon groups of two, three, or four judges to share the honor, the obligation, and the pain of decision. When we recognize the burden and the pain of judging, we might uncover one element of adjudication that exists but is relatively unacknowledged: Much "adjudication" is not a win/lose proposition but an effort at accommodation, with judges and juries responding to both sides but currently without vocabulary or permission to express empathy with competing claims. Many verdicts allocate victory to both sides, but our tradition is to mask that allocation rather than to endorse the practice of seeing multiple claims of right. Feminism may help bolster our trust in practice and permit us to remove the facades of total victory and defeat.

A third problem with revising the list of aspirations for our judges is one of meaning and application. Care, connection, nurturance, identification are distinct qualities, each in need of contextual examination. If we simply stipulate to an expanded list of qualities for judges, we slip back into the universalism that feminist vantage points have taught us to suspect. Moreover, courts have claimed to be nurturant in the past; the juvenile court and intermediate sentencing were both based upon arguments of an obligation to be responsive to the needs of the populations presumably being served. Maternal thinking is appealing as a model, but many accounts of juvenile court and intermediate sentencing suggest that parenting modes are profoundly disabling to those parented. Where does "attentive love" come from in a society as heterogeneous as ours? Communitarianism is a popular word in legal academe today, but the word is used without much attention paid to the fact of a multitude of extant communities, with competing modes of being. . . .

One might then return to the argument . . . [t]hat . . . feminism and adjudication may simply be incompatible. [But] I am suspicious of a response in the name of feminism, that declines to accept power, authority and responsibility. Sara Ruddick is instructive here; maternal thinking is predicated upon the practice of adults caring for children. The fact of power, and an acceptance of the obligation to exercise it, comes from the social practice of caretaking. Because current social practice demands ongoing relationships between mother and child, the power is tempered with compassion, the authority with affection. Because the parenting exists in a context of a dangerous world, the mother holds her power with the painful self-consciousness of the limits of her powers. . . .

NOTE ON FEMININE JUDGING

One of the first legal scholars to bring Gilligan's work to bear on judging was Suzanna Sherry. Sherry argued that there is a "feminine" jurisprudence that is apparent even among conservative female judges such as Justice Sandra Day O'Connor. This assertedly feminine jurisprudence bears some similarity to civic republicanism, which is characterized by a focus on responsibility and human interdependence rather than abstract universal principles. See Suzanna Sherry, Civil Virtue and the Feminine Voice in Constitutional Adjudication, 72 Va. L. Rev. 543 (1986). Many have questioned her analysis. See, e.g., Mary Joe Frug, Progressive Feminist Legal Scholarship: Can We Claim "A Different Voice"?, 15 Harv. Women's L.J. 37, 44-46 (1992); Sue Davis, The Voice of Sandra Day O'Connor, 77 Judicature 134 (Nov.-Dec. 1993). Consider Justice O'Connor's opinions in *J.E.B.*, set forth at page 893, and Harris v. Forklift Systems, Inc., set forth at page 548. Consider also Justice Ginsburg's opinion in United States v. Virginia, set forth at page 382. To what extent do Justice O'Connor and Justice Ginsburg speak with the same voice?

The hypothesis that women judges reason differently than their male colleagues is a difficult one to test. Studies of voting behavior of women judges have come at the problem in different ways, none with very conclusive results. In summarizing these studies, the ABA Commission on Women notes:

> [The reliability of the studies] is sometimes limited by small sample sizes and inadequate controls for factors other than gender. Early studies tended to find no significant gender differences in judicial rulings, even on women's rights issues. By contrast, some more recent studies have found differences at least on certain issues, although not always on women's rights or on matters traditionally thought to inspire feminine compassion [such as death penalty sentences].
>
> An equally critical question is the extent to which women judges have used their leadership to press for changes in the judicial process that would

make it more responsive to the needs of women. Here again, the evidence is mixed. In some respects, as Judge Gladys Kessler notes, "There has truly been a 'revolutionary reform' of the justice system's response to women's concerns" in areas such as domestic violence, child support, and gender bias. Much of this change has resulted from efforts by female judges, not only through their rulings but also through their work in organizations like the National Association of Women Judges.

Yet as Kessler also observes, many women leaders have "become the victims of [their] own success." They have so many individual opportunities and claims on their time that their collective reform efforts are suffering from a "fading sense of urgency, diminishing energy, and a loss of commitment." Many pressing needs of women in the justice system remain unmet, and not all women judges and bar leaders have joined forces to respond.

ABA Commission on Women in the Profession, The Unfinished Agenda: A Report on the Status of Women in the Legal Profession 30-31 (2001); Michael E. Solimine & Susan E. Wheatley, Rethinking Feminist Judging, 70 Ind. L.J. 891 (1995); Theresa M. Beiner, What Will Diversity on the Bench Mean for Justice?, 6 Mich. J. Gender & L. 113 (1999) (suggesting some differences on civil rights suits); Sue Davis et al., Voting Behavior and Gender on the U.S. Court of Appeals, 77 Judicature 129 (1993) (finding some differences in employment discrimination and search and seizure cases, but not in obscenity cases); Jennifer A. Segal, The Decision Making of Clinton's Nontraditional Judicial Appointees, 80 Judicature 279 (1997) (finding differences on individual liberties and criminal procedure, but not on women's issues); Jeffrey Toobin, Women in Black, New Yorker, Oct. 30, 2000, at 48 (finding greater severity in enforcement of the criminal laws in general and the death penalty in particular by Texas's female judges than by male judges).

In challenging the judicial norm of "impartiality," Resnik is not claiming a "feminine" style of judging, but she does seem to make a normative claim about the virtues associated with the values women might bring to judging. Along these lines, see Robin West, Caring for Justice 24 (1997) ("Judges should aim for justice, but if they hope to achieve it, then they must *also* aim for care.").

Resnik assumes also that greater female representation of women on the judiciary will make a difference. Can we expect women judges to be more favorable to women parties in some contexts? Would this be bias? Suppose that female judges on average gave more generous financial awards to displaced homemakers in divorce cases than their male judges, and were less likely to grant summary judgment for defendants in gender discrimination cases. Would this establish bias? By which judges? Are there any contexts in which the group identity of the judge should be a ground for disqualification?

In Black v. Sullivan & Cromwell, 418 F. Supp. 1 (1975), Judge Constance Baker Motley denied a motion seeking her recusal on grounds that her sex and prior experience as a civil rights attorney would bias her in favor of the plaintiff in a gender discrimination case. In rejecting that motion, the court ruled that if the "background or sex or race of each judge were, by definition, sufficient grounds for removal, no judge on this court could hear this case, or many others, by virtue of the fact that all of them were attorneys, or a sex, often with distinguished law firms or public service backgrounds." Id. at 4. To what extent do we want judges to build on their experience of group membership in deciding cases? Where is the line between empathy and partiality? Is it coherent to claim both that women have a "different voice" and that they bring no bias to their own decisionmaking?

5. Women as Parties, Witnesses, and Litigators

In re Marriage of Iverson
15 Cal. Rptr. 2d 70 (Ct. App. 1992)

SILLS, P. J.

Cheryl Iveron appeals from a judgment dissolving her marriage of 15 years to George Chick Iverson. Primarily she challenges the trial court's finding that a premarital agreement signed by the parties was valid.

The oral statement of decision of the judge who presided over the trial of the validity of the premarital agreement — and who acted as trier of fact in that proceeding — is so replete with gender bias that we are forced to conclude Cheryl could not have received a fair trial. Accordingly, we must reverse and direct the matter be retried before a different judge

. . . During the trial, Chick testified he did not want to get married, told Cheryl he did not want to get married, and made it clear to his associates he was perfectly happy not getting married.

Cheryl told a somewhat different story. Chick first brought up the subject of marriage. He asked her to marry him in front of the late actor John Wayne, just after Chick had asked Wayne to be his best man. Marriage was the reason she moved in with Chick. He told her he wanted the couple to live together and be married.

The testimony also differed on the circumstances surrounding Cheryl's signing of the agreement. Chick presented the testimony of Rita Cruikshank, wife of the late William Cruikshank, Chick's attorney. She testified that in June 1972, Cheryl and Chick met on her husband's boat. William Cruikshank read the agreement to them. He asked if they understood what he was reading to them. They answered yes. This happened several times while he was reading the agreement. After he finished, he turned to Cheryl and told her, "Cheryl, I think maybe it's advisable you see another attorney, make sure this is what you want to do." Cheryl said, "No, no, no. Whatever Chick wants." He then handed Cheryl a pen. She signed.

Cheryl testified she never discussed the contents of the agreement with an attorney before she signed it. Nor could she recall even being advised by any attorney about her rights to property that might be acquired during her marriage to Chick. She had no recollection of ever signing the agreement (though she acknowledged signing it, because her name was on it).

After the testimony was finished, the trial judge noted there was "too much money" involved in the case "for it not to be appealed." He then said, "I want whoever reviews this to be able to have the benefit of my reasoning for how I get to where I got." He then elaborated:

> One of the things that struck me, first of all, was that the petitioner in this case, Cheryl Iverson, only had five or six luncheon dates with Chick Iverson before she decided to move into his home. Now, he sure as heck does not look like John Wayne and he doesn't look like John Derek. And even if we take 17 years off him, I don't think he looks like Adonis.
>
> And, so, we have a situation in the beginning where we have a girl who has been testified to [sic] was lovely, and is lovely, but who did not have much of an education, and did not have much of a background in business, and did not have much by way of material wealth. Had nothing going for her except for her physical attractiveness. Who, somehow or other, comes to the attention of Mr. Iverson and, after five or six luncheon dates, is invited to move into his home.
>
> It seems to me that the process of marrying is one in which there is some mutual advantages from the act of getting married, maybe different ones from the act of establishing a relationship, a live-in type, spousal-type relationship.
>
> But, in light of the testimony that Mr. Iverson had come out of a very unpleasant, very unhappy marriage, his statement that he was reluctant to get married again adds some dimension here. "Once burned, twice cautious." He had just gone through a divorce which cost him a million dollars. He does not want to get in one of those things again. He has talked to his important friends in the film industry and other areas, where living together is the common situation rather than marriage. And, so, decides that's the best thing for him. He makes an offer to petitioner, who thinks it's good. And then she moves in.
>
> I cannot accept the fact that, as she said, he was the one that proposed marriage to her. That would be the last thing that would be on his mind. And why, in heaven's name, do you buy the cow when you get the milk free, as we used to say. And, so, he's getting the milk free. And Cheryl is living with him in his home.
>
> And the impetus for marriage must be coming from her side, because there's nothing Mr. Iverson is going to get out of it. Marriage is a drag on the market. It's a deprivation of his freedom. He's got everything that he would want out of a relationship with none of the obligations. Now, I am of the opinion that the impetus for the marriage in the home, prior to the incident of the birthday party for John Wayne, came almost entirely from the petitioner in this case, resisted by respondent.

Catchpole v. Brannon
42 Cal. Rptr. 2d 440 (Ct. App. 1995)

KLINE, P.J.

This case presents the unusual question whether the alleged gender bias of the trial judge requires us to set aside his judgment.

Appellant, Marie Catchpole, commenced this litigation in the Superior Court of Humboldt County, asserting claims of sexual harassment, assault and battery, and intentional and negligent infliction of emotional distress against respondents [who were her employers at Burger King (EBK)]. . . . Judgment against appellant was rendered by a superior court judge sitting without a jury. . . .

Appellant testified she was subjected to a hostile work environment at EBK, in which supervisors, particularly Brannon, encouraged employees to discuss sexual matters, to touch each other, and to "rate" customers' attractiveness. Several former employees also testified that Brannon flirted with female employees, talked about their bodies, showed them lingerie magazines and ads for X-rated strip shows, offered unsolicited "advice" about sexual matters, and touched them inappropriately. In addition, a former employee and two female friends testified that they had gone to Brannon's home on numerous occasions, where Brannon and his wife provided alcohol and marijuana and showed them pornographic movies. EBK had a nonfraternization policy, which prohibited managers from associating with employees away from EBK. Brannon had earlier been reprimanded for inviting employees to his house in violation of that policy. Melody Rane, Greenhalgh, and several EBK employees testified that appellant was difficult to get along with and rude to other employees.

Appellant testified that in the early morning of December 11, 1987, at Brannon's insistence, she went to his home after work to discuss her problems with coworkers. Brannon forcibly removed her clothes and performed an act of oral sex on her, after which he forced her to orally copulate him.

Nearly two months later, on February 2, 1988, appellant mentioned the assault to another EBK employee, who then reported it to the assistant manager on duty. . . . Brannon was fired the next day. . . .

After appellant reported Brannon's assault, she was allegedly subjected to retaliatory harassment by numerous employees at EBK who blamed her for his dismissal. These acts of retaliation, about which she complained repeatedly, were assertedly never adequately addressed by management. . . .

The trial judge's lengthy interrogation of [the plaintiff] differed markedly from the treatment he accorded others who testified, most of whom, including respondent Brannon, were asked no questions. The court's initial questions set the tone for what was to follow:

> THE COURT: Okay. No doubt this particular lawsuit has been difficult
> for you, and embarrassing for you, and I assume a lot of people in your

position would have chosen to not go forward with a lawsuit of this sort. Can you tell me why you decided to do it?

THE WITNESS [appellant]: Yes. Because I felt I needed to do something to get in control of the situation. I felt so humiliated and so down trodden, that I needed a way to overcome this. Um, I wanted to set right what was wrong. I — I wanted to, um, be able to have a chance to say what I felt was wrong; what had been done to me, and the injustices I felt at the time. I — I felt they were never addressed, and now is my chance to address them. Whether I win or not, I'm still going to win in my heart, because I was able to sit here and address the people that wronged me.

THE COURT: Okay. You indicated in your testimony . . . that your father, to this day, feels that you shouldn't have been where you were on December the 11th. He somehow blames you for what happened; is that right?

THE WITNESS: Did I say that in my testimony?

THE COURT: I thought you did.

THE WITNESS: Um —

THE COURT: At least that's what I got out of what you said.

THE WITNESS: My — my father felt — um, he — he didn't understand how I had gotten into this mess. And — and, um, he is very upset about it. And I don't know whether he thinks I should have been or should not have been.

THE COURT: Okay. Um, maybe I assumed something that a father might feel that way. . . . Is this suit in any way connected with how your father feels about the situation? You want to prove something to him?

THE WITNESS: I — I never thought of that.

THE COURT: Okay. Fine. You understand that regardless of what the motivations are within yourself, that the allegations that you made against these people are very serious allegations?

THE WITNESS: Yes.

THE COURT: Okay. Fine. And you understand that if Mr. Brannon's opening statement is correct, he has already lost, I guess, quite a bit of money, and been subject to certain trials and tribulations as a result of those allegations, correct?

THE WITNESS: Yes.

THE COURT: Okay. Likewise, I assume that you understand that Ken and the Ranes and the other crew members have been subjected to the claims of harassment; um, that they either harassed you or failed to prevent the harassment, and I assume you understand that in many ways it's going to be your word against all of those other people?

THE WITNESS: No.

THE COURT: You don't understand that?

THE WITNESS: No, I —

THE COURT: Okay. Go ahead.

THE WITNESS: Um, I have corroboration.

THE COURT: Okay. I'm not saying you don't, I'm just saying that you need — I assume that you understand that the Brannons are going to say you weren't at their house on December 11th; that Kent's going to say

that most of what you said about him is incorrect, and probably a lot of
these crew members are going to come in here and say they didn't do
anything wrong, either. So in some ways, um, absent — I don't know
what corroboration you have, but absent that corroboration, it's still a lot
of your word against their word. Do you understand that?
THE WITNESS: Yes.
THE COURT: Okay. So you understand that your testimony is going to
be looked at very carefully, and that you can't simply tell me that the
conversation on November 19th, 1987 was A, B, C and D. If you can't
remember that conversation, in total — in other words, you can't just
paraphrase a conversation. Do you understand that?
THE WITNESS: Yes. . . .

[I]mmediately following the opening statements of counsel, the judge
asked appellant's counsel how long the trial was going to take.

MR. ZIGLER: I think we're going to have trouble finishing next week,
Your Honor.
THE COURT: Well, how many witnesses do you have?
MR. ZIGLER: Potentially twenty-two, Your Honor.
THE COURT: Jesus Christ. Well, there is a limited amount of judicial
resource here. If you think it's worth it, Mr. Zigler, you may proceed. . . .

. . . The following exchange . . . pertains to appellant's acceptance of
Brannon's invitation to come to his house to discuss the problems she was
having at work. . . .

THE COURT: Um, as I understand your testimony, even though you
liked to work [Brannon's] shift, you didn't like his sexualization of the
work place; is that right?
THE WITNESS: Yes.
THE COURT: Why did you go to his house?
THE WITNESS: I just — I have said previously that I had gone to him
about that, and had [sic] apologized.
THE COURT: But I don't understand. If you were —
THE WITNESS: I had forgiven him. I didn't hold a grudge. And then he
told me he had a wife. I mean, all fear's [sic] flew out of my head then. To
me, a wife and kids meant a complete family, um, safety, and he was just
inviting me over to —
THE COURT: But couldn't you have easily said, "No, not tonight. I'm
tired. I have got to go to school tomorrow. I'll talk about it later." Why
not? Why didn't you say that?
THE WITNESS: I —
THE COURT: You don't know?
THE WITNESS: I didn't feel that I could.
THE COURT: Okay. How about —
THE WITNESS: I didn't want to offend him.

THE COURT: When you went back to Burger King that night, and whatever he did in there, he was doing, um, why didn't you just get in your car at that point and drive home, and say, "I'll see you to [sic] tomorrow. I don't have time to wait around here while you do that for your wife."

THE WITNESS: My car wasn't there. It was at his house.

THE COURT: What I'm saying is, why didn't you say, "Sorry, Rudy. I can't go back with you. I'm too tired. I'm going now."

THE WITNESS: Well, we were at the store, and then we drove back to his house.

THE COURT: I understand you went to his house. What I'm saying is, before you went back to the store to get whatever he got, why didn't you just say, you know, "It's too late. I can't wait around here any more."

THE WITNESS: He said he really wanted to discuss it with me that night, and that I needed to stay. I said I would listen.

THE COURT: When his wife went to bed at 2:30 that morning, you were still concerned about school the next day, correct?

THE WITNESS: Yes.

THE COURT: Why didn't you leave then?

THE WITNESS: He began—he said that he hadn't really gotten a chance to talk to me. He was going to stay up and do his paperwork.

THE COURT: I understand that. But, you know, when do you assert yourself? Why didn't you just say, "Hey, I don't care whether you talked to me or not, I'm tired."

THE WITNESS: I couldn't assert myself.

THE COURT: You couldn't?

THE WITNESS: No, he—he was a—he was my manager. I didn't—if he said I had to discuss something with him, I needed to. That didn't mean that I wanted to stay and have sex with him.

THE COURT: Do you think—well, I'm not saying it meant anything. Do you think he could have fired you if you had walked out at that point?

THE WITNESS: Yes.

THE COURT: Okay. Why did you take a second drink when you were tired and wanted to go home?

THE WITNESS: A second drink of juice?

THE COURT: Whatever it was. I don't know what it was. Why did you take one if you wanted to go home? Why didn't you just say, "No, I'm tired. I have got to go home."

THE WITNESS: I said I was tired; I said, "I want to go home." And he said, "I'm just"—like I said, he said he wanted to talk to me about this, and he was going to be doing his paperwork, and he went and got me a drink. I mean, I didn't refuse. I just said, "Sure."

THE COURT: Um, somehow he managed to hold you and take your clothes off. How did that happen; do you recall?

THE WITNESS: Yeah.

THE COURT: Okay. How?

THE WITNESS: He had a steal [sic] grip on my arm. Um, the blouse was snapped. He took and unsnapped it. Um, he—he was scaring me with the tone of his voice, and, um, at that point he shook me. Um—

THE COURT: Okay.

THE WITNESS: He unsnapped my pants. He still had a steal [sic] grip on me, and unbuttoned his shirt.

THE COURT: There was no time between this entire process that he didn't have his — a steal [sic] grip? You —

THE WITNESS: Exactly.

THE COURT: What about the time you testified to when he was performing oral sex on you, and had his hands on your breasts?

THE WITNESS: His arms were very large and he — he had them very heavily on me.

THE COURT: Okay.

THE WITNESS: I felt I had no choice. And if I made a move, his wife would come out.

THE COURT: I guess I understand that, that you were afraid that his wife would just add to your problems, but why didn't you tell him, "Okay. I'm going to scream loud enough to wake up your kids." That would sort of put him in a pickle, wouldn't it?

THE WITNESS: I didn't think about that.

THE COURT: Okay. Where was the phone?

THE WITNESS: I don't know. In the kitchen, I guess. I — I didn't see a phone.

THE COURT: You didn't see a phone in the living room?

THE WITNESS: No.

THE COURT: You stated at one point, and I don't know where this was, during the events of that morning, that once he had taken your clothes off, that you were constantly trying to get them on and leave. Did you ever consider just leaving without your clothes?

THE WITNESS: No.

THE COURT: That wouldn't be something that you would want to do?

THE WITNESS: No.

THE COURT: Okay. Um, another thing you mentioned, that at some point during the course of the assault upon you, that you said, "I don't want to do this. I don't want to get pregnant." Was pregnancy really something that crossed your mind at this point?

THE WITNESS: Yes, it was, because he said he wanted to get into my cherry. I was trying to —

THE COURT: You weren't worried about your — your physical safety at this point?

THE WITNESS: Yes, I was worried about my physical safety. I was trying to deter him. I was trying to give him a reason not to.

THE COURT: Okay. How long, once he inserted his penis into your mouth, was that in your mouth?

THE WITNESS: A few minutes.

THE COURT: After all of this happened, and you left about 6:30, did you go to class that day?

THE WITNESS: Well, I — I went to the dorms and slept for a few hours. And then I did, yes.

THE COURT: After you had a chance to think about what had
    happened to you that morning, did you blame yourself for letting this
    happen?
THE WITNESS: I didn't blame myself. I — I was angry for — um, with
    myself for not, um, getting out of it. That I couldn't get out of it. I — I
    was in a — that I was in a bind. That — a bind that humiliated me so
    much.
THE COURT: So you were concerned that you weren't in control, is
    that right?
THE WITNESS: In control of Rudy?
THE COURT: Of the event.
THE WITNESS: No, I certainly wasn't in control.
THE COURT: Well, isn't that what you just said, you were angry with
    yourself for letting — putting yourself in the position where you didn't
    have control?
THE WITNESS: I was angry with myself that it happened; I was angry
    with my body; I was angry that I even agreed to go over there.
THE COURT: Well, I can understand that. And the reason you brought
    this lawsuit was to gain some control, right?
THE WITNESS: Yes. To gain some control in my life, and not falsely.
    [. . .]

    . . . In his Notice of Tentative Decision, the trial judge rejected out of
hand "the basic scenario of an alleged sexual assault away from the work
place, where the victim waits for an hour to accompany her alleged attacker,
and then allows a four hour attack to occur in a residence with the attacker's
family at home. . . ." For this reason, the court rhetorically inquired, "'Why
was it necessary to use up the court system with a case which was, so
obviously, one which could only be detrimental to everyone concerned?'
Attorneys have a duty to evaluate their cases and present claims which have
at least marginal merit. This case was clearly not one which should have been
filed or tried. If sanctions could be imposed for this misuse of resource they
would be imposed here."
    While we cannot say as a matter of law that appellant was entitled to
judgment in her favor, the court's characterization of the case distorts the
record. . . . The implication that appellant invited Brannon's sexual attention
or consented to his advances was never advanced by respondents; nor did
respondents seriously dispute that the assault, which was corroborated by
Officer Parris, actually took place; their chief contention was simply that it
was not work related. Nor does the record suggest appellant "sought the
attention of Mr. Brannon." Among other things, Dr. Berg's testimony that
appellant was "passive" and usually avoided "personal interactions" was
never contradicted. The emphasis the court placed on appellant's failure to
"scream" at the time of the assault so as to alert Brannon's wife ignores
appellant's uncontradicted testimony that Brannon had told her that if his
wife woke she "wouldn't be mad at all, and wouldn't help me at all. That

she — she would, in fact, like to join in. And I took that as a threat, because if she came out there, then I would have two against me. Two big people against me instead of one." Though, as we have said, many of appellant's factual claims were contested, the court appears to have been almost entirely indifferent to evidence corroborating her fundamental contentions regarding the sexualization of her workplace, the harassment she experienced there, and the assault itself. Among other things, the court completely brushed aside Brannon's failure on the stand to explicitly deny the assault and the sexual harassment attributed to him and others by appellant. In short, the court's treatment of the evidence does not appear to have been even-handed.

[T]he judgment seems to have improperly turned on stereotypes about women rather than a realistic evaluation of the facts . . . , a problem apparently all too common in sexual harassment cases. The court's disparagement of appellant's credibility on the grounds that she accepted Brannon's invitation to come to his house, remained alone with him, and did not resist his assault more forcibly is based on an unrealistic and gender-biased standard of reasonableness. Among other things, the court appears oblivious to appellant's dependence on her assailant for her job and scholarship and the need to placate him for those reasons. The court was equally indifferent to the intimidation a woman in appellant's position would likely experience. . . .

NOTE ON BIAS IN THE COURTROOM

Do you agree that *Iverson* and *Catchpole* exhibit judicial bias? Was the response by the appellate court adequate?

The kinds of explicit gender stereotypes in these excerpts are unusual. But other forms of gender bias are not. Beginning in 1982, courts began establishing gender bias task forces. Some jurisdictions also established separate commissions on racial and ethnic bias or gave one commission responsibility to consider all diversity-related issues. By the turn of the twenty-first century, some 65 state and federal courts had issued reports on bias in the justice system. ABA Commission on Women, Unfinished Agenda, supra, at 20. The ABA had also amended both the ABA Model Code of Judicial Conduct, Section 3B(6), and the Model Rules of Professional Conduct, Rule 8.4, to include prohibitions on gender bias in the courtroom.

The extent of bias is difficult to measure. Published reports have relied on some mix of quantitative and qualitative approaches, and have considered issues such as the demographics of the bench, bar, and court personnel; the outcomes for male and female litigants in areas like bail, sentencing, and custody awards; and the perceptions of participants in the justice system. The

ABA Commission on Women in the Profession summarizes the problems exemplified by these studies and the reforms necessary to address them.

. . . Between two thirds and three quarters of women report experiencing bias, while only a quarter to a third of men report observing it and far fewer report experiencing it. Women are also more likely than men to believe that bias is a significant problem and that female attorneys are treated less favorably than male attorneys by judges and opposing counsel. Two-thirds of African American lawyers, but less than a fifth of white lawyers, report witnessing racial bias in the justice system in the last three years. About forty percent of surveyed lawyers report witnessing or experiencing sexual orientation bias in professional settings, even in jurisdictions that have ordinances prohibiting it. Between about a quarter to a half of lawyers with disabilities also experience various forms of bias in the legal system. . . .

Demeaning conduct takes a variety of forms. To be sure, gender bias rules and educational programs have reduced the most egregious problems. Female lawyers no longer routinely cope with labels such as "pretty girl," "little lady," "lawyerette," "baby doll," "sweetie" and "attorney generalette." Nor do women frequently encounter questions such as whether they "really understand all the economics involved in this [antitrust] case," or whether their clients are "satisfied with the representation [they] had at trial even though [the lawyer] was a woman."

However, some of these problems persist, particularly those involving disrespectful forms of address. Female lawyers, administrative personnel, and witnesses are still addressed by their first names, while male counterparts are not. . . .

Women also report recurring instances of being ignored, interrupted, or mistaken for nonprofessional support staff. And support staff, for their part, often experience similarly demeaning comments and have been expected to perform menial personal services, such as making coffee or running non-work related errands.

Such problems persist partly because they are not acknowledged as problems. Many white men, who have not been on the receiving end of systematic bias, tend to discount its significance. The gender gap in experience is striking. For example, in the District of Columbia Circuit survey of lawyers, only 3 percent of white men, but over a third of white women and half of women of color, had been mistaken for non-lawyers by other counsel.

When men observe such incidents, they often seem like isolated, idiosyncratic, or inadvertent slights. A common reaction is that women should just "grow up and stop whining." Such reactions both silence and stigmatize complainants. Many women are unwilling to jeopardize a client's case or their own career prospects by antagonizing decision makers or earning a reputation as "humorless," "oversensitive," or a "troublemaker." . . .

A common finding of gender bias studies is that the credibility of female lawyers, litigants, and witnesses is often discounted. Examples range from the occasional overt comment, such as "Shut up. Let's hear what the men have to say," to the much more common and subtle patterns of devaluation, such as openly ignoring or trivializing claims.

In some instances, judicial attitudes are tied to perceptions about the substantive rights or injuries at issue. Claims involving violence, acquaintance rape, sexual harassment, and employment discrimination face special skepticism. In New Jersey's recent follow-up survey of gender bias, about 60 to 70 percent of women (compared with about a quarter of men) reported that victims of domestic violence and sex harassment had less credibility than other victims.

ABA Commission on Women in the Profession, The Unfinished Agenda: A Report on the Status of Women in the Legal Profession 20-21 (2001).

For further discussion, see Judith Resnik, Asking About Gender in Courts, 21 Signs 952 (Summer 1996) (summarizing bias issues and citing to reports); Jennifer F. Sweet, Gender Bias at the Heart of Justice: An Empirical Study of State Task Forces, 6 S. Cal. Rev. L. & Women's Stud. 1 (1996); Deborah R. Hensler & Judith Resnik, Contested Identities: Task Forces on Gender, Race, and Ethnic Bias and the Obligations of the Legal Profession, in Ethics in Practice, supra, at 240-263; Lynn Hecht Schafran & Norma J. Wikler, National Judicial Education Program, Gender Fairness in the Courts: Action in the New Millennium (2001). For a catalog of proposed remedies, see Key Components to Achieve and Secure Gender Fairness in the Courts, reprinted Judith McConnell & Kathleen F. Sikora, Gender Bias and the Institutionalization of Change: Lessons from the California, in 39 Judges' J. 12, 16 (Spring 2000).

Putting Theory into Practice

5-8. A defense attorney in New Mexico says in open court, referring to the woman prosecutor, "Ladies and gentlemen, can you believe this pretty little thing is an assistant attorney general?" New Mexico law prohibits "intentionally manifesting . . . bias or prejudice" on the basis of sex in judicial or quasi-judicial proceedings. See N.M. Rule of Professional Conduct 16-300 (1996). (The quote is borrowed from Lynn Hecht Schafran, Eve, Mary, Superwoman: How Stereotypes About Women Influence Judges, 24 Judges' J. 12, 15 (1985).) How should the prosecutor respond? How should the court?

5-9. Defense attorney Dennis Scheib filed a motion in a criminal case asking the judge to order prosecutor Nancy Grace not to wear scoop necks, skirts shorter than one inch above the knee, or dresses slit up the sides, on the grounds such dress would be distracting to the jury and would give her an unfair advantage in court. See Martha Ezzard, And No Scoop Necks, Please: Courtroom Sexism: The "Southern Belle" Charge, Atlanta Const., Nov. 6, 1995, at 12A.

Should he prevail? Is his motion an example of gender bias? What about judicial orders directing women lawyers not to wear pants in open court on the ground that they fail to show sufficient respect for the dignity of judicial proceedings?

5-10. David Margolick reports that Judge Paula Lapossa cried when the victim of a shooting and rape testified at the sentencing hearing of the defendant that she sought no vengeance and that she hoped that her assailant could be rehabilitated rather than imprisoned for 25 years as the prosecution sought. The judge tried to explain, "All of you know that I am crying, and I want you to know the reason is because of her forgiving nature. . . . It is unusual for a victim of such a vicious crime to have such a forgiving attitude. And I think that that reflects all the best that there is in human nature." To the defense counsel and the defendant, the judge is reported to have said, "I want Mr. Glazier and Mr. Cook to realize, that even though I'm emotional and I'm crying, that you will have nothing to fear." Nonetheless, the defense asked the judge to recuse herself. The motion was denied, and the defendant was sentenced to 80 years in prison.

Can you defend the judge's decision not to recuse herself?

5-11. In a New York case, a judge reportedly denied a defense lawyer's request for a delay in the selection of a jury so that the defendant could see her doctor about a growth that the lawyer said "may be malignant." The doctor could not see the defendant on Friday, when the court was not in session. In denying the motion, the judge said, "If this doctor is so booked up that he cannot see an emergency patient, then I repeat, there are many, many doctors available, and we don't have to delay the justice system because one doctor takes that attitude." The judge also stated to the defense attorney, "I cannot believe the doctor, if told the facts you have recited, would refuse to see her on Friday even for five minutes." See Lisa W. Foderaro, Defendant in Westchester Murder May Have Cancer, Lawyer Says, N.Y. Times, Jan. 16, 1992, at A16. Is this gender bias?

6. Gender and Juries

≣ *J.E.B. v. Alabama ex rel. T.B.*
≣ 511 U.S. 127 (1994)

Justice BLACKMUN delivered the opinion of the Court[, in which STEVENS, O'CONNOR, SOUTER, and GINSBURG, JJ., joined].

I

On behalf of [the mother of a minor child], respondent State of Alabama filed a complaint for paternity and child support against petitioner J.E.B. in the District Court of Jackson County, Alabama. . . . The trial court assembled a panel of 36 potential jurors, 12 males and 24 females. After the court excused three jurors for cause, only 10 of the remaining 33 jurors were male. The State then used 9 of its 10 peremptory strikes to remove male jurors; petitioner used all but one of his strikes to remove female jurors. As a result, all the selected jurors were female.

Before the jury was empaneled, petitioner objected to the State's peremptory challenges on the ground that they were exercised against male jurors solely on the basis of gender, in violation of the Equal Protection Clause. . . . Petitioner argued that the logic and reasoning of Batson v. Kentucky, [476 U.S. 79 (1986),] which prohibits peremptory strikes solely on the basis of race, similarly forbids intentional discrimination on the basis of gender. The court rejected petitioner's claim and empaneled the all-female jury. The jury found petitioner to be the father of the child and the court entered an order directing him to pay child support. . . .

. . . Today we reaffirm what, by now, should be axiomatic: Intentional discrimination on the basis of gender by state actors violates the Equal Protection Clause, particularly where, as here, the discrimination serves to ratify and perpetuate invidious, archaic, and overbroad stereotypes about the relative abilities of men and women.

II

Discrimination on the basis of gender in the exercise of peremptory challenges is a relatively recent phenomenon. Gender-based peremptory strikes were hardly practicable for most of our country's existence, since, until the 19th century, women were completely excluded from jury service. So well-entrenched was this exclusion of women that in 1880 this Court, while finding that the exclusion of African-American men from juries violated the Fourteenth Amendment, expressed no doubt that a State "may confine the selection [of jurors] to males." Strauder v. West Virginia, [100 U.S. 303, 310 (1880)].

Many States continued to exclude women from jury service well into the present century, despite the fact that women attained suffrage upon ratification of the Nineteenth Amendment in 1920.[3] States that did permit women to serve on juries often erected other barriers, such as registration requirements and automatic exemptions, designed to deter women from exercising their right to jury service. . . .

The prohibition of women on juries was derived from the English common law which, according to Blackstone, rightfully excluded women from juries under "the doctrine of *propter defectum sexus,* literally, the

---

3. . . . As late as 1961, three States, Alabama, Mississippi, and South Carolina, continued to exclude women from jury service. See Hoyt v. Florida, [368 U.S. 57, 62 (1961)]. Indeed, Alabama did not recognize women as a "cognizable group" for jury-service purposes until after the 1966 decision in White v. Crook, 251 F. Supp. 401 (M.D. Ala.) (three-judge court).

'defect of sex.'" United States v. De Gross, 960 F.2d 1433, 1438 (9th Cir. 1992) (en banc), quoting 2 W. Blackstone, Commentaries *362.[4] In this country, supporters of the exclusion of women from juries tended to couch their objections in terms of the ostensible need to protect women from the ugliness and depravity of trials. Women were thought to be too fragile and virginal to withstand the polluted courtroom atmosphere. See Bailey v. State, 215 Ark. 53, 61 (1949) ("[c]riminal court trials often involve testimony of the foulest kind, and they sometimes require consideration of indecent conduct, the use of filthy and loathsome words, references to intimate sex relationships, and other elements that would prove humiliating, embarrassing, and degrading to a lady"). . . .

This Court in Ballard v. United States, [329 U.S. 187 (1946)], first questioned the fundamental fairness of denying women the right to serve on juries. Relying on its supervisory powers over the federal courts, it held that women may not be excluded from the venire in federal trials in States where women were eligible for jury service under local law. In response to the argument that women have no superior or unique perspective, such that defendants are denied a fair trial by virtue of their exclusion from jury panels, the Court explained:

> It is said . . . that an all male panel drawn from the various groups within a community will be as truly representative as if women were included. The thought is that the factors which tend to influence the action of women are the same as those which influence the action of men — personality, background, economic status — and not sex. Yet it is not enough to say that women when sitting as jurors neither act nor tend to act as a class. Men likewise do not act like a class. . . . The truth is that the two sexes are not fungible; a community made up exclusively of one is different from a community composed of both; the subtle interplay of influence one on the other is among the imponderables. To insulate the courtroom from either may not in a given case make an iota of difference. Yet a flavor, a distinct quality is lost if either sex is excluded.

[Id. at 193-194.]

Fifteen years later, however, the Court still was unwilling to translate its appreciation for the value of women's contribution to civic life into an enforceable right to equal treatment under state laws governing jury service. In Hoyt v. Florida, [368 U.S. 57, 61 (1961)], the Court found it

---

4. In England there was at least one deviation from the general rule that only males could serve as jurors. If a woman was subject to capital punishment, or if a widow sought postponement of the disposition of her husband's estate until birth of a child, a *writ de ventre inspiciendo* permitted the use of a jury of matrons to examine the woman to determine whether she was pregnant. But even when a jury of matrons was used, the examination took place in the presence of 12 men, who also composed part of the jury in such cases. The jury of matrons was used in the United States during the Colonial period, but apparently fell into disuse when the medical profession began to perform that function. See Note, Jury Service for Women, 12 U. Fla. L. Rev. 224-225 (1959).

reasonable, "despite the enlightened emancipation of women," to exempt women from mandatory jury service by statute, allowing women to serve on juries only if they volunteered to serve. The Court justified the differential exemption policy on the ground that women, unlike men, occupied a unique position "as the center of home and family life." [Id. at 62].

In 1975, the Court finally repudiated the reasoning of *Hoyt* and struck down, under the Sixth Amendment, an affirmative registration statute nearly identical to the one at issue in *Hoyt.* See Taylor v. Louisiana, [419 U.S. 522 (1975)]. We explained: "Restricting jury service to only special groups or excluding identifiable segments playing major roles in the community cannot be squared with the constitutional concept of jury trial." [Id. at 530]. The diverse and representative character of the jury must be maintained "'partly as assurance of a diffused impartiality and partly because sharing in the administration of justice is a phase of civic responsibility.'" [Id. at 530-531].

III

Taylor relied on Sixth Amendment principles, but the opinion's approach is consistent with the heightened equal protection scrutiny afforded gender-based classifications. . . .

While the prejudicial attitudes toward women in this country have not been identical to those held toward racial minorities, the similarities between the experiences of racial minorities and women, in some contexts, "over-power those differences." Note, Beyond *Batson*: Eliminating Gender-Based Peremptory Challenges, 105 Harv. L. Rev. 1920, 1921 (1992). . . .

Certainly, with respect to jury service, African-Americans and women share a history of total exclusion, a history which came to an end for women many years after the embarrassing chapter in our history came to an end for African-Americans.

We need not determine, however, whether women or racial minorities have suffered more at the hands of discriminatory state actors during the decades of our Nation's history. It is necessary only to acknowledge that "our Nation has had a long and unfortunate history of sex discrimination," [id. at 684], a history which warrants the heightened scrutiny we afford all gender-based classifications today. Under our equal protection jurisprudence, gender-based classifications require "an exceedingly persuasive justification" in order to survive constitutional scrutiny. See Personnel Administrator of Massachusetts v. Feeney, [442 U.S. 256, 273 (1979)]. . . . Thus, the only question is whether discrimination on the basis of gender in jury selection substantially furthers the State's legitimate interest in achieving a fair and impartial trial. In making this assessment, we do not weigh the value of peremptory challenges as an institution against our asserted commitment to eradicate invidious discrimination from the courtroom. Instead, we consider whether peremptory challenges based on gender stereotypes provide substantial aid to a litigant's effort to secure a fair and impartial jury.

Far from proffering an exceptionally persuasive justification for its gender-based peremptory challenges, respondent maintains that its decision to strike virtually all the males from the jury in this case "may reasonably have been based upon the perception, supported by history, that men otherwise totally qualified to serve upon a jury might be more sympathetic and receptive to the arguments of a man alleged in a paternity action to be the father of an out-of-wedlock child, while women equally qualified to serve upon a jury might be more sympathetic and receptive to the arguments of the complaining witness who bore the child." Brief for Respondent.[9]

We shall not accept as a defense to gender-based peremptory challenges "the very stereotype the law condemns." Powers v. Ohio, [499 U.S. 400, 410 (1991)]. Respondent's rationale, not unlike those regularly expressed for gender-based strikes, is reminiscent of the arguments advanced to justify the total exclusion of women from juries.[10] Respondent offers virtually no support for the conclusion that gender alone is an accurate predictor of juror's attitudes; yet it urges this Court to condone the same stereotypes that justified the wholesale exclusion of women from juries and the ballot box. Respondent seems to assume that gross generalizations that would be deemed impermissible if made on the basis of race are somehow permissible when made on the basis of gender.

Discrimination in jury selection, whether based on race or on gender, causes harm to the litigants, the community, and the individual jurors who are wrongfully excluded from participation in the judicial process. The

9. Respondent cites one study in support of its quasi-empirical claim that women and men may have different attitudes about certain issues justifying the use of gender as a proxy for bias. See R. Hastie, S. Penrod & N. Pennington, Inside the Jury 140 (1983). The authors conclude: "Neither student nor citizen judgments for typical criminal case material have revealed differences between male and female verdict preferences. . . . The picture differs [only] for rape cases, where female jurors appear to be somewhat more conviction-prone than male jurors." The majority of students suggest that gender plays no identifiable role in juror attitudes. See, e.g., V. Hans & N. Vidmar, Judging the Jury 76 (1986). . . .

10. A manual formerly used to instruct prosecutors in Dallas, Texas, provided the following advice: "I don't like women jurors because I can't trust them. They do, however, make the best jurors in cases involving crimes against children. It is possible that their 'women's intuition' can help you if you can't win your case with the facts." Alschuler, The Supreme Court and the Jury: Voir Dire, Peremptory Challenges, and the Review of Jury Verdicts, 56 U. Chi. L. Rev. 153, 210 (1989). Another widely circulated trial manual speculated:

> If counsel is depending upon a clearly applicable rule of law and if he wants to avoid a verdict of "intuition" or "sympathy," if his verdict in amount is to be proved by clearly demonstrated blackboard figures for example, generally he would want a male juror. . . .
> [But women] are desired jurors when the plaintiff is a man. A woman juror may see a man impeached from the beginning of the case to the end, but there is at least the chance with the woman juror (particularly if the man happens to be handsome or appealing) [that] the plaintiff's derelictions in and out of court will be overlooked. A woman is inclined to forgive sin in the opposite sex; but definitely not her own. . . . 3 M. Belli, Modern Trials 51.67 and 51.68, pp. 446-447 (2d ed. 1982).

litigants are harmed by the risk that the prejudice which motivated the discriminatory selection of the jury will infect the entire proceedings. . . . The community is harmed by the State's participation in the perpetuation of invidious group stereotypes and the inevitable loss of confidence in our judicial system that state-sanctioned discrimination in the courtroom engenders.

When state actors exercise peremptory challenges in reliance on gender stereotypes, they ratify and reinforce prejudicial views of the relative abilities of men and women. Because these stereotypes have wreaked injustice in so many other spheres of our country's public life, active discrimination by litigants on the basis of gender during jury selection "invites cynicism respecting the jury's neutrality and its obligation to adhere to the law." Powers v. Ohio, [499 U.S. at 412]. The potential for cynicism is particularly acute in cases where gender-related issues are prominent, such as cases involving rape, sexual harassment, or paternity. . . .

In recent cases we have emphasized that individual jurors themselves have a right to nondiscriminatory jury selection procedures. . . . Contrary to respondent's suggestion, this right extends to both men and women. . . . All persons, when granted the opportunity to serve on a jury, have the right not to be excluded summarily because of discriminatory and stereotypical presumptions that reflect and reinforce patterns of historical discrimination. Striking individual jurors on the assumption that they hold particular views simply because of their gender is "practically a brand upon them, affixed by law, an assertion of their inferiority." Strauder v. West Virginia, [100 U.S. at 308]. It denigrates the dignity of the excluded juror, and, for a woman, reinvokes a history of exclusion from political participation.[14] The message it sends to all those in the courtroom, and all those who may later learn of the discriminatory act, is that certain individuals, for no reason other than gender, are presumed unqualified by state actors to decide important questions upon which reasonable persons could disagree.[15]

---

14. The popular refrain is that all peremptory challenges are based on stereotypes of some kind, expressing various intuitive and frequently erroneous biases. But where peremptory challenges are made on the basis of group characteristics other than race or gender (like occupation, for example), they do not reinforce the same stereotypes about the group's competence or predispositions that have been used to prevent them from voting, participating on juries, pursuing their chosen professions, or otherwise contributing to civic life. . . .

15. Justice Scalia argues that there is no "discrimination and dishonor" in being subject to a race- or gender-based peremptory strike. . . . The only support Justice Scalia offers for his conclusion is the fact that race- and gender-based peremptory challenges have a long history in this country. . . . We do not dispute that this Court long has tolerated the discriminatory use of peremptory challenges, but this is not a reason to continue to do so. Many of "our people's traditions," such as de jure segregation and the total exclusion of women from juries, are now unconstitutional even though they once co-existed with the Equal Protection Clause.

IV

Our conclusion that litigants may not strike potential jurors solely on the basis of gender does not imply the elimination of all peremptory challenges. . . . Parties still may remove jurors whom they feel might be less acceptable than others on the panel; gender simply may not serve as a proxy for bias. Parties may also exercise their peremptory challenges to remove from the venire any group or class of individuals normally subject to "rational basis" review. . . . Even strikes based on characteristics that are disproportionately associated with one gender could be appropriate, absent a showing of pretext.[16]

If conducted properly, voir dire can inform litigants about potential jurors, making reliance upon stereotypical and pejorative notions about a particular gender or race both unnecessary and unwise. Voir dire provides a means of discovering actual or implied bias and a firmer basis upon which the parties may exercise their peremptory challenges intelligently. . . .

Failing to provide jurors the same protection against gender discrimination as race discrimination could frustrate the purpose of *Batson* itself. Because gender and race are overlapping categories, gender can be used as a pretext for racial discrimination.[18] Allowing parties to remove racial minorities from the jury not because of their race, but because of their gender, contravenes well-established equal protection principles and could insulate effectively racial discrimination from judicial scrutiny.

V

Equal opportunity to participate in the fair administration of justice is fundamental to our democratic system.[19] It not only furthers the goals of

---

16. For example, challenging all persons who have had military experience would disproportionately affect men at this time, while challenging all persons employed as nurses would disproportionately affect women. Without a showing of pretext, however, these challenges may well not be unconstitutional, since they are not gender- or race-based. . . .

18. The temptation to use gender as a pretext for racial discrimination may explain why the majority of the lower court decisions extending *Batson* to gender involve the use of peremptory challenges to remove minority women. All four of the gender-based peremptory cases to reach the federal courts of appeals . . . involved the striking of minority women.

19. This Court almost a half century ago stated:

The American tradition of trial by jury, considered in connection with either criminal or civil proceedings, necessarily contemplates an impartial jury drawn from a cross-section of the community. . . . This does not mean, of course, that every jury must contain representatives of all the economic, social, religious, racial, political and geographical groups of the community; frequently such complete representation would be impossible. But it does mean that prospective jurors shall be selected by court officials without systematic and intentional exclusion of any of these groups. Recognition must be given to the fact that those eligible for jury service are to be found in every stratum of society. Jury competence is an individual rather than a group or class matter. That fact lies at the very heart of the jury system. To disregard it is to open the door to class distinctions and discriminations which are abhorrent to the democratic ideals of trial by jury.

the jury system. It reaffirms the promise of equality under the law — that all citizens, regardless of race, ethnicity, or gender, have the chance to take part directly in our democracy. . . .

Justice O'CONNOR, concurring.

I agree with the Court that the Equal Protection Clause prohibits the government from excluding a person from jury service on account of that person's gender. . . . But today's important blow against gender discrimination is not costless. I write separately to discuss some of these costs, and to express my belief that today's holding should be limited to the government's use of gender-based peremptory strikes.

Batson v. Kentucky . . . itself was a significant intrusion into the jury selection process. *Batson* mini-hearings are now routine in state and federal trial courts, and *Batson* appeals have proliferated as well. . . . In further constitutionalizing jury selection procedures, the Court increases the number of cases in which jury selection — once a sideshow — will become part of the main event.

For this same reason, today's decision further erodes the role of the peremptory challenge. The peremptory challenge is "a practice of ancient origin" and is "part of our common law heritage." Edmonson v. Leesville Concrete Co., [500 U.S. 614, 639 (1991)] (O'Connor, J., dissenting). The principal value of the peremptory is that it helps produce fair and impartial juries. Swain v. Alabama, [380 U.S. 202, 218-219 (1965)]. . . .

Moreover, "[t]he essential nature of the peremptory challenge is that it is one exercised without a reason stated, without inquiry and without being subject to the court's control." [*Swain*, 380 U.S. at 220]. Indeed, often a reason for it cannot be stated, for a trial lawyer's judgments about a juror's sympathies are sometimes based on experienced hunches and educated guesses, derived from a juror's responses at voir dire or a juror's "'bare looks and gestures.'" [Id.] That a trial lawyer's instinctive assessment of a juror's predisposition cannot meet the high standards of a challenge for cause does not mean that the lawyer's instinct is erroneous. . . . Our belief that experienced lawyers will often correctly intuit which jurors are likely to be the least sympathetic, and our understanding that the lawyer will often be unable to explain the intuition, are the very reason we cherish the peremptory challenge. But, as we add, layer by layer, additional constitutional restraints on the use of the peremptory, we force lawyers to articulate what we know is often inarticulable.

In so doing we make the peremptory challenge less discretionary and more like a challenge for cause. We also increase the possibility that biased jurors will be allowed onto the jury, because sometimes a lawyer will be unable to provide an acceptable gender-neutral explanation even though the

---

Thiel v. Southern Pacific Co., [328 U.S. 217, 220 (1946)].

lawyer is in fact correct that the juror is unsympathetic. Similarly, in jurisdictions where lawyers exercise their strikes in open court, lawyers may be deterred from using their peremptories, out of the fear that if they are unable to justify the strike the court will seat a juror who knows that the striking party thought him unfit. Because I believe the peremptory remains an important litigator's tool and a fundamental part of the process of selecting impartial juries, our increasing limitation of it gives me pause.

Nor is the value of the peremptory challenge to the litigant diminished when the peremptory is exercised in a gender-based manner. We know that like race, gender matters. A plethora of studies make clear that in rape cases, for example, female jurors are somewhat more likely to vote to convict than male jurors. See R. Hastie, S. Penrod, & N. Pennington, Inside the Jury 140-141 (1983). . . . Moreover, though there have been no similarly definitive studies regarding, for example, sexual harassment, child custody, or spousal or child abuse, one need not be a sexist to share the intuition that in certain cases a person's gender and resulting life experience will be relevant to his or her view of the case. "'Jurors are not expected to come into the jury box and leave behind all that their human experience has taught them.'" Beck v. Alabama, [447 U.S. 625, 642 (1980)]. Individuals are not expected to ignore as jurors what they know as men — or women.

Today's decision severely limits a litigant's ability to act on this intuition, for the import of our holding is that any correlation between a juror's gender and attitudes is irrelevant as a matter of constitutional law. But to say that gender makes no difference as a matter of law is not to say that gender makes no difference as a matter of fact. I previously have said with regard to Batson: "That the Court will not tolerate prosecutors' racially discriminatory use of the peremptory challenge, in effect, is a special rule of relevance, a statement about what this Nation stands for, rather than a statement of fact." Brown v. North Carolina, [479 U.S. 940, 941-942 (1986)] (O'Connor, J., concurring in denial of certiorari). Today's decision is a statement that, in an effort to eliminate the potential discriminatory use of the peremptory, . . . gender is now governed by the special rule of relevance formerly reserved for race. Though we gain much from this statement, we cannot ignore what we lose. In extending Batson to gender we have added an additional burden to the state and federal trial process, taken a step closer to eliminating the peremptory challenge, and diminished the ability of litigants to act on sometimes accurate gender-based assumptions about juror attitudes.

These concerns reinforce my conviction that today's decision should be limited to a prohibition on the government's use of gender-based peremptory challenges. The Equal Protection Clause prohibits only discrimination by state actors. . . .

Accordingly, I adhere to my position that the Equal Protection Clause does not limit the exercise of peremptory challenges by private civil litigants and criminal defendants. This case itself presents no state action dilemma, for here the State of Alabama itself filed the paternity suit on behalf of petitioner. But what of the next case? Will we, in the name of fighting gender discrimination, hold that the battered wife — on trial for wounding her abusive husband — is a state actor? Will we preclude her from using her peremptory challenges to ensure that the jury of her peers contains as many women members as possible? I assume we will, but I hope we will not.

Justice KENNEDY, concurring in the judgment.

I am in full agreement with the Court. . . .

The importance of individual rights to our analysis prompts a further observation concerning what I conceive to be the intended effect of today's decision. We do not prohibit racial and gender bias in jury selection only to encourage it in jury deliberations. Once seated, a juror should not give free rein to some racial or gender bias of his or her own. The jury system is a kind of compact by which power is transferred from the judge to jury, the jury in turn deciding the case in accord with the instructions defining the relevant issues for consideration. The wise limitation on the authority of courts to inquire into the reasons underlying a jury's verdict does not mean that a jury ought to disregard the court's instructions. A juror who allows racial or gender bias to influence assessment of the case breaches the compact and renounces his or her oath.

In this regard, it is important to recognize that a juror sits not as a representative of a racial or sexual group but as an individual citizen. Nothing would be more pernicious to the jury system than for society to presume that persons of different backgrounds go to the jury room to voice prejudice. . . . The jury pool must be representative of the community, but that is a structural mechanism for preventing bias, not enfranchising it. . . . Thus, the Constitution guarantees a right only to an impartial jury, not to a jury composed of members of a particular race or gender. . . .

Justice SCALIA, with whom THE CHIEF JUSTICE and Justice THOMAS join, dissenting.

Today's opinion is an inspiring demonstration of how thoroughly up-to-date and right-thinking we Justices are in matters pertaining to the sexes (or as the Court would have it, the genders), and how sternly we disapprove the male chauvinist attitudes of our predecessors. The price to be paid for this display — a modest price, surely — is that most of the opinion is quite irrelevant to the case at hand. The hasty reader will be surprised to learn, for example, that this lawsuit involves a complaint about the use of peremptory challenges to exclude men from a petit jury. To be sure, petitioner, a man, used all but one of his peremptory strikes to remove women from the jury (he used his last challenge to strike the sole remaining male from the pool), but the validity of his strikes is not before us. Nonetheless, the Court treats itself to an extended discussion of the historic exclusion of women not only from jury service, but also from service at the bar (which is rather like jury service, in that it involves going to the courthouse a lot). All this, as I say, is irrelevant, since the case involves state action that allegedly discriminates against men. The parties do not contest that discrimination on the basis of sex[1] is subject to what our cases call "heightened scrutiny," and the citation of one of those cases (preferably one involving men rather than women, see, e.g., Mississippi Univ. for Women v. Hogan, [458 U.S. 718, 723-724 (1982),] is all that was needed.

The Court also spends time establishing that the use of sex as a proxy for particular views or sympathies is unwise and perhaps irrational. The opinion stresses the lack of statistical evidence to support the widely held belief that, at least in certain types of cases, a juror's sex has some statistically significant predictive value as to how the juror will behave. This assertion seems to place the Court in opposition to its earlier Sixth Amendment "fair cross-section" cases. See, e.g., Taylor v. Louisiana, [419 U.S. 522, 532 n.12 (1975)] ("Controlled studies . . . have concluded that women bring to juries their own perspectives and values that influence both jury deliberation and result"). But times and trends do change, and unisex is unquestionably in fashion. Personally, I am less inclined to demand statistics, and more inclined to credit the perceptions of experienced litigators who have had money on the line. But it does not matter. The Court's fervent defense of the proposition *il n'y a pas de différence entre les hommes et les femmes* (it stereotypes the opposite view as hateful "stereotyping") turns out to be, like its recounting of the history of sex discrimination against women, utterly irrelevant. Even if sex was a remarkably good predictor in certain cases, the Court would find its use in peremptories unconstitutional. . . .

Of course the relationship of sex to partiality would have been relevant if the Court had demanded in this case what it ordinarily demands: that the complaining party have suffered some injury. Leaving aside for the moment the reality that the defendant himself had the opportunity to strike women from the jury, the defendant would have some cause to complain about the prosecutor's striking male jurors if male jurors tend to be more favorable towards defendants in paternity suits. But if men and women jurors are (as the Court thinks) fungible, then the only arguable injury from the prosecutor's "impermissible" use of male sex as the basis for his peremptories is injury to the stricken juror, not to the defendant. . . . This case illustrates why making restitution to Paul when it is Peter who has been robbed is such a bad idea. Not only has petitioner, by implication of the Court's own reasoning, suffered no harm, but the scientific evidence

---

1. Throughout this opinion, I shall refer to the issue as sex discrimination rather than (as the Court does) gender discrimination. The word "gender" has acquired the new and useful connotation of cultural or attitudinal characteristics (as opposed to physical characteristics) distinctive to the sexes. That is to say, gender is to sex as feminine is to female and masculine to male. The present case does not involve peremptory strikes exercised on the basis of femininity or masculinity (as far as it appears, effeminate men did not survive the prosecution's peremptories). The case involves, therefore, sex discrimination plain and simple.

presented at trial established petitioner's paternity with 99.92% accuracy. Insofar as petitioner is concerned, this is a case of harmless error if there ever was one; a retrial will do nothing but divert the State's judicial and prosecutorial resources, allowing either petitioner or some other malefactor to go free.

The core of the Court's reasoning is that peremptory challenges on the basis of any group characteristic subject to heightened scrutiny are inconsistent with the guarantee of the Equal Protection Clause. That conclusion can be reached only by focusing unrealistically upon individual exercises of the peremptory challenge, and ignoring the totality of the practice. Since all groups are subject to the peremptory challenge (and will be made the object of it, depending upon the nature of the particular case) it is hard to see how any group is denied equal protection. . . . That explains why peremptory challenges coexisted with the Equal Protection Clause for 120 years. This case is a perfect example of how the system as a whole is even-handed. While the only claim before the Court is petitioner's complaint that the prosecutor struck male jurors, for every man struck by the government petitioner's own lawyer struck a woman. To say that men were singled out for discriminatory treatment in this process is preposterous. The situation would be different if both sides systematically struck individuals of one group, so that the strikes evinced group-based animus and served as a proxy for segregated venire lists. See Swain v. Alabama, [80 U.S. 202, 223-224 (1965)]. The pattern here, however, displays not a systemic sex-based animus but each side's desire to get a jury favorably disposed to its case. That is why the Court's characterization of respondent's argument as "reminiscent of the arguments advanced to justify the total exclusion of women from juries" is patently false. Women were categorically excluded from juries because of doubt that they were competent; women are stricken from juries by peremptory challenge because of doubt that they are well disposed to the striking party's case. . . . There is discrimination and dishonor in the former, and not in the latter — which explains the 106-year interlude between our holding that exclusion from juries on the basis of race was unconstitutional, Strauder v. West Virginia, [supra], and our holding that peremptory challenges on the basis of race were unconstitutional, Batson v. Kentucky, supra.

Although the Court's legal reasoning in this case is largely obscured by anti-male-chauvinist oratory, to the extent such reasoning is discernible it invalidates much more than sex-based strikes. . . . [The Court's analysis] places all peremptory strikes based on any group characteristic at risk, since they can all be denominated "stereotypes." Perhaps, however (though I do not see why it should be so), only the stereotyping of groups entitled to heightened or strict scrutiny constitutes "the very stereotype the law condemns" — so that other stereotyping (e.g., wide-eyed blondes and football players are dumb) remains OK. Or perhaps when the Court refers to "impermissible stereotypes," it means the adjective to be limiting rather than descriptive — so that we can expect to learn from the Court's peremptory/stereotyping jurisprudence in the future which stereotypes the Constitution frowns upon and which it does not. . . .

[M]ake no mistake about it: there really is no substitute for the peremptory. Voir dire (though it can be expected to expand as a consequence of today's decision) cannot fill the gap. The biases that go along with group characteristics tend to be biases that the juror himself does not perceive, so that it is no use asking about them. It is fruitless to inquire of a male juror whether he harbors any subliminal prejudice in favor of unwed fathers. . . .

In order, it seems to me, not to eliminate any real denial of equal protection, but simply to pay conspicuous obeisance to the equality of the sexes, the Court imperils a practice that has been considered an essential part of fair jury trial since the dawn of the common law. The Constitution of the United States neither requires nor permits this vandalizing of our people's traditions.

For these reasons, I dissent.

Carol Weisbrod, Images of the Woman Juror
9 Harv. Women's L.J. 59, 70-76 (1986)

Proponents of women's suffrage and jury service argued that giving political responsibility to women would allow them to contribute to the public world the special beneficial influence they wielded in the home. Believing that the benefits women gave to the home could readily be transferred to the public world, their goal was, as Frances Willard put it in 1888, "to make the whole world homelike." As stated by a judge in 1884, just as women make the home a special place where goodness reigns, their involvement in the public sphere would raise the moral level of society: "[I]n political as well as household affairs, 'it is not good that man should be alone.' Vices that one sex will tolerate, both sexes, if together, will abominate and punish." A suffragist at the turn of the century perhaps best summarized the point by saying that "the feminine heart, the maternal influence, are needed in the court-room as well as in the home."

The perceptive capacities of women were sometimes seen as superior to men's in a way particularly relevant to jury service. Supporters of women's jury service thought domestic virtue gave women a heightened ability to sense the truth. A state official in 1884 offered the following in favor of women jurors: "They do not reason like men upon the evidence, but, being possessed of a higher quality of intellectuality, i.e., keen perceptions, they see the truth of the thing at a glance." Proponents also argued that, once having determined the truth, women would hold fast to their positions, ensuring a just verdict.

Supporters of women's jury service also argued that women's heightened perceptions included the ability to understand other women, whether as witnesses or defendants, better than men could. Thus, one author claimed that in most criminal cases where women are involved, women could "be of immense service in clearing up evidence, and showing to the male jurors on the panel the absurdity or impossibility of some of the statements." . . .

Inherent in some of these arguments is not only the idea that women could better understand and therefore better judge other women, but also the assumption that women may judge each other according to a different standard than men would use. The 1917 Susan Glaspell story, A Jury of Her Peers [reprinted in The Best Short Stories of 1917, at 256-282 (E.J. O'Brien ed., 1918)] illustrates both of these ideas. The story describes a visit to a farm in which a man has been found strangled. His wife, Minnie, is in jail, accused of the murder. Three men, including the sheriff and the county attorney, visit the couple's home, accompanied by two women: one, the sheriff's wife, a woman "married to the law," the other, a neighbor of Minnie. The men are looking for evidence of motive but are unsuccessful. The women look at various domestic items and discover the motive. . . . The facts noticed by the women relate to exclusively female and domestic matters, such as housekeeping and sewing. Thus, tiny domestic hints discovered by other women's unique perceptive abilities provide the critical missing evidentiary link relating to motive. The motive relates broadly to Minnie's unhappiness with her husband, a cold man whose temperament is suggested by the fact that he broke open the bird cage and strangled Minnie's songbird. Minnie, like the canary, had sung when she was a young girl — "He killed that too."

The "judgment of her peers" is to keep silent about the evidence they uncovered. Since the men pay little attention to Minnie's domestic items — and would probably not have recognized their meaning even if they had — the effect of the women's silence is to keep the men ignorant of the motive. Without such evidence, the men fear that the jury will tend to acquit ("you know how these juries are with women"). The men are identified with the law, and the story assumes that the (presumably male) jury of the outside world would have judged the wife guilty of her husband's murder despite any amount of provocation or derangement. The women are identified as love or forgiveness, but also perhaps as a kind of higher law or higher justice.

The story thus contains both of the assumptions found in the historical literature: that women see things that men do not see, at least in relation to other women, and that women and men evaluate those discoveries differently. Although the murder is excused by the female jury of peers, the story suggests that it would not be justified in the actual judicial system. The women are not merely more sensitive than men in what they see about the woman defendant; they also seem to operate under a different moral code. As the story is told, the crimes of neglecting Minnie, destroying her spirit and happiness, and killing her songbird are all related to her crime of killing her husband. These crimes by her husband are offered as moral justification when the jury of women decides, in effect, to acquit a murderess.

≣≣≣≣
≣≣≣≣
≣≣≣≣
≣≣≣≣
≣≣≣≣
≣≣≣≣
Cristina M. Rodriguez, Note, Clearing the Smoke-Filled Room: Women Jurors and the Disruption of an Old-Boys' Network in Nineteenth-Century America
108 Yale L.J. 1805, 1806-1807, 1812-1814, 1816-1819 (1999)

To comprehend why jury service had a social significance distinct from suffrage, rather than consider nineteenth-century women jurors as variations on women voters, the former should be seen in the same context as women who sought access to the bar. Both women lawyers and women jurors can be understood as outsiders who invaded the space of the courtroom and challenged the masculinist legal culture that operated according to the internal logic of an "old-boys" or insiders' network. Opposition to women jurors did flow in part from traditional objections to changes in the legal status of women; not only would women be distracted from their domestic duties, but the status of juror did not befit feminine nature. The primary opposition, however, emanated from a desire to preserve a particular legal culture. The mixed jury experiments in the Wyoming and Washington Territories suggest that women jurors introduced into the fluid legal culture of post-Civil War America a concept of a "gendered justice," or the belief that women as women would perform their duties as jurors differently from their male counterparts. By disrupting the status quo of the male-dominated legal profession, the possibility of a gendered justice fueled opposition to female jury service, even as female suffrage remained grudgingly accepted. . . .

. . . Proponents of the experiments projected that if women could be persuaded to sit on juries, they would operate unconstrained by the same external conditions that beset male jurors and would act as their judgment and consciences dictated. Justice Howe [presiding over the mixed juries] concluded that by serving on juries, women would have the best possible opportunity to "aid in suppressing the dens of infamy which curse the country." In his remarks to the first mixed jury, Howe characterized the experiment as a test of the women jurors' power to defend themselves against crime. He counseled the women to immunize themselves against the hostile public and assured them that they would be protected, in body and reputation, from the improprieties that the public feared, as well as from the public itself. . . .

The first mixed petit jury presided over the celebrated murder trial of Andrew Howie. During the trial itself, the attorneys in the case turned their tactics to what they thought would be the tendencies of the six female jurors. The lawyers believed that women would know nothing of the dangers that confronted men in the territories — dangers that sometimes demanded men to kill in self-defense. Defense attorneys therefore sought to appeal to the women jurors' sympathies, rather than their reasonable intuitions about what kinds of actions might be justified. . . . The matter-of-course way in which the trial proceeded deflated the opposition's predictions of the law's decline and neutralized whatever apprehensions remained among the public — at least for a time. . . .

Whereas a branch of separate spheres ideology dictated that women would be too sympathetic to serve as qualified jurors, the Howie trial revealed that the variable of the women juror was not a predictable one: As the experiments unfolded, the content of feminized justice evolved from "too soft" to "too hard" and severe. . . .

Critics also argued that women in the courtroom would distract men by changing the legal discussion into "a charming tete-a-tete with the best looking young man on the jury. . . . Session[s] . . . would witness a delightful but wicked flirtation between good-looking juryman and the volatile wife." Unable to focus on the "legal harangue," women jurors would instead introduce frivolous conversation, emblematic of their domestic sphere, into the sober proceedings. . . .

Across the country, journalists and concerned citizens, . . . pondered what "female justice" meant. The *New Orleans Times* wrote that the confusion of "dress" and "rights" brought on by the mingling of the sexes in the courtroom threatened to obliterate distinctions between men and women. The daily charged that the jury experiment was premised on a fictitious female "masculinity," concluding that the mixed jury would actually yield beneficial results by proving women to be incapable of sitting "as the peers of men without setting at defiance all the laws of delicacy and propriety."

The *Philadelphia Press* offered an alternative view consistent with the outcome of the Howie trial. The paper asserted that women, by nature, moralized excessively and therefore did not belong as decisionmakers in a legal system that depended on discovering nuances and gradations in responsibility. "Is it possible for a jury of women, carrying with them all their sensitiveness, sympathies, predilections, jealousies, prejudices, hatreds, to reach an impartial verdict?" Regardless of whether opponents believed the woman juror to be "too soft" or "too hard," a consistent argument ran through all of the criticism: The woman juror, by defying the separate spheres construct, dangerously conflated gender roles in a manner incompatible with prevailing legal culture. . . .

In the end, media accounts abounded with five predictable conclusions: (1) women's exalted moral natures rendered them ill-suited for the dirty world of the courtroom; (2) the characteristic emotions that made women good mothers would operate to cloud their judgment; (3) incapable of apprehending abstractions, women would be unable to decipher the technicalities of the law and intricacies of evidence; (4) inherently frivolous, women jurors would be too distracted to perform their duties, distracting male jurors in the process; and (5) the demands of women's domestic responsibilities made jury service a logistical impossibility. . . .

The results of the jury experiments confirmed that women would change the nature of the justice dispensed in court. Those who had anticipated that women jurors would advance a law-and-order had most accurately predicted the effects of gendered justice. . . .

. . . That the women jurors handed down verdicts that defied the initial expectation that women would be too weak-willed to be good jurors only enlarged the threat they posed to the conventional administration of justice.

Joan W. Howarth, Deciding to Kill: Revealing the Gender in the Task Handed to Capital Jurors
1994 Wis. L. Rev. 1345, 1371, 1376-1378, 1394, 1398-1403, 1407-1408

The "guided discretion" of capital decisionmaking is a battleground of context versus principle. If contextual reasoning is associated with a feminine mode of decisionmaking, the decision to impose death is a startlingly feminine moment at the heart of capital punishment jurisprudence. Indeed, the capital decision stands today as an island of indeterminacy in an ocean of determinate sentencing. . . .

Many jurors who use their discretion to impose death do not recognize that they had a choice to do otherwise. Jurors want the instructions to tell them whether to sentence to life or death, so that is how they understand the instructions. . . . Although each had participated in a relatively open-ended weighing process, juror after juror told me that the judge's instructions required them to impose death. "The instructions that we received . . . didn't leave any room for choices." . . .

One juror reported, "I didn't want to do it, but I had to." Another explained, "You can feel sorry and sadness for what you have to do but you still have to do it. That is part of discipline." These accounts confirm the hypothesis of social scientists that jurors who had imposed death would readily characterize the decision as one required by the applicable law in order to minimize their sense of personal responsibility.

Thus, jurors approach open-ended weighing as if rules provided answers; as if the task were finding facts, not supplying a moral response. . . .

The preference for certainty and principled decisionmaking is so well-entrenched that even the members of the Court who recognize that contextualized discretion is necessary choose language to describe capital decisionmaking that hides the uncertainty of discretion behind the soothing language of certainty and predictability. The Court indulges in the comforting words of legal determinacy, calling the decisions made through individualized discretion nothing less than "reliable" and "accurate," as if capital sentences were somehow comparable to brand name appliances. . . .

Those who fear that the feminist call for connectedness could result in longer and harsher sentences for defendants are describing a condition that already exists. Several jurors told me that they felt closest to victims of the defendant who testified during the penalty phase. One juror characterized his reaction to the victims' testimony as establishing a "strong connection." Another explained that the most moving portion of the trial was the penalty testimony of a rape victim of the defendant: "Whatever doubts we had about the guilt phase went away. We went back to that jury room [with] a sense of relief." . . .

Capital jurisprudence denies its emotional component. Jurors learn to fight authentic emotional response, and therefore distrust open appeals to emotion. . . . Although appeals to emotions are the most prevalent type of argument, "transparent" appeals to the emotions of jurors constitute misconduct, which can lead to reversal of a resultant death sentence. The court consistently describes capital punishment law as unsullied by the taint of emotion. This rhetorical stance is most evident in the court's treatment of no-sympathy instructions, its use of the reasonable juror for appellate review of penalty determinations, and its assessment of victim-impact evidence. . . .

. . . In California v. Brown, [479 U.S. 538 (1987),] the court upheld a death sentence imposed by a jury that been instructed not to be swayed by "mere sympathy." . . . Justice O'Connor provided a majority to affirm the death sentence with a concurrence that upheld the no-sympathy instruction because it enabled the jurors to make their moral decision based on reason, not emotion: "[T]he sentence imposed . . . should reflect a reasoned moral response to the defendant's background, character, and crime rather than mere sympathy or emotion." [479 U.S. at 542-543.] Brown counsels that forbidding the capital jury to rely on sentiment or sympathy increases the reliability of the sentence that results. . . .

A more subtle manifestation of the Court's routine erasure of emotionality from the jury's decision to impose death is its use of the "reasonable juror" standard for appellate review of trial court error that may have contributed to a jury verdict for death. In Sawyer v. Whitley, [507 U.S. 968 (1992)], the Court held that a capital defendant who claims actual innocence in a successive habeas petition must show by clear and convincing evidence that, but for constitutional error, no reasonable juror would have found petitioner eligible for the death penalty under applicable state law.

The hypothetical "reasonable juror" is, of course, a staple of appellate oversight of jurors' factfinding abilities throughout civil and criminal procedure. . . . The use of the fictional "reasonable juror" makes the most sense when . . . factfinding is at issue.

The capital sentence, however, is fundamentally about values and conscience, not merely facts. The weight of the decision itself imposes emotion on the determination. But the Court's choice of the "reasonable juror" standard . . . removes the emotion, conscience, and mercy from the determination. By narrowing the "gut-level hunch" to a matter of reason, the Court cleans the emotion out of the process. . . .

The denial of emotion in capital jurisprudence is also evident in the series of recent decisions related to victim-impact evidence. . . . Booth v. Maryland, [482 U.S. 496 (1987),] and South Carolina v. Gathers, [490 U.S. 805 (1989),] . . . which barred the admission of victim-impact evidence and argument . . . were both decided in part on the principle that the decision to sentence to death must be based on reason rather than emotion. [Even in overruling these decisions,] Payne v. Tennessee, [501 U.S. 808 (1991),] . . . contains not a hint about any positive virtues emotion may contribute to achieving a moral decision. The single reference to the role of emotion is made in Justice O'Connor's concurrence, which suggests that the emotionally moving [testimony] . . . was harmlessly cumulative [and] "did not inflame [the jurors'] passions more than did the facts of the crime. . . ." [Id. at 832]. . . .

The very reason for having a jury is to bring personal values and experiences into decisionmaking. Handing off the task of capital sentencing to juries is justified by the benefit of giving this task to people for whom it will be a personal, not a professional decision. Part of personalizing a decision is bringing emotion to it. . . .

Notes

1. Equality and Impartiality: Can Both Goals Be Achieved in Jury Selection? The jury system reflects a tension between the ideals of impartiality, on the one hand, and the right to be judged by one's peers, on the other. When Gwendolyn Hoyt unsuccessfully challenged a jury selection system that gave automatic exemptions to women, she was seeking to obtain a jury of her peers to judge the charge against her that she had murdered her abusive husband.

> [T]he affair occurred in the context of a marital upheaval involving, among other things, the suspected infidelity of the appellant's husband, and culminating in the husband's final rejection of his wife's efforts at reconciliation. It is claimed, in substance, that women jurors would have been more understanding or compassionate than men in assessing the quality of appellant's act and her defense of "temporary insanity."

Hoyt v. Florida, 368 U.S. 57, 58 (1961). The court upheld the broad statutory exemption to women "whether born of the State's historic public policy or of a determination that it would not be administratively feasible to decide in each individual instance whether the family responsibilities of a prospective female juror were serious enough to warrant an exemption." Id. at 63.

Hoyt v. Florida was overruled by Taylor v. Louisiana, 419 U.S. 522 (1975), on the basis of the defendant's Sixth Amendment right to a jury trial. The reasoning was mixed, however, combining concern both for "diffused impartiality," on the one hand, and for the importance of "sharing in the administration of justice [as] a phase of civic responsibility," on the other. Id. at 530-531. The concern for the fairness of the defendant's trial, protected by the Sixth Amendment, assumes that women and men may offer different perspectives; the concern for the equal protection right of prospective jurors to be treated as equals is based on equality and civic responsibility and suggests there are no significant sex-based differences.

Was *J.E.B.* correctly decided? Prohibiting sex-based peremptories limits the exercise of bias based on the assumption that only women have gender. See Martha Minow, Stripped Down Like a Runner or Enriched by Experience, 33 Wm. & Mary L. Rev. 1201 (1992). On the other hand, it also prohibits litigation strategies that might otherwise be used to curtail bias against women. As Justice O'Connor notes, there are some cases in which gender does make a difference. Does pretending otherwise improve the accuracy of the jury system?

J.E.B. applies on its facts only to the government's use of gender-based peremptory challenges. Notwithstanding Justice O'Connor's hope that it be so limited, most believe that now that Batson v. Kentucky has been extended to sex-based challenges, so will the rules prohibiting the exercise of race-based peremptories by private civil litigants and criminal defendants. See Edmonson v. Leesville Concrete Co., 500 U.S. 614 (1991) (*Batson* applied to civil cases); Georgia v. McCollum, 505 U.S. 42 (1992) (*Batson* applied to criminal defendants).

Would you expect a greater proportion of men, or women, to benefit from *J.E.B.*? (Is this even a meaningful question?) One study of the District of Columbia District Court jury pool from January to June of 1993 showed that while the proportion of jurors either excused for cause or not used was roughly equivalent to the overall composition of the jury pool, peremptory strikes were used disproportionately against men. Although the defense exercised slightly more of its strikes against women, in total 29.7 percent of all women who reported for service were struck by either the defense or the government in both civil and criminal trials, while 35.5 percent of all men were struck. See Karen L. Cipriani, The Numbers Don't Add Up: Challenging the Premise of J.E.B. v. Alabama ex rel. T.B., 31 Am. Crim. L. Rev. 1253, 1265-1267 (1994). In criminal cases alone, men and women were struck in roughly equal numbers, again with the defense striking a somewhat higher proportion of women than men. Id. at 1267 n.82. In the criminal cases recorded during this period, while 76.4 percent of the attorneys and defendants were male, the seated juries were 56 percent female. Id. at 1275. What conclusions, if any, do you draw from these figures?

What exactly does impartiality mean in the context of a jury of peers? Is it that a potential juror should have no views on any relevant subject? Or that jury perspectives in some sense should be drawn from a cross-section of the community, and "not arbitrarily skewed for or against any particular group or characteristic"? See Holland v. Illinois, 493 U.S. 474, 515 (1990) (Stevens, J., dissenting). Should the goal be proportional representation on juries? See Kenneth S. Klein & Theodore D. Klastorin, Do Diverse Juries Aid or Impede Justice?, 1999 Wis. L. Rev. 553 (1999); Deborah L. Forman, What Difference Does It Make? Gender and Jury Selection, 2 UCLA Women's L.J. 35, 83 (1992).

If gender-based peremptory strikes are not allowed, how about strikes based on an individual's sexual orientation? Would challenge for cause ever be appropriate based on sexual orientation? See Vanessa H. Eisemann, Striking a Balance of Fairness: Sexual Orientation and Voir Dire, 13 Yale J.L. & Feminism 1 (2001) (arguing that sexual orientation should be treated like race, religion, ethnicity, and gender for the purposes of what is a permissible basis for a peremptory strike).

2. Discretion and Different Voice Theory. Should juries be given more or less discretion? Professor Howarth seems to assume that greater emotion in capital sentencing by juries is associated with women's different voice, and a positive thing that the law should face up to and embrace, not hide or try to wring out of the system. Is she right? For a similar perspective from a feminist criminal defense lawyer on the need for juries "to hear about the social misery that underlies crime," including "the conditions under which deprived inner-city youth and battered women live," see Abbe Smith, Criminal Responsibility, Social Responsibility, and Angry Young Men: Reflections of a Feminist Criminal Defense Lawyer, 21 N.Y.U. Rev. L. & Soc. Change 433, 489 (1994-1995).

Would greater discretion favor women? It may depend upon the crime and the circumstances. See Andrea Shapiro, Unequal Before the Law: Men, Women and the Death Penalty, 8 Am. U. J. Gender Soc. Pol'y & L. 427, 469 (2000) (women who maintain "the image of a 'real' woman will be spared from the ultimate sentence of death," while those who "blatantly and explicitly disturb society's notions of the 'real' woman will not); Victor L. Streib, Death Penalty for Female Offenders, 58 U. Cin. L. Rev. 845, 868, 877-878 (1990) (while juries and judges are both more lenient toward female offenders, executed women are likely to be very poor and uneducated individuals who "committed shockingly 'unladylike' behavior, allowing the sentencing judges and juries to put aside any image of them as 'the gentler sex' and to treat them as 'crazed monsters' deserving nothing more than extermination"); Elizabeth Rapaport, Some Questions About Gender and the Death Penalty, 20 Golden Gate U. L. Rev. 501 (1990) (greater opprobrium normally attaches to the killing of strangers than to the killing of intimates, which "is chivalrous to women as perpetrators, since such a high percentage of the homicides women commit are domestic; but it is not chivalrous to women as victims"); see also Elizabeth Rapaport, Staying Alive: Executive Clemency, Equal Protection, and the Politics of Gender in Women's Capital Cases, 4 Buff. Crim. L. Rev. 967, 968 (2001) (women sentenced to death are more likely to receive executive clemency than death row men); Jenny E. Carroll, Images of Women and Capital Sentencing Among Female Offenders: Exploring the Outer Limits of the Eighth Amendment and Articulated Theories of Justice, 75 Tex. L. Rev. 1413 (1997). The question of gender bias in criminal sentencing is pursued in the next section, beginning at page 908.

Note that Howarth wishes to encourage juries to use their emotions not only in favor of defendants, but in favor of victims as well. The Supreme Court, reversing its prior decisions in the area, held that victim impact statements are constitutionally allowed in capital murder proceedings as a means of showing the "uniqueness" of each individual and hence the specific harm caused by the crime. See Payne v. Tennessee, 501 U.S. 808 (1991). Thirty-one states have now added victims' rights amendments to their constitutions. See Jennifer J. Stearman, An Amendment to the Constitution of the United States to Protect the Rights of Crime Victims: Exploring the Effectiveness of State Efforts, 30 U. Balt. L.F. 43 (1999). A federal constitutional Victims' Rights Amendment has been proposed, the most recent version of which guarantees crime victims the following rights: ". . . to notice of, and not to be excluded from, all public proceedings relating to the crime; to be heard, if present, and to submit a written statement at a public pretrial or trial proceeding to determine a release from custody, an acceptance of a negotiated plea, or a sentence; to [these rights] at a public parole proceeding, or at a non-public parole proceeding, to the extent they are afforded to the convicted offender; to notice of a release pursuant to a public or parole proceeding or an escape; to a final disposition . . . free from unreasonable delay; to an order to restitution from the convicted offender; to consideration for the safety of the victim in determining any release from custody; and to notice of the rights established by this article. . . ." See S.J. Res. 3, 106th Cong. (1999). In September 1999, the Senate Judiciary Committee approved this version of the Victims' Rights Amendment by a 12-5 vote, and the issue remains current in both houses of Congress. The Amendment is fiercely opposed by civil rights advocates. See, e.g., Robert P. Mosteller & H. Jefferson Powell, With Disdain for the Constitutional Craft: The Proposed Victims' Rights Amendment, 78 N.C. L. Rev. 371 (2000); Rachel King, Why a Victims' Rights Constitutional Amendment Is a Bad Idea: Practical Experiences from Crime Victims, 68 U. Cin. L. Rev. 357 (2000). What are the likely results of such contextualized focus on victims? Are women likely to benefit? Minorities?

Would you apply Howarth's analysis to wrongful acquittals? Does the "ethic of care" support jury nullification? Most feminist scholars say not. Susan Bandes, for example, explains how empathy and narrative, in the context of victim impact statements, is a political tool for dehumanizing the defendant in order to more easily cast him out of the human community. Bandes, Empathy, Narrative, and Victim Impact Statements, 63 U. Chi. L. Rev. 361, 412 (1996). Anne Bowen Poulin, also arguing within the terms of different voice theory but resisting the kinds of conclusions drawn from it by Howarth, argues that we should "acknowledge more openly the role we ask the jury to play — injecting a different voice into our system of rational rules," but that jury nullification is not justified and should be controlled through such measures as clearer oral and written instructions to juries, special interrogatories, permission to take notes and ask questions, and trial transcripts. Poulin, The Jury: The Criminal Justice System's Different Voice, 62 U. Cin. L. Rev. 1377, 1410-1423 (1994).

7. Women and Criminal Sentencing

≡≡≡ *United States v. Handy*
≡≡≡ 752 F. Supp. 561 (E.D.N.Y. 1990)

GLASSER, District Judge:

. . . Ms. Handy pleaded guilty to a single count indictment charging her with conspiring with William Johnson to distribute and possess with intent to distribute cocaine. The events leading up to her arrest describe a reverse buy — that is to say — the defendants were not selling cocaine to an undercover officer or to a confidential informant, but were negotiating to buy cocaine for a stated price. The money with which to consummate the purchase was in a handbag on the floor near Ms. Handy and totaled $75,000. Also in her handbag were a diluent used to "cut" cocaine and glassine envelopes.

Johnson was, for the preceding five years, Handy's boyfriend. On the day prior to her arrest, he requested her to accompany him to New York City to buy narcotics. She agreed to accompany him and to carry the purchase money. She denied ever having done so before. She admitted to knowing for at least two years of Johnson's involvement in illegal activity based upon the inconsistency between his lifestyle and his earnings as a meat cutter and she suspected that the illegal activity was drug related.

The facts which identify this defendant as Nadine Handy, a person, rather than an objective manifestation of discrete criteria to which are assigned numbers which, when added together yield a sentencing result, are as follows:

She was born in Baltimore, Maryland, thirty-six years ago. She was one of ten children whose father died when she was three and whose mother died at the age of forty when the defendant was fifteen years old. She is the mother of three out-of-wedlock children. She gave birth to her first child when she was seventeen and still in high school. He is now nineteen years old and is a strong candidate for a basketball scholarship to college with aspirations of playing professional basketball thereafter. She gave birth to her second child, a daughter, two years later and left high school. This child is now sixteen, is enrolled in the "gifted and talented" class in her local high school and is the likely recipient of a $1,000 annual college scholarship. She gave birth to her second daughter who is now eight years old and in the third grade. All the children live with her. She has no prior criminal record.

Ms. Handy has been gainfully employed for the past thirteen years. For the past eight years she has been employed by the same firm, Farm Fresh Food, Inc. in Baltimore to which she returned to resume her work when released on bail. She has borne the sole responsibility for rearing her three children and supporting them without public assistance. She also undertook to care for the two children of her boyfriend, Johnson, when they came to Baltimore from California. Letters written on behalf of Ms. Handy describe her selflessness in that regard and the positive influence she has had on their lives.

The picture of Ms. Handy portrayed by the salient facts I summarized and by the many letters on her behalf, is of a young woman born into and reared in poverty in an urban environment which is a socio-economic minefield through which she threaded her way and emerged unscathed, relatively speaking. That is to say, she abjured the suffocating effects of the world of welfare for the independence and dignity-reinforcing world of work and has been steadily and gainfully employed for thirteen years. She has single-handedly and successfully guided three children through the socio-economic minefield of a not atypically treacherous urban environment. Letters addressed to the court attest to the high regard in which she is held at work and in her community. What then brings her before the court? The explanation which is all but inescapable is that this single parent fell in love with the co-defendant, William Johnson and despite her many other strengths did not have the strength to say "no" to him. The story is as old as the story of civilization — he offered her an apple and she did eat. That the government did not view her as a sophisticated, knowledgeable drug dealer is indicated by its stipulation at the time of her plea not to oppose a four point guideline reduction for her minimal role in the offense. There is no indication that the defendant was drawn to trafficking in drugs by the lure of the huge sums of money incident to such traffic. Were that the case it would be reasonable to assume that she would not persist in working as a meat wrapper at an average salary of approximately $250 per week.

Is a downward modification appropriate and justified by the statutes and the guidelines promulgated pursuant thereto? I believe it is. I believe that the conclusion I reach is one a sentencing judge is permitted to reach within the framework of the guidelines. I do not depart as an expression of general dissatisfaction with the guidelines. It is rather late in the day for that and would be tilting at windmills. . . .

I find the circumstances related to family ties and relationships and to previous and current employment record to be sufficiently extraordinary to warrant a downward departure for the following reasons. Although ordinarily an employment record is not relevant in determining whether a sentence should be outside the guidelines, U.S.S.G. §5H1.5, the continuous employment for thirteen years of this single parent of three teenage children is extraordinary. That factor, coupled with the fact that an exceptionally promising future of the older two children would be threatened by the prolonged incarceration of this mother drives the court to conclude that a downward departure is warranted. . . .

Lest the decision in this case is sought to be regarded as authority for a downward departure in every case of a single parent, or in every case in which a defendant has been gainfully employed, I emphasize that it is not so intended. The decision in this case is intensely fact specific. I also wish to emphasize that although passing references have been made in the course of this opinion to the socio-economic background of the defendant and to the fact that she is a first offender, those factors were not regarded as factors warranting a downward departure. . . .

Notes

1. Federal Sentencing Reform.   In an effort to eliminate unwarranted sentencing disparity, Congress passed the Sentencing Reform Act of 1984, Pub. L. No. 98-473, tit. 11, ch. 2, 98 Stat. 1987 (1984) (codified at 18 U.S.C. §§3551-3673; 28 U.S.C. §§991-998). The Act was meant to promote the goals of honesty, uniformity, and proportionality in sentencing by mandating "real time," uniform sentences for similar conduct. The Federal Sentencing Commission established the Federal Sentencing Guidelines in order to shift the focus of punishment away from the characteristics of the defendant to the characteristics of the crime.

Until the promulgation of sentencing guidelines, the individual circumstances of the defendant were regularly considered by judges when determining punishment. The Guidelines now forbid consideration of traditional "individualizing" factors, except in "extraordinary" situations, and specify that family ties and responsibilities are not ordinarily relevant. See U.S. Sentencing Guidelines Manual §5H1.10 (1997).

Handy demonstrates the difficulties of staying within the boundaries set by the sentencing guideline reforms. The judge makes four references to the defendant's background, six to her status as a single parent, six to the defendant being gainfully employed and/or not on welfare, four to the defendant's "exceptionally promising" children, and three to the defendant's relationship with the co-defendant. It would seem the judge was impressed by the defendant's life choices, choices made despite being "reared in poverty in an urban environment which is a socio-economic minefield." Are these the kind of "extraordinary" contextual considerations allowed under the Federal Sentencing Guidelines or the kind of information about family ties and responsibility that should not be relevant? Do you think the outcome of the case would have been different had all else been the same, except that the defendant had no children? That she had been a man? Should it be?

The focus on neutrality in sentencing is said to have disproportionately affected women, who prior to the Act had generally received more lenient sentences than men who committed similar crimes. See, e.g., Ilene H. Nagel & Barry L. Johnson, The Role of Gender in a Structured Sentencing System: Equal Treatment, Policy Choices, and the Sentencing of Female Offenders Under the United States Sentencing Guidelines, 85 J. Crim. L. & Criminology 181, 185-189 (1994); Myrna S. Raeder, Gender and Sentencing: Single Moms, Battered Women, and Other Sex-Based Anomalies in the Gender-Free World of the Federal Sentencing Guidelines, 20 Pepp. L. Rev. 905, 922-929 (1993). However, recent studies reveal that women still receive more lenient sentencing than men due to downward judicial departures from the Sentencing Guidelines. See, e.g., David B. Mustard, Racial, Ethnic, and Gender Disparities in Sentencing: Evidence from the U.S. Federal Courts, 44 J.L. & Econ. 285 (2001). Recall a similar pattern in jury sentencing. See pages 900-901 and 906-907, supra (women are sentenced to death less often and receive executive clemency more often than men although they may face more severe penalties when their crimes seem particularly "unladylike").

As for sentencing of women in state courts, some debate has focused on whether women receive higher sentences than men for violent crimes against their spouses. Debate was fueled by two Baltimore County, Maryland, sentences handed down on the same day in 1994. In one case, a judge sentenced a man to 18 months in prison for killing his wife, whom he found in bed with another man; in the other case, a woman was sentenced to three years in prison for killing her abusive husband. These cases, and the conflicting studies on disparate sentencing, are reviewed in Wendy Keller, Disparate Treatment of Spouse Murder Defendants, 6 S. Cal. Rev. L. & Women's Stud. 255 (1996).

Criticism of sentencing reform has also focused on its detrimental impact on members of racial minority groups. Specifically on the impact of sentencing reform on African-American women, see Paula C. Johnson, At the Intersection of Injustice: Experiences of African-American Women in Crime and Sentencing, 4 Am. U. J. Gender & L. 1, 9 (1995) (arguing that the "progression toward mandatory sentencing . . . perpetuates the historically devalued status of African American women, construing them as undeserving of social benefits and as intrinsically incorrigible," and also violates the Eighth Amendment).

2. Sentencing and Motherhood. Approximately 80 percent of women in federal prisons have young children. About two-thirds of them are single parents. During their parents' incarceration, 91 percent of the children of men prisoners are cared for by their mothers, but only about 33 percent of the children of women prisoners are cared for by their fathers. See Patricia M. Wald, "What About the Kids?": Parenting Issues in Sentencing, 8 Fed. Sent. Rep. 137 (1995). Thus, although incarceration obviously takes men away from their children, "neutral" sentencing has a different impact on women (and their children) than on men (and their children). See Lanette P. Dalley, Imprisoned Mothers and Their Children: Their Often Conflicting Legal Rights, 22 Hamline J. Pub. L. & Pol'y 1 (2000). Does the failure of the Sentencing Guidelines to take parental responsibility into account therefore constitute gender bias against women offenders?

Consider the following:

> The purpose of just punishment emphasizes consistency in sentencing. If the "same" sentence has an inconsistent impact on two different defendants, then considering the two sentences as equivalent is unjust. An incarcerative sentence may have a distinctly different impact on a parent than it has on a non-parent. For example, in many states incarceration constitutes a ground for termination of parental rights. A two year prison sentence does not equal two years in prison accompanied by permanent loss of child custody. . . .

Eleanor Bush, Considering the Defendant's Children at Sentencing, 2 Fed. Sent. Rep. 194, 194 (1990); see also Raeder, Gender and Sentencing, supra, at 961 (blindly imposing equal treatment on parents at sentencing when the rest of society does not "makes a mockery of so-called gender neutrality in sentencing").

Senior United States District Court Judge Jack Weinstein agrees. Weinstein argues that, while the motivation behind gender-neutral sentencing guidelines may have been commendable, the results have often been nonsensical. "[O]stensibly gender-neutral provisions do not lead to gender-neutral results in a society in which many male and female experiences with crime, family life, and community differ." Jack Weinstein, The Effect of Sentencing on Women, Men, the Family, and the Community, 5 Colum. J. Gender & L. 169, 181 (1996). Weinstein advocates an approach to sentencing that incorporates consideration of the effect of a parent's incarceration on her children.

> The lack of parental supervision resulting from incarceration of heads of households can lead into a vicious downward spiral of criminal activity, jail sentences, and possible death for [children of incarcerated parents] at a young age. . . . Avoiding punitive solutions based solely on incarceration for defendants who are heads of households may prevent the children from being victimized because of their parents' acts while at the same time it may

guarantee a certain degree of stability that can encourage a home environment where the children can pursue alternatives beyond criminal activity.

Id. at 179.

Yet, it is argued that a policy of across-the-board mitigation of sentences for offenders with primary child care responsibilities would reinforce gender stereotypes.

> Such a policy would effectively use the criminal law to reward women for their status as mothers (or, alternatively, to punish women for not having children). It would say in effect, "you have violated the criminal law, but we'll overlook that so you can do what you are supposed to do — care for your children." This denies single-mother offenders the status of full moral agents and disregards the social contributions of childless women, whose employment and community ties are not given the same consideration in sentencing.

Nagel & Johnson, supra, at 208.

Courts that have specifically addressed the issue of parental responsibility at sentencing have generally decided that motherhood itself is not an extraordinary circumstance and thus, without more, is not a valid basis for a downward departure.

> A sole, custodial parent is not a rarity in today's society, and imprisoning such a parent will by definition separate the parent from the children. It is apparent that in many cases the other parent may be unable or unwilling to care for the children, and that the children will have to live with relatives, friends, or even in foster homes. . . . This situation, though unfortunate, is simply not out of the ordinary.

United States v. Brand, 907 F.2d 31, 33 (4th Cir.), cert. denied, 498 U.S. 1014 (1990). In practice, however, recent research indicates that judges in fact do take into account the extralegal factor of motherhood in determining sentences. See Sean B. Berberian, Protecting Children: Explaining Disparities in the Female Offender's Pretrial Process, and Policy Issues Surrounding Lenient Treatment of Mothers, 10 Hastings Women's L.J. 369 (1999) (finding that women with children were significantly more likely to receive pretrial release and lower bail/bond amounts).

On June 27, 1994, President Nelson Mandela of the Republic of South Africa signed a Presidential Act providing an early release from prison for certain categories of prisoners, including "all mothers in prison on 10 May 1994, with minor children under the age of twelve (12) years." Fathers were not included. In his statement in support of the Act, President Mandela stated that he was motivated predominantly by a concern for children who had been deprived of the nurturing and care that their mothers would ordinarily have provided.

. . . Having spent many years in prison myself, I am well aware of the hardship which flows from incarceration. I am also well aware that imprisonment inevitably has harsh consequences for the family of the prisoner.

Account was taken of the special role I believe that mothers play in the care and nurturing of younger children. . . .

I have had an on-going concern about the general plight of young children in South Africa. . . .

In my experience there are only a minority of fathers who are actively involved in nurturing and caring for their children. . . .

President of the Republic of South Africa v. Hugo, 1997 (4) SA 1 (CC).

A father with a child under the age of 12 who was not entitled to early release under the order challenged his exclusion under the anti-discrimination provisions of the interim South African Constitution. Is there any question about how this case would be decided in the United States? A majority of the South African Constitutional Court rejected the challenge on the grounds that the early release order was not "unfair discrimination." One justice dissented, and another determined that although the Act constituted "unfair discrimination," it was justified. See id.

3. Sentencing and Pregnancy. Whether pregnancy is considered in relation to family ties of the defendant or as a physical condition, the Federal Sentencing Guidelines prohibit departures unless extraordinary situations exist. See U.S.S.G. §§5H1.4, 5H1.6. Federal judges can, at their discretion, postpone a defendant's sentence until after she gives birth, sentence the offender to incarceration in a facility that can attend to her medical needs, or by similar means otherwise accommodate her pregnancy while remaining within the Guideline ranges.

Case law concerning downward departures for pregnancy is limited. Two concerns seem to be common in these few cases: whether the defendant was pregnant at the time of the crime and whether pregnancy is in fact an extraordinary situation. In United States v. Pozzy, 902 F.2d 133, 138-139 (1st Cir.), cert. denied, 498 U.S. 943 (1990), the court noted that "pregnancy of convicted female felons is neither atypical nor unusual." Myrna Raeder calls this conclusion "suspect," pointing out that while pregnant *female* felons may not be unusual, pregnant *felons* are, and that by confining the sample to women, the 1st Circuit violated the Sentencing Commission's ban on consideration based on sex. Raeder, Gender and Sentencing, supra, at 947. Is this sound analysis?

The Court in *Pozzy* also expressed concern that giving a downward departure for pregnancy would send "an obvious message to all female defendants that pregnancy is 'a way out.'" 902 F.2d at 139. The D.C. Circuit vacated a sentence based on a downward departure given to a pregnant woman who conceived after her arrest. United States v. Dyce, 91 F.3d 1462 (D.C. Cir. 1996), cert. denied, 519 U.S. 1018 (1996). But see United States v. Arize, 792 F. Supp. 920 (E.D.N.Y. 1992) (defendant's unknown pregnancy at time of offense a valid basis for downward departure because of the potential that defendant would permanently lose custody of the child); United States v. Pokuaa, 782 F. Supp. 747 (E.D.N.Y. 1992) (downward departure given to defendant who was in seventh month of pregnancy at time of sentencing and who was experiencing complications with the pregnancy).

4. Sentencing and Prior Abuse. One of the factors "not ordinarily relevant" to determining whether to depart from the Federal Sentencing Guidelines is a defendant's mental or emotional condition. U.S. Sentencing Guidelines Manual §5H1.3 (1997). This provision has been allowed to authorize departure for extraordinary conditions involving abused female offenders, provided the defendant can establish a nexus between the abuse and the offense. In this regard, the Guidelines are in line with traditional sentencing assessments of an individual defendant's blameworthiness. What about when the abuse isn't current, but may have affected, at least indirectly, defendant's ability to control her behavior?

In October of 1994, only two weeks after being granted custody of her two children, Susan Smith of Union, South Carolina, loaded her young sons into her car, drove to a nearby lake, pointed the car toward the lake, and then released the hand brake and jumped out. After a nine-day search for the black carjacker who Smith told police drove off with her children, Smith admitted she had killed her sons. Her capital murder trial was short, and during the penalty phase, her attorneys argued for leniency based on a history of depression brought on in large part by sexual abuse she suffered as a child. The jury sentenced her to life imprisonment, sparing her the death penalty. See Chris Burritt & Jack Warner, The Susan Smith Trial, Atlanta Const., July 22, 1995, at C8; Jurors in Susan Smith Trial Say They Don't Have Any Regrets, Atlanta Const., Aug. 28, 1995, at C6.

Smith was tried in a state court, but past victimization has been found as a basis for downward departure from the Federal Sentencing Guidelines as well. In United States v. Roe, 976 F.2d 1216, 1218 (9th Cir. 1992), the court found that a history of abuse so severe that the defendant was "virtually a mind puppet" was extraordinary and that a downward departure was not forbidden by the Guidelines. Similarly, in United States v. Gaviria, 804 F. Supp. 476, 477 (E.D.N.Y. 1992), the sentencing judge granted a downward departure to a woman who, according to a psychiatrist, "reflect[ed] the stigmata of an abused person." See also United States v. Delgado, 994 F. Supp. 143 (E.D.N.Y. 1998) (granting a downward departure in part because of the childhood abuse suffered by the female defendant and because of her "difficult" life). Other federal courts have insisted that there be a causal link or nexus between the defendant's condition and the crime. See, e.g., United States v. Perkins, 963 F.2d 1523, 1528 (D.C. Cir. 1992) (reversing and remanding a downward departure from the Guidelines for a woman diagnosed with "dependent personality disorder" because the sentencing judge failed to find a nexus between the defendant's condition and the crime she committed). Nagel and Johnson assert that this nexus requirement is essential to the preservation of women's autonomy: "If the defendant's victimization did not influence the offense behavior, any departure is merely a 'victim' discount, imposed out of pity for the defendant, rather than out of a sense that a lesser sentence is deserved. Such departures would undermine the moral agency of their recipients. . . ." Nagel & Johnson, supra, at 211.

5. Sentencing and Dominance by Male Intimates. Should sentencing be affected by a woman's involvement in a controlling relationship? This issue arises most often in the context of drug conspiracies. The war on drugs has had a marked influence on the number of women sentenced in federal courts. One commentator argues that if the extent to which women have been victims of male domination and coercion is not taken into account, their sentences will not correlate with their "actual blameworthiness." Nora V. Demleitner, Women, Men, Gender, Sex, Congress and the Guidelines, 8 Fed. Sent. Rep. 132 (1995). See also Myrna Raeder, The Forgotten Offender: The Effect of the Sentencing Guidelines and Mandatory Minimums on Women and Their Children, 8 Fed. Sent. Rep. 157, 160 (1995) (given that females have been socialized more toward dependent relationships, departures from Sentencing Guidelines are necessary to recognize the gendered nature of some female crime). Furthermore, women may be more likely to receive harsher sentences for their participation in drug rings because of their refusal to snitch, out of either loyalty or fear, on their drug-dealing boyfriends. See Joe Rigert, Drug Sentences Often Stacked Against Women, Minneapolis Star Trib., Dec. 14, 1997, at 1A.

The Guidelines do not specifically consider the possibility that a defendant's conduct may be the result of some form of dominance that falls short of physical abuse or duress. Courts have occasionally granted downward departures based on a perceived subservience in a female defendant. For instance, in United States v. Naylor, 735 F. Supp. 928 (D. Minn. 1990), the court found the defendant deserving of a downward departure because of her romantic relationship with a manipulative, much older co-defendant. The court determined that while Naylor's co-defendant did not physically abuse her, he used his relationship with her purposefully to exploit her and manipulate her into involvement in a cocaine distribution conspiracy. Compare United States v. Guiro, 887 F. Supp. 66, 67 (E.D.N.Y. 1995) (defendant "drawn into the drug conspiracy through her romantic attachment to a drug dealer") with United States v. Thomas, 181 F.3d 870 (7th Cir. 1999) (denying a downward departure for a female defendant who claimed she committed tax fraud because of the abuse she suffered at the hands of her husband and because of her dependent personality). Is allowing leniency for subservience a mark of paternalism, or is it simply factoring an important element of an individual's human existence into the sentencing equation?

Will recognition of the control of women by their boyfriends or husbands reinforce stereotypical assumptions that women are led astray by men? The case of the "Miss America Bandit" illustrates the potential danger of allowing departures based on an individual judge's paternalistic instincts. In United States v. Mast, No. CR-88-0720-AAH-1 (C.D. Cal. 1989), rev'd on other grounds, 925 F.2d. 1472 (9th Cir. 1991), a young woman was convicted of a string of bank robberies. At sentencing, the judge ordered a downward departure based on the defendant's domination by her boyfriend, even though there were no indications of physical abuse. The judge's comments during the sentencing hearing included: "men have exercised traditional control over the activities of women, and I'm not going to ignore that, no matter how much flak I get from women's lib," and "I think it's a fact of life that men can exercise a Svengali influence over women," and "women are a soft touch, particularly if sex is involved." See John Griffith, Woman Faces Counts in Bank Case, Oregonian, Feb. 4, 1992, at C8; Kim Murphy, "Soft Touch" Bandit Gets a Break from Judge on Term, L.A. Times, May 13, 1989. Is this judge really taking the social reality of the defendant into consideration, or is he instead imposing his own views of reality on the situation? How much of a factor did the defendant's relationship with her boyfriend appear to be in the *Handy* sentence?

8. Women and Civil Remedies

Lucinda M. Finley, Female Trouble: The Implications of Tort Reform for Women
64 Tenn. L. Rev. 847, 847-857, 861-866, 870 (1997)

Tort reform, particularly in products liability actions, has been on the federal legislative burner for over a decade. Its latest incarnation, the Common Sense Product Liability Legal Reform Act of 1996, came within a presidential veto of enactment during the recently concluded 104th Congress. Legislatures in various states have also passed or proposed reform measures, including limitations on nonpecuniary loss and punitive damages. . . .

This article analyzes these proposals and their possible adverse impact on women and women's health. . . .

[C]riticisms leveled at nonpecuniary loss damages and their underlying value judgements are seriously questionable, if not fundamentally flawed. . . .

. . . It is hardly value neutral to privilege those activities or types of loss that have a market price over those that are seriously undervalued or not readily valued by the market. Money is not the measure of all human value;

activities or losses that are not easily fungible with money are not, therefore, unimportant or unreal. . . .

. . . How many people would give up their fertility, sexual functioning, ability to relate to people and enjoy human interaction, and their favorite activities in exchange for a guaranteed income stream to cover wages and medical bills? . . . [Arguing that the tort system which trades in money should only try to replace lost funds] ignores or underestimates the social function of tort law — signaling and reinforcing messages about the aspects of human life and types of people that our society values and deems worth protecting. . . .

. . . There are several prevalent types of injuries that disproportionately happen to women, and cause harms considered to be nonpecuniary loss. These injuries include: hostile environment sexual harassment; sexual assault or coercive sexual abuse from teachers, parents, and health care providers; reproductive harm, such as infertility caused by a drug or contraceptive, like DES or Dalkon Shield, used only by women in connection with sex or reproduction; and the painful disfigurement of capsular contracture of the breasts caused by a highly gendered product like breast implants. All of these injuries can certainly adversely impact a woman's earnings potential and cause her to incur medical expenses. However, the primary impact of these injuries is in eviscerating self-esteem, dignity, or a sense of security; causing physical and psychic pain; or impairing sexual or relationship fulfillment. Reproductive or sexual harm caused by drugs and medical devices has a highly disproportionate impact on women, because far more drugs and devices have been devised to control women's fertility or bodily functions associated with sex and childbearing than have been devised for men. These drugs and devices have harmed women by rendering them infertile, causing malformed reproductive organs, causing miscarriages or septic abortions, or causing menstrual chaos.

These harms represent aspects of life and human wholeness that either have little or no value in the marketplace or that society feels most uncomfortable about commodifying by assigning a market value. . . .

Another reason why nonpecuniary loss damages remain particularly important for women is that the pecuniary harm caused by many types of injuries that disproportionately affect women is not readily appreciated or is easily overlooked by lawyers, judges, and juries. For example, when a woman has to endure a sexually hostile environment at work, and suffers the accompanying elevated stress and erosion of dignity and self-esteem, her productivity, work performance, career aspirations, and promotion or relocation prospects will all be adversely affected. . . .

The disparate impact of market-based damage measurement is derived from two principal sources: (1) the generally lower value the market assigns to women's work and to women wage earners and (2) the market's failure to recognize or value many productive activities in which women engage when those activities, such as household management and caretaking, are performed in the private realm. Damages for past lost income simply replicate the unequal wage rates of the market, and thus make assessments about the relative worth of human lives that many people would find distasteful. . . .

Courts often calculate damages for projected future income or lost earning capacity by using gender and race based earnings tables. These tables lock tort damages into the assumptions that past inequities will continue unabated into the future, and that no woman or person of color will ever break out of stereotypical patterns for her gender or race. In addition, courts frequently discount projections of women's future earning capacity by incorporating gender-biased assumptions about the effect of marriage and childbearing on women's work force participation, advancement, and earnings.

Pecuniary loss calculations usually fail to recognize or assess adequately the productive economic value of women's household and caretaking activities. For example, if a woman wage earner is injured, the calculation of pecuniary loss damages rarely includes the lost value of her ability to clean and manage the home or to care for family members, despite the productiveness and economic importance of these services. Similarly, if a family member requires extensive caretaking services, that person will be able to recover something for the market value of such services. However, if another family member, more often a female, leaves or curtails her job to provide this care, neither she nor the injured person will be able to recover the caretaker's lost market income, even though the economic unit of which the injured person is a part has undoubtedly suffered a pecuniary loss. Even when courts do acknowledge the economic value of household services, as they are not likely to do when calculating pecuniary loss damages for the wrongful death or disability of a homemaker, the market assigns much lower values to these activities than their true social importance or value, precisely because they are "women's work." . . .

. . . Several empirical studies and evaluations of case reports have demonstrated that women's tort recoveries, particularly for pecuniary loss, are on average well below recoveries for men. These studies magnify the importance of the nonpecuniary loss category of damages for women. . . .

. . . Any limitation that focuses on health care liability will disproportionately affect women simply because, overall, women consume more health care services than men and women comprise the majority of malpractice plaintiffs. . . .

Proposals that would link punitive damages only to economic loss . . . are particularly problematic from the perspective of gender equity. . . . If only the economic loss component of damages counts towards assessing punitive damages, then higher wage earners injured primarily in ways that affect their earning capacity will be able to recover significant punitive damages, without regard to the gravity of the defendant's conduct. . . . Those who are injured primarily in nonpecuniary ways, such as women who have suffered reproductive or sexual injuries, will rarely be able to recover more than the amount of the cap, no matter how egregious the defendant's disregard of health and safety. . . .

. . . The incentives to take women's sexual and reproductive health more seriously will be seriously undermined if a potential injurer knows that the punitive damages . . . will rarely exceed a readily manageable amount such as $250,000.

For example, A.H. Robins continued to market the Dalkon Shield IUD, despite mounting reports of pelvic inflammatory disease, perforated uteruses, infertility, septic abortions and internal corporate reports acknowledging that the infection causing propensity of the product could be greatly reduced for a cost of a few cents per device. . . . A.H. Robins did not urge physicians and women to remove the Dalkon Shields, until the company was assessed punitive damage awards in excess of one million dollars in cases that otherwise had low compensatory damages that averaged $11,000 to $40,000. . . .

An FDA-approval defense from punitive damages should be of particular concern to women. An unusually high number of the drugs and devices that have gone wrong and become alarming public health problems have been gender-specific products for use in women's bodies [including DES, the early versions of birth control pills, IUDs such as the Dalkon Shield and Copper-7, Parlodel, Ritodine, and silicone gel breast implants.]

Notes

1. The Relationship between Tort Remedies and Earnings. A significant component of the undervaluation of women's claims in tort law is their lower assumed, and actual, level of earnings. This factor also affects members of other groups, such as racial minorities. For an analysis of the race and gender effects of using the standard economic data in setting tort recovery awards, see Martha Chamallas, The Architecture of Bias: Deep Structures in Tort Law, 146 U. Pa. L. Rev. 463 (1998). Other sources on gender bias in tort recovery awards include Thomas Koenig & Michael Rustad, His and Her Tort Reform: Gender Injustice in Disguise, 70 Wash. & Lee L. Rev. 1 (1995); Elaine Gibson, The Gendered Wage Dilemma in Personal Injury Damages, in Tort Theory 185 (Ken Cooper-Stephenson & Elaine Gibson eds., 1983); Jane Goodman et al., Money, Sex, and Death: Gender Bias in Wrongful Death Damage Awards, 25 Law & Soc'y Rev. 263 (1991).

Another component is the devaluation of what women do outside of paid employment. For an exhaustive analysis of the many ways in which the law devalues household labor, see Katharine Silbaugh, Turning Labor into Love: Housework and the Law, 91 Nw. U. L. Rev. 1 (1996); see also Nancy C. Staudt, Taxing Housework, 84 Geo. L.J. 1571 (1996) (considering appropriate treatment of home labor in tax law). For a more detailed analysis of the devaluation of women's labor, see pages 342-364 in Chapter 3.

There is some tension between those seeking realistic valuation of household work and those seeking to bring nonmarket understandings to bear on market activities. See, e.g., Margaret Jane Radin, Contested Commodities (1996). Will efforts to quantify and value the contributions that women make to keeping house and raising children actually cheapen, by commodifying, these activities? Is this to women's advantage? Katharine Silbaugh answers this challenge by arguing that economic understandings of housework are not to the exclusion of other understandings, but in addition to them. Silbaugh, Commodification and Women's Household Labor, 9 Yale J.L. & Feminism 81, 95 (1997). In any event, she argues, recognition of the value of household work is urgent with respect to how women on public welfare (and thus the public welfare system) are perceived, how much domestic workers are paid and whether they are covered by various labor laws and workers' compensation programs, women's Social Security entitlements, the enforcement of contracts having to do with caretaking and homemaking, and the treatment of women at divorce. Id. at 110-119.

2. Bias and Remedies. In addition to the disparity in men's and women's earnings and the undervaluation of women's services, Finley points to the failure of judges and juries to understand the kinds of non-economic losses that women experience. Is the problem that women value non-economic loss more than men? See Elizabeth Handsley, Mental Injury Occasioned by Harm to Another: A Feminist Critique, 14 Law & Ineq. 391 (1996) (tort law should recognize greater value women tend to place on relationships, caring, and connection by giving greater recognition to mental injury suffered when others are injured or killed). Or is it instead, or also, that women experience non-economic losses that men simply do not experience?

Bias may also come into play in evaluating defenses to tort actions. For example, many tort actions by women have been dismissed, or no damages found, on the grounds that the injuries alleged by the plaintiff, such as nervous symptoms, pain, emotional distress, and sexual dysfunction were a result of menopause rather than the wrongful conduct of the defendant. These cases are summarized in Phyllis T. Bookspan & Maxine Kline, On Mirrors and Gavels: A Chronicle of How Menopause Was Used as a Legal Defense Against Women, 32 Ind. L. Rev. 1267 (1999).

3. Care as Remedy? Leslie Bender argues that financial responsibility is inadequate recognition for the types of harm flowing from mass torts committed by corporate officers and that remedies should respond to the victims' need for community, care, and relationships by requiring that individual corporate defendants perform the physical and emotional work of caregiving for injured plaintiffs. See Bender, Feminist (Re)Torts: Thoughts on the Liability Crisis, Mass Torts, Power, and Responsibilities, 1990 Duke L.J. 848. Does the impracticality of this proposal suggest how, or why, incompatible caregiving principles are so foreign to our legal system?

Putting Theory into Practice

5-12. The following case is not a sex discrimination case in the ordinary sense, nor are either of the opinions written by a woman judge. Do the opinions reflect any of the characteristics associated with women's "different voice"? Does any of the legal reasoning used or legal precedents distinguished mask assumptions that are biased against women?

Note especially the different fact statements of the two opinions. What accounts for the different choice of facts? Different decisions about relevance? Different methods of legal reasoning? Are these differences ones of "substance" or "method"? How might you rewrite the opinion to better reflect what is meant in this chapter by women's "different voice"?

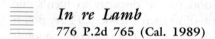

In re Lamb
776 P.2d 765 (Cal. 1989)

BY THE COURT:

Petitioner Laura Beth Lamb was admitted to practice in December 1983. She has no prior record of discipline. On November 13, 1986, she pled nolo contendere to two felony counts of false personation to obtain a benefit. (Pen. Code, §529, subd. 3.) The charges arose from allegations that petitioner took the July 1985 bar examination for her husband.

Upon receiving the record of conviction, we referred the matter to the State Bar for a determination whether the misconduct involved moral turpitude and, if so, what discipline should be imposed. Among other things, the parties stipulated before the State Bar Court that moral turpitude was involved. The hearing officer proposed disbarment, and the review department concurred. Petitioner sought review.

Petitioner's case has sympathetic aspects, and her expressions of contrition seem genuine. Nonetheless, her deceitful crime was exceptionally serious. Considering the public danger inherent in bar exam cheating, and the criminal dishonesty and moral turpitude involved, "[o]nly . . . the most compelling mitigating circumstances" could prevent disbarment. (See Rules Proc. of State Bar, div. V, Stds. for Atty. Sanctions for Prof. Misconduct, std. 3.2 ["Standards"].) Moreover, despite her intellectual promise, the psychological problems which led to petitioner's moral misjudgment cast continuing doubt upon her fitness to practice law. Under the circumstances, we adopt the State Bar Court's proposal and disbar petitioner.

Facts

Before the State Bar Court, the parties stipulated as follows: Petitioner posed as her husband Morgan Lamb in a photograph submitted to the State Bar as identification for the July 1985 bar examination. She later appeared at the examination and represented herself as her husband. To avoid detection, she deliberately smeared her thumbprint and forged her husband's signature on the admission card. Petitioner then took the examination in her husband's place, signing his name on the examination booklets. She passed the examination. An anonymous telephone tip to the State Bar in November 1985 triggered an investigation which led to the current proceeding. The stipulation concedes that petitioner's misconduct involved moral turpitude and constituted a willful violation of her oath and duties as an attorney. . . .

[D]ocumentary evidence originally presented to the criminal court on the issue of sentence was introduced in the State Bar disciplinary proceeding for purposes of mitigation. These documents indicate that petitioner's troubled background led her to value family life and marital harmony at all costs. From 1983 to 1985, after their graduation from law school, petitioner's husband suffered a series of professional setbacks, including loss of employment and bar exam failures in both Texas and California. He reacted with violent rage and depression, and the marriage deteriorated rapidly. Meanwhile, petitioner became pregnant in late 1984. Her pregnancy and general health were endangered by serious complications of her chronic diabetes. The confluence of emotional and physical stress caused petitioner to conclude that her only hope for her unborn child was to accede to her husband's pleas that she take the July 1985 exam in his place.[65]

After her arrest in April 1986, petitioner was fired from her position as an enforcement attorney for the Securities and Exchange Commission. Petitioner initially sought a new job as a lawyer, but ultimately refrained from law practice after her arrest. Petitioner works as a legal secretary. She and her husband are now divorced.

After petitioner's arrest, her criminal counsel referred her to a psychiatrist, Dr. Faerstein, for evaluation and treatment. Dr. Faerstein saw her on three occasions, for a total of five and one-half hours, between May and July 1986. In a February 1987 letter to the superior court, he opined that petitioner's immature personality and physical illness led her to have unrealistic goals, deny her marital problems, and make irrational life judgments. According to Dr. Faerstein, petitioner's misconduct stemmed from "a misguided and psychologically pathological attempt" at saving her marriage.

---

65. Though seven months pregnant and seriously ill when she took the exam, petitioner managed to receive the ninth highest score in the state for July 1985. She entered the hospital immediately after completing the exam. When her condition became life-threatening, labor was induced, and a healthy daughter was born prematurely.

Dr. Faerstein found petitioner genuinely contrite and "amenable to therapy" for her "long-term psychological problems." With an "adequate course of psychotherapy," he concluded, "she may be able to function with sufficient social judgment, restraint and appropriateness as to be able to function as a member of the bar. Such a decision would clearly depend on future opinions from her treating therapist."

In a letter to the court dated February 17, 1987, Francine Bartfield, a licensed clinical social worker, stated that she had been treating petitioner since December 2, 1986. Bartfield confirmed that petitioner was "a confused, socially naive, immature young woman, who [exercised] poor judgment, and acted [not from antisocial motives but from] a distorted notion that she could save her marriage." According to Bartfield, petitioner was contrite, understood her misconduct was "seriously pathological," and was unlikely to "do anything remotely like this again." Petitioner's "prognosis for the future is good," Bartfield wrote, "provided she remains in therapy long enough to develop the psychic structures that have not, yet, matured. . . . This will require a long term commitment. . . ."

Finally, the stipulated record includes letters from relatives, friends, classmates, and professional colleagues. These attest to petitioner's exceptional character, her legal ability, and her life difficulties.

The State Bar Court hearing occurred on November 9, 1987. The parties stipulated to petitioner's completion of 132 community-service hours during the first six months of her probation. . . . In a brief statement, petitioner declared, "I just want to assure you that I'm sorry for what happened, and I wish I could have thought of a better way to handle my problems, but at the time, I just couldn't, and I'm so sorry."

The hearing officer issued his decision on January 25, 1988. In recommending disbarment, the hearing officer reasoned as follows: Because petitioner had committed crimes involving moral turpitude, disbarment was required unless "the most compelling mitigating circumstances clearly predominate. . . ." (Std. 3.2.) In aggravation, the case involved multiple acts of wrongdoing or demonstrated a pattern of misconduct (std. 1.2(b)(ii)), involved dishonesty and concealment (std. 1.2(b)(iii)), and significantly harmed the public and the administration of justice (std. 1.2(b)(iv)). While petitioner's "predicament" was "extreme," her emotional inability to see "ethical options" endangered the public.[66] Despite petitioner's need for long-term treatment to overcome her emotional problems, there was no evidence she had committed "voluntarily" to therapy or had continued it

---

66. In the hearing officer's view, "She could have gone to a battered women's shelter or to any of the persons who wrote letters on her behalf, including her mother, her father, or her sister, for advice, shelter, and, if necessary, for protection against her husband. Her expressed motivation for the impersonation, the protection of her unborn child, is most noble, but placing herself under the stress of the impersonation actually endangered the health of the fetus, as she admits. . . ."

after termination of her probation condition. Hence, mere suspension with a therapy condition would not adequately protect the public.

On February 8, 1988, petitioner moved to reopen proceedings before the hearing officer and to submit additional evidence of her commitment to therapy. (Rules Proc. of State Bar, rule 562.) The motion was denied. . . .

On August 2, 1988, the review department unanimously adopted the hearing officer's disbarment recommendation. This petition followed. . . .

Discussion . . .

Petitioner's deceitful acts were of exceptional gravity. Her conduct threatened innumerable clients with significant injury through unknowing exposure to an unqualified practitioner. It undermined the integrity of the State Bar's admission system, on which public confidence in the competence of attorneys is founded. Substantial harm to "the public [and] the administration of justice" (std. 1.2(b)(iv)) was averted only by an anonymous tip. And, though it did not directly occur in petitioner's "practice" of law, her misconduct evidenced her disregard of the State Bar's admission rules and directly "relate[d]" to her obligations as an attorney. (Cf. std. 2.3.)

As the State Bar suggests on review, because petitioner's criminal breach of professional standards was so morally serious and so dangerous, only the most overwhelming evidence of mitigation could prevent her disbarment in the public interest. Petitioner fails to sustain that heavy burden.

Petitioner urges that her misconduct stemmed from overwhelming physical and psychological pressures. The Standards provide that "extreme emotional difficulties or physical disabilities" at the time of the misconduct may sometimes serve as mitigating circumstances. However, because of the need for public protection against unfit practitioners, a member subject to discipline must first establish "through clear and convincing evidence that he or she no longer suffers from such difficulties or disabilities." (Std. 1.2(e)(iv).) Considering the magnitude of petitioner's misconduct, and its pertinence to her fitness as an attorney, proof of her complete and sustained recovery and rehabilitation must be exceptionally strong. (See std. 1.2(e)(viii).)

We find no such proof here. Petitioner claims the State Bar Court ignored up-to-date evidence of her sincerity and continuing progress in therapy.[5] However, professional evaluations conducted the previous year

---

5. As noted above, the hearing officer denied petitioner's post hearing motion to submit additional evidence of commitment to therapy. Petitioner's counsel claims no documentary evidence "updating" petitioner's progress was presented at the hearing itself because it was assumed that the oral "stipulation" to that effect . . . would suffice. However, it appears that documentary evidence was omitted by the oversight of petitioner's counsel; in the oral

uniformly found a guarded prognosis dependent on a long-term treatment program. Though replete with testimonials to her talent and general character, the record contains, and petitioner submitted, no "clear and convincing" indication of petitioner's *sustained and complete* rehabilitation from chronic personal problems which led to her catastrophic misjudgment. (See In re Conflenti, [624 P.2d 253 (Cal. 1981)].) Thus we, like the State Bar Court, cannot be sure of petitioner's ability to avoid comparable mistakes in her future practice.[6]

Petitioner emphasizes that she has ended the marriage which contributed to her acute stress. She also points out that diabetes, though sometimes controllable, cannot be cured. Thus, she urges, she has done everything possible to eliminate the causes of her misconduct.

However, the consensus of mental health professionals was that petitioner suffered a *chronic emotional disability, independent* of her marital and physical problems, which contributed substantially to her disastrous misjudgment. As noted, we have no convincing evidence that her susceptibility in this regard has ended.

Petitioner appends to her reply brief *in this court* a letter *to us*, dated December 10, 1988, from Francine Bartfield. Bartfield reports that she continued to treat petitioner weekly until July 1988, when loss of insurance coverage forced petitioner to seek less expensive psychological counseling. Bartfield's letter claims petitioner participated sincerely in therapy, gained insight, made personality changes which ensure her misconduct will not recur, has an "excellent" prognosis, and appears fit to practice law "in an ethical and lawful manner." Bartfield states her understanding that petitioner remains in counseling and has no plans to terminate her treatment.

In general, this court does not consider evidence other than that which was before the State Bar Court. ". . . We are particularly wary of extrinsic evidence consisting of 'opinions about petitioner's mental attitude [that are] based largely on petitioner's own out-of-court statements. Such evidence is virtually impossible to evaluate in the absence of cross-examination.' (In re Possino, [689 P.2d 115 (Cal. 1984)].) [Bartfield's December 1988 letter is] inherently unreliable under this test. The [letter merely reflects] personal

---

stipulation, counsel referred merely to a "letter" or "letters" which "your Honor will read." . . .

6. Petitioner notes cases in which we have considered personal, psychological, or physical problems in mitigation without requiring complete recovery or rehabilitation. . . . The only *criminal-conviction* case cited, however, In re Nadrich, [747 P.2d 1146 (Cal. 1988)], involved circumstances not present here. In 1982, Nadrich sustained a federal conviction for distributing LSD in interstate commerce. While serious, Nadrich's conduct was thus less closely related to his honesty, oath, and duties as an attorney than petitioner's here. Moreover, evidence showed that Nadrich became a drug courier to subsidize his involuntary, medically-induced Percodan addiction. He had continued in psychotherapy since 1982, and had abstained from drugs for the intervening six years. Our case law generally supports the view that physical, mental, or emotional problems do not excuse, and may indeed require, discipline necessary for the protection of the public. . . .

beliefs in petitioner's . . . recovery, and [is] based exclusively upon conversations or interviews with [her]. . . ." [quoting Rosenthal v. State Bar, 738 P.2d 740, 742 (Cal. 1987)].

In any event, considering the magnitude of petitioner's transgression, the 1988 Bartfield letter is insufficient evidence of her recovery. The legal, ethical, and moral pressures of daily practice come in many forms. Besides raw avarice and self-aggrandizement, they may include the sincere but misguided desire to please a persuasive or overbearing client. . . . Petitioner's proffered evidence fails to demonstrate the sustained recovery which would satisfy us of her ability to withstand such stresses.

Petitioner appears to exhibit genuine remorse, and she presents numerous testimonials to her integrity. The parties stipulate to her candor and cooperation in the State Bar investigation. These factors may be deemed mitigating in appropriate circumstances. (See std. 1.2(e)(v), (vi), (vii).) Her youth and her apparent absence of antisocial motive also weigh in her favor.[7] Considering the seriousness of petitioner's misconduct, however, this evidence is not sufficient to overturn the disbarment recommendation absent a showing of complete and sustained rehabilitation. . . .

Despite our sympathetic feelings, our paramount duty is to protect the public, the courts, and the profession. Accordingly we, like the State Bar Court, believe that reinstatement proceedings are the means by which petitioner should demonstrate her clear rehabilitation after "the passage of considerable time." (Std. 1.2(e)(viii).) We therefore adopt the State Bar Court's recommendation that petitioner be disbarred. . . .

The Rules of Procedure of the State Bar specify that a petition for reinstatement may not be filed "within five years after the effective date of interim suspension or disbarment or resignation whichever first occurred. . . ."

KAUFMAN, Justice, dissenting.

I dissent.

There was public danger inherent in petitioner's serious misconduct, but the circumstances that gave rise to that misconduct were unique and no longer exist. Contrary to the majority's premise, there is no danger to the public or anyone else from petitioner's one-time, aberrational conduct stemming from circumstances that no longer exist and as to which there is not the slightest possibility of recurrence. Thus, while disbarment in this case will doubtlessly be applauded in some circles, it is wholly unwarranted. It serves only to punish an apparently talented lawyer whose misconduct resulted from the most desperate, life-threatening circumstances. Indeed,

---

7. On the other hand, the absence of a prior disciplinary record counts for little where, as here, the attorney has been in practice only a short time and the current misconduct is serious. (E.g., In re Schwartz[, 644 P.2d 833 (Cal. 1982)]; std. 1.2(e)(i).) Nor is petitioner's community service, imposed as a condition of probation, a substantial mitigating factor.

such drastic discipline serves the public interest less well than would a long period of probation on appropriate conditions, including proof of fitness before returning to the practice of law.

The record discloses the following uncontroverted facts: After adamantly refusing several times her then-husband's insistent demands that she take the bar examination for him, petitioner eventually did so only when she was so desperately physically ill and overwhelmingly mentally intimidated by his barbaric threats and conduct that she felt she had no alternative but to do so, or lose the unborn child with which she was then many months pregnant. The child has long since been born and petitioner's marriage to her former husband has been dissolved. The circumstances were absolutely unique and could not possibly recur.

Petitioner is an insulin-dependent diabetic. When she became pregnant, her physician advised her the pregnancy and its anticipated complications would be life threatening and recommended that she have the pregnancy aborted. She refused. What ensued was nightmarish.

The physician's predictions proved all too true. Petitioner's pregnancy was extremely difficult and provoked severe complications of her diabetes, resulting in substantial, even life-threatening risks to her and her unborn child.

Hormonal changes because of the pregnancy made petitioner's diabetes difficult to control. Yet the doctors told petitioner that inadequate control could result in an overly large baby or render the mother unable to properly nourish the baby. Petitioner was compelled to maintain a strict dietary regimen and to undergo multiple blood tests and insulin injections each day; still, she was unable to achieve control of her diabetic condition. The unstable diabetes produced a toxic substance, acetone, in petitioner's body. She became so weak and dizzy she could hardly hold her head up. Petitioner's physicians told her that the heavy levels of acetone in her body could cause severe spinal deformities or other handicapping or fatal defects in the baby.

Petitioner developed toxemia and proteinuria, both kidney malfunctions, early in her pregnancy. Toxemia raises the blood pressure and can kill the mother, or the fetus, or both. Petitioner's blood pressure was elevated to dangerous levels for both her and her child.

Proteinuria caused her kidneys to over-eliminate protein from the body, depriving it of needed nourishment for herself and the fetus. Petitioner was required to lie still and not to exert herself to avoid expending her slender protein resources. The proteinuria also resulted in massive edema (swelling). Petitioner's legs became so swollen that her skin was split and bleeding. Her attending physicians feared the swelling would enter the womb and threaten the life of the fetus. The proteinuria further exacerbated petitioner's already dangerously high blood pressure. To alleviate the proteinuria, petitioner entered the hospital to receive intravenous blood protein. She also required two blood transfusions.

Petitioner was also hospitalized numerous times during her pregnancy because of uncontrollable vomiting and a dangerous insulin reaction.

In addition, petitioner suffered from proliferative diabetic retinopathy, a condition which causes hemorrhaging of blood vessels in the eyes and can result in blindness. The pregnancy further weakened the blood vessels in petitioner's eyes and increased the risk of blindness.

The complications of the pregnancy not only stripped petitioner of her physical resources, but the extreme stress of the pregnancy, her inability to control her diabetes, and the effects of the acetone, high blood pressure and protein deficiency fundamentally affected petitioner's mental and emotional health as well. She lived in fear that as a result of the pregnancy there was a good chance that she would become blind, the baby would be severely handicapped, or that death would result for either petitioner, the baby, or both. In short, petitioner was mentally and emotionally distraught and confused.

In addition to the overwhelming physical and emotional problems of her pregnancy, petitioner's marriage and home life had become nothing short of a disaster.

Petitioner had met Morgan Lamb in law school. In 1983, after their graduation from law school, Morgan accepted employment at a prestigious law firm in Houston. Petitioner joined Morgan in Houston and they were married in October 1983. After passing the California bar examination, petitioner was hired as an attorney in the Houston office of the Securities and Exchange Commission (SEC). Soon after, however, things began to fall apart.

Morgan failed the Texas bar examination. He began to act depressed and moody. He would cry, hide in bed, or watch television. He also became violently argumentative.

Morgan retook the Texas bar examination. He was so convinced he would fail again that he became hysterical. Although he did pass, he was fired by his law firm. His reactions became more extreme, violent and unpredictable. He would shout and throw things, and even abused petitioner physically.

After these setbacks, petitioner and her husband attempted a new start. They moved to Los Angeles where Morgan had secured a position with a prominent law firm. Petitioner was able to transfer to the Los Angeles office of the SEC.

Morgan sat for the February 1985 California bar examination. By this time, petitioner was pregnant and already so ill she had to take a leave of absence from her job. Then, within a short space of time, Morgan was fired from his position with the Los Angeles law firm and he received a letter notifying him that he had failed the California bar examination. After that, he lost any semblance of self-control. He threw heavy objects and furniture. He smashed large lamps and tore down the curtain rods. He screamed at petitioner and pushed her violently. He threatened to kill himself. He threatened to kill petitioner and the baby. Petitioner was so frightened she removed a gun he kept near the bed. Members of petitioner's family who visited her saw broken glass on the floor, smashed lamps, holes in the wall and bits of food plastered on the wall. Petitioner lived in fear of her husband's violent tantrums.

Petitioner desperately wanted to save her marriage and the lives of herself and her baby. The stress of her home situation placed an intolerable stress on the unborn baby because of petitioner's extremely high blood pressure and physical illnesses. Her doctors told her she had to alleviate the stress or risk the life of her baby or herself. Petitioner was required to lie still because of her dangerous protein deficiency. At times, however, Morgan would shake her and force her to get up and do housework and take care of him.

Morgan became convinced he could not pass the bar examination and repeatedly importuned petitioner to take it for him. She refused numerous times, although she was afraid of what he might do to her or to himself if she did not relent. Each time she refused he would fly into a rage. Finally, in her weak and confused state, petitioner gave in to her husband's demands that she take the exam for him because she could not think of any way to refuse without endangering herself or the baby. She submitted her photograph with his application to take the July 1985 bar examination. Even thereafter, she attempted to convince her husband to take the examination himself and studied with him so that he would be prepared for the examination. For a short time, that plan seemed to be working, but then Morgan began to find more and more excuses not to study. Ultimately, petitioner succumbed to the overwhelming pressures and took the examination posing as her husband.

Immediately upon completing the bar examination, petitioner entered the hospital, where her doctors urged her to have the baby delivered at once or risk the death of both herself and her baby. Petitioner refused because the baby's lungs were too underdeveloped for it to survive outside her body. Petitioner underwent experimental treatments to help the baby's lungs develop. She herself was on the verge of death and required intensive care. After ten days, labor was induced and a healthy baby girl was born, two months prematurely.

Petitioner does not claim that her conduct was justified or legally excused by these circumstances. She in fact stipulated her conduct involved moral turpitude and accepts responsibility for it. Rather, the issue is what discipline is appropriate for petitioner's conduct.

In fastening upon disbarment as the appropriate discipline the majority give insufficient consideration to the mitigating circumstances in this case. The majority discount petitioner's evidence in mitigation because they do not find it "clear and convincing" that she no longer suffers from the extreme emotional and physical difficulties which contributed to her misconduct. (Rules Proc. of State Bar, div. V, Stds. for Atty. Sanctions for

Prof. Misconduct, std. 1.2(e)(iv).) They, like the hearing officer and the review department, reach this conclusion on the basis that petitioner's problems require long-term ongoing psychological therapy, and that she has failed to demonstrate a commitment to such counseling.

Petitioner's "long-term" psychological problems relate to her childhood in a dysfunctional family where one parent abused drugs and all the family members became withdrawn and isolated. Yet it is uncontroverted that, despite the psychological shortcomings attributable to her past, petitioner had always been able to conform her conduct to the highest ethical standards. The record shows that the conduct leading to this offense was completely aberrational and out of character. It was only in the unique combination of situational circumstances here, in which she was on the verge of complete physical, mental and emotional collapse, that she engaged in these bizarre acts.

Petitioner has shown, not only clearly and convincingly, but beyond question, that she has done everything possible to eliminate the extreme emotional and physical difficulties that led to the misconduct. She is, of course, no longer pregnant and no longer suffers the dire complications brought on by the combination of pregnancy and her diabetes. She has ended her marriage to Morgan Lamb. Though she cannot change the fact of her diabetes, she has brought it under control. And she has committed to voluntary, long-term therapy to overcome her problems. A fair reading of the record shows that the hearing officer had before him significant evidence that, despite her need for therapy to overcome her past problems, her therapist was of the opinion that it was extremely unlikely that petitioner "will do anything remotely like this again." In addition, petitioner's probation after her criminal conviction was terminated early, based in part on her success in ongoing therapy. The hearing officer's concern that petitioner would not continue in therapy absent the compulsion of probation has been answered. Petitioner has voluntarily continued in therapy after termination of her probation, and she has submitted a letter to this court from her therapist documenting her continued progress in therapy.[1]

The circumstances established by the record are clearly overwhelmingly mitigating and demand a discipline less severe than disbarment. This court has imposed less severe discipline in cases where the mitigating circumstances were far less compelling and where the misconduct was at least as egregious.

In the recent case of In re Mostman, [765 P.2d 448 (Cal. 1989)], an attorney solicited another person to kill or do bodily injury to a former client. The mitigating circumstances included initial refusals to engage in

---

1. The majority's rejection of this letter is improvident, indeed, inexplicable, in view of the fact the hearing officer's recommendation of disbarment was based almost solely on the alleged lack of demonstrated commitment to therapy, yet he denied petitioner's motion to reopen to submit further evidence on the question.

misconduct, the conduct did not stem from the attorney's practice of law, the attorney was in great emotional distress because he believed the former client had engaged in a campaign of intimidation and harassment against him, and he had been remorseful and cooperative concerning his conviction. Although the attorney had been twice disciplined before, we imposed five years' probation and an actual suspension of two years. In In re Nadrich, [747 P.2d 1146 (Cal. 1988)], an attorney was convicted of possessing, with intent to distribute, 30 grams of LSD. In mitigation, the attorney's addiction to an opiate-based prescription medication, the abrupt cutting-off of his prescription and his withdrawal from law practice had "create[d] an overwhelming financial pressure." We ordered five years' probation with one-year actual suspension. In In re Higbie, [493 P.2d 97 (Cal. 1972)], an attorney conspired to smuggle marijuana into the country. We ordered a two-year suspension with one-year actual suspension, rather than disbarment, because the primary motivation for the wrongful behavior was not personal profit (the attorney acted at the insistence of a friend — a pilot — that the attorney help him find employment, but the pilot was really "setting him up" to claim a bounty) and because of the attorney's prior good record. In In re Kreamer, [535 P.2d 728 (Cal. 1975)], an attorney was convicted of illegal possession of marijuana and of conspiracy to distribute the marijuana. Chronic depression brought on by a breakup with his fiancee led the attorney to use marijuana and to withdraw from his law practice. He turned to drug dealing when faced with mounting debts. We ordered three years' probation and no actual suspension. In In re Jones, [487 P.2d 1016 (Cal. 1971)], an attorney was convicted of subornation of perjury and submission of false evidence. In mitigation he offered his lack of prior disciplinary record, his previous good reputation, his age (66), his difficulty in securing employment to support his 10-year-old twins, and financial difficulties resulting from his criminal and bar proceedings. We imposed three years' probation with one-year actual suspension. (See also Frazer v. State Bar, [737 P.2d 1338 (Cal. 1987),] in which an attorney committed multiple acts of willful misconduct, abandoning clients to their prejudice, obtaining substantial loans under unfair terms and pursuant to misrepresentations, and ultimately losing the money without making any repayment. On the basis of the attorney's agoraphobia as a mitigating factor we ordered five years' probation with actual suspension for eighteen months and until restitution had been made. In Maltaman v. State Bar, [741 P.2d 185 (Cal. 1987)], an attorney willfully disobeyed important court orders and attempted deliberately to mislead a judicial officer. He also lied on several occasions during his disciplinary proceedings. We imposed five years' probation with one-year actual suspension.)

The failure of this court to accord petitioner in this case at least as favorable consideration is to me inexplicable. Petitioner's conduct here was highly situational and a complete departure from her normal conduct. It resulted from an unfortunate and unique coincidence of circumstances, as to which there is virtually no chance of recurrence. Her actions were devoid of any motivation of venality or baseness.

We have often reiterated that the primary purpose of discipline is the protection of the public, the profession and the courts rather than punishment of the attorney. (In re Severo, [714 P.2d 1244 (Cal. 1986)].) Disbarment here serves only to punish petitioner. An alternative is available which would, in my view, far better serve the public, the profession and the courts. To the extent necessary, we may impose conditions of probation which will ensure that the attorney is rehabilitated and the public is protected. I would impose a lengthy probation, with a substantial term of actual suspension and with appropriate probationary conditions, including continued therapy and a demonstration of fitness before returning to the practice of law.

6

Autonomy

Many legal standards assume that individuals are capable of formulating a specific "intent" to act, of exercising free "choice" or "consent," and of behaving as a "reasonable" person. Women's rights advocates make similar assumptions when they argue that women should have greater personal autonomy, more freedom to make their own choices, and sufficient power to control their own lives.

Recent "postmodern" currents in social theory challenge these assumptions and call into question both the capacity of individuals to act independently of societal influences and the capacity of the law to make objective determinations about individuals' intent, consent, and rationality.[1] Postmodern theorists reject the Enlightenment view of the stable, autonomous self, capable of "privileged insight into its own processes and into the 'laws of nature.'" Jane Flax, Postmodernism and Gender Relations in Feminist Theory, in Feminism/Postmodernism 39, 41 (Linda J. Nicholson ed., 1990). As an alternative, these theorists offer a more complicated view of individuals with multiple sources of identity, shaped by institutional and ideological forces that overlap, intersect, and sometimes contradict each other. These structures produce a person's experience of identity and autonomy, but that experience can be misleading. Under the postmodern view, the self is a product of fluctuating possibilities, and individual perceptions of motives and interests are in part socially constructed and constrained.

These and related themes gained influence in law during the 1980s through what became known as the critical legal studies movement (CLS). This loose coalition of progressive academic scholars worked on multiple

---

1. In addition to the legal themes associated with postmodernism that are developed in this chapter, postmodernism has been associated with critiques of the law's rationality, determinacy, and neutrality, which were developed in Chapter 4, and anti-essentialism, which is examined in Chapter 7.

fronts to challenge the law's claim to neutrality, rationality, and objectivity and to seek ways of building a more egalitarian, humane, and collaborative social order. In some respects, however, CLS critiques bumped up against obstacles of their own making. Their assault on the objective foundations of liberal legal thought seemed to undermine any foundations for an alternative framework as well. If neutrality, objectivity, and autonomy were impossible, how could CLS justify its own reform agenda? How could "critics build a unified political and analytic stance from women's varying perceptions of their varying experiences? And what entitles that stance to special authority?" Deborah L. Rhode, Feminist Critical Theories, 42 Stan. L. Rev. 617, 622 (1990).

For advocates of women's rights, however, postmodern and CLS insights have left a productive legacy. A better understanding of the limits of individual autonomy and objectivity can lead to better strategies for expanding perspectives and challenging constraints. Translated into practical terms, postmodern theory makes clear that choice is a relative concept and that in some matters at least, more is better than less. All perspectives are partial, but some are more complete than others — more consistent, coherent, inclusive, and self-critical. On this understanding, autonomy becomes a relative concept that includes not simply freedom from interference by others, but also the ability to flourish among and in relation to others. This chapter, by focusing on legal issues concerned with rape, prostitution, pregnancy, abortion, and welfare, explores these new meanings of autonomy.

A. SEX AND CONSENT

1. "Statutory" Rape: The (Ir)relevance of Consent

≡ *Michael M. v. Superior Court of Sonoma County*
450 U.S. 464 (1981)

Justice REHNQUIST announced the judgment of the Court and delivered an opinion, in which THE CHIEF JUSTICE, Justice STEWART, and Justice POWELL joined.

The question presented in this case is whether California's "statutory rape" law, §261.5 of the Cal. Penal Code Ann. (West Supp. 1981), violates the Equal Protection Clause of the Fourteenth Amendment. Section 261.5 defines unlawful sexual intercourse as "an act of sexual intercourse accomplished with a female not the wife of the perpetrator, where the female is under the age of 18 years." The statute thus makes men alone criminally liable for the act of sexual intercourse.

In July 1978, a complaint was filed in the Municipal Court of Sonoma County, Cal., alleging that petitioner, then a 17½-year-old male, had had unlawful sexual intercourse with a female under the age of 18, in violation of §261.5. The evidence, adduced at a preliminary hearing showed that at approximately midnight on June 3, 1978, petitioner and two friends approached Sharon, a 16½-year-old female, and her sister as they waited at a bus stop. Petitioner and Sharon, who had already been drinking, moved away from the others and began to kiss. After being struck in the face for rebuffing petitioner's initial advances, Sharon submitted to sexual inter-course with petitioner. Prior to trial, petitioner sought to set aside the information on both state and federal constitutional grounds, asserting that §261.5 unlawfully discriminated on the basis of gender. The trial court and the California Court of Appeal denied petitioner's request for relief and petitioner sought review in the Supreme Court of California.

The Supreme Court held that "section 261.5 discriminates on the basis of sex because only females may be victims, and only males may violate the section." [601 P.2d 572, 574 (Cal. 1979).] The court then subjected the classification to "strict scrutiny," stating that it must be justified by a compelling state interest. It found that the classification was "supported not by mere social convention but by the immutable physiological fact that it is the female exclusively who can become pregnant." [Id.] Canvassing "the tragic human costs of illegitimate teenage pregnancies," including the large number of teenage abortions, the increased medical risk associated with teenage pregnancies, and the social consequences of teenage childbearing, the court concluded that the State has a compelling interest in preventing such pregnancies. Because males alone can "physiologically cause the result which the law properly seeks to avoid," the court further held that the gender classification was readily justified as a means of identifying offender and victim. For the reasons stated below, we affirm the judgment of the California Supreme Court.

As is evident from our opinions, the Court has had some difficulty in agreeing upon the proper approach and analysis in cases involving challenges to gender-based classifications. . . .

Underlying these decisions is the principle that a legislature may not "make overbroad generalizations based on sex which are entirely unrelated to any differences between men and women or which demean the ability or social status of the affected class." Parham v. Hughes, [441 U.S. 347, 354 (1979)] (plurality opinion of Stewart, J.). But because the Equal Protection Clause does not "demand that a statute necessarily apply equally to all persons" or require "'things which are different in fact . . . to be treated in law as though they were the same,'" Rinaldi v. Yeager, [384 U.S. 305, 309 (1966)], quoting Tigner v. Texas, [310 U.S. 141, 147 (1940)], this Court has consistently upheld statutes where the gender classification is not invidious, but rather realistically reflects the fact that the sexes are not similarly situated in certain circumstances. Parham v. Hughes, supra;

Califano v. Webster, [430 U.S. 313 (1977)]; Schlesinger v. Ballard, [419 U.S. 498 (1975)]; Kahn v. Shevin, [416 U.S. 351 (1974)]. As the Court has stated, a legislature may "provide for the special problems of women." Weinberger v. Wiesenfeld, [420 U.S. 636, 653 (1975)].

Applying those principles to this case, the fact that the California Legislature criminalized the act of illicit sexual intercourse with a minor female is a sure indication of its intent or purpose to discourage that conduct. Precisely why the legislature desired that result is of course somewhat less clear. This Court has long recognized that "[i]nquiries into congressional motives or purposes are a hazardous matter," . . . and the search for the "actual" or "primary" purpose of a statute is likely to be elusive. . . . Here, for example, the individual legislators may have voted for the statute for a variety of reasons. Some legislators may have been concerned about preventing teenage pregnancies, others about protecting young females from physical injury or from the loss of "chastity," and still others about promoting various religious and moral attitudes towards premarital sex.

The justification for the statute offered by the State, and accepted by the Supreme Court of California, is that the legislature sought to prevent illegitimate teenage pregnancies. That finding, of course, is entitled to great deference. . . . And although our cases establish that the State's asserted reason for the enactment of a statute may be rejected, if it "could not have been a goal of the legislation," Weinberger v. Wiesenfeld, supra, [420 U.S. at 648, n.16], this is not such a case.

We are satisfied not only that the prevention of illegitimate pregnancy is at least one of the "purposes" of the statute, but also that the State has a strong interest in preventing such pregnancy. At the risk of stating the obvious, teenage pregnancies, which have increased dramatically over the last two decades, have significant social, medical, and economic consequences for both the mother and her child, and the State. Of particular concern to the State is that approximately half of all teenage pregnancies end in abortion. And of those children who are born, their illegitimacy makes them likely candidates to become wards of the State.[6]

---

6. The policy and intent of the California Legislature evinced in other legislation buttresses our view that the prevention of teenage pregnancy is a purpose of the statute. The preamble to the Pregnancy Freedom of Choice Act, for example, states: "The legislature finds that pregnancy among unmarried persons under 21 years of age constitutes an increasing social problem in the State of California." Cal. Welf. & Inst. Code Ann. §16145 (West 1980).

Subsequent to the decision below, the California Legislature considered and rejected proposals to render §261.5 gender neutral, thereby ratifying the judgment of the California Supreme Court. That is enough to answer petitioner's contention that the statute was the "'accidental by-product of a traditional way of thinking about females.'" Califano v. Webster, [430 U.S. 313, 320 (1977)] (quoting Califano v. Goldfarb, [430 U.S. 199, 223 (1977)] (Stevens, J., concurring in judgment)). Certainly this decision of the California Legislature is as good a source as is this Court in deciding what is "current" and what is "outmoded" in the perception of women.

We need not be medical doctors to discern that young men and young women are not similarly situated with respect to the problems and the risks of sexual intercourse. Only women may become pregnant, and they suffer disproportionately the profound physical, emotional and psychological consequences of sexual activity. The statute at issue here protects women from sexual intercourse at an age when those consequences are particularly severe.

The question thus boils down to whether a State may attack the problem of sexual intercourse and teenage pregnancy directly by prohibiting a male from having sexual intercourse with a minor female.[8] We hold that such a statute is sufficiently related to the State's objectives to pass constitutional muster.

Because virtually all of the significant harmful and inescapably identifiable consequences of teenage pregnancy fall on the young female, a legislature acts well within its authority when it elects to punish only the participant who, by nature, suffers few of the consequences of his conduct. It is hardly unreasonable for a legislature acting to protect minor females to exclude them from punishment. Moreover, the risk of pregnancy itself constitutes a substantial deterrence to young females. No similar natural sanctions deter males. A criminal sanction imposed solely on males thus serves to roughly "equalize" the deterrents on the sexes.

We are unable to accept petitioner's contention that the statute is impermissibly underinclusive and must, in order to pass judicial scrutiny, be *broadened* so as to hold the female as criminally liable as the male. It is argued that this statute is not *necessary* to deter teenage pregnancy because a gender-neutral statute, where both male and female would be subject to prosecution, would serve that goal equally well. The relevant inquiry, however, is not whether the statute is drawn as precisely as it might have been, but whether the line chosen by the California Legislature is within constitutional limitations.

In any event, we cannot say that a gender-neutral statute would be as effective as the statute California has chosen to enact. The State persuasively contends that a gender-neutral statute would frustrate its interest in effective enforcement. Its view is that a female is surely less likely to report violations of the statute if she herself would be subject to criminal prosecution. In an area already fraught with prosecutorial difficulties, we decline to hold that the Equal Protection Clause requires a legislature to enact a statute so broad that it may well be incapable of enforcement.

---

8. We do not understand petitioner to question a State's authority to make sexual intercourse among teenagers a criminal act, at least on a gender-neutral basis. In Carey v. Population Services International, [431 U.S. 678, 694, n.17 (1977)] (plurality opinion of Brennan, J.), four Members of the Court assumed for the purposes of that case that a State may regulate the sexual behavior of minors, while four other Members of the Court more emphatically stated that such regulation would be permissible. . . .

We similarly reject petitioner's argument that §261.5 is impermissibly overbroad because it makes unlawful sexual intercourse with prepubescent females, who are, by definition, incapable of becoming pregnant. Quite apart from the fact that the statute could well be justified on the grounds that very young females are particularly susceptible to physical injury from sexual intercourse, . . . it is ludicrous to suggest that the Constitution requires the California Legislature to limit the scope of its rape statute to older teenagers and exclude young girls.

There remains only petitioner's contention that the statute is unconstitutional as it is applied to him because he, like Sharon, was under 18 at the time of sexual intercourse. Petitioner argues that the statute is flawed because it presumes that as between two persons under 18, the male is the culpable aggressor. We find petitioner's contentions unpersuasive. Contrary to his assertions, the statute does not rest on the assumption that males are generally the aggressors. It is instead an attempt by a legislature to prevent illegitimate teenage pregnancy by providing an additional deterrent for men. The age of the man is irrelevant since young men are as capable as older men of inflicting the harm sought to be prevented.

In upholding the California statute we also recognize that this is not a case where a statute is being challenged on the grounds that it "invidiously discriminates" against females. To the contrary, the statute places a burden on males which is not shared by females. But we find nothing to suggest that men, because of past discrimination or peculiar disadvantages, are in need of the special solicitude of the courts. Nor is this a case where the gender classification is made "solely for . . . administrative convenience," as in Frontiero v. Richardson, [411 U.S. 677, 690 (1973)] (emphasis omitted), or rests on "the baggage of sexual stereotypes" as in Orr v. Orr, [440 U.S. 268, 283 (1979)]. As we have held, the statute instead reasonably reflects the fact that the consequences of sexual intercourse and pregnancy fall more heavily on the female than on the male.

Accordingly, the judgment of the California Supreme Court is Affirmed.

[The concurring opinion of Justice Stewart is omitted.]

Justice BLACKMUN, concurring in the judgment.

It is gratifying that the plurality recognizes that "[a]t the risk of stating the obvious, teenage pregnancies . . . have increased dramatically over the last two decades" and "have significant social, medical, and economic consequences for both the mother and her child, and the State." . . . There have been times when I have wondered whether the Court was capable of this perception, particularly when it has struggled with the different but not unrelated problems that attend abortion issues. See, for example, the opinions (and the dissenting opinions) in Beal v. Doe, [432 U.S. 438 (1977)]; Maher v. Roe, [432 U.S. 464 (1977)]; Poelker v. Doe, [432 U.S.

519 (1977)]; Harris v. McRae, [448 U.S. 297 (1980)]; Williams v. Zbaraz, [448 U.S. 358 (1980)]; and today's opinion in H.L. v. Matheson, [450 U.S. 398 (1980)].

Some might conclude that the two uses of the criminal sanction — here flatly to forbid intercourse in order to forestall teenage pregnancies, and in *Matheson* to prohibit a physician's abortion procedure except upon notice to the parents of the pregnant minor — are vastly different proscriptions. But the basic social and privacy problems are much the same. Both Utah's statute in *Matheson* and California's statute in this case are legislatively created tools intended to achieve similar ends and addressed to the same societal concerns: the control and direction of young people's sexual activities. . . .

I, however, cannot vote to strike down the California statutory rape law, for I think it is a sufficiently reasoned and constitutional effort to control the problem at its inception. For me, there is an important difference between this state action and a State's adamant and rigid refusal to face, or even to recognize, the "significant . . . consequences" — to the woman — of a forced or unwanted conception. I have found it difficult to rule constitutional, for example, state efforts to block, at that later point, a woman's attempt to deal with the enormity of the problem confronting her, just as I have rejected state efforts to prevent women from rationally taking steps to prevent that problem from arising. See, e.g., Carey v. Population Services International, [431 U.S. 678 (1977)]. See also Griswold v. Connecticut, [381 U.S. 479 (1965)]. In contrast, I am persuaded that, although a minor has substantial privacy rights in intimate affairs connected with procreation, California's efforts to prevent teenage pregnancy are to be viewed differently from Utah's efforts to inhibit a woman from dealing with pregnancy once it has become an inevitability. . . .

I think, too, that it is only fair, with respect to this particular petitioner, to point out that his partner, Sharon, appears not to have been an unwilling participant in at least the initial stages of the intimacies that took place the night of June 3, 1978.* Petitioner's and Sharon's nonacquaintance with

---

*Sharon at the preliminary hearing testified as follows: "Q. [by the Deputy District Attorney]. On June the 4th, at approximately midnight — midnight of June the 3rd, were you in Rohnert Park? "A. [by Sharon]. Yes. "Q. Is that in Sonoma County? "A. Yes. "Q. Did anything unusual happen to you that night in Rohnert Park? "A. Yes. "Q. Would you briefly describe what happened that night? Did you see the defendant that night in Rohnert Park? "A. Yes. "Q. Where did you first meet him? "A. At a bus stop. "Q. Was anyone with you? "A. My sister. "Q. Was anyone with the defendant? "A. Yes. "Q. How many people were with the defendant? "A. Two. "Q. Now, after you met the defendant, what happened? "A. We walked down to the railroad tracks. "Q. What happened at the railroad tracks? "A. We were drinking at the railroad tracks and we walked over to this bush and he started kissing me and stuff, and I was kissing him back, too, at first. Then, I was telling him to stop — "Q. Yes. "A. — and I was telling him to slow down and stop. He said, 'Okay, okay.' But then he just kept doing it. He just kept doing it and then my sister and two other guys came over to where we were and my sister said — told me to get up and come home. And then I didn't — "Q. Yes. "A. — and then my sister and — "Q. All right. "A. — David, one of the boys that were there, started walking home and we stayed there and then later — "Q. All right. "A. — Bruce left Michael, you know. "The Court: Michael being the defendant? "The Witness: Yeah. We was lying there

each other before the incident; their drinking; their withdrawal from the others of the group; their foreplay, in which she willingly participated and seems to have encouraged; and the closeness of their ages (a difference of only one year and 18 days) are factors that should make this case an unattractive one to prosecute at all, and especially to prosecute as a felony, rather than as a misdemeanor chargeable under §261.5. But the State has

---

and we were kissing each other, and then he asked me if I wanted to walk him over to the park; so we walked over to the park and we sat down on a bench and then he started kissing me again and we were laying on the bench. And he told me to take my pants off. I said, 'No,' and I was trying to get up and he hit me back down on the bench and then I just said to myself, 'Forget it,' and I let him do what he wanted to do and he took my pants off and he was telling me to put my legs around him and stuff—

"Q. Did you have sexual intercourse with the defendant? "A. Yeah. "Q. He did put his penis into your vagina? "A. Yes. "Q. You said that he hit you? "A. Yeah. "Q. How did he hit you? "A. He slugged me in the face. "Q. With what did he slug you? "A. His fist. "Q. Where abouts in the face? "A. On my chin. "Q. As a result of that, did you have any bruises or any kind of an injury? "A. Yeah. "Q. What happened? "A. I had bruises. "The Court: Did he hit you one time or did he hit you more than once? "The Witness: He hit me about two or three times.

"Q. Now, during the course of that evening, did the defendant ask you your age? "A. Yeah. "Q. And what did you tell him? "A. Sixteen. "Q. Did you tell him you were sixteen? "A. Yes. "Q. Now, you said you had been drinking, is that correct? "A. Yes. "Q. Would you describe your condition as a result of the drinking? "A. I was a little drunk." App. 20-23.

CROSS-EXAMINATION "Q. Did you go off with Mr. M. away from the others? "A. Yeah. "Q. Why did you do that? "A. I don't know. I guess I wanted to. "Q. Did you have any need to go to the bathroom when you were there. "A. Yes. "Q. And what did you do? "A. Me and my sister walked down the railroad tracks to some bushes and went to the bathroom. "Q. Now, you and Mr. M., as I understand it, went off into the bushes, is that correct? "A. Yes. "Q. Okay. And what did you do when you and Mr. M. were there in the bushes? "A. We were kissing and hugging. "Q. Were you sitting up? "A. We were laying down. "Q. You were lying down. This was in the bushes? "A. Yes. "Q. How far away from the rest of them were you? "A. They were just bushes right next to the railroad tracks. We just walked off into the bushes; not very far.

"Q. So your sister and the other two boys came over to where you were, you and Michael were, is that right? "A. Yeah. "Q. What did they say to you, if you remember? "A. My sister didn't say anything. She said, 'Come on, Sharon, let's go home.' "Q. She asked you to go home with her? "A. (Affirmative nod.) "Q. Did you go home with her? "A. No. "Q. You wanted to stay with Mr. M.? "A. I don't know. "Q. Was this before or after he hit you? "A. Before.

"Q. What happened in the five minutes that Bruce stayed there with you and Michael? "A. I don't remember. "Q. You don't remember at all? "A. (Negative head shake.) "Q. Did you have occasion at that time to kiss Bruce? "A. Yeah. "Q. You did? You were kissing Bruce at that time? "A. (Affirmative nod.) "Q. Was Bruce kissing you? "A. Yes. "Q. And were you standing up at this time? "A. No, we were sitting down.

"Q. Okay. So at this point in time you had left Mr. M. and you were hugging and kissing with Bruce, is that right? "A. Yeah. "Q. And you were sitting up. "A. Yes. "Q. Was your sister still there then? "A. No. Yeah, she was at first. "Q. What was she doing? "A. She was standing up with Michael and David. "Q. Yes. Was she doing anything with Michael and David? "A. No, I don't think so. "Q. Whose idea was it for you and Bruce to kiss? Did you initiate that? "A. Yes. "Q. What happened after Bruce left? "A. Michael asked me if I wanted to go walk to the park. "Q. And what did you say? "A. I said, 'Yes.' "Q. And then what happened? "A. We walked to the park.

"Q. How long did it take you to get to the park? "A. About ten or fifteen minutes. "Q. And did you walk there? "A. Yes. "Q. Did Mr. M. ever mention his name? "A. Yes." Id., at 27-32.

chosen to prosecute in that manner, and the facts, I reluctantly conclude, may fit the crime.

Justice BRENNAN, with whom Justices WHITE and MARSHALL join, dissenting. . . .

. . . I fear that the plurality opinion and Justices Stewart and Blackmun reach the opposite result by placing too much emphasis on the desirability of achieving the State's asserted statutory goal — prevention of teenage pregnancy — and not enough emphasis on the fundamental question of whether the sex-based discrimination in the California statute is substantially related to the achievement of that goal. . . .

[E]ven assuming that prevention of teenage pregnancy is an important governmental objective and that it is in fact an objective of §261.5 . . . , California still has the burden of proving that there are fewer teenage pregnancies under its gender-based statutory rape law than there would be if the law were gender neutral. To meet this burden, the State must show that because its statutory rape law punishes only males, and not females, it more effectively deters minor females from having sexual intercourse.[5]

The plurality assumes that a gender-neutral statute would be less effective than §261.5 in deterring sexual activity because a gender-neutral statute would create significant enforcement problems. . . . However, a State's bare assertion that its gender-based statutory classification substantially furthers an important governmental interest is not enough to meet its burden of proof under Craig v. Boren. Rather, the State must produce evidence that will persuade the court that its assertion is true. See Craig v. Boren, [429 U.S. 190, 200-204 (1976)].

The State has not produced such evidence in this case. Moreover, there are at least two serious flaws in the State's assertion that law enforcement problems created by a gender-neutral statutory rape law would make such a statute less effective than a gender-based statute in deterring sexual activity.

First, the experience of other jurisdictions, and California itself, belies the plurality's conclusion that a gender-neutral statutory rape law "may well be incapable of enforcement." There are now at least 37 States that have enacted gender-neutral statutory rape laws. Although most of these laws protect young persons (of either sex) from the sexual exploitation of older

---

5. Petitioner has not questioned the State's constitutional power to achieve its asserted objective by criminalizing consensual sexual activity. However, I note that our cases would not foreclose such a privacy challenge. The State is attempting to reduce the incidence of teenage pregnancy by imposing criminal sanctions on those who engage in consensual sexual activity with minor females. We have stressed, however, that "[i]f the right of privacy means anything, it is the right of the individual, married or single, to be free from unwarranted governmental intrusion into matters so fundamentally affecting a person as the decision whether to bear or beget a child." Eisenstadt v. Baird, [405 U.S. 438, 453 (1972)] (footnote omitted). Minors, too, enjoy a right of privacy in connection with decisions affecting procreation. Carey v. Population Services International, [431 U.S. 678, 693 (1977)]. Thus, despite the suggestion of the plurality to the contrary . ·. . , it is not settled that a State may rely on a pregnancy-prevention justification to make consensual sexual intercourse among minors a criminal act.

individuals, the laws of Arizona, Florida, and Illinois permit prosecution of both minor females and minor males for engaging in mutual sexual conduct. California has introduced no evidence that those States have been handicapped by the enforcement problems the plurality finds so persuasive.[7] Surely, if those States could provide such evidence, we might expect that California would have introduced it.

In addition, the California Legislature in recent years has revised other sections of the Penal Code to make them gender-neutral. For example, Cal. Penal Code Ann. §286(b)(1) and §288a(b)(1) (West Supp. 1981), prohibiting sodomy and oral copulation with a "person who is under 18 years of age," could cause two minor homosexuals to be subjected to criminal sanctions for engaging in mutually consensual conduct. Again, the State has introduced no evidence to explain why a gender-neutral statutory rape law would be any more difficult to enforce than those statutes.

The second flaw in the State's assertion is that even assuming that a gender-neutral statute would be more difficult to enforce, the State has still not shown that those enforcement problems would make such a statute less effective than a gender-based statute in deterring minor females from engaging in sexual intercourse.[8] Common sense, however, suggests that a gender-neutral statutory rape law is potentially a greater deterrent of sexual activity than a gender-based law, for the simple reason that a gender-neutral law subjects both men and women to criminal sanctions and thus arguably has a deterrent effect on twice as many potential violators. Even if fewer persons were prosecuted under the gender-neutral law, as the State suggests, it would still be true that twice as many persons would be subject to arrest. The State's failure to prove that a gender-neutral law would be a less effective deterrent than a gender-based law, like the State's failure to prove that a gender-neutral law would be difficult to enforce, should have led this Court to invalidate §261.5.

---

7. There is a logical reason for this. In contrast to laws governing forcible rape, statutory rape laws apply to consensual sexual activity. Force is not an element of the crime. Since a woman who consents to an act of sexual intercourse is unlikely to report her partner to the police — whether or not she is subject to criminal sanctions — enforcement would not be undermined if the statute were to be made gender neutral. . . .

8. As it is, §261.5 seems to be an ineffective deterrent of sexual activity. . . . According to statistics provided by the State, an average of only 61 juvenile males and 352 adult males were arrested for statutory rape each year between 1975 and 1978. . . . During each of those years there were approximately one million Californian girls between the ages of 13-17. . . . Although the record in this case does not indicate the incidence of sexual intercourse involving those girls during that period, the California State Department of Health estimates that there were almost 50,000 pregnancies among 13-to-17-year-old girls during 1976. . . . I think it is fair to speculate from this evidence that a comparison of the number of arrests for statutory rape in California with the number of acts of sexual intercourse involving minor females in that State would likely demonstrate to a male contemplating sexual activity with a minor female that his chances of being arrested are reassuringly low. I seriously question, therefore, whether §261.5 as enforced has a substantial deterrent effect. . . .

III

Until very recently, no California court or commentator had suggested that the purpose of California's statutory rape law was to protect young women from the risk of pregnancy. Indeed, the historical development of §261.5 demonstrates that the law was initially enacted on the premise that young women, in contrast to young men, were to be deemed legally incapable of consenting to an act of sexual intercourse.[9] Because their chastity was considered particularly precious, those young women were felt to be uniquely in need of the State's protection.[10] In contrast, young men were assumed to be capable of making such decisions for themselves; the law therefore did not offer them any special protection.

It is perhaps because the gender classification in California's statutory rape law was initially designed to further these outmoded sexual stereotypes,

9. California's statutory rape law had its origins in the Statutes of Westminster enacted during the reign of Edward I at the close of the 13th century (3 Edw. 1, ch. 13 (1275); 13 Edw. 1, ch. 34 (1285)). The age of consent at that time was 12 years, reduced to 10 years in 1576 (18 Eliz. 1, ch. 7, 4). This statute was part of the common law brought to the United States. Thus, when the first California penal statute was enacted, it contained a provision (1850 Cal. Stats., ch. 99, §47, p. 234) that proscribed sexual intercourse with females under the age of 10. In 1889, the California statute was amended to make the age of consent 14 (1889 Cal. Stats., ch. 191, §1, p. 223). In 1897, the age was advanced to 16 (1897 Cal. Stats., ch. 139, §1, p. 201). In 1913 it was fixed at 18, where it now remains (1913 Cal. Stats., ch. 122, §1, p. 212).

Because females generally have not reached puberty by the age of 10, it is inconceivable that a statute designed to prevent pregnancy would be directed at acts of sexual intercourse with females under that age.

The only legislative history available, the draftsmen's notes to the Penal Code of 1872, supports the view that the purpose of California's statutory rape law was to protect those who were too young to give consent. The draftsmen explained that the "[statutory rape] provision embodies the well settled rule of the existing law; that a girl under ten years of age is incapable of giving any consent to an act of intercourse which can reduce it below the grade of rape." Code Commissioners' note, subd. 1, following Cal. Penal Code, p. 111 (1st ed. 1872). There was no mention whatever of pregnancy prevention. . . .

10. Past decisions of the California courts confirm that the law was designed to protect the State's young females from their own uninformed decisionmaking. In People v. Verdegreen, 106 Cal. 211, 214-215, 39 P. 607, 608-609 (1895), for example, the California Supreme Court stated: "The obvious purpose of [the statutory rape law] is the protection of society by protecting from violation the virtue of young and unsophisticated girls. . . . It is the insidious approach and vile tampering with their persons that primarily undermines the virtue of young girls, and eventually destroys it; and the prevention of this, as much as the principal act, must undoubtedly have been the intent of the legislature." As recently as 1964, the California Supreme Court decided People v. Hernandez, [393 P.2d 674], in which it stated that the under-age female "is presumed too innocent and naive to understand the implications and nature of her act. . . . The law's concern with her capacity or lack thereof to so understand is explained in part by a popular conception of the social, moral and personal values which are preserved by the abstinence from sexual indulgence on the part of a young woman. An unwise disposition of her sexual favor is deemed to do harm both to herself and the social mores by which the community's conduct patterns are established. Hence the law of statutory rape intervenes in an effort to avoid such a disposition."

It was only in deciding *Michael M.* that the California Supreme Court decided for the first time in the 130-year history of the statute, that pregnancy prevention had become one of the purposes of the statute.

rather than to reduce the incidence of teenage pregnancies, that the State has been unable to demonstrate a substantial relationship between the classification and its newly asserted goal. . . .

I would hold that §261.5 violates the Equal Protection Clause of the Fourteenth Amendment, and I would reverse the judgment of the California Supreme Court.

Justice STEVENS, dissenting.

Local custom and belief — rather than statutory laws of venerable but doubtful ancestry — will determine the volume of sexual activity among unmarried teenagers.[1] The empirical evidence cited by the plurality demonstrates the futility of the notion that a statutory prohibition will significantly affect the volume of that activity or provide a meaningful solution to the problems created by it. Nevertheless, as a matter of constitutional power, unlike my Brother Brennan . . . , I would have no doubt about the validity of a state law prohibiting all unmarried teenagers from engaging in sexual intercourse. The societal interests in reducing the incidence of venereal disease and teenage pregnancy are sufficient, in my judgment, to justify a prohibition of conduct that increases the risk of those harms.

My conclusion that a nondiscriminatory prohibition would be constitutional does not help me answer the question whether a prohibition applicable to only half of the joint participants in the risk-creating conduct is also valid. It cannot be true that the validity of a total ban is an adequate justification for a selective prohibition; otherwise, the constitutional objection to discriminatory rules would be meaningless. The question in this case is whether the difference between males and females justifies this statutory discrimination based entirely on sex.

The fact that the Court did not immediately acknowledge that the capacity to become pregnant is what primarily differentiates the female from the male does not impeach the validity of the plurality's newly found wisdom. I think the plurality is quite correct in making the assumption that the joint act that this law seeks to prohibit creates a greater risk of harm for the female than for the male. But the plurality surely cannot believe that the risk of pregnancy confronted by the female — any more than the risk of venereal disease confronted by males as well as females — has provided an effective deterrent to voluntary female participation in the risk-creating conduct. Yet the plurality's decision seems to rest on the assumption that the California Legislature acted on the basis of that rather fanciful notion.

---

1. "Common sense indicates that many young people will engage in sexual activity regardless of what the New York Legislature does; and further, that the incidence of venereal disease and premarital pregnancy is affected by the availability or unavailability of contraceptives. Although young persons theoretically may avoid those harms by practicing total abstention, inevitably many will not." Carey v. Population Services International, [431 U.S. 678, 714] (Stevens, J., concurring in part and in judgment).

In my judgment, the fact that a class of persons is especially vulnerable to a risk that a statute is designed to avoid is a reason for making the statute applicable to that class. The argument that a special need for protection provides a rational explanation for an exemption is one I simply do not comprehend.[6]

In this case, the fact that a female confronts a greater risk of harm than a male is a reason for applying the prohibition to her — not a reason for granting her a license to use her own judgment on whether or not to assume the risk. Surely, if we examine the problem from the point of view of society's interest in preventing the risk-creating conduct from occurring at all, it is irrational to exempt 50% of the potential violators. . . . And, if we view the government's interest as that of a *parens patriae* seeking to protect its subjects from harming themselves, the discrimination is actually perverse. Would a rational parent making rules for the conduct of twin children of opposite sex simultaneously forbid the son and authorize the daughter to engage in conduct that is especially harmful to the daughter? That is the effect of this statutory classification.

If pregnancy or some other special harm is suffered by one of the two participants in the prohibited act, that special harm no doubt would constitute a legitimate mitigating factor in deciding what, if any, punishment might be appropriate in a given case. But from the standpoint of fashioning a general preventive rule — or, indeed, in determining appropriate punishment when neither party in fact has suffered any special harm — I regard a total exemption for the members of the more endangered class as utterly irrational.

In my opinion, the only acceptable justification for a general rule requiring disparate treatment of the two participants in a joint act must be a legislative judgment that one is more guilty than the other. The risk-creating conduct that this statute is designed to prevent requires the participation of two persons — one male and one female.[7] In many situations it is probably true that one is the aggressor and the other is either an unwilling, or at least a less willing, participant in the joint act. If a statute authorized punishment

6. A hypothetical racial classification will illustrate my point. Assume that skin pigmentation provides some measure of protection against cancer caused by exposure to certain chemicals in the atmosphere and, therefore, that white employees confront a greater risk than black employees in certain industrial settings. Would it be rational to require black employees to wear protective clothing but to exempt whites from that requirement? It seems to me that the greater risk of harm to white workers would be a reason for including them in the requirement — not for granting them an exemption.

7. In light of this indisputable biological fact, I find somewhat puzzling the California Supreme Court's conclusion, quoted by the plurality . . . that males "are the *only* persons who may physiologically cause the result which the law properly seeks to avoid." [601 P.2d 572, 575 (1979)] (emphasis in original). Presumably, the California Supreme Court was referring to the equally indisputable biological fact that only females may become pregnant. However, if pregnancy results from sexual intercourse between two willing participants — and the California statute is directed at such conduct — I would find it difficult to conclude that the pregnancy was "caused" solely by the male participant.

of only one participant and required the prosecutor to prove that that participant had been the aggressor, I assume that the discrimination would be valid. Although the question is less clear, I also assume, for the purpose of deciding this case, that it would be permissible to punish only the male participant, if one element of the offense were proof that he had been the aggressor, or at least in some respects the more responsible participant in the joint act. The statute at issue in this case, however, requires no such proof. The question raised by this statute is whether the State, consistently with the Federal Constitution, may always punish the male and never the female when they are equally responsible or when the female is the more responsible of the two.

It would seem to me that an impartial lawmaker could give only one answer to that question. The fact that the California Legislature has decided to apply its prohibition only to the male may reflect a legislative judgment that in the typical case the male is actually the more guilty party. Any such judgment must, in turn, assume that the decision to engage in the risk-creating conduct is always — or at least typically — a male decision. If that assumption is valid, the statutory classification should also be valid. But what is the support for the assumption? It is not contained in the record of this case or in any legislative history or scholarly study that has been called to our attention. I think it is supported to some extent by traditional attitudes toward male-female relationships. But the possibility that such a habitual attitude may reflect nothing more than an irrational prejudice makes it an insufficient justification for discriminatory treatment that is otherwise blatantly unfair. For, as I read this statute, it requires that one, and only one, of two equally guilty wrongdoers be stigmatized by a criminal conviction. . . .

[I do not] find at all persuasive the suggestion that this discrimination is adequately justified by the desire to encourage females to inform against their male partners. Even if the concept of a wholesale informant's exemption were an acceptable enforcement device, what is the justification for defining the exempt class entirely by reference to sex rather than by reference to a more neutral criterion such as relative innocence? Indeed, if the exempt class is to be composed entirely of members of one sex, what is there to support the view that the statutory purpose will be better served by granting the informing license to females rather than to males? If a discarded male partner informs on a promiscuous female, a timely threat of prosecution might well prevent the precise harm the statute is intended to minimize.

Finally, even if my logic is faulty and there actually is some speculative basis for treating equally guilty males and females differently, I still believe that any such speculative justification would be outweighed by the paramount interest in evenhanded enforcement of the law. A rule that authorizes punishment of only one of two equally guilty wrongdoers violates the essence of the constitutional requirement that the sovereign must govern impartially.

I respectfully dissent.

Wendy W. Williams, *The Equality Crisis: Some Reflections on Culture, Courts, and Feminism*
7 Women's Rts. L. Rep. 175, 185-187, 200 (1982)

The original statutory rape laws were quite explicitly based on [a view of the man as aggressor in sex]. Then, as is true even today, men were considered the natural and proper initiators of sex. In the face of male sexual initiative, women could do one of two things, yield or veto, "consent" or decline. What normal women did not, *should* not, do was to initiate sexual contact, to be the sexual aggressor. The premise underlying statutory rape laws was that young women's chastity was precious and their naivete enormous. Their inability knowingly to consent to sexual intercourse meant that they required protection by laws which made their consent irrelevant but punished and deterred the "aggressive" male. . . .

Statutory rape is, in criminal law terms, a clear instance of a victimless crime, since all parties are, by definition, voluntary participants. In what sense, then, can Rehnquist assert that the woman is victim and the man offender? One begins to get an inkling when, later, the Justice explains that the statutory rape law is "protective" legislation: "The statute here protects women from sexual intercourse at an age when those consequences are particularly severe." [*Michael M.*, 450 U.S. 464, 471-472 (1981).] His preconceptions become manifest when, finally, Rehnquist on one occasion calls the statute a "rape" statute [id. at 475] — by omitting the word "statutory" inadvertently exposing his hidden assumptions and underlining the belief structure which the very title of the crime, "statutory rape," lays bare.

. . . The notion that men are frequently the sexual aggressors and that the law ought to be able to take that reality into account in very concrete ways is hardly one that feminists could reject out of hand (I'm thinking here of sexual harassment and forcible rape, among other things); it is therefore an area . . . in which we need to pay special attention to our impulses lest we inadvertently support and give credence to the very social constructs and behaviors we so earnestly mean to oppose. . . . At this point, we need to think as deeply as we can about what we want the future of women and men to be. De we want equality of the sexes — or do we want justice for two kinds of human beings who are fundamentally different?

Notes

1. Consent and Statutory Rape. Technically, consent is not an element of statutory rape. Does it follow, however, as Williams maintains, that the offense is "a clear instance of a victimless crime since all parties are, by definition, voluntary participants"? Do the facts presented in Justice Rehnquist's and Justice Blackmun's opinions suggest that the willingness of the victim's participation in the events giving rise to the prosecution might have had some relevance to the case? Notice that these two Justices reach the same conclusion in the case, but apparently based on different views about Sharon's level of consent. From Justice Rehnquist, all we know is that Sharon was "struck in the face" for "rebuffing" Michael's advances and then she "submitted" to sexual intercourse. Such factual situations support a common justification for statutory rape law: that underage girls "consent" to sexual relationships that we, as a society, can and should recognize as exploitative. Michelle Oberman, Statutory Rape Laws, A.B.A. J., Aug. 1996, at 86. However, the Court does not defend the result on this ground. Would such a rationale be convincing?

Under Justice Blackmun's reasoning, Sharon's "not unwilling" participation in the incident suggests that it wasn't *real* rape but a lesser, "statutory" version. Do you agree with Justice Blackmun that Sharon was not an unwilling participant? What consequences should follow from your answer?

If Sharon was "willing," what does this say about the majority's justification for the sex-based statute — that the fear of pregnancy is an effective deterrent?

California revised its statutory rape law in 1993. Like many other jurisdictions, California now imposes liability for consensual sex only if there is a gap in age between the parties and the victim is under the statutory age of consent. See Cal. Penal Code §261.5 (West 2001) (any person who engages in unlawful sexual intercourse with a minor who is not more than three years older or three years younger than the perpetrator is guilty of a misdemeanor, whereas any person over the age of 21 years who engages in unlawful sexual intercourse with a minor under 16 years of age may be guilty of either a misdemeanor or a felony). The reform occurred after several women who pressured teenage boys into sex received light penalties for other offenses. Susannah Miller, Note, The Overturning of *Michael M.*: Statutory Rape Law Becomes Gender-Neutral in California, 5 UCLA Women's L. J. 289, 292 (1994).

As noted above, California's statute, like those of all but 15 states, is now sex-neutral. Oberman, supra, at 32. One commentator, Susannah Miller, asserts that the legislative motivation behind the change is not recognition of female sexual autonomy, but instead recognition of changing societal attitudes toward male sexuality — attitudes that realize that boys, as well as girls, are vulnerable to sexual exploitation by older people. Miller, supra, at 297. According to Miller and other commentators, although the reform was motivated by concerns about sexual exploitation of boys and not the sexual autonomy of girls, the revised statute is a positive step for women because, on its face, it takes a more equal stance toward the sexes. First, the new §261.5 recognizes that women, as well as men, can be sexually aggressive. Second, it acknowledges that boys, as well as girls, can be emotionally traumatized by statutory rape. Thus, under the language of the law, the sexes are treated equally. Id. at 298-299. What concept of equality underpins this reform? Is the empirical assumption on which it is based more accurate than the empirical assumptions reflected in the earlier statute? Are there other equal protection issues implicated by statutory rape laws?

Beginning in the mid-1990s, California and several other states launched a campaign to toughen enforcement of statutory rape laws and to publicize the illegality of sex with minors. Congress encouraged such policies under the 1996 welfare law. Public health agency reports indicate that a majority of births to teen mothers involve fathers 20 years old or older. Cheryl Wetzstein, California Fights Statutory Rape with Media, Cops, Wash. Times, Sept. 13, 1997, at A2. According to then-Governor Wilson, punishing "gross irresponsibility" among older men was an important part of the effort to "attack [unwed childbearing] on all fronts." Id. Critics, however, pointed out that only 8 percent of the mothers had partners who were five years older and who would be subject to statutory rape prohibitions. Id.; Judith Havermann, Statutory Rape-Pregnancy Link Reassessed, Wash. Post, Apr. 16, 1999, at A3. Some of these critics also charged that statutory rape laws have been selectively enforced against men who are "particularly unpopular, socially unacceptable, of the wrong color, or who make the mistake of having intercourse with a woman from a socially upstanding (and well connected) family. . . . [Such laws] are both paternalistic and patriarchal and should be firmly resisted." Richard Delgado, Selective Enforcement Targets "Unpopular" Men, A.B.A. J., Aug. 1996, at 87.

How should prosecutors decide whether to pursue statutory rape violations? Should the key factors be consent, age, pregnancy, or abuse of position (e.g., teachers or athletic coaches)? Would it be legitimate to target enforcement resources against men who father children and who end up on welfare? What about using fornication laws in an effort to "restore disgrace to teenage pregnancy"? James Brooke, An Old Law Chastising Pregnant Teenagers, N.Y. Times, Oct. 28, 1996, at A1. Such statutes remain on the books in about ten states, but are very rarely used. Richard A. Posner & Katharine B. Silbaugh, A Guide to America's Sex Laws (1996).

How should courts and/or legislatures respond to a practice of allowing men arrested for statutory rape to marry their pregnant partners in lieu of jail time. Ellen Goodman, A Criminal Record — Or a Wedding Band?, Boston Globe, Sept. 12, 1996, at A15. If the mother wants to marry and lacks alternative sources of economic support, does it make sense to create a "family out of a felony"? Id. If the premise of statutory rape laws is that a minor below a certain age is not mature enough to consent to sex, is she mature enough to consent to marriage?

Some states have abolished the separate crime of statutory rape altogether. Illinois, for example, criminalizes acts of sexual penetration "by the use of force or threat of force," without proof of nonconsent. 720 Ill. Comp. Stat. Ann. 5/12-13(1) (West Supp. 2001). Consent is an affirmative defense, which "means a freely given agreement to the act of sexual penetration or sexual conduct in question. Lack of verbal or physical resistance or submission by the victim resulting from the use of force or threat of force by the accused shall not constitute consent." 720 Ill. Comp. Stat. Ann. 5-12/17(a) (West 1993). Would a conviction be justified under this statute against the defendant in *Michael M.*?

How about a promiscuity defense? As Michelle Oberman explains:

> [A]t common law, the accused was permitted a complete defense if he could demonstrate credible evidence of prior promiscuous behavior on the part of the minor. The Model Penal Code's statutory rape provision preserves this defense, noting in the commentary that prior sexual promiscuity "rebuts the presumption of naivete and inexperience" that justifies the criminal nature of statutory rape. . . .
>
> Not all jurisdictions maintain the promiscuity defense, and among those that do, not all equate promiscuity with non-virginity. Yet even in those cases which attempt to differentiate promiscuity from non-virginity, the ambiguous nature of the term "promiscuous" results in an intrusive and value-laden inquiry into the victim's sexual past.

Michelle Oberman, Turning Girls into Women: Re-Evaluating Modern Statutory Rape Law, 85 J. Crim. L. & Criminology 15, 32-33 (1994). Oberman argues that the promiscuity defense introduces the issue of consent into statutory rape law: when the girl has had previous sexual experience, prosecutors do not press charges, juries do not convict, or sentences are light. Id. at 53.

What is the nature of the "consent" to sex demonstrated by girls like Sharon? Oberman argues:

> [E]ven assuming that girls do experience sexual pleasure and desire, these are only two of a multiplicity of factors which induce their consent to sex.
>
> The stories girls tell about the "consensual" sex in which they engage reflect a poignant subtext of hope and pain. Girls express longing for emotional attachment, romance, and respect. At the same time, they suffer enormous insecurity and diminished self-image. These two factors are clearly interrelated — the worse girls feel about themselves, the more they look to males for ratification of the women that they are becoming. The importance of being attractive to males takes on a central role in many girls' lives. This may be evidenced by seemingly innocuous behaviors such as increased bathroom time in the morning before school, and wearing make-up and padded bras, but it is

also seen in the epidemic of dieting among girls, and the devastating toll taken by the eating disorders that result from distorted body image. Teenage girls recognize that they are, or at least that they should be, objects of desire. The romantic aspirations which girls report reflect these insecurities. Girls want boyfriends, relationships, or somebody who will hold them and tell them that they are wanted.

Girls negotiate access to the fulfillment of these emotional needs by way of sex. A girl who wants males to find her attractive, who wants acceptance and popularity, might reasonably consent to sex with a popular boy, to multiple popular boys, or with any partner who can persuade her that she is attractive and desirable. Males recognize, and occasionally exploit, girls' insecurity. Thus, it is no coincidence that the ubiquitous "pick up" line almost always plays to a female's desire for acceptance. . . .

Id. at 65-66. Oberman concludes:

> Modern statutory rape law . . . classifies intercourse as either consensual sex or rape. However, from the girl's vantage point, her consent may have been so fraught with ambivalence that it was meaningless. This search for evidence of nonconsent (or force) causes the finder of fact to turn away from the story told by the girl in order to evaluate the story from a "neutral" vantage point.
>
> As a result, the legal system never comes to terms with the ambiguity inherent in the sexual choices made by teenage girls. . . . If girls' autonomy is to be taken seriously, the law must evaluate the sexual decisions they make, and formulate a legal response which enhances the likelihood that those decisions are autonomous ones.

Id. at 70. Can you imagine a "legal response which enhances the likelihood that [teenage girls' decisions to have sex] are autonomous ones"? The dilemma of desire and exploitation is heightened for girls who have developmental disabilities. See Sherene Razack, From Consent to Responsibility, From Pity to Respect: Subtexts in Cases of Sexual Violence Involving Girls and Women with Developmental Disabilities, 19 Law & Soc. Inquiry 891 (1994). Do statutory rape laws contribute to the ideology of women as sexual victims, thereby disempowering young women from taking an active part in defining their own sexuality?

Would a preferable alternative to heightened statutory rape prosecution be school-based health programs providing contraception and birth control information, thus "empower[ing] young women to be responsible as participants or not in heterosexual relations" rather than as victims who must be taught "only how to respond to heterosexual male questions — Yes or No . . ."? Michelle Fine & Nancie Zane, Bein' Wrapped Too Tight: When Low-Income Women Drop Out of High School, in Dropouts from School: Issues, Dilemmas, and Solutions 23, 41-42 (Lois Weis, Eleanor Farrar, & Hugh G. Petrie eds., 1989). Is teenage pregnancy an indication of failure or an indication of teenage girls exercising their own autonomous choices? See excerpts of Regina Austin, Sapphire Bound?, 1989 Wis. L. Rev.

539 (arguing that efforts to curb teenage pregnancy represent imposition of white, middle-class values on black teenagers).

2. Statutory Rape: A Violent Crime?   Although statutory rape cases are generally viewed as instances of consensual sexual activity, at least one court has held that nonforcible statutory rape of a 13-year-old girl is in fact a violent crime for purposes of determining sentencing for an unrelated federal criminal offense. In United States v. Shannon, 110 F.3d 382, 389 (7th Cir. 1996), cert. denied, 522 U.S. 888 (1997), Judge Posner, writing for the majority, upheld a district court's determination that the defendant's prior conviction for nonforcible statutory rape was a crime of violence within the meaning of the Federal Sentencing Guidelines. The Guidelines define a crime of violence as a felony that either involves force, attempted force, or threat of force, or involves conduct that presents a serious potential risk of physical injury to the victim. U.S.S.G. §4B1.2(1). Judge Posner examined the Wisconsin statutory rape law in question to determine "whether the conduct punished by the . . . law under which the defendant was convicted involves a serious risk of physical injury." 110 F.3d at 386. The Wisconsin statute criminalizes "sexual contact or sexual intercourse with a person who has not attained the age of 16." Wis. Stat. Ann. §948.02(2) (West 2000). According to Posner,

> . . . The Wisconsin statute covers a lot of ground, and some of it may not be crime of violence ground. But sexual intercourse with a 13-year-old is in our view a crime of violence within the meaning of the guidelines, because it does present a serious risk of physical injury. A 13-year-old is unlikely to have a full appreciation of the disease and fertility risks of intercourse, and accurate knowledge of contraceptive and disease-preventive measures, and the maturity to make a rational comparison of the costs and benefits of premarital intercourse. . . . Furthermore, a very young girl who becomes pregnant is quite likely not to take good care of herself and her fetus, making the pregnancy more dangerous to both. . . .
>
> To the extent that a 13-year-old is incapable of appreciating the full risk and consequences of sexual intercourse, her ensuing pregnancy and parturition (or abortion) must be considered at least quasi-involuntary and could be considered, therefore, a physical injury even if the pregnancy is normal. And sex with a 13-year-old creates a significant risk of pregnancy. . . . The pregnancy of a 13-year-old is arguably a physical injury in itself and clearly creates a substantial risk of secondary physical injury to mother or fetus from complications of the pregnancy. . . .

110 F.3d at 387-388.

Judge Posner's opinion leaves open the question of whether sexual intercourse with a 14- or 15-year-old or sexual contact short of intercourse with a younger girl would necessarily constitute a crime of violence. Would these facts change the discussion?

The Wisconsin statute above is sex-neutral. Would a rape of a 13-year-old boy by a woman teacher be a crime of violence, assuming the facts of the indictment show the sexual acts to be "consensual"? Should it make a difference if the defendant is male or female?

Putting Theory into Practice

6-1. A law in State X defines statutory rape as sexual intercourse with a child under the age of 16. Colleen, age 20, gives birth to a baby fathered by 16-year-old Shane, who at the time of conception was 15. Colleen was, for several years, Shane's babysitter; their sexual relationship began when Shane was 12, and Shane never complained to his parents about the sexual liaison with Colleen. Colleen is charged with statutory rape, but pleads to the lesser crime of contributing to a child's misconduct. Colleen applies for public assistance, and the Department of Social Services petitions the court to order Shane to contribute to the child's financial support. The Parentage Act of State X, which mandates that parents provide support for their children, makes no exception for parents who are minors. What result? See State ex rel. Hermesmann v. Speyer, 847 P.2d 1273 (Kan. 1993) (minor parent is liable for child support despite status as victim of statutory rape).

2. Rape: Distinguishing Consent and Nonconsent

≡ *Catharine A. MacKinnon, Toward a Feminist*
Theory of the State
172-178 (1989)

Under law, rape is a sex crime that is not regarded as a crime when it looks like sex. The law, speaking generally, defines rape as intercourse with force or coercion and without consent. . . .

Rape cases finding insufficient evidence of force reveal that acceptable sex, in the legal perspective, can entail a lot of force. This is both a result of the way specific facts are perceived and interpreted within the legal system and the way the injury is defined by law. The level of acceptable force is adjudicated starting just above the level set by what is seen as normal male sexual behavior, including the normal level of force, rather than at the victim's, or women's, point of violation. In this context, to seek to define rape as violent not sexual is as understandable as it is futile. . . .

The point of defining rape as "violence not sex" has been to claim an ungendered and nonsexual ground for affirming sex (heterosexuality) while rejecting violence (rape). The problem remains what it has always been: telling the difference. The convergence of sexuality with violence, long used at law to deny the reality of women's violation, is recognized by rape survivors with a difference: where the legal system has seen the intercourse in rape, victims see the rape in intercourse. . . . To know what is wrong with rape, [we must] know what is right about sex. If this, in turn, proves difficult, the difficulty is as instructive as the difficulty men have in telling the difference when women see one. Perhaps the wrong of rape has proved so difficult to define because the unquestionable starting point has been that rape is defined as distinct from intercourse, while for women it is difficult to distinguish the two under conditions of male dominance. . . .

The law of rape divides women into spheres of consent according to indices of relationship to men. Which category of presumed consent a woman is in depends upon who she is relative to a man who wants her, not what she says or does. These categories tell men whom they can legally fuck, who is open season and who is off limits, not how to listen to women. The paradigm categories are the virginal daughter and other young girls, with whom all sex is proscribed, and the whorelike wives and prostitutes, with whom no sex is proscribed. Daughters may not consent; wives and prostitutes are assumed to, and cannot. Actual consent or nonconsent, far less actual desire, is comparatively irrelevant. If rape laws existed to enforce women's control over access to their sexuality, as the consent defense implies, no would mean no, marital rape would not be a widespread exception, and it would not be effectively legal to rape a prostitute. . . .

The adjudicated line between rape and intercourse commonly centers on some assessment of the woman's "will." But how should the law or the accused know a woman's will? . . .

The deeper problem is that women are socialized to passive receptivity; may have or perceive no alternative to acquiescence; may prefer it to the escalated risk of injury and the humiliation of a lost fight; submit to survive. Also, force and desire are not mutually exclusive under male supremacy. So long as dominance is eroticized, they never will be. Some women eroticize dominance and submission; it beats feeling forced. Sexual intercourse may be deeply unwanted, the woman would never have initiated it, yet no force may be present. So much force may have been used that the woman never risked saying no. Force may be used, yet the woman may prefer the sex — to avoid more force or because she, too, eroticizes dominance. Women and men know this. Considering rape as violence not sex evades, at the moment it most seems to confront, the issue of who controls women's sexuality and the dominance/submission dynamic that has defined it. When sex is violent, women may have lost control over what is done to them, but absence of force does not ensure the presence of that control. Nor, under conditions of male dominance, does the presence of force make an interaction nonsexual. If sex is normally something men do to women, the issue is less whether there was force than whether consent is a meaningful concept.

≣ *Federal Rule of Evidence 412*

(a) Evidence generally inadmissible. — The following evidence is not admissible in any civil or criminal proceeding involving alleged sexual misconduct except as provided in subdivisions (b) and (c):

(1) Evidence offered to prove that any alleged victim engaged in other sexual behavior.

(2) Evidence offered to prove any alleged victim's sexual predisposition.

(b) Exceptions. —

(1) In a criminal case, the following evidence is admissible, if otherwise admissible under these rules:

> (A) evidence of specific instances of sexual behavior by the alleged victim offered to prove that a person other than the accused was the source of semen, injury or other physical evidence;
>
> (B) evidence of specific instances of sexual behavior by the alleged victim with respect to the person accused of the sexual misconduct offered by the accused to prove consent or by the prosecution; and
>
> (C) evidence the exclusion of which would violate the constitutional rights of the defendant.

State v. Colbath
540 A.2d 1212 (N.H. 1988)

SOUTER, Justice. . . .

During the noon hour of June 28, 1985, the defendant, Richard Colbath, went with some companions to the Smokey Lantern tavern in Farmington, where he became acquainted with the female complainant. There was evidence that she directed sexually provocative attention toward several men in the bar, with whom she associated during the ensuing afternoon, the defendant among them. He testified that he had engaged in "feeling [the complainant's] breasts [and] bottom [and that she had been] rubbing his crotch" before the two of them eventually left the tavern and went to the defendant's trailer. It is undisputed that sexual intercourse followed; forcible according to the complainant, consensual according to the defendant. In any case, before they left the trailer the two of them were joined unexpectedly by a young woman who lived with the defendant, who came home at an unusual hour suspecting that the defendant was indulging in faithless behavior. With her suspicion confirmed, she became enraged, kicked the trailer door open and went for the complainant, whom she assaulted violently and dragged outside by the hair. It took the intervention of the defendant and a third woman to bring the melee to an end.

As soon as the complainant returned to town she accused the defendant of rape, and the police promptly arrested and charged him accordingly. During the initial investigation on the evening of June 28, Candice Lepene, the daughter of the tavern's owner, told the police that she had seen the complainant leave the tavern with the defendant during the afternoon. In a subsequent written statement, however, she said that she did not know whether the complainant had left with a companion or alone, but she described the complainant prior to her departure as "a girl with dark hair hanging all over everyone and making out with Richard Colbath and a few others." The police did not disclose this statement to the defense prior to trial, although defense counsel knew that Lepene had given a statement and subpoenaed her to testify at trial. . . .

. . . The trial itself focused on the defense of consent, which the defendant addressed by his own testimony about the complainant's behavior with him at the bar and at the trailer, and by seeking to elicit exculpatory evidence that the complainant had appeared to invite sexual advances from other men as well as from himself in the hours preceding the incident. Some of this evidence was excluded and some admitted. During the charge, however, the judge instructed the jury, subject to the defendant's objection, that evidence of the complainant's behavior with other men was irrelevant to the issues before them. This appeal followed the verdict of guilty. . . .

[The issue in this appeal is] raised by the defendant's objection to the jury instruction that evidence of the complainant's behavior with men other than the defendant in the hours preceding the incident was immaterial, or irrelevant, to the question of the defendant's guilt or innocence. . . .

The trial judge first allowed the defense to elicit testimony from the complainant that at one point during the afternoon she had been sitting in the lap of one of the defendant's companions named Gillis. Shortly after that testimony, and before the defendant had called any witnesses, the State moved for a ruling *in limine* to prohibit defense witnesses from testifying about the complainant's behavior in the tavern with any other men than the defendant. . . . [The court issued] a ruling granting the prosecution's motion, for the stated reason that the complainant's "conduct with others is not material on the issue of whether or not she consented to have sexual intercourse with" the defendant. The court later supplemented this reason with the alternative grounds that the testimony in question was inadmissible as evidence of character, and inadmissible as well under the rape shield law, [N.H. Rev. Stat. Ann. 632-A:6 (1988)], which bars evidence of "[p]rior consensual sexual activity between the victim and any person other than" the defendant, when offered to prove an offense under . . . chapter 632-A.

This ruling did not end the matter, however. Although the court had ordered defense counsel not to ask his own witnesses about the complainant's behavior with third parties, further evidence of such activity did come in through the State's next witness, Candice Lepene. She testified on direct examination that the complainant had left the tavern in the company of various men several times during the afternoon, and the court admitted her statement to the police, quoted above, that she had seen "a girl with dark hair hanging all over everyone and making out with Richard Colbath and a few others." On cross-examination Lepene was permitted to testify further about her earlier statement.

When it came time for jury instructions, however, the court's charge reflected its earlier ruling on the motion *in limine*. First, the judge reminded the jurors that he had received evidence of the complainant's public activities with various men on the afternoon of the 28th, including her own admission that she had engaged in close physical contact with at least one man besides the defendant. Then the judge explained that he had allowed the jury to hear this testimony only to provide background information, and he went on to instruct the jurors plainly that the complainant's "conduct with other individuals is not relevant on the issue of whether or not she gave consent to sexual intercourse." . . .

The defendant has suggested that we address this issue simply as one of statutory construction [of the rape shield law's bar against admitting evidence of "prior consensual sexual activity between the victim and any person other than the defendant," N.H. Rev. Stat. Ann. §632-A:6 (1988)], by holding that the shield law's mandate to exclude evidence of "consensual sexual activity" with others can have no application to overt sexual activity of the complainant in a bar open to the public. This was, indeed, the position taken by defendant's trial counsel, who relied on prior construction of the act as intended to honor the complainant's interest in preserving the privacy of intimate activity. See, e.g., State v. Howard, [426 A.2d 457, 461 (N.H. 1981)]; Berger, Man's Trial, Woman's Tribulation: Rape Cases in the Courtroom, 77 Colum. L. Rev. 1, 41 (1977) ("[T]he trauma of baring one's intimate past to the eyes of the world — turning one's bedroom into a showcase — overshadows the usual discomfort of testifying . . . to one's biases, lies or even convictions of criminal acts." (footnote omitted)).

While we do not reject this argument, we are not disposed to rule on it here. The State did not address the argument's merits at all in its brief, and we prefer not to rule on a legal position so little remarked upon by one side of the case when, as here, existing precedent provides a clear conceptual framework for the resolution of the issue before us.

That framework began to emerge in the first appeal to question the applicability of the shield law after its enactment in 1975. See 1975 N.H. Laws 302:1; State v. Howard, [supra]. Despite the absolute terms of the shield law's prohibition, our cases have consistently reflected the common recognition that such a statute's reach has to be limited by a defendant's State and national constitutional rights to confront the witnesses against him and to present his own exculpatory evidence. N.H. Const. pt. I, art. 15; State v. Howard, [supra]; U.S. Const. amend. VI. . . . Thus, this court has held that a rape defendant must be given an opportunity to demonstrate that the "probative value [of the statutorily inadmissible evidence] in the context of that particular case outweighs its prejudicial effect on the prosecutrix." State v. Howard, [426 A.2d at 461]. But see Tanford and Bocchino, Rape Victim Shield Laws and the Sixth Amendment, 128 U. Pa. L. Rev. 544, 570 (1980) (countervailing prejudice is risk of jury irrationality, not harm to victim's feelings). . . .

As soon as we address this process of assigning relative weight to prejudicial and probative force, it becomes apparent that the public character of the complainant's behavior is significant. On the one hand, describing a complainant's open, sexually suggestive conduct in the presence of patrons of a public bar obviously has far less potential for damaging the sensibilities than revealing what the same person may have done in the company of another behind a closed door. On the other hand, evidence of public displays of general interest in sexual activity can be taken to indicate a contemporaneous receptiveness to sexual advances that cannot be inferred from evidence of private behavior with chosen sex partners. See State v. Goulet, [529 A.2d 879, 881 (1987)] (evidence of sexual promiscuity not necessarily admissible in spite of shield law); State v. Shute, [446 A.2d 1162 (1982)] (evidence of mere predilection for promiscuity too remote).

In this case, for example, the jury could have taken evidence of the complainant's openly sexually provocative behavior toward a group of men as evidence of her probable attitude toward an individual within the group. Evidence that the publicly inviting acts occurred closely in time to the alleged sexual assault by one such man could have been viewed as indicating the complainant's likely attitude at the time of the sexual activity in question. It would, in fact, understate the importance of such evidence in this case to speak of it merely as relevant. We should recall that the fact of intercourse was not denied, and that the evidence of assault was subject to the explanation that the defendant's jealous living companion had inflicted the visible injuries. The companion's furious behavior had a further bearing on the case, as well, for the jury could have regarded her attack as a reason for the complainant to regret a voluntary liaison with the defendant, and as a motive for the complainant to allege rape as a way to explain her injuries and excuse her undignified predicament. With the sex act thus admitted, with the evidence of violence subject to exculpatory explanation, and with a motive for the complainant to make a false accusation, the outcome of the prosecution could well have turned on a very close judgment about the complainant's attitude of resistance or consent.

Because little significance can be assigned here either to the privacy interest or to a fear of misleading the jury, the trial court was bound to recognize the defendant's interest in presenting probably crucial evidence of the complainant's behavior closely preceding the alleged rape. Thus, the facts of this case well illustrate the court's previous observation that the sexual activities of a complainant immediately prior to an alleged rape may well be subject to a defendant's constitutional right to present evidence. . . . The demand of the Constitutions is all the clearer when those activities were carried on in a public setting. Because the jury instruction effectively excluded the evidence in question, the conviction must be reversed and the case remanded for a new trial.

Reversed and remanded.

Susan Estrich, Rape
95 Yale L.J. 1087, 1102-1105 (1986)

My view is that . . . a "negligent rapist" should be punished, albeit — as in murder — less severely than the man who acts with purpose or knowledge, or even knowledge of the risk. First, he is sufficiently blame-worthy for it to be just to punish him. Second, the injury he inflicts is sufficiently grave to deserve the law's prohibition.

The traditional argument against negligence liability is that punishment should be limited to cases of choice, because to punish a man for his stupidity is unjust and, in deterrence terms, ineffective. Under this view, a man should only be held responsible for what he does knowingly or purposely or at least while aware of the risks involved. . . .

If inaccuracy or indifference to consent is [the best that a man can do] because he lacks the capacity to act reasonably, then it might well be unjust and ineffective to punish him for it. But such men will be rare . . . at least as long as voluntary drunkenness is not equated with inherent lack of capacity. More common is the case of the man who could have done better but didn't; could have paid attention, but didn't; heard her say no, or saw her tears, but decided to ignore them. Neither justice nor deterrence argues against punishing this man.

Certainly, if the "reasonable" attitude to which a male defendant is held is defined according to a "no means yes" philosophy that celebrates male aggressiveness and female passivity, there is little potential for unfairness in holding men who fall below *that* standard criminally liable. Under such a low standard of reasonableness, only a very drunk man could honestly be mistaken as to a woman's consent, and a man who voluntarily sheds his capacity to act and perceive reasonably should not be heard to complain here — any more than with respect to other crimes — that he is being punished in the absence of choice.

But even if reasonableness is defined — as I argue it should be — according to a rule that "no means no," it is not unfair to hold those men who violate the rule criminally responsible, provided that there is fair warning of the rule. I understand that some men in our society have honestly believed in a different reality of sexual relations, and that many may honestly view such situations differently than women. But, it is precisely because men and women may perceive these situations differently, and because the injury to women stemming from the different male perception may be grave, that it is necessary and appropriate for the law to impose a duty upon men to act with reason, and to punish them when they violate that duty.

In holding a man to such a standard of reasonableness, the law signifies that it considers a woman's consent to sex to be significant enough to merit a man's reasoned attention. In effect, the law imposes a duty on men to open their eyes and use their heads before engaging in sex — not to read a woman's mind, but to give her credit for knowing her own mind when she speaks it. The man who has the inherent capacity to act reasonably, but fails to do so, has made the blameworthy choice to violate this duty. While the injury caused by purposeful conduct may be greater than that caused by negligent acts, being negligently sexually penetrated without one's consent remains a grave harm, and being treated like an object whose words or actions are not even worthy of consideration adds insult to injury. This dehumanization exacerbates the denial of dignity and autonomy which is so much a part of the injury of rape, and it is equally present in both the purposeful and negligent rape.

By holding out the prospect of punishment for negligence, the law provides an additional motive for men to "take care before acting, to use their faculties and draw on their experience in gauging the potentialities of contemplated conduct." We may not yet have reached the point where men are required to ask verbally. But if silence does not negate consent, at least the word "no" should, and those who ignore such an explicit sign of non-consent should be subject to criminal liability.

Notes

1. Rape in the United States. By even the most conservative estimates, the United States has the highest rate of reported rape in the Western industrial world. According to governmental and crime center research, one out of every six U.S. women and one out of 33 U.S. men have experienced an attempted or completed rape as a child and/or adult. 2000 National Victim Assistance Academy, www.ojp.usdoj.gov/ovc/assist/nvaa2000/academy/J-10-SA.htm. A longitudinal survey of a national probability sample of adult women found that approximately 13 percent of adult women have been victims of completed rape during their lifetime. Id. (citing this and other studies). About 8 percent of U.S. adolescents have been victims of at least one sexual assault. Id. More than 52 percent of all rape and sexual assault victims are females younger than 25. Id. (citing studies). See also National Victim Center and Crime Victims Research and Treatment Center, Rape in America: A Report to the Nation 2 (1992).

These estimates are, however, widely believed to grossly understate the number of actual sexual assaults because victims' fear, humiliation, and doubts about being believed make rape the most unreported felony. See U.S. Senate, Committee on the Judiciary, Majority Staff Report, 103rd Cong., 1st Sess., The Response to Rape: Detours on the Road to Equal Justice (1994). Complaints of rape made to law enforcement agencies, like complaints of other crimes, can be deemed false or baseless by police investigators. These offenses are called "unfounded" and are excluded from crime counts. The "unfounded" rate for forcible rape is higher than for any other violent crime; for example, in 1995, 8 percent of forcible rape complaints were "unfounded," while the average for all violent crimes reported to the Federal Bureau of Investigation for its Crime Index was 2 percent. Crime in the United States 1995: Uniform Crime Reports 24 (1996).

Problems in police handling of rape complaints have recently received national attention, partly as a result of path-breaking investigative journalism by the Philadelphia Inquirer. Its investigation revealed that a third of the cases reported to the police unit handling sexual assaults were classified as 2701, a code calling for further investigation in matters not designated a crime. Because 2701 calls need not be reported as part of crime statistics, there is no way to tell if any further investigation is conducted. Follow-ups of these cases revealed that many had been botched by an underfunded, poorly trained, and inadequately monitored sex crimes unit. Public hearings led the police department to invite women and children's advocacy groups to form an oversight committee for 2701 cases. About a third of those cases were determined to be rapes and another quarter to be sexual crimes. Although Philadelphia no longer uses that coding, other jurisdictions continue to use similar systems, as do many college campuses, for confidential reports that complainants never take to police. See A Philadelphia Story, Ms., June/July 2001, at 24; Mark Fazlollah, National Rape Statistics Highly Suspect, Women's Enews, http://www.womensenews.org, Jan. 8, 2001. Such practices underscore the need for greater internal and external monitoring of law enforcement practices. Relying on trained female officers to take rape reports can also be highly effective in reducing disproportionate rates of unfounded charges. Beverly J. Ross, Does Diversity in Legal Scholarship Make a Difference: A Look at the Law of Rape, 100 Dick. L. Rev. 795, 812 (1996).

2. The Causes of Rape. Explanations for rape fall along three main dimensions: individual, sociobiological, and cultural. At the individual level:

> Profiles of rapists indicate that many are primarily attracted to power; they want the feeling of domination, adventure, and self-esteem that comes from coercive sex. Other men emphasize anger; rape is a means to punish or avenge some wrong by a particular woman, women in general, or another adversary. Most rapists blame their victims, and some stress situational influences such as peer pressure or drug and alcohol abuse. Exposure to family violence during childhood increases the likelihood that men will engage in sexually violent activities as adults.

Deborah L. Rhode, Speaking of Sex 121 (1997). See Diana Scully, Understanding Sexual Violence: A Study of Convicted Rapists (1990).

At the sociobiological level, some theorists suggest evolutionary causes for male sexual assault. In essence, these theorists maintain that for men, having intercourse with a large number of fertile females has "favorable reproductive consequences." For men who have difficulty attracting willing partners, coercive sex is "adaptive" and likely to be favored by natural selection. Randy Thornhill & Craig T. Palmer, A Natural History of Rape: Biological Bases of Sexual Coercion 190-191 (2000); Neil M. Malamuth, The Confluence Model of Sexual Aggression: Feminist and Evolutionary Perspectives, in Sex, Power, Conflict: Evolutionary and Feminist Perspectives 269 (David M. Buss & Neil M. Malamuth eds., 1996). According to sociobiologists, an evolutionary theory is necessary to explain why reproductive-age women are so overrepresented among rape victims, why penile-vaginal rape is disproportionately likely with these women, and why rape so rarely results in other physical injury or death. Owen Jones, Sex, Culture and the Biology of Rape: Toward Explanation and Prevention, 87 Cal. L. Rev. 827, 897-899 (1999). From this perspective, contemporary feminists appear on the wrong track when they claim that rape is more about power than sex and when they downplay the relevance of women's dress as a precipitating cause. Thornhill & Palmer, supra, at 182-183.

Most feminists, for their part, have found these sociobiological accounts inadequate in several respects, as have other experts from within the scientific community. Not only is the evidentiary basis for many of their claims extremely weak or highly contested, but also their accounts fail to explain many key facts. If rape is so adaptive and genetically hardwired, why is there so much cultural variation in attitudes toward rape, and why are there societies in which rape is so rare? See Peggy Reeves Sanday, Female Power and Male Dominance: On the Origins of Sexual Inequality (1981) (comparative anthropological study of male and female power in various cultures). If rape is primarily a reproductive strategy, why are about a third of victims too young or old to reproduce, and why are nonvaginal assaults so common? And if rape is predominantly about sex, not power, and sexually alluring dress is such a significant contributing factor, what accounts for the massive rape of women in wartime? Bosnian women were not wearing miniskirts. Martin Miller, Rape, L.A. Times, Feb. 20, 2000, at E1; Frans B.M. de Waal, Survival of the Rapist, N.Y. Times, Apr. 2, 2000, §7, at 24.

3. Rape Law Reform. To date, rape law reform in this country has come in two waves: (1) the Model Penal Code (MPC) revision of the 1950s and (2) laws responding to the feminist critique of rape laws, which began in the 1970s. The MPC, which stimulated statutory reform in many states, abolished a common provision requiring the victim to offer the "utmost" or "reasonable" resistance. This reform refocused the crime from the consent of the woman to the conduct of the defendant. To increase the likelihood of convictions and to reduce the scope for idiosyncratic or biased judgments, the MPC also divided rape into three categories. First-degree felony rape was reserved for life-threatening conduct where the parties were strangers or where the defendant inflicted serious bodily harm. Life-threatening rape between acquaintances was a second-degree felony. Less serious abuses were grouped under a new third-degree felony of "gross sexual imposition." See

Stephen J. Schulhofer, Taking Sexual Autonomy Seriously, 11 Law & Phil. 35, 36-38 (1992).

In the next wave of law reform, new legislation, such as rape shield statutes, was designed to protect the victims as well as to obtain convictions. By the close of the 1990s, only Utah and Arizona had not enacted such statutes, but both had recognized a rape shield doctrine by means of the common law. See State v. Johns, 615 P.2d 1260, 1263 (Utah 1980); State ex rel. Pope v. Superior Court, 545 P.2d 946, 953 (Ariz. 1976). In addition, in 1994, Congress enacted Federal Rule of Evidence 413 as part of the Violent Crime Control and Law Enforcement Act. Under Rule 413, evidence of the defendant's prior instances of sexual violence is admissible in a federal sexual assault trial, even if relevant only as evidence of his disposition or propensity to engage in such conduct. The rule, because it carves out an exception to the usual doctrine that prior similar acts are inadmissible to show propensity, has generated controversy. See Mark A. Sheft, Federal Rule of Evidence 413: A Dangerous New Frontier, 33 Am. Crim. L. Rev. 57 (1995).

Other reforms spurred by women's rights advocates included further refinements in the grading systems for sexual offenses, reformulation of statutory provisions with gender-neutral language, elimination or relaxation of the marital rape exemption, and alterations in the substantive require-ments of force and nonconsent to facilitate convictions. Schulhofer, supra, at 38-39. Professor Estrich's proposal to require holding a defendant responsi-ble for rape when the woman has said "no" represents an effort to further consent standards. Does it go too far? Far enough? Would it meet MacKinnon's concern about the hazy line between sex and rape? What proposal would meet MacKinnon's concern?

Although definitive studies have not been done to measure the effects of rape law reform in all jurisdictions, existing research suggests that the effects have been fairly modest. For example, one of the most comprehensive studies, which investigated the impact of rape law reform in three "strong" and three "weak" jurisdictions, concluded that many of the desired improvements were modest or nonexistent. See generally Cassia Spohn & Julia Horney, Rape Law Reform: A Grassroots Revolution and Its Impact (1992); see also Cassia Spohn & Julie Horney, The Impact of Rape Law Reform on the Processing of Simple and Aggravated Rape Cases, 86 J. Crim. L. 861 (1996) (finding little or no change in rape reports, arrests, or convictions but some improvement in the treatment of complaints); Ronet Bachman & Raymond Paternoster, A Contemporary Look at the Effects of Rape Law Reform: How Far Have We Really Come?, 84 J. Crim. L. & Criminology 554, 574 (1993) (finding little effect on either victim behavior reports or rates of imprisonment as a result of statutory rape law reform). According to Gregory Matoesian, "[W]hile rape reform has had some symbolic impact on society, such legislation has not increased overall rates of conviction or plea bargains substantially, nor has rape shield legislation, which was designed to prohibit introduction of the victim's sexual history during the trial, affected defense attorneys' trial tactics." Matoesian, Reproducing Rape: Domination Through Talk in the Courtroom 17 (1993). How important are "symbolic" impacts, compared to material impacts? Does the fault lie in the inadequacy of reform measures or in the strength of underlying rape "myths" and "narratives" in the wider culture as well as in the legal culture?

4. Consent and Gender. Nowhere, perhaps, are views about the meaning of consent as divided as in the context of rape: perspectives range from Justice Souter's assumption that consent can be determined by "evidence of public displays of general interest in sexual activity" to Catharine MacKinnon's claim that consent is merely a label placed on the kind of sex of which the law approves under conditions of gender inequality. Note that Justice Souter's view presupposes the greatest amount of female self-control, MacKinnon's the least. Which understanding is likely to lead to rules giving women greater sexual autonomy?

Rape is not the only area of the law in which the issue of consent may be influenced by gendered understandings of individual autonomy and consent. Jane Aiken groups rape with sexual harassment, battering, and dispropor-tionate family burdens as all part of a system of "double binds," produced by the assumption that women consent to behaviors that would otherwise be considered moral and legal harms. Jane Harris Aiken, Intimate Violence and the Problem of Consent, 48 S.C. L. Rev. 615 (1997); see also Martha Chamallas, Consent, Equality, and the Legal Control of Sexual Conduct, 61 S. Cal. L. Rev. 777 (1988), and the discussion of surrogate parenting contracts at pages 1116-1134.

Much of the recent debate on rape law has centered on how or whether to redefine consent. Susan Estrich, for example, proposes that the law should focus on the reasonableness of the defendant's intent and should assume that a reasonable man understands "no" to mean "no." Other feminists worry that such a reformulation would fail to protect a woman frightened into passivity. They would focus on the coerciveness of the man's conduct or require an affirmative yes. See, e.g., Lynne Henderson, What Makes Rape a Crime, 3 Berkeley Women's L.J. 193, 216-217 (1988); Lani Anne Remick, Read Her Lips: An Argument for a Verbal Consent Standard on Rape, 141 U. Pa. L. Rev. 1103 (1993). Steven Schulhofer argues that the focus of criminal prohibitions should be protecting women's autonomy — her physical integrity and her capacity to choose, unconstrained by impermissi-ble pressures and limitations. Schulhofer, supra at, 71-72; Schulhofer, Unwanted Sex: The Culture of Intimidation and the Failure of Law (2000). To that end, Schulhofer proposes a crime of nonviolent sexual misconduct for invading women's bodily integrity in the face of ambivalence, objection, or silence. Such a statute would encompass economic pressure or other coercive behavior to obtain sex. See also Linda R. Hirshman & Jane E.

Larson, Hard Bargains: The Politics of Sex 268-272 (1998) (arguing that by forcing the stronger partner to bargain with the weaker for explicit consent, we begin to ensure mutuality in adult sexual relationships).

How would you evaluate these proposals? Would they be fair to defendants? Are they consistent with cultural practices? Consider the findings of one 1988 study in which a third of surveyed college women admitted that they had sometimes said no to sex when they meant yes, largely out of a desire to avoid appearing promiscuous. Charlotte Muehlenhard & I. Hollabaugh, Do Women Sometimes Say No When They Mean Yes?: The Prevalence and Correlates of Women's Token Resistance to Sex, 54 J. Personality & Soc. Psychol. 872 (1988). See also Andrew E. Taslitz, Patriarchal Stories I: Cultural Rape: Narratives in the Courtroom 5 S. Cal. Rev. L. & Women's Stud. 389, 468 (1996) (reporting 1991 study in which one third of surveyed college students believed that women who say no often mean maybe or yes). Do you think a study today would yield similar findings? To what extent should the criminal law seek to change rather than reflect attitudes about sexual abuse?

How should the law assess consent in these contexts? Must it be viewed as an either/or proposition — either present or absent? Are there alternative ways of viewing consent? If the law recognized consent to be a relative term, would it be possible to differentiate acceptable and abusive sex?

5. Cultural Attitudes and "Rape Myths." What assumptions underlie the court's analysis in *Colbath*? Do any of these assumptions reflect "rape myths"?

The classic rape myths fall into four main categories: (1) only certain women (i.e., those with "bad" reputations) are raped; (2) only certain men (i.e., psychopaths) rape; (3) women invite or deserve rape by their appearance and behavior; and (4) women fantasize or fabricate rape, motivated by desire, revenge, blackmail, jealousy, guilt, or embarrassment. Rhode, Speaking of Sex, supra, at 120-121; Mary Koss et al., No Safe Haven: Male Violence Against Women at Home, at Work, and in the Community 7-17, 185-87 (1994); Morrison Torrey, When Will We Be Believed? Rape Myths and the Idea of a Fair Trial in Rape Prosecutions, 24 U.C. Davis L. Rev. 1013, 1025 (1991). These myths help to explain both legal doctrines that treat rape differently from other crimes and decisionmaking by judges, juries, and law enforcement personnel that impedes prosecution of rape cases.

Susan Estrich attributes the strict requirements of resistance, corroboration, and prompt complaint to the male "nightmare" of being accused of rape. Estrich, supra, at 1140-1141. She also charges that the resistance requirement judges women by a male standard — that of "a reasonable person . . . who does not scare easily, one who does not feel vulnerability, one who is not passive, one who fights back, not cries. The reasonable woman, it seems, is not a schoolboy 'sissy.' She is a real man." Id. at 1114.

Other commentators stress deeper causes. For example, Lynne Henderson maintains that "the hatred of women, the devaluation of women, and the patriarchal structure that has silenced women and promoted male aggression seem to be preferable places to search for an explanation." Henderson, supra, at 197. In accounting for the persistence of these myths, commentators stress both cultural influences and individual traits. The eroticization of male aggression in popular films, television, fiction, and video games, together with gender stereotypes in media coverage of sexual assault, plays a role. See Rhode, Speaking of Sex, supra, at 83-85, 128; Helen Benedict, Virgin or Vamp: How the Press Covers Sex Crimes (1992). Studies of rape myths held by women also find that lack of empathy for victims is correlated with low levels of self-esteem, happiness, and satisfaction, as well as with emotional dependence on men. Gloria Cowan, Women's Hostility Toward Women and Rape and Sexual Harassment Myths, 6 Violence Against Women, 238 244 (2000).

Despite the persistence of rape myths, there is little evidence to support them. For example, studies find that the vast majority of complainants have "good" reputations (four-fifths in one District of Columbia survey) and that many "normal" men have engaged in nonconsensual sex. Virtually every study of male college students has found that a substantial number, typically around a third and sometimes close to half, acknowledge that they would commit rape if they could be sure of not being caught. A majority also report engaging in some sexually coercive behavior; Torrey, supra, at 1023-1024; Lynne Henderson, Rape and Responsibility, 11 Law & Phil. 127, 170 (1993); Susan Basow, Gender: Stereotypes and Roles 318 (1992). Studies of convicted rapists also reveal that few are "deviant," depraved, or deprived in the conventional sense; the vast majority are involved in consensual sexual relationships and are more sexually active than the average male. Rhode, Speaking of Sex, supra, at 121. Contrary to widespread belief, false reports are no higher for rape than for other crimes. Estimated rates are around 2 percent. Torrey, supra, at 1028. Given the humiliation, intrusiveness, and trauma associated with bringing charges, underreporting, and not overclaiming, is the far greater problem in cases of sexual assault.

Despite their lack of empirical foundations, these rape myths continue to have a powerful influence on the attitudes of offenders, complainants, police, prosecutors, jurors, and judges. Such cultural narratives shape decisions about whether to report or prosecute a crime, whether to convict or acquit a defendant, how to treat a complainant, and how to sentence a defendant. Andrew E. Taslitz, Patriarchal Stories I: Cultural Rape Narratives in the Courtroom, 5 S. Cal. Rev. L. & Women's Stud. 387, 393 (1996); Sherene Razack, From Consent to Responsibility, from Pity to Respect: Subtexts in Cases of Sexual Violence Involving Girls and Women with Developmental Disabilities, 19 Law & Soc. Inquiry 891 (1995); Lisa A. Binder, "With more than admiration he admired": Images of Beauty and Defilement in Judicial Narratives of Rape, 18 Harv. Women's L.J. 265

(1995); Alinor C. Sterling, Undressing the Victim: The Intersection of Evidentiary and Semiotic Meanings of Women's Clothing in Rape Trials, 7 Yale J.L. & Feminism 87 (1995); Susan F. Hirsch, Interpreting Media Representations of a "Right of Madness": Law and Culture in the Construction of Rape Identities, 19 Law & Soc. Inquiry 1023 (1994); Karen M. Kramer, Rule by Myth: The Social and Legal Dynamics Governing Alcohol-Related Acquaintance Rapes, 47 Stan. L. Rev. 115 (1994); Kevin Brown, The Social Construction of a Rape Victim: Stories of African American Males About the Rape of Desiree Washington, 1992 U. Ill. L. Rev. 997 (1992).

Consider the following examples:

- Parents who shrugged off the rapes of high school girls by the Los Angeles "Spur Posse" (whose members competed with each other for sexual conquests) on the ground that "those girls were trash." Emily Jaffe, Girls Who Go Too Far, Newsweek, July 22, 1991, at 58.

- A juror who voted to acquit William Kennedy Smith of the rape of a woman he picked up in a bar because "he's too charming and too good-looking to have to resort to violence for a night out." Lynn Hecht Schafran, The Importance of Voir Dire in Rape Trials, Trial, Aug. 1992, at 26.

- A judge who referred to a 12-year-old victim as an "unusually promiscuous young lady." Lynn Hecht Schafran, Documenting Gender Bias in the Courts, 70 Judicature 280, 289 (1987).

- A juror who voted to acquit three St. John's University fraternity brothers of a widely publicized gang rape on the assumption that "Hell hath no fury like a woman scorned." Peggy Reeves Sanday, A Woman Scorned: Acquaintance Rape on Trial 238 (1996).

- Sports fans who labeled Desiree Washington, the complainant who brought rape charges against Mike Tyson, as a "gold digger" who needlessly destroyed a revered role model for conduct that she had invited by going to his hotel room alone. Brown, supra.

- A judge who voted to overturn a rape conviction on the theory that "when an adult woman goes to a man's room, [she certainly has] to realize that they [are] not going upstairs to play Scrabble." State v. Rusk, 424 A.2d 720, 733-734 (Cole, J., dissenting).

How would you respond to such views? Many experts have concluded that rape law reforms are unlikely to be effective without challenging such cultural attitudes. See, e.g., Elizabeth Iglesias, Rape, Race, and Representation, 49 Vand. L. Rev. 869, 887 (1996) ("feminists must target the social spaces where dominant cultural narratives actually influence the decisions made at different points in the case processing system"); Lisa Frohmann &

Elizabeth Mertz, Legal Reform and Social Construction: Violence, Gender, and the Law, 19 Law & Soc. Inquiry 829, 835 (1995) ("[t]o effectuate social change through legal reform . . . , more formal attempts to alter statutes and policies must be supplemented by analysis of the social and cultural patterns that shape the implementation, interpretation, and effect of law"). If these experts are correct, what can lawyers and scholars do to assist the process?

6. Rape Trauma Syndrome. To what extent can experts be helpful in determining the question of consent? In the course of improving clinical treatment for rape victims, researchers have developed a profile of rape victims known as the "rape trauma syndrome." The syndrome is character-ized by two phases: Phase I or the "acute phase" is a period of disorganization in which the victim is either emotionally out of control — crying, sobbing, restless, or tense — or extraordinarily controlled — calm, composed, or subdued. Headaches, fatigue, sleep problems, and gastrointes-tinal and genitourinary disturbances are common during this period. Phase II or the "long-term reorganization process" is a period of nightmares, phobic reactions, sexual fears, and changes in routine. See Ann Wolbert Burgess & Lynda Lytle Holmstrom, Rape Trauma Syndrome, in Forcible Rape: The Crime, the Victim, and the Offender 315 (Duncan Chappell et al., eds. 1977).

Some courts have approved use of expert testimony about rape trauma syndrome to help prove that a forcible assault, rather than consensual sex, occurred. State v. Marks, 647 P.2d 1292, 1299 (Kan. 1982); Street v. United States, 602 A.2d 141 (D.C. 1992). Typically, admissibility of this testimony is limited to rehabilitating the victim's credibility rather than proving the prosecution's case-in-chief. See, e.g., People v. Hampton, 746 P.2d 947 (Colo. 1987) (evidence admissible to explain delay in reporting); People v. Reid, 475 N.Y.S.2d 741 (Sup. Ct. 1984) (evidence admissible to explain retraction of accusations). Several cases have held that the evidence cannot be introduced to prove that the rape occurred, on the theory that this evades the fact-finding province of the jury. See, e.g., State v. Saldana, 324 N.W.2d 227 (Minn. 1982); People v. Bledsoe, 681 P.2d 291 (Cal. 1984) (expert testimony not admissible on guilt of defendant because the syndrome was developed for therapeutic reasons rather than to verify that rape occurred). See also State v. Alexander, 401 S.E.2d 146 (S.C. 1991) (evidence of post-rape behavior of victims relevant to guilt but too prejudicial to be admissible). For analysis of these cases, and an argument that any tendency to overvalue expert testimony can be corrected by cross-examination, see Toni M. Massaro, Experts, Psychology, Credibility, and Rape: The Rape Trauma Syndrome Issue and Its Implications for Expert Psychological Testimony, 69 Minn. L. Rev. 395 (1985).

If evidence of rape trauma syndrome is admissible to show lack of consent, should it also be admissible to show that an alleged victim's behavior was not consistent with a "normal" rape victim and, thus, that the rape did not really occur? The Indiana Supreme Court reversed one court's exclusion of such evidence, finding it relevant because it made it less probable that a rape had occurred. Henson v. State, 535 N.E.2d 1189 (Ind. 1989) (evidence offered to show victim who returned to bar where rape allegedly occurred was not in fact raped). For a critical view of this case, see Nicole Rosenberg Economou, Note, Defense Expert Testimony on Rape Trauma Syndrome: Implications for the Stoic Victim, 42 Hastings L.J. 1143, 1154-1155 (1991) (arguing that court both misapplied the medical data and failed to recognize that even if victim's actions did not fit the syndrome, this fact would not be probative of whether rape occurred). What assumptions about rape victims does this use of evidence imply? Would it be fair to the defendant to allow the evidence when it favors the prosecution and not when it favors him?

Like battered women's syndrome, rape trauma syndrome has come under fire by feminists who argue that it has been used to re-pathologize women. Susan Stefan argues, for example, that labeling rape survivors as victims of a "syndrome" encourages juries and judges to think of them as crazy and helpless, and their responses to having been raped as symptoms of mental disorder rather as normal reactions to violence.

> Focusing on rape trauma syndrome in a criminal trial shifts attention from the defendant's actions to the victim's reactions. The use of rape trauma syndrome to explain "counterintuitive" reactions — such as a woman's delay in reporting rape — in terms of her pathology, precludes explaining these reactions as sensible behavior in the context of endemic male violence against women. The use of rape trauma syndrome evidence also threatens to reintroduce the parade of horribles women worked so hard to eliminate for the last twenty years: psychiatric examination of the rape victim, defendants' access to the woman's medical and psychiatric records, admission of evidence of the victim's past sexual behavior, and even corroboration requirements. It is understandable that prosecutors use rape trauma syndrome evidence in court because it may increase the chance of conviction, but its use is no feminist victory.

Susan Stefan, The Protection Racket: Rape Trauma Syndrome, Psychiatric Labeling, and Law, 88 Nw. U. L. Rev. 1271, 1274-1275 (1994).

3. Rape and Lawyers' Ethical Responsibilities

American Bar Association Standards on the Criminal Defense Function
Standard 4-7.6(b) (3d ed. 1993)

A lawyer's belief or knowledge that the witness is telling the truth does not preclude cross-examination.

≣≣ ## Model Code of Professional Responsibility
≣≣ DR 7-106(c) (1983)

(c) In appearing in his professional capacity before a tribunal, a lawyer shall not: . . .

(2) Ask any question that he has no reasonable basis to believe is relevant to the case and that is intended to degrade a witness or other person.

≣≣ ## Model Code of Professional Responsibility
≣≣ DR 7-101 (1983)

(A) A lawyer shall not intentionally:

(1) Fail to seek the lawful objectives of his client through reasonably available means permitted by law and the Disciplinary Rules, except as provided by DR 7-101(B). A lawyer does not violate this Disciplinary Rule, however, by acceding to reasonable requests of opposing counsel which do not prejudice the rights of his client, by being punctual in fulfilling all professional commitments, by avoiding offensive tactics, or by treating with courtesy and consideration all persons involved in the legal process.

≣≣ ## Model Rules of Professional Conduct
≣≣ Rule 4.4: Respect for Rights of Third Persons (1994)

In representing a client, a lawyer shall not use means that have no substantial purpose other than to embarrass, delay, or burden a third person, or use methods of obtaining evidence that violate the legal rights of such a person.

≣≣ ## Cookie Ridolfi, Statement on Representing Rape Defendants
≣≣ (July 26, 1989) (unpublished manuscript, on file with author at Santa Clara Law School)

I have never felt conflicted about what side I stand on in a criminal trial. My political sensibilities keep me firmly planted on the side of the defendant. As a public defender for nearly seven years, I have seen that my clients are victims of poverty, racism, and a criminal justice system that, despite its lofty ideals, presumes guilt, not innocence. My experience has shown me that the system is stacked against an accused and doubly stacked against those who are not white or are poor. . . .

However, my role as a defender in sexual assault cases is not clear or simple. These cases frequently require that I, a feminist who rejects harmful stereotypes of women, exploit those same stereotypes in defense of my client. In the majority of sexual assault cases, the complainant and defendant know one another and fabrication or consent is raised as a defense. . . . As a consequence, in most sex cases, my role is to charge the complainant with having agreed to the sexual encounter, or having asked for it, or of being a woman scorned whose feelings of rejection caused her to cry rape as an act of revenge.

Some defense attorneys believe that effective cross-examination can be done in a way that does not demean the complainant. I disagree. No matter what tone of voice is used or how politely the questions are put, a good cross-examination must still ultimately demonstrate that the complaining witness is a liar. . . . An attorney who is concerned about a complainant's feelings necessarily compromises her client's right to an advocate with exclusive loyalty.

In the conflict between my commitment to defender work and my increasing distress over what is required of me in a sex case, the fact that my own gender is also an issue at trial weighs heavily. Last year I defended a man charged with assault and rape. He and the complainant were dance partners in a club featuring provocative "live dancing." She testified that the defendant appeared at her door late one night, forced his way inside, then dragged her into the basement where he viciously raped and beat her. The client said that he had been invited into the house for sex which was interrupted when the complainant's husband came home; it was her husband who beat her, not him.

After more than a week of trial where emotions ran high for everyone, the jury acquitted him. Afterwards, I met with jurors. One woman juror told me that she believed in his innocence because she was certain that I could not have fought for him in the way that I did had he committed that crime. . . . I later learned that he was arrested and convicted in two new rape/assault cases similar to the one I had tried. . . . [T]hat trial and that complainant still haunt me. I think of the horror described from the witness stand and I believe now that it is true. I think about the fact that the defendant left the courthouse a free man and returned to a community that pitied him as a victim and despised her as the victimizer. I think about the two women that were beaten and raped by him just a few months later. Finally, I think about my role in that.

Despite this experience and my growing discomfort with my own participation in the defense of rape cases, I remain firm in my belief that every person, no matter what the charge or circumstances of the case, deserves dedicated and competent counsel. I also know that some men are victims of a woman's false charges of rape and agree strongly that this defense must be pursued when a defendant makes this claim. I am not critical of any other woman who chooses to defend a man charged with rape. But for all of the reasons I have given, I would find it difficult to again be in the position where I would have to challenge a woman's claim of rape knowing that what she claims may be true.

Notes

1. The Scope of Rape Shield Statutes. In *Colbath*, the defendant sought evidence of the victim's previous behavior with other men on the same day the alleged crime took place. Without ruling directly on the defendant's construction of the rape shield statute, Justice Souter states that there are other constitutional principles that control the case, namely, the defendant's right to "confront the witnesses against him and to present his own exculpatory evidence." These principles give the defendant "an opportunity to demonstrate that the 'probative value [of the statutorily inadmissible evidence] in the context of that particular case outweighs its prejudicial effect on the prosecutrix.'" Under what standards is the court to balance these interests? Does this approach adequately take into account the purpose of the rape shield statute?

Most states have rape shield laws. About half the states bar admission of sexual history evidence except for relations with the accused and an explanation of physical evidence (such as the presence of semen). Evidence introduced under these exceptions must first be subject to an in camera determination of admissibility. About a fifth of the states permit the admission of sexual history evidence if the judge makes an in camera determination of relevance. The remaining jurisdictions have some variations on these provisions. In all but four states, proof of a victim's prior relations with the rapist is admissible on a minimal showing that its probative value outweighs its prejudice. In these four states, it is admissible subject to certain requirements. In interpreting these provisions, courts are likely to resolve doubts on the side of admissibility because exclusionary rulings that prejudice defendants may result in reversals on appeal, while admission of evidence that harms victims and results in acquittal will be insulated from review. See Linda Robayo, Note, The Glen Ridge Trial: New Jersey's Cue to Amend Its Rape Shield Statute, 19 Seton Hall Legis. J. 272 (1994).

Rape shield statutes have drawn criticism from all sides. Civil libertarians and criminal defense counsel often claim that the protections compromise defendants' rights to a fair trial. By contrast, many feminists claim that the exemptions compromise complainants' rights to privacy and deter other victims from reporting the crime. Shawn J. Wallace, Note, Rape Shield Laws: Protecting the Victim at the Expense of the Defendant's Constitutional Rights, 97 N.Y.L. Sch. J. Hum. Rts. 485 (1997); Peter M. Hazelton, Note, Rape Shield Laws: Limits on Zealous Advocacy, 19 Am. J. Crim. L. 35 (1991).

Does Federal Rule of Evidence 412 strike the right balance? To justify admission, should evidence of prior sexual history be not just "relevant" but "highly relevant" *and* have probative value that "substantially outweighs" its potential prejudice or invasion of privacy? See Robayo, supra (discussing reforms in New Jersey's rape law following a celebrated rape trial at which evidence of a retarded girl's history was used to exonerate perpetrators of a brutal gang rape). If the evidence is offered to show prior sexual activity with the defendant, should the defendant have to establish that the prior activity led him to believe that the alleged assault occurred "with what a reasonable person would believe to be affirmative and freely given permission. . . ."? Id. at 301-319.

2. Ethical Responsibilities in Criminal Defense. The role of defense counsel in rape cases often raises fundamental questions of legal ethics:

- What are lawyers' responsibilities when they believe that their clients are guilty or wish to assert positions that are factually untrue?

- Are clients entitled to a defense that includes impeaching a witness whom the lawyer believes is telling the truth?

- Should lawyers' obligations take into account the costs to potential witnesses? If so, does rape stand on a different footing from other civil or criminal proceedings? Alternatively, does any matter involving particularly vulnerable victims present special considerations?

- Should the lawyer's gender affect resolution of these issues? Does a defendant gain an extra and unwarranted advantage from representation by a female attorney in a case where the sexual history of a witness is relevant? Might a juror assume that no woman would zealously attack another woman's credibility without a belief that she was testifying untruthfully?

- Do the bar's ethical rules provide adequate guidance on these questions?

The American bar's prevailing view is that a lawyer's belief that a client is guilty or that an opposing witness is truthful should not prevent efforts to present the most persuasive possible case, which may include impeaching that witness. In essence, the justification for a vigorous defense in criminal contexts is that the system cannot guarantee due process if attorneys deny adequate representation to any clients they assume are guilty. The only way to ensure that the state has met its burden of proof is for lawyers to put questions that might raise a reasonable doubt, irrespective of their personal beliefs in the truth of the witnesses' account. So, too, the only way to ensure trust and candor in attorney-client relationships is to avoid penalizing clients for compromising disclosures. Many commentators take the position that criminal defense entails special obligations of zealous advocacy, both because of the potential for abusive state power and because of the special stakes for the defendant whose liberty, reputation, and sometimes life may be at risk. See Deborah L. Rhode, In the Interests of Justice 54-56, 73-74 (2001);

David Luban, Are Criminal Defenders Different?, 91 Mich. L. Rev. 1729 (1993).

To some commentators, however, impeachment of truthful witnesses is especially problematic in rape cases. Zealous advocacy in that context may carry special costs because of the particularly grave potential for humiliation; the deterrence that invasive cross-examination creates for reporting rapes; and the societal impact of sanctioning "rape myths," suggesting that complainants provoke, desire, or deserve what they get. Lawyers' appeals to such myths are often effective. Jurors are less likely to convict a defendant if evidence suggests that the victim engaged in nonmarital sex, drank, used drugs, dressed "provocatively," or knew the defendant, however brief their acquaintance. The same information affects judicial decisionmaking, and racial bias amplifies these effects when the complainant is a woman of color. Rhode, Speaking of Sex, supra, at 121-127; Hazelton, supra. In addition, rape victims often suffer from rape trauma syndrome, which may lead them to suppress details of an assault. Zealous cross-examination on such details may unduly discredit a victim's basically accurate account.

Exploitation of rape complainants' special vulnerability can have a corrosive impact on the entire law enforcement system. Rape is the most underreported felony, in part because of a further victimization of victims that rape shield statutes have only partially addressed. To commentators such as David Luban, such considerations suggest limits on lawyers' roles:

> The real value underlying the advocate's role is the protection of individuals against institutions that pose chronic threats to their well-being. The state is the most conspicuous of these, but in point of fact no institution has ever posed a more chronic and pervasive threat to the well-being of individual women than that of patriarchy, the network of cultural expectations and practices that engenders and encourages male sexual violence. . . . Thus, the moral limits to the advocate's role in rape cases must be designed to maximize the protection of jeopardized individuals against both these threatening institutions. Placing the brutal cross-examination of the truthful victim off limits serves precisely that function.
>
> Matters would be different if rape were rare and false accusations of rape occurred regularly. Then the advocate's role would properly focus on the vulnerability of men, not of women. Suffice it to say that the world is not this way. . . . In my view, then, the advocate's role should stop well short of an all-out assault on the prosecutrix. . . . The lawyer can ask the victim whether she consented. The lawyer can also argue reasonable doubt to the jury. What she cannot do is cross-examine her to make her look like a whore.

David Luban, Partisanship, Betrayal, and Autonomy: A Reply to Stephen Ellman, 90 Colum. L. Rev. 1004, 1029-1031 (1990).

Does Luban sufficiently consider the costs to male defendants who may misjudge consent? Given the brutal conditions of this nation's prisons and the permanent stigma that may attach to rape convictions, should defendants be entitled to have the jury see the case from their perspective? Compare the view of one public defender:

> The effect of the women's movement on me has been as strong as on anyone else, but I'm no one special; I try to win my cases. If I could get my client off by appealing to the jury's sexism I probably would because I'd be more concerned with this one guy and his freedom than the ethical issue of sexism.

Timothy Beneke, Men on Rape 104-105 (1982). Is this responsible? Is it unethical? Would it be ethical to do otherwise?

3. The Rape Crisis Counselor Privilege. A related issue is whether a rape complainant should have the right to shield disclosures made to rape crisis counselors. About half the states have enacted privilege statutes that protect such information. Most of these extend an absolute privilege: about eight have provided a qualified privilege. See E.B. Warren, She's Got to Have It: A Qualified Rape Crisis Counselor Privilege, 17 Cardozo L. Rev. 141, 148 (1995). The justifications for such a privilege are obvious. The injuries of a sexual assault may be compounded by public disclosure of intimate details from therapeutic sessions. Knowledge that conversations can be revealed may inhibit the trust and candor necessary for effective counseling.

The justifications for allowing defendants access to therapeutic records are equally obvious. In some rape cases, the boundaries of consent and coercion are blurred at best, and subtle, even unintended, encouragement by rape counselors to define an interaction as rape may affect how a complainant later recalls the event. See Rachel Capoccia, Piercing the Veil of Tears: The Admission of Rape Crisis Counselors' Records in Acquaintance Rape Trials, 68 S. Cal. L.J. 1335, 1342 (1995). Other relevant details in therapeutic records may include the complainant's prior involvement with the accused and a history of mental health problems. Given the enormous costs to the defendant of an unjust conviction, some relinquishment of the complainant's privacy interests may appear reasonable.

How would you strike the balance? Would a justifiable compromise be to allow the judge to review the materials in camera to determine if their probative value is sufficient to outweigh the complainant's interest in confidentiality? Or would this solution compromise both competing principles, particularly since the judge must typically make the determination without knowing the nature of the case?

4. Racial Bias. At one time, rape of a nonwhite woman was not a crime. See George v. State, 37 Miss. 316 (1859). See also A. Leon Higginbotham, Jr., & Anne F. Jacobs, The "Law Only as an Enemy": The Legitimization of Racial Powerlessness Through the Colonial Laws of Virginia, 70 N.C. L. Rev. 969, 1056 (1992) (rape of black slave women not a crime in Mississippi, Missouri, and Virginia before the Civil War). By contrast, the rape of a white woman by a black man was long considered the most horrendous possible offense. The most common justification for lynching a black man was that he had raped a white woman. While in colonial Virginia men of both races faced the death penalty for rape of a white woman, black men were far more likely to be convicted and to receive the harshest penalties. At various times, the law required that blacks convicted of raping white women be castrated. Higginbotham & Jacobs, supra, at 1055-1060. See also Jennifer Wriggins, Rape, Racism, and the Law, 6 Harv. Women's L.J. 103 (1983).

Racial bias in rape cases remains pervasive. Although most rapes, like most other crimes, are intraracial rather than interracial, rapes in which black men are the perpetrators and white women the victims continue to receive the greatest attention and the most serious sanctions. One study of Indianapolis rape cases found that "most of the reported rapes involved Black suspects and Black victims. The second largest category involved white suspects on white victims, while Black on white rapes constituted the smallest group of reported rapes. As these cases progressed through the system, however, the percentage of cases involving Black suspects and white victims steadily increased, the percentage of Black intra-racial assaults steadily decreased, and the percentage of white on white rapes remained relatively constant." Elizabeth Iglesias, Rape, Race, and Representation: The Power of Discourse, Discourses of Power, and the Reconstruction of Heterosexuality, 49 Vand. L. Rev. 869, 881 (1996) (citing Gary D. LaFree, Rape and Criminal Justice: The Social Construction of Sexual Assault (1989)). LaFree's data also indicated that in cases where sentences of six or more years in the penitentiary were imposed on the offenders, 50 percent of the cases involved white victims, while only 16.7 percent involved black victims. Id. at 882 n.26. A Texas study similarly found that the median sentence for a black man who raped a white woman was 19 years. For a white man who raped a white woman, it was five years. Ray F. Herndon, Race Tilts the Scales of Social Justice, Dallas Times Herald, Aug. 9, 1990, at A1.

Racism also affects the choice of victims. A recent widely publicized example involved the kidnapping, rape, and torture of college exchange students from Japan, who were selected, according to one of the defendants, on the assumption that Japanese women were "submissive" and would not risk the "shame and dishonor" of reporting the incident. Nicholas K. Geranios, Abduction and Rape of 2 Japanese Students Outrages Spokane, L.A. Times, Dec. 31, 2000, at 133; Kevin Blocker, Man Pleads Guilty to

Abductions, Spokane Rev., May 26, 2001, at A1. The facts in the case highlight one strategy for challenging such stereotypes. The women did come forward, and every effort was then made to shield their identity from the media. Students and faculty were prohibited from discussing the case, and court documents identified the complainants only by initial.

Elizabeth Iglesias argues that facts like these reflect a culture in which gender and racial subordination interact to produce "rules of sexual accessibility." Under these rules, according to Iglesias, "all men must have sexual access to at least some women," "some women are sexually accessible to only some men" (that is, white women are to be sexually accessible only to white men), "all women must be sexually accessible to at least some men," and "some women are sexually accessible to all men" (for example, prostitutes and women of color). Iglesias, supra, at 884-885. How should the criminal law respond to these dynamics? Should the punishment for white men who rape black women be increased, or should the punishment for black men who rape white women be reduced?

5. Rape in Prison. Prison inmates are among the least sympathetic and most vulnerable victims of sexual assault. The precise extent of the problem is difficult to gauge because almost half the states do not collect statistics on prison rape and many inmates have learned that there is often little to be gained and more to be lost by reporting it. However, most recent surveys find that at least a fifth of the nation's two million inmates report experiencing forced sexual contact during incarceration. Tamar Lewin, Little Sympathy or Remedy for Inmates Who Are Raped, N.Y. Times, Apr. 15, 2001 at 1.

The problems are pervasive for both male and female prisoners because the circumstances of incarceration create many opportunities for abuse and few avenues of escape. The power disparities between guards and inmates, the use of body frisks as security checks, the ability of authorities to confer or withhold privileges, and the culture of violence among many offenders all increase the likelihood of abuse. As a Human Rights Watch report summarized the problem:

> Our findings indicate that being a woman prisoner in U.S. state prisons can be a terrifying experience. If you are sexually abused, you cannot escape from your abuser. Grievance or investigatory procedures, where they exist, are often ineffectual, and correctional employees continue to engage in abuse because they believe they will rarely be held accountable, administratively or criminally. Few people outside the prison walls know what is going on or care if they do know. Fewer still do anything to address the problem. . . .

We found that male correctional employees have vaginally, anally, and orally raped female prisoners and sexually assaulted and abused them. We found that in the course of committing such gross misconduct, male officers have not only used actual or threatened physical force, but have also used their near total authority to provide or deny goods and privileges to female prisoners to compel them to have sex or, in other cases, to reward them for having done so.

Human Rights Watch, Abuse, All Too Familiar, Sexual Abuse of Women in U.S. State Prisons (1996); Angela Y. Davis, Public Imprisonment and Private Violences: Reflection on the Hidden Punishment of Women, 24 New Eng. J. Crim. & Civ. Confinement 339, 347 (1998).

For male prisoners, the problems arise more from inmates than staff and from the unwillingness of authorities to intervene. Human Rights Watch, No Escape: Male Rape in U.S. Prisons (2001). For prisoners of both sexes, the result in some institutions has been widespread systems of sexual slavery and forced prostitution. Id.; Lewin, supra; Mark Hansen, Brutal Findings, 87 A.B.A. J., July 2001, at 16.

Despite the pervasiveness of sexual abuse, sanctions are extremely rare. Part of the reason involves the difficulties of proof, the inadequacy of legal standards, and the lack of access to legal representation. Much sexual abuse occurs in private or in the presence of witnesses who are reluctant to risk retaliation by corroborating the victim's account. According to Amnesty International's recent report, many jurisdictions lack appropriate criminal penalties. Five states have no law prohibiting sexual relations between correction officials and inmates. Seven states make custodial sexual misconduct a misdemeanor, not a felony. Only ten states have statutes covering all prison staff, and almost half exclude at least some correctional facilities. Amnesty International, Fear, Shame, and Impunity: Sexual Abuse of Women in Custody (2001); see also Amnesty International, Not Part of My Sentence: Violations of the Human Rights of Women in Custody (1999). Although prisoners may also challenge sexually exploitative conditions of confinement as cruel and unusual punishment under the Eighth Amendment, they must establish that prison officials had actual knowledge of the alleged deprivation and responded with deliberate indifference. See Wilson v. Seiter, 501 U.S. 294, 302-304 (1991); Farmer v. Brennan, 511 U.S. 825 (1994); Hovater v. Robinson, 1 F.3d 1063 (10th Cir. 1993). An unfortunate byproduct of this standard is the disincentive it creates for prison officials to inform themselves about abuse. Hansen, supra, at 17. Even where the conditions are sufficiently egregious to establish a violation, prisoners may be unable to find lawyers to bring a claim. Federally funded legal services agencies may no longer represent prisoners, and the private bar has been uninterested in pursuing such cases, which are known as being difficult to win and seldom lucrative. Hansen, supra, at 18. However, as experts in the area note, although rape is now a predictable part of prison life, it is not an inevitable one, and officials could do much more to provide sexual abuse training, independent complaint channels, segregation of vulnerable or dangerous inmates, and adequate penalties for negligent or abusive conduct by prison staff. How could such reforms be achieved?

6. Rape in Wartime: Violence against Women as a Human Rights Issue. Women have historically been the targets of mass rape during wartime. As Cynthia Enloe notes:

> Stories of the rapes of Belgian women by German soldiers in World War I and of rapes of Chinese women by Japanese soldiers and of German women by Russian soldiers in World War II became so widely known as to affect the international politics of each of these conflicts. In scores of civil and interstate conflicts, from ancient Greece through the period of white American westward expansion and into the recent era of disputes over ideology and sovereignty in Bangladesh, Sri Lanka, Mozambique, and El Salvador, stories of rape have been a staple of war reporting. "Murder, pillage, and rape" is a litany that has been repeated over and over by war reporters as if rape naturally accompanied pillaging. Moreover, in all these conflicts tales of rape have been instruments wielded overwhelmingly by men, especially by those men positioned to shape the larger political conflict. The rapes have been reported as violations of "our" women's honor, as threats to "our" manhood as fathers, husbands, and sons, challenges to "our" collective masculinized honor as an ethnic community, as a nation.

Cynthia Enloe, Afterword: Have the Bosnian Rapes Opened a New Era of Feminist Consciousness?, in Mass Rape: The War Against Women in Bosnia-Herzegovina 219-220 (Alexandra Stiglmayer ed., Marion Faber trans., 1994) (hereinafter Mass Rape); see also Susan Brownmiller, Against Our Will: Men, Women and Rape 31-113 (1975).

Although some charges of rape were brought following World War II, the vast majority of sexual assaults went unnoticed and unpunished. The International Military Tribunal for Nuremberg and the Far East did not include rape as a crime against humanity. Rather, it was subsumed under the general category of inhumane acts, and it was not a focus of prosecution or distinct findings by the Tribunal. Allies did not indict Japanese military or political leaders for the notorious rapes and enforced prostitution of some 100,000 to 200,000 Korean and Filipina "comfort women." Patricia Viseur Sellers, Arriving at Rwanda: Extension of Sexual Assault Prosecution Among the Statutes of the Ad Hoc International Criminal Tribunals, 90 Am. Soc. Int'l L. Proc. 605 (1996).

A half century later, the international community began to recognize rape as a human rights violation, largely in response to the atrocities committed in Rwanda and Yugoslavia during the early 1990s. Estimates of the number of rapes that occurred during the Yugoslavian war vary from 20,000 to 50,000; Bosnian Muslim women were apparently the primary victims. See Alexandra Stiglmayer, The Rapes in Bosnia-Herzegovina, in Mass Rape, supra, at 85. Moreover, rape appears to have been used as a method of "ethnic cleansing" in the former Yugoslavia. For example, Muslim and Croatian women were sometimes raped and then killed, sometimes raped in order to defile them in their own eyes and the eyes of their countrymen, and sometimes deliberately impregnated by Serbian soldiers in order to "produce Serbian babies." These rapes were systematic rather than random. Women reported being held in "rape camps" throughout Bosnia-Herzegovina, and on a smaller scale on the Muslim-Croatian side, where adults and girls alike were raped repeatedly, the latter often until they died. See id. In Rwanda, rape was systematically carried out against Tutsi women. Kate Nahapetian, Selective Justice: Prosecuting Rape in the International Criminal Tribunal for the Former Yugoslavia and Rwanda, 14 Berkeley Women's L.J. 126 (1999).

Catharine MacKinnon has noted that the rapes in Bosnia-Herzegovina were simultaneously crimes against women and a form of genocide. Speaking of the practice of forced impregnation, MacKinnon observes:

> If this were racial rape, as Americans are familiar with it, the children would be regarded as polluted, dirty, and contaminated, even as they are sometimes given comparative privileges based on "white" blood. But because this is ethnic rape, lacking racial markers, the children are regarded by the aggressors as somehow clean and purified, as "cleansed" ethnically. The babies made with Muslim and Croatian women are regarded as Serbian babies. The idea seems to be to create a fifth column within Muslim and Croatian society of children — all sons — who will rise up and join their fathers. Much Serbian fascist ideology simply adopts and adapts Nazi views. This one is the ultimate achievement of the Nazi ideology that culture is genetic.

Catharine A. MacKinnon, Rape, Genocide, and Women's Human Rights, in Mass Rape, supra, at 183, 191-192.

Despite the horror, such practices are nothing new in wartime. See Fionnuala Ni Aolain, The Entrenchment of Systematic Abuse: Mass Rape in Former Yugoslavia, 8 Harv. Hum. Rts. J. 285, 295 (1995). What *is* new is the emergence of a feminist voice chronicling and condemning wartime rape. Women are finally being heard denouncing not only the rapes but also the cultural contexts that license such abuse. Enloe points out:

> [T]he rapes in Bosnia have been documented by women's organizations, organizations that are primarily concerned with the raped women's own welfare. Furthermore, these women's organizations have helped create an international political network of feminists who are using news of the Bosnian women's victimization not to institutionalize women as victims, not to incite men to more carnage, but to explain anew how war makers rely on peculiar ideas about masculinity. Finally, they are documenting these rapes so that internationally recognized human rights can be redefined in women's favor.

And this time the feminist reporters are using news of wartime sexual assaults by male soldiers to rethink the very meanings of both sovereignty and national identity as each is protected — or challenged — by the workings of the international community.

Enloe, supra, at 220.

A torrent of Western feminist legal writing has, accordingly, sought to reframe wartime rape as a crime against women, not merely a crime against "our" or "their" women, and to recognize genocidal rape as a unique crime against humanity punishable under international human rights law. See, e.g., Amy Ray, The Shame of It: Gender-Based Terrorism in the Former Yugoslavia, 46 Am. U. L. Rev. 793 (1997); Scott Splittgerber, The Need for Greater Regional Protection for the Human Rights of Women: The Cases of Rape in Bosnia and Guatemala, 15 Wis. Int'l L.J. 185 (1996); Siobhan K. Fisher, Occupation of the Womb: Forced Impregnation as Genocide, 46 Duke L.J. 91 (1996); Linda A. Malone, Beyond Bosnia and In re Kasinga: A Feminist Perspective on Recent Developments in Protecting Women from Sexual Violence, 14 B.U. Int'l L.J. 319 (1996); Sharon Healey, Prosecuting Rape Under the Statute of the War Crimes Tribunal for the Former Yugoslavia, 21 Brooklyn J. Int'l L. 327 (1995); Catharine Niarchos, Women, War, and Rape: Challenges Facing the International Tribunal for the Former Yugoslavia, 17 Hum. Rts. Q. 649 (1995); Adrien K. Wing & Sylke Merchan, Rape, Ethnicity, and Culture: Spirit Injury from Bosnia to Black America, 25 Colum. Hum. Rts. L. Rev. 1 (1993).

The efforts of the international women's rights community helped to ensure that when the United Nations Security Council established the International Criminal Tribunal for the former Yugoslavia (ICTY) and the International Criminal Tribunal for Rwanda (ICTR), rape was explicitly included as a crime against humanity within these Tribunals' jurisdiction. Nahapetian, supra, at 128. Both have established some important precedents for the prosecution of rape as a war crime. In the first trial (of Dusko Tadic), the ICTY held that aiding and abetting could establish criminal liability if the acts alleged had a direct and substantial affect on the commission of the rapes. The Tribunal subsequently found that "sexual enslavement," including nightly assaults or "rape camps," constituted a crime against humanity (Dragoljub Kunarac, Radamir Kovac). The Tribunal also for the first time indicted a former head of government, Yugoslavia leader Slobodan Milosevic, for crimes against humanity, including mass rapes of Bosnian women. Catharine MacKinnon, along with the National Organization for Women, has brought suit on behalf of the raped women of Bosnia-Herzegovina against Bosnian Serb leader Radovan Karadzic for genocide, rape, and torture. In the first international war crime trial for genocide (Jean-Paul Akayesu), the ICTR found that "[s]exual violence was an integral part of the destruction of the Tutsi group — destruction of the spirit, of the will to live, and of life itself." Judgment, Prosecutor v. Akayesu, No. ICTR-96-4-1,

¶¶731-732 (Sept. 2, 1998). See Patricia H. Davis, The Politics of Prosecuting Rape as a War Crime, 34 Int'l L. 1223 (Winter 2000).

Should the genocidal rapes in Bosnia be viewed as simply an extreme example of the routinely anti-female culture of the military? See Madeline Morris, By Force of Arms: Rape, War, and Military Culture, 45 Duke L.J. 651 (1996). To what extent do wartime rapes mirror, or dwarf, the everyday "private," domestic rapes of women and children?

4. Marital Rape

Kizer v. Commonwealth of Virginia
321 S.E.2d 291 (Va. 1984)

COMPTON, Justice.

Indicted for the rape of his wife in violation of Code §18.2-61, Edward Alan Kizer was found guilty in a bench trial and sentenced on September 9, 1983 to confinement in the penitentiary for a term of 20 years. Execution of 15 years of the sentence was suspended and the defendant was placed on probation for life. . . . [We reverse the conviction.]

The facts mainly are undisputed. Defendant and his wife, Jeri, were married in June of 1981 in Texas. The couple moved to Norfolk where defendant, age 20, was stationed aboard ship as an enlisted man in the Navy. They occupied rented quarters ashore that were leased in both names. Following the birth of a child, the couple began having marital difficulties. In September of 1982, about six months before the incident in question, the wife returned to Texas briefly. According to her testimony, the purpose of the trip was "to visit" her parents for two weeks; the visit was not "a separation" from her husband.

During the "middle of February" 1983, about three weeks before the alleged offense, the defendant "moved back to the ship." The wife continued to reside in the apartment with the child. According to the wife's testimony, the separation occurred because "[t]he marriage was over and I did not want the marriage to be any longer. . . ." The wife added that she "wanted to be separated and in the process to file for divorce after the legal separation in Virginia." The defendant testified that the parties were not "legally separated" and that he moved to the ship "to avoid any other arguing with my wife . . . in front of our son because we did not want to subject him to arguing between me and my wife, Jeri."

Previously, the wife had left the husband from "about the first of January to about the middle of February" 1983. After the parties "had talked to each other," she returned to the marital home, saying to the husband, "I want to make it work but I do not love you." The defendant had suspected his wife of "fooling around" while he was on duty at sea, but testified that he "still loved the girl" and wanted the marriage "to work."

During the three-week period from the middle of February to the date of the incident, the defendant came to the apartment to visit the child pursuant to an oral agreement with the wife. She estimated he made "a couple" visits. The defendant testified that he "tried" to visit the boy "seven or eight times." The parties had agreed that the defendant would notify the wife in advance of a planned visit so that she would not be in the apartment when he arrived.

On March 5, the day before the incident in question, the defendant came to the apartment without notifying the wife. She refused to allow him to enter the premises during the morning and again during the afternoon. Still later in the day, she permitted him to see the child as the wife, accompanied by a male friend, left the apartment on the friend's motorcycle. She returned to the apartment about five hours later, at 11:30 P.M., but did not remain. The defendant told her he was staying at the marital abode because he did not want to return to the ship due to the lateness of the hour.

The evidence showed that the parties did not engage in sexual intercourse during the period from September 1982, when she visited her parents in Texas, until the date of the incident in question. During a portion of this time, the defendant was aboard ship at sea.

Prior to the alleged offense, the defendant filed a petition in court seeking an award of custody of his child. In addition, the parties decided in February to consult a lawyer "about getting a legal separation." As the parties were en route to an attorney's office, the wife told defendant that she had changed her mind and that she did not want to separate "right now." He said, "Are you sure?" and she responded, "Yes." They returned to their apartment. The wife testified that she decided to discontinue the trip to the attorney because the defendant had just received notification that his father was very ill and she did not want to put more "pressure" on him at that time.

The evidence showed that before the day of the alleged offense, the defendant discussed "the rape laws of Virginia" with a friend. The defendant had said that "he [the defendant] was kind of hard up for sex" and that he thought he "ought to go over there and rip her clothes off of her and take it."

On the day in question, March 6, the defendant had been visiting friends in an apartment "across the hall" from the marital home. He knocked on the door to his apartment about 6:00 P.M. and asked his wife to allow him to use the shower. She refused because she was afraid to be in the premises alone with him. The defendant insisted on gaining entry and, as the wife tried to lock the front door to the apartment, he kicked the door twice. The door "came open and the frame came off the door," according to the wife's testimony. The defendant took the child from the mother's arms and placed him on the floor. The defendant picked up the wife, carried her to the bedroom, ripped off her clothing, and forcibly had sexual intercourse with her. During this time, she was screaming, scratching, kicking, and pulling defendant's hair. At one point during the 45-minute episode, the wife broke away from the defendant and rushed to the bedroom window, screaming for help. After the assault, the wife ran from the apartment and reported the incident to a police officer who was in the area.

The defendant was arrested on a warrant that day about 9:45 P.M., after earlier having confessed to the acts essentially as related by the wife. About three weeks after the incident, and before the rape trial, the defendant was awarded custody of his son following a hearing.

On appeal, the question presented is whether, under this evidence, the Commonwealth established beyond a reasonable doubt the elements necessary to sustain a conviction for marital rape. In such a case, under [Weishaupt v. Commonwealth, 315 S.E.2d 847 (Va. 1984)], the prosecution, in addition to establishing a violation of the general rape statute, Code 18.2-61, must prove beyond a reasonable doubt that the wife unilaterally had revoked her implied consent to marital intercourse. [315 S.E.2d at 855.] The wife's revocation of consent must be demonstrated by a manifest intent "to terminate the marital relationship." [Id.] The facts necessary to show this intention to terminate must reveal that the wife: has lived separate and apart from the husband; has refrained from voluntary sexual intercourse with her husband; and, "in light of all the circumstances," has conducted herself "in a manner that establishes a de facto end to the marriage." [Id.] In this context, "de facto" means "in fact," or "actually." Black's Law Dictionary 375 (5th ed. 1979).

In the present case, the evidence shows, first, a violation of the rape statute sufficient to sustain a conviction of the defendant for the rape of a female not his wife. Second, the evidence establishes that the parties lived separate and apart. Third, the proof shows that the wife refrained from voluntary sexual intercourse with the defendant. The evidence fails, however, to show beyond a reasonable doubt the wife conducted herself in a manner that established an actual end to the marriage, in light of all the circumstances.

Significantly, the wife's marital conduct during the six-month period before the assault was equivocal, ambivalent, and ambiguous. Prior to September 1982, the parties had been having domestic difficulties but apparently had been living together as husband and wife. She left Norfolk and went to Texas to "visit" her parents. But she testified that this was not a "separation" in the divorce sense. She returned from Texas and during part of the September-January period, the husband was on shipboard duty at sea. In January, the wife left again but returned after the parties "talked." She stated at the time that she wanted to make the marriage "work." In February, she terminated a planned trip with her husband to a divorce lawyer, advising the husband that she had changed her mind and did not wish to separate "right now." Finally, about three weeks before the alleged offense, the husband began living aboard ship in port. At the time, the wife considered the marriage to be "over."

Evaluating the foregoing circumstances in the light most favorable to the Commonwealth, we think it is apparent that the wife subjectively considered the marriage fractured beyond repair when the parties separated in February. Nevertheless, we cannot say that this subjective intent was manifested objectively to the husband, in view of the wife's vacillating conduct, so that he perceived, or reasonably should have perceived, that the marriage actually was ended.

The facts in *Weishaupt*, upon which the Attorney General relies in urging affirmance, are in sharp contrast to the circumstances of the present case. There, the wife moved out of the marital abode, taking with her the infant child of the parties. At the time of the offense, the parties had been separated continuously for 11 months and had not engaged in sexual relations during the period. There was no contact between the parties during the separation except telephone conversations concerning the child and chance meetings in public. During the period, the wife had consulted a divorce attorney who advised waiting until the parties were separated for a full year before filing suit for divorce. In sum, unlike the present case, the wife's marital conduct in *Weishaupt* during the pertinent period, viewed objectively, was unequivocal, definite, and certain; her conduct manifestly demonstrated that the marriage was in fact at an end and evidenced that the wife unilaterally had revoked her implied consent to marital intercourse. In *Weishaupt*, unlike this case, the Commonwealth proved beyond a reasonable doubt that the husband knew, or reasonably should have known, that the marriage was terminated de facto.

Accordingly, the judgment of conviction in this case will be reversed and the indictment will be dismissed.

THOMAS, Justice, dissenting.

The victim in this case took a horrible beating. The integrity of her body was brutally invaded by her estranged husband. The facts in this appeal are such that the majority concedes that had the victim not been married to the assailant, the assailant would have been guilty of rape. Nevertheless, in an opinion which fails to give due precedential weight to the Court's recent decision in Weishaupt v. Commonwealth, [315 S.E.2d 847 (Va. 1984)], the majority concludes, in essence, that Edward Kizer had a right to do what he did. The majority opinion marks a retreat from the principles announced in *Weishaupt*. . . .

According to the majority, before a husband can be found guilty of raping his wife, the wife must make "manifest objectively to the husband" the wife's view that the marriage is at an end. *Weishaupt* nowhere requires that the wife make manifest to her husband that the marriage is at an end. *Weishaupt* requires only that the wife make manifest to an objective observer "her intent to terminate the marital relationship." The difference is that, under the majority view, the trial court must place itself in the position of the estranged husband to determine whether the husband should have known that his wife considered the marriage over. Under *Weishaupt*, the court was not required to place itself in the husband's shoes; instead, it was called upon to occupy the more traditional posture of looking at the facts from the perspective of an objective observer to determine whether from that perspective the wife conducted herself in a manner that showed the marriage to be over. . . .

When viewed properly, the evidence shows the following: the couple was married on June 20, 1981. One child was born of the marriage. In September 1982, the couple began to experience marital difficulties. The couple did not engage in voluntary sexual relations from September 1982 through the attack which occurred in March 1983, a period of six months. The husband moved out of the marital abode in the middle of February, 1983. From that time to the attack there was neither sexual nor social contact between the parties. At the time the husband moved out, the parties discussed obtaining a legal separation. They even started on their way to visit a lawyer. The only reason they did not consult with a lawyer at that time was the fact that during the car ride the husband advised his estranged wife that his father was seriously ill. The wife decided to postpone the visit to the lawyer so as not to place an additional emotional burden upon her estranged husband while he tried to handle the problems associated with his father's illness. Further, prior to the attack, the husband filed suit to secure custody of the couple's child.

In my view, the foregoing facts meet either the original *Weishaupt* test or the modified test contained in the majority opinion. The single salient fact among all the facts and circumstances, and the one which makes this a stronger case for conviction than *Weishaupt*, is the husband's attempt to secure the custody of the couple's child. The majority mentions this fact but makes nothing of it, thus glossing over a very critical point.

In the normal course of events, husbands do not file custody suits unless they consider their marriages to be over. It is unrealistic to believe that the husband in this case would have sued for the custody of his child unless he thought the relationship with his wife was at an end. This husband demonstrated by his action in filing a custody suit that it was manifest to him that his marriage was over. The pendency of the custody suit added to the six-month absence of sexual relations and the one-month separation would lead any objective husband or impartial observer to conclude that the marriage in question was at an end.

Thus, in my opinion, the conviction for rape should be affirmed.

CARRICO, C.J., joins in this dissent.

Notes

1. The Common Law Marital Rape Exemption. The common law marital rape exemption is credited to Sir Matthew Hale, 1 History of the

Pleas of the Crown 628 (1st American ed. 1847). It was based on the assumption that in marriage the wife gave her irrevocable consent to intercourse with her husband. The notion of irrevocable consent appears to have been a euphemism for the deeper underlying notion that a woman is the property of a man — first her father and then her husband. See People v. Liberta, 474 N.E.2d 567, 576 (N.Y. 1984), cert. denied, 471 U.S. 1020 (1985). Moreover, at common law, the concept of marital unity viewed husband and wife as one, and a married man, therefore, could not be liable for raping himself.

As those rationales grew increasingly anachronistic, commentators supplied various policy arguments, some inconsistent. One commentator assumed that marital rape occurred so infrequently that legal remedies were unnecessary. Others assumed that it occurred so frequently that any remedial structure would be overwhelmed by complaints, as women seeking divorces would file complaints to blackmail their husbands in order to obtain better settlements in divorce. Deborah L. Rhode, Justice and Gender 250 (1988). The Model Penal Code commentary to §213.1 reasons that courts should not intrude on the "privacy" of the family relationship, that a husband's use of force against his wife is not as harmful as other kinds of forced sex, and that spousal rape presents greater evidentiary problems than other rapes. What deeper assumptions underlie these rationales? See, e.g., Anne C. Dailey, Note, To Have and to Hold: The Marital Rape Exemption and the Fourteenth Amendment, 99 Harv. L. Rev. 1255, 1268-1269 (1986). On what basis is it supposed that rape is falsely charged more often than other crimes or that wives are even more likely than other women to fabricate charges of rape?

2. Reform of the Marital Rape Exemption. No state has retained the full common law exemption for rape, and by the mid-1990s, about half of the states no longer recognized any form of marital rape exemption. See Lisa R. Eskow, Note, The Ultimate Weapon? Demythologizing Spousal Rape and Reconceptualizing Its Prosecution, 48 Stan. L. Rev. 677, 682 (1996). The rule has been eliminated or qualified, in some states, by judicial decision and, in other states, by statute.

Among the judicial decisions eliminating or modifying the exemption, some have concentrated on the changing role of women in this society and the inconsistency between this role and the "chattel" role assumed at common law. See, e.g., State v. Smith, 426 A.2d 38 (N.J. 1981). Others have drawn on constitutional principles, finding the exemption a violation of equal protection. See, e.g., People v. Liberta, supra. Still others have interpreted state statutory revisions broadly in light of changing circumstances. See, e.g., Commonwealth v. Chretian, 417 N.E.2d 1203, 1208 (Mass. 1981); State v. Rider, 449 So. 2d 903 (Fla. Dist. Ct. App. 1984), appeal dismissed, 470 U.S. 1075 (1985). The case discussed in *Kizer*, Weishaupt v. Commonwealth, 315 S.E.2d 847, 855 (Va. 1984), had pursued this last approach, interpreting the common law together with various statutory changes to conclude that no marital exemption existed when the wife had "manifested an intent to terminate the marital relationship."

Statutory reform efforts also have taken a variety of approaches. For example, the Violence Against Women Act (discussed in Chapter 4, at pages 675-692) recognizes no exemption for marital rape. Many states have eliminated the exemption altogether. See, e.g., N.C. Gen. Stat. §14-27.8 (2000); Wis. Stat. Ann. §940.225(6) (West 1996); N.M. Stat. Ann. §30-9-11 (Michie 1994); Utah Code Ann. §76-5-402 (1999). Other states have eliminated the exemption only in cases in which the parties are living apart or have legally separated or filed for divorce or for an order of protection. See, e.g., La. Rev. Stat. Ann. §14.43(B) (West 1997) (must have judgment of separation or, if not legally separated, must have obtained a temporary restraining order or injunction); Md. Ann. Code art. 27, §464D (1996) (must have lived separate and apart either with written separation agreement or limited divorce decree or for at least three months prior to assault).

Many laws reforming the marital rape exemption have preserved a form of the exemption for lesser forms of sexual assault but eliminated it for some aggravated assaults. Missouri, for example, allows conviction of a spouse for "forcible rape," but allows marriage to the victim as an affirmative defense for lesser forms of sexual assault. See Mo. Ann. Stat. §566.023 (West 1999). What is the justification for this approach?

Would a preferable approach be to treat marital rape by a husband as a crime, but as a lesser or different crime than one committed by a stranger? California and Tennessee take this approach. In Tennessee, spousal rape is only a class C felony, as opposed to rape by a stranger, which is a class B felony. Tenn. Code Ann. §39-13-507 (Michie 2001). California has a separate crime called "Rape of a Spouse" with different reporting requirements and sentencing provisions than those applying to stranger rape. Cal. Penal Code §§261, 262 (West 2001). Compare Model Penal Code §213.1(c) (1980) (forced sexual intercourse by man against his wife cannot be rape unless there is a judicial separation decree, but it may constitute some other crime, like assault).

Is there a convincing argument that marital rape should be treated as a more, not a less, serious crime? Empirical research indicates that the greatest adverse psychological effects on women who have been raped are those resulting from sexual assaults by a husband or a relative. In one study, 52 percent of women raped by a husband and 52 percent of women raped by a relative reported long-term effects on their lives. For women raped by a stranger, the figure was 39 percent; for women raped by an acquaintance, 25 percent; and for women raped by a friend, date, or lover, 22 percent. Diana E. H. Russell, Rape in Marriage 192-193 (rev. ed. 1990). See also research cited in Rhode, Justice and Gender, supra, at 251, and David Finkelhor & Kersti Yllo, License to Rape: Sexual Abuse of Wives 137, 140 (1985) (finding long-term injury to self-confidence and self-esteem). A few courts have specifically rejected the rationale that marital rape is less traumatic than stranger rape. See, e.g., People v. M.D., 595 N.E.2d 702, 712 (Ill. App. Ct.), app. denied, 602 N.E.2d 467 (Ill. 1992).

Still another statutory variation adds the requirement that a wife file a complaint of rape within a shortened period of time. South Carolina has a 30-day reporting requirement, S.C. Code Ann. §16-3-658 (Law Co-op. Supp. 2000), and in California, a report must be made within one year unless independent admissible evidence exists. Cal. Penal Code §262 (West Supp. 2001). What assumptions does such a requirement reflect? Are they justified?

Some legislative reforms have actually broadened, rather than narrowed, the marital rape exemption. Some states, for example, recognize some form of an exemption for parties living together who are not legally married to one another. See, e.g., Conn. Gen. Stat. Ann. §53(a)-67(b) (West 2001); Minn. Stat. Ann. §609.349 (West 1987). A few states downgrade to a lesser offense a rape committed by a "voluntary social companion" of the victim. See, e.g., 11 Del. Code Ann. §775(a)(2) (Michie 2000) (provides an exemption for cases where "defendant [is] victim's voluntary social companion on the occasion of the crime" if victim "permitted the defendant sexual intercourse within the previous 12 months"); Mont. Code Ann. §45-5-511(2) (2001) (evidence of victim's past sexual conduct with offender is admissible for defense). What assumptions do these defenses reflect? Are they justified?

Kizer illustrates just one of the possible loopholes in such "liberalized" approaches to marital rape. What is the purpose of the requirement that the wife objectively manifest an unequivocal intent that the marriage is over? If you disagree with the reversal of the conviction, is it because you object to the standard or to the way it was applied in the case? What do you make of Justice Thomas's point that the only reason the wife did not pursue a legal separation was that she was concerned about the potential added strain on her estranged husband because of his father's illness? Should this be relevant to the defendant's criminal liability for rape? Since *Kizer*, Virginia has amended its statute so that a husband is not immune from rape charges if the spouses were living apart at the time of the offense or if the husband caused serious physical injury by the use of force or violence. See Va. Code Ann. §18.2-61 (Michie 2001). Are these amendments sufficient? According to one commentator, criminalizing marital rape is "an important instrument of social change that will eventually force husbands to reevaluate their thoughts and decisions about rape and marriage." Rebecca M. Ryan, The Sex Right: A Legal History of the Marital Rape Exemption, 20 Law & Soc. Inquiry 941 (1995). If this is true, which legal approaches are most appropriate?

3. The Constitutionality of Marital Rape Exemptions. As noted above, a few courts have found that the marital rape exemption is unconstitutional. These courts concluded that the exemption violates the equal protection clause because there is no rational basis for distinguishing between marital and nonmarital rape. See, e.g., People v. M.D., 595 N.E.2d 702 (Ill. App. Ct.), appeal denied, 602 N.E.2d 467 (Ill. 1992); People v. Liberta, 474 N.E.2d 567 (N.Y. 1984), cert. denied, 471 U.S. 1020 (1985). One commentator argues that the marital rape exemption also violates the woman's constitutional right to privacy in that it "conditions the benefit of marriage upon women's forfeiture of their rights to bodily integrity, procreative freedom, and individual autonomy" and "condition[s] the benefit of protection from rape upon women's forfeiture of their fundamental right to marriage." Anne C. Dailey, Note, To Have and to Hold: The Marital Rape Exemption and the Fourteenth Amendment, 99 Harv. L. Rev. 1255, 1264 (1986). Dailey prefers the equal protection claim to a privacy theory, however, because it better draws attention to the "reality of collective power relations" between men and women. Id. at 1267-1273. Recall MacKinnon's critique of equality analysis at pages 536-539. Does it apply here?

Pursuing the equal protection line of analysis, Robin West describes three different approaches:

(1) a rationality model, which targets legislative classifications that are irrational or irrelevant to legitimate state goals; (2) an anti-subordination model, which targets legislation that substantively contributes to the subordination of one group by another; and (3) a pure protection model, which targets a state's failure to grant protection of its law to all citizens equally, thus failing to ensure that all citizens are subject equally to one and only one sovereign, namely the sovereignty of the rule of law.

West, Equality Theory, Marital Rape, and the Promise of the Fourteenth Amendment, 42 Fla. L. Rev. 45, 71 (1990). West criticizes the rationality model because it identifies the wrong problem about marital rape exemptions:

. . . The evil flaw of these exemptions is not that they irrationally treat married couples differently from cohabitants, or married women differently from unmarried women, or husbands differently from rapists unacquainted with their victims, or women differently from men. The evil is that they legalize, and hence legitimate, a form of violence that does inestimable damage to all women. . . .

. . . The antisubordination model and pure protection interpretations of the equal protection clause, by contrast, precisely highlight the most offensive features of marital rape exemptions — not [their irrationality], but their legitimation of a regime of private force and organized violence that creates and encourages the male subordination of women and the insulation of a separate and sovereign political regime through which that subordination is effectuated.

Id. at 69, 71. West equates the anti-subordination model with substantive equality in that it seeks an end result in which men and women are social equals. Id. at 60. The pure protection model has a slightly different focus, in that it

> envisions a world in which the state is the sole, legitimate repositor of organized force exercised by some individuals against others. The equal protection clause would not tolerate the existence of separate "regimes" of sovereignty, backed by unchecked and private systems of organized violence. The pure protection model requires that we live under only one sovereign — the state. Any other exercise of violence and power by one group of citizens over another is criminal, and the state is constitutionally obligated to guard its citizens against such domination. . . .

Id. at 62-63. West proposes that, to implement her pure protection view of the equal protection clause, Congress pass a statute, a "Married Women's Privacy Act," that specifically guarantees to all women protection against violent sexual assaults, prohibits states from insulating the "sexualized social, private or intimate subordination of women by men," and guarantees that no state denies to women protection of the state against private criminality. Id. at 76. In order for constitutional authority to exist, such legislation must be viewed as a reasonable means of securing Fourteenth Amendment guarantees against state action. See Katzenbach v. Morgan, 384 U.S. 641, 650 (1966). Is it clear that this requirement can be met by the proposed act? What if a state decided to decriminalize rape or marital rape altogether? Could Congress prohibit it from doing so?

5. Acquaintance Rape: Constructing Consent from Conflicting Truths

Karen M. Kramer, Note, Rule by Myth: The Social and Legal Dynamics Governing Alcohol-Related Acquaintance Rapes
47 Stan. L. Rev. 115, 141-143 (1994)

[The following account is taken from a supplemental report prepared by Detective Tim Frecceri in the case of State v. Thomas, No. B9198729, Palo Alto Mun. Ct. Preliminary Examination, Nov. 13, 1991; see also Cal. Super. Ct. Sentencing Proceedings, Jan. 31, 1992, State v. Thomas, No. 151643.]

Anne had arrived as a freshman at [Stanford] University a few days before the incident. While meeting other residents in her dorm, Anne stopped in Thomas's room because she heard him playing music she liked. After visiting other people, she returned to his room later that evening and Thomas offered her a beer. Although Anne had only drunk alcohol once before, she accepted the beer. Other students who had been in Thomas's room when Anne arrived left for a different party. In the period of two hours, Thomas gave Anne half a beer and eight drinks of peppermint schnapps, all of which she drank. Anne asked Thomas, "if he was trying to get her drunk, but he told her he was not, and assured her that everything was O.K."

After consuming the alcohol, Anne "didn't feel too good, so she laid down . . . on his bed." When asked if she had any intention of teasing or seducing Thomas, she emphatically said, "no." To the contrary, "because of alcohol's effect on her, she had to lay down and didn't do a lot of talking." After a while, she and Thomas began to kiss; soon he had completely undressed her.

In her conversation with the detective, Anne explained that she didn't feel any pressure from the suspect, and that he didn't make any verbal threats to her as he undressed her. However, she said, she felt a certain coercion from [Thomas's] presence, coupled with the fact that her condition and judgment had been impaired by alcohol. She mentioned [Thomas's] physical size as part of this coercion, estimating that he is at least 6' 04" or more, and has a muscular build. She also mentioned the manner in which [Thomas] spoke to her as part of this coercion, recalling that from when he began providing her with alcohol to when they were having sexual intercourse, he kept saying to her in a calm, soothing voice, statements like, "It's O.K. You can do what you want, no one has to know, I won't hurt you," among other things. . . . When she became aware that things were going beyond holding and kissing, she indicated to [Thomas] that he should stop. . . . [Anne] told him, "I can't do this, I have a boyfriend." [Thomas] responded by saying, "It's O.K., he doesn't have to know." [Anne] then told [Thomas] that she was a virgin and that she was only seventeen years old. [Thomas] responded by saying something similar to, "It's O.K. No one has to know, your family doesn't have to find out, this can be between you and me. If you want it, it's O.K. I won't hurt you." [Anne] recalled that she protested more than once; she is certain that she told [Thomas] several times that she couldn't do it because she was a virgin and because she was only seventeen years old. [However, Thomas] proceeded to have sexual intercourse with [her]. . . . [Anne] felt sharp vaginal pain and said, "Ow, stop." [Thomas] stopped for a minute or so and continued to lay next to [Anne], kissing and touching her. As she became aware that he was preparing to have sexual intercourse again, she again told the suspect, "I can't, I'm a virgin." . . . Nevertheless, [Thomas] positioned himself above [Anne], as she lay on her back, and again inserted his erect penis into her vagina. Once again, after a few moments of [Thomas] pushing his penis into [Anne's] vagina, she felt a sharp vagina[l] pain, so she said, "Ow, stop." [Anne] thinks she might have told [Thomas], "that hurts," as well. . . . [Thomas] then asked her, "If you don't want it in you, will you at least kiss it?" [Anne] complied. . . . She could not recall her frame of mind at this time, though she did feel somewhat obligated to do this to the suspect. She indicated that because she was intoxicated and had impaired judgement, because [Thomas] was unable to continue intercourse with her, due to her vagina[l] pain, and because of his physical presence, she was aware of implied coercion.

After Thomas had an orgasm, Anne dressed and left the room, leaving behind several personal items, including her wallet, glasses, and shoes.

Beverly Balos & Mary Louise Fellows, Guilty of the Crime of Trust: Nonstranger Rape
75 Minn. L. Rev. 599, 601-602 (1991)

Current law allows defendants to use a preexisting relationship to give credibility to a defense of consent or reasonable, good faith belief of consent. If courts applied the doctrine of confidential relationship, evidence of the relationship would impose upon the defendant a heightened duty of care to the victim.

Imposing the heightened duty of care associated with the confidential relationship doctrine makes three distinct changes to the prosecution of nonstranger rapes. First, it changes the mental element of the crime because the heightened duty of care requires that the defendant be found blameworthy for being inattentive to the victim's words or conduct indicating nonconsent, and for failing to obtain consent through positive words or positive actions. Second, the heightened duty changes the definition of consent to mean positive words or positive action indicating a freely given agreement to have sexual contact. Third, this heightened duty deters the defendant from introducing evidence of the prior relationship or prior conduct between the victim and the defendant as relevant to showing consent to sexual contact during the disputed incident. Instead, the prosecution may introduce evidence of the prior relationship and conduct in order to impose on the defendant a heightened duty to obtain consent.

Katherine Roiphe, The Morning After: Fear, Sex, and Feminism on College Campuses
66-68 (1993)

By viewing rape as encompassing more than the use or threat of physical violence to coerce someone into sex, rape-crisis feminists reinforce tradition-al views about the fragility of the female body and will. Today's definition of date or acquaintance rape stretches beyond acts of violence or physical force. According to common definitions of date rape, even verbal coercion or manipulation constitutes rape. Verbal coercion is defined as "a woman's consenting to unwanted sexual activity because of a man's verbal arguments not including verbal threats of force." The belief that verbal coercion is rape extends beyond official definitions; it pervades workshops, counseling sessions, and student opinion pieces. In Harvard's moderate feminist magazine, the *Lighthouse*, a student wrote an impassioned piece about the prevalence of what she considered emotional rape.

In an essay entitled "Nonviolent Sexual Coercion," psychologists Charlene Muelenhard and Jennifer Schrag include the remarks, "He said he'd break up with me if I didn't," "He said I was frigid," and "He said everyone's doing it" in the category of verbal coercion. They go on to explain that "a woman with low self-esteem might feel that if she refuses her partner's sexual advances she will lose him, and her value will be lessened because she is no longer associated with him." This is a portrait of the cowering woman, knocked on her back by the barest feather of peer pressure. Solidifying this image of women into policy implies an acceptance of the passive role. By protecting women against verbal coercion, these feminists are promoting the view of women as weak-willed, alabaster bodies, whose virtue must be protected from the cunning encroachments of the outside world. The idea that women can't withstand verbal or emotional pressure infantilizes them. The suggestion lurking behind this definition of rape is that men are not just physically but intellectually and emotionally more powerful than women. Printing pamphlets about verbal coercion institutionalizes an unacceptable female position.

We should not nurture this woman on her back, her will so mutable, so easily shaped; we should not support her in her passivity. We are not this woman on her back. We do not have the mind of an eleven-year-old in the body of a twenty-year-old. All competent female college students are compromised by the association of gullibility, low self-esteem, and the inability to assert ourselves with our position in relation to men. We should not be pressured and intimidated by words like "I'll break up with you if you don't" — and anyone who is intimidated should be recognized as the exception, not the rule. Allowing verbal coercion to constitute rape is a sign of tolerance toward the ultra feminine stance of passivity. The brand of "low self-esteem" these psychologists describe should not be tolerated, it should be changed. Whether or not we feel pressured, regardless of our level of self-esteem, the responsibility for our actions is still our own.

Neil Gilbert, *The Phantom Epidemic of Sexual Assault*
103 The Public Interest 54, 55, 58-61 (1991)

Mary Koss's survey of 6,159 college students, sponsored by Ms. magazine, is the most widely cited study of sexual assault on campus. Her findings . . . reveal that at some time in their lives, 15 percent of the female students had been raped and another 11 percent had experienced an attempted rape, usually by an acquaintance. Forty-one percent of the women raped were virgins at the time of the attack. Less frequently cited is the finding that in just one year on college campuses, the 3,187 female respondents in the survey reported suffering 862 incidents of rape or attempted rape. While many of these women experienced more than one episode, this annual count represents a level of sexual assault that would claim victim to the vast majority of women at some point in their college careers. . . .

[In her survey,] Mary Koss was guided by what she calls a strict legal definition of rape: acts that involve the penetration of a woman "against consent through the use of force or threat of bodily harm, or intentional incapacitation of the victim." To identify victims of rape by this definition, survey respondents were asked ten questions about their sexual experiences, a few of which follow:

Have you had sexual intercourse when you didn't want to, because you were overwhelmed by a man's continual arguments and pressure? Because a man gave you alcohol or drugs? Because a man threatened or used some degree of physical force to compel you?

The report that one out of three female Stanford students has experienced date rape derives from a survey in which respondents revealed that they had "full sexual activity when they did not want to."

The results of these surveys, however, are misleading: in their efforts to capture the full extent of sexual molestation, the studies cast a large, tightly-woven net that snares the minnows with the sharks. If unwanted hugs and kisses are equated with the sexual abuse of children, we have all been victims. . . . [Other definitions include] conduct that ranges from attempted petting to any kind of exploitatve sexual contact. . . .

Mary Koss's view of rape is limited to sexual behavior that involves penetration. Koss, however, takes a strict legal definition and gives it a loose empirical interpretation. For example, if a woman said that she had had sexual intercourse when she did not want to, because a man gave her alcohol or drugs, Koss would label her a victim of rape. Presumably this is a case of "intentional incapacitation of the victim." Still, circumstances matter: what makes a difference are what the man's intention was, how much alcohol the woman had ingested, and whether and how she expressed her lack of consent. Fifty-five percent of the women identified by Koss as rape victims had been drinking or taking drugs just before the episode. Did the man order a beer or a bottle of wine during dinner? Did she select the brand and split the bill? Was she too intoxicated to reason with the man? Did she physically resist his advances or run away?

The behavioral referents for Koss's classification of attempted rape are equally ambiguous. Consider the following case. After having a drink, a young man and woman are sitting on a couch kissing in a tight embrace; she offers no objection, perhaps she even offers some encouragement. As he embraces her, with the thought of having intercourse in mind, the man touches the woman's genitals. She pushes his hand away and breaks out of the embrace. Although the man then stops and sheepishly apologizes, he has already committed a sexual act that involves alcohol, force, intent to penetrate, and lack of consent. Many would say that the young man misbehaved. As Koss would have it, this encounter qualifies as attempted rape.

Koss's empirical definitions of rape and attempted rape imply an understanding of sexual encounters that does not square with human attitudes and experiences. According to this view, a young woman who embraces a man who attracts her must know decisively whether or not she wants to have sexual intercourse at every given movement. Moreover, she must communicate these sentiments explicitly before any physical contact occurs. This perception does not allow for the modesty, emotional confusion, ambivalence, and vacillation that inexperienced young people may feel during the initial stages of sexual intimacy. (Remember that 41 percent of the women defined as victims of rape were virgins at the time of the incident.)

According to Koss, respondents were identified as victims of "sexual coercion" if they had engaged in sexual intercourse because they were "overwhelmed by a man's continual arguments and pressure." The conventional script of nagging and pleading — "Everyone does it," "If you really love me, you'd do it," "We did it last night," "You will like it" — is transformed into a version of sexual assault.

Under these definitions of rape and sexual coercion, the kaleidoscope of intimate discourse — passion, emotional turmoil, entreaties, flirtation, provocation, demureness — must give way to cool-headed contractual sex. "Will you do it, yes or no? Please sign on the line below."

How do reasonable women view this matter? Most of the female students surveyed disagreed with the operational definition of rape in the *Ms.* study. Seventy-three percent of those who the researcher defined as having been raped did not perceive of themselves as victims. Indeed, 42 percent of the women who were defined as having been raped had sex again with the men who had supposedly raped them. Among the college men surveyed, 84 percent of those identified as having committed rape disagreed with the researcher's interpretation of the incidents. Evidently, so did the women with whom they were involved, as 55 percent of these men had sex again with their putative victims. . . .

The feminist prescription redefines conventional morality so as to give women complete control of physical intimacy between the sexes. Advances by males, in almost any form, that do not receive clear and explicit consent are deemed coercive or assaultive. Passion, spontaneity, and the smile or not that implies assent are all ruled out of intimate discourse to be replaced by rational calculation and formal understanding. The awesome complexity of human interaction is reduced to "No means no" (even though "yes" may also mean "no").

Kim Lane Scheppele, *The Re-Vision of Rape Law*
54 U. Chi. L. Rev. 1095, 1108-1113 (1987)

[Individual perceptions of events are inevitably shaped by social context and experience.] Where a [rape] victim and defendant were previously friendly or where the disputed event occurred while they were dating or in another potentially intimate setting, perceptions of the victim and defendant about what really happened may diverge. . . . What seems to matter . . . is the opportunity for cue swapping, in which the potential for very different perceptions emerges. Once there is a question that the woman could have done something perceived by the man as a come on, the rape becomes less clear-cut in law. Again, this is not to say that the woman did not experience a rape. It's just that in circumstances like this, her definition of what has happened to her may not accord with the interpretations others may have of the same event. From what we know about the different perceptions of women and men, this should not be surprising.

Social psychological research shows that men often tend to read sexual intent into women's behavior when that intent is not there, but women do not seem to do the same with men. Men see women's friendliness as evidence of seductiveness and promiscuity when the women themselves think they're merely being polite. When given the same cues in a story about a friendship or a dating context, men are more likely than women to see the relationship as potentially sexual and to expect more sexual activity to be forthcoming. Men seem to sexualize their descriptions of women and of social situations, seeing women as being sexually receptive and as leading men on even with the most meager evidence.

And these attitudes are not just harmless pictures of the world, but frames within which men act. A study of a small number of convicted rapists indicates that they were very confused by women's signals in social or sexual situations and that they did not perceive what, to the women, were clear rejections of sexual advances as negative cues. After examining a group of studies in which men have been asked to report their likelihood of raping, Malamuth reports that about 35 percent of men indicated some chance that they would rape a woman if they could be assured that they would not be caught and punished. And those men who reported a higher likelihood of raping women were more accepting of a series of rape myths, such as the views that women want to be raped, that they ask for rape by the way they dress and act, that they are indicating they want to have sex if they invite men to their apartments or engage in kissing or touching of any sort. Studies of the sexual activity of college students conducted periodically since the 1950s indicate that between one-fourth and one-fifth of college women reported that they have been forced into sexual activity and recent studies show that between one-quarter and one-third of college men admit to using coercive methods to force women into sex. Men who engage in such coercive sexual activity are more likely to see women as adversaries and to have a value system that legitimizes aggression, particularly toward women.

The social psychological evidence reveals that, where men and women have a chance to interact and exchange cues about their intentions, men are frequently likely to be wrong about what the woman thinks is going on. Where perceptions diverge in this way, a woman may experience a rape that a man thought was just the normal aggression needed to overcome what he saw was the "no" that meant "yes." The social psychological evidence gives us reason to believe that these perceptual fault lines are deep, enduring, and of enormous consequence in daily life.

What is the law to do? The situation that confronts courts is not just the difficult matter of separating truth from falsehood, determining whether someone in the rape case is lying or whether there is enough evidence to sustain a conviction. Both judges and juries must face the fact that there often will be conflicting true versions of the same event and that what is true for one of the parties may not be true for the other. The only evidence we have consists of perceptions, whether they are the reports of the victim and defendant (filtered through the perceptions of judge and jury) or the ways judges' and juries' first-hand perceptions lead them to interpret the physical evidence and testimony available. There is no such thing as a value-neutral fact. All facts are made meaningful and "real" against a backdrop of expectations and interpretive conventions. Given the current state of divergent perceptions of men and women, the more troubling question for law is not the question of truth and falsehood, but instead the question of which true version of a particular story should be adopted as the official version of what happened.

Here, the obvious solutions of farming factual problems out to juries or putting more women on the bench are unlikely to settle the question satisfactorily, but not for the obvious reason. One might think that with the evidence presented here, it will be impossible for juries composed of men and women ever to agree on anything or that female judges necessarily will reach different conclusions from male judges, destroying whatever coherence exists in law. But we know from experience, at least with juries, that this is not so.[58] In addition, surveys of the general public indicate that men and women are not significantly different in many of their attitudes toward the appropriate legal standards for judging rape. When asked about whether the degree of a woman's resistance should be the major factor determining whether a rape has occurred, whether a delay in reporting means a rape probably didn't happen, and whether convicted rapists should get long sentences, men and women reveal almost identical attitudes.[59] Other questions, such as whether it would do some women good to be raped or

---

58. In [one] study of jurors in rape trials, no sex differences were found in the likelihood of voting for conviction. Hubert S. Field and Leigh B. Bienen, Jurors and Rape 121 (1980).
59. Field and Bienen, Jurors and Rape, supra, at 50-51.

whether a woman provokes a rapist by her appearance, do provoke different responses from women and men, but it is significant that in most of the questions where the subject is the correct legal standard there is substantial agreement. It is not impossible or even difficult to get agreement about the relevant legal standards against which particular cases should be judged and there seems to be substantial agreement about the correct legal result in particular cases. The perceptual fault lines between women and men do not seem to carry over into the context of law.

That is exactly the problem. Women and men do have very different perceptions of experience, but in the context of law one set of perceptions is hidden. Michel Foucault speaks of subjugated knowledge to describe such buried views. What remains — the perceptions acknowledged, recognized, and seen in law — is the socially constructed "objective" point of view against which both men's and women's actions are judged by both men and women. The point of view is the law. But it is not the point of view of all.

Notes

1. The Frequency of Acquaintance Rape. In a recent study by the Harvard School of Public Health, about a fifth of some 2,000 high school students surveyed report being a victim of sexual violence in a dating relationship, including being hit, slapped, or forced into sexual activity. Amy Dickinson, When Dating Is Dangerous, Time, Aug. 27, 2001, at 63. Statistics collected by the Bureau of Justice and National Institute of Justice similarly indicate that over a quarter of some 4,000 surveyed college-age women had experienced rape, attempted rape, unwanted sexual contact, or stalking during the seven-month period preceding the survey. Almost half the women who were identified by the researcher as having been raped did not consider it to be a rape. Over 40 percent did not report it because they did not think it was serious and were not sure a crime had been committed. Over 13 percent did not know how to make a report. Another 20 percent who were raped did not report it because they anticipated harsh or dismissive treatment by others in the justice system. Women had been taking drugs or alcohol in about 40 percent of the rape cases. Bureau of Justice Statistics, http://www.ojp.usdoj.gov/bjs.abstract.svew.htm (visited Feb. 19, 2001).

2. Consent and Responsibility. If the problem of acquaintance rape is largely a problem of unmatched perceptions and expectations, what responsibility, if any, do women share in perpetuating misconceptions and misunderstandings? Surveys of college students find that neither men nor women have complete confidence that a woman's "no" means "no" in a sexual situation. Kramer reports that in a survey by the Stanford University Rape Education Project, "[t]he 1,190 male and female students who responded overwhelmingly reported that when they say 'no' in a sexual situation, they mean it. Yet both men and women rated a 'no' from others as less meaningful than their own. Particularly striking was the belief among women that they mean no when they say 'no,' but that other women often do not." Kramer, supra, 47 Stan. L. Rev. at 118. Indeed, some college women admit to engaging in "token resistance," defined as "saying 'no' when they mean 'yes.'" In the study previously noted on the discussion of consent at page 967, about a third of the women admitted to having said "no" when they meant "yes." Charlene L. Muehlenhard & Lisa C. Hollabaugh, Do Women Sometimes Say No When They Mean Yes?: The Prevalence and Correlates of Women's Token Resistance to Sex, 54 J. Personality & Soc. Psychol. 872, 872 (1988).

How would you respond to Gilbert's claim that the feminist position on date rape unreasonably gives women complete control to define, after the fact, what is or is not acceptable, consensual sex? Is his point that whether rape has occurred should (continue to?) be judged by men's understandings? That men and women should have equal control? What rape rules would put men and women on an "equal" footing?

The study by Mary Koss to which Gilbert responds is analyzed in Robin Warshaw, I Never Called It Rape (1988). The methodology is described in detail in an afterword written by Dr. Koss. What do you make of her findings, described by Gilbert, that 42 percent of the women who were raped said they had sex again with the men who assaulted them?

> Because the rape victim doesn't believe that what has happened to her is rape, she sometimes decides to give her attacker another chance. After all, he's nice-looking, has a good job, or belongs to the right fraternity, and everyone else seems to think he's a great guy.
>
> What happens? Often, the same thing: He rapes her again. That's when most women bail out of continuing to see the men involved. In the Ms. survey, women who were raped had a mean average of 2.02 episodes. . . .
>
> Sometimes a woman sees the man who raped her again in order to turn the rape into an experience of sexual intercourse that happened in the context of an ongoing relationship and, therefore, to make it acceptable. For example, after being raped by a man she had dated for three weeks, Bonnie then had intercourse with him (she had been a virgin at the time of the rape). She explains her action as an attempt to "sort of legitimize what happened."

Id. at 63. If an adult woman doesn't realize she has been raped, to what extent is there a harm the law should recognize?

As noted earlier at page 966, Stephen J. Schulhofer argues that the harm is to women's autonomy and that individuals should have the right "to act freely on their own unconstrained conception of what their bodies and their sexual capacities are for." Schulhofer, Taking Sexual Autonomy Seriously, 11 Law & Phil. 35, 70 (1992). In his view, intercourse, without a clear declaration of consent by the woman, should be punishable as "nonviolent sexual misconduct." Id. at 77. Does this new criminal prohibition solve or compound the problems that Gilbert, Roiphe, and Scheppele discuss? Is there any room left for misunderstandings or mistakes of fact? Would you find the solution a satisfactory one? Would most Americans? If not, what would be satisfactory?

John Leo captures widespread concerns in objecting even to the "no means no" formula in consent because "no can mean 'maybe', 'convince me', 'back off a while', or 'get lost'. The mating game does not proceed by words alone." John Leo, Two Steps Ahead of the Thought Police 247 (1994). In Leo's view, the "demonization" of men that is common in feminists' writing on date rape is profoundly unjust. If women cannot be clear about their preferences, men should not pay the price.

Given the enormous physical, psychological, and social consequences that accompany conviction as a sex offender, who should bear the risk of misunderstood signals? How much responsibility should women have to prevent such misunderstandings?

Do you share Roiphe's concern that the notion of "verbal coercion" presents women as passive, innocent, and "ultra feminine," incapable of taking responsibility for their own actions? Was the Stanford student in Kramer's article raped? What do you make of the "coercion" she says she experienced? Kramer reports that the police detective investigating the case recommended that the district attorney prosecute Thomas on several charges, including statutory rape and a violation of California Penal Code §261.3, which defines an act as rape when "a person is prevented from resisting by any intoxicating or anesthetic substance, or any controlled substance, administered by or with the privity of the accused." The district attorney concluded that there was insufficient evidence to charge forcible rape and decided to charge Thomas only with statutory rape. Kramer, supra, 47 Stan. L. Rev. at 143. Would Thomas have been charged under Schulhofer's proposal?

Do the issues of consent and coercion in acquaintance rape mask other cultural dynamics? Roiphe argues that fears about "verbal coercion" and concerns about "miscommunication" between men and women in sexual situations disguise deeper, unarticulated fears about class and racial mixing on college campuses: "The conservative thrust of the movement against date rape is that women need to be protected from men who don't share their social background." Roiphe, The Morning After, supra, at 79. Karen Kramer argues that cases of acquaintance rape are complicated by social expectations about alcohol: it is widely believed in our society that "alcohol increases sexual arousal, loosens women's sexual inhibitions, and increases men's feelings of power and dominance." Kramer, supra, at 120; see also Caroline Knapp, Drinking: A Love Story (1996) (arguing that for many women, drinking is a way to engage in sexual behavior without taking responsibility for it). How should the law respond?

3. Institutional Responsibilities. What are the responsibilities of educational institutions to prevent and remedy sexual assault? In 1990, as part of an effort to increase accountability for student safety, Congress passed the Campus Security Act. It requires all colleges and universities receiving federal funds to report campus crime statistics, including all forcible or nonforcible sexual offenses. 20 U.S.C §1092(f)(1)(F)(i)(II) (2001). Failure to report can result in fines up to $25,000 or other enforcement action by the U.S. Department of Education.

Despite this requirement, many sexual assaults go unreported, partly because institutions are reluctant to disclose anything that would alarm prospective students and their families. Robyn Gearey, College Cop Out: Closing the Books on Campus Crime, The New Republic, Nov. 10, 1997, at 21. Schools have an additional reason to avoid reporting when an incident of sexual assault involves a star athelete whose eligibility might be compromised. Paul McEnroe & Chris Ison, Taking a Chance on Athletes, Star-Tribune (Minneapolis, MN), Dec. 17, 1999, at 1A; Deborah Reed, Where's the Penalty Flag: A Call for the NCAA to Promulgate an Eligibility Rule Revoking a Male Student-Athlete's Eligibility to Participate in Intercollegiate Athletics for Committing Violent Acts Against Women, 21 Women's Rights L. Rep. 41 (1999); Margaret Fosmoe, Prosecutions Rare in Student Assault Cases, South-Bend Tribune, May 1, 2000, at A1. School administrators often encourage complainants to rely on confidential campus complaint procedures rather than on formal police reports that would need to be included in annual crime statistics. A case in point involved Christy Brzonkala, the student whose claim under the Violence Against Women Act resulted in Supreme Court review. See United States v. Morrison, excerpted on pages 675-686, supra. Virginia Tech failed to disclose her complaint of rape by two prominent football players and attempted to dissuade her from making any public disclosures. Brzonkala, Sept. 11, 1996, <http://campus-safety. org/publicpolicy/congress1104/brzonkala470.html>. See also United States v. Miami University, 91 F. Supp. 2d 1132 (S.D. Ohio 2000) (student disciplinary records are "education records" protected by the Family Educational Rights and Privacy Act, and thus may not be released to media).

How should the law respond to these enforcement failures? Should Congress amend the Campus Security Act to include a private right of action for monetary damages if a school negligently fails to report abuse? What other prevention and remedial measures might be appropriate? Are women ever justified in resorting to "self-help?" Consider, for example, the widely criticized practice of students who, frustrated by administrative inaction, responded by naming their alleged assailants on bathroom walls. See William Celis 3d Date Rape and a List at Brown, N.Y. Times, Nov. 18, 1990, at 26. Are rape education programs the preferable alternative? Some evidence finds that well-designed programs can alter attitudes about sexual aggression, but little effort has been made to assess long-term behavioral changes. See

Kimberly A. Hanson & Christine A. Gidycz, Evaluation of a Sexual Assault Prevention Program, 61 J. Counseling & Clinical Psychol. 1046 (1993); Patrick J. Harrison, Jeannette Downes, & Michael D. Williams, Data and Acquitable Rape: Perceptions and Attitude Change Strategies, 32 College Student Rev. 31 (1991).

4. Law and Social Change. To what extent is the criminal law an appropriate tool for changing sexual attitudes? In the debates over greater use of the criminal law to control family violence, Franklin E. Zimring raises the "tactical question [of] whether stretching retributive limits will underscore the seriousness of spousal exploitation rather than produce disrespect and rejection of the legal result." Zimring, Legal Perspectives on Family Violence, 75 Cal. L. Rev. 521, 538 (1987). Is the criminal law likely to be effective in deterring the behavior of men who engage in behavior that they perceive as welcome?

What are the hazards of the criminal law being "too far out in front" of public attitudes about the contact that it seeks to prohibit? Consider the following portion of a letter to the editor of the Duke University student newspaper:

> I am sick of a bunch of whining women who place blame for social evils on the nearest scapegoat, and I am tired of these women pointing their fingers at me and all other males.

Tony Leung, Don't Assign Blame for Rape So Quickly, Chronicle, Mar. 28, 1990, at 8, cols. 3-4. Is there a reasoned response to this complaint?

Putting Theory into Practice

6-2. Should sexual intercourse under the following circumstances constitute a crime?*

a. A welfare-dependent mother of three young children who can't seem to make ends meet succumbs to the sexual pressures of a man who is willing to provide her the financial support she needs if she does so.

b. A successful attorney agrees to have sex with a politician who appears willing to help him land a much-coveted political appointment if he does so.

c. A struggling law student agrees to have sex with a fellow student so that she will have his assistance in publishing an acceptable law review note and in running for an officer position on the review.

---

*Circumstances (a) and (b) were inspired by hypotheticals discussed in Schulhofer, Taking Sexual Autonomy Seriously, supra, at 84.

6. Prostitution: Consent under Conditions of Constraint

≣
≣
≣
Margaret Jane Radin, The Pragmatist and the Feminist
63 S. Cal. L. Rev. 1699, 1699-1701 (1990)

If the social regime permits buying and selling of sexuality . . . , thereby treating [it] as a fungible market commodit[y] given the capitalistic understandings of monetary exchange, there is a threat to the personhood of women, who are the "owners" of these "commodities." The threat to personhood from commodification arises because essential attributes are treated as severable fungible objects, and this denies the integrity and uniqueness of the self. But if the social regime prohibits this kind of commodification it denies women the choice to market their sexual . . . services, and given the current feminization of poverty and lack of avenues for free choice for women, this also poses a threat to the personhood of women. The threat from enforced noncommodification arises because narrowing women's choices is a threat to liberation, and because their choices to market sexual . . . services, even if nonideal, may represent the best alternatives available to those who would choose them.

Thus the double bind: both commodification and noncommodification may be harmful. Harmful, that is, under our current social conditions. Neither one need be harmful in an ideal world. The fact that money changes hands need not necessarily contaminate human interactions of sharing, nor must the fact that a social order makes nonmonetary sharing its norm necessarily deprive or subordinate anyone. That commodification now tends toward fungibility of women and noncommodification now tends toward their domination and continued subordination are artifacts of the current social hierarchy. In other words, the fact of oppression is what gives rise to the double bind.

Thus, it appears that the solution to the double bind is not to solve but to dissolve it: remove the oppressive circumstances. But in the meantime, if we are practically limited to those two choices, which are we to choose? I think that the answer must be pragmatic. We must look carefully at the nonideal circumstances in each case and decide which horn of the dilemma is better (or less bad), and we must keep re-deciding as time goes on.

To generalize a bit, it seems that there are two ways to think about justice. One is to think about justice in an ideal world, the best world that we can now conceive. The other is to think about nonideal justice; given where we now find ourselves, what is the better decision? In making this decision, we think about what actions can bring us closer to ideal justice. For example, if we allow commodification, we may push further away any ideal of a less commodified future. But if we enforce noncommodification, we may push further away any ideal of a less dominated future. In making our decisions of nonideal justice, we must also realize that these decisions will help to reconstitute our ideals. For example, if we commodify all attributes of personhood, the ideal of personhood we now know will evolve into another one that does not conceive fungibility as bad. The double bind, then, is a problem involving nonideal justice, and I think its only solution can be pragmatic. There is no general solution; there are only piecemeal, temporary solutions.

Holly B. Fechner, Three Stories of Prostitution in the West: Prostitutes' Groups, Law, and Feminist "Truth"
4 Colum. J. Gender & L. 26, 33, 34, 37, 40-45, 47-50 (1994)

The Red Thread (DeRode Draad), founded in the Netherlands in 1985 by prostitutes and ex-prostitutes, organizes women in prostitution to assert their civil rights. It educates the public, provides legal and health education to prostitutes, acts as a community center for women in prostitution, and advocates for decriminalization of prostitution for all parties.

The English Collective of Prostitutes [ECP] argues that poverty is the cause of prostitution and that women need other economic options. It was founded in 1975 by prostitutes and ex-prostitutes. . . . The ECP concentrates on public education through numerous campaigns for decriminalization of prostitution and improved social services for women.

Women Hurt in Systems of Prostitution Engaged in Revolt [WHISPER], begun in 1985 by survivors of prostitution and women's advocates, views prostitution as violence against women and children that constitutes an integral part of a pervasive system of sex discrimination. WHISPER educates the public and women in prostitution and advocates for social services for women attempting to escape sexual exploitation. It supports strengthened legal penalties against pimps and tricks and expanded civil rights remedies for women and children. . . .

Women of color disproportionately comprise the clientele of each group, mirroring their overrepresentation in lesser paid forms of prostitution in each country. . . .

The Red Thread employs a liberal feminist analysis of prostitution. It is affiliated with the International Committee for Prostitutes' Rights (ICPR) and various sister organizations in the United States, particularly COYOTE in San Francisco. Four themes pervade the Red Thread's materials and campaigns: prostitution as work, improving prostitutes' working conditions, maximizing and validating women's choices, and eradicating the social stigma of prostitution through such methods as public education and decriminalization of prostitution. Consistent with fundamental principles of liberalism, the Red Thread's story describes prostitution in terms of rights, independence, autonomy and self-fulfillment. The Red Thread's vision of equality insists that prostitution is work and that prostitutes deserve the same rights as other workers. . . . The Red Thread attempts to convey a sense of dignity and sophistication about the "profession" of prostitution to the world and to women working in prostitution. . . .

The [ECP] represents prostitutes' interests based on social feminist theories. . . . It advocates economic justice for all women and abolition of all laws against prostitution. . . . Three themes pervade its materials and organizing efforts: poverty is the cause of prostitution, women (particularly women of color and lesbians) are often poor, and the government supports these conditions by its inaction. Poverty forces women into the sex industry, argues the ECP. "This is what prostitution is about — money and the lack of it," its leaders exclaim. "That lack, that poverty, is what is immoral and criminal." By positing poverty as the cause of prostitution, the ECP argues that women are not free to choose prostitution as a work option: "Sex is supposed to be personal, always a free choice, different from work. But it's not a free choice when we are dependent on men for money." Poverty turns sex into work out of necessity.

The ECP offers a feminist critique of capitalism that views sexuality as merely one more commodity to be sold on the market. "[S]exuality is a commodity all women are forced to 'sell' in one way or another. Our poverty as women leaves us little choice." . . . Prostitutes refuse to accept their poverty by making money from what most women give to men for free.
. . .

In this way, prostitution is a form of protest. . . . In the view of the ECP, the government is implicated in the oppression of women by failing to provide adequate social services and failing to value women's contributions to society. The government, the ECP claims, is the biggest pimp of all by taking advantage of women's labor (in the form of emotional and sexual services to men and physical and emotional care of families) and failing to compensate them for it as other services are compensated within a social welfare state. . . .

Increased social welfare benefits, increased wages for work by women, and wages for housework so that no woman is forced into prostitution form the basis for the ECP's solution. . . .

The ECP favors decriminalization — the compete abolition of all laws against prostitution. It perceives prostitution laws as punishing women for their refusal to be poor. . . .

. . . WHISPER . . . asserts that prostitution is a system of exploitation and violence that differentially harms women. Because women suffer the harms of prostitution, WHISPER proposes social and legal reforms to shift the burden to men who benefit from it, particularly pimps and tricks. It endorses the abolition of all laws that penalize women and children in prostitution and supports enhanced penalties for pimps and tricks, including new civil rights causes of action for women and children used in prostitution.

It opposes what it views as the sexual liberals' promotion of, and apology for, the commercial exploitation of women.

. . . "The real harm of prostitution," its leaders claim, is that it allows men to use women as sexual objects, [in] a rape-like mentality." Prostitution makes all women objects for men's use and abuse. . . . Prostitution allows men unconditional sexual access to women and children limited solely by their ability to pay for it.

The mere exchange of money, claims WHISPER, cannot change acts of violence against women into work. . . . WHISPER argues that addressing prostitution as if it were an occupation buys into the myth perpetuated by men that women are available to serve men's sexual desires.

By documenting the violence and manipulation used to recruit and trap women in the sex industry, we've come to realize that prostitution is not a "career choice" or a "victimless crime," but rather prostitution creates an environment in which crimes against women and children are defined as a commercial enterprise. Women cannot choose or consent to prostitution under current conditions of sex inequality, claims WHISPER. . . .

Notes

1. **Historical Background.** Prostitution has long been a focus of feminist concern:

> . . . During most of its first century, the American women's movement viewed prostitution as the preeminent metaphor for sexual oppression. The "social evil," variously defined, became the symbol of female subordination.
>
> In explaining that focus, historians have identified a complex set of forces. Until the antebellum period, prostitution remained an unobtrusive presence on the social and legal landscape. Early-nineteenth-century common law did not criminalize prostitution per se, although it could be prosecuted under other offenses such as lewdness, fornication, adultery, or disorderly conduct. The shortage of women and the tight-knit character of American communities worked against commercial vice. Much of the adult sexual exploitation that occurred involved slaves and domestic servants rather than an independent class of prostitutes. With industrialization, urbanization, and western migration, prostitution became more visible. As single men moved to the frontier, they decreased the supply of eligible bachelors in established communities and increased the demand for sexual outlets in unsettled regions. Markets also emerged near military camps and seaports. Women, particularly immigrants and women of color, who could find neither husbands nor adequate employment, were increasingly likely to conclude that the "wages of sin" were better than any available alternative. The relative anonymity of urban areas, the growing secularization of American society, and the tacit tolerance of law-enforcement officials accelerated such trends. Despite occasional "whorehouse riots," in which an aroused citizenry torched local brothels, the tendency was

> toward peaceful coexistence as long as prostitutes kept within accepted
> geographic and social bounds.

Deborah L. Rhode, Justice and Gender 253 (1989). The first major
challenges to this regime, variously characterized as "moral reform" and
"social purity" campaigns, began in the 1830s and resurfaced in the late
nineteenth and early twentieth centuries. At the outset, the leaders of these
initiatives were mainly male clergy and philanthropists, but women's
organizations soon joined the crusade. Their goals were to reform
prostitutes and to discourage men from employing or recruiting them. Id. at
254-255; Elizabeth Pleck, Feminist Responses to "Crimes Against Wom-
en," 1868-1896, 8 Signs 451 (1983). These efforts led to expanded criminal
prohibitions and enforcement strategies.

The criminalization of prostitution has been justified on multiple
grounds: promoting conventional morality, protecting public health, avoiding public nuisance, and preventing sexual exploitation and abuse. Class,
race, and ethnic prejudice also underpinned many of the early "antivice"
campaigns. Many moral reformers were particularly concerned by the vision
of husbands of white women consorting with lower-class immigrants and
women of color. Rhode, Justice and Gender, supra, at 256; Mark Thomas
Connelly, The Response to Prostitution in the Progressive Era 50-69, 97
(1980).

In 1908, the Supreme Court articulated the central moral argument for
criminal sanctions:

> The lives and example of such persons are in hostility to "the idea of the family,
> as consisting in the springing from the union for life of one man and one
> woman in the holy estate of matrimony; the sure foundation of all that is stable
> and noble in our civilization, the best guaranty of that reverent morality which
> is the source of all beneficent progress in social and political improvement."

United States v. Bitty, 208 U.S. 393, 401 (1908) (quoting Murphy v.
Ramsey, 114 U.S. 15, 45 (1885)). Should this view inform current policy?

2. The Legal Status of Prostitution. The legal status of prostitution
varies considerably. Most countries either prohibit or regulate the sale of sex,
but the scope of permissible behavior, the severity of penalties, and the
practices of enforcement agencies vary widely. In this country, every state
but Nevada prohibits engaging in sexual intercourse for money or offering
to do so. Every state but Nevada also makes it a crime knowingly to
encourage or compel a person to sell sex for money (pandering) or to receive
"something of value" knowing that it was earned through an act of
prostitution (pimping). Sylvia Law, Commercial Sex: Beyond Decriminalization, 73 S. Cal. L. Rev. 523, 530 (2000). Most jurisdictions classify first-
time offenses as misdemeanors, but typically punish repeat behavior as a
felony. Joann Miller, Prostitution in Contemporary American Society, in

Sexual Coercion: A Sourcebook on Its Nature, Causes and Prevention 45, 53 (Elizabeth Grauerholz & Mary Koralewski eds., 1991). About half of all states have a "patron clause," which subjects customers to the same penalty as prostitutes. Id. at 53, 57 n.9. Other jurisdictions classify patronizing a prostitute as a less serious offense.

Nevada permits prostitution in counties with populations under 200,000 persons, subject to highly restrictive licensing conditions. Prostitutes must be registered and fingerprinted by the police and must work in brothels where they typically have no control over their hours or customers. County police have broad discretion to regulate the conditions under which commercial sex is permissible. For example, prostitutes generally may not have their children live in the same community in which they work, drive a car in city limits, or be on the streets after 5 P.M. Law, supra, at 560. Although the system has effectively reduced street solicitation and incidental crime in areas surrounding brothels and has largely eliminated the risks of sexually transmitted diseases, it has failed to curtail illegal prostitution elsewhere in the state. About a thousand women work in 33 licensed brothels and account for only a small percentage of those estimated to be working in Nevada. Id.

Experience in other countries with licensure systems is comparable. Most European countries, following the United Nations recommendations, have repealed prohibitions on engaging in prostitution but have retained laws against soliciting, pimping, pandering, running a disorderly house, or transporting a woman across national boundaries for purposes of prostitution. See United Nations Study on Profits in Persons and Prostitution (1959). Other restrictions range from fairly laissez-faire approaches in countries like Denmark to tightly controlled zoning systems for licensed brothels in many German cities. See Law, supra, at 552-554; Priscilla Alexander, Prostitution: A Difficult Issue for Feminists, in Sex Work: Writings by Women in the Sex Industry 184 (Frédérique Delacoste & Priscilla Alexander eds., 2d ed. 1987). Even where commercial sex is legal and taxable, workers often lack basic rights and benefits, such as pensions, health insurance, and unemployment benefits. "Jasmin", Prostitution Is Work, 37 Social Text 33 (1993). The same is true in Nevada, where prostitutes are classified as independent contractors rather than employees. Law, supra, at 543.

In other countries, particularly those in Asia, South America, and the Mideast, prostitution remains a criminal offense. The prohibitions in some tradition-oriented societies are quite severe. In other nations, a de facto licensing system has evolved despite formal prohibitions. Such patterns are especially common in areas around military installations and other predominantly male work sites. In some countries, the United States armed forces have worked with local authorities to promote "safe" but accessible sex for overseas servicemen. United States bases have attracted large concentrations of "bar girls" or "hospitality women," sometimes 10,000 to 20,000 per base. Women not complying with registration requirements (including periodic medical exams) are subject to arrest, and employers with a specified percentage of unregistered workers may be declared off-limits to servicemen. Cynthia Enloe, The Morning After, 118-120, 142-160 (1993); Saundra Pollock Sturdevant & Brenda Stoltzfus, Olongopo: The Bar System, in Let the Good Times Roll: Prostitution and the United States Military in Asia 45 (Saundra Pollock Sturdevant & Brenda Stoltzfus, eds. 1992); Tong du Chun: The Bar System, in id. at 176. Through de facto or de jure licensing structures, a growing number of Asian and European countries are also developing sex tourism industries. See Section B.4.

In this country, there have been frequent legal challenges to prostitution statutes but infrequent successes. Some courts have struck down, on equal protection grounds, statutes that apply only to female prostitutes. Plas v. State, 598 P.2d 966 (Alaska 1979). Other judges have upheld gender-specific laws on the theory that women are subject to greater risks, such as pregnancy. See Flute v. State, 282 S.E.2d 112, 113 (Ga. 1981) (upholding pandering law applicable only to male pandering of females). Courts have also rejected challenges based on state or federal privacy guarantees on the ground that sexual freedom is not a right that is fundamental or implicit in the concept of ordered liberty. Hawaii v. Mueller, 671 P.2d 1351 (Haw. 1983).

Although most statutes are now gender-neutral in form, they do not work out that way in fact, largely because law enforcement officials rarely prosecute customers or pimps. For example, over a two-year period in New York, which has a statute punishing both parties who engage in commercial sex, customers accounted for only about 1 percent of all arrests. The percentage of pimps among those arrested was even lower. Miller, supra at 52. A Boston survey reveals similar patterns. See Minouche Kandel, Whores in Court: Judicial Processing of Prostitutes in the Boston Municipal Court in 1990, 4 Yale J.L. & Feminism 333 (1992) (finding 263 arrests of female prostitutes and 8 of male pimps; half of the 8 were dismissed).

Efforts to challenge such discriminatory enforcement patterns have been largely unsuccessful. In some jurisdictions, the reasoning is that no impermissible discrimination occurs as long as male and female prostitutes are treated alike. People v. Superior Court of Alameda County, 562 P.2d 1315, 1321 (Cal. 1977). In other jurisdictions, the rationale is that sellers of sex constitute a "greater danger to society" than buyers or that prostitutes and customers are violating different laws. State v. Tookes, 699 P.2d 983, 988 (Haw. 1985); State v. Hicks, 360 A.2d 150 (Del. Super. Ct. 1976), aff'd, 373 A.2d 205 (Del. 1977); People v. Nelson, 427 N.Y.S.2d 194, 197 (N.Y. City Ct. 1980); Commonwealth v. King, 372 N.E.2d 196 (Mass. 1977). In addition, courts have often concluded that "concentrating . . . enforcement effort on the 'profiteer,' rather than the customer, of commercial vice" is a way for a police department "to efficiently utilize its limited resources. . . ." People v. Superior Court of Alameda County, supra,

562 P.2d at 1320, 1321 (1977) (upholding police practice of employing more males than females as decoys for solicitation). From this perspective, enforcement priorities concerning prostitution appear similar to those concerning narcotic traffic, where "no one seriously suggests that it is inappropriate . . . to concentrate on the profiteer. . . ." Id. at 1321.

In drug transactions, police often use arrests of street dealers as a way to obtain evidence against those higher up in drug conspiracies. As is clear from the studies cited above, law enforcement officials seldom rely on this strategy in prostitution cases; enforcement focuses largely on streetwalkers, yet the most substantial profits from prostitution are obtained not by these workers, the main targets of arrests, but by pimps and other middlemen such as operators of massage parlors and escort services. Should this fact be relevant in assessing equal protection claims? Consider the experience of the Oakland Police Department during the mid-1970s, when it was briefly compelled by court order to employ female decoys and arrest male customers. This practice reportedly resulted in a "devastating" reduction in prostitution-related offenses. People v. Superior Court of Alameda County, supra, 562 P.2d at 1325 (Tobriner, J., dissenting). Similar reductions have resulted in other jurisdictions that targeted customers. Id.

In Commonwealth v. An Unnamed Defendant, 492 N.E.2d 1184 (Mass. App. Ct. 1986), a Massachusetts appellate court held that a local police department policy to arrest female but not male streetwalkers or male customers failed to satisfy strict scrutiny under the state's Equal Rights Amendment. One stated reason for the policy was that the citizens complained only about the women, and they were more recognizable to the officers. Is that rationale more objectionable than the one in Oakland? Is it a more plausible explanation for selective enforcement policies? If patrons faced a substantial risk of arrest, could the resulting stigma have a significant deterrent effect on the trade? Would that be in "women's interests"? Which women? See Julie Lefler, Shining the Spotlight on Johns: Moving Toward Equal Treatment of Male Customers and Female Prostitutes, 10 Hastings L.J. 11 (1999), and discussion below.

3. The Market for Prostitution. There are no reliable estimates of the amount of prostitution worldwide. However, what limited data are available suggest a market of "staggering dimensions," Laura Reanda, Prostitution as a Human Rights Question: Problems and Prospects of United Nations Action, 13 Hum. Rights Q. 202, 205 (1991). For example, Brazil reportedly has five million female prostitutes, many of them children. Id. Estimates of the number of women in this country whose primary source of income is prostitution range from 250,000 to 1.3 million. See Law, supra, at 527; Catharine A. MacKinnon, Sex Equality 1384 (2001). Other research suggests that roughly one in six men has been a client in the past five years. Robert T. Michael et al., Sex in America: A Definitive Study 63 (1994); Legalized Prostitution: Street Cleaning, The Economist, Sept. 7, 1991, at

A28. Over a hundred thousand individuals are arrested for prostitution each year. About 10 percent of those arrests are of customers and 20 percent are of male prostitutes, although in some jurisdictions the percentages are far lower. Alexander, supra, at 205. Commercial sex accounts for a larger number of female arrests than any other crime.

The market for prostitution is highly stratified, with street workers at the bottom of the occupational hierarchy. They account for 85 to 90 percent of all prostitution arrests, but only about 10 to 20 percent of all prostitutes. Prostitution also occurs through massage parlors, bars, and cafes. Brothels are establishments specifically devoted to prostitution. Countries with legalized brothels often confine them to particular districts. Call girl or escort services account for the most sex work in this country.

Traditionally, call girls worked independently, but escort services are increasingly making initial connections between customers and sex workers, who then arrange their own meetings. Other categories of sex work that overlap or are closely allied with prostitution involve some forms of live sexual entertainment, domestic work that includes sexual relations with employers, and mail-order bride purchases.

The prostitution industry is also stratified by race, class, gender, and sexual orientation. In this, as in many countries, racism is apparent both in the demographics of employment and in law enforcement responses. Women of color account for an estimated 40 percent of street prostitutes in the United States, 50 percent of those who are arrested, and 85 percent of those who receive jail sentences. Ann M. Lucas, Race, Class, Gender and Deviancy: The Criminalization of Prostitution, 10 Berkeley Women's L.J. 47, 49 (1995); Vednita Nelson, Prostitution: Where Racism and Sexism Intersect, 1 Mich. J. Gender & L., 81, 85 (1993). Women of color also pay higher fines and serve longer jail time than their white counterparts. Id. As the discussion below notes, racist marketing and enforcement strategies are also common in other nations.

Prostitution directed at gay, lesbian, and straight women customers occupies a relatively small but growing share of the domestic and global market. Some escort services provide sexual as well as social companions for heterosexual women, while prostitution for lesbians is connected with a modest number of bars. See Joan Nestle, Lesbians and Prostitutes: A Historical Sisterhood, in Good Girls/Bad Girls: Feminists and Sex Trade Workers Face to Face 131 (Laurie Bell ed., 1987). Gay men constitute a larger market and generally seek boys or transvestites. From the Floor, in id. at 126.

4. Alternative Regulatory Structures. Few, if any, feminists support America's current approach to prostitution, but they differ widely over what would be an acceptable alternative. Early in this century, British feminist Sylvia Pankhurst captured the essence of what is objectionable about criminalization of commercial sex: legislation that "was passed ostensibly to protect women [has been used] to punish them." Rhode, Justice and Gender, supra, at 257 (quoting Pankhurst). The current system is objectionable on multiple grounds. It stigmatizes and degrades certain women, predominantly poor women and women of color, for doing overtly what many women have always done covertly: trade sex for material advantages. Criminalizing commercial sex increases women's vulnerability to physical abuse and economic coercion. Studies of streetwalkers typically find that about two-thirds to four-fifths are subject to physical assault and to extremely high rates of rape and murder. See sources cited in Law, supra, at 533; Deborah L. Rhode, Speaking of Sex 82 (1997); Alexander, supra, at 184; MacKinnon, Sex Equality, supra, at 1410-1419. Women are reluctant to report activities that could lead to prosecution, and police systematically fail to pursue complaints by sex workers. Law, supra, at 533. Arrest records heighten women's difficulties in moving to alternative work and often force them to rely on pimps and middlemen to screen customers or provide money for bail and fines. Rhode, Justice and Gender, supra, at 260-261.

It is not only prostitutes that bear the costs of largely ineffective enforcement efforts. The United States spends upward of $10 million yearly in prostitution arrests that seldom target the main profiteers: men who are pimps or who operate brothels, massage parlors, and escort services. Julie Pearl, The Highest Paying Customers: America's Cities and the Costs of Prostitution Control, 38 Hastings L.J. 797 (1987); Rhode, Speaking of Sex, supra, at 82. It costs over $2,000 to prosecute a single woman offender, who typically returns almost immediately to the streets. Id.; San Francisco Task Force on Prostitution, Final Report Submitted to the Board of Supervisors of the City and County of San Francisco (1996).

The most commonly proposed alternatives to the current system are

- full decriminalization, i.e., removal of penalties from all consensual sexual activities and related commercial practices;

- partial decriminalization, i.e., removal of penalties from the sale of sexual services but not from other related activities such as purchasing, pimping, pandering, soliciting, or advertising; and

- regulation, i.e., removal of penalties from activities that meet state-imposed requirements, such as zoning restrictions, licensing regulations, and health exams.

Most organizations of sex workers, such as The Red Thread and COYOTE, support full decriminalization and take the left-liberal view that any activity should be legal so long as it is not coerced. In their view, the legalization of victimless crimes would better enable the state to regulate coercion and other abuses. Jody Freeman sets out the arguments that prostitution rights groups make within this general framework in The Feminist Debate over Prostitution Reform: Prostitutes' Rights Groups,

Radical Feminists, and the (Im)possibility of Consent, 5 Berkeley Women's L.J. 75, 90 (1989-1990). Similarly, the ECP views the coercion involved in prostitution as economic in nature, with the only effective remedies being economic as well. From this perspective, prostitution is simply one form of the exploitation fostered by advanced capitalism.

WHISPER, like the ECP, finds prostitution rooted deeply in a comprehensive, pervasive system of exploitation. For WHISPER, however, the coercion is fundamentally sexual, rather than economic, and it supports only partial decriminalization.

> Prostitution isn't like anything else. Rather everything else is like prostitution, because it is the model for women's condition, for gender stratification and its logical extension, sex discrimination.

Sarah Wynter, WHISPER: Women Hurt in Systems of Prostitution Engaged in Revolt, in Sex Work, supra, at 266, 268. WHISPER's objective is to shift the burden of prostitution from women to the men who benefit from it. In addition to greater use of criminal sanctions against "pimps" and "johns," one strategy is to publish names and pictures of prostitutes' patrons in local newspapers. This practice is described and analyzed, on both policy and constitutional grounds, in Courtney Guyton Persons, Sex in the Sunlight: The Effectiveness, Efficiency, Constitutionality, and Advisability of Publishing Names and Pictures of Prostitutes' Patrons, 49 Vand. L. Rev. 1525 (1996) (concluding that the practice is not likely to be effective and, when occurring before conviction, violates defendants' fair trial rights).

A related strategy, exemplified in a Florida statute, is to create civil remedies, including compensatory and punitive damages and attorney's fees, for women and girls compelled to participate in prostitution through such means as threats, extortion, promise of legal benefit or rewards such as an acting or modeling contract, promise of marriage, threat of legal interference with the woman's relationship with her children, and exploitation of a developmental disability or substance dependency or of a woman's need for food, shelter, safety, or affection. Fla. Stat. Ann. §796.09 (West 2000). The statute is discussed by one of its drafters in Margaret A. Baldwin, Strategies of Connection: Prostitution and Feminist Politics, 1 Mich. J. Gender & L. 65 (1993). One action under the statute was brought against a car salesman and his dealership when the salesman allegedly coerced the plaintiff, whose credit was said not to be good enough to get a car loan, into having sex as a condition of obtaining a car.

Such approaches are supported by many feminists, but opposed by most organizations of current sex workers. From their perspective, anything that interferes with the ability of prostitutes to profit from sex work or limits the ways that they can use their profits, including support of pimps, is a violation of women's rights to control their own sexuality. Where all of these groups converge is in opposing criminal penalties for workers themselves and in supporting strategies that would ensure their safety. According to most feminists and sex workers, the way for society to minimize the harms associated with prostitution is to maximize women's employment choices, increase their access to social services, improve the working conditions of prostitution, and eliminate the social stigma associated with consensual commercial sex. As Carlin Meyer puts it:

> [C]riminalization and regulation of prostitution, far more than prostitution itself, institutionalizes male sexual domination and social control of women. . . . When society regulates prostitutes, it ideologizes and enforces a pervasive system of control of women's bodies, not merely through direct control of "bad girls," but by establishing indirect and rigid codes for "good girls."

Carlin Meyer, Decriminalizing Prostitution: Liberation or Dehumanization?, 1 Cardozo Women's L.J. 105, 108 (1993). See also Catharine A. MacKinnon, Prostitution and Civil Rights, 1 Mich. J. Gender & L. 13, 20 (1996) (claiming that criminal laws against prostitution are a form of sex discrimination, in that they represent "legal victimization piled on top of social victimization," which legitimates women's subordination).

Most feminists and sex workers are also united in opposing regulation as an alternative to decriminalization. Workers generally object to the highly restrictive conditions imposed by licensing structures and to the large share of profits taken by brothel owners (typically 50 percent). Law, supra, at 561; Rebecca Mead, American Pimp, New Yorker, Apr. 23 and 30, 2001, at 74, 78. It is telling that only a small percentage of Nevada's prostitutes work in licensed brothels despite the relatively substantial incomes available. Women in small establishments can net up to $1,500 a week after room and board, while women in large establishments make substantially more. As independent contractors, prostitutes generally set their own prices for different services, and customers at establishments like the Moonlight Bunnyranch pay from $100 to several thousand dollars for their experience. Mead, supra, at 82.

Is the profitability of such forms of prostitution part of the problem rather than the solution? To what extent would legalization of prostitution represent state collaboration in the exploitation and commodification of female sexuality?

5. Prostitution and the Autonomy of Women. At issue in debates over prostitution are fundamental issues about the meaning of consent and the nature of sexual expression under circumstances of true equality. Among the most divisive issues are whether any women who engage in commercial sex have made truly free choices to do so and whether sex work is work like any other and preferable along some dimensions. What complicates the debate are the diversity of experiences among women engaged in commercial sex and the inadequate or conflicting data concerning their experiences.

The objective conditions and subjective perceptions of prostitutes vary considerably. As one worker put it, "[s]ome [women] feel they are victims. Some *are* victims. And then there are others who have made that choice and celebrate that choice." Sex Trade Workers and Feminists: Myths and Illusions, in Good Girls/Bad Girls: Feminists and Sex Trade Workers 202 (Laurie Bell ed., 1987).

Studies of U.S. prostitutes generally do not find high levels of dissatisfaction or sexual impairment. Almost three-quarters of those surveyed in one midwestern city believed their lives were better after entering prostitution; another study found that two-thirds had no regrets about their choice of work. John Decker, Prostitution: Regulation and Control 89, 114, 142 (1979); Jennifer Jones, Motivations for Entrance into Prostitution, in The Female Offender (Laura Crites ed., 1976); Gilbert Geis, One-Eyed Justice: An Examination of Homosexuality, Abortion, Prostitution, Narcotics, and Gambling in the U.S. 175-181 (1974); Gail Sheehy, Hustling: Prostitution in Our Wide-Open Society 104 (1973). Compared with the generally low-paying and tedious jobs otherwise available to them, prostitution often promises more money, excitement, independence, flexibility, and control. Eleanor Miller, Street Women 139-164 (1986); Margo St. James, The Reclamation of Whores, in Good Girls/Bad Girls, supra, at 81, 84. As one commentator notes:

> Some prostitutes may find the work emotionally taxing or disagreeable. They may have violent confrontations with their clients or pimps. However, some of these lamentable conditions are also shared by women who are in violent noncommercial relationships. Many women are forced to work in sweatshops . . . are sexually exploited by their bosses or are in abusive marriages. There is potential for coercion in any relationship. Nevertheless, it would be imprudent to suggest that such unpleasantness be resolved by prohibiting these relationships altogether.

Norma Jean Almodovar, For Their Own Good: The Results of the Prostitution Laws as Enforced by Cops, Politicians and Judges, 10 Hastings Women's L.J. 119, 123 (1999).

Some prostitutes also claim that the first time they felt powerful was the first time they turned a trick. Alexander, supra, at 188; Gail McPherson, The Whore Stigma: Female Disorder and Male UnWorthiness, 37 Social Text 39, 54 (1993). According to one worker:

> [B]eing able to earn [a substantial income] is a blessing . . . I have no regret for my experiences. Prostitution brought me social life, money, sex and entertainment. . . . I was alone in college, on welfare with a son. He wanted football clothes. He got them. . . .

Anonymous, Prostitution: A Narrative by a Former "Call Girl," 1 Mich. J. Gender & L. 105 (1993). One prostitute who had previously worked in a male-dominated occupation servicing telephone lines recalled that "I came home exhausted every day plus I was harassed by guys on the job. Working as a prostitute in a massage parlor is far less draining and I still get that kick of being an assertive woman." McPherson, supra, at 57. For at least some women, generally independent call girls, sex work can carry substantial economic rewards with relatively little risk of prosecution or disease.

Even for these women, however, many feminists question whether prostitution represents the kind of free, informed, individual choice that is worthy of respect. Consider the position as set forth by Dorchen Leidhodt, Associate Director of the Coalition Against Traffic in Women, a nongovernmental organization with consultative status to the United Nations Economic and Social Council:

> Prostitution is not about women making money. It is about other people — usually men — making money off women's bodies. Pimps, brothel owners, club owners, hotel chains, travel agencies, pornographers, organized crime syndicates, and governments are the real economic beneficiaries of the sex trade in women. . . .
>
> Prostitution is not about individuals. It is an institution of male dominance, and it is also a global industry in which the prostituting of women is constantly being packaged in new ways, using new forms of technology, tapping new markets: sex-tourism, mail-order bride selling, sex entertainment, sex immigration, dial-a-porn, computer pornography.
>
> Just as prostitution isn't about individuals, it isn't about choice. Instead, prostitution is about the absence of meaningful choices; about having alternative routes to survival cut off or being in a situation where you don't have options to begin with. . . . [T]he majority of women in prostitution in the country — most studies estimate 60-70 percent — have histories of sexual abuse in childhood. . . . Add to this the reality that the population targeted by pimps and traffickers is teenagers. It becomes clear that the majority of prostitutes are socialized into "sex work" in childhood and adolescence when consent is meaningless and choice an illusion.
>
> Then there are the related factors of poverty, lack of education, and homelessness. Women in prostitution, with few exceptions, are not people who debated between the advantages of going to law school or working at the X-tasy Massage Parlor. The average education level of a sample of Portland, Oregon [prostitutes] was tenth grade. . . .
>
> Choice vanishes when, in order to endure the prostitution, women become addicted to alcohol or drugs, or become prostitutes to support their addiction. In the Portland, Oregon, study, 85% of the women were drug or alcohol abusers.
>
> Nor is choice present when a woman is so traumatized by having stranger after stranger use her body as a seminal spittoon that she accepts prostitution as her destiny.
>
> Just as prostitution is not about choice, it's not about work. Or if it is, it is work in the same way that slavery or bonded labor is work — work that violates human dignity and every other human right. What other kind of work has as job training years of being sexually abused in childhood? What other job has as

its working conditions: rape . . . beatings . . . and premature death and murder.
. . . .

Dorchen Liedholt, Prostitution: A Violation of Women's Human Rights, 1 Cardozo Women's L.J. 133, 136-141 (1993). Catharine MacKinnon adds: "Women's precluded options in societies that discriminate on the basis of sex, including in employment, are fundamental to the prostitution context. If prostitution is a free choice, why are the women with the fewest choices the ones most often found doing it?" MacKinnon, Prostitution and Civil Rights, 1 Mich. J. Gender & L. 13, 27-28 (1996).

According to some sociologists, when prostitutes give favorable accounts of their experience, they are engaging in "neutralizing techniques":

> Sociologists use the term to describe the way in which socially despised and marginalized groups survive their marginal condition. Such techniques may be employed because the only alternative available may be the painful one of self-contempt. The idea that prostitution is freely chosen is such a technique.

Sheila Jeffreys, The Idea of Prostitution 137 (1997).

In response to such claims, defenders of sex work often note that survey research is usually based on street workers and prostitutes serving prison sentences, which overrepresent particularly vulnerable groups such as teenagers and drug users. According to these commentators, generalizations based on such groups are a "gross distortion." McPherson, supra, at 53. Many sex workers are also offended by the dismissal of their own perceptions as false consciousness. As members of one Canadian organization of sex workers put it:

> When you are a prostitute that says, "Well, I don't agree with the way you're interpreting my life, I don't feel oppressed or I don't feel exploited in the way that you're saying," they say things like "she's too blinded to her own oppression to see her experience for what it really is, and it really is the patriarchy." They find it necessary to interpret prostitutes' experience of their lives and then feed it back to the prostitutes to tell them what's really happening, whereas they wouldn't dare be so condescending or patronizing with any other group of women.

Realistic Feminists: An Interview with Valerie Scott, Peggy Miller, and Ryan Hotchkiss of the Canadian Organization for the Rights of Prostitutes, in Good Girls/Bad Girls, supra, at 204, 213.

Is it necessary to accept either the liberal notion that individuals can exercise free choice over matters of sexuality or the radical feminist position that they cannot? Is it possible to join Peggy Radin and other feminists who view the individual subject in postmodern terms — simultaneously an agent and a product of contingencies and constraints over which she has little control or even of which she may have little, if any, awareness? Within this view, choice is not an either/or proposition, but rather a range of points along a continuum. Keep this perspective in mind as you study the remainder of topics in this chapter.

6. Prostitution in the Ideal World. Apart from the issue of whether women under current conditions of inequality can freely choose sex work, a related question is whether there are alternative conditions in which they ought to be able to do so. In a world of true equality, would commercial sex be inherently exploitative?

Some feminists and some sex workers attribute the degraded aspects of current prostitution to its social and legal status, not to its intrinsic nature. As Ann McClintock notes,

> "anti sex-work feminists argue that to support sex worker rights is tantamount to supporting men's indiscriminate access to the sexuality of women . . . 'under any conditions and any terms men choose.'" Sex workers argue precisely the opposite. A central tenet of the prostitution movement is the demand that sex workers be given the right to exchange sexual services on *their* terms and on *their* conditions, not on the terms of the state, the police, pimps, male managers, or clients.

Ann McClintock, Sex Workers and Sex Work, 37 Social Text 1, 2 (1993). Underlying this view is the assumption that commercial intimacy is not intrinsically exploitative. One member of the Canadian Organization for the Rights of Prostitutes summarizes that position:

> Anonymous sex has validity in its own right. Since when is sex only acceptable and valid and good sex if it's linked to love or linked to someone that they have invested in, in terms of a relationship? There are a lot of people who feel unwilling or reluctant or unable to express a lot of pockets of their sexuality and their sexual needs unless it is with someone they don't have to look at afterwards. There's an excitement that goes with a new person, a novelty. Needing novelty is perfectly acceptable around other needs that we have. . . . Humanity benefits from giving legitimacy to all kinds of needs as long as they're consensual. . . . [Prostitutes'] ideal situation is like anybody else's — that we have control over our work environment. . . .

Realistic Feminists, in Good Girls/Bad Girls, supra, at 206, 209. See also "Barbara," It's a Pleasure Doing Business with You, 37 Social Text, 11, 12 (1993) (stressing call girls' ability to help men who are confused and repressed).

A related view is that prostitution may not be necessary or desirable in an ideal world, but that it is a justifiable response to certain "ubiquitous and permanent imperfections of actual human societies." Lars O. Ericsson, Charges Against Prostitution: An Attempt at a Philosophical Assessment, 90 Ethics 335, 366 (1980). As philosopher Lars Ericsson summarizes the argument, voluntary sex work involves the sale of persons' services, not their bodies. Id. at 341. While "mercenary sex" is not of the same value as "romantic sex" between parties who "love and care for one another," neither is the commercial version without value. Id. at 339. In essence, philosophers like Ericsson dismiss anti-commodification arguments as "sentimental" — the product of cultural double standards and sexual taboos that restrict rather than liberate female sexuality. In their view, a world of gender equality would present women with the same opportunities as men to be purchasers of nonstigmatized sexual services.

Other feminists stake out an intermediate position between absolute denunciation and categorical vindication of commercial sex. Some commentators are agnostic, or at least willing to keep open the question about the role of such sexuality in an ideal world. Carlin Meyer explains:

> We need to reflect on whether romantic love is really the only valid foundation for sexual interaction; to question the view that "legitimate" sexual intimacy must be tied to spiritual connection. All too many of us seem to have swallowed wholesale this ideology: we abhor . . . "impersonal" sex; we yearn for intimate "pillow talk;" we disdain the prostitute for engaging in sex without "real connection." (Which of us hasn't engaged in sex without connection? It wasn't prostitutes who told their daughters to "close your eyes and think . . . [of the Empire"]). . . .
>
> Dworkin suggests that men's incapacity to see sex partners as "whole" is necessarily — in her words — a "paralyzation of individuality." Must we all learn to see the subjects of our sexual desire as whole, equal, non-partial, and unsegmented? Even were it desirable, *can* we eliminate inequality in the realm of the intimate? Can we do so before we eliminate pervasive economic and social inequality? And if not, what do we do in the meantime?

Carlin Meyer, Decriminalizing Prostitution: Liberation or Dehumanization? 1 Cardozo Women's L.J. 105, 117 (1993). How would you respond?

7. Prostitution, Capitalism, and the International Traffic in Women. Global trafficking in women has become one of the world's most serious and pervasive human rights violations. Most governmental and nongovernmental organizations estimate that somewhere between one and four million women and girls are trafficked globally, with annual profits approaching $7 billion. About 50,000 are brought into the United States each year, largely from Southeast Asia, Russia, and Latin America. Catharine A. MacKinnon, Sex Equality 1385 (2001); Amy O'Neil Richard, International Trafficking in Women to the United States: A Contemporary Manifestation of Slavery and Organized Crime (1999); Becki Young, Trafficking of Humans Across United States Borders: How United States Laws Can Be Used to Punish Traffickers and Protect Victims, 13 Geo. Immigration L.J. 73 (1998).

Trafficking encompasses a range of crimes, including sex tourism, debt bondage, involuntary servitude, forced prostitution, and rape. The United Nations Convention for the Suppression of the Traffic in Persons and of the Exploitation of the Prostitution of Others (1949) defines trafficker as "any person who, to gratify the passions of another: 1) procures, entices or leads away, for purposes of prostitution another person, even with the consent of that person; [or] exploits the prostitution of another person, even with the consent of that person." The 2000 United Nations Convention Against Transnational Organized Crime; Protocol to Prevent, Suppress, and Punish Trafficking in Persons, Especially Women and Children, includes as trafficking "the recruitment, transportation, transfer, harboring or receipt of persons, by means of the threat or use of force or other forms of coercion, of abduction, of fraud, of deception, of the abuse of power or of a position of vulnerability or of the giving or receiving of payments or benefits to achieve the consent of a person having control over another person, for the purposes of exploitation." Exploitation includes "the prostitution of others or other forms of sexual exploitation, forced labor or services, slavery, or practices similar to slavery, servitude, or the removal of organs." The United States has adopted a similar definition in the Victims of Trafficking and Violence Protection Act of 2000, which prohibits "(A) sex trafficking in which a commercial sex is induced by force, fraud, or coercion, or in which the person induced to perform such an act has not attained 18 years of age; or (B) the recruitment, harboring, transportation, provision, or obtaining a person for labor or services, through the use of force, fraud, or coercion for the purpose of subjection to involuntary servitude, peonage, debt bondage, or slavery." Pub. L. No. 106-386, 114 Stat. 1464, §103(8).

Trafficking and enforced prostitution have been long-standing problems, particularly during wartime, but until recently they have seldom been subject to prosecution. No government took action to address the violation of the thousands of Indonesian, Korean, Chinese, Malaysian, Taiwanese, and Japanese "comfort women," who were forced into brothels by Japanese military forces during World War II. MacKinnon, supra, at 1389; George Hicks, The Comfort Women: Japan's Brutal Regime of Enforced Prostitution in the Second World War (1994). Only a few prosecutions for such offenses occurred under international war crimes tribunals, and it was not until 50 years later that several South Korean women won civil damages from a Japanese court. The United War Crimes Commission, 13 Law Reports of Trials of War Criminals 57-58 (1949); Taihei Okada (translator), The "Comfort Women" Case: Judgment of April 27, 1998, Shimonoseki Branch, Yamaguchi Prefectural Court, Japan, 8 Pac. Rim. L. & Pol'y J. 63 (1999). As noted in the previous discussion of rape as a war crime, the international tribunal for the former Yugoslavia is now actively prosecuting enforced prostitution that occurred as part of ethnic cleansing efforts during the recent conflict.

Much of the current trafficking industry involves deception, kidnapping, or outright purchase of women and girls for work in the sex trade. Some women or their families are duped by advertisements or personal solicitations for jobs such as waitresses, au pairs, sales clerks, actresses, and exotic dancers. Other women are drugged or kidnapped and smuggled across state lines. Many are then resold to brothels and kept against their will by a variety of methods. Typically, women are taken to a city or foreign country where they lack marketable skills and familiarity with the language and legal culture. Their passports and other forms of identification are removed, and they are threatened with assault, murder, or prosecution by local authorities if they try to escape. Once women have entered the sex trade, the social stigma they encounter further restricts their employment and marriage options. See U.S. Department of State, Francis T. Miko, Trafficking in Women and Children: The U.S. and International Response (1999); Organization for Security and Cooperation in Europe, Office for Democratic Institutions and Human Rights, Trafficking in Human Beings, Implications for the OSCE (September 1999); Margot Hornblower, The Skin Trade, Time, June 21, 1993, at 44.

Some women are promised freedom after they have earned enough to repay their travel, purchase price, room and board, and interest on these debts. Often, however, such promises are never kept or the costs remain prohibitive. Pasuk Phongpaichit, Trafficking in People in Thailand, in Illegal Immigration and Commercial Sex: The New Slave Trade 84-85 (Phil Williams ed., 1999). Women who refuse to work are often raped, physically assaulted, denied food, or forcibly restrained from leaving houses of prostitution. In one notorious case, sex workers chained to their beds died in a Thailand brothel fire. Charlotte Bunch, Women's Rights as Human Rights: Toward a Re-Vision of Human Rights, in Gender Violence: A Development and Human Rights Issue 8 (Charlotte Bunch & Roxanna Carrillo eds., 1991).

Most working conditions are highly exploitative. Many prostitutes have 10- to 18-hour shifts in squalid conditions with no choice of customers and little birth control or health care. Siriporn Sakhrobanek, Nataya Boonpakdee, & Chutima Jantateero, The Traffic in Women: Human Realities of the International Sex Trade 4-5 (1997); Hornblower, supra. In some areas, AIDS rates are epidemic and education/prevention efforts are minimal or nonexistent. See P. Estebanez, K. Fuch, & R. Najera, HIV and Female Sex Workers, World Health Organization Bulletin 397 (1993). The rising rate of sexually transmitted disease, coupled with long-standing beliefs about the value of intercourse with virgins, has heightened demand for ever younger partners of both sexes, and purchase of preteens and adolescents has become increasingly common. Marlise Simons, The Littlest Prostitutes, N.Y. Times, Jan. 16, 1994, at 31 (Magazine); Ngo Vinh Long, Vietnam, in Prostitution: An International Handbook on Trends, Problems and Policies (Nanette J. Davis ed., 1993); Trafficking of Women and Children in the International

Sex Trade: Hearing Before the House Subcomm. on International Operations and Human Rights of the Comm. on International Relations, 106th Cong. 10 (1999); E.T. Berkman, Note, Responses to the International Child Sex Tourism Trade, 19 B.C. Int'l & Comp. L. Rev. 347 (1996); D. Hodgson, Combatting the Organized Sexual Exploitation of Asian Children: Recent Developments and Prospects, 9 Int'l J.L. & Fam. 23 (1995). In one representative case, a young woman from Nepal was sold for $1,000 when she was 12 to traders promising her work as a housemaid in Bombay. Instead, she was taken to a brothel and required to repay her purchase price as well as rent, food, and clothing expenses. Seven years later she still owed $300. She did not, however, see alternatives: "In Nepal you do not get enough to eat. One can endure anything except hunger." Hornblower, supra. See also Janie Chuang, Redirecting the Debate over Trafficking in Women: Definitions, Paradigms, and Contexts, 11 Harv. Hum. Rts. J. 69, 69 (1998) (discussing the dynamics of poverty that encourage sales of daughters).

A related and rapidly increasing industry involves sex tourism. In the United States, some 25 companies offer "sex tours" to countries such as Thailand and the Philippines, where purchasers have ready access to bars and brothels. A representative California travel agency ad reads: "Sex Tours to Thailand, Real Girls, Real Sex, Real Cheap. These women are the most sexually available in the world. Did you know you can actually buy a virgin girl for as little as $200? You could fuck a different girl for the rest of your life." The agency offers a prize to the man who has sex with the most girls on the tour.

To what extent is such prostitution a reflection of racist as well as sexist dynamics? Laurie Shrage observes that "when we look at sex commerce cross-culturally and historically, one thing that stands out but stands unexplained is that a large percentage of sex customers seek (or sought) sex workers whose racial, ethnic, national, or class identities are (or were) different from their own." Shrage, Moral Dilemmas of Feminism: Prostitution, Adultery, and Abortion 142 (1994); see also Vednita Nelson, Prostitution: Where Racism and Sexism Intersect, 1 Mich. J. Gender & L. 81 (1993). Shrage continues:

> [I]f we do not assume that racism and xenophobia have diminished, then we might wonder how inter-ethnic "sex tourism" manages to be compatible with the ongoing existence of racial and national hatreds and fears — especially when such sentiments create barriers to intermarriage and, in general, to greater social cohesion in most areas of our lives. How does sex trading overcome these hostile sentiments? Or, if it does not, does interracial prostitution reflect an interracial rape mentality more than one of interracial respect?

Shrage, supra, at 144. Shrage suggests that more research is necessary on "whether the behavior of white American and European males who frequent female sex providers of African, Asian, Latin American, and Native American descent can be explained in part by culturally produced racial fantasies concerning the sexuality of these women." Id. at 148. For further discussion of race and sex in the context of harassment, pornography, and prostitution, see pages 1202-1206.

Several scholars have made the case for treating forced prostitution as a form of slavery. See, e.g., Kathleen Barry, Female Sexual Slavery (1979); Neal Devins, Men Who Own Women: A Thirteenth Amendment Critique of Forced Prostitution, 103 Yale L.J. 791 (1993). Here again, however, the line between "voluntary" and "forced" prostitution is complex and at times contested. When prostitution appears to be the only way a woman can support her family, has she made a free and rational choice to become a prostitute, or should it be said that she was coerced? See Nora V. Demleitner, Forced Prostitution: Naming an International Offense, 18 Fordham Int'l L.J. 163, 187 (1994) (noting that critics, including feminist critics, have taken both sides on the debate).

What other strategies might be most effective in curbing sex trafficking and tourism? The U.S. State Department, as well as most experts in the field, has advocated a three-pronged approach: prevention, punishment, and protection. U.S. State Department, Francis T. Miko Trafficking in Women and Children, supra. From the standpoint of prevention, more effort could focus on challenging the cultural devaluation of women, expanding their education and employment opportunities, and reducing poverty in the countries that supply the global trade. Vulnerable groups also could use better information about the strategies of traffickers and the legal remedies available. Id.; Coalition Against Trafficking in Women, Declaration of Rights for Women in Conditions of Sex Trafficking and Prostitution (Jan. 19, 1999).

From the standpoint of punishment, the vast majority of countries could increase the sanctions for trafficking and the frequency with which they are imposed. Part of the reason that the global sex trade has become such an expanding vehicle for international crime, second only to drugs and guns, is that the penalties are often lighter. For example, in the United States, the maximum federal penalty for dealing in a kilogram of heroin is life in prison; the mandatory minimum for crack cocaine is five years. By contrast, sex trackers, who procure women for compulsory sex and assist their imprisonment, have received sentences as light as one to four years. Richards, supra, at 13; United States v. Casteneda, 239 F.3d 978 (9th Cir. 2001). In many foreign countries, enforcement of anti-trafficking laws remains grossly inadequate due to lack of resources and training, corruption of police and immigration officials, and governmental ambivalence about curtailing profitable sex tourism activities. See Kelly E. Hyland, The Impact of the Protocol to Prevent, Suppress, and Punish Trafficking in Persons, Especially Women and Children, 8 Hum. Rts. Brief 30, 30-31 (2001).

The recently enacted Victims of Trafficking and Violence Protection Act of 2000, supra, attempts to respond to these problems by increasing the maximum penalties for trafficking to 20 years, providing a civil damages remedy for victims, increasing assistance to international law enforcement efforts, and giving the President discretionary power to impose sanctions on nations that fail to meet minimum standards for enforcement of anti-trafficking prohibitions. Pub. L. No. 106-386, 114 Stat. 1464, §§109, 110(d), 112(a), and 112(a)(2).

The Act also addresses the third area in which increased efforts are necessary: protection of victims. Traditionally, the targets of trafficking have often been punished more harshly than the traffickers themselves. Id. at §§112(a), 14, 17. Women have been subject to immediate deportation, which deters reporting and cooperation with enforcement efforts. Under the new Act, some 5,000 "T" visas will now be available each year for women who are assisting investigators or who would "suffer extreme hardship" if deported. Id. at §107(e). So too, the recently adopted U.N. Protocol to Prevent, Suppress, and Punish Trafficking in Perrsons, Especially Women and Children (supplementing the United Nations Convention against Transnational Organized Crime), contained in Annex II of the Report of the Ad Hoc Committee on the Elaboration of a Convention Against Transnational Organized Crime on the Work of its First to Eleventh Sessions, U.N. Doc. A/55/383 (2000), directs signatory nations to consider implementing measures to assist victims, such as medical, psychological, and counseling services, and employment, education, and training opportunities.

The effectiveness of this Protocol and of the U.S. Act remains to be seen. United Nations conventions have no enforcement mechanism, and the most important penalty, sanctioning, and the victim protection provisions of the U.S. legislation incorporate substantial room for discretion in implementation. Legal responses to the sex tourism industry are notable for their absence, and other responses, such as airport protests against tour participants, are only beginning to develop. Coalition Against Trafficking in Women, Holding Men Accountable in Los Angeles (Apr. 18, 1998). Progress in curtailing the global sex trade thus depends on whether courts and law enforcement officials begin to treat enforced prostitution as a serious human rights violation and whether the public and government leaders begin to see the issue as a critical international priority. Are there other strategies you can envision that would encourage such responses?

Putting Theory into Practice

6-3. The last quarter century has witnessed the growth of a new "mail-order bride" industry that sells addresses of eligible women to men seeking companions or wives. The World Association of Introduction Agencies recognizes some 2,700 agencies worldwide, which broker an estimated 4,000 marriages annually. Kathryn A. Lloyd, Wives for Sale: The Modern International Mail-Order Bride Industry, 20 J. Int'l L. Bus. 341, 343 (2000).

This industry represents a modern variation on an earlier tradition of picture brides, a system in which individual families arranged marriages between their daughters and men of the same racial or ethnic groups abroad. That practice was encouraged by restrictive immigration laws, such as U.S. anti-Asian immigrant exclusion acts, which largely restricted legal immigration status to male laborers and prevented them from traveling back and forth to their native lands to arrange their own marriages. Once a picture bride was selected, the marriage would be legalized in Asia, and the wife would be eligible to immigrate to the United States. Christine S.Y. Chun, The Mail Order Bride Industry: The Perpetuation of Transnational Economic Inequalities and Stereotypes, 17 U. Pa. J. Int'l Econ. L. 1155, 1157-1158 (1996). The practice died out in the mid-20th century as a result of the repeal of the exclusion acts and the growth of the Asian population in the United States. However, a superficially similar practice resurfaced in the 1970s in the form of a mail-order bride industry.

Contemporary bridal agencies generally recruit potential candidates from economically disadvantaged countries through newspaper and magazine advertisements. Women from the Philippines and Latin America account for a large percentage of the prospective brides because many speak English, are familiar with the United States, live in poverty, and are aware that marriage is the easiest way to obtain American citizenship. An increasing number of women are from the former Soviet Union and Eastern Europe. Vanessa B.M. Vergara, Abusive Mail-Order Bride Marriage and the Thirteenth Amendment, 94 Nw. U. L. Rev. 1547, 1560 (2000).

Mail-order bride agencies compile catalogs with photographs and descriptions of each woman that they recruit. The catalogs are highly salable in and of themselves, as they feature very attractive women and provide "a fantasy for American men who have been unlucky in love." Some agencies verify the information provided and require detailed disclosures such as whether the woman has "flat, medium, or full breasts," whether she has experienced premarital sex, and what kind of underwear she likes to wear. Lisa Belkin, The Mail Order Bride Business, N.Y. Times, May 11, 1986, at E28. The November/December 1995 issue of Cherry Blossoms, for example, has 22 pages displaying 500 full-body photographs and head shots of women along with statistics.

The women are typically portrayed as exotic, dutiful, and accommodating. A typical entry reads:

> Maria Claire (19) Philippines/5'3"; 105; hospital attendant (nursing aide grad). Catholic. "I'm kind, honest, and humble to everybody and most of all loving and caring. Never been touch and never been kiss except to the one I'm looking to. In shorts, single and still negotiable."

Another catalog features candidates "docile, exotic, and available as bed partners and domestic help at the same time." Eddy Meng, Mail-Order Brides: Gilded Prostitution and the Legal Response, 28 U. Mich. J.L. Ref. 197, 205 (1995). Each of these women is painted as an "eternal treasure . . . whose main objective in life is to please her husband." Id.

The catalogs are targeted to white men from industrialized countries such as the United States, Australia, and Canada. The typical client in search of a foreign bride is older than the potential bride, a college graduate, and politically conservative. For a fee, men buy the addresses of the women they select from the catalogs. After a man obtains the addresses, he mails letters to potential brides. Firms advise men not to limit their options and to write to as many women as possible, even the "less attractive" applicants. After selecting the most promising candidate, the man typically travels to the home country of the potential bride, often on one of the tour packages offered by the agency. If, after meeting, the couples agree to marry, the wedding occurs in the woman's home country or the husband-to-be applies for a fiancée visa, which allows the prospective bride to travel to the man's country. United States immigration law requires the couple to marry within 90 days. Once they are married, the bride obtains resident status on a two-year conditional basis. Ninety days before the expiration of the two-year period, the couple must jointly petition for unrestricted permanent residency status for the wife. The burden of proof is on the couple to establish that the marriage is viable and was not fraudulently arranged to evade immigration restrictions. Immigration Marriage Fraud Amendments of 1986, Pub. L. No. 99-639, 100 Stat. 3537, 8 U.S.C.A. §1184(d).

The total cost to the men typically ranges from $5,000 to $15,000. Vergara, supra, at 1558. The agencies do not screen their male customers or provide any assistance to brides once they reach their new home country, and no governmental or nongovernmental organizations monitor the experience of these women. Donna Lee, Mail Fantasy: Global Sexual Exploitation in the Mail-Order Bride Industry and Proposed Legal Solutions, 5 Asian L.J. 139, 144 (1998).

Expectations are frequently disappointed. Although the practice appeals to men seeking submissive wives, the women who participate often do so in order to take control over their own lives and do not fit the stereotype of the docile wife. In turn, many of these women have been led to believe, on the basis of books they have read and movies they have seen, that American men are wealthy and treat their wives better than men in their home countries. The men seeking foreign brides through this mail-order practice, however, often have highly negative attitudes toward women. Many have experienced a bitter divorce or break-up, and most of the men find women in their own country to be too aggressive, too demanding, and too devoted to their own careers. A substantial number of these men become physically and emotionally abusive toward their new wives.

Once in the United States, the mail-order brides find themselves completely separated from their cultural network and family support. Unlike the traditional picture-bride structure, where the foreign brides lived in a substitute immigrant culture with husbands of their own ethnic and racial background, the modern mail-order bride typically enters an almost completely white community, to which the man she married is her only connection. She must count on her husband for support and has no funds to obtain legal help or to buy a plane ticket to return home. See Chun, supra.

In response to these problems, the U.S. Immigration and Nationality Act and the Violence Against Women Act provide for a waiver of the joint petition requirement for permanent residency in certain circumstances, including spousal abuse. See Lisa C. Ikemoto, Mail Fraud, 3 J. Gender, Race & Justice 511, 541 (2000). However, many women are unaware of their legal rights or afraid to exercise them for fear of deportation or violent retaliation by their husbands. Many are too afraid or ashamed to report their abuse and therefore cannot provide the documentation necessary to qualify for the domestic violence waiver. Vergara, supra, at 1567. The Illegal Immigration Reform and Immigrant Responsibility Act of 1996 attempts to address some of these problems by requiring international matchmaking agencies to provide potential brides information in their native language about U.S. permanent residence status, the battered spouse waiver, and the unregulated nature of the industry. 8 U.S.C. §1375; Lee, supra, at 167. However, many women have difficulty understanding these disclosures and lack legal assistance to pursue their rights.

Should the contemporary mail-order bride industry be further regulated by law? If so, what should the regulations be?

6-4. A group of women students at a state law school decide to organize a conference to draw attention to the harmful effects of prostitution and the extent to which it perpetuates male subordination.

a. The organizers have lined up a number of highly prominent participants, all of whom oppose decriminalization of most prostitution-related activities. The students also intend to ask some well-known scholars to present alternative points of view on prostitution, including support of decriminalization. The leading anti-prostitution speakers refuse to participate if "pro-prostitution" advocates are present. How should the students proceed? What legal, moral, or policy considerations are relevant?

b. Conference organizers agree not to invite the activists favoring decriminalization. However, the students arrange with a local artist to present an exhibit expressing their views. The exhibit includes a videotape featuring works by and about prostitutes, and footage from sexually explicit films in which sex workers appear. Two of the conference speakers demand that the videotape be removed because they feel, "based on their experiences at other events, that the tape would be a threat to their safety." Tamar Lewin, Furor on Exhibit at Law School Splits Feminists, N.Y. Times, Nov.

13, 1992, at B9. Students remove the tape, at which point the artist withdraws the entire exhibit.

Complaints are then made that the conference organizers' action constitutes censorship of speech in violation of the First Amendment. One professor, who was not involved in the decision to remove the tape, responds: "I don't see this as a fight within feminism but a fight between those who wish to end male supremacy and those who wish to do better under it." Id.

How would you have handled the incident if you had been one of the student leaders? How should the dean and university legal counsel respond to the First Amendment claims?

B. PREGNANCY AND AUTONOMY

1. Control of Conception and Other Aspects of Women's Health

≡≡
≡≡   *Griswold v. Connecticut*
≡≡   381 U.S. 479 (1965)

Mr. Justice DOUGLAS delivered the opinion of the court.

[Appellants, Planned Parenthood personnel who prescribed contraceptives for "married persons," were charged as accessories to the violation of the Connecticut statute prohibiting the use of contraceptives. The Court first held that they had standing to assert their patients' privacy rights.]

[W]e are met with a wide range of questions that implicate the Due Process Clause of the Fourteenth Amendment. Overtones of some arguments suggest that Lochner v. New York, 198 U.S. 45 [(1905)], should be our guide. But we decline that invitation. . . . We do not sit as a super-legislature to determine the wisdom, need, and propriety of laws that touch economic problems, business affairs, or social conditions. This law, however, operates directly on an intimate relation of husband and wife and their physician's role in one aspect of that relation.

The association of people is not mentioned in the Constitution nor in the Bill of Rights. The right to educate a child in a school of the parents' choice — whether public or private or parochial — is also not mentioned. Nor is the right to study any particular subject or any foreign language. Yet the First Amendment has been construed to include certain of those rights.
. . .

By Pierce v. Society of Sisters, [268 U.S. 510 (1925)], the right to educate one's children as one chooses is made applicable to the States by the force of the First and Fourteenth Amendments. By Meyer v. Nebraska, [262 U.S. 390 (1923)], the same dignity is given the right to study the German language in a private school. In other words, the State may not, consistently with the spirit of the First Amendment, contract the spectrum of available knowledge. . . .

In NAACP v. Alabama, 357 U.S. 449, 462 [(1958)], we protected the "freedom to associate and privacy in one's associations," noting that freedom of association was a peripheral First Amendment right. Disclosure of membership lists of a constitutionally valid association, we held, was invalid "as entailing the likelihood of a substantial restraint upon the exercise by petitioner's members of their right to freedom of association." Ibid. In other words, the First Amendment has a penumbra where privacy is protected from governmental intrusion. In like context, we have protected forms of "association" that are not political in the customary sense but pertain to the social, legal, and economic benefit of the members. In Schware v. Board of Bar Examiners, 353 U.S. 232 [(1957)], we held it not permissible to bar a lawyer from practice, because he had once been a member of the Communist Party. The man's "association with that Party" was not shown to be "anything more than a political faith in a political party" (id., at 244) and was not action of a kind proving bad moral character. Id. at 245-246. . . .

The foregoing cases suggest that specific guarantees in the Bill of Rights have penumbras, formed by emanations from those guarantees that help give them life and substance. Various guarantees create zones of privacy. The right of association contained in the penumbra of the First Amendment is one, as we have seen. The Third Amendment in its prohibitions against the quartering of soldiers "in any house" in time of peace without the consent of the owner is another facet of that privacy. The Fourth Amendment explicitly affirms the "right of the people to be secure in their persons, houses, papers, and effects, against unreasonable searches and seizures." The Fifth Amendment in its Self-Incrimination Clause enables the citizen to create a zone of privacy which government may not force him to surrender to his detriment. The Ninth Amendment provides: "The enumeration in the constitution, of certain rights, shall not be construed to deny or disparage others retained by the people."

The Fourth and Fifth Amendments were described in Boyd v. United States, 116 U.S. 616, 630 [(1886)], as protection against all governmental invasions "of the sanctity of a man's home and the privacies of life." We recently referred in Mapp v. Ohio, 367 U.S. 643, 656 [(1961)], to the Fourth Amendment as creating a "right to privacy, no less important than any other right carefully and particularly reserved to the people."

We have had many controversies over these penumbral rights of "privacy and repose." These cases bear witness that the right of privacy which presses for recognition here is a legitimate one.

The present case, then, concerns a relationship lying within the zone of privacy which, in forbidding the use of contraceptives rather than regulating their manufacture or sale, seeks to achieve its goals by . . . having a maximum destructive impact upon that relationship. Such a law cannot stand in light of the familiar principle, so often applied by the Court, that a "governmental purpose to control or prevent activities constitutionally subject to state regulation may not be achieved by means which sweep unnecessarily broadly and thereby invade the area of protected freedoms." NAACP v. Alabama, [377 U.S. 288, 307 (1964)]. Would we allow the police to search the sacred precincts of marital bedrooms for telltale signs of the use of contraceptives? The very idea is repulsive to the notions of privacy surrounding the marriage relationship.

We deal with a right of privacy older than the Bill of Rights — older than our political parties, older than our school system. Marriage is a coming together for better or worse, hopefully enduring, and intimate to the degree of being sacred. It is an association that promotes a way of life, not causes; a harmony in living, not political faiths; a bilateral loyalty, not commercial or social projects. Yet it is an association for as noble a purpose as any involved in our prior decisions.

Reversed.

Mr. Justice GOLDBERG, whom THE CHIEF JUSTICE and Mr. Justice BRENNAN join, concurring. . . .

[I]t should be said of the Court's holding today that it in no way interferes with a State's proper regulation of sexual promiscuity or misconduct. As my Brother Harlan so well stated in his dissenting opinion in Poe v. Ullman, [361 U.S. 497, 553 (1961)]:

> Adultery, homosexuality and the like are sexual intimacies which the State forbids . . . but the intimacy of husband and wife is necessarily an essential and accepted feature of the institution of marriage, an institution which the State not only must allow, but which always and in every age it has fostered and protected. It is one thing when the State exerts its power either to forbid extra-marital sexuality . . . or to say who may marry, but it is quite another when, having acknowledged a marriage and the intimacies inherent in it, it undertakes to regulate by means of the criminal law the details of that intimacy.

In sum, I believe that the right of privacy in the marital relation is fundamental and basic — a personal right "retained by the people" within the meaning of the Ninth Amendment. Connecticut cannot constitutionally abridge this fundamental right, which is protected by the Fourteenth Amendment from infringement by the States. I agree with the Court that petitioners' convictions must therefore be reversed.

Eisenstadt v. Baird
405 U.S. 438 (1972)

Mr. Justice BRENNAN delivered the opinion of the Court.

Appellee William Baird was convicted at a bench trial in the Massachusetts Superior Court under Massachusetts General Laws Ann., c.272, §21, first, for exhibiting contraceptive articles in the course of delivering a lecture on contraception to a group of students at Boston University and, second, for giving a young woman a package of Emko vaginal foam at the close of his address. The Massachusetts Supreme Judicial Court unanimously set aside the conviction for exhibiting contraceptives . . . but . . . sustained the conviction for giving away the foam. [Baird then obtained a writ of habeas corpus in federal court, and the state appealed.] We affirm.

Massachusetts General Laws Ann., c.272, §21, under which Baird was convicted, provides a maximum five-year term of imprisonment for "whoever . . . gives away . . . any drug, medicine, instrument or article whatever for the prevention of conception," except as authorized in §21A. Under §21A, "[a] registered physician may administer to or prescribe for any married person drugs or articles intended for the prevention of pregnancy or conception. [And a] registered pharmacist actually engaged in the business of pharmacy may furnish such drugs or articles to any married person presenting a prescription from a registered physician." As interpreted by the State Supreme Judicial Court, these provisions make it a felony for anyone, other than a registered physician or pharmacist acting in accordance with the terms of §21A, to dispense any article with the intention that it be used for the prevention of conception. The statutory scheme distinguishes among three distinct classes of distributees — first, married persons may obtain contraceptives to prevent pregnancy, but only from doctors or druggists on prescription; second, single persons may not obtain contraceptives from anyone to prevent pregnancy; and, third, married or single persons may obtain contraceptives from anyone to prevent, not pregnancy, but the spread of disease. This construction of state law is, of course, binding on us.

The legislative purposes that the statute is meant to serve are not altogether clear. In Commonwealth v. Baird, [247 N.E.2d 574 (1969)], the Supreme Judicial Court noted only the State's interest in protecting the health of its citizens: "(T)he prohibition in §21," the court declared, "is directly related to" the State's goal of "preventing the distribution of articles designed to prevent conception which may have undesirable, if not dangerous, physical consequences," [247 N.E.2d at 578]. In a subsequent decision, Sturgis v. Attorney General, [260 N.E.2d 687, 690 (Mass. 1970)], the court, however, found "a second and more compelling ground for upholding the statute" — namely, to protect morals through "regulating the private sexual lives of single persons."[3] The Court of Appeals, for

---

3. Appellant suggests that the purpose of the Massachusetts statute is to promote marital fidelity as well as to discourage premarital sex. Under §21A, however, contraceptives may be made available to married persons without regard to whether they are living with their spouses or the uses to which the contraceptives are to be put. Plainly the legislation has no deterrent effect on extramarital sexual relations.

reasons that will appear, did not consider the promotion of health or the protection of morals through the deterrence of fornication to be the legislative aim. Instead, the court concluded that the statutory goal was to limit contraception in and of itself—a purpose that the court held conflicted "with fundamental human rights" under Griswold v. Connecticut, [381 U.S. 479 (1965)], where this Court struck down Connecticut's prohibition against the use of contraceptives as an unconstitutional infringement of the right of marital privacy. [Baird v. Eisenstadt, 429 F.2d 1398, 1401-1402 (1st Cir. 1970).]

We agree that the goals of deterring premarital sex and regulating the distribution of potentially harmful articles cannot reasonably be regarded as legislative aims of §21 and §21A. And we hold that the statute, viewed as a prohibition on contraception per se, violates the rights of single persons under the Equal Protection Clause of the Fourteenth Amendment. . . .

II

The basic principles governing application of the Equal Protection Clause of the Fourteenth Amendment are familiar. . . . The question for our determination in this case is whether there is some ground of difference that rationally explains the different treatment accorded married and unmarried persons. . . .[7] For the reasons that follow, we conclude that no such ground exists.

First. . . . Conceding that the State could, consistently with the Equal Protection Clause, regard the problems of extramarital and premarital sexual relations as "[e]vils . . . of different dimensions and proportions, requiring different remedies," Williamson v. Lee Optical Co., [348 U.S. 483, 489 (1955)], we cannot agree that the deterrence of premarital sex may reasonably be regarded as the purpose of the Massachusetts law.

It would be plainly unreasonable to assume that Massachusetts has prescribed pregnancy and the birth of an unwanted child as punishment for fornication, which is a misdemeanor under Massachusetts [law]. Aside from the scheme of values that assumption would attribute to the State, it is abundantly clear that the effect of the ban on distribution of contraceptives to unmarried persons has at best a marginal relation to the proffered objective. What Mr. Justice Goldberg said in Griswold v. Connecticut, supra, at 498 (concurring opinion), . . . is equally applicable here. "The rationality of this justification is dubious, particularly in light of the admitted

7. Of course, if we were to conclude that the Massachusetts statute impinges upon fundamental freedoms under *Griswold*, the statutory classification would have to be not merely rationally related to a valid public purpose but necessary to the achievement of a compelling state interest. E.g., Shapiro v. Thompson, [394 U.S. 618 (1969)]; Loving v. Virginia, [388 U.S. 1 (1967)]. But just as in Reed v. Reed, [404 U.S. 71 (1971)], we do not have to address the statute's validity under that test because the law fails to satisfy even the more lenient equal protection standard.

widespread availability to all persons in the State of Connecticut, unmarried as well as married, of birth-control devices for the prevention of disease, as distinguished from the prevention of conception." Like Connecticut's laws, §21 and §21A do not at all regulate the distribution of contraceptives when they are to be used to prevent, not pregnancy, but the spread of disease. Nor, in making contraceptives available to married persons without regard to their intended use, does Massachusetts attempt to deter married persons from engaging in illicit sexual relations with unmarried persons. Even on the assumption that the fear of pregnancy operates as a deterrent to fornication, the Massachusetts statute is thus so riddled with exceptions that deterrence of premarital sex cannot reasonably be regarded as its aim.

Moreover, §21 and §21A on their face have a dubious relation to the State's criminal prohibition on fornication. As the Court of Appeals explained, "Fornication is a misdemeanor [in Massachusetts], entailing a thirty dollar fine, or three months in jail. Violation of the present statute is a felony, punishable by five years in prison. . . ." 429 F.2d at 1401. Even conceding the legislature a full measure of discretion in fashioning means to prevent fornication, and recognizing that the State may seek to deter prohibited conduct by punishing more severely those who facilitate than those who actually engage in its commission, we, like the Court of Appeals, cannot believe that in this instance Massachusetts has chosen to expose the aider and abetter who simply gives away a contraceptive to 20 times the 90-day sentence of the offender himself. . . .

Second. . . . The Supreme Judicial Court in Commonwealth v. Baird, supra, held that the purpose of the [law in question] was to serve the health needs of the community by regulating the distribution of potentially harmful articles.

[The Court here concludes that it would be irrational for a law grounded on health needs to distinguish between married and unmarried persons, since their health needs would be identical.]

Third. If the Massachusetts statute cannot be upheld as a deterrent to fornication or as a health measure, may it, nevertheless, be sustained simply as a prohibition on contraception? . . . We need not and do not, however, decide that important question in this case because, whatever the rights of the individual to access to contraceptives may be, the rights must be the same for the unmarried and the married alike.

If under *Griswold* the distribution of contraceptives to married persons cannot be prohibited, a ban on distribution to unmarried persons would be equally impermissible. It is true that in *Griswold* the right of privacy in question inhered in the marital relationship. Yet the marital couple is not an independent entity with a mind and heart of its own, but an association of two individuals each with a separate intellectual and emotional makeup. If the right of privacy means anything, it is the right of the individual, married or single, to be free from unwarranted governmental intrusion into matters so fundamentally affecting a person as the decision whether to bear or beget a child.

On the other hand, if *Griswold* is no bar to a prohibition on the distribution of contraceptives, the State could not, consistently with the Equal Protection Clause, outlaw distribution to unmarried but not to married persons. In each case the evil, as perceived by the State, would be identical, and the underinclusion would be invidious. . . . The judgment of the Court of Appeals is affirmed.

Mr. Justice POWELL and Mr. Justice REHNQUIST took no part in the consideration or decision of this case.

[The concurring opinion of Mr. Justice Douglas is omitted.]

[The concurring opinion of Mr. Justice White, with whom Mr. Justice Blackmun joined, is omitted.]

[The dissenting opinion of Mr. Chief Justice Burger is omitted.]

Erickson v. Bartell Drug Co.
141 F. Supp. 2d 1266 (W.D. Wash. 2001)

Robert S. LASNIK, Judge.

The parties' cross-motions for summary judgment in this case raise an issue of first impression in the federal courts whether the selective exclusion of prescription contraceptives from defendant's generally comprehensive prescription plan constitutes discrimination on the basis of sex.[1] In particular, plaintiffs assert that Bartell's decision not to cover prescription contraceptives such as birth control pills, Norplant, Depo-Provera, intra-uterine devices, and diaphragms under its Prescription Benefit Plan for non-union employees violates Title VII, 42 U.S.C. §2000e et seq., as amended by the Pregnancy Discrimination Act, 42 U.S.C. §2000e(k).

This matter is proceeding as a class action on behalf of "all female employees of Bartell who at any time after December 29, 1997, were enrolled in Bartell's Prescription Benefit Plan for non-union employees while using prescription contraceptives."

---

1. Bartell's benefit plan is self-insured and covers all prescription drugs, including a number of preventative drugs and devices, such as blood-pressure and cholesterol-lowering drugs, hormone replacement therapies, prenatal vitamins, and drugs to prevent allergic reactions, breast cancer, and blood clotting. The plan specifically excludes from coverage a handful of products, including contraceptive devices, drugs prescribed for weight reduction, infertility drugs, smoking cessation drugs, dermatologicals for cosmetic purposes, growth hormones, and experimental drugs.

A. APPLICATION OF TITLE VII . . .

. . . The legislative history of Title VII does not forecast how the law was to be interpreted by future courts faced with specific examples of allegedly discriminatory conduct. . . . What is clear from the law itself, its legislative history, and Congress' subsequent actions, is that the goal of Title VII was to end years of discrimination in employment and to place all men and women, regardless of race, color, religion, or national origin, on equal footing in how they were treated in the workforce.

In 1978, Congress had the opportunity to expound on its view of sex discrimination by amending Title VII to make clear that discrimination because of "pregnancy, childbirth, or related medical conditions" is discrimination on the basis of sex. 42 U.S.C. §2000e(k). The amendment, known as the Pregnancy Discrimination Act ("PDA"), was not meant to alter the contours of Title VII: rather, Congress intended to correct what it felt was an erroneous interpretation of Title VII by the United States Supreme Court in General Elec. Co. v Gilbert, 429 U.S. 125 (1976). In *Gilbert*, the Supreme Court held that an otherwise comprehensive short-term disability policy that excluded pregnancy-related disabilities from coverage did not discriminate on the basis of sex. The *Gilbert* majority based its decision on two findings: (a) pregnancy discrimination does not adversely impact all women and therefore is not the same thing as gender discrimination; and (b) disability insurance which covers the same illnesses and conditions for both men and women is equal coverage. To the *Gilbert* majority, the fact that pregnancy-related disabilities were an uncovered risk unique to women did not destroy the facial parity of the coverage. The dissenting justices, Justice Brennan, Justice Marshall, and Justice Stevens, took issue with these findings, arguing that: (a) women, as the only sex at risk for pregnancy, were being subjected to unlawful discrimination; and (b) in determining whether an employment policy treats the sexes equally, the court must look at the comprehensiveness of the coverage provided to each sex. It was the dissenters' interpretation of Title VII which ultimately prevailed in Congress H.R. Rep. No. 95-948, at 2 (1978) ("Justice Brennan . . . pointed out that since the plan included comprehensive coverage for males and failed to provide comprehensive coverage for females, the majority erred in finding that the exclusion of pregnancy disability coverage was a nondiscriminatory policy. Furthermore, Justice Stevens, in his dissenting opinion, argued that 'it is the capacity to become pregnant which primarily differentiates the female from the male.' It is the committee's view that the dissenting Justices correctly interpreted the Act.").

The language of the PDA was chosen in response to the factual situation presented in *Gilbert*, namely a case of overt discrimination toward pregnant employees. Not surprisingly, the amendment makes no reference whatsoever to prescription contraceptives. Of critical importance to this case, however, is the fact that, in enacting the PDA, Congress embraced the

dissent's broader interpretation of Title VII which not only recognized that there are sex-based differences between men and women employees, but also required employers to provide women-only benefits or otherwise incur additional expenses on behalf of women in order to treat the sexes the same.
. . .

Although this litigation involves an exclusion for prescription contraceptives rather than an exclusion for pregnancy-related disability costs, the legal principles established by *Gilbert* and its legislative reversal govern the outcome of this case. An employer has chosen to offer an employment benefit which excludes from its scope of coverage services which are available only to women. All of the services covered by the policy are available to both men and women, so, as was the case in *Gilbert*, "there is no risk from which men are protected and women are not. Likewise, there is no risk from which women are protected and men are not." *Gilbert*, 429 U.S. at 135 (quoting Geduldig v. Aiello, 417 U.S. 484, 496-97 (1974). Nevertheless, the intent of Congress in enacting the PDA, even if not the exact language used in the amendment, shows that mere facial parity of coverage does not excuse or justify an exclusion which carves out benefits that are uniquely designed for women. . . .

The other tenet reaffirmed by the PDA (i.e., that discrimination based on any sex-based characteristic is sex discrimination) has also been considered by the courts. The Supreme Court has found that classifying employees on the basis of their childbearing capacity, regardless of whether they are, in fact, pregnant, is sex-based discrimination. International Union, United Automobile, Aerospace and Agricultural Implement Workers of Am. v. Johnson Controls, Inc., 499 U.S. 187, 197-98 (1991). The court's analysis turned primarily on Title VII's prohibition on sex-based classifications, using the PDA merely to bolster a conclusion that had already been reached. To the extent that a woman's ability to get pregnant may not fall within the literal language of the PDA, the court was not overly concerned. Rather, the court focused on the fact that disparate treatment based on unique, sex-based characteristics, such as the capacity to bear children, is sex discrimination prohibited by Title VII.

Having reviewed the legislative history of Title VII and the PDA, the language of the statute itself, and the relevant case law, the Court finds that Bartell's exclusion of prescription contraception from its prescription plan is inconsistent with the requirements of federal law. The PDA is not a begrudging recognition of a limited grant of rights to a strictly defined group of women who happen to be pregnant. Read in the context of Title VII as a whole, it is a broad acknowledgment of the intent of Congress to outlaw any and all discrimination against any and all women in the terms and conditions of their employment, including the benefits an employer provides to its employees. Male and female employees have different, sex-based disability and healthcare needs, and the law is no longer blind to the fact that only women can get pregnant, bear children, or use prescription contraception. The special or increased healthcare needs associated with a woman's unique sex-based characteristics must be met to the same extent, and on the same terms, as other healthcare needs. Even if one were to assume that Bartell's prescription plan was not the result of intentional discrimination,[7] the exclusion of women-only benefits from a generally comprehensive prescription plan is sex discrimination under Title VII.

Title VII does not require employers to offer any particular type or category of benefit. However, when an employer decides to offer a prescription plan covering everything except a few specifically excluded drugs and devices, it has a legal obligation to make sure that the resulting plan does not discriminate based on sex-based characteristics and that it provides equally comprehensive coverage for both sexes. . . . In light of the fact that prescription contraceptives are used only by women, Bartell's choice to exclude that particular benefit from its generally applicable benefit plan is discriminatory.[8]

B. SPECIFIC ARGUMENTS RAISED BY DEFENDANT-EMPLOYER . . .

An underlying theme in Bartell's argument is that a woman's ability to control her fertility differs from the type of illness and disease normally treated with prescription drugs in such significant respects that it is permissible to treat prescription contraceptives differently than all other prescription medicines. The evidence submitted by plaintiffs shows, however, that the availability of affordable and effective contraceptives is of great importance to the health of women and children because it can help to prevent a litany of physical, emotional, economic, and social consequences. See Sylvia A. Law, Sex Discrimination and Insurance for Contraception, 73 Wash. L. Rev. 363, 364-68 (1998).

[T]he adverse economic and social consequences of unintended pregnancies fall most harshly on women and interfere with their choice to participate fully and equally in the "marketplace and the world of ideas."

---

7. There is no evidence or indication that Bartell's coverage decisions were intended to hinder women in their ability to participate in the workforce or to deprive them of equal treatment in employment or benefits. The most reasonable explanation for the current state of affairs is that the exclusion of women-only benefits is merely an unquestioned holdover from a time when employment-related benefits were doled out less equitably than they are today. The lack of evidence of bad faith or malice toward women does not affect the validity of plaintiffs' Title VII claim. Where a benefit plan is discriminatory on its face, no inquiry into subjective intent is necessary. . . .

8. Bartell's argument that its prescription plan is not discriminatory because the female dependants of male employees are subject to the same exclusions as are female employees is unavailing. First, discriminating against a protected class cannot be justified through consistency. Second, Bartell ignores the clear import of Congress' repudiation of *Gilbert*: a policy which uses sex-based characteristics to limit benefits, thereby creating a plan which is less comprehensive for one sex than the other, violates Title VII.

Stanton v. Stanton, 421 U.S. 7, 14-15 (1975). See also Planned Parenthood v. Casey, 505 U.S. 833, 856 (1992) ("The ability of women to participate equally in the economic and social life of the nation has been facilitated by their ability to control their reproductive lives.").

The availability of a reliable, affordable way to prevent unintended pregnancies would go a long way toward ameliorating the ills described above. Although there are many factors which help explain the unusually high rate of unintended pregnancies in the United States, an important cause is the failure to use effective forms of birth control. Alan Guttmacher Institute, Contraception Counts: State-by-State Information 1 (May 1997). Insurance policies and employee benefit plans which exclude coverage for effective forms of contraception contribute to the failure of at-risk women to seek a physician's assistance in avoiding unwanted pregnancies. . . .

The fact that prescription contraceptives are preventative appears to be an irrelevant distinction in this case: Bartell covers a number of preventative drugs under its plan. The fact that pregnancy is a "natural" state and is not considered a disease or illness is also a distinction without a difference. Being pregnant, though natural, is not a state that is desired by all women or at all points in a woman's life. Prescription contraceptives, like all other preventative drugs, help the recipient avoid unwanted physical changes. As discussed above, identifying and obtaining an effective method of contraception is a primary healthcare issue throughout much of a woman's life and is, in many instances, of more immediate importance to her daily healthcare situation than most other medical needs. . . . Although there are some distinctions that can be drawn between prescription contraceptives and the other prescription drugs covered by Bartell's plan, none of them is substantive or otherwise justifies the exclusion of contraceptives from a generally comprehensive healthcare plan. . . .

Defendant argues that the exclusion of prescription contraceptives from defendant's prescription benefit plan does not run afoul of the PDA and is not, therefore, unlawful. . . . The Court finds that, regardless of whether the prevention of pregnancy falls within the phrase "pregnancy, childbirth, or related medical conditions," Congress' decisive overruling of General Elec. Co. v. Gilbert, 429 U.S. 125 (1976), evidences an interpretation of Title VII which necessarily precludes the choices Bartell has made in this case. . . .

Bartell also suggests that it should be permitted to limit the scope of its employee benefit programs in order to control costs. Cost is not, however, a defense to allegations of discrimination under Title VII. See Los Angeles Dept. of Water & Power v. Manhart, 435 U.S. 702, 716-17 (1978); 29 C.F.R. §1604.9(e). While it is undoubtedly true that employers may cut benefits, raise deductibles, or otherwise alter coverage options to comply with budgetary constraints, the method by which the employer seeks to curb costs must not be discriminatory. Bartell offers its employees an admittedly generous package of healthcare benefits, including both third-party healthcare plans and an in-house prescription program. It cannot, however, penalize female employees in an effort to keep its benefit costs low. The cost savings Bartell realizes by excluding prescription contraceptives from its healthcare plans are being directly borne by only one sex in violation of Title VII. Although Bartell is permitted, under the law, to use non-discriminatory cuts in benefits to control costs, it cannot balance its benefit books at the expense of its female employees. . . .

Prescription contraceptives are not the only drugs or devices excluded from coverage under Bartell's benefit plan. Bartell argues that it has chosen to exclude from coverage all drugs for "family planning," and that this exclusion is neutral and non-discriminatory. There is no "family planning" exclusion in the benefit plan, however, and the contours of such a theoretical exclusion are not clear. On the list of excluded drugs and devices, contraceptive devices and infertility drugs are the two categories which might be considered "family planning" measures. Contrary to defendant's explanation, there appear to be some drugs which fall under the "family planning" rubric which are covered by the plan. Prenatal vitamins, for example, are frequently prescribed in anticipation of a woman becoming pregnant and are expressly covered under the plan. And although both parties agree that Bartell's plan excludes coverage for Viagra, an impotency drug, it is not clear that it falls into any of the excluded categories.

Even if the Court were able to identify a consistent theory to explain the various exclusions and inclusions in Bartell's plan, the exclusion of prescription contraceptives, alone or in combination with the exclusion of infertility drugs, is in no way neutral or equal. Although the issue is not before the Court, there is at least an argument that the exclusion of infertility drugs applies equally to male and female employees, making the coverage offered to all employees less comprehensive in roughly the same amount and manner. The additional exclusion of prescription contraceptives, however, reduces the comprehensiveness of the coverage offered to female employees while leaving the coverage offered to male employees unchanged. As discussed above, such inequities are discriminatory and violate Title VII.

Employers in general, and Bartell in particular, might justifiably wonder why, when Title VII has been on the books for thirty-seven years, this Court is only now holding that it includes a right to prescription contraceptives in certain circumstances. The answer, of course, is that until this case, no court had been asked to evaluate the common practice of excluding contraceptives from a generally comprehensive health plan under Title VII. While there are a number of possible explanations for the lack of litigation over this issue, none of them changes the fact that, having now been properly raised as a matter of statutory construction, this Court is constitutionally required to rule on the issue before it.

Although the Court's decision is a matter of first impression for the judiciary, it is not the first tribunal to consider the lawfulness of a contraception exclusion. On December 14, 2000, the EEOC made a finding of reasonable cause on the same issue which is entitled to some deference.

. . . As the Commission found, the exclusion of prescription contraceptives from a generally comprehensive insurance policy constitutes sex discrimination under Title VII because the employers "have circumscribed the treatment options available to women, but not to men." This unequal treatment is an unlawful employment practice under Title VII of the Civil Rights Act of 1964. . . .

. . . Plaintiffs' motion for summary judgment on their disparate treatment claim is granted. Bartell is hereby ordered to cover each of the available options for prescription contraception to the same extent, and on the same terms, that it covers other drugs, devices, and preventative care for non-union employees. It is further ordered that Bartell shall offer coverage for contraception-related services, including the initial visit to the prescribing physician and any follow-up visits or outpatient services, to the same extent, and on the same terms, as it offers coverage for other outpatient services for its non-union employees. . . .

Notes

1. The Constitutional Right to Contraception. The Court in *Griswold* attempts to distinguish its decision from Lochner v. New York and other discredited early-twentieth-century cases overturning economic legislation on grounds such legislation infringed upon the freedom of contract of property owners and their employees. The distinction the Court offers is that *Griswold* "operates directly on an intimate relation of husband and wife and their physician's role in one aspect of that relation," rather than "economic problems, business affairs, or social conditions." Is the distinction successful? Some have argued not, including one scholar and former judge whose Supreme Court nomination failed perhaps principally because he argued that there was inadequate constitutional grounding for the right recognized in *Griswold*. See Robert Bork, Neutral Principles and Some First Amendment Problems, 47 Ind. L. Rev. 1 (1971); Mark Gitenstein, Matters of Principle: An Insider's Account of America's Rejection of Robert Bork's Nomination to the Supreme Court 322 (1992).

The right in *Griswold* was based squarely on the special status of marriage in this society. How could it follow, then, as the Court in Eisenstadt v. Baird concludes, that the right protected covers unmarried as well as married persons? Could it also follow that the right to contraception extends to minors? In invalidating a New York law criminalizing the distribution of contraceptives by anyone other than a licensed pharmacist, and the distribution, advertisement, or display of contraceptives by anyone to minors, the Supreme Court sidestepped this question. Carey v. Population Serv. Int'l, 431 U.S. 678, 694 n.17 (1977) (plurality opinion). Justice Powell in his concurring opinion argued, however, that "there is . . . no justification for subjecting restrictions on the sexual activity of the young to heightened judicial review." Id. at 705 (Powell, J., concurring).

Does a line between access to contraceptives and right to have sex make any sense? Compare Bruce C. Hafen, The Constitutional Status of Marriage, Kinship, and Sexual Privacy — Balancing the Individual and Social Interests, 81 Mich. L. Rev. 463, 531 (1983) ("[c]ontraception and sexual relations are simply two different things, one of which can be given legal protection without protecting the other") with Brenda D. Hofman, Note, The Squeal Rule: Statutory Resolution and Constitutional Implication — Burdening the Minor's Right of Privacy, 1984 Duke L.J. 1325, 1339 ("the decision to engage in sexual activity logically precedes — and is therefore implied in — the decision to use a contraceptive"). As to consenting adults, the question of a right to sexual activity has not been resolved, except as to same-sex couples. See Bowers v. Hardwick, 478 U.S. 186 (1986), discussed at pages 752, 783.

2. Contraception as a Source of Subordination. Whose autonomy interests are protected by the Supreme Court's decisions guaranteeing legal access to contraceptives? Women's autonomy, to be sure, but this autonomy must be understood in the broader contexts within which decisions about sexuality and reproduction are made. For example, while contraception facilitates control over reproductive decisions, it may actually lessen the control women have over decisions about whether to engage in sexual intercourse. It could be possible, indeed, that under conditions of male dominance, contraception makes women more available for sex. Catharine A. MacKinnon makes this point with respect to abortion:

> So long as women do not control access to our sexuality, abortion facilitates women's heterosexual availability. In other words, under conditions of gender inequality, sexual liberation in this sense does not free women; it frees male sexual aggression. The availability of abortion removes the one remaining legitimized reason that women have had for refusing sex besides the headache.

MacKinnon, Feminism Unmodified: Discourses on Life and Law 99 (1987). The fact that women do not control the meanings attached to contraception also limits the autonomy it might otherwise give them:

> . . . [W]omen often do not use birth control because of its social meaning, a meaning we did not create. Using contraception means acknowledging and planning the possibility of intercourse, accepting one's sexual availability, and appearing non-spontaneous. It means appearing available to male incursions.

Id. at 95.

Historian Linda Gordon underlines the class dimensions of birth control, explaining how men, particularly among the poor, tend to associate masculinity with sexual images of potence, which is undercut by the use of contraception "because it introduces calculation and negotiation with women into sexual relations," while among the prosperous, masculinity is associated to a greater extent with earning power, responsibility, children's high achievement, and other goals that tend to be served by contraceptive use. Gordon, Woman's Body, Woman's Right: Birth Control in America 480 (updated ed. 1990). Among women in lower socioeconomic classes, raising children can be drudgery, but "less alienat[ing] and more creative than most alternatives; it offers many others at least a semblance of control over their working conditions and goals." Id. Race is a further complicating factor. At various times and circumstances, racial pride might stimulate fertility or it might stimulate greater use of contraception. Race also affects the availability of competing opportunities to motherhood and thus the motivation to reproduce. Id. at 481.

For a perceptive historical analysis of how the different stages of the birth control movement in this country reflected the interests of different classes of women, whose autonomy was articulated in quite different terms, see id. at xix-xxi.

3. Medical Technology and Women's Health Autonomy. The health risks associated with the use of contraceptives by women impose another limitation on the autonomy that women derive from the legal availability of these resources. Women have successfully sued manufacturers for inadequate warnings about the risks of birth control pills, see, e.g., MacDonald v. Ortho Pharmaceutical Corp., 475 N.E.2d 65 (Mass.), cert. denied, 474 U.S. 920 (1985), and for failure to give proper instructions for use of diaphragms, see, e.g., Baroldy v. Ortho Pharmaceutical Corp., 760 P.2d 574 (Ariz. Ct. App. 1988), and spermicidal jelly, see, e.g., Wells v. Ortho Pharmaceutical Corp., 788 F.2d 741 (11th Cir.), cert. denied, 479 U.S. 950 (1986).

The most widespread damage to women as a result of dangerous contraceptives related to the negligent design and manufacturing problems of some intrauterine contraceptive devices (IUDs). Litigation over injuries caused by the Dalkon Shield device, including ectopic pregnancy, septic abortion, birth defects, infant death, infertility, and pelvic inflammatory disease, began in the 1970s, and by 1985, the sole manufacturer, A.H. Robins Co., had disposed of more than 9,000 claims and faced an additional 5,000. Robins filed for bankruptcy and had all claims consolidated in federal court, where a "bar date" was established by which all individuals with potential claims had to present them (April 30, 1986), along with a closed fund of over $2.4 billion out of which all claims were to be paid. See In re A.H. Robins, Inc., 880 F.2d 694 (4th Cir.), cert. denied, 493 U.S. 959 (1989). The complicated three-tiered plan under which claims were to be processed is described in detail in Kenneth R. Feinberg, The Dalkon Shield Claimants Trust, 53 Law & Contemp. Probs. 79 (1990). For a history of the

Dalkon Shield litigation as an example of contemporary women's protest against medical violence against women, see Karen M. Hicks, Surviving the Dalkon Shield IUD: Women v. The Pharmaceutical Industry (1994).

The great promise of the Dalkon Shield was that it located responsibility for contraception in medical technology rather than in women, who might forget or misuse other forms of reproductive control. Does such a reliance on technology rather than on women themselves represent a step forward or backward for women's autonomy? For a history and critique of the development and marketing of the Dalkon Shield, which argues in favor of woman-centered methods for reproductive choice, see Nicole J. Grant, The Selling of Contraception: The Dalkon Shield Case, Sexuality, and Women's Autonomy (1992).

The Dalkon Shield litigation and high damages awards in other contraceptive cases have been blamed for a narrowing of reproductive choices for American women, on the theory that they have made drug manufacturers reluctant to pursue alternatives available widely in other countries. One of these alternatives, Depo-Provera, is injected into the arm every three months to suppress ovulation through release of hormones. It costs about $120 and is 99 percent effective. Worries have surfaced, however, that forms of contraception like Depo-Provera, over which a woman has less short-term control, will be too easily imposed on her, turning a source of woman's autonomy into a means of control over her. See Philip J. Hilts, Panel Urges Contraceptive's Approval, N.Y. Times, June 20, 1992, at A6. Ironically, new forms of the IUD have been developed, and extensive studies have demonstrated that they are safe and effective, but memories of the Dalkon Shield cause women, physicians, and sex educators to avoid them. Sylvia A. Law, Tort Liability and the Availability of Contraceptive Drugs and Devices in the United States, 23 N.Y.U. Rev. L. & Soc. Change 339, 383-385 (1997).

Norplant raises similar possibilities of control over, rather than by, women. Norplant is a birth control system comprised of six matchstick-size silicone capsules implanted beneath the skin of a woman's upper arm that suppress ovulation and inhibit fertilization through the gradual release of synthetic hormones. In 1993, Norplant cost $365, plus up to $500 for the implantation procedure. It is 99 percent effective, and remains effective for up to five years. See Reshma Menon Yaqub, The Double-Edged Sword of Norplant, Chi. Trib., Jan. 24, 1993, at 11. There are, however, some potential medical side effects, including headaches, depression, nervousness, enlargement of the ovaries and/or fallopian tubes, inflammation of the skin, weight gain, inflammation of the cervix, nausea, dizziness, acne, abnormal hair growth, tenderness of the breasts, and prolonged or irregular bleeding. Norplant is contraindicated for women with certain medical conditions, such as heart, kidney, and liver disease; diabetes; and high blood pressure. Norplant capsules that are not removed after five years put the woman at risk of ectopic pregnancy. See Catherine Albiston, The Social Meaning of the

Norplant Condition: Constitutional Considerations of Race, Class, and Gender, 9 Berkeley Women's L.J. 9, 10 (1994). Unlike sterilization, it can be reversed, id. at 12, but it has to be removed by doctors, which not all women can afford. As a result of numerous health issues and the necessity of having doctors rather than women themselves remove it, Norplant was withdrawn from sale in the United Kingdom in 1999. Barbara Seaman, Under My Skin: Lessons from the Demise of Norplant, In These Times, Jan. 8, 2001, at 19. For a review of the medical issues concerning Norplant, which contends that Norplant was better tested than the Dalkon Shield and other devices made available to women, see Law, Tort Liability, supra, at 385-389.

The health implications of RU-486, described on pages 1091-1092, have also concerned many advocates. For example, the Institute on Women and Technology at the Massachusetts Institute of Technology denounced the drug as yet another example of a dubious contraceptive being promoted as an instrument of reproductive freedom. Brae Canlen, The Long Labor of RU 486, Cal. Law., May 1997, at 34, 85. See also pages 1154-1155 (discussing use of Norplant as a condition of probation).

Another disadvantage of female contraceptive alternatives is that most do not protect against AIDS and other sexually transmitted diseases. Male condom use has increased dramatically, relied upon by 13 percent of women of reproductive age in 1995, as compared to 17.8 percent of women using female sterilization, 17.3 percent using birth control pills, 7 percent using male sterilization, 1.9 percent using injectable contraceptives, 1.2 percent using diaphragms, and .5 percent using IUDs. See National Center for Health Statistics, Fertility, Family Planning and Women's Health: The 1995 National Survey of Family Growth 51 (1997). Female condoms now exist, but few women use them. Id.

Do women benefit from being the ones primarily responsible for birth control? On the one hand, of course, female contraception allows women to maintain greater control over their reproductive decisions. On the other hand, what is the broader impact of viewing contraception as a "woman's problem"?

The concern that disseminators of female contraception and other medical advances for women are not as attentive to health risks as those that serve men is part of a broader set of complaints against the medical establishment alleging discriminatory or abusive treatment of women. These complaints include concern over an unnecessary number of Caesarean section operations, see Leslie G. Espinoza, Dissecting Women, Dissecting Law: The Court-Ordering of Caesarean Section Operations and the Failure of Informed Consent to Protect Women of Color, 13 Nat'l Black L.J. 211 (1994); Margaret M. Donohoe, Our Epidemic of Unnecessary Caesarean Sections: The Role of the Law in Creating It, The Role of the Law in Stopping It, 11 Wis. Women's L.J. 197 (1996); Nancy Ehrenreich, The Colonization of the Womb, 43 Duke L.J. 492 (1993); Mary Gabay &

Sidney M. Wolfe, Unnecessary Caesarean Sections: Curing a National Epidemic (1994); the prosecution of midwives for the unlawful practice of medicine, compare, e.g., State Board of Nursing v. Ruebke, 913 P.2d 142 (Kan. 1996) (midwifery does not entail the unlawful practice of medicine) with State ex rel. Missouri State Bd. v. Southworth, 704 S.W.2d 219 (Mo. 1986) (state statute prohibits the unlicensed practice of medicine or midwifery); and the disproportionate exclusion of women from medical research and drug test trials, see, e.g., Keville, supra; Karen H. Rothenberg, Gender Matters: Implications for Clinical Research and Women's Health Care, 32 Hous. L. Rev. 1210 (1996). The NIH Revitalization Act of 1993, 42 U.S.C. §289a-2 (1994), requires the National Institutes of Heath of the Department of Heath and Human Services to include women and minorities as subjects of clinical research. Criticism of the guidelines issued under this legislation can be found in Jonathan M. Eisenberg, NIH Promulgates New Guidelines for the Inclusion of Women and Minorities in Medical Research, 10 Berkeley Women's L.J. 183 (1995).

Of the medical products released on the market for use by women, few have caused damage as widespread and intensive as DES, a synthetic estrogen hormone prescribed between 1940 and 1970 to prevent miscarriages and now linked to cancer and birth defects that become increasingly severe with each new generation. Women's success in recovering damages for DES-related injuries has been mixed. Compare Brown v. Superior Court, 751 P.2d 470 (Cal. 1988) (under circumstances in which women not aware of which manufacturer made the DES they were prescribed, court upheld "market share" liability among all companies that manufactured the drug) with Payton v. Abbott Labs, 437 N.E.2d 171 (Mass. 1982) (rejecting market share liability theory) and O'Brien v. Eli Lilly & Co., 668 F.2d 704 (3d Cir. 1981) (holding that two-year statute of limitations for claim against DES manufacturer began running from date plaintiff daughter read magazine article describing connections between drug and cancer, after which if she had exercised due diligence, she would have determined that her mother had taken the drug that arguably caused her subsequent cancer). For a history of DES and its physical and psychological effects, see Roberta J. Apfel & Susan M. Fisher, To Do No Harm: DES and the Dilemmas of Modern Medicine (1984). See also O'Gilvie v. International Playtex, Inc., 821 F.2d 1438 (10th Cir. 1987), cert. denied, 486 U.S. 1032 (1988) (upholding jury verdict for over $1.5 million in actual damages and $10 million in punitive damages for death from toxic shock syndrome caused by tampons); Dralle v. Ruder, 500 N.E.2d 514 (Ill. Ct. App. 1986) (upholding strict liability and negligence action against manufacturer of Bendectin, an anti-nausea medication prescribed during pregnancy that was found to cause birth defects), judgment rev'd, 529 N.E.2d 209 (Ill. 1988) (no loss of companionship damages); Oxendine v. Merrell Dow Pharmaceuticals, Inc., 506 A.2d 1100 (D.C. 1986) (reversing jnov for defendant after jury awarded $750,000 in compensatory damages for birth defects caused by Bendectin, and remanding for trial on punitive damages).

Another example of medical technology that may not have been adequately tested is silicone gel-filled breast implants, used by women cancer patients who have had mastectomies and by hundreds of thousands more women who have sought to attain the perfect breast size. While the harm of breast implants is highly disputed, the rupture and leakage of silicone from implants have been associated with very serious arthritic and auto-immune disorders. With a number of cases in the early 1990s yielding multi-million-dollar verdicts (one for $25 million, including $20 million in punitive damages), in late 1992 the Food and Drug Administration (FDA) withdrew approval for silicone breast implants except for "urgent need" patients who had had mastectomies. See 21 C.F.R. pt. 821; David E. Bernstein, The Breast Implant Fiasco (Review Essay), 87 Cal. L. Rev. 457, 479 (1999). Despite various settlement efforts, thousands of individual cases were litigated in state and federal courts; according to one commentator, defendants have won the "vast majority" of cases since 1994. Bernstein, supra, at 484. Several federal cases were particularly significant, having enlisted high-profile expert panels to advise the court on the scientific basis for the plaintiffs' claims and, on the basis of advice received from these panels, rejected the plaintiffs' expert testimony about the harms of silicone-gel breast implants under Federal Rule of Evidence 706. One judge held that the plaintiffs were required to prove a "relative risk of greater than 2.0" and that the epidemiological evidence did not prove causation to that degree. As a result, plaintiffs could not introduce evidence of causation in their own individual cases. See Hall v. Baxter Healthcare Corp., 947 F. Supp. 1387 (D. Or. 1996) (ruling against admission of certain expert testimony, but deferring effective date of ruling until reports of national Rule 706 panel). This case was followed in In re Silicone Gel Breast Implants Products Litigation, 11 F. Supp. 2d 1217 (D. Colo. 1998), which held that unless plaintiffs can show that women as a group who use silicone-gel breast implants are at least 50 percent more likely to have the symptoms in question, they could not try to show, individually, that their illnesses are attributable to the breast implants. See Lucinda M. Finley, Guarding the Gate to the Courthouse: How Trial Judges Are Using Their Evidentiary Screening Role to Remake Tort Causation Rules, 49 DePaul L. Rev. 335, 357 (1999). See also Allison v. McGhan Med. Corp, 184 F.3d 1300 (11th Cir. 1999) (affirming summary judgment on strict liability and fraud/misrepresentation claims for maker of silicone-gel breast implants because plaintiff could not prove that the implants caused her injuries, after district court excluded testimony of her experts under *Daubert*). The methodologies for each of these panels are described and analyzed by the authors of a fuller report prepared for the Judicial Conference of the United States, in Laurel L. Hooper, Joe S. Cecil, & Thomas E. Willging, Assessing

Causation in Breast Implant Litigation: The Role of Science Panels, 64 Law & Contemp. Probs. 139 (2001).

It is reported that the former silicone implant makers have spent more than $6 billion to settle about 370,000 of the claims filed by U.S. and foreign implant recipients. Greg Gordon, Debate on Breast Implants Focusing on Different Toxin: Some Scientists Say Platinum Poses More Risks than Silicone, Star Trib. (Minneapolis), Dec. 18, 2000, at 1A.

Commentators disagree vehemently about the science underlying the breast implant cases and the most appropriate method to handle that science in the legal process. Compare Bernstein, supra, at 476 (summarizing litigated cases and scientific studies, and claiming that the FDA "seems to have succumbed to severe political and media pressure" when it banned breast implants except for reconstructive surgery) and Marcia Angell, Science on Trial: The Clash of Medical Evidence and the Law in the Breast Implant Case (1996) (criticizing legal system for allowing jury verdicts in breast implant cases when the scientific basis for such claims did not establish causal link between implants and injuries claimed) with Finley, supra, at 373 (criticizing cases that rejected expert testimony on causation, arguing that they confused general and specific causation and that the heightened requirements that these cases imposed for proof of causation are "likely" to have "significant gender, race, and class implications") and Rebecca S. Dresser et al., Breast Implants Revisited: Beyond *Science on Trial*, 1997 Wis. L. Rev. 705 (arguing that rather than criticizing the science of plaintiffs in breast implant cases, manufacturers should have used better science themselves to assess their risks before promoting breast implants).

Issues also arise over whether women are more likely to be undertreated for diseases than men. One study of 139,000 Medicare patients, for example, found that women were 7 percent less likely to receive clot-dissolving drugs in the first hour of treatment for heart attacks; had fewer catheterizations, which determine if angioplasty or heart-bypass operations are needed; and in other ways received a lesser level of care. See Sandra C. Gan et al., Treatment of Acute Myocardial Infarction Among Men and Women, 343 New Eng. J. Med. 8 (July 2000). Another study found that emergency rooms incorrectly sent home a disproportionate number of women and blacks with the warning signs of heart attacks. See J. Hector Pope et al., Missed Diagnoses of Acute Cardiac Ischemia in the Emergency Department, 342 New Eng. J. Med. 1163 (Apr. 2000). One-third of women in another study did not receive all of the treatment that was warranted for breast cancer. Denise Grady, Incomplete Breast Cancer Care Found, N.Y. Times, Sept. 29, 2000, at A21. See also Terri D. Keville, The Invisible Woman: Gender Bias in Medical Research, 15 Women's Rts. L. Rep. 123, 129 (Winter 1993/Spring 1994) (noting failure to diagnose and treat women with certain diseases such as heart disease and lung cancer as aggressively as men, and less access to kidney transplants); Carol Jonann Bess, Gender Bias in Health Care: A Life or Death Issue for Women with

Coronary Heart Disease, 6 Hastings Women's L.J. 41 (1995) (charging gender bias in treatment for coronary heart disease).

4. Insurance and Women's Health. Other issues raising suggestions of discriminatory health treatment for women concern the coverage of health care insurance. Is *Bartell* correctly decided? Where, exactly, is the discrimination? Is it because the exclusion of contraceptives (oral conceptives cost about $300 per year) mean that women's out-of-pocket costs for prescription drugs average 68 percent more than men's? Lila Arzua, Why Cover Contraceptives, Wash. Post, Aug. 2, 2000, at A31; Julie F. Kay, Prescription Drug Plans Discriminate Against Women, Reproductive Freedom News, Oct. 2000, at 3. Is it because other drugs used only by men, such as Viagra, which promotes male sexual performance, often (although apparently not under the facts in *Bartell*) are covered by insurance?

A number of states mandate that insurance companies offer contraceptive coverage in their prescription drug plans. Id. (reporting 12 states in 2000). Should the court in *Bartell* have waited for other states to act? What about the specificity of the court's order? Is it an indication that the court is legislating, rather than acting in a proper judicial role? Or is it the only way to correct the discrimination in this case?

Does it follow from *Bartell* that infertility treatments should also be covered? Previous to *Bartell*, courts had not compelled such coverage. See, e.g., Krauel v. Iowa Methodist Med. Ctr., 95 F.3d 674, 679-680 (8th Cir. 1996); Saks v. Franklin Covey Co., 117 F. Supp. 2d 318, 328-329 (S.D.N.Y. 2000). Bartell explicitly recognizes the decisions, without disapproval. 141 F. Supp.2d at 1275 n.14.

Whether various medical procedures are "standard" treatments, covered by health plans, or "experimental or investigational," and thus not covered, may also raise issues of sex discrimination, although in litigation the cases focus on how to interpret insurance policies rather than whether the policies are discriminatory. See, e.g., Smith v. Office of Civilian Health and Medical Programs of the Uniformed Services, 97 F.3d 950 (7th Cir. 1996) (high-dose chemotherapy still an experimental treatment for breast cancer, and coverage properly denied); Henderson v. Bodine Aluminum, Inc., 70 F.3d 958 (8th Cir. 1995) (covered); Wilson v. Office of Civilian Health and Medical Programs of the Uniformed Services, 65 F.3d 361 (4th Cir. 1995) (covered). See also Bullwinkel v. New England Mutual Life Ins. Co., 18 F.3d 429 (7th Cir. 1994) (breast lump that was diagnosed and treated before health insurance policy became effective, but that was not diagnosed or treated as cancer, was pre-existing condition and thus excluded from the coverage when later turned out to be cancer). For an analysis of various issues relating to insurance coverage for treatment of breast cancer, see Julia Anastasio, Legislative Developments in the Regulation of Insurance Coverage: Will These New Regulations Benefit Women with Breast Cancer?, 7

Am. U. J. Gender, Soc. Pol'y & L. 56 (1998-1999) (summarizing and analyzing proposed legislation).

Insurance coverage for women after a normal childbirth delivery of one overnight stay is also the subject of considerable controversy. See Tracy Wilson Smirnoff, "Drive-Through Deliveries": Indiscriminate Postpartum Early Discharge Practices Presently Necessitate Legislation Mandating Minimum Inpatient Hospital Stays, 44 Clev. St. L. Rev. 231 (1996).

5. Involuntary Contraception. Coercion has also been an issue in contraception, especially with respect to mental "incompetents" and poor and minority women. In Buck v. Bell, 274 U.S. 200 (1927), the Supreme Court upheld a Virginia sterilization law that allowed the superintendent of an institution for the mentally disabled to compel the sterilization of a female inmate. In defense of the decision, Justice Holmes wrote:

> We have seen more than once that the public welfare may call upon the best citizens for their lives. It would be strange if it could not call upon those who already sap the strength of the State for these lesser sacrifices, in order to prevent our being swamped with incompetence. . . . Three generations of imbeciles is enough.

Id. at 207.

The view of the Supreme Court toward compulsory sterilization changed in Skinner v. Oklahoma ex rel. Williamson, 316 U.S. 535 (1942), which held that it was a violation of equal protection for the state to sterilize a man convicted of some specific felonies (grand larceny and larceny by trespass) but not others (embezzlement). However, some states continue to authorize compulsory sterilization under some circumstances, such as conviction for certain crimes, see, e.g., Cal. Penal Code §645 (West 1999) (authorizing sterilization of person convicted of rape of children under the age of 13); Wash. Rev. Code §9.92.100 (1998) (authorizing sterilization for persons convicted of sex with female under age ten), and for the benefit of mentally ill or mentally incompetent persons, see, e.g., Vt. Stat. Ann. tit. 18, §8712(c) (2000) (court may order sterilization of an incompetent person if it is in the best interests of the person); Conn. Gen. Stat. §45a-699 (1993) (court may consent to sterilization if presented with clear and convincing evidence that it is in the best interests of the individual).

Sterilization abuse has been well documented, impacting disproportionately on poor and minority women whose welfare benefits in some cases have been conditioned on "consenting" to sterilization. See, e.g., Relf v. Weinberger, 372 F. Supp. 1196, 1199 (D.D.C. 1974), on remand sub nom. Relf v. Mathews, 403 F. Supp. 1235 (D.D.C. 1975), vacated sub nom. Relf v. Weinberger, 565 F.2d 722 (D.C. Cir. 1977) (two black girls, ages 12 and 14, were sterilized at a federally funded clinic in Alabama without their knowledge or the knowledge of their parents); Madrigal v. Quilligan, No.

CV 75-2057-JWC (C.D. Cal. June 30, 1978), reported in Joelle S. Weiss, Controlling HIV-Positive Women's Procreative Destiny: A Critical Equal Protection Analysis, 2 Const. L.J. 643, 663-664 (1992) (ten non-English-speaking Chicanas sued doctors for coercing their consent to sterilization by withholding medication during intensive labor; court held sterilization performed with the bona fide belief that women had voluntarily submitted); Stump v. Sparkman, 435 U.S. 349 (1978) (judge ordered sterilization of 15-year-old girl who was told only that her appendix was being removed, pursuant to petition by girl's mother that she was mildly retarded; judge held absolutely immune from liability); Harris v. Karam, No. CIV 78-601 (D. Ariz. 1979), described in Dick Grosboll, Sterilization Abuse: Current State of the Law and Remedies for Abuse, 10 Golden Gate U. L. Rev. 1147, 1155-1156 (1980) (county officials conditioned medical services on the patient's consent to birth control, sterilization, or abortion); Walker v. Pierce, 560 F.2d 609 (4th Cir. 1977), cert. denied, 434 U.S. 1075 (1978) (civil rights action against obstetrician who refused to treat Medicaid patients who already had two children if they failed to consent to a tubal ligation; dismissed on the grounds that he was not acting under color of state law); Avery v. County of Burke, 660 F.2d 111, 115 (4th Cir. 1981) (county agency induced teenage girl to undergo unwanted sterilization on the basis of misrepresentation that she had sickle cell trait).

Federal regulations and state laws are designed to protect against such abuses. Statutes setting forth specific criteria generally use those similar to the ones set forth in In re Grady, 426 A.2d 467 (N.J. 1981), discussed in note 6, below. See, e.g., Utah Code Ann. §62A-6-108 (Michie 1997). Older cases upholding involuntary sterilization statutes include In re Sterilization of Moore, 221 S.E.2d 307 (N.C. 1976) (upholding constitutionality of sterilization statute, with procedural safeguards, to prevent the procreation of children by a mentally ill or retarded individual who would probably be unable to care for a child or who would procreate a child with serious physical, mental, or nervous diseases or deficiencies); Cook v. Oregon, 495 P.2d 768 (Or. Ct. App. 1972) (upholding constitutionality of state statute allowing state agency to order sterilization upon finding that procreation would produce a child or children "who would become neglected or dependent children as a result of the parent's inability by reason of mental illness or mental retardation to provide adequate care").

Many states require the appointment of a special guardian ad litem for the incompetent individual to represent that individual's interests before sterilization will be allowed. See, e.g., In re Sterilization of Moore, 221 S.E.2d 307; In re Grady, 426 A.2d 467 (N.J. 1981). What should be the role of that guardian? One scholar argues that the guardian always should oppose sterilization. See George Annas, Sterilization of the Mentally Retarded: A Decision for the Courts, 1981 Hastings Cent. Rep. 19 (Aug.). Does this position attach too great an importance to procreative "autonomy"? Or too little?

The issue of "forced" sterilization in the context of conditions of probation in connection with criminal charges of child abuse or neglect is explored in Section B of this chapter.

6. A Right to Sterilization?   As stated in note 3, above, sterilization is currently the most widely used birth control technique — the option of 26 percent of American women of reproductive age and 10 percent of men.

Consensual sterilization is generally available, notwithstanding some early official efforts to limit it. Courts are tending to apply increasingly liberal standards of competency to mentally disabled adults, leaving up to the woman herself the choice of whether or not to be sterilized. How difficult should it be to obtain the sterilization of a woman who is deemed incompetent to make the decision on her own? See in re Romero, 790 P.2d 819 (Colo. 1990) (to sterilize woman without her consent, need to prove incompetency by clear and convincing evidence). Should there be a constitutional right to be sterilized where sterility is the condition likely to maximize the woman's ability to live a relatively autonomous life? Over dissents by some of its most liberal members, the California Supreme Court held that a statutory prohibition on elective sterilization of developmentally disabled persons on whose behalf sterilization is sought by a parent or guardian violates "privacy and liberty interests protected by the Fourteenth Amendment." See Conservatorship of Valerie N., 707 P.2d 760, 772 (Cal. 1985).

Even if there is a constitutional right to sterilization, difficult issues remain as to when that right may be exercised on behalf of an incompetent individual. A 1981 New Jersey case raised this issue with respect to a 19-year-old woman, Lee Ann Grady, who as a result of Down's syndrome had very limited intellectual capacities and understanding. According to the court:

> . . . She has no significant understanding of sexual relationships or marriage. If she became pregnant, she would neither understand her condition nor be able to make decisions about it. Her lack of awareness could lead to severe health problems. It is uncontradicted that she would not be able to care for a baby alone. Indeed, she will probably need lifetime supervision to care for her own needs.
>
> Recognizing her sexual growth, the Gradys [her parents] have provided birth control pills for the past four years. Although there is no evidence that Lee Ann has engaged in sexual activity or has any interest in doing so, her parents believe that contraception is an appropriate precaution to exercise under the circumstances of their daughter's life.
>
> As Lee Ann has approached the age of 20 — when she will leave her special class in the public school system — the Gradys . . . fear they will predecease their daughter and she will be unable to live independently. Thus they have sought to attain for her a life less dependent on her family. The Gradys wish to place Lee Ann in a sheltered work group and eventually in a

group home for retarded adults. But the parents see dependable and continuous contraception as a prerequisite to any such change in their daughter's environment. With the advice of their doctor, they sought to have Lee Ann sterilized. . . . The hospital refused to permit the operation.

In re Grady, 426 A.2d 467, 470 (N.J. 1981).

What standard should the court apply to the parents' request? Does Lee Ann Grady meet this standard? Should it be enough that a woman will be unable to care for any children she might conceive? In *Grady*, the court held that sterilization of an "incompetent" person could be allowed only if there was clear and convincing proof that sterilization is in the incompetent person's best interests, taking into account such factors as the possibility of pregnancy, the likelihood of sexual intercourse, the possibility of trauma or psychological damage (both with and without sterilization), the inability of the individual to understand reproduction or contraception, the availability of less drastic means, the advisability of delay, the ability of the individual to care for a child, the possibility of improvement in the individual's condition, and the good faith of those seeking to have the sterilization procedures performed. Id. at 483. Is this too strict a standard? Strict enough? Cf. In re Hayes, 608 P.2d 635 (Wash. 1980) (under a similar test, finding that burden not met in case in which 16-year-old child was severely mentally retarded and sexually active and whose parents had unsuccessfully attempted alternative means of contraception); Conservatorship of Valerie N., 707 P.2d 760 (Cal. 1998) (holding that evidence insufficient to show sterilization required or that less intrusive means of contraception not presently available). Why shouldn't the parents of an incompetent be able to make the decision about sterilization on their own? See Elizabeth S. Scott, Sterilization of Mentally Retarded Persons: Reproductive Rights and Family Privacy, 1986 Duke L.J. 806, 865 (arguing that for retarded persons who cannot make their own decisions, "parents — not courts — are the best surrogates").

A few courts have followed a "substituted judgement" test, whereby the court attempts to ascertain "what decision would be made by the incompetent person if he or she were competent." In re Moe, 432 N.E.2d 712, 720 (Mass. 1982). Is this a workable standard? How would it be applied to the *Grady* facts?

Putting Theory into Practice

6-5. In 1995, an estimated 85,000 women underwent a mastectomy as part of their treatment for breast cancer. About half of them opted for breast reconstruction. The availability of breast reconstruction after a mastectomy, studies have shown, encourages women to obtain early treatment because it makes the prospect of breast cancer less frightening and mutilating than it would otherwise be. A recent survey found that over 100 health insurance companies nationwide have either denied or restricted coverage for breast reconstruction. For example, some companies do not cover reconstruction of the second breast that the woman may choose to have removed as a preventative measure.

Is this an equality issue? What if penile implants are covered, to achieve sexual functioning for men, and not breast reconstruction for women? See Cristine Nardi, Comment, When Health Insurers Deny Coverage for Breast Reconstructive Surgery: Gender Meets Disability, 1997 Wis. L. Rev. 777 (summarizing relevant state legislation and federal legislative proposals, and urging a national standard).

2. Abortion

a. The Legal Framework

Roe v. Wade
410 U.S. 113 (1973)

Justice BLACKMUN delivered the opinion of the Court. . . .

I

[Texas law makes] it a crime to "procure an abortion," as therein defined, or to attempt one, except with respect to "an abortion procured or attempted by medical advice for the purpose of saving the life of the mother." Similar statutes are in existence in a majority of the States. . . .

II

Jane Roe, a single woman who was residing in Dallas County, Texas, instituted this federal action in March 1970 [seeking] a declaratory judgment that the Texas criminal abortion statutes were unconstitutional on their face, and an injunction restraining the defendant from enforcing the statutes. . . .

V

The principal thrust of appellant's attack on the Texas statutes is that they improperly invade a right, said to be possessed by the pregnant woman, to choose to terminate her pregnancy. Appellant would discover this right in the concept of personal "liberty" embodied in the Fourteenth Amendment's Due Process Clause; or in personal, marital, familial, and sexual privacy said to be protected by the Bill of Rights or its penumbras, see

Griswold v. Connecticut, 381 U.S. 479 (1965); Eisenstadt v. Baird, 405 U.S. 438 (1972); id., at 460 (White, J., concurring in result); or among those rights reserved to the people by the Ninth Amendment, Griswold v. Connecticut, 381 U.S., at 486 (Goldberg, J., concurring). . . .

VII

Three reasons have been advanced to explain historically the enactment of criminal abortion laws in the 19th century and to justify their continued existence.

It has been argued occasionally that these laws were the product of a Victorian social concern to discourage illicit sexual conduct. Texas, however, does not advance this justification in the present case. . . .

A second reason is concerned with abortion as a medical procedure. When most criminal abortion laws were first enacted, the procedure was a hazardous one for the woman. . . .

Modern medical techniques have altered this situation. . . .

The third reason is the State's interest — some phrase it in terms of duty — in protecting prenatal life. Some of the argument for this justification rests on the theory that a new human life is present from the moment of conception. The State's interest and general obligation to protect life then extends, it is argued, to prenatal life. Only when the life of the pregnant mother herself is at stake, balanced against the life she carries within her, should the interest of the embryo or fetus not prevail. Logically, of course, a legitimate state interest in this area need not stand or fall on acceptance of the belief that life begins at conception or at some other point prior to live birth. In assessing the State's interest, recognition may be given to the less rigid claim that as long as at least *potential* life is involved, the State may assert interests beyond the protection of the pregnant woman alone. . . .

VIII

The Constitution does not explicitly mention any right of privacy. In a line of decisions, however, going back perhaps as far as Union Pacific R. Co. v. Botsford, 141 U.S. 250, 251 (1891), the Court has recognized that a right of personal privacy, or a guarantee of certain areas or zones of privacy, does exist under the Constitution. In varying contexts, the Court or individual Justices have, indeed, found at least the roots of that right in the First Amendment . . . ; in the Fourth and Fifth Amendments . . . ; in the penumbras of the Bill of Rights . . . ; or in the concept of liberty guaranteed by the first section of the Fourteenth Amendment. . . . These decisions make it clear that only personal rights that can be deemed "fundamental" or "implicit in the concept of ordered liberty," Palko v. Connecticut, 302 U.S. 319, 325 (1937), are included in this guarantee of personal privacy. They also make it clear that the right has some extension to activities relating to marriage, Loving v. Virginia, 388 U.S. 1, 12 (1967); procreation, Skinner v. Oklahoma, 316 U.S. 535, 541-542 (1942); contraception, Eisenstadt v. Baird, 405 U.S., at 453-454; id., at 460, 463-465 (White, J., concurring in result); family relationships, Prince v. Massachusetts, 321 U.S. 158, 166 (1944); and child rearing and education, Pierce v. Society of Sisters, 268 U.S. 510, 535 (1925), Meyer v. Nebraska, supra.

This right of privacy, whether it be founded in the Fourteenth Amendment's concept of personal liberty and restrictions upon state action, as we feel it is, or, as the District Court determined, in the Ninth Amendment's reservation of rights to the people, is broad enough to encompass a woman's decision whether or not to terminate her pregnancy. The detriment that the State would impose upon the pregnant woman by denying this choice altogether is apparent. Specific and direct harm medically diagnosable even in early pregnancy may be involved. Maternity, or additional offspring, may force upon the woman a distressful life and future. Psychological harm may be imminent. Mental and physical health may be taxed by child care. There is also the distress, for all concerned, associated with the unwanted child, and there is the problem of bringing a child into a family already unable, psychologically and otherwise, to care for it. In other cases, as in this one, the additional difficulties and continuing stigma of unwed motherhood may be involved. All these are factors the woman and her responsible physician necessarily will consider in consultation.

On the basis of elements such as these, appellant and some *amici* argue that the woman's right is absolute and that she is entitled to terminate her pregnancy at whatever time, in whatever way, and for whatever reason she alone chooses. With this we do not agree. Appellant's arguments that Texas either has no valid interest at all in regulating the abortion decision, or no interest strong enough to support any limitation upon the woman's sole determination, are unpersuasive. The Court's decisions recognizing a right of privacy also acknowledge that some state regulation in areas protected by that right is appropriate. As noted above, a State may properly assert important interests in safeguarding health, in maintaining medical standards, and in protecting potential life. At some point in pregnancy, these respective interests become sufficiently compelling to sustain regulation of the factors that govern the abortion decision. The privacy right involved, therefore, cannot be said to be absolute. . . .

We, therefore, conclude that the right of personal privacy includes the abortion decision, but that this right is not unqualified and must be considered against important state interests in regulation.

IX. . . .

A

The appellee and certain *amici* argue that the fetus is a "person" within the language and meaning of the Fourteenth Amendment. In support of this, they outline at length and in detail the well-known facts of fetal development. If this suggestion of personhood is established, the appellant's case, of course, collapses, for the fetus' right to life would then be guaranteed specifically by the Amendment. . . .

The Constitution does not define "person" in so many words. Section 1 of the Fourteenth Amendment contains three references to "person." The first, in defining "citizens," speaks of "persons born or naturalized in the United States." The word also appears both in the Due Process Clause and in the Equal Protection Clause. "Person" is used in other places in the Constitution. . . . [I]n nearly all these instances, the use of the word is such that it has application only postnatally. None indicates, with any assurance, that it has any possible pre-natal application.

All this, together with our observation . . . that throughout the major portion of the 19th century prevailing legal abortion practices were far freer than they are today, persuades us that the word "person," as used in the Fourteenth Amendment, does not include the unborn. . . .

B

The pregnant woman cannot be isolated in her privacy. She carries an embryo and, later, a fetus, if one accepts the medical definitions of the developing young in the human uterus. . . . The situation therefore is inherently different from marital intimacy, or bedroom possession of obscene material, or marriage, or procreation, or education, with which *Eisenstadt* and *Griswold, Stanley, Loving, Skinner,* and *Pierce* and *Meyer* were respectively concerned. As we have intimated above, it is reasonable and appropriate for a State to decide that at some point in time another interest, that of health of the mother or that of potential human life, becomes significantly involved. The woman's privacy is no longer sole and any right of privacy she possesses must be measured accordingly.

Texas urges that, apart from the Fourteenth Amendment, life begins at conception and is present throughout pregnancy, and that, therefore, the State has a compelling interest in protecting that life from and after conception. We need not resolve the difficult question of when life begins. When those trained in the respective disciplines of medicine, philosophy, and theology are unable to arrive at any consensus, the judiciary, at this point in the development of man's knowledge, is not in a position to speculate as to the answer. . . .

In areas other than criminal abortion, the law has been reluctant to endorse any theory that life, as we recognize it, begins before live birth or to accord legal rights to the unborn except in narrowly defined situations and except when the rights are contingent upon live birth. For example, the traditional rule of tort law denied recovery for prenatal injuries even though the child was born alive. That rule has been changed in almost every jurisdiction. In most States, recovery is said to be permitted only if the fetus was viable, or at least quick, when the injuries were sustained, though few courts have squarely so held. In a recent development, generally opposed by the commentators, some States permit the parents of a stillborn child to maintain an action for wrongful death because of prenatal injuries. Such an action, however, would appear to be one to vindicate the parents' interest and is thus consistent with the view that the fetus, at most, represents only the potentiality of life. Similarly, unborn children have been recognized as acquiring rights or interests by way of inheritance or other devolution of property, and have been represented by guardians *ad litem*. Perfection of the interests involved, again, has generally been contingent upon live birth. In short, the unborn have never been recognized in the law as persons in the whole sense.

X

In view of all this, we do not agree that, by adopting one theory of life, Texas may override the rights of the pregnant woman that are at stake. We repeat, however, that the State does have an important and legitimate interest in preserving and protecting the health of the pregnant woman, whether she be a resident of the State or a nonresident who seeks medical consultation and treatment there, and that it has still *another* important and legitimate interest in protecting the potentiality of human life. These interests are separate and distinct. Each grows in substantiality as the woman approaches term and, at a point during pregnancy, each becomes "compelling."

With respect to the State's important and legitimate interest in the health of the mother, the "compelling" point, in the light of present medical knowledge, is at approximately the end of the first trimester. This is so because of the now-established medical fact . . . that until the end of the first trimester mortality in abortion may be less than mortality in normal childbirth. It follows that, from and after this point, a State may regulate the abortion procedure to the extent that the regulation reasonably relates to the preservation and protection of maternal health. Examples of permissible state regulation in this area are requirements as to the qualifications of the person who is to perform the abortion; as to the licensure of that person; as to the facility in which the procedure is to be performed, that is, whether it must be a hospital or may be a clinic or some other place of less-than-hospital status; as to the licensing of the facility; and the like.

This means, on the other hand, that, for the period of pregnancy prior to this "compelling" point, the attending physician, in consultation with his patient, is free to determine, without regulation by the State, that, in his medical judgment, the patient's pregnancy should be terminated. If that decision is reached, the judgment may be effectuated by an abortion free of interference by the State.

With respect to the State's important and legitimate interest in potential life, the "compelling" point is at viability. This is so because the fetus then presumably has the capability of meaningful life outside the mother's womb. State regulation protective of fetal life after viability thus has both logical and biological justifications. If the State is interested in protecting fetal life after viability, it may go so far as to proscribe abortion during that period, except when it is necessary to preserve the life or health of the mother.

Measured against these standards, [Texas law], in restricting legal abortions to those "procured or attempted by medical advice for the purpose of saving the life of the mother," sweeps too broadly. The statute makes no distinction between abortions performed early in pregnancy and those performed later, and it limits to a single reason, "saving" the mother's life, the legal justification for the procedure. The statute, therefore, cannot survive the constitutional attack made upon it here. . . .

[The concurring opinion of Justice Stewart is omitted.]

[The dissenting opinion of Justice Rehnquist is omitted.]

Planned Parenthood of Southeastern Pennsylvania v. Casey
505 U.S. 833 (1992)

Justice O'CONNOR, Justice KENNEDY, and Justice SOUTER announced the judgment of the Court and delivered the opinion of the Court with respect to Parts I, II, III, V-A, V-C, and VI, in which Justice BLACKMUN and Justice STEVENS join, an opinion with respect to Part V-E, in which Justice STEVENS joins, and an opinion with respect to Parts IV, V-B, and V-D.

I

Liberty finds no refuge in a jurisprudence of doubt. Yet 19 years after our holding that the Constitution protects a woman's right to terminate her pregnancy in its early stages, Roe v. Wade, 410 U.S. 113 (1973), that definition of liberty is still questioned. Joining the respondents as amicus curiae, the United States, as it has done in five other cases in the last decade, again asks us to overrule *Roe*. . . .

At issue in these cases are five provisions of the Pennsylvania Abortion Control Act of 1982 as amended in 1988 and 1989. 18 Pa. Cons. Stat. §§3203-3220 (1990). . . . The Act requires that a woman seeking an abortion give her informed consent prior to the abortion procedure, and specifies that she be provided with certain information at least 24 hours before the abortion is performed. §3205. For a minor to obtain an abortion, the Act requires the informed consent of one of her parents, but provides for a judicial bypass option if the minor does not wish to or cannot obtain a parent's consent. §3206. Another provision of the Act requires that, unless certain exceptions apply, a married woman seeking an abortion must sign a statement indicating that she has notified her husband of her intended abortion. §3209. The Act exempts compliance with these three require- ments in the event of a "medical emergency," which is defined in §3203 of the Act. See §§3203, 3205(a), 3206(a), 3209(c). In addition to the above provisions regulating the performance of abortions, the Act imposes certain reporting requirements on facilities that provide abortion services. §§3207(b), 3214(a), 3214(f). . . .

After considering the fundamental constitutional questions resolved by Roe, principles of institutional integrity, and the rule of *stare decisis*, we are led to conclude this: the essential holding of Roe v. Wade should be retained and once again reaffirmed.

It must be stated at the outset and with clarity that *Roe*'s essential holding, the holding we reaffirm, has three parts. First is a recognition of the right of the woman to choose to have an abortion before viability and to obtain it without undue interference from the State. Before viability, the State's interests are not strong enough to support a prohibition of abortion or the imposition of a substantial obstacle to the woman's effective right to elect the procedure. Second is a confirmation of the State's power to restrict abortions after fetal viability, if the law contains exceptions for pregnancies which endanger a woman's life or health. And third is the principle that the State has legitimate interests from the outset of the pregnancy in protecting the health of the woman and the life of the fetus that may become a child. These principles do not contradict one another; and we adhere to each.

II

Constitutional protection of the woman's decision to terminate her pregnancy derives from the Due Process Clause of the Fourteenth Amendment. It declares that no State shall "deprive any person of life, liberty, or property, without due process of law." . . .

Neither the Bill of Rights nor the specific practices of States at the time of the adoption of the Fourteenth Amendment marks the outer limits of the substantive sphere of liberty which the Fourteenth Amendment protects. See U.S. Const., Amend. 9. As the second Justice Harlan recognized: "[T]he full scope of the liberty guaranteed by the Due Process Clause cannot be found in or limited by the precise terms of the specific guarantees elsewhere provided in the Constitution. This 'liberty' is not a series of isolated points pricked out in terms of the taking of property; the freedom of speech, press, and religion; the right to keep and bear arms; the freedom from unreasonable searches and seizures; and so on. It is a rational continuum which, broadly speaking, includes a freedom from all substantial arbitrary impositions and purposeless restraints, . . . and which also recognizes, what a reasonable and sensitive judgment must, that certain interests require particularly careful scrutiny of the state needs asserted to justify their abridgment." Poe v. Ullman, [367 U.S. 497, 543 (1961) (Harlan, J., dissenting)]. . . .

Our law affords constitutional protection to personal decisions relating to marriage, procreation, contraception, family relationships, child rearing, and education. . . . These matters, involving the most intimate and personal choices a person may make in a lifetime, choices central to personal dignity and autonomy, are central to the liberty protected by the Fourteenth Amendment. At the heart of liberty is the right to define one's own concept of existence, of meaning, of the universe, and of the mystery of human life. Beliefs about these matters could not define the attributes of personhood were they formed under compulsion of the State.

These considerations begin our analysis of the woman's interest in terminating her pregnancy but cannot end it, for this reason: though the abortion decision may originate within the zone of conscience and belief, it is more than a philosophic exercise. Abortion is a unique act. It is an act fraught with consequences for others: for the woman who must live with the implications of her decision; for the persons who perform and assist in the procedure; for the spouse, family, and society which must confront the knowledge that these procedures exist, procedures some deem nothing short of an act of violence against innocent human life; and, depending on one's beliefs, for the life or potential life that is aborted. Though abortion is conduct, it does not follow that the State is entitled to proscribe it in all instances. That is because the liberty of the woman is at stake in a sense unique to the human condition and so unique to the law. The mother who carries a child to full term is subject to anxieties, to physical constraints, to pain that only she must bear. That these sacrifices have from the beginning of the human race been endured by woman with a pride that ennobles her in the eyes of others and gives to the infant a bond of love cannot alone be grounds for the State to insist she make the sacrifice. Her suffering is too intimate and personal for the State to insist, without more, upon its own vision of the woman's role, however dominant that vision has been in the course of our history and our culture. The destiny of the woman must be shaped to a large extent on her own conception of her spiritual imperatives and her place in society.

It should be recognized, moreover, that in some critical respects the abortion decision is of the same character as the decision to use contraception, to which Griswold v. Connecticut, [381 U.S. 479 (1965),] Eisenstadt v. Baird, [405 U.S. 438 (1972),] and Carey v. Population Services International, [431 U.S. 678 (1977),] afford constitutional protection. We have no doubt as to the correctness of those decisions. They support the reasoning in *Roe* relating to the woman's liberty because they involve personal decisions concerning not only the meaning of procreation but also human responsibility and respect for it. As with abortion, reasonable people will have differences of opinion about these matters. One view is based on such reverence for the wonder of creation that any pregnancy ought to be welcomed and carried to full term no matter how difficult it will be to provide for the child and ensure its well-being. Another is that the inability to provide for the nurture and care of the infant is a cruelty to the child and an anguish to the parent. These are intimate views with infinite variations, and their deep, personal character underlay our decisions in *Griswold*, *Eisenstadt*, and *Carey*. The same concerns are present when the woman confronts the reality that, perhaps despite her attempts to avoid it, she has become pregnant.

It was this dimension of personal liberty that *Roe* sought to protect. . . .

[T]he reservations any of us may have in reaffirming the central holding of *Roe* are outweighed by the explication of individual liberty we have given combined with the force of *stare decisis*. . . .

III

A

[W]hen this Court reexamines a prior holding, its judgment is customarily informed by a series of prudential and pragmatic considerations designed to test the consistency of overruling a prior decision with the ideal of the rule of law, and to gauge the respective costs of reaffirming and overruling a prior case. Thus, for example, we may ask whether the rule has proved to be intolerable simply in defying practical workability . . . ; whether the rule is subject to a kind of reliance that would lend a special hardship to the consequences of overruling and add inequity to the cost of repudiation . . . ; whether related principles of law have so far developed as to have left the old rule no more than a remnant of abandoned doctrine . . . ; or whether facts have so changed or come to be seen so differently, as to have robbed the old rule of significant application or justification. . . .

Although *Roe* has engendered opposition, it has in no sense proven "unworkable," . . . representing as it does a simple limitation beyond which a state law is unenforceable. . . .

The inquiry into reliance counts the cost of a rule's repudiation as it would fall on those who have relied reasonably on the rule's continued application. Since the classic case for weighing reliance heavily in favor of following the earlier rule occurs in the commercial context, see Payne v. Tennessee, [501 U.S. 808 (1991)], where advance planning of great precision is most obviously a necessity, it is no cause for surprise that some would find no reliance worthy of consideration in support of *Roe*.

. . . Abortion is customarily chosen as an unplanned response to the consequence of unplanned activity or to the failure of conventional birth control, and except on the assumption that no intercourse would have occurred but for *Roe*'s holding, such behavior may appear to justify no reliance claim. Even if reliance could be claimed on that unrealistic assumption, the argument might run, any reliance interest would be *de minimis*. This argument would be premised on the hypothesis that reproductive planning could take virtually immediate account of any sudden restoration of state authority to ban abortions.

To eliminate the issue of reliance that easily, however, one would need to limit cognizable reliance to specific instances of sexual activity. But to do this would be simply to refuse to face the fact that for two decades of economic and social developments, people have organized intimate relationships and made choices that define their views of themselves and their places in society, in reliance on the availability of abortion in the event that contraception should fail. The ability of women to participate equally in the economic and social life of the Nation has been facilitated by their ability to control their reproductive lives. . . . The Constitution serves human values, and while the effect of reliance on *Roe* cannot be exactly measured, neither can the certain cost of overruling *Roe* for people who have ordered their thinking and living around that case be dismissed.

No evolution of legal principle has left *Roe*'s doctrinal footings weaker than they were in 1973. No development of constitutional law since the case was decided has implicitly or explicitly left *Roe* behind as a mere survivor of obsolete constitutional thinking.

It will be recognized, of course, that *Roe* stands at an intersection of two lines of decisions, but in whichever doctrinal category one reads the case, the result for present purposes will be the same. The *Roe* Court itself placed its holding in the succession of cases most prominently exemplified by *Griswold* . . . see *Roe*, 410 U.S., at 152-153. When it is so seen, *Roe* is clearly in no jeopardy. . . .

Roe . . . may be seen [also] . . . as a rule (whether or not mistaken) of personal autonomy and bodily integrity, with doctrinal affinity to cases recognizing limits on governmental power to mandate medical treatment or to bar its rejection. If so, our cases since *Roe* accord with *Roe*'s view that a State's interest in the protection of life falls short of justifying any plenary override of individual liberty claims. Cruzan v. Director, Missouri Dept. of Health, 497 U.S. 261, 278 (1990). . . .

Finally, one could classify *Roe* as *sui generis*. If the case is so viewed, then there clearly has been no erosion of its central determination. The original holding resting on the concurrence of seven Members of the Court in 1973 was expressly affirmed by a majority of six in 1983, see Akron v. Akron Center for Reproductive Health, Inc., 462 U.S. 416 (1983) (*Akron I*), and by a majority of five in 1986, see Thornburgh v. American College of Obstetricians and Gynecologists, 476 U.S. 747 (1986), expressing adherence to the constitutional ruling despite legislative efforts in some States to test its limits. More recently, in Webster v. Reproductive Health Services,

492 U.S. 490 (1989), although two of the present authors questioned the trimester framework in a way consistent with our judgment today [Kennedy, J., and O'Connor, J.], a majority of the Court either decided to reaffirm or declined to address the constitutional validity of the central holding of *Roe*. . . .

. . . If indeed the woman's interest in deciding whether to bear and beget a child had not been recognized as in *Roe*, the State might as readily restrict a woman's right to choose to carry a pregnancy to term as to terminate it, to further asserted state interests in population control, or eugenics, for example. Yet *Roe* has been sensibly relied upon to counter any such suggestions. E.g., Arnold v. Board of Education of Escambia County, Ala., 880 F.2d 305, 311 (11th Cir. 1989) (relying upon *Roe* and concluding that government officials violate the Constitution by coercing a minor to have an abortion); Avery v. County of Burke, 660 F.2d 111, 115 (4th Cir. 1981) (county agency inducing teenage girl to undergo unwanted sterilization on the basis of misrepresentation that she had sickle cell trait). . . .

We have seen how time has overtaken some of *Roe*'s factual assumptions: advances in maternal health care allow for abortions safe to the mother later in pregnancy than was true in 1973, see *Akron I*, [462 U.S.] at 429, n.11, and advances in neonatal care have advanced viability to a point somewhat earlier. . . . But these facts go only to the scheme of time limits on the realization of competing interests, and the divergences from the factual premises of 1973 have no bearing on the validity of *Roe*'s central holding, that viability marks the earliest point at which the State's interest in fetal life is constitutionally adequate to justify a legislative ban on nontherapeutic abortions. The soundness or unsoundness of that constitutional judgment in no sense turns on whether viability occurs at approximately 28 weeks, as was usual at the time of *Roe*, at 23 to 24 weeks, as it sometimes does today, or at some moment even slightly earlier in pregnancy, as it may if fetal respiratory capacity can somehow be enhanced in the future. Whenever it may occur, the attainment of viability may continue to serve as the critical fact, just as it has done since *Roe* was decided; which is to say that no change in *Roe*'s factual underpinning has left its central holding obsolete, and none supports an argument for overruling it.

. . . Within the bounds of normal *stare decisis* analysis, then, and subject to the considerations on which it customarily turns, the stronger argument is for affirming *Roe*'s central holding, with whatever degree of personal reluctance any of us may have, not for overruling it. . . .

C

. . . The Court's power lies . . . in its legitimacy, a product of substance and perception that shows itself in the people's acceptance of the Judiciary as fit to determine what the Nation's law means and to declare what it demands. . . .

. . . The Court must take care to speak and act in ways that allow people to accept its decisions on the terms the Court claims for them, as grounded truly in principle, not as compromises with social and political pressures having, as such, no bearing on the principled choices that the Court is obliged to make. . . .

. . . Where, in the performance of its judicial duties, the Court decides a case in such a way as to resolve the sort of intensely divisive controversy reflected in *Roe* and those rare, comparable cases, its decision has a dimension that the resolution of the normal case does not carry. It is the dimension present whenever the Court's interpretation of the Constitution calls the contending sides of a national controversy to end their national division by accepting a common mandate rooted in the Constitution.

The Court is not asked to do this very often, having thus addressed the Nation only twice in our lifetime, in the decisions of Brown v. Board of Education, 347 U.S. 483 (1954) and *Roe*. But when the Court does act in this way, its decision requires an equally rare precedential force to counter the inevitable efforts to overturn it and to thwart its implementation. Some of those efforts may be mere unprincipled emotional reactions; others may proceed from principles worthy of profound respect. But whatever the premises of opposition may be, only the most convincing justification under accepted standards of precedent could suffice to demonstrate that a later decision overruling the first was anything but a surrender to political pressure, and an unjustified repudiation of the principle on which the Court staked its authority in the first instance. So to overrule under fire in the absence of the most compelling reason to reexamine a watershed decision would subvert the Court's legitimacy beyond any serious question. . . .

. . . Some cost will be paid by anyone who approves or implements a constitutional decision where it is unpopular, or who refuses to work to undermine the decision or to force its reversal. The price may be criticism or ostracism, or it may be violence. An extra price will be paid by those who themselves disapprove of the decision's results when viewed outside of constitutional terms, but who nevertheless struggle to accept it, because they respect the rule of law. To all those who will be so tested by following, the Court implicitly undertakes to remain steadfast, lest in the end a price be paid for nothing. The promise of constancy, once given, binds its maker for as long as the power to stand by the decision survives and the understanding of the issue has not changed so fundamentally as to render the commitment obsolete. . . .

. . . Like the character of an individual, the legitimacy of the Court must be earned over time. So, indeed, must be the character of a Nation of people who aspire to live according to the rule of law. Their belief in themselves as such a people is not readily separable from their understanding of the Court invested with the authority to decide their constitutional cases and speak before all others for their constitutional ideals. If the Court's legitimacy should be undermined, then, so would the country be in its very ability to see itself through its constitutional ideals. The Court's concern with legitimacy is not for the sake of the Court but for the sake of the Nation to which it is responsible.

. . . A decision to overrule *Roe*'s essential holding under the existing circumstances would address error, if error there was, at the cost of both profound and unnecessary damage to the Court's legitimacy, and to the Nation's commitment to the rule of law. It is therefore imperative to adhere to the essence of *Roe*'s original decision, and we do so today.

IV . . .

The woman's right to terminate her pregnancy before viability is the most central principle of Roe v. Wade. It is a rule of law and a component of liberty we cannot renounce.

On the other side of the equation is the interest of the State in the protection of potential life. The *Roe* Court recognized the State's "important and legitimate interest in protecting the potentiality of human life." *Roe*, supra, at 162. . . .

. . . That portion of the decision in *Roe* has been given too little acknowledgment and implementation by the Court in its subsequent cases. Those cases decided that any regulation touching upon the abortion decision must survive strict scrutiny, to be sustained only if drawn in narrow terms to further a compelling state interest. See, e.g., *Akron I*, 462 U.S. at 427. Not all of the cases decided under that formulation can be reconciled with the holding in *Roe* itself. . . .

Roe established a trimester framework to govern abortion regulations. Under this elaborate but rigid construct, almost no regulation at all is permitted during the first trimester of pregnancy; regulations designed to protect the woman's health, but not to further the State's interest in potential life, are permitted during the second trimester; and during the third trimester, when the fetus is viable, prohibitions are permitted provided the life or health of the mother is not at stake. *Roe*, [410 U.S.] at 163-166. . . .

The trimester framework no doubt was erected to ensure that the woman's right to choose not become so subordinate to the State's interest in promoting fetal life that her choice exists in theory but not in fact. We do not agree, however, that the trimester approach is necessary to accomplish this objective. A framework of this rigidity was unnecessary and in its later interpretation sometimes contradicted the State's permissible exercise of its powers.

Though the woman has a right to choose to terminate or continue her pregnancy before viability, it does not at all follow that the State is prohibited from taking steps to ensure that this choice is thoughtful and informed. Even in the earliest stages of pregnancy, the State may enact rules and regulations designed to encourage her to know that there are philosophic and social arguments of great weight that can be brought to bear in favor of continuing the pregnancy to full term and that there are procedures and institutions to allow adoption of unwanted children as well as a certain degree of state assistance if the mother chooses to raise the child herself. "'[T]he Constitution does not forbid a State or city, pursuant to democratic processes, from expressing a preference for normal childbirth.'" Webster v. Reproductive Health Services, 492 U.S. at 511. . . . It follows that States are free to enact laws to provide a reasonable framework for a woman to make a decision that has such profound and lasting meaning. This, too, we find consistent with *Roe*'s central premises, and indeed the inevitable consequence of our holding that the State has an interest in protecting the life of the unborn.

We reject the trimester framework, which we do not consider to be part of the essential holding of *Roe*. . . .

. . . Numerous forms of state regulation might have the incidental effect of increasing the cost or decreasing the availability of medical care, whether for abortion or any other medical procedure. The fact that a law which serves a valid purpose, one not designed to strike at the right itself, has the incidental effect of making it more difficult or more expensive to procure an abortion cannot be enough to invalidate it. Only where state regulation imposes an undue burden on a woman's ability to make this decision does the power of the State reach into the heart of the liberty protected by the Due Process Clause. . . .

A finding of an undue burden is a shorthand for the conclusion that a state regulation has the purpose or effect of placing a substantial obstacle in the path of a woman seeking an abortion of a nonviable fetus. A statute with this purpose is invalid because the means chosen by the State to further the interest in potential life must be calculated to inform the woman's free choice, not hinder it. . . .

Some guiding principles should emerge. What is at stake is the woman's right to make the ultimate decision, not a right to be insulated from all others in doing so. Regulations which do no more than create a structural mechanism by which the State, or the parent or guardian of a minor, may express profound respect for the life of the unborn are permitted, if they are not a substantial obstacle to the woman's exercise of the right to choose. . . . Unless it has that effect on her right of choice, a state measure designed to persuade her to choose childbirth over abortion will be upheld if reasonably related to that goal. Regulations designed to foster the health of a woman seeking an abortion are valid if they do not constitute an undue burden. . . .

These principles control our assessment of the Pennsylvania statute, and we now turn to the issue of the validity of its challenged provisions.

V...

A

[The Court upholds the medical emergency definition, as construed by the court of appeals to include three conditions — preeclampsia, inevitable abortion, and premature ruptured membrane — that the district court had found were not covered by the statute.]

B

. . . Except in a medical emergency, the statute requires that at least 24 hours before performing an abortion a physician inform the woman of the nature of the procedure, the health risks of the abortion and of childbirth, and the "probable gestational age of the unborn child." The physician or a qualified nonphysician must inform the woman of the availability of printed materials published by the State describing the fetus and providing information about medical assistance for childbirth, information about child support from the father, and a list of agencies which provide adoption and other services as alternatives to abortion. An abortion may not be performed unless the woman certifies in writing that she has been informed of the availability of these printed materials and has been provided them if she chooses to view them. . . .

To the extent *Akron I*[, 462 U.S. 416 (1983),] and *Thornburgh*[, 476 U.S. at 762,] find a constitutional violation when the government requires, as it does here, the giving of truthful, nonmisleading information about the nature of the procedure, the attendant health risks and those of childbirth, and the "probable gestational age" of the fetus, those cases go too far, are inconsistent with *Roe*'s acknowledgment of an important interest in potential life, and are overruled. . . . It cannot be questioned that psychological well-being is a facet of health. Nor can it be doubted that most women considering an abortion would deem the impact on the fetus relevant, if not dispositive, to the decision. In attempting to ensure that a woman apprehend the full consequences of her decision, the State furthers the legitimate purpose of reducing the risk that a woman may elect an abortion, only to discover later, with devastating psychological consequences, that her decision was not fully informed. If the information the State requires to be made available to the woman is truthful and not misleading, the requirement may be permissible.

We also see no reason why the State may not require doctors to inform a woman seeking an abortion of the availability of materials relating to the consequences to the fetus, even when those consequences have no direct relation to her health. An example illustrates the point. We would think it constitutional for the State to require that in order for there to be informed consent to a kidney transplant operation the recipient must be supplied with information about risks to the donor as well as risks to himself or herself. . . .

[I]t is worth noting that the statute now before us does not require a physician to comply with the informed consent provisions "if he or she can demonstrate by a preponderance of the evidence, that he or she reasonably believed that furnishing the information would have resulted in a severely adverse effect on the physical or mental health of the patient." 18 Pa. Cons. Stat. §3205 (1990). In this respect, the statute does not prevent the physician from exercising his or her medical judgment. . . .

. . . The idea that important decisions will be more informed and deliberate if they follow some period of reflection does not strike us as unreasonable, particularly where the statute directs that important information become part of the background of the decision. The statute, as construed by the Court of Appeals, permits avoidance of the waiting period in the event of a medical emergency and the record evidence shows that in the vast majority of cases, a 24-hour delay does not create any appreciable health risk. In theory, at least, the waiting period is a reasonable measure to implement the State's interest in protecting the life of the unborn, a measure that does not amount to an undue burden.

Whether the mandatory 24-hour waiting period is nonetheless invalid because in practice it is a substantial obstacle to a woman's choice to terminate her pregnancy is a closer question. The findings of fact by the District Court indicate that because of the distances many women must travel to reach an abortion provider, the practical effect will often be a delay of much more than a day because the waiting period requires that a woman seeking an abortion make at least two visits to the doctor. The District Court also found that in many instances this will increase the exposure of women seeking abortions to "the harassment and hostility of anti-abortion protestors demonstrating outside a clinic." [Planned Parenthood v. Casey, 744 F. Supp. 1323, 1351 (E.D. Pa. 1990).] As a result, the District Court found that for those women who have the fewest financial resources, those who must travel long distances, and those who have difficulty explaining their whereabouts to husbands, employers, or others, the 24-hour waiting period will be "particularly burdensome." Id. at 1352.

These findings are troubling in some respects, but they do not demonstrate that the waiting period constitutes an undue burden. We do not doubt that, as the District Court held, the waiting period has the effect of "increasing the cost and risk of delay of abortions," id. at 1378, but the District Court did not conclude that the increased costs and potential delays amount to substantial obstacles. . . .

C

Section 3209 of Pennsylvania's abortion law provides, except in cases of medical emergency, that no physician shall perform an abortion on a married woman without receiving a signed statement from the woman that she has notified her spouse that she is about to undergo an abortion. The woman has the option of providing an alternative signed statement certifying that her husband is not the man who impregnated her; that her husband could not be located; that the pregnancy is the result of spousal sexual assault which she has reported; or that the woman believes that notifying her husband will cause him or someone else to inflict bodily injury upon her. A physician who performs an abortion on a married woman without receiving the appropriate signed statement will have his or her license revoked, and is liable to the husband for damages.

[The District Court findings, with respect to the reasons some women do not consult their husbands about the decision to obtain an abortion, including domestic violence, sexual abuse, rape, and sexual mutilation, are omitted.] . . .

This information and the District Court's findings reinforce what common sense would suggest. In well-functioning marriages, spouses discuss important intimate decisions such as whether to bear a child. But there are millions of women in this country who are the victims of regular physical and psychological abuse at the hands of their husbands. Should these women become pregnant, they may have very good reasons for not wishing to inform their husbands of their decision to obtain an abortion. Many may have justifiable fears of physical abuse, but may be no less fearful of the consequences of reporting prior abuse to the Commonwealth of Pennsylvania. Many may have a reasonable fear that notifying their husbands will provoke further instances of child abuse; these women are not exempt from §3209's notification requirement. Many may fear devastating forms of psychological abuse from their husbands, including verbal harassment, threats of future violence, the destruction of possessions, physical confinement to the home, the withdrawal of financial support, or the disclosure of the abortion to family and friends. These methods of psychological abuse may act as even more of a deterrent to notification than the possibility of physical violence, but women who are the victims of the abuse are not exempt from §3209's notification requirement. And many women who are pregnant as a result of sexual assaults by their husbands will be unable to avail themselves of the exception for spousal sexual assault, §3209(b)(3), because the exception requires that the woman have notified law enforcement authorities within 90 days of the assault, and her husband will be notified of her report once an investigation begins. §3128(c). If anything in this field is certain, it is that victims of spousal sexual assault are extremely reluctant to report the abuse to the government; hence, a great many spousal rape victims will not be exempt from the notification requirement imposed by §3209.

The spousal notification requirement is thus likely to prevent a significant number of women from obtaining an abortion. It does not merely make abortions a little more difficult or expensive to obtain; for many women, it will impose a substantial obstacle. We must not blind ourselves to the fact that the significant number of women who fear for their safety and the safety of their children are likely to be deterred from procuring an abortion as surely as if the Commonwealth had outlawed abortion in all cases. . . .

This conclusion is in no way inconsistent with our decisions upholding parental notification or consent requirements. See, e.g., *Akron II* [Ohio v. Akron Center for Reproductive Health, 497 U.S. 502, 520 (1990)]; Bellotti v. Baird, 443 U.S. 622 (1979) (*Bellotti II*); Planned Parenthood of Central Mo. v. Danforth, [428 U.S. 52, 74 (1976)]. Those enactments, and our judgment that they are constitutional, are based on the quite reasonable assumption that minors will benefit from consultation with their parents and that children will often not realize that their parents have their best interests at heart. We cannot adopt a parallel assumption about adult women.

We recognize that a husband has a "deep and proper concern and interest . . . in his wife's pregnancy and in the growth and development of the fetus she is carrying." *Danforth*, [428 U.S.] at 69. With regard to the children he has fathered and raised, the Court has recognized his "cognizable and substantial" interest in their custody. Stanley v. Illinois, 405 U.S. 645, 651-652 (1972). . . . If this case concerned a State's ability to require the mother to notify the father before taking some action with respect to a living child raised by both, therefore, it would be reasonable to conclude as a general matter that the father's interest in the welfare of the child and the mother's interest are equal.

Before birth, however, the issue takes on a very different cast. It is an inescapable biological fact that state regulation with respect to the child a woman is carrying will have a far greater impact on the mother's liberty than on the father's. The effect of state regulation on a woman's protected liberty is doubly deserving of scrutiny in such a case, as the State has touched not only upon the private sphere of the family but upon the very bodily integrity of the pregnant woman. . . . The Court has held that "when the wife and the husband disagree on this decision, the view of only one of the two marriage partners can prevail. Inasmuch as it is the woman who physically bears the child and who is the more directly and immediately affected by the pregnancy, as between the two, the balance weighs in her favor." *Danforth*, [428 U.S.] at 71. . . .

There was a time, not so long ago, when a different understanding of the family and of the Constitution prevailed. In Bradwell v. Illinois, 16 Wall. 130 (1873), three Members of this Court reaffirmed the common-law principle that "a woman had no legal existence separate from her husband, who was regarded as her head and representative in the social state; and, notwithstanding some recent modifications of this civil status, many of the special rules of law flowing from and dependent upon this cardinal principle still exist in full force in most States." Id. at 141 (Bradley, J., joined by Swayne and Field, JJ., concurring in judgment). Only one generation has passed since this Court observed that "woman is still regarded as the center of home and family life," with attendant "special responsibilities" that precluded full and independent legal status under the Constitution. Hoyt v. Florida, 368 U.S. 57, 62 (1961). . . .

Section 3209 embodies a view of marriage consonant with the common-law status of married women but repugnant to our present understanding of marriage and of the nature of the rights secured by the Constitution. Women do not lose their constitutionally protected liberty when they marry. The Constitution protects all individuals, male or female, married or unmarried, from the abuse of governmental power, even where that power is employed for the supposed benefit of a member of the individual's family. These considerations confirm our conclusion that §3209 is invalid.

D

[The parental consent provision, requiring consent to an abortion, except in a medical emergency, for an unemancipated young woman under 18, unless the court determines that that the young woman is mature and capable of giving informed consent and has in fact given her informed consent, or that an abortion would be in her best interests, is constitutional.]

Justice STEVENS, concurring in part and dissenting in part. . . .

II . . .

. . . The State may promote its preferences by funding childbirth, by creating and maintaining alternatives to abortion, and by espousing the virtues of family; but it must respect the individual's freedom to make such judgments. . . .

In my opinion . . . [the sections of the Pennsylvania statute requiring] a physician or counselor to provide the woman with a range of materials clearly designed to persuade her to choose not to undergo the abortion [are unconstitutional]. While the State is free, pursuant to §3208 of the Pennsylvania law, to produce and disseminate such material, the State may not inject such information into the woman's deliberations just as she is weighing such an important choice.

Under this same analysis . . . [those sections requiring] the physician to inform a woman of the nature and risks of the abortion procedure and the medical risks of carrying to term, are neutral requirements comparable to those imposed in other medical procedures. Those sections indicate no effort by the State to influence the woman's choice in any way. If anything, such requirements enhance, rather than skew, the woman's decisionmaking.

III

The 24-hour waiting period required by §3205(a)(1)-(2) of the Pennsylvania statute raises even more serious concerns. Such a requirement arguably furthers the State's interests in two ways, neither of which is constitutionally permissible.

First, it may be argued that the 24-hour delay is justified by the mere fact that it is likely to reduce the number of abortions, thus furthering the State's interest in potential life. But such an argument would justify any form of coercion that placed an obstacle in the woman's path. The State cannot further its interests by simply wearing down the ability of the pregnant woman to exercise her constitutional right.

Second, it can more reasonably be argued that the 24-hour delay furthers the State's interest in ensuring that the woman's decision is informed and thoughtful. But there is no evidence that the mandated delay benefits women or that it is necessary to enable the physician to convey any relevant information to the patient. The mandatory delay thus appears to rest on outmoded and unacceptable assumptions about the decisionmaking capacity of women. . . .

In the alternative, the delay requirement may be premised on the belief that the decision to terminate a pregnancy is presumptively wrong. This premise is illegitimate. . . .

The counseling provisions are similarly infirm. Whenever government commands private citizens to speak or to listen, careful review of the justification for that command is particularly appropriate. . . . I conclude that the information requirements . . . do not serve a useful purpose and thus constitute an unnecessary — and therefore undue — burden on the woman's constitutional liberty to decide to terminate her pregnancy.

Justice BLACKMUN, concurring in part, concurring in the judgment in part, and dissenting in part.

I join parts I, II, III, V-A, V-C, and VI of the joint opinion of Justices O'Connor, Kennedy, and Souter. . . .

II

Today, no less than yesterday, the Constitution and decisions of this Court require that a State's abortion restrictions be subjected to the strictest of judicial scrutiny. Our precedents and the joint opinion's principles require us to subject all non-*de minimis* abortion regulations to strict scrutiny. Under this standard, the Pennsylvania statute's provisions requiring content-based counseling, a 24-hour delay, informed parental consent, and reporting of abortion-related information must be invalidated. . . .

A . . .

State restrictions on abortion violate a woman's right of privacy in two ways. First, compelled continuation of a pregnancy infringes upon a woman's right to bodily integrity by imposing substantial physical intrusions and significant risks of physical harm. . . .

Further, when the State restricts a woman's right to terminate her pregnancy, it deprives a woman of the right to make her own decision about reproduction and family planning — critical life choices that this Court long has deemed central to the right to privacy. The decision to terminate or continue a pregnancy has no less an impact on a woman's life than decisions about contraception or marriage. [*Roe* at 153.] Because motherhood has a dramatic impact on a woman's educational prospects, employment opportunities, and self-determination, restrictive abortion laws deprive her of basic control over her life. For these reasons, "the decision whether or not to beget or bear a child" lies at "the very heart of this cluster of constitutionally protected choices." Carey v. Population Services International, 431 U.S. 678, 685 (1977).

A State's restrictions on a woman's right to terminate her pregnancy also implicate constitutional guarantees of gender equality. State restrictions on abortion compel women to continue pregnancies they otherwise might terminate. By restricting the right to terminate pregnancies, the State conscripts women's bodies into its service, forcing women to continue their pregnancies, suffer the pains of childbirth, and in most instances, provide years of maternal care. The State does not compensate women for their services; instead, it assumes that they owe this duty as a matter of course. This assumption — that women can simply be forced to accept the "natural" status and incidents of motherhood — appears to rest upon a conception of women's role that has triggered the protection of the Equal Protection Clause. See, e.g., Mississippi Univ. for Women v. Hogan, 458 U.S. 718, 724-726 (1982); Craig v. Boren, 429 U.S. 190, 198-199 (1976). The joint opinion recognizes that these assumptions about women's place in society "are no longer consistent with our understanding of the family, the individual, or the Constitution." . . .

[The opinion of Chief Justice Rehnquist, with whom Justice White, Justice Scalia, and Justice Thomas join, concurring in the judgment in part and dissenting in part, and urging that Roe v. Wade be overruled, is omitted.]

Justice SCALIA, with whom THE CHIEF JUSTICE, Justice WHITE, and Justice THOMAS join, concurring in the judgment in part and dissenting in part.
. . . The States may, if they wish, permit abortion-on-demand, but the Constitution does not require them to do so. The permissibility of abortion, and the limitations upon it, are to be resolved like most important questions in our democracy: by citizens trying to persuade one another and then voting. . . .

That is, quite simply, the issue in this case: not whether the power of a woman to abort her unborn child is a "liberty" in the absolute sense; or even whether it is a liberty of great importance to many women. Of course it is both. The issue is whether it is a liberty protected by the Constitution of the United States. I am sure it is not. I reach that conclusion not because of anything so exalted as my views concerning the "concept of existence, of meaning, of the universe, and of the mystery of human life." . . . Rather, I reach it for the same reason I reach the conclusion that bigamy is not constitutionally protected — because of two simple facts: (1) the Constitution says absolutely nothing about it, and (2) the longstanding traditions of American society have permitted it to be legally proscribed. *Akron II*, [497 U.S.] at 520 (Scalia, J., concurring). . . .

The Court's reliance upon stare decisis can best be described as contrived. . . .

. . . I have always thought, and I think a lot of other people have always thought, that the arbitrary trimester framework, which the Court today discards, was quite as central to *Roe* as the arbitrary viability test, which the Court today retains. It seems particularly ungrateful to carve the trimester framework out of the core of *Roe*, since its very rigidity (in sharp contrast to the utter indeterminability of the "undue burden" test) is probably the only reason the Court is able to say, in urging stare decisis, that *Roe* "has in no sense proven 'unworkable.'" . . . [T]he following portions of *Roe* have not been saved:

> Under *Roe*, requiring that a woman seeking an abortion be provided truthful information about abortion before giving informed written consent is unconstitutional, if the information is designed to influence her choice, *Thornburgh*, 476 U.S. at 759-765; *Akron I*, 462 U.S. at 442-445. Under the joint opinion's "undue burden" regime (as applied today, at least) such a requirement is constitutional. . . .
>
> Under *Roe*, requiring that information be provided by a doctor, rather than by nonphysician counselors, is unconstitutional, *Akron I*, [462 U.S.] at 446-449. Under the "undue burden" regime (as applied today, at least) it is not. . . .
>
> Under *Roe*, requiring a 24-hour waiting period between the time the woman gives her informed consent and the time of the abortion is unconstitutional, *Akron I*, [462 U.S.] at 449-451. Under the "undue burden" regime (as applied today, at least) it is not. . . .
>
> Under *Roe*, requiring detailed reports that include demographic data about each woman who seeks an abortion and various information about each abortion is unconstitutional, *Thornburgh*, [476 U.S.] at 765-768. Under the "undue burden" regime (as applied today, at least) it generally is not. . . .

The Court's description of the place of *Roe* in the social history of the United States is unrecognizable. Not only did *Roe* not, as the Court suggests, resolve the deeply divisive issue of abortion; it did more than anything else to nourish it, by elevating it to the national level where it is infinitely more difficult to resolve. National politics were not plagued by abortion protests, national abortion lobbying, or abortion marches on Congress, before Roe v. Wade was decided. Profound disagreement existed among our citizens over the issue — as it does over other issues, such as the death penalty — but that disagreement was being worked out at the state level. As with many other issues, the division of sentiment within each State was not as closely balanced as it was among the population of the Nation as a whole, meaning not only that more people would be satisfied with the results of state-by-state resolution, but also that those results would be more stable. Pre-*Roe*, moreover, political compromise was possible.

Roe's mandate for abortion-on-demand destroyed the compromises of the past, rendered compromise impossible for the future, and required the entire issue to be resolved uniformly, at the national level. At the same time, *Roe* created a vast new class of abortion consumers and abortion proponents by eliminating the moral opprobrium that had attached to the act. ("If the Constitution *guarantees* abortion, how can it be bad?" — not an accurate line of thought, but a natural one.) Many favor all of those developments, and it is not for me to say that they are wrong. But to portray *Roe* as the statesmanlike "settlement" of a divisive issue, a jurisprudential Peace of Westphalia that is worth preserving, is nothing less than Orwellian. *Roe* fanned into life an issue that has inflamed our national politics in general, and has obscured with its smoke the selection of Justices to this Court in particular, ever since. And by keeping us in the abortion-umpiring business, it is the perpetuation of that disruption, rather than of any *pax Roeana*, that the Court's new majority decrees. . . .

[W]hether it would "subvert the Court's legitimacy" or not, the notion that we would decide a case differently from the way we otherwise would have in order to show that we can stand firm against public disapproval is frightening. It is a bad enough idea, even in the head of someone like me, who believes that the text of the Constitution, and our traditions, say what they say and there is no fiddling with them. But when it is in the mind of a Court that believes the Constitution has an evolving meaning . . . ; that the Ninth Amendment's reference to "othe[r]" rights is not a disclaimer, but a charter for action . . . ; and that the function of this Court is to "speak before all others for [the people's] constitutional ideals" unrestrained by meaningful text or tradition — then the notion that the Court must adhere to a decision for as long as the decision faces "great opposition" and the Court is "under fire" acquires a character of almost czarist arrogance. We are offended by these marchers who descend upon us, every year on the anniversary of *Roe*, to protest our saying that the Constitution requires what our society has never thought the Constitution requires. These people who refuse to be "tested by following" must be taught a lesson. We have no Cossacks, but at least we can stubbornly refuse to abandon an erroneous opinion that we might otherwise change — to show how little they intimidate us. . . .

In truth, I am as distressed as the Court is . . . about the "political pressure" directed to the Court: the marches, the mail, the protests aimed at inducing us to change our opinions. How upsetting it is, that so many of our citizens (good people, not lawless ones, on both sides of this abortion issue, and on various sides of other issues as well) think that we Justices should properly take into account their views, as though we were engaged not in ascertaining an objective law but in determining some kind of social consensus. The Court would profit, I think, from giving less attention to the fact of this distressing phenomenon, and more attention to the *cause* of it. That cause permeates today's opinion: a new mode of constitutional adjudication that relies not upon text and traditional practice to determine the law, but upon what the Court calls "reasoned judgment," . . . which turns out to be nothing but philosophical predilection and moral intuition. . . .

. . . As long as this Court thought (and the people thought) that we Justices were doing essentially lawyers' work up here — reading text and discerning our society's traditional understanding of that text — the public pretty much left us alone. Texts and traditions are facts to study, not convictions to demonstrate about. But if in reality our process of constitutional adjudication consists primarily of making *value judgments* . . . then a free and intelligent people's attitude towards us can be expected to be (*ought* to be) quite different. The people know that their value judgments are quite as good as those taught in any law school — maybe better. If, indeed, the "liberties" protected by the Constitution are, as the Court says, undefined and unbounded, than the people *should* demonstrate, to protest that we do not implement their values instead of *ours*. . . .

We should get out of this area, where we have no right to be, and where we do neither ourselves nor the country any good by remaining.

Notes

1. Stare Decisis, Reliance, and Autonomy. The joint O'Connor/Kennedy/Souter opinion accepts the conventional wisdom that the strongest reliance interests, for stare decisis purposes, are in commercial cases. What values does this assumption reflect?

What is the nature of the reliance interests at stake in this case? In what sense can it be said that women have come to "rely upon" the right to choose abortion? One possibility is that they are accustomed to being reckless in using birth control in the knowledge that abortion exists as a "back-up." Can this be what the three Justices have in mind? Another possibility takes a broader view of both reliance and the interests protected by *Roe*: women have come to see themselves as having some control and autonomy in personal decisionmaking, which *Roe* has come to symbolize, and it is this sense of background autonomy that enables them to see and plan their lives — their occupational lives as well as their reproductive lives — in long-range terms. Can *this* be what they have in mind? If so, this reasoning is specifically rejected by Justice Rehnquist writing for four Justices:

> The joint opinion . . . turns to what can only be described as an unconventional — and unconvincing — notion of reliance, a view based on the surmise that the availability of abortion since *Roe* has led to "two decades of economic and social developments that would be undercut if the error of *Roe* were recognized." . . . The joint opinion's assertion of this fact is undeveloped and totally conclusory. In fact, one can not be sure to what economic and social developments the opinion is referring. Surely it is dubious to suggest that women have reached their "places in society" in reliance upon *Roe*, rather than as a result of their determination to obtain higher education and compete with men in the job market, and of society's increasing recognition of their ability to fill positions that were previously thought to be reserved only for men.

Planned Parenthood v. Casey, 505 U.S. at 956, 957 (Rehnquist, C.J., dissenting). What different assumptions about individual autonomy and choice do Chief Justice Rehnquist and the authors of the joint opinion make?

2. Spousal Notice and Consent Provisions. In Planned Parenthood v. Danforth, 428 U.S. 52 (1976), the Supreme Court struck down Missouri's spousal consent provisions, concluding that the goal of fostering mutuality and trust in a marriage cannot reasonably be advanced by giving the husband a veto power over the abortion decision. Some lower court decisions had distinguished spousal consent from spousal notification and upheld the presumably less intrusive notification requirements. See, e.g., Scheinberg v. Smith, 659 F.2d 476 (5th Cir. Unit B), reh'g denied en banc, 667 F.2d 93 (5th Cir. 1981). This distinction paralleled the distinction the Supreme Court had made with respect to abortions by minors. Compare Bellotti v. Baird, 443 U.S. 622 (1979) (invalidating parental consent provisions without judicial bypass to permit mature minors and minors whose best interests so required to obtain an abortion) with Hodgson v. Minnesota, 497 U.S. 417 (1990) (upholding two-parent notification requirement with judicial bypass provision, five Justices indicating approval of one-parent notification provision without judicial bypass). In *Casey*, at least with respect to spousal interference, the Court seems to have decided to treat consent and notification alike.

What seems to be the concern of state legislators in attempting to mandate spousal notification? Is it simply one more barrier to abortion designed to curtail the number of abortions that occur in the state? Is it possible that the legislators have in mind some particular scenarios in which an abortion, without spousal notification, would be the wrong decision even from the woman's point of view? What if, for example, the woman decided in favor of an abortion, despite her wishes for a child, because she believed (wrongly) that her husband did not want another child but did not want to put him in the position of supporting an abortion? What if she believed (again, wrongly) that another child would create too much economic pressure on her husband but that his moral scruples opposing abortion would not permit him to take that economic pressure into account in advising her about whether to have an abortion? Chief Justice Rehnquist appears to have in mind these kinds of fact patterns. See *Casey*, 505 U.S. at 973 n.2 (Rehnquist, C.J., dissenting). Is it impermissible for a state legislature to attempt to protect a woman from these possible misperceptions? Or is the problem that in doing so it cannot infringe too greatly on the rights of women whose circumstances did not fit these patterns?

Casey effectively shut down state efforts to impose spousal notification or consent provisions, at least for the time being, although litigation by husbands or boyfriends seeking to protect their interests in a fetus continues to be filed. In one highly publicized case, a Scotland court responded to one father's petition by entering an interim order banning a woman from carrying out her plans to have an abortion. The ban was later lifted. See Bruce McKain, Lords Bid Is Abandoned, The Herald (Glasgow), May 28, 1997, at 5. Arguing for greater rights on the part of the father, see Mary A. Totz, Note, What's Good for the Goose Is Good for the Gander: Toward Recognition of Men's Reproductive Rights, 15 N. Ill. L. Rev. 141 (1994) (present reproductive law, by binding the potential father to the decisions of the pregnant woman, deprives men of their fundamental right to choose whether to beget a child); see also Kevin M. Apollo, Comment, The Biological Father's Right to Require a Pregnant Women to Undergo Medical Treatment Necessary to Sustain Fetal Life, 94 Dick. L. Rev. 199 (1989) (arguing for fathers' rights in context of forced medical treatment for pregnant women when necessary to protect fetus).

3. Parental Notice and Consent Requirements. The parental consent with judicial bypass provision upheld in *Casey* essentially confirms the Court's prior decisions in *Danforth* and *Bellotti*, referred to above. In Hodgson v. Minnesota, 497 U.S. 417 (1990), the Court also considered a challenge to a judicial bypass provision accompanying a parental notification requirement, as applied, which alleged that the bypass provision imposes additional trauma on minors, causes delays and hence increases the health risks of the procedure, and compels many minors to travel out of state to avoid the provision. In Minnesota, as well as in Pennsylvania, waiting periods aggravate the burdens caused by the notification/judicial bypass requirement. See 497 U.S. at 464, 467-468 (Marshall, J., dissenting). To the dissenters in *Hodgson*, these burdens seemed particularly pointless in that the bypass, for those with the stamina and resources to pursue the procedures, was in effect a "rubber stamp," with only an "extremely small" number of petitions denied: "Although they represent substantial intrusion on minors' privacy and take up significant amounts of court time, there is no evidence that they promote more reasoned decisionmaking or screen out adolescents who may be particularly immature or vulnerable." Id. at 477. This conclusion conforms with ten years of experience in Massachusetts, in which of 9,000 bypass petitions, all but 13 were granted, and of these 13, all but one was successfully appealed; in the one remaining case, the parents eventually gave consent, and the minor obtained the abortion. American Academy of Pediatrics v. Lungren, 912 P.2d 1148 (Cal. 1996).

Does this "rubber stamp" argument strengthen or weaken the state's case for parental notification requirements? If judges were more scrupulous in determining either that a minor is mature or that an abortion is in her best interests, would the integrity, and thus the legitimacy, of the process be improved? See Gene Lindsey, The Viability of Parental Abortion Notification and Consent Statutes: Assessing Fact and Fiction, 38 Am. U. L. Rev. 881, 917-918 (1989) (Supreme Court should either clarify standards to curtail rejection of bypass petitions on impermissible grounds, or reconsider parental consent and notification requirements, and by-pass provisions).

What information should judges seek in conducting a meaningful review of a minor's maturity or best interests? Under what circumstances would an abortion desired by a minor not be in her best interests? Short of a rule that amounted to a "rubber stamp," is this a question that judges can answer through determinate standards?

In a case argued and decided along with *Hodgson*, Ohio v. Akron Center for Reproductive Health, 497 U.S. 502 (1990), the Court upheld an Ohio parental notification requirement with a judicial bypass procedure that required the minor to prove by clear and convincing evidence that (1) she is mature; (2) she has experienced a pattern of physical, emotional, or sexual abuse by one of her parents; or (3) notice is not in her best interests. Confronted with an attack to the statute on its face, the Court upheld the rule, concluding that allegations that the bypass procedure could delay an abortion 22 days did not render the statute unconstitutional. Parental notification and consent statutes continue to be upheld in the federal courts, and in most states, so long as they contain adequate judicial bypass provisions. See, e.g., Lambert v. Wicklund, 520 U.S. 292 (1997) (per curiam) (upholding parental notification statute with judicial bypass available when notification not in minor's best interest); Barnes v. Mississippi, 992 F.2d 1335 (5th Cir.), cert. denied, 510 U.S. 976 (1993) (upholding Mississippi parental consent statute with judicial bypass provision); Florida v. North Florida Women's Health and Counseling Services, No. 1D00-1983, 2001 Fla. App. Lexis 1217 (Feb. 9, 2001) (upholding parental notification provision with judicial bypass provision); Pro-Choice Mississippi v. Fordice, 716 So. 2d 645 (Miss. 1998) (upholding two-parent consent requirement with judicial bypass). See also Causeway Medical Suite v. Ieyoub, 109 F.3d 1096 (5th Cir. 1997), cert. denied, 522 U.S. 943 (1997) (invalidating Louisiana parental consent statute that granted judges discretion to deny abortion even when minor is found to be mature and abortion is in her best interests, and failed to specify time frame within which decision must be rendered); Planned Parenthood, Sioux Falls Clinic v. Miller, 63 F.3d 1452 (8th Cir. 1995), cert. denied sub nom. Janklow v. Planned Parenthood, Sioux Falls Clinic, 517 U.S. 1174 (1996) (affirming district court's holding that requirement that physician notify a pregnant minor's parent 48 hours before the abortion was unconstitutional because no judicial bypass procedure was available); In re Anonymous, 558 N.W.2d 784 (Neb. 1997) (upholding denial of minor to obtain abortion under judicial bypass procedure after court found minor not sufficiently mature to avoid notification requirement, and modifying provision to require notification of only one parent).

A few state courts, however, have struck down parental consent or parental notification statutes, even when judicial bypass provisions were provided. See, e.g., Planned Parenthood League of Massachusetts v. Attorney General, 677 N.E.2d 101 (Mass. 1997) (on state constitutional grounds, invalidating two-parent consent requirement, even though it had a judicial bypass provision, because no state interest served). A California parental consent requirement with a judicial bypass provision was invalidated by the California Supreme Court, based on the reasoning that the state's contention of a strong state interest in the physical and emotional health of the minor was undermined by the circumstance that the state does not require parental consent "for a minor to obtain medical care and make other important decisions in analogous contexts that pose at least equal or greater risks to the physical, emotional and psychological health of a minor and her child as those posed by the decision to terminate pregnancy." Academy of Pediatrics v. Lungren, 940 P.2d 797, 826 (Cal. 1997). The same reasoning was adopted by the New Jersey Supreme Court in invalidating a parental notification provision that was shown to impose substantial costs in terms of delay, financial cost, and foregone abortions. See Planned Parenthood of Central New Jersey v. Farmer, 762 A.2d 620 (N.J. 2000).

Notwithstanding the evidence in *Hodgson* that the judicial bypass procedure was a pointless procedure, bypass requests by minors are occasionally denied. In one case, reported in American Civil Liberties Union, Reproductive Freedom Project, 2 Reproductive Rights Update 3 (Thanksgiving 1990, No. 21), an Ohio judge denied a request, finding that "if [the minor in this case] was mature, she would have notified her parents." This case was later affirmed by the Ohio Supreme Court:

> On the one hand, appellant is a senior in high school who plans to attend college, and is a person who had a prior experience in the termination of a pregnancy. On the other hand, appellant testified that she had an abortion in June 1990 and is seeking to have another one performed less than a year later. Moreover, appellant testified that each pregnancy was the result of intercourse with a different man. . . . [A]ppellant was on a program of birth control, but discontinued it. In light of [this evidence], it was not unreasonable, arbitrary or unconscionable for the trial judge to dismiss the complaint by essentially

finding that appellant did not prove her "maturity" allegation by clear and convincing evidence.

In re Jane Doe 1, 566 N.E.2d 1181 (Ohio 1991). See also In re Anonymous, 650 So. 2d 919 (Ala. Civ. App. 1994) (upholding trial court's denial of petition for judicial bypass when minor's primary reason for seeking bypass was to avoid disappointing her mother); In re T.H., 484 N.E.2d 568 (Ind. 1985) (affirming trial court's denial of petition of 14-year-old in custody of state where state refused consent but had offered to cover minor's medical expenses and assist with adoption placement, despite testimony by foster mother, welfare supervisor, and minor herself that minor was sufficiently mature to make abortion decision herself). What assumptions do these cases reflect?

As part of the Adolescent Family Life Act, enacted to promote the involvement of parents and religious and charitable organizations in family planning services for adolescents, any grantee under the Act must obtain permission from a minor's parents before providing family planning services to her. 42 U.S.C. §300z-5(a)(22)(A)(i) (1982). Since *Hodgson* requires that a two-parent notification requirement be accompanied by a judicial bypass provision, is there a constitutional question about such a condition, which has no such bypass procedure? Given the distinction the Supreme Court has made between a woman's constitutional right to choose an abortion and her right to obtain state funds in order to exercise that choice, discussed in note 5, below, the provision is almost certainly constitutional. Other provisions of the Act have been upheld from challenge under the establishment clause in Bowen v. Kendrick, 487 U.S. 589 (1988), and counseling restrictions applicable to programs funded by Title X were upheld in the face of a broader First Amendment challenge in Rust v. Sullivan, 500 U.S. 173 (1991), discussed below at page 1089. The First Amendment arguments against restrictions on teaching and counseling services for adolescents by family planning programs receiving federal funds are reviewed in Janet Benshoof, The Chastity Act: Government Manipulation of Abortion Information and the First Amendment, 101 Harv. L. Rev. 1916 (1988).

For a state-by-state compendium of laws relating to abortion, see NARAL & NARAL Foundation, Who Decides? A State-by-State Review of Abortion and Reproductive Rights (10th ed. Jan. 2001).

Adolescent pregnancy poses additional issues in terms of race and social class, which are explored in note 5, below, and in the section on statutory rape beginning on page 936.

4. Litigating under the "Undue Burden" Test. State legislatures continue to be active in passing abortion regulation, and pro-choice advocates have continued to oppose it. The main areas in contention include who can perform abortions, what information a state can require women seeking abortions to be furnished, how long a waiting period states can incorporate into their procedures, and at what point abortion can be prohibited except in extreme circumstances relating to saving a woman's life. As of February 2000, 13 states enforced mandatory delays in connection with the provision of certain required information, most of which imposed 24-hour delays. In a number of other states, mandatory delay and information statutes are enjoined, stayed, or not enforced. See Ann Farmer, Double Roadblock to Reproductive Rights, 9 Reproductive Freedom News 4, 5 (May 2000) (newsletter of The Center for Reproductive Law & Policy). The outcomes of challenges brought in federal court not been the same. For example, a Wisconsin law requiring physicians who perform abortions to meet with their patients at least 24 hours before the procedure to provide the patients with specific oral and printed information, except when the physician in his or her "reasonable medical judgment" determines that there is a "medical emergency," was upheld. Karlin v. Foust, 188 F.3d 446 (7th Cir. 1999). On the other hand, an Indiana statute requiring that medical personnel provide certain information "in the presence of" the pregnant woman 18 hours before the procedure was found to be unconstitutional, based on a showing that the "in the presence" requirement was likely to prevent abortions for approximately 10 to 13 percent of Indiana women who would otherwise choose to have an abortion, or about 1,300 to 1,700 women per year. See A Woman's Choice — East Side Women's Clinic v. Newman, 132 F. Supp. 2d 1150 (S.D. Ind. 2001). See also Fargo Women's Health Organization v. Schafer, 18 F.3d 526 (8th Cir. 1994) (North Dakota regulation requiring abortion providers to furnish women seeking abortion with information 24 hours prior to procedure does not pose an undue burden by requiring multiple visits because statute does not require that this information be given in person); Preterm Cleveland v. Voinovich, 627 N.E.2d 570 (Ohio Ct. App.), motion to certify record overruled, 624 N.E.2d 194 (Ohio 1993), reh'g denied, 626 N.E.2d 693 (1994) (Ohio statute requiring physician to furnish "objective and nonjudgmental" information to women seeking abortion does not infringe on freedom of speech or equal protection guarantees, and does not pose an undue burden).

Part of the factual showing in A Woman's Choice — East Side Women's Clinic was a study of the effects of a Mississippi law requiring that a woman seeking an abortion receive information in person from a health care provider 24 hours before the procedure. This study, published in 1997 in the Journal of the American Medical Association, compared abortion rates in the year before and the year after the 1992 Mississippi law, which was the first mandatory delay law to go into effect in any state. It found that the total rate of abortions for Mississippi residents decreased by approximately 16 percent; that the proportion of Mississippi residents traveling to other states to obtain abortions increased 37 percent (from 18.6 percent to 25.4 percent); and that the proportion of second-trimester abortions among all Mississippi women obtaining abortions increased 40 percent (from 10.4 percent to 14.5 percent). 132 F. Supp. at 1161. See Theodore Joyce et al.,

The Impact of Mississippi's Mandatory Delay Law on Abortions and Births, 278 JAMA 653, 655 (1997). A more recent study showed that the rate of second-trimester abortions in Mississippi after enactment of the law increased by 53 percent (from 7.5 percent of abortions to 11.5 percent) among women whose closest health care provider is in-state, while it increased by only 8 percent (from 10.5 percent to 11.3 percent) among women whose closest provider was across the Mississippi border. All in all, this second study concluded that the mandatory delay law increased the mean gestational age of the fetus at the time of the procedure by approximately four days. Women living closest to abortion providers in other states were relatively unaffected by the law. See Ted Joyce & Robert Kaestner, The Impact of Mississippi's Mandatory Delay Law on the Timing of Abortion, 32 Family Planning Perspectives 4 (2000). This issue is further explored in note 5, infra.

Other abortion regulations have focused on licensing and other requirements for abortion providers not imposed on other types of medical facilities. Greenville Women's Clinic v. Bryant, 222 F.3d 157 (4th Cir. 2000), cert. denied, 531 U.S. 1191 (2001), upheld an extensive set of regulations in South Carolina that were imposed specifically on clinics performing any second-semester abortions or more than five first-trimester abortions, holding that the regulation did not strike at the abortion right itself and that any increased costs to women were modest and not shown to burden the ability of a woman to make the decision to have an abortion. But see The Women's Center v. Tennessee, No. 3:99-0465, 2000 U.S. Dist. LEXIS 20198 (M.D. Tenn. Apr. 17, 2000) (issuing preliminary injunction against enforcement of Tennessee statute that imposed additional regulations upon ambulatory surgical treatment centers in which a "substantial number of medical or surgical pregnancy terminations are performed," on grounds that statute will likely be found to be unconstitutionally vague, although plaintiffs did not show that the regulations will impose an "undue burden" on women seeking an abortion). In Mazurek v. Armstrong, 520 U.S. 968 (1997), the United States Supreme Court vacated an injunction against enforcement of a Montana statute limiting performance of abortions to physicians, a limitation similar to rules that exist in 40 other states. The court of appeals had thought such an injunction appropriate based on evidence that the motive for the Montana legislation was to make abortions more difficult, by preventing the sole physician's assistant performing abortions in the state from doing so. The Supreme Court held that even if the law targeted this single individual, there was insufficient evidence that the law created a substantial obstacle to abortion. Id. at 973-974.

Another site for litigation over abortion rights is state regulation prohibiting a particular method of late-term (or so-called partial-birth) abortions. In 1997, over 14 states had such statutes, a number of which were challenged as violative of the woman's right to abortion. In 2000, the United States Supreme Court held unconstitutional a Nebraska statute banning partial-birth abortions, which lacked any exception for the preservation of the mother's health and proscribed the dilation and evacuation method used in most second-trimester abortions as well as the infrequently used dilation and extraction procedure. Stenberg v. Carhart, 530 U.S. 914 (2000). Federal legislation (the Partial-Birth Abortion Ban Act) has been pending since 1997, but it has not been enacted into law. See also Jane L. v. Bangerter, 102 F.3d 1112 (10th Cir. 1996), cert. denied sub nom. Leavitt v. Jane L., 520 U.S. 1274 (1997) (Utah statute allowing abortions to be performed after 20 weeks gestational age only to save the woman's life, prevent grave damage to her health, or prevent the birth of a child with grave defects found to impose an unconstitutional undue burden on right to abortion).

In addressing these challenges to abortion statutes, there has been some confusion about what standard is appropriate to *facial* challenges to abortion legislation. In United States v. Salerno, 481 U.S. 739, 745 (1987), the Court had stated that to bring a successful facial challenge, the challenger must demonstrate that no set of circumstances exists under which the statute would be valid. Justice O'Connor's opinion in *Casey*, however, concluded that the spousal notification provision was invalid, even though some women would be able to notify their husbands without adverse consequences, so long as in a "large fraction of cases" it will operate as a substantive obstacle. 505 U.S. at 893-895. This analysis was reiterated in a subsequent O'Connor opinion, see Fargo Women's Health Organization v. Schafer, 507 U.S. 1013 (mem. opinion by O'Connor, J., joined by Souter, J., concurring in denial of certiorari), and debated without resolution in Janklow v. Planned Parenthood, Sioux Falls Clinic, 517 U.S. 1174 (1996) (compare mem. opinion denying application for stay and injunction pending appeal by Stevens, J., which noted that *Salerno*'s "rigid and unwise dictum has been properly ignored," 517 U.S. at 1175, with dissenting opinion by Scalia, J., endorsing *Salerno* language, 517 U.S. at 1178-1181). For an analysis of the different approaches courts have taken in the midst of uncertainty over this question, and criticism for failing to analyze factual evidence relating to a challenged regulation in determining whether it causes an undue burden in the particular state in question, see Sandra Lynne Tholen & Lisa Baird, Con Law Is as Con Law Does: A Survey of Planned Parenthood v. Casey in the State and Federal Courts, 28 Loy. L.A. L. Rev. 971, 1003-1017, 1022-1029 (1995); see also John Christopher Ford, Note, The *Casey* Standard for Evaluating Facial Attacks on Abortion Statutes, 95 Mich. L. Rev. 1443 (1997) (urging development of the "large fraction" test suggested in *Casey*).

5. The Class and Race Dimensions of the Abortion Right.   Other limitations on the abortion right include public funding restrictions. In the first decade after *Roe*, the Supreme Court upheld the withdrawal of funding for elective (i.e., not "medically necessary") abortions obtained by Medicaid-eligible, indigent clients, see Beal v. Doe, 432 U.S. 438 (1977), and Maher v. Roe, 432 U.S. 464 (1977), as well as annual federal funding legislation, known each year as the "Hyde Amendment," which limits federal reimbursement for abortions to very narrow exceptions, such as when necessary to save the life of the mother or to end pregnancies resulting from rape or incest. See Harris v. McRae, 448 U.S. 297 (1980). Federal courts have held generally that state efforts to get around the federal Hyde Amendment restrictions are invalid, under the federal preemption clause. See, e.g., Elizabeth Blackwell Health Center for Women v. Knoll, 61 F.3d 170 (3d Cir.), reh'g en banc denied (1995), cert. denied, 516 U.S. 1093 (1996). Federal funding restrictions do not affect any rights that might be established to state funds, under state law. See, e.g., Low-Income Women of Texas v. Bost, 38 S.W.3d 689 (Tex. Ct. App. 2000) (failure to fund medically necessary abortions for the poor under state's Medicaid program violates state Equal Rights Amendment); Dalton v. Little Rock Family Planning Servs., 516 U.S. 474 (1996) (per curiam) (Hyde Amendment does not apply if compensation program entirely state-funded). But some states have interpreted their own state constitutions to require no more than the U.S. Constitution. See, e.g., Renee B. v. Florida Agency for Health Care Administration, 790 So. 2d 1036 (Fla. 2001) (failure to fund medically necessary abortions that are not required to save the life of the mother or to terminate a pregnancy caused by rape or incest does not violate Florida state constitution). For an inventory of state statutes relating to Medicaid funding for abortions, as well as parental involvement statutes and other matters, see Jon F. Merz, Catherine A. Jackson, & Jacob A. Klerman, A Review of Abortion Policy: Legality, Medicaid Fund, and Parental Involvement, 17 Women's Rts. L. Rep. 1 (1995).

It is clear that even restrictions that do not directly concern funding are especially disadvantageous to poor women.

> A forty-eight hour waiting period . . . may not be an "undue burden" for affluent professional women, and a hospitalization requirement may only serve to make her abortion more expensive. But for an 18-year-old girl in the rural South, unmarried, pregnant, hoping to finish school and build a decent life, who has little or no access to transportation, a hospitalization requirement can mean an abortion that will cost nearly one-thousand dollars and involve a trip of hundreds of miles; a waiting period can mean two long trips and an overnight stay in a strange and distant city.

Walter Dellinger & Gene B. Sperling, Abortion and the Supreme Court: The Retreat from Roe v. Wade, 138 U. Pa. L. Rev. 83, 102 (1989). The financial and logistical problems for many women delay many abortions into the second trimester, where they are more expensive, more dangerous, and more morally objectionable to many individuals. Lack of funds alone can mean significant delays; it has been estimated that 22 percent of the

Medicaid-eligible women who had a second-trimester abortion would have had a first-trimester abortion if they could have afforded it. Senate Committee on Labor and Human Resources, The Freedom of Choice Act of 1992, S. Rep. No. 102-321, 102d Cong., 2d Sess. 24 (July 15, 1992) (citing Alan Guttmacher Institute, Abortion in the United States (June 1, 1991)). For many, such restrictions necessitate an illegal abortion, from which women of color are far more likely to die than white women. Id. at 22 (between 1972 and 1974, two-thirds of women who died from illegal abortions were women of color). See also Laurie Nsiah-Jefferson, Reproductive Laws, Women of Color and Low-Income Women, 11 Women's Rts. L. Rep. 15 (1989) (citing data demonstrating that poor women and women of color are disproportionately affected by legal restrictions on abortion). The special medical risks of teenage pregnancy are examined in Teenage Pregnancy: Developing Strategies for Change in the Twenty-First Century (Dionne J. Jones & Stanley F. Battle eds., 1990); see especially John M. Taborn, Adolescent Pregnancy: A Medical Concern, at 91-100, and Alva P. Barnett, Factors That Adversely Affect the Health and Well-Being of African-American Adolescent Mothers and Their Infants, at 101-109.

For a time, access to abortion by poor women was further impeded by a federal regulation prohibiting federally funded facilities from engaging in counseling, referral, or other activities to inform their clients about abortion. In the face of statutory and constitutional challenges, this regulation was upheld by the Supreme Court in Rust v. Sullivan, 500 U.S. 173 (1991), but in one of his first official acts as president, Bill Clinton lifted the so-called gag rule by executive order. See Karen Tumulty & Marlene Cimons, Clinton Revokes Abortion Curbs, L.A. Times, Jan. 23, 1993, at A1.

What it means to be an unwed, pregnant woman, especially perhaps a teenage girl, may say much about the basic social structure of a society. One recent detailed analysis has shown how unwed, pregnant mothers were used in the pre-*Roe* years as a "social resource" to structure alternatives and policies based on gender, class, and race. According to this study, the babies of white girls, whose virtue was privately stained but publicly to be protected, were used to fill the needs of white childless couples. The "illegitimate" children of black girls, who became highly visible welfare dependents, were proof of the irresponsibility and the decay of the black community — scapegoats for society's ills:

> In 1957, Sally Brown was 16. Just before Thanksgiving, she missed her period for the second month in a row. She concluded, in terror, that she was pregnant. Sally was a white girl, the elder daughter of the owners of a small drycleaning establishment in a medium-sized city in western Pennsylvania. The Friday after Thanksgiving, she told her mother. Mrs. Brown told Mr. Brown. Both parents were horrified — furious at Sally and particularly at her boyfriend, Tim, a local "hood" they thought they had forbidden Sally to date. In October, Sally told Tim about the first missed period and in November, the

second. It was obvious to Sally that Tim's interest in her was dwindling rapidly. She felt heartsick and scared.

Mr. Brown, a businessman for twenty years with deep roots in his community, was bitterly obsessed with what the neighbors, the community and their friends at church would say if they knew about Sally. He proposed a sensible solution: to send Sally away and tell the townspeople that she was dead. The Monday following Thanksgiving, however, Mrs. Brown put her own plan into action. She contacted the high school and informed the principal that Sally would not be returning for the second half of her junior year because she'd been offered the wonderful opportunity to spend the Spring semester with relatives in San Diego. She then called up the Florence Crittenton Home in Philadelphia and arranged for Sally to move in after Christmas vacation.

Before Sally began to "show," she left home, having spent six weeks with parents who alternately berated her and refused to speak to her. They also forbid her to leave the house.

At the maternity home, Sally took classes in good grooming, sewing, cooking and charm. In her meetings with the Home's social worker, Sally insisted over and over that she wanted to keep her baby. The social worker diagnosed Sally as borderline schizophrenic with homosexual and masochistic tendencies. She continued to see Sally on a weekly basis.

In mid-June, after the birth of a 7 pound 14 ounce boy, Sally told her social worker that she wanted to put the baby up for adoption because, "I don't think any unmarried girl has the right to keep her baby. I don't think it's fair to the child. I know I don't have the right."

On June 21, Sally's baby was claimed and later adopted by a Philadelphia lawyer and his infertile wife. Before Sally's 17th birthday in July, she was back home anticipating her senior year in high school. She had been severely warned by the social worker and her parents never, ever, to tell anyone of this episode and to resume her life as if it had never happened. . . .

In February, 1957, Brenda Johnson was 16 and expecting a baby. Brenda was black. She lived near Morningside Park in upper Manhattan with her mother, and older sister, and two younger brothers. Brenda hadn't had to tell anyone about her pregnancy. Her mother had picked up on it in September when Brenda was beginning her third month. Mrs. Johnson had been concerned and upset about the situation, sorry Brenda would have to leave school and disgusted that her daughter was thinking about marrying Robert, her 19-year-old boyfriend. On the day she discovered the pregnancy, she said to Brenda, "It's better to be an unwed mother than an unhappy bride. You'll never be able to point your finger at me and say, 'If it hadn't been for her.'"

In October, Brenda had been called into the Dean of Girls' office at school, expelled and told not to plan on coming back.

At first, Robert stayed around the neighborhood. He continued to be friendly, and he and Brenda spent time together during the first half of Brenda's pregnancy. As she got bigger, though, she felt sure that Robert was spending time with other girls too.

During the winter, Brenda hung around her family's apartment, ran errands and helped her mother who worked as a domestic for a middle-class family downtown. She went for her first pre-natal examination at seven months.

As Brenda got close to her due date, she worried how she would take care of a baby. There was no extra space in the apartment and no extra money in the family budget for a baby. Brenda asked her mother and her older sister about giving the baby up, maybe to her mother's relative in South Carolina, but her mother told her firmly, "You put your child away, you might as well kill him. He'll think no one wants him."

In early March, Brenda had a girl she named Jean in the maternity ward of the local public hospital. Brenda told the nurse, "I love the baby as much as if I was married." Having no money of her own, and having been offered little help from Robert who she heard had left for Florida to find work, Brenda went to the Welfare Office. There she received a long, sharp lecture about young girls having sex that taxpayers have to bear the costs of. She was told she would have to find Robert if she wanted to get on welfare and that the welfare people would be watching her apartment building for him. The welfare worker asked Brenda if she knew what happened in some places to girls in her situation who got a second baby. The worker told her that in some states, a girl with a second illegitimate child would lose her welfare grant. She also said that some people liked the idea of putting a repeater in jail or making it impossible for her to have any more bastards.

Rickie Solinger, Wake Up, Little Susie: Single Pregnancy and Race Before Roe v. Wade 1-3 (1992).

To what extent do you think the different race-based responses to teenage pregnancy described by Solinger still exist today?

6. Between Contraception and Abortion: New Medical Options Blurring the Line. The Court in *Casey* notes that the decision to have an abortion is "in some critical respects . . . of the same character as the decision to use contraception." 505 U.S. at 852. The fact remains that Griswold v. Connecticut, 381 U.S. 479 (1965), Eisenstadt v. Baird, 405 U.S. 438 (1972), and Carey v. Population Servs. Int'l, 431 U.S. 678 (1977), discussed in the previous section beginning on page 1031, limit the state's ability to regulate contraception to a far greater degree than its ability to regulate abortion. The distinction is based presumably on the understanding that contraception prevents pregnancy, while abortion terminates it. Before conception occurs, the state is presumed to have no interest in potential human life, and thus may regulate contraception only as a health and safety matter; after conception, the state's interest in potential life identified in *Roe* commences.

The demarcation between contraception and abortion may make some sense with respect to barrier methods of birth control, where (if the method is successful) conception does not occur, but methods that operate after a fertilized egg has implanted itself in the uterine wall might be said to implicate the same state interest in potential life that has been recognized in the abortion context. Some methods long treated as contraceptives such as the interuterine devices (IUD's) and some birth control pills allow conception to occur, but prevent pregnancy by altering the uterine environment and defeating its ability to sustain pregnancy. See Annemarie Brennan, Note, Is All Privacy Created Equal?, 20 Vt. L. Rev. 815, 818 (1996). Newer medical technologies, such as RU-486, make even more problematic the difficulty of drawing a line between contraception and abortion. RU-486 is a combination of two drugs in pill form. Mifepristone is taken in pill form within the first nine weeks of pregnancy and when followed within 48 hours with another drug, prostaglandin, in most cases causes a miscarriage. Is this a form of contraception, so that only health and safety regulations are appropriate (which may include supervision in a health care facility and other measures), or is it a form of abortion, so that the state may require additional measures addressed to the state's interest in potential life, such as waiting periods and mandatory "informed consent" provisions? See Gwendolyn Prothro, RU 486 Examined: Impact of a New Technology on an Old Controversy, 30 U. Mich. J.L. Ref. 715 (1997) (urging recognition of a continuum between contraception and abortion, along which the woman's right to make her procreative decisions without interference by the state gradually decreases). After years of legal wrangling, RU-486 was finally approved by the FDA in September 2000, under strict conditions requiring at least three doctor's visits. Because of the restrictions and fear of anti-abortion reprisals, few doctors are expected to offer the procedure. Serge F. Kovaleski & Susan Okie, Doctors' Fears May Limit Use of Abortion Pill, Wash. Post, Oct. 1, 2000, at A1.

b. Probing the Theoretical Foundations for an Abortion Right

Reva Siegel, Reasoning from the Body: A Historical Perspective on Abortion Regulation and Questions of Equal Protection
44 Stan. L. Rev. 261, 267-268, 273-277, 332, 350-351, 354, 357-363, 370 (1992)

Social forces play a powerful part in shaping the process of reproduction. Social forces define the circumstances under which a woman conceives a child, including how voluntary her participation in intercourse may be. Social forces determine whether a woman has access to methods of preventing and terminating a pregnancy, and whether it is acceptable for her to use them. Social forces determine the quality of health care available to a woman during pregnancy, and they determine whether a pregnant woman will be able to support herself throughout the term of gestation, or instead will be forced to depend on others for support. Social relations determine who cares for a child once it is born, and what resources, rewards, and penalties attend the work of gestating and nurturing human life.

Thus, human reproduction is not simply a physiological process; like eating and dying, it is a social process, occurring in and governed by culture. In each culture, norms and practices of the community, including those of family, market, medicine, church, and state, combine to shape the social relations of reproduction. If physiological forces seem to define the process of reproduction, it is because most cultures reason about the social relations of reproduction as part of the physical relations of reproduction, that is, as unalterable aspects of nature; ideologies of gender sustain these habits of thought. Ideological norms and institutional practices pertaining to repro-duction play a central part in defining women's status, the dignity they are accorded, the degradations to which they are subjected, and the degree of autonomy they are allowed or dependency they must suffer. These norms and practices affect women who are mothers most intensely, but in one way or another they affect all women.

These observations, tenets of anthropological and feminist critical thought, do not inform the reasoning of those charged with interpreting the Constitution. In crafting equal protection and due process doctrine concerning reproductive regulation, the Court has typically reasoned from the premise that women's reproductive role is dictated by nature, and that regulation of women's reproductive conduct can be evaluated by consulting facts of nature. The result is that social relations enforced by the body politic often find constitutional justification in the organization of the female body itself. . . .

Given the time and circumstances of authorship, *Roe* describes a woman's interest in terminating a pregnancy in an attentive and empathetic fashion. The opinion notes many factors that may cause women to seek an abortion. It recognizes that "[s]pecific and direct harm medically diagnosa-ble even in early pregnancy may be involved" and that "[p]sychological harm may be imminent"; it further observes that "[m]aternity, or additional offspring, may force upon the woman a distressful life and future," that a woman's "[m]ental and physical health may be taxed by child care," and that pregnancy may result in a child a family is "unable, psychologically or otherwise, to care for" or "the additional difficulties and continuing stigma of unwed motherhood." The opinion suggests that, in making the decision whether to terminate a pregnancy, "[a]ll these are factors the woman and her responsible physician necessarily will consider in consultation." [Roe v. Wade, 410 U.S. 113, 153 (1973).]

Roe describes a woman's interest in terminating a pregnancy in terms consonant with the logic of the therapeutic exception, which was expanding at the time of the Court's decision. Consequently, the opinion presents decisions about motherhood as a private dilemma to be resolved by a woman and her doctor: a "woman's problem," in which the social organization of motherhood plays little part. In *Roe*, the Court repeatedly suggests that states should defer to private decisions respecting abortion because they reflect the expertise of a medical professional, not because the community owes any particular deference to women's decisions about whether to assume the obligations of motherhood. Because *Roe* and its progeny treat pregnancy as a physiological problem, they obscure the extent to which the community that would regulate a woman's reproductive choices is in fact implicated in them, responsible for defining motherhood in ways that impose material deprivations and dignitary injuries on those who perform its work. Analyzed within a medical framework, exclusion from employment, denial of unemployment and health insurance benefits, the stigma of unwed motherhood, and other of pregnancy's "natural sanctions" appear as consequences of a woman's body — not practices of the community that would regulate her conduct. *Roe*'s account of the abortion decision invites criticism of the abortion right as an instrument of feminine expedience (i.e. abortion "for convenience" or "on demand") because it presents the burdens of motherhood as woman's destiny and dilemma — a condition for which no other social actor bears responsibility. . . .

Roe justifies the state's interest in regulating abortion by adopting, quite explicitly, a purely medical definition of pregnancy:

> The pregnant woman cannot be isolated in her privacy. She carries an embryo and, later, a fetus, if one accepts the medical definitions of the developing young in the human uterus. See Dorland's Illustrated Medical Dictionary 478-479, 547 (24th ed. 1965). The situation therefore is inherently different from [all other privacy precedents]. . . . [410 U.S. at 159.]

When the Court considers the pregnant woman from what it conceives to be a strictly physiological standpoint, in *Roe*, just as in equal protection cases like *Geduldig* [v. Aiello, 417 U.S. 484 (1974)], it sees her "situation [as] inherently different" from that of other citizens. The Court asserts that the pregnant woman's privacy rights are defeasible, without devoting a single sentence to explaining why this is so. The Court simply assumes that the existence of the embryo/fetus is sufficient to explain and justify the state's interest in regulating abortion; the opinion nowhere addresses the possibility that public interest in restricting abortion might be shaped by social judgments about the pregnant woman herself. As in its equal protection jurisprudence, the Court reasons from the premise that the physical reality of pregnancy can objectively substantiate public regulatory judgments concerning the pregnant woman.

Consistent with the manner in which it justifies the state's interest in regulating abortion, *Roe* defines the circumstances in which the state may regulate abortion in terms of medical facts concerning gestation. The opinion's "trimester framework" allows the state to regulate abortion in the interests of maternal health in the second trimester of pregnancy, when mortality in abortion exceeds mortality in childbirth, and allows regulation in the interests of potential life in the third trimester of pregnancy, at the point of fetal viability. According to *Roe*, the concept of viability supplies "logical and biological justifications" for "[s]tate regulation protective of fetal life" because "the fetus then presumably has the capability of meaningful life outside the mother's womb."

Roe thus holds that the state has an interest in potential life which becomes compelling at the point of viability. It defines this regulatory interest in potential life physiologically, without reference to the sorts of constitutional considerations that normally attend the use of state power against a citizen. In the Court's reasoning, facts concerning the physiological development of the unborn provide "logical and biological justifications" both limiting and legitimating state action directed against the pregnant woman. Because *Roe* analyzes an exercise of state power from a medical, rather than a social, point of view, it authorizes state action against the pregnant woman on the basis of physiological criteria, requiring no inquiry into the state's reasons for acting against the pregnant woman, or the impact of its actions on her. Indeed, *Roe* analyzes the state's interest in potential life as a benign exercise of state power for the protection of the unborn, and not as a coercive exercise of state power against pregnant women, often reasoning as if the state's interest in protecting potential life scarcely pertained to the pregnant woman herself. Thus, in the course of justifying its decision to protect the abortion decision as a right of privacy, the Court recognized an antagonistic state interest in restricting women's access to abortion on which it imposed temporal, but few principled, restraints.

To the extent that *Roe* relied upon physiological reasoning to define the state's interest in potential life, it unleashed a legal discourse of indeterminate content and scope — one legitimating boundless regulation of women's reproductive lives should the Court abandon the trimester framework that presently constrains it. In recognizing the state's interest in potential life, the Court ignored a simple social fact that should be of critical constitutional significance: When a state invokes an interest in potential life to justify fetal-protective regulation, the proposed use of public power concerns not merely the unborn, but women as well. Abortion-restrictive regulation is sex-based regulation, the use of public power to force women to bear children. Yet, the Court has never described the state's interest in protecting potential life as an interest in forcing women to bear children. *Roe*'s physiological reasoning obscures that simple social fact. "[I]f one accepts the medical definitions of the developing young in the human uterus" as a sufficient, objective, and authoritative framework for evaluating the state's regulatory interest in abortion — as *Roe* did — state action compelling women to perform the work of motherhood can be justified without ever acknowledging that the state is enforcing a gender status role. In part, this is because analyzing abortion-restricting regulation within physiological paradigms obscures its social logic, but also, and as importantly, it is because physiological reasons for regulating women's conduct are already laden with socio-political import: Facts about women's bodies have long served to justify regulation enforcing judgments about women's roles. . . .

If physiological reasoning still plays an important part in justifying diverse forms of reproductive regulation, it plays an especially pronounced role in the jurisprudence of fetal-protective regulation. To justify such regulation, it is wholly unnecessary to appeal to considerations of maternal duty — or of religion, class, and race — as physicians did a century ago. From the standpoint of law, the fact that unborn life exists from the point of conception is sufficient to explain social interest in protecting it, and the fact that women alone may gestate life provides sufficient and unimpeachable reason for regulating their conduct. In law, it now appears a mere happenstance of nature that women's conduct must be regulated to protect unborn life. . . .

Abortion-restrictive regulation is state action compelling pregnancy and motherhood, and this simple fact cannot be evaded by invoking nature or a woman's choices to explain the situation in which the pregnant woman subject to abortion restrictions finds herself. A pregnant woman seeking an abortion has the practical capacity to terminate a pregnancy, which she would exercise but for the community's decision to prevent or deter her. If the community successfully effectuates its will, it is the state, and not nature, which is responsible for causing her to continue the pregnancy. Similarly, a woman's choice to engage in sexual relations is no longer significant as a cause of pregnancy, if she would terminate that pregnancy, but for the interposition of communal force. A woman's "choice" to engage in (protected or unprotected) sex may be relevant to the state's justifications for enacting abortion-restrictive regulation, but it does not absolve the state from responsibility for compelling the pregnancy of a woman it prevents from obtaining an abortion. Indeed, if nature or a woman's "choices" play a prominent role in the state's justifications for imposing motherhood upon her, such explanations will obscure the fact that the state's decision to enact abortion restrictions rests on social judgments about the pregnant woman, just as they obscure the fact that such restrictions are an act of communal force against her. The significant role that arguments about women's nature and choices have played in rationalizing abortion-restrictive regulation, today and in the past, should raise suspicions about them: Both types of explanations express normative judgments about women, and do not eliminate the task of analyzing abortion-restrictive regulation as an act of state force against women. . . .

In analyzing abortion-restrictive regulation from an antidiscrimination standpoint, I premise my discussion on the assumption that laws forbidding or impairing women's practical access to abortion are sex-based. I assume, as most commentators have, that when the Court revisits Geduldig v. Aiello, it should modify it to accord with the common social understanding and the amended terms of the Civil Rights Act of 1964, that regulation concerning women's capacity to gestate categorically differentiates on the basis of sex, and so is facially sex-based. . . .

Is the purpose of abortion-restrictive regulation a legitimate one? *Roe* describes a legislature's purpose in restricting women's access to abortion as protecting unborn life. Yet, from a social standpoint, that purpose can be differently described. A legislature's purpose in enacting restrictions on abortion is to pressure or compel women to carry a pregnancy to term which they would otherwise terminate — as the Court has acknowledged in the funding cases.

It is by no means clear that this legislative purpose is legitimate under equal protection doctrine. A legislature's effort to force women to bear children could easily be characterized as a "statutory objective [that] reflects archaic and stereotypic notions" about women. Motherhood is the role upon which this society has traditionally predicated "gross, stereotyped distinctions between the sexes." Thus, the objective of abortion-restrictive regulation is to force women to assume the role and perform the work that has traditionally defined their secondary social status. More particularly, the purpose of abortion-restrictive regulation appears constitutionally suspect if one considers (1) the role that stereotypes of women as "childrearers" played in the history of coerced childbearing (including laws criminalizing both abortion and contraception), (2) the role these same stereotypes played in justifying restrictions on women's participation in the workforce and the political arena during the era that federal and state law denied women access to abortion and contraception, and (3) the exclusions and indignities this society still inflicts upon women who gestate and nurture human life. . . .

. . . Examining the relationship between a legislature's ends and means will identify stereotypical reasoning where the legislature misattributes characteristics of some group members to the group as a whole, and thus employs "gender as an inaccurate proxy for other, more germane bases of classification." But because a state's decision to save fetal life by compelling pregnancy entails a purely functional use of the pregnant woman, any traditional sex-role assumptions that may inform or prompt this regulatory decision cannot be detected by examining how closely the state's means are related to its ends. Rather, one has to ask, in what ways might assumptions about the proper roles of men and women have moved the state to engage in fetal life-saving by compelling pregnancy? What view of women prompted the state's decision to use them as a means to an end? Given the constitutionally suspect means that laws restricting abortion employ to promote the state's interest in potential life, and especially given their history of overt gender-based justifications, it is patently unreasonable to assume *a priori* that they are adopted by a process of legislative deliberation free from constitutionally illicit judgments about women.

[T]here is strong evidence that the attitudes which first prompted enactment of abortion-restrictive regulation still persist. Although the separate spheres tradition no longer receives official public sanction, the sex-role concepts it fostered continue to play a crucial part in the abortion controversy, supplying norms of sexual and maternal comportment for women that inform public judgments about the propriety of abortion. For example, in Louisiana, where the legislature recently attempted to enforce the state's nineteenth century criminal abortion statute and then enacted severe restrictions on abortion, a poll of the state's residents indicated they favored providing women access to abortion when pregnancy occurred because of incest or rape (89 percent); when the child is likely to have serious birth defects (67 percent); when childbirth might endanger a woman's health (64 percent), or when childbirth might endanger a woman's mental health (64 percent); but 79 percent of respondents were opposed to abortion "when childbirth might interrupt the woman's career." . . . National polls and sociological research confirm that such attitudes are widespread. . . .

Thus, today, as in the nineteenth century, legislators enacting restrictions on abortion may act from judgments about the sexual and maternal conduct of the women they are regulating, and not merely from a concern about the welfare of the unborn. Legislators may condemn abortion because they assume that any pregnant woman who does not wish to be pregnant has committed some sexual indiscretion properly punishable by compelling pregnancy itself. Popular support for excusing women who are victims of rape or incest from the proscriptions of criminal abortion laws demonstrates that attitudes about abortion do indeed rest on normative judgments about women's sexual conduct. Opinion polls like Louisiana's suggest that the public assumes a woman can be coerced into continuing a pregnancy because the pregnancy is her sexual "fault."

Along distinct, but related lines, legislators may view abortion as repellant because it betrays a lack of maternal solicitude in women, or otherwise violates expectations of appropriately nurturing female conduct. If legislators assume that women are "child-rearers," they will take for granted the work women give to motherhood and ignore what it takes from them, and so will view women's efforts to avoid some two decades of life-consuming work as an act of casual expedience or unseemly egoism. Thus, they will condemn women for seeking abortion "on demand," or as a mere "convenience," judging women to be unnaturally egocentric because they do not give their lives over to the work of bearing and nurturing children — that is, because they fail to act like mothers, like normal women should. . . .

. . . Even if state actors have adopted restrictions on abortion out of a genuine and single-minded concern for the welfare of the unborn, archaic or stereotypical assumptions about women may nonetheless deeply bias their deliberations, making fetal life-saving by compelled pregnancy seem reasonable where otherwise it would not. A legislature's attitudes about women may cause it to underestimate or disregard the burdens it would impose on them by compelling pregnancy. A latent assumption that motherhood is women's "normal" condition can easily render state actors oblivious to the life-consuming consequences of forcing women to perform its work — just as a latent assumption that motherhood is women's "deserved" condition will cause indifference to the burdens the legislation will inflict. In short, a legislature may not decide that it is reasonable to save unborn life by compelling pregnancy, "but for" the archaic or stereotypic assumptions about women it holds. If restrictions on abortion are adopted in these circumstances, they offend constitutional guarantees of equal protection. . . .

[S]tate action restricting abortion injures women. . . . First, restrictions on abortion do not merely force women to bear children; powerful gender norms in this society ensure that almost all women who are forced to bear children will raise them as well, a result that legislatures adopting restrictions on abortion both desire and expect. Second, the work legislatures would force women to perform defines women's social status along predictable, gender-delineated lines. Women who perform the socially essential labor of bearing and rearing children face diverse forms of stigmatization and injury, none of which is ordained by the physiology of gestation, and all of which is the doing of the society that would force women to bear children. Third, when states adopt restrictions on abortion, they compel women to become mothers, while in no respect altering the conditions that make the institution of motherhood a principal cause of women's subordinate social status. When the gender-based impositions of abortion-restrictive regulation are considered in light of the forms of gender bias that may animate it, it is clear abortion-restrictive regulation is and remains caste legislation which subordinates women in ways that offend constitutional guarantees of equal protection. . . .

Robin West, The Supreme Court 1989 Term, Foreword: Taking Freedom Seriously
104 Harv. L. Rev. 43, 81-85 (1990)

[T]he standard liberal legalist argument for reproductive rights . . . may threaten our reproductive responsibilities. It is central to the liberal understanding of rights, including the right to an abortion, that the possession of a right insulates both the right-holder and the act that the right protects from the community's scrutiny, judgment, and understanding. Although the scope of the right may be limited by a compelling state interest, once the right is recognized, its exercise is no longer scrutinized for the moral quality of its exercise in any particular situation. In the reproductive context, then, the woman's "right" to exercise her choice to continue or terminate her pregnancy, assuming she has such a right, insulates her motives, reasons, or needs for doing so. Thus, the now standard liberal legalist argument for reproductive freedom rests on the claim that some pre-existing fundamental right — the right to privacy, the right to bodily integrity, or the right to nonsubordination — protects from majoritarian infringement a woman's decision either to carry a fetus to term or to abort and that state limits on that right are consequently invalid unless "compelling." The significance of the right is precisely that the reason for exercising it is not relevant to its existence.

The insularity of the decision to abort accorded by the liberal notion of "right" obviously broadens and deepens the scope of reproductive freedoms, *so long as the right is protected.* The clarity of the "rule" recognized in *Roe* consequently strengthens reproductive freedom. The insularity of the abortion decision accorded by the right also, however, has a cost: it obfuscates the moral quality of most abortion decisions. For that very reason, the standard liberal legalist understanding of the right to abort may become a liability in a world in which the public and state legislatures, rather than Herculean Supreme Court Justices, are the guardians of individual freedom. By insisting that the "right" to an abortion, like all rights, is not contingent on the morality of the right-holder or the moral quality of the conduct the right protects, the liberal legalist understanding may inadvertently bolster rather than challenge the pernicious and false claims that the decision to abort is more often than not based on nothing more than a woman's "convenience," is generally necessitated by her sexual promiscuity, and, at the extreme, is the moral equivalent of the decision to commit a premeditated murder. The overriding "insulating" logic of rights, generally embraced by the prochoice movement, that rights insulate conduct and the actor from scrutiny so that they can better protect the "worst of us" as well as the "worst in us" — may reinforce the damaging misperception that the demand for abortion reflects the irresponsible worst of us and worst within us. In a world, fast approaching since *Webster* and *Hodgson*, in which legislators, not courts, must bear the burden of decision in the reproductive field, that misperception may arguably do as much harm as the current conservative Court's continuing, interstitial retreat from the broad liberal promises of *Roe.*

From a postdemocratic liberal perspective, support for reproductive freedom — like all freedom — should rest on the demonstrated capacity of pregnant women to decide whether to carry a fetus to term or to abort responsibly. Correlatively, support for expanded reproductive freedom should rest on the claim that only by accepting the responsibility to make these judgments do women manifest their freedom to pursue their authentically chosen and desired life goals. . . . [W]hat a rights-focused liberalism obscures is that the meaningful distinction between murder and abortion is not in the nominal and question-begging difference between a "fetus" and a "baby," but rather in the moral quality of the underlying decision that liberal legalism insulates from scrutiny. Unlike the homicidal decision to take another's life, the decision to abort is more often than not a morally responsible decision. The abortion decision typically rests not on a desire to destroy fetal life but on a responsible and moral desire to ensure that a new life will be borne only if it will be nurtured and loved.

Such a shift in the focus of the abortion debate, however, does carry with it very real dangers. First, by resting the case for reproductive freedom on responsibility and rights, prochoice advocates would introduce a level of complexity to the debate that lacks the security of a clear constitutional rule. Like all freedoms, its security would rest on citizens' understanding that it is deserved, rather than on the legalistic ground that it is a right simply possessed regardless of the contrary whims or convictions of the community. Second and more important, explicitly basing reproductive freedom on the responsibility as well as the rights of women seems to invite a world in which each woman's decision to terminate her pregnancy would be monitored for compliance with some sort of responsibility-based moral code. . . . [F]rom a feminist perspective, no less than a Western liberal one, this solution looks like a *reductio ad absurdum*. In the very real world in which we live, . . . the good faith of any such relationship is likely to be — not just might be — badly tainted by the bias and simple meanness of a society still crippled by misogynist and racist perceptions of women. "Rights," by definition, insulate the individual and her freedom against this very danger. Responsibility-based arguments for reproductive freedom, on the other hand, seem to invite it.

A failure to rest reproductive freedom on a theory of responsibilities may ensure the complete erosion of the right, however. The Court's manifest ambivalence over the constitutional status of the right to privacy that undergirds reproductive freedom has compromised the persuasiveness of the appeal to rights and constitutional authority that has to date characterized the prochoice movement. Prochoice groups consequently must turn their attention away from courts and to the legislatures and the public who will increasingly be responsible for either protecting or obliterating this individual liberty. As the audience of the "prochoice/prolife" debate shifts away from courts and to legislatures, it may be prudent — whether or not philosophically wise — to focus attention on reproductive responsibility as well as on reproductive rights. If the premise of the rights-based argument — a Court willing to guard the individual liberty protected by the right against even well-intended state infringement — ceases to exist, the argument must change. Liberals and feminists must develop alternative, public-regarding arguments supporting those rights and the liberty they protect that transcend the circular and increasingly false insistence that they simply exist.

Minimally, a responsibility-based argument for reproductive freedom that would justify rather than supplant the rights-based claim of Roe v. Wade would more accurately correspond to the experience of women. Women need the freedom to make reproductive decisions not merely to vindicate a right to be left alone but often to strengthen their ties to others: to plan responsibly and have a family for which they can provide, to pursue professional or work commitments made to the outside world, or to continue supporting their families or communities. At other times the decision to abort is necessitated not by a murderous urge to end life, but by the harsh reality of a financially irresponsible partner, a society indifferent to the care of children, and a workplace incapable of accommodating or supporting the needs of working parents. At many other times the need to abort follows directly from a violent sexual assault. When made for any of these reasons, the decision to abort is not one made in an egoistic private vacuum. Whatever the reason, the decision to abort is almost invariably made within a web of interlocking, competing, and often irreconcilable responsibilities and commitments.

By focusing on the moral quality of reproductive decisions rather than insulating them from understanding, liberals could redirect societal attention toward this web of shared responsibilities and societal failures. We might then begin to recognize that we have a collective responsibility to address the variable causes that result in unwanted pregnancies, from the pervasive acceptance of sexual violence in our culture to our collective refusal to provide meaningful material assistance for the nurturing of children and families. Whatever the fate of *Roe*, widespread understanding of the moral nature of the abortion decision, the profound sense of responsibility that often accompanies it, and the societal failure to assume responsibility for the causes and effects of unwanted pregnancy, childbirth, and motherhood would strengthen, not weaken, the case for abortion rights and the freedoms those rights ought to protect. Without a Court willing to protect those rights in the face of societal opposition, however, that understanding may be necessary to the liberty's very existence.

Eileen L. McDonagh, My Body, My Consent: Securing the Constitutional Right to Abortion Funding
62 Alb. L. Rev. 1057, 1061, 1068, 1072-1076, 1083-1088, 1090-1091 (1999)

The Supreme Court has ruled that a person's constitutional right to liberty protected by the Due Process Clause includes the right to bodily integrity. The right to bodily integrity and liberty is a cornerstone of common law, legislative statutes (positive law), and constitutional law. Although not widely understood, there are in fact two components to the right to bodily integrity and liberty: the right of a person to choose how to live her own life and the right of a person to consent to the effects of a private party on her bodily integrity and liberty. In the context of constitutional guarantees, a person's right to consent to "what is done" to her body is an even stronger right than a person's right to choose "what to do" with her life. For example, the Court has ruled that no one has a constitutional right to choose a medical treatment with the intention of ending one's life, even if terminally ill. Yet the Court has ruled that a person does have a constitutional right to consent to medical treatment, which includes the right to refuse medical treatment necessary to sustain one's life.

Since there are two components to the right to bodily integrity and liberty — choice and consent — once the state designates the fetus as an entity separate from the woman, her right to terminate pregnancy stems not only from her right to make a choice about her liberty, but more fundamentally, from her right to consent to how the fetus, as another entity, affects her body and liberty. . . .

In over twenty-five years of reasoning about abortion rights . . . the Court has failed to acknowledge that pregnancy is a condition in a woman's body resulting from the fetus. This is evident in *Casey* by the Court's statement that the "mother who carries a child to full term is subject to anxieties, to physical constraints, to pain that only she must bear." The Court's passive attribution, "is subject," neglects to recognize medical and legal attribution of the condition of pregnancy — including its pain — to the fertilized ovum and later the fetus. Due to this oversight, the Court at best, incompletely, and at worst, incorrectly, specifies the right to an abortion as the right of a woman to choose what to do with her own body without government interference rather than as a woman's right to consent to the massive burdens and pains of pregnancy that result from a separate entity, the fetus. . . .

[T]he consent foundation for abortion rights reinterprets what is happening when a woman seeks an abortion. As Robin West, a constitutional law scholar, notes, the fetus is not merely an innocent and passive by-product of pregnancy, an entity at rest that is merely carried by the woman who is pregnant and necessarily destroyed by her decision to exercise her right of privacy to make a choice about her own life without state interference. To the contrary: the principle of consent identifies the fetus as seriously harming a woman if she does not consent to its effects on her body and liberty. . . .

Medical professionals refer to even a normal pregnancy as an extraordinary condition in which "[t]he physiological alterations" resulting from the fetus "in all organ systems in the pregnant woman are among the most remarkable events in normal biology." One medical dictionary defines pregnancy as a condition that "sets up great changes, not only in the womb, but throughout the whole body." While most of the changes resulting from the fetus's effects on a woman's body subside about a month after birth, a "few minor alterations persist throughout life." In a medically normal pregnancy some hormones in a woman's body rise to 400 times their base level; a new organ, the placenta, grows in her body; all of her blood is rerouted to be available to the growing fetus; her blood plasma and cardiac volume increase forty percent; and her heart rate increases fifteen percent.

The changes in a woman's cardiovascular system resulting from the fetus can lead to serious symptoms that mimic heart disease, such as a decrease in cardiac output. When a woman is in a supine position, this decrease in cardiac output can lead to a decrease in blood pressure, which causes such symptoms as "lightheadedness, nausea, and even syncope." In some cases the cardiovascular changes of normal pregnancy can aggravate an underlying heart condition, and then a normal pregnancy can become an abnormal pregnancy threatening a woman's life. Another potentially fatal problem associated with the changes wrought by the fetus is thromboembolic disease, the "leading cause of nonobstetric postpartum maternal mortality." The risk of deep vein thrombophlebitis is five times higher for pregnant women than for nonpregnant ones. A normal pregnancy can also become life-threatening if septic pelvic vein thrombophlebitis develops.

Furthermore, even in a medically normal pregnancy the fetus massively affects a woman's liberty every minute, every hour, every day, every week, and every month for nine months. A woman must bring the fetus with her wherever she goes. Her option to associate or not with the fetus is nonexistent. In this way, even a medically normal pregnancy affects a woman's right to liberty, in the sense of her right to control her own body and to associate with whom she chooses. . . .

Thus, the more fundamental right underpinning a woman's right to choose an abortion is her right to bodily integrity and liberty, including her right to defend herself with deadly force against the serious harm of even a medically normal pregnancy resulting from a fetus. The law's recognition of people's right to use deadly force in their self-defense encompasses a wider latitude of harm than only imminent death itself. The massive way even a medically normal pregnancy affects a woman's body and liberty corresponds with standards in the law for the use of deadly force to defend one's bodily integrity and liberty in relation to a born person who is protected by the Fourteenth Amendment. . . .

All states affirm the right of people to use deadly force when threatened with absolute injuries that can cause death. Medically abnormal pregnancies thus meet the standard in the law for using deadly force to stop a fetus from harming a woman's body in a way that threatens her life. States also affirm that people have a right to use deadly force to stop a born person from imposing serious injuries, even if those injuries fall short of actually threatening death. Forty-two states have passed statutes explicitly affirming people's

> right to use deadly force when another private party threatens them with a sufficient quantity of bodily injury, referred to variously as "serious bodily harm," "serious physical injury," "great bodily harm," "great personal injury," "in peril of bodily harm," "grievous bodily harm," or as in the case of Michigan, brutality."

[Eileen L. McDonagh, Breaking the Abortion Deadlock: From Choice to Consent 93 (1996).] The Model Penal Code defines a serious bodily injury as an injury "which creates a substantial risk of death or which causes serious, permanent disfigurement, or protracted loss or impairment of the function of any bodily member or organ," where protracted means as long as four weeks.

The massive effects of a fetus on a woman's body correspond to the level of injury justifying the use of deadly force, if a woman does not consent to those effects. If a born person were to affect another born person's body in even a fraction of the ways a fetus affects a woman's body, the magnitude of the injury would be easy to recognize. Imagine a born person who injected into another's body, without consent, hormones 400 times their normal level, or someone who, without consent, took over the blood system of another to meet her own personal use, or someone who, without consent, grew a new organ in that person's body. . . .

The fundamental rights line of analysis can be applied to abortion rights by establishing the following: Bodily integrity and liberty are a fundamental right. When a woman does not consent to pregnancy, the fetus situates her similarly to other victims of harm to their bodily integrity and liberty. To the degree that the state protects people from legal and medical harm to their bodily integrity and liberty, the Equal Protection Clause mandates the state to protect a woman from the legal and/or medical harm of a nonconsensual pregnancy. State failure to do so deprives a woman of her constitutional right to equal protection and her fundamental right to bodily integrity and liberty. . . .

The key question, therefore, is with whom is a woman similarly situated when she suffers the harm of a nonconsensual pregnancy resulting from a fetus? There are four possible situations in which she might be situated. . . .

> Situation 1. The harm that a woman suffers is similar to harm resulting from a person inflicting harm on her/himself, such as someone choking on a piece of food.

> Situation 2. The harm that a woman suffers is similar to harm resulting from a living organism not under state protection, such as cancer or a virus, harming a person.

> Situation 3. The harm that a woman suffers is similar to harm resulting from a living organism that is not a person but is under state protection, such as wolves, grizzly bears, or other protected species of wildlife, harming a person.

> Situation 4. The harm that a woman suffers is similar to harm resulting from a mentally incompetent person harming another person.
> . . .

[O]ne can rule out Situation 1 because a woman who is pregnant is not similarly situated with a person who is alone, making a choice about what book to read, whether to use a contraceptive, or whether to remove a piece of food on which she is choking. Even if the pregnant woman were to be viewed as responsible for the harm of a nonconsensual pregnancy — for example, because she consented to sexual intercourse as a prerequisite of that harm — the harm itself results from a separate entity: the fetus.

Situation 2 can also be ruled out because it is constitutional for the state to protect the fetus from the moment of conception. The Court has recognized the constitutional legitimacy of a state having a profound interest in protecting the fetus before viability and a compelling interest after viability. Since states do protect the fetus, a woman suffering the harm of a nonconsensual pregnancy resulting from a fetus is not similarly situated with people in Situation 2 who suffer harm from entities that are not under state protection.

Since, according to the Court, it is unknown whether the fetus is a person, a woman suffering the harm of a nonconsensual pregnancy resulting from a fetus could be similarly situated with people in Situation 3 or Situation 4.

If the fetus is not a person, pregnancy resulting from it situates a woman similarly with other victims of harm resulting from state-protected living entities, such as wildlife, as in Situation 3. State policies assist people when they are threatened by harm resulting from state-protected entities, such as grizzly bears and wolves. This is the case even when the state has a legitimate interest in protecting wildlife. The state's introduction of wolves into Yellowstone National Park and their protection, for example, does not preclude protecting people from harm to their property, much less their bodily integrity and liberty, resulting from such wolves. Not only does the state protect people's bodily integrity and liberty from harm resulting from wolves by killing or removing wolves that threaten or create such harm, but the state also routinely economically compensates people whose livestock is harmed by wolves.

Thus, state policies that protect living, but non-human, entities, such as wildlife, include provisions for protecting people's property, bodily integrity, and liberty from adverse effects of those entities. The state thereby assists people in their self-defense against harm resulting from non-human entities under state protection, such as wildlife. If the fetus is legally constructed to be a non-person under state protection, the Equal Protection Clause mandates that the state assist a pregnant woman in her self-defense against the harm resulting from the fetus, since the state offers assistance to similarly situated people suffering from harm resulting from living, state-protected entities that are not persons. A state's failure to do so deprives a pregnant woman suffering the harm of a nonconsensual pregnancy resulting from a fetus of equal protection of her bodily integrity and liberty.

According to Situation 4, if the fetus is a person, pregnancy resulting from it situates a woman similarly with other victims of harm resulting from people. In this case, the fetus would be like a person who is mentally incompetent, due to age or lack of mental functioning, and thus lacking the mens rea to be held legally responsible for harm resulting from it. The state assists people in their self-defense against harm to their bodily integrity and liberty resulting from mentally incompetent people. Thus, if the fetus were legally constructed to be a person, albeit a mentally incompetent one, the state would need to offer assistance to a woman against the harm resulting from a fetus similar to the way the state assists other people who are victims of harm resulting from mentally incompetent people. State failure to do so would deprive a pregnant woman suffering the harm of a nonconsensual pregnancy resulting from a fetus of equal protection of her bodily integrity and liberty. . . .

Some may object that if a woman consents to sexual intercourse (action X), then by extension she has consented to pregnancy (condition Y) as a foreseeable consequence of sexual intercourse. However, the law does not assume that if action X causes condition Y, then consent to action X constitutes consent to condition Y, even if condition Y is a foreseeable consequence of action X. As law scholar Robin West notes, a woman may retain a right to consent to pregnancy, even when she has consented to an action, sexual intercourse, that entails the condition of pregnancy as a foreseeable risk. Moral responsibility for a condition and consent to a condition must be distinguished. A person who consents to an action that has the foreseeable risk of a subsequent condition may be held morally responsible for that condition, should it occur, but that person is not presumed by law to have consented to the condition itself. A person who voluntarily smokes (action X), for example, may be considered responsible for the subsequent condition of lung cancer (condition Y), should it occur, but the person is not required to consent to the presence of the cancer in her body. So, too, with pregnancy. A woman who voluntarily engages in sexual intercourse (action X), may be partially morally responsible for the condition of pregnancy (condition Y), should it occur, but it does not follow that she is legally required to consent to that condition.

Notes

1. The Right to Abortion as an Equality Right. *Casey* grounds the abortion right as a liberty interest, protected by the due process clause of the Fourteenth Amendment. This grounding represented somewhat of an advance over the right to privacy relied upon in Roe v. Wade itself, a right not stated expressly in the United States Constitution but rather articulated in "a line of decisions" based on the First, Fourth, Fifth, Ninth, and Fourteenth Amendments (and their "penumbras") defining those personal rights that are "implicit in the concept of ordered liberty." Roe v. Wade, 410 U.S. 113, 152 (1973) (citation omitted).

As the discussion in *Casey* suggests, the privacy theory of *Roe* has probably received more criticism than any other single example of constitutional jurisprudence. Critics have pointed to the absence of support for a

1108 ≡ 6. *Autonomy*

privacy-based abortion right in the text of the Constitution and the failure of *Roe*'s trimester system to acknowledge the state's interest in protecting unborn life. See, e.g., John Hart Ely, The Wages of Crying Wolf: A Comment on Roe v. Wade, 82 Yale L.J. 920 (1973); Robert H. Bork, The Tempting of America: The Political Seduction of the Law 111-116 (1990); Richard A. Epstein, Substantive Due Process by Any Other Name: The Abortion Cases, 1973 Sup. Ct. Rev. 159. Many who support a constitutional right to abortion criticize *Roe*'s failure to acknowledge the social dimensions of women's reproduction and note the meaninglessness of a privacy right for women who have insufficient power and resources to exercise it. See, e.g., Rosalind Petchesky, Abortion and Women's Choice: The State, Sexuality and Reproductive Freedom (rev. ed. 1990).

The equality principle, explored in the Siegel reading, above, has become the theoretical foundation for the abortion right that is favored by many commentators. See, e.g., Sylvia A. Law, Rethinking Sex and the Constitution, 132 U. Pa. L. Rev. 955, 1013-1028 (1984); Ruth Colker, An Equal Protection Analysis of United States Reproductive Health Policy: Gender, Race, Age, and Class, 1991 Duke L.J. 324. The Supreme Court has nodded a few times in the direction of equality analysis, without fully adopting it. See, e.g., Thornburgh v. American College of Obstetricians and Gynecologists, 476 U.S. 747, 772 (1986) ("promise that a certain private sphere of individual liberty will be kept largely beyond the reach of government . . . extends to women as well as men"); Webster v. Reproductive Health Servs., 492 U.S. 490, 538 (1989) (Blackmun, J., concurring in part and dissenting in part) (discussing both liberty and equality concerns); Bray v. Women's Health Clinic, 506 U.S. 263, 322-326 (1993) (Stevens, J., dissenting) (abortion protestors are motivated by discriminatory animus toward women). Do you find any traces of equal protection analysis in *Casey*?

Any equality-based theory, of course, would have to get around Geduldig v. Aiello, 417 U.S. 484 (1974), discussed in Chapter 3 at pages 332-336, and later in this chapter at pages 1111-1113. Under *Geduldig*, restrictions on a pregnant woman's choice to have an abortion would not amount to sex discrimination, since pregnancy is unique and thus there is not a sense in which similarly situated men are better treated vis-à-vis such restrictions. Siegel assumes that *Geduldig,* if looked at today, would — or at least should — be modified "to accord with the common social understanding and the amended terms of the Civil Rights Act of 1964, that regulation concerning women's capacity to gestate categorically differentiates on the basis of sex, and so is facially sex-based." Siegel, supra, 44 Stan. L. Rev. at 354. That remains, of course, to be seen. See Bray v. Alexandria Women's Health Clinic, 506 U.S. 263 (1993), described in note 4, below.

Setting *Geduldig* aside, is Siegel's analysis a sound application of equality analysis? Formal or substantive equality? Is dominance theory more apt? Does her critique of *Roe* apply equally well to *Casey*?

Can the woman's right to choose an abortion rest entirely on the equality principle? Stephen J. Schnably argues that both privacy and equality analyses are necessary; equality analysis is necessary to understand that the right to make reproductive decisions is fundamentally a problem of unequal power, but that the end goal remains private decisionmaking. See Schnably, Beyond Griswold: Foucauldian and Republican Approaches to Privacy, 23 Conn. L. Rev. 861, 932-934 (1991).

2. The Right to Abortion and Relational Feminism. Another theoretical foundation for the abortion right, of which the West reading is an example, is drawn from relational/different voice feminism. Other examples include Donald P. Judges, Taking Care Seriously: Relational Feminism, Sexual Difference, and Abortion, 73 N.C. L. Rev. 1323 (1995); Julia E. Hanigsberg, Homologizing Pregnancy and Motherhood: A Consideration of Abortion, 94 Mich. L. Rev. 371 (1995); Ruth Colker, Abortion and Dialogue (1992); Robert D. Goldstein, Mother-Love and Abortion (1988). Is a responsibility-based theory sound in this context?

Some dodge the ultimate foundation question, arguing instead that, for strategic reasons, advocates of a woman's right to choose abortion should underscore the moral difficulties for women faced with the abortion choice and the reverence for human life that typically accompanies that choice because tying the right to the liberal notion of choice implies autonomous, self-interested individuals and thus feeds into the unattractive image of mothers pursuing their own self-interest, thus sowing the seeds for undercutting that right. See Joan C. Williams, Gender Wars: Selfless Women in the Republic of Choice, 66 N.Y.U. L. Rev. 1559, 1561 (1991). Is West's argument also a strategic argument, or is her claim that the abortion right is more defensible as a theoretical matter from a responsibility-based perspective?

Other feminists are troubled, on principle as well as on strategy grounds, about the limitations of autonomy approaches to abortion. Marjorie M. Shultz, for example, worries that the "uncritical embrace of extreme autonomy rhetoric and *exclusively* woman-regarding positions . . . undermine[s] our persuasiveness, [renders] us vulnerable on grounds of principle, and [damages] our aspirations for a humane and responsible world." Shultz, Abortion and the Maternal-Fetal Conflict: Broadening Our Concerns, 1 S. Cal. Rev. L. & Women's Stud. 79, 81 (1992). Shultz raises concerns that an unrestricted autonomy-based right would affect other legal principles in an undesirable way, such as undercutting the responsibility of doctors and employers to take reasonable measures to protect the safety of a fetus. Id.

Linda C. McClain cautions against responsibility-based theories for the abortion right, whether strategic or principled, claiming such theories will trigger too much second-guessing of women's decisions, without adequate societal or governmental commitment to reproductive health and to families. At the same time, it will also leave women vulnerable to charges of irresponsibility. Even the most compelling cases of constraint will still be found by some abortion opponents to be instances of mere "convenience." McClain, The Poverty of Privacy?, 3 Colum. J. Gender & L. 119, 173 (1992). See also Pamela S. Karlan & Daniel R. Ortiz, In a Diffident Voice: Relational Feminism, Abortion Rights, and the Feminist Legal Agenda, 87 Nw. U. L. Rev. 858 (1993) (criticizing relational approach to abortion as strategically defective).

Groups such as Feminists for Life of America (FFLA), who base their opposition to the woman's right to an abortion on the principles of relational feminism, illustrate McClain's argument. FFLA rejects the argument that abortion rights are necessary for women's equality and opposes abortion as a "quick fix," as oppressive of women, and as discriminatory against unborn children whom it is in women's interests to protect. The arguments of this organization are detailed and critiqued in Linda C. McClain, Equality, Oppression, and Abortion: Women Who Oppose Abortion Rights in the Name of Feminism, in Feminist Nightmares: Women at Odds 159 (Susan Ostrov Weisser & Jennifer Fleischner, eds. 1994).

3. The Right to Abortion and Freedom from Bodily Invasion. The reading by Eileen McDonagh builds on one of the most well-known philosophical arguments in favor of the abortion right, offered by Judith Jarvis Thomson. Thomson presents the following hypothetical:

> You wake up in the morning and find yourself back to back in bed with an unconscious violinist. A famous unconscious violinist. He has been found to have a fatal kidney ailment, and the Society of Music Lovers has canvassed all the available medical records and found that you alone have the right blood type to help. They have therefore kidnapped you, and last night the violinist's circulatory system was plugged into yours, so that your kidneys can be used to extract poisons from his blood as well as your own. The director of the hospital now tells you, "Look, we're sorry the Society of Music Lovers did this to you — we would never have permitted it if we had known. But still, they did it, and the violinist now is plugged into you. To unplug you would be to kill him. But never mind, it's only for nine months. By then he will have recovered from his ailment, and can safely by unplugged from you."

Thomson, A Defense of Abortion, 1 Phil. & Pub. Affairs 47, 48-49 (1971).

What arguments in support of the woman's right to an abortion does this hypothetical suggest? Does it suggest limits to that right? Does McDonagh's argument have any appeal? Robin West believes so:

> It is a liberal and individualistic argument, respectful of the institutions as well as the moral precommitments of liberal legal jurisprudence. It could conceivably find its way into the Court's reasoning over the next few years.

West, Liberalism and Abortion, 87 Geo. L.J. 2117, 2119 (1999). West also finds parallels between McDonagh's argument and the work of both John Stuart Mill and Catharine MacKinnon:

> All three social critics have argued the moral necessity of women's consent to the justice of a defining institution, have then highlighted the present lack of it, have emphasized that the lack of a woman's consent implies an act of violence upon her, which had theretofore been unrecognized or unacknowledged but which carries substantial psychic and physical harms, and then have tried to hold that violence and the unacknowledged and uncompensated harm it causes to the critical light of the demands of justice. In all three cases, furthermore, the responses by critics to these arguments have been . . . met first with the claim that the institution, convention, or condition so targeted — patriarchal marriage, sex, pregnancy — is a *natural* condition, or at any rate impervious to change, and then with the claim that the alleged harms the institutional purportedly visits upon women are in any event trivial or nonexistent. Accordingly, in all three cases, the argument for liberal reform has been dependent upon both a clear showing that the institution in question is nonconsensual, harmful, and changeable, and a resolute insistence that liberalism demands that the state take the harm seriously.

Id. at 2121. Is the consent argument a simple extension of the liberal privacy jurisprudence of *Roe*, depending less on conceptual leap than on a greater understanding of the potential harms of pregnancy to the woman?

Building on the consent model, some have argued that restrictions on a woman's right to choose an abortion amount to involuntary servitude, in violation of the Thirteenth Amendment. See, e.g., Andrew Koppelman, Forced Labor: A Thirteenth Amendment Defense of Abortion, 84 Nw. U.L. Rev. 480 (1990); Donald H. Regan, Rewriting Roe v. Wade, 77 Mich. L. Rev. 1569, 1619 (1979). Does this principle add to the other theories already presented? See also Susan E. Looper-Friedman, "Keep your laws off my body": Abortion Regulation and the Takings Clause, 29 New Eng. L. Rev. 253 (1995) (arguing that abortion is a property right, protected under the takings clause). For the argument that the slavery analogy is racist and polarizing, see Debora Threedy, Slavery Rhetoric and the Abortion Debate, 2 Mich. J. Gender & L. 3 (1994).

4. Anti-Abortion Activism. The right to abortion is increasingly contested through activities and initiatives designed to discourage women from seeking abortions, and doctors from providing them. In an effort to stop demonstrations at abortion clinics in the Washington, D.C., area, various clinics sued to enjoin Operation Rescue from trespassing on, and obstructing general access to, the premises of abortion clinics under 42 U.S.C. §1985(3), which provides a federal cause of action for private conspiracies to interfere with the civil rights of others. The Supreme Court in a 5-4 decision in Bray v. Alexandria Women's Health Clinic, 506 U.S. 263 (1993), concluded that plaintiffs had not established an animus against women based on their sex and that abortion is not "such an irrational object of disfavor" as to justify a presumption that opposition to that activity also constituted opposition to those who engage in that activity (i.e., women). Id. at 270. It also concluded that the deprivation of the right to abortion — unlike, say, the right to travel (as to which the Court said women's traveling interstate to reach the clinics was not enough to implicate in this case) — was not sufficient to constitute the object of a purely private conspiracy under §1985. Id. at 274-278.

What differentiates the activities of Operation Rescue from the mass "sit-ins" that were conducted for the purpose of promoting desegregation in the South in the 1960s? According to Justice Scalia in *Bray*, only a strictly construed race- or class-based animus requirement would prevent §1985(3) from being used against such protests. Id. at 263. Justice Stevens disagreed, stating that at dispute is not the existence of a class-based animus requirement, but how to interpret it.

> [T]he demonstrations in the 1960's were motivated by a desire to extend the equal protection of the laws to all classes — not to impose burdens on any disadvantaged class. Those who engaged in the nonviolent "sit-ins" to which the Court refers were challenging "a political and economic system that had denied them the basic rights of dignity and equality that this country had fought a Civil War to secure." NAACP v. Claiborne Hardware Co., 458 U.S. 886, 918 (1982).

Id. at 344 (Stevens, J., dissenting). Assume that the 1960s sit-ins, like Operation Rescue's activities, violated state trespass laws. Is Justice Stevens's response anything more than a subjective judgment that some mass violations of law, because they promote some higher purpose, are beyond the reach of anti-conspiracy laws, while others are not?

Rehearsed in *Bray* are the arguments over whether discrimination affecting a characteristic or activity unique to women constitutes discrimination based on sex. Recall Geduldig v. Aiello, 417 U.S. 484 (1974), discussed in Chapter 3, beginning at page 332, which held that singling out pregnancy as the only "disability" not covered by a state disability insurance plan discriminated between pregnant persons and nonpregnant persons, i.e., not on the basis of sex. *Geduldig* has never been overruled as a matter of constitutional law; the effects of the ruling were reversed only in the employment context when Congress amended Title VII with the enactment of the Pregnancy Discrimination Act. Does it follow from *Geduldig* that activities aimed against persons seeking abortions are not discrimination based on sex? What should be the relevance of Justice Scalia's observation that the activities are aimed also at those seeking to assist "persons" obtaining abortions (some of whom are men)? That there are other reasons for opposing abortion besides animus toward women?

Does the respondents' position that §1985(3) should be available to help secure the autonomy of women in obtaining abortions require a state endorsement of abortion? As Justice Scalia points out, the Supreme Court's decisions upholding government abortion-funding restrictions, see note 5, above, affirm that state policies disfavoring abortion are not necessarily unconstitutional. But to Justice Stevens, this observation misses the point, which is not whether the federal government is obligated to protect one right or another, but whether in enacting §1985(3), it has attempted to do so. The question, in other words, is one of statutory construction.

Are there any additional facts that might have led Justice Scalia to find a violation of §1985(3) in this case?

Bray remains important as an expression of the current fault lines in the Court's understanding of what constitutes discrimination based on sex and what constitutes discriminatory intent with regard to sex. See Tracy E. Higgins, "By Reason of Their Sex": Feminist Theory, Postmodernism, and Justice, 80 Cornell L. Rev. 1536 (1995) (analyzing how both sides in *Bray* selectively and inconsistently used the biological sex of the actors to support their own positions on these issues). *Bray*'s impact on the federal remedies available to combat clinic violence, however, has been substantially altered by the 1994 passage of the Freedom of Access to Clinic Entrances Act (FACE). FACE allows for civil remedies and/or criminal penalties against anyone who

> by force or threat of force or by physical obstruction, intentionally injures, intimidates or interferes with or attempts to injure, intimidate or interfere with any person because that person is or has been, or in order to intimidate such person . . . from, obtaining or providing reproductive health services.

18 U.S.C. §248(a)(1) (1994). Violators are subject to one year in prison or up to $10,000 in fines, or both, for the first violation, and up to three years in prison and up to $25,000 in fines for the second. If bodily injury or death results, other penalties are possible. The Act also authorizes a private right of action in favor of physicians, clinic staff, and patients who are injured by conduct proscribed by the Act. For a fuller discussion of the Act, including criticisms that the Act does not offer enough protection for those injured by aggressive anti-abortion movement tactics, see Evelyn Figueroa & Mette Kurth, *Madsen* and the FACE Act: Abortion Rights or Traffic Control, 5 UCLA Women's L.J. 247 (1994).

FACE has survived numerous constitutional attacks at the federal appellate level based on the First Amendment, the Eighth Amendment, the Tenth Amendment, and the Religious Freedom Restoration Act. See, e.g., United States v. Gregg, 226 F.3d 253 (3d Cir. 2000), cert. denied, 121 S. Ct. 855 (2001); United States v. Scott, 187 F.3d 282 (2d Cir. 1999); Terry v. Reno, 101 F.3d 1412 (D.C. Cir. 1996), cert. denied, 520 U.S. 1264 (1997); United States v. Wilson, 73 F.3d 675 (7th Cir. 1995), cert. denied,

519 U.S. 806 (1996); Cheffer v. Reno, 55 F.3d 1517 (11th Cir. 1995); American Life League v. Reno, 47 F.3d 642 (4th Cir.), cert. denied, 516 U.S. 809 (1995). For overview and commentary, see Lan Hoang, Note, Freedom of Access to Clinic Entrances Act, 18 U.S.C. §248: The Controversy Behind the Remedy, 20 Seton Hall Legis. J. 128 (1996); Kristine L. Sendek, Comment, "FACE"-ing the Constitution: The Battle over the Freedom of Access to Clinic Entrances Shifts from Reproductive Health Facilities to the Federal Courts, 46 Cath. U. L. Rev. 165 (1996). For fuller explanation of the substance of the challenges, see Benjamin W. Roberson, Abortion as Commerce: The Impact of United States v. Lopez on Freedom of Access to Clinic Entrances Act of 1994, 50 Vand. L. Rev. 239 (1997) (arguing that FACE exceeds limits of the commerce clause and that state laws are better suited to deal with violent anti-abortion protests); Jill W. Rose & Chris Osborn, Note, FACE-ial Neutrality: A Free Speech Challenge to the Freedom of Access to Clinic Entrances Act, 80 Va. L. Rev. 1505 (1995) (arguing that FACE is a viewpoint-based regulation of speech and thus a violation of the First Amendment).

In addition to FACE, the Supreme Court has held that the Racketeer Influenced and Corrupt Organizations Act (RICO), 18 U.S.C. §1961 et seq. (1994), does not require an economic motive. RICO may thus provide federal remedies, including treble damages, for some organized obstructions of health clinics involving extortion or actual or threatened violence. See, e.g., National Organization for Women v. Scheidler, 510 U.S. 249, reh'g denied, 510 U.S. 1215 (1994). Certiorari in *Scheidler* was not granted as to whether in this context an antitrust claim under the Sherman Act, 15 U.S.C. §§1-7 (1997), could be stated. 968 F.2d 612, 623 (7th Cir. 1992), cert. denied on that question, 508 U.S. 971 (1993), dismissal reaffirmed, 25 F.3d 1053 (7th Cir. 1994); see also Northeast Women's Center v. McMonagle, 670 F. Supp. 1300 (E.D. Pa. 1987) (dismissing antitrust claim).

In addition to federal remedies, as the Court in *Bray* points out, state laws provide some protection for health care providers and for women seeking abortions. These include trespass laws and the possibility of tort actions for tortious interference with business, false imprisonment, intentional infliction of emotional distress, and other legally recognized wrongs. Some large verdicts have been obtained, including an award of $204,585 in actual damages and $1,010,000 in punitive damages against Operation Rescue-National, Rescue America, and other anti-abortion groups, for interference with access to ten women's clinics in Houston during the time of the 1992 Republican National Convention. See Operation Rescue v. Planned Parenthood, 937 S.W.2d 60 (Tex. Ct. App. 1996) (affirming award). See also Planned Parenthood v. Life Activists, 23 F. Supp.2d 1182 (D. Or. 1998) (in action brought under FACE, jury awarded $107 million to a group of doctors/health care providers whose names were posted on the Nuremberg Files Website), award vacated on appeal, 244 F.3d 1007, (9th Cir. 2001).

Some states, in apparent recognition that existing trespass laws may be insufficiently specific to address the problem of organized interference with abortion facilities, have passed special statutes directed at physical acts intended to interfere with an individual entering or exiting a health care facility. See, e.g., Cal. Penal Code §602.11 (West 1999). Some have urged that the application of various privacy torts in state court, such as intrusion upon seclusion, false light, and the public disclosure of private facts, be vitalized to give some protection, especially to abortion-providing doctors who are targeted for vicious publicity campaigns by anti-abortion activists. See, e.g., Angela Christina Couch, Wanted: Privacy Protection for Doctors Who Perform Abortions, 4 Am. U. J. Gender & L. 361 (1996).

When injunctions are sought under either federal or state law, the Supreme Court has held that they must "burden no more speech than necessary to serve a significant government interest." Madsen v. Women's Health Center, Inc., 512 U.S. 753, 765 (1994). In *Madsen* itself, a 300-foot no-approach zone in which all uninvited approaches were prohibited was struck down, but the Court upheld a 36-foot buffer zone, prohibiting congregating or picketing around the property line of the clinic and prohibiting "singing, chanting, whistling, shouting, yelling, use of bull-horns, auto horns, sound amplification equipment, or other sounds or images observable to or within earshot of the patients inside the Clinic" during the hours of surgical procedures and recovery periods. A subsequent case upheld a 15-foot zone around a clinic from which protesters had to remain free and a "cease and desist" provision allowing patients to require sidewalk counselors to retreat, but invalidated an injunction creating floating 15-foot buffer zones around people and vehicles seeking access to the clinic. Schenck v. Pro-Choice Network of Western New York, 519 U.S. 357 (1997). Still more recently, in 2000, the Court upheld a Colorado statute making it unlawful for any person within 100 feet of a health care facility's entrance to "knowingly approach" within 8 feet of another person without that person's consent with leaflets, handbills, or signs or to engage in oral protest, education, or counseling with that person. Hill v. Colorado, 530 U.S. 703 (2000).

Putting Theory into Practice

6-6. a. Through amniocentesis, the sex of a fetus may be determined during the second trimester in time to obtain a legal abortion. Illinois law prohibits abortions that are performed "with knowledge that the pregnant woman is seeking the abortion solely on account of the sex of the fetus." 720 Ill. Ann. Stat. 510/6(8) (West 1993). See also 18 Pa. Cons. Stat. Ann. §3204(a) & (c) (1994) (providing that "[no] abortion which is sought solely because of the sex of the unborn child shall be deemed a necessary abortion"). Are these laws constitutional? Should they be?

b. How about a law prohibiting sex selection in in vitro fertilization? One survey of readers of Lamaze Family magazine showed that of the 41 percent of parents who would opt to choose the baby's sex, both mothers and fathers would pick a boy over a girl by nearly a 2:1 ratio. See Out of the Box, Brandweek, Apr. 19, 1999, at 34. Other research shows consistently that boys are preferred to girls, especially as first or only children. See April L. Cherry, A Feminist Understanding of Sex-Selective Abortion: Solely a Matter of Choice?, 10 Wis. Women's L.J. 161, 171-172 (1995). As a feminist legislator, would you oppose, or support, the prohibition?

Consider in your analysis the fact that one fertility clinic in Fairfax, Virginia, which boasts a 93 percent success rate for couples seeking to conceive a daughter (as compared to a rate of 73 percent in other clinics and a rate in the low 80s for boys in other clinics), gets about twice as many requests for girls as for boys. A couple must have at least one child to be eligible for the program and, if they wish to specify a sex, may only specify the "nondominant" sex in their family. See Lisa Belkin, Getting the Girl, N.Y. Times, July 25, 1999, at 26 (Magazine). What does the experience of this clinic suggest about the nature of the demand for girls?

For efforts to weigh the harms of allowing sex selection to women's interests against the harms of prohibiting the practice, see Cherry, supra; Jodi Danis, Sexism and "The Superfluous Female": Arguments for Regulating Pre-Implantation Sex Selection, 18 Harv. Women's L.J. 219 (1995).

c. There is some evidence that males are conceived more often if intercourse occurs on the day of ovulation, while females are more likely to be conceived if intercourse occurs 36 to 48 hours prior to ovulation. Id. at 227. Should the law attempt to regulate intentional sex selection based on this information?

6-7. A comparison of the strictness of states' anti-abortion laws and their spending on at-risk children showed that states with strong anti-abortion laws spent less money on a per child basis for foster care, for parents who adopt children with special needs, and for poor women with dependent children than did states with strong abortion rights laws. Jean Schroedel, Is the Fetus a Person: A Comparison of Policies Across the Fifty States (2000). What explains this correlation? After you have identified the explanation that makes the most sense to you, formulate arguments that undercut your explanation.

3. Pregnancy and Contractual Autonomy

In re Baby M.
525 A.2d 1128 (N.J. Super. Ct. Ch. Div. 1987), rev'd, 537 A.2d 1227 (N.J. 1988)

SORKOW, J.S.C., Presiding Judge.

. . . This litigation began on May 5, 1986, when Mr. and Mrs. William Stern filed an ex-parte application for an order to show cause why this court should not issue an order for a summary judgment to enforce a surrogate-parenting contract. . . .

[A] verified complaint was filed seeking to enforce a surrogate-parenting agreement, compel the surrender to plaintiffs of the infant child born to Mrs. Mary Beth Whitehead, restrain any interference with plaintiffs' custody of the infant, terminate Mrs. Whitehead's parental rights and allow adoption of the child by Mrs. Stern. . . .

On February 6, 1986, Mr. Stern and Mr. and Mrs. Whitehead signed the surrogate parenting agreement. It was in all material respects the same contract [as one] that Mrs. Whitehead signed in the Spring of 1984. Mrs. Whitehead testified that her obligation was to attempt conception by artificial insemination, upon conception to carry the child to term, deliver and surrender the child to Mr. Stern renouncing at that time all of her parental rights and acknowledging that doing so would be in the child's best interest. It was also agreed that Mr. Stern's name would appear on the child's birth certificate.

In addition, the contract provided the following: Mrs. Whitehead would assume the risks of the pregnancy and child birth. She would submit to a psychiatric evaluation for which Mr. Stern would pay. Mr. Stern had the right to name the child. That in the event of the death of Mr. Stern, the child would be placed in the custody of Mr. Stern's wife. Mrs. Whitehead would not abort the child. In addition, she would undergo amniocentesis; and if the child was found to have a genetic or congenital abnormality, it would be aborted if Mr. Stern requested it.

That in the event the child possessed genetic or congenital abnormalities William Stern would assume legal responsibility for the child once it was born. . . .

The Whiteheads and the Sterns clearly understood the terms of the agreement and their obligations. . . .

Mrs. Whitehead was to be paid $10,000 and all medical expenses including dental expenses for performing her contractual obligations. . . .

. . . The court was further told by the parties that they all understood their obligations under the contract. . . . Mrs. Stern, it must be noted, is not a party to the contract. This was to avoid any possible inference that there is a violation of N.J.S.A. 9:3-54 (which prohibits giving a consideration to obtain an adoptable child). Mr. Whitehead signed a certification pursuant to

N.J.S.A. 9:17-44 establishing his non-paternity. Mr. Stern agreed to pay Mrs. Whitehead $10,000 for conceiving and bearing his child.

Fundamentally, when there were no time constraints, when Mrs. Whitehead was not pregnant, when each party had the opportunity to obtain advice (legal, medical and/or psychological), the parties expressed their respective offers and acceptances to each other and reduced their understanding to a writing. If the mutual promises were not sufficient to establish a valid consideration, then certainly there was consideration when there was conception. The male gave his sperm; the female gave her egg in their preplanned effort to create a child — thus, a contract.

For the past year, there has been a child in being. She is alive and well. She is tangible proof of that which the Whiteheads and Mr. Stern in concert agreed to do. The child was conceived with a mutual understanding by the parties of her future life. Except that now, Mrs. Whitehead has failed to perform one of her last promises, which was to surrender the child and renounce parental rights. . . .

It is argued that Mrs. Whitehead should have a time period after delivery to determine if she wants to surrender the child. Such a rule has been developed in Kentucky by the use of Kentucky's private placement adoption statute. Use of laws not intended for their intended purpose creates forced and confusing results. . . . [T]here is no law governing surrogacy contracts in New Jersey and . . . the laws of adoption do not apply to surrogacy contracts. The sole legal concepts that control are parens patriae and best interests of the child. To wait for birth, to plan, pray and dream of the joy it will bring and then be told that the child will not come home, that a new set of rules applies and to ask a court to approve such a result deeply offends the conscience of this court. A person who has promised is entitled to rely on the concomitant promise of the other promisor. This court holds therefore that . . . once conception has occurred the parties' rights are fixed, the terms of the contract are firm and performance will be anticipated with the joy that only a newborn can bring. . . .

Defendants argue unconscionability. They claim the terms are manifestly unfair or oppressive. These terms were known to Mrs. Whitehead from her earlier surrogate contracting experience. She read the second contract, albeit briefly, prior to signing it. She was aware of her compensation. She had been pregnant before and had to be aware of the risks of pregnancy. Her obligation included physical examination for her own welfare as well as the welfare of the fetus. Mrs. Whitehead says that Mr. Stern undertook no risks. To compare the risk of pregnancy in a woman to the donation of sperm by the man would be unconscionable. This, however, is the bargain Mrs. Whitehead sought and obtained. Mr. Stern did take a risk, however, whether the child would be normal or abnormal, whether accepted or rejected he would have a lifetime obligation and responsibility to the child as its natural and biological father.

To the issue of unconscionability, defendants fail to show proof of overreaching or disproportionate bargaining that result in an unfair contract. Mrs. Whitehead was anxious to contract. At the New Brunswick meeting, she pressed for a definitive statement by the Sterns. She knew just what she was bargaining for. This court finds that she has changed her mind, reneged on her promise and now seeks to avoid her obligations. Unconscionability claims arise, more often than not, in consumer contracts for products or services. The seller is in the dominant position and the buyer must comply or there is no deal. Not so here — either party could have walked away from the other. Either party would then have continued on [the Infertility Clinic of New York's] roster of available surrogates and childless families seeking a surrogate. They chose not to do so. The bargain here was one for totally personal service. It was a very scarce service Mrs. Whitehead was providing. Indeed, it might even be said she had the dominant bargaining position for without her Mr. Stern had no other immediate source available. Each party sought each other to fulfill their needs.

It is argued by *amicus* that the $10,000 to be paid Mrs. Whitehead is so low as to be unconscionable. In counterpoint, it is stated that not all services can be compensated by money. Millions of men and women work for each other in their marital relationship. There may even be mutual inequality in the value of the work performed but the benefits obtained from the relationship serve to reject the concept of equating societal acts to a monetary balancing. Perhaps the risk was great for the money to be paid but the risk was what Mrs. Whitehead chose to assume and at the agreed upon fee. And it is assumed she received other intangible benefits and satisfaction from doing what she did. Her original application set forth her highly altruistic purpose. Notwithstanding *amicus'* position, all in this world cannot be equated to money. . . .

It is further argued that the contract is illusory; that is to say, that only one of the parties has an obligation, the other only benefits, that there is no mutuality of obligation. . . . Such is not the case. Mr. Stern gave his sperm; Mrs. Whitehead gave her egg. Together the miracle of a new life was obtained. Mrs. Whitehead argues Mr. Stern does not have to take the child under certain circumstances which have not happened and are not before this court. She is arguing hypothetically, "if." It is suggested again that the court is dealing with the facts before it. Even assuming arguendo, that the court were to address the issue of the illusory contract as stated by the defendants, the conclusion would be the same. The Whiteheads argue that Mr. Stern does not have to take the baby if it is imperfect; but the fact is the contract does provide that there is obligation and responsibility, that there is a life long responsibility by Mr. Stern for the child's support and welfare. The contract is not illusory. . . .

An agreement between parents is inevitably subservient to the considerations of best interests of the child. The welfare of a child cannot be subscribed by an agreement of the parents. . . . It must follow that "best interests" are paramount to the contract and this court must answer a best interests inquiry if it is to specifically perform the surrogate parenting agreement.

What does "best interests of the child" mean? . . . It has many meanings for it is a concept general in meaning but specific in application. . . .

[P]erhaps Dr. Salk gives the most quantified definition. He establishes nine criteria in defining "best interests of a child."

1) Was the child wanted and planned for? We now know the Sterns desperately wanted a child. They intended by the contract to have a child. They previously planned for the child by considering Mrs. Stern's own capability, inquiring about adoption and exploring surrogacy. They resolved in favor of surrogacy as the only viable vehicle for them to have a family. Mr. and Mrs. Stern contracted for Mrs. Whitehead's services. They created a nursery and made new wills to provide for the expected child. Mrs. Whitehead wanted to carry a child for a childless couple. It is clear that the Sterns planned for and wanted the child. Mrs. Whitehead did not. Her testimony is quite to that effect.

2) What is the emotional stability of the people in the child's home environment? The Sterns are found to have a strong and mutually supportive relationship. Any familial difficulties are handled through rational decision making. This is good evidence of mutual respect and empathy. Each recognizes and respects the other's needs, desires and goals. There is evidence of successful cooperative parenting of the infant child.

The Whiteheads appear to have a stable marriage now. It was earlier plagued with separations, domestic violence and severe financial difficulties requiring numerous house moves. There was a bankruptcy. Mrs. Whitehead dominates the family. Mr. Whitehead is clearly in a subordinate role. He has little to do with the subject child. Mrs. Whitehead is found to be thoroughly enmeshed with Baby M, unable to separate out her own needs from the baby's. This overbearing could inhibit the child's development of independence. The mental health professionals called by the guardian *ad litem* agree that Mrs. Whitehead may have trouble subordinating her own needs to the child's needs. Mrs. Whitehead has been shown, by clear and convincing proof to this court's satisfaction, to be impulsive, as shown by her unplanned future when dropping out of high school, the removal of her son from a second grade classroom without first making inquiry of the teacher and principal. Another example of impulsiveness is her flight to Florida in violation of a court order. She has been shown, by clear and convincing proof to this court's satisfaction, to be manipulative . . . [and] exploitive also. She uses her children for her own ends: witness the bringing of her older daughter to court where the child was terrorized by the crush of media, by her fawning use of the media to her own narcissistic ends. It appears she totally failed to consider the impact of the false sex abuse charge on her daughter. The placement of an infant's crib in Tuesday's room is without sensitivity or regard to Tuesday's feelings.

3) What is the stability and peacefulness of the families? Again, the Sterns are found to be living private unremarkable lives. The Whiteheads have known marital discord, domestic violence and many residential moves, although things are tranquil now.

4) What is the ability of the subject adults to recognize and respond to the child's physical and emotional needs? This court finds from clear and convincing proofs presented to it that Mrs. Whitehead has been shown to impose herself on her children. Her emphasis with the infant may impair the parenting of her other two children for whom she has been, with limited exception until now, a good mother. She exhibits an emotional overinvestment. It was argued by defendant's counsel that Mrs. Whitehead loves her children too much. This is not necessarily a strength. Too much love can smother a child's independence. Even an infant needs her own space.

The Sterns show sensitivity to the child's needs but at the same time allow her to develop independently. Both families recognize and satisfy the infant's physical needs.

5) What are the family attitudes towards education and their motivation to encourage curiosity and learning? The Sterns have demonstrated the strong role that education has played in their lives. They both hold doctoral degrees in the sciences. Mrs. Stern is a medical doctor. Mrs. Whitehead dropped out of the 10th grade in high school. Mr. Whitehead graduated high school doing enough, as he said, "to get by." Mrs. Whitehead has interposed herself in her son's education, denying the finding of a professional child study team and rejecting their recommendations.

6) What is the ability of the adults to make rational judgments? Mr. Whitehead permits his wife to make most of the important decisions in their family. His active participation in the May 5, 1986 elopement is hardly evidence of cogent thought. Mrs. Whitehead is found to be impulsive especially in crisis circumstances or moments of heightened concern. She doesn't think of the consequences: at age 15½ she drops out of school, she withdraws her son from second grade for what she perceives to be an affront to him without first inquiring of the teacher or principal, she elopes to Florida in direct violation of a court order, without considering the economic and emotional consequences. She impulsively, not to say maliciously, makes an untruthful allegation about Mr. Stern. Mr. and Mrs. Stern have shown a capability to make logical reasoned decisions in all circumstances.

7) What is the capacity of the adults in the child's life to instill positive attitudes about matters concerning health? It is already noted that Mrs. Stern is a pediatrician. The court assumes her skill can but benefit the child. Other than failing to have the child vaccinated when Mrs. Whitehead was in Florida for the first few months of the child's life, which is not to be minimized, there is no evidence that she would convey poor health habits to the child. Mr. Whitehead has been shown to be an episodic alcoholic "binging" for two week periods approximately every six months. He is

doing nothing to eliminate this concern. To infuse a child into such a milieu is problematic.

8) What is the capacity of the adults in the baby's life to explain the circumstance of origin with least confusion and greatest emotional support? Mrs. Whitehead being the parent most invested with the infant's care, in all likelihood would be charged with the task of telling the child of her origins. This court doubts her capability to truthfully report Baby M's origin. She has shown little empathy for the Sterns and their role and even less ability to acknowledge the facts surrounding the original contract. Insofar as emotional support is concerned, the court doubts Mrs. Whitehead could or would subordinate herself for the child's benefit where there is a conflictual circumstance such as relating the child's origins to her. To this day she still appears to reject any role Mr. Stern played in the conception. She chooses to forget that but for him there would be no child. The quality of her reporting capabilities have been tested in these proceedings and found generally wanting. The Sterns have indicated a willingness to obtain professional advice on how and when to tell his daughter. Important in this equation is the child's trust that will have been constructed between custodial parent and child.

9) Which adults would better help the child cope with her own life? It has been shown that Mrs. Whitehead has trouble coping in crisis. She can manage the routine. The Sterns have shown no aberration in either circumstance.

The court also evaluates the climate to which the child may be exposed with the Whiteheads. In addition to a history of economic and domestic instability with another house move imminent, in addition to the reduced level of importance given to education in the Whitehead home and in addition to the character trait problems defined by almost all the mental health professionals including Mrs. Whitehead's own chosen experts, Mrs. Whitehead has a genuine problem in recognizing and reporting the truth.

While we here address best interest it is relevant to her entire posture before the court. Doctor Klein, her own expert, said she lies under stress. Dr. Schecter said she is a faulty reporter because of her "I don't know, I can't recall" answers; especially the number of such answers. The court found this to be so to such an extent it became apparent that Mrs. Whitehead testified to what she chose to, exercising a selective memory, intentionally not recalling or outright lying on the witness stand. This court is thoroughly satisfied that Mrs. Whitehead fully knew of the contents of this court's May 5, 1986 order [to show cause why the surrogate-parenting contract should not be enforced]. She testified on oath to the contrary but the content of her father's letter and [the letter of a witness, Hergenhan, who lied to the court] prove the contrary and it is Hergenhan's letter that also mitigates against Mrs. Whitehead for Mrs. Whitehead knew a lie was being perpetrated on the court; she knew it, participated in it and never acknowledged it. This fundamental inability to speak the truth establishes a tarnished Whitehead environment.

The foregoing recital shows that Mr. Whitehead is a benign force in the Whitehead household. The drive and direction are solely Mrs. Whitehead's prerogatives. This court is satisfied by clear and convincing proofs that Mrs. Whitehead is unreliable insofar as her promise is concerned. She breached her contract without regard to her legal obligations. There has been domestic violence in her household that she could not recall until the court documents refreshed her recollection. She should have known of these facts as she is the one who called the police. There were many house moves in the earlier years of marriage and another move appears imminent. The Whiteheads have had severe economic difficulties including a bankruptcy. In those court papers there appears to be a flawed statement of assets in that the Whiteheads omitted two assets thus misleading the court and their creditors. Mrs. Whitehead has been found too enmeshed with this infant child and unable to separate her own needs from those of the child. She tends to smother the child with her presence even to the exclusion of access by her other two children. She does not have the ability to subordinate herself to the needs of this child. The court is satisfied that based on the details above, Mrs. Whitehead is manipulative, impulsive and exploitive. She is also for the most part, untruthful choosing only to remember what may enhance her position, or altering the facts about which she is testifying or intentionally not remembering. Education plays a subordinate role in the Whiteheads' milieu. The judgment-making ability of Mrs. Whitehead is sorely tested. One outstanding example was her decision to run away in the face of a court order. While she claims fear of the system made her do it this court sees it, minimally, as a disregard of her legal and civic obligation to respond to a court's order, and, maximally, as a contempt of the court order. She does not concern herself with consequences of her acts. Her lack of candor makes her a poor candidate to report to the child in an age appropriate manner and time, the facts of the child's origins. She is a woman without empathy. She expresses none for her husband's problems with alcohol and her infusion of her other children into this process, exposing them rather than protecting them from the searing scrutiny of the media, mitigates against her claim for custody. She is a good mother for and to her older children. She would not be a good custodian for Baby M. . . .

Now having found that the best interest of the child will be enhanced and served in paternal custody, that there is no evidence of fraud, overreaching or violation of any other principle of equity by Mr. Stern, this court having evaluated the equities finds them weighted in favor of Mr. Stern. Enforcing the contract will leave Mr. and Mrs. Whitehead in the same position that they were in when the contract was made. To not enforce the contract will give them the child and deprive Mr. Stern of his promised benefits. This court therefore will specifically enforce the surrogate-parenting agreement to compel delivery of the child to the father and to terminate the mother's parental rights.

Notes

1. *Baby M.* Reversed. The trial court opinion set forth above was reversed by the New Jersey Supreme Court in In re Baby M., 537 A.2d 1227 (N.J. 1988). The court concluded that the surrogacy contract was invalid because it conflicted with state statutes the trial court had found inapplicable — statutes prohibiting the payment of money for adoption, statutes requiring consent of a birth mother to adoption *after* the birth of the child and regulating adoption in other ways, and statutes requiring proof of parental unfitness or abandonment before termination of parental rights. The court also held that the surrogate contract violated the public policy that "to the extent possible, children should remain with and be brought up by both of their natural parents." Id. at 1246-1247. The court proceeded to resolve the dispute as a custody dispute between two "natural" parents, awarding custody to Mr. Stern and visitation to Mrs. Whitehead. When faced with a similar legal issue, a California appellate court also found a surrogate parenting agreement unenforceable. Applying custody doctrine governing disputes between two legal parents, the court awarded joint physical and legal custody to the biological father and the surrogate mother. See In re Marriage of Moschetta, 30 Cal. Rptr. 2d 893 (Ct. App. 1994).

Although the trial court in *Baby M.* found the contract enforceable and the New Jersey Supreme Court did not, the end results were similar: Mr. Stern was awarded custody of the child. This is because, ultimately, both courts arrived at a best-interests-of-the-child analysis, and the courts agreed that the Sterns would offer the child a more stable upbringing. What do you think of the best-interests analysis applied by the trial court in the case? What assumptions underlie the analysis? The supreme court was more sympathetic to Mrs. Whitehead, stating that "given her predicament, Mrs. Whitehead was rather harshly judged." 537 A.2d at 1259. At the same time, in awarding custody to Mr. Stern, it relied on the same kinds of factors noted by the trial court. Using the facts provided in the opinion, is it possible to write a persuasive opinion, focused on the best interests of the child, to reach the opposite result?

2. An Intent-Based Approach to New Reproductive Arrangements. Approximately one in five couples in the United States with a woman of childbearing age is infertile. Christine L. Kerian, A Last Resort Alternative for Infertile Women or a Commodification of Women's Bodies and Children?, 12 Wis. Women's L.J. 113 (1997). The conventional, autonomy-based defense of enforcement of surrogate contracts and other arrangements for alternative reproduction is set forth in John A. Robertson,

Children of Choice: Freedom and the New Reproductive Technologies (1994).

Feminist scholars have divided over the issue of surrogacy generally and in particular over how the issue of autonomy should be analyzed. The principal feminist defense of surrogate contracts is that they credit a woman's expression of intent about her parental status and avoid stereotypes about women as instinctive mothers that contribute to limiting gender roles. Surrogate contracts also assume, and thus reinforce, interest in and responsibility for parenting by both mothers and fathers:

> [L]egal rules . . . should recognize the importance and the legitimacy of individual efforts to project intentions and decisions into the future. Where such intentions are deliberate, explicit and bargained for, where they are the catalyst for reliance and expectations, as is the case in technologically-assisted reproductive arrangements, they should be honored. . . .
>
> By embracing the emerging opportunities provided by advancing technology, the law would enhance individual freedom, fulfillment and responsibility. Important additional gains would also accrue. Rules that would determine legal parenthood on the basis of individual intentions about procreation and parenting — at least in the context of reproductive technology — would recognize, encourage and reinforce men's choices to nurture children. By adopting a sex-neutral criterion such as intention, the law would partially offset the biological disadvantages men experience in accessing child-nurturing opportunities. The result would parallel recent legal efforts to offset the burdens that childbearing imposes on women who seek equal access to market employment.

Marjorie Maguire Shultz, Reproductive Technology and Intent-Based Parenthood: An Opportunity for Gender Neutrality, 1990 Wis. L. Rev. 297, 302-303. Note the objectives Shultz favors: individual freedom, sex neutrality, and offsetting the "biological disadvantages men experience in accessing child-nurturing opportunities." With which version of equality is this proposal most consistent?

Other commentators agreeing that intent of the parties should be the primary determinative factor when disputes regarding surrogacy contracts arise, so long as traditional contract law protections (including unconscionability) are part of the analysis, include Malina Coleman, Gestation, Intent, and the Seed: Defining Motherhood in the Era of Assisted Human Reproduction, 17 Cardozo L. Rev. 497 (1996); Kerian, supra. See also Shoshana L. Gillers, Note, A Labor Theory of Legal Parenthood, 110 Yale L.J. 691 (2001) (arguing for a labor theory for determining parenthood that would allow a woman to contract out her reproductive labor through a surrogacy agreement that expresses the woman's intent to gestate a fetus for another); Carmel Shalev, Birth Power: The Case for Surrogacy 146-166 (1989) (allowing women to direct the use of their reproductive labor communicates self-determining images of women). For the argument that the intent-based analysis should be expanded to allow alternative definitions of legal parenthood with respect to surrogacy and other forms of "collaborative reproduction," including partial parenting status and multiple parents, see Alison Harvison Young, Reconceiving the Family: Challenging the Paradigm of the Exclusive Family, 8 Am. U. J. Gender, Social Pol'y & L. 505 (1998); Alexa E. King, Solomon Revisited: Assigning Parenthood in the Context of Collaborative Reproduction, 5 UCLA Women's L.J. 329 (1995).

Many question an intent-based approach to surrogacy arrangements. See, e.g., Marsha Garrison, Law Making for Baby Making: An Interpretive Approach to the Determination of Legal Parentage, 113 Harv. L. Rev. 835 (2000) (arguing that a newly developing and highly specialized judicial test to deal with new reproductive technologies creates inconsistencies with well-established family law doctrine, which is adequate to handle new issues); Ilana Hurwitz, Collaborative Reproduction: Finding the Child in the Maze of Legal Motherhood, 33 Conn. L. Rev. 127 (2000) (best interests of the child, not intent of the contracting adults, should determine legal parentage in nontraditional reproduction cases). See also Janet L. Dolgin, The "Intent" of Reproduction: Reproductive Technologies and the Parent-Child Bond, 26 Conn. L. Rev. 1261, 1262-1264 (1994) (intent-based approach to surrogacy arrangements unconsciously and unsuccessfully attempts to reconcile status and contract approaches to family law).

Can a mother giving meaningful consent to serve as a surrogate and give up all rights after the birth of the child? Consider the New Jersey Supreme Court's concern:

> Under the contract, the natural mother is irrevocably committed before she knows the strength of her bond with her child. She never makes a totally voluntary, informed decision, for quite clearly any decision prior to the baby's birth is, in the most important sense, uninformed, and any decision after that, compelled by a pre-existing contractual commitment, the threat of a lawsuit, and the inducement of a $10,000 payment, is less than totally voluntary.

537 A.2d at 1248. Among courts that have followed this line of analysis, see R.R. v. M.H., 689 N.E.2d 790 (Mass. 1998) (surrogacy agreement unenforceable unless surrogate mother has a "reasonable" waiting period during which she could change her mind). Is it "good" for women for the law to assume that the surrogate mother cannot know her mind ahead of time or that the instincts of motherhood may be beyond her control?

An additional question is whether economic constraints undermine the woman's ability to make a binding contract. These constraints, along with the "equation of (valued) femaleness with selflessness and motherhood, would seem to provide just the motivation necessary to cause a woman to enter into a contract that pays the equivalent of $1.57 per hour for nine months of life- and health-endangering, emotionally difficult work." Nancy

Ehrenreich, Surrogacy as Resistance? The Misplaced Forces on Choice in the Surrogacy and Abortion Funding Contexts, 41 DePaul L. Rev. 1369, 1380-1381 (1992) (review essay). Other critics of surrogacy agreements who have stressed the potential exploitation of poor women include Judith Areen, *Baby M.* Reconsidered, 76 Geo. L.J. 1741, 1750-1752 (1988); George Annas, The Baby Broker Boom, Hastings Center Rep., June 1986, at 30-31; Shari O'Brien, Commercial Conceptions: A Breeding Ground for Surrogacy, 65 N.C. L. Rev. 127, 142-143 (1986); Derek Morgan, Making Motherhood Male: Surrogacy and the Moral Economy of Women, 12 J.L. & Soc'y 219, 232 (1985). See also Angie Godwin McEwen, Note, So You're Having Another Woman's Baby: Economics and Exploitation in Gestational Surrogacy, 32 Vand. J. Transnat'l L. 271 (1999) (reviewing arguments on both sides of the exploitation debate).

Commentators opposing the enforcement of surrogate contracts have also emphasized how surrogacy arrangements support ideological messages about having a child "of one's own" that have reinforced male dominance and women's sense of obligation to bear children:

> Given the discourse surrounding this issue, which treats infertility as a human tragedy of immense proportions and child rearing as an inviolable right, enforcing such contracts would seem to suggest that it is absolutely essential for women to become mothers by whatever means possible.

Ehrenreich, supra, at 1376. See also Barbara Katz Rothman, Recreating Motherhood: Ideology and Technology in a Patriarchal Society (1989); Nadine Taub, Surrogacy: Sorting Through the Alternatives, 4 Berkeley Women's L.J. 285, 291 (1989-1990) (arguments against surrogacy based on lack of consent tend to glorify pregnancy and denigrate the importance of relationships not based on gestational bonding).

In her intent-based defense of enforcing surrogate contracts, Shultz does not ignore the constraints within which women make reproductive decisions or the negative ideological messages associated with surrogacy. She argues, however, that the risks of assuming universal consent must be weighed against the risks of assuming universal nonconsent:

> At best, sexist scripting is complex and contradictory. Who is to say what is merely "adaptive" and what is "free" choice? In the surrogacy example, which is the sexist conditioned script? A surrogate's wanting another child? Her feeling that she can give the ultimate altruistic gift of life? Her panic that it is unnatural to "give up" "her" child? Her belief that her gestational and genetic services are of major value and therefore might sell in the world? Is the intending mother controlled by sexist scripting in wanting to bring her husband's genetic child into their family? Or are her critics following a sexist script in feeling she deserves to be punished by losing the child she wanted to mother because she did not give up or postpone her career? Or because she was reluctant to risk her health to have her "own" baby? Similarly, is the

intending father acting out a male chauvinist vanity in wanting a child that is "his," or is he expressing a male commitment to nurturing a child?

The insight that choices may be adaptive is a useful theoretical construct; it challenges received ideas and aids reflection. But we still have functional and policy decisions to make. When a given choice is said to be adaptive, what should be done? Can we envision some pristine and separate self not shaped by outside persons, events and circumstances? The self is inevitably interactive and permeable. Identifying some pure component called individual will, unswayed and untainted by social, psychological or cultural conditioning is an illusion.

If uncritically accepted to resolve conflicts over policy, the adaptive choice argument obscures as well as illumines. Identifying which pressures create "unfree choices" in order that individuals not be held accountable for them is a recurrent necessity in contract law. Doctrines like duress, coercion, lack of capacity and unconscionability establish criteria under which particular choices can be treated as voluntary exercises of meaningful choice or not. However, where an adaptive choice argument is used to justify a categorical bar on enforcement of all procreational or parenthood agreements — for example all surrogacy agreements — something different is happening. Given that pressures on such choices, as on all human choices, are uneven and multidirectional, if no possibility of a freely chosen surrogacy arrangement is envisioned, then the argument is not really about pressured choice. Rather, it is either about surrogacy per se, or about women as a group lacking the capacity for free decision-making.

Under the first branch, if it is argued that surrogacy would never be agreed to by an autonomous and reasonable person, then a species of substantive unconscionability is being alleged. An argument that the transaction is unacceptable as a matter of substantive policy is simply framed as an argument that the choice is "adaptive" rather than "free." The real conclusion — that surrogacy is bad — is, then, not articulated; it is assumed rather than demonstrated. The conclusion that surrogacy is unacceptable, however, is precisely the question to which the adaptive choice argument was addressed. Under the banner of respect for individuals, the adaptive choice argument, pressed to its logical conclusion, embraces the very evil it assails; prohibiting an entire category of individual choices on the ground that those choices are adaptive rather than free becomes a justification for substituting one's own judgment about the underlying value issue for that of others.

On the second branch of the argument, the assumption is that because of dominance of women by men, women as a group lack meaningful choice; *their* choices are especially likely to be adaptive. [Gender issues aside,] constrictions that grow from sexist conditions and conditioning provide compelling reasons to work against sex discrimination and dominance, and for expanded opportunities for women. They are also reasons to examine *particular* agreements for evidence of duress, unconscionability, lack of capacity, etc. Analysis of these standard defenses would be improved by greater sensitivity to gender as a factor that, like poverty or lack of education, can reduce the meaningfulness of a particular woman's particular choice. But the reality of sex discrimination is not a reason to presume categorically that women are unable to act freely and responsibly with reference to decisions about procreation and parental intentions. Otherwise, again, the result is self-defeating. In the name of protecting their freedom, individual women are treated as non-autonomous persons.

Finally, there is a general symbolic as well as a specific outcome-determinative dimension to the issue of free versus adaptive choice. To be sure, there is a cognizable risk of papering over systemic duress with the ideology of free choice. But there is also a danger of undermining both the perception and the experience of responsible freedom through constant reiterations of determinism, however well-intentioned. The matter comes down to which risks one prefers.

Shultz, supra, at 353-355.

Lori B. Andrews, who has vigorously defended surrogacy contracts, is also concerned about the implications of assuming that women cannot make responsible reproductive decisions:

> Some feminists are comfortable with advocating disparate treatment on the grounds that gestation is such a unique experience that it has no male counterpart at law and so deserves a unique legal status. The special nature of gestation, according to this argument, gives rise to special rights — such as the right for the surrogate to change her mind and assert her legal parenthood after the child is born.
>
> The other side of the gestational coin, which has not been sufficiently addressed by these feminists, is that with special rights come special responsibilities. If gestation can be viewed as unique in surrogacy, then it can be viewed as unique in other areas. Pregnant women could be held to have responsibilities that other members of society do not have — such as the responsibility to have a Cesarean section against their wishes in order to protect the health of a child (since only pregnant women are in the unique position of being able to influence the health of the child).
>
> Some feminists have criticized surrogacy as turning participating women, albeit with their consent, into reproductive vessels. I see the danger of the anti-surrogacy arguments as potentially turning *all* women into reproductive vessels, without their consent, by providing government oversight for women's decisions and creating a disparate legal category for gestation.

Andrews, Surrogate Motherhood: The Challenge for Feminists, 16 Law, Med. & Health Care 72, 78 (1988).

To what extent does the debate over surrogacy echo familiar disputes among feminists between formal and substantive equality?

Perhaps because of the dilemma posed by the problematic concept of choice, many feminists who have written on the subject of surrogacy advocate a middle ground, such as that followed by the New Jersey Supreme Court in *Baby M.*, whereby surrogacy contracts are neither illegal nor enforceable. See, e.g., Taub, supra, at 296-299; Martha Field, Surrogate Motherhood (1988); Janet L. Dolgin, Status and Contract in Surrogate Motherhood: An Illumination of the Surrogacy Debate, 38 Buff. L. Rev.

515 (1990); Katharine T. Bartlett, Re-Expressing Parenthood, 98 Yale L.J. 293, 326-337 (1988).

3. The Commodification Critique. Alongside specific concerns about lack of consent and the potential exploitation of particular women surrogates, some commentators have focused on the more general dangers to society of conceiving of personal attributes as fungible objects. Doing so, Margaret Jane Radin argues, "detaches from the person that which is integral to the person." Radin, Market-Inalienability, 100 Harv. L. Rev. 1849, 1881 (1987).

> . . . In our understanding of personhood we are committed to an ideal of individual uniqueness that does not cohere with the idea that each person's attributes are fungible, that they have a monetary equivalent, and that they can be traded off against those of other people. . . .
>
> . . . Market rhetoric invites us to see the person as a self-interested maximizer in all respects. Freedom or autonomy, therefore, is seen as individual control over how to maximize one's overall gains. . . . [I]t is not satisfactory to think that marketing whatever one wishes defines freedom.

Id. at 1885. Applying the pragmatic analysis described earlier in this chapter at page 1006, Radin vacillates between an "incomplete commodification" approach and a "market-inalienable" approach to surrogacy, balancing the destructive effects that paid surrogacy has to understandings of human flourishing against the benefits, under the non-ideal circumstances of this world, for women's empowerment. See id. at 1928-1936. See also Elizabeth S. Anderson, Is Women's Labor a Commodity?, 19 Phil. & Pub. Aff. 71 (1990) (supporting a more decisive conclusion that surrogacy constitutes an unconscionable commodification of children and women's reproductive capacities). For a case against surrogacy contracts based on commitments to more traditional ideals of the family, in contrast to Radin's emphasis on individual flourishing, see William Joseph Wagner, The Contractual Reallocation of Procreative Resources and Parental Rights: The Natural Endowment Critique, 41 Case W. Res. L. Rev. 1 (1990).

4. Gestational Surrogacy. In *Baby M.*, Mary Beth Whitehead was the child's biological mother, both because of her genetic contribution to the child and because she carried the child in her womb. Because she was the mother, after the New Jersey Supreme Court determined that her rights could not be terminated on the basis of a contract signed before the birth of the child, the custody of the child was adjudicated between her and the child's biological father under the customary test applied in custody disputes between biological parents: the best-interests-of-the-child test.

When the genetic and gestational functions are bifurcated, the issues become more complicated. In Johnson v. Calvert, 19 Cal. Rptr. 2d 494 (Cal. 1993), the gestational mother asserted parental rights against the contract parents, who were also the genetic parents of the child. The California Supreme Court, interpreting the state's version of the Uniform Parentage Act to permit a finding of parenthood on either genetic or gestational grounds, concluded that "when the two means do not coincide in one woman, she who intended to procreate the child — that is, she who intended to bring about the birth of a child that she intended to raise as her own — is the natural mother under California law." Id. at 500. In so doing, the court adopted the approach advocated by Professor Shultz, outlined in note 2, above. As for the concern expressed by the New Jersey Supreme Court in *Baby M.* about when a prebirth contract could be truly voluntary, the court responded:

> The argument that a woman cannot knowingly and intelligently agree to gestate and deliver a baby for intending parents carries overtones of the reasoning that for centuries prevented woman from attaining equal economic rights and professional status under the law. To resurrect this view is both to foreclose a personal and economic choice on the part of the surrogate mother, and to deny intending parents what may be their only means of procreating a child of their own genes.

Id. at 503.

In a subsequent California case involving another surrogate who was not the genetic mother, it was not the surrogate but the intended father who changed his mind, deciding he no longer wished to be either married or a father. In re Marriage of Buzzanca, 61 Cal. Rptr. 2d 280 (Ct. App. 1998). In this case, as well, the intentional parenthood approach prevailed, and the father was held responsible for child support. Id.

5. The Gender and Race Critique of Surrogacy Arrangements. Is the question of parenthood a scientific question or a social/political one? Some have stated that the woman who contributes the egg is deemed the mother in the Johnson v. Calvert context because that contribution is most analogous to the male contribution of sperm.

> In Western, patriarchal societies, the classic where-do-babies-come-from tale we tell children is a variation on "Daddy planted a seed in Mommy." Contrast this with a tale Pearl Buck wrote for children. Johnny wants to know where he came from. You were in me, his mother explains. But BEFORE, Johnny wants to know. You were *always* in me, his mother explains. When I was in my mother, you were in me. When she was in her mother, you were in me. You were always in me. . . .
> . . . In a mother-based system, a person is what mothers grow. People are made of the care and nurturance that bring a baby forth into the world and turn that baby into a member of society. In a patriarchal system, a person is what grows out of a seed; originally a man's seed, but now expanded in the sex-neutral language of "gametes." The essence of what a person is, in patriarchal thinking, is there when the seed is planted. Motherhood becomes,

in such thinking, a place. Providing the place becomes a service. Under patriarchy, the place in which the seed grows does not really matter. It can be a wife, a "surrogate," or an artificial womb.

Barbara Katz Rothman, Daddy Plants a Seed, 47 Hastings L.J. 1241, 1244-1245 (1996). See also Rothman, Recreating Motherhood: Ideology and Technology in a Patriarchal Society 45 (1989) ("[W]hat makes a child one's own is the seed, the genetic tie, the 'blood.' And the blood they mean is not the real blood of pregnancy and birth, not the blood of the pulsing core, the bloody show, the blood of birth, but the metaphorical blood of the genetic tie."); Katha Pollitt, When Is a Mother Not a Mother: Surrogate Mother Case of Anna Johnson, The Nation, Dec. 31, 1990, at 825 ("[the] decision follows the general pattern of our society, in which women's experiences are recognized to the extent that they are identical with men's, and devalued or ignored to the extent that they are different"); Janet Dolgin, Just a Gene: Judicial Assumptions About Parenthood, 40 UCLA L. Rev. 637, 687 (1993) (*Calvert* case decided so as to strengthen value of traditional, middle-class family).

Race-sensitive perspectives have also produced harsh criticism of the *Calvert* case.

> Minority women increasingly will be sought to serve as "mother machines" for embryos of middle and upper-class clients. It's a new, virulent form of racial and class discrimination. Within a decade, thousands of poor and minority women will be used as a "breeder class" for those who can afford $30,000 to $40,000 to avoid the inconvenience and danger of pregnancy.

Anita L. Allen, The Black Surrogate Mother, 8 Harv. Blackletter J. 17, 30 (1991). See also April L. Cherry, Nurturing the Service of White Culture: Racial Subordination, Gestational Surrogacy, and the Ideology of Motherhood, 10 Tex. J. Women & L. 83 (2001) (arguing that gestational surrogacy arrangements serve to reinforce notions of black women as nurturers of white children, while continuing to deny them legal rights as parents); Dorothy E. Roberts, Race and the New Reproduction, 47 Hastings L.J. 935 (1996) (new reproductive technologies reflect and reinforce racial hierarchy in America); George Annas, Fairy Tales Surrogate Mothers Tell, 16 Law, Med. & Health Care 27 (1988) (charging that surrogate motherhood is both classist and sexist). What factors relating to poor and minority women might point in the opposite direction? Is this the same debate that prostitution raises?

From a law and economics or efficiency analysis, the financial constraints that push a woman toward becoming a surrogate are the same considerations as motivate all kinds of decisionmaking throughout the economy. See, e.g., Richard A. Posner, The Ethics and Economics of Enforcing Contracts of Surrogate Motherhood, 5 J. Contemp. Health L. & Pol'y 21, 26 (1989) (just as only wealthy people can afford butlers and expensive cars, so only wealthy people will be able to afford surrogate mothers); see also Louis Michael Seidman, *Baby M.* and the Problem of Unstable Preferences, 76 Geo. L.J. 1829 (1988) (conflicts in individual objectives better resolved through market ordering than through government regulation). This is essentially the approach taken by the *Calvert* court:

> Although common sense suggests that women of lesser means serve as surrogate mothers more often than do wealthy women, there has been no proof that surrogacy contracts exploit poor women to any greater degree than economic necessity in general exploits them by inducing them to accept lower-paid or otherwise undesirable employment.

Johnson v. Calvert, 19 Cal. Rptr. 494, 503 (Cal. 1993).

6. Surrogacy and Legal Reform. A sampling of state statutes dealing with surrogate parenting contracts can be found in Christine L. Kerian, Surrogacy: A Last Resort Alternative for Infertile Women or a Commodification of Women's Bodies and Children?, 12 Wis. Women's L.J. 113 (1997). Some states still make surrogacy illegal, with either criminal or civil sanctions. See, e.g., Mich. Comp. Laws Ann. §722.859 (West 1993) (procurement of surrogacy agreement is a misdemeanor or a felony); N.Y. Dom. Rel. Law §123 (McKinney 1999) (civil penalty for entering into surrogacy agreement); Utah Code Ann. §76-7-204(1)(d) (1999) (misdemeanor); Wash. Rev. Code Ann. §26.26.250 (West 1997) (gross misdemeanor).

The District of Columbia, Indiana, Kentucky, Louisiana, Michigan, Nebraska, and Washington make surrogacy contracts entered into for compensation unenforceable. Kerian, supra, at 145. Arizona, New York, and Utah prohibit enforcement of paid and unpaid surrogacy contracts. Id. at 146. Most other states that have addressed the issue have adopted a more neutral ground, allowing for the enforceability of surrogacy arrangements in some form or another. Id. at 146-147. Florida expressly permits gestational surrogacy agreements; Nevada, New Hampshire and Virginia allow them if the intended parents are married and money is paid only for medical and necessary living expenses. Lisa C. Ikemoto, The In/Fertile, the Too Fertile, and the Dysfertile, 47 Hastings L.J. 1007, 1032 (1996). Washington does not require that the intended parents be married, and only Arkansas expressly provides for the possibility of unmarried men, but not women, becoming parents through a surrogacy arrangement. Id.

The Uniform Status of Children of Assisted Conception Act, 9B U.L.A. 102-117 (Supp. 1988), adopted by the National Conference of Commissioners on Uniform State Law in 1988, gives jurisdictions a choice about whether to allow or disallow surrogacy arrangements. Alternative A spells out the terms under which surrogacy arrangements should be allowed. It requires that all relevant parties, including the husband of the surrogate mother, be parties to the agreement and that they obtain court approval of the agreement prior to conception. The court must find that the intended mother is unable to bear a child, that the surrogate has had at least one pregnancy prior to this arrangement and can have another child without unreasonable risk, that the parties have received counseling, and that home studies of the intended parents and the surrogate have been performed. Without court approval, the contract is void, and the woman who gives birth is the child's mother. A surrogate may change her mind and terminate the agreement without liability to the intended parents within six months of the last insemination. If she does not, the agreement is enforceable, and the intended parents are the legal parents. Under Alternative B of the Uniform Act, surrogacy agreements are void and unenforceable. North Dakota has adopted Alternative B of the Act, and Virginia has adopted some parts of Alternative A. See Kerian, supra, at 143-144 & n.216.

The Family Law Section of the American Bar Association approved a Model Surrogacy Act, which makes surrogacy agreements lawful and enforceable by specific performance. Under this Model Act, the allowable compensation to the surrogate ranges from $7,500 to $12,500. The surrogate may not renege on the agreement, but she may abort the pregnancy. The intended parents must be infertile. The Act substitutes a simplified procedure for the customary adoption requirements. Id. at 144-145.

One question that is likely to arise more frequently in the tort context is what duty doctors and lawyers who participate in surrogacy arrangements have to prevent harm to the participants. See, e.g., Stiver v. Parker, 975 F.2d 261 (6th Cir. 1992) (in case in which baby born with severe disorders, surrogacy "broker" has duty to act with a "high degree of diligence" in protecting the parties from harm).

7. Frozen "Pre-embryos": Balancing Wanted and Unwanted Parenthood. Legal disputes among couples arising over frozen embryos not yet implanted raise slightly different issues. One couple who had planned on using frozen embryos to start a family divorced before a pregnancy had been achieved, at which point the wife sought custody of the embryos for possible future implantation and the husband sought authority to prevent implantation. The trial court declared that the embryos were "human beings" and awarded custody to the wife on the grounds that such action was the most likely to protect their best interests. Davis v. Davis, 1989 Tenn. App. LEXIS 641 (Blount County Cir. Ct., Sept. 26, 1989). The Tennessee Court of Appeals reversed, concluding that the parties shared an equal interest in the embryos, that the husband had a constitutionally protected right not to beget a child where no pregnancy had yet taken place, and that there was no compelling state interest to justify implantation against the will of either party. Davis v. Davis, 1990 Tenn. App. LEXIS 642 (Sept. 13, 1990).

On appeal to the state supreme court, the wife changed her position, deciding that rather than using the embryos to become pregnant herself, she wanted to donate them to a childless couple. The court rejected the approaches of both the trial court and the court of appeals, holding that "preembryos are not, strictly speaking, either 'persons' or 'property,' but occupy an interim category that entitles them to special respect because of their potential for human life." Davis v. Davis, 842 S.W.2d 588, 597 (Tenn. 1992), cert. denied sub nom. Stowe v. Davis, 507 U.S. 911 (1993). If possible, the court stated, a contest over pre-embryos should be resolved according to prior agreement. Id. Where no such agreement exists, each party's constitutional privacy interests require that their particular positions, burdens, and interests in a particular case be weighed against the other's and the disposition ordered that avoids the most harm. Id. at 603-604. The court balanced the interests as follows:

Beginning with the burden imposed on Junior Davis, we note that the consequences are obvious. Any disposition which results in the gestation of the preembryos would impose unwanted parenthood on him, with all of its possible financial and psychological consequences. The impact that this unwanted parenthood would have on Junior Davis can only be understood by considering his particular circumstances, as revealed in the record.

Junior Davis testified that he was the fifth youngest of six children. When he was five years old, his parents divorced, his mother had a nervous breakdown, and he and three of his brothers went to live at a home for boys run by the Lutheran Church. Another brother was taken in by an aunt, and his sister stayed with her mother. From that day forward, he had monthly visits with his mother but saw his father only three more times before he died in 1976. Junior Davis testified that, as a boy, he had severe problems caused by separation from his parents. He said that it was especially hard to leave his mother after each monthly visit. He clearly feels that he has suffered because of his lack of opportunity to establish a relationship with his parents and particularly because of the absence of his father.

In light of his boyhood experiences, Junior Davis is vehemently opposed to fathering a child that would not live with both parents. Regardless of whether he or Mary Sue had custody, he feels that the child's bond with the non-custodial parent would not be satisfactory. He testified very clearly that his concern was for the psychological obstacles a child in such a situation would face, as well as the burdens it would impose on him. Likewise, he is opposed to donation because the recipient couple might divorce, leaving the child (which he definitely would consider his own) in a single-parent setting.

Balanced against Junior Davis's interest in avoiding parenthood is Mary Sue Davis's interest in donating the preembryos to another couple for implantation. Refusal to permit donation of the preembryos would impose on her the burden of knowing that the lengthy IVF procedures she underwent were futile, and that the preembryos to which she contributed genetic material would never become children. While this is not an insubstantial emotional burden, we can only conclude that Mary Sue Davis's interest in donation is not as significant as the interest Junior Davis has in avoiding parenthood. If she were allowed to donate these preembryos, he would face a lifetime of either wondering about his parental status or knowing about his parental status but having no control over it. He testified quite clearly that if the preembryos were brought to term he would fight for custody of his child or children. Donation, if a child came of it, would rob him twice — his procreational autonomy would be defeated and his relationship with his offspring would be prohibited.

The case would be closer if Mary Sue Davis were seeking to use the preembryos herself, but only if she could not achieve parenthood by any other reasonable means. We recognize the trauma that Mary Sue has already experienced and the additional discomfort to which she would be subjected if she opts to attempt IVF again. Still, she would have a reasonable opportunity, through IVF, to try once again to achieve parenthood in all its aspects — genetic, gestation, bearing, and rearing.

Further, we note that if Mary Sue Davis were unable to undergo another round of IVF, or opted not to try, she could still achieve the child-rearing aspects of parenthood through adoption. The fact that she and Junior Davis pursued adoption indicates that, at least at one time, she was willing to forego genetic parenthood and would have been satisfied by the child-rearing aspects of parenthood alone.

Id.

Is this an example of the kind of contextualized legal reasoning discussed in Chapter 5? Is it an application of the "ethic of care"? Pragmatism? Stereotyped thinking? Resistance to stereotypes?

Mary Sue Davis was unable to conceive children through the usual means because after six painful tubal pregnancies, both of her fallopian tubes were inoperative. Each of the six IVF attempts involved a month of subcutaneous injections to shut down her pituitary gland and eight days of intermuscular injections to stimulate her ovaries to produce ova. She was anesthetized five times for the aspiration procedure and then returned for the transfer back to her uterus 48 to 72 hours later. Should this wear and tear and pain be considered in the balancing of interests? Compare Mario J. Trespalacios, Comment, Frozen Embryos: Towards an Equitable Solution, 46 U. Miami L. Rev. 803 (1992) (mothers' physical investment or "sweat equity" should count) with Kristine E. Luongo, The Big Chill: Davis v. Davis and the Protection of "Potential Life," 29 New Eng. L. Rev. 1011, 1043-1043 (1995) (although court overly trivialized Mary Sue's sweat equity, there is not the same reason to favor her interest over Junior's interest as there is in the abortion context).

Is it clear to you why Junior Davis's strong feelings about not fathering children he could not raise himself in a nuclear family weighed more heavily than Mary Sue Davis's wish to succeed in her efforts to produce one or more children for herself or for others? The court stated that "[o]rdinarily, the party wishing to avoid procreation should prevail, assuming that the other party has a reasonable possibility of achieving parenthood by means other than use of the preembryos in question." 842 S.W.2d at 604. The court seemed to suggest that further IVF procedures or adoption would offer reasonable possibilities for Mary Sue Davis to achieve parenthood. What's going on here? How do you think the equities would be balanced if Junior Davis had wanted the embryos for implantation in his new wife and Mary Sue Davis had wanted the embryos discarded?

While the law is still emerging in this area, the trend seems to be, as in *Davis*, to favor the right not to procreate over the right to procreate. This usually, although not always, means finding the agreement the couple signed before the assisted reproductive procedures to be unenforceable. See, e.g., J.B. v. M.B., 2001 N.J. LEXIS 955 (Aug. 14, 2001) (at divorce, wife entitled to have frozen embryos destroyed, notwithstanding agreement in contract to relinquish them to in vitro fertilization program if their marriage dissolved, because such contracts are contrary to public policy); A.Z. v. B.Z., 725 N.E.2d 1051 (Mass. 2000) (agreement that embryos would be wife's if the parties separated was unenforceable as a type of forced procreation; likewise, parenthood should not be forced on husband, notwithstanding his prior consent, once he objects to such an undertaking); Kass v. Kass, 696 N.E.2d 174 (N.Y. 1998) (enforcing preconception agreement expressing intention of parties to donate any disputed embryos to the IVF program for research purposes, notwithstanding woman's dispute of the agreement and desire to implant the embryos). What, precisely, is the gender issue raised by the frozen embryo cases? See Judith F. Daar, Assisted Reproductive Technologies and the Pregnancy Process: Developing an Equality Model to Protect Reproductive Liberties, 25 Am J.L. & Med. 455, 457 (1999) (arguing that a woman using assisted reproductive technologies "should have the same right to control the fate of her unimplanted embryos as she would have to control her early fetus in traditional pregnancy" and that deciding in favor of the partner who wants to destroy the pre-embryos deprives the woman of her constitutional right to control her reproductive autonomy).

A few states have enacted statutes addressing the status or use of cryopreserved pre-embryos. See Fla. Stat. Ann. §742.17 (West 1997) (requiring couples and IVF programs to agree in advance about the disposition of pre-embryos in the event of a divorce or the death of a spouse); La. Rev. Stat. §9:121 et seq. (West 2000) (requiring the treatment of pre-embryos as "juridical persons" and prohibiting destruction of pre-embryos or their use for research purposes); N.H. Rev. Stat. Ann. §168-B:13 to 168-B:15 (1994) (regulating in vitro fertilization and pre-embryo transfer).

4. The Pregnant Woman and Fetus as Adversaries

Dorothy E. Roberts, Punishing Drug Addicts Who Have Babies: Women of Color, Equality, and the Right of Privacy
104 Harv. L. Rev. 1419, 1428-1432, 1453-1455, 1462-1463 (1991)

A. The Crack Epidemic and the State's Response

Crack cocaine appeared in America in the early 1980s, and its abuse has grown to epidemic proportions. Crack is especially popular among inner-city women. Indeed, evidence shows that, in several urban areas in the United States, more women than men now smoke crack. Most crack-addicted women are of childbearing age, and many are pregnant. This phenomenon has contributed to an explosion in the number of newborns affected by maternal drug use. Some experts estimate that as many as 375,000 drug-exposed infants are born every year. In many urban hospitals, the number of these newborns has quadrupled in the last five years. A widely cited 1988 study conducted by the National Association for Prenatal Addiction Research and Education (NAPARE) found that eleven percent of newborns in thirty-six hospitals surveyed were affected by their mothers' illegal-drug use during pregnancy. . . . In several hospitals, the proportion of drug-exposed infants was as high as fifteen and twenty-five percent.

Babies born to drug-addicted mothers may suffer a variety of medical, developmental, and behavioral problems, depending on the nature of their mother's substance abuse. Immediate effects of cocaine exposure can include premature birth, low birth weight, and withdrawal symptoms. Cocaine-exposed children have also exhibited neurobehavioral problems such as mood dysfunction, organizational deficits, poor attention, and impaired human interaction, although it has not been determined whether these conditions are permanent. Congenital disorders and deformities have also been associated with cocaine use during pregnancy. According to NAPARE, babies exposed to cocaine have a tenfold greater risk of suffering sudden infant death syndrome (SIDS).

Data on the extent and potential severity of the adverse effects of maternal cocaine use are controversial. The interpretation of studies of cocaine-exposed infants is often clouded by the presence of other fetal risk factors, such as the mother's use of additional drugs, cigarettes, and alcohol and her socioeconomic status. For example, the health prospects of an infant are significantly threatened because pregnant addicts often receive little or no prenatal care and may be malnourished. Moreover, because the medical community has given more attention to studies showing adverse effects of cocaine exposure than to those that deny these effects, the public has a distorted perception of the risks of maternal cocaine use. Researchers have not yet authoritatively determined the percentage of infants exposed to cocaine who actually experience adverse consequences. . . .

The most common penalty for a mother's prenatal drug use is the permanent or temporary removal of her baby. Hospitals in a number of states now screen newborns for evidence of drugs in their urine and report positive results to child welfare authorities. Some child protection agencies institute neglect proceedings to obtain custody of babies with positive toxicologies based solely on these tests. More and more government authorities are also removing drug-exposed newborns from their mothers immediately after birth pending an investigation of parental fitness. In these investigations, positive neonatal toxicologies often raise a strong presumption of parental unfitness, which circumvents the inquiry into the mother's ability to care for her child that is customarily necessary to deprive a parent of custody.

A second form of punishment is the "protective" incarceration of pregnant drug addicts charged with unrelated crimes. In 1988, a Washington, D.C. judge sentenced a thirty-year-old woman named Brenda Vaughn, who pleaded guilty to forging $700 worth of checks, to jail for the duration of her pregnancy. The judge stated at sentencing that he wanted to ensure that the baby would be born in jail to protect it from its mother's drug abuse. . . .

Finally, women have been prosecuted after the birth of their children for having exposed the fetuses to drugs or alcohol. . . .

Poor Black women bear the brunt of prosecutors' punitive approach. These women are the primary targets of prosecutors, not because they are more likely to be guilty of fetal abuse, but because they are Black and poor. Poor women, who are disproportionately Black, are in closer contact with government agencies, and their drug use is therefore more likely to be detected. Black women are also more likely to be reported to government authorities, in part because of the racist attitudes of health care professionals. Finally, their failure to meet society's image of the ideal mother makes their prosecution more acceptable. . . .

[A] New England Journal of Medicine study of pregnant women in Pinellas County [Florida] . . . found that only about twenty-six percent of those who used drugs were Black. [Ira J. Chasnoff et al., The Prevalence of Illicit-Drug or Alcohol Use During Pregnancy and Discrepancies in Mandatory Reporting in Pinellas County, Florida, 322 New Eng. J. Med. 1201, 1204 (table 2) (1990).] Yet over *ninety percent* of Florida prosecutions for drug abuse during pregnancy have been brought against Black women. [The study found] . . . that despite similar rates of substance abuse, Black women were ten times more likely than white women to be reported to public health authorities for substance abuse during pregnancy. In addition, . . . both health care professionals and prosecutors wield a great deal of discretion in selecting women to be subjected to the criminal justice system. [Id. at 1202-1205.]

The prosecution of drug-addicted mothers demonstrates the inadequacy of antidiscrimination analysis and the superiority of the antisubordination approach. Rather than conform Black women's experiences to the intent standard, we can use those experiences to reveal the narrowmindedness of the Court's view of equality. First, the antidiscrimination approach may not adequately protect Black women from prosecutions' infringement of equality, because it is difficult to identify individual guilty actors. Who are the government officials motivated by racial bias to punish Black women? The hospital staff who test and report mothers to child welfare agencies? The prosecutors who develop and implement policies to charge women who use drugs during pregnancy? Legislators who enact laws protecting the unborn?

It is unlikely that any of these individual actors intentionally singled out Black women for punishment based on a conscious devaluation of their motherhood. The disproportionate impact of the prosecutions on poor Black women does not result from such isolated, individualized decisions. Rather, it is a result of two centuries of systematic exclusion of Black women from tangible and intangible benefits enjoyed by white society. Their exclusion is reflected in Black women's reliance on public hospitals and public drug treatment centers, in their failure to obtain adequate prenatal care, in the more frequent reporting of Black drug-users by health care professionals, and in society's acquiescence in the government's punitive response to the problem of crack-addicted babies.

More generally, the antidiscrimination principle mischaracterizes the role of social norms in perpetuating inequality. This view of equality perceives racism as disconnected acts by individuals who operate outside of the social fabric. . . .

The prosecutions of drug-addicted mothers demonstrated how dramatically this perspective departs from reality. It is precisely a shared societal norm — the devaluation of Black motherhood — that perpetuates the social conditions discussed above and explains why Black women are particularly susceptible to prosecution. The Court's vision of equality acquiesces in racist norms and institutions by exempting them from a standard that requires proof of illicit motive on the part of an individual governmental actor. The inability to identify and blame an individual government actor allows society to rationalize the disparate impact of the prosecutions as the result of the mothers' own irresponsible actions. Formal equality theory thus legitimates the subordination of Black women.

In contrast to the antidiscrimination approach, antisubordination theory mandates that equal protection law concern itself with the concrete ways in which government policy perpetuates the inferior status of Black women. The law should listen to the voices of poor Black mothers and seek to eliminate their experiences of subordination. From this perspective, the prosecutions of crack-addicted mothers are unconstitutional because they reinforce the myth of the undeserving Black mother by singling out — whether intentionally or not — Black women for punishment. The government's punitive policy reflects a long history of denigration of Black mothers dating back to slavery, and it serves to perpetuate that legacy of unequal respect. The prosecutions should therefore be upheld only if the state can demonstrate that they serve a compelling interest that could not be achieved through less discriminatory means. . . .

Understanding the prosecution of drug-addicted mothers as punishment for having babies clarifies the constitutional right at stake. The woman's right at issue is not the right to abuse drugs or to cause the fetus to be born with defects. It is the right to choose to be a mother that is burdened by the criminalization of conduct during pregnancy. This view of the constitutional issue reveals the relevance of race to the resolution of the competing interests. Race has historically determined the value society places on an individual's right to choose motherhood. Because of the devaluation of Black motherhood, protecting the right of Black women to choose to bear a child has unique significance.

≣ *Ferguson v. City of Charleston*
≣ 532 U.S. 67 (2001)

Justice STEVENS delivered the opinion of the Court.

In this case, we must decide whether a state hospital's performance of a diagnostic test to obtain evidence of a patient's criminal conduct for law enforcement purposes is an unreasonable search if the patient has not consented to the procedure. More narrowly, the question is whether the interest in using the threat of criminal sanctions to deter pregnant women from using cocaine can justify a departure from the general rule that an official nonconsensual search is unconstitutional if not authorized by a valid warrant.

I

In the fall of 1988, staff members at the public hospital operated in the city of Charleston by the Medical University of South Carolina (MUSC) became concerned about an apparent increase in the use of cocaine by patients who were receiving prenatal treatment. In response to this perceived increase, as of April 1989, MUSC began to order drug screens to be performed on urine samples from maternity patients who were suspected of using cocaine. If a patient tested positive, she was then referred by MUSC staff to the county substance abuse commission for counseling and treatment. However, despite the referrals, the incidence of cocaine use among the patients at MUSC did not appear to change.

Some four months later, Nurse Shirley Brown, the case manager for the MUSC obstetrics department, heard a news broadcast reporting that the police in Greenville, South Carolina, were arresting pregnant users of cocaine on the theory that such use harmed the fetus and was therefore child abuse. Nurse Brown discussed the story with MUSC's general counsel, Joseph C. Good, Jr., who then contacted Charleston Solicitor Charles Condon in order to offer MUSC's cooperation in prosecuting mothers whose children tested positive for drugs at birth.

After receiving Good's letter, Solicitor Condon took the first steps in developing the policy at issue in this case. He organized the initial meetings, decided who would participate, and issued the invitations, in which he described his plan to prosecute women who tested positive for cocaine while pregnant. The task force that Condon formed included representatives of MUSC, the police, the County Substance Abuse Commission and the Department of Social Services. Their deliberations led to MUSC's adoption of a 12-page document entitled "POLICY M-7," dealing with the subject of "Management of Drug Abuse During Pregnancy."

The first three pages of Policy M-7 set forth the procedure to be followed by the hospital staff to "identify/assist pregnant patients suspected of drug abuse." The first section, entitled the "Identification of Drug Abusers," provided that a patient should be tested for cocaine through a urine drug screen if she met one or more of nine criteria.[4] It also stated that a chain of custody should be followed when obtaining and testing urine samples, presumably to make sure that the results could be used in subsequent criminal proceedings. The policy also provided for education and referral to a substance abuse clinic for patients who tested positive. Most important, it added the threat of law enforcement intervention that "provided the necessary 'leverage' to make the policy effective." That threat was, as respondents candidly acknowledge, essential to the program's success in getting women into treatment and keeping them there.

The threat of law enforcement involvement was set forth in two protocols, the first dealing with the identification of drug use during pregnancy, and the second with identification of drug use after labor. Under the latter protocol, the police were to be notified without delay and the patient promptly arrested. Under the former, after the initial positive drug

---

4. Those criteria were as follows:
1. No prenatal care
2. Late prenatal care after 24 weeks gestation
3. Incomplete prenatal care
4. Abruptio placentae
5. Intrauterine fetal death
6. Preterm labor "of no obvious cause"
7. IUGR [intrauterine growth retardation] "of no obvious cause"
8. Previously known drug or alcohol abuse
9. Unexplained congenital anomalies.

test, the police were to be notified (and the patient arrested) only if the patient tested positive for cocaine a second time or if she missed an appointment with a substance abuse counselor.[5] In 1990, however, the policy was modified at the behest of the solicitor's office to give the patient who tested positive during labor, like the patient who tested positive during a prenatal care visit, an opportunity to avoid arrest by consenting to substance abuse treatment.

The last six pages of the policy contained forms for the patients to sign, as well as procedures for the police to follow when a patient was arrested. The policy also prescribed in detail the precise offenses with which a woman could be charged, depending on the stage of her pregnancy. If the pregnancy was 27 weeks or less, the patient was to be charged with simple possession. If it was 28 weeks or more, she was to be charged with possession and distribution to a person under the age of 18 — in this case, the fetus. If she delivered "while testing positive for illegal drugs," she was also to be charged with unlawful neglect of a child. Under the policy, the police were instructed to interrogate the arrestee in order "to ascertain the identity of the subject who provided illegal drugs to the suspect." Other than the provisions describing the substance abuse treatment to be offered to women who tested positive, the policy made no mention of any change in the prenatal care of such patients, nor did it prescribe any special treatment for the newborns.

II

Petitioners are 10 women who received obstetrical care at MUSC and who were arrested after testing positive for cocaine. Four of them were arrested during the initial implementation of the policy; they were not offered the opportunity to receive drug treatment as an alternative to arrest. The others were arrested after the policy was modified in 1990; they either failed to comply with the terms of the drug treatment program or tested positive for a second time. Respondents include the city of Charleston, law enforcement officials who helped develop and enforce the policy, and representatives of MUSC.

Petitioners' complaint challenged the validity of the policy under various theories, including the claim that warrantless and nonconsensual drug tests conducted for criminal investigatory purposes were unconstitutional searches. Respondents advanced two principal defenses to the constitutional claim: (1) that, as a matter of fact, petitioners had consented to the searches; and (2) that, as a matter of law, the searches were reasonable, even absent consent, because they were justified by special non-

---

5. Despite the conditional description of the first category, when the policy was in its initial stages, a positive test was immediately reported to the police, who then promptly arrested the patient.

law-enforcement purposes. The District Court rejected the second defense because the searches in question "were not done by the medical university for independent purposes. [Instead,] the police came in and there was an agreement reached that the positive screens would be shared with the police." Accordingly, the District Court submitted the factual defense to the jury with instructions that required a verdict in favor of petitioners unless the jury found consent. The jury found for respondents.

Petitioners appealed. . . . The Court of Appeals for the Fourth Circuit affirmed, but without reaching the question of consent. 186 F.3d 469 (1999). Disagreeing with the District Court, the majority of the appellate panel held that the searches were reasonable as a matter of law under our line of cases recognizing that "special needs" may, in certain exceptional circumstances, justify a search policy designed to serve non-law-enforcement ends. On the understanding "that MUSC personnel conducted the urine drug screens for medical purposes wholly independent of an intent to aid law enforcement efforts," the majority applied the balancing test used in Treasury Employees v. Von Raab, 489 U.S. 656 (1989), and Vernonia School Dist. 47J v. Acton, 515 U.S. 646 (1995), and concluded that the interest in curtailing the pregnancy complications and medical costs associated with maternal cocaine use outweighed what the majority termed a minimal intrusion on the privacy of the patients. . . .

We granted certiorari . . . to review the appellate court's holding on the "special needs" issue. Because we do not reach the question of the sufficiency of the evidence with respect to consent, we necessarily assume for purposes of our decision — as did the Court of Appeals — that the searches were conducted without the informed consent of the patients. We conclude that the judgment should be reversed and the case remanded for a decision on the consent issue.

III

Because MUSC is a state hospital, the members of its staff are government actors, subject to the strictures of the Fourth Amendment. . . . Moreover, the urine tests conducted by those staff members were indisputably searches within the meaning of the Fourth Amendment. . . . Neither the District Court nor the Court of Appeals concluded that any of the nine criteria used to identify the women to be searched provided either probable cause to believe that they were using cocaine, or even the basis for a reasonable suspicion of such use. Rather, the District Court and the Court of Appeals viewed the case as one involving MUSC's right to conduct searches without warrants or probable cause.

Because the hospital seeks to justify its authority to conduct drug tests and to turn the results over to law enforcement agents without the knowledge or consent of the patients, this case differs from the four previous cases in which we have considered whether comparable drug tests "fit within the closely guarded category of constitutionally permissible suspicionless searches." . . . In three of those cases, we sustained drug tests for railway employees involved in train accidents, Skinner v. Railway Labor Executives' Assn., 489 U.S. 602 (1989), for United States Customs Service employees seeking promotion to certain sensitive positions, [*Von Raab*, supra], and for high school students participating in interscholastic sports, [*Vernonia School Dist.*, supra]. In the fourth case, we struck down such testing for candidates for designated state offices as unreasonable. Chandler v. Miller, 520 U.S. 305 (1997).

In each of those cases, we employed a balancing test that weighed the intrusion on the individual's interest in privacy against the "special needs" that supported the program. As an initial matter, we note that the invasion of privacy in this case is far more substantial than in those cases. In the previous four cases, there was no misunderstanding about the purpose of the test or the potential use of the test results, and there were protections against the dissemination of the results to third parties. The use of an adverse test result to disqualify one from eligibility for a particular benefit, such as a promotion or an opportunity to participate in an extracurricular activity, involves a less serious intrusion on privacy than the unauthorized dissemination of such results to third parties. The reasonable expectation of privacy enjoyed by the typical patient undergoing diagnostic tests in a hospital is that the results of those tests will not be shared with nonmedical personnel without her consent. . . . In none of our prior cases was there any intrusion upon that kind of expectation.[14]

The critical difference between those four drug-testing cases and this one, however, lies in the nature of the "special need" asserted as justification for the warrantless searches. In each of those earlier cases, the "special need" that was advanced as a justification for the absence of a warrant or individualized suspicion was one divorced from the State's general interest in law enforcement. . . . In this case, however, the central and indispensable feature of the policy from its inception was the use of law enforcement to coerce the patients into substance abuse treatment. This fact distinguishes this case from circumstances in which physicians or psychologists, in the course of ordinary medical procedures aimed at helping the patient herself, come across information that under rules of law or ethics is subject to reporting requirements, which no one has challenged here. See, e.g., Council on Ethical and Judicial Affairs, American Medical Association, Policy Finder, Current Opinions E-5.05 (2000) (requiring reporting where "a patient threatens to inflict serious bodily harm to another person or to him or herself and there is a reasonable probability that the patient may carry out the threat"); Ark. Code Ann. §12-12-602 (1999) (requiring reporting

---

14. In fact, we have previously recognized that an intrusion on that expectation may have adverse consequences because it may deter patients from receiving needed medical care. Whalen v. Roe, 429 U.S. 589, 599-600 (1977). . . .

of intentionally inflicted knife or gunshot wounds); Ariz. Rev. Stat. Ann. §13-3620 (Supp. 2000) (requiring "any . . . person having responsibility for the care or treatment of children" to report suspected abuse or neglect to a peace officer or child protection agency).

Respondents argue in essence that their ultimate purpose — namely, protecting the health of both mother and child — is a beneficent one. In *Chandler,* however, we did not simply accept the State's invocation of a "special need." Instead, we carried out a "close review" of the scheme at issue before concluding that the need in question was not "special," as that term has been defined in our cases. 520 U.S. at 322. . . .

While the ultimate goal of the program may well have been to get the women in question into substance abuse treatment and off of drugs, the immediate objective of the searches was to generate evidence for law enforcement purposes in order to reach that goal. The threat of law enforcement may ultimately have been intended as a means to an end, but the direct and primary purpose of MUSC's policy was to ensure the use of those means. In our opinion, this distinction is critical. Because law enforcement involvement always serves some broader social purpose or objective, under respondents' view, virtually any nonconsensual suspicionless search could be immunized under the special needs doctrine by defining the search solely in terms of its ultimate, rather than immediate, purpose. Such an approach is inconsistent with the Fourth Amendment. Given the primary purpose of the Charleston program, which was to use the threat of arrest and prosecution in order to force women into treatment, and given the extensive involvement of law enforcement officials at every stage of the policy, this case simply does not fit within the closely guarded category of "special needs."

Accordingly, the judgment of the Court of Appeals is reversed, and the case is remanded for further proceedings consistent with this opinion.

The concurring opinion by Justice Kennedy is omitted.

Dissenting opinion by Justice SCALIA, with whom THE CHIEF JUSTICE and Justice THOMAS join as to Part II.

There is always an unappealing aspect to the use of doctors and nurses, ministers of mercy, to obtain incriminating evidence against the supposed objects of their ministration — although here, it is correctly pointed out, the doctors and nurses were ministering not just to the mothers but also to the children whom their cooperation with the police was meant to protect. But whatever may be the correct social judgment concerning the desirability of what occurred here, that is not the issue in the present case. The Constitution does not resolve all difficult social questions, but leaves the vast majority of them to resolution by debate and the democratic process — which would produce a decision by the citizens of Charleston, through their elected representatives, to forbid or permit the police action at issue here. The question before us is a narrower one: whether, whatever the desirability of this police conduct, it violates the Fourth Amendment's prohibition of unreasonable searches and seizures. In my view, it plainly does not.

I

The first step in Fourth Amendment analysis is to identify the search or seizure at issue. What petitioners, the Court, and to a lesser extent the concurrence really object to is not the urine testing, but the hospital's reporting of positive drug-test results to police. But the latter is obviously not a search. At most it may be a "derivative use of the product of a past unlawful search," which, of course, "works no new Fourth Amendment wrong" and "presents a question, not of rights, but of remedies." United States v. Calandra, 414 U.S. 338, 354 (1974). There is only one act that could conceivably be regarded as a search of petitioners in the present case: the taking of the urine sample. I suppose the testing of that urine for traces of unlawful drugs could be considered a search of sorts, but the Fourth Amendment protects only against searches of citizens' "persons, houses, papers, and effects"; and it is entirely unrealistic to regard urine as one of the "effects" (i.e., part of the property) of the person who has passed and abandoned it. . . . Some would argue, I suppose, that testing of the urine is prohibited by some generalized privacy right "emanating" from the "penumbras" of the Constitution (a question that is not before us); but it is not even arguable that the testing of urine that has been lawfully obtained is a Fourth Amendment search. (I may add that, even if it were, the factors legitimizing the taking of the sample, which I discuss below, would likewise legitimize the testing of it.)

It is rudimentary Fourth Amendment law that a search which has been consented to is not unreasonable. There is no contention in the present case that the urine samples were extracted forcibly. The only conceivable bases for saying that they were obtained without consent are the contentions (1) that the consent was coerced by the patients' need for medical treatment, (2) that the consent was uninformed because the patients were not told that the tests would include testing for drugs, and (3) that the consent was uninformed because the patients were not told that the results of the tests would be provided to the police. . . .

Under our established Fourth Amendment law, the last two contentions would not suffice, even without reference to the special-needs doctrine. The Court's analogizing of this case to Miranda v. Arizona, 384 U.S. 436 (1966), and its claim that "standards of knowing waiver" apply are flatly contradicted by our jurisprudence, which shows that using lawfully (but deceivingly) obtained material for purposes other than those represented, and giving that material or information derived from it to the police, is not unconstitutional. . . .

Until today, we have never held — or even suggested — that material which a person voluntarily entrusts to someone else cannot be given by that person to the police, and used for whatever evidence it may contain. Without so much as discussing the point, the Court today opens a hole in our Fourth Amendment jurisprudence, the size and shape of which is entirely indeterminate. Today's holding would be remarkable enough if the confidential relationship violated by the police conduct were at least one protected by state law. It would be surprising to learn, for example, that in a State which recognizes a spousal evidentiary privilege the police cannot use evidence obtained from a cooperating husband or wife. But today's holding goes even beyond that, since there does not exist any physician-patient privilege in South Carolina. See, e.g., Peagler v. Atlantic Coast R.R. Co., 101 S.E.2d 821 (S.C. 1958). Since the Court declines even to discuss the issue, it leaves law enforcement officials entirely in the dark as to when they can use incriminating evidence obtained from "trusted" sources. Presumably the lines will be drawn in the case-by-case development of a whole new branch of Fourth Amendment jurisprudence, taking yet another social judgment (which confidential relationships ought not be invaded by the police) out of democratic control, and confiding it to the uncontrolled judgment of this Court — uncontrolled because there is no common-law precedent to guide it. I would adhere to our established law, which says that information obtained through violation of a relationship of trust is obtained consensually, and is hence not a search.

II

I think it clear, therefore, that there is no basis for saying that obtaining of the urine sample was unconstitutional. The special-needs doctrine is thus quite irrelevant, since it operates only to validate searches and seizures that are otherwise unlawful. In the ensuing discussion, however, I shall assume (contrary to legal precedent) that the taking of the urine sample was (either because of the patients' necessitous circumstances, or because of failure to disclose that the urine would be tested for drugs, or because of failure to disclose that the results of the test would be given to the police) coerced. Indeed, I shall even assume (contrary to common sense) that the testing of the urine constituted an unconsented search of the patients' effects. On those assumptions, the special-needs doctrine would become relevant; and, properly applied, would validate what was done here.

The conclusion of the Court that the special-needs doctrine is inapplicable rests upon its contention that respondents "undertook to obtain [drug] evidence from their patients" not for any medical purpose, but "for the specific purpose of incriminating those patients." In other words, the purported medical rationale was merely a pretext; there was no special need. . . . This contention contradicts the District Court's finding of fact that the goal of the testing policy "was not to arrest patients but to facilitate their treatment and protect both the mother and unborn child." . . . This finding is binding upon us unless clearly erroneous, see Fed. Rule

Civ. Proc. 52(a). Not only do I find it supportable; I think any other finding would have to be overturned.

The cocaine tests started in April 1989, neither at police suggestion nor with police involvement. Expectant mothers who tested positive were referred by hospital staff for substance-abuse treatment — an obvious health benefit to both mother and child. . . . And, since "infants whose mothers abuse cocaine during pregnancy are born with a wide variety of physical and neurological abnormalities," . . . which require medical attention, . . . the tests were of additional medical benefit in predicting needed postnatal treatment for the child. Thus, in their origin — before the police were in any way involved — the tests had an immediate, not merely an "ultimate," . . . purpose of improving maternal and infant health. Several months after the testing had been initiated, a nurse discovered that local police were arresting pregnant users of cocaine for child abuse, the hospital's general counsel wrote the county solicitor to ask "what, if anything, our Medical Center needs to do to assist you in this matter," . . . (South Carolina law requires child abuse to be reported, see S.C. Code Ann. §20-7-510), the police suggested ways to avoid tainting evidence, and the hospital and police in conjunction used the testing program as a means of securing what the Court calls the "ultimate" health benefit of coercing drug-abusing mothers into drug treatment. . . . Why would there be any reason to believe that, once this policy of using the drug tests for their "ultimate" health benefits had been adopted, use of them for their original, immediate, benefits somehow disappeared, and testing somehow became in its entirety nothing more than a "pretext" for obtaining grounds for arrest? On the face of it, this is incredible. The only evidence of the exclusively arrest-related purpose of the testing adduced by the Court is that the police-cooperation policy itself does not describe how to care for cocaine-exposed infants. . . . But of course it does not, since that policy, adopted months after the cocaine testing was initiated, had as its only health object the "ultimate" goal of inducing drug treatment through threat of arrest. Does the Court really believe (or even hope) that, once invalidation of the program challenged here has been decreed, drug testing will cease?

In sum, there can be no basis for the Court's purported ability to "distinguish this case from circumstances in which physicians or psychologists, in the course of ordinary medical procedures aimed at helping the patient herself, come across information that . . . is subject to reporting requirements," . . . unless it is this: That the addition of a law-enforcement-related purpose to a legitimate medical purpose destroys applicability of the "special-needs" doctrine. But that is quite impossible, since the special-needs doctrine was developed, and is ordinarily employed, precisely to enable searches by law enforcement officials who, of course, ordinarily have a law enforcement objective. . . .

As I indicated at the outset, it is not the function of this Court — at least not in Fourth Amendment cases — to weigh petitioners' privacy interest against the State's interest in meeting the crisis of "crack babies" that developed in the late 1980's. I cannot refrain from observing, however, that the outcome of a wise weighing of those interests is by no means clear. The initial goal of the doctors and nurses who conducted cocaine-testing in this case was to refer pregnant drug addicts to treatment centers, and to prepare for necessary treatment of their possibly affected children. When the doctors and nurses agreed to the program providing test results to the police, they did so because (in addition to the fact that child abuse was required by law to be reported) they wanted to use the sanction of arrest as a strong incentive for their addicted patients to undertake drug-addiction treatment. And the police themselves used it for that benign purpose, as is shown by the fact that only 30 of 253 women testing positive for cocaine were ever arrested, and only 2 of those prosecuted. . . . It would not be unreasonable to conclude that today's judgment, authorizing the assessment of damages against the county solicitor and individual doctors and nurses who participated in the program, proves once again that no good deed goes unpunished.

But as far as the Fourth Amendment is concerned: There was no unconsented search in this case. And if there was, it would have been validated by the special-needs doctrine. For these reasons, I respectfully dissent.

Notes

1. Criminal Prosecutions of Drug-Abusing Pregnant Women. While the degree of harm is still under study, there is no doubt that drug abuse by a pregnant woman enhances certain serious risks to the unborn child. Justice Kennedy in his concurring opinion in *Ferguson* summarizes some of the recent research:

> . . . Infants whose mothers abuse cocaine during pregnancy are born with a wide variety of physical and neurological abnormalities. See Chiriboga, Brust, Bateman, & Hauser, Dose-Response Effect of Fetal Cocaine Exposure on Newborn Neurologic Function, 103 Pediatrics 79 (1999) (finding that, compared with unexposed infants, cocaine-exposed infants experienced higher rates of intrauterine growth retardation, smaller head circumference, global hypertonia, coarse tremor, and extensor leg posture). Prenatal exposure to cocaine can also result in developmental problems which persist long after birth. See Arendt, Angelopoulos, Salvator, & Singer, Motor Development of Cocaine-exposed Children at Age Two Years, 103 Pediatrics 86 (1999) (concluding that, at two years of age, children who were exposed to cocaine in utero exhibited significantly less fine and gross motor development than those not so exposed); Chasnoff et al., Prenatal Exposure to Cocaine and Other Drugs: Outcome at Four to Six Years, 846 Annals of the New York Academy of Sciences 314, 319-320 (J. Harvey and B. Kosofsky eds. 1998) (finding that

four to six year olds who were exposed to cocaine in utero exhibit higher instances of depression, anxiety, social, thought, and attention problems, and delinquent and aggressive behaviors than their unexposed counterparts). There can be no doubt that a mother's ingesting this drug can cause tragic injury to a fetus and a child. There should be no doubt that South Carolina can impose punishment upon an expectant mother who has so little regard for her own unborn that she risks causing him or her lifelong damage and suffering. The State, by taking special measures to give rehabilitation and training to expectant mothers with this tragic addiction or weakness, acts well within its powers and its civic obligations.

121 S.Ct. 1281, 1294-1295 (Kennedy, J., concurring)

In light of these risks, pregnant women have been criminally charged under two different theories: delivery of a controlled substance to a minor and child abuse or endangerment. Courts have rejected the drug delivery theory on the grounds that the statutes under which charges were brought were not intended to apply to delivery of a controlled substance to a minor by way of the umbilical cord. See, e.g., Johnson v. State, 602 So. 2d 1288 (Fla. 1992); People v. Hardy, 469 N.W.2d 50 (Mich. Ct. App. 1990); see also State v. Luster, 419 S.E.2d 32 (Ga. Ct. App. 1992) ("person" does not include fetus). Most courts have also rejected the child abuse theory, on the grounds that a fetus is not a living child or "person" protected by child abuse statutes. See, e.g., Sheriff v. Encoe, 885 P.2d 596 (Nev. 1994); Commonwealth v. Welch, 864 S.W.2d 280 (Ky. 1993); State v. Gray, 584 N.E.2d 710 (Ohio 1993); Reyes v. Superior Court, 141 Cal. Rptr. 912 (Ct. App. 1977).

One state supreme court has upheld such a prosecution. See Whitner v. State, 492 S.E.2d 777 (S.C. 1997), cert. denied, 523 U.S. 1145 (1998). In *Whitner*, the defendant pled guilty to charges of child neglect after smoking crack while pregnant, on advice of counsel who promised to get her into a drug treatment plan so that she could be reunited with her children. The judge, however, sentenced her to an eight-year prison term. After serving 19 months of her sentence, the local ACLU managed to get her conviction set aside, on grounds the statute under which she was convicted punished the unlawful neglect of a child, not a fetus. See Dorothy E. Roberts, Unshackling Black Motherhood, 95 Mich. L. Rev. 938, 944-945 (1997). In reinstating the conviction, the *Whitner* court reasoned that if wrongful death claims involving viable fetuses and criminal prosecutions for feticide against parties other than the mother can be sustained, it was not "absurd," as the defendant had contended, to sustain prosecutions of drug-abusing mothers as well. 492 S.E.2d at 781-782. The court did not feel itself bound by the fact that the legislature failed on 11 occasions to pass proposed bills specifically addressing drug abuse during pregnancy. Id. at 787 (Moore, J., dissenting). South Carolina continues "a prosecutorial campaign against pregnant crack addicts." See Roberts, Unshackling Black Motherhood, supra, at 941-946.

While most prosecutors have not been successful in using criminal actions against drug-abusing pregnant women, some commentators strongly favor it. "If substance abuse during pregnancy is prosecuted," the argument goes, "society sends out a clear message that it will condemn and punish those responsible for the harms caused by the substance abuse. . . . [P]rospective jail terms will motivate drug-addicted women either to seek treatment prior to becoming pregnant, or if already pregnant, to obtain what treatment is still available to them before giving birth and to continue treatment for future pregnancies after delivery." Michael T. Flannery, Court-Ordered Prenatal Intervention: A Final Means to the End of Gestational Substance Abuse, 30 J. Fam. L. 519, 574-575 (1991-1992). Other commentators urging aggressive use of criminal child abuse statutes include Kathryn Schierl, Note, A Proposal to Illinois Legislators: Revise the Illinois Criminal Code to Include Criminal Sanctions Against Prenatal Substance Abusers, 23 J. Marshall L. Rev. 393 (1990); Sam S. Balisy, Note, Maternal Substance Abuse: The Need to Provide Legal Protection for the Fetus, 60 S. Cal. L. Rev. 1209 (1987); Tom Rickhoff & Curtis L. Cukjati, Protecting the Fetus from Maternal Drug and Alcohol Abuse: A Proposal for Texas, 21 St. Mary's L.J. 259 (1989).

Does this reasoning extend to criminalizing abuse of alcohol or tobacco during pregnancy? See James Drago, One for My Baby, One More for the Road: Legislation and Counseling to Prevent Prenatal Exposure to Alcohol, 7 Cardozo Women's L.J. 163 (2001) (reviewing legislation and case law, and recommending a combination of "a low level of criminal sanctions" and education); Lynn M. Paltrow, When Becoming Pregnant Is a Crime, 9 Crim. Just. Ethics 41, 43 (1990) (describing prosecutions of pregnant women for activities such as drinking alcohol and having sex against a doctor's advice). Research shows that among women who drink at the same rate, children born to low-income women have a 70.9 percent rate of fetal alcohol syndrome, compared to a 4.5 percent rate for those of upper-income women. Roberts, Unshackling Black Motherhood, supra, at 953 n.93 (citing Nesrin Bingol et al., The Influence of Socioeconomic Factors on the Occurrence of Fetal Alcohol Syndrome, 6 Advances in Alcohol & Substance Abuse 105 (1987)). The difference is explained on the basis of the better nutrition of the wealthier women. Id. at 953-954. A Northwestern University study also suggests that outcomes in pregnancies complicated by cocaine abuse may be improved by comprehensive prenatal care. Id. at 953 (citing Scott N. MacGregor et al., Cocaine Abuse During Pregnancy: Correlation Between Prenatal Care and Perinatal Outcome, 74 Obstetrics & Gynecology 882, 885 (1989)). How, if at all, does this research affect your analysis of the policy issues entailed in regulating pregnant women who abuse alcohol or cocaine?

How about driving too fast when pregnant, or failing to wear a seat belt, or working against the advice of one's doctor? If the law regulates abuse of cocaine during pregnancy, should it also regulate these activities?

See Dawn Johnsen, From Driving to Drugs: Governmental Regulation of Pregnant Women's Lives After *Webster*, 138 U. Pa. L. Rev. 179 (1989) (arguing on constitutional and policy grounds that in all of these contexts the government should treat a pregnant woman as a single legal entity and help her to further her own strong interest in a healthy baby, rather than as a separate legal entity from the fetus).

Since the difficulty with prosecuting drug-abusing women has been the absence of clear legislative intent to cover drug abuse during pregnancy as a form of drug delivery or a form of child endangerment, presumably a statute clearly directed at such conduct would provide a basis for such prosecutions. Efforts to pass specific legislation directed at pregnant women have been largely unsuccessful, however. Does this surprise you?

What do you make of the fact that despite similar rates of substance abuse, black women are ten times more likely than white women to be reported to government authorities? See Roberts, Unshackling Black Motherhood, supra, at 947-948 (citing Ira J. Chasnoff et al., The Prevalence of Illicit-Drug or Alcohol Use During Pregnancy and Discrepancies in Mandatory Reporting in Pinellas County, Florida, 322 New Eng. J. Med. 1201, 1204 (1990)).

Can the state's coercive powers be effective in changing the behavior of pregnant women and causing them to act more responsibly? Roberts argues that use of the law punitively is counterproductive in that it deters pregnant women from seeking much-needed medical treatment. In this regard, the state treats women as having the autonomy to choose to use, or not to use, drugs when the only choice they may experience is whether to seek, or not to seek, drug abuse treatment. Even so, is it clear that use of the criminal law in this context will not have *any* effect on deterring drug abuse by pregnant women?

What about the role of doctors in the prosecution of pregnant women? Viewing the issue in the larger context of all forms of legal intervention that might be sought by doctors to compel pregnant women to accept recommended medical treatment on behalf of their unborn children, Michelle Oberman argues that "maternal-fetal" conflicts are actually conflicts between the women and their doctors, in which the doctors violate their fiduciary duty to their pregnant patients. See Oberman, Mothers and Doctors' Orders: Unmasking the Doctor's Fiduciary Role in Maternal-Fetal Conflicts, 94 Nw. U. L. Rev. 451 (2000). Does this argument apply also to interventions initiated by doctors against their drug-abusing pregnant patients? Or should this be a special case?

Drug-addicted women seem to epitomize the paradoxical nature of choice displayed in many other contexts in this chapter: the legal constraints placed upon them as if they were autonomous actors activate decisions other than those contemplated by the law (i.e., avoiding medical care). Pragmatically, what legal approach in this area best recognizes the realities of drug-addicted women? For analysis of how the law might incorporate a treatment-centered, rather than a punitive, model, see note 4, infra.

2. Probationary Conditions and Civil Commitment. An alternative that some courts have pursued for controlling the reproductive decisions of women who are deemed irresponsible with respect to such matters is to order a woman not to become pregnant as a condition of probation. In some cases, such conditions have been imposed for crimes unrelated to the woman's childbearing or childrearing conduct. See Stacey L. Arthur, The Norplant Prescription: Birth Control, Woman Control, or Crime Control?, 40 UCLA L. Rev. 1, 11-13 (1992) (describing California trial court case in which a defendant was ordered "not to get pregnant" as condition of probation for drug-related offenses). These orders have not fared well on appeal if the condition is not reasonably related to the crime committed or to the goal of rehabilitation. See, e.g., Thomas v. State, 519 So. 2d 1113 (Fla. Dist. Ct. App. 1988) (invalidating probationary condition that defendant not become pregnant unless married, after conviction for grand theft and battery); State v. Norman, 484 So. 2d 953 (La. Ct. App. 1986) (same, after conviction for forgery); People v. Dominguez, 64 Cal. Rptr. 290 (Ct. App. 1967) (same, after conviction for second-degree robbery).

When the underlying conviction is for child abuse or neglect, some trial courts have ordered women, as a condition of probation, either not to conceive or to use birth control. Appellate courts have overturned many of these cases as well, either on privacy grounds or on the grounds that such conditions are not reasonably related to the legitimate purposes of probation. See Kansas v. Mosburg, 768 P.2d 313 (Kan. Ct. App. 1989) (probationary condition that defendant refrain from getting pregnant violates defendant's privacy interests); People v. Pointer, 199 Cal. Rptr. 357 (Ct. App. 1984) (invalidating no-conception term of probation for defendant convicted of felony child endangerment after her children were severely and irreparably harmed by her fanatical adherence to macrobiotic diet, on grounds less restrictive alternatives were available, including periodic pregnancy tests followed by prenatal monitoring if she became pregnant, and removal of the child from the defendant after birth if circumstances warranted); Rodriguez v. State, 378 So. 2d 7 (Fla. Dist. Ct. App. 1979) (condition that defendant not marry or become pregnant did nothing to decrease possibility of further child abuse); State v. Livingston, 372 N.E.2d 1335 (Ohio Ct. App. 1976) (probationary condition that defendant not have another child violates defendant's constitutional privacy rights and not reasonably related to future criminality).

In some cases, defendants have declined to appeal for fear of receiving a harsher penalty. See Arthur, supra, at 11-21. What outcome would you expect on appeal in a Tennessee case in which a woman and her husband were both convicted of molesting the woman's two sons and ordered to serve 20 years in prison, with the alternative of probation for both if the woman agreed to sterilization by tubal ligation? The woman accepted the terms. See AP, Woman Who Molested Sons Agrees to Sterilization, N.Y. Times, Jan. 31, 1993, at A29. If appeal had been sought, does the woman have a sex discrimination claim?

By the end of 1993, six women convicted of child abuse or child abandonment had been ordered to use Norplant as a condition of probation. See Sarah Gill, Discrimination, Historical Abuse, and the New Norplant Problem, 16 Women's Rts. L. Rep. 43, 46 (Fall 1994) (citing Women's Legal Defense Fund, Norplant Legislation and Litigation — 1993 (Jan. 1994)). (Norplant is discussed earlier in this chapter, at pages 1046-1047.) Is it in women's interests, at least those without the relevant health risks, to be able to choose probation on condition that they receive the Norplant treatment, after appropriate notice and consent? Defendants may well find these conditions preferable to the sentencing alternatives available to them. See Arthur, supra, at 95 (probational conditions requiring use of birth control should be allowed in some circumstances, as long as special care is taken to ensure that defendants understand and genuinely consent); Thomas E. Bartrum, Note, Birth Control as a Condition of Probation — A New Weapon in the War Against Child Abuse, 80 Ky. L.J. 1037, 1039 (1991-1992) (imposition of birth control as a condition of probation "can represent a legitimate balance between a state's interest in the protection of society and a probationer's right of procreative liberty"). Most commentators, however, have opposed the imposition of probationary conditions, especially Norplant. See, e.g., Albiston, supra (the Norplant condition systematically reinforces social biases and racial stereotypes of poor women of color as "welfare queens" and inadequate mothers); Darci Elaine Burrell, The Norplant Solution: Norplant and the Control of African-American Motherhood, 5 UCLA Women's L.J. 401 (1995) (Norplant proposals directed at curtailing reproduction by poor women based on same view of African-American women as the views upon which slavery, the eugenics movement, and the sterilization abuses of the 1970s were based); Tracy Ballard, The Norplant Conditions: One Step Forward or Two Steps Back?, 16 Harv. Women's L.J. 139 (1993) (Norplant conditions violate equal protection by discriminating on the basis of gender, race, and status, and also the Eighth Amendment's prohibition against cruel and unusual punishment); Megan J. Ballard, Comment, A Practical Analysis of the Constitutional and Legal Infirmities of Norplant as a Condition of Probation, 7 Wis. Women's L.J. 85 (1992-1993) (Norplant condition constitutes possible violation of constitutional rights of privacy, free exercise of religion, equal protection, and freedom from cruel and unusual punishment, and also may violate common law right to refuse medical treatment).

What about a form of "civil commitment" for women who are in grave danger of drug abuse during a pregnancy? In 1998, South Dakota became the first state to require pregnant women who abuse alcohol or drugs to be taken into custody and undergo mandatory rehabilitation. Wisconsin soon followed, and several other states introduced legislation adopting a similar approach to the problem. See Christa J. Richer, Note, Fetal Abuse Law: Punitive Approach and the Honorable Status of Motherhood, 50 Syracuse L. Rev. 1127 (2000). An Illinois court ordered a 25-year-old pregnant cocaine addict to a drug treatment center for the duration of her pregnancy when she failed to make regular visits to the center in violation of her probation for earlier charges of disorderly conduct. See Court Confines Pregnant Woman to Drug Treatment Center, 3 Reproductive Rights Update (No. 8), Apr. 19, 1991, at 5. Does such an approach present any different issues from those presented by imposing treatment, or isolation, as a condition of probation? For the case in favor of the approach, see Deborah Mathieu, Mandating Treatment for Pregnant Substance Abusers: A Compromise, 14 Pol. & Life Sciences 199, 204 (Aug. 1995) (recommending use of traditional civil commitment process, after refusal to receive treatment voluntarily in an outpatient program). Courts have not been as enthusiastic. See, e.g., State ex rel. Angela M.W. v. Kruzicki, 561 N.W.2d 729 (Wis. 1997) (state was not authorized, under statute protecting child in need of protection, to keep pregnant woman who had repeatedly used cocaine in protective custody).

3. Civil Child Abuse and Neglect. Use of a state's civil child abuse and neglect statutes is an alternative to criminal measures designed to control drug abuse by pregnant women. However these statutes, too, will be applied only if the courts conclude they were intended to apply to prenatal conduct. See, e.g., In re Valerie D., 613 A.2d 748, 755, 758-762 (Conn. 1992) (maternal substance abuse constitutes parental neglect, but legislature did not intend for the termination statute to apply to prenatal parental conduct). Legislatures, again, are free to amend their statutes. Some have done so. See, e.g., Fla. Stat. Ann. §415.503(9)(g)(1) (West 1998) (neglect of child includes "[u]se by the mother of a controlled substance or alcohol during pregnancy when the child, at birth, is demonstrably adversely affected by such usage"); 705 Ill. Comp. Stat. Ann. §405/2-18(c) & (d) (West 1999) (proof of fetal alcohol syndrome or "a medical diagnosis at birth of withdrawal symptoms from narcotics or barbituates" is prima facie evidence of child neglect); Nev. Rev. Stat. Ann. §432B.330(1)(b) (Michie 2000) (child is "in need of protection" if "he is suffering from congenital drug addiction or the fetal alcohol syndrome, because of the faults or habits of a person responsible for his welfare").

If drug abuse during pregnancy constitutes child neglect, what dispositions are most appropriate? Removal of the child from the parent and even termination of parental rights may seem the most likely options. What will happen then, however, to the child? Babies who test positive for drugs are poor health risks, and disproportionately nonwhite, which means they are not strong adoption candidates and may face repeated recycling through the overloaded foster care system. See Michelle Oberman, Sex, Drugs, Pregnancy, and the Law: Rethinking the Problems of Pregnant Women Who Use Drugs, 43 Hastings L.J. 505, 525 (1992); see also Bonnie I. Robin-Vergeer, The Problem of the Drug-Exposed Newborn: A Return to Principled Intervention, 42 Stan. L. Rev. 745 (1990) (analyzing intervention alternatives for babies born with positive drug tests, based on various risk factors).

4. The Treatment Alternative. Several of the women facing well-publicized prosecutions for criminal child abuse for using drugs during pregnancy had sought treatment during pregnancy but found either that waiting lists were long or that the drug treatment programs would not accept pregnant women. See Eileen McNamara, Fetal Endangerment Cases on the Rise, Boston Globe, Oct. 3, 1989, at 1. A survey of 85 percent of the drug treatment programs in New York City found that 54 percent categorically exclude pregnant women, 67 percent exclude pregnant women on Medicaid, and 87 percent have no services for crack-addicted pregnant women on Medicaid. Janet R. Fink, Effects of Crack and Cocaine on Infants: A Brief Review of the Literature, 24 Clearinghouse Rev. 460, 463-464 (Special Issue 1990) (citing testimony given to the House Select Committee on Children, Youth, and Families by Dr. Wendy Chavkin).

At least one lawsuit has challenged successfully the practices of substance abuse treatment programs that exclude pregnant women as sex-based discrimination under a state public accommodations statute. See Elaine W. v. Joint Diseases North General Hosp., Inc., 613 N.E.2d 523 (N.Y. 1993). In *Elaine W.*, the hospital had claimed that there were medical reasons for not providing drug detoxification treatment to pregnant women, but the court held, in the face of contrary evidence, that the defense was inadequate. A copy of the *amicus* brief filed in the case on behalf of the American Public Health Association has been published. See Nadine Taub et al., The Case of Elaine W. v. Joint Diseases North General Hospital, Inc.: When Treating Women Equally Means Equal Access to Treatment, 3 Colum. J. Gender & L. 301 (1992).

In partial response to this problem, Congress passed the Alcohol, Drug Abuse, and Mental Health Administration Reorganization Act, Pub. L. No. 102-321, 106 Stat. 323 (codified as amended in scattered sections of 42 U.S.C.A. §§201-300 (West Supp. 1993)). This legislation expands block grants provided to states for drug treatment programs, including money targeted at addressing the particular needs of pregnant, drug-addicted women. The Act is discussed in Alys I. Cohen, Challenging Pregnancy Discrimination in Drug Treatment: Does the ADAMHA Reorganization Act Provide an Answer?, 6 Yale J.L. & Feminism 91 (1994). Some states, including Maryland, Oregon, Washington, and Wisconsin, earlier had enacted legislation to target treatment services for drug-addicted pregnant women. These programs are discussed in Page McGuire Linden, Drug

Addiction During Pregnancy: A Call for Increased Social Responsibility, 4 Am. U. J. Gender & L. 105, 136-137 (1995).

It remains to be seen how realistic alternative drug treatment plans are. The cost for drug treatment programs for a pregnant cocaine addict is staggering; in the Chicago area, the minimum price tag is $12,000 per month, and none of the programs investigated accepted Medicaid. Michelle Oberman, Sex, Drugs, Pregnancy, and the Law: Rethinking the Problems of Pregnant Women Who Use Drugs, 43 Hastings L.J. 505, 517 (1992). Addicts are unlikely to have private insurance that covers these expenses. Id. at 544 (citing Committee to Study Outreach for Prenatal Care, Institute of Medicine, Prenatal Care: Reaching Mothers, Reaching Infants 56 (Sarah B. Brown ed., 1988) (more than a quarter of the women in this country have no health insurance for maternity care; two-thirds of these women lack any medical insurance whatsoever)).

Cost is not the only impediment. Even advocates of the treatment alternatives point out that "there are few established methods for treating the addictions themselves, let alone for addressing the effect on the fetus of withdrawal from these drugs." Id. at 516. In addition to the medical complications associated with drug addiction, including a higher risk of contracting HIV, pregnant addicts are said to be poor patients, for example, missing almost 38 percent of their scheduled medical appointments. Id. at 518-519.

On the other hand, there seems little doubt that prenatal treatment for a drug-addicted woman is highly beneficial. From an economic perspective, the National Association for Perinatal Addiction Research and Education (NAPARE) estimates the prenatal costs of a cocaine-addicted woman at $7,000 (including maternal hospital stay and two days of neonatal care), while the costs incurred by an addict who fails to obtain prenatal care average $31,000, due to the increased need for neonatal intensive care. Oberman, supra, at 514-515 (citing Missing Links: Coordinating Federal Drug Policy for Women, Infants and Children: Hearing Before the Senate Comm. on Governmental Affairs, 101st Cong., 1st Sess. 75 (1989) (statement of Dr. Ira Chasnoff, president, NAPARE)).

Further commentary favoring treatment approaches for drug-abusing pregnant women include David C. Brody & Heidee McMillin, Combating Fetal Substance Abuse and Governmental Foolhardiness Through Collaborative Linkages, Therapeutic Jurisprudence and Common Sense: Helping Women Help Themselves, 12 Hastings Women's L.J. 243 (2001) (advocating "therapeutic jurisprudence" model); Dawn Johnsen, Shared Interests: Promoting Healthy Births Without Sacrificing Women's Liberty, 43 Hastings L.J. 569 (1992) (arguing for a "facilitative" approach).

Putting Theory into Practice

6-8. A foster parent who often cares for babies born to drug-addicted mothers decides to institute a novel program to prevent the birth of more drug-affected children, by founding a private nonprofit organization called Children Requiring A Caring Kommunity (C.R.A.C.K.) with the objective of "offering effective prevention measures to reduce the tragedy of numerous drug affected pregnancies." C.R.A.C.K. offers $200 to females who promise to be sterilized or receive long-term birth control. The cash payment is made upon the showing of a certificate that the procedure has been performed. Is there any legal theory that would preclude this transaction? See Juli Horka-Ruiz, Note, Preventing the Birth of Drug-Addicted Babies Through Contract: An Examination of the C.R.A.C.K. Organization, 7 Wm. & Mary J. Women & L. 473 (2001) (arguing that the C.R.A.C.K. program creates a legally enforceable contract); Jennifer Mott Johnson, Reproductive Ability for Sale, Do I Hear $200?: Private Cash-for-Contraception Agreements as an Alternative to Maternal Substance Abuse, 43 Ariz. L. Rev. 205 (2001) (weighing competing constitutional and policy considerations and concluding that the scheme has merit). Is this any different or better than the court-mandated probation conditions discussed previously?

6-9. In February 1994, researchers at the National Institute of Allergy and Infectious Diseases determined that a regimen of antepartum, intrapartum, and neonatal AZT treatment reduced the rate of vertical (mother-to-child) HIV transmission by approximately two-thirds, from 25.05 percent to 8.3 percent. See Edward M. Connor et al., Reduction of Maternal-Infant Transmission of Human Immunodeficiency Virus Type I with Zidovudine Treatment, 331 New Eng. J. Med. 1173, 1176, 1178 (1994), cited in David Lowe, HIV Study Raises Ethical Concerns for the Treatment of Pregnant Women, 10 Berkeley Women's L.J. 176, 176, 178 (1995). On the basis of this research, the legislative committee proposes to mandate AZT treatment of pregnant HIV-positive women. Through further research, you determine that (1) the prognosis is probably not as good as the figures above indicate, since women in more advanced stages of the disease, and those with more prolonged exposure to AZT, were not included in the study; (2) the long-term effects of AZT are not known, but potentially include cancer and adverse effects on certain tissues and the reproductive system; (3) the use of AZT during pregnancy could create a resistance to the drug, which may lessen the drug's therapeutic benefit for the woman when it is needed for her own health; and (4) the measure will disproportionately affect women of color, who comprise 73 percent of all women diagnosed with AIDS in the United States. See Lowe, supra, at 176-179. On the basis of this information, how would you analyze the proposed mandatory treatment proposal? Compare Colin Crawford, An Argument for Universal Pediatric

HIV Testing, Counseling and Treatment, 3 Cardozo Women's L.J. 31 (1996) with Elizabeth B. Cooper, Why Mandatory HIV Testing of Pregnant Women and Newborns Must Fail: A Legal, Historical, and Public Policy Analysis, 3 Cardozo Women's L.J. 13 (1996) and Jean R. Sternlight, Mandatory Non-Anonymous Testing of Newborns for HIV: Should It Ever Be Allowed?, 27 J. Marshall L. Rev. 373 (1994).

6-10.　Since the age of 13, Jewel has suffered from cancer, for which she underwent major surgery several times, together with multiple radiation treatments and chemotherapy. At age 17, while her cancer was temporarily in remission, she became pregnant. During the 25th week of her pregnancy, she was diagnosed with an inoperable tumor in her right lung, from which her health quickly declined. Informed of her options, Jewel agreed to "palliative treatment" to extend her life until her 28th week of pregnancy to give her fetus a better chance of survival. Jewel expressed her wish "to live long enough to hold that baby." Jewel declined even more rapidly than was predicted, however, and in her 26th week, the attending doctors sought to deliver the fetus surgically. The doctors believed that while a "normal" 26-week fetus had a 50-60 percent chance of survival, the chance of survival of Jewel's fetus would be less than 20 percent because of the mother's condition and that the chances dropped virtually to zero if the surgery was not done immediately. Doctors also believed that the mother would probably die in the next couple of days without surgical intervention to deliver the child and that the surgery would accelerate her death. Jewel is semi-comatose and not competent to give consent to immediate surgery.

What legal standard should determine whether surgery should be permitted by a court in this case? What additional facts would be needed to apply this standard?

What if Jewel made it clear that she would not consent to surgery before the 28th week? Do the circumstances presented — with surgery, the fetus's chance of survival moves from zero to slight; Jewel's death is accelerated from two days to one — justify surgery over her objections? See In re A.C., 573 A.2d 1235 (D.C. 1990). Sources on forced Caesarean sections are listed on pages 1047-1048. On the father's asserted rights, see the discussion at pages 1080-1081.

C. ECONOMIC AUTONOMY AND WOMEN'S POVERTY

Martha Albertson Fineman, Cracking the Foundational Myths: Independence, Autonomy, and Self-Sufficiency
8 Am. U. J. Gender Soc. Pol'y & L. 13, 14, 16-26 (2000)

. . . The assumed family is a specific ideological construct with a particular population and a gendered form that allows us to privatize individual dependency and pretend that it is not a public problem. [T]he gendered nature of this assumed family is essential to the maintenance and continuance of our foundational myths of individual independence, autonomy, and self-sufficiency. This assumed family also masks the dependency of society and all its public institutions on the uncompensated and unrecognized dependency work assigned to caretakers within the private family. . . .

Perhaps the most important task for those concerned with the welfare of poor mothers and their children, as well as other vulnerable members of society, is the articulation of a theory of collective responsibility for dependency. The idea of collective responsibility must be developed as a claim of "right" or entitlement to support and accommodation on the part of caretakers. It must be grounded on an appreciation of the value of caretaking labor. A further important concern is to ensure that any theory of collective responsibility not concede the right of collective control over individual intimate decisions, such as whether and when to reproduce or how to form one's family.

The rhetorical and ideological rigidity with which contemporary policy debates have been conducted makes the claim of collective responsibility a particularly difficult task at the end of the Twentieth Century. Core components of America's founding myths, such as the sacredness of individual independence, autonomy, and self-sufficiency have been ossified, used as substitutes for analysis, and eclipsed rather than illuminated debate.

I do not reject these core concepts. I do, however, insist that we have a responsibility to reexamine them in the context of our present society and the needs and aspirations of people today. . . .

Historic ideals of independence and self-sufficiency are complementary themes in our political discourse. These aspirational ideals are applied to individuals as well as to families. Their dichotomous terms, dependence and subsidy, are also complementary, viewed as occurring in tandem. Both dependence and subsidy have been successfully used in a simplistic and divisive manner by politicians, social conservatives, and advocates of small government to control and limit contemporary policy discussions.

Dependence is negatively compared with the desirable status of independence — subsidy with the meritorious self-sufficiency. Independence and self-sufficiency are set up as transcendent values, attainable aspirations for all members of society. Simplified pejorative notions of dependence and subsidy are joined, and condemnation or pity are considered appropriate responses for those unable to live up to the ideals, particularly those who are dependent and in need of subsidy. . . .

It is puzzling, as well as paradoxical, that the term dependency has such negative connotations. Its very existence prompts and justifies mean spirited and ill-conceived political responses, such as the recent welfare "reform." Far from being pathological, avoidable, and the result of individual failings, dependency is a universal and inevitable part of the human development. It is inherent in the human condition.

All of us were dependent as children, and many of us will be dependent as we age, become ill, or suffer disabilities. In this sense, dependency is "inevitable" and not deserving of condemnation or stigma. Note that the examples I have chosen to illustrate this category of inevitable dependency are biological or physical in nature. Biological dependencies, however, do not exhaust the potential range of situations of dependence. For example, in addition to biological dependence, one may be psychologically or emotionally dependent on others. In fact, these other forms of dependence may even accompany the physiological or biological dependence, which I have labeled inevitable. But economic, psychological, and emotional dependency are not generally understood to be universally experienced. As a result, assertions about their inevitability in each individual's life would be controversial. It is the characteristic of universality (which indisputably accompanies inevitable dependence) that is central to my argument for societal or collective responsibility. In other words, the realization that biological dependency is both inevitable and universal is theoretically important. Upon this foundational realization is built my claim for justice — the demand that society value and accommodate the labor done by the caretakers of inevitable dependants.

I argue that the caretaking work creates a collective or societal debt. Each and every member of society is obligated by this debt. Furthermore, this debt transcends individual circumstances. In other words, we need not be elderly, ill, or children any longer to be held individually responsible. Nor can we satisfy or discharge our collective responsibility within our individual, private families. Merely being financially generous with our own mothers or duly supporting our own wives will not suffice to satisfy our share of the societal debt generally owed to all caretakers.

My argument that the caretaking debt is a collective one is based on the fact that biological dependency is inherent to the human condition, and therefore, of necessity of collective or societal concern. Just as individual dependency needs must be met if an individual is to survive, collective dependency needs must be met if a society is to survive and perpetuate itself. The mandate that the state (collective society) respond to dependency, therefore, is not a matter of altruism or empathy (which are individual responses often resulting in charity), but one that is primary and essential because such a response is fundamentally society-preserving.

If infants or ill persons are not cared for, nurtured, nourished, and perhaps loved, they will perish. We can say, therefore, that they owe an individual debt to their individual caretakers. But the obligation is not theirs alone — nor is their obligation confined only to their own caretakers. A sense of social justice demands a broader sense of obligation. Without aggregate caretaking, there could be no society, so we might say that it is caretaking labor that produces and reproduces society. Caretaking labor provides the citizens, the workers, the voters, the consumers, the students, and others who populate society and its institutions. The uncompensated labor of caretakers is an unrecognized subsidy, not only to the individuals who directly receive it, but more significantly, to the entire society. . . .

Society preserving tasks, like dependency work, are commonly delegated. The delegation is accomplished through the establishment and maintenance of societal institutions. For example, the armed services are established to attend to the collective need for national defense. But delegation is not the same thing as abandonment. The armed services are structured simultaneously as both the responsibility of only some designated members (volunteers or draftees) and of all members of society (taxpayers and voters).

This dual and complementary responsibility is consistent with our deeply held beliefs about how rights and obligations are accrued and imposed in a just society — collective obligations have both an individual and a collective dimension. Certain members of society may be recruited, volunteer, or even be drafted for service, but they have a right to be compensated for their services from collective resources. They also have a right to the necessary tools to perform their assigned tasks and to guarantees that they will be protected by rules and policies that facilitate their performance. Caretakers should have the same right to have their society-preserving labor supported and facilitated. Provision of the means for their task should be considered the responsibility of the collective society.

Society has not, however, responded this way to caretaking. The most common form of social accommodation for dependency has been its assignment to the institution of the private family. Within that family, dependency has been further delegated as the individual responsibility of the family equivalent of volunteer or draftee — the person in the gendered role of mother (or grandmother or daughter or daughter-in-law or wife or sister). But the resources necessary for caretaking have not been considered to be the responsibility of the collective society. Instead, each individual private family is ideally and ideologically perceived as responsible for its own members and their dependency. A need to call on collective resources, such as welfare assistance, is considered a family as well as an individual failure, deserving of condemnation and stigma. . . .

The assignment of responsibility for the burdens of dependency to the family in the first instance, and within the family to women, operates in an unjust manner because this arrangement has significant negative material consequences for the caretaker. This obvious observation allows me to introduce an additional, but often overlooked, form of dependency into the argument — "derivative dependency." Derivative dependency arises on the part of the person who assumes responsibility for the care of the inevitable dependent person. I refer to this form of dependency as derivative to capture the very simple point that those who care for others are themselves dependent on resources in order to undertake that care. Caretakers have a need for monetary or material resources. They also need recourse to institutional supports and accommodation, a need for structural arrangements that facilitate caretaking.

Currently, neither the economic nor the structural supports for caretaking are adequate. Many caretakers and their dependents find themselves impoverished or severely economically compromised. Some of their economic problems stem from the fact that within families, caretaking work is unpaid and not considered worthy of social subsidies. There are also, however, direct costs associated with caretaking. Caretaking labor interferes with the pursuit and development of wage labor options. Caretaking labor saps energy and efforts from investment in career or market activities, those things that produce economic rewards. There are foregone opportunities and costs associated with caretaking, and even caretakers who work in the paid labor force typically have more tenuous ties to the public sphere because they must also accommodate caretaking demands in the private. These costs are not distributed among all beneficiaries of caretaking (institutional or individual). Unjustly, the major economic and career costs associated with caretaking are typically borne by the caretaker alone. . . .

As it now stands in this society, derivative dependents are expected to get both economic and structural resources within the family. The market is unresponsive and uninvolved, and the state is perceived as a last resort for financial resources, the refuge of the failed family. A caretaker who must resort to governmental assistance may do so only if she can demonstrate that she is needy in a highly stigmatized process. . . .

In popular and political discourse, the idea of "subsidy" is viewed as an equally negative companion to dependence, the opposite of the ideal of self-sufficiency. But a subsidy is nothing more than the process of allocating collective resources to some persons or endeavors rather than other persons or endeavors because a social judgment is made that they are in some way "entitled" or the subsidy is justified. Entitlement to subsidy is asserted through a variety of justifications, such as the status of the persons receiving the subsidy, their past contributions to the social good, or their needs. Often, subsidy is justified because of the position the subsidized persons hold or the potential value of the endeavor they have undertaken to the larger society.

Typically, subsidy is thought of as the provision of monetary or economic assistance. But subsidy can also be delivered through the organization of social structures and norms that create and enforce expectations. Taking this observation into account, along with the earlier discussion of inevitable and derivative dependency, it seems obvious that we must conclude that subsidy is also universal. We all exist in context, in social and cultural institutions, such as families, which facilitate, support and subsidize us and our endeavors.

In complex modern societies no one is self-sufficient, either economically or socially. We all live subsidized lives. Sometimes the benefits we receive are public and financial, such as in governmental direct transfer programs to certain individuals like farmers or sugar growers. Public subsidies can also be indirect, such as the benefits given in tax policy. Private economic subsidy systems work in the forms of foundations, religions and charities. But a subsidy can also be non-monetary, such as the subsidy provided by the uncompensated labor of others in caring for us and our dependency needs.

It seems clear that all of us receive one or the other or both types of subsidy throughout our lives. The interesting question in our subsidy shaped society, therefore, has to be why only some subsidies are differentiated and stigmatized while others are hidden. In substantial part, subsidies are hidden when they are not called subsidy (or welfare, or the dole), but termed "investments," "incentives," or "earned" when they are supplied by government, and called "gifts," "charity," or the product of familial "love" when they are contributions of caretaking labor. . . .

As a result of such discussion, the very terms of independence and self-sufficiency might well be redefined or re-imagined in the public mind. Independence is not the same as being unattached. Independence from subsidy and support is not attainable, nor is it desirable — we want and need the contexts that sustain us. A different understanding of independence is needed and attainable. Independence is gained when an individual has the basic resources that enable her or him to act consistent with the tasks and expectations imposed by the society. This form of independence should be every citizen's birthright, but independence in this sense can only be achieved when individual choices are relatively unconstrained by inequalities, particularly those inequalities that arise from poverty. Independence, as well as justice, requires that those who are assigned a vital societal function are also provided with the wherewithal to do those tasks. This is a state or collective responsibility and may not be relegated to potentially exploitative private institutions. . . .

Shannon DeRouselle, Welfare Reform and the Administration for Children's Services: Subjecting Children and Families to Poverty and Then Punishing Them for It
25 N.Y.U. Rev. L. & Soc. Change 403, 405-413, 416, 424-426, 432 (1999)

... I. Federal and New York Welfare Reform

Tammy is a single, twenty-three-year-old mother of two children, Carl Jr. and Keisha, and has intermittently received AFDC benefits for the past seven years. Tammy became pregnant with Carl Jr. during her junior year of high school, and she subsequently dropped out of school during the summer before her senior year to take care of him. Tammy received AFDC benefits for Carl Jr. while living at home with her mother and three younger sisters. Carl Jr.'s father provided no financial or emotional support. A year later, Tammy became pregnant again. Tammy's mother refused to allow her to continue to live at home since she already had several children to support herself. Keisha's father also was not present in his child's life. Tammy and her children moved to a one bedroom apartment in the projects of East New York, Brooklyn.

Tammy's welfare caseworker told her that she would have to find a job or would have her benefits terminated pursuant to the new welfare reform work requirements that went into effect earlier that month. Tammy searched for, and eventually found a job as a part-time salesclerk at a local supermarket. She has worked in the past, but since she has no high school diploma and few skills, her previous jobs paid only slightly above minimum wage. Her current job pays the same. Tammy works from 3 p.m. to 9 p.m., five days a week. Tammy's mother and sisters help her by looking after her children when she is at work. This is a blessing, because she could not otherwise afford child care. But after Tammy had worked a few weeks at the supermarket, her caseworker informed her that she no longer qualified for cash assistance since her earnings were now just above the income eligibility maximum for a family of three. Tammy, confused, did not understand why her benefits were canceled, especially after she had complied with the new welfare rules and began her life as an independent, self-sufficient mother. Assuming that her loss of benefits also meant that she no longer qualified for Food Stamps and Medicaid, Tammy did not reapply for either program and has struggled to make ends meet ever since.

A. The Personal Responsibility and Work Opportunity Act of 1996

In August 1996, the 104th Congress ended the Aid to Families with Dependent Children [(AFDC)] program, which since 1935 had provided cash benefits to economically disadvantaged families with children who lacked the support of one or both parents. Under AFDC, states were reimbursed by federal matching funds for a portion of the benefits provided to eligible families with dependent children. [The Personal Responsibility and Work Opportunity Act of 1996 (PRA), Pub. L. No. 104-193, 110 Stat. 2105 (1996)] replaced AFDC with block grants to states under the Temporary Assistance for Needy Families (TANF) program.

The PRA responded to several years of political debate over the direction of public assistance policy in the United States. Reform supporters celebrated the change as a much-needed renovation of a system that created a cycle of welfare dependency. The old system, critics asserted, offered aid recipients more incentives to continue receiving benefits than it did inducements to remove themselves from the welfare rolls. Opponents of the reform criticized some of its provisions for relying on misleading stereotypes and conjectures. These opponents argued that pervasive notions of the African-American "Welfare Queen" who has additional children in order to receive an extra welfare check from the government were warped and misleading.

In the legislation, Congress concluded that "marriage is the foundation of a successful society." Accordingly, PRA seeks to encourage marriage, prevent out-of-wedlock pregnancies and reduce out-of-wedlock births. In addition, PRA institutes work requirements that are intended to end the dependence of needy parents on government benefits by promoting job preparation and work.

PRA amendments transformed previous welfare law. The amendments most relevant to this article are the provisions for termination of benefits to families based on either new time limits or a parent's failure to comply with program rules. Under AFDC, states were restrained, with few exceptions, from terminating benefits on the basis of sanctions or time limits. Instead, prior law required states to provide aid to all individuals whose income and assets fell within a state's prescribed range in order for the state to continue to receive federal funding for AFDC. Benefits were thus akin to an entitlement to qualifying individuals; a family with dependent children was eligible for monetary benefits so long as it could demonstrate need.

The PRA required every state to design a plan outlining how it proposed to accomplish the goal of ending dependence on government benefits by promoting job preparation, work, and marriage. TANF provides each state increased flexibility to implement programs designed to achieve these objectives and address the individual needs of the particular state. The amount of each state's federal block grant is tied to its performance with respect to annual target rates of state employment percentages, teenage and out-of-wedlock pregnancy statistics, and welfare roll reduction figures set by Congress. However, the state block grant is capped at $16.4 billion and will not increase until fiscal year 2002. Hence, a state must reach these federal goals in order to avoid having its level of federal funding for public assistance reduced. Unfortunately, the incentive for states to maintain their levels of federal funding has resulted in stringent provisions which have already disqualified millions of needy families from welfare.

Under PRA, a family is excluded from TANF-funded aid if it includes an adult who has received any TANF-funded assistance in any state for a cumulative period of sixty months. The sixty month limit is the federal maximum and does not prohibit individual states from setting shorter time eligibility limit boundaries. In other words, the federal government will refuse to provide assistance under the TANF program to needy families that include members who have received a total of five years of benefits over their adult lifetime, regardless of individual circumstances or hardships. PRA allows a state to exempt a maximum of 20% of its average monthly caseload from the sixty month time limit due to hardship or if the family includes an individual who has been battered or subjected to extreme cruelty. Nevertheless, even this limited provision has been subject to political criticism, raising questions as to whether Congress included this stipulation out of genuine concern for those families facing the most dire of circumstances, or because of political compromise.

In addition to the eligibility time limits, adult recipients are now required to be employed no later than twenty-four months after they begin receiving benefits. Although welfare-to-work programs were initiated for certain categories of recipients as early as 1968, failure to comply with requirements in the past could only result in the reduction, not termination, of benefits. The federal government has now set minimum participation rates (25% of TANF's single parent family population in 1997, 30% in 1998, 35% in 1999, 40% in 2000, 45% in 2001, and 50% in 2002), and weekly hours requirements (twenty hours for families with dependent children in 1997 and 1998, twenty-five hours in 1999, and thirty hours in 2000) and has specified a list of permitted work activities. A state must reach the required participation rates and ensure that benefit recipients are employed in appropriate types of work for the requisite number of hours to avoid a reduction in federal funding. A recipient must demonstrate that she is actively trying to find work or improve her employability, and must accept any offer of lawful employment, regardless of the salary, to avoid having her benefits terminated. Despite a recipient's employability and individual circumstances, she may be ineligible for an exemption and, if she is unable or unwilling to find continuous work after twenty-four months, assistance will be terminated.

PRA further prohibits assistance for teenage parents not living in an adult-supervised setting or attending high school or an equivalent training program. State officials must determine that extenuating circumstances exist in order for a teen parent to be exempt from this rule. Excusing factors include either that (1) the teen parent has no living parent, legal guardian, or other appropriate adult relative with whom to live; (2) such persons will not allow the teen to live with them; or (3) the teen parent has been, is, or may be subject to physical or emotional abuse in such person's home.

Sanctions follow for failure to comply with the new rules. A recipient who exceeds her time eligibility limit or violates any requirement set forth above receives a pro rata reduction or complete termination of benefits. . . .

Through December 1996, three states — Iowa, Massachusetts, and Wisconsin — accounted for 13,000, or 72%, of the 18,000 terminations nationwide under the section 1315 waiver provision. A General Accounting Office (GAO) study found that failure to comply with work requirements was the most common reason for benefit termination in these three states. Hurried terminations resulted in high rates of error — in some states, more than half of the case terminations were reversed on appeal. In addition, the GAO found that a significant portion of the terminated families did not continue to receive Food Stamps and Medicaid, even though they might have remained eligible for these programs. . . . Explanations for this drop include the failure by many families to take the steps necessary to maintain eligibility and the doubt of many families that eligibility continued or was worth the effort. . . .

B. New York's Welfare Reform Act of 1997

New York's welfare reform strategy, enacted to comply with the federal law, is known as the Welfare Reform Act of 1997 (NYRA). NYRA went into effect November 1, 1997.

The rules of NYRA generally coincide with corresponding federal requirements. NYRA's sixty month eligibility limit, adult work requirement, and teenage parent residency and school requirements incorporate the terms of PRA. But NYRA adds another restriction: a two year limit for state funded benefits, called Safety Net Assistance — receipt of which also counts toward the sixty month federal limit. Welfare recipients who have exceeded the time limit are permanently terminated from TANF-funded benefits. A benefit recipient who quits or reduces work hours without good cause becomes ineligible for benefits until she is willing to comply with work requirements. For a "second offense," she automatically becomes ineligible for benefits for at least three months — longer if she does not comply with the requirements. For a "third offense," she loses her benefits for a minimum of six months. NYRA exempts the following classifications of individuals from work requirements: the ill, incapacitated, elderly, disabled, caretakers of ill or incapacitated members of the household, parents and caretakers of children under the age of one, and pregnant women after the eighth month of pregnancy. Significantly, NYRA eliminates past exemptions for people without access to transportation and for teens who have been out of the house for more than a year.

C. Welfare Reform: Evaluations

Sponsors of welfare reform point to reports of shrinking welfare rolls and caseloads across the country as evidence of success. Welfare reform proponents boast that the current percentage of people in the United States on welfare is the lowest in thirty years. Fourteen months after the enactment of PRA, welfare rolls had fallen nationally by more than 1.7 million people.

Most reports claim that welfare rolls have diminished considerably because former recipients have moved from welfare into the workplace and no longer rely on public assistance. However, not all persons leaving welfare have made the transition to work—the reduction is largely the result of recipients who no longer qualify for aid for other reasons. In fact, the GAO findings indicate that more families in Iowa, Massachusetts, and Wisconsin had earnings before benefit termination than afterwards.

Legislators must look beyond the figure reduction rhetoric and recognize . . . [that the] . . . simple removal of families from welfare rolls [is not a] reliable indicator that these families are now self-sufficient. It is simply implausible that the threat of termination of benefits engenders economic independence. . . .

. . . Many families will be much worse off after benefit termination, yet these cases are frequently overlooked by reports that praise welfare reform.

Even when families do move from welfare to work, evidence indicates that reform gains are still tenuous. . . . Studies of the short-term effects of welfare-to-work programs found only moderate differences in earnings between program participants and control groups. In a study of the five-year impacts of four welfare-to-work programs, the Manpower Demonstration Research Corporation found somewhat more substantial gains in earnings for welfare-to-work program participants, but the greatest improvement was only $2076 annually. Moreover, once reductions in cash assistance are accounted for, the overall income of participants improved in only two of the four programs. Policy-makers can easily reduce welfare rolls, but the challenges for PRA and NYRA are to permanently keep the rolls low and reduce poverty at the same time. The failure to accomplish these objectives is a failure of welfare reform. . . .

II. New York City's Child Welfare System . . .

Tammy, in need of additional income since losing her public assistance, convinced the manager of the supermarket where she worked to increase her hours. The only problem was that the extra hours were during the day, which required her to find someone else to watch her children. The only person that she could afford had to leave one and a half hours before she returned home on Tuesdays. Tammy tried to work something out, but the babysitter had other obligations and could not stay until Tammy got home. Her options were to find another babysitter, or to ask the babysitter to have the kids take a nap before leaving, and to hope that nothing happened to them before she got home. Since Tammy barely had enough money for rent, bills, clothes and food, she reluctantly chose to leave the kids unattended. . . .

III. Tensions between [the Administration for Children's Services (ACS)] and Welfare Reform Policies

Three weeks later, on a Tuesday, Keisha woke up before Tammy came home. Scared, Keisha began to cry loudly for about a half-hour before a neighbor heard her screams. The neighbor, acting out of concern, immediately called the police, who then contacted ACS. Two officers and an ACS caseworker entered the apartment and found Carl Jr. and Keisha alone and frightened. In all of the commotion, during which onlookers had gathered to see what was going on, Tammy returned from work. Terrified that something had happened to her children, she rushed into the apartment. After the caseworker determined that Tammy had left the young children at home alone, the officers arrested her for endangering the children. Although unharmed, both children were immediately removed from Tammy's custody and placed in a foster care facility where they currently remain pending a family court hearing. Tammy also faces criminal charges.

A. Increased Child Maltreatment Allegations

It is my contention that ACS [New York's agency in charge of child protection] will see an increase in the number of abuse and neglect cases as a result of the changed welfare law. In 1991, the Los Angeles County Department of Children and Family Services found that "child abuse and neglect referrals jumped 12 percent following a 2.7 percent decrease in the state's AFDC grant and another 20 percent following AFDC cuts totaling 5.8 percent in 1992." Moreover, the National Incidence Study of Child Abuse and Neglect reports that children in families with incomes under $15,000 a year are twenty-two times more likely to experience maltreatment than children in families with incomes over $30,000. Finally, since PRA denies legal immigrants Food Stamp benefits and gives states the option to deny them TANF cash assistance, Medicaid, and child care services as well, many legal immigrant families are at risk of becoming involved with the child welfare system. States across the country with large immigrant populations will face particular challenges to meet these families needs, and to assess the impact of welfare reform on the child welfare system. Fortunately, New York has not exercised its option to eliminate TANF cash assistance to legal immigrants.

Families whose benefits are cut off may have no other resources on which to survive. The lack of alternative sources of income will result in a dangerously lower standard of living for thousands of families. Without monetary assistance or Food Stamps, parents will not be able to meet the nutritional needs of their children. Parents will barely, if at all, be able to afford living expenses such as rent and utilities. The incidence of parents leaving children unattended or in the hands of unqualified caretakers will become more frequent given that affordable quality child care is already virtually nonexistent. Combined, these financial strictures will have the effect of subjecting poor families to the threat of state intervention for neglect. Furthermore, the current trend towards the criminalization of neglect cases will result in poor women being inordinately penalized by the law. . . .

An increased number of neglect cases will cause an already overloaded child welfare system in New York City to serve children and families in a narrower capacity than it already does. Since the quality of ACS's work already falls below legal standards and standards of good practice, more children will be put in peril. The heightened risk affects children who are in danger but are judged not in need of removal, children whose danger persists but whose cases are improperly closed, and children who are erroneously removed from their families and consequently encounter the threat of abuse and neglect, including psychological harm in foster care settings.

B. Impairment of PRA Objectives

. . . Even assuming the validity of the premises which form the basis of the need for welfare reform, the inconsistencies between the two social welfare policies become obvious. Family structure and self-sufficiency are not promoted when parents are compelled to work in low-skill, low-wage, transitory jobs. Instead, the strict work requirements and aggressive child protection discourage family cohesiveness by leaving families in poverty and subsequently removing children for neglect when their parents are unable to provide for their care. The most likely scenario is that some public assistance recipients will be unable to obtain employment because jobs are not available or a benefit recipient's employability proves to be non-competitive in the market. Terminating benefits will leave these families in a dire predicament. PRA and NYRA eliminate the "financial" and the TANF-funded "other reasonable" means named in section 1012(f)(i)(A) of the New York Family Court Act that ACS has available to offer to poor families. As a result, this statutory provision has even less protective force, since welfare reform eliminates even the option to provide poor parents with the means by which they can give their children adequate housing, food, clothing, and child care. . . .

IV. Suggestions for Improvement . . .

In a better ending, the ACS caseworker, recognizing the vulnerability of Tammy's family, and following the agency's policy of family permanency, would suggest a plan for services for the family before removing Carl Jr. and Keisha and having Tammy arrested. The ACS caseworker would then call Tammy's welfare caseworker and the New York City Department of Social Services to get financial assistance and vouchers for child care at one of the city-funded daycare centers, and to have Tammy re-registered for Food Stamps and Medicaid. Even though Tammy would not be eligible for financial assistance under the state's new strict welfare law, at least the law did include a provision whereby Tammy could receive vouchers for Carl Jr. and Keisha to obtain daycare, clothes, and other basic necessities — an allowance proposed by a joint commission comprised of legislators, child protective services officials, welfare caseworkers, child and family advocates, and community representatives. Tammy could therefore go back to work at the supermarket and no longer rely on cash assistance. Most importantly, Carl Jr. and Keisha could be at home with their loving mother.

≣ *Vicki Schultz, Life's Work*
≣ 100 Colum. L. Rev. 1881, 1914-1917, 1928-1935 (2000)

[T]raditional welfare strategies can be detrimental to women. . . . Joint property approaches [whereby individual men pay their partners for taking care of the house and children] rely on individual breadwinners to fund household labor, while welfare strategies rely on the state. State funding is advantageous for women, because it frees them from serving individual men and sheds class bias by funding household work at a uniform level regardless of the earnings of the family members who support it. Nonetheless, by paying women to stay home with their children rather than providing real support for parents (especially single parents) to work at paid jobs, welfare strategies still encourage women to invest in homemaking and caregiving to the exclusion of their job skills — which may harm women and their families in the long run. For this reason, in the wake of changes to the traditional Aid to Families with Dependent Children (AFDC) system, a number of feminists are proposing alternatives designed to enable low-income mothers and fathers — along with their middle-class counterparts — to participate in parenting and paid work at the same time, and to improve the status of the work they do.

Feminist economist Barbara Bergmann, for example, has criticized the traditional AFDC program for creating a disincentive to employment that hurts women in the long run.[128] She advocates a system more like the French system, which eliminates this disincentive by providing single parents with better support for working at a job while parenting. In France, according to Bergmann, a single mother who takes a job can do far better than her American counterpart — and better, too, than her French counterpart who stays home full-time to care for her children. In addition to

---

128. In the United States, under AFDC, according to Bergmann, a low-skilled single parent had no incentive to leave AFDC for a paid job. After paying for child care, the mother would earn no more — and might even earn less — than she did on welfare. In addition, if she went out to work, she would lose her health insurance, and her job would not be likely to provide it. The result is a real risk that a serious illness would place her family in financial ruin. See [Bergmann, Saving Our Children from Poverty: What the United States Can Learn from France 12-13, 91-94 (1996).]

receiving a comparatively higher wage than in the U.S. (due to a higher minimum wage), the French mother who goes to work will not lose her health insurance, and she will pay little or nothing for high-quality child care that is coveted even by the middle classes. In France, says Bergmann, "[a] single mother and her children do not have to live in poverty. With a job, she can support them at a decent standard."[129]

Bergmann's analysis shows that, despite its facial neutrality, the traditional American welfare approach has harmful class and gender effects. Single mothers are likely to remain poor no matter what they do, whether they work at paid jobs or not. In addition, Bergmann points out, paying single mothers to care for their children raises demands to support married middle-class women's homemaking, which only exacerbates class differentials and further reinforces the gender-based division of labor.[130] To move the United States in a more promising direction, Bergmann has proposed a program called "Help for Working Parents," which would provide low-income parents (single or married) the resources to combine paid work with parenting. The program would provide universal health insurance (on a sliding scale), child care vouchers (for public or private forms of child care), food stamps, and expanded housing assistance for high-cost areas. Perhaps most importantly, it would also provide government subsidies to bring individual earnings above the poverty level.[131] The proposal contemplates that, like most fathers, mothers will engage in full-time work; however, full-time work is defined as thirty hours a week — a substantial reduction from the current norm for American men and women.[132]

Feminist political theorist Nancy Fraser has also criticized the welfare model for reasons that are remarkably similar to Bergmann's, despite their different points of departure.[133] Fraser even takes issue with a remarkably utopian version of the welfare approach — one more generous than we have come close to achieving in the United States — that she calls a "Caregiver Parity" model. As Fraser describes the model:

129. Id. at 12.
130. See id. at 123-24.
131. See id. at 124-30.
132. See id. Bergmann's program was developed jointly with feminist Heidi Hartmann, the head of the Women's Public Policy Institute. See Barbara Bergmann & Heidi Hartmann, A Welfare Reform Based on Help for Working Parents, 1 Feminist Econ. 85 (1995).
133. Fraser criticizes what she calls a "Universal Breadwinner" model, which encourages women to work the same full-time hours as men, on the ground that it reinforces androcentric breadwinner norms and reduces time for leisure and civic activities for everyone. See [Nancy Fraser, Justice Interruptus: Critical Reflections on the "Postsocialist" Condition 51-55 (1997).] Bergmann does not advance a similar critique; her work might even be said to embody Fraser's Universal Breadwinner approach. . . . [H]owever, I think Fraser and Bergmann are closer to each other than they are to many other feminists. Both understand the significance of paid work to women's lives; and both take seriously the need to dismantle gender-based patterns of paid work in order to achieve a more egalitarian society.

The point is to enable women with significant domestic responsibilities to support themselves and their families either through carework alone or through carework plus part-time employment. . . . Thus, childbearing, child rearing, and informal domestic labor are to be elevated to parity with formal paid labor. . . .

To this end, several major new programs are necessary. One is a program of caregiver allowances to compensate childbearing, child rearing, housework, and other forms of socially necessary domestic labor; the allowances must be sufficiently generous at the full-time rate to support a family. . . . Also required is a program of workplace reforms [to] facilitate the possibility of combining supported carework with part-time employment and of making transitions between different life-states.[135]

Like Bergmann, Fraser condemns even such a well-intentioned model on the ground that it reinforces the gender-based division of labor in ways that harm poor women the most, but ultimately hurt all women. "Although the system of allowances-plus-wages provides the equivalent of a basic minimum breadwinner wage, it also institutes a 'mommy track' in employment — a market in flexible, noncontinuous full- and/or part-time jobs [which] will pay considerably less even at the full-time rate than comparable breadwinner-track jobs." As a result, Fraser concludes, the model will perpetuate current patterns of income inequality. Even though the model, according to Fraser, aims to "make difference costless," the model actually promotes women's marginalization by reproducing the link between caregiving and femininity, on the one hand, and breadwinning and masculinity, on the other.[138]

Thus, both political theorist Nancy Fraser and economist Barbara Bergmann are concerned that even a generous welfare model would replicate the undesirable features of the old family-wage system. Both believe we can do better by creating social systems that enable people to combine paid work with caregiving and improve and desegregate low-wage work. Like Bergmann, Fraser advocates vigorous steps to eliminate the gender segregation of jobs and to provide generous social support for job-holding. Her vision is similar to Bergmann's, except that Fraser argues explicitly for reducing the amount of time both men and women devote to paid work so that we can all be more active participants in family life, political activity, and civic endeavors. Fraser quotes approvingly from the Swedish Ministry of Labor:

---

135. Id. at 55-56.
138. As Fraser puts it:

By supporting women's informal carework, it reinforces the view of such work as women's work and consolidates the gender division of domestic labor. By consolidating dual labor markets for breadwinners and caregivers, moreover, the model marginalizes women within the employment sector. By reinforcing the association of caregiving with femininity, finally, it may also impede women's participation in other spheres of life, such as politics and civil society.
Id. at [55-58].

"To make it possible for both men and women to combine parenthood and gainful employment, a new view of the male role and a radical change in the organization of working life are required." In such a world, the "employment sector would not be divided into two different tracks; all jobs would be designed for workers who are caregivers, too; all would have a shorter workweek than full-time jobs have now; and all would have the support of employment-enabling services."[140] Creating such a world would require us to dismantle the gendered association of men with paid work and women with child care and housework. It would require us to fully envision men as committed caregivers and women as authentic workers — something which even some feminists, let alone many other men and women, have not yet been able to do.

This is unsurprising, for family-wage ideology is such a deeply-ingrained part of our heritage that it remains difficult to recast women's (and men's) roles as workers and citizens in such transformative terms. As historian Linda Gordon has shown, even most late nineteenth and early twentieth-century women's rights activists who were instrumental in creating the modern welfare state were "maternalists" who based their approach on the family-wage system.[141] These feminists' acceptance of a gendered system of labor limited their vision of "welfare" to a system that paid women to stay home and take care of children (such a system was understood to be temporary, anyway, since the beneficiaries were imagined to be widows who would eventually remarry), rather than a system that enabled both women — and men — to take care of their families while at the same time engaging in paid work. Some reformers understood that the family wage was a myth, and that "mothers' aid would be only a poor substitute for insisting on decent wages" for working women.[142] But the most prominent activists' adherence to family-wage ideology blinded them to the need for broader governmental policies that would enable women to work to support families on our own, such as better jobs and job training, wage subsidies, and collectivized child care. It was left to less mainstream activists to call for these and other measures that envisioned wage work as an important component of women's lives and identities, and, more radical still, of their independence from men.

. . . I realize that work alone is no panacea. It is the platform on which equal citizenship should be built, not the entire edifice. Still, the importance of work to the future cannot be overemphasized; abandoning work as a political and cultural ideal would be a serious mistake. People need more

---

140. Id. at [61-62].

141. See [Linda Gordon, Pitied but Not Entitled: Single Mothers and the History of Welfare 1890-1935, at 53-59 (1994)]; see also Sonya Michel, The Limits of Maternalism: Policies Toward American Wage-Earning Mothers During the Progressive Era, in Mothers of a New World: Maternalist Politics and the Origins of Welfare States 277, 277-78 (Seth Koven & Sonya Michel eds., 1993) (discussing maternalist political activism). . . .

142. Gordon, supra, at 62.

than money or property: We need life projects. We need goals and activities to which we can commit our hearts, minds, and bodies. We need to struggle with our capacities and our limits, in sustained ways in stable settings. We need to work alongside others in pursuit of common goals. We need to feel that we are contributing to something larger than ourselves and our own families. Most of us even need something that requires regular rhythms and structure, and provides a mechanism for deferring gratification. We need to feel that we are earning our keep — that we have a source of wherewithal that is our own. We also need public recognition for our labors. It is difficult to imagine any single activity that can fulfill all these purposes for the vast majority of people other than working. We have seen what happens to people when they don't have work to give life structure and meaning, and it is not exemplary. There is a reason why democratic societies have organized themselves as employment societies. Paid work is the only institution that can be sufficiently widely distributed to provide a stable foundation for a democratic order. It is also one of the few arenas — perhaps the only one — in which diverse groups of people can come together and develop respect for each other through shared experience. Can we think of a society anywhere in the world we would want to emulate in which most people do not work for a living?

In contrast to such a work-centered approach, some important thinkers have proposed that we abandon our historic emphasis on work and create alternative paths to the good life. Bruce Ackerman and Anne Alstott envision a "stakeholder society," for example, in which investment rather than working becomes the means of securing the good life. Rather than making sure that each citizen has access to a decent job, they would distribute to each citizen a sum of money to invest. They believe it is property that is crucial to citizenship, so it doesn't really matter whether people have a vocation to which they can devote themselves, or something else, such as a hobby, so long as they have an income and a stake in the polity that provides it.[187] Indeed, in rhetoric that harkens back to nineteenth-century characterizations of paid work as wage slavery, Ackerman and Alstott even hint that work is inconsistent with liberal notions of freedom.

Other thinkers have gone so far as to celebrate the end of work. Feminist Carole Pateman has hinted, for example, that in the future, democratic citizenship will not be premised on paid work. This is a good thing, she suggests, for it alleviates the gender dilemma in that equation, given that women have been associated with domesticity as opposed to wage work and hence seen as incapable of equal citizenship. Rather than addressing this predicament by democratizing work, Pateman suggests that we resolve it by eroding men's attachment to wage work (as women's attachment is presumed to have been), and basing citizenship on something

---

187. See Bruce Ackerman & Anne Alstott, The Stakeholder Society 11 (1999).

like our common dependency, rather than on the notion that work can ever make any of us "independent."[189]

Even though work alone can never make us independent, that does not mean we can do without it. Ordinary people understand the significance of work and have demanded access to work in broad, inclusive terms. Indeed, over the past forty years, all the major social movements have focused on obtaining equal access to work for those excluded from its rewards. The civil rights movement's demand for jobs (along with peace and freedom) found expression in Title VII of the Civil Rights Act of 1964, which promised to integrate African-Americans into all the best forms of work in our economy. William Julius Wilson's current emphasis on jobs for the dispossessed resonates with the language of the 1968 Kerner Commission Report, which pronounced unemployment one of the most significant problems facing poor black communities. The Kerner report emphasized male unemployment, but, even at the time, women (of all races) were demanding to be taken seriously as workers. The emphasis on work has been crucial to Second Wave feminism, which was born in part out of the recognition that even relatively well-off, white middle-class women were united with their minority, poor, and working-class sisters in the experience of being marginalized in the world of work — which in turn disempowered them in politics and in private life.

Older Americans have also demanded recognition as valid workers, and they won it in the Age Discrimination in Employment Act (ADEA). . . .

The disability rights movement has also emphasized access to work, and they won an important victory with the Americans with Disabilities Act (ADA). . . .

We can also view the transition from welfare to work as part of this trend. I realize that the impetus for welfare-to-work programs has come from the political right, who may not have the best interests of poor people at heart. But it would be a mistake to attribute all of the new emphasis on work to conservatives alone. Some of the demand has come from members of the working poor who do not receive welfare, and who do not have the luxury of keeping a parent at home to take care of their own children. . . .

. . . Poor single parents have long expressed a desire for work that will allow them to support their children; they know that a decent job is the only path that provides real hope for their empowerment in the long run. Most people who receive welfare payments have been working for pay all along, as they must in order to ensure the survival of their families. But, partly because so many of them are women and racial minorities, single parents have not been perceived as "authentic" workers who have the capacity to contribute to productive endeavors beyond raising their own children. Women who

---

189. See [Carole Pateman, The Patriarchal Welfare State, in Democracy and the Welfare State 231, 238 (Amy Gutmann ed., 1988).]

draw on welfare are overrepresented among classic contingent workers, who fare worse on a variety of dimensions than people in more permanent employment. This is the legacy of the fact that our welfare system has been based on a family-wage model that sees women as inauthentic workers and cannot imagine mothers in economically-powerful provider roles.

Even if many welfare-to-work programs have been adopted for the wrong reasons, their existence does provide a political opening to turn things around. Not only is paid work important to people's ability to get ahead and their sense of community and self-esteem; it is also a more easily politicized setting than the privatized home. By creating social systems that allow poor (and other) parents to combine caregiving with stable employment, we enable them to move into the workforce — a space in which they can more easily engage in collective action to improve their situation. . . .

Viewed from this perspective, the best welfare-to-work programs push in the direction of a more expansive set of social programs that guarantee and support a right to work for everyone. If work is to provide the foundation for citizenship (as welfare-to-work programs imply), then everyone must have access to a suitable job, as well as the training and education needed to do the job. There is no reason to find or create jobs exclusively for people who have drawn on welfare, when so many others are struggling to find jobs, often under fiercely competitive conditions. The goal should be to ensure that everyone — mothers on welfare, fathers struggling to pay child support, poor women and men without children, people with disabilities, middle-class homemakers or divorcees, people in temporary jobs who want steady employment, older people, youth who are trying to finance continuing education, and, yes, even well educated displaced workers — has work. . . .

Notes

1. From Worthy Mothers to Deviant Ones. Welfare began in the United States as state programs establishing "mother's pensions" for destitute mothers and their children. Use of the term "pension" connoted that the payment was a substitute for money that might otherwise be received in paid employment and contributed to the notion inherent in these early programs that motherhood was a job and that a mother's devotion to the care of her children was important. See Jill Duerr Berrick, From Mother's Duty to Personal Responsibility: The Evolution of AFDC, 7 Hastings Women's L.J. 257, 258-259 (1996).

The initial purpose was to relieve impoverishment caused by mothers having been abandoned, or left widowed, by their husband — i.e., worthy mothers. From the very beginning, blacks, immigrants, and unwed mothers were systematically excluded, either by the failure to establish programs in locations where these populations were concentrated or through discriminatory eligibility requirements. In 1931, the first national survey of mother's pensions broken down by race found that only 3 percent of recipients were black. See Linda Gordon, Pitied but Not Entitled: Single Mothers and the History of Welfare 48 (1994).

With the Civil Rights movement of the 1960s and the elimination by courts of welfare criteria that excluded African Americans from participation, including moral criteria and residency requirements, an increasingly larger proportion of welfare recipients were never married, non-Caucasian, and adolescent. By 1992, over 60 percent of welfare recipients were women of color. As this demographic transformation occurred, women on welfare were no longer viewed as worthy mothers, but as women engaged in sexually deviant behavior. Accordingly, attention was focused less on the children in their care than on their sexual and procreative practices. Berrick, supra, at 264.

There are a number of excellent histories of the U.S. welfare system. See Gordon, supra; Gwendolyn Mink, The Wages of Motherhood: Inequality in the Welfare State, 1917-1942 (1995); Theda Skocpol, Protecting Soldiers and Mothers: The Political Origins of Social Policy in the United States (1992); Joel F. Handler & Yeheskel Hasenfeld, The Moral Construction of Poverty: Welfare Reform in America (1991); Edward D. Berkowitz, America's Welfare State: From Roosevelt to Reagan (1991); Michael B. Katz, The Undeserving Poor: From the War on Poverty to the War of Welfare (1989); Mimi Abramovitz, Regulating the Lives of Women: Social Welfare Policy from Colonial Times to the Present (1988); Frances Piven & Richard Cloward, Regulating the Poor: The Functions of Public Welfare (1971). Specifically on the relationship between welfare and race, see Jill Quadagno, The Color of Welfare: How Racism Undermined the War on Poverty (1994); Dorothy E. Roberts, Welfare and the Problem of Black Citizenship, 105 Yale L.J. 1563 (1996) (book review).

2. Welfare Reform and Its Critics. The DeRouselle reading describes the major overhaul of the U.S. welfare system that occurred with the passage of the Personal Responsibility and Work Opportunity Reconciliation Act of 1996, Pub. L. No. 104-193, 110 Stat. 2105 (codified as amended in various sections of 42 U.S.C.), which replaced the Aid to Families with Dependent Children program (AFDC), the Job Opportunity and Basic Skills program (JOBS), and emergency assistance programs, with the Temporary Assistance for Needy Families Block Grant program (TANF), effective July 1, 1997. Under the Act, individuals and families no longer have any entitlement to federal assistance. Instead, TANF makes federal monies available to the states, roughly in proportion to prior federal spending in the various federal welfare programs, to distribute according to their own eligibility rules. Based on 1994 spending levels, states are required to spend a certain amount of their own funds as well, but subject to certain federal limitations, they retain control over how these funds and the federal block grants are to be spent. Among the federal limitations, states must require recipients to work within two years of receiving assistance and must terminate benefits subsidized by TANF funds after five years. Work participation rates with which states must comply are phased in; by the year 2002, for example, 50 percent of all families must satisfy the specified work requirement. Minor parents may not be assisted unless they are attending school and living at home or in an adult-supervised living arrangement. Assistance must be limited if an individual in the family is not cooperating with child support-related requirements. In addition, TANF recipients are not automatically eligible for Medicaid, as AFDC recipients were in the past. These and other provisions are outlined in Center for Law and Social Policy, The Temporary Assistance for Needy Families Block Grant, 4 Geo. J. Fighting Poverty 311 (1997).

Many have questioned the workability of the new federal restrictions. As for the work requirement that applies after a recipient has been on welfare for two years, for example, Neil Gilbert points out that those unemployed after two years are likely to be the least skilled and least motivated. Thirty-seven percent of AFDC mothers in 1994, based on self-report data, were addicted to alcohol and drugs. Estimates of the reading level of the typical AFDC mother range from below sixth grade to the eighth grade level. Neil Gilbert, Welfare Reform: Implications and Alternatives, 7 Hastings Women's L.J. 323, 332 (1996). Gilbert suggests that some sort of public works program would be necessary to employ the unemployed beyond the two-year limit. But such a program, taking into account the cost of supervision and daycare, would essentially double the cost of welfare without increasing the amount of a recipient's grant. No one has been willing to answer the question of what happens to recipients who refuse either to work or to participate in training programs or public works programs. Id. "The five-year limit, particularly, is stone silent regarding the fate of children once benefits are terminated." Id. at 333.

At the same time, some of those most likely to leave the welfare rolls include many with difficulties, including drug abuse, and serious health problems that make them more likely to violate the stricter reform rules. See Nina Bernstein, Studies Dispute 2 Assumptions About Welfare Overhaul, N.Y. Times, Dec. 12, 2000, at A18. One comprehensive 1998-1999 study of 40,000 households by the Urban Institute found that 29 percent of those who left welfare in 1995 and 22 percent of those who left welfare in 1997 were back on welfare. About one-third of women who were no longer on welfare said they had to cut the size of meals, or skip meals, because they did not have enough money for food, and about half reported that they either often or sometimes run out of food and do not have money to buy more. Id. (citing Pamela J. Loprest & Sheila R. Zedlewski, Current and Former Welfare Recipients: How Do They Differ? (1999)).

Another complaint raised about welfare reform is the failure to inform families of their eligibility for child care assistance, health insurance, and food stamps. See Lolly Bowean, Children Are Uninsured Because Parents Don't Know They Qualify, Reports Says, Wall St. J., Aug. 10, 2000, at 12 (citing study by Robert Wood Johnson Foundation showing that six out of ten children are uninsured because their parents think that because they work and aren't on welfare, their children don't qualify for insurance); Roslyn Powell & Mia Cahill, Nowhere to Turn: New York City's Failure to Inform Parents on Public Assistance About Their Child Care Rights, 7 Geo. J. Poverty L. & Pol'y 363 (2000); see also Sharon K. Long et al., Child Care Assistance Under Welfare Reform: Early Responses by the States, Assessing the New Federalism (Apr. 1998), at http://newfederalism.urban.org/html/occ15.html (and other items at this site).

It is still too early to tell whether welfare reform will lead, as DeRouselle suggests, to more child abuse and neglect. One study would seem to say not. Somini Sengupta, No Rise in Child Abuse Seen in Welfare Shift, N.Y.Times, Aug. 10, 2000, at 1 (citing Forum on Child and Family Statistics, America's Children: Key National Indicators of Well-Being (2000) (showing decline in child maltreatment cases from over 1 million in 1993, 969,000 in 1996, and 903,000 in 1998)). What factors would you expect to influence whether child abuse and neglect cases rise as a result of welfare reform?

3. The Goals of Welfare Reform. An important objective of the Personal Responsibility and Work Opportunity Reconciliation Act of 1996 is the reduction of out-of-wedlock pregnancies and childbirths. Amy L. Wax argues that this is a legitimate goal. See Wax, The Two-Parent Family in the Liberal State: The Case for Selective Subsidies, 1 Mich. J. Race & L. 491, 494 (1996). Do you agree? Census data show that five years after the overhaul of the welfare system, the proportion of black children living with two married parents increased from 34.8 percent to 38.9 percent. Blaine Harden, 2-Parent Families Rise After Change in Welfare Laws, N.Y. Times, Aug. 12, 2001, at A1. Is this good news? The proportion of white children living with two married parents remained stable at 78.2 percent, just slightly down from 78.5 percent. Id. What conclusions might we draw, if any, from this statistic?

Charles Murray in 1984 stated the basic case for conservative welfare reform, arguing that welfare entrenched, rather than cured, poverty. Like all people, Murray argued, the poor make rational choices based on the existing incentive structures. Welfare rewarded having out-of-wedlock children, and thus increased it. Murray not only defended shutting down the then-existing welfare system. He also supported public blame of the lazy and praise of the self-sufficient. Without the threat of degradation — i.e., without a distinction between the deserving and the undeserving poor — the poor, Murray argued, would have no reason to take responsibility for themselves and their families as best they could. See Murray, Losing Ground: American Social Policy 1950-1980, at 154-162, 178-181 (1984).

Note the importance of individual agency in Murray's line of analysis. The poor are capable of acting rationally; as individual agents, they are also blameworthy when they choose an option that is immoral. The degree of choice exercised by the poor is, of course, a contested empirical fact. Murray assumes that the poor could work if only they chose to, while others describe an economic structure in which the opportunities for self-sufficiency, notwithstanding increasingly positive economic indicators for the "haves," are steadily worsening for the "have-nots." See, e.g., Joel E. Handler, Women, Families, Work and Poverty: A Cloudy Future, 6 UCLA Women's L.J. 375 (1996); Deborah Jones Merritt, Ending Poverty by Cutting Teenaged Births: Promise, Failure, and Paths to the Future, 57 Ohio St. L.J. 441, 453 (1996) (United States has most unequal distribution of both wealth and income in the Western world; based on U.S. Census data, top fifth of American families took home 49.1 percent of the country's aggregate income in 1994 and bottom fifth took home 3.6 percent of that income; top 1 percent of American families control nearly 40 percent of nation's wealth). See also data in note 4, infra.

Murray also assumes that the availability of welfare on a per-child basis increases the incentive for welfare mothers to have large families. Linda McClain questions the assumption that the poor have this degree of agency in their reproductive lives. She points to research showing that women do not make reproductive decisions based on the availability of welfare benefits. See McClain, "Irresponsible" Reproduction, 47 Hastings L.J. 339, 383 n.179 (1996) (citing studies); see also Lucy A. Williams, The Ideology of Division: Behavior Modification Welfare Reform Proposals, 102 Yale L.J. 719, 739-741 (1992) (citing research documenting lack of correlation between receipt of welfare funds and childbearing decisions of unmarried women). Research specifically on the experience of New Jersey with its family cap provisions indicates no statistically significant difference between birth rates of women who are subject to the cap and those who are not. McClain, supra, at 383 n.181 (citing research).

In addition to the empirical debate about the effects of the U.S. welfare system on economic dependency, there is disagreement over the normative implications of poverty. Conservative scholars and policymakers see fundamental gender differences that make the heterosexual, patriarchal family necessary to the preservation of social order. As McClain notes, conservatives tend to view mothering and domestic life as things that come naturally to women. In contrast, responsible fatherhood must be socially prescribed for men, or they will follow their natural inclinations toward violence, lawlessness, and promiscuity. McClain summarizes this argument: "By facilitating women's ability to maintain a family independent of men's financial support, welfare is harmful because it renders men unnecessary, depriving them of their cultural role of provider and leading them to seek satisfaction in predatory, promiscuous, and irresponsible sex — including 'irresponsible father of random progeny,' children they will not support."

McClain, supra, at 386 (citing conservative theorists Irving Kristol and George Gilder). Feminists (including McClain) generally reject this picture of domesticity as "natural" to women and foreign to men. In work written earlier than the excerpt provided in this section, Martha L. Fineman rejects the patriarchal view that associates degeneracy with single motherhood and insists on the presence of a responsible male breadwinner for functional family life. She urges that family be defined, protected, and promoted, in the first instance, in terms of the mother-child relationship rather than the husband-wife couple. See Martha Albertson Fineman, The Neutered Mother, the Sexual Family and Other Twentieth Century Tragedies (1995). What changes in current law would follow from the reconception of family as the mother-child dyad, rather than the traditional two-parent family, and by Fineman's analysis of the reciprocal dependence of family and state? What further changes would be required in the excerpt provided in this section?

Diana M. Pearce offers a line of analysis compatible with Fineman's. Pearce argues that the core of the "welfare problem" is the devaluation of women's work and the "false distinction between independent and dependent workers":

> . . . Frequently [the] contrast is drawn between women whose work is in the home, either unpaid or poorly paid (such as housekeepers and child-care workers), versus those whose work is in the marketplace, including some women as well as most men. Those in paid employment outside the home environment could not be "independent" without the support system provided by the home or its surrogates, such as "housewives" and day-care centers. Such workers' "independence" could not occur without the hidden and unrecognized dependence these workers have on others. . . .
> . . . In concrete terms, as long as we accept the denigration of women who take care of dependent children as "dependent," and as long as the welfare problem is termed one of "dependency," then the policy choices are constrained to a set of equally impossible choices for a single mother. . . .

Pearce, Welfare Is Not for Women: Why the War on Poverty Cannot Conquer the Feminization of Poverty, in Women, the State, and Welfare 265, 275 (Linda Gordon ed., 1990). See also McClain, supra (poor blamed for "irresponsible" reproduction, meaning raising children without being dependent on a man); Nancy Fraser & Linda Gordon, A Genealogy of Dependency: Tracing a Keyword of the U.S. Welfare State, 19 Signs 309 (1994) (analyzing changing connotations of "dependency" in social policy rhetoric).

A number of commentators have highlighted the subsidies for the non-poor, which seem to have increasing public support, even as Congress has pulled the plug on "welfare." See, e.g., Martha T. McCluskey, Subsidized Lives and the Ideology of Efficiency, 8 Am. U. J. Gender Soc. Pol'y & L. 115 (2000); Martha T. McCluskey, Whose Risk, Whose Security?, Am.

Prospect 38 (Jan. 31, 2000). Is there a justification for this apparent contradiction?

As the Vicki Schultz reading makes clear, critics of contemporary welfare reform do not agree on the appropriate alternative. In addition to the differences described in that reading, feminist scholars disagree about whether welfare should be more conspicuously enlarged to include the middle classes or whether it should be restricted to the truly needy. Linda Gordon, building from the premise that a bigger welfare state is likely to be a more popular one, advocates more universal solutions, such as national health insurance and child allowances for children in all families, such as those provided in many European countries. Gordon, Pitied but Not Entitled, supra, at 305; see also Stephen D. Sugarman, Financial Support of Children and the End of Welfare As We Know It, 81 Va. L. Rev. 2523 (1995) (advocating child support assurance scheme). Dorothy Roberts, on the other hand, objects to such approaches, questioning the extent of "trickle-up" benefits to the poor, the failure to "dismantle the institutional-ized impediments to Blacks' social and economic citizenship," and the insufficiency of the appeal to Americans' individual self-interest in resolving the problems of the poor. Roberts favors solutions that directly confront issues of race and class justice. See Dorothy E. Roberts, Welfare and the Problem of Black Citizenship, 105 Yale L.J. 1563, 1588-1592 (1996). Which side is most appealing?

Women's advocates have expressed concern that women will be more vulnerable to domestic abuse as a result of both the emphasis in welfare reform on ending illegitimacy and the time limits on welfare, which may force women back into dependency upon an abusive mate. Among articles discussing how the risks should be addressed, see Patricia Cole & Sarah M. Buel, Safety and Financial Security for Battered Women: Necessary Steps for Transitioning from Welfare to Work, 7 Geo. J. Poverty & Pol'y 307 (2000).

Another possible unintended consequence of welfare reform is an increased rate of pregnancy termination. Susan Frelich Appleton argues that welfare reform, including federal bonuses to states that reduce the out-of-wedlock birth rate, encourages abortion among rational actor recipients. See Appleton, When Welfare Reforms Promote Abortion: "Personal Responsi-bility," "Family Values," and the Right to Choose, 85 Geo. L.J. 155 (1996).

For a discussion of the issue of teenage pregnancy and an examination of the relationship between the age of the mother and child outcomes, see Deborah Jones Merritt, Ending Poverty by Cutting Teenaged Births: Promise, Failure, and Paths to the Future, 57 Ohio St. L.J. 441 (1996).

4. Women and Poverty. More women live in poverty than men, in both absolute numbers and proportionally. The gap increases with age. Roughly 17 percent of children live in poverty. By age 65 and over, less than 7 percent of men live in poverty, as compared to 12 percent of women. U.S.

Census Bureau, Current Population Survey, Special Populations Branch, Table 16 (Poverty Status of the Population in 1999 by Age and Sex: March 2000) (Mar. 2000).

As noted on page 1182, supra, the data show a widening gap between the rich and the poor. From 1988 to 1998, the earnings of the poorest fifth of American families rose less than 1 percent (to $12,990), while the earnings of the richest fifth jumped 15 percent (to $137,480). See Center on Budget and Policy Priorities and the Economic Policy Institute, State Income Inequality Continued to Grow in Most States in the 1990s (Jan. 2000). In fact, in the two-year period immediately following welfare reform, the income of the poorest 20 percent of female-headed families fell by an average of $580 per family. Kathy Sawyer, Poorest Families Are Losing Ground: Female-Headed Households' Gains Erode as Welfare Reform Starts, Study Says, Wash. Post, Aug. 22, 1999, at A7.

5. Women and Social Security, Unemployment Insurance, and Minimum Wage. It is estimated that without social security, more than half of women over the age of 65 would live in poverty. Currently, if a woman spends most of her career raising her family, her social security benefit is half of her husband's and, when her husband dies, she gets 100 percent of his benefits. As a result of social security caps, the benefit structure is weighted in favor of low-wage workers, who get a larger percentage of preretirement earnings than do workers with higher wages. In addition, women are far less likely than men to have pension, or 401(k) plans. Since low-wage workers are less apt to save and invest, women's advocates have tended to oppose proposals to privatize social security. See Trudy Lieberman, Social Security for Women: Privatization Will Hurt Retired Women, The Nation, July 19, 1999, at 6. Instead, they have favored proposals to improve social security, from which women receive only about half what men do. Among these proposed improvements are being able to drop out two years of low earnings for each biological child, a family service credit of $5,000 per year for up to ten years for the family's lower-earning member with children under six years old, and an increase in benefits based on the former spouse's benefit from 50 to 75 percent. Judy Mann, Advocating for a Family Service Credit, Wash. Post, Aug. 6, 1999; see also Institute for Women's Policy Research, Social Security for Women: Proposals for Change, IWPR Pub. No. D436 (Oct. 1999) (summarizing these and other proposals).

Some advocates also propose the expansion of unemployment insurance for women who work part-time or who leave work for family-related reasons. See Testimony of Vicky Lovell, Institute for Women's Policy Research, Policy Alternatives for Improving Access to Unemployment Insurance for Women, Low-Wage and Part-Time Workers: The Case of Georgia, IWPR Pub. No. B236 (Dec. 15, 2000). For a draft paper arguing that unemployment insurance is a poor vehicle for the kind of wealth distribution that low-wage and marginal working women may require, see Gillian Lester, Unemployment Insurance and Wealth Redistribution, at http://papers.ssrn.com/paper.taf?abstract_id=264550.

Raising the minimum wage is also a working women's issue. One recent nationwide study showed that those leaving welfare between 1997 and 1999 earned a median wage of $7.15 an hour. Even with the earned income tax credit and food stamps, their median annual earnings were only $17,388. Gertrude Schaffner Goldberg & Sheila Collins, Reform Should Mean Entitlement to Work, Welfare, at http://www.womensnews.org/index.cfm. For facts and figures, and the argument that an increase in the minimum wage does not, as critics suggest, force employers to fire or hire fewer workers, see Jared Bernstein, Heidi Hartmann, & John Schmitt, The Minimum Wage Increase: A Working Woman's Issue, Economic Policy Institute Issue Brief No. 133 (Sept. 16, 1999).

Putting Theory Into Practice

6-11. How do you evaluate the wisdom and legality of state legislation providing for a $500 cash payment to welfare mothers who agree to the implantation of Norplant, the insertion of an IUD, or the use of some alternative form of contraception that does not require that they remember to take daily medication or use a contraceptive at the time of sexual intercourse. See Meredith Blake, Welfare and Coerced Contraception: Morality Implications of State Sponsored Reproductive Control, 34 J. Fam. L. 311, 319 n.57 (1995-1996) (describing proposed legislation in Kansas). From the point of view of women's autonomy interests, is this proposal sound? What are its strengths and weaknesses?

6-12. Another proposal would give individuals and couples an annual tax deduction, or fixed benefits if they do not pay taxes, for periodically attending responsible parenting classes and counseling sessions. See Douglas A. Berman, The Rights and Wrongs of Norplant Offers, 3 S. Cal. Rev. L. & Women's Stud. 1, 11 (1993). Is this a better approach than the Kansas Norplant proposal?

6-13. West Virginia offers a $100 monthly cash incentive payment to married couples who receive welfare checks in order to encourage two-parent families. Jessica Thompson, In Marriage Debates, No Love Is Lost; Lawmakers' Matrimony Movement Has Critics Aplenty, Star Trib. (Minneapolis), Aug. 13, 2001, at 1A. Is this good policy? For whom?

D. RECONCEIVING AUTONOMY

Kathryn Abrams, Sex Wars Redux: Agency and Coercion in Feminist Legal Theory
95 Colum. L. Rev. 304, 351-352, 338, 345, 352, 374-376
(1995)

[L]aw tends most frequently to assume a simplified version of the liberal subject: a subject capable of uncompromised agentic self-determination, to whom legal authorities ascribe full responsibility for actions taken, and on whose behalf they are generally reluctant to intervene. The strength of these assumptions has often required lawyers seeking to depart from them to describe a sharply contrasting legal subject. In justifying legal intervention or a mitigation of legal sanction, lawyers have described, and judges have acknowledged, a female subject wholly incapable of self-direction, whom the law must rescue from her plight or relieve of responsibility for her actions. The pragmatic interest of feminist lawyers in securing positive outcomes for their clients has often made them complicit in this dichotomizing tendency. They have stressed the extent of their clients' subordination and constraint in ways that have muted any capacity for self-direction of agency.

Most forms of partial agency . . . stand outside this Manichean view of legal subjectivity. [One example is Susan Keller's analysis of the variability that exists in the gaps between viewers' interpretation of a pornographic representation and their application of the representation in their own erotic lives, a variability which can serve as a salient route to self-exploration as well as a viable form of resistance and a way to problematize dominant sexual arrangements. Another example is Martha Mahoney's proposal that the unitary images of battered women offered by dominance theory be supplemented by accounts that incorporate the daily acts of self-preservation, familial protection, and outright resistance that she sees in the narrative of battered women. The works of both Keller and Mahoney] suggest a subject who is neither as unencumbered as the law's traditional subject nor as immobilized as the exceptional subject of the law's protection. If properly understood, these accounts not only have the potential to communicate new images of women living under conditions of oppression, but rather to revise the imagery, assumptions, and even the outcomes reflected in several areas of gender-related law. . . .

. . . Powerlessness is the description through which many legal proceedings simultaneously exonerate and stigmatize "good" victims of sexualized injury, those who conform to traditional gender roles. "Irresponsibility" — or full agency, culpably exercised — is the term with which legal authorities sanction non-conforming women: those who are sexually active, sexually aggressive, live outside the boundaries, or challenge the conventions of mainstream heterosexual family life. A similar form of policing is frequently accomplished by means of the dichotomy between the wholly autonomous subject and the wholly compromised victim. Assimilation to the image of the wholly compromised or constructed victim is a price that women may be asked to pay for legal intervention in interactions or circumstances that were formerly not the province of law. Women may assert their divergence from unremitting victimization, but only at the risk of being assimilated to the autonomous subject who does not require, or requires considerably less, legal intervention. Highlighting this disciplinary use of the dichotomy may help some legal decisionmakers learn to see what exists of the human spectrum between those abstract poles: claimants who are functional and at least minimally self-directing, but also injured and in need of some degree of legal assistance. . . .

. . . Dominance feminists' critics have sought to vindicate the submerged or repressed elements of the dominance vision: the partial agency women retain and the sexual pleasure we might hope to enjoy as we struggle toward greater equality. By framing these two positions not as mutual antagonists but as parts of a single program whose elements are sometimes in sync and sometimes in tension, women can secure our future power without sacrificing the quality or misrepresenting the character of our present lives.

Jennifer Nedelsky, Reconceiving Autonomy: Sources, Thoughts, and Possibilities
1 Yale J.L & Feminism 7, 21, 32-33 (1989)

There is . . . a twofold objective in reconceiving autonomy: (1) to recognize that the irreducible tension between the individual and the collective makes choices or trade-offs necessary; and (2) at the same time, to move beyond a conception of human beings which sees them exclusively as separate individuals and focuses on the threat of the community. The collective is not simply a potential threat to individuals, but is constitutive of them, and thus is a source of their autonomy as well as a danger to it. . . . The task . . . is to think of autonomy in terms of the forms of human interactions in which it will develop and flourish. . . .

It is hardly surprising that a tradition which has conceived of the relationship between the individual and the collective primarily in terms of the threat of the latter does not provide an adequate basis for defining individual rights in the context of affirmative responsibilities of the state. The dichotomy between individual rights and state power has meant that the courts have particular trouble in cases which require them both to accept the state's intrusion into a previously private sphere and to develop a useful framework of individual rights.

Wyman v. James[, 400 U.S. 309 (1971),] dramatically illustrates the justices' inability to analyze rights in the context of dependence. The Supreme Court held that a social worker did not need a warrant for a "home visit" to a woman receiving Aid for Families with Dependent Children.

Justice Blackmun's underlying argument for the majority was essentially this: in accepting the state's offer of responsibility for the welfare of her child, Mrs. James had declared her home life to be the state's business. She could not then turn around and stand on the traditional rights of individuals against state intrusion. In dissent, Justice Douglas made an impassioned argument against the state's capacity to "buy up" rights when it distributes largesse and convincingly argued that if Mrs. James were a businessman objecting to administrative searches, she would win. But Douglas showed virtually no acknowledgement of the ways in which traditional rights may have to be reconceived as the state takes on responsibilities that transform its relations to the individual. Neither approach seems to recognize that the task is to think creatively about the protections of autonomy given the realities of overlapping spheres of public and private interest. Neither a denial of rights nor a denial of realities can solve the problem.

Even when courts do try to protect individual rights in the face of collective power, they tend to use a private-rights model to define and justify the rights in question. Thus Goldberg v. Kelly[, 397 U.S. 254 (1970),] uses the concept of "new property" to explain why welfare recipients are entitled to pretermination hearings. The choice of property is understandable, but particularly unfortunate. . . . [C]haracterizing dependents' rights as property invites a focus on entitlement that misses the point and facilitates retrenchment. Property also carries with it a powerful tradition of inequality which should not be incorporated into new conceptions of autonomy.

But the problem with the concept of new property is more general. It is a mistake to tie protections for citizens' autonomy to particular substantive rights. The objective is to protect the autonomy of citizens in their interactions with government. The appropriate forms of those interactions may vary depending on the kind of interest involved. But the entitlement to autonomy, and to bureaucratic encounters conducive to autonomy, should not depend upon or be deduced from the particular interest at stake. What is at issue here is autonomy and democratic citizenship, which are not relevant only to particular rights.

NOTE ON RECONCEIVING AUTONOMY

The readings offer different, although not contradictory, reconceptualizations of autonomy. The Abrams reading challenges both the liberal legal assumption of the dichotomized legal subject — one who is either autonomous or coerced, freely acting or incapable of self-direction, responsible or irresponsible — and dominance feminism's definition of woman as victim, which fails to move outside the liberal dichotomy. Abrams suggests a more complicated view of the subject, as an individual both free and constrained. Among other feminist scholars who have developed analyses along these lines, see Jane E. Larson, "Women Understand So Little, They Call My

Good Nature 'Deceit'": A Feminist Rethinking of Seduction, 93 Colum. L. Rev. 374 (1993); Katharine T. Bartlett, Minow's Social Relations Approach: Unanswering the Unasked, 17 Law & Soc. Inquiry 437, 464-469 (1992); Martha Minow: Choices and Constraints: For Justice Thurgood Marshall, 80 Geo. L.J. 2093 (1992); Martha Mahoney, Legal Images of Battered Women: Redefining the Issue of Separation, 90 Mich. L. Rev. 1 (1991); see also Kathryn Abrams, Ideology and Women's Choices, 24 Ga. L. Rev. 761 (1990). What are the implications of the shift from the dichotomous view of the subject to the more complicated view that Abrams has in mind? This line of analysis is further developed in Chapter 7.

The Nedelsky reading addresses the premise of individual autonomy, which puts it into competition with, or in adversarial relationship to, the collective community. Nedelsky urges a shift from the conventional understanding of separate individuals whose interests are necessarily threatened by the collective power of the community, to a view in which the community is viewed as facilitative of individual flourishing and autonomy, and the obligations of government do not depend on the pre-identification of discrete individual rights. Linda C. McClain pursues a similar theme when she explores alternative, non-atomistic definitions of autonomy, including autonomy as self-government, which she explains may coexist with and include many forms of connection among citizens. See McClain, "Atomistic Man" Revisited: Liberalism, Connection, and Feminist Jurisprudence, 65 S. Cal. L. Rev. 1171, 1190 (1992). For the development of a concept of "narrative autonomy," in which persons connect action and identity through a process of continual interpretation and reinterpretation of their experiences in light of their relational commitments and communities, see Susan H. Williams, A Feminist Reassessment of Civil Society, 72 Ind. L.J. 417 (1997).

Once separation from others is no longer viewed as the central premise of autonomy, the way is cleared for still a third reconceptualization of autonomy, one which views individual rights claims as claims not by an isolated, rights-bearing individual, but by an individual who is deeply interconnected with and dependent upon others.

> . . . As I see it, individual autonomy is a capacity, not a static human characteristic to be posited as a presupposition of legal or political theory. This capacity must be developed; it can flourish or become moribund. What is essential to the development of autonomy is not protection against intrusion but constructive relationship. The central question for inquiries into autonomy (legal or otherwise) is then how to structure relationships so that they foster rather than undermine autonomy. . . .
>
> . . . If we understand autonomy as made possible by relationship rather than by exclusion, we can better understand the genuine problem of autonomy in the modern state. Our central problem today is not maintaining a sphere into which the state cannot penetrate but fostering autonomy where people are already within the sphere of state control or responsibility. The problem is best

addressed by focusing on how the interactions between state and citizen are structured.

Jennifer Nedelsky, Law, Boundaries, and the Bounded Self, 30 Representations 162, 168-169 (1990).

Martha Minow and Mary Lyndon Shanley define relational rights in terms of "the claims that arise out of relationships of human interdependence." See Minow & Shanley, Relational Rights and Responsibilities: Revisioning the Family in Liberal Political Theory and Law, 11 Hypatia 4, 23 (Winter 1996). See also Martha Minow, Interpreting Rights; An Essay for Robert Cover, 96 Yale L.J. 1860, 1888 (1987) (rights claims express relationships and interconnections at the very moment that the individual asserts his or her autonomy); Susan G. Kupfer, Autonomy and Community in Feminist Legal Thought, 22 Golden Gate U. L. Rev. 583 (1992) (reformulating autonomy in light of West's notion of the "authentic self" and feminist commitment to community); Anne C. Dailey, Feminism's Return to Liberalism, 102 Yale L.J. 1265, 1267 (1993) (book review) (describing shift in legal feminism to a "redeemed liberalism in which the philosophy of possessive individualism characteristic of classical liberalism has been tempered by a principle of empathy"); Joanna K. Weinberg, Poverty, Reproduction, and Autonomy: Some Thoughts on the Ethics of Social Policy Legislation, 3 Colum. J. Gender & L. 375 (1992) (comparing "traditional" autonomy and "relational" autonomy).

How does formulating the issue of autonomy in terms of the connections and relationships it enables make a difference to any of the issues raised in this chapter? Does the concept of relational autonomy avoid the problems of indeterminacy inherent in relational feminism more generally?

7
Anti-Essentialism

Feminist legal scholars in the United States have primarily struggled as women for "equality" with men. As this book illustrates, equality in this context has had many meanings: identical treatment for men and women under the law; "special treatment" for women when women's experiences diverge biologically or culturally from those of men; the re-valorization of stereotypically "female" practices and qualities; the end of male domination; the achievement of autonomy. The struggle for equality as women, however, necessarily assumes that all women have some important commonalities, and feminists have periodically called the extent of these commonalities into question. During feminism's first wave, as section C of Chapter 1 illustrates, African-American feminists such as Sojourner Truth called attention to the difference race makes in women's experience. Beginning in the 1980s, some feminist legal scholars began to ask again whether the pursuit of equality as women had wrongly left differences among women — especially differences of race, ethnicity, sexuality, nation, ability, and class — in the background. Meanwhile, others wondered whether "women" is ever a useful concept, and used postmodern theory to subject the term to critique. This chapter pursues these concerns at a theoretical level, concerns that are often grouped together under the term "anti-essentialism."

"Essentialism" in feminist legal literature has come to refer to several related but distinct problems. One is a tendency in feminist theorizing to focus only on what all women have in common: their subordination to men. One critique of this kind of analysis is that women are never just women; they are lesbians, black, Asian American, disabled or able-bodied, poor, and middle-class. A second critique is that men are never just men, either: not all men have equal access to "male" power. One response to these criticisms is that all women *do* share certain commonalities; that is what makes the category "women" socially salient. Another is that the demand to incorporate race, ethnicity, class, sexuality, disability, and so forth into every feminist analysis makes rigorous analysis — not to mention deciding antidiscrimination claims — impossible. A third response might be that feminism must focus on women, not men, because gender ultimately works to the benefit of men and the detriment of women. To what extent and in what contexts can we usefully generalize about all women? What alternatives are there to using "women" as a central organizing category? Does feminism rightly or wrongly ignore gender as a system of practices and ideologies that structure and sometimes burden the lives of men?

A second, related meaning of "essentialism" is the problem of false universalism, in which the experience of a privileged subset of a group is treated as characteristic of all members of the group. For example, feminists whose work appears throughout this book have often claimed that legal standards purporting to be neutral and objective are actually tailored to men's lives, priorities, and experiences. False universalism is a critique that can be extended to feminist theory itself. Thus, several feminist commentators have argued that feminist scholarship is too often centered around the needs and desires of white, middle class, heterosexual, able-bodied, and otherwise privileged women.

The problem of false universalism takes on additional complexity when Western feminism travels abroad. How, for example, should Western feminists respond to practices like clitoridectomy, veiling, or gender-based access to rights and privileges when they occur in a non-Western context? When feminists challenge such practices, are they inappropriately importing Western conceptions of gender oppression? When feminists defer to such practices in the name of respecting indigenous "cultures," are they complicit with oppression? Which should take precedence when feminism and anti-colonialism or multiculturalism seem to be at odds?

A third meaning of the term "essentialism" might be called the "naturalist" error. From a critical legal perspective, to commit the naturalist error is to assume that certain aspects of the sex/gender system are given by nature rather than being "socially constructed." Feminist scholars have consistently argued, for example, that women are not "naturally" more emotional, better suited to care for children, or less intelligent than men. (The tension between feminism and sociobiology is explored in Section B of Chapter 5.) Within feminist scholarship, the effort to avoid the naturalist error has led to debates about whether the distinction between "sex" and "gender" is itself meaningful. Is "sex" — a term often employed to describe the biological basis on which social "gender" is constructed — itself a socially constructed concept? Do people really come in just two kinds, male and female? Should feminists encourage the blurring of these categories?

A fourth meaning of the term "essentialism" points at a problem located in the process of categorization itself. Human cognition inevitably involves categorization, yet every category is inevitably underinclusive and overinclusive. Every category is useful for some purposes and not for others. When categories are both assumed to be fixed and treated as extremely important to social life, as "gender" is, what are the consequences for resisting injustice? Is it possible to escape categories altogether? Would trying to do so make thought, or collective action, impossible? Is it possible to learn to think of our categories as provisional instead of unalterable, socially created rather than inherent in nature? Are we, as humans, essentially "essentialist"?

Finally, a fifth connotation of the term "essentialism" involves the vexed relationship between feminism and the cross-disciplinary academic movement known as "postmodernism." Postmodern theory seeks to undermine ordinary assumptions about truth and power by suggesting that truth and power are interrelated. Relations of power help determine what a society takes to be "true," and power thus has its most pervasive effects when it determines what we think we know. Some anti-essentialist commentators argue that feminists should be receptive to postmodernist theory, because both feminists and postmodernists are skeptical of claims about universal truth, which have often been used to justify women's oppression. Other feminists, however, argue that postmodern theory is dangerous because it suggests that people can simply "think" themselves free of oppression, and because it leads to moral relativism — the position that any world view or opinion is as good as any other because none can be proven to be universally "true." Another criticism of postmodern theory is that its corrosive skepticism of all concepts and categories ultimately disables political action. The encounter between feminism and postmodernism has led to many debates within feminist theory, some of them focusing on how knowledge is produced and others focusing on what "power" means. Can feminists seek to change the world without being committed to the belief that there are ultimate truths? What is "power," and what constitutes resistance to power? What does women's "liberation" mean in a world saturated with power relations?

The last section of the chapter asks how the theoretical insights developed by anti-essentialist thinkers can be lived in a feminist legal practice. These readings also bring us back to some of the questions raised at the beginning of this book. Is it possible for an individual or a group of people to be oppressed in some ways and privileged in others? Is it possible for a person to benefit from oppression without actively or even knowingly being "an oppressor?" What struggles are most important in a world troubled by all sorts of injustice? How should one conduct oneself in the world as a feminist and a lawyer?

Although the term "essentialism" can refer to many different things, within recent feminist theory the term consistently is a derogatory label. As you work through this section of the chapter, ask yourself whether it is always bad to be an essentialist. Are some forms of essentialism worse than others? Are some kinds of essentialism necessary or appropriate in certain contexts?

A. ANTI-ESSENTIALISM IN FEMINIST LEGAL THEORY

1. Critiques of Single-Axis Theorizing

a. Differences among Women

> ## Judy Scales-Trent, Black Women and the Constitution: Finding Our Place, Asserting Our Rights
> 24 Harv. C.R.-C.L. L. Rev. 9, 9-11, 16-17, 18-20, 23, 35-39 (1989)

The economic, political, and social situation of black women in America is bad, and has been bad for a long time. Historically, they have borne both the disabilities of blacks and the disabilities which inhere in their status as women. These two statuses have often combined in ways which are not only additive, but synergistic — that is, they create a condition for black women which is more terrible than the sum of their two constituent parts. The result is that black women are the lowest paid group in America today when compared to white women, black men or white men. They also face significantly higher unemployment rates than any of those groups. The poverty rates for black women, even controlling for age and education, are higher than the poverty rates for white women and black men. By the beginning of this decade seventy percent of all poor black families were supported by black women. Not surprisingly, studies have shown that when compared to whites and black men, black women lack an overall sense of well-being and satisfaction, while possessing a strong sense of powerlessness and lack of control over their lives.

Despite, or perhaps because of, this dual disability and its negative effects on life opportunities for black women, the problems of black women often go unrecognized. Black women have not been seen as a discrete group with a unique history, unique strengths and unique disabilities. By creating two separate categories for its major social problems — "the race problem," and "the women's issue" — society has ignored the group which stands at the interstices of these two groups, black women in America. For example, social reformist discussion tends to focus on the need to protect "minorities and women" from the hardships of discrimination. Although this term is intended to be inclusive, in fact, it misleads by overlooking those Americans who are both "minorities" and "women." A more accurate approach would be to use terms such as "male minorities and women," or "minorities and white women." These phrases acknowledge that other groups, including black women, do exist and that their problems can be addressed separately.

The legal system has incorporated the same dichotomous system — "minorities" and "women" — into its way of analyzing problems. Thus, the legal system, which is trying to protect the rights of "blacks" and "women," when faced with the existence of "black women," sometimes has difficulty categorizing this group. For example, during the debates over the employment discrimination provision of the 1964 Civil Rights Act, legislators discussed whether or not to add a prohibition against sex discrimination to the bill. Since the bill clearly would prohibit discrimination in employment based on race, there was some confusion and disagreement as to whether black women were going to be treated as blacks or as women for the purposes of obtaining the protection of the statute. During the House debates, Rep. Griffiths, a white woman, expressed her concern that black women would be protected by the Act based on their race, whereas white women would have no protection unless sex were added as a prohibited basis of discrimination. She stated: "If you do not add sex to this bill . . . you are going to try to take colored men and colored women and give them equal employment rights, and down at the bottom of the list is going to be a white woman with no rights at all." Rep. Celler, a white man, tried to clarify the issue by noting that black women would be protected only on the basis of race, not sex. He explained, "if the Negress who applied for the job was disqualified because of the pigmentation of her skin, because she was colored, the act would apply." The consensus was, however, that this distinction would not hold up in real employment situations. The clear distinctions the legislators wanted to make between race and sex discrimination became unclear once black women had to be categorized.

Although the legal system has a framework for analyzing legal issues involving black Americans, and a framework for analyzing legal issues involving American women, the system is not clear on how to analyze issues involving black American women — standing, as they do, with a foot in each camp. . . .

When groups allege employment discrimination based upon group status, often that discrimination is based upon one characteristic, such as religion, sex, or race. However, employers who discriminate do not always do so in such neat categories. Just as widespread discrimination against black women as a class has always existed in American society, widespread employment discrimination against the class has existed as well. Since the enactment of Title VII, black women have gone to court claiming discrimination, as individuals and as a group, based on their distinct identity as black women. In 1980, the Fifth Circuit became the first court of appeals to rule on the issue of whether black women are protected as a discrete class under Title VII, in Jefferies v. Harris Cty. Community Action Association.[32] The court held that they are so protected, noting that discrimination against

32. 615 F.2d 1025 (5th Cir. 1980).

black females can exist even in the absence of discrimination against black men or white women. The court further stated:

> In the absence of a clear expression by Congress that it did not intend to provide protection against discrimination directed especially toward black women as a class separate and distinct from the class of women and the class of blacks, we cannot condone a result which leaves black women without a viable Title VII remedy.[34]

The Jefferies court found further support for this position in the Supreme Court's holdings and analysis in the "sex plus" cases. In those cases the Court found that discrimination against certain subclasses of women violated Title VII.[35] Since then, every court which has ruled on the issue has agreed that black women can claim, as a distinct group, Title VII protection against discrimination based on the race/sex dual status. . . .

Black women have sought to claim this distinct status in court because it is often the only way that they can prove that they have been victims of remediable harm. The facts of the Jefferies case provide one example of the importance of how the claimant presents herself and her claim. In that case, Jefferies alleged that the employer discriminated in failing to promote her to the position of Field Representative in a county agency. The person who was promoted into the job she sought was a black man. Jefferies was therefore not able to prove race discrimination. Moreover, since statistical proof showed that one of the previous Field Representatives had been a woman, and that almost half of the supervisory positions within the agency were held by women, the plaintiff could not prove sex discrimination. However, the evidence showed that every position for which she had applied had been filled either by men or white women. Therefore, she could logically claim that the employer had been discriminating against black women as a class. Thus Jeffries was able to focus the proof of discrimination on the harm committed against her as a black woman. Similarly, in Lewis v. Bloomsburg Mills,[43] the plaintiffs were able to show a hiring rate of black women in the range of five to eight standard deviations below the "expected" level. They were able, therefore, to make a prima facie showing of discrimination. If, however, they had been required to commingle their statistical hiring data with the hiring data for either black men or white women, the standard deviation might well have been lower, thereby masking the harm they had suffered, and making their argument weaker. . . .

. . . The major difference, for the purposes of this Article, between Title VII and the Constitution is that under Title VII, protected groups are always treated in the same manner. . . . The Equal Protection Clause differs from

---

34. Id. at 1032.
35. [For more on "sex-plus" analysis under Title VII, see Chapter 2.]
43. 773 F.2d 561 (4th Cir. 1985).

Title VII in that the level of protection changes depending upon which group is presenting the equal protection claim, and depending upon how much protection the Court thinks is warranted based on that group's social and historical status. Thus, under Title VII, black women assert their rights as a separate group in order to focus the evidence on the particular harm where that harm is to black women as a class. Under an equal protection analysis, black women might proceed as a separate group not only to focus the evidence with particularity on the harm done to black women, but also in order to get the court to assess the evidence within a framework which offers more protection to black women than it might to white women or to black men. It is because of this difference between Title VII and the Constitution that a new analysis is required to situate the group "black women" within the Equal Protection Clause, and to consider how this group should be treated by the courts. . . .

There are three possible ways to protect black women within the equal protection framework. The first is to treat black women as a subset of blacks or of women, and to grant their claims the level of protection accorded that group under the current tripartite analysis of the Court. The second is to treat black women as a discrete group seeking protection under the Constitution, and to assess that group on its own merits to determine the level of protection it should be afforded. One might analyze the situation of black women in this society as that of a "discrete and insular" minority which is unable to enjoy the benefits of full citizenship, and thus entitled to strict scrutiny protection under the Equal Protection Clause. Third, one might argue that since black women carry the burden of membership in the black group, which is already entitled to strict scrutiny protection, and in the disfavored female group, they should be entitled to more than strict scrutiny protection by the courts. . . .

[Scales-Trent reviews the legal history of the United States to support her argument that black women constitute a discrete and insular group defined by immutable characteristics, historically subject to prejudice, and characterized by political powerlessness.]

This Article argues that black women can be viewed as a subset of blacks, and are therefore entitled to the highest level of constitutional protection by virtue of their membership in the black class. It further argues that based on their history and position in society, black women can be seen as a discrete group which can be assessed on its own for purposes of determining the level of protection it should receive under the Equal Protection Clause. These conclusions raise new questions about the further direction of developments under the Equal Protection Clause, questions which are addressed in this section.

The first question concerns the theory that black women are a subset of the black group, and therefore qualify for the highest level of protection based on that status. If this theory applies, does it follow that other subsets of black groups, with secondary characteristics which do not warrant the highest level of protection (i.e., aged, retarded), merit the same consideration as black women? That is, should the black aged and the black retarded also be treated as the black female group?

The answer is yes. Subsets, such as the black aged and the black retarded, are in the same analytical position as black women for purposes of the Equal Protection Clause, and should be treated the same way. Since the stigma of race always exists in these instances, the level of protection accorded the race group must also be granted to subsets of that group.

In its decision on "dual discrimination" claims brought under Title VII of the Civil Rights Act of 1964, the Fifth Circuit maintained, in dicta, that such claims should be limited to those groups sharing two immutable traits, such as race and sex.[133] That analysis applied here would distinguish between, on the one hand, black women or the black retarded (all immutable traits), and on the other, the black aged (age, though irreversible, is not immutable). Such distinctions could be made, but would make no analytical sense. . . .

A second issue is raised by the argument that black women can be considered a discrete group for purposes of the Equal Protection Clause. If this is true, what about Asian women and Hispanic women? Where do these double categories stop?

In Judge v. Marsh the district court allowed a group of black women to bring a Title VII claim based on their status as black women, but expressed concern that creating such subgroups turned the statute into a "many-headed Hydra."[136] The court was concerned that subgroups for every possible combination of race, color, sex, national origin, and religion could be created, and wondered "whether any employer could make an employment decision under such a regime without incurring a volley of discrimination charges." The concern, then, is with the "slippery slope": What are we letting ourselves in for if we start down this path? In a recent case which raised similar "slippery slope" concerns, the Court stated that the petitioner lost the case because there was "no limiting principle" to the type of challenge he brought to the Court.[138] The task here, then, is to see if there is a "limiting principle" to the notion that groups may define themselves in different ways for purposes of constitutional protection.

In reality, because of the way the Equal Protection Clause has developed, it is already self-limiting. A group demanding recognition and protection from the Court must show that it is discrete, insular and powerless. It must show as well that this group definition is causing it to be denied the equal protection of the laws. To the extent that other "dual" groups — Asian women, for example — could show a group identity and

---

133. Jefferies v. Harris City Community Action Association, 615 F.2d 1025, 1033-34 (5th Cir. 1980).

136. 649 F. Supp. 770, 780 (D.D.C. 1986).

138. McCleskey v. Kemp, 481 U.S. 279, 283 (1987).

harm to the group based on that identity, it is hard to see why they should not be equally protected. There is no way to read the language of the Equal Protection Clause to limit the scope of its protection to a small number of groups.

Another approach to the "many-headed Hydra" problem would be to imagine the worst possible scenario if this type of group redefinition were permitted. Again, it is instructive to look at the concerns raised by courts under Title VII as a starting point. In Judge v. Marsh, the court was concerned that an employer would not be able to make any employment decision at all without fear of facing a discrimination claim if the claims of subgroups were allowed. Despite the court's concern about the future, this statement reflects today's reality. The Supreme Court has already decided that Title VII's prohibition of race discrimination protects white workers as well as black, and that its prohibition against sex discrimination protects male workers as well as female. If an employer is covered by Title VII, it is true at present that she cannot make any employment decision at all without considering the possibility of a Title VII charge. Similarly, every citizen is protected by the Equal Protection Clause. Ultimately, any "dual discrimination" claim raises issues of proof. The question then becomes whether the group alleging harm will be allowed to focus the proof on the harm caused them by their dual status and thus be able to receive a remedy.

[This article argues that] whether viewed as a subset of the black group, or as a distinct group in itself, black women are entitled to the "strict scrutiny" level of constitutional protection. Although the subset argument might well be the stronger one, due to the clarity of the Court's recognition of race as a particularly unjustifiable mode of classification, this Article maintains that black women also have a strong argument that they are a "discrete and insular" minority, that they are the object of historical prejudice and stereotypes, and that this prejudice and insularity affect their ability to use the political processes to protect their interests. From the colonial period to the present, various state and private actors have singled them out for treatment different than that meted out to white women or black men. This has resulted in the creation of a group which is overrepresented among those living in poverty, and underrepresented among those who influence the political process. It is a group which carries the degraded statuses of both blacks and women, and finds its life chances thereby doubly limited. Any state action which burdens this group should be subject to at least strict scrutiny under the Equal Protection Clause. This Article suggests that because black women are stigmatized by race plus another stigma (sex), they should be entitled to a strict scrutiny level of review (race) plus additional protection in the form of, for example, an eased burden of proof.

Sumi K. Cho, *Converging Stereotypes in Racialized Sexual Harassment: Where the Model Minority Meets Suzie Wong*
1 J. Gender Race & Just. 177, 181, 190-194 (1997)

. . . At almost every campus where I have been, both as a student and faculty member, I have encountered appalling cases of sexual harassment against Asian Pacific and Asian Pacific American (APA) women.

In this Article, I hope to reveal how converging racial and gender stereotypes of APA women help constitute what I refer to as "racialized (hetero)sexual harassment." This form of harassment denotes a particular set of injuries resulting from the unique complex of power relations that APA women experience in the workplace. . . .

[T]he process of objectification that women in general experience takes on a particular virulence with the overlay of race upon gender stereotypes. Generally, objectification diminishes the contributions of all women, reducing their worth to male perceptions of female sexuality. In the workplace, objectification comes to mean that the value of women's contributions will be based not on their professional accomplishments or work performance, but on male perceptions of their vulnerability to harassment. Asian Pacific women suffer greater harassment exposure due to racialized ascriptions (for example, they are exotic, hyper-eroticized, masochistic, desirous of sexual domination, etc.) that set them up as ideal gratifiers of western neocolonial libidinal formations. In a 1990 Gentleman's Quarterly article entitled "Oriental Girls," Tony Rivers rehearsed the racialized particulars of the "great western male fantasy":

> Her face — round like a child's, . . . eyes almond-shaped for mystery, black for suffering, wide-spaced for innocence, high cheekbones swelling like bruises, cherry lips. . . .
>
> When you get home from another hard day on the planet, she comes into existence, removes your clothes, bathes you and walks naked on your back to relax you. . . . She's fun you see, and so uncomplicated. She doesn't go to assertiveness-training classes, insist on being treated like a person, fret about career moves, wield her orgasm as a non-negotiable demand. . . .
>
> She's there when you need shore leave from those angry feminist seas. She's a handy victim of love or a symbol of the rape of third world nations, a real trouper.[52]

---

52. Tony Rivers, Oriental Girls, Gentleman's Q. (British ed.), Oct. 1990, at 158, 161, 163. . . .

There is a booming sub-genre in pornography involving Asian Pacific women, but I was unable to stomach this research after one attempt to document some of the material. This sub-genre is replete with the submissive stereotype and frequently uses Asian Pacific women in particularly masochistic and demeaning forms of pornography. Researchers who have investigated this sub-genre report video titles such as "Asian Anal Girls, Asian Ass, Asian Slut, Asian Suck Mistress, Banzai Ass, China deSade, Oriental Encounters, Oriental Sexpress, Oriental Lust, Oriental Callgirls, Oriental Sexpot, Oriental Squeeze, Oriental Taboo, and

As the passage demonstrates, Asian Pacific women are particularly valued in a sexist society because they provide the antidote to visions of liberated career women who challenge the objectification of women. In this sense, this gender stereotype also assumes a "model minority" function, for it deploys this idea of Asian Pacific women to "discipline" white women, just as Asian Pacific Americans in general are frequently used in negative comparisons with their "non-model" counterparts, African Americans.

The passage is also a telling illustration of how colonial and military domination are interwoven with sexual domination to create the "great western male fantasy." Military involvement in Asia, colonial and neocolonial history, and the derivative Asian Pacific sex tourism industry have established power relations between Asia and the West that in turn have shaped stereotypes of Asian Pacific women. Through mass media and popular culture, these stereotypes are internationally transferred so that they apply to women both in and outside of Asia. As his article continues, Rivers suggests that the celluloid prototype of the "Hong Kong hooker with a heart of gold" (from the 1960 film, The World of Suzie Wong) may be available in one's own hometown: "Suzie Wong was the originator of the modern fantasy. . . . Perhaps even now, . . . on the edge of a small town, Suzie awaits a call." These internationalized stereotypes, combined with the inability of U.S. Americans to distinguish between Asian Pacific foreigners

---

Oriental Techniques of Pain and Pleasure." James S. Moy, Marginal Sights: Staging the Chinese in America 136-37 (1993) (citing Final Report of the Attorney General's Commission on Pornography 388-433 (1986)). See also Diana Russell, Against Pornography 53-55, 61-62, 64, 102-05 (1993) (observing that pornographic portrayals of Asian Pacific women reveal "common racist stereotypes about Asian women as extremely submissive and knowledgeable about how to serve and 'please a man,'" and documenting the considerable use of bondage and torture in this sub-genre that caters to male arousal through domination of women); Michael Stein, The Ethnography of an Adult Bookstore: Private Scenes, Public Spaces 60-61 (1990), cited in Eddy Meng, Note, Mail Order Brides: Gilded Prostitution and the Legal Response, 28 U. Mich. J.L. Reform 197 n.204 (1994) (citing magazines such as Oriental Pussy and Hong Kong Hookers, in addition to pornographic video titles). Meng also uncovered an Internet service entitled "Oriental Fetish" that encourages users to "learn the secrets of Oriental Sexuality." Id. at 230 n.206.

In addition to the pornography industry, there are semi-pornographic portrayals of Asian Pacific women in other more "respectable" outlets. Sweeps week often features sensational "exposés" of sex tourism industries in Bangkok, Thailand or in the Philippines for talk shows and local news stations. Teaser ads for these "news" segments typically expose as much Asian Pacific skin as is allowed on television. The advertising industry has bestowed the Clio, its highest award, on a commercial campaign for Singapore Airlines that consisted solely of smiling flight attendants in traditional dress and soft focus with the tag line, "Singapore Girl, You're a great way to fly." For a more in-depth description of this ad campaign, see infra. A recent CD cover for New York recording artist John Zorn displays sadomasochistic images taken from Japanese pornographic films of Japanese women bound and suspended by ropes. Elisa Lee, Uprooting the Garden of Torture, Third Force, Nov.-Dec. 1994, at 18. Mail-order bride industries posing as matchmaking businesses with names such as Cherry Blossoms or Lotus Blossoms also exploit stereotypical images of willing, pliant and impoverished Asian Pacific sex partners for middle-aged American males disenchanted by "liberated" American women. See Venny Villapando, The Business of Selling Mail-Order Brides, in Making Waves: An Anthology of Writings By and About Asian American Women 319-20 (Asian Women United of Cal. ed., 1989).

and Asian Pacific Americans, result in a globalized dimension to the social construction of APA women.

Given this cultural backdrop of converging racial and gender stereotypes in which the model minority meets Suzie Wong, so to speak, APA women are especially susceptible to racialized sexual harassment. . . .

Notes

1. Anti-Discrimination Law and the Problem of Intersectionality. How should courts resolve the equal protection issue Scales-Trent raises? Should discrimination against women of color receive strict scrutiny or intermediate scrutiny? Should each subgroup be examined by courts to see whether it constitutes a "discrete and insular minority"? Will such specificity make the equal protection clause jurisprudence unworkable? Do you agree that a "many-headed Hydra" threatens to emerge from the "subset" approach?

2. Conceptualizing Discrimination and the Problem of Intersectionality. Does the doctrinal problem reveal a deeper philosophical problem in anti-discrimination jurisprudence? Kimberlé Crenshaw, who coined the term "intersectionality" in her article Demarginalizing the Intersection of Race and Sex: A Black Feminist Critique of Antidiscrimination Doctrine, Feminist Theory, and Antiracist Politics, believes so:

> According to the dominant view, a discriminator treats all people within a race or sex category similarly. Any significant experiential or statistical variation within this group suggests either that the group is not being discriminated against or that conflicting interests exist which defeat any attempts to bring a common claim. Consequently, one generally cannot combine these categories. Race and sex, moreover, become significant only when they operate to explicitly *disadvantage* the victims; because the *privileging* of whiteness or maleness is implicit, it is generally not perceived at all. . . .
>
> Because the scope of antidiscrimination law is so limited, sex and race discrimination have come to be defined in terms of the experiences of those who are privileged *but for* their racial or sexual characteristics. Put differently, the paradigm of sex discrimination tends to be based on the experiences of white women; the model of race discrimination tends to be based on the experiences of the most privileged Blacks. Notions of what constitutes race and sex discrimination are, as a result, narrowly tailored to embrace only a small set of circumstances, none of which include discrimination against Black women.
> . . .
>
> If any real efforts are to be made to free Black people of the constraints and conditions that characterize racial subordination, then theories and strategies purporting to reflect the Black community's needs must include an analysis of sexism and patriarchy. Similarly, feminism must include an analysis of race if it hopes to express the aspirations of non-white women. Neither

Black liberationist politics nor feminist theory can ignore the intersectional experiences of those whom the movements claim as their respective constituents.

1989 U. Chi. Legal. F. 150-51, 166.

Does Cho's argument about the "racialized sexual harassment" to which Asian-American women are subjected suggest that the law of sexual harassment has been based on the experiences of white women? Might sexual harassment law be analyzed differently if Asian American women's experiences were considered paradigmatic?

Analyzing EEOC data on sexual harassment charges brought against employers from 1992 through 1999, Tanya Hernandez found that women of color brought disproportionately more sexual harassment claims than white women. Tanya Kateri Hernandez, Sexual Harassment and Racial Disparity: The Mutual Construction of Gender and Race, 4 J. Gender Race & Justice 183, 186-87 (2001); see also Kimberlé Crenshaw, Race, Gender, and Sexual Harassment, 65 S. Cal. L. Rev. 1467, 1470 (1992) (speculating that women of color's experiences with racism may make it easier for them than for white women to challenge sexual harassment). Hernandez suggests that the racialized sexual harassment of women of color has much in common with sex tourism, in which men go to "exotic" locales in search of racially "different" women. She concludes:

> [R]egardless of whether a separate cause of action is developed for racialized sexual harassment or whether the current sexual harassment cause of action is modified to explicitly permit evidence of racial harassment as part of the sexual harassment claim, the joint analysis of sex tourism and sexual harassment charges reveals the need to begin to infuse sexual harassment law with a deeper understanding of the ways in which gender is racialized. In short, an understanding of the globalized stereotypes of women of color as sexual commodities must begin to be incorporated into the construction of sexual harassment claims, thereby beginning to get at the root of how gender is racialized generally. A globalized understanding of sexual harassment, for instance, would require that the element of "unwelcomeness" be informed by the knowledge that harassers perceive "welcomeness" to sexual overtures just by virtue of a woman's race or ethnicity. This gives even more meaning to Catharine MacKinnon's observation . . . that sexual harassment is, in essence, a solicitation for prostitution.
>
> Educating the judiciary and public of all the ways in which gender is racially constructed and maintained should begin with the observation that racialized sexual harassment is what happens to White women even if they are not cognizant of it in that way. The sex tourism context highlights this premise nicely with its positioning of subjugated "natives" in opposition to emasculating White American "woman-libbers" in the construction of gender. Accordingly, White women's stories of sexual harassment, like the stories of women of color, should start to be analyzed as part of the process of racialization in addition to being viewed as a form of sex discrimination. Using a racial lens to

assess all women's stories of sexual harassment may be helpful in the continuing project of making the legal claim of sexual harassment more responsive to the lives of real women.

Hernandez, supra, at 213-14. Is the sexual harassment of white women racialized? For the previous discussion of this issue, see pages 587-596 and 1022-1030.

b. Patriarchy, Feminism, and Men

Note, Invisible Man: Black and Male under Title VII
104 Harv. L. Rev. 749, 750-54, 755-56, 763-65, 766-67 (1991)

The law has not recognized that the black male gender, rather than providing privileges in the workplace normally associated with being male, signals a unique basis of vulnerability to employment discrimination. Reasoning that black men's experience of being male represents a mere racial variation on the white male experience, courts incorrectly assume that black men suffer from discrimination only because they are black and not because they are black men. Conceptualizing separate and overlapping black and male categories, judges are unable to recognize the distinctive features of being black and male that serve as the target for discrimination. When an employer hires or promotes only white men and black women, therefore, black men currently have no remedy for disparate impact under Title VII. . . .

. . . Discrimination cannot be adequately analyzed by placing people in simple gender or racial categories and then arguing that some belong to multiple groups. Categorization leads judges to misunderstand how employers act upon both black men and women in ways arising from an inseparable combination of race and sex — that black men, like black women, experience discrimination that is peculiar to their history and social position. Once Title VII doctrine recognizes that black men stand alone in their experience, the status of black women and white men in the defendant's workplace will no longer be dispositive. To address the claims of black men, judges should thus use a framework that takes into account the complex interplay between sex and race — one that parallels the framework increasingly used to analyze black women's claims.

Many employers refuse to extend equal employment opportunities to black men. Black men are disproportionately unemployed in most fields, both those with high threshold qualifications and those requiring a low or no particular level of education. Currently, the government estimates that black men have an unemployment rate of 12.2%, compared with 11.5% for black women and only 4.4% for white men and 4.9% for white women.

Those black men who do work are overwhelmingly found in low-status labor occupations, fields with the highest levels of unemployment. In these occupations, desegregation has been slow and difficult, and statistics indicate that black men work significantly longer hours than white men in the same positions.

Although proportionately fewer black than white workers as a group are eligible for professional positions under current criteria, black men are at a particular disadvantage even in these male-dominated fields. Only 14% of working black men are employed in managerial and professional jobs, as compared with 18.2% of working black women, 26.4% of white men, and 26.5% of white women. Indeed, of the top ten job categories to which black men belong, none are professional. Similarly, of the black men who are employed, only 16.7% work in the female-dominated technical, sales, and administrative support services, compared with 38.8% for black women, 19.6% for white men, and 45.3% for white women. White men are thus better represented in the upper-level than mid-level white-collar fields, while black men are not, and in fact are the least represented overall.

Educational disadvantage is an inadequate explanation for these occupational distributions and the corresponding unemployment rates. According to a government study, black men who are eligible only for positions not requiring a high school diploma had significantly higher unemployment than did white men with similar profiles. Therefore, because blue-collar jobs generally do not have educational requirements, the educational disadvantages black men face cannot explain the disparity between black and white men in these occupations. Although an unequal educational background may explain in part the status of black men in high-level professions — white men are twice as likely to graduate from college as are black men, and three black women graduate each year for every two black men — even black men who achieve the qualifications necessary for positions offering upward mobility are disproportionately unemployed. Statistics indicate that black men who have attended college have a higher level of unemployment — and earn less — than white high school dropouts.

. . . .

In white- and blue-collar fields, then, explaining the low rates of work force participation requires a particularized account of the black male experience. Certainly, serious social factors not directly attributable to discrimination work to remove black men from the realm of employability. These include incarceration and early death; currently, there are several hundred thousand more black women in the United States than there are black men. Nevertheless, unemployment figures reflect only those individuals eligible and looking for work; factors compromising employability do not address the concern that those black men who are seeking jobs do not find them. In trying to understand why the unemployment disparities are so stark, comparisons between black men on one hand and white women, white men, and black women on the other reveal that assigning privilege and disadvantage to simple gender and racial categories only promotes confusion. For example, although black men have a lower representation in the professional workforce than black women, black men enjoy a higher median income. Black men's status, therefore, is different from that which results from averaging the statuses of white men and black women. Because employer discrimination is the only remaining explanation for the black male variance in unemployment, an individualized, distinctive conception of the existing barriers black men face must be developed. . . .

[The author states that "no published opinion has permitted a black man to prevail in a sex-and-race discrimination suit," and suggests that since the doctrinal foundation for such a claim exists, courts must experience some problem in applying it to black men.]

Sex-plus analysis seems at first inapt when applied to black men, whose sex seems to connote privilege rather than disadvantage. The intuitive contradiction of a claim of sex discrimination against men makes it difficult for judges to place black men's claims in the framework used to assess other dual discrimination claims because courts fail to recognize that black men stand in a unique social position. The unique position of other groups, such as black women, is easier to identify because each component of black women's disenfranchisement is commonly recognized as creating a protected class; taken together, two traditionally suspect categories create a super-suspect category that is easy to see. Yet black men do not benefit in employment from privilege by gender; rather, they are totally separated from white men when blackness, a traditionally disenfranchised category, is combined with maleness, normally considered a privileged one.

Suspicious of black men's claims of distinctive race-and-sex discrimination, courts demand proof of gender-neutral racism before or instead of additionally addressing the male sex discrimination claim. Courts have thus erred in two different ways. First, contrary to the line of Title VII jurisprudence involving black women, some courts refuse even to reach the merits of the sex discrimination claim unless the plaintiff has established a firm foundation of race discrimination. In Robinson v. Adams,[122] for example, the Ninth Circuit rejected the argument that a black man had established a prima facie case of sex-and-race discrimination against Orange County, which employed many black people but almost no black men. The court wrote:

> Conceivably, the absence of any Black male employees could result from racial stereotyping or have some other link to racial discrimination. . . . [The plaintiff's] showing that Black males are statistically underrepresented cannot, standing alone, show a racially discriminatory impact when there is clearly no racially discriminatory impact on Blacks as a whole.

122. 847 F.2d 1315 (9th Cir. 1987).

Whereas black women need not show generic race discrimination to state a Title VII claim, to require such proof of black men may effectively bar them from bringing their claims.

The second consequence of the limited analysis applied to black men is that, because courts gauge social difference using white male workers as the standard, they simply do not address black male claims of sexism when the plaintiff has alleged both types of discrimination. Judges instead subsume one claim into the other. Reviewing an appeal in the Ninth Circuit, the court in a footnote prefatorily dismissed an effort by a black man to bring a race-and-sex discrimination claim: "[The plaintiff] generally alleged that the [defendant] discriminated against him on the basis of race, color, sex, and national origin. His essential complaint, however, appears to be that the Board denied him a license because he is black."[126] Other courts have similarly narrowed their inquiries by examining only the racial discrimination component of race-and-sex claims.

Courts are not alone in overlooking the possibility of sex discrimination against black men. Part of the responsibility for the absence of case law entertaining race-and-sex discrimination claims by black men lies with the black male plaintiffs and their own normative male focus. The availability of relief is largely influenced by the content of the pleaded complaint: courts will not respond to claims that are not before them. Black men often may not conceive of the discrimination they experience as calling for a distinctive assessment and may thus bring claims of racial discrimination alone when claims of race-and-sex discrimination would be more appropriate. As the primary framers of legal rules, men universalize from the male experience in critiquing social and economic structures. Thus, when black men experience discrimination — even if black women could not have had the same experience — they are likely to describe the discrimination as relating only to their race. . . .

There is a logical necessity to the application of Title VII to the claims of black men. Rejecting categorization means that discrimination against each group takes a unique form — being black as a categorical experience inaccurately depicts actual circumstance. Just as black women are discriminated against because they are black women, black men are discriminated against because they are black men and not merely because they are black. Certainly, the empirical evidence supports this latter contention; both objective and subjective hiring criteria work against black men in ways that they do not against other groups. If sex-plus and race-plus analyses are understood to connote that employment discrimination cannot be severed into independent forces, black men can begin to obtain the relief necessary to bring them within the realm of equalized opportunity.

---

126. Haddock v. Board of Dental Examiners, 777 F.2d 462, 463 n.1 (9th Cir. 1985).

Nancy Levit, Feminism for Men: Legal Ideology and the Construction of Maleness
43 UCLA L. Rev. 1037, 1038-41 (1996)

It may seem a little odd to suggest that feminist theory has overlooked men. In varying ways, liberal feminism, difference theory, dominance theory, and postmodern feminism have analyzed, objectified, vilified, and deconstructed men as a population, male as a gender and constellation of role expectations and typical behaviors, and men as historical crafters of doctrine, theory, and language. Yet, in several important respects, apart from the crucial role of culprit, men have been largely omitted from feminism.

Feminist legal theorists have paid mild attention to whether men could embrace feminist objectives — the "Can men be feminists?" question. This issue is treated as a relatively unimportant one, usually relegated to footnotes. Legal literature has given relatively modest and incidental attention to how a wide variety of gender role stereotypes harm men, and how legal constructs perpetuate these stereotypes. The negative effect gender role stereotypes have on men is typically subsidiary to the main focus of feminist legal literature, which has concentrated on documenting the patterns of subordination of women. Inquiry in feminist legal theory has focused instead on questions of feminist ideology, epistemology, and political philosophy. Theorists in disciplines other than law have demonstrated significantly more interest in constructs of masculinity. Perhaps most significantly, though, men have been omitted as participants in the reconstructive project.

The primary purpose of this Article is to suggest that feminist legal theory needs to turn its attention to issues of relational justice: avoiding gender role stereotyping in both directions. To this end, the Article evaluates how the different strands of feminist legal theory treat men. Over the course of the development of equal treatment theory, special treatment theory, radical feminism, and postmodern feminism, men have been treated as objects of analysis, as "other," as oppressors, or have simply been omitted. In significant part, the inattention to the situations of men was understandable. Perhaps to come into being, feminist theory was necessarily exclusionary, carving out its own space. On the theoretical level, feminism is ready to take the next step and inclusively invite men into the discourse.

The second objective of this Article is to explore the ways in which men are harmed by gender stereotypes. The Article applies insights from feminist thought to situations in which gender role stereotypes operate to the detriment of men. Thus, the Article considers the ways in which legal constructs and methods of analysis have helped to shape masculinity. Maleness has been constructed in a number of ways by statutes, judicial decisions, and legal reasoning. I suggest that one component of male aggression has been legal doctrines that shape concepts of personhood by dictating who society's criminals and warriors are. The image of masculinity is also formed by legal responses to areas in which men suffer injuries. Laws preventing male plaintiffs from suing for same-sex sexual harassment, and analysts' lack of interest in male rape and spousal battery of men contribute to a climate in which men are taught to suffer in silence. In the areas of parental leave and child custody, men are socially and legally excluded from caring and nurturing roles. Various legal doctrines send distinct messages about what it means to be male. This cumulative legal ideology of masculinity is under-explored.

Finally, this Article will suggest ways that men and women can reconstruct a social world in which traditional gender roles diminish in importance. The point here is not simply that feminist discourse can be powerful without being a conversation of exclusion, but that for feminist objectives to succeed, they must become more all-encompassing. This Article argues that it is not only possible for men to become feminists, but imperative that they do. By demonstrating some of the ways patriarchy harms men, I hope to encourage men to care about, and to work toward, the dismantling of patriarchy.

I should start with a caveat and a couple of disclaimers. First, it may seem harsh to criticize feminist theory for succeeding, for doing what it set out to do: to thoroughly document the persistence of patriarchy across time and cultures. But this is not the nature of my critique. This Article argues that feminism has stalled in an important way by not reaching far enough.

One fear I have in embarking on this essay is that the project of cataloguing the omission of men from feminist theory might be seen as an attempt to diminish the centuries of horrors experienced by women. My purpose is quite the contrary. Instead, I hope to advance the cause of feminism by pointing out the more universal harms of gender role stereotyping. This Article is intended as a sympathetic critique, offered from the perspective of a feminist who is deeply troubled by the bipolar nature of the sameness-difference debate. A second concern is that exploring the treatment of men in and by feminist theory will itself foster both polarization of the gender categories "male" and "female" as well as an essentialist approach. Gay and lesbian legal theories remind us of how incomplete and unnuanced any dichotomous male/female analysis of gender is. A related concern is that the identification of gender stereotypes might reinscribe them. Finally, I worry that some of the substance of this piece will be coopted by those who would misuse the arguments toward antifeminist ends: either to deny the necessity of feminist legal theory or to distort the historical treatment of women. Yet this Article was largely impelled by the lessons of feminist theory itself—not to allow issues to remain silenced and to "question everything."

Notes

1. Men and the Intersection of Gender and Race. Is the subordinated status of men of color a feminist issue? Like the author of the student note excerpted above, Floyd Weatherspoon argues that African-American men suffer from a combination of race and gender discrimination both in employment and in the criminal justice system. See Floyd D. Weatherspoon, Remedying Employment Discrimination Against African American Males, 36 Washburn L.J. 23 (1996); Floyd D. Weatherspoon, The Devastating Impact of the Justice System on the Status of African-American Males: An Overview Perspective, 23 Cap. U. L. Rev. 23 (1994). In contrast, Devon Carbado asserts that "Heterosexual Black men occupy a privileged victim status in antiracist discourse.":

> A central project of antiracist discourse is to reveal the extent to which Black men are victims of a racist criminal justice system. Given the statistics for Black male incarceration and the problems of discrimination in the criminal justice system, this project is undeniably important.
>
> Nevertheless, as a result of this focus on Black men without a similar focus on Black women, Black men are perceived to be significantly more vulnerable and significantly more "endangered" than Black women. Black men become the quintessential example of the effects of racial subordination. . . .
>
> As a consequence of this myth of racial authenticity and the currency of the endangered Black male trope, when an individual Black man is on trial for some criminal offense, the Black community sees first and foremost his status as a racial victim. Furthermore, when the alleged crime involves violence against women, the fact that a Black female or a woman of any race may be the victim of Black male aggression is subordinate to the concern that a Black man may be the victim of a racist criminal justice system.

Devon W. Carbado, Men in Black, 3 J. Gender, Race & Justice 427, 429 (2000); see also Kevin Brown, The Social Construction of a Rape Victim: Stories of African American Males About the Rape of Desireé Washington, in Black Men on Race, Gender, and Sexuality: A Critical Reader (Devon W. Carbado ed. 1999). Could Weatherspoon and Carbado both be correct? How should feminists conceptualize the relationship between women of color and men of color in a society that is both racist and sexist?

2. Feminist Theory and Men. Does feminist theory, as Nancy Levit suggests, wrongly ignore the distinctive burdens faced by men in a gendered society? A few high-profile books for a popular audience have recently tried to explore issues of masculinity in contemporary social life. See Susan Faludi, Stiffed: The Betrayal of the American Man (2000); Christina Hoff Sommers, The War Against Boys: How Misguided Feminism Is Harming Our Young (2000). Similarly, a few legal theorists have suggested that understanding and combating violence against women necessitates attention to social norms of masculinity. See Katharine K. Baker, Sex, Rape, and Shame, 79 B.U. L. Rev. 663 (1999); Angela P. Harris, Gender, Violence, Race, and Criminal Justice, 52 Stan. L. Rev. 777 (2000). Is exploration of patriarchy's burdens on heterosexual men a fruitful avenue for feminist theorizing? If so, what are those burdens? Levit names a few: the law encourages and condones male aggressive and violent behavior; the courts reinforce the social expectation that men should "suffer in silence" by trivializing men's experiences of rape and sexual harassment; and family law reinforces the stereotype that men do not belong in nurturing roles. Levit, supra, at 1055-1079. Do you agree? Are there other burdens?

Has feminism encouraged male-bashing? The Roper Organization conducted surveys in 1970 and 1990 in which they asked 3,000 American women and 1,000 American men a set of questions about their perceptions of men.[1] In the 1970 survey, two-thirds of those questioned agreed that men were basically kind, gentle, and thoughtful. In 1990, only fifty-one percent agreed. In 1970, forty-one percent of those surveyed thought that all men wanted from a date was to go to bed; in 1990, fifty-four percent reached that conclusion. In 1970, thirty-two percent believed that men were basically selfish and self-centered; in 1990, forty-two percent agreed. In 1970, forty-nine percent believed that men's egos require that they put women down; in 1990, fifty-five percent agreed. In 1970, thirty-nine percent believed that men were interested only in their work, and not really interested in their families. By 1990, after two decades of a fatherhood revolution, fifty-three percent of those surveyed believed that men were only interested in their work, a fourteen percent increase. Michael S. Kimmel, Issues for Men in the 1990s, 46 U. Miami L. Rev. 671, (1992). Are these shifts in views by women the healthy result of consciousness-raising? Or do they suggest a problematic willingness to blame "men" for complex structural problems?

The new "men's movement" may contribute to the sense of "gender war" described by Kimmel and such writers as Susan Faludi. See Faludi, Backlash: The Undeclared War Against American Women (1991). The most prominent spokesman for this movement, Robert Bly, urges that men "retreat from the world of women to temporary male sanctuaries in order to recapture some 'deep' or 'wild' masculinity that has become dormant in today's modern technological society in which women actively participate." Kimmel, supra, at 672, citing Robert Bly, Iron John: A Book About Men 6, 222-237, 244-249 (1990). Is there anything wrong with male "consciousness-raising"? What destructive, or constructive, impact might such a movement have on the role of gender in this society?

---

1. See Roper Organization, Opinions About Men, in The 1990 Virginia Slims Opinion Poll: A 20-Year Perspective of Women's Issues 54 (1990).

3. The Construction of Masculinity. In academic disciplines outside law, studies on masculinity have begun to emerge. See, e.g., R.W. Connell, Masculinities (1995); Lynne Segal, Slow Motion: Changing Masculinity, Changing Men (1990); Michael Kimmel, Manhood in America: A Cultural History (1996). Should legal theory follow suit, as Levit suggests? Is feminist legal theory the place for such investigation? Or is there reason for feminist legal theory to continue to focus on "women" (with all the definitional problems we have seen this entails)? Richard Delgado's fictional character, "Rodrigo Crenshaw," argues:

> [O]ne should never adopt the perspective of the more powerful group, even strategically. Adopting another's perspective is always a mistake. One starts out thinking one can go along with the more numerous, better organized, and more influential group — say, white women in the case of sisters of color — and reap some benefits. You think that you can jump nimbly aside before the inevitable setbacks, disappointments and double crosses set in. But you can't. You will march strongly and determinedly in the wrong direction, alienating yourself in the process. You'll end up having the newly deployed rights cut back in your case, perhaps being criticized as irresponsible when you try to exercise them. Moreover, any small suggestion for deviation in the agenda, any polite request that the larger group consider your own concerns, will bring quick denunciation. You are being divisive. You are weakening the movement.

Richard Delgado, Rodrigo's Sixth Chronicle: Intersections, Essences, and the Dilemma of Social Reform, 68 N.Y.U. L. Rev. 639, 657 (1993). Is this an argument against coalition building? Does it suggest that trying to include men in feminism is a bad idea? If Delgado is correct, should white women and women of color work together? Is Rodrigo's argument "essentialist" in assuming there are clear distinctions between groups?

For another take on the usefulness of taking "women" as the primary subject of feminism, see Christine A. Littleton, Does It Still Make Sense To Talk About "Women?" 1 UCLA Women's L.J. 15 (1991) (focusing on women avoids false inclusivity and gender "neutrality" that obscures continuing female subordination).

2. False Universalisms

Martinez v. Santa Clara Pueblo
402 F. Supp. 5 (D.N.M. 1975), rev'd and remanded, 540 F.2d 1039 (10th Cir. 1976), rev'd, 436 U.S. 49 (1978)

MECHEM, District Judge.

Julia Martinez and her daughter Audrey Martinez bring this suit, each individually and as the representative of a class, against the Santa Clara Pueblo and Governor Lucario Padilla, individually and in his capacity as governor of the Pueblo. Plaintiffs claim that a portion of a tribal ordinance which denies Pueblo membership to the children of female but not male members of the Pueblo who marry non-members of the Pueblo, violates 25 U.S.C. §1302(8), which prohibits a tribal government in the exercise of its powers of self-government from denying "to any persons within its jurisdiction the equal protection of its laws or depriv(ing) any person of liberty or property without due process of law." Plaintiffs seek an injunction against the further enforcement of the ordinance.

[25 U.S.C. §1302, the Indian Civil Rights Act, was enacted by Congress in 1968. The purpose of the Act was to "single out the more important civil rights contained in the Constitution and to render those applicable to tribal members who reside on the reservation," Martinez v. Santa Clara Pueblo, 540 F.2d 1039, 1042 (1976). Congress made some effort to square these new rights with existing tribal law and custom; for example, the Fifteenth Amendment and the nonestablishment clause of the First Amendment were omitted from the Act. Moreover, courts have held that the requirements of the ICRA are not necessarily coextensive with the requirements of the U.S. Constitution. See, e.g., Howlett v. The Salish and Kootenai Tribes, 529 F.2d 233 (9th Cir. 1976). Nevertheless, many Indian nations, including the Pueblo, were opposed to the ICRA, seeing it as an effort to undermine tribal law. Martinez v. Santa Clara Pueblo, 540 F.2d at 1045.]

The ordinance, passed in 1939, reads as follows: . . .

1. All children born of marriage between members of the Santa Clara Pueblo shall be members of the Santa Clara Pueblo.

2. All children born of marriage between male members of the Santa Clara Pueblo and non-members shall be members of the Santa Clara Pueblo.

3. Children born of marriage between female members of the Santa Clara Pueblo and non-members shall not be members of the Santa Clara Pueblo.

4. Persons shall not be naturalized as members of the Santa Clara Pueblo under any circumstances.

Plaintiffs attack subparts two and three of the ordinance. . . .

The social and political organization of the Pueblo must be discussed first. Santa Clara Pueblo was founded around 1300 A.D. The Pueblo now covers roughly 48,000 acres, held by the United States in trust for the Pueblo. Approximately 1,200 recognized members and between 150 and 200 non-members currently live on the Pueblo. Approximately 150 recognized members live elsewhere, one-third of them in other locations in New Mexico, and the rest scattered across twenty-two different states.

In its early days, Santa Clara culture made no distinction between what Anglo-Americans would term "political" and "religious" matters. However, with the Spanish invasion in the early seventeenth century, the Pueblo instituted a "secular" government to distract Spanish attention from the caciques (religious leaders) who were the real authorities in the Pueblo. The distinction between religious and secular spheres is now well established in the Santa Clara culture.

The membership of the Pueblo is and has been organized into what the anthropologists refer to as "moieties," specifically the Winter people and the Summer people. Each moiety is led by a cacique; and each is further divided into factions. The precise function and significance of moiety membership is not clear on the record; it is, however, clear that it is primarily a religious grouping. The caciques are still the dominant authorities in the Pueblo, nominating the candidates for secular office and exercising an effective veto by influence over the actions of the secular government.

The division of the moieties into factions is a relatively recent development. During the early part of the twentieth century sharp conflicts developed in the Pueblo over the importance of traditional customs and values in the life of the Pueblo. For example, a major source of controversy was whether the Governor should be an older, highly respected man who was well versed in the traditional ways, or a younger man, educated in Anglo-American schools, who could speak English and would be able to deal more effectively with non-Pueblo society. The disagreement literally split the Pueblo, and during the late 1920s and early 1930s the Pueblo had two governors, neither of whom recognized the authority of the other, and two separate Winter and Summer moieties. The Bureau of Indian Affairs (BIA) staff in Washington offered to arbitrate the dispute. The entire Pueblo agreed that the BIA officials from Washington were irrelevant.

[The members of the Pueblo] did agree to have the resident BIA agent, Elizabeth Sargent, help settle the difference. At her suggestion, and after much discussion, the Pueblo organized pursuant to the authority of the Wheeler-Howard Act, 25 U.S.C. §476, and adopted a Constitution and By-Laws in 1935. As reorganized the secular government retained many of its traditional institutions, such as the unity of the legislative and "appellate" judicial functions in the Council, while at the same time incorporating and instituting certain Anglo-American institutions, principally voting for secular officials. Thus, the present Pueblo government is neither wholly traditional nor wholly anglicized.

Under the Constitution and By-Laws there is a single governing body, the Council, which possesses both legislative and "appellate" judicial powers. Santa Clara Constitution, Article IV, Sections 1 and 2. The Council consists of the secular officers of the Pueblo — the Governor, the Lieutenant Governor, the Secretary, the Treasurer, the Interpreter, and the Sheriff — and eight representatives. Santa Clara Constitution, Article III, Sections 1 and 5. As a matter of custom and practice, the representatives represent the factions, which still exist.

The Governor is the chief executive of the Pueblo charged with enforcing the law "civil and criminal, written and unwritten." Santa Clara Constitution, Article V; Santa Clara By-Laws, Article 1, Section 1. In addition he appears to have the initial responsibility for settling controversies among and concerning the members of the Pueblo. A person aggrieved by a ruling of the Governor may appeal to the Council, id., at which time the Governor may vote only to break a tie. Santa Clara Constitution, Article IV, Section 2.

All other secular governmental power and responsibility is vested in the Council, including the power to enact ordinances governing Pueblo life, Santa Clara Constitution, Article IV, Section 1, Subsection 5. Most important for the present case, the Constitution specifically grants the Council the power to determine which children of mixed marriages shall be recognized as members of the Pueblo, Santa Clara Constitution, Article II, Section 2, and to determine who is a member for purposes of dealings in land and land use rights, Santa Clara Constitution, Article VII, Section 1. The 1939 Ordinance was enacted by the Council pursuant to these powers, and is agreed by all parties to be in force at this time.

The factual development of the equal protection claims of the parties is best begun by identifying the interests of plaintiffs and defendants affected or served by the Ordinance.

. . . Audrey Martinez is the daughter of the marriage of plaintiff Julia Martinez, a recognized member of the Pueblo and Myles Martinez, a non-member of the Pueblo. It is undisputed that the 1939 Ordinance bars recognition of Audrey as a member of the Pueblo. If Myles were a member of the Pueblo and Julia Martinez were not — or if Julia were not married, and Audrey had been born out of wedlock, the Ordinance would not bar her recognition as a member and the Council would in fact so recognize her.

Julia Martinez has lived at the Pueblo all her life, with the exception of a relatively brief absence to further her education. Myles Martinez has lived at the Pueblo ever since his marriage to Julia, with the exception of a relatively brief absence while serving in the armed forces. Audrey Martinez grew up on the Pueblo, although she does leave to pursue her education. Aside from the fact that she is not recognized as a member of the Pueblo and is therefore denied certain rights, she has been raised in the culture of Santa Clara, speaks Tewa, the traditional language, and clearly considers herself to be a Santa Claran.

As a factual matter, recognition as a member of the Pueblo would give Audrey Martinez three distinct types of rights which she is presently denied. First, she would gain political rights, primarily the right to vote, to take matters before the Pueblo Council, and the qualification to hold office as a secular official.

Secondly, she would be entitled to share in the material benefits of Pueblo membership. The most important of the material benefits is that referred to as land use rights. . . . Other material benefits and privileges include the right to hunt and fish on the land, the use of irrigation water, and an equal share in any distribution of pecuniary benefits made by the Pueblo, or any other programs, present or future, undertaken by the Pueblo for the benefit of its members.

Third, as members, Audrey and other children similarly situated would as of right be able to continue living at the Pueblo. While it is true that the Martinez family and a number of other families in their position live at the Pueblo, this is not as a matter of right. If and when Mrs. Martinez dies, the rest of the family, as non-members would not have the right to continue living on the Pueblo, though it is not now known whether they would be forced to leave. Furthermore, under the Santa Clara Constitution, Article IV, Section 1, Subsection 5, non-members and only non-members may be expelled from the Pueblo for violating a Pueblo Ordinance.

Lack of membership does not now affect entitlement to federal benefits accorded Indians generally, or participation in the religious life of the Pueblo. In 1968, Mr. and Mrs. Martinez obtained BIA census numbers for their children, and since then the children have received all federal benefits generally available to Indians, including educational and medical benefits. As to religion, Audrey Martinez is already allowed to participate in Pueblo religious ceremonies to the same extent that she would be if she were a recognized member of the Pueblo. Thus, the question presented is one of membership in the Pueblo for purposes of purely internal, secular, rights and privileges. . . .

In addition to these relatively precise and legally protectible interests, Julia and Audrey Martinez and many of those similarly situated share a strong emotional involvement with the Pueblo. Regardless of official definitions of membership, Julia Martinez feels that her children, having grown up in Santa Clara, should be recognized as Santa Clarans. Audrey Martinez, despite official definitions, clearly considers herself to be a Santa Clara Indian. While the law may not recognize or protect these interests, it would be foolish to pretend that they do not exist.

While the factual context of the legal claims made by Audrey and Julia Martinez differs, it is clear that both ultimately present the same legal question — whether the 1939 Ordinance violates their rights to equal protection of tribal laws, as secured to them by the Indian Civil Rights Act, 25 U.S.C. §1302(8).

The specific interests of the Pueblo in membership policies generally and in the particular policy of the 1939 Ordinance are of concern as well. Since 1680 the Pueblo has existed as a conquered people, identifiable as a group but surrounded by an alien culture, first Spanish and later American. From a practical political standpoint, the result has been a tension in the life of the Pueblo between traditional Pueblo customs and values and the "modern" customs and values of Anglo-American society. As noted above, this tension was once so acute that the Pueblo became divided against itself. The differences were eventually resolved by the adoption of the Constitution, which drew upon both traditional Pueblo and modern Anglo-American institutions, synthesizing them into a unique structure neither wholly traditional nor wholly modern.

The function of membership policies must be examined within this context. . . . [Membership policies] are no more or less than a mechanism of social, and to an extent psychological and cultural, self-definition. The importance of this to Santa Clara or to any other Indian tribe cannot be overstressed. In deciding who is and who is not a member, the Pueblo decides what it is that makes its members unique, what distinguishes a Santa Clara Indian from everyone else in the United States. If its ability to do this is limited or restricted by an external authority, then a new definition of what it is to be a Santa Claran is imposed, and the culture of Santa Clara is inevitably changed.

The second major interest served by membership policies, and by the particular policy of the 1939 Ordinance, is that of economic survival of the tribal unit. As plaintiffs have demonstrated, the adoption of the 1939 Ordinance was in response to a sudden increase in mixed marriages, which had resulted in a proportionate strain on the economic resources of the Pueblo. Plaintiffs argue that economic integrity of the Pueblo is less important than cultural autonomy. The difficulty with this position is that the two are not easily separable. The ability of the Pueblo to control the use and distribution of its resources enhances its ability to maintain its cultural autonomy.

Plaintiffs do not challenge the power of the Pueblo, as delegated to and exercised by the Council, to make and enforce rules concerning membership. Their attack on the Ordinance is solely aimed at the criteria employed as to children of mixed marriages.

At trial the defendants sought to prove that the Ordinance was merely the written embodiment of ancient custom, or alternatively, that the Ordinance regulated membership for religious as well as secular purposes. The Ordinance does not regulate religious as well as political membership. As noted above, Audrey Martinez, although not a recognized member of the Pueblo, is allowed to participate in religious ceremonies to the same extent she would be if she were a member. While there is a relationship between religious life and secular, political life at Santa Clara, the distinction has been clear for nearly four hundred years. The Ordinance neither pertains to religious membership, nor necessarily affects it.

Whether or not the Ordinance is an embodiment of pre-existing ancient Pueblo custom is less clear. Before 1939 mixed marriages were relatively rare in the Pueblo, and consequently there was no need for a hard and fast rule concerning membership; rather, the Council considered each case separately.

In that sense, the establishment of any one rule must be seen as a break with tradition.

On the other hand, the criteria employed in classifying children of mixed marriages as members or non-members are rooted in certain traditional values. It appears that Santa Clara was traditionally patrilineal and patrilocal — in other words, that kinship, name and location of residence generally were expected to follow the male rather than the female line. These cultural expectations have lost much of their force, but they are not entirely vitiated. . . . Furthermore, it is apparent that membership of the parents and marriage, either within or out of the Pueblo, has always been considered a highly significant factor in membership determinations as opposed to other possible criteria such as degree of Santa Clara ancestry. When a member of the Pueblo married a non-member, the status of children of the marriage was questionable. Consonant with this, children born to an unmarried Santa Clara woman traditionally have been and still are recognized as members, regardless of who the father is or might be.

It is clear that the interests of plaintiffs and defendants in the 1939 Ordinance are vitally important. Indeed, they are fundamentally the same. Both sides have political and property rights which are affected by the Ordinance. Both sides also have a deep psychological and cultural interest in the membership Ordinance which, if not legally quantifiable, cannot be ignored. . . .

Courts faced with the necessity of construing 25 U.S.C. §1302(8) have consistently held that the equal protection guarantee of the Indian Civil Rights Act is not identical to the constitutional guarantee of equal protection. . . . Instead, the Act and its equal protection guarantee must be read against the background of tribal sovereignty and interpreted within the context of tribal law and custom. Crowe v. Eastern Band of Cherokee Indians etc., 506 F.2d 1231 (4th Cir. 1974). . . . Unfortunately, this principle does not answer questions so much as teach the terms in which they must be asked. . . .

. . . [T]here is authority to the effect that where a tribe has departed from traditional methods of choosing tribal officials and adopted Anglo-American voting procedures, the equal protection clause of the Act will incorporate the constitutional equal protection standard of Baker v. Carr, 369 U.S. 186 (1962), and, if necessary, courts will enforce that standard by ordering reapportionment of tribal voting districts. White Eagle v. One Feather, 478 F.2d 1311 (8th Cir. 1973). . . . Even in this situation, however, the courts have viewed the matter of reapportionment as an aspect of equal enforcement of already existing tribal law, and have refused to interpret the equal protection clause of 25 U.S.C. §1302(8) in a manner that would require the enfranchisement of a new class of the tribal population, Wounded Head v. Tribal Council of Oglala Sioux Tribe, 507 F.2d 1079, 1083 (8th Cir. 1975), on the grounds that such an action would come

dangerously close to substituting Anglo-American culture for tribal culture.
. . .

Plaintiffs do not suggest that the Indian Civil Rights Act should be interpreted in a manner which would impose an Anglo-American equal protection standard on tribes in derogation of their traditional values. To the contrary, they have consistently argued, as have the defendants, that the Act should be interpreted in such a manner as to preserve the cultural identity of Indian tribes in general and of Santa Clara in particular. Plaintiffs instead point out that the sex of the parent who is a member of the Pueblo bears little or no relationship to the strength of the parent's identification with traditional Santa Clara culture or the likelihood that the parent will attempt to pass the traditional cultural values on to the child. They point out, quite correctly, that Audrey Martinez and many other children similarly situated have been brought up on the Pueblo, speak the Tewa language, participate in its life, and are, culturally, for all practical purposes, Santa Clara Indians. On the other hand, there are certainly instances of children whose fathers are members of Santa Clara, but who have been raised far from the Pueblo, who cannot speak the language, who have not participated in the life of the Pueblo, and who know nothing of its values, customs and traditions, yet who are, under the 1939 Ordinance, recognized as members. Plaintiffs contend that this is not only irrational but actively destructive of the cultural identity of the Pueblo.

Even assuming plaintiffs are correct, the equal protection guarantee of the Indian Civil Rights Act should not be construed in a manner which would require or authorize this Court to determine which traditional values will promote cultural survival and therefore should be preserved and which of them are inimical to cultural survival and should therefore be abrogated. Such a determination should be made by the people of Santa Clara; not only because they can best decide what values are important, but also because they must live with the decision every day. Obviously they can and should be the judges of whether a particular rule is beneficial or inimical to their survival as a distinct cultural group.

Much has been written about tribal sovereignty. If those words have any meaning at all, they must mean that a tribe can make and enforce its decisions without regard to whether an external authority considers those decisions wise. To abrogate tribal decisions, particularly in the delicate area of membership, for whatever "good" reasons, is to destroy cultural identity under the guise of saving it. Congress has not indicated that it intended the Indian Civil Rights Act to be interpreted in such a manner.

Leti Volpp, Feminism Versus Multiculturalism
101 Colum. L. Rev. 1181, 1181-1183, 1184, 1204, 1205-1209, 1218 (2001)

The political theorist Susan Moller Okin recently posed the provocative question: Is multiculturalism bad for women?[1] According to Okin, until the past few decades minorities were expected to assimilate; now such assimilation is "considered oppressive." This, she suggests, raises a dilemma: What should be done when claims of minority cultures or religions contradict the norm of gender equality that is at least formally endorsed by liberal states?

As examples of the clash of cultures that can ensue, Okin proffers Muslim schoolchildren wearing head scarves, polygamous marriages in African immigrant communities, and female clitoridectomy in African immigrant communities in France and the United States. In addition, Okin describes four other types of cases that have surfaced in the United States. These are the marriages of children or marriages that are otherwise coerced (which she illustrates with an example involving Iraqi immigrants), Hmong marriage by capture, parent-child suicide by Japanese and Chinese immigrants, and "wife-murder by immigrants from Asian and Middle Eastern countries whose wives have either committed adultery or treated their husbands in a servile way."

Faced with this list, Okin concludes that we have too quickly assumed that feminism and multiculturalism are both good things that are easily reconciled. While she does acknowledge that "Western cultures, of course, still practice many forms of sex discrimination," and notes that "virtually all of the world's cultures have distinctly patriarchal pasts," she asserts that some cultures — mostly, she says, Western liberal cultures — 'have departed far further from [these pasts] than others." Her conclusion: Female members of "a more patriarchal minority culture" may "be much better off if the culture into which they were born were either to become extinct (so that its members would become integrated into the less sexist surrounding

---

1. Susan Moller Okin, Is Multiculturalism Bad for Women?, in Is Multiculturalism Bad for Women? 7, 9 (Joshua Cohen et al. eds., 1999) [hereinafter Is Multiculturalism Bad for Women?]. Okin's essay first appeared in the Boston Review, and was subsequently republished in a volume with responses by Katha Pollitt, Will Kymlicka, Bonnie Honig, Azizah Y. al-Hibri, Yael Tamir, Sander L. Gilman, Abdullahi An-Na'im, Robert Post, Bhikhu Parekh, Saskia Sassen, Homi K. Bhabha, Cass R. Sunstein, Joseph Raz, Janet E. Halley, and Martha C. Nussbaum. Is Multiculturalism Bad for Women?, supra, at v-vi. Of these respondents, Honig, Gilman, and Bhabha question Okin's fundamental premise that Western liberal societies are definitionally less gender-subordinating than minority immigrant communities, as I do in this paper. Homi K. Bhabha, Liberalism's Sacred Cow, in Is Multiculturalism Bad for Women?, supra, at 79, 79-80; Sander L. Gilman, "Barbaric" Rituals?, in Is Multiculturalism Bad for Women?, supra, at 53, 57-58; Bonnie Honig, "My Culture Made Me Do It," in Is Multiculturalism Bad for Women?, supra, at 35, 36-37, 40; Okin, supra, at 22-23. An-Na'im similarly raises the issue of Okin's failure to address economic rights, although he separates the question of economic rights from the issue of gender. Abdullahi An-Na'im, Promises We Should All Keep in Common Cause, in Is Multiculturalism Bad for Women?, supra, at 59, 61-62.

culture),'' or if the culture were "encouraged to alter itself so as to reinforce the equality of women. . . .''

But is Okin correct to posit multiculturalism and feminism as contradictory? I argue here that posing multiculturalism and feminism as oppositional results in a discourse of "feminism versus multiculturalism" that is premised on serious and fundamental logical flaws. Such a discourse relies upon a particular subject, the immigrant woman victim of minority culture. In examining how the figure of the immigrant woman victim is constructed, I address both the theoretical bases of the feminism versus multiculturalism discourse and the disturbing consequences of its adoption.

. . . The thrust of my argument is not that we ought to eliminate or dismiss feminist values, but to suggest they will broaden and shift when we examine immigrant and Third World women in a more accurate light. . . .

Society's excessive focus on minority and Third World sex-subordinating cultural practices has four detrimental effects. . . .

First, in concealing structural forces that shape cultural practices, what can be erased are forces that make culture. Specific cultural practices are connected to forces that deny women economic and political agency. These forces include global inequalities; new articulations of patriarchies in specific regions that are, for example, the result of emerging religious fundamentalisms; the legacies of colonialism and racism; and the flows of transnational capital. Our culture is not constructed within "hermetically sealed" boxes that travel with us from cradle to grave. While culture is often represented as the product of timeless ritual insular to particular communities, such forces profoundly shape culture.

As an example, the historical practice of sati — immolation of a widow on her husband's funeral pyre — is consistently singled-out as an expression of Indian culture or Hindu religion, and is often described as caused by religious and wifely devotion. But sati was not constituted as a practice through "Indian culture" or "Hindu religion" alone. Feminist theorist Lata Mani has examined how the "tradition" of sati was constructed through the collaboration of British colonial officials and Hindu pundits who attempted to find a religious basis for the practice as the colonial government sought to determine the appropriate legislative response. Officials and missionaries constructed such a basis by ignoring and marginalizing anything that did not accord with their presumptions. In individual descriptions of sati, even while European observers wrote of "wifely devotion" and a superstitious and barbarous religion, nothing in the widows' explanations pointed to a religious basis for sati. Instead, their explanations consisted of concerns for future subsistence and financial support, concerns that were explicitly material and social. However, with the involvement of the British colonial government, religion and culture were given the force of explanation, obscuring material reasons for the practice. Sati continues to be so understood, and in fact, is very often utilized in philosophical discourse to represent extreme cultural difference.

As another example, amid the concern about gender apartheid under the Taliban, there has been little focus on the relationship between the intensification of religious fundamentalism and geopolitical economics. The United States gave aid to various mujahideen forces inAfghanistan to fight the Soviets. From these mujahideen groups, the Taliban emerged. The United States aided General Zia of Pakistan — whose government adopted the notorious hudood ordinances that among other provisions criminalized extramarital sex, so that women who accuse men of rape or become pregnant risk punishment for adultery — for the same reason. Feminists in the United States need to think critically about the relationship of this aid to states with policies inimical to women's concerns, instead of abstractly condemning Islam as the font of patriarchal oppression. At the same time, it is crucial for feminists to examine the importance of Christian fundamentalism within the United States and its effect on the lives of millions of women around the world through funding and development that structure reproductive practices and politics. Such an examination would lead to a more nuanced analysis of differential birth rates in the global North and South than afforded by the often cited explanation that birth rates are the product of differing cultural valuations about the worth of male children.

The second point is that the extreme focus on what is commonly conceptualized as cultural violence or subordination makes it difficult to see forces beyond culture. There are other important social, political, and economic issues affecting women's lives other than the cultural practices that garner so much attention. Only certain problems receive coverage or generate concern, namely those used to illustrate the alien and bizarre oppression of women of color; for example, sati, dowry death, veiling, female genital surgeries, female infanticide, marriage by capture, purdah, polygamy, footbinding, and arranged marriages. Other problems — which raise questions of the role of dominant individuals, communities or states in shaping gendered subordination, such as ongoing relationships of economic inequity, development and community policies, exploitation by transnational corporations, or racism — are ignored.

As an illustration of this, Alice Walker and Pratibha Parmar made a film critical of female genital surgeries called "Warrior Marks," which has been the target of both intense praise and criticism. In the book they wrote to accompany the film, they recount an anecdote that describes a meeting between the filmmakers and a group of women who run a collective garden. Asked about their feelings about "female genital mutilation," the response of these women is to:

> ask[ ] the "rich Americans" for a refrigerated truck they need badly to get their produce to outlying areas. The filmmakers, who do not perceive themselves as "rich" by their own cultural standards, joke that they could probably only pay for one tire for such a truck. The request for a truck is not mentioned again.

The issues affecting immigrant or Third World women that receive the greatest attention are those that appear most easily identifiable as concerns to relatively privileged women in the West. These concerns include violations that threaten the freedom of movement, freedom of dress, freedom of bodily integrity, and freedom of control over one's sexuality, rather than violations of the right to shelter or basic sustenance. Thus, self-conception, in terms of what one fears for oneself, may play a role in generating concern about specific violations of women's rights.

The decision to focus on the issue of the cultural origins of violence against women rather than their material well-being also reflects a specific history. The focus on violence was a strategic one made by the "women's rights as human rights" movement. Male violence against women was believed to be the universal experience that could tie together women across the world, in the face of North-South divides that presented too much conflict among women regarding the issue of transnational economic equality. But the enormous success in creating a transnational "women's rights as human rights" movement that coalesced around the problem of the woman subject to male violence has served to shape what we envision as gender subordination. This strategy may contain limits as to what gains it can produce.

The insistent focus on immigrant and Third World women as victims also leads many to deny the existence of agency within patriarchy, ignoring that these women are capable of emancipatory change on their own behalf. The binary assumption that women in the West have choice, and that those in immigrant and Third World contexts have none, in part reflects the limits of our language in describing choice: Either one is an agent, or one is a victim. This binary also reflects historical representations of the West as the site of rugged individualism, and the East as the repository of passivity and culture. Furthermore, it reflects a legacy of feminist politics and theory that presents Third World women as bound by culture, as described above. This conceptualization has bled into discourses that can deny the subjectivity of immigrant and Third World women, both in terms of feminist empowerment and in terms of their enjoyment of pleasure.

A fourth effect of this intense focus on other women's sexist cultures is that it obscures violence at home, namely specific practices of violence against women within the United States, including those perpetrated by the state. The First World is seldom depicted as a violator in discussions of women's international human rights. For example, the obsessive focus on Muslim countries' "Islamic" reservations to the Convention on the Elimination of All Forms of Discrimination Against Women obscures the fact that the U.S. government has made reservations in the same manner. Both Muslim countries and the United States have entered sweeping reservations based on domestic law to the principle of equality — Muslim countries on the basis of Islamic law, and the United States on the basis of the U.S. Constitution. The United States has specifically interpreted broader treaty obligations that would require establishing the doctrine of comparable worth, introducing paid maternity leave, and promoting the full development of women and prohibiting discrimination, as enforceable only to the extent required by the U.S. Constitution. Although the specific reservations made are not identical to those made by Muslim countries, it has been argued that through these reservations, both countries refuse to recognize international obligations due to a domestic "sacred law." The "sacred law" of the United States is the U.S.Constitution, which, by treating sex discrimination as less serious and harmful than racial discrimination, is used to deny the treaty obligations of international law.

Thus, the excessive focus on the cultural devaluing of "other" women obviates the fact of sexism among majority communities or in Western states. The negative image of "other" women is used as a mirror of progress, so comparisons between women, as opposed to comparisons with men, become the relevant frame of reference for the discussion of human rights. By accepting the contention that their lives are superior to the lives of women from "other" cultures, the attention of many women is diverted from the fact that they continue to be subordinate to men within their own culture. . . .

It does not seem coincidental that the way some feminists have depicted gender oppression in immigrant and Third World communities reflects a failure to think about how women's concerns in those communities might implicate their own identities. There is a strong desire for innocence in many strands of feminist politics, supported by the definition of the essential female identity of woman as victim of male violence. But an individual can be subordinated in one social relation and dominant in another. There is an ease with which one slips into a position of subordination, for example, as a woman subject to the discrimination of the glass ceiling, without seeing how this very subordinate location may simultaneously reflect privilege, for example, as one that relies on domestic labor and child care by immigrant women of color. The missionary impulse to save immigrant and Third World women from their subordination is rarely turned to uplift domestic workers from exploitative work situations. The repressive cultures of these women, on the other hand, are a subject of feminist concerns. Thus, women in the First World can feel as though they have autonomy and agency in contrast to women in the Third World, at the same time that they feel victimized by men in the First, but will not conceptualize themselves to be agents of subordinating practices. This absolution of responsibility rests on the assumption that relations between women are presumed to be non-oppressive, whereas the bonds of race are presumed to oppress women of color. But this ignores the oppression of race and class among women. While to some extent this is understood in the context of the domestic politics of the United States, the innocence of the category "woman" seems to have been repackaged in the wrapping of the discourses of feminism versus multiculturalism and transnational women's rights.

A missionary feminist effort assuming West is Best incurs a defensive reaction from members of criticized communities, and thus plays into the hands of those who choose to defend sex subordinating behavior in the name of cultural nationalism. The cultural nationalist response to imperialist descriptions of other women functions as a problematic mirror image. Resistance becomes configured as the necessity of preserving culture, leading to the freezing of particular identifications of culture, which keeps women trapped within the binary logic. Blanket condemnation is less helpful in engendering dialogue than acknowledging that women in the West also have a problem with epidemic rates of male violence against women, sharing strategies that have been attempted to combat this violence, and asking how immigrant and Third World women are grappling with violence in their own communities. And beyond the mere equivalence of universal gender subordination, we also must understand and confront how gender subordination is related to other forces of subordination — including racism and transnational economic inequalities. This means paying attention to context, to the meaning of difference, and to global disparities of power. . . .

We will not reach new possibilities through a simplistic and binary freezing of difference and sameness, of women vis-á-vis men, and of "us" vis-á-vis minority and Third World communities. We need to learn to see and challenge the multiple, overlapping, and discrete oppressions that occur both within and across white/Western and Third World/nonwhite communities. Otherwise, we remain mired in the battle of feminism versus multiculturalism.

Notes

1. *Martinez* Reversed. The Tenth Circuit Court of Appeals reversed the decision in *Martinez* on the merits; the court held that "there could have been a solution without discrimination." Santa Clara Pueblo v. Martinez, 540 F.2d 1039, 1047 (10th Cir. 1976). The Supreme Court reversed the decision of the Tenth Circuit, not on the merits, but on the grounds that Congress had failed to provide remedies for violation of the Indian Civil Rights Act other than habeas corpus. Santa Clara Pueblo v. Martinez, 436 U.S. 49 (1978).

Did the district court rule correctly on the merits? Consider Catharine MacKinnon's reflections on the case:

I am told that the rule was made in 1939 after the General Allotment Act divided up communal lands into individually held parcels, in something like an attempt to make Indians into proper agrarians. . . . It appeared to the governing body of the Tribe that the offspring of mixed marriages threatened to swell the population of the Pueblo and diminished individual shares of the property. If this were the pressing problem it could have been solved without resorting to discrimination by simply excluding the offspring of both sexes where the parent, either male or female, married outside the Pueblo. . . .

Given this history, which the tribe did not choose or make, I imagine the tribe saying, we need this rule. I imagine Julia Martinez replying: I understand that history, it is also my history, but this is a male supremacist solution to a problem male supremacy created. . . . Why is it seen as a matter of cultural survival when men guarantee exclusive access to Indian women as a requirement of tribal membership, but when an Indian woman attempts to claim that her family is an Indian family, to choose who to make a family with, it's called a threat to cultural survival? Whose culture is this culture? Is male supremacy sacred because it has become a tribal tradition?

Catharine A. MacKinnon, Feminism Unmodified: Discourses on Life and Law 66-67 (1987).

Consider the case from each of the major perspectives developed in this book. Does support of Julia Martinez's challenge to the tribal rule necessarily mean giving gender justice priority over anti-colonial struggle? Do Volpp's essay and MacKinnon's comments suggest alternatives to pitting gender justice against anti-colonialism?

2. Feminist Theory and Deconstructing "Culture." Volpp suggests that one problem with a focus on "culture" is that it obscures the economic and political determinants of social behavior. Genevieve Chato and Christine Conte, in similar fashion, argue that the *Martinez* ordinance can better be understood when Indian nations are viewed as internal colonies of the United States, just as many "Third World" nations are former colonies of European powers. Genevieve Chato and Christine Conte, The Legal Rights of American Indian Women, in Readings in American Indian Law: Recalling the Rhythm of Survival 252 (Jo Carrillo ed., 1998). Using the Navajo nation as an example, they argue that economic underdevelopment has hindered Navajo women's pursuit of equality in several interrelated ways. First, demographic pressure on a fixed land base has reduced the importance of livestock raising and farming, the traditional bases of Navajo women's authority in the household, and increased the incidence of welfare dependence. Id. at 259. Second, the economic marginalization of the Navajo has meant that most available jobs involve construction and other types of manual labor, job categories in which men are given preference. Id. As in the U.S. economy, women are clustered in low-paying, often part-time "pink collar" jobs.

Third, Chato and Conte argue that in response to pressure from the United States government, the Navajo Nation adopted a political and judicial system on the model of the federal government. "This was a practical response providing parallel structures to negotiate sovereignty issues and resource royalties for the tribe. However, this model has also been extended into the realm of discrimination against women in the political and legal arenas. Navajo women are dismally underrepresented on the Navajo Tribal Council and in the judicial system." Id at 260.

Last and most importantly, according to Chato and Conte, "traditional Navajo beliefs against female leadership outside of the household have been reinforced by discriminatory Anglo norms." Id. Navajo women thus face a double struggle for equality. How should Pueblo law respond? How should United States law respond?

3. Cultural Identity vs. Women's Autonomy. Application of the Indian Child Welfare Act of 1978 (ICWA), 25 U.S.C. §§1901-1963 (1982), presents another context in which rules designed to protect the cultural identity of American Indian nations may substantially curtail rights that women would otherwise possess. The ICWA is a jurisdictional act codifying previous state and federal law that requires, among other things, proceedings relating to the neglect, custody, or adoption of children of the tribe to be adjudicated in tribal courts. The Act was in response to the removal or placement of many Indian children away from Indian communities, which continues to threaten the survival of Indian culture. See Donna J. Goldsmith, Individual vs. Collective Rights: The Indian Child Welfare Act, 13 Harv. Women's L.J. 1, 4-5 (1990); Rennard Strickland, Genocide at Law: An Historic and Contemporary View of the Native American Experience, 34 U. Kan. L. Rev. 713 (1986).

In Mississippi Choctaw Band of Indians v. Holyfield, 490 U.S. 30 (1989), the United States Supreme Court considered a case under the ICWA in which a Choctaw mother and father, who were unmarried, sought to place their newborn twins for adoption with a non-Indian family living off the reservation, in order that the children would have opportunities that the tribe would not be able to provide. The mother lived on the reservation at the time, but because there were no hospitals there, the children were born off the reservation. A Mississippi trial court, affirmed by the state supreme court, granted the adoption. The Supreme Court overruled on the grounds that because the mother was domiciled on the reservation, under the ICWA the state court had no jurisdiction to decide the adoption petition.

The effect of *Holyfield* was to preempt the desire of the mother (as well as the father) to put her children up for adoption outside the reservation. Should the tribe's interest in its own continued survival supersede that desire? Feminist method has urged the consideration of legal problems from the point of view of the outsider, whose perspective the law often fails to see. Is it clear which perspective is the outsider one in *Holyfield?* How should the conflict between the mother's right to exercise her autonomy to do what she thinks is best for her children and the tribe's right to maintain its cultural identity be resolved?

4. Feminist Analyses of the "Cultural Defense." Another area of conflict among feminists has to do with the so-called cultural defense in criminal law, or the use of evidence describing the culture of an immigrant defendant's native country in order to bolster a claim of justification or excuse. Two of the most-discussed examples are People v. Chen, No. 87-7774 (N.Y. Sup. Ct. Dec. 2, 1988) and People v. Wu, 286 Cal. Rptr. 868 (Ct. App. 1991) (discussed in Leti Volpp, (Mis)Identifying Culture: Asian Women and the "Cultural Defense," 17 Harv. Women's L.J. 57 (1994)). In *Chen*, the defendant was a 54-year-old Chinese immigrant who killed his wife by smashing her skull with a claw hammer. Chen argued that he lacked the intent to kill but rather had acted under "extreme emotional disturbance" in part because of his Chinese cultural values. Chen had become suspicious that his wife was having an affair, and attacked her after she admitted that she was seeing another man. Chen's attorney introduced an expert witness, a white anthropologist named Burton Pasternak, who testified that "In general terms, I think that one could expect a Chinese to react in a much more volatile, violent way to those circumstances than someone from our own society. I think there's no doubt about it." Pasternak elaborated by stating that social control is more strict and unchanging in China than in the West; that a Chinese man whose wife had committed adultery would be dishonored and that both parties would have difficulty remarrying; and that in the United States a Chinese "adulteress" would have no problem establishing a relationship with a white man, whereas a Chinese man whose wife had committed adultery would be considered a "pariah" among Chinese women and would have no chance finding a white woman. On cross-examination, Pasternak strongly contrasted Chinese people with "the average American," whom he described as a white professional male, and argued that Chinese immigrants assimilated into American society "very slowly, if ever." Impressed by this testimony, the trial judge found Chen guilty of manslaughter rather than murder and sentenced him to five years probation instead of time in prison.

In *Wu*, the defendant, who grew up in China, became romantically involved with a man, Gary Wu, who emigrated to the United States and married another woman. Many years later, however, he contacted the defendant and told her he was unhappily married and that if Helen emigrated to the United States he would marry her and she could bear a child for him. Helen did emigrate to the United States, but Gary did not offer to marry her, even after the two of them had a child, a son named Sidney. Gary did divorce his wife, but did not tell Helen.

Helen, who was unable to speak English or drive a car, was unhappy in the United States, and eventually told Gary she would return to Macau. She did so without Sidney, but for the next eight years repeatedly asked Gary to visit her with Sidney. Gary continually asked for money, at one point proposing marriage after Helen showed him a certificate of deposit for a million Hong Kong dollars. Finally, Helen returned to the United States, where Gary's ailing mother said Helen should take Sidney when she died because Gary would not take good care of him. Helen and Gary were married in Las Vegas, but when pressed Gary would not say whether he had married her for her money. Shortly thereafter, Helen saw Gary beating their son, and Sidney told her the house they were staying in belonged to another woman, who was Gary's girlfriend. At that point, Helen told Sidney she wanted to die and asked if he would go too. He clung to her neck and cried. Helen cut the cord off a window blind and strangled her son. She then attempted to kill herself by slashing her wrist with a kitchen knife, but she was revived at the local emergency room.

At the murder trial, the judge refused to instruct the jurors that they could choose to consider Helen's cultural background in determining the presence or absence of malice, and Wu was convicted of murder. On appeal, the California Court of Appeals reversed, holding that evidence of her cultural background was relevant to the issues of premeditation and deliberation and could potentially reduce the murder charge to one of voluntary manslaughter. The experts in this case were not anthropologists but "transcultural psychologists," who explained that Helen's behavior represented love and maternal altruism: " . . . in her own culture, in her own mind, there are no other options but to, for her at the time, but to kill herself and take the son along with her so that they could sort of step over to the next world where she could devote herself, all of herself to the caring of the son, caring of Sidney. . . . Her purpose . . . in many ways . . . is a benevolent one."

Leti Volpp, commenting on these cases, rejects the notion of a formalized "cultural defense" as likely to promote stereotyping, but also rejects the position that cultural evidence should never be admissible to support a defendant's claim. She argues that the admission of cultural evidence was wrong in the *Chen* case, but correct in the *Wu* case, justifying this outcome by appealing to the value of "antisubordination." More specifically, Volpp offers guidelines for the admission of cultural evidence:

> There must be an acknowledgement of the fluid and interdynamic nature of cultures. Information that explains the actions of a defendant should be articulated by community members who are sensitive to the dynamics of power and subordination within the community of the defendant. . . . Information about the defendant's culture should never be reduced to stereotypes about a community but rather should concretely address the individual defendant's location in her community, her location in the diaspora and her history. The information should be provided so as to give insight into an individual's thoughts, and should not be used for purposes of explaining how an individual fits into stereotypes of group behavior.

Volpp, (Mis)Identifying Culture, supra, at 100. Are these guidelines workable in practice? Do they distinguish between the cultural evidence in *Chen* and in *Wu*?

Most of the "cultural defense" cases involve Asian immigrants. Daina Chiu argues that the debate over the "cultural defense" itself is in large part a debate over the place of Asian Americans. In her view, the debate illustrates three different modes of "managing Asian difference" in American society. Those who argue for a cultural defense to protect immigrants recognize cultural difference but use it as a reason for "special treatment," thereby preserving Americanness as white. Chiu calls this the "exclusion" approach to Asian Americans, and argues that it harms Asian women in particular, who have traditionally played a subordinate role in Asian culture. The position rejecting any cultural defense reflects the "assimilation" approach, which demands conformity to dominant norms. And the intermediate position, which would admit cultural evidence to show state of mind or mitigate punishment, reflects what Chiu calls "guilty liberalism." Chiu argues that the intermediate position necessarily fails because "the defendant benefits only to the extent that she shares the same values as dominant white culture. Therefore, white society is able to reinforce its prejudices through the other culture while purporting to act in tolerance of difference. In particular, this approach allows white society to reify sexism and reconstruct the subordination of women through the medium of another culture." Daina C. Chiu, The Cultural Defense: Beyond Exclusion, Assimilation, and Guilty Liberalism, 82 Cal. L. Rev. 1053, 1057 (1994). Chiu argues that the Chen case is an example of guilty liberalism. The judge in that case, she argues, reduced Chen's culpability not because he was acting under "different" cultural values, but because he held the "same" cultural values as Americans: "The subordination of women and the privileging of the male sex-right are common to both cultures." Id. at 1114.

If Chiu is correct, can the state possibly respond in a constructive way? Is the criminal justice system in a no-win situation?

The "cultural defense" has been controversial among feminists. For further commentary, see Donna Kay Maeda, Subject to Justice: The "Cultural Defense" and Legal Constructions of Race, Culture, and Nation, in Postcolonial America 81 (C. Richard King ed. 2000); Doriane Lambelet Coleman, Individualizing Justice Through Multiculturalism: The Liberals' Dilemma, 96 Colum. L. Rev. 1093 (1996); Leti Volpp, Talking "Culture": Gender, Race, Nation, and the Politics of Multiculturalism, 96 Colum. L. Rev. 1573 (1996) (responding to Coleman); Holly Maguigan, Cultural Evidence and Male Violence: Are Feminist and Multiculturalist Reformers on a Collision Course in Criminal Courts?, 70 N.Y.U. L. Rev. 36 (1995) (rejecting all-or-nothing approach to cultural evidence and advocating its admissibility as to defendant's mental state, subject to refutation through conventional avenues); Deirdre Evans-Pritchard and Alison Dundes Renteln, The Interpretation and Distortion of Culture: A Hmong "Marriage by Capture" Case in Fresno, CA, 4 S. Cal. Interdisc. L.J. 1 (1995); Alice S. Gallin, Note, The Cultural Defense: Undermining the Policies Against Domestic Violence, 35 B.C. L. Rev. 723 (1994); Taryn F. Goldstein, Cultural Conflicts in Court: Should the American Criminal Justice System Formally Recognize a "Cultural Defense?" 99 Dick. L. Rev. 141 (1994);

Alison D. Renteln, A Justification of the Cultural Defense as Partial Excuse, 2 S. Cal. Rev. L. & Women's Stud. 437 (1993); Nilda Rimonte, A Question of Culture: Cultural Approval of Violence Against Women in the Pacific-Asian Community and the Cultural Defense, 43 Stan. L. Rev. 1311 (1991); Melissa Spatz, Note, A "Lesser" Crime: A Comparative Study of Legal Defenses for Men Who Kill Their Wives, 24 Colum. J.L. & Soc. Probs. 597 (1991); Carolyn Choi, Note, Application of a Cultural Defense in Criminal Proceedings, 8 UCLA Pac. Basin L.J. 80 (1990).

5. Religious Freedom and Gender Equality in the United States. In EEOC v. Catholic University of America, 83 F.3d 455 (D.C. Cir. 1996), Sister Elizabeth McDonough, a Dominican nun and the first woman to be appointed to the canon law faculty at Catholic University, was denied tenure and filed discrimination charges with the EEOC against the university, arguing that Catholic University had engaged in sex discrimination and retaliatory conduct in violation of Title VII. The district judge dismissed the case without reaching the merits, holding that applying Title VII would violate both the free exercise and the establishment clauses of the First Amendment, because Sister McDonough's primary role in the Department of Canon Law was the functional equivalent of the task of a minister. EEOC v. Catholic University of America, 856 F. Supp. 1, 10 (D.D.C. 1994). The D.C. Circuit affirmed, taking note of a long line of cases holding that the free exercise clause exempts the selection of clergy from Title VII and similar statutes. In addition, the appellate court held that a substantive judicial review of Sister McDonough's case would entangle the court in religious matters in violation of the establishment clause. Indeed, the court rebuked the EEOC for having conducted its investigation and brought suit in the first place. 83 F.3d at 467. Concurring in the opinion, Judge Karen Henderson nevertheless observed that Catholic University had not itself viewed the investigation as an infringement upon its religious freedom until the district court's post-trial request for briefing on the issue: "From the beginning — now, over eight years ago — CUA, an indisputably sectarian institution (and no stranger to litigation), viewed Sister McDonough's quest for tenure as an academic matter." 83 F.3d at 471 (Henderson, J., concurring).

On the other hand, in a case involving allegations of sexual harassment by a novice of the Society of Jesus against various superiors at two Jesuit institutions (who plaintiff claimed sent him pornographic material, made unwelcome sexual advances, and engaged him in inappropriate and unwelcome sexual discussions), the Ninth Circuit Court of Appeals held that the ministerial exception to Title VII did not apply because the church was "neither exercising its constitutionally protected prerogative to choose its ministers nor embracing the behavior at issue as a constitutionally protected religious practice." Bollard v. California Province of the Soc'y of Jesus, 196

F.3d 940, 944 (9th Cir. 1999), reh'g en banc denied, 211 F.3d 1331 (9th Cir. 2000).

Are the issues in EEOC v. Catholic University the same as in *Martinez*?

Does current sex discrimination law assume not only a white, middle-class, heterosexual woman, but also a woman without religious commitments? For the argument that employment discrimination law should apply to religious organizations, see Jane Rutherford, Equality as the Primary Constitutional Value: The Case for Applying Employment Discrimination Laws to Religion, 81 Cornell L. Rev. 1049 (1996); see also Linda L. Ammons, What's God Got To Do With It? Church and State Collaboration in the Subordination of Women and Domestic Violence, 51 Rutgers L. Rev. 1207 (1999); Keith E. Sealing, Polygamists Out of the Closet: Statutory and State Constitutional Prohibitions Against Polygamy Are Unconstitutional Under the Free Exercise Clause, 17 G. St. U. L. Rev. 691 (2001); see generally Cass Sunstein, Should Sex Equality Law Apply to Religious Institutions? in Is Multiculturalism Bad for Women? (Susan Moller Okin, Joshua Cohen, Matthew Howard, and Martha C. Nussbaum eds., 1999).

6. Religious Freedom, Gender Equality, and International Human Rights. How should international human rights law, and non-government organizations like women's rights organizations, respond to non-liberal regimes that both embrace religious fundamentalism and place special burdens on women? Some feminists emphasize the need for national laws incorporating religious fundamentalist concepts that subordinate women to be subject to the human rights provisions of the United Nations Charter, the Women's Convention, and other international law principles. See, e.g., Ann Elizabeth Mayer, A "Benign" Apartheid: How Gender Apartheid Has Been Rationalized, 5 UCLA J. Int'l L. & Foreign Aff. 237 (2000-2001); Bahia Tahzib-Lie, Applying a Gender Perspective in the Area of the Right to Freedom of Religion or Belief, 2000 BYU L. Rev. 967; Courtney W. Howland, The Challenge of Religious Fundamentalism to the Liberty and Equality Rights of Women: An Analysis under the United Nations Charter, 35 Colum. J. Transnat'l. L. 271 (1997); Urfan Khaliq, Beyond the Veil?: An Analysis of the Provisions of the Women's Convention and the Law as Stipulated in Shari'ah, 2 Buff. J. Int'l L. 1 (1995). Other feminist writers are concerned that human rights approaches may treat women from fundamentalist religious traditions as helpless victims rather than strategic actors who may embrace aspects of fundamentalist practice. See e.g., Shefali Desai, Hearing Afghan Women's Voices: Feminist Theory's Reconceptualization of Women's Human Rights 16 Ariz. J. Int'l & Comp. L. 805 (1999). Still others take the tack that fundamentalist regimes such as the Taliban in Afghanistan do not conform to Islamic law itself, and for that reason should not receive international recognition. Marjon E. Ghasemi, Islam, International Human Rights & Women's Equality: Afghan Women Under Taliban Rule, 8 S. Cal. Rev. L. & Women's Stud. 445 (1999).

The terrorist attack on the World Trade Center in September 2001, attributed to Osama bin Laden, brought to prominence the Taliban's treatment of women in particular, and the situations of Middle Eastern women, especially Muslim, more generally. For various perspectives on women, gender, and feminism in Muslim nations, see Arab Women: Between Defiance and Restraint (Suha Sabbagh ed., 1996); Islam, Gender, and Social Change (Yvonne Yazbeck Haddad and John L. Esposito eds., 1998); Faith and Freedom: Women's Human Rights in the Muslim World (Mahnaz Afkhami ed., 1995); Leila Ahmed, Women and Gender in Islam: Historical Roots of a Modern Debate (1992); Fatima Mernissi, The Veil and the Male Elite: A Feminist Interpretation of Women's Rights in Islam (Mary Jo Lakeland trans., 1991).

3. The Naturalist Error: Critiquing Biological Definitions of "Women"

≡ *Littleton v. Prange*
≡ 9 S.W.3d 223 (1999)

HARDBERGER, Chief Justice.

This case involves the most basic of questions. When is a man a man, and when is a woman a woman? Every schoolchild, even of tender years, is confident he or she can tell the difference, especially if the person is wearing no clothes. These are observations that each of us makes early in life and, in most cases, continue to have more than a passing interest in for the rest of our lives. It is one of the more pleasant mysteries.

The deeper philosophical (and now legal) question is: can a physician change the gender of a person with a scalpel, drugs and counseling, or is a person's gender immutably fixed by our Creator at birth? The answer to that question has definite legal implications that present themselves in this case involving a person named Christie Lee Littleton. . . .

Christie is a transsexual. She was born in San Antonio in 1952, a physically healthy male, and named after her father, Lee Cavazos. At birth, she was named Lee Cavazos, Jr. (Throughout this opinion Christie will be referred to as "She." This is for grammatical simplicity's sake, and out of respect for the litigant, who wishes to be called "Christie," and referred to as "she." It has no legal implications.)

At birth, Christie had the normal male genitalia: penis, scrotum and testicles. Problems with her sexual identity developed early though. Christie testified that she considered herself female from the time she was three or four years old, the contrary physical evidence notwithstanding. Her distressed parents took her to a physician, who prescribed male hormones. These were taken, but were ineffective. Christie sought successfully to be excused from sports and physical education because of her embarrassment over changing clothes in front of the other boys.

By the time she was 17 years old, Christie was searching for a physician who would perform sex reassignment surgery. At 23, she enrolled in a program at the University of Texas Health Science Center that would lead to a sex reassignment operation. For four years Christie underwent psychological and psychiatric treatment by a number of physicians, some of whom testified in this case.

On August 31, 1977, Christie's name was legally changed to Christie Lee Cavazos. Under doctor's orders, Christie also began receiving various treatments and female hormones. Between November of 1979 and February of 1980, Christie underwent three surgical procedures, which culminated in a complete sex reassignment. Christie's penis, scrotum and testicles were surgically removed, and a vagina and labia were constructed. Christie additionally underwent breast construction surgery.

Dr. Donald Greer, a board certified plastic surgeon, served as a member of the gender dysphoria team at UTHSC in San Antonio, Texas during the time in question. Dr. Paul Mohl, a board certified psychiatrist, also served as a member of the same gender dysphoria team. Both participated in the evaluation and treatment of Christie. The gender dysphoria team was a mutli-disciplinary team that met regularly to interview and care for transsexual patients.

The parties stipulated that Dr. Greer and Dr. Mohl would testify that their background, training, education and experience is consistent with that reflected in their curriculum vitaes, which were attached to their respective affidavits in Christie's response to the motions for summary judgment. In addition, Dr. Greer and Dr. Mohl would testify that the definition of a transsexual is someone whose physical anatomy does not correspond to their sense of being or their sense of gender, and that medical science has not been able to identify the exact cause of this condition, but it is in medical probability a combination of neuro-biological, genetic and neonatal environmental factors. Dr. Greer and Dr. Mohl would further testify that in arriving at a diagnosis of transsexualism in Christie, the program at UTHSC was guided by the guidelines established by the Johns Hopkins Group and that, based on these guidelines, Christie was diagnosed psychologically and psychiatrically as a genuine male to female transsexual. Dr. Greer and Dr. Mohl also would testify that true male to female transsexuals are, in their opinion, psychologically and psychiatrically female before and after the sex reassignment surgery, and that Christie is a true male to female transsexual.

On or about November 5, 1979, Dr. Greer served as a principal member of the surgical team that performed the sex reassignment surgery on Christie. In Dr. Greer's opinion, the anatomical and genital features of Christie, following that surgery, are such that she has the capacity to function sexually as a female. Both Dr. Greer and Dr. Mohl would testify that, in their opinions, following the successful completion of Christie's participation in UTHSC's gender dysphoria program, Christie is medically a woman.

Christie married a man by the name of Jonathon Mark Littleton in Kentucky in 1989, and she lived with him until his death in 1996. Christie filed a medical malpractice suit under the Texas Wrongful Death and Survival Statute in her capacity as Jonathon's surviving spouse. The sued doctor, appellee here, filed a motion for summary judgment. The motion challenged Christie's status as a proper wrongful death beneficiary, asserting that Christie is a man and cannot be the surviving spouse of another man.

The trial court agreed and granted the summary judgment. . . . In her affidavit, Christie states that Jonathon was fully aware of her background and the fact that she had undergone sex reassignment surgery.

Can there be a valid marriage between a man and a person born as a man, but surgically altered to have the physical characteristics of a woman?

This is a case of first impression in Texas. The underlying statutory law is simple enough. Texas (and Kentucky, for that matter), like most other states, does not permit marriages between persons of the same sex. See Tex. Fam. Code Ann. §2.001(b) (Vernon 1998); Ky. Rev. Stat. Ann. §402.020(1)(d) (Banks-Baldwin 1999). In order to have standing to sue under the wrongful death and survival statues, Christie must be Jonathon's surviving spouse. Tex. Civ. Prac. & Rem. Code Ann. §§71.004, 71.021 (Vernon 1977). The defendant's summary judgment burden was to prove she is not the surviving spouse. Referring to the statutory law, though, does not resolve the issue. This court, as did the trial court below, must answer this question: Is Christie a man or a woman? There is no dispute that Christie and Jonathon went through a ceremonial marriage ritual. If Christie is a woman, she may bring this action. If Christie is a man, she may not.

Christie is medically termed a transsexual, a term not often heard on the streets of Texas, nor in its courtrooms. If we look at other states or even other countries to see how they treat marriages of transsexuals, we get little help.

Only a handful of other states, or foreign countries, have even considered the case of the transsexual. The opposition to same-sex marriages, on the other hand, is very wide spread. Only one state has ever ruled in favor of same-sex marriage: Hawaii, in the case of Baehr v. Lewin, 74 Haw. 530, 852 P.2d 44 (1993). All other cases soundly reject the concept of same-sex marriages. See, e.g., Dean v. District of Columbia, 653 A.2d 307 (D.C. 1995); Jones v. Hallahan, 501 S.W.2d 588 (Ky. 1973); Baker v. Nelson, 291 Minn. 310, 191 N.W.2d 185 (1971), aff'd, 409 U.S. 810, 93 S.Ct. 37, 34 L.Ed.2d 65 (1972); Singer v. Hara, 11 Wash. App. 247, 522 P.2d 1187 (1974). Congress has even passed the Defense of Marriage Act (DOMA), just in case a state decides to recognize same-sex marriages.

DOMA defines marriage for federal purposes as a "legal union between one man and one woman," and provides that no state "shall be required to give effect to any public act, record, or judicial proceeding of any other state respecting a relationship between persons of the same sex that is treated as a marriage under the laws of such other State . . . or a right or claim arising from such relationship." Defense of Marriage Act, Pub.L. No. 104-109, §2(a), 110 Stat. 2419 (1996) (codified as amended at 28 U.S.C.A. §1738C (West Supp. 1997). So even if one state were to recognize same-sex marriages it would not need to be recognized in any other state, and probably would not be. Marriage is tightly defined in the United States: "a legal union between one man and one woman." See id. §3(a).

Public antipathy toward same-sex marriages notwithstanding, the question remains: is a transsexual still the same sex after a sex-reassignment operation as before the operation? A transsexual, such as Christie, does not consider herself a homosexual because she does not consider herself a man. Her self-identity, from childhood, has been as a woman. Since her various operations, she does not have the outward physical characteristics of a man either. Through the intervention of surgery and drugs, Christie appears to be a woman. In her mind, she has corrected her physical features to line up with her true gender.

"Although transgenderism is often conflated with homosexuality, the characteristic, which defines transgenderism, is not sexual orientation, but sexual identity. Transgenderism describes people who experience a separation between their gender and their biological/anatomical sex." Mary Coombs, Sexual Dis-Orientation: Transgendered People and Same-Sex Marriage, 8 UCLA Women's L.J. 219, 237 (1998).

Nor should a transsexual be confused with a transvestite, who is simply a man who attains some sexual satisfaction from wearing women's clothes. Christie does not consider herself a man wearing women's clothes; she considers herself a woman wearing women's clothes. She has been surgically and chemically altered to be a woman. She has officially changed her name and her birth certificate to reflect her new status. But the question remains whether the law will take note of these changes and treat her as if she had been born a female. To answer this question, we consider the law of those jurisdictions who have previously decided it. . . .

[The court examines four judicial decisions in England and the United States, three of which held that, in the court's words, "once a man, always a man," as well as an unreported New Zealand decision holding that "a fully transitioned transsexual should be permitted to marry as a member of his new sex because the alternative [an apparent same-sex marriage] would be more disturbing," see Mary Coombs, Sexual Dis-Orientation: Transgendered People and Same-Sex Marriage, 8 UCLA Women's L.J 219, 250 & n.137 (1998) (citing M. v. M. (unreported) May 30, 1991, S. Ct. of New Zealand), and notes the existence of an Oregon statute permitting a person who has undergone a sex change to alter his or her birth certificate to reflect the new designation.]

In our system of government it is for the legislature, should it choose to do so, to determine what guidelines should govern the recognition of marriages involving transsexuals. The need for legislative guidelines is particularly important in this case, where the claim being asserted is statutorily-based. The statute defines who may bring the cause of action: a surviving spouse, and if the legislature intends to recognize transsexuals as surviving spouses, the statute needs to address the guidelines by which such recognition is governed. When or whether the legislature will choose to address this issue is not within the judiciary's control.

It would be intellectually possible for this court to write a protocol for when transsexuals would be recognized as having successfully changed their sex. Littleton has suggested we do so, perhaps using the surgical removal of the male genitalia as the test. As was pointed out by Littleton's counsel, "amputation is a pretty important step." Indeed it is. But this court has no authority to fashion a new law on transsexuals, or anything else. We cannot make law when no law exists: we can only interpret the written word of our sister branch of government, the legislature. Our responsibility in this case is to determine whether, in the absence of legislatively-established guidelines, a jury can be called upon to decide the legality of such marriages. We hold they cannot. In the absence of any guidelines, it would be improper to launch a jury forth on these untested and unknown waters. . . .

Christie was created and born a male. Her original birth certificate, an official document of Texas, clearly so states. During the pendency of this suit, Christie amended the original birth certificate to change the sex and name. Under section 191.028 of the Texas Health and Safety Code she was entitled to seek such an amendment if the record was "incomplete or proved by satisfactory evidence to be inaccurate." Tex. Health & Safety Code Ann. §191.028 (Vernon 1992). The trial court that granted the petition to amend the birth certificate necessarily construed the term "inaccurate" to relate to the present, and having been presented with the uncontroverted affidavit of an expert stating that Christie is a female, the trial court deemed this satisfactory to prove an inaccuracy. However, the trial court's role in considering the petition was a ministerial one. It involved no fact-finding or consideration of the deeper public policy concerns presented. No one claims the information contained in Christie's original birth certificate was based on fraud or error. We believe the legislature intended the term "inaccurate" in section 191.028 to mean inaccurate as of the time the certificate was recorded; that is, at the time of birth. At the time of birth, Christie was a male, both anatomically and genetically. The facts contained in the original birth certificate were true and accurate, and the words contained in the amended certificate are not binding on this court.

There are some things we cannot will into being. They just are.

We hold, as a matter of law, that Christie Littleton is a male. As a male, Christie cannot be married to another male. Her marriage to Jonathon was invalid, and she cannot bring a cause of action as his surviving spouse.

We affirm the summary judgment granted by the trial court.

Karen Angelini, Justice, concurring. . . .

According to Chief Justice Hardberger, . . . biological considerations are preferable to psychological factors as tools for making the decision we must make. In this case, I must agree.

I note, however, that "real difficulties . . . will occur if these three criteria [chromosomal, gonadal and genital tests] are not congruent." Corbett v. Corbett, 2 All E.R. 33, 48 (P.1970). We must recognize the fact that, even when biological factors are considered, there are those individuals whose sex may be ambiguous. See Julie A. Greenberg, Defining Male and Female: Intersexuality and the Collision Between Law and Biology, 41 Ariz. L. Rev. 265 (1999). Having recognized this fact, I express no opinion as to how the law would view such individuals with regard to marriage. We are, however, not presented with such a case at this time. See Corbett, 2 All E.R. at 48-49. . . .

Alma L. Lopez, Justice, dissenting. . . .

In this case, the court is required to determine as a matter of law whether Christie is Jonathon's surviving spouse, not to speculate on the legalities of public policies not yet addressed by our legislature. Under a focused review of this case, a birth certificate reflecting the birth of a male child named Lee Cavazos does not prove that Christie Littleton is not the surviving spouse of Jonathan Littleton. Having failed to prove that Christie was not Jonathon's surviving spouse, Dr. Prange was not entitled to summary judgment. Because Christie's summary judgment evidence raises a genuine question of material fact about whether she is the surviving spouse of Jonathon Littleton, I respectfully dissent.

≡≡≡ *Rosa v. Park West Bank & Trust Co.*
≡≡≡ 214 F.3d 213 (1st Cir. 2000)

LYNCH, Circuit Judge. . . .

According to the complaint, which we take to be true for the purpose of this appeal, . . . on July 21, 1998, [Lucas] Rosa came to the Bank to apply for a loan. A biological male, he was dressed in traditionally feminine attire. He requested a loan application from Norma Brunelle, a bank employee. Brunelle asked Rosa for identification. Rosa produced three forms of photo identification: (1) a Massachusetts Department of Public Welfare Card; (2) a Massachusetts Identification Card; and (3) a Money Stop Check Cashing ID Card. Brunelle looked at the identification cards and told Rosa that she would not provide him with a loan application until he "went home and changed." She said that he had to be dressed like one of the identification cards in which he appeared in more traditionally male attire before she would provide him with a loan application and process his loan request.

Rosa sued the Bank for violations of the [Equal Credit Opportunity Act (ECOA)] and various Massachusetts antidiscrimination statutes. Rosa charged that "[b]y requiring [him] to conform to sexstereotypes before proceeding with the credit transaction, [the Bank] unlawfully discriminated against [him] with respect to an aspect of a credit transaction on the basis of sex." He claims to have suffered emotional distress, including anxiety, depression, humiliation, and extreme embarrassment. Rosa seeks damages, attorney's fees, and injunctive relief.

Without filing an answer to the complaint, the Bank moved to dismiss pursuant to Federal Rule of Civil Procedure 12(b)(6). The district court granted the Bank's motion. The court stated:

> [T]he issue in this case is not [Rosa's] sex, but rather how he chose to dress when applying for a loan. Because the Act does not prohibit discrimination based on the manner in which someone dresses, Park West's requirement that Rosa change his clothes does not give rise to claims of illegal discrimination. Further, even if Park West's statement or action were based upon Rosa's sexual orientation or perceived sexual orientation, the Act does not prohibit such discrimination.

Price Waterhouse v. Hopkins, 490 U.S. 228, 109 S.Ct. 1775, 104 L. Ed.2d 268 (1988), which Rosa relied on, was not to the contrary, according to the district court, because that case "neither holds, nor even suggests, that discrimination based merely on a person's attire is impermissible."

On appeal, Rosa says that the district court "fundamentally misconceived the law as applicable to the Plaintiff's claim by concluding that there may be no relationship, as a matter of law, between telling a bank customer what to wear and sex discrimination." Rosa also says that the district court misapplied Rule 12(b)(6) when it, allegedly, resolved factual questions.

The Bank says that Rosa loses for two reasons. First, citing cases pertaining to gays and transsexuals, it says that the ECOA does not apply to crossdressers. Second, the Bank says that its employee genuinely could not identify Rosa, which is why she asked him to go home and change.

. . . In interpreting the ECOA, this court looks to Title VII case law, that is, to federal employment discrimination law. The Bank itself refers us to Title VII case law to interpret the ECOA.

The ECOA prohibits discrimination, "with respect to any aspect of a credit transaction[,] on the basis of race, color, religion, national origin, sex or marital status, or age." 15 U.S.C. §1691(a). Thus to prevail, the alleged discrimination against Rosa must have been "on the basis of . . . sex." See Oncale v. Sundowner Offshore Servs., Inc., 523 U.S. 75, 78, 118 S.Ct. 998, 140 L.Ed.2d 201 (1998). The ECOA's sex discrimination prohibition "protects men as well as women." Id.

While the district court was correct in saying that the prohibited bases of discrimination under the ECOA do not include style of dress or sexual orientation, that is not the discrimination alleged. It is alleged that the Bank's actions were taken, in whole or in part, "on the basis of . . . [the appellant's] sex." The Bank, by seeking dismissal under Rule 12(b)(6), subjected itself to rigorous standards. . . . Whatever facts emerge, and they may turn out to have nothing to do with sex-based discrimination, we cannot say at this point that the plaintiff has no viable theory of sex discrimination consistent with the facts alleged.

The evidence is not yet developed, and thus it is not yet clear why Brunelle told Rosa to go home and change. It may be that this case involves an instance of disparate treatment based on sex in the denial of credit. . . . It is reasonable to infer that Brunelle told Rosa to go home and change because she thought that Rosa's attire did not accord with his male gender: in other words, that Rosa did not receive the loan application because he was a man, whereas a similarly situated woman would have received the loan application. That is, the Bank may treat, for credit purposes, a woman who dresses like a man differently than a man who dresses like a woman. If so, the Bank concedes, Rosa may have a claim. Indeed, under Price Waterhouse, "stereotyped remarks [including statements about dressing more 'feminine-ly'] can certainly be evidence that gender played a part." Price Waterhouse, 490 U.S. at 251, 109 S.Ct. 1775. It is also reasonable to infer, though, that Brunelle refused to give Rosa the loan application because she thought he was gay, confusing sexual orientation with cross-dressing.[1] If so, Rosa concedes, our precedents dictate that he would have no recourse under the federal Act. . . . It is reasonable to infer, as well, that Brunelle simply could not ascertain whether the person shown in the identification card photographs was the same person that appeared before her that day. If this were the case, Rosa again would be out of luck. It is reasonable to infer, finally, that Brunelle may have had mixed motives, some of which fall into the prohibited category.

It is too early to say what the facts will show; it is apparent, however, that, under some set of facts within the bounds of the allegations and non-conclusory facts in the complaint, Rosa may be able to prove a claim under the ECOA. . . .

≣≣≣ *Elvia R. Arriola, Law and the Gendered Politics
of Identity: Who Owns the Label "Lesbian"?*
8 Hastings Women's L.J. 1, 1-3, 5-6, 8-9 (1997)

Several years ago, I was a member of a predominantly lesbian women's support group. The group offered a "womanspace" for individuals who

---

1. Massachusetts law, the subject of the pendent state law claims, does prohibit discrimination based on sexual orientation. See Mass. Gen. Laws ch. 272, §§92A, 98; id. ch. 151B, §4(14).

wanted to share their experiences, strength, and hope as survivors of rape and sexual abuse. On a weekly basis, anywhere from fifteen to thirty women of all racial, ethnic and social backgrounds, who knew each other only by first name, rented a meeting room from a community church and shared stories of sexual victimization and abuse, with the singular goal of healing themselves through mutual support. . . . In the company of other survivors, the women felt safe enough, sometimes for the first time in their adult lives, to weep or get angry; for in this safe space they trusted that their companions would not mock, negate, or minimize their feelings. Of course, the critical sense of safety was ensured by the practice of someone standing guard at the door to make sure no man accidentally walked into the rented rooms. If that happened, all talk would suspend until the man was gone. This ground rule grew out of the plainly obvious fact that this was a meeting for women healing from sexual abuse by the men in their lives; only an all-women atmosphere could guarantee an emotionally safe environment.

Imagine, then, the turmoil created in this "womanspace" when one day a tall, quiet woman who had shown up regularly at meetings for several weeks suddenly came out to the group as a transsexual female. Not only that, she was a transsexual female who identified as a lesbian. Suddenly "Micki," who had simply appeared as an unusually tall, rather quiet and professionally dressed woman, looked very different to the group's members. Some of the women were too involved with their own issues to take in immediately what had just happened. In the following weeks, however, a few women, both lesbian and not, reacted strongly, sharing that they felt threatened by Micki's continued presence. Micki's feminine appearance bore witness to the wonders of modern medicine, but to some she was nothing but a fake. Her revelation explained at last the slightly masculine build around the shoulders and neck: this supposed woman was a man, or at least had been born male. Further, although she had given up her male identity, Micki's self confident demeanor betrayed residual hints of her socialization as a privileged white male.

Her chosen identity as a lesbian posed another gender and sexuality enigma. Having castrated "his" penis while leaving "his" sexual orientation unscathed, to what label was s/he entitled? The choice of a lesbian identity to express her (his) new identity as a "woman-loving-woman" communicated an unfamiliar sex and gender ambiguity. For some, the ambiguity only generated feelings of hostility and feelings of mockery for this once-man's appropriation of a label — lesbian — which they felt belonged only to "real women."

In the conflict and confusion that surfaced for several weeks after her coming out, Micki encountered both support and prejudice from fellow members of the incest survivors' group. A few sought out Micki's friendship, trying to assure her that she was welcome. Others kept their distance and in private conversations voiced their distrust and interest in removing Micki from the group. They felt abandoned by their group, angry and enraged that not everyone agreed that Micki should leave. Too many individuals supported Micki to force a formal demand that she leave and not come back. The resistors expressed a sense of betrayal by the group's unwillingness to oust Micki, whose perceived crime was in once having had a penis and now being viewed as neither truly female, nor woman, nor lesbian. She was at best a not-man. Eventually, the conflict led to a split, as Micki's resistors formed their own group, with membership limited to women who had been born into a female body. Micki herself eventually left the group. She ultimately formed her own support group, focusing on gender identity and abuse issues. . . .

. . . By leaving to form another support group, Micki opened the door for healing from incest and sexual abuse to other transsexual females. Yet, the women who separated from the original group never had to examine the source of their fears. No one thought to ask whether some of their reactions to Micki, based upon preconceived ideas about the meaning of sex, gender or sexuality, might have stemmed from the same hetero-patriarchal value system which accounted for their own sexual victimization. Certainly no one felt the need to understand or address the unique form of gender oppression that leads an individual to such a drastic measure as sex reassignment surgery (SRS). The fact that Micki's recovery involved stories of how s/he had been shamed and traumatized from the time of his (her) childhood for engaging in gender-nonconforming behavior did not interest her opponents. Yet I wonder how the group never questioned the inclusion of "butchy" lesbians, some of whom dressed in very masculine attire, and who described similar childhood examples of abusive treatment for their own gender-nonconforming behavior. I have asked and answered my own question: it is all gender-based oppression. . . .

I have often wondered what would have happened in that group if Micki had not left. In the few weeks she was there, did it make any difference for someone like Micki, who had been raised as a boy and had become a man, to hear the depth of anger experienced by women who had survived male rape or incest and who now felt desperate at being unable to escape even a hint of residual male energy in a transgender female? Was it unreasonable for the women-from-birth to see Micki as a burden, rather than as someone who might help their healing by vouching as a once-man for the reality of abusive male power, and affirming to them, "yes, this is what men do and you were unjustly violated?" Could either side have seen the source of their fears and their unjust experiences as rooted in societal attitudes based on male power and privilege which continue to induce heightened levels of female sexual victimization, or which so oppress some boys/men that their only escape is to castrate the physical signs of the male gender identity they were assigned at birth?

Notes

1. What Is a Woman, Anyway? Was "Micki" a woman? Was Christie Littleton? What factors should determine the answer to that question? On what factors did the court in *Littleton* rely?

The judge in *Littleton* described sexual difference as "the most basic of questions," one that "every schoolchild, even of tender years," can confidently answer. But is sexual difference really so easy to discern? One issue of definition, as in the *Littleton* case, is how to classify persons who take medical steps to alter their physiognomy and hormonal makeup, in order to align their public appearance with their psychological self-conceptions. Another issue concerns how to classify persons who, by medical definitions, are neither completely "male" nor "female." According to Julie Greenberg, "Recent medical literature indicates that approximately one to four percent of the world's population may be intersexed and have either ambiguous or noncongruent sex features." Julie A. Greenberg, Defining Male and Female: Intersexuality and the Collision Between Law and Biology, 41 Ariz. L. Rev. 265, 267 (1999).

Indeed, if medical science is taken seriously, is the widespread social assumption that there are only two sexes — "male" and "female" — justified? Consider Anne Fausto-Sterling's argument that there are really five sexes, not two:

> For some time medical investigators have recognized the concept of the intersexual body. But the standard medical literature uses the term intersex as a catch-all for three major subgroups with some mixture of male and female characteristics: the so-called true hermaphrodites, whom I call herms, who possess one testis and one ovary (the sperm- and egg-producing vessels, or gonads); the male pseudohermaphrodites (the "merms"), who have testes and some aspects of the female genitalia but no ovaries; and the female pseudohermaphrodites (the "ferms"), who have ovaries and some aspects of the male genitalia but lack testes. Each of those categories is in itself complex; the percentage of male and female characteristics, for instance, can vary enormously among members of the same subgroup. Moreover, the inner lives of the people in each subgroup — their special needs and their problems, attractions and repulsions — have gone unexplored by science. But on the basis of what is known about them I suggest that the three intersexes, herm, merm and ferm, deserve to be considered additional sexes each in its own right. Indeed, I would argue further that sex is a vast, infinitely malleable continuum that defies the constraints of even five categories.

Anne Fausto-Sterling, The Five Sexes: Why Male and Female Are Not Enough, The Sciences, March/April 1993, 20, 21. See also Arriola, Law and the Gendered Politics of Identity, supra, 8 Hastings Women's L.J. at 19-20 (listing eight assumptions about sexual difference that feminists have failed to think through); Greenberg, supra, at 268 (pointing out that statutes like the federal Defense of Marriage Act that restrict marriage to relationships between "males" and "females" potentially create problems for people who are not, scientifically speaking, clearly either male or female).

The term "transgender" has emerged to cover a range of such sex/gender identities. The San Francisco Human Rights Commission Report, for example, defines it this way:

> [T]he term Transgender is used as an umbrella term that includes male and female cross dressers, transvestites, female and male impersonators, pre-operative and post-operative transsexuals, and transsexuals who choose not to have genital reconstruction, and all persons whose perceived gender and anatomic sex may conflict with the gender expression, such as masculine-appearing women and feminine-appearing men. . . .
>
> All other terms — cross-dresser, transvestite, transsexual — are subsets of the umbrella term transgender.

Jamison Green & Larry Brinkin, Investigation into Discrimination Against Transgendered People: A Report by the Human Rights Commission City and County of San Francisco, 1994 Proc. from the Third Int'l Conf. on Transgender Law & Emp. Pol'y M-13, cited in Phyllis Randolph Frye, The International Bill of Gender Rights vs. the Cider House Rules: Transgenders Struggle With the Courts over What Clothing They Are Allowed to Wear on the Job, Which Restroom They Are Allowed to Use on the Job, Their Right to Marry, and the Very Definition of Their Sex, 7 Wm. & Mary J. Women & L. 133, 154 (2000). What is the relationship between a "transgender person" and a "woman"? Does it depend on who is making the determination and for what purpose? On what factors should feminists rely in deciding who is a woman?

2. Transgender Identity and Discrimination Based on "Sex." Until very recently, courts have refused to recognize discrimination against transgender people as legally cognizable. As Paisley Currah and Shannon Minter observe:

> The impact of these judicial exclusions has been particularly stark in sex discrimination cases. Thus, although it is difficult to see how an employer's decision to terminate an employee for undergoing sex-reassignment could plausibly be deemed anything other than a form of sex-based discrimination, courts have adopted the Orwellian notion that there is a meaningful legal distinction between discrimination because of sex and discrimination because of a change of sex. In Holloway v. Arthur Anderson & Co.,[14] for example, Ramona Holloway was fired for transitioning from male to female on the job. The Ninth Circuit held that Holloway was not discriminated against "because she is male or female, but rather because she is a transsexual who chose to change her sex. This type of claim is not actionable under Title VII." Similarly,

---

14. 566 F.2d 659 (9th Cir. 1977).

in Underwood v. Archer Management Services, Inc.,[17] the plaintiff alleged that she had been terminated from her job because, as a transsexual woman, she retained some masculine traits. The court held that insofar as "she was discriminated against because . . . she transformed herself into a woman" rather than "because she is a woman," she had failed to state a viable sex discrimination claim.

The incoherence of this purportedly meaningful distinction (between sex and change of sex) is apparent the moment one imagines a court applying a similar distinction in a case involving discrimination on any other ground. It is unlikely, for example, that an employer who terminated an employee for changing her religious affiliation or nationality would be absolved of liability on the ground that he did not object to the employee's new religion or national origin, but only to the change of religion or national origin. Yet, the only difference between these situations and that of a transsexual person is that while changing one's religion or nationality is generally considered to be a legitimate personal choice, "the very idea that one sex can change into another" is likely to engender "ridicule and horror."

Paisley Currah and Shannon Minter, Unprincipled Exclusions: The Struggle to Achieve Judicial and Legislative Equality for Transgender People, 7 Wm. & Mary J. Women & L. 37, 40-41 (2000). Similarly, courts have refused to recognize discrimination against transgender people as a form of anti-gay discrimination or as a form of discrimination against people with disabilities. Id.

More recently, however, courts have begun to rely on the Supreme Court's decisions in Price Waterhouse v. Hopkins, 490 U.S. 228 (1989) and Oncale v. Sundowner Offshore Servs., Inc., 523 U.S. 75, 79-80 (1998), to find that sex stereotyping is a form of sex discrimination prohibited under Title VII. See Chai Feldblum and Lisa Mottet, Gay People, Trans People, Women: Is It All About Gender? 17 N.Y.L. Sch. J.. Hum. Rts. 623, 642-47 (2000). The sex stereotyping article supports the claims of gender-nonconforming people; the *Rosa* case is one example. There is also movement in some states to recognize discrimination against transgender people as discrimination based on sex. For example, Feldblum and Mottet report:

[I]n November 2000, the Connecticut Commission on Human Rights and Opportunities issued a declaratory ruling that discrimination against an individual based on transgender status constituted discrimination based on sex under Connecticut law. The Commission had received a petition on behalf of John/Jane Doe requesting such a declaratory ruling, and several groups intervened to support the petition. The Commission adopted a definition of transgender people, which includes transsexuals (both pre-and post-operative), intersexed people, anyone whose self-described gender identity is other than their sexual identity at birth (regardless of whether such individuals have had hormonal treatment or surgery), and also apparently effeminate men and

17. 857 F. Supp. 96 (D.D.C. 1994).

masculine women. With regard to all such individuals, the reasoning of the Connecticut Commission was straightforward. As the Commission noted, quite succinctly, "more and more courts have ruled that having specific expectations that a person will manifest certain behavior based upon his or her gender is not only conceptually outmoded sexual stereotyping, but also an unlawful form of sex discrimination."

Id. at 647-48.

3. "Sex," "Gender," and Feminist Theory. Is feminist theory well suited to address the struggles of "Micki," Christie Littleton, or Lucas Rosa? Should feminists be concerned with their struggles? If so, is that because transgender people and people with gender-atypical appearances suffer from sex discrimination, or because they suffer forms of discrimination that are related to, but distinct from, sex discrimination? Part of the answer to this question turns on feminist conceptions of terms like "sex" and "gender." Feminist theorist Linda Nicholson argues that feminists have used the word "gender" in two distinct ways.

> On the one hand, gender was developed and is still often used as a contrasting term to sex, to depict that which is socially constructed as opposed to that which is biologically given. On this usage, gender is typically thought to refer to personality traits and behavior in distinction from the body. Here, gender and sex are thought to be distinct. On the other hand, gender has increasingly become used to refer to any social construction having to do with the male/female distinction, including those constructions that separate "female" bodies from "male" bodies. This latter usage emerged when many came to realize that society not only shapes personality and behavior, it also shapes the ways in which the body appears. But if the body is itself always seen through social interpretation, then sex is not something that is separate from gender but is, rather, that which is subsumable under it.

Linda Nicholson, Interpreting Gender, 20 Signs 79 (1994). For other descriptions and critiques of the uses of "gender" in feminist theory, see Mary Hawkesworth, Confounding Gender, 22 Signs 649 (1997); Joan Wallach Scott, Gender and the Politics of History 42-49 (1988).

Which conception of gender is more appropriate for feminism? Nicholson argues for the second. In her view, treating gender as something distinct from sex assumes that there is something called sexual difference that is always the same across cultures; this belief she calls "biological foundationalism." Id. at 82. Nicholson argues that biological foundationalism is inappropriate for feminists because it assumes without proof that all cultures experience sexual and bodily difference in the same way. Id. Similarly, Katherine Franke argues that it is gender that determines sex, and not the other way around. In Franke's view, "sexual equality jurisprudence has uncritically accepted the validity of biological sexual differences. By accepting these biological differences, equality jurisprudence reifies as foundational fact that which is really an effect of normative gender ideology." See Katherine M. Franke, The Central Mistake of Sex Discrimination Law: The Disaggregation of Sex from Gender, 144 U. Pa. L. Rev. 1, 2 (1995). Therefore, discrimination against transgender people should be understood as a form of sex discrimination.

Nicholson's and Franke's arguments seem to suggest that the distinction between "sex" and "gender" is not a useful one. Mary Anne Case argues, to the contrary, that unless sex and gender are "disaggregated," forms of discrimination that turn on gender role expectations rather than the physical attributes of sex will not be readily recognized. Case argues that Price Waterhouse v. Hopkins, set forth at pages 181-186, *VMI*, set forth at pages 382-398, and numerous cases in which effeminate men have been penalized for breaching gender norms, are cases of gender, not sex, discrimination. Case, Disaggregating Gender from Sex and Sexual Orientation: The Effeminate Man in the Law and Feminist Jurisprudence, 105 Yale L.J. 1 (1995). Among the effeminate men cases she discusses is Smith v. Liberty Mutual Ins. Co., 569 F.2d 325 (5th Cir. 1978) (Title VII cannot be "strained" to cover a male applicant who, though admittedly qualified for the position sought, was not hired because the interviewer found him "effeminate"). Case, supra, at 50-54. See generally Francisco Valdes, Queers, Sissies, Dykes, and Tomboys: Deconstructing the Conflation of "Sex," "Gender," and "Sexual Orientation" in Euro-American Law and Society, 83 Cal. L. Rev. 1 (1995) (arguing that Anglo-American law and society regularly conflate "sex," "gender," and "sexual orientation'); compare Richard Epstein, Gender Is for Nouns, 41 DePaul L. Rev. 981, 982 (1992) (objecting to the shift from "sex" to "gender" discrimination because it strengthens the case for viewing sex discrimination as socially-created and thus arbitrary, rather than biologically based).

Judges as well as academic feminists disagree about the proper relationship between the concepts of "sex" and "gender." Some members of the Supreme Court have begun using the terms "sex" and "gender" interchangeably. The issue became a matter of discussion between the justices in J.E.B. v. Alabama (set forth on page 886-898). The opinion for the court written by Justice Blackmun, along with separate concurring opinions by Justice O'Connor and Justice Kennedy and a dissenting opinion by Justice Rehnquist, all addressed whether the practice of making peremptory strikes of jurors based on whether they were men or women constitutes gender discrimination. Justice Scalia ridicules the change in terminology and uses the term "sex discrimination," explaining his usage as follows:

> [G]ender is to sex as feminine is to female and masculine to male. The present case does not involve peremptory strikes exercised on the basis of femininity or masculinity (as far as it appears, effeminate men did not survive the

prosecution's peremptories). The case involves, therefore, sex discrimination plain and simple.

511 U.S. 127, 157 n.1 (1994) (Scalia, J., dissenting).

Justice Ginsburg had made the move from sex to gender by 1975, when she decided that the word "sex" was too disturbing in that it "may conjure up improper images" of what occurs in porno theaters. See Ruth Bader Ginsburg, Gender in the Supreme Court: The 1973 and 1974 Terms, 1975 Sup. Ct. Rev. 1, n.1.

In what direction should the law go?

4. Our Categories, Ourselves

Linda Hamilton Krieger, The Content of Our Categories
47 Stan. L. Rev. 1161, 1188-90 (1995)

Every person, and perhaps even every object that we encounter in the world, is unique, but to treat each as such would be disastrous. Were we to perceive each object sui generis, we would rapidly be inundated by an unmanageable complexity that would quickly overwhelm our cognitive processing and storage capabilities. Similarly, if our species were "programmed" to refrain from drawing inferences or taking action until we had complete, situation-specific data about each person or object we encountered, we would have died out long ago. To function at all, we must design strategies for simplifying the perceptual environment and acting on less-than-perfect information. A major way we accomplish both goals is by creating categories. As cognitive psychologist Eleanor Rosch wrote in 1977, "Since no organism can cope with infinite diversity, one of the most basic functions of all organisms is the cutting up of the environment into classifications by which nonidentical stimuli can be treated as equivalent." Categories and categorization permit us to identify objects, make predictions about the future, infer the existence of unobservable traits or properties, and attribute the causation of events.

What happens when we group objects into categories? First, we tend to perceive members of the same category as being more similar to each other, and members of different categories as more dissimilar to each other, than when all the objects are viewed in aggregate. The same results adhere when the "objects" we categorize are other human beings.

This should come as no surprise. Categories are guardians against complexity. Their purpose is to simplify the perceptual field by distorting it, so that we experience it as less complex and more predictable than it actually is. . . . Categorical structures can simplify the perceptual environment only if "fuzzy" differences are transformed into clear-cut distinctions. Complexity continually threatens the balance of our categorical structures. Assimilation and enhancement of contrast "guard the guardians." Thus, with object and social categories, one can predict a tendency towards thinking that "all x's are alike."

Second, although some debate exists on this issue, it appears that we create a mental prototype, often visual, of the "typical" category member. To determine whether an item is a member of a particular category, we match the object perceived with the category prototype and determine the "distance" between the two. We experience an object first as a member of its "basic" category — the category most accessible at the moment. Only with additional mental processing do we identify it as a member of its superordinate or subordinate categories. According to this view, we carry in our heads images of the "typical letter a," the "typical chair," the "typical law school professor," and the "typical urban gang member."

Cognitive psychologists refer to these categorical structures as "schemas." . . .

Schemas, like other categorical structures, "enable the perceiver to identify stimuli quickly, . . . fill in information missing from the stimulus configuration, and select a strategy for obtaining further information, solving a problem, or reaching a goal." But the price of this cognitive economy is that categorical structures — whether prototypes, stereotypes, or schemas — bias what we see, how we interpret it, how we encode and store it in memory, and what we remember about it later. In intergroup relations, these biases, mediated through perception, inference, and judgment, can result in discrimination, whether we intend it or not, whether we know it or not.

≣ **Mary Coombs, *Interrogating Identity***
≣ 11 Berkeley Women's L.J. 222, 223, 241-246 (1996)

By identity construction, I refer both to the creation of socially-defined identity categories such as race, sexual orientation, and religion, and to the process of classifying individuals within and among these categories. In analyzing these processes, it is helpful to recognize four structural aspects of identity construction, which operate concurrently: category construction, intersectionality, classificatory authority, and context. First, each identity category is properly constructed not as a dichotomy, but at least as a continuum. Indeed, some categories, such as race, are perhaps more accurately seen as a three-dimensional field. Second, all individuals exist at the intersection of multiple identity categories, such as that of "black woman," though for most of us some of these are the less-visible categories of privilege. Third, the authority to classify a particular person as either black or white, for example, is often contested. Such attribution may be done by the person herself, or by others, and the others may classify a person inclusively (she is "one of us") or exclusively (she is "other"). Finally, one's identity is always contingent and contextual. Identity is not fixed or absolute; rather, it is determined by particular persons for particular purposes at particular times in a process in which the person identified participates with varying degrees of freedom. . . .

What are the implications of recognizing the multiplicity, complexity, and fictitious nature of identity? It means, first, that identity can be deployed strategically and politically. I do not mean that one can simply choose one's identity. One's sense of identity is highly constrained. As [Judy] Scales-Trent says, she wears the label black both "to show solidarity" and because it is "really mine and no one may take it from me." Nor can we simply wish away such identity-based phenomena as race or racism. Racial identity is both real and unreal, both "all smoke and mirrors" and "profoundly serious, because so many fall for the trick." Nonetheless, identities are not essential and unchangeable; they are subject to collective and perhaps individual recon-ceptualization. As we claim identities, we reshape the meanings of the categories we use. Consider four newer categories that are still under construction: "people of color," "mixed-race" or "biracial," "bisexual," and "queer."

The notion of an identity as a person of color (or its feminist counterpart, "woman of color") is, I believe, a relatively recent phenome-non. It is a means of conscious coalition building and an intellectual commitment to examining the commonalities and differences among people who share this umbrella identity. . . . Because the category is consciously and explicitly coalitional, it makes obvious a truth about every identity category: its overinclusiveness. No matter how narrowly the category is defined, it treats as similar people who are always more than their common identity as, say, black female North American middle-class middle-aged heterosexual law professors.

The politics of a biracial or mixed-race category are quite different from those of a people of color category. If a mixed-race category were to be generally recognized, it would require us to focus on the different criteria by which we make racial categorizations. . . .

. . . What cost might there be to those who identify as black (the vast majority of whom are genetically mixed-race) if the census added a mixed-race category? Does the mixed-race category make sense as a new racial or ethnic category, or is it simply a way of avoiding the implications of being (seen as) black? Will the recognition of a mixed-race category erode or entrench the white racism embedded in the existing categories and the means by which people are assigned to them?

In effect, . . . people seeking recognition as mixed-race are seeking to secede, as individuals, from blackness. Simultaneously, they call into question the boundaries that have been drawn around the country of whiteness, by questioning the credentials of many of its citizens. When and how and to what extent such secession should be recognized is a political and strategic question, not merely one of discovering and proclaiming the truth of an identity.

The categories bisexual and queer have emerged in reaction to oversimplified dichotomies of sex, gender and sexual orientation. Just as essentialist racial identities do not capture many individuals' sense of themselves, the dichotomies male/female, masculine/feminine, and straight/gay do not accurately reflect many persons' self-identity. . . .

. . . Bisexuality . . . threatens the boundaries of both the heterosexual and the homosexual communities. Again, the less favored group, who see recognition of their identity as more fragile, may be particularly hostile. The lesbian and gay community often sees the claim to be a "bi" as embodying selfishness or false consciousness in denying one's "true" gay identity. As with biracial identity claims, it is an open question what the political impact of category reconceptualization might be. Multi-racial people might join under an umbrella of people of color; bisexuals, along with gays, lesbians and transgendered persons might define themselves collectively as queer.

Both race and sexual orientation are rooted in part in biological facts like skin color or genitalia, but these are of no more inherent significance than the color of one's eyes or the shape of one's ears. The identity categories that have such pervasive political and cultural significance are socially constructed, not biological, facts. "One must learn to be 'black' in this society, precisely because 'blackness' is a socially produced category." The active nature of this identity construction is especially evident in the context of sexual orientation. The acts of "outing" and "flaunting" and "closeting" — concepts developed to describe the processes of gay identity formation — have resonances for the meaning of one's racial or ethnic or religious identity. The burgeoning literature of queer theory provides a new understanding of identity that can be applied in other contexts. In particular, queer theory has engaged with the tension of simultaneously using and deconstructing identity categories.

Queer theory helps us understand how all identity categories are created rather than simply revealed. For many people, . . . race seems obvious and fixed, even if the significance attributed to it is socially constructed. But, at least in any culture where we do not walk around naked, gender and sexual orientation are always recognized as performative. We are all always demonstrating who we are by what we do. Sexual identity is a practice, not a thing. Some scholars recognize that racial identity is also a practice. As Scales-Trent says, "'race' . . . is a continuing act of imagination. It is a very demanding verb." Our identity, both as we understand it and as it is perceived by others, is the result of a series of actions we take in particular contexts, with varying (often very narrow) degrees of freedom.

Notes

1. Category Construction and Anti-Discrimination Law. Krieger suggests that category construction, despite its limitations, is an inherent feature of human cognition. If this is true, can its troubling implications for justice be surmounted? Krieger's article examines how Title VII doctrine, in particular, fails to recognize that invidious discrimination often occurs at the cognitive (unconscious) rather than the intentional level, and suggests ways to reform Title VII doctrine to bring it into line with what is known about human cognition. Might more knowledge about cognition have implications for other areas of legal doctrine as well? In this context, recall the materials about employment discrimination and Title VII, examined in Chapter 2.

In contrast, Coombs' discussion of category construction assumes that identity categories are consciously and strategically created, even "performed." Could both Krieger and Coombs be right?

2. From "Intersectionality" to "Multidimensionality" in Feminist and Queer Legal Thought. Recently, scholars who write about the complex interrelations of race and sexuality have utilized early feminist legal theories of "intersectionality," seeking ways to conceptualize "the inherent complexity of systems of oppression . . . and the social identity categories around which social power and disempowerment are distributed." Darren Lenard Hutchinson, Ignoring the Sexualization of Race: Heteronormativity, Critical Race Theory, and Anti-Racist Politics, 47 Buff. L. Rev. 1, 9 (1999). These scholars seek to extend the concept of intersectionality to incorporate all the multiple categories to which people assign themslves and are assigned by others. See generally Darren Lenard Hutchinson, Identity Crisis: "Intersectionality," "Multidimensionality," and the Development of an Adequate Theory of Subordination, 6 Mich. J. Race & L. 285, 309-316 (2001) (surveying recent theoretical developments and arguing for "multidimensionality" as a helpful way to analyze oppression); Francisco Valdes, Beyond Sexual Orientation in Queer Legal Theory: Majoritarianism, Multidimensionality, and Responsibility in Social Justice Scholarship or Legal Scholars as Cultural Warriors, 75 Denv. U. L. Rev. 1409, 1415 (1998) ("Multidimensionality tends to promote awareness of patterns as well as particularities in social relations by studying in an interconnected way the specifics of subordination."); Elvia R. Arriola, Gendered Inequality: Lesbians, Gays, and Feminist Legal Theory, 9 Berkeley Women's L.J. 103, 139-141 (1994) (urging a "holistic" examination of subordination); Peter Kwan, Complicity and Complexity: Cosynthesis and Praxis, 49 DePaul L. Rev. 673, 688 (2000) (using "cosynthesis" to describe a "mutually defining, synergistic, and complicit relationship between identity categories" that "denies the priority of the deconstructive concerns of class over race, of race over gender, or of gender over sexual orientation, of anything over anything else.").

If oppression is always multidimensional, is feminist theory distinct from other anti-subordination theory at all?

3. Sex and the Social Construction of Identity Categories. Coombs suggests that sexual and racial identities are "practices" rather than things. Is sexual identity also a practice? Take a moment to consult your own experience. What kinds of social practices signal sexual identity in the dominant U.S. culture? In subcultures within the United States? How do these practices vary by race, sexual orientation, religion, ethnicity, age, class? Have your personal and political commitments affected how you "perform" your gender?

Coombs' reference to "performance" refers to Judith Butler's famous assertion that sexual identity is "performative." Judith Butler, Gender Trouble: Feminism and the Subversion of Identity (1990). Butler is often identified as a postmodern theorist; for more on postmodernism and feminism, see section 5, below.

5. Postmodernist Theory and Feminist Theory

Tracy E. Higgins, "By Reason of Their Sex":
Feminist Theory, Postmodernism, and Justice
80 Cornell L. Rev. 1536, 1537-39, 1560-63, 1568-72 (1995)

"Woman" is a troublesome term, in feminism and in law. The category is neither consistently nor coherently constituted in linguistic, historical, or legal contexts. Yet the framework through which women have sought (and gained) improvements in their legal, economic, and social status depends upon the ascription of meaning to the term. Each claim under the Equal Protection Clause or civil rights statutes implies an affirmative (though perhaps unstated) "redescription" of the category. Feminist theorists, in turn, offer alternative redescriptions of the term as a critique of categories within both law and feminism. As multiple redescriptions of woman compete for acceptance in law and in feminist legal theory, the question of the authority of the descriptive voice arises. Wherein lies the legitimacy of any particular claim about woman? Is there a transcendent truth, a "metanarrative" of sexual difference, that is, a narrative that exists outside of contingent, historical notions of gender, against which we may measure the validity of such a claim? If not, upon what basis are we to choose among competing redescriptions?

Both the Supreme Court's jurisprudence of gender and feminist legal theory have generally assumed that some identifiable and describable category of woman exists prior to the construction of legal categories. For the Court, this woman — whose characteristics admittedly have changed over time — serves as the standard against which gendered legal classifications are measured. For feminism, her existence has served a different but equally important purpose as the subject for whom political goals are pursued. To the extent that the definitions of the category diverge, the differences among definitions are played out in feminist critiques of the Court's gender jurisprudence, and, occasionally, in the Court's response to those critiques.

Despite such differences, both the Supreme Court and its feminist critics have largely treated the analysis of gender categories as a problem of accuracy. For the Court, the validity of gender classifications depends upon their correspondence to a set of gendered norms that the Court accepts as true or real or in some sense independent of legal categories. The response of feminist legal theorists to this analysis has been either to challenge the Court's conclusions about the accuracy of the correspondence or more recently, to challenge the set of norms against which the gender categories are measured. Neither response displaces the Court's basic construction of the problem as one of assessing the accuracy of a particular account of gender difference. Indeed, feminist efforts to offer truer or better stories of women's experience — and to justify those stories through feminist method — assume that there is an underlying truth to be told.

To the extent that these legal accounts of gender, both mainstream and feminist, endeavor to assess the accuracy of gender categories, they represent a mode of argument that tracks foundationalist or objectivist assumptions about knowledge. That is, their authority or persuasiveness rests upon their perceived correspondence to a reality that exists independent of legal discourse. These accounts depend therefore upon the identification of secure foundations for (gender) knowledge that are in some sense free of historical, political, or social contingency. Such modernist or objectivist assumptions have been under attack for decades within the academy. More recently, leftist legal critics have borrowed the insights and tools of antifoundationalist philosophy to call into question law's claim to rationality and legitimacy. Even more recently, some scholars have begun to question whether the postmodern or antifoundationalist view of knowledge as contingent promotes or threatens progressive social movements such as feminism, whatever its usefulness in challenging the validity of existing legal norms. . . .

Just as the Supreme Court has shifted its ideology of gender difference over time, feminist legal theorists have defined their subject woman in various ways, both tracking and determining the nature of legal claims raised on her behalf. The earliest claims for "simple equality" — equal treatment, equal pay, equal opportunity — depended only on defining woman as like man but excluded. Such a definition simultaneously avoided the complexities of gender difference and rhetorically eliminated any justification for different treatment. This claim of simple equality was consistent with the Supreme Court's early approach to gender classifications — the identification and elimination of false stereotypes. As the limitations of this approach were exposed, the definition of woman and explanations of the nature of her inequality or oppression became more complicated. Indeed, the Court's decisions in *Geduldig*[26] and *Michael M.*[27] highlighted the complexity of the equality puzzle. Efforts to translate needs surrounding pregnancy, reproductive freedom, and the threat of sexual violence into claims of right have required more complicated theories of difference.

Even as particular feminist theories of gender difference have evolved, feminist legal theorists have generally assumed that there exists some identity, described by the category of woman, that serves as the source of feminist goals within law and politics and as the subject of theory. Indeed, the structure of identity politics seemingly necessitates such an assumption, underlying as it does feminism's claim to speak as and for the group women. In the legal realm, the group-based nature of civil rights claims has required increasingly complex theories of what it might mean to discriminate "by reason of her sex." Feminist legal theorists therefore have been compelled to develop a notion of womanhood that can simultaneously describe the collective experiences of women and translate that description into legal claims. Such general accounts or "metanarratives" of gender have lent political coherence to feminism and have served as a basis for expanding the substantive scope of equality claims for women.

Despite the temptation, and arguably the necessity, of articulating generalizable claims about women, feminist legal theorists have divided over the content of such claims and have struggled to locate an account of gender that is credible. Just as the Supreme Court has attempted to ground its gender analysis outside the contestable realm of law and culture, feminist theorists have sought some coherent and convincing basis for offering better accounts of women's lives. Like the Court, some feminists, including feminist legal theorists, seem to be motivated in this endeavor by a desire to root gender outside of politics, to describe a connection among women that precedes feminism.

Although feminist legal theorists have effectively criticized the Court's approach to gender by exposing the partiality of its assumptions, they have frequently done so by offering a fuller theory of gender difference, an alternative "metanarrative" that does not rely on a problematic privileging of biology. In so doing feminists have faced their own crisis of authority, one that stems from the problem of accounting for differences among women rather than differences between men and women. Among women, indeed among feminists, who has authority to speak on woman's behalf? . . .

[Higgins describes "the mothering story" as the effort of cultural feminists to place care work at the center of women's experience (explored in Chapter 5), and "the dominance story" as the effort of dominance feminists to place sexual violence at the center of women's experience (explored in

26. [Geduldig v. Aiello, 417 U.S. 484 (1974); see p. 333.]
27. [Michael M. v. Superior Court of Sonoma County, 450 U.S. 464 (1981); see pp. 936-949.]

Chapter 4), and notes that both efforts have been controversial among feminists.] In addition to fostering the very divisiveness they are intended to quell, both the mothering story and the dominance story operate to naturalize a particular type of women's experience. For example, the mothering story explains gender difference by privileging a traditional Western, heterosexual experience of motherhood within the nuclear family. Similarly, the dominance story privileges women's accounts of sexual violence while discounting accounts of sexual pleasure as problematic, compromised, or even products of false consciousness. To the extent that one account or the other becomes the "official" feminist story of gender difference, it constitutes the category woman in a particular way, accepting some experiences as definitive while excluding others. When feminists aspire to account for women's oppression through claims of cross-cultural commonality, they construct the feminist subject through exclusions and, as Judith Butler has observed, "those excluded domains return to haunt the integrity and unity of the feminist 'we'."[164] . . .

The divisions within feminism surrounding various metanarratives of women's oppression suggest that any effort to give specific content to the category woman will inevitably generate disagreement among women. This realization forces reconsideration not only of the way gender categories are constituted but also of the way in which we think about the constitution of such categories. Questioning the idea of woman's identity as such, some feminists have begun to reexamine the quest for a general account of oppression. Although many feminist legal theorists have remained concerned with the imperatives of identity politics, feminist philosophers and political theorists have been more willing to challenge the coherence of the category. In so doing, they have turned increasingly to the antifoundationalist stance of postmodernism as a basis for social criticism.

Postmodernism, broadly defined, rejects the role of philosophy as a foundation for social criticism. For example, Jean-Francois Lyotard defines the postmodern condition as one in which the "grand narratives" of legitimation, including narratives of historical progress, scientific rationality, reason, and justice, are no longer credible.[166] These modern or Enlightenment accounts yield to a new "postmodern" view in which social criticism, including moral judgment, exists independent of any universalist theoretical ground. As Nancy Fraser and Linda Nicholson explain, "No longer anchored philosophically, the very shape or character of social criticism changes; it becomes more pragmatic, ad hoc, contextual, and local." [167]

164. Judith Butler, Contingent Foundations: Feminism and the Question of "Postmodernism," in Feminists Theorize the Political 3, 14 (Judith Butler & Joan Scott eds., 1992).
166. [See Jean-Francois Lyotard, The Postmodern Condition: A Report on Knowledge 12 (Geoff Bennington & Brian Massumi trans., 1984).]
167. [Nancy Fraser & Linda J. Nicholson, Social Criticism Without Philosophy, in Feminism/Postmodernism 26 (Linda J. Nicholson ed., 1990).]

This wide-ranging attack on metaphysics has led to skepticism of any overarching theory of justice and a call for what Lyotard describes as a "justice of multiplicities."

The postmodern skepticism of grand theory resonates with feminist legal theory's increasing distrust of universal claims about women. Postmodernism suggests that the problem lies not in ensuring that the representation of women's experience is accurate, but rather in the concept of representation itself. Sexual difference, however it may be measured, is irretrievably bound up with gender. In short, gender itself is a product of power and language and social institutions, including law, not a reality that preexists those structures. Thus, for postmodern feminist theorists, the problem of accounting for a range of feminist views and experiences is less an ontological than an epistemological difficulty.

At the same time, postmodernism apparently undermines the central goal of feminism and other forms of social criticism: the identification and critique of inequality and injustice that transcend cultural, political, and geographic boundaries. As Fraser and Nicholson have argued, Lyotard's justice of multiplicities not only calls into question universalist notions of justice but also renders problematic feminist critique of legal institutions and legal reform outside of narrow, localized experience. To the extent that postmodernism questions the use of cross-cultural categories, it threatens to undermine the identification of broad structures of inequality premised on gender.

Thus, postmodernism is at once promising and threatening for feminism. Divisions within feminism over descriptions of women's experience, coupled with the risk of reinforcing traditional gender roles, have continued to draw feminists away from broad theories of gender difference and towards a recognition of the contingency and partiality of any particular account of gender. By questioning the possibility of true accounts and emphasizing the constitutive role of language, postmodernism resonates with feminist critiques of legal accounts of womanhood.

At the same time, if postmodernism disables truth claims feminists themselves cannot claim to tell true stories of women's experience. It is for this reason that some feminists have been ambivalent about embracing fully the implications of antifoundationalism. Feminists, along with other groups on the margin of power, are reluctant to relinquish the hope that resort to some standard independent of politics and culture will strengthen their claims. Those who have been excluded from power continue to rely upon the possibility that those empowered who purport to respect that standard will respond to arguments for their inclusion. Although women have been largely excluded from the development of Western notions of justice (and indeed at times assumed incapable of reason), resort to claims of justice and equality has led to identifiable legal gains for women. Feminists therefore may fear that without an objectively defensible basis for distinguishing between truth and falsehood, women are left only with power to dictate the outcome of competing claims of truth. That prospect most frightens those who are oppressed. As Sabina Lovibond has asked, "How can any one ask me to say goodbye to 'emancipatory metanarratives' when my own emancipation is still such a patchy, hit-or-miss affair?"[175]

Feminists may also be reluctant to embrace postmodernism because, despite the difficulty of giving content to the category "woman," that category seems necessary to feminist political advocacy. In other words, the lingering essentialism and tendency toward universalizing theoretical claims in feminist legal theory result, at least in part, from the political utility of making specific claims about women as a group. The perceived strategic cost of surrendering the claim to narrative authority is a product not only of the political structure but of the legal structure as well: the protection of civil rights laws is premised on the allegation of a group-based harm, thereby requiring an argument structured in terms of the characteristics, needs, and vulnerabilities of that group. These laws require feminist advocates not only to structure claims based on an allegation of harm to a particular woman but also to link that harm to the condition of women as a group.

Confronted with both the need to offer an authoritative account of women's experience and the consequences of exclusion implicit in offering such an account, feminist legal theorists have hoped for a middle path between postmodernism and foundationalism. They have revealed and criticized the partiality of law's description of womanhood while maintaining the possibility of a truer description, one freer from distortion and exclusion. In this sense, feminists' movement between critique and reaffirmation of gender categories parallels the Court's continuing quest for a principled basis for reviewing gender classifications. In sorting true from false accounts, however, feminists and the Court face a crisis of authority: Whose descriptions are valid? From what standpoint can mainstream accounts be criticized as incomplete?

≣
≣   ### Katharine T. Bartlett, Feminist Legal Methods
≣   103 Harv. L. Rev. 829, 880-885 (1990)

Positionality is a stance from which a number of apparently inconsistent feminist "truths" make sense. The positional stance acknowledges the existence of empirical truths, values and knowledge, and also their contingency. It thereby provides a basis for feminist commitment and political action, but views these commitments as provisional and subject to further critical evaluation and revision.

. . . . [P]ositionality retains a concept of knowledge based upon experience. Experience interacts with an individual's current perceptions to

---

175. [Sabina Lovibond, Feminism and Postmodernism, in New Left Review 12 (Nov./Dec. 1989).]

reveal new understandings and to help that individual, with others, make sense of those perceptions. Thus, from women's position of exclusion, women have come to "know" certain things about exclusion: its subtlety; its masking by "objective" rules and constructs; its pervasiveness; its pain; and the need to change it. These understandings make difficult issues decidable and answers non-arbitrary.

Like the postmodern [stance], however, positionality rejects the perfectibility, externality, or objectivity of truth. Instead, the positional knower conceives of truth as situated and partial. Truth is situated in that it emerges from particular involvements and relationships. These relationships, not some essential or innate characteristics of the individual, define the individual's perspective and provide the location for meaning, identity, and political commitment. Thus, for example, the meaning of pregnancy derives not just from its biological characteristics, but from the social place it occupies — how workplace structures, domestic arrangements, tort systems, high schools, prisons, and other societal institutions construct its meaning.

Truth is partial in that the individual perspectives that yield and judge truth are necessarily incomplete. No individual can understand except from some limited perspective. Thus, for example, a man experiences pornography as a man with a particular upbringing, set of relationships, race, social class, sexual preference, and so on, which affect what "truths" he perceives about pornography. A woman experiences pregnancy as a woman with a particular upbringing, race, social class, set of relationships, sexual preference, and so on, which affect what "truths" she perceives about pregnancy. As a result, there will always be "knowers" who have access to knowledge that other individuals do not have, and no one's truth can be deemed total or final.

Because knowledge arises within social contexts and in multiple forms, the key to increasing knowledge lies in the effort to extend one's limited perspective. Self-discipline is crucial. My perspective gives me a source of special knowledge, but a limited knowledge that I can improve by the effort to step beyond it, to understand other perspectives, and to expand my sources of identity. To be sure, I cannot transcend my perspective; by definition, whatever perspective I currently have limits my view. But I can improve my perspective by stretching my imagination to identify and understand the perspectives of others.

Positionality's requirement that other perspectives be sought out and examined checks the characteristic tendency of all individuals — including feminists — to want to stamp their own point of view upon the world. This requirement does not allow certain feminist positions to be set aside as immune from critical examination. When feminists oppose restrictive abortion laws, for example, positionality compels the effort to understand those whose views about the sanctity of potential human life are offended by assertion of women's unlimited right to choose abortion. When feminists debate the legal alternative of joint custody at divorce, positionality compels appreciation of the desire by some fathers to be responsible, co-equal parents. And (can it get worse?) when feminists urge drastic reform of rape laws, positionality compels consideration of the position of men whose social conditioning leads them to interpret the actions of some women as "inviting" rather than discouraging sexual encounter.

Although I must consider other points of view from the positional stance, I need not accept their truths as my own. Positionality is not a strategy of process and compromise that seeks to reconcile all competing interests. Rather, it imposes a twin obligation to make commitments based on the current truths and values that have emerged from methods of feminism, and to be open to previously unseen perspectives that might come to alter these commitments. As a practical matter, of course, I cannot do both simultaneously, evenly, and perpetually. Positionality, however, sets an ideal of self-critical commitment whereby I act, but consider the truths upon which I act subject to further refinement, amendment, and correction.

Some "truths" will emerge from the ongoing process of critical reexamination in a form that seems increasingly fixed or final. Propositions such as that I should love my children, that I should not murder others for sport, or that democracy is as a general matter better than authoritarianism seem so "essential" to my identity and my social world that I experience them as values that can never be overridden, even as standards by which I may judge others. These truths, indeed, seem to confirm the view that truth does exist (it must; these things are true) if only I could find it. For feminists, the commitment to ending gender-based oppression has become one of these "permanent truths." The problem is the human inclination to make this list of "truths" too long, to be too uncritical of its contents, and to defend it too harshly and dogmatically.

Positionality reconciles the existence of reliable, experience-based grounds for assertions of truth upon which politics should be based, with the need to question and improve these grounds. The understanding of truth as "real," in the sense of produced by the actual experiences of individuals in their concrete social relationships, permits the appreciation of plural truths. By the same token, if truth is understood as partial and contingent, each individual or group can approach its own truths with a more honest, self-critical attitude about the value and potential relevance of other truths.

The ideal presented by the positionality stance makes clear that current disagreements within society at large and among feminists — disagreements about abortion, child custody, pornography, the military, pregnancy, motherhood, and the like — reflect value conflicts basic to the terms of social existence. If resolvable at all, these conflicts will not be settled by reference to external or pre-social standards of truth. From the positional stance, any resolutions that emerge are the products of human struggles about what social realities are better than others. Realities are deemed better not by comparison to some external, "discovered" moral truths or "essential" human characteristics, but by internal truths that make the most sense of experienced, social existence. Thus, social truths will emerge from social relationships and what, after critical examination, they tell social beings about what they want themselves, and their social world, to be. . . .

In this way, feminist positionality resists attempts at classification either as essentialism . . . or relativistic. . . . Positionality is both nonrelative and nonarbitrary. It assumes some means of distinguishing between better and worse understanding; truth claims are significant or "valid" for those who experience that validity. But positionality puts no stock in fixed, discoverable foundations. If there is any such thing as ultimate or objective truth, I can never, in my own lifetime, be absolutely sure that I have discovered it. I can know important and non-arbitrary truths, but these are necessarily mediated through human experiences and relationships. There can be no universal, final, or objective truth; there can be only "partial, locatable, critical knowledges"; [241] no aperspectivity — only improved perspectives. . . .

Notes

1. Postmodernism in Feminist Legal Theory. As Maxine Eichner notes, postmodern theory (also referred to as poststructuralist theory) has "profoundly changed the ways that scholars in many disciplines approach the study of their fields." Maxine Eichner, On Postmodern Feminist Legal Theory, 36 Harv. C.R.-C.L. L. Rev. 1, 2 (2001). These fields include English, comparative literature, women's studies, "anthropology, art history, history, philosophy, political theory, sociology, and even the philosophy of science." Eichner, supra, at 2. Postmodernism has been slower, however, to make a mark on legal studies. Eichner speculates that this may be so because postmodern theory is better suited for critique than for building positive theory, and/or because the discipline of law — which relies on fixed categories and either/or logic — is "so closely associated with the vision of modernity against which postmodernists are reacting." Id. at 4.

Nevertheless, postmodernism has begun to creep into feminist legal scholarship. For some theorists, postmodernist analytic techniques offer feminists the opportunity to radically "change how people think." Thus, Marie Ashe argues that "[t]he great relevance of poststructuralism for jurisprudence . . . is that it throws into question the categories and classifications upon which law has uncritically supported exercises of power that have silenced and opposed in the name of nature or in the name of practical necessity. . . . Law's recognition of its own limitation may open its ears to hearing the namings, the self-definitions, and the claims of oppressed persons, and more significantly, may permit Law's recognition that its customary namings and classifications have no greater claim to validity than

241. [Donna Haraway, Situated Knowledges: The Science Question in Feminism and the Privilege of Partial Perspective, 14 Feminist Stud. 575, 584 (1988).]

do the self-narratives of those whom it has kept in silence." Marie Ashe, Mind's Opportunity: Birthing a Poststructuralist Feminist Jurisprudence, in Legal Studies as Cultural Studies: A Reader in (Post)Modern Critical Theory 116-117 (Jerry Leonard ed. 1995). Joan Williams argues that postmodernism can help theorists move beyond the sameness/difference debate in feminist legal theory. See Joan C. Williams, Dissolving the Sameness/Difference Debate: A Post-Modern Path Beyond Essentialism in Feminist and Critical Race Theory, 1991 Duke L.J. 296.

Some legal scholars have used postmodernist theory to construct positive programs for doctrinal reform. Drucilla Cornell has used the work of psychoanalyst Jacques Lacan to argue for doctrines affecting abortion, pornography, and sexual harassment that will protect women's freedom to exercise their sexual imaginations, thus sheltering women's right to imagine themselves as persons. See Drucilla Cornell, The Imaginary Domain: Abortion, Pornography, & Sexual Harassment (1995); see also Drucilla Cornell, At the Heart of Freedom: Feminism, Sex, and Equality (1998) (arguing that freedom, not equality with men, is what women need). Zillah Eisenstein uses postmodernist theory to argue for reforming the workplace in light of "the family and women's place in it," with special attention to the pregnant body. See Zillah R. Eisenstein, The Female Body and the Law (1988). Maxine Eichner identifies four propositions that emerge for her from postmodernist theory:

> First, . . . postmodern feminists must use the link that they have so clearly demonstrated between power and identity to encourage women to resist dominant notions of gender roles.
>
> Second, . . ., feminist legal theory should take to heart postmodern feminist insights regarding the importance of seeking more fluid notions of gender identity that are less closely linked to a particular sex. . . .
>
> Third, insofar as differences between women and men exist, feminist legal theorists should hesitate before celebrating them and touting their recognition as a mode of accepting "the Other." . . . [A] postmodernist legal theory must distinguish between traits and characteristics it seeks to revalue and those it seeks to make disappear through the elimination of oppression.
>
> Fourth, and finally, a postmodern feminism based on differences and heterogeneity must ultimately be grounded in a politics of material equality. Only within a system in which certain basic equalities exist can differences truly be valued rather than represent the visible scars of oppression.

Maxine Eichner, supra, at 65-66. Based on these principles, Eichner identifies an agenda for legal reform:

> [F]eminists must locate and support the legal conditions that would promote "subaltern counterpublics," and shield them from the pressure of dominant discourses emanating from the state, the market, and culture. These legal conditions would include allowing people the time and resources for social/civic participation through paid child-care benefits, shorter mandatory

working hours, paid parental leave, and the deductibility of expenses for civic organizations, in addition to currently available tax deductions for donations to such organizations. . . .

Postmodern feminist theory should . . . place a high priority on broadening the definition of family beyond the stereotypical model (composed of a heterosexual adult male breadwinner and a heterosexual adult female caretaker along with their biological children), and on creating a network of protections that makes it costless for families to diverge from this model. . . .

. . . [A] postmodern feminist agenda could seek laws to require television stations that receive public funding to produce programs featuring divergent depictions of gender roles. Similarly, postmodern feminists could seek to ensure that alternative gender discourses are communicated to children and young adults through federal or local mandates that require schools to expose students to examples of those who diverge from standard gender depictions of women and men. Such a requirement would go beyond simply presenting jobs and qualities in sex-neutral terms. Instead, students would be exposed to women and men in nontraditional occupations.

Id. at 68-69, 71. In addition, Eichner uses postmodern theory to argue for sex-neutral laws and rules whenever possible; for protection against domestic and street violence; for women's control over their bodies; for campaign finance laws that will make significant economic redistribution possible; for a progressive tax structure and a living wage; and for benefits for part-time workers. Id. at 72-76.

How does this agenda differ (if at all) from agendas that might emerge from the other varieties of feminist legal theory we have examined in this book?

2. Postmodern Theory and the Problem of Knowledge. Bartlett's description of positionality draws from work in other disciplines on the problem of feminism and knowledge. See especially Linda Alcoff, Cultural Feminism Versus Post-Structuralism: The Identity Crisis in Feminist Theory, 13 Signs 405 (1988); Mary Hawkesworth, Knowers, Knowing, Known: Feminist Theory and Claims of Truth, 14 Signs 533 (1989); and Donna Haraway, cited in footnote 241 of the Higgins excerpt above. Is Bartlett's conception of positionality helpful? Does it differ from postmodernism as described by Higgins?

Is worrying about epistemological questions of identity and truth a luxury for the epistemologically privileged? bell hooks makes this suggestion, but then suggests that African Americans have much to gain from challenging the essentialist claims of those in authority. Patricia J. Williams has addressed this same issue with a bifurcated strategy. At times she has challenged the critical approaches that undermine the legal constructions that members of minority groups might use to improve their own status in existing society, such as individual rights. See, e.g., Williams, Alchemical Notes: Reconstructing Ideals from Deconstructed Rights, 22 Harv. C.R.-

C.L. L. Rev. 401 (1987). At other times, she has struck piercing blows to the possibility of unified conceptions of identity that might be thought necessary to support any meaningful concept of individual rights. See, e.g., Williams, On Being the Object of Property, 14 Signs 5 (1988). Mari J. Matsuda's scholarship combines a similar set of political commitments with a contingent approach to questions of gender and race identity that challenges unitary foundations for such commitments. Compare, e.g., Matsuda, Looking to the Bottom: Critical Legal Studies and Reparations, 22 Harv. C.R.-C.L. L. Rev. 323 (1987), with Matsuda, When the First Quail Calls: Multiple Consciousness as Jurisprudential Method, 11 Women's Rts. L. Rep. 7 (1989). For an exploration of the need for a double, or integrated, strategy in the context of international women's rights issues, see Tracy E. Higgins, Anti-Essentialism, Relativism, and Human Rights, 19 Harv. Women's L.J. 89, 119 (1996) (urging a brand of "cross-cultural feminism" in which "[f]alse consciousness should be measured not against true consciousness (objective, absolute, pre-political) but against feminist consciousness (subjective, contested, political) and that "[f]eminist consciousness . . . must be understood as consisting of multiple and sometimes competing critical stances toward cultural oppression").

3. Postmodernism and "Strategic Essentialism." Some scholars argue that presenting claims about women's experience as if they represented the unambiguous truth is more a strategic choice than an intellectual commitment. Frances Olsen, for example, writes that the uncompromising or "grand theory" character of MacKinnon's claims has galvanized feminism, helped to break habits of thought, and made feminism more understandable than would be possible through more complex explanations of women's subordination. See Olsen, Feminist Theory in Grand Style (book review), 89 Colum. L. Rev. 1147, 1170-1177 (1989). Outside legal discourse, Gayatri Spivak has famously endorsed "strategic essentialism" in pursuit of specific political goals. See Gayatri Spivak, Outside in the Teaching Machine 1-5 (1993); see also Diana Fuss, Essentially Speaking: Feminism, Nature and Difference 20 (1989) (essentialism may have strategic or interventionary value).

The problem, argues Kathryn Abrams, is that many essentialist claims that have been made by feminists — for example, the claim that women's "voluntary" desire for heterosexual sex is not real but, rather, an ideologically determined response to oppression, which then contributes to that oppression — are not good strategy. They are not good strategy because they offend women and distance them from feminist struggles, ignore the complicated responses of women that contain both compromise and resistance, and perpetuate the notion that women cannot be rational decisionmakers. See Abrams, Ideology and Women's Choices, 24 Ga. L. Rev. 761, 777-792 (1990).

4. Feminist Voices against Postmodernism. Might postmodern critique be dangerous for feminism? Robin West argues that feminists should be wary of recent critical social theory, including postmodern theory. She identifies four central themes of critical social theory — ideas concerning power, knowledge, morality, and the self. With respect to power, West criticizes the idea — usually attributed to Foucault — that power should not be seen as only or primarily repressive, but rather as "productive." Foucauldian theorists focus particularly on the ways that power relations produce and shape what is officially understood to be truth. West argues, however, that patriarchal power is not productive but repressive and violent. "If feminist legal theorists want to understand, much less challenge, patriarchal power, we need to come to grips with its utterly non-discursive and silencing violence." West, Feminism in the Law: Theory, Practice and Criticism, 1989 U. Chi. Legal F. 59, 62. Focusing on the ideologies that justify this violence, West argues, encourages male blindness to the violence that marks women's lives. Moreover, whereas critical social theorists see the ideological aspects of power as invisible and hence needing exposure, in patriarchy it is violence, not ideology, that tends to be invisible and hence should be exposed. Id. at 63.

With respect to knowledge, West argues that critical social theorists' focus on knowledge, texts, and ideology — what has been said about the world — is misplaced when it comes to patriarchal power. "Patriarchy has mostly produced silence from women, and it is for precisely that reason that feminists not yet taken by social theory have theorized so extensively about women's silence rather than women's discourse. . . . So long as silence rather than discourse remains the primary product of modern patriarchy, then whatever else it has going for it, the social theorist's focus on discourse and speech is an entirely misguided entry into the study of modern women's lives. We ought instead study the production of silence." Id. at 66.

With respect to morality, West criticizes critical legal theorist Roberto Unger, who argues that the direction of progressive social action should be toward increased autonomy and away from hierarchy. West points out that inequality is an inherent aspect of the relationship between women and children, and this is not the same as domination.

> Women of all cultures routinely, although not always, respond to their utterly unequal and hierarchic relationships with their infants and children with nurturance, care and love, rather than power, narcissism and the imposition for the sake of ego-gratification of the stronger's will upon the weaker's fate. The nurturant response the infant engenders in the mother seeks the fulfillment of the needs of the weaker party; it does not seek to recreate or reinvent the weak in the image desired by the strong. From a truly woman-and child-centered perspective, the bare fact of physical inequality takes on an entirely different hue from that projected by modern social theory: The physically unequal mother in all cultures typically breast feeds and protects, rather than bullies or browbeats, the vulnerable infant and child. The powerful mother nurtures so as

to give life and create growth in the weak. She does not impose so as to inscribe her will.

West, 1989 U. Chi. Legal F. at 80. West further points out that morality is not located solely in speech, but also in nonverbal and preverbal instincts and intuitions that stem from the experience of being cared for. Finally, West argues that women's experience has an important role to play in the shaping of morality: "There is surely no way to know with any certainty whether women have a privileged access to a way of life that is more nurturant, more connected, more natural, more loving, and thereby more moral than the principled lives which both men and women presently pursue in the public sphere, including the sphere of legal practice, theory and pedagogy. But it does suggest that whether by reason of sociological role, psychological upbringing or biology, women are closer to such a life." Id. at 83.

Finally, West is critical of recent social theorizing about the self. Postmodern social theorists have argued that the contemporary idea of "the self" — isolated, autonomous, able to know the world and itself — is actually a fairly recent historical construction. West agrees with this claim and adds that feminists claim that this notion of the "self" reflects the experiences of men and is as such a patriarchal construct. Although there are some tensions between these claims, West argues that a deeper tension between feminists and postmodernists has to do with the nature of "selfhood" more generally. As West characterizes the postmodernist claim, "any description of a concrete, given, natural, precultural self is delusional, and . . . our only true inner nature is one of instability, potentiality, negative capability and susceptibility to change — that our inessentialism is our essence." West argues that this is not women's experience. Rather, women have been socialized not to experience self at all, but a sense of selflessness. Feminist consciousness raising seeks to help women reclaim an inner self, whereas postmodern theorists wish to lose theirs.

> The critical female self knows herself as a fantastic, unlived, unspeakable, unspoken alternative which cannot render itself more concrete, and which is known in large part through its absence from cultured life. . . . This anti-symbolic, uncultured, natural, loving, female self knows herself often and tragically as that which is feared, repressed, despised, raped, abused and killed by the vicious side of patriarchy. She knows herself even more often as that which is trivialized, fantasized and rendered unreal, untrustworthy, irrational and ultimately nonexistent by the cultured side of patriarchy. It is no wonder that she hates and disowns herself. But paradoxically, she also knows herself, at times, as exceedingly, painfully, achingly real. She knows herself as joyful, living, loving and real, even as she knows herself as only dimly perceived, because she is so universally denied. She knows herself, miraculously if only on occasion, not as the hated, feared, denied, trivialized and trampled upon, but as worthy and beautiful, and as one who must be reclaimed from denial, fear, oppression and loathing. . . .

Feminist legal theories in particular should stay true to these glimpsed and occasional experiences of the self within. If we want an ideal to guide a critique of law that is total, if we want a source of light to guide legal reforms that are truly progressive, if we want to understand how we should begin to remake and reclaim the world in a way that is more loving and more holistic, then we should be extremely wary of the postmodern, poststructuralist and social-theoretic claim that this non-discursive, woman-bonded, creative, erotic and quietly rebellious self within is but another product of a political, patriarchal, liberal and societal discourse. We should instead seek to protect and nurture and give voice to that most tentative, intuitive, unschooled and above all else undisciplined female self that lies within. For it is that self who will show us truly new ways to judge, new ways to legislate, and new ways to order.

Id. at 95-96. See also West, Caring for Justice (1997) (making a similar argument against postmodernist theory); Catharine A. MacKinnon, Points Against Postmodernism, 75 Chi.-Kent L. Rev. 687, 703 (2000) (arguing that postmodern theory, by erasing the distinction between truth and lies, makes it impossible for feminists to speak the truth about women's lives and be heard); but see Katherine C. Sheehan, Caring for Deconstruction, 12 Yale J.L. & Feminism 85 (2000) (criticizing West's understanding of postmodernism and arguing that deconstruction in the manner of Jacques Derrida can be useful for feminists).

B. TOWARD AN ANTI-ESSENTIALIST FEMINIST LEGAL PRACTICE

Mari J. Matsuda, Beside My Sister, Facing the Enemy: Legal Theory Out of Coalition
43 Stan. L. Rev. 1183, 1189-1191 (1993)

The way I try to understand the interconnection of all forms of subordination is through a method I call "ask the other question." When I see something that looks racist, I ask, "Where is the patriarchy in this?" When I see something that looks sexist, I ask, "Where is the heterosexism in this?" When I see something that looks homophobic, I ask, "Where are the class interests in this?" Working in coalition forces us to look for both the obvious and non-obvious relationships of domination, helping us to realize that no form of subordination ever stands alone.

If this is true, we've asked each other, then isn't it also true that dismantling any one form of subordination is impossible without dismantling every other? And more and more, particularly in the women of color movement, the answer is that "no person is free until the last and the least of us is free."

In trying to explain this to my own community, I sometimes try to shake people up by suggesting that patriarchy killed Vincent Chin.[1] Most people think racism killed Vincent Chin. When white men with baseball bats, hurling racist hate speech, beat a man to death, it is obvious that racism is a cause. It is only slightly less obvious, however, when you walk down the aisles of Toys "R" Us, that little boys grow up in this culture with toys that teach dominance and aggression, while little girls grow up with toys that teach about being pretty, baking, and changing a diaper. And the little boy who is interested in learning how to nurture and play house is called a "sissy." When he is a little older he is called a "f-g." He learns that acceptance for men in this society is premised on rejecting the girl culture and taking on the boy culture, and I believe that this, as much as racism, killed Vincent Chin. I have come to see that homophobia is the disciplinary system that teaches men that they had better talk like 2 Live Crew or someone will think they "aren't real men," and I believe that this homophobia is a cause of rape and violence against women. I have come to see how that same homophobia makes women afraid to choose women, sending them instead into the arms of men who beat them. I have come to see how class oppression creates the same effect, cutting off the chance of economic independence that could free women from dependency upon abusive men.

I have come to see all of this from working in coalition: from my lesbian colleagues who have pointed out homophobia in places where I failed to see it; from my Native American colleagues who have said, "But remember that we were here first," when I have worked for the rights of immigrant women; from men of color who have risked my wrath to say, "But racism is what is killing us. Why can't I put that first on my agenda?"

The women of color movement has, of necessity, been a movement about intersecting structures of subordination. This movement suggests that anti-patriarchal struggle is linked to struggle against all forms of subordination. It has challenged communities of color to move beyond race alone in the quest for social justice. . . .

These are threatening suggestions for many of us who have worked primarily in organizations forged in the struggle for racial justice. Our political strength and our cultural self-worth is often grounded in racial pride. Our multi-racial coalitions have, in the past, succeeded because of a unifying commitment to end racist attacks on people of color. Moving beyond race to include discussion of other forms of subordination risks breaking coalition. Because I believe that the most progressive elements of

---

1. [Vincent Chin was a Chinese-American man living in Detroit who was murdered by several young white men armed with baseball bats after an exchange of invective. Possibly mistaking him for Japanese, the men attacked him with claims that he was "taking their jobs." See generally Paula C. Johnson, The Social Construction of Identity in Criminal Cases: Cinema Verite and the Pedagogy of Vincent Chin, 1 Mich. J. Race & L. 347 (1996).]

any liberation movement are those who see the intersections (and the most regressive are those who insist on only one axis), I am willing to risk breaking coalition by pushing intersectional analysis.

An additional and more serious risk is that intersectional analysis done from on high, that is, from outside rather than inside a structure of subordination, risks misunderstanding the particularity of that structure. Feminists have spent years talking about, experiencing, and building theory around gender. Native Americans have spent years developing an understanding of colonialism and its effect on culture. That kind of situated, ground-up knowledge is irreplaceable. A casual effort to say, "Okay, I'll add gender to my analysis," without immersion in feminist practice, is likely to miss something. Adding on gender must involve active feminists, just as adding on considerations of indigenous peoples must include activists from native communities. Coalition is the way to achieve this inclusion.

It is no accident that women of color, grounded as they are in both feminist and anti-racist struggle, are doing the most exciting theoretical work on race-gender intersections. It is no accident that gay and lesbian scholars are advancing social construction theory and the analysis of sexuality in subordination. In raising this I do not mean that we cannot speak of subordination second-hand. Rather, I wish to encourage us to do this, and to suggest that we can do this most intelligently in coalition, listening with special care to those who are actively involved in knowing and ending the systems of domination that touch their lives.

Isabelle R. Gunning, Arrogant Perception, World-Travelling, and Multicultural Feminism: The Case of Female Genital Surgeries
23 Colum. Hum. Rts. L. Rev. 189, 197-205 (1991-1992)

Our very desire as Western feminists to "do something" about the lives of other women exposes the fact that we do all live in an increasingly shrinking global village. We are different but not entirely dissimilar; we are independent beings but not without interconnectedness and overlaps. One feminist scholar has described a method by which feminists of various colors can learn to identify their interconnectedness even as they respect independence: world-travelling. [See Maria Lugones, Playfulness, World-Traveling and Perception, 2 Hypatia 3 (1987).]

World-travelling has been described by women of color, in jest, as "schizophrenia." One moves or travels among different "worlds." "Worlds" are any social situations ranging from "an incomplete visionary utopia" to a subculture or community within a larger dominant community to a "traditional construction of life." "Travelling" is the shift from being one person in one world to a different person in another world. But the "difference" is part of a coherent whole; one does not act or pose as someone else.

One analogous example of the lowest level kind of "travelling" is the "travelling" an adult child does from her world as grown up law professor, law student, worker, to the world of visiting her parents. . . .

The travelling that women and men of color must do from their various sub-communities or "worlds" to the dominant culture or "world" is a more conscious kind of travelling. For the woman of color to survive she may have to acquire very consciously a different language and set of norms to become a fluent speaker. . . .

The consciousness requires that one not just "speak" the language. Understanding the norms requires a sense of how this world comprehends or constructs you regardless of your own self-construction. For example, I am an African-American female law professor. In the world of academia I am a fairly fluent speaker, and I have a shared history with other law professors: that of attending prestigious universities for my training. Those are the things that I share with my white counterparts. But for me to survive, I need to understand the norms of academia completely, especially those that flow from the fact that academia has only recently defined itself as including either African-Americans or women of any race. I cannot just walk into the library or stand in front of a classroom and blithely expect the accord generally given a "professor" without understanding that there is likely to be a hesitation, if not an outright challenge as the white person I confront grapples with the incongruity of my position.

This personal survival skill employed by women and men of color is a method that can be used in cross cultural understanding or analysis to understand the context and condition of the "other." However, one must perform the task with "playfulness." Playfulness is a term used less to connote joy than to make an important distinction. One does not travel in order to judge ("this is a terrible place to be"), because that suggests that one has engaged in the enterprise with a fixed, self-important sense of self, and with an eye towards winning over losing; this is dangerously close to imperialism. Rather "playfulness" is used to describe an openness in travelling, an attitude that rejects rules and structure and a willingness to engage in a reconstruction of self without a concern for competence. . . . At the end of a playful journey, one finds that the victims of arrogant perception are really "subjects, lively beings, resistors," [and] "constructors of [their own] visions." One can recognize and respect their independence and yet understand their interconnectedness with oneself. . . .

The recognition of both independence and interconnectedness is essential for cross cultural understanding. I suggest a three-pronged approach to creating that recognition. In order to understand the independence of the "other" one needs to be clear about one's own boundaries. One has to be clear about the cultural influences and pressures that are inextricably involved in one's own sense of self. This requires understanding oneself in one's own historical context with an emphasis on the overlaps, influences and conditions which one is observing in the "other." Recognizing interconnectedness requires two additional approaches. The first is to understand one's historical relationship to the "other" and to approach that understanding from the "other's" perspective, i.e., to see the self as the "other" might see you. Second, one must see the "other" in her own cultural context as she sees herself. This prong requires both an in-depth look at one's own complex cultural context in search of analogues to culturally challenging practices in the "other's" culture, as well as an in-depth look at the rich cultural context of the other woman's life.

Judy Scales-Trent, Equal Rights Advocates: Addressing the Legal Issues of Women of Color
13 Berkeley Women's L.J. 34, 34-36, 55-56, 65-66 (1998)

On February 21, 1991, reporters and television cameras crowded into a small conference room in San Francisco to hear an announcement by representatives of three local public interest law firms — Asian Law Caucus ("ALC"), Mexican American Legal Defense and Education Fund ("MAL-DEF"), and Equal Rights Advocates ("ERA"). The media had come to hear about the firms' victory in a case that would affect the rights of hundreds of thousands of workers in America. At the request of these attorneys, a federal district judge in Fresno had just ruled that undocumented workers in this country were protected by federal civil rights law. At the press briefing, the decision was announced and explained in English, Spanish, and Chinese. The story was covered not only by Bay area reporters, but also by Univision, a television station that broadcasts in Spanish throughout North and South America.

For Alicia Castrejon, an undocumented worker who was fired when she became pregnant, the victory meant that she might regain her job and receive back pay. But the decision had importance far beyond the particularities of her case. As one of the first federal rulings on the rights of undocumented workers in America, the case — EEOC v. Tortilleria "La Mejor" — sent a signal to those workers, and to their employers, that discrimination against undocumented workers would not be tolerated. [1]

This was also an important moment in the life of ERA, a small public interest law firm in San Francisco. Since its creation in 1973, the firm had been addressing women's legal issues in a variety of ways, with an emphasis on employment discrimination law. ERA attorneys had taken many cases, including those involving sexual harassment, discriminatory wages, and the exclusion of women from nontraditional jobs. The case of Tortilleria "La Mejor," however, represented the more specialized focus on the legal issues

---

1. [EEOC v. Tortilleria "La Mejor," 758 F.Supp. 585 (E.D. Cal. 1991).]

of women of color — Latinas, Asian-American women, Native women, and African-American women — that the firm had come to adopt.

ERA's focus on women of color developed because of the continuing marginalization of these groups of women. In this country, it is common to speak about "women's issues" or "the race problem," and one often hears the phrase "minorities and women." Categorizing people this way obscures the fact that some minorities are women, and some women are members of minority groups. Because women who are minorities ("women of color") are not even visible in common parlance, their very real existence is obscured and their issues remain unaddressed.

Unfortunately, the invisibility of women of color persists even within the public interest law movement. Of the nearly 300 public interest legal organizations in this country, approximately seventeen, like the Women's Legal Defense Fund, were created to address women's legal issues, while approximately eleven others, like MALDEF, focus on those issues affecting a particular ethnic/racial group. These firms do, of course, perform work that has enormous value for women of color. When MALDEF wins a voting rights case, the importance of that victory for those Mexican Americans who are women cannot be understated. Similarly, the Women's Legal Defense Fund played a crucial role in getting Congress to pass the Pregnancy Discrimination Act, which prohibits discrimination in the workplace on the basis of pregnancy. Clearly, an important percentage of the women who benefit from this statute are African-American, Latina, Asian-American, and/or Native women. Yet the major focus of these groups is not the effect of the intersection of gender and race/ethnicity on the lives of these women. Thus, issues that arise at this juncture are sometimes not even seen, or are rejected as unimportant or irrelevant.

One notable example of this phenomenon is the case of Webster v. Reproductive Health Services.[4] In 1988, as the Supreme Court was preparing to hear the case, many women's rights groups began to prepare briefs outlining their arguments for the continued protection of women's constitutional right to abortion. Because the National Association for the Advancement of Colored People ("NAACP") Legal Defense Fund had been a major public interest law firm for so long, and because of its national reputation as an important fighter for the oppressed, many activists thought that its support for the issue would send a powerful message to the Court. However, despite active lobbying by representatives of women's groups, the NAACP Legal Defense Fund refused to sign on to any of the briefs. In its view, abortion was a women's issue, not a race issue, and the NAACP Legal Defense Fund addressed only issues of race. Arguments that approximately half of all African Americans are women and that reproductive rights should,

---

4. 492 U.S. 490 (1989).

therefore, be important to an organization that cares about the lives of African Americans were to no avail.

Given this context, ERA's unique willingness and ability to see and explore the complications that arise at the intersection of gender and race/ethnicity in American society, and thus in American law, is of great importance. . . .

[Scales-Trent describes the origins of ERA's "Women of Color Project" and the 1983 hiring of Terisa Chaw, ERA's first woman of color attorney.]

When Chaw joined ERA to begin the Women of Color Project, she did not know what this work would involve. However, she did know that she needed to start by contacting the many organizations in the area that addressed issues of race and ethnicity—organizations such as the ALC and La Raza Centro Legal. She also had the impression that many of these organizations did not know about ERA, primarily because they somehow did not see women's issues as connected with issues of race and ethnicity. She needed to increase ERA's visibility in minority communities. . . .

Because of Chaw's contacts within the Asian community in the Bay area, the ALC asked ERA if it wanted to join them as co-counsel in a case involving the wages of some of the garment workers against Fritzi Manufacturing Company, a major San Francisco women's clothing manufacturer, and its contractor, T & W Fashions. ALC was representing thirteen former and present garment workers, all Chinese men and women. During this period, there were approximately 20,000 garment workers in the Bay area, most of whom worked in the 100 garment shops in Chinatown. The majority of these workers were immigrants who did not speak English and therefore had limited marketable skills, as well as little understanding of their employment rights. As a result, many of the workers received neither the minimum wage nor the overtime pay required by law.

When Chaw suggested that ERA join the ALC in this litigation, the other ERA attorneys and senior staff initially did not understand why the case might involve gender discrimination. Even if the majority of the class members were women, how could there be gender discrimination if both men and women were aggrieved by these practices? Why should a law firm created to address women's issues represent men? What would be the ramifications if it did?

Chaw conceptualized this case as a women's issue well-suited for ERA. She explained to the ERA staff and legal committee that the garment workers were primarily women—poor women of color who, because they spoke only Chinese, were even more vulnerable than other women. Because of their particular vulnerability, they were being exploited by the manufacturer. As a result of Chaw's persuasive arguments, ERA decided to join the ALC in representing these garment workers. . . .

After only one year, Chaw left ERA in July of 1984. Her outreach efforts and public education campaign had made ERA more visible within communities of color in the Bay area, and had established important contacts for the firm. More importantly, she had helped the ERA staff begin to reconceptualize how they thought about women's issues. In a case where most of those harmed were women, it would no longer matter whether or not men were included in the client group: it was the harmful impact on women that had to be addressed. Also, ERA, which had previously focused on employment discrimination, now included the minimum wage as one of its issues.

As Chaw was leaving, Shauna Marshall, an African-American attorney, arrived at ERA. Because of her extensive litigation background at the Justice Department, Marshall immediately became involved in several ongoing cases. . . . Six months later, in early 1985, ERA hired Marjorie Fujiki as director of the Women of Color Project. For the first time in the history of ERA, two of the three staff attorneys — the people who led the ERA program — were women of color.

Fujiki immediately began working with Marshall and the ALC on the garment workers' case. She had already worked with ALC as a law student and appreciated its approach to litigation, which was based in community education. The community education approach to litigation mirrored Fujiki's ideas, drawing her to ERA, where the attorneys spent approximately three-fourths of their time on litigation and the rest on community education. According to Fujiki, this community-based litigation was one of ERA's greatest strengths.

Consistent with this community-based approach, the attorneys not only held bi-weekly meetings with their clients during the litigation, but they also provided community education on the rights of garment workers as part of the Garment Workers' Educational Project created by ALC. . . .

[A]t the close of this three-year struggle, both the contractor and the manufacturer settled the case for $172,000.00. It was the first time that a garment manufacturer had been forced to pay damages for labor violations to the workers of one of its contractors. . . .

Several ERA projects grew out of the garment workers' case. After seeing how little money their clients received in the settlement, the ERA staff had a stronger understanding of how low the minimum wage was and of how legal work to increase the minimum wage could be a gender issue. As a result, ERA involved itself in the Coalition for a Fair Minimum Wage. According to former executive director Davis, ERA would never have seen this as a women's issue before its involvement in the garment workers' case. . . .

Another offshoot of the garment workers' case was ERA's decision to take an active role in opposing Proposition 63, which would amend the state constitution to declare English the official language of California. Again, it was Fujiki who saw this as a gender issue that ERA should address. She pointed out that it is mainly the women in immigrant communities who bring their families to social services and that these women often speak no

English. Therefore, any requirement limiting access to social services to those who speak English would adversely affect immigrant women, as well as their families. In California, most of these women are Latinas and Asian-American women. . . .

With regard to defining issues, the impact of the garment workers' case on ERA was much larger than any monetary award it won for its clients. As Davis noted: "[this case] really broadened our thinking considerably." This was the case that opened up for the law firm both how they defined gender issues, and how ERA would provide services to its constituents. From now on ERA would conceptualize issues as "women's issues" when it could see an adverse impact on a group of women. They no longer would think that gender issues had to include only women, and exclude men. Also, ERA would no longer be limited to discrimination issues: it now understood that unfair labor practices, for example, could also be women's issues.

With respect to how ERA conducted its work, the impact of the garment workers' case was two-fold. First, ERA would no longer pursue litigation for its own sake, but would view litigation as a stepping stone to open up a range of other activity. Second, ERA would now be more involved in coalition work. Serving as co-counsel with ALC and the Employment Law Center on the garment workers' case led ERA to work in broad-based community coalitions to address the low minimum wage and the English-only referendum. Indeed, when Fujiki left ERA in late 1986, the ERA newsletter noted that her work had not only helped ERA forge strong relationships with the minority women's community, but had also given ERA the opportunity to build "long-lasting alliances" with various communities within the Bay area. . . .

In her 1987 "Message from the Executive Director," Davis noted the transformation of ERA from a law firm specializing in sex discrimination to a law firm that "is dedicated to combating aggressively and affirmatively the disenfranchisement of women, especially low-income women and women of color." She continued:

> Easily the single most important factor in our metamorphosis was the establishment in 1983 of our Women of Color Project. The Project, more than any other aspect of ERA's program, compelled us to look at the phenomenon now known as the "feminization of poverty." The problems facing minority women are problems related to race, sex and class. For ERA, tackling these problems has meant working in coalitions with a broad range of organizations. Typically, these organizations were established to work on issues of race alone or race and class. Sex, if addressed at all, was a peripheral issue. In many instances, ERA has been the only feminist organization initiating contacts and participating in these coalitions and, as such, has served as a bridge linking the women's movement to the civil rights movement. . . .

The impact of the Women of Color Project extends beyond ERA's legal and policy work to influence the work of other groups in the larger community in at least two ways. First, other groups in the community have begun to see the intersection of sex and race/ethnicity in their own work and to act upon that new knowledge. Second, other groups have been empowered to act by their relationship with ERA.

For example, it became clear that Spanish radio and television had begun to see women's issues within the larger problem of ethnicity when they began to contact ERA for information. Kaufman noted that the Spanish-language media in the Bay area had never covered a story on abortion. But when ERA did work on abortion rights, Spanish radio and television contacted ERA for information and ran stories on this issue. Blanco points out that legal advocacy groups like MALDEF or ALC, which focus on issues of race/ethnicity, now see the related gender issues and refer these cases to ERA.

Another example of the effect that ERA's work has had on other community groups can be seen in Marshall's status as the only non-Chinese member of the twenty-five-member board of Chinese for Affirmative Action. When asking her to join the board, group members explained that they wanted her help in addressing black-Asian tensions within the community, and help in understanding both their own racism and the fact that the civil rights movement they are now a part of "was built on the backs of African Americans." Marshall noted that at one meeting, the board discussed what position they should take on the nomination of Clarence Thomas to the Supreme Court. She thought it significant that the board recognized this as an important question for an Asian advocacy group to consider. Marshall understood that the group wanted her on the board so she could push them to broaden their perspective on civil rights issues, as including women of color had helped ERA broaden its perspective on gender issues. Marshall continued, "[T]hey didn't ask one of our Asian staff or former staff members to be on the board . . . . They made a decision to really expand themselves and to push."

≣≣≣≣
L. Amede Obiora, Feminism, Globalization, and Culture: After Beijing
4 Ind. J. Global Legal Stud. 355, 357-364 (1997)

As they witness radical changes that are calling into question the validity of conventional categories on the heels of globalization, conscientious feminists extol the virtues of attention to specifics. Thus, it is now quite popular in feminist circles to critique essentialism and the obliteration of what some are gradually recuperating as redeeming borders. Opposing these critical feminist posturings are trends in the realms of law, politics, and the economy which decidedly favor the conflation of boundaries.

Both the global and feminist trends are fraught with contradictions. Despite claims of the growing emergence of a unified self and locus in the aftermath of globalization, the world economic order and sociopolitical climate remain characterized by polarizations and insistent tensions between the center and the periphery. The global landscape continues to be defined by a constellation of dependent relationships, and intractable forces of change continue to create inequities. The rich get richer as the poor toil and languish; repressive regimes wax stronger as reformists agitate for accountable and representative governance; the credibility and momentum of the rule of law appear to be eroding as it recurrently proves impotent to alleviate aggravated sufferings and oppressions around the globe. This is occurring, ironically, at precisely the moment in history that a proliferation of human rights campaigns enunciate the basic requirements of a good life and aspire to them as a threshold prerequisite for the protection of human dignity.

For their part, feminist revisionists have achieved some recognition for their homage to diversity and pluralism at the same time that the manipulation and deployment of cultural difference to sexist ends renders certain regimes suspicious. Feminist concerns to respect difference and counter efforts to guard against the aberration of difference are mutually reinforcing. Yet they often engender conflicting responses. One critical question revolves around how best to reconcile the conflicts. The insight, "the personal is political" has animated the platform of the feminist movement since its renaissance. The force of feminist epistemology and praxis rests in part on the celebration of the personal. Yet this same strength has sometimes operated as a blinder to fundamental differences. . . .

In The Second Sex, Simone de Beauvoir observed that women were not savvy and resourceful enough to extensively engage in political activity. She suggested that the problem could be attributed to the fact that women lived apart from one another; they were divided by race and class; and they have been unable to see beyond their own quite particular situations. In other words, they too often lacked "the sense of the universal," approaching the world instead as "a confused conglomeration of special cases." Women have come a long way since de Beauvoir wrote, as demonstrated particularly by evidence emanating from the proceedings at the Fourth United Nations World Conference on Women in Action for Equality, Development and Peace, which was held in Beijing.

Eyewitness and other accounts of the U.N. Conference were rather inspiring. It was most interesting to learn of how the zeal of women was translated and amplified by sophisticated technology. One of the most phenomenal aspects of the Conference revolved around the instrumentality of the information age and electronic media in the mobilization of women and in the facilitation of the Conference agenda. From many indications, these devices brought home the notion of a "global village" and lent credence to the folk wisdom "unity is strength." Conglomerating in cyberspace, prior to, in the course of, and following the Conference, scores of women seemed to have transcended immense odds — sparse material resources, temporal and spatial constraints, and the like — to interact and share, brainstorm, network, and strategize. In the process, many of the women discovered, engaged, and came to a deeper understanding of their differences and commonalties. Invariably, their inclination to struggle for the common cause of eliminating gender-based inequities was reinforced, irrespective of their often divergent points of emphasis and departure. In the ensuing interchanges, these women illuminated the ubiquitous and abiding faces of structured patriarchy. Their sentiments resonated in the Platform for Action articulated at the Conference.

Observers of the evolution of the United Nations World Conferences on Women would attest that building a consensus for resolutions has not come easily at many of these forums. At the First World Conference on Women, held in Mexico City in 1975, the agenda was ensnared in a power struggle regarding who should define its focus and parameters. The second conference in Copenhagen in 1980 and the conference in Nairobi in 1985 were equally mired by controversy. The objectives of women from the so-called Third World countries, more preoccupied with the ravages of specific patterns of economic marginalization, debt crises, restrictive monetary policies, and militarization, were perceived by some women from the more privileged regions as overly-broad and diversionary. The responses of many women from Third World countries to Western feminists' demands for sexual rights were equally dismissive. Ela Bhatt subsequently formulated the crux of the matter thus: "they ask for abortion rights; we ask for safe drinking water and basic health care." Criticizing the Western domination of earlier conferences, Asma Jahangir, chair of Pakistan's Human Rights Commission, remarked, "I am beginning to think that Western women lack a deep understanding and global perspective of women's issues."

The Beijing meetings mirrored the traditional pattern of disagreements, gridlocks, dialogues and eventual reconciliations and resolutions. In fact, when delegates arrived in Beijing for the Conference, they had merely a draft document adorned with parentheses indicating texts still subject to negotiation and consensual approval. After sustained deliberations, the Conference culminated in the adoption of a landmark resolution. In and of itself, the achievement of a consensus on the Beijing Platform of Action was an historic accomplishment. In fairness to the people who labored on the preceding conferences, however, it is important to note that Beijing built on the gains of past conferences, especially on the breakthroughs which distinguished the 1985 Nairobi Conference and brought it recognition as the "birth of global feminism."

But what is this so-called "global feminism?" For our immediate purposes, we could assume that it speaks, among other things, of the permeation and reinforcement of preexisting feminist proclivities, currents, and movements in some quarters or of the inception and intensification of a global momentum. "Global Feminism" could also signify a vindication of core insights which were embedded in some of the issues pioneered by Third World women at the Mexico Conference in 1975. In illuminating the vicious and cyclical dynamics of gender bias, asymmetry, and oppression, these women voiced concerns about the increasingly totalizing complexities of patriarchal hegemony. The Mexico Conference eventually concluded that "women's roles are closely linked to the political, economic, social, and cultural conditions that constrain them from advancement and that factors determining the economic exploitation and marginalization of women stem from chronic inequalities . . . [and] injustices" of material conditions at most levels across the globe.

A cursory review of the Declaration and Platform for Action which was unanimously adopted by representatives of 189 countries participating in the Fourth World Conference on Women reflects a reaffirmation of the Mexico findings. The Platform for Action concentrated on some of the key issues identified as representing fundamental obstacles to the advancement of the majority of women in the world. One of the chief concerns addressed in Beijing was the question of the increasing feminization of poverty. In this age of tremendous global transformations, and radical transformations which have meant plenty for many in terms of market potentials and returns, women predominantly remain on the lowest rung of the economic ladder. These global trends have precipitated grave ramifications for the totality of the lives of many women. To weather the harsh realities of adversities induced by capitalist globalization, many women have had to double their work efforts. At the same time, they are reducing their food rations and enduring deprivations of essential social services and health care in proportions that diminish their productivity and life expectancy. The impoverishment of women is most intense in, although not peculiar to, the developing countries in the Southern hemisphere and the Eastern European economies in transition. The world over, women disproportionately bear the brunt of structural adjustment programs, industrial reorganizations, and the woes of "Failed States" in general.

Deliberations in Beijing were so broad that Noeleen Heyzer, the director of the United Nations Fund for Women, commented that the Conference should have been called "the women's conference on the world." In the same vein, the Secretary-General of the U.N. confirmed that "all of the great global concerns — the environment, human rights, population, social development — directly affect the situation of women. . . . Equally, improvements in the situation of women will bring positive change in each of the great global issues." Echoing a similar sentiment, Ms. Gertrude Mongella, Secretary-General of the Fourth World Conference on Women, stated that "there is no women's agenda as such. There is just one national, one global agenda. But women will put different emphases and different priorities on the issues based on where they come from and where they want to go."

Thus, true to the fundamental feminist critique, "the personal is political," the Beijing Platform emphasized the intricate link between the personal circumstances of women and public structures, and prescribed pertinent political solutions. Its global perspective not only served to attenuate the relevance of the public-private divide and reinstitute the wisdom of "the personal is political" as a rallying point. It also served to narrow the gap between the North-South perspectives in the international women's movement. As indicated earlier, the dichotomization of issues of sexuality and subsistence characterized international women's forums at the outset. Campaigns for sexual rights and freedoms were disparaged as the trite obsession of privileged Western feminists by some feminists who preferred to emphasize economic concerns. These predominantly Third World feminists were in turn dismissed as falsely conscious by some of their Western counterparts who failed to understand why they would minimize the importance of sexual rights, plagued as they are by a multitude of sexual dilemmas and offenses deriving from patriarchal cultural traditions.

The dichotomization of issues among women necessarily persists in the contemporary era, albeit differently and in somewhat less polarized proportions. Many women now more holistically comprehend the intimate relationship between women's economic dependence and the various manifestations of sexual violence. But to what extent have they achieved consensus on what constitutes violence? Few would deny that the world seems to be inching closer more than ever to acknowledging a more universal feminist agenda, even if demarcating its contours generates charged controversy. The Beijing imperative expresses a commitment to a global framework, attesting to the fact that the women's movement has matured to a considerable extent. In material respects, the imperative seems to herald the beginning of a new era in the globalization of feminism.

However, can one speak meaningfully today of global feminism? What is the context for and the content of such a claim? Does appropriating a global framework marginalize feminist issues or are feminist issues intrinsically global? Could the impetus for global feminism derive from the disparate impact of global issues and globalization on women as a discrete group? Considering the controversies among women, do postulations of global feminism risk essentializing to an absurd extent? Or will the realization of a global feminist agenda invariably entail watering issues down to achieve consensus and arrive at the path of least resistance which may be devoid of significance in the final analysis?

Is globalization a value-free process? What voices are entombed in the process of globalization? If the least empowered voices are in danger of exclusion, can we afford to take solace in claims which demonstrate that women have ample capacity for empathy and expect that the outcome will be different here? A central element of the global feminist agenda is the recognition of the human rights of women. What is the scope and substance of these rights? Is it obvious that the perspectives of the West and the "Rest" converge on questions of the constituent elements of women's human rights, or is there a danger of glorifying the views and ways of the West as the norms and rights of the world? Given the advantage of hindsight and the wealth of literature that suggest the incommensurability of norms, values, and standards, what then? Is "global feminism" a quaint nomenclature that disguises women-on-women enactments of power and hegemony?

Putting Theory into Practice

7-1. You and your three best friends from law school decide to start a "feminist law firm." What kinds of work will you seek out? Whom will you seek to hire? What clients and communities do you hope to serve? Will your firm have the conventional status hierarchies between attorneys, paralegals, support staff, and maintenance workers? If not, what relationships will you create? Will your firm pursue litigation, community organizing, legislative work, direct action, some or all of the above? What principles will you adopt to keep true to your vision? Write a mission statement for your firm.

7-2. Consider the various approaches to feminist legal theory surveyed in this book. What would be a just world according to each perspective? Do these visions of justice differ from one another? Can the approaches we have studied be combined, or are some of them mutually exclusive?

7-3. Are women an oppressed group? In what way(s)? How does the law contribute to their oppression? Can the law challenge that oppression? In what way(s)? Is law enough? If not, what more is needed for women's liberation?

7-4. What, if anything, is unique about the oppression of women compared to the oppression of other social groups? Is "women" a useful category? From a feminist point of view, what is a woman? Are there oppressions that all women share? Should these be the basis for "global feminism"? If not, what should global feminism look like?

7-5. What, if any, progress has been made in your lifetime for women? In what ways, if any, has life gotten worse for women? What issues will face a baby girl born today? Can you answer that question without specifying her race-ethnicity, language group, class, nation, sexuality, physical ability?

7-6. To what critiques explored in this chapter is this casebook vulnerable? Have the casebook authors engaged in any version of essentialism? Should they or could they have avoided it?

Statutory Appendix

Civil Rights Act of 1870†
42 U.S.C. (1994)

§1981. Equal rights under the law

(a) Statement of equal rights

All persons within the jurisdiction of the United States shall have the same right in every State and Territory to make and enforce contracts, to sue, be parties, give evidence, and to the full and equal benefit of all laws and proceedings for the security of persons and property as is enjoyed by white citizens, and shall be subject to like punishment, pains, penalties, taxes, licenses, and exactions of every kind, and to no other.

(b) "Make and enforce contracts" defined*

For purposes of this section, the term "make and enforce contracts" includes the making, performance, modification, and termination of contracts, and the enjoyment of all benefits, privileges, terms, and conditions of the contractual relationship.

(c) Protection against impairment*

The rights protected by this section are protected against impairment by nongovernmental discrimination and impairment under color of State law.

---

†Paragraphs of this statute that reflect amendments or additions contained in the Civil Rights Act of 1991, Pub. L. 102-166, 102d Cong., Nov. 21, 1991, 105 Stat. 1071, are marked with an asterisk (*).

Civil Rights Act of 1871
42 U.S.C. (1994)

§1983. Civil action for deprivation of rights

Every person who, under color of any statute, ordinance, regulation, custom, or usage, of any State or Territory or the District of Columbia, subjects, or causes to be subjected, any citizen of the United States or other person within the jurisdiction thereof to the deprivation of any rights, privileges, or immunities secured by the Constitution and laws, shall be liable to the party injured in an action at law, suit in equity, or other proper proceeding for redress. . . .

Civil Rights of 1871
42 U.S.C. (1994)

§1985. Conspiracy to interfere with civil rights . . .

(3) Depriving persons of rights or privileges

If two or more persons in any State or Territory conspire or go in disguise on the highway or on the premises of another, for the purpose of depriving, either directly or indirectly, any person or class of persons of the equal protection of the laws, or of equal privileges and immunities under the laws; or for the purpose of preventing or hindering the constituted authorities of any State or Territory from giving or securing to all persons within such State or Territory the equal protection of the laws; or if two or more persons conspire to prevent by force, intimidation, or threat, any citizen who is lawfully entitled to vote, from giving his support or advocacy in a legal manner, toward or in favor of the election of any lawfully qualified person as an elector for President or Vice President, or as a Member of Congress of the United States; or to injure any citizen in person or property on account of such support or advocacy; in any case of conspiracy set forth in this section, if one or more persons engaged therein do, or cause to be done, any act in furtherance of the object of such conspiracy, whereby another is injured in his person or property, or deprived of having and exercising any right or privilege of a citizen of the United States, the party so injured or deprived may have an action for the recovery of damages occasioned by such injury or deprivation, against any one or more of the conspirators.

The Equal Pay Act of 1963
29 U.S.C. (1994)

§206(d)

(1) No employer having employees subject to any provisions of this section shall discriminate, within any establishment in which such employees are employed, between employees on the basis of sex by paying wages to employees in such establishment at a rate less than the rate at which he pays wages to employees of the opposite sex in such establishment for equal work on jobs the performance of which requires equal skill, effort, and responsibility, and which are performed under similar working conditions, except where such payment is made pursuant to (i) a seniority system; (ii) a merit system; (iii) a system which measures earnings by quantity or quality of production; or (iv) a differential based on any other factor other than sex: *Provided,* That an employer who is paying a wage rate differential in violation of this subsection shall not, in order to comply with the provisions of this subsection, reduce the wage rate of any employee.

(2) No labor organization, or its agents, representing employees of an employer having employees subject to any provisions of this section shall cause or attempt to cause such an employer to discriminate against an employee in violation of paragraph (1) of this subsection.

(3) For purposes of administration and enforcement, any amounts owing to any employee which have been withheld in violation of this subsection shall be deemed to be unpaid minimum wages or unpaid overtime compensation under this Act.

(4) As used in this subsection, the term "labor organization" means any organization of any kind, or any agency or employee representation committee or plan, in which employees participate and which exists for the purpose, in whole or in part, of dealing with employers concerning grievances, labor disputes, wages, rates of pay, hours of employment, or conditions of work.

Title VII of the Civil Rights Act of 1964†
42 U.S.C. (1994)

§2000e. Definitions

For the purposes of this subchapter—

(a) The term "person" includes one or more individuals, governments, governmental agencies, political subdivisions, labor unions, partnerships,

†Paragraphs of this statute that reflect amendments or additions contained in the Civil Rights Act of 1991, Pub. L. 102-166, 102d Cong., Nov. 21, 1991, 105 Stat. 1071, are marked with an asterisk (*).

associations, corporations, legal representatives, mutual companies, joint-stock companies, trusts, unincorporated organizations, trustees, trustees in cases under Title 11, or receivers.

(b) The term "employer" means a person engaged in an industry affecting commerce who has fifteen or more employees for each working day in each of twenty or more calendar weeks in the current or preceding calendar year, and any agent of such a person, but such term does not include (1) the United States, a corporation wholly owned by the Government of the United States, an Indian tribe, or any department of agency of the District of Columbia subject by statute to procedures of the competitive service (as defined in section 2102 of Title 5), or (2) a bona fide private membership club (other than a labor organization) which is exempt from taxation under section 501(c) of Title 26, except that during the first year after March 24, 1972, persons having fewer than twenty-five employees (and their agents) shall not be considered employers. . . .

(d) The term "labor organization" means a labor organization engaged in an industry affecting commerce, and any agent of such an organization, and includes any organization of any kind, any agency, or employee representation committee, group, association, or plan so engaged in which employees participate and which exists for the purpose, in whole or in part, of dealing with employers concerning grievances, labor disputes, wages, rates of pay, hours, or other terms or conditions of employment, and any conference, general committee, joint or system board, or joint council so engaged which is subordinate to a national or international labor organization. . . .

(f) The term "employee" means an individual employed by an employer, except that the term "employee" shall not include any person elected to public office in any State or political subdivision of any State by the qualified voters thereof, or any person chosen by such officer to be on such officer's personal staff, or an appointee on the policy making level or an immediate adviser with respect to the exercise of the constitutional or legal powers of the office. The exemption set forth in the preceding sentence shall not include employees subject to the civil service laws of a State government, governmental agency or political subdivision. With respect to employment in a foreign country, such term includes an individual who is a citizen of the United States.*

(g) The term "commerce" means trade, traffic, commerce, transportation, transmission, or communication among the several States; or between a State and any place outside thereof; or within the District of Columbia, or a possession of the United States; or between points in the same State but through a point outside thereof. . . .

(i) The term "State" includes a State of the United States, the District of Columbia, Puerto Rico, the Virgin Islands, American Samoa, Guam, Wake Island, the Canal Zone, and Outer Continental Shelf lands defined in the Outer Continental Shelf Lands Act.

(j) The term "religion" includes all aspects of religious observance and practice, as well as belief, unless an employer demonstrates that he is unable to reasonably accommodate to an employee's or prospective employee's religious observance or practice without undue hardship on the conduct of the employer's business.

(k) The terms "because of sex" or "on the basis of sex" include, but are not limited to, because of or on the basis of pregnancy, childbirth, or related medical conditions; and women affected by pregnancy, childbirth, or related medical conditions shall be treated the same for all employment-related purposes, including receipt of benefits under fringe benefit programs, as other persons not so affected but similar in their ability or inability to work, and nothing in section 2000e-2(h) of this title shall be interpreted to permit otherwise. This subsection shall not require an employer to pay for health insurance benefits for abortion, except where the life of the mother would be endangered if the fetus were carried to term, or except where medical complications have arisen from an abortion: *Provided,* That nothing herein shall preclude an employer from providing abortion benefits or otherwise affect bargaining agreements in regard to abortion.

(l) The term "complaining party" means the [Equal Employment Opportunity Commission (the "Commission")], the Attorney General, or a person who may bring an action or proceeding under this subchapter.*

(m) The term "demonstrates" means meets the burdens of production and persuasion.*

(n) The term "respondent" means an employer, employment agency, labor organization, joint labor-management committee controlling apprenticeship or other training or retraining program, including an on-the-job training program, or Federal entity subject to section 2000e-16 of this title.*

§2000e-1. Applicability to Foreign and religious employment*

(a) Inapplicability of subchapter to certain aliens and employees of religious entities

This subchapter shall not apply to an employer with respect to the employment of aliens outside any State, or to a religious corporation, association, educational institution, or society with respect to the employment of individuals of a particular religion to perform work connected with the carrying on by such corporation, association, educational institution, or society of its activities.

(b) Compliance with statute as violative of foreign law

It shall not be unlawful under section 2000e-2 or 2000e-3 of this title for an employer (or a corporation controlled by an employer), labor organization, employment agency, or joint labor-management committee controlling apprenticeship or other training or retraining (including on-the-job training programs) to take any action otherwise prohibited by such section, with respect to an employee in a workplace in a foreign country if compliance with such section would cause such employer (or such corporation), such organization, such agency, or such committee to violate the law of the foreign country in which such workplace is located.

(c) Control of corporation incorporated in a foreign country

(1) If an employer controls a corporation whose place of incorporation is a foreign country, any practice prohibited by section 2000e-2 or 2000e-3 of this title engaged in by such corporation shall be presumed to be engaged in by such employer.

(2) Sections 2000e-2 and 2000e-3 of this title shall not apply with respect to the foreign operations of an employer that is a foreign person not controlled by an American employer.

(3) For purposes of this subsection, the determination of whether an employer controls a corporation shall be based on —
    (A) the interrelation of operations;
    (B) the common management;
    (C) the centralized control of labor relations; and
    (D) the common ownership or financial control, of the employer and the corporation.

§2000e-2. Unlawful employment practices

(a) Employer practices

It shall be an unlawful employment practice for an employer —

(1) to fail or refuse to hire or to discharge any individual, or otherwise to discriminate against any individual with respect to his compensation, terms, conditions, or privileges of employment, because of such individual's race, color, religion, sex, or national origin; or

(2) to limit, segregate, or classify his employees or applicants for employment in any way which would deprive or tend to deprive any individual of employment opportunities or otherwise adversely affect his status as an employee, because of such individual's race, color, religion, sex, or national origin.

(b) Employment agency practices

It shall be an unlawful employment practice for an employment agency to fail or refuse to refer for employment, or otherwise to discriminate against, any individual because of his race, color, religion, sex, or national origin, or to classify or refer for employment any individual on the basis of his race, color, religion, sex, or national origin.

(c) Labor organization practices

It shall be an unlawful employment practice for a labor organization —

(1) to exclude or to expel from its membership, or otherwise to discriminate against, any individual because of his race, color, religion, sex, or national origin;

(2) to limit, segregate, or classify its membership or applicants for membership, or to classify or fail or refuse to refer for employment any individual, in any way which would deprive or tend to deprive any individual of employment opportunities, or would limit such employment opportunities or otherwise adversely affect his status as an employee or as an applicant for employment, because of such individual's race, color, religion, sex, or national origin; or

(3) to cause or attempt to cause an employer to discriminate against an individual in violation of this section.

(d) Training programs

It shall be an unlawful employment practice for any employer, labor organization, or joint labor-management committee controlling apprenticeship or other training or retraining, including on-the-job training programs to discriminate against any individual because of his race, color, religion, sex, or national origin in admission to, or employment in, any program established to provide apprenticeship or other training.

(e) Businesses or enterprises with personnel qualified on basis of religion, sex, or national origin; educational institutions with personnel of particular religion

Notwithstanding any other provision of this subchapter, (1) it shall not be an unlawful employment practice for an employer to hire and employ employees, for an employment agency to classify, or refer for employment any individual, for a labor organization to classify its membership or to classify or refer for employment any individual, or for an employer, labor organization, or joint labor-management committee controlling apprenticeship or other training or retraining programs to admit or employ any individual in any such program, on the basis of his religion, sex, or national origin in those certain instances where religion, sex, or national origin is a bona fide occupational qualification reasonably necessary to the normal operation of that particular business or enterprise, and (2) it shall not be an unlawful employment practice for a school, college, university, or other educational institution or institution of learning to hire and employ employees of a particular religion if such school, college, university, or other educational institution or institution of learning is, in whole or in substantial part, owned, supported, controlled, or managed by a particular religion or by a particular religious corporation, association, or society, or if the curriculum of such school, college, university, or other educational institution or institution of learning is directed toward the propagation of a particular religion. . . .

(h) Seniority or merit system; quantity or quality of production; ability tests; compensation based on sex and authorized by minimum wage provisions

Notwithstanding any other provision of this subchapter, it shall not be an unlawful employment practice for an employer to apply different standards of compensation, or different terms, conditions, or privileges of employment pursuant to a bona fide seniority or merit system, or a system which measures earnings by quantity or quality of production or to employees who work in different locations, provided that such differences are not the result of an intention to discriminate because of race, color, religion, sex, or national origin, nor shall it be an unlawful employment practice for an employer to give and to act upon the results of any professionally developed ability test provided that such test, its administration or action upon the results is not designed, intended or used to discriminate because of race, color, religion, sex, or national origin. It shall not be an unlawful employment practice under this subchapter for any employer to differentiate upon the basis of sex in determining the amount of the wages or compensation paid or to be paid to employees of such employer if such differentiation is authorized by the provisions of section 206(d) of Title 29.

(i) Businesses or enterprises extending preferential treatment to Indians

Nothing contained in this subchapter shall apply to any business or enterprise on or near an Indian reservation with respect to any publicly announced employment practice of such business or enterprise under which a preferential treatment is given to any individual because he is an Indian living on or near a reservation.

(j) Preferential treatment not to be granted on account of existing number or percentage imbalance

Nothing contained in this subchapter shall be interpreted to require any employer, employment agency, labor organization, or joint labor-management committee subject to this subchapter to grant preferential treatment to any individual or to any group because of the race, color, religion, sex, or national origin of such individual or group on account of an imbalance which may exist with respect to the total number or percentage of persons of any race, color, religion, sex, or national origin employed by any employer, referred or classified for employment by any employment agency or labor organization, admitted to membership or classified by any labor organization, or admitted to, or employed in, any apprenticeship or other training program, in comparison with the total number or percentage of persons of such race, color, religion, sex, or national origin in any community, State, section, or other area, or in the available work force in any community, State, section, or other area.

(k) Burden of proof in disparate impact cases*

(1)(A) An unlawful employment practice based on disparate impact is established under this subchapter only if—

(i) a complaining party demonstrates that a respondent uses a particular employment practice that causes a disparate impact on the basis of race, color, religion, sex, or national origin and the respondent fails to demonstrate that the challenged practice is job related for the position in question and consistent with business necessity; or

(ii) the complaining party makes the demonstration described in subparagraph (C) with respect to an alternative employment practice and the respondent refuses to adopt such alternative employment practice.

(B)(i) With respect to demonstrating that a particular employment practice causes a disparate impact as described in subparagraph (A)(i), the complaining party shall demonstrate that each particular challenged employment practice causes a disparate impact, except that if the complaining party can demonstrate to the court that the elements of a respondent's decisionmaking process are not capable of separation for analysis, the decisionmaking process may be analyzed as one employment practice.

(ii) If the respondent demonstrates that a specific employment practice does not cause the disparate impact, the respondent shall not be required to demonstrate that such practice is required by business necessity.

(C) The demonstration referred to by subparagraph (A)(ii) shall be in accordance with the law as it existed on June 4, 1989, with respect to the concept of "alternative employment practice."

(2) A demonstration that an employment practice is required by business necessity may not be used as a defense against a claim of intentional discrimination under this subchapter.

(3) Notwithstanding any other provision of this subchapter, a rule barring the employment of an individual who currently and knowingly uses or possesses a controlled substance, as defined in schedules I and II of section 102(6) of the Controlled Substances Act (21 U.S.C. 802(6)),

other than the use or possession of a drug taken under the supervision of a licensed health care professional, or any other use or possession authorized by the Controlled Substances Act or any other provision of Federal law, shall be considered an unlawful employment practice under this subchapter only if such rule is adopted or applied with an intent to discriminate because of race, color, religion, sex, or national origin.

(l) Prohibition of discriminatory test scores*

It shall be an unlawful employment practice for a respondent, in connection with the selection or referral of applicants or candidates for employment or promotion, to adjust the scores of, use different cutoff scores for, or otherwise alter the results of, employment related tests on the basis of race, color, religion, sex, or national origin.

(m) Impermissible consideration of race, color, religion, sex, or national origin in employment practices*

Except as otherwise provided in this subchapter, an unlawful employment practice is established when the complaining party demonstrates that race, color, religion, sex, or national origin was a motivating factor for any employment practice, even though other factors also motivated the practice.

(n) Resolution of challenges to employment practices implementing litigated or consent judgments or orders*

(1)(A) Notwithstanding any other provision of law, and except as provided in paragraph (2), an employment practice that implements and is within the scope of a litigated or consent judgment or order that resolves a claim of employment discrimination under the Constitution or Federal civil rights laws may not be challenged under the circumstances described in subparagraph (B).

(B) A practice described in subparagraph (A) may not be challenged in a claim under the Constitution or Federal civil rights laws—

(i) by a person who, prior to the entry of the judgment or order described in subparagraph (A), had—

(I) actual notice of the proposed judgment or order sufficient to apprise such person that such judgment or order might adversely affect the interests and legal rights of such person and that an opportunity was available to present objections to such judgment or order by a future date certain; and

(II) a reasonable opportunity to present objections to such judgment or order; or

(ii) by a person whose interests were adequately represented by another person who had previously challenged the judgment or order on the same legal grounds and with a similar factual situation, unless there has been an intervening change in law or fact.

(2) Nothing in this subsection shall be construed to —

(A) alter the standards for intervention under rule 24 of the Federal Rules of Civil Procedure or apply to the rights of parties who have successfully intervened pursuant to such rule in the proceeding in which the parties intervened;

(B) apply to the rights of parties to the action in which a litigated or consent judgment or order was entered, or of members of a class represented or sought to be represented in such action, or of members of a group on whose behalf relief was sought in such action by the Federal Government;

(C) prevent challenges to a litigated or consent judgment or order on the ground that such judgment or order was obtained through collusion or fraud, or is transparently invalid or was entered by a court lacking subject matter jurisdiction; or

(D) authorize or permit the denial to any person of the due process of law required by the Constitution.

(3) Any action not precluded under this subsection that challenges an employment consent judgment or order described in paragraph (1) shall be brought in the court, and if possible before the judge, that entered such judgment or order. Nothing in this subsection shall preclude a transfer of such action pursuant to section 1404 of Title 28.

§2000e-3. Other unlawful employment practices

(a) Discrimination for making charges, testifying, assisting, or participating in enforcement proceedings

It shall be an unlawful employment practice for an employer to discriminate against any of his employees or applicants for employment, for an employment agency, or joint labor-management committee controlling apprenticeship or other training or retraining, including on-the-job training programs, to discriminate against any individual, or for a labor organization to discriminate against any member thereof or applicant for membership, because he has opposed any practice made an unlawful employment practice by this subchapter, or because he has made a charge, testified, assisted, or participated in any manner in an investigation, proceeding, or hearing under this subchapter.

(b) Printing or publication of notices or advertisements indicating prohibited preference, limitation, specification, or discrimination; occupational qualification exception

It shall be an unlawful employment practice for an employer, labor organization, employment agency, or joint labor-management committee controlling apprenticeship or other training and retraining, including on-the-job training programs, to print or publish or cause to be printed or published any notice or advertisement relating to employment by such an employer or membership or in any classification or referral for employment by such a labor organization, or relating to any classification or referral for employment by such an employment agency, or relating to admission to, or employment in, any program established to provide apprenticeship or other training by such a joint labor-management committee, indicating any preference, limitation, specification, or discrimination, based on race, color, religion, sex, or national origin, except that such a notice or advertisement may indicate a preference, limitation, specification, or discrimination based on religion, sex, or national origin when religion, sex, or national origin is a bona fide occupational qualification for employment.

§2000e-5. Enforcement provisions* . . .

(g) Injunctions; appropriate affirmative action; equitable relief; accrual of back pay; limitations on judicial orders

(1) If the court finds that the respondent has intentionally engaged in or is intentionally engaging in an unlawful employment practice charged in the complaint, the court may enjoin the respondent from engaging in such unlawful employment practice, and order such affirmative action as may be appropriate, which may include, but is not limited to, reinstatement or hiring of employees, with or without back pay (payable by the employer, employment agency, or labor organization, as the case may be, responsible for the unlawful employment practice), or any other equitable relief as the court deems appropriate. Back pay liability shall not accrue from a date more than two years prior to the filing of a charge with the Commission. Interim earnings or amounts earnable with reasonable diligence by the person or persons discriminated against shall operate to reduce the back Bay otherwise allowable.

(2)(A) No order of the court shall require the admission or reinstatement of an individual as a member of a union, or the hiring, reinstatement, or promotion of an individual as an employee, or the payment to him of any back pay, if such individual was refused admission, suspended, or expelled, or was refused employment or advancement or was suspended or discharged for any reason other than discrimination on account of race, color, religion, sex, or national origin or in violation of section 2000e-3(a) of this title.

(B) On a claim in which an individual proves a violation under section 2000e-2(m) of this title and a respondent demonstrates that the respondent would have taken the same action in the absence of the impermissible motivating factor, the court —

(i) may grant declaratory relief, injunctive relief (except as provided in clause (ii)), and attorney's fees and costs demonstrated to be directly attributable only to the pursuit of a claim under section 2000e-2(m) of this title; and

(ii) shall not award damages or issue an order requiring any admission, reinstatement, hiring, promotion, or payment, described in subparagraph (A).

(k) Attorney's fee; liability of Commission and United States for costs

In any action or proceeding under this subchapter the court, in its discretion, may allow the prevailing party, other than the Commission or the United States, a reasonable attorney's fee (including expert fees) as part of the costs, and the Commission and the United States shall be liable for costs the same as a private person.

§2000e-11. Veterans' special rights or preference

Nothing contained in this subchapter shall be construed to repeal or modify any Federal, State, territorial, or local law creating special rights or preference for veterans.

§2000e-16. Employment by Federal Government

(a) Discriminatory practices prohibited; employees or applicants for employment subject to coverage

All personnel actions affecting employees or applicants for employment (except with regard to aliens employed outside the limits of the United States) in military departments as defined in section 102 of Title 5, in executive agencies as defined in section 105 of Title 5 (including employees and applicants for employment who are paid from nonappropriated funds), in the United States Postal Service and the Postal Rate Commission, in those units of the Government of the District of Columbia having positions in the competitive service, and in those units of the legislative and judicial branches of the Federal Government having positions in the competitive service, and in the Library of Congress shall be made free from any discrimination based on race, color, religion, sex, or national origin.

Civil Rights Act of 1991†
42 U.S.C. (1994)

§1981a. Damages in cases of intentional discrimination in employment

(a) Right of recovery

(1) Civil rights

In an action brought by a complaining party under section 706 or 717 of the Civil Rights Act of 1964 (42 U.S.C. 2000e-5) [42 U.S.C.A. §2000e-5; 42 U.S.C.A. §2000e-16] against a respondent who engaged in unlawful intentional discrimination (not an employment practice that is unlawful because of its disparate impact) prohibited under section 703, 704, or 717 of the Act [42 U.S.C.A. §2000e-2, §2000e-3, §2000e-16], and provided that the complaining party cannot recover under section 1981 of this title, the complaining party may recover compensatory and punitive damages as allowed in subsection (b) of this section, in addition to any relief authorized by section 706(g) of the Civil Rights Act of 1964 from the respondent. . . .

(b) Compensatory and punitive damages

(1) Determination of punitive damages

A complaining party may recover punitive damages under this section against a respondent (other than a government, government agency or political subdivision) if the complaining party demonstrates that the respondent engaged in a discriminatory practice or discriminatory practices with malice or with reckless indifference to the federally protected rights of an aggrieved individual.

(2) Exclusions from compensatory damages

Compensatory damages awarded under this section shall not include backpay, interest on backpay, or any other type of relief authorized under section 706(g) of the Civil Rights Act of 1964 [42 U.S.C.A. §2000e-5(g)].

(3) Limitations

The sum of the amount of compensatory damages awarded under this section for future pecuniary losses, emotional pain, suffering, inconvenience, mental anguish, loss of enjoyment of life, and other nonpecuniary losses, and the amount of punitive damages awarded under this section, shall not exceed, for each complaining party—

†Other provisions of the Civil Rights Act of 1991 are incorporated in the Civil Rights Act of 1870, 42 U.S.C. §1981 (1994), and Title VII of the Civil Rights Act of 1964, 42 U.S.C. §2000e et seq. (1994), supra in this Appendix.

(A) in the case of a respondent who has more than 14 and fewer than 101 employees in each of 20 or more calendar weeks in the current or preceding calendar year, $50,000;

(B) in the case of a respondent who has more than 100 and fewer than 201 employees in each of 20 or more calendar weeks in the current or preceding calendar year, $100,000; and

(C) in the case of a respondent who has more than 200 and fewer than 501 employees in each of 20 or more calendar weeks in the current pr preceding calendar year, $200,000; and

(D) in the case of a respondent who has more than 500 employees in each of 20 or more calendar weeks in the current or preceding calendar year, $300,000.

(4) Construction

Nothing in this section shall be construed to limit the scope of, or the relief available under, section 1981 of this title.

(c) Jury trial

If a complaining party seeks compensatory or punitive damages under this section —

(1) any party may demand a trial by jury; and

(2) the court shall not inform the jury of the limitations described in subsection (b)(3) of this section.

(d) Definitions

As used in this section:

(1) Complaining party

The term "complaining party" means —

(A) in the case of a person seeking to bring an action under subsection (a)(1) of this section, the Equal Employment Opportunity Commission, the Attorney General, or a person who may bring an action or proceeding under title VII of the Civil Rights Act of 1964 (42 U.S.C. 2000e et seq.). . . .

(2) Discriminatory practice

The term "discriminatory practice" means the discrimination described in paragraph (1), or the discrimination or the violation described in paragraph (2), of subsection (a) of this section.

⟰ *Title IX of the Education Amendments of 1972†*
20 U.S.C. (1994)

§1681. Sex

(a) Prohibition against discrimination; exceptions

No person in the United States shall, on the basis of sex, be excluded from participation in, be denied the benefits of, or be subjected to discrimination under any education program or activity receiving Federal financial assistance, except that:

(1) Classes of educational institutions subject to prohibition
in regard to admissions to educational institutions, this section shall apply only to institutions of vocational education, professional education, and graduate higher education, and to public institutions of undergraduate higher education;

(2) Educational institutions commencing planned change in admissions
in regard to admissions to educational institutions, this section shall not apply (A) for one year from June 23, 1972, nor for six years after June 23, 1972, in the case of an educational institution which has begun the process of changing from being an institution which admits only students of one sex to being an institution which admits students of both sexes, but only if it is carrying out a plan for such a change which is approved by the Secretary of Education or (B) for seven years from the date an educational institution begins the process of changing from being an institution which admits only students of only one sex to being an institution which admits students of both sexes, but only if it is carrying out a plan for such a change which is approved by the Secretary of Education, whichever is the later;

(3) Educational institutions of religious organizations with contrary religious tenets
this section shall not apply to an educational institution which is controlled by a religious organization if the application of this subsection would not be consistent with the religious tenets of such organization;

(4) Educational institutions training individuals for military services or merchant marine
this section shall not apply to an educational institution whose primary purpose is the training of individuals for the military services of the United States, or the merchant marine;

†Sections 1687 and 1688 were added by the Civil Rights Restoration Act of 1987, Pub. L. 100-259, §§3a, 3b, Mar. 22, 1988, 102 Stat. 28, 29.

(5) Public educational institutions with traditional and continuing admissions policy

in regard to admissions this section shall not apply to any public institution of undergraduate higher education which is an institution that traditionally and continually from its establishment has had a policy of admitting only students of one sex;

(6) Social fraternities or sororities; voluntary youth service organizations

this section shall not apply to membership practices —

(A) of a social fraternity or social sorority which is exempt from taxation under section 501(a) of Tide 26, the active membership of which consists primarily of students in attendance at an institution of higher education, or

(B) of the Young Men's Christian Association, Young Women's Christian Association, Girl Scouts, Boy Scouts, Camp Fire Girls, and voluntary youth service organizations which are so exempt, the membership of which has traditionally been limited to persons of one sex and principally to persons of less than nineteen years of age;

(7) Boy or Girl conferences

this section shall not apply to —

(A) any program or activity of the American Legion undertaken in connection with the organization or operation of any Boys State conference, Boys Nation conference, Girls State conference, or Girls Nation conference; or

(B) any program or activity of any secondary school or educational institution specifically for —

(i) the promotion of any Boys State conference, Boys Nation conference, Girls State conference, or Girls Nation conference; or

(ii) the selection of students to attend any such conference;

(8) Father-son or mother-daughter activities at educational institutions

this section shall not preclude father-son or mother-daughter activities at an educational institution, but if such activities are provided for students of one sex, opportunities for reasonably comparable activities shall be provided for students of the other sex; and

(9) Institution of higher education scholarship awards in "beauty" pageants

this section shall not apply with respect to any scholarship or other financial assistance awarded by an institution of higher education to any individual because such individual has received such award in any pageant in which the attainment of such award is based upon a combination of factors related to the personal appearance, poise, and talent of such individual and in which participation is limited to individuals of one sex only, so long as such pageant is in compliance with other nondiscrimination provisions of Federal law.

(b) Preferential or disparate treatment because of imbalance in participation or receipt of Federal benefits; statistical evidence of imbalance

Nothing contained in subsection (a) of this section shall be interpreted to require any educational institution to grant preferential or disparate treatment to the members of one sex on account of an imbalance which may exist with respect to the total number or percentage of persons of that sex participating in or receiving the benefits of any federally supported program or activity, in comparison with the total number or percentage of persons of that sex in any community, State, section, or other area: *Provided,* That this subsection shall not be construed to prevent the consideration in any hearing or proceeding under this chapter of statistical evidence tending to show that such an imbalance exists with respect to the participation in, or receipt of the benefits of, any such program or activity by the members of one sex.

(c) "Educational institution" defined

For purposes of this chapter an educational institution means any public or private preschool, elementary, or secondary school, or any institution of vocational, professional, or higher education, except that in the case of an educational institution composed of more than one school, college, or department which are administratively separate units, such term means each such school, college, or department.

§1685. Authority under other laws unaffected

Nothing in this chapter shall add to or detract from any existing authority with respect to any program or activity under which Federal financial assistance is extended by way of a contract of insurance or guaranty.

§1686. Interpretation with respect to living facilities

Notwithstanding anything to the contrary contained in this chapter, nothing contained herein shall be construed to prohibit any educational institution receiving funds under this Act, from maintaining separate living facilities for the different sexes.

§1687. Interpretation of "program or activity"

For the purposes of this chapter, the term[s] "program or activity" and "program" mean all of the operations of—

    (1)(A) a department, agency, special purpose district, or other instrumentality of a State or of a local government; or

(B) the entity of such State or local government that distributes such assistance and each such department or agency (and each other State or local government entity) to which the assistance is extended, in the case of assistance to a State or local government;

(2)(A) a college, university, or other postsecondary institution, or a public system of higher education; or

(B) a local educational agency (as defined in section 8801 of this title), system of vocational education, or other school system;

(3)(A) an entire corporation, partnership, or other private organization, or an entire sole proprietorship —

(i) if assistance is extended to such corporation, partnership, private organization, or sole proprietorship as a whole; or

(ii) which is principally engaged in the business of providing education, health care, housing, social services, or parks and recreation; or

(B) the entire plant or other comparable, geographically separate facility to which Federal financial assistance is extended, in the case of any other corporation, partnership, private organization, or sole proprietorship; or

(4) any other entity which is established by two or more of the entities described in paragraph (1), (2), or (3);

any part of which is extended Federal financial assistance, except that such term does not include any operation of an entity which is controlled by a religious organization if the application of section 1681 of this title to such operation would not be consistent with the religious tenets of such organization.

§1688. Neutrality with respect to abortion

Nothing in this chapter shall be construed to require or prohibit any person, or public or private entity, to provide or pay for any benefit or service, including the use of facilities, related to an abortion. Nothing in this section shall be construed to permit a penalty to be imposed on any person or individual because such person or individual is seeking or has received any benefit or service related to a legal abortion.

National Defense Authorization Act for Fiscal Year 1994

10 U.S.C. §654 (2000)

§654. Policy concerning homosexuality in the armed forces

(a) Findings. Congress makes the following findings:

(1) Section 8 of article I of the Constitution of the United States commits exclusively to the Congress the powers to raise and support armies, provide and maintain a Navy, and make rules for the government and regulation of the land and naval forces.

(2) There is no constitutional right to serve in the armed forces.

(3) Pursuant to the powers conferred by section 8 of article I of the Constitution of the United States, it lies within the discretion of the Congress to establish qualifications for and conditions of service in the armed forces.

(4) The primary purpose of the armed forces is to prepare for and to prevail in combat should the need arise.

(5) The conduct of military operations requires members of the armed forces to make extraordinary sacrifices, including the ultimate sacrifice, in order to provide for the common defense.

(6) Success in combat requires military units that are characterized by high morale, good order and discipline, and unit cohesion.

(7) One of the most critical elements in combat capability is unit cohesion, that is, the bonds of trust among individual service members that make the combat effectiveness of a military unit greater than the sum of the combat effectiveness of the individual unit members.

(8) Military life is fundamentally different from civilian life in that —

(A) the extraordinary responsibilities of the armed forces, the unique conditions of military service, and the critical role of unit cohesion, require that the military community, while subject to civilian control, exist as a specialized society; and

(B) the military society is characterized by its own laws, rules, customs, and traditions, including numerous restrictions on personal behavior, that would not be acceptable in civilian society.

(9) The standards of conduct for members of the armed forces regulate a member's life for 24 hours each day beginning at the moment the member enters military status and not ending until that person is discharged or otherwise separated from the armed forces.

(10) Those standards of conduct, including the Uniform Code of Military Justice, apply to a member of the armed forces at all times that the member has a military status, whether the member is on base or off base, and whether the member is on duty or off duty.

(11) The pervasive application of the standards of conduct is necessary because members of the armed forces must be ready at all times for worldwide deployment to a combat environment.

(12) The worldwide deployment of United States military forces, the international responsibilities of the United States, and the potential for involvement of the armed forces in actual combat routinely make it necessary for members of the armed forces involuntarily to accept living conditions and working conditions that are often spartan, primitive, and characterized by forced intimacy with little or no privacy.

(13) The prohibition against homosexual conduct is a long-standing element of military law that continues to be necessary in the unique circumstances of military service.

(14) The armed forces must maintain personnel policies that exclude persons whose presence in the armed forces would create an unacceptable risk to the armed forces' high standards of morale, good order and discipline, and unit cohesion that are the essence of military capability.

(15) The presence in the armed forces of persons who demonstrate a propensity or intent to engage in homosexual acts would create an unacceptable risk to the high standards of morale, good order and discipline, and unit cohesion that are the essence of military capability.

(b) Policy. A member of the armed forces shall be separated from the armed forces under regulations prescribed by the Secretary of Defense if one or more of the following findings is made and approved in accordance with procedures set forth in such regulations:

(1) That the member has engaged in, attempted to engage in, or solicited another to engage in a homosexual act or acts unless there are further findings, made and approved in accordance with procedures set forth in such regulations, that the member has demonstrated that —

(A) such conduct is a departure from the member's usual and customary behavior;

(B) such conduct, under all the circumstances, is unlikely to recur;

(C) such conduct was not accomplished by use offeree, coercion, or intimidation;

(D) under the particular circumstances of the case, the member's continued presence in the armed forces is consistent with the interests of the armed forces in proper discipline, good order, and morale; and

(E) the member does not have a propensity or intent to engage in homosexual acts.

(2) That the member has stated that he or she is a homosexual or bisexual, or words to that effect, unless there is a further finding, made and approved in accordance with procedures set forth in the regulations, that the member has demonstrated that he or she is not a person who engages in, attempts to engage in, has a propensity to engage in, or intends to engage in homosexual acts.

(3) That the member has married or attempted to marry a person known to be of the same biological sex. . . .

(f) Definitions. In this section:

(1) The term "homosexual" means a person, regardless of sex, who engages in, attempts to engage in, has a propensity to engage in, or intends to engage in homosexual acts, and includes the terms "gay" and "lesbian."

(2) The term "bisexual" means a person who engages in, attempts to engage in, has a propensity to engage in, or intends to engage in homosexual and heterosexual acts.

(3) The term "homosexual act" means —

(A) any bodily contact, actively undertaken or passively permitted, between members of the same sex for the purpose of satisfying sexual desires; and

(B) any bodily contact which a reasonable person would understand to demonstrate a propensity or intent to engage in an act described in subparagraph (A).

Table of Cases

Principal cases are in italics.

Index

1319